Customary International Humanitarian Law

INTERNATIONAL COMMITTEE OF THE RED CROSS

CUSTOMARY INTERNATIONAL HUMANITARIAN LAW

VOLUME I

RULES

Jean-Marie Henckaerts and Louise Doswald-Beck
With contributions by Carolin Alvermann,
Knut Dörmann and Baptiste Rolle

CAMBRIDGE
UNIVERSITY PRESS

PUBLISHED BY THE PRESS SYNDICATE OF THE UNIVERSITY OF CAMBRIDGE
The Pitt Building, Trumpington Street, Cambridge, United Kingdom

CAMBRIDGE UNIVERSITY PRESS
The Edinburgh Building, Cambridge, CB2 2RU, UK
40 West 20th Street, New York, NY 10011–4211, USA
477 Williamstown Road, Port Melbourne, VIC 3207, Australia
Ruiz de Alarcón 13, 28014 Madrid, Spain
Dock House, The Waterfront, Cape Town 8001, South Africa

http://www.cambridge.org

First published 2005

Printed in the United Kingdom at the University Press, Cambridge

Typeface Trump Medieval 10/13 pt.   *System* LaTeX 2_ε [TB]

A catalogue record for this book is available from the British Library

ISBN 0 521 80899 5 hardback
ISBN 0 521 00528 0 paperback

Hardback also available as:
ISBN 0 521 53925 0 set including Volume II

CONTENTS

FOREWORD BY DR. JAKOB KELLENBERGER
President of the International Committee of the Red Cross

The laws of war were born of confrontation between armed forces on the battle-field. Until the mid-nineteenth century, these rules remained customary in nature, recognised because they had existed since time immemorial and because they corresponded to the demands of civilisation. All civilisations have developed rules aimed at minimising violence – even this institution-alised form of violence that we call war – since limiting violence is the very essence of civilisation.

By making international law a matter to be agreed between sovereigns and by basing it on State practice and consent, Grotius and the other founding fathers of public international law paved the way for that law to assume uni-versal dimensions, applicable both in peacetime and in wartime and able to transcend cultures and civilizations. However, it was the nineteenth-century visionary Henry Dunant who was the true pioneer of contemporary interna-tional humanitarian law. In calling for "some international principle, sanc-tioned by a Convention and inviolate in character" to protect the wounded and all those trying to help them, Dunant took humanitarian law a decisive step forward. By instigating the adoption, in 1864, of the Geneva Convention for the amelioration of the condition of the wounded and sick in armed forces in the field, Dunant and the other founders of the International Committee of the Red Cross laid the cornerstone of treaty-based international humanitarian law.

This treaty was revised in 1906, and again in 1929 and 1949. New conventions protecting hospital ships, prisoners of war and civilians were also adopted. The result is the four Geneva Conventions of 1949, which constitute the foundation of international humanitarian law in force today. Acceptance by the States of these Conventions demonstrated that it was possible to adopt, in peacetime, rules to attenuate the horrors of war and protect those affected by it.

Governments also adopted a series of treaties governing the conduct of hostil-ities: the Declaration of St Petersburg of 1868, the Hague Conventions of 1899 and 1907, and the Geneva Protocol of 1925, which bans the use of chemical and bacteriological weapons.

These two normative currents merged in 1977 with the adoption of the two Protocols additional to the 1949 Geneva Conventions, which brought up to date both the rules governing the conduct of hostilities and those protecting war victims.

More recently, other important conventions were added to this already long list of treaties, in particular the 1980 Convention on Certain Conventional Weapons and its five Protocols, the 1997 Ottawa Convention on the Prohibition of Anti-Personnel Landmines, the 1998 Statute of the International Criminal Court, the 1999 Protocol to the 1954 Convention for the Protection of Cultural Property in the Event of Armed Conflict and the 2000 Optional Protocol on the Involvement of Children in Armed Conflict.

This remarkable progress in codifying international humanitarian law should not, however, cause us to ignore customary humanitarian law. There are three reasons why this body of law remains extremely important.

First, while the Geneva Conventions enjoy universal adherence today, this is not yet the case for other major treaties, including the Additional Protocols. These treaties apply only between or within States that have ratified them. Rules of customary international humanitarian law on the other hand, sometimes referred to as "general" international law, bind all States and, where relevant, all parties to the conflict, without the need for formal adherence.

Second, international humanitarian law applicable to non-international armed conflict falls short of meeting the protection needs arising from these conflicts. As admitted by the diplomatic conferences that adopted them, Article 3 common to the Geneva Conventions and Protocol II additional to those Conventions represent only the most rudimentary set of rules. State practice goes beyond what those same States have accepted at diplomatic conferences, since most of them agree that the essence of customary rules on the conduct of hostilities applies to *all* armed conflicts, international and non-international.

Last, customary international law can help in the interpretation of treaty law. It is a well-established principle that a treaty must be interpreted in good faith and with due regard for all relevant rules of international law.

With this in mind, one better understands the mandate assigned to the ICRC by the 26th International Conference of the Red Cross and Red Crescent (Geneva, 1995), when the organization was asked to:

prepare, with the assistance of experts in international humanitarian law representing various geographical regions and different legal systems, and in consultation with experts from governments and international organisations, a report on customary rules of international humanitarian law applicable in international and non-international armed conflicts, and to circulate the report to States and competent international bodies.

The ICRC accepted this mandate with gratitude and humility – gratitude because it appreciates the international community's confidence in it as symbolised by this assignment, and humility since it was fully aware of the difficulty involved in describing the present state of customary international law on the basis of all available sources.

The ICRC charged two members of its Legal Division with the task of carrying out this study. Under the guidance of a Steering Committee composed of 12 experts of international repute, the ICRC engaged in a large-scale consultation process involving over 100 eminent authorities. Considering this report primarily as a work of scholarship, the ICRC respected the academic freedom both of the report's authors and of the experts consulted, the idea being to capture the clearest possible "photograph" of customary international humanitarian law as it stands today.

The ICRC believes that the study does indeed present an accurate assessment of the current state of customary international humanitarian law. It will therefore duly take the outcome of this study into account in its daily work, while being aware that the formation of customary international law is an ongoing process. The study should also serve as a basis for discussion with respect to the implementation, clarification and development of humanitarian law.

Lastly, the ICRC is pleased that this study has served to emphasise the universality of humanitarian law. All traditions and civilizations have contributed to the development of this law, which is today part of the common heritage of mankind.

The ICRC would like to express its deep gratitude to the experts who gave freely of their time and expertise, to the staff of its Legal Division, and in particular to the authors, who, in bringing this unique project to its conclusion, refused to be discouraged by the enormity of the task.

In presenting this study to the States party to the Geneva Conventions, to National Red Cross and Red Crescent Societies and other humanitarian organisations, to judges and scholars and to other interested parties, the ICRC's sincere hope is that it will clarify the meaning and significance of a number of rules of international humanitarian law and that it will ensure greater protection for war victims.

FOREWORD BY DR. ABDUL G. KOROMA
Judge at the International Court of Justice

Sadly, it cannot be said that the incidence of armed conflict has become any rarer since the end of the Second World War. Rather, a host of conflicts across the world, both international and non-international, have highlighted as never before the extent to which civilians have become targets and the growing need to ensure the protection of the wounded, the sick, detainees and the civilian population afforded to them by the rules of international humanitarian law. Opinions vary as to the reason for the increasing number of violations of international humanitarian law. Is it a lack of awareness of the rules on the part of those who should observe them? Is it the inadequacy of the rules even where they are known? Is it weak mechanisms for enforcing the rules? Or is it sheer disregard for the rules? To some extent, there is truth in each. For international humanitarian law to be more effective, not one but all of these facets of the problem need to be addressed. Clearly, the first step in achieving the goal of universal respect for humanitarian rules must be the articulation of what the rules require; only then can the question of how to improve upon them be considered.

This study of customary international humanitarian law and its role in protecting the victims of war is both timely and important for a number of reasons. The relevant treaty law covers a wide variety of aspects of warfare, but treaty law, by its very nature, is unable to provide a complete picture of the state of the law. While treaties bind those States that have adhered to them, without the existence of customary law, non-parties would be free to act as they wished. In addition, because they are written down, treaty rules are well defined and must be clear as to the standard of conduct they require; but since a treaty is the result of an agreement between the parties, the instruction provided by a treaty rule is only as useful as the degree of genuine agreement achieved. Written rules cannot be vague or open to divergent interpretations. Customary international law, while being notorious for its imprecision, may be no less useful than treaty law, and may in fact actually have certain advantages over it. For example, it is widely accepted that general customary international law binds States that have not persistently and openly dissented in relation to a rule while that rule was in the process of formation. Also, one of the most important bases for the success of a treaty regime is the extent of the political will to achieve the

xii

purposes of that treaty, and that is as important, if not more so, than the need for the rules to be in written form.

Accordingly, this study, which aims to articulate the existing customary rules on the subject, can only help improve respect for international humanitarian law and offer greater protection to victims of war. Knowledge of the relevant customary law on the part of the various actors involved in its application, dissemination and enforcement, such as military personnel, governmental authorities, courts and tribunals and governmental and non-governmental organisations, is a vital first step towards enhancing the effectiveness of international humanitarian law. This study is an invaluable contribution to that goal.

FOREWORD BY DR. YVES SANDOZ

Member of the International Committee of the Red Cross; former Director of the ICRC Department of International Law and Policy; Lecturer, Universities of Geneva and Fribourg

The decision to go ahead with a study on customary international humanitarian law depended primarily on the answer to two questions – how useful it would be and how much it would cost – which together give us the famous cost-effectiveness ratio, something that must be taken into account in any undertaking, even if its purpose is humanitarian.

To be sure, applying the criterion of cost-effectiveness is not necessarily appropriate for humanitarian work since it would be cynical to attach a financial price to life and well-being. Nevertheless, those who run an organisation like the ICRC have a moral duty to seek maximum efficiency in the use to which they put their human and financial resources (while seeking to increase those resources). For, as long as there are wars, it will never be possible to do enough, or to do it well enough, to protect and assist those affected.

The international community has given the ICRC the onerous mandate to "work for the faithful application of international humanitarian law". This imposes a duty of constant vigilance. For the ICRC, impartiality means not only avoiding discrimination between the different victims of a given conflict, but also constantly striving to ensure that all the victims of all the conflicts on the planet are treated equitably, without regional or ethnic preference and independently of the emotions sparked by media-selected images.

This concern to avoid discrimination and to ensure impartiality on a global scale guides the ICRC in choosing its activities. When the time comes to make these choices, meeting the victims' urgent need for food and medical care logically remains the priority and claims far and away the largest part of the organisation's budget. How could paying for a meeting of experts take precedence over delivering sacks of flour?

The choices, however, are not that stark. Experience has shown that nothing is to be gained by swinging blindly into action when the fighting starts. Many organisations have learned the hard way that you cannot be effective without first understanding the situation in which you are working, the mentality of those involved in the conflict and the society and culture of those you seek to aid. And if you must first understand, you must also be understood, not only by the combatants – who must know and accept the red cross and red crescent emblems and the principles of humanity, impartiality and neutrality symbolised by that emblem – but also by your intended beneficiaries.

The ICRC's long experience has convinced it that in order to be effective it has to engage in a wide range of activities, activities that must not be viewed in isolation but rather in relation to one another. The complementary nature of those activities has grown ever clearer with the passing years.

Each of these activities is linked to other activities, all fitting together to form a coherent edifice. That is, humanitarian action in the field prompts discussion, which then develops in meetings of experts of various kinds before eventually taking the form of treaty provisions or new international institutions such as the International Criminal Court, whose Statute was adopted in 1998. The next task is to work towards universal acceptance of the new rules by convincing the States through their governments, their parliaments, their senior officials, etc. of the importance of respecting such rules. Lastly, individual States must be encouraged to adopt national laws incorporating the new rules into domestic legislation, to ensure that the public knows and understands basic humanitarian principles, to ensure that international humanitarian law is adequately taught in schools and universities, and to integrate the subject into military training. The ultimate goal of all this work is to benefit the victims of war and facilitate the task of those seeking to help them.

But it will never be enough. War will remain cruel and there will never be adequate compliance with rules aimed at curbing that cruelty. New problems will arise requiring new forms of action and new discussion about the adequacy of existing rules or their application to new realities. And so the great wheel of law and humanitarian endeavour will continue to turn in the direction of a goal that may never be fully attained, that is, an end to armed conflict. Indeed, that goal sometimes seems to recede amid the pain and anguish of countless wars; but we must always struggle back towards it.

A lawyer in an office working on the development of international humanitarian law is doing a job different from that of the surgeon treating wounded people or a nutritionist in a refugee camp. But all three are in fact pursuing the same objective, each with his or her own place in the indispensable circle of law and humanitarian action.

Ascertaining the role played by legal experts is nevertheless not enough to justify a study on customary international humanitarian law. As part of the process outlined above, the ICRC has in recent years devoted significant resources to considering the state of the law and to spreading knowledge of it. But those resources are limited and choices must therefore be made between various options within the legal domain. Should priority be given to developing new law, promoting national legislation, clarifying certain aspects of practical implementation, consulting experts on sensitive questions, training the miliitary or mobilising public opinion as a means of bringing about greater compliance? All these activities are necessary to some extent, but the question is where the priority belongs. The singular thing about the proposed study on customary law was that it was ill-suited to compromise and to half-measures. The choice was between doing it – and ensuring that one had the means to do it well – and foregoing it on the grounds that its value would rely totally on its credibility.

The decision was eventually taken to go ahead with the project. The ICRC's Legal Division was assigned this difficult task and given the means to do a thorough job. Lavish means were not necessary because the ICRC is lucky enough to be able to count on volunteer work by a wide range of the world's leading experts. And we cannot thank them enough for their generosity and commitment. But the administrative work involved and the tasks of organising meetings and translating a number of texts all obviously cost money, as does tapping the sources, in all corners of the world, on which the study is based.

How then can such an investment be justified? Why devote large-scale resources to clarifying what is customary in a branch of law that is so widely codified and by whose treaties the vast majority of States are bound? Many reasons can be given for this, but I will cite two which seem to me essential.

The first is that, despite everything, there remain in international humanitarian law vast but little-known reaches that it is important to explore more fully. This is particularly the case for the rules restricting the use of certain means and methods of warfare. These rules, which were laid down in the Additional Protocols of 1977, very directly concern the military, since it is they who have to implement these rules. If they are sometimes rather vague, this is because at the time of their adoption it was not possible for everyone to agree on a more precise formulation.

The problem is all the more sensitive as the great majority of modern-day armed conflicts are internal, while most of the rules in question are formally applicable only to international conflicts. For the average person, this is completely absurd. Indeed, how can one claim the right to employ against one's own population means of warfare which one has prohibited for use against an invader? Nevertheless, for historical reasons, precisely this distinction has been made. To be sure, treaties drawn up today tend to soften the effects of this distinction. It exists all the same, and the study on customary law makes it possible to ascertain the extent to which it has been blurred in practice and according to the *opinio juris* of the States.

The ICRC study also represents an excellent opportunity to view international humanitarian law in its entirety, asking what purpose it has served and how it has been applied, studying the relevance of its various provisions and determining whether some of the problems encountered today do not call for a fresh look at this or that provision.

The study plays a capital role in answering these questions, especially as the problem is not to know whether given rules exist or not but rather how to interpret them. But this is no easy matter. Whatever else, the study's conclusions will serve as a valuable basis for identifying areas in the law that should be clarified or developed and for engaging in whatever dialogue or negotiation is necessary to strengthen the coherence of military doctrines and those of the jurisprudence of national and international courts, present or future. Therefore, coherence is indispensable to international humanitarian law's credibility.

The second reason is to be found not so much in the results of the study but in the study itself. Doing research throughout the world to find out how the rules are complied with, translated, taught and applied, then collating that information in order to ascertain both the successes and the remaining gaps – is all this not the best way to ensure more effective application of these rules, to stimulate interest, research and new ideas and, above all, to encourage dialogue between the world's different cultures? This undertaking has particular significance at a time of renewed tension for humanity when religious and cultural frictions are being exploited for violent ends. The Geneva Conventions have been universally embraced. The rules of international humanitarian law represent a kind of common heritage of mankind, with its roots in all human cultures. They can therefore be viewed as a cement between different cultures. It is thus essential to remind people of those rules and persuade them to comply. The study has been a golden opportunity to do this.

With the fruit of this enormous labour before us, one might think that the circle has been closed. The contrary is the case, however, and I would like to conclude by stressing that this study will have achieved its goal only if it is considered not as the end of a process but as a beginning. It reveals what has been accomplished but also what remains unclear and what remains to be done.

The study is a still photograph of reality, taken with great concern for absolute honesty, that is, without trying to make the law say what one wishes it would say. I am convinced that this is what lends the study international credibility. But though it represents the truest possible reflection of reality, the study makes no claim to be the final word. It is not all-encompassing – choices had to be made – and no one is infallible. In the introduction to *De jure belli ac pacis*, Grotius says this to his readers: "I beg and adjure all those into whose hands this work shall come, that they assume towards me the same liberty which I have assumed in passing upon the opinions and writings of others." What better way to express the objective of those who carried out this study? May it be read, discussed and commented on. May it prompt renewed examination of international humanitarian law and of the means of bringing about greater compliance and of developing the law. Perhaps it could even help go beyond the subject of war and spur us to think about the value of the principles on which the law is based in order to build universal peace – the utopian imperative – in the century on which we have now embarked.

The study on customary international humanitarian law is more than the record of a worthy project – it is above all a challenge for the future.

ACKNOWLEDGEMENTS

The realisation of this study would not have been possible without the hard work and commitment of many. Persons from all corners of the globe and with different areas of expertise contributed to the study in the form of research, drafting, reviewing, fact-checking, editing, proofreading and expert advice. We are profoundly grateful to all of them for their dedication, support and assistance. While we have attempted to list each person individually, we are conscious there are also many unnamed persons who have helped in the accomplishment of this work. To all of them, we would also like to express our sincere gratitude and apologise in advance for any inadvertent omissions.

National Research Teams

The reports on State practice were prepared by the following teams:

Algeria: Professor Ahmed Laraba

Angola: Professor Maurice Kamto, with the assistance of Albert Hilaire Anoubon Momo and André Ndomikolayi

Argentina: Professor Raúl Emilio Vinuesa, with the assistance of Silvina Sandra Gonzalez Napolitano and Marta María Pastor

Australia: Professor Timothy McCormack, with the assistance of Gideon Boas, Malcolm Langford, Colin Andrew Hatcher, Virginia Newell and Shahyar Rousha

Belgium: Professor Eric David, with the assistance of Isabelle Kuntziger, Garlone Egels and Robert Remacle
   The financial contribution of the Belgian Red Cross is gratefully acknowledged.

Bosnia and Herzegovina: Colonel Mugo Geć (Federation of Bosnia and Herzegovina) and Professor Liljana Mijović, with the assistance of Nedeljko Milijević (Republika Srpska)

Botswana: Professor Oagile Key Dingake

Brazil: Professor Antônio Augusto Cançado Trindade

Canada: Professor Katia Boustany (deceased), with the assistance of Maria Molina

Chile: Professor Hernán Salinas Burgos, with the assistance of Daniela Kravetz

China: Professor Tieya Wang (deceased), with the assistance of Professor Yong Zhang

Colombia: Fabricio López Sacconi, with the assistance of Raúl Hernández, Magaly Ramos, Sonia Torres and Mauricio Reyes

Croatia: Professor Maja Seršić, with the assistance of Professor Ksenija Turković, Davorin Lapas and Ivica Kinder

Cuba: Doctora María de los Angeles de Varona Hernández

Egypt: Professor Ahmed Abou El Wafa

El Salvador: Professor Antônio Augusto Cançado Trindade, with the assistance of Cristina Zeledon

Ethiopia: Professor Andreas Eshete, with the assistance of Alemu Brook

France: Professor Paul Tavernier, with the assistance of Eloi Fillion, Claire Servoin, Karine Mollard-Bannelier, Davide Ferrarini, Dr. Béatrice Maurer, Karine Christakis, Isabelle Capette, François Darribehaude, Sonia Parayre and Marianne Saracco

Germany: Professor Horst Fischer, with the assistance of Dr. Gregor Schotten and Dr. Heike Spieker

India: Professor Nripendra Lal Mitra, with the assistance of Dr. Umesh Veeresh Kadam (research coordinator), Dr. M. K. Nawaz, Dr. S. V. Joga Rao, Dr. V. Vijaya Kumar, M. K. Balachandran, T. S. Matilal and Rekha Chaturvedi

Indonesia: Professor G. P. H. Haryomataram, with the assistance of Fadillah Agus, Kushartoyo Budisantoso, Arlina Permanasari, Andrey Sujatmoko and Aji Wibowo

Iran: Professor Djamchid Momtaz, with the assistance of Farah Rahmani

Iraq: Professor Mohammed Abdallah Ad-Douri, with the assistance of Dr. Janan Sukker

Israel: Professor Yoram Dinstein, with the assistance of Dr. Fania Domb

Italy: Professor Gabriella Venturini, Professor Paolo Benvenuti, with the assistance of Dr. Enrico Casalini and Dr. Marco Graziani

Japan: Professor Hisakazu Fujita, with the assistance of Professor Akira Mayama, Yukiko Takashiba and Hiromi Yoshino

Jordan: Professor Mohamed Yousef Olwan, with the assistance of Lieutenant-Colonel Muhannad Hijazi and Dr. Ghazi Ar-Rashdan

Korea (Republic of): Professor Jae-Ho Sung, with the assistance of Dr. Min-Hyo Lee

Kuwait: Professor Eisa Al-Enezi

Lebanon: Professor Hassan Kassem Jouni, with the assistance of George Khalil Saad and Abdelrahman Makki

Malaysia: Professor Nurhalida binti Mohamed Khalil, with the assistance of Zalina binti Abdul Halim

Netherlands: Anna Nuiten, under the supervision of Dr. Gerard Tanja, Professor Frits Kalshoven, Hans Boddens Hosang, Katrien Coppens, Dr. Liesbeth Lijnzaad and Hanneke van Sambeek

The financial contribution of the T. M. C. Asser Institute is gratefully acknowledged.

Nicaragua: Professor Antônio Augusto Cançado Trindade, with the assistance of Cristina Zeledon

Nigeria: Professor Amechi Uchegbu, with the assistance of Dr. B. O. Okere and Muhammed T. Ladan, Esq.

Pakistan: Ahmar Bilal Soofi, Esq.

Peru: Professor Raúl Emilio Vinuesa, with the assistance of Silvina Sandra Gonzalez Napolitano, Marta María Pastor and Yesenia J. Cabezas Anicama

Philippines: Professor Alberto T. Muyot, with the assistance of Joel P. Raquedan and Vincent Pepito F. Yambao, Jr.

Russian Federation: Professor Igor Pavlovitch Blishchenko (deceased), with the assistance of Professor Aslan Abashidze

Rwanda: Professor Félicité Karomba, with the assistance of Straton Nsengiyumva

South Africa: Professor Michael Cowling

Spain: Dr. José Luis Rodríguez-Villasante y Prieto, with the assistance of Manuel Fernández Gómez, Professor Dr. Julio Jorge Urbina, Juan Manuel García Labajo, Juan Carlos González Barral, Vicente Otero Solana, Dr. Gonzalo Jar Couselo, David Suárez Leoz, Dr. Francisco Alonso Pérez, Sonia Hernández Prada, Professor Dr. Manuel Pérez González, Fernando Pignatelli Meca, Javier Guisández Gómez and Federico Bordas

Syria: Professor Muhammad Aziz Shukri, with the assistance of Dr. Amal Yaziji and Maan Mahasen

United Kingdom: Professor Françoise Hampson, with the assistance of Dr. Jenny Kuper.

The financial contributions of the British Red Cross and the Foreign and Commonwealth Office are gratefully acknowledged.

United States of America: Burrus M. Carnahan, with the assistance of Michael H. Hoffman and Professor Theodor Meron

Uruguay: Professor Raúl Emilio Vinuesa, with the assistance of Silvina Sandra Gonzalez Napolitano and Marta Maria Pastor

Yugoslavia: Professor Milan Šahović, with the assistance of Dejan Šahović, Dr. Miodrag Starčević and Dr. Bosko Jakovljević

Zimbabwe: Professor Joel Zowa, with the assistance of Dr. Lovemore Madhuku

International Research Teams

The international research teams collected practice from international sources, consolidated their research with those of the national research teams and prepared the first draft of the study. The researchers are Richard Desgagné, Camille Giffard, Gustaf Lind, Gregor Schotten, Heike Spieker and Jean-François Quéguiner.

These researchers worked under the supervision of the Rapporteurs who presented a first assessment of customary international humanitarian law at the meetings of the Steering Committee and a second assessment during the consultations with academic and governmental experts. The Rapporteurs are Professors Georges Abi-Saab, Ove Bring, Eric David, Horst Fischer, Françoise Hampson and Theodor Meron.

The financial contributions of the British and Swedish Red Cross Societies and of the Swedish Ministry of Foreign Affairs towards the work of Professors Hampson and Bring respectively are gratefully acknowledged.

Steering Committee

The study was carried out under the guidance and with the advice of the Steering Committee, whose members are Professors Georges Abi-Saab, Salah El-Din Amer, Ove Bring, Eric David, John Dugard, Florentino Feliciano, Horst Fischer, Françoise Hampson, Theodor Meron, Djamchid Momtaz, Milan Šahović and Raúl Emilio Vinuesa.

Academic and Governmental Experts

The experts invited to comment on the first assessment provided by the international research teams are Abdallah Ad-Douri, Paul Berman, Sadi Çaycý, Michael Cowling, Edward Cummings, Antonio de Icaza, Yoram Dinstein, Jean-Michel Favre, William Fenrick, Dieter Fleck, Juan Carlos Gómez Ramírez, Jamshed A. Hamid, Arturo Hernández-Basave, Ibrahim Idriss, Hassan Kassem Jouni, Kenneth Keith, Githu Muigai, Rein Müllerson, Bara Niang, Mohamed Olwan, Raul C. Pangalangan, Stelios Perrakis, Paulo Sergio Pinheiro, Arpád Prandler, Pemmaraju Sreenivasa Rao, Camilo Reyes Rodríguez, Itse E. Sagay, Harold Sandoval, Somboon Sangianbut, Marat A. Sarsembayev, Muhammad Aziz Shukri, Parlaungan Sihombing, Geoffrey James Skillen, Guoshun Sun, Bakhtyar Tuzmukhamedov and Karol Wolfke.

ICRC Research Team

Numerous persons at the ICRC have worked on the study doing research, checking information and providing editorial assistance, in particular for Volume II. Etienne Antheunissens and Tudor Hera carried out research into the ICRC archives. Carolin Alvermann, Sarah Avrillaud, Gilles Benedick, Joanna Bourke-Martignioni, Angela Cotroneo, Eloi Fillion, Emanuela-Chiara Gillard, Neal Gilmore, Antoine Grand, Valérie Houetz, David Kootz, Carine Nassif, Anna Nuiten, Aurélie Legrand, François Moreillon, Stéphane Ojeda, Guilhem Ravier, Baptiste Rolle, Ion Smochina, Nadine Thwaites, Huyghen van den Eertwegh and Barbara Van der Beken contributed to the final version of

Volume II during different stages of the long writing process. In so doing, they benefited from the assistance of Laila Bahaa-el-Din, Namuezi Fedi, Tristan Ferraro, Marie-Eve Friedrich, Francisco-Javier Leon-Diaz and Nathalie Stadelmann and from numerous ICRC staff members in the field who provided additional information on national legislation and case-law. Jérémie Labbe Grenier, Yasmine Hadjoudj, Haleh Mehran and Tobias Schaffner completed the final arduous task of checking the footnotes of Volume I. All these people amply deserve a heartfelt "thank you".

Research would not have been possible without the assistance of Monica Cometti, Magalie Develon, Florence Gaspar, Brigitte Gremaud and Jean Perrenoud at the ICRC Information and Documentation Center, as well as all the staff at the UN Library in Geneva, in particular Werner Simon, and Jan Hladík at UNESCO Headquarters in Paris.

In addition, we would like to thank Patricia Barbey, Lydie Beguelin, Vojislava Bursac, Renée Bretton, Séverine Mueller-Moine, Christine Pellaton, Janine Rossier, Elodie Straub, Sandrine Wagner and Nina Zufferey for providing indispensable administrative support.

We are also very grateful to all our colleagues, and former colleagues, at the ICRC who so generously gave of their time to review the drafts of Volume I and who provided many insightful comments, including Raoul Bittel, Serge Bourgeois, Laurent Colassis, Isabelle Daoust, Richard Desgagné, Annemarie Dick, Knut Dörmann, María Teresa Dutli, Alexandre Faite, Emanuela-Chiara Gillard, Thomas Graditzky, Paul Hardy, Peter Herby, Rikke Ishøy, Bertrand Levrat, Charlotte Lindsey-Curtet, Barbara Jaeggi, Isabelle Kuntziger, Jean-Philippe Lavoyer, Kathleen Lawand, Dominique Loye, Louis Maresca, Nils Melzer, Laura Olson, Jelena Pejic, Cristina Pellandini, Gabor Rona, Anne Ryniker, Silvia Schaller, Anna Segall, Philip Spoerri, Sylvie van Lammeren and Ameur Zemmali.

A very special word of thanks is due to Knut Dörmann, Emanuela-Chiara Gillard, Laura Olson, Gabor Rona and Jelena Pejic who read and commented on all the drafts and provided invaluable support throughout the writing process.

We owe a special debt of gratitude for the advice and constructive criticism from Maurice Mendelson and Karol Wolfke, who reviewed the introductory part on the assessment of customary international law, and from Sadi Çaycý, Edward Cummings, Eric David, Yoram Dinstein, William Fenrick, Dieter Fleck, Juan Carlos Gómez Ramírez, Michael Meyer, Theodor Meron, Raul Pangalangan, Peter Rowe, Milan Šahović, Marat Sarsembaev, Helen Upton, Elizabeth Wilmshurst and Karol Wolfke for their comments on different drafts of Volume I and Jan Hladík at UNESCO for reviewing the draft chapter on cultural property.

Special thanks are also due to Knut Dörmann, Horst Fischer, Theodor Meron, the Mines and Arms Unit of the ICRC led by Peter Herby, William Fenrick and Antonio Cassese for reviewing Parts I–VI of Volumes I and II respectively.

The authors express their genuine appreciation to François Bugnion, Jean-Philippe Lavoyer and Yves Sandoz for their advice, comments and support throughout the genesis of this study.

Lastly our sincere gratitude goes to Christina Grisewood for the monumental task of copy-editing both Volumes I and II, to Philippa Youngman, who prepared the copy for typesetting, and the staff at Cambridge University Press, in particular Finola O'Sullivan for supervising publication and Neil de Cort and Alison Powell for overseeing the production.

This study would not have been possible without the patience, support and encouragement of Mei and Josef.

Geneva, August 2004

Jean-Marie Henckaerts
Louise Doswald-Beck

INTRODUCTION

International humanitarian law has its origins in the customary practices of armies as they developed over the ages and on all continents. The "laws and customs of war", as this branch of international law has traditionally been called, was not applied by all armies, and not necessarily vis-à-vis all enemies, nor were all the rules the same. However, the pattern that could typically be found was restraint of behaviour vis-à-vis combatants and civilians, primarily based on the concept of the soldier's honour. The content of the rules generally included the prohibition of behaviour that was considered unnecessarily cruel or dishonourable, and was not only developed by the armies themselves, but was also influenced by the writings of religious leaders.

The most significant landmark from the point of view of cataloguing these customs in one document was the drafting by Professor Francis Lieber of the Instructions for the Government of Armies of the United States in the Field, promulgated as General Order No. 100 by President Lincoln in 1863 during the American Civil War. The Lieber Code, as it is now known, strongly influenced the further codification of the laws and customs of war and the adoption of similar regulations by other States. Together, they formed the basis of the draft of an international convention on the laws and customs of war presented to the Brussels Conference in 1874. Although this conference did not adopt a binding treaty, much of its work was later used in the development of the 1899 and 1907 Hague Conventions and Declarations. These treaties did not codify all aspects of custom, but its continued importance was reaffirmed in the so-called "Martens clause", first inserted in the preamble to the 1899 Hague Convention (II), which provides that:

Until a more complete code of the laws of war is issued, the High Contracting Parties think it right to declare that in cases not included in the Regulations adopted by them, populations and belligerents remain under the protection and empire of the principles of international law, as they result from the usages established between civilized nations, from the laws of humanity and the requirements of the public conscience.

The importance attributed to customary law, despite, or because of, its partial codification, was most clearly seen in the reliance placed on it by the various war crimes trials after both the First and Second World Wars.[1]

---

[1] See Knut Dörmann, *Elements of War Crimes under the Rome Statute of the International Criminal Court: Sources and Commentary*, Cambridge University Press, 2003.

The driving force behind the development of international humanitarian law has been the International Committee of the Red Cross (ICRC), founded in 1863. It initiated the process which led to the conclusion of the Geneva Conventions for the protection of the victims of war of 1864, 1906, 1929 and 1949. It was at the origin of the 1899 Hague Convention (III) and 1907 Hague Convention (X), which adapted, respectively, the 1864 and 1906 Geneva Conventions to maritime warfare and were the precursors of the Geneva Convention for the Amelioration of the Condition of the Wounded, Sick and Shipwrecked Members of Armed Forces at Sea of 1949. It took the initiative to supplement the Geneva Conventions that led to the adoption in 1977 of two Additional Protocols. The ICRC has both encouraged the development of and been involved in the negotiation of numerous other treaties, such as the 1980 Convention on Certain Conventional Weapons, the 1997 Ottawa Convention banning anti-personnel landmines and the 1998 Statute of the International Criminal Court. Recognition of this role is reflected in the mandate given to the ICRC by the international community to work for "the faithful application of international humanitarian law applicable in armed conflicts" and for "the understanding and dissemination of knowledge of international humanitarian law applicable in armed conflicts and to prepare any development thereof".[2]

More than 50 years have now passed since the Geneva Conventions of 1949 were adopted and almost 30 years since the adoption of their Additional Protocols. These years have, unfortunately, been marked by a proliferation of armed conflicts affecting every continent. Throughout these conflicts, the Geneva Conventions – and in particular Article 3 common to the four Conventions, applicable in non-international armed conflicts – together with their Additional Protocols have provided legal protection to war victims, namely persons who do not or no longer participate in hostilities (the wounded, sick and shipwrecked, persons deprived of their liberty for reasons related to the conflict, and civilians). Nevertheless, there have been countless violations of these treaties and of basic humanitarian principles, resulting in suffering and

---

[2] Statutes of the International Red Cross and Red Crescent Movement, adopted by the 25th International Conference of the Red Cross, Geneva, 23–31 October 1986, Article 5(2)(c) and (g) respectively. The Statutes were adopted by the States party to the Geneva Conventions and the members of the International Red Cross and Red Crescent Movement. This mandate was first given to the ICRC by Article 7 of the Statutes of the International Red Cross adopted by the 13th International Conference of the Red Cross, The Hague, 23–27 October 1928, according to which "all complaints in regard to alleged violations of the international Conventions, and in general, all questions calling for examination by a specifically neutral body, shall remain the exclusive province of the International Committee of the Red Cross". Subsequently, Article 6(4) and (7) of the Statutes of the International Red Cross adopted by the 18th International Conference of the Red Cross, Toronto, 22 July–8 August 1952, stated that the ICRC "undertakes the tasks incumbent on it under the Geneva Conventions, works for the faithful application of these Conventions and takes cognizance of complaints regarding alleged breaches of the humanitarian Conventions" and "works for the continual improvement and diffusion of the Geneva Conventions".

death which might have been avoided had international humanitarian law been respected.

The general opinion is that violations of international humanitarian law are not due to the inadequacy of its rules, but rather to a lack of willingness to respect them, to a lack of means to enforce them and to uncertainty as to their application in some circumstances, but also to ignorance of the rules on the part of political leaders, commanders, combatants and the general public.

The International Conference for the Protection of War Victims, convened in Geneva from 30 August to 1 September 1993, discussed, in particular, ways and means to address violations of international humanitarian law but did not propose the adoption of new treaty provisions. Instead, in its Final Declaration, adopted by consensus, the Conference reaffirmed "the necessity to make the implementation of humanitarian law more effective" and called upon the Swiss government "to convene an open-ended intergovernmental group of experts to study practical means of promoting full respect for and compliance with that law, and to prepare a report for submission to the States and to the next session of the International Conference of the Red Cross and Red Crescent".[3]

To this end, the Intergovernmental Group of Experts for the Protection of War Victims met in Geneva in January 1995 and adopted a series of recommendations aimed at enhancing respect for international humanitarian law, in particular by means of preventive measures that would ensure better knowledge and more effective implementation of the law. Recommendation II of the Intergovernmental Group of Experts proposed that:

The ICRC be invited to prepare, with the assistance of experts in IHL [international humanitarian law] representing various geographical regions and different legal systems, and in consultation with experts from governments and international organisations, a report on customary rules of IHL applicable in international and non-international armed conflicts, and to circulate the report to States and competent international bodies.[4]

In December 1995, the 26th International Conference of the Red Cross and Red Crescent endorsed this recommendation and officially mandated the ICRC to prepare a report on customary rules of international humanitarian law applicable in international and non-international armed conflicts.[5] The present study is the outcome of the research carried out pursuant to this mandate.

---

[3] International Conference for the Protection of War Victims, Geneva, 30 August–1 September 1993, Final Declaration, *International Review of the Red Cross*, No. 296, 1993, p. 381.

[4] Meeting of the Intergovernmental Group of Experts for the Protection of War Victims, Geneva, 23–27 January 1995, Recommendation II, *International Review of the Red Cross*, No. 310, 1996, p. 84.

[5] 26th International Conference of the Red Cross and Red Crescent, Geneva, 3–7 December 1995, Resolution 1, International humanitarian law: From law to action; Report on the follow-up to the International Conference for the Protection of War Victims, *International Review of the Red Cross*, No. 310, 1996, p. 58.

Purpose of the study

International humanitarian treaty law is well developed and covers a wide variety of aspects of warfare, offering protection to victims of war and limiting permissible means and methods of warfare. The four Geneva Conventions of 1949 and their Additional Protocols of 1977 provide an extensive regime for the protection of persons who do not or no longer participate in armed conflict. The regulation of the means and methods of warfare in treaty law goes back to the 1868 St. Petersburg Declaration, the 1899 and 1907 Hague Conventions and the 1925 Geneva Gas Protocol and has most recently been addressed in the 1972 Biological Weapons Convention, the 1977 Additional Protocols, the 1980 Convention on Certain Conventional Weapons and its five Protocols, the 1993 Chemical Weapons Convention and the 1997 Ottawa Convention banning anti-personnel landmines. The protection of cultural property in the event of armed conflict is regulated in detail in the 1954 Hague Convention and its two Protocols. The 1998 Statute of the International Criminal Court contains a list of war crimes subject to its jurisdiction.

There are, however, two important impediments to applying these treaties to current armed conflicts. First, treaties apply only to the States that have ratified them. This means that different treaties of international humanitarian law apply to different armed conflicts depending on which treaties the States involved have ratified. While nearly all States have ratified the four Geneva Conventions of 1949, Additional Protocol I has not yet gained universal adherence. As the Protocol is applicable only between parties to a conflict that have ratified it, its efficacy today is limited because several States that have been involved in international armed conflicts are not a party to it. Similarly, Additional Protocol II is only applicable in armed conflicts taking place on the territory of a State that has ratified it. While some 150 States have ratified this Protocol, several States in which non-international armed conflicts are taking place have not. In these non-international armed conflicts, common Article 3 of the four Geneva Conventions often remains the only applicable treaty provision.

Secondly, this wealth of treaty law does not regulate a large proportion of today's armed conflicts in sufficient detail. The primary reason for this is that the majority of current armed conflicts are non-international, which are subject to far fewer treaty rules than international conflicts, although their number is increasing. In fact, only a limited number of treaties apply to non-international armed conflicts, namely the Convention on Certain Conventional Weapons, as amended, the Statute of the International Criminal Court, the Ottawa Convention banning anti-personnel landmines, the Chemical Weapons Convention, the Hague Convention for the Protection of Cultural Property and its Second Protocol and, as already mentioned, Additional Protocol II and Article 3 common to the four Geneva Conventions. While common Article 3 is of fundamental importance, it only provides a rudimentary framework of minimum standards and does not contain much detail. Additional Protocol II usefully supplements common Article 3, but it is still less detailed than the rules governing international armed conflicts contained in Additional Protocol I.

Additional Protocol II contains a mere 15 substantive articles, whereas Additional Protocol I has more than 80. These figures may not be all important, but they nonetheless show that there is a significant difference in terms of regulation between international and non-international armed conflicts, with the latter suffering from a lack of rules, definitions, details and requirements in treaty law. This is the prevailing situation, even though the majority of armed conflicts today are non-international.

Specifically, Additional Protocol II contains only a very rudimentary regulation of the conduct of hostilities. Article 13 provides that "the civilian population as such, as well as individual civilians, shall not be the object of attack . . . unless and for such time as they take a direct part in hostilities". Unlike Additional Protocol I, Additional Protocol II does not contain, however, specific rules and definitions with respect to the principles of distinction and proportionality.

Common sense would suggest that such rules, and the limits they impose on the way war is waged, should be equally applicable in international and non-international armed conflicts. The fact that in 2001 the Convention on Certain Conventional Weapons was amended to extend its scope to non-international armed conflicts is an indication that this notion is gaining currency within the international community.

This study provides evidence that many rules of customary international law apply in both international and non-international armed conflicts and shows the extent to which State practice has gone beyond existing treaty law and expanded the rules applicable to non-international armed conflicts. In particular, the gaps in the regulation of the conduct of hostilities in Additional Protocol II have largely been filled through State practice, which has led to the creation of rules parallel to those in Additional Protocol I, but applicable as customary law to non-international armed conflicts.

Knowledge of the rules of customary international law is therefore of use to the many actors involved in the application, dissemination and enforcement of international humanitarian law, such as governmental authorities, arms bearers, international organisations, components of the International Red Cross and Red Crescent Movement and non-governmental organisations. A study on customary international humanitarian law may also be helpful in reducing the uncertainties and the scope for argument inherent in the concept of customary international law.

Knowledge of the rules of customary international law may also be of service in a number of situations where reliance on customary international law is required. This is especially relevant for the work of courts and international organisations. Indeed, courts are frequently required to apply customary international law. This is the case, for example, for the International Criminal Tribunal for the Former Yugoslavia which, pursuant to Article 3 of its Statute, has jurisdiction over violations of the laws and customs of war. As a result, the Tribunal has had to determine whether certain violations of international humanitarian law were violations under customary international law over which the Tribunal has jurisdiction. In addition, in many countries, customary international law is a source of domestic law and can be invoked before and adjudicated by national courts. Customary international law is also relevant to the work of international organisations in that it generally represents the law binding upon all member States.

Scope of the study

This study has not sought to determine the customary nature of each treaty rule of international humanitarian law and, as a result, does not necessarily follow the structure of existing treaties. Rather, it has sought to analyse issues in order to establish what rules of customary international law can be found inductively on the basis of State practice in relation to these issues. As the approach chosen does not analyse each treaty provision with a view to establishing whether or not it is customary, it cannot be concluded that any particular treaty rule is *not* customary merely because it does not appear as such in this study. In this regard, it is important to note that the great majority of the provisions of the Geneva Conventions of 1949, including common Article 3, are considered to be customary law, and the same is true for the 1907 Hague Regulations (see *infra*). Furthermore, given that the Geneva Conventions have now been ratified by 192 States, they are binding on nearly all States as a matter of treaty law.

It was decided not to research customary law applicable to naval warfare as this area of law was recently the subject of a major restatement, namely the San Remo Manual on Naval Warfare.[6] The general rules contained in the manual were nevertheless considered useful for the assessment of the customary nature of rules that apply to all types of warfare.

A number of topics could not be developed in sufficient detail for inclusion in this edition, but they might be included in a future update. These include, for example, the Martens clause, identification of specifically protected persons and objects, and civil defence.

Where relevant, practice under international human rights law has been included in the study. This was done because international human rights law

---

[6] Louise Doswald-Beck (ed.), *San Remo Manual on International Law Applicable to Armed Conflicts at Sea*, Prepared by international lawyers and naval experts convened by the International Institute of Humanitarian Law, Cambridge University Press, 1995.

continues to apply during armed conflicts, as indicated by the express terms of the human rights treaties themselves, although some provisions may, subject to certain conditions, be derogated from in time of public emergency. The continued applicability of human rights law during armed conflict has been confirmed on numerous occasions by the treaty bodies that have analysed State behaviour, including during armed conflict, and by the International Court of Justice (see introduction to Chapter 32). This study does not purport, however, to provide an assessment of customary human rights law. Instead, human rights law has been included in order to support, strengthen and clarify analogous principles of international humanitarian law. In addition, while they remain separate branches of international law, human rights law and international humanitarian law have directly influenced each other, and continue to do so, and this for mainly three reasons. First, an assessment of conformity with human rights law at times involves a determination of respect for or breach of international humanitarian law. For example, measures taken in states of emergency will be unlawful under human rights law if, *inter alia*, they violate international humanitarian law.[7] Conversely, international humanitarian law contains concepts the interpretation of which needs to include a reference to human rights law, for example, the provision that no one may be convicted of a crime other than by a "regularly constituted court affording all the judicial guarantees which are recognised as indispensable".[8] Secondly, human rights-type provisions are to be found in international humanitarian law, for example, Article 75 of Additional Protocol I and Articles 4 and 6 of Additional Protocol II, and humanitarian law-type provisions are to be found in human rights law, for example, the provisions on child soldiers in the Convention on the Rights of the Child and its Protocol on the Involvement of Children in Armed Conflict. Thirdly, and most significantly, there is extensive practice by States and by international organisations commenting on the behaviour of States during armed conflict in the light of human rights law.[9]

Assessment of customary international law

The Statute of the International Court of Justice describes customary international law as "a general practice accepted as law".[10] It is generally agreed that

---

[7] Article 4 of the International Covenant on Civil and Political Rights, Article 15 of the European Convention on Human Rights and Article 27 of the American Convention on Human Rights all state that derogation measures by States must not be "inconsistent with their other obligations under international law". The African Charter on Human and Peoples' Rights does not allow for derogation.

[8] Common Article 3(1)(d) of the Geneva Conventions of 1949.

[9] See, in particular, Chapter 32 on Fundamental Guarantees.

[10] ICJ Statute, Article 38(1)(b).

the existence of a rule of customary international law requires the presence of two elements, namely State practice (*usus*) and a belief that such practice is required, prohibited or allowed, depending on the nature of the rule, as a matter of law (*opinio juris sive necessitatis*). As the International Court of Justice stated in the *Continental Shelf case*: "It is of course axiomatic that the material of customary international law is to be looked for primarily in the actual practice and *opinio juris* of States."[11] The exact meaning and content of these two elements has been the subject of much academic writing. The approach taken in this study to determine whether a rule of general customary international law exists is a classic one, set out by the International Court of Justice in a number of cases, in particular in the *North Sea Continental Shelf cases*.[12]

State practice

In the assessment of State practice, two separate issues need to be addressed, namely the selection of practice that contributes to the creation of customary international law and the assessment of whether this practice establishes a rule of customary international law.

Selection of State practice

The practice collected for the purpose of this study, and which is summarised in Volume II, was selected on the basis of the following criteria.

(i) Both physical and verbal acts of States constitute practice that contributes to the creation of customary international law. Physical acts include, for example, battlefield behaviour, the use of certain weapons and the treatment provided to different categories of persons. Verbal acts include military manuals, national legislation, national case-law, instructions to armed and security forces, military communiqués during war, diplomatic protests, opinions of official legal advisers, comments by governments on draft treaties, executive decisions and regulations, pleadings before international tribunals, statements in international organisations and at international conferences and government positions taken with respect to resolutions of international organisations.

The approach to consider both physical and verbal acts as practice follows that taken by leading bodies in the field of international law and by States themselves. The International Court of Justice has taken into consideration official statements as State practice in a number of cases, including the *Fisheries*

---

[11] ICJ, *Continental Shelf case (Libyan Arab Jamahiriya v. Malta)*, Judgement, 3 June 1985, *ICJ Reports 1985*, pp. 29–30, § 27.
[12] ICJ, *North Sea Continental Shelf cases*, Judgement, 20 February 1969, *ICJ Reports 1969*, p. 3.

Jurisdiction cases,[13] the *Nicaragua case*,[14] and the *Gabčíkovo-Nagymaros Project case*.[15]

The International Law Commission has similarly considered verbal acts of States as contributing towards the creation of customary international law. It did so, for example, in the context of the Draft Articles on State Responsibility where it considered the concept of a "state of necessity" to be customary.[16]

The International Criminal Tribunal for the Former Yugoslavia has stated that in appraising the formation of customary rules of international human-itarian law, "reliance must primarily be placed on such elements as official pronouncements of States, military manuals and judicial decisions".[17]

The International Law Association considers that "verbal acts, and not only physical acts, of States count as State practice" and points out that "the practice of the international tribunals is replete with examples of verbal acts being treated as examples of practice. Similarly, States regularly treat this sort of act in the same way."[18]

Whether physical or verbal, relevant practice only consists of *official* practice. Hence, the physical acts of parties to armed conflicts contribute only to the

---

[13] ICJ, *Fisheries Jurisdiction case (United Kingdom v. Iceland)*, Joint separate opinion of Judges Forster, Bengzon, Jiménez de Aréchaga, Singh and Ruda, 25 July 1974, *ICJ Reports 1974*, p. 47; Separate opinion of Judge Dillard, 25 July 1974, *ICJ Reports 1974*, pp. 56–58; Separate opinion of Judge De Castro, 25 July 1974, *ICJ Reports 1974*, pp. 81–88; Separate opinion of Judge Waldock, 25 July 1974, *ICJ Reports 1974*, pp. 119–120; Dissenting opinion of Judge Gros, 25 July 1974, *ICJ Reports 1974*, p. 135; Dissenting opinion of Judge Petrén, 25 July 1974, *ICJ Reports 1974*, p. 161. The judges inferred the existence of customary rules from claims made to areas of the sea, without considering whether they had been enforced; see also the opinions of the same judges in the *Fisheries Jurisdiction case (Federal Republic of Germany v. Iceland)*, 25 July 1974, *ICJ Reports 1974*, p. 175.

[14] ICJ, *Case concerning Military and Paramilitary Activities in and against Nicaragua (Nicaragua v. United States)*, Merits, Judgement, 27 June 1986, *ICJ Reports 1986*, p. 100, § 190. The Court found further confirmation of the validity as customary international law of the principle of the prohibition of the use of force expressed in Article 2(4) of the UN Charter in the fact that it was "frequently referred to in statements by State representatives as being not only a principle of customary international law but also a fundamental or cardinal principle of such law".

[15] ICJ, *Case concerning the Gabčíkovo-Nagymaros Project (Hungary v. Slovakia)*, Judgement, 25 September 1997, *ICJ Reports 1997*, pp. 39–46, §§ 49–58. The Court declared the customary nature of the concept of a "state of necessity", which could preclude the wrongfulness of an act not in conformity with international law. In so doing, the Court relied on materials, including many official statements, used by the ILC in drafting the corresponding article of the Draft Articles on State Responsibility.

[16] ILC, Draft Articles on State Responsibility, *Yearbook of the ILC*, 1980, Vol. II, Part 2, UN Doc. A/CN.4/SER.A/1980/Add.1 (Part 2), 1980, pp. 34–52. The ILC based its conclusions on statements of government representatives or lawyers. For another example, see *Yearbook of the ILC*, 1950, Vol. II, pp. 368–372. The Commission referred to the following categories of evidence of customary international law: international instruments, decisions of national and international courts and national legislation, as well as to diplomatic correspondence, opinions of national legal advisers and the practice of international organisations.

[17] ICTY, *Tadić case*, Case No. IT-94-AR72, Decision on the defence motion for interlocutory appeal on jurisdiction, 2 October 1995, § 99.

[18] ILA, Final Report of the Committee on the Formation of Customary (General) International Law, Statement of Principles Applicable to the Formation of General Customary International Law, Report of the Sixty-Ninth Conference, London, 2000, Principle 4 and commentary (a) thereto, pp. 725–726 (hereinafter "ILA Report").

creation of rules of customary international law as long as they represent official practice.

Abstention from certain conduct is also noted where relevant. Such omissions will be discussed in more detail below.

(ii) The practice of the executive, legislative and judicial organs of a State can contribute to the formation of customary international law. The State comprises the executive, legislative and judicial branches of government. The organs of these branches can engage the international responsibility of the State and adopt positions that affect its international relations.[19] In case of conflict between the positions of various organs of a State, the practice is considered internally inconsistent and does not contribute to the formation of customary law.

(iii) Acts do not contribute to the formation of customary international law if they are never disclosed.[20] This is so as long as such acts are not known to other States and, consequently, do not give them an opportunity, if they so wished, to react to them. In order to count, practice has to be public or communicated to some extent. This does not necessarily mean that the practice has to be published or communicated to the whole world, but at least it should be communicated to one other State or relevant international organisation, including the ICRC. States communicate with the ICRC in the context of its international mandate to assist in the implementation of international humanitarian law and the fact that it may "take cognizance of any complaints based on alleged breaches of [international humanitarian law]".[21] Hence, communications to the ICRC, while often confidential, are not purely private acts and count as State practice.

(iv) Although decisions of international courts are subsidiary sources of international law,[22] they do not constitute State practice. This is because, unlike national courts, international courts are not State organs. Their decisions have nevertheless been included because a finding by an international court that a rule of customary international law exists constitutes persuasive evidence to that effect. In addition, because of the precedential value of their decisions, international courts can also contribute to the emergence of a rule of customary international law by influencing the subsequent practice of States and international organisations.

---

[19] For a more elaborate reasoning and references to international case-law on this point, see ILA Report, *supra* note 18, Principle 9, pp. 728–729, referring to PCIJ, *Nottebohm case (second phase) (Liechtenstein v. Guatemala)*, Judgement, 6 April 1955, *ICJ Reports 1955*, p. 22 and the *Lotus case (France v. Turkey)*, Judgement, 7 September 1927, PCIJ Ser. A, No. 10, pp. 23, 26 and 28–29.

[20] See, e.g., ILA Report, *supra* note 18, Principle 5, p. 726.

[21] Statutes of the International Red Cross and Red Crescent Movement, *supra* note 2, Article 5(2)(c).

[22] ICJ Statute, Article 38(1)(d).

What States claim before international courts, however, is clearly a form of State practice.

(v) International organisations have international legal personality and can participate in international relations in their own capacity, independently of their member States. In this respect, their practice can contribute to the formation of customary international law.[23] Therefore, this study has included, for example, the UN Secretary-General's Bulletin on observance by United Nations forces of international humanitarian law as relevant practice, in particular because "the instructions in the Bulletin reflect the quintessential and most fundamental principles of the laws and customs of war", even though it is recognised that "the Secretary-General did not consider himself necessarily constrained by the customary international law provisions of the Conventions and Protocols as the lowest common denominator by which all national contingents would otherwise be bound".[24]

In addition, official ICRC statements, in particular appeals and memoranda on respect for international humanitarian law, have been included as relevant practice because the ICRC has international legal personality.[25] The practice of the organisation is particularly relevant in that it has received an official mandate from States "to work for the faithful application of international humanitarian law applicable in armed conflicts and . . . to prepare any development thereof".[26] The view that ICRC practice counts is also adopted by the International Criminal Tribunal for the Former Yugoslavia, which has regarded the organisation's practice as an important factor in the emergence of customary rules applicable to non-international armed conflicts.[27] In addition, the official reactions which ICRC statements elicit are State practice.

(vi) The negotiation and adoption of resolutions by international organisations or conferences, together with the explanations of vote, are acts of the States involved. With a few exceptions, it is recognised that resolutions are normally not binding in themselves and therefore the value accorded to any particular resolution depends on its content, its degree of acceptance and the

---

[23] See, e.g., ICJ, *Case concerning Reservations to the Convention on Genocide*, Advisory Opinion, 28 May 1951, *ICJ Reports 1951*, p. 25. The Court took into account the depository practice of the UN Secretary-General.

[24] Daphna Shraga, "UN Peacekeeping Operations: Applicability of International Humanitarian Law and Responsibility for Operations-Related Damage", *American Journal of International Law*, Vol. 94, 2000, p. 408.

[25] See, e.g., ICTY, *The Prosecutor v. Blagoje Simić et al.*, Case No. IT-95-9-PT, Decision on the prosecution motion under Rule 73 for a ruling concerning the testimony of a witness, 27 July 1999, released as a public document by Order of 1 October 1999, § 46 and footnote 9.

[26] Statutes of the International Red Cross and Red Crescent Movement, *supra* note 2, Article 5(2)(c) and (g).

[27] ICTY, *Tadić case*, *supra* note 17, § 109.

consistency of State practice outside it.[28] The greater the support for the resolution, the more importance it is to be accorded. Information on reasons for abstentions or negative votes is therefore indicated in this study where relevant, for such votes are often based on disagreement with certain parts of the resolution and not necessarily with the resolution as a whole. Likewise, statements made by States during debates on the drafting of resolutions constitute State practice and have been included where relevant.

(vii) The practice of armed opposition groups, such as codes of conduct, commitments made to observe certain rules of international humanitarian law and other statements, does not constitute State practice as such. While such practice may contain evidence of the acceptance of certain rules in noninternational armed conflicts, its legal significance is unclear and it has therefore been listed under "Other Practice" in Volume II.

Assessment of State practice
State practice has to be weighed to assess whether it is sufficiently "dense" to create a rule of customary international law.[29] To establish a rule of customary international law, State practice has to be virtually uniform, extensive and representative. Although some time will normally elapse before there is sufficient practice to satisfy these criteria, no precise amount of time is required. As stated by the International Court of Justice in the *North Sea Continental Shelf cases*:

Although the passage of only a short period of time is not necessarily, or of itself, a bar to the formation of a new rule of customary international law on the basis of what was originally a purely conventional rule, an indispensable requirement would be that within the period in question, short though it might be, State practice, including that of States whose interests are specially affected, should have been both extensive and virtually uniform in the sense of the provision invoked; and should moreover have occurred in such a way as to show a general recognition that a rule of law or legal obligation is involved.[30]

(i) The first requirement for State practice to create a rule of customary international law is that it must be *virtually uniform*. Different States must not have engaged in substantially different conduct, some doing one thing and some another. In the *Asylum case*, the International Court of Justice was presented with a situation in which practice was not sufficiently uniform to establish a rule of customary international law with respect to the exercise of diplomatic asylum. In this respect, it stated that:

---

[28] The importance of these conditions was stressed by the ICJ in the *Nuclear Weapons case*, Advisory Opinion, 8 July 1996, *ICJ Reports 1996*, pp. 254–255, §§ 70–73.

[29] The expression comes from Sir Humphrey Waldock, "General Course on Public International Law", *Collected Courses of the Hague Academy of International Law*, Vol. 106, 1962, p. 44.

[30] ICJ, *North Sea Continental Shelf cases, supra* note 12, p. 43, § 74.

The facts brought to the knowledge of the Court disclose so much uncertainty and contradiction, so much fluctuation and discrepancy in the exercise of diplomatic asylum and in the official views expressed on various occasions, there has been so much inconsistency in the rapid succession of conventions on asylum, ratified by some States and rejected by others, and the practice has been so much influenced by considerations of political expediency in the various cases, that it is not possible to discern in all this any constant and uniform usage, accepted as law.[31]

In the *Fisheries case*, the International Court of Justice dealt with a similar situation with respect to a ten-mile closing line for bays in which it considered that, although such a line had

been adopted by certain States both in their national law and in their treaties and conventions, and although certain arbitral decisions have applied it as between these States, other States have adopted a different limit. Consequently, the ten-mile rule has not acquired the authority of a general rule of international law.[32]

However, the Court in this case also considered that "too much importance need not be attached to a few uncertainties or contradictions, real or apparent" in a State's practice when making an evaluation.[33] It is enough that the practice is sufficiently similar. It was on the basis of such sufficient similarity that the International Court of Justice found in the *Continental Shelf cases* that the concept of the exclusive economic zone had become part of customary law. Even though the various proclamations of such a zone were not identical, they were sufficiently similar for the Court to reach this conclusion.[34]

The jurisprudence of the International Court of Justice shows that contrary practice which, at first sight, appears to undermine the uniformity of the practice concerned, does not prevent the formation of a rule of customary international law as long as this contrary practice is condemned by other States or denied by the government itself and therefore does not represent its *official* practice. Through such condemnation or denial, the original rule is actually confirmed. The International Court of Justice dealt with such a situation in the *Nicaragua case* in which it looked at the customary nature of the principles of non-use of force and non-intervention, stating that:

It is not to be expected that in the practice of States the application of the rules in question should have been perfect, in the sense that States should have refrained, with complete consistency, from the use of force or from intervention in each other's internal affairs. The Court does not consider that, for a rule to be established as customary, the corresponding practice must be in absolute rigorous conformity with

---

[31] ICJ, *Asylum case (Colombia v. Peru)*, Judgement, 20 November 1950, *ICJ Reports 1950*, p. 277.

[32] ICJ, *Fisheries case (United Kingdom v. Norway)*, Judgement, 18 December 1951, *ICJ Reports 1951*, p. 131.

[33] *Ibid.* p. 138.

[34] ICJ, *Continental Shelf case (Tunisia v. Libyan Arab Jamahiriya)*, Judgement, 24 February 1982, *ICJ Reports 1982*, p. 74, § 100 and *Continental Shelf case, supra* note 11, p. 33, § 34.

the rule. In order to deduce the existence of customary rules, the Court deems it sufficient that the conduct of States should, in general, be consistent with such rules, and that instances of State conduct inconsistent with a given rule should generally have been treated as breaches of that rule, not as indications of the recognition of a new rule. If a State acts in a way prima facie incompatible with a recognized rule, but defends its conduct by appealing to exceptions or justifications contained within the rule itself, then whether or not the State's conduct is in fact justifiable on that basis, the significance of that attitude is to confirm rather than to weaken the rule.[35]

This finding is particularly relevant for a number of rules of international humanitarian law where there is overwhelming evidence of verbal State practice supporting a certain rule found alongside repeated evidence of violations of that rule. Where this has been accompanied by excuses or justifications by the actors and/or condemnations by other States, such violations are not of a nature to challenge the existence of the rule in question. States wishing to change an existing rule of customary international law have to do so through their *official* practice and claim to be acting *as of right*.

(ii) The second requirement for a rule of general customary international law to come into existence is that the State practice concerned must be both *extensive and representative*. It does not, however, need to be universal; a "general" practice suffices.[36] No precise number or percentage of States is required. One reason why it is impossible to put a precise figure on the extent of participation required is that the criterion is in a sense *qualitative* rather than quantitative. That is to say, it is not simply a question of how many States participate in the practice, but also *which* States.[37] In the words of the International Court of Justice in the *North Sea Continental Shelf cases*, the practice must "include that of States whose interests are specially affected".[38]

This consideration has two implications: (1) if all "specially affected States" are represented, it is not essential for a majority of States to have actively participated, but they must have at least acquiesced in the practice of "specially affected States"; (2) if "specially affected States" do not accept the practice, it cannot mature into a rule of customary international law, even though unanimity is not required as explained.[39] Who is "specially affected" will vary according to circumstances. Concerning the question of the legality of the use of blinding laser weapons, for example, "specially affected States" include those identified as having been in the process of developing such weapons. In the area of humanitarian aid, States whose population is in need of such aid or States which

---

[35] ICJ, *Case concerning Military and Paramilitary Activities in and against Nicaragua, supra* note 14, p. 98, § 186.

[36] ILA Report, *supra* note 18, Principle 14, p. 734.

[37] ILA Report, *supra* note 18, commentary (d) and (e) to Principle 14, pp. 736–737.

[38] ICJ, *North Sea Continental Shelf cases, supra* note 12, p. 43, § 74.

[39] ILA Report, *supra* note 18, commentary (e) to Principle 14, p. 737.

frequently provide such aid are to be considered "specially affected". With respect to any rule of international humanitarian law, countries that participated in an armed conflict are "specially affected" when their practice examined for a certain rule was relevant to that armed conflict. Notwithstanding the fact that there are specially affected States in certain areas of international humanitarian law, it is also true that all States have a legal interest in requiring respect for international humanitarian law by other States, even if they are not a party to the conflict (see the commentary to Rule 144). As a result, the practice of all States must be considered, whether or not they are "specially affected" in the strict sense of that term.

This study has taken no view as to whether it is legally possible to be a "persistent objector" in relation to customary rules of international humanitarian law. Apart from the fact that many authorities believe that this is not possible in the case of rules of *jus cogens*, there are also authorities that doubt the continued validity of this doctrine.[40] If one accepts that it is legally possible to be a persistent objector, the State concerned must have objected to the emergence of a new norm during its formation and continue to object afterwards; it is not possible to be a "subsequent objector".

(iii) The third requirement is related to the time necessary to form a rule of customary international law through the adoption of virtually uniform, extensive and representative practice. As indicated above, while some time will normally elapse before there is sufficient practice to satisfy these criteria, there is no specific time requirement. It is all a question of accumulating a practice of sufficient density, in terms of uniformity, extent and representativeness.[41]

Opinio juris

The second requirement for the existence of a rule of customary international law, *opinio juris*, relates to the need for the practice to be carried out *as of right*. The particular form in which the practice and this legal conviction needs to be expressed may well differ depending on whether the rule involved contains a prohibition, an obligation or merely a right to behave in a certain manner.

Practice establishing the existence of a prohibition, for example, the rule that it is prohibited to declare that no quarter will be given (see Rule 46), includes not only statements that such behaviour is prohibited and condemnations of instances where the prohibited behaviour did take place, possibly combined with justifications or excuses from the criticised State, but also physical practice abstaining from the prohibited behaviour. If the practice largely consists of abstention combined with silence, there will need to be some indication

---

[40] For an in-depth discussion of this issue, see Maurice H. Mendelson, "The Formation of Customary International Law", *Collected Courses of the Hague Academy of International Law*, Vol. 272, 1998, pp. 227–244.

[41] ILA Report, *supra* note 18, commentary (b) to Principle 12, p. 731.

that the abstention is based on a legitimate expectation to that effect from the international community.

Practice establishing the existence of an obligation, for example, the rule that the wounded and sick must be cared for (see Rule 110), can be found primarily in behaviour in conformity with such a requirement. The fact that it is a legal requirement, rather than one reflecting courtesy or mere comity, can be found by either an expression of the need for such behaviour, or by criticism by other States in the absence of such behaviour. It may also be that, following criticism by other States, the criticised State will explain its abstinence by seeking justification within the rule.

Practice establishing the existence of a rule that allows a certain conduct, for example, the rule that States have the right to vest universal jurisdiction in their courts over war crimes (see Rule 157), can be found in acts that recognise the right to behave in such a way without actually requiring such behaviour. This will typically take the form of States undertaking such action, together with the absence of protests by other States.

During work on the study it proved very difficult and largely theoretical to strictly separate elements of practice and legal conviction. More often than not, one and the same act reflects practice and legal conviction. As the International Law Association has pointed out, the International Court of Justice "has not in fact said in so many words that just because there are (allegedly) distinct elements in customary law the same conduct cannot manifest both. It is in fact often difficult or even impossible to disentangle the two elements."[42] This is particularly so because verbal acts count as State practice and often reflect the legal conviction of the State involved at the same time.

When there is sufficiently dense practice, an *opinio juris* is generally contained within that practice and, as a result, it is not usually necessary to demonstrate separately the existence of an *opinio juris*. *Opinio juris* plays an important role, however, in certain situations where the practice is ambiguous, in order to decide whether or not that practice counts towards the formation of custom. This is often the case with omissions, when States omit to act or react but it is not clear why. An example of such a situation was analysed by the Permanent Court of International Justice in the *Lotus case* in which France disputed Turkey's right to prosecute for a collision on the high seas. France argued that the absence of such prosecutions proved a prohibition under customary international law to prosecute, except by the flag State of the ship on board which the wrongful act took place. The Court, however, disagreed because it was not clear whether other States had abstained from prosecuting because they thought they had no right to do so or because of some other reason, for example, lack of interest or belief that a court of the flag State is a more

---

[42] ILA Report, *supra* note 18, § 10(c), p. 718. For an in-depth analysis, see Peter Haggenmacher, "La doctrine des deux éléments du droit coutumier dans la pratique de la Cour internationale", *Revue générale de droit international public*, Vol. 90, 1986, p. 5.

convenient forum. The Court stated there was no evidence of any "consci-ous[ness] of having a duty to abstain".[43]

Another situation of ambiguity was analysed by the International Court of Justice in the *North Sea Continental Shelf cases* in which Denmark and the Netherlands argued that a customary rule existed requiring a continental shelf to be delimited on the basis of the equidistance principle, *inter alia*, because a number of States had done so. The Court considered that the basis of the action of those States remained speculative and that no inference could be drawn that they believed themselves to be applying a rule of customary international law.[44] In other words, the States that had delimited their continental shelf on the basis of the equidistance principle had behaved in accordance with that principle but nothing showed that they considered themselves bound by it. It is basically in such cases, where practice is ambiguous, that both the International Court of Justice and its predecessor, the Permanent Court of International Justice, have looked in particular at whether they could separately establish the existence of an *opinio juris* that would indicate that the ambiguous practice in fact counted towards the establishment of customary international law.[45]

In the area of international humanitarian law, where many rules require abstention from certain conduct, omissions pose a particular problem in the assessment of *opinio juris* because it has to be proved that the abstention is not a coincidence but based on a legitimate expectation. When such a requirement of abstention is indicated in statements and documents, the existence of a *legal* requirement to abstain from the conduct in question can usually be proved. In addition, such abstentions may also occur after the behaviour in question created a certain controversy, which also helps to prove that the abstention was not coincidental, although it is not always easy to conclude that the absten-tion occurred because of a sense of legal obligation. A particular example of this problem is abstention from certain conduct in non-international armed conflicts when a clear rule to abstain from such conduct can only be found in treaty law applicable to international armed conflicts. This is, for example, the case for abstention from the use of certain weapons in non-international armed conflicts, when the prohibition of the use of these weapons was agreed to by treaty a long time ago when rules in relation to non-international armed conflicts were not as readily thought about or accepted as they are now. Absten-tion from such use or of prohibited behaviour is not likely to lead other States to comment, and this is particularly the case in relation to non-international armed conflicts in which other States are not directly affected. The process of claim and counterclaim does not produce as much clarity with respect to non-international armed conflicts as it does with respect to international armed conflicts because in the latter case, two or more States are directly affected

---

[43] PCIJ, *Lotus case, supra* note 19, p. 28.
[44] ICJ, *North Sea Continental Shelf cases, supra* note 12, pp. 43–44, §§ 76–77.
[45] ILA Report, *supra* note 18, Principle 17(iv) and commentary.

by each other's behaviour, while in the former case, usually only one State is directly affected.

It appears that international courts and tribunals on occasion conclude that a rule of customary international law exists when that rule is a desirable one for international peace and security or for the protection of the human person, provided that there is no important contrary *opinio juris*.[46] Examples of such conclusions are the finding by the International Military Tribunal at Nuremberg that the Hague Conventions of 1907 had hardened into customary law,[47] and the finding by the International Court of Justice in the *Nicaragua case* that the rule of non-intervention in the internal and external affairs of other States was part of customary international law.[48] However, when there was clear evidence of contrary *opinio juris* by a number of States, including specially affected ones, international case-law has held that the existence of a rule of customary international was not proven, for example, the advisory opinion of the International Court of Justice in the *Nuclear Weapons case* on the issue of whether the use of nuclear weapons was illegal,[49] and the ruling of the sole arbitrator in the *Texaco v. Libya case* on the issue of a possible change in the law relating to compensation for expropriation.[50]

This aspect of the assessment of customary law is particularly relevant for international humanitarian law, given that most of this law seeks to regulate behaviour for humanitarian reasons. In some instances, it is not yet possible to find a rule of customary international law even though there is a clear majority practice in favour of the rule and such a rule is very desirable.

Impact of treaty law

Treaties are also relevant in determining the existence of customary international law because they help assess how States view certain rules of international law. Hence, the ratification, interpretation and implementation of a

---

[46] For an analysis of this phenomenon in the behaviour of international courts, see Frederic L. Kirgis, "Custom on a Sliding Scale", *American Journal of International Law*, Vol. 81, 1987, p. 146.

[47] International Military Tribunal at Nuremberg, *Case of the Major War Criminals*, Judgement, 1 October 1946, *Official Documents*, Vol. I, pp. 253–254.

[48] ICJ, *Case concerning Military and Paramilitary Activities in and against Nicaragua*, *supra* note 14, pp. 106–110, §§ 202–209.

[49] ICJ, *Nuclear Weapons case*, *supra* note 28, p. 255, § 73. This finding of the ICJ was in relation to an analysis of whether there was sufficiently consistent *opinio juris*. In this context, the Court found, with respect to UN General Assembly resolutions which stated that the use of nuclear weapons was illegal and which were adopted by a large majority of States, that they did not create sufficient *opinio juris* to establish a rule of customary law because of the large number of negative votes and abstentions.

[50] *Texaco Overseas Petroleum Company and California Asiatic Oil Company v. Libyan Arab Republic*, Arbitral Award, 19 January 1977, §§ 80–91, reprinted in *International Legal Materials*, Vol. 17, 1978, pp. 27–31. The sole arbitrator found that there was insufficient support by one group of specially affected States for the Charter of Economic Rights and Duties of States and for the Declaration on the Establishment of a New International Economic Order.

treaty, including reservations and statements of interpretation made upon ratification, are included in the study. In the *North Sea Continental Shelf cases*, the International Court of Justice clearly considered the degree of ratification of a treaty to be relevant to the assessment of customary law. In that case, the Court stated that "the number of ratifications and accessions so far secured [39] is, though respectable, hardly sufficient", especially in a context where practice outside the treaty was contradictory.[51] Conversely, in the *Nicaragua case*, the Court placed a great deal of weight, when assessing the customary status of the non-intervention rule, on the fact that the UN Charter was almost universally ratified and that relevant UN General Assembly resolutions had been widely approved, in particular Resolution 2625 (XXV) on friendly relations between States, which was adopted without a vote.[52] It can even be the case that a treaty provision reflects customary law, even though the treaty is not yet in force, provided that there is sufficiently similar practice, including by specially affected States, so that there remains little likelihood of significant opposition to the rule in question.[53]

In practice, the drafting of treaty norms helps to focus world legal opinion and has an undeniable influence on the subsequent behaviour and legal conviction of States. This reality was recognised by the International Court of Justice in the *Continental Shelf case*:

It is of course axiomatic that the material of customary international law is to be looked for primarily in the actual practice and *opinio juris* of States, even though multilateral conventions may have an important role to play in recording and defining rules deriving from custom, or indeed in developing them.[54]

The Court thus recognised that treaties may codify pre-existing customary international law but may also lay the foundation for the development of new customs based on the norms contained in those treaties. The Court has even gone so far as to state that "it might be that . . . a very widespread and representative participation in [a] convention might suffice of itself, provided it included that of States whose interests were specially affected".[55]

The International Law Association has summarised this case-law, stating that a (multilateral) treaty may thus interact in four different ways with custom: it can provide evidence of existing custom; it can provide the inspiration or model for the adoption of new custom through State practice; it can assist in the so-called "crystallisation" of emerging custom; and it can even give rise to new custom of "its own impact" if the rule concerned is of a fundamentally

[51] ICJ, *North Sea Continental Shelf cases, supra* note 12, p. 42, § 73.
[52] ICJ, *Case concerning Military and Paramilitary Activities in and against Nicaragua, supra* note 14, pp. 99–100, § 188.
[53] ICJ, *Continental Shelf case, supra* note 11, p. 33, § 34. The number of claims to an exclusive economic zone had risen to 56, which included several specially affected States.
[54] ICJ, *Continental Shelf case, supra* note 11, pp. 29–30, § 27.
[55] ICJ, *North Sea Continental Shelf cases, supra* note 12, p. 42, § 73.

norm-creating character and is widely adopted by States with a view to creating a new general legal obligation. There can be no presumption that any of these interactions has taken place and in each case it is a matter of examining the evidence.[56]

This study takes the cautious approach that widespread ratification is only an indication and has to be assessed in relation to other elements of practice, in particular the practice of States not party to the treaty in question. Consistent practice of States not party has been considered as important positive evidence. Contrary practice of States not party, however, has been considered as important negative evidence. The practice of States party to a treaty vis-à-vis States not party is also particularly relevant.

This study has not, however, limited itself to the practice of States not party to the relevant treaties of international humanitarian law. To limit the study to a consideration of the practice of only the 30-odd States that have not ratified the Additional Protocols, for example, would not comply with the requirement that customary international law be based on widespread and representative practice. Therefore, the assessment of the existence of customary law takes into account the fact that, at the time of writing, Additional Protocol I has been ratified by 162 States and Additional Protocol II by 157 States. Similarly, the assessment of customary law also takes into account the fact that the Geneva Conventions have been ratified by 192 States and this is not repeated in the commentaries.

Lastly, the most important judicial decisions on the customary nature of humanitarian law provisions are not repeated in the commentaries which cite the rules held to be customary. This applies in particular to the finding by the International Military Tribunal at Nuremberg that the 1907 Hague Regulations "undoubtedly represented an advance over existing international law at the time of their adoption . . . but by 1939 these rules laid down in the Convention were recognized by all civilized nations, and were regarded as being declaratory of the laws and customs of war".[57] It also applies to the *Nicaragua case*, in which the International Court of Justice held that common Article 3 of the Geneva Conventions reflected "elementary considerations of humanity" constituting a "minimum yardstick" applicable to all armed conflicts.[58] It further applies to the finding of the International Court of Justice in the *Nuclear Weapons case* that the great majority of the provisions of the 1949 Geneva Conventions represent customary international law.[59] In the same vein, it is important to stress, though it is not repeated in the commentaries, that with regard to the Statute of the International Criminal Court, there was a "general

---

[56] ILA Report, *supra* note 18, Principles 20–21, 24, 26 and 27, pp. 754–765.
[57] International Military Tribunal at Nuremberg, *Case of the Major War Criminals, supra* note 47.
[58] ICJ, *Case concerning Military and Paramilitary Activities in and against Nicaragua, supra* note 14, p. 114, § 218.
[59] ICJ, *Nuclear Weapons case, supra* note 28, pp. 257–258, §§ 79 and 82.

agreement that the definitions of crimes in the ICC Statute were to reflect existing customary international law, and not to create new law".[60]

Organisation of the study

To determine the best way of fulfilling the mandate entrusted to it, the ICRC consulted a group of academic experts in international humanitarian law who formed the Steering Committee of the study. The Steering Committee consisted of Professors Georges Abi-Saab, Salah El-Din Amer, Ove Bring, Eric David, John Dugard, Florentino Feliciano, Horst Fischer, Françoise Hampson, Theodor Meron, Djamchid Momtaz, Milan Šahović and Raúl Emilio Vinuesa. The Steering Committee adopted a Plan of Action in June 1996 and research started in October 1996. Pursuant to the Plan of Action, research was conducted using both national and international sources reflecting State practice. Research into these sources focused on the six parts of the study as identified in the Plan of Action:

- Principle of distinction
- Specifically protected persons and objects
- Specific methods of warfare
- Weapons
- Treatment of civilians and persons *hors de combat*
- Implementation

The measure of access to national and international sources largely explains the research method adopted.

Research in national sources of practice

Since national sources are more easily accessible from within a country, it was decided to seek the cooperation of national researchers. To this end, nearly 50 countries were selected (9 in Africa, 15 in Asia, 11 in Europe, 11 in the Americas and 1 in Australasia) and in each a researcher or group of researchers was identified to report on State practice (see Annex I). The Steering Committee selected the countries on the basis of geographic representation, as well as recent experience of different kinds of armed conflicts in which a variety of methods of warfare had been used. The result was a series of reports on State practice. Significant practice of other countries was identified through research into international sources and ICRC archives (see *infra*).

The sources of State practice collected by the national researchers include military manuals, national legislation, national case-law, instructions to armed

---

[60] Philippe Kirsch, "Foreword", in Knut Dörmann, *Elements of War Crimes under the Rome Statute of the International Criminal Court: Sources and Commentary*, *supra* note 1, p. xiii; see also Report of the Preparatory Committee on the Establishment of an International Criminal Court, Vol. I, Proceedings of the Preparatory Committee during March–April and August 1996, *UN General Assembly Official Records*, UN Doc. A/51/22, 13 September 1996, § 54.

and security forces, military communiqués during war, diplomatic protests, opinions of official legal advisers, comments by governments on draft treaties, executive decisions and regulations, pleadings before international tribunals, statements in international organisations and at international conferences and government positions taken with respect to resolutions of international organisations.

The military manuals and national legislation of countries not covered by the reports on State practice were also researched and collected. This work was facilitated by the network of ICRC delegations around the world and the extensive collection of national legislation gathered by the ICRC Advisory Service on International Humanitarian Law. The purpose of the additional research was also to make sure that the study would be as up-to-date as possible and would, to the extent possible, take into account developments up to 31 December 2002. In some cases, it has been possible to include more recent practice.

Research in international sources of practice

State practice gleaned from international sources was collected by six teams, each of which concentrated on one part of the study. These teams consisted of the following persons:

Part I. Principle of distinction
Rapporteur: Georges Abi-Saab
Researcher: Jean-François Quéguiner
Part II. Specifically protected persons and objects
Rapporteur: Horst Fischer
Researchers: Gregor Schotten and Heike Spieker
Part III. Specific methods of warfare
Rapporteur: Theodor Meron
Researcher: Richard Desgagné
Part IV. Weapons
Rapporteur: Ove Bring
Researcher: Gustaf Lind
Part V. Treatment of civilians and persons hors de combat
Rapporteur: Françoise Hampson
Researcher: Camille Giffard
Part VI. Implementation
Rapporteur: Eric David
Researcher: Richard Desgagné

These teams researched practice in the framework of the United Nations and of other international organisations, in particular the African Union (formerly the Organization of African Unity), Council of Europe, Gulf Cooperation Council, European Union, League of Arab States, Organization of American

States, Organization of the Islamic Conference and Organization for Security and Cooperation in Europe. The practice of the Commonwealth of Independent States, Inter-Parliamentary Union and Non-Aligned Movement was also researched. Access to the practice of these organisations was facilitated by the ICRC delegations which maintain contacts with them.

State practice at the international level is reflected in a variety of sources, including in resolutions adopted in the framework of the United Nations, in particular by the Security Council, General Assembly and Commission on Human Rights, ad hoc investigations conducted by the United Nations, the work of the International Law Commission and comments it elicited from governments, the work of the committees of the UN General Assembly, reports of the UN Secretary-General, thematic and country-specific procedures of the UN Commission on Human Rights, reporting procedures before the Human Rights Committee, the Committee against Torture, the Committee on the Elimination of Discrimination Against Women and the Committee on the Rights of the Child, *travaux préparatoires* of treaties, and State submissions to international and regional courts.

International case-law was also collected to the extent that it provides evidence of the existence of rules of customary international law.

Research in ICRC archives

To complement the research into national and international sources, the ICRC looked into its own archives relating to nearly 40 recent armed conflicts, some 20 of which occurred in Africa, 8 in Asia, 8 in Europe and 2 in the Americas (see Annex II). In general, these conflicts were selected so that countries and conflicts not yet dealt with by a report on State practice would also be covered.

The result of this three-pronged approach – that is, research into national, international and ICRC sources – is that practice from all parts of the world is cited. In the nature of things, however, this research cannot purport to be complete. Research for the study focused in particular on practice from the last 30 years to ensure that the result would be a restatement of contemporary customary international law, but, where still relevant, older practice has also been cited.

Consolidation of research results

Upon completion of the research, all practice gathered was summarised and consolidated into separate parts covering the different areas of the study. This work was carried out by the six international research teams for the part which concerned them. The chapters containing this consolidated practice were subsequently edited, supplemented and updated by a group of ICRC researchers, and are published in Volume II, "Practice". The reason for publishing such voluminous chapters is twofold. First, those consulting the study should be able to verify the basis in State practice for each rule of customary international law. Each rule in Volume I refers to the chapter and section in Volume II where the practice on which that rule is based can be found. Secondly, it was considered useful to publish the wealth of information that has been compiled. Many practitioners and scholars will thus be able to use the practice gathered for their own professional purposes.

Expert consultations

In a first round of consultations, the ICRC invited the international research teams to produce an "executive summary" containing a preliminary assessment of customary international humanitarian law on the basis of the practice collected. These executive summaries were discussed within the Steering Committee at three meetings in Geneva (see Annex III). On the basis of this first round of consultations, the "executive summaries" were updated, and during a second round of consultations, they were submitted to a group of academic and governmental experts from all the regions of the world invited in their personal capacity by the ICRC to attend two meetings with the Steering Committee (see Annex III). During these two meetings in Geneva, the experts helped to evaluate the practice collected and indicated particular practice that had been missed.

Writing of the report

The assessment by the Steering Committee, as reviewed by the group of academic and governmental experts, served as a basis for the writing of the final report. The authors of the study re-examined the practice, reassessed the existence of custom, reviewed the formulation and the order of the rules, and drafted the commentaries. The draft texts were submitted to the ICRC Legal Division, whose members provided extremely helpful comments and insights. Moreover, each Part was reviewed by an additional reader: Maurice Mendelson for the introductory part on the assessment of customary international law, Knut Dörmann for Part I, Theodor Meron for Part II, Horst Fischer for Part III, the Mines and Arms Unit of the ICRC led by Peter Herby for Part IV, William Fenrick for Part V and Antonio Cassese for Part VI. On the basis of their comments and those of the ICRC Legal Division, a second draft was prepared, which was submitted for written consultation to the Steering Committee, the group of academic and governmental experts and the ICRC Legal Division. The text was further updated and finalised taking into account the comments received.

This study was initiated under the supervision of Louise Doswald-Beck, then Deputy Head and later Head of the ICRC Legal Division. Jean-Marie Henckaerts has been responsible for the overall management of the study and drafted Parts I, II, III and V of Volume I. Louise Doswald-Beck drafted Parts IV and VI, as well as Chapters 14 and 32, of Volume I. The introductory parts were drafted by both of them. In drafting the text they received important contributions from Carolin Alvermann, Knut Dörmann and Baptiste Rolle. The authors, jointly, bear the sole responsibility for the content of the study.

Annex I. National research

On the basis of geographical representation and experience of armed conflict, the following States were selected for an in-depth study of national practice on international humanitarian law by a local expert. Significant practice of other States was found in international sources and the ICRC's archives.

Africa
Algeria, Angola, Botswana, Egypt, Ethiopia, Nigeria, Rwanda, South Africa, Zimbabwe.

Asia
China, India, Indonesia, Iran, Iraq, Israel, Japan, Jordan, Republic of Korea, Kuwait, Lebanon, Malaysia, Pakistan, Philippines, Syria.

Australasia
Australia.

Europe
Belgium, Bosnia and Herzegovina, Croatia, France, Germany, Italy, Netherlands, Russian Federation, Spain, United Kingdom, Yugoslavia.

Americas
Argentina, Brazil, Canada, Chile, Colombia, Cuba, El Salvador, Nicaragua, Peru, United States of America, Uruguay.

Annex II. Research in the ICRC archives

The conflicts for which research was carried out in the ICRC archives were chosen in order to include States and territories not covered by a report on State practice.

Africa
Angola, Burundi, Chad, Chad–Libya, Democratic Republic of the Congo, Djibouti, Eritrea–Yemen, Ethiopia (1973–1994), Liberia, Mozambique, Namibia,

Nigeria–Cameroon, Rwanda, Senegal, Senegal–Mauritania, Sierra Leone, Somalia, Somalia–Ethiopia, Sudan, Uganda, Western Sahara.

Asia
Afghanistan, Cambodia, India (Jammu and Kashmir), Papua New Guinea, Sri Lanka, Tajikistan, Yemen, Yemen–Eritrea (also under Africa).

Europe
Armenia–Azerbaijan (Nagorno-Karabakh), Cyprus, Former Yugoslavia (conflict in Yugoslavia (1991–1992), conflict in Bosnia and Herzegovina (1992–1996), conflict in Croatia (Krajinas) (1992–1995)), Georgia (Abkhazia), Russian Federation (Chechnya), Turkey.

Americas
Guatemala, Mexico.

Annex III. Expert consultations

1. Consultation with the Steering Committee (1998)
First meeting, 28 April–1 May 1998: Specific methods of warfare; Weapons.
Second meeting, 16–18 August 1998: Principle of distinction; Specifically protected persons and objects.
Third meeting, 14–17 October 1998: Treatment of civilians and persons *hors de combat*; Implementation.
The Steering Committee consisted of Professors Georges Abi-Saab, Salah El-Din Amer, Ove Bring, Eric David, John Dugard, Florentino Feliciano, Horst Fischer, Françoise Hampson, Theodor Meron, Djamchid Momtaz, Milan Šahović and Raúl Emilio Vinuesa.

2. Consultation with academic and governmental experts (1999)
First meeting, 4–8 January 1999: Specific methods of warfare; Weapons; Specifically protected persons and objects.
Second meeting, 1–5 May 1999: Principle of distinction; Treatment of civilians and persons *hors de combat*; Implementation.
The following academic and governmental experts were invited by the ICRC, in their personal capacity, to participate in this consultation:
Abdallah Ad-Douri (Iraq), Paul Berman (United Kingdom), Sadi Çaycý (Turkey), Michael Cowling (South Africa), Edward Cummings (United States of America), Antonio de Icaza (Mexico), Yoram Dinstein (Israel), Jean-Michel Favre (France), William Fenrick (Canada), Dieter Fleck (Germany), Juan Carlos Gómez Ramírez (Colombia), Jamshed A. Hamid (Pakistan), Arturo Hernández-Basave (Mexico), Ibrahim Idriss (Ethiopia), Hassan Kassem Jouni (Lebanon), Kenneth Keith (New Zealand), Githu Muigai (Kenya), Rein Müllerson (Estonia), Bara Niang (Senegal), Mohamed Olwan (Jordan), Raul C. Pangalangan (Philippines),

Stelios Perrakis (Greece), Paulo Sergio Pinheiro (Brazil), Arpád Prandler (Hungary), Pemmaraju Sreenivasa Rao (India), Camilo Reyes Rodríguez (Colombia), Itse E. Sagay (Nigeria), Harold Sandoval (Colombia), Somboon Sangianbut (Thailand), Marat A. Sarsembayev (Kazakhstan), Muhammad Aziz Shukri (Syria), Parlaungan Sihombing (Indonesia), Geoffrey James Skillen (Australia), Guoshun Sun (China), Bakhtyar Tuzmukhamedov (Russia) and Karol Wolfke (Poland).

3. Written consultation with the academic and governmental experts (2002–2004)

The experts listed above were invited to comment on two drafts, and a number of them provided written comments which were taken into account.

ABBREVIATIONS

CCW	Convention on Prohibitions or Restrictions on the Use of Certain Conventional Weapons which may be deemed to be Excessively Injurious or to have Indiscriminate Effects (1980)
CDDH	Diplomatic Conference on the Reaffirmation and Development of International Humanitarian Law Applicable in Armed Conflicts (Geneva, 1974–1977)
CIS	Commonwealth of Independent States
CSCE	Conference on Security and Cooperation in Europe
ECOSOC	United Nations Economic and Social Council
ENMOD Convention	Convention on the Prohibition of Military or Any Other Hostile Use of Environmental Modification Techniques (1976)
EC	European Community
EU	European Union
FMLN	Farabundo Martí para la Liberación Nacional (Farabundo Martí National Liberation Front, El Salvador)
FRY	Federal Republic of Yugoslavia
ICC	International Criminal Court
ICJ	International Court of Justice
ICJ Reports	International Court of Justice, Reports of Judgments, Advisory Opinions and Orders
ICRC	International Committee of the Red Cross
ICTR	International Criminal Tribunal for Rwanda
ICTY	International Criminal Tribunal for the Former Yugoslavia
IHL	International humanitarian law
ILA	International Law Association
ILC	International Law Commission
IMT	International Military Tribunal
LTTE	Liberation Tigers of Tamil Eelam (Sri Lanka)
NATO	North Atlantic Treaty Organisation
OAS	Organization of American States

OAU	Organization of African Unity (now African Union)
OIC	Organization of the Islamic Conference
OSCE	Organization for Security and Cooperation in Europe
PCIJ	Permanent Court of International Justice
POW	Prisoner of war
SFRY	Socialist Federal Republic of Yugoslavia
SPLM/A	Sudan People's Liberation Movement/Army
UN	United Nations
UNESCO	United Nations Education, Scientific and Cultural Organization
UNHCR	United Nations High Commissioner for Refugees
UN Sub-Commission on Human Rights	United Nations Sub-Commission on the Promotion and Protection of Human Rights (formerly the Sub-Commission on Prevention of Discrimination and Protection of Minorities)
USSR	Union of Soviet Socialist Republics
UK	United Kingdom of Great Britain and Northern Ireland
US	United States of America
YPA	Yugoslav People's Army

PART I

THE PRINCIPLE OF DISTINCTION

DISTINCTION BETWEEN CIVILIANS AND COMBATANTS

Rule 1. The parties to the conflict must at all times distinguish between civilians and combatants. Attacks may only be directed against combatants. Attacks must not be directed against civilians.

Practice

Volume II, Chapter 1, Section A.

Summary

State practice establishes this rule as a norm of customary international law applicable in both international and non-international armed conflicts. The three components of this rule are interrelated and the practice pertaining to each of them reinforces the validity of the others. The term "combatant" in this rule is used in its generic meaning, indicating persons who do not enjoy the protection against attack accorded to civilians, but does not imply a right to combatant status or prisoner-of-war status (see Chapter 33). This rule has to be read in conjunction with the prohibition to attack persons recognised to be *hors de combat* (see Rule 47) and with the rule that civilians are protected against attack unless and for such time as they take a direct part in hostilities (see Rule 6). Belligerent reprisals against civilians are discussed in Chapter 41.

International armed conflicts

The principle of distinction between civilians and combatants was first set forth in the St. Petersburg Declaration, which states that "the only legitimate object which States should endeavour to accomplish during war is to weaken the military forces of the enemy".[1] The Hague Regulations do not as such specify that a distinction must be made between civilians and combatants, but Article 25, which prohibits "the attack or bombardment, by whatever means, of towns, villages, dwellings, or buildings which are undefended", is based on this principle.[2] The principle of distinction is now codified in Articles 48, 51(2)

---

[1] St. Petersburg Declaration, preamble (cited in Vol. II, Ch. 1, § 83).
[2] Hague Regulations, Article 25.

and 52(2) of Additional Protocol I, to which no reservations have been made.[3] According to Additional Protocol I, "attacks" means "acts of violence against the adversary, whether in offence or in defence".[4]

At the Diplomatic Conference leading to the adoption of the Additional Protocols, Mexico stated that Articles 51 and 52 of Additional Protocol I were so essential that they "cannot be the subject of any reservations whatsoever since these would be inconsistent with the aim and purpose of Protocol I and undermine its basis".[5] Also at the Diplomatic Conference, the United Kingdom stated that Article 51(2) was a "valuable reaffirmation" of an existing rule of customary international law.[6]

The prohibition on directing attacks against civilians is also laid down in Protocol II, Amended Protocol II and Protocol III to the Convention on Certain Conventional Weapons and in the Ottawa Convention banning anti-personnel landmines.[7] In addition, under the Statute of the International Criminal Court, "intentionally directing attacks against the civilian population as such or against individual civilians not taking direct part in hostilities" constitutes a war crime in international armed conflicts.[8]

Numerous military manuals, including those of States not, or not at the time, party to Additional Protocol I, stipulate that a distinction must be made between civilians and combatants and that it is prohibited to direct attacks against civilians.[9] Sweden's IHL Manual identifies the principle of distinction as laid down in Article 48 of Additional Protocol I as a rule of customary international law.[10] In addition, there are numerous examples of national legislation which make it a criminal offence to direct attacks against civilians, including the legislation of States not, or not at the time, party to Additional Protocol I.[11]

In the *Kassem case* in 1969, Israel's Military Court at Ramallah recognised the immunity of civilians from direct attack as one of the basic rules of international humanitarian law.[12] There are, moreover, many official statements which invoke the rule, including by States not, or not at the time, party to

---

[3] Additional Protocol I, Article 48 (adopted by consensus) (cited in Vol. II, Ch. 1, § 1), Article 51(2) (adopted by 77 votes in favour, one against and 16 abstentions) (*ibid.*, § 154) and Article 52(2) (adopted by 79 votes in favour, none against and 7 abstentions) (*ibid.*, § 85).

[4] Additional Protocol I, Article 49.

[5] Mexico, Statement at the Diplomatic Conference leading to the adoption of the Additional Protocols (cited in Vol. II, Ch. 1, §§ 146, 307, 536 and 800).

[6] United Kingdom, Statement at the Diplomatic Conference leading to the adoption of the Additional Protocols (*ibid.*, §§ 319, 537 and 803).

[7] Protocol II to the CCW, Article 3(2) (*ibid.*, § 157); Amended Protocol II to the CCW, Article 3(7) (*ibid.*, § 157); Protocol III to the CCW, Article 2(1) (*ibid.*, § 158); Ottawa Convention, preamble (*ibid.*, § 3).

[8] ICC Statute, Article 8(2)(b)(i) (*ibid.*, § 160).

[9] See military manuals (*ibid.*, §§ 10–34 and 173–216), in particular the manuals of France (*ibid.*, §§ 21 and 188), Indonesia (*ibid.*, § 192), Israel (*ibid.*, §§ 25 and 193–194), Kenya (*ibid.*, § 197), United Kingdom (*ibid.*, §§ 212–213) and United States (*ibid.*, §§ 33–34 and 214–215).

[10] Sweden, *IHL Manual* (*ibid.*, § 29).

[11] See legislation (*ibid.*, §§ 217–269), in particular the legislation of Azerbaijan (*ibid.*, §§ 221–222), Indonesia (*ibid.*, § 243) and Italy (*ibid.*, § 245).

[12] Israel, Military Court at Ramallah, *Kassem case* (*ibid.*, § 271).

Additional Protocol I.[13] The rule has also been invoked by parties to Additional Protocol I against non-parties.[14]

In their pleadings before the International Court of Justice in the *Nuclear Weapons case*, many States invoked the principle of distinction.[15] In its advisory opinion in the *Nuclear Weapons case*, the Court stated that the principle of distinction was one of the "cardinal principles" of international humanitarian law and one of the "intransgressible principles of international customary law".[16]

When the ICRC appealed to the parties to the conflict in the Middle East in October 1973, i.e., before the adoption of Additional Protocol I, to respect the distinction between combatants and civilians, the States concerned (Egypt, Iraq, Israel and Syria) replied favourably.[17]

Non-international armed conflicts

Article 13(2) of Additional Protocol II prohibits making the civilian population as such, as well as individual civilians, the object of attack.[18] The prohibition on directing attacks against civilians is also contained in Amended Protocol II to the Convention on Certain Conventional Weapons.[19] It is also set forth in Protocol III to the Convention on Certain Conventional Weapons, which has been made applicable in non-international armed conflicts pursuant to an amendment of Article 1 of the Convention adopted by consensus in 2001.[20] The Ottawa Convention banning anti-personnel landmines states that the Convention is based, *inter alia*, on "the principle that a distinction must be made between civilians and combatants".[21]

Under the Statute of the International Criminal Court, "intentionally directing attacks against the civilian population as such or against individual civilians not taking direct part in hostilities" constitutes a war crime in non-international armed conflicts.[22] In addition, this rule is included in other instruments pertaining also to non-international armed conflicts.[23]

---

[13] See, e.g., the statements of Azerbaijan (*ibid.*, § 273), China (*ibid.*, § 279), France (*ibid.*, §§ 41 and 285), Germany (*ibid.*, §§ 290–291 and 293), Iran (*ibid.*, §§ 296–297), Iraq (*ibid.*, § 298), Pakistan (*ibid.*, §§ 311–312), South Africa (*ibid.*, § 49), United Kingdom (*ibid.*, § 321) and United States (*ibid.*, §§ 51–53 and 322–329).

[14] See, e.g., the statements of Germany vis-à-vis Turkey (*ibid.*, § 292) and Iraq (*ibid.*, § 293), of Lebanon (*ibid.*, § 304) and Pakistan (*ibid.*, § 312) vis-à-vis Israel, and of Spain vis-à-vis Iran and Iraq (*ibid.*, § 315).

[15] See the statements of Ecuador (*ibid.*, § 39), Egypt (*ibid.*, §§ 40 and 283), India (*ibid.*, § 42), Japan (*ibid.*, § 43), Netherlands (*ibid.*, § 309), New Zealand (*ibid.*, § 45), Solomon Islands (*ibid.*, § 48), Sweden (*ibid.*, § 316), United Kingdom (*ibid.*, §§ 50 and 321) and United States (*ibid.*, § 329).

[16] ICJ, *Nuclear Weapons case* (*ibid.*, § 434).

[17] See ICRC, The International Committee's Action in the Middle East (*ibid.*, § 445).

[18] Additional Protocol II, Article 13(2) (adopted by consensus) (*ibid.*, § 156).

[19] Amended Protocol II to the CCW, Article 3(7) (*ibid.*, § 157).

[20] Protocol III to the CCW, Article 2(1) (*ibid.*, § 158).

[21] Ottawa Convention, preamble (*ibid.*, § 3).

[22] ICC Statute, Article 8(2)(e)(i) (*ibid.*, § 160).

[23] See, e.g., Memorandum of Understanding on the Application of IHL between Croatia and the SFRY, para. 6 (*ibid.*, §§ 6, 97 and 167); Agreement on the Application of IHL between the Parties

Military manuals which are applicable in or have been applied in non-international armed conflicts specify that a distinction must be made between combatants and civilians to the effect that only the former may be targeted.[24] To direct attacks against civilians in any armed conflict is an offence under the legislation of numerous States.[25] There are also a number of official statements pertaining to non-international armed conflicts invoking the principle of distinction and condemning attacks directed against civilians.[26] States' submissions to the International Court of Justice in the *Nuclear Weapons case* referred to above were couched in general terms applicable in all armed conflicts.

No official contrary practice was found with respect to either international or non-international armed conflicts. This rule is sometimes expressed in other terms, in particular as the principle of distinction between combatants and non-combatants, whereby civilians who do not take a direct part in hostilities are included in the category of non-combatants.[27]

to the Conflict in Bosnia and Herzegovina, para. 2.5 (*ibid.*, § 7, 98 and 168); San Remo Manual, paras. 39 and 41 (*ibid.*, §§ 8 and 99); UN Secretary-General's Bulletin, Section 5.1 (*ibid.*, §§ 9, 100 and 171); Cairo Declaration on Human Rights in Islam, Article 3(a) (*ibid.*, § 165); Hague Statement on Respect for Humanitarian Principles (*ibid.*, § 166); UNTAET Regulation 2000/15, Section 6(1)(e)(i) (*ibid.*, § 172).

[24] See, e.g., the military manuals of Argentina (*ibid.*, § 173), Benin (*ibid.*, § 177), Cameroon (*ibid.*, § 178), Canada (*ibid.*, § 179), Colombia (*ibid.*, §§ 181–182), Germany (*ibid.*, § 189), Netherlands (*ibid.*, § 201), New Zealand (*ibid.*, § 203), Philippines (*ibid.*, § 205), Togo (*ibid.*, § 211) and Yugoslavia (*ibid.*, 216).

[25] See, e.g., the legislation of Armenia (*ibid.*, § 218), Australia (*ibid.*, § 220), Azerbaijan (*ibid.*, §§ 221–222), Belarus (*ibid.*, § 223), Belgium (*ibid.*, § 224), Bosnia and Herzegovina (*ibid.*, § 225), Canada (*ibid.*, § 228), Colombia (*ibid.*, § 230), Democratic Republic of the Congo (*ibid.*, § 231), Congo (*ibid.*, § 232), Croatia (*ibid.*, § 234), Estonia (*ibid.*, § 239), Georgia (*ibid.*, § 240), Germany (*ibid.*, § 241), Ireland (*ibid.*, § 244), Lithuania (*ibid.*, § 248), Netherlands (*ibid.*, § 250), New Zealand (*ibid.*, § 252), Niger (*ibid.*, § 254), Norway (*ibid.*, § 255), Slovenia (*ibid.*, § 257), Spain (*ibid.*, § 259), Sweden (*ibid.*, § 260), Tajikistan (*ibid.*, § 261), United Kingdom (*ibid.*, § 265), Vietnam (*ibid.*, § 266), Yemen (*ibid.*, § 267) and Yugoslavia (*ibid.*, § 268); see also the legislation of the Czech Republic (*ibid.*, § 237), Hungary (*ibid.*, § 242), Italy (*ibid.*, § 245) and Slovakia (*ibid.*, § 256), the application of which is not excluded in time of non-international armed conflict, and the draft legislation of Argentina (*ibid.*, § 217), Burundi (*ibid.*, § 226), El Salvador (*ibid.*, § 238), Jordan (*ibid.*, § 246), Nicaragua (*ibid.*, § 253) and Trinidad and Tobago (*ibid.*, § 262).

[26] See, e.g., the statements of Belgium (*ibid.*, § 274), France (*ibid.*, §§ 286 and 288–289), Germany (*ibid.*, §§ 294–295), Malaysia (*ibid.*, § 306), Netherlands (*ibid.*, § 308), Philippines (*ibid.*, § 47), Slovenia (*ibid.*, § 314) and Uganda (*ibid.*, § 317).

[27] See, e.g., the military manuals of Croatia (*ibid.*, § 718), Dominican Republic (*ibid.*, §§ 185, 583 and 720), Ecuador (*ibid.*, §§ 20 and 721), Hungary (*ibid.*, § 724), Sweden (*ibid.*, § 733) and United States (*ibid.*, §§ 34 and 737); Israel, Military Court at Ramallah, *Kassem* case (*ibid.*, § 271); the statements of Belgium (*ibid.*, § 274), Colombia (*ibid.*, § 840), Egypt (*ibid.*, § 40), India (*ibid.*, § 42), Iran (*ibid.*, § 296), Japan (*ibid.*, § 43), South Korea (*ibid.*, § 302), Solomon Islands (*ibid.*, § 48) and United States (*ibid.*, §§ 53, 328); UN Security Council, Res. 771 (*ibid.*, § 337) and Res. 794 (*ibid.*, § 338); UN Commission on Human Rights, Res. 1992/S-1/1 (*ibid.*, § 388); UN Secretary-General, Report on protection for humanitarian assistance to refugees and others in conflicts situations (*ibid.*, § 57); Report pursuant to paragraph 5 of Security Council resolution 837 (1993) on the investigation into the 5 June 1993 attack on United Nations forces in Somalia conducted on behalf of the UN Security Council (*ibid.*, § 58); ICJ, *Nuclear Weapons case*, Advisory Opinion (*ibid.*, § 61). For other formulations, see, e.g., the military manuals of Belgium (*ibid.*, § 12) (distinction between "the civilian population and those participating in hostilities") and Sweden (*ibid.*, § 29) (distinction between "persons participating in hostilities and

Alleged violations of this rule have generally been condemned by States, irrespective of whether the conflict was international or non-international.[28] Similarly, the UN Security Council has condemned or called for an end to alleged attacks against civilians in the context of numerous conflicts, both international and non-international, including in Afghanistan, Angola, Azerbaijan, Burundi, Georgia, Lebanon, Liberia, Rwanda, Sierra Leone, Somalia, Tajikistan, the former Yugoslavia and the territories occupied by Israel.[29]

As early as 1938, the Assembly of the League of Nations stated that "the intentional bombing of civilian populations is illegal".[30] The 20th International Conference of the Red Cross in 1965 solemnly declared that governments and other authorities responsible for action in all armed conflicts should conform to the prohibition on launching attacks against a civilian population.[31] Subsequently, a UN General Assembly resolution on respect for human rights in armed conflicts, adopted in 1968, declared the principle of distinction to be applicable in all armed conflicts.[32] The Plan of Action for the years 2000–2003, adopted by the 27th International Conference of the Red Cross and Red Crescent in 1999, requires that all parties to an armed conflict respect "the total ban on directing attacks against the civilian population as such or against civilians not taking a direct part in hostilities".[33] In a resolution adopted in 2000 on protection of civilians in armed conflicts, the UN Security Council reaffirmed its strong condemnation of the deliberate targeting of civilians in all situations of armed conflict.[34]

The jurisprudence of the International Court of Justice in the *Nuclear Weapons case*, of the International Criminal Tribunal for the Former

---

who are thereby legitimate objectives, and members of the civilian population"); the statement of New Zealand (*ibid.*, § 45) (distinction between "combatants and those who are not directly involved in armed conflict"); UN General Assembly, Res. 2444 (XXIII) (*ibid.*, § 55) (distinction between "persons taking part in the hostilities and members of the civilian population") and Res. 2675 (XXV) (*ibid.*, § 56) (distinction between "persons actively taking part in the hostilities and civilian populations").

[28] See, e.g., the statements of Australia (*ibid.*, § 272), Bosnia and Herzegovina (*ibid.*, § 276), China (*ibid.*, § 279), Croatia (*ibid.*, § 281), France (*ibid.*, §§ 284, 286 and 288–289), Germany (*ibid.*, §§ 290 and 292–295), Iran (*ibid.*, § 297), Kazakhstan (*ibid.*, § 301), Lebanon (*ibid.*, § 305), Netherlands (*ibid.*, § 308), Pakistan (*ibid.*, §§ 311–312), Slovenia (*ibid.*, § 314), Spain (*ibid.*, § 315), Uganda (*ibid.*, § 317) and Yugoslavia (*ibid.*, § 331).

[29] See, e.g., UN Security Council, Res. 564 (*ibid.*, § 336), Res. 771 (*ibid.*, § 337), Res. 794 (*ibid.*, § 338), Res. 819 (*ibid.*, § 339), Res. 853 (*ibid.*, § 340), Res. 904 (*ibid.*, § 341), Res. 912 (*ibid.*, § 342), Res. 913 (*ibid.*, § 343), Res. 918, 925, 929 and 935 (*ibid.*, § 344), Res. 950 (*ibid.*, § 345), Res. 978 (*ibid.*, § 346), Res. 993 (*ibid.*, § 347), Res. 998 (*ibid.*, § 348), Res. 1001 (*ibid.*, § 349), Res. 1019 (*ibid.*, § 350), Res. 1041 (*ibid.*, § 351), Res. 1049 and 1072 (*ibid.*, § 352), Res. 1052 (*ibid.*, § 353), Res. 1073 (*ibid.*, § 354), Res. 1076 (*ibid.*, § 355), Res. 1089 (*ibid.*, § 356), Res. 1161 (*ibid.*, § 357), Res. 1173 and 1180 (*ibid.*, § 358) and Res. 1181 (*ibid.*, § 359).

[30] League of Nations, Assembly, Resolution adopted on 30 September 1938 (*ibid.*, § 378).

[31] 20th International Conference of the Red Cross, Res. XXVIII (*ibid.*, §§ 60 and 429).

[32] UN General Assembly, Res. 2444 (XXIII) (adopted by unanimous vote of 111 in favour, none against and no abstentions) (*ibid.*, §§ 55 and 379).

[33] 27th International Conference of the Red Cross and Red Crescent, Plan of Action for the years 2000–2003 (adopted by consensus) (*ibid.*, § 433).

[34] UN Security Council, Res. 1296 (*ibid.*, § 361).

Yugoslavia, in particular in the *Tadić case, Martić case* and *Kupreškić case,* and of the Inter-American Commission on Human Rights in the case relative to the events at La Tablada in Argentina provides further evidence that the obligation to make a distinction between civilians and combatants is customary in both international and non-international armed conflicts.[35]

The ICRC has called on parties to both international and non-international armed conflicts to respect the distinction between combatants and civilians.[36]

Rule 2. Acts or threats of violence the primary purpose of which is to spread terror among the civilian population are prohibited.

Practice

Volume II, Chapter 1, Section B.

Summary

State practice establishes this rule as a norm of customary international law applicable in both international and non-international armed conflicts.

International armed conflicts

Article 51(2) of Additional Protocol I prohibits "acts or threats of violence the primary purpose of which is to spread terror among the civilian population".[37] No reservations have been made to this provision. At the Diplomatic Conference leading to the adoption of the Additional Protocols, Mexico stated that Article 51 of Additional Protocol I was so essential that it "cannot be the subject of any reservations whatsoever since these would be inconsistent with the aim and purpose of Protocol I and undermine its basis".[38] Also at the Diplomatic Conference, the United Kingdom stated that Article 51(2) was a "valuable reaffirmation" of an existing rule of customary international law.[39]

The prohibition of acts or threats of violence aimed at terrorising the civilian population is set forth in a large number of military manuals.[40] Violations of this

---

[35] ICJ, *Nuclear Weapons case*, Advisory Opinion (*ibid.*, §§ 61 and 434); ICTY, *Tadić case*, Interlocutory Appeal (*ibid.*, §§ 435, 625, 750 and 882), *Martić case*, Review of the Indictment (*ibid.*, §§ 437 and 552) and *Kupreškić case*, Judgement (*ibid.*, §§ 441 and 883); Inter-American Commission on Human Rights, *Case 11.137 (Argentina)* (*ibid.*, §§ 64, 443 and 810).

[36] See, e.g., the practice of the ICRC (*ibid.*, §§ 67–75).

[37] Additional Protocol I, Article 51(2) (adopted by 77 votes in favour, one against and 16 abstentions) (*ibid.*, § 477).

[38] Mexico, Statement at the Diplomatic Conference leading to the adoption of the Additional Protocols (*ibid.*, §§ 146, 307, 536 and 800).

[39] United Kingdom, Statement at the Diplomatic Conference leading to the adoption of the Additional Protocols (*ibid.*, §§ 319, 537 and 803).

[40] See, e.g., the military manuals of Argentina (*ibid.*, § 489), Australia (*ibid.*, § 490), Belgium (*ibid.*, §§ 491–492), Benin (*ibid.*, § 493), Cameroon (*ibid.*, § 494), Canada (*ibid.*, § 495), Colombia (*ibid.*, § 496), Croatia (*ibid.*, § 497), Ecuador (*ibid.*, § 498), France (*ibid.*, § 499), Germany (*ibid.*, § 500),

rule are an offence under the legislation of numerous States.[41] The prohibition is also supported by official statements.[42] This practice includes that of States not, or not at the time, party to Additional Protocol I.[43] States party to Additional Protocol I have also invoked this rule against States not party.[44]

When the ICRC appealed to the parties to the conflict in the Middle East in October 1973, i.e., before the adoption of Additional Protocol I, to respect the prohibition of "methods intended to spread terror among the civilian population", the States concerned (Egypt, Iraq, Israel and Syria) replied favourably.[45]

It can be argued that the prohibition of acts or threats of violence aimed at terrorising the civilian population is further supported by the wider prohibition of "all measures of intimidation or of terrorism" in Article 33 of the Fourth Geneva Convention.[46] Prior to the adoption of this provision, the Report of the Commission on Responsibility set up after the First World War listed "systematic terror" as a violation of the laws and customs of war.[47]

Non-international armed conflicts

Article 13(2) of Additional Protocol II prohibits acts or threats of violence the primary purpose of which is to spread terror among the civilian population.[48] In addition, the prohibition is included in other instruments pertaining also to non-international armed conflicts.[49]

The prohibition of acts or threats of violence aimed at terrorising the civilian population is set forth in military manuals which are applicable in or have been applied in non-international armed conflicts.[50] Violations of this rule in any

Hungary (*ibid.*, § 501), Kenya (*ibid.*, § 502), Netherlands (*ibid.*, § 503), New Zealand (*ibid.*, § 504), Nigeria (*ibid.*, § 505), Russia (*ibid.*, § 506), Spain (*ibid.*, § 507), Sweden (*ibid.*, § 508), Switzerland (*ibid.*, § 509), Togo (*ibid.*, § 510), United States (*ibid.*, §§ 511–512) and Yugoslavia (*ibid.*, § 513).

[41] See, e.g., the legislation of Argentina (*ibid.*, § 514), Australia (*ibid.*, § 515), Bangladesh (*ibid.*, § 516), Bosnia and Herzegovina (*ibid.*, § 517), China (*ibid.*, § 518), Colombia (*ibid.*, § 519), Côte d'Ivoire (*ibid.*, § 520), Croatia (*ibid.*, § 521), Czech Republic (*ibid.*, § 522), Ethiopia (*ibid.*, § 523), Ireland (*ibid.*, § 524), Lithuania (*ibid.*, § 525), Netherlands (*ibid.*, § 526), Norway (*ibid.*, § 527), Slovakia (*ibid.*, § 528), Slovenia (*ibid.*, § 529), Spain (*ibid.*, § 530) and Yugoslavia (*ibid.*, § 531).

[42] See, e.g., the statements of Israel (*ibid.*, § 534), Lebanon (*ibid.*, § 535) and United States (*ibid.*, §§ 538–540).

[43] See, e.g., the practice of France (*ibid.*, § 499), Israel (*ibid.*, § 534), Kenya (*ibid.*, § 502) and United States (*ibid.*, §§ 511–512 and 538–540).

[44] See, e.g., the statement of Lebanon vis-à-vis Israel (*ibid.*, § 535).

[45] See ICRC, The International Committee's Action in the Middle East (*ibid.*, § 556).

[46] Fourth Geneva Convention, Article 33 (*ibid.*, § 476). The relevance of this provision to the present rule is explained in Yves Sandoz, Christophe Swinarski, Bruno Zimmermann (eds.), *Commentary on the Additional Protocols*, ICRC, Geneva, 1987, § 4538.

[47] Report of the Commission on Responsibility (cited in Vol. II, Ch. 1, § 481).

[48] Additional Protocol II, Article 13(2) (adopted by consensus) (*ibid.*, § 479).

[49] See, e.g., Memorandum of Understanding on the Application of IHL between Croatia and the SFRY, para. 6 (*ibid.*, § 485); Agreement on the Application of IHL between the Parties to the Conflict in Bosnia and Herzegovina, para. 2.5 (*ibid.*, § 486).

[50] See, e.g., the military manuals of Argentina (*ibid.*, § 489), Australia (*ibid.*, § 490), Benin (*ibid.*, § 493), Cameroon (*ibid.*, § 494), Canada (*ibid.*, § 495), Colombia (*ibid.*, § 496), Croatia (*ibid.*, § 497), Ecuador (*ibid.*, § 498), Germany (*ibid.*, § 500), Hungary (*ibid.*, § 501), Kenya (*ibid.*, § 502), Netherlands (*ibid.*, § 503), New Zealand (*ibid.*, § 504), Russia (*ibid.*, § 506), Spain (*ibid.*, § 507), Togo (*ibid.*, § 510) and Yugoslavia (*ibid.*, § 513).

armed conflict are an offence under the legislation of many States.[51] There are also official statements pertaining to non-international armed conflicts invoking this rule.[52]

It can be argued that the prohibition of acts or threats of violence aimed at terrorising the civilian population is further supported by the wider prohibition of "acts of terrorism" in Article 4(2)(d) of Additional Protocol II.[53] "Acts of terrorism" are specified as war crimes under the Statutes of the International Criminal Tribunal for Rwanda and of the Special Court for Sierra Leone.[54] In his report on the establishment of a Special Court for Sierra Leone, the UN Secretary-General noted that violations of Article 4 of Additional Protocol II have long been considered crimes under customary international law.[55]

No official contrary practice was found with respect to either international or non-international armed conflicts. Alleged violations of this rule have generally been condemned by States.[56] Similarly, the UN General Assembly and UN Commission on Human Rights have adopted several resolutions condemning the terrorisation of the civilian population in the conflicts in the former Yugoslavia.[57] Furthermore, the indictments in the Đukić case, Karadžić and Mladić case and Galić case before the International Criminal Tribunal for the Former Yugoslavia included charges of terrorising the civilian population in violation of the laws and customs of war, in the first two cases as part of charges of unlawful attack.[58] In its judgement in the Galić case in 2003, the Trial Chamber found the accused guilty of "acts of violence the primary purpose of which is to spread terror among the civilian population, as set forth in Article 51 of Additional Protocol I, as a violation of the laws or customs of war under Article 3 of the Statute of the Tribunal".[59]

---

[51] See, e.g., the legislation of Bosnia and Herzegovina (ibid., § 517), Colombia (ibid., § 519), Croatia (ibid., § 521), Ethiopia (ibid., § 523), Ireland (ibid., § 524), Lithuania (ibid., § 525), Norway (ibid., § 527), Slovenia (ibid., § 529), Spain (ibid., § 530) and Yugoslavia (ibid., § 531); see also the legislation of the Czech Republic (ibid., § 522) and Slovakia (ibid., § 528), the application of which is not excluded in time of non-international armed conflict, and the draft legislation of Argentina (ibid., § 514).

[52] See, e.g., the statements of Botswana (ibid., § 533) and United States (ibid., § 540).

[53] Additional Protocol II, Article 4(2)(d) (adopted by consensus) (ibid., § 478). The relevance of this provision to the present rule is explained in Yves Sandoz, Christophe Swinarski, Bruno Zimmermann (eds.), Commentary on the Additional Protocols, ICRC, Geneva, 1987, § 4538.

[54] ICTR Statute, Article 4(d) (cited in Vol. II, Ch. 1, § 487); Statute of the Special Court for Sierra Leone, Article 3(d) (ibid., § 480).

[55] UN Secretary-General, Report on the establishment of a Special Court for Sierra Leone (ibid., § 545).

[56] See, e.g., the statements of Israel (ibid., § 534), Lebanon (ibid., § 535) and United States (ibid., § 540).

[57] See, e.g., UN General Assembly, Res. 49/196 (ibid., § 541) and Res. 53/164 (ibid., § 542); UN Commission on Human Rights, Res. 1992/S-2/1, 1993/7, 1994/72 and 1995/89 (ibid., § 543).

[58] ICTY, Đukić case, Initial Indictment (ibid., § 551), Karadžić and Mladić case, First Indictment (ibid., § 553) and Galić case, Initial Indictment (ibid., § 554).

[59] ICTY, Prosecutor v. Stanislav Galić, Case No. IT-98-29-T, Judgement and Opinion, 5 December 2003, § 769.

The ICRC has reminded parties to both international and non-international armed conflicts of the prohibition on terrorising the civilian population.[60]

Examples

Examples of acts of violence cited in practice as being prohibited under this rule include offensive support or strike operations aimed at spreading terror among the civilian population,[61] indiscriminate and widespread shelling,[62] and the regular bombardment of cities,[63] but also assault, rape, abuse and torture of women and children,[64] and mass killing.[65] The indictments on the grounds of terrorising the civilian population in the above-mentioned cases before the International Criminal Tribunal for the Former Yugoslavia concerned deliberate and indiscriminate firing on civilian targets,[66] unlawful firing on civilian gatherings,[67] and a protracted campaign of shelling and sniping upon civilian areas.[68] These examples show that many acts violating the prohibition of acts or threats of violence aimed at terrorising the civilian population are also covered by specific prohibitions.

Rule 3. All members of the armed forces of a party to the conflict are combatants, except medical and religious personnel.

Practice

Volume II, Chapter 1, Section C.

Summary

State practice establishes this rule as a norm of customary international law in international armed conflicts. For purposes of the principle of distinction (see Rule 1), members of State armed forces may be considered combatants in both international and non-international armed conflicts. Combatant status, on the other hand, exists only in international armed conflicts (see introductory note to Chapter 33).

---

[60] See, e.g., the practice of the ICRC (cited in Vol. II, Ch. 1, §§ 556–558 and 561).
[61] Australia, *Defence Force Manual* (*ibid.*, § 490).
[62] UN General Assembly, Res. 53/164 (*ibid.*, § 542).
[63] UN Commission on Human Rights, Special Rapporteur on the Situation of Human Rights in the Former Yugoslavia, Report (*ibid.*, § 546).
[64] UN High Commissioner for Human Rights, Report on systematic rape, sexual slavery and slavery-like practices during armed conflicts (*ibid.*, § 547).
[65] OSCE, Kosovo/Kosova, as seen as told, An analysis of the human rights findings of the OSCE Kosovo Verification Mission (*ibid.*, § 549).
[66] ICTY, *Đukić case*, Initial Indictment (*ibid.*, § 551).
[67] ICTY, *Karadžić and Mladić case*, First Indictment (*ibid.*, § 553).
[68] ICTY, *Galić case*, Initial Indictment (*ibid.*, § 554).

International armed conflicts

This rule goes back to the Hague Regulations, according to which "the armed forces of the belligerent parties may consist of combatants and non-combatants".[69] It is now set forth in Article 43(2) of Additional Protocol I.[70]

Numerous military manuals contain this definition of combatants.[71] It is supported by official statements and reported practice.[72] This practice includes that of States not, or not at the time, party to Additional Protocol I.[73]

No official contrary practice was found.

Non-international armed conflicts

Common Article 3 of the Geneva Conventions and Additional Protocol II refer to "armed forces" and Additional Protocol II also to "dissident armed forces and other organized armed groups". These concepts are not further defined in the practice pertaining to non-international armed conflicts. While State armed forces may be considered combatants for purposes of the principle of distinction (see Rule 1), practice is not clear as to the situation of members of armed opposition groups. Practice does indicate, however, that persons do not enjoy the protection against attack accorded to civilians when they take a direct part in hostilities (see Rule 6).

Persons taking a direct part in hostilities in non-international armed conflicts are sometimes labelled "combatants". For example, in a resolution on respect for human rights in armed conflict adopted in 1970, the UN General Assembly speaks of "combatants in all armed conflicts".[74] More recently, the term "combatant" was used in the Cairo Declaration and Cairo Plan of Action for both types of conflicts.[75] However, this designation is only used in its generic meaning and indicates that these persons do not enjoy the protection against attack accorded to civilians, but does not imply a right to combatant status or prisoner-of-war status, as applicable in international armed conflicts (see Chapter 33).

---

[69] Hague Regulations, Article 3 (*ibid.*, § 571).

[70] Additional Protocol I, Article 43(2) (adopted by consensus) (*ibid.*, § 572).

[71] See, e.g., the military manuals of Argentina (*ibid.*, § 574), Australia (*ibid.*, § 575), Belgium (*ibid.*, § 576), Benin (*ibid.*, § 577), Cameroon (*ibid.*, § 578), Canada (*ibid.*, § 579), Colombia (*ibid.*, § 580), Croatia (*ibid.*, §§ 581–582), Dominican Republic (*ibid.*, § 583), Ecuador (*ibid.*, § 584), France (*ibid.*, §§ 585–586), Germany (*ibid.*, § 587), Hungary (*ibid.*, § 588), Indonesia (*ibid.*, § 589), Israel (*ibid.*, § 590), Italy (*ibid.*, §§ 591–592), Kenya (*ibid.*, § 593), South Korea (*ibid.*, § 594), Madagascar (*ibid.*, § 595), Netherlands (*ibid.*, § 596), New Zealand (*ibid.*, § 597), Russia (*ibid.*, § 598), South Africa (*ibid.*, § 599), Spain (*ibid.*, § 600), Sweden (*ibid.*, § 601), Togo (*ibid.*, § 602), United Kingdom (*ibid.*, § 603) and United States (*ibid.*, §§ 604–606).

[72] See, e.g., the practice of Argentina (*ibid.*, 611), India (*ibid.*, § 612), Iraq (*ibid.*, § 613), Japan (*ibid.*, § 614), Jordan (*ibid.*, § 615) and Syria (*ibid.*, § 619).

[73] See, e.g., the practice of France (*ibid.*, § 585), Indonesia (*ibid.*, § 589), Israel (*ibid.*, § 590), Kenya (*ibid.*, § 593), United Kingdom (*ibid.*, § 603) and United States (*ibid.*, §§ 604–606).

[74] UN General Assembly, Res. 2676 (XXV), 9 December 1970, preamble and § 5.

[75] Cairo Declaration, Sections 68–69, and Cairo Plan of Action, Section 82, both adopted at the Africa-Europe Summit held under the Aegis of the Organization of African Unity and the European Union, 3–4 April 2000.

The lawfulness of direct participation in hostilities in non-international armed conflicts is governed by national law. While such persons could also be called "fighters", this term would be translated as "combatant" in a number of languages and is therefore not wholly satisfactory either.

Treaty provisions use different designations that can apply to "fighters" in the context of non-international armed conflicts, including: persons taking active part in the hostilities;[76] members of dissident armed forces or other organized armed groups;[77] persons who take a direct part in hostilities;[78] civilians who take a direct part in hostilities;[79] civilians taking direct part in hostilities;[80] and combatant adversary.[81] The uncertainty about the qualification of members of armed opposition groups is further addressed in the commentaries to Rules 5 and 6.

Interpretation

According to this rule, when military medical and religious personnel are members of the armed forces, they are nevertheless considered non-combatants. According to the First Geneva Convention, temporary medical personnel have to be respected and protected as non-combatants only as long as the medical assignment lasts (see commentary to Rule 25).[82] As is the case for civilians (see Rule 6), respect for non-combatants is contingent on their abstaining from taking a direct part in hostilities.

The military manuals of Germany and the United States point out that there can be other non-combatant members of the armed forces besides medical and religious personnel. Germany's Military Manual explains that "combatants are persons who may take a direct part in hostilities, i.e., participate in the use of a weapon or a weapon-system in an indispensable function", and specifies, therefore, that "persons who are members of the armed forces but do not have any combat mission, such as judges, government officials and blue-collar workers, are non-combatants".[83] The US Naval Handbook states that "civil defense personnel and members of the armed forces who have acquired civil defense status" are non-combatants, in addition to medical and religious personnel.[84]

Non-combatant members of the armed forces are not to be confused, however, with civilians accompanying armed forces who are not members of the armed forces by definition.[85]

---

[76] Geneva Conventions, common Article 3.
[77] Additional Protocol II, Article 1(1) (adopted by 58 votes in favour, 5 against and 29 abstentions) (cited in Vol. II, Ch. 1, § 633).
[78] Additional Protocol II, Article 4(1) (adopted by consensus).
[79] Additional Protocol II, Article 13(3) (adopted by consensus) (*ibid.*, § 756).
[80] ICC Statute, Article 8(2)(e)(i).   [81] ICC Statute, Article 8(2)(e)(ix).
[82] First Geneva Convention, Article 25 (cited in Vol. II, Ch. 7, § 7).
[83] Germany, *Military Manual* (cited in Vol. II, Ch. 1, § 587).
[84] United States, *Naval Handbook* (*ibid.*, § 605).
[85] See Third Geneva Convention, Article 4(A)(4).

While in some countries, entire segments of the population between certain ages may be drafted into the armed forces in the event of armed conflict, only those persons who are actually drafted, i.e., who are actually incorporated into the armed forces, can be considered combatants. Potential mobilisation does not render the person concerned a combatant liable to attack.[86]

Rule 4. The armed forces of a party to the conflict consist of all organised armed forces, groups and units which are under a command responsible to that party for the conduct of its subordinates.

Practice

Volume II, Chapter 1, Section D.

Summary

State practice establishes this rule as a norm of customary international law applicable in international armed conflicts. For purposes of the principle of distinction, it may also apply to State armed forces in non-international armed conflicts.[87]

International armed conflicts

This rule is set forth in Article 43(1) of Additional Protocol I.[88]

Many military manuals specify that the armed forces of a party to the conflict consist of all organised armed groups which are under a command responsible to that party for the conduct of its subordinates.[89] This definition is supported by official statements and reported practice.[90] Practice includes that of States not, or not at the time, party to Additional Protocol I.[91]

---

[86] This conclusion is based on discussions during the second consultation with academic and governmental experts in the framework of this study in May 1999 and the general agreement among the experts to this effect. The experts also considered that it may be necessary to consider the legislation of a State in determining when reservists actually become members of the armed forces.

[87] See CDDH, *Official Records*, Vol. X, CDDH/I/238/Rev. 1, pp. 93–94; see also Yves Sandoz, Christophe Swinarski, Bruno Zimmermann (eds.), *Commentary on the Additional Protocols*, ICRC, Geneva, 1987, § 4462.

[88] Additional Protocol I, Article 43(1) (adopted by consensus) (cited in Vol. II, Ch. 1, § 631).

[89] See, e.g., the military manuals of Argentina (*ibid.*, § 637), Australia (*ibid.*, § 638), Canada (*ibid.*, § 642), Croatia (*ibid.*, § 644), Germany (*ibid.*, § 647), Hungary (*ibid.*, § 648), Italy (*ibid.*, § 651), Kenya (*ibid.*, § 652), Netherlands (*ibid.*, § 654), New Zealand (*ibid.*, § 655), Nigeria (*ibid.*, § 656), Russia (*ibid.*, § 657), Spain (*ibid.*, § 659), Sweden (*ibid.*, § 660) and United Kingdom (*ibid.*, § 662).

[90] See, e.g., the practice of Belgium (*ibid.*, § 670), France (*ibid.*, § 671), Germany (*ibid.*, § 672), Iran (*ibid.*, § 673), Netherlands (*ibid.*, § 676) and Syria (*ibid.*, § 677).

[91] See, e.g., the practice of France (*ibid.*, § 671), Kenya (*ibid.*, § 652), United Kingdom (*ibid.*, § 662) and United States (*ibid.*, § 665).

In essence, this definition of armed forces covers all persons who fight on behalf of a party to a conflict and who subordinate themselves to its command. As a result, a combatant is any person who, under responsible command, engages in hostile acts in an armed conflict on behalf of a party to the conflict. The conditions imposed on armed forces vest in the group as such. The members of such armed forces are liable to attack.

This definition of armed forces builds upon earlier definitions contained in the Hague Regulations and the Third Geneva Convention which sought to determine who are combatants entitled to prisoner-of-war status. Article 1 of the Hague Regulations provides that the laws, rights and duties of war apply not only to armies, but also to militia and volunteer corps fulfilling four conditions:

1. to be commanded by a person responsible for his subordinates;
2. to have a fixed distinctive emblem recognizable at a distance;
3. to carry arms openly; and
4. to conduct their operations in accordance with the laws and customs of war.

It further specifies that in countries where militia or volunteer corps (so-called "irregular" armed forces) constitute the army, or form part of it, they are included under the denomination "army".[92] This definition is also used in Article 4 of the Third Geneva Convention, with the addition of organised resistance movements.[93] The Hague Regulations and the Third Geneva Convention thus consider all members of armed forces to be combatants and require militia and volunteer corps, including organised resistance movements, to comply with four conditions in order for them to be considered combatants entitled to prisoner-of-war status. The idea underlying these definitions is that the regular armed forces fulfil these four conditions *per se* and, as a result, they are not explicitly enumerated with respect to them. The definition contained in Additional Protocol I does not distinguish between the regular armed forces and other armed groups or units, but defines all armed forces, groups and units which are under a command responsible to a party for the conduct of its subordinates as armed forces of that party. Both definitions express the same idea, namely that all persons who fight in the name of a party to a conflict – who "belong to" a party in the words of Article 4 of the Third Geneva Convention – are combatants. The four conditions contained in the Hague Regulations and the Third Geneva Convention have been reduced to two conditions, the main difference being the exclusion of the requirements of visibility for the definition of armed forces as such. The requirement of visibility is relevant with respect to a combatant's entitlement to prisoner-of-war status (see Rule 106). Additional Protocol I, therefore, has lifted this requirement from the definition of armed

---

[92] Hague Regulations, Article 1 (*ibid.*, § 628).
[93] Third Geneva Convention, Article 4 (*ibid.*, § 630).

forces (Article 43) and placed it in the provision dealing with combatants and prisoner-of-war status (Article 44).

In addition, Article 43 of Additional Protocol I does not mention the requirement to respect the laws and customs of war but includes a requirement to have an internal disciplinary system to enforce compliance with international humanitarian law, but this change does not substantially alter the definition of armed forces for the purposes of determining those combatants entitled to prisoner-of-war status. The requirement of an internal disciplinary system supplements the provisions concerning command responsibility (see Rules 152–153) and is a corollary to the obligation to issue instructions which comply with international humanitarian law (see commentary to Rule 139).[94]

Articles 43 and 44 of Additional Protocol I reaffirm what was already stated in Article 85 of the Third Geneva Convention, namely that "prisoners of war prosecuted under the laws of the Detaining Power for acts committed prior to capture shall retain, even if convicted, the benefits of the present Convention", that is to say that they retain their status. These provisions "thus preclude any attempt to deny prisoner of war status to members of independent or regular armed forces on the allegation that their force does not enforce some provision of customary or conventional law of armed conflict (as construed by the Detaining Power)".[95] Only the failure to distinguish oneself from the civilian population (see Rule 106) or being caught as a spy (see Rule 107) or a mercenary (see Rule 108) warrants forfeiture of prisoner-of-war status.

The definition in Article 43 of Additional Protocol I is now generally applied to all forms of armed groups who belong to a party to an armed conflict to determine whether they constitute armed forces. It is therefore no longer necessary to distinguish between regular and irregular armed forces. All those fulfilling the conditions in Article 43 of Additional Protocol I are armed forces.

Incorporation of paramilitary or armed law enforcement agencies into armed forces

Specific practice was found concerning the incorporation of paramilitary or armed law enforcement agencies, such as police forces, *gendarmerie* and constabulary, into armed forces.[96] Examples of such paramilitary agencies incorporated into the armed forces of a State include the Special Auxiliary Force attached to Bishop Muzorewa's United African National Congress in Zimbabwe, which was integrated into the national army after the Bishop became

---

[94] See Yves Sandoz, Christophe Swinarski, Bruno Zimmermann (eds.), *Commentary on the Additional Protocols*, ICRC, Geneva, 1987, § 1675.

[95] Michael Bothe, Karl Josef Partsch, Waldemar A. Solf, *New Rules for Victims of Armed Conflicts*, Martinus Nijhoff, The Hague, 1982, p. 239.

[96] See, e.g., the practice of Argentina (cited in Vol. II, Ch. 1, § 688), Belgium (*ibid.*, § 685), Canada (*ibid.*, § 689), France (*ibid.*, § 686), Germany (*ibid.*, § 690), Netherlands (*ibid.*, § 691), New Zealand (*ibid.*, § 692), Spain (*ibid.*, §§ 693 and 696) and Philippines (*ibid.*, § 695) and the reported practice of India (*ibid.*, § 698), South Korea (*ibid.*, § 699), Syria (*ibid.*, § 700) and Zimbabwe (*ibid.*, § 697).

Prime Minister, and India's Border Security Force in Assam.[97] Examples of armed law enforcement agencies being incorporated into the armed forces include the Philippine Constabulary and Spain's Guardia Civil.[98]

Incorporation of paramilitary or armed law enforcement agencies into armed forces is usually carried out through a formal act, for example, an act of parliament. In the absence of formal incorporation, the status of such groups will be judged on the facts and in the light of the criteria for defining armed forces. When these units take part in hostilities and fulfil the criteria of armed forces, they are considered combatants. In addition, Additional Protocol I requires a party to the conflict to notify such incorporation to the other parties to the conflict.[99] Belgium and France issued a general notification to this effect to all States party upon ratification of Additional Protocol I.[100] This method of satisfying the requirement of notification was explicitly recognised by the Rapporteur of the Working Group at the Diplomatic Conference leading to the adoption of the Additional Protocols.[101] In the light of the general obligation to distinguish between combatants and civilians (see Rule 1), such notification is important because members of the armed forces of each side have to know who is a member of the armed forces and who is a civilian. Confusion is particularly likely since police forces and *gendarmerie* usually carry arms and wear a uniform, although in principle their uniforms are not the same as those of the armed forces proper. While notification is not constitutive of the status of the units concerned, it does serve to avoid confusion and thus enhances respect for the principle of distinction.

Rule 5. Civilians are persons who are not members of the armed forces. The civilian population comprises all persons who are civilians.

Practice

Volume II, Chapter 1, Section E.

Summary

State practice establishes this rule as a norm of customary international law applicable in international armed conflicts. It also applies to non-international armed conflicts although practice is ambiguous as to whether members of armed opposition groups are considered members of armed forces or civilians.

---

[97] These examples are quoted in New Zealand, *Military Manual* (*ibid.*, § 692).

[98] Philippines, *Decree on the Constitution of the Integrated National Police* (*ibid.*, § 695); Spain, *Military Criminal Code* (*ibid.*, § 696).

[99] Additional Protocol I, Article 43(3) (adopted by consensus) (*ibid.*, § 684).

[100] Belgium, Interpretative declarations made upon ratification of Additional Protocol I (*ibid.*, § 685); France, Reservations and declarations made upon ratification of Additional Protocol I (*ibid.*, § 686).

[101] Yves Sandoz, Christophe Swinarski, Bruno Zimmermann (eds.), *Commentary on the Additional Protocols*, ICRC, Geneva, 1987, § 1682.

International armed conflicts

The definition of civilians as persons who are not members of the armed forces is set forth in Article 50 of Additional Protocol I, to which no reservations have been made.[102] It is also contained in numerous military manuals.[103] It is reflected in reported practice.[104] This practice includes that of States not, or not at the time, party to Additional Protocol I.[105]

In its judgement in the *Blaškić case* in 2000, the International Criminal Tribunal for the Former Yugoslavia defined civilians as "persons who are not, or no longer, members of the armed forces".[106]

No official contrary practice was found. Some practice adds the condition that civilians are persons who do not participate in hostilities. This additional requirement merely reinforces the rule that a civilian who participates directly in hostilities loses protection against attack (see Rule 6). However, such a civilian does not thereby become a combatant entitled to prisoner-of-war status and, upon capture, may be tried under national law for the mere participation in the conflict, subject to fair trial guarantees (see Rule 100).

Exception

An exception to this rule is the *levée en masse*, whereby the inhabitants of a country which has not yet been occupied, on the approach of the enemy, spontaneously take up arms to resist the invading troops without having time to form themselves into an armed force. Such persons are considered combatants if they carry arms openly and respect the laws and customs of war (see commentary to Rule 106). This is a long-standing rule of customary international humanitarian law already recognised in the Lieber Code and the Brussels Declaration.[107] It is codified in the Hague Regulations and the Third Geneva Convention.[108] Although of limited current application, the *levée en masse* is still repeated in many military manuals, including very recent ones.[109]

---

[102] Additional Protocol I, Article 50 (adopted by consensus) (cited in Vol. II, Ch. 1, § 705).

[103] See, e.g., the military manuals of Argentina (*ibid.*, § 712), Australia (*ibid.*, § 713), Benin (*ibid.*, § 714), Cameroon (*ibid.*, § 715), Canada (*ibid.*, § 716), Colombia (*ibid.*, § 717), Croatia (*ibid.*, §§ 718–719), Dominican Republic (*ibid.*, § 720), Ecuador (*ibid.*, § 721), France (*ibid.*, §§ 722–723), Hungary (*ibid.*, § 724), Indonesia (*ibid.*, § 725), Italy (*ibid.*, § 727), Kenya (*ibid.*, § 728), Madagascar (*ibid.*, § 729), Netherlands (*ibid.*, § 730), South Africa (*ibid.*, § 731), Spain (*ibid.*, § 732), Sweden (*ibid.*, § 733), Togo (*ibid.*, § 734), United Kingdom (*ibid.*, § 735), United States (*ibid.*, §§ 736–737) and Yugoslavia (*ibid.*, § 738).

[104] See, e.g., the reported practice of Israel (*ibid.*, § 726), Jordan (*ibid.*, § 743), Rwanda (*ibid.*, § 746) and Syria (*ibid.*, § 747).

[105] See, e.g., the practice of France (*ibid.*, § 722), Indonesia (*ibid.*, § 725), Israel (*ibid.*, § 726), Kenya (*ibid.*, § 728), United Kingdom (*ibid.*, § 735) and United States (*ibid.*, §§ 736–737).

[106] ICTY, *Blaškić case*, Judgement (*ibid.*, § 751).

[107] Lieber Code, Articles 49 and 51; Brussels Declaration, Article 10.

[108] Hague Regulations, Article 2; Third Geneva Convention, Article 4(A)(6).

[109] See, e.g., the military manuals of Benin (cited in Vol. II, Ch. 1, § 714), Cameroon (*ibid.*, § 715), Canada (*ibid.*, § 764), Kenya (*ibid.*, § 728), Madagascar (*ibid.*, § 729), South Africa (*ibid.*, § 731) and Togo (*ibid.*, § 734).

Non-international armed conflicts

The definition that "any person who is not a member of armed forces is considered to be a civilian" and that "the civilian population comprises all persons who are civilians" was included in the draft of Additional Protocol II.[110] The first part of this definition was amended to read that "a civilian is anyone who is not a member of the armed forces or of an organized armed group" and both parts were adopted by consensus in Committee III of the Diplomatic Conference leading to the adoption of the Additional Protocols.[111] However, this definition was dropped at the last moment of the conference as part of a package aimed at the adoption of a simplified text.[112] As a result, Additional Protocol II does not contain a definition of civilians or the civilian population even though these terms are used in several provisions.[113] It can be argued that the terms "dissident armed forces or other organized armed groups . . . under responsible command" in Article 1 of Additional Protocol II inferentially recognise the essential conditions of armed forces, as they apply in international armed conflict (see Rule 4), and that it follows that civilians are all persons who are not members of such forces or groups.[114] Subsequent treaties, applicable to non-international armed conflicts, have similarly used the terms civilians and civilian population without defining them.[115]

While State armed forces are not considered civilians, practice is not clear as to whether members of armed opposition groups are civilians subject to Rule 6 on loss of protection from attack in case of direct participation or whether members of such groups are liable to attack as such, independently of the operation of Rule 6. Although the military manual of Colombia defines the term civilians as "those who do not participate directly in military hostilities (internal conflict, international conflict)",[116] most manuals define civilians negatively with respect to combatants and armed forces and are silent on the status of members of armed opposition groups.

Rule 6. Civilians are protected against attack unless and for such time as they take a direct part in hostilities.

Practice

Volume II, Chapter 1, Section F.

---

[110] Draft Additional Protocol II submitted by the ICRC to the Diplomatic Conference leading to the adoption of the Additional Protocols, Article 25 (*ibid.*, § 706).
[111] Draft Additional Protocol II, Article 25 as adopted by Committee III (*ibid.*, § 706).
[112] See *ibid.*, § 706.
[113] Additional Protocol II, Articles 13–15 and 17–18.
[114] Michael Bothe, Karl Joseph Partsch, Waldemar A. Solf (eds.), *New Rules for Victims of Armed Conflicts*, Martinus Nijhoff, The Hague, 1982, p. 672.
[115] See, e.g., Amended Protocol II to the CCW, Article 3(7)–(11); Protocol III to the CCW, Article 2; Ottawa Convention, preamble; ICC Statute, Article 8(2)(e)(i), (iii) and (viii).
[116] Colombia, *Instructors' Manual* (*ibid.*, § 717).

Summary

State practice establishes this rule as a norm of customary international law applicable in both international and non-international armed conflicts. The use of human shields is the subject of Rule 97.

International armed conflicts

The rule whereby civilians lose their protection against attack when and for such time as they take a direct part in hostilities is contained in Article 51(3) of Additional Protocol I, to which no reservations have been made.[117] At the Diplomatic Conference leading to the adoption of the Additional Protocols, Mexico stated that Article 51 of Additional Protocol I was so essential that it "cannot be the subject of any reservations whatsoever since these would be inconsistent with the aim and purpose of Protocol I and undermine its basis".[118] Also at the Diplomatic Conference, the United Kingdom stated that the exception to the civilian immunity from attack contained in Article 51(3) was a "valuable reaffirmation" of an existing rule of customary international law.[119] Upon ratification of the Convention on Certain Conventional Weapons, the United Kingdom declared that civilians enjoyed the protection of the Convention "unless and for such time as they take a direct part in hostilities".[120]

Numerous military manuals state that civilians are not protected against attack when they take a direct part in hostilities.[121] The rule is supported by official statements and reported practice.[122] This practice includes that of States not, or not at the time, party to Additional Protocol I.[123] When the ICRC appealed to the parties to the conflict in the Middle East in October 1973, i.e., before the adoption of Additional Protocol I, to respect civilian immunity from

---

[117] Additional Protocol I, Article 51(3) (adopted by 77 votes in favour, one against and 16 abstentions) (*ibid.*, § 755).

[118] Mexico, Statement at the Diplomatic Conference leading to the adoption of the Additional Protocols (*ibid.*, § 800).

[119] United Kingdom, Statement at the Diplomatic Conference leading to the adoption of the Additional Protocols (*ibid.*, § 803).

[120] United Kingdom, Declaration made upon ratification of the CCW (*ibid.*, § 757).

[121] See, e.g., the military manuals of Australia (*ibid.*, § 762), Benin (*ibid.*, § 763), Canada (*ibid.*, § 764), Colombia (*ibid.*, § 765), Croatia (*ibid.*, § 766), Dominican Republic (*ibid.*, § 767), Ecuador (*ibid.*, § 768), France (*ibid.*, § 769), Germany (*ibid.*, § 770), India (*ibid.*, § 771), Indonesia (*ibid.*, § 772), Italy (*ibid.*, § 773), Kenya (*ibid.*, § 774), Madagascar (*ibid.*, § 775), Netherlands (*ibid.*, §§ 776–777), New Zealand (*ibid.*, § 778), Nigeria (*ibid.*, §§ 779–780), South Africa (*ibid.*, § 781), Spain (*ibid.*, § 782), Sweden (*ibid.*, § 783), Togo (*ibid.*, § 784), United Kingdom (*ibid.*, § 786), United States (*ibid.*, §§ 787–788) and Yugoslavia (*ibid.*, § 789).

[122] See, e.g., the statements of Belgium (*ibid.*, § 792) and United States (*ibid.*, §§ 804–806) and the reported practice of Chile (*ibid.*, § 793), Jordan (*ibid.*, § 796), Malaysia (*ibid.*, § 799) and United States (*ibid.*, § 807).

[123] See, e.g., the practice of France (*ibid.*, § 769), India (*ibid.*, § 771), Indonesia (*ibid.*, § 772), Kenya (*ibid.*, § 774), Malaysia (*ibid.*, § 799), Nigeria (*ibid.*, § 779), United Kingdom (*ibid.*, § 786) and United States (*ibid.*, §§ 787–788 and 804–807).

attack, unless and for such time as they took a direct part in hostilities, the States concerned (Egypt, Iraq, Israel and Syria) replied favourably.[124]

Non-international armed conflicts

Pursuant to Article 13(3) of Additional Protocol II, civilians are immune from direct attack "unless and for such time as they take a direct part in hostilities".[125] In addition, this rule is set forth in other instruments pertaining also to non-international armed conflicts.[126]

The rule that civilians are not protected against attack when they take a direct part in hostilities is included in many military manuals which are applicable in or have been applied in non-international armed conflicts.[127]

In the case concerning the events at La Tablada in Argentina, the Inter-American Commission on Human Rights held that civilians who directly take part in fighting, whether singly or as members of a group, thereby become legitimate military targets but only for such time as they actively participate in combat.[128]

To the extent that members of armed opposition groups can be considered civilians (see commentary to Rule 5), this rule appears to create an imbalance between such groups and governmental armed forces. Application of this rule would imply that an attack on members of armed opposition groups is only lawful for "such time as they take a direct part in hostilities" while an attack on members of governmental armed forces would be lawful at any time. Such imbalance would not exist if members of armed opposition groups were, due to their membership, either considered to be continuously taking a direct part in hostilities or not considered to be civilians.

It is clear that the lawfulness of an attack on a civilian depends on what exactly constitutes direct participation in hostilities and, related thereto, when direct participation begins and when it ends. As explained below, the meaning of direct participation in hostilities has not yet been clarified. It should be noted, however, that whatever meaning is given to these terms, immunity from attack does not imply immunity from arrest and prosecution.

---

[124] See ICRC, The International Committee's Action in the Middle East (*ibid.*, § 813).

[125] Additional Protocol II, Article 13(3) (adopted by consensus) (*ibid.*, § 756).

[126] See, e.g., Memorandum of Understanding on the Application of IHL between Croatia and the SFRY, para. 6 (*ibid.*, § 759); Agreement on the Application of IHL between the Parties to the Conflict in Bosnia and Herzegovina, para. 2.5 (*ibid.*, § 760); UN Secretary-General's Bulletin, Section 5.2 (*ibid.*, § 761).

[127] See, e.g., the military manuals of Australia (*ibid.*, § 762), Benin (*ibid.*, § 763), Colombia (*ibid.*, § 765), Croatia (*ibid.*, § 766), Ecuador (*ibid.*, § 768), Germany (*ibid.*, § 770), Italy (*ibid.*, § 773), Kenya (*ibid.*, § 774), Madagascar (*ibid.*, § 775), Netherlands (*ibid.*, § 776), Nigeria (*ibid.*, § 779), South Africa (*ibid.*, § 781), Spain (*ibid.*, § 782), Togo (*ibid.*, § 784) and Yugoslavia (*ibid.*, § 789).

[128] Inter-American Commission on Human Rights, *Case 11.137 (Argentina)* (*ibid.*, § 810).

Definition

A precise definition of the term "direct participation in hostilities" does not exist. The Inter-American Commission on Human Rights has stated that the term "direct participation in hostilities" is generally understood to mean "acts which, by their nature or purpose, are intended to cause actual harm to enemy personnel and *matériel*".[129] Loss of protection against attack is clear and uncontested, as evidenced by several military manuals, when a civilian uses weapons or other means to commit acts of violence against human or material enemy forces.[130] But there is also a lot of practice which gives little or no guidance on the interpretation of the term "direct participation", stating, for example, that the assessment of direct participation has to be made on a case-by-case basis or simply repeating the general rule that direct participation causes civilians to lose protection against attack.[131] The military manuals of Ecuador and the United States give several examples of acts constituting direct participation in hostilities, such as serving as guards, intelligence agents or lookouts on behalf of military forces.[132] The Report on the Practice of the Philippines similarly considers that civilians acting as spies, couriers or lookouts lose their protection against attack.[133]

In a report on human rights in Colombia, the Inter-American Commission on Human Rights sought to distinguish "direct" from "indirect" participation:

Civilians whose activities merely support the adverse party's war or military effort or otherwise only indirectly participate in hostilities cannot on these grounds alone be considered combatants. This is because indirect participation, such as selling goods to one or more of the armed parties, expressing sympathy for the cause of one of the parties or, even more clearly, failing to act to prevent an incursion by one of the armed parties, does not involve acts of violence which pose an immediate threat of actual harm to the adverse party.[134]

---

[129] Inter-American Commission on Human Rights, Third report on human rights in Colombia (*ibid.*, § 811).
[130] See, e.g., the military manuals of Australia (*ibid.*, § 820), Belgium (*ibid.*, § 821), Ecuador (*ibid.*, § 822), El Salvador (*ibid.*, § 823), India (*ibid.*, § 824), Netherlands (*ibid.*, § 825), United States (*ibid.*, §§ 827 and 830) and Yugoslavia (*ibid.*, § 831).
[131] See, e.g., Geneva Conventions, Common Article 3 (*ibid.*, § 754); Additional Protocol I, Article 51(3) (adopted by 77 votes in favour, one against and 16 abstentions) (*ibid.*, § 755); Additional Protocol II, Article 13(3) (adopted by consensus) (*ibid.*, § 756); Memorandum of Understanding on the Application of IHL between Croatia and the SFRY, para. 6 (*ibid.*, § 759); Agreement on the Application of IHL between the Parties to the Conflict in Bosnia and Herzegovina, para. 2.5 (*ibid.*, § 760); UN Secretary-General's Bulletin, Section 5.2 (*ibid.*, § 761); the practice of Australia (*ibid.*, § 762), Belgium (*ibid.*, § 792), Benin (*ibid.*, § 763), Canada (*ibid.*, § 764), Colombia (*ibid.*, § 765), Croatia (*ibid.*, § 766), Dominican Republic (*ibid.*, § 767), Ecuador (*ibid.*, § 768), France (*ibid.*, § 769), Germany (*ibid.*, § 770), India (*ibid.*, § 771), Indonesia (*ibid.*, § 772), Italy (*ibid.*, § 773), Jordan (*ibid.*, § 796), Kenya (*ibid.*, § 774), Madagascar (*ibid.*, § 775), Malaysia (*ibid.*, § 799), Netherlands (*ibid.*, § 776), New Zealand (*ibid.*, § 778), Spain (*ibid.*, § 782), Sweden (*ibid.*, § 783), Togo (*ibid.*, § 784), United Kingdom (*ibid.*, §§ 757 and 786), United States (*ibid.*, §§ 787–788 and 804–806), Yugoslavia (*ibid.*, § 789); Inter-American Commission on Human Rights, *Case 11.137 (Argentina)* (*ibid.*, § 810).
[132] Ecuador, *Naval Manual* (*ibid.*, § 822); United States, *Naval Handbook* (*ibid.*, § 830).
[133] Report on the Practice of the Philippines (*ibid.*, § 849).
[134] Inter-American Commission on Human Rights, Third report on human rights in Colombia (*ibid.*, § 811).

The distinction between direct and indirect participation had previously been developed by the Special Representative of the UN Commission on Human Rights for El Salvador.[135] It is clear, however, that international law does not prohibit States from adopting legislation that makes it a punishable offence for anyone to participate in hostilities, whether directly or indirectly.

The Report on the Practice of Rwanda makes a distinction between acts that constitute direct participation in international and non-international armed conflicts and excludes logistical support in non-international armed conflicts from acts that constitute direct participation. According to the responses of Rwandan army officers to a questionnaire referred to in the report, unarmed civilians who follow their armed forces during an international armed conflict in order to provide them with food, transport munitions or carry messages, for example, lose their status as civilians. In the context of a non-international armed conflict, however, unarmed civilians who collaborate with one of the parties to the conflict always remain civilians. According to the report, this distinction is justified by the fact that in internal armed conflicts civilians are forced to cooperate with the party that holds them in its power.[136]

It is fair to conclude, however, that outside the few uncontested examples cited above, in particular use of weapons or other means to commit acts of violence against human or material enemy forces, a clear and uniform definition of direct participation in hostilities has not been developed in State practice.[137]

Several military manuals specify that civilians working in military objectives, for example, munitions factories, do not participate directly in hostilities but must assume the risks involved in an attack on that military objective.[138] The injuries or death caused to such civilians are considered incidental to an attack upon a legitimate target which must be minimised by taking all feasible precautions in the choice of means and methods, for example, by attacking at night (see Rule 17). The theory that such persons must be considered quasi-combatants, liable to attack, finds no support in modern State practice.

Situations of doubt as to the character of a person

The issue of how to classify a person in case of doubt is complex and difficult. In the case of international armed conflicts, Additional Protocol I has sought to resolve this issue by stating that "in case of doubt whether a person is a

---

[135] UN Commission on Human Rights, Special Representative on the Situation of Human Rights in El Salvador, Final Report (*ibid.*, § 853).
[136] Report on the Practice of Rwanda (*ibid.*, § 850).
[137] The ICRC has sought to clarify the notion of direct participation by means of a series of expert meetings that began in 2003.
[138] See, e.g., the military manuals of Australia (cited in Vol. II, Ch. 2, § 635), Canada (*ibid.*, § 636), Colombia (*ibid.*, § 637), Croatia (*ibid.*, § 638), Ecuador (*ibid.*, § 639), Germany (*ibid.*, § 640), Hungary (*ibid.*, § 641), Madagascar (*ibid.*, § 642), Netherlands (*ibid.*, § 643), New Zealand (*ibid.*, § 644), Spain (*ibid.*, §§ 645–646), Switzerland (*ibid.*, § 647) and United States (*ibid.*, § 648).

civilian, that person shall be considered to be a civilian".[139] Some States have written this rule into their military manuals.[140] Others have expressed reservations about the military ramifications of a strict interpretation of such a rule. In particular, upon ratification of Additional Protocol I, France and the United Kingdom expressed their understanding that this presumption does not override commanders' duty to protect the safety of troops under their command or to preserve their military situation, in conformity with other provisions of Additional Protocol I.[141] The US Naval Handbook states that:

Direct participation in hostilities must be judged on a case-by-case basis. Combatants in the field must make an honest determination as to whether a particular civilian is or is not subject to deliberate attack based on the person's behavior, location and attire, and other information available at the time.[142]

In the light of the foregoing, it is fair to conclude that when there is a situation of doubt, a careful assessment has to be made under the conditions and restraints governing a particular situation as to whether there are sufficient indications to warrant an attack. One cannot automatically attack anyone who might appear dubious.

In the case of non-international armed conflicts, the issue of doubt has hardly been addressed in State practice, even though a clear rule on this subject would be desirable as it would enhance the protection of the civilian population against attack. In this respect, the same balanced approach as described above with respect to international armed conflicts seems justified in non-international armed conflicts.

---

[139] Additional Protocol I, Article 50(1) (adopted by consensus) (cited in Vol. II, Ch. 1, § 887).
[140] See, e.g., the military manuals of Argentina (*ibid.*, § 893), Australia (*ibid.*, § 894), Cameroon (*ibid.*, § 895), Canada (*ibid.*, § 896), Colombia (*ibid.*, § 897), Croatia (*ibid.*, § 898), Hungary (*ibid.*, § 900), Kenya (*ibid.*, § 901), Madagascar (*ibid.*, § 902), Netherlands (*ibid.*, § 903), South Africa (*ibid.*, § 904), Spain (*ibid.*, § 905), Sweden (*ibid.*, § 906) and Yugoslavia (*ibid.*, § 908).
[141] France, Declarations and reservations made upon ratification of Additional Protocol I (*ibid.*, § 888); United Kingdom, Declarations and reservations made upon ratification of Additional Protocol I (*ibid.*, § 889).
[142] United States, *Naval Handbook* (*ibid.*, § 830).

DISTINCTION BETWEEN CIVILIAN OBJECTS AND MILITARY OBJECTIVES

Rule 7. The parties to the conflict must at all times distinguish between civilian objects and military objectives. Attacks may only be directed against military objectives. Attacks must not be directed against civilian objects.

Practice

Volume II, Chapter 2, Section A.

Summary

State practice establishes this rule as a norm of customary international law applicable in both international and non-international armed conflicts. The three components of this rule are interrelated and the practice pertaining to each reinforces the validity of the others. Belligerent reprisals against civilian objects are discussed in Chapter 41.

International armed conflicts

This rule is codified in Articles 48 and 52(2) of Additional Protocol I, to which no reservations have been made.[1] At the Diplomatic Conference leading to the adoption of the Additional Protocols, Mexico stated that Article 52 was so essential that it "cannot be the subject of any reservations whatsoever since these would be inconsistent with the aim and purpose of Protocol I and undermine its basis".[2] The prohibition on directing attacks against civilian objects is also set forth in Amended Protocol II and Protocol III to the Convention on Certain Conventional Weapons.[3] In addition, under the Statute of the International Criminal Court, "intentionally directing attacks against civilian objects, that is, objects which are not military objectives", constitutes a war crime in international armed conflicts.[4]

---

[1] Additional Protocol I, Article 48 (adopted by consensus) (cited in Vol. II, Ch. 2, § 1) and Article 52(2) (adopted by 79 votes in favour, none against and 7 abstentions) (*ibid.*, § 50).
[2] Mexico, Statement at the Diplomatic Conference leading to the adoption of the Additional Protocols (*ibid.*, § 79).
[3] Amended Protocol II to the CCW, Article 3(7) (*ibid.*, § 107); Protocol III to the CCW, Article 2(1) (*ibid.*, § 106).
[4] ICC Statute, Article 8(2)(b)(ii) (*ibid.*, § 108).

The obligation to distinguish between civilian objects and military objectives and the prohibition on directing attacks against civilian objects is contained in a large number of military manuals.[5] Sweden's IHL Manual, in particular, identifies the principle of distinction as set out in Article 48 of Additional Protocol I as a rule of customary international law.[6] Many States have adopted legislation making it an offence to attack civilian objects during armed conflict.[7] There are also numerous official statements invoking this rule.[8] This practice includes that of States not, or not at the time, party to Additional Protocol I.[9]

In their pleadings before the International Court of Justice in the *Nuclear Weapons case*, several States invoked the principle of distinction between civilian objects and military objectives.[10] In its advisory opinion, the Court stated that the principle of distinction was one of the "cardinal principles" of international humanitarian law and one of the "intransgressible principles of international customary law".[11]

When the ICRC appealed to the parties to the conflict in the Middle East in October 1973, i.e., before the adoption of Additional Protocol I, to respect the distinction between civilian objects and military objectives, the States concerned (Egypt, Iraq, Israel and Syria) replied favourably.[12]

Non-international armed conflicts

The distinction between civilian objects and military objectives was included in the draft of Additional Protocol II but was dropped at the last moment as

---

[5] See, e.g., the military manuals of Argentina, Australia, Belgium, Benin, Cameroon, Canada, Croatia, France, Germany, Hungary, Israel, Netherlands, New Zealand, Nigeria, Philippines, Spain, Sweden, Switzerland, Togo and United States (*ibid.*, § 7), Indonesia (*ibid.*, § 8), Sweden (*ibid.*, § 9), Argentina, Australia, Belgium, Benin, Cameroon, Canada, Colombia, Croatia, Ecuador, France, Germany, Italy, Kenya, Lebanon, Madagascar, Netherlands, New Zealand, Nigeria, South Africa, Spain, Togo, United Kingdom, United States and Yugoslavia (*ibid.*, § 115), Argentina (*ibid.*, § 116) and United States (*ibid.*, § 117).

[6] Sweden, *IHL Manual* (*ibid.*, § 9).

[7] See, e.g., the legislation of Australia (*ibid.*, § 119), Azerbaijan (*ibid.*, § 120), Canada (*ibid.*, § 122), Congo (*ibid.*, § 123), Croatia (*ibid.*, § 124), Estonia (*ibid.*, § 126), Georgia (*ibid.*, § 127), Germany (*ibid.*, § 128), Hungary (*ibid.*, § 129), Ireland (*ibid.*, § 130), Italy (*ibid.*, § 131), Mali (*ibid.*, § 132), Netherlands (*ibid.*, § 133), New Zealand (*ibid.*, § 134), Norway (*ibid.*, § 136), Slovakia (*ibid.*, § 137), Spain (*ibid.*, § 138), United Kingdom (*ibid.*, § 140) and Yemen (*ibid.*, § 141); see also the draft legislation of Argentina (*ibid.*, § 118), Burundi (*ibid.*, § 121), El Salvador (*ibid.*, § 125), Nicaragua (*ibid.*, § 135) and Trinidad and Tobago (*ibid.*, § 139).

[8] See, e.g., the statements of Croatia (*ibid.*, 145), Egypt (*ibid.*, § 146), EC and its member States, USSR and United States (*ibid.*, § 147), France (*ibid.*, § 148), Iran (*ibid.*, § 149), Iraq (*ibid.*, § 150), Mexico (*ibid.*, § 151), Mozambique (*ibid.*, § 152), Slovenia (*ibid.*, § 155), Sweden (*ibid.*, § 156), United Arab Emirates (*ibid.*, § 157), United Kingdom (*ibid.*, §§ 158–159) and United States (*ibid.*, §§ 160–163).

[9] See, e.g., the practice of Egypt (*ibid.*, § 146), France (*ibid.*, §§ 7, 115 and 148), Indonesia (*ibid.*, § 8), Iran (*ibid.*, § 149), Iraq (*ibid.*, § 150), Kenya (*ibid.*, § 115), United Kingdom (*ibid.*, §§ 115 and 158–159) and United States (*ibid.*, §§ 7, 115, 117 and 160–163).

[10] See the pleadings before the ICJ in the *Nuclear Weapons case* by Egypt (*ibid.*, § 16), Iran (*ibid.*, § 23), Japan (*ibid.*, § 25), Sweden (*ibid.*, § 156) and United Kingdom (*ibid.*, § 32).

[11] ICJ, *Nuclear Weapons case*, Advisory Opinion (*ibid.*, § 179).

[12] See ICRC, The International Committee's Action in the Middle East (*ibid.*, § 102).

part of a package aimed at the adoption of a simplified text.[13] As a result, Additional Protocol II does not contain this principle nor the prohibition on directing attacks against civilian objects, even though it has been argued that the concept of general protection in Article 13(1) of Additional Protocol II is broad enough to cover it.[14] The prohibition on directing attacks against civilian objects has, however, been included in more recent treaty law applicable in non-international armed conflicts, namely Amended Protocol II to the Convention on Certain Conventional Weapons.[15] This prohibition is also contained in Protocol III to the Convention on Certain Conventional Weapons, which has been made applicable in non-international armed conflicts pursuant to an amendment of Article 1 of the Convention adopted by consensus in 2001.[16] In addition, the Second Protocol to the Hague Convention for the Protection of Cultural Property uses the principle of distinction between civilian objects and military objectives as a basis to define the protection due to cultural property in non-international armed conflicts.[17]

The Statute of the International Criminal Court does not explicitly define attacks on civilian objects as a war crime in non-international armed conflicts. It does, however, define the destruction of the property of an adversary as a war crime unless such destruction be "imperatively demanded by the necessities of the conflict".[18] Therefore, an attack against a civilian object constitutes a war crime under the Statute inasmuch as such an attack is not imperatively demanded by the necessities of the conflict. The destruction of property is subject to Rule 50 and the practice establishing that rule also supports the existence of this rule. It is also relevant that the Statute defines attacks again installations, material, units or vehicles involved in a humanitarian assistance or peacekeeping mission as a war crime in non-international armed conflicts, as long as these objects "are entitled to the protection given to ... civilian objects under the international law of armed conflict".[19]

In addition, the prohibition on directing attacks against civilian objects is included in other instruments pertaining also to non-international armed conflicts.[20]

---

[13] Draft Additional Protocol II submitted by the ICRC to the Diplomatic Conference leading to the adoption of the Additional Protocols, Article 24(1) (*ibid.*, § 2).

[14] Michael Bothe, Karl Joseph Partsch, Waldemar A. Solf (eds.), *New Rules for Victims of Armed Conflicts*, Martinus Nijhoff, The Hague, 1982, p. 677.

[15] Amended Protocol II to the CCW, Article 3(7) (cited in Vol. II, Ch. 2, § 107).

[16] Protocol III to the CCW, Article 2(1) (*ibid.*, § 106).

[17] Second Protocol to the Hague Convention for the Protection of Cultural Property, Article 6(a) (cited in Vol. II, Ch. 12, § 21).

[18] ICC Statute, Article 8(2)(e)(xii).   [19] ICC Statute, Article 8(2)(e)(iii).

[20] See, e.g., Memorandum of Understanding on the Application of IHL between Croatia and the SFRY, para. 6 (cited in Vol. II, Ch. 2, §§ 3, 60 and 111); Agreement on the Application of IHL between the Parties to the Conflict in Bosnia and Herzegovina, para. 2.5 (*ibid.*, §§ 4, 61 and 112); San Remo Manual, paras. 39 and 41 (*ibid.*, §§ 5 and 62); UN Secretary-General's Bulletin, Section 5.1 (*ibid.*, §§ 6, 63 and 113); Cairo Declaration on Human Rights in Islam, Article 3(b) (*ibid.*, § 109); Hague Statement on Respect for Humanitarian Principles (*ibid.*, § 110).

The obligation to distinguish between civilian objects and military objectives and the prohibition on directing attacks against civilian objects is included in military manuals which are applicable in or have been applied in non-international armed conflicts.[21] Numerous States have adopted legislation making it an offence to attack civilian objects during any armed conflict.[22] There is also some national case-law based on this rule.[23] There are, furthermore, a number of official statements pertaining to non-international armed conflicts which refer to this rule.[24] The statements before the International Court of Justice in the *Nuclear Weapons case* referred to above were couched in general terms applicable in all armed conflicts.

No official contrary practice was found with respect to either international or non-international armed conflicts. States and international organisations have generally condemned alleged attacks against civilian objects, for example, during the conflicts in Bosnia and Herzegovina, Lebanon, Sudan and between Iran and Iraq.[25] As early as 1938, the Assembly of the League of Nations stated that "objectives aimed at from the air must be legitimate military objectives and must be identifiable".[26] More recently, in a resolution on protection of civilians in armed conflicts adopted in 1999, the UN Security Council strongly condemned all "attacks on objects protected under international law".[27]

The jurisprudence of the International Court of Justice and of the International Criminal Tribunal for the Former Yugoslavia provides further evidence that the prohibition on attacking civilian objects is customary in both international and non-international armed conflicts.[28]

---

[21] See, e.g., the military manuals of Benin, Croatia, Germany, Nigeria, Philippines and Togo (*ibid.*, § 7) and Benin, Colombia, Croatia, Ecuador, Germany, Italy, Kenya, Lebanon, Madagascar, South Africa, Togo and Yugoslavia (*ibid.*, § 115).

[22] See, e.g., the legislation of Australia (*ibid.*, § 119), Azerbaijan (*ibid.*, § 120), Canada (*ibid.*, § 122), Congo (*ibid.*, § 123), Croatia (*ibid.*, § 124), Estonia (*ibid.*, § 126), Georgia (*ibid.*, § 127), Germany (*ibid.*, § 128), New Zealand (*ibid.*, § 134), Norway (*ibid.*, § 136), Spain (*ibid.*, § 138) and United Kingdom (*ibid.*, § 140); see also the legislation of Hungary (*ibid.*, § 129), Italy (*ibid.*, § 131) and Slovakia (*ibid.*, § 137), the application of which is not excluded in time of non-international armed conflict, and the draft legislation of Argentina (*ibid.*, § 118), Burundi (*ibid.*, § 121), El Salvador (*ibid.*, § 125), Nicaragua (*ibid.*, § 135) and Trinidad and Tobago (*ibid.*, § 139).

[23] See, e.g., Colombia, *Administrative Case No. 9276* (*ibid.*, § 142); Croatia, *RA. R. case* (*ibid.*, § 143).

[24] See the statements of the EC and its member States (*ibid.*, § 147) and of Mozambique (*ibid.*, § 152), Slovenia (*ibid.*, § 155), USSR (*ibid.*, § 147) and United States (*ibid.*, § 147).

[25] See, e.g., the statements of the EC and its member States (*ibid.*, § 147) and of Croatia (*ibid.*, § 145), Egypt (*ibid.*, § 146), Iran (*ibid.*, § 149), Slovenia (*ibid.*, § 155), USSR (*ibid.*, § 147), United States (*ibid.*, § 147) and United Kingdom (*ibid.*, § 159); UN Security Council, Res. 1052 (*ibid.*, § 164); UN General Assembly, Res. 50/193 (*ibid.*, 168) and Res. 51/112 (*ibid.*, § 169); UN Commission on Human Rights, Res. 1993/7 (*ibid.*, § 170), Res. 1994/75 (*ibid.*, § 171) and Res. 1995/89 (*ibid.*, § 173); Contact Group of the OIC (Egypt, Iran, Pakistan, Saudi Arabia, Senegal and Turkey), Letter to the President of the UN Security Council (*ibid.*, § 177).

[26] League of Nations, Assembly, Resolution adopted on 30 September 1938 (*ibid.*, § 167).

[27] UN Security Council, Res. 1265 (*ibid.*, § 165).

[28] ICJ, *Nuclear Weapons case*, Advisory Opinion (*ibid.*, § 179); ICTY, *Kupreškić case*, Judgement (*ibid.*, § 180) and *Kordić and Čerkez case*, Decision on the Joint Defence Motion and Judgement (*ibid.*, § 182).

The Plan of Action for the years 2000–2003, adopted by the 27th International Conference of the Red Cross and Red Crescent in 1999, requires that all parties to an armed conflict respect "the total ban on directing attacks ... against civilian objects".[29] The ICRC has called on parties to both international and non-international armed conflicts to respect the distinction between civilian objects and military objectives and not to direct attacks at civilian objects.[30]

Interpretation

Several States have stressed that the rule contained in Article 52(2) of Additional Protocol I, which provides that "attacks shall be limited strictly to military objectives", only prohibits direct attacks against civilian objects and does not deal with the question of incidental damage resulting from attacks directed against military objectives.[31] The purpose of these statements is to emphasise that an attack which affects civilian objects is not unlawful as long as it is directed against a military objective and the incidental damage to civilian objects is not excessive. This consideration is taken into account in the formulation of the current rule by the use of the words "attacks *directed* against". The same consideration applies *mutatis mutandis* to Rule 1.

Rule 8. In so far as objects are concerned, military objectives are limited to those objects which by their nature, location, purpose or use make an effective contribution to military action and whose partial or total destruction, capture or neutralisation, in the circumstances ruling at the time, offers a definite military advantage.

Practice

Volume II, Chapter 2, Section B.

Summary

State practice establishes this rule as a norm of customary international law applicable in both international and non-international armed conflicts.

---

[29] 27th International Conference of the Red Cross and Red Crescent, Plan of Action for the years 2000–2003 (adopted by consensus) (*ibid.*, § 178).
[30] See, e.g., the practice of the ICRC (*ibid.*, §§ 185–186 and 188–193).
[31] See the reservations and declarations made upon ratification of the Additional Protocols and other statements by Australia (*ibid.*, § 51), Canada (*ibid.*, §§ 52 and 71), France (*ibid.*, § 53), Federal Republic of Germany (*ibid.*, § 75), Italy (*ibid.*, § 54), Netherlands (*ibid.*, § 80), New Zealand (*ibid.*, § 55), United Kingdom (*ibid.*, §§ 56 and 86) and United States (*ibid.*, § 92).

International armed conflicts

This definition of military objectives is set forth in Article 52(2) of Additional Protocol I, to which no reservations have been made.[32] At the Diplomatic Conference leading to the adoption of the Additional Protocols, Mexico stated that Article 52 was so essential that it "cannot be the subject of any reservations whatsoever since these would be inconsistent with the aim and purpose of Protocol I and undermine its basis".[33] The definition has been used consistently in subsequent treaties, namely in Protocol II, Amended Protocol II and Protocol III to the Convention on Certain Conventional Weapons, as well as in the Second Protocol to the Hague Convention for the Protection of Cultural Property.[34]

Numerous military manuals contain this definition of military objectives.[35] It is supported by official statements.[36] This practice includes that of States not, or not at the time, party to Additional Protocol I.[37]

This definition of military objectives was found to be customary by the Committee Established to Review the NATO Bombing Campaign Against the Federal Republic of Yugoslavia.[38]

Non-international armed conflicts

Although this definition of military objectives was not included in Additional Protocol II, it has subsequently been incorporated into treaty law applicable in non-international armed conflicts, namely Amended Protocol II to the Convention on Certain Conventional Weapons and the Second Protocol to the Hague Convention for the Protection of Cultural Property.[39] It is also contained in Protocol III to the Convention on Certain Conventional Weapons,

---

[32] Additional Protocol I, Article 52(2) (adopted by 79 votes in favour, none against and 7 abstentions) (*ibid.*, § 319).

[33] Mexico, Statement at the Diplomatic Conference leading to the adoption of the Additional Protocols (*ibid.*, § 353).

[34] Protocol II to the CCW, Article 2(4) (*ibid.*, § 321); Amended Protocol II to the CCW, Article 2(6) (*ibid.*, § 321); Protocol III to the CCW, Article 1(3) (*ibid.*, § 321); Second Protocol to the Hague Convention for the Protection of Cultural Property, Article 1(f) (*ibid.*, § 322).

[35] See, e.g., the military manuals of Argentina, Australia, Belgium, Benin, Cameroon, Canada, Colombia, Croatia, France, Germany, Hungary, Italy, Kenya, Madagascar, Netherlands, New Zealand, South Africa, Spain, Sweden, Togo, United Kingdom and United States (*ibid.*, § 328), Ecuador (*ibid.*, § 331), Indonesia (*ibid.*, § 333), United States (*ibid.*, § 339) and Yugoslavia (*ibid.*, § 340).

[36] See, e.g., the statements of France (*ibid.*, § 364), Iran (*ibid.*, § 347), Iraq (*ibid.*, § 348), Israel (*ibid.*, § 364), Jordan (*ibid.*, § 351), Syria (*ibid.*, § 355), Turkey (*ibid.*, § 364) and United States (*ibid.*, §§ 350, 360 and 364).

[37] See, e.g., the practice of France (*ibid.*, § 364), Iran (*ibid.*, § 347), Iraq (*ibid.*, § 348), Israel (*ibid.*, § 364), Kenya (*ibid.*, § 328), Turkey (*ibid.*, § 364), United Kingdom (*ibid.*, § 328) and United States (*ibid.*, §§ 328, 350, 360 and 364).

[38] Committee Established to Review the NATO Bombing Campaign Against the Federal Republic of Yugoslavia, Final Report (*ibid.*, § 365).

[39] Amended Protocol II to the CCW, Article 2(6) (*ibid.*, § 321); Second Protocol to the Hague Convention for the Protection of Cultural Property, Article 1(f) (*ibid.*, § 322).

which has been made applicable in non-international armed conflicts pursuant to an amendment of Article 1 of the Convention adopted by consensus in 2001.[40]

Military manuals which are applicable in or have been applied in non-international armed conflicts incorporate this definition of military objectives.[41] It is also contained in some national legislation.[42] In addition, the definition is included in official statements pertaining to non-international armed conflicts.[43]

No contrary practice was found with respect to either international or non-international armed conflicts in the sense that no other definition of a military objective has officially been advanced. The Report on US Practice explains that the United States accepts the customary nature of the definition contained in Article 52(2) of Additional Protocol I and that the formulation used in the US Naval Handbook, namely effective contribution to "the enemy's war-fighting or war-sustaining capability", reflects its position that this definition is a wide one which includes areas of land, objects screening other military objectives and war-supporting economic facilities.[44]

Interpretation

Several States have indicated that in their target selection they will consider the military advantage to be anticipated from an attack as a whole and not from parts thereof.[45] The military manuals of Australia, Ecuador and the United States consider that the anticipated military advantage can include increased security for the attacking forces or friendly forces.[46]

Many military manuals state that the presence of civilians within or near military objectives does not render such objectives immune from attack.[47] This is the case, for example, of civilians working in a munitions factory. This practice indicates that such persons share the risk of attacks on that military objective

---

[40] Protocol III to the CCW, Article 1(3) (*ibid.*, § 321).
[41] See, e.g., the military manuals of Benin, Canada, Colombia, Croatia, Germany, Italy, Kenya, Madagascar, South Africa and Togo (*ibid.*, § 328), Ecuador (*ibid.*, § 331) and Yugoslavia (*ibid.*, § 340).
[42] See, e.g., the legislation of Italy (*ibid.*, § 341) and Spain (*ibid.*, § 342).
[43] See, e.g., the statements of Colombia (*ibid.*, § 346) and Philippines (*ibid.*, § 354).
[44] Report on US Practice (*ibid.*, § 361) referring to United States, *Naval Handbook* (*ibid.*, § 339).
[45] See the statements of Australia (*ibid.*, § 329), Canada (*ibid.*, § 320), France (*ibid.*, § 320), Germany (*ibid.*, § 332), Italy (*ibid.*, § 334), New Zealand (*ibid.*, § 336), Spain (*ibid.*, §§ 320 and 337) and United States (*ibid.*, § 359).
[46] See the military manuals of Australia (*ibid.*, § 329), Ecuador (*ibid.*, § 331) and United States (*ibid.*, § 339).
[47] See, e.g., the military manuals of Australia (*ibid.*, § 635), Canada (*ibid.*, § 636), Colombia (*ibid.*, § 637), Croatia (*ibid.*, § 638), Ecuador (*ibid.*, § 639), Germany (*ibid.*, § 640), Hungary (*ibid.*, § 641), Madagascar (*ibid.*, § 642), Netherlands (*ibid.*, § 643), New Zealand (*ibid.*, § 644), Spain (*ibid.*, §§ 645–646), Switzerland (*ibid.*, § 647) and United States (*ibid.*, § 648).

but are not themselves combatants. This view is supported by official state-ments and reported practice.[48] Such attacks are still subject to the principle of proportionality (see Rule 14) and the requirement to take precautions in attack (see Rules 15–21). The prohibition on using human shields is also relevant to this issue (see Rule 97).

Examples

State practice often cites establishments, buildings and positions where enemy combatants, their materiel and armaments are located, and military means of transportation and communication as examples of military objectives.[49] As far as dual-use facilities are concerned, such as civilian means of transportation and communication which can be used for military purposes, practice consid-ers that the classification of these objects depends, in the final analysis, on the application of the definition of a military objective.[50] Economic targets that effectively support military operations are also cited as an example of military objectives, provided their attack offers a definite military advantage.[51] In addi-tion, numerous military manuals and official statements consider that an area of land can constitute a military objective if it fulfils the conditions contained in the definition.[52]

Rule 9. Civilian objects are all objects that are not military objectives.

Practice

Volume II, Chapter 2, Section C.

Summary

State practice establishes this rule as a norm of customary international law applicable in both international and non-international armed conflicts. The definition of civilian objects has to be read together with the definition of military objectives: only those objects that qualify as military objectives may be attacked; other objects are protected against attack.

---

[48] See, e.g., the statements of Belgium (*ibid.*, § 651) and United States (*ibid.*, §§ 652–653).
[49] See the practice cited in *ibid.*, §§ 417–492.
[50] See the practice cited in *ibid.*, §§ 493–560.
[51] See the practice cited in *ibid.*, §§ 561–596.
[52] See, e.g., the military manuals of Australia (*ibid.*, § 601), Belgium (*ibid.*, §§ 602–604), Benin (*ibid.*, § 605), Ecuador (*ibid.*, § 608), France (*ibid.*, § 609), Italy (*ibid.*, §§ 610–611), Madagascar (*ibid.*, § 612), Netherlands (*ibid.*, § 613), New Zealand (*ibid.*, § 614), Spain (*ibid.*, § 615), Sweden (*ibid.*, § 616), Togo (*ibid.*, § 617), United Kingdom (*ibid.*, § 618) and United States (*ibid.*, § 619) and the statements of Belgium (*ibid.*, § 622), Canada (*ibid.*, §§ 597 and 623), Federal Republic of Germany (*ibid.*, §§ 597 and 624), France (*ibid.*, § 598), Italy (*ibid.*, § 597), Netherlands (*ibid.*, §§ 597, 599 and 625), New Zealand (*ibid.*, § 597), Pakistan (*ibid.*, § 599), Spain (*ibid.*, § 597), United Kingdom (*ibid.*, §§ 597, 599 and 626) and United States (*ibid.*, §§ 599 and 627–628).

International armed conflicts

This definition of civilian objects is set forth in Article 52(1) of Additional Protocol I, to which no reservations have been made.[53] At the Diplomatic Conference leading to the adoption of the Additional Protocols, Mexico stated that Article 52 was so essential that it "cannot be the subject of any reservations whatsoever since these would be inconsistent with the aim and purpose of Protocol I and undermine its basis".[54] The same definition has been used consistently in subsequent treaties, namely in Protocol II, Amended Protocol II and Protocol III to the Convention on Certain Conventional Weapons.[55] Upon signature of the Statute of the International Criminal Court, Egypt declared that the term "civilian objects" in the Statute must be understood in accordance with the definition provided in Additional Protocol I.[56]

Numerous military manuals contain this definition of civilian objects,[57] including those of States not, or not at the time, party to Additional Protocol I.[58]

Non-international armed conflicts

Although this definition was not included in Additional Protocol II, it has subsequently been incorporated into treaty law applicable in non-international armed conflicts, namely Amended Protocol II to the Convention on Certain Conventional Weapons.[59] This definition of civilian objects is also contained in Protocol III to the Convention on Certain Conventional Weapons, which has been made applicable in non-international armed conflicts pursuant to an amendment of Article 1 of the Convention adopted by consensus in 2001.[60]

This definition of civilian objects is also set forth in military manuals which are applicable in or have been applied in non-international armed conflicts.[61]

---

[53] Additional Protocol I, Article 52(1) (adopted by 79 votes in favour, none against and 7 abstentions) (*ibid.*, § 660).

[54] Mexico, Statement at the Diplomatic Conference leading to the adoption of the Additional Protocols (*ibid.*, § 679).

[55] Protocol II to the CCW, Article 2(5) (*ibid.*, § 661); Amended Protocol II to the CCW, Article 2(7) (*ibid.*, § 661); Protocol III to the CCW, Article 1(4) (*ibid.*, § 662).

[56] Egypt, Declarations made upon signature of the ICC Statute (*ibid.*, § 663).

[57] See, e.g., the military manuals of Argentina, Australia, Cameroon, Canada, Colombia, Kenya, Madagascar, Netherlands, South Africa, Spain, United Kingdom and United States (*ibid.*, § 665), Benin (*ibid.*, § 666), Croatia (*ibid.*, § 667), Ecuador (*ibid.*, § 668), France (*ibid.*, § 669), Italy (*ibid.*, § 670), Sweden (*ibid.*, § 671), Togo (*ibid.*, § 672), United States (*ibid.*, § 673) and Yugoslavia (*ibid.*, § 674).

[58] See, e.g., the military manuals of France (*ibid.*, § 669), Kenya (*ibid.*, § 665), United Kingdom (*ibid.*, § 665) and United States (*ibid.*, § 665).

[59] Amended Protocol II to the CCW, Article 2(7) (*ibid.*, § 661).

[60] Protocol III to the CCW, Article 1(4) (*ibid.*, § 662).

[61] See, e.g., the military manuals of Colombia, Kenya, Madagascar and South Africa (*ibid.*, § 665), Benin (*ibid.*, § 666), Croatia (*ibid.*, § 667), Ecuador (*ibid.*, § 668), Italy (*ibid.*, § 670), Togo (*ibid.*, § 672) and Yugoslavia (*ibid.*, § 674).

No contrary practice was found with respect to either international or non-international armed conflicts in the sense that no other definition of civilian objects has officially been advanced. Some military manuals define civilian objects as "objects that are not used for military purposes".[62] This definition is not incompatible with this rule but rather underlines the fact that civilian objects lose their protection against attack if they are used for military purposes and, because of such use, become military objectives (see Rule 10).

Examples

State practice considers civilian areas, towns, cities, villages, residential areas, dwellings, buildings and houses and schools,[63] civilian means of transportation,[64] hospitals, medical establishments and medical units,[65] historic monuments, places of worship and cultural property,[66] and the natural environment[67] as *prima facie* civilian objects, provided, in the final analysis, they have not become military objectives (see Rule 10). Alleged attacks against such objects have generally been condemned.[68]

Rule 10. Civilian objects are protected against attack, unless and for such time as they are military objectives.

Practice

Volume II, Chapter 2, Section D.

Summary

State practice establishes this rule as a norm of customary international law applicable in both international and non-international armed conflicts.

International and non-international armed conflicts

Loss of protection of civilian objects must be read together with the basic rule that only military objectives may be attacked. It follows that when a civilian object is used in such a way that it loses its civilian character and qualifies as a military objective, it is liable to attack. This reasoning can also be found in the Statute of the International Criminal Court, which makes it a war crime

---

[62] See the military manuals of Benin (*ibid.*, § 666), Croatia (*ibid.*, § 667), France (*ibid.*, § 669), Italy (*ibid.*, § 670) and Togo (*ibid.*, § 672).
[63] See the practice cited in *ibid.*, §§ 199–264.   [64] See the practice cited in *ibid.*, §§ 265–315.
[65] See the practice cited in Vol. II, Ch. 7.   [66] See the practice cited in Vol. II, Ch. 12.
[67] See the practice cited in Vol. II, Ch. 14.
[68] See, e.g., the statements of Croatia (cited in Vol. II, Ch. 2, § 145), Egypt (*ibid.*, § 146), EC and its member States, USSR and United States (*ibid.*, § 147), Mozambique (*ibid.*, § 152), Slovenia (*ibid.*, § 155), United Arab Emirates (*ibid.*, § 157) and United Kingdom (*ibid.*, § 159).

to intentionally direct attacks against civilian objects, provided they "are not military objectives".[69]

Numerous military manuals contain the rule that civilian objects lose their protection against attack when and for such time as they are military objectives.[70] In this context, loss of protection of civilian objects is often referred to in terms of objects being "used for military purposes" or of objects being "used for military action".[71] These expressions are not incompatible with this rule and, in any case, they are used by States that have accepted the definition of military objectives contained in Rule 8.

Situations of doubt as to the character of an object

The issue of how to classify an object in case of doubt is not entirely clear. Additional Protocol I formulates an answer by providing that "in case of doubt whether an object which is normally dedicated to civilian purposes, such as a place of worship, a house or other dwelling or a school, is being used to make an effective contribution to military action, it shall be presumed not to be so used".[72] No reservations have been made to this provision. Indeed, at the Diplomatic Conference leading to the adoption of the Additional Protocols, Mexico stated that Article 52 was so essential that it "cannot be the subject of any reservations whatsoever since these would be inconsistent with the aim and purpose of Protocol I and undermine its basis".[73] The principle of presumption of civilian character in case of doubt is also contained in Amended Protocol II to the Convention on Certain Conventional Weapons.[74]

The presumption of civilian character of an object formulated in Additional Protocol I is also contained in numerous military manuals.[75] While the US

---

[69] ICC Statute, Article 8(2)(b)(ii); see also Article 8(2)(b)(ix) and (e)(iv) (concerning attacks against buildings dedicated to religion, education, art, science or charitable purposes, historic monuments, hospitals and places where the sick and wounded are collected) and Article 8(2)(b)(v) (concerning attacks against towns, villages, dwellings or buildings which are undefended).

[70] See, e.g., the military manuals of Australia (cited in Vol. II, Ch. 2, § 687), Belgium (*ibid.*, § 688), Cameroon (*ibid.*, § 689), Canada (*ibid.*, § 690), Colombia (*ibid.*, § 691), Croatia (*ibid.*, § 692), France (*ibid.*, § 693), Israel (*ibid.*, § 694), Italy (*ibid.*, § 695), Kenya (*ibid.*, § 696), Madagascar (*ibid.*, § 697), Netherlands (*ibid.*, §§ 698–700), New Zealand (*ibid.*, § 701), Russia (*ibid.*, § 702), Spain (*ibid.*, § 703) and United States (*ibid.*, §§ 704–705).

[71] See, e.g., the practice of Australia (*ibid.*, § 687), Canada (*ibid.*, § 690), Netherlands (*ibid.*, § 700), Russia (*ibid.*, § 702) and United States (*ibid.*, §§ 705 and 710–711).

[72] Additional Protocol I, Article 52(3) (adopted by 79 votes in favour, none against and 7 abstentions) (*ibid.*, § 719).

[73] Mexico, Statement at the Diplomatic Conference leading to the adoption of the Additional Protocols (*ibid.*, § 751).

[74] Amended Protocol II to the CCW, Article 3(8)(a) (*ibid.*, § 720).

[75] See, e.g., the military manuals of Argentina (*ibid.*, § 725), Australia (*ibid.*, § 726), Benin (*ibid.*, § 727), Cameroon (*ibid.*, § 728), Canada (*ibid.*, § 729), Colombia (*ibid.*, § 730), Croatia (*ibid.*, § 731), France (*ibid.*, § 732), Germany (*ibid.*, § 733), Hungary (*ibid.*, § 734), Israel (*ibid.*, § 735), Kenya (*ibid.*, § 736), Madagascar (*ibid.*, § 737), Netherlands (*ibid.*, § 738), New Zealand (*ibid.*, § 739), Spain (*ibid.*, § 741), Sweden (*ibid.*, § 742), Togo (*ibid.*, § 743) and United States (*ibid.*, § 744).

Air Force Pamphlet contains this rule,[76] a report submitted to Congress by the US Department of Defence in 1992 states that the rule is not customary and is contrary to the traditional law of war because it shifts the burden of determining the precise use of an object from the defender to the attacker, i.e., from the party controlling that object to the party lacking such control. This imbalance would ignore the realities of war in demanding a degree of certainty of the attacker that seldom exists in combat. It would also encourage the defender to ignore its obligations to separate civilians and civilian objects from military objectives.[77] According to the Report on the Practice of Israel, Israel is of the view that this presumption only applies when the field commander considers that there is a "significant" doubt and not if there is merely a slight possibility of being mistaken. Accordingly, the decision whether or not to attack rests with the field commander who has to determine whether the possibility of mistake is significant enough to warrant not launching the attack.[78]

In the light of the foregoing, it is clear that, in case of doubt, a careful assessment has to be made under the conditions and restraints governing a particular situation as to whether there are sufficient indications to warrant an attack. It cannot automatically be assumed that any object that appears dubious may be subject to lawful attack. This is also consistent with the requirement to take all feasible precautions in attack, in particular the obligation to verify that objects to be attacked are military objectives liable to attack and not civilian objects (see Rule 16).

---

[76] United States, *Air Force Pamphlet* (*ibid.*, § 744).
[77] United States, Department of Defense, Final Report to Congress on the Conduct of the Persian Gulf War (*ibid.*, § 752).
[78] Report on the Practice of Israel (*ibid.*, § 749).

CHAPTER 3

INDISCRIMINATE ATTACKS

Rule 11. Indiscriminate attacks are prohibited.

Practice

Volume II, Chapter 3, Section A.

Summary

State practice establishes this rule as a norm of customary international law applicable in both international and non-international armed conflicts.

International armed conflicts

The prohibition of indiscriminate attacks is set forth in Article 51(4) of Additional Protocol I.[1] At the Diplomatic Conference leading to the adoption of the Additional Protocols, France voted against Article 51 because it deemed that paragraph 4 by its "very complexity would seriously hamper the conduct of defensive military operations against an invader and prejudice the inherent right of legitimate defence recognized in Article 51 of the Charter of the United Nations".[2] Upon ratification of Additional Protocol I, however, France did not enter a reservation with respect to the prohibition of indiscriminate attacks. At the Diplomatic Conference leading to the adoption of the Additional Protocols, Mexico stated that Article 51 was so essential that it "cannot be the subject of any reservations whatsoever since these would be inconsistent with the aim and purpose of Protocol I and undermine its basis".[3] The prohibition of indiscriminate attacks is also contained in Protocol II and Amended Protocol II to the Convention on Certain Conventional Weapons.[4]

---

[1] Additional Protocol I, Article 51(4) (adopted by 77 votes in favour, one against and 16 abstentions) (cited in Vol. II, Ch. 3, § 1).

[2] France, Statement at the Diplomatic Conference leading to the adoption of the Additional Protocols (*ibid.*, § 73).

[3] Mexico, Statement at the Diplomatic Conference leading to the adoption of the Additional Protocols (*ibid.*, § 228).

[4] Protocol II to the CCW, Article 3(3) (*ibid.*, § 4); Amended Protocol II to the CCW, Article 3(8) (*ibid.*, § 4).

A large number of military manuals specify that indiscriminate attacks are prohibited.[5] Numerous States have adopted legislation making it an offence to carry out such attacks.[6] The prohibition is supported by official statements and reported practice.[7] This practice includes that of States not, or not at the time, party to Additional Protocol I.[8]

In their pleadings before the International Court of Justice in the *Nuclear Weapons case* and *Nuclear Weapons (WHO) case*, several States invoked the prohibition of indiscriminate attacks in their assessment of whether an attack with nuclear weapons would violate international humanitarian law.[9]

When the ICRC appealed to the parties to the conflict in the Middle East in October 1973, i.e., before the adoption of Additional Protocol I, to respect the prohibition of indiscriminate attacks, the States concerned (Egypt, Iraq, Israel and Syria) replied favourably.[10]

Non-international armed conflicts

The prohibition of indiscriminate attacks was included in the draft of Additional Protocol II but was dropped at the last moment as part of a package aimed at the adoption of a simplified text.[11] As a result, Additional Protocol II does not contain this rule as such, even though it has been argued that it is

---

[5] See, e.g., the military manuals of Argentina (*ibid.*, §§ 12–13), Australia (*ibid.*, §§ 12 and 14), Belgium (*ibid.*, § 12), Benin (*ibid.*, § 12), Cameroon (*ibid.*, § 15), Canada (*ibid.*, §§ 12 and 16), Ecuador (*ibid.*, § 17), France (*ibid.*, § 12), Germany (*ibid.*, § 18), India (*ibid.*, § 19), Indonesia (*ibid.*, § 12), Israel (*ibid.*, §§ 12 and 21), Italy (*ibid.*, § 22), Kenya (*ibid.*, § 12), Netherlands (*ibid.*, §§ 12 and 23), New Zealand (*ibid.*, §§ 12 and 24), Russia (*ibid.*, § 26), South Africa (*ibid.*, §§ 12 and 27), Spain (*ibid.*, § 12), Sweden (*ibid.*, § 12), Switzerland (*ibid.*, § 29), Togo (*ibid.*, § 12) and United Kingdom (*ibid.*, § 12).

[6] See, e.g., the legislation of Armenia (*ibid.*, § 32), Australia (*ibid.*, § 34), Belarus (*ibid.*, § 35), Belgium (*ibid.*, § 36), Bosnia and Herzegovina (*ibid.*, § 37), Canada (*ibid.*, § 38), China (*ibid.*, § 39), Colombia (*ibid.*, § 40), Cook Islands (*ibid.*, § 41), Croatia (*ibid.*, § 42), Cyprus (*ibid.*, § 43), Estonia (*ibid.*, § 45), Georgia (*ibid.*, § 46), Indonesia (*ibid.*, § 47), Ireland (*ibid.*, § 48), Lithuania (*ibid.*, § 51), Netherlands (*ibid.*, § 52), New Zealand (*ibid.*, § 53), Niger (*ibid.*, § 55), Norway (*ibid.*, § 56), Slovenia (*ibid.*, § 57), Spain (*ibid.*, § 58), Sweden (*ibid.*, § 59), Tajikistan (*ibid.*, § 60), United Kingdom (*ibid.*, § 61), Yugoslavia (*ibid.*, § 62) and Zimbabwe (*ibid.*, § 63); see also the draft legislation of Argentina (*ibid.*, § 32), El Salvador (*ibid.*, § 44), Jordan (*ibid.*, § 49), Lebanon (*ibid.*, § 50) and Nicaragua (*ibid.*, § 54).

[7] See, e.g., the statements of Bosnia and Herzegovina (*ibid.*, § 66), Botswana (*ibid.*, § 67), Finland (*ibid.*, § 72), Monitoring Group on the Implementation of the 1996 Israel-Lebanon Ceasefire Understanding, consisting of France, Israel, Lebanon, Syria and United States (*ibid.*, § 75), Germany (*ibid.*, § 76), Iran (*ibid.*, § 79), Iraq (*ibid.*, §§ 80–81), Malaysia (*ibid.*, § 83), Poland (*ibid.*, § 89), Slovenia (*ibid.*, § 91), South Africa (*ibid.*, § 92), Sweden (*ibid.*, § 93), Syria (*ibid.*, § 94), United Kingdom (*ibid.*, §§ 95–97), United States (*ibid.*, § 98) and Yugoslavia (*ibid.*, § 100) and the reported practice of Malaysia (*ibid.*, § 84).

[8] See, e.g., the practice of China (*ibid.*, § 39), France (*ibid.*, § 74), India (*ibid.*, § 19), Indonesia (*ibid.*, § 12), Iran (*ibid.*, § 79), Iraq (*ibid.*, § 80), Israel (*ibid.*, §§ 12 and 21), Kenya (*ibid.*, § 12), Malaysia (*ibid.*, §§ 83–84), South Africa (*ibid.*, § 92), United Kingdom (*ibid.*, §§ 12 and 953–97) and United States (*ibid.*, §§ 30 and 98).

[9] See. e.g., the pleadings of Australia (*ibid.*, § 65), India (*ibid.*, § 77), Mexico (*ibid.*, § 85), New Zealand (*ibid.*, § 86) and United States (*ibid.*, § 99).

[10] See ICRC, The International Committee's Action in the Middle East (*ibid.*, § 139).

[11] Draft Additional Protocol II submitted by the ICRC to the Diplomatic Conference leading to the adoption of the Additional Protocols, Article 26(3) (*ibid.*, § 3).

included by inference within the prohibition against making the civilian population the object of attack contained in Article 13(2).[12] This rule has been included in more recent treaty law applicable in non-international armed conflicts, namely Amended Protocol II to the Convention on Certain Conventional Weapons.[13] In addition, the prohibition has been included in other instruments pertaining also to non-international armed conflicts.[14]

Military manuals which are applicable in or have been applied in non-international armed conflicts specify the prohibition of indiscriminate attacks.[15] Numerous States have adopted legislation making it an offence to carry out such attacks in any armed conflict.[16] A number of official statements pertaining to non-international armed conflicts refer to this rule.[17] The pleadings before the International Court of Justice in the *Nuclear Weapons case* referred to above were couched in general terms applicable in all armed conflicts.

No official contrary practice was found with respect to either international or non-international armed conflicts. Alleged violations of this rule have generally been condemned by States, irrespective of whether the conflict was international or non-international.[18] The United Nations and other international organisations have also condemned violations of this rule, for example, in the context of the conflicts in Afghanistan, Bosnia and Herzegovina, Burundi, Chechnya, Kosovo, Nagorno-Karabakh and Sudan.[19]

---

[12] Michael Bothe, Karl Joseph Partsch, Waldemar A. Solf (eds.), *New Rules for Victims of Armed Conflicts*, Martinus Nijhoff, The Hague, 1982, p. 677.

[13] Amended Protocol II to the CCW, Article 3(8) (cited in Vol. II, Ch. 3, § 4).

[14] See, e.g., Memorandum of Understanding on the Application of IHL between Croatia and the SFRY, para. 6 (*ibid.*, § 6); Agreement on the Application of IHL between the Parties to the Conflict in Bosnia and Herzegovina, para. 2.5 (*ibid.*, § 7); San Remo Manual, para. 42 (*ibid.*, § 8); Comprehensive Agreement on Respect for Human Rights and IHL in the Philippines, Part III, Article 2(4) (*ibid.*, § 10); UN Secretary-General's Bulletin, Section 5.5 (*ibid.*, § 11).

[15] See, e.g., the military manuals of Australia (*ibid.*, §§ 12 and 14), Benin (*ibid.*, § 12), Ecuador (*ibid.*, § 17), Germany (*ibid.*, § 18), India (*ibid.*, §§ 19–20), Italy (*ibid.*, § 22), Kenya (*ibid.*, § 12), South Africa (*ibid.*, §§ 12 and 27) and Togo (*ibid.*, § 12).

[16] See, e.g., the legislation of Armenia (*ibid.*, § 33), Belarus (*ibid.*, § 35), Belgium (*ibid.*, § 36), Bosnia and Herzegovina (*ibid.*, § 37), Colombia (*ibid.*, § 40), Croatia (*ibid.*, § 42), Estonia (*ibid.*, § 45), Georgia (*ibid.*, § 46), Lithuania (*ibid.*, § 51), Niger (*ibid.*, § 55), Norway (*ibid.*, § 56), Slovenia (*ibid.*, § 57), Spain (*ibid.*, § 58), Sweden (*ibid.*, § 59), Tajikistan (*ibid.*, § 60) and Yugoslavia (*ibid.*, § 62); see also the draft legislation of Argentina (*ibid.*, § 32), El Salvador (*ibid.*, § 44), Jordan (*ibid.*, § 49) and Nicaragua (*ibid.*, § 54).

[17] See, e.g., the statements of Germany (*ibid.*, § 76), India (*ibid.*, §§ 77–78), Malaysia (*ibid.*, §§ 83–84) and Slovenia (*ibid.*, § 91).

[18] See, e.g., the statements of Bosnia and Herzegovina (*ibid.*, § 66), Botswana (*ibid.*, § 67), Iran (*ibid.*, § 79), Iraq (*ibid.*, §§ 80–81), Malaysia (*ibid.*, § 83), Slovenia (*ibid.*, § 91), South Africa (*ibid.*, § 92), United Kingdom (*ibid.*, §§ 95–97), United States (*ibid.*, § 98) and Yugoslavia (*ibid.*, § 100).

[19] See, e.g., UN Security Council, Res. 1199 (*ibid.*, § 102) and Statement by the President (*ibid.*, § 103); UN General Assembly, Res. 40/137 (*ibid.*, § 106), Res. 48/153, 49/196 and 50/193 (*ibid.*, § 107), Res. 51/112 (*ibid.*, § 108), Res. 53/164 (*ibid.*, § 109), Res. 55/116 (*ibid.*, § 110); UN Commission on Human Rights, Res. 1987/58 and 1995/74 (*ibid.*, § 111), Res. 1992/S-2/1 and 1993/7 (*ibid.*, § 112), Res. 1994/75 and 1995/89 (*ibid.*, § 113), Res. 1995/77, 1996/73, 1997/59 and

The jurisprudence of the International Criminal Tribunal for the Former Yugoslavia provides further evidence of the customary nature of the prohibition of indiscriminate attacks in both international and non-international armed conflicts.[20]

The 25th International Conference of the Red Cross in 1986 deplored "the indiscriminate attacks inflicted on civilian populations . . . in violation of the laws and customs of war".[21] The ICRC has reminded parties to both international and non-international armed conflicts of their duty to abstain from indiscriminate attacks.[22]

Rule 12. Indiscriminate attacks are those:

(a) **which are not directed at a specific military objective;**
(b) **which employ a method or means of combat which cannot be directed at a specific military objective; or**
(c) **which employ a method or means of combat the effects of which cannot be limited as required by international humanitarian law;**

and consequently, in each such case, are of a nature to strike military objectives and civilians or civilian objects without distinction.

Practice

Volume II, Chapter 3, Section B.

Summary

State practice establishes this rule as a norm of customary international law applicable in both international and non-international armed conflicts.

International armed conflicts

This definition of indiscriminate attacks is set forth in Article 51(4)(a) of Additional Protocol I.[23] France voted against Article 51 at the Diplomatic Conference leading to the adoption of the Additional Protocols because it deemed

---

1998/67 (*ibid.*, § 114), Res. 1998/82 (*ibid.*, § 115), Res. 2000/58 (*ibid.*, § 116); Council of Europe, Committee of Ministers, Declaration on Nagorno-Karabakh (*ibid.*, § 125) and Declaration on Bosnia and Herzegovina (*ibid.*, § 126); Council of Europe, Parliamentary Assembly, Res. 1055 (*ibid.*, § 127); EC, Ministers of Foreign Affairs, Declaration on Yugoslavia (*ibid.*, § 128); EC, Statement on the bombardment of Goražde and Declaration on Yugoslavia (*ibid.*, § 129); EU, Council of Ministers, Council Regulation EC No. 1901/98 (*ibid.*, § 130); European Council, SN 100/00, Presidency Conclusions (*ibid.*, § 131).
20 ICTY, *Tadić case*, Interlocutory Appeal (*ibid.*, § 134) *Kordić and Čerkez case*, Decision on the Joint Defence Motion (*ibid.*, § 136) and *Kupreškić case*, Judgement (*ibid.*, § 137).
21 25th International Conference of the Red Cross, Res. I (*ibid.*, § 133).
22 See, e.g., the practice of the ICRC (*ibid.*, §§ 139–142, 144–154 and 156–157).
23 Additional Protocol I, Article 51(4)(a) (adopted by 77 votes in favour, one against and 16 abstentions) (*ibid.*, § 164).

that paragraph 4 by its "very complexity would seriously hamper the conduct of defensive military operations against an invader and prejudice the inherent right of legitimate defence".[24] Upon ratification of Additional Protocol I, however, France did not enter a reservation to this provision. At the Diplomatic Conference leading to the adoption of the Additional Protocols, Mexico stated that Article 51 was so essential that it "cannot be the subject of any reservations whatsoever since these would be inconsistent with the aim and purpose of Protocol I and undermine its basis".[25] A report on the work of Committee III of the Diplomatic Conference stated that there was general agreement that a proper definition of indiscriminate attacks included the three types of attack set down in this rule.[26] With the exception of subparagraph (c), this definition of indiscriminate attacks is also contained in Protocol II and Amended Protocol II to the Convention on Certain Conventional Weapons.[27]

A large number of military manuals contain this definition of indiscriminate attacks, in whole or in part.[28] It has similarly been relied upon in official statements.[29] This practice includes that of States not party to Additional Protocol I.[30]

Non-international armed conflicts

Additional Protocol II does not contain a definition of indiscriminate attacks, even though it has been argued that subsections (a) and (b) of the definition contained in this rule are included by inference within the prohibition contained in Article 13(2) on making the civilian population the object of attack.[31]

---

[24] France, Statement at the Diplomatic Conference leading to the adoption of the Additional Protocols (*ibid.*, § 73).

[25] Mexico, Statement at the Diplomatic Conference leading to the adoption of the Additional Protocols (*ibid.*, §§ 228 and 268).

[26] Report on the work of Committee III of the Diplomatic Conference leading to the adoption of the Additional Protocols (*ibid.*, § 200).

[27] Protocol II to the CCW, Article 3(3)(a) (*ibid.*, § 165); Amended Protocol II to the CCW, Article 3(8)(a) (*ibid.*, § 166).

[28] See, e.g., the military manuals of Australia (*ibid.*, §§ 170, 212 and 256), Belgium (*ibid.*, §§ 170, 212 and 256), Benin (*ibid.*, § 171), Canada (*ibid.*, §§ 170, 212 and 256), Ecuador (*ibid.*, §§ 172 and 213), Germany (*ibid.*, §§ 170, 212 and 256), Israel (*ibid.*, §§ 173, 214 and 257), Kenya (*ibid.*, § 174), Netherlands (*ibid.*, §§ 170, 212 and 256), New Zealand (*ibid.*, §§ 170, 212 and 256), Nigeria (*ibid.*, § 175), South Africa (*ibid.*, § 176), Spain (*ibid.*, §§ 170, 212 and 256), Sweden (*ibid.*, §§ 170, 212 and 256), Togo (*ibid.*, § 177), United Kingdom (*ibid.*, § 178), United States (*ibid.*, §§ 179–180, 215–217 and 258) and Yugoslavia (*ibid.*, § 259); see also the draft legislation of El Salvador (*ibid.*, §§ 181, 218 and 260) and Nicaragua (*ibid.*, §§ 182, 219 and 261).

[29] See, e.g., the statements of Canada (*ibid.*, § 221), Colombia (*ibid.*, § 184), Federal Republic of Germany (*ibid.*, § 222), German Democratic Republic (*ibid.*, § 223), India (*ibid.*, §§ 185 and 224), Iraq (*ibid.*, § 225), Italy (*ibid.*, § 226), Jordan and United States (*ibid.*, §§ 186 and 227), Mexico (*ibid.*, §§ 188 and 228–229), Nauru (*ibid.*, § 230), Rwanda (*ibid.*, § 190), Sri Lanka (*ibid.*, § 231), United Kingdom (*ibid.*, §§ 191 and 232) and United States (*ibid.*, §§ 192–195 and 233–237).

[30] See, e.g., the practice of India (*ibid.*, §§ 185, 224 and 265) and United States (*ibid.*, §§ 186, 227 and 267).

[31] Michael Bothe, Karl Joseph Partsch, Waldemar A. Solf (eds.), *New Rules for Victims of Armed Conflicts*, Martinus Nijhoff, The Hague, 1982, p. 677.

With the exception of subsection (c), this definition has also been included in more recent treaty law applicable in non-international armed conflicts, namely Amended Protocol II to the Convention on Certain Conventional Weapons.[32] In addition, the definition is included in other instruments pertaining also to non-international armed conflicts.[33]

This definition of indiscriminate attacks is also set forth in military manuals which are applicable in or have been applied in non-international armed conflicts.[34] It is supported by official statements.[35]

The 24th International Conference of the Red Cross in 1981 urged parties to armed conflicts in general "not to use methods and means of warfare that cannot be directed against specific military targets and whose effects cannot be limited".[36]

Further evidence of the customary nature of the definition of indiscriminate attacks in both international and non-international armed conflicts can be found in the jurisprudence of the International Court of Justice and of the International Criminal Tribunal for the Former Yugoslavia. In its advisory opinion in the *Nuclear Weapons case*, the International Court of Justice stated that the prohibition of weapons that are incapable of distinguishing between civilian and military targets constitutes an "intransgressible" principle of customary international law. The Court observed that, in conformity with this principle, humanitarian law, at a very early stage, prohibited certain types of weapons "because of their indiscriminate effect on combatants and civilians".[37] In its review of the indictment in the *Martić case* in 1996, the International Criminal Tribunal for the Former Yugoslavia examined the legality of the use of cluster bombs according to customary international law, including the prohibition of indiscriminate attacks involving a means or method of warfare which cannot be directed at a specific military objective.[38]

No official contrary practice was found. No other definition of indiscriminate attacks has officially been advanced, and the statements made with respect to indiscriminate attacks in general under Rule 11 may be based in some or more instances on an understanding of indiscriminate attacks as contained in Rule 12, especially since no other definition exists.

---

[32] Amended Protocol II to the CCW, Article 3(8)(a) (cited in Vol. II, Ch. 3, § 166).

[33] See, e.g., Memorandum of Understanding on the Application of IHL between Croatia and the SFRY, para. 6 (*ibid.*, §§ 167, 209 and 253); Agreement on the Application of IHL between the Parties to the Conflict in Bosnia and Herzegovina, para. 2.5 (*ibid.*, §§ 168, 210 and 254); San Remo Manual, para. 42(b) (*ibid.*, §§ 169, 211 and 255).

[34] See, e.g., the military manuals of Australia (*ibid.*, §§ 170, 212 and 256), Benin (*ibid.*, § 171), Ecuador (*ibid.*, §§ 172 and 213), Germany (*ibid.*, §§ 170, 212 and 256), Kenya (*ibid.*, § 174), Nigeria (*ibid.*, § 175), Togo (*ibid.*, § 177) and Yugoslavia (*ibid.*, § 259).

[35] See, e.g., the statements of India (*ibid.*, §§ 185, 224 and 265), Jordan (*ibid.*, §§ 186, 227 and 267) and United States (*ibid.*, §§ 186, 195, 227, 236 and 267); see also the draft legislation of El Salvador (*ibid.*, §§ 181, 218 and 260) and Nicaragua (*ibid.*, §§ 182, 219 and 261).

[36] 24th International Conference of the Red Cross, Res. XIII (*ibid.*, §§ 242 and 279).

[37] ICJ, *Nuclear Weapons case* (*ibid.*, § 243).

[38] ICTY, *Martić case*, Review of the Indictment (*ibid.*, § 246).

Interpretation

This definition of indiscriminate attacks represents an implementation of the principle of distinction and of international humanitarian law in general. Rule 12(a) is an application of the prohibition on directing attacks against civilians (see Rule 1) and the prohibition on directing attacks against civilian objects (see Rule 7), which are applicable in both international and non-international armed conflicts. Rule 12(b) is also an application of the prohibition on directing attacks against civilians or against civilian objects (see Rules 1 and 7). The prohibition of weapons which are by nature indiscriminate (see Rule 71), which is applicable in both international and non-international armed conflicts, is based on the definition of indiscriminate attacks contained in Rule 12(b). Lastly, Rule 12(c) is based on the logical argument that means or methods of warfare whose effects cannot be limited as required by international humanitarian law should be prohibited. But this reasoning begs the question as to what those limitations are. Practice in this respect points to weapons whose effects are uncontrollable in time and space and are likely to strike military objectives and civilians or civilian objects without distinction. The US Air Force Pamphlet gives the example of biological weapons.[39] Even though biological weapons might be directed against military objectives, their very nature means that after being launched their effects escape from the control of the launcher and may strike both combatants and civilians and necessarily create a risk of excessive civilian casualties.

Rule 13. Attacks by bombardment by any method or means which treats as a single military objective a number of clearly separated and distinct military objectives located in a city, town, village or other area containing a similar concentration of civilians or civilian objects are prohibited.

Practice

Volume II, Chapter 3, Section C.

Summary

State practice establishes this rule as a norm of customary international law applicable in both international and non-international armed conflicts.

International armed conflicts

According to Additional Protocol I, an attack by bombardment by any method or means which treats as a single military objective a number of clearly separated and distinct military objectives located in a city, town, village or

---

[39] United States, *Air Force Pamphlet* (*ibid.*, § 258).

other area containing a similar concentration of civilians or civilian objects, so-called "area bombardments", are indiscriminate and, as such, prohibited.[40]

The prohibition of "area bombardment" is contained in numerous military manuals.[41] These include manuals of States not, or not at the time, party to Additional Protocol I.[42]

When the ICRC appealed to the parties to the conflict in the Middle East in October 1973, i.e., before the adoption of Additional Protocol I, to respect the prohibition of "area bombardment", the States concerned (Egypt, Iraq, Israel and Syria) replied favourably.[43]

Non-international armed conflicts

The prohibition of "area bombardment" was included in the draft of Additional Protocol II but was dropped at the last moment as part of a package aimed at the adoption of a simplified text.[44] As a result, Additional Protocol II does not contain this rule as such, even though it has been argued that it is included by inference within the prohibition contained in Article 13(2) on making the civilian population the object of attack.[45] The prohibition is set forth in more recent treaty law applicable in non-international armed conflicts, namely Amended Protocol II to the Convention on Certain Conventional Weapons.[46] In addition, it has been included in other instruments pertaining also to non-international armed conflicts.[47]

Military manuals which are applicable in or have been applied in non-international armed conflicts specify the prohibition of "area bombardment".[48]

The conclusion that this rule is customary in non-international armed conflicts is also supported by the argument that because so-called "area bombardments" have been considered to constitute a type of indiscriminate attack,

---

[40] Additional Protocol I, Article 51(5)(a) (adopted by 77 votes in favour, one against and 16 abstentions) (ibid., § 283).

[41] See, e.g., the military manuals of Australia (ibid., §§ 290–291), Belgium (ibid., § 292), Benin (ibid., § 293), Canada (ibid., § 294), Croatia (ibid., § 295), Germany (ibid., § 296), Israel (ibid., § 297), Italy (ibid., § 298), Kenya (ibid., § 299), Madagascar (ibid., § 300), Netherlands (ibid., § 301), New Zealand (ibid., § 302), Spain (ibid., § 303), Sweden (ibid., § 304), Switzerland (ibid., § 305), Togo (ibid., § 306), United Kingdom (ibid., § 307) and United States (ibid., § 308).

[42] See the military manuals of Israel (ibid., § 297), Kenya (ibid., § 299), United Kingdom (ibid., § 307) and United States (ibid., § 308).

[43] See ICRC, The International Committee's Action in the Middle East (ibid., § 321).

[44] Draft Additional Protocol II submitted by the ICRC to the Diplomatic Conference leading to the adoption of the Additional Protocols, Article 26(3)(a) (ibid., § 284).

[45] Michael Bothe, Karl Joseph Partsch, Waldemar A. Solf (eds.), New Rules for Victims of Armed Conflicts, Martinus Nijhoff, The Hague, 1982, p. 677.

[46] Amended Protocol II to the CCW, Article 3(9) (cited in Vol. II, Ch. 3, § 285).

[47] See, e.g., Memorandum of Understanding on the Application of IHL between Croatia and the SFRY, para. 6 (ibid., § 288); Agreement on the Application of IHL between the Parties to the Conflict in Bosnia and Herzegovina, para. 2.5 (ibid., § 289).

[48] See, e.g., the military manuals of Australia (ibid., § 290), Benin (ibid., § 293), Croatia (ibid., § 295), Germany (ibid., § 296), Italy (ibid., § 298), Kenya (ibid., § 299), Madagascar (ibid., § 300) and Togo (ibid., § 306).

and because indiscriminate attacks are prohibited in non-international armed conflict, it must follow that "area bombardments" are prohibited in non-international armed conflicts.

No official contrary practice was found with respect to either international or non-international armed conflicts.

Interpretation

At the Diplomatic Conference leading to the adoption of the Additional Protocols, the United States specified that the words "clearly separated" in the definition of area bombardments required a distance "at least sufficiently large to permit the individual military objectives to be attacked separately".[49] This view was supported by some other States.[50]

---

[49] United States, Statement at the Diplomatic Conference leading to the adoption of the Additional Protocols (*ibid.*, § 315).
[50] See the statements at the Diplomatic Conference leading to the adoption of the Additional Protocols made by Canada (*ibid.*, § 311), Egypt (*ibid.*, § 312) and United Arab Emirates (*ibid.*, § 314).

PROPORTIONALITY IN ATTACK

Rule 14. Launching an attack which may be expected to cause incidental loss of civilian life, injury to civilians, damage to civilian objects, or a combination thereof, which would be excessive in relation to the concrete and direct military advantage anticipated, is prohibited.

Practice

Volume II, Chapter 4.

Summary

State practice establishes this rule as a norm of customary international law applicable in both international and non-international armed conflicts.

International armed conflicts

The principle of proportionality in attack is codified in Article 51(5)(b) of Additional Protocol I, and repeated in Article 57.[1] At the Diplomatic Conference leading to the adoption of the Additional Protocols, France voted against Article 51 because it deemed that paragraph 5 by its "very complexity would seriously hamper the conduct of defensive military operations against an invader and prejudice the inherent right of legitimate defence".[2] Upon ratification of Additional Protocol I, however, France did not enter a reservation to this provision. At the Diplomatic Conference leading to the adoption of the Additional Protocols, Mexico stated that Article 51 was so essential that it "cannot be the subject of any reservations whatsoever since these would be inconsistent with the aim and purpose of Protocol I and undermine its basis".[3] Also at the Diplomatic Conference, several States expressed the view that the principle of proportionality contained a danger for the protection of the civilian population

---

[1] Additional Protocol I, Article 51(5)(b) (adopted by 77 votes in favour, one against and 16 abstentions) (cited in Vol. II, Ch. 4, § 1) and Article 57(2)(a)(iii) (adopted by 90 votes in favour, none against and 4 abstentions) (cited in Vol. II, Ch. 5, § 325).

[2] France, Statement at the Diplomatic Conference leading to the adoption of the Additional Protocols (cited in Vol. II, Ch. 4, § 89).

[3] Mexico, Statement at the Diplomatic Conference leading to the adoption of the Additional Protocols (cited in Vol. II, Ch. 1, § 307).

but did not indicate an alternative solution to deal with the issue of inciden-tal damage from attacks on lawful targets.[4] The United Kingdom stated that Article 51(5)(b) was "a useful codification of a concept that was rapidly becom-ing accepted by all States as an important principle of international law relating to armed conflict".[5]

The principle of proportionality in attack is also contained in Protocol II and Amended Protocol II to the Convention on Certain Conventional Weapons.[6] In addition, under the Statute of the International Criminal Court, "intentionally launching an attack in the knowledge that such attack will cause incidental loss of life or injury to civilians or damage to civilian objects . . . which would be clearly excessive in relation to the concrete and direct overall military advan-tage anticipated" constitutes a war crime in international armed conflicts.[7]

A large number of military manuals lay down the principle of proportional-ity in attack.[8] Sweden's IHL Manual, in particular, identifies the principle of proportionality as set out in Article 51(5) of Additional Protocol I as a rule of cus-tomary international law.[9] Numerous States have adopted legislation making it an offence to carry out an attack which violates the principle of proportion-ality.[10] This rule is supported by official statements.[11] This practice includes that of States not, or not at the time, party to Additional Protocol I.[12] When the ICRC appealed to the parties to the conflict in the Middle East in October 1973,

---

[4] See the statements at the Diplomatic Conference leading to the adoption of the Additional Protocols made by the German Democratic Republic (cited in Vol. II, Ch. 4, § 90), Hungary (*ibid.*, § 93), Poland (*ibid.*, § 105), Romania (*ibid.*, § 106) and Syria (*ibid.*, § 112).

[5] United Kingdom, Statement at the Diplomatic Conference leading to the adoption of the Addi-tional Protocols (*ibid.*, § 114).

[6] Protocol II to the CCW, Article 3(3) (*ibid.*, § 4); Amended Protocol II to the CCW, Article 3(8) (*ibid.*, § 4).

[7] ICC Statute, Article 8(2)(b)(iv) (*ibid.*, § 5); see also UNTAET Regulation 2000/15, Section 6(1)(b)(iv) (*ibid.*, § 13).

[8] See, e.g., the military manuals of Australia (*ibid.*, § 14), Belgium (*ibid.*, § 15), Benin (*ibid.*, § 16), Cameroon (*ibid.*, § 17), Canada (*ibid.*, §§ 18–19), Colombia (*ibid.*, § 20), Croatia (*ibid.*, § 21), Ecuador (*ibid.*, § 22), France (*ibid.*, §§ 23–24), Germany (*ibid.*, §§ 25–26), Hungary (*ibid.*, § 27), Indonesia (*ibid.*, § 28), Israel (*ibid.*, §§ 29–30), Kenya (*ibid.*, § 31), Madagascar (*ibid.*, § 32), Netherlands (*ibid.*, § 33), New Zealand (*ibid.*, § 34), Nigeria (*ibid.*, §§ 35–36), Philippines (*ibid.*, § 37), South Africa (*ibid.*, § 38), Spain (*ibid.*, § 39), Sweden (*ibid.*, § 40), Switzerland (*ibid.*, § 41), Togo (*ibid.*, § 42), United Kingdom (*ibid.*, § 43) and United States (*ibid.*, §§ 44–48).

[9] Sweden, *IHL Manual* (*ibid.*, § 40).

[10] See, e.g., the legislation of Armenia (*ibid.*, § 50), Australia (*ibid.*, §§ 51–52), Belarus (*ibid.*, § 53), Belgium (*ibid.*, § 54), Canada (*ibid.*, §§ 57–58), Colombia (*ibid.*, § 59), Congo (*ibid.*, § 60), Cook Islands (*ibid.*, § 61), Cyprus (*ibid.*, § 62), Georgia (*ibid.*, § 64), Germany (*ibid.*, § 65), Ireland (*ibid.*, § 66), Mali (*ibid.*, § 68), Netherlands (*ibid.*, § 69), New Zealand (*ibid.*, §§ 70–71), Niger (*ibid.*, § 73), Norway (*ibid.*, § 74), Spain (*ibid.*, § 75), Sweden (*ibid.*, § 76), United Kingdom (*ibid.*, §§ 78–79) and Zimbabwe (*ibid.*, § 80); see also the draft legislation of Argentina (*ibid.*, § 49), Burundi (*ibid.*, § 56), El Salvador (*ibid.*, § 63), Lebanon (*ibid.*, § 67), Nicaragua (*ibid.*, § 72) and Trinidad and Tobago (*ibid.*, § 77).

[11] See, e.g., the statements of Australia (*ibid.*, § 82), Germany (*ibid.*, § 92), Jordan and the United States (*ibid.*, § 97), United Kingdom (*ibid.*, §§ 114–117), United States (*ibid.*, §§ 119–125) and Zimbabwe (*ibid.*, § 129) and the reported practice of the United States (*ibid.*, § 127).

[12] See, e.g., the practice of Indonesia (*ibid.*, § 28), Iraq (*ibid.*, § 96), Israel (*ibid.*, §§ 29–30), Kenya (*ibid.*, § 31), Philippines (*ibid.*, § 37), United Kingdom (*ibid.*, §§ 114–117) and United States (*ibid.*, §§ 44–48, 97 and 119–125) and the reported practice of the United States (*ibid.*, § 127).

i.e., before the adoption of Additional Protocol I, to respect the principle of proportionality in attack, the States concerned (Egypt, Iraq, Israel and Syria) replied favourably.[13]

In their submissions to the International Court of Justice in the *Nuclear Weapons case* and *Nuclear Weapons (WHO) case*, numerous States, including States not, or not at the time, party to Additional Protocol I, invoked the principle of proportionality in their assessments of whether an attack with nuclear weapons would violate international humanitarian law.[14] In its advisory opinion, the Court acknowledged the applicability of the principle of proportionality, stating that "respect for the environment is one of the elements that go to assessing whether an action is in conformity with the principles of necessity and proportionality".[15]

Non-international armed conflicts

While Additional Protocol II does not contain an explicit reference to the principle of proportionality in attack, it has been argued that it is inherent in the principle of humanity which was explicitly made applicable to the Protocol in its preamble and that, as a result, the principle of proportionality cannot be ignored in the application of the Protocol.[16] The principle has been included in more recent treaty law applicable in non-international armed conflicts, namely Amended Protocol II to the Convention on Certain Conventional Weapons.[17] In addition, it is included in other instruments pertaining also to non-international armed conflicts.[18]

Military manuals which are applicable in or have been applied in non-international armed conflicts specify the principle of proportionality in attack.[19] Many States have adopted legislation making it an offence to violate the principle of proportionality in attack in any armed conflict.[20] In the *Military Junta case* in 1985, the National Appeals Court of Argentina considered the

---

[13] See ICRC, Memorandum on the Applicability of International Humanitarian Law (*ibid.*, § 148).

[14] See the statements of Egypt (*ibid.*, § 87), India (*ibid.*, § 94), Iran (*ibid.*, § 95), Malaysia (*ibid.*, § 100), Netherlands (*ibid.*, § 101), New Zealand (*ibid.*, § 102), Solomon Islands (*ibid.*, § 109), Sweden (*ibid.*, § 111), United Kingdom (*ibid.*, § 118), United States (*ibid.*, § 126) and Zimbabwe (*ibid.*, § 129).

[15] ICJ, *Nuclear Weapons case* (*ibid.*, § 140).

[16] Michael Bothe, Karl Joseph Partsch, Waldemar A. Solf (eds.), *New Rules for Victims of Armed Conflicts*, Martinus Nijhoff, The Hague, 1982, p. 678.

[17] Amended Protocol II to the CCW, Article 3(8)(c) (cited in Vol. II, Ch. 4, § 4).

[18] See, e.g., Memorandum of Understanding on the Application of IHL between Croatia and the SFRY, para. 6 (*ibid.*, § 8); Agreement on the Application of IHL between the Parties to the Conflict in Bosnia and Herzegovina, para. 2.5 (*ibid.*, § 9); San Remo Manual, para. 46(d) (*ibid.*, § 10); UN Secretary-General's Bulletin, Section 5.5 (*ibid.*, § 12).

[19] See, e.g., the military manuals of Benin (*ibid.*, § 16), Canada (*ibid.*, § 19), Colombia (*ibid.*, § 20), Croatia (*ibid.*, § 21), Ecuador (*ibid.*, § 22), Germany (*ibid.*, §§ 25–26), Kenya (*ibid.*, § 31), Madagascar (*ibid.*, § 32), Nigeria (*ibid.*, § 35), Philippines (*ibid.*, § 37), South Africa (*ibid.*, § 38) and Togo (*ibid.*, § 42).

[20] See, e.g., the legislation of Armenia (*ibid.*, § 50), Belarus (*ibid.*, § 53), Belgium (*ibid.*, § 54), Colombia (*ibid.*, § 59), Germany (*ibid.*, § 65), Niger (*ibid.*, § 73), Spain (*ibid.*, § 75) and Sweden

principle of proportionality in attack to be part of customary international law.[21] There are also a number of official statements pertaining to armed conflicts in general or to non-international armed conflicts in particular that refer to this rule.[22] The pleadings of States before the International Court of Justice in the *Nuclear Weapons case* referred to above were couched in general terms applicable in all armed conflicts.

The jurisprudence of the International Criminal Tribunal for the Former Yugoslavia and a report of the Inter-American Commission on Human Rights provide further evidence of the customary nature of this rule in non-international armed conflicts.[23]

No official contrary practice was found with respect to either international or non-international armed conflicts. Alleged violations of the principle of proportionality in attack have generally been condemned by States.[24] The United Nations and other international organisations have also condemned such violations, for example, in the context of the conflicts in Chechnya, Kosovo, the Middle East and the former Yugoslavia.[25]

The ICRC has reminded parties to both international and non-international armed conflicts of their duty to respect the principle of proportionality in attack.[26]

Interpretation

Several States have stated that the expression "military advantage" refers to the advantage anticipated from the military attack considered as a whole and not only from isolated or particular parts of that attack.[27] The relevant provision in the Statute of the International Criminal Court refers to the civilian injuries, loss of life or damage being excessive "in relation to the concrete and direct

---

(*ibid.*, § 76); see also the draft legislation of Argentina (*ibid.*, § 49), Burundi (*ibid.*, § 56), El Salvador (*ibid.*, § 63) and Nicaragua (*ibid.*, § 72).

[21] Argentina, National Appeals Court, *Military Junta case* (*ibid.*, § 81).

[22] See, e.g., the statements of Jordan (*ibid.*, § 97), Nigeria (*ibid.*, § 103), Rwanda (*ibid.*, § 108), Spain (*ibid.*, § 110) and United States (*ibid.*, § 97).

[23] ICTY, *Martić case*, Review of the Indictment (*ibid.*, § 139) and *Kupreškić case*, Judgement (*ibid.*, § 140); Inter-American Commission on Human Rights, Third report on human rights in Colombia (*ibid.*, § 138).

[24] See, e.g., the statements of Rwanda (*ibid.*, § 106) and Spain (*ibid.*, § 108) and the reported practice of Kuwait (*ibid.*, § 97) and Nigeria (*ibid.*, § 101).

[25] See, e.g., UN Security Council, Res. 1160 and 1199 (*ibid.*, § 132) and Res. 1322 (*ibid.*, § 133); UN Commission on Human Rights, Res. 2000/58 (*ibid.*, § 134); EC, Ministers of Foreign Affairs, Declaration on Yugoslavia (*ibid.*, § 137).

[26] See, e.g., the practice of the ICRC (*ibid.*, §§ 146 and 148–152).

[27] See the practice of Australia (*ibid.*, §§ 161 and 167), Belgium (*ibid.*, §§ 162, 168 and 177), Canada (*ibid.*, §§ 162, 169 and 178), France (*ibid.*, §§ 162 and 165), Germany (*ibid.*, §§ 162, 170 and 179), Italy (*ibid.*, §§ 162 and 180), Netherlands (*ibid.*, §§ 162 and 181), New Zealand (*ibid.*, §§ 161 and 171), Nigeria (*ibid.*, § 172), Spain (*ibid.*, §§ 162 and 173), United Kingdom (*ibid.*, §§ 162 and 182) and United States (*ibid.*, §§ 174 and 183).

overall military advantage anticipated" (emphasis added).[28] The ICRC stated at the Rome Conference on the Statute of the International Criminal Court that the addition of the word "overall" to the definition of the crime could not be interpreted as changing existing law.[29] Australia, Canada and New Zealand have stated that the term "military advantage" includes the security of the attacking forces.[30]

Upon ratification of Additional Protocol I, Australia and New Zealand stated that they interpreted the term "concrete and direct military advantage antici-pated" as meaning that there is a *bona fide* expectation that the attack would make a relevant and proportional contribution to the objective of the military attack involved.[31] According to the Commentary on the Additional Protocols, the expression "concrete and direct" military advantage was used in order to indicate that the advantage must be "substantial and relatively close, and that advantages which are hardly perceptible and those which would only appear in the long term should be disregarded".[32]

Numerous States have pointed out that those responsible for planning, decid-ing upon or executing attacks necessarily have to reach their decisions on the basis of their assessment of the information from all sources which is available to them at the relevant time.[33] These statements were generally made with reference to Articles 51–58 of Additional Protocol I, without excluding their application to the customary rule.

---

[28] ICC Statute, Article 8(2)(b)(iv) (*ibid.*, § 5).
[29] ICRC, Paper submitted to the Working Group on Elements of Crimes of the Preparatory Commission for the International Criminal Court (*ibid.*, § 190).
[30] See the practice of Australia (*ibid.*, §§ 161 and 167), Canada (*ibid.*, § 169) and New Zealand (*ibid.*, § 161).
[31] Australia, Declarations made upon ratification of Additional Protocol I (*ibid.*, § 161); New Zealand, Declarations made upon ratification of Additional Protocol I (*ibid.*, § 161).
[32] Yves Sandoz, Christophe Swinarski, Bruno Zimmermann (eds.), *Commentary on the Additional Protocols*, ICRC, Geneva, 1987, § 2209.
[33] See the practice of Algeria (cited in Vol. II, Ch. 4, § 193), Australia (*ibid.*, §§ 194 and 207), Austria (*ibid.*, § 195), Belgium (*ibid.*, §§ 196, 208 and 214), Canada (*ibid.*, §§ 197, 209 and 215), Ecuador (*ibid.*, § 210), Egypt (*ibid.*, § 198), Germany (*ibid.*, §§ 199 and 216), Ireland (*ibid.*, § 200), Italy (*ibid.*, § 201), Netherlands (*ibid.*, §§ 202 and 217), New Zealand (*ibid.*, § 203), Spain (*ibid.*, § 204), United Kingdom (*ibid.*, §§ 205 and 218) and United States (*ibid.*, §§ 211 and 219).

PRECAUTIONS IN ATTACK

Rule 15. In the conduct of military operations, constant care must be taken to spare the civilian population, civilians and civilian objects. All feasible precautions must be taken to avoid, and in any event to minimise, incidental loss of civilian life, injury to civilians and damage to civilian objects.

Practice

Volume II, Chapter 5, Section A.

Summary

State practice establishes this rule as a norm of customary international law applicable in both international and non-international armed conflicts. The two components of this rule are interrelated and the practice pertaining to each reinforces the validity of the other. This is a basic rule to which more content is given by the specific obligations contained in Rules 16–21. The practice collected in terms of those specific obligations is also relevant to prove the existence of this rule and *vice versa*.

International armed conflicts

The principle of precautions in attack was first set out in Article 2(3) of the 1907 Hague Convention (IX), which provides that if for military reasons immediate action against naval or military objectives located within an undefended town or port is necessary, and no delay can be allowed the enemy, the commander of a naval force "shall take all due measures in order that the town may suffer as little harm as possible".[1] It is now more clearly codified in Article 57(1) of Additional Protocol I, to which no reservations have been made.[2]

The obligation to take constant care and/or to take precautions to avoid or minimise incidental civilian losses is contained in numerous military

---

[1] 1907 Hague Convention (IX), Article 2(3) (cited in Vol. II, Ch. 5, § 63).
[2] Additional Protocol I, Article 57(1) (adopted by 90 votes in favour, none against and 4 abstentions) (*ibid.*, § 1).

manuals.[3] It is also supported by official statements and reported practice.[4] This practice includes that of States not, or not at the time, party to Additional Protocol I.[5] When the ICRC appealed to the parties to the conflict in the Middle East in October 1973, i.e., before the adoption of Additional Protocol I, to respect the obligation to take precautions in attack, the States concerned (Egypt, Iraq, Israel and Syria) replied favourably.[6]

Non-international armed conflicts

The requirement to take precautions in attack was included in the draft of Additional Protocol II but was dropped at the last moment as part of a package aimed at the adoption of a simplified text.[7] As a result, Additional Protocol II does not explicitly require such precautions. Article 13(1), however, requires that "the civilian population and individual civilians shall enjoy general protection against the dangers arising from military operations", and it would be difficult to comply with this requirement without taking precautions in attack.[8] More recent treaty law applicable in non-international armed conflicts, namely Amended Protocol II to the Convention on Certain Conventional Weapons and the Second Protocol to the Hague Convention for the Protection of Cultural Property, does spell out the requirement of precautions in attack.[9] In addition, this requirement is contained in other instruments pertaining also to non-international armed conflicts.[10]

[3] See, e.g., the military manuals of Australia (*ibid.*, §§ 6 and 71), Belgium (*ibid.*, §§ 7 and 72), Benin (*ibid.*, §§ 8 and 73), Cameroon (*ibid.*, § 9), Canada (*ibid.*, §§ 10 and 74), Croatia (*ibid.*, §§ 11 and 75–76), Ecuador (*ibid.*, §§ 12 and 77), France (*ibid.*, §§ 13 and 78), Germany (*ibid.*, §§ 14 and 79), Hungary (*ibid.*, §§ 15 and 80), Israel (*ibid.*, § 16), Italy (*ibid.*, §§ 17 and 81), Kenya (*ibid.*, § 82), Madagascar (*ibid.*, §§ 18 and 83), Netherlands (*ibid.*, §§ 19–20 and 84), New Zealand (*ibid.*, §§ 21 and 85), Nigeria (*ibid.*, §§ 22–23 and 86), Philippines (*ibid.*, § 87), Romania (*ibid.*, § 24), Spain (*ibid.*, §§ 25 and 88), Sweden (*ibid.*, § 26), Switzerland (*ibid.*, § 89), Togo (*ibid.*, §§ 27 and 90), United Kingdom (*ibid.*, § 91) and United States (*ibid.*, §§ 28–29 and 92–94).
[4] See, e.g., the statements of Costa Rica (*ibid.*, § 99), Israel (*ibid.*, § 101), Liberia (*ibid.*, § 36), Netherlands (*ibid.*, §§ 38 and 105), Saudi Arabia (*ibid.*, § 106), South Africa (*ibid.*, § 39), United Kingdom (*ibid.*, §§ 41 and 108–111) and United States (*ibid.*, §§ 42 and 112–124) and the reported practice of Indonesia (*ibid.*, §§ 35 and 100), Israel (*ibid.*, § 102), Jordan (*ibid.*, § 103), Malaysia (*ibid.*, §§ 37 and 104), Syria (*ibid.*, §§ 40 and 107), United States (*ibid.*, § 125) and Zimbabwe (*ibid.*, § 126).
[5] See, e.g., the practice and reported practice of Indonesia (*ibid.*, §§ 35 and 100), Israel (*ibid.*, §§ 16 and 101–102), Kenya (*ibid.*, § 82), Malaysia (*ibid.*, §§ 37 and 104), Philippines (*ibid.*, § 87), South Africa (*ibid.*, § 39), United Kingdom (*ibid.*, §§ 41, 91 and 108–111) and United States (*ibid.*, §§ 28–29, 42, 92–94 and 112–125).
[6] See ICRC, The International Committee's Action in the Middle East (*ibid.*, § 51).
[7] Draft Additional Protocol II submitted by the ICRC to the Diplomatic Conference leading to the adoption of the Additional Protocols, Article 24(2) (*ibid.*, § 3).
[8] Additional Protocol II, Article 13(1) (adopted by consensus) (*ibid.*, § 2).
[9] Amended Protocol II to the CCW, Article 3(10) (cited in Vol. II, Ch. 28, § 4); Second Protocol to the Hague Convention for the Protection of Cultural Property, Article 7 (cited in Vol. II, Ch. 5, § 208).
[10] See, e.g., Memorandum of Understanding on the Application of IHL between Croatia and the SFRY, para. 6 (*ibid.*, §§ 4 and 67); Agreement on the Application of IHL between the Parties to the Conflict in Bosnia and Herzegovina, para. 2.5 (*ibid.*, §§ 5 and 68); CSCE Code of Conduct, para. 36 (*ibid.*, § 69); UN Secretary-General's Bulletin, Section 5.3 (*ibid.*, § 70).

The obligation to take constant care and/or to take precautions to avoid or minimise incidental civilian losses is contained in military manuals which are applicable in or have been applied in non-international armed conflicts.[11] There are a number of official statements pertaining to armed conflicts in general or to non-international armed conflicts in particular that refer to this requirement.[12]

In 1965, the 20th International Conference of the Red Cross adopted a resolution calling on governments and other authorities responsible for action in all armed conflicts to spare the civilian population as much as possible.[13] This was subsequently reaffirmed by the UN General Assembly in a resolution on respect for human rights in armed conflict adopted in 1968.[14] Furthermore, in a resolution adopted in 1970 on basic principles for the protection of civilian populations in armed conflicts, the General Assembly required that "in the conduct of military operations, every effort should be made to spare civilian populations from the ravages of war, and all necessary precautions should be taken to avoid injury, loss or damage to civilian populations".[15]

The jurisprudence of the International Criminal Tribunal for the Former Yugoslavia in the *Kupreškić case* and the Inter-American Commission on Human Rights in the case concerning the events at La Tablada in Argentina provides further evidence of the customary nature of this rule in both international and non-international armed conflicts.[16] In the *Kupreškić case*, the Tribunal found the requirement to take precautions in attack to be customary because it specified and fleshed out general pre-existing norms.[17] It can be argued indeed that the principle of distinction, which is customary in international and non-international armed conflicts, inherently requires respect for this rule. The Tribunal also relied on the fact that the rule had not been contested by any State.[18] This study found no official contrary practice either.

The ICRC has appealed to parties to both international and non-international armed conflicts to respect the requirement to take precautions in attack.[19]

---

[11] See, e.g., the military manuals of Benin (*ibid.*, §§ 8 and 73), Croatia (*ibid.*, §§ 11 and 75), Ecuador (*ibid.*, §§ 12 and 77), Germany (*ibid.*, §§ 14 and 79), Italy (*ibid.*, §§ 17 and 81), Madagascar (*ibid.*, §§ 18 and 83), Nigeria (*ibid.*, §§ 22–23 and 86) and Togo (*ibid.*, §§ 27 and 90).

[12] See, e.g., the statements of Bosnia and Herzegovina, Republika Srpska (*ibid.*, § 34), Colombia (*ibid.*, § 98), Liberia (*ibid.*, § 36), Malaysia (*ibid.*, § 104), United Kingdom (*ibid.*, § 41) and United States (*ibid.*, § 42).

[13] 20th International Conference of the Red Cross, Res. XXVIII (*ibid.*, § 48).

[14] UN General Assembly, Res. 2444 (XXIII) (adopted by unanimous vote of 111 votes in favour to none against) (*ibid.*, § 45).

[15] UN General Assembly, Res. 2675 (XXV) (adopted by 109 votes in favour, none against and 8 abstentions) (*ibid.*, § 46).

[16] ICTY, *Kupreškić case*, Judgement (*ibid.*, §§ 49 and 132); Inter-American Commission on Human Rights, *Case 11.137 (Argentina)* (*ibid.*, § 133).

[17] ICTY, *Kupreškić case*, Judgement (*ibid.*, §§ 49 and 132).

[18] ICTY, *Kupreškić case*, Judgement (*ibid.*, §§ 49 and 132).

[19] See, e.g., the practice of the ICRC (*ibid.*, §§ 51, 53–61 and 135–142).

Feasibility of precautions in attack

The obligation to take all "feasible" precautions has been interpreted by many States as being limited to those precautions which are practicable or practically possible, taking into account all circumstances ruling at the time, including humanitarian and military considerations.[20] Protocols II and III and Amended Protocol II to the Convention on Certain Conventional Weapons define feasible precautions in the same terms.[21]

Upon ratification of Additional Protocol I, Switzerland stated that the obligation imposed by Article 57(2) on "those who plan or decide upon an attack" to take the specific precautionary measures set out in the article creates obligations only for "commanding officers at the battalion or group level and above".[22] It previously expressed its concern at the Diplomatic Conference leading to the adoption of the Additional Protocols that the wording in the chapeau of Article 57(2) was ambiguous and "might well place a burden of responsibility on junior military personnel which ought normally to be borne by those of higher rank".[23] Also at the Diplomatic Conference, Austria expressed the same concern that "junior military personnel could not be expected to take all the precautions prescribed, particularly that of ensuring respect for the principle of proportionality during an attack".[24] Upon ratification of Additional Protocol I, the United Kingdom made a similar point with respect to the obligation to cancel or suspend an attack if it becomes clear that the target is not a military objective or that its attack is likely to cause excessive civilian damage (see Rule 19) to the effect that this obligation only applied to "those who have the authority and practical possibility to cancel or suspend the attack".[25]

Information required for deciding upon precautions in attack

Numerous States have expressed the view that military commanders and others responsible for planning, deciding upon or executing attacks necessarily have to reach decisions on the basis of their assessment of the information from all

---

[20] See the practice of Algeria (*ibid.*, § 147), Argentina (*ibid.*, § 160), Australia (*ibid.*, § 161), Belgium (*ibid.*, § 148), Canada (*ibid.*, §§ 149, 162 and 168), France (*ibid.*, §150), Germany (*ibid.*, §§ 151 and 169), India (*ibid.*, § 170), Ireland (*ibid.*, § 152), Italy (*ibid.*, §§ 153 and 171), Netherlands (*ibid.*, §§ 154, 163 and 172), New Zealand (*ibid.*, § 164), Spain (*ibid.*, § 155), Turkey (*ibid.*, § 174), United Kingdom (*ibid.*, § 157) and United States (*ibid.*, § 175).

[21] Protocol II to the CCW, Article 3(4) (cited in Vol. II, Ch. 28, § 4); Protocol III to the CCW, Article 1(5) (cited in Vol. II, Ch. 30, § 109); Amended Protocol II to the CCW, Article 3(10) (cited in Vol. II, Ch. 28, § 4).

[22] Switzerland, Declaration made upon signature and reservation made upon ratification of Additional Protocol I (cited in Vol. II, Ch. 5, § 156).

[23] Switzerland, Statement at the Diplomatic Conference leading to the adoption of the Additional Protocols (*ibid.*, § 173).

[24] Austria, Statement at the Diplomatic Conference leading to the adoption of the Additional Protocols (*ibid.*, § 167).

[25] United Kingdom, Reservations and declarations made upon ratification of Additional Protocol I (*ibid.*, § 158).

sources which is available to them at the relevant time.[26] At the same time, many military manuals stress that the commander must obtain the best possible intelligence, including information on concentrations of civilian persons, important civilian objects, specifically protected objects, the natural environment and the civilian environment of military objectives.[27]

Rule 16. Each party to the conflict must do everything feasible to verify that targets are military objectives.

Practice

Volume II, Chapter 5, Section B.

Summary

State practice establishes this rule as a norm of customary international law applicable in both international and non-international armed conflicts.

International armed conflicts

The obligation to do everything feasible to verify that targets are military objectives is set forth in Article 57(2)(a) of Additional Protocol I, to which no reservations relevant to this rule have been made.[28]

This obligation is included in numerous military manuals.[29] It is supported by official statements and reported practice.[30] This practice includes that of States not, or not at the time, party to Additional Protocol I.[31] When the ICRC appealed to the parties to the conflict in the Middle East in October 1973,

---

[26] See Ch. 4, footnote 33.
[27] See, e.g., the military manuals of Australia (cited in Vol. II, Ch. 5, § 185), Benin (*ibid.*, § 186), Croatia (*ibid.*, § 188), France (*ibid.*, § 190), Italy (*ibid.*, § 191), Madagascar (*ibid.*, § 192), Nigeria (*ibid.*, § 194), Spain (*ibid.*, § 195), Sweden (*ibid.*, § 196) and Togo (*ibid.*, § 197).
[28] Additional Protocol I, Article 57(2)(a) (adopted by 90 votes in favour, none against and 4 abstentions) (*ibid.*, § 207).
[29] See, e.g., the military manuals of Argentina (*ibid.*, § 213), Australia (*ibid.*, § 214), Belgium (*ibid.*, § 215), Benin (*ibid.*, § 216), Cameroon (*ibid.*, § 217), Canada (*ibid.*, § 218), Croatia (*ibid.*, §§ 219–220), Ecuador (*ibid.*, § 221), France (*ibid.*, § 222), Germany (*ibid.*, § 223), Hungary (*ibid.*, § 224), Israel (*ibid.*, § 225), Italy (*ibid.*, § 226), Kenya (*ibid.*, § 227), Madagascar (*ibid.*, § 228), Netherlands (*ibid.*, § 229), New Zealand (*ibid.*, § 230), Nigeria (*ibid.*, § 231), Philippines (*ibid.*, § 232), Spain (*ibid.*, § 233), Sweden (*ibid.*, § 234), Switzerland (*ibid.*, § 235), Togo (*ibid.*, § 236), United Kingdom (*ibid.*, § 237), United States (*ibid.*, §§ 238–240) and Yugoslavia (*ibid.*, § 241).
[30] See, e.g., the statements of Indonesia (*ibid.*, § 246), Iraq (*ibid.*, § 248), Jordan (*ibid.*, § 250), Netherlands (*ibid.*, § 252) and United Kingdom (*ibid.*, § 254) and the reported practice of Iran (*ibid.*, § 247), Israel (*ibid.*, § 249), Malaysia (*ibid.*, § 251), Syria (*ibid.*, § 253), United States (*ibid.*, § 255) and Zimbabwe (*ibid.*, § 256).
[31] See, e.g., the practice of Indonesia (*ibid.*, § 246), Iraq (*ibid.*, § 248), Israel (*ibid.*, § 225), Kenya (*ibid.*, § 227), United Kingdom (*ibid.*, §§ 237 and 254) and United States (*ibid.*, §§ 238–240) and the reported practice of Iran (*ibid.*, § 247), Israel (*ibid.*, § 249), Malaysia (*ibid.*, § 251) and United States (*ibid.*, § 255).

i.e., before the adoption of Additional Protocol I, to respect the obligation to do everything feasible to verify that targets are military objectives, the States concerned (Egypt, Iraq, Israel and Syria) replied favourably.[32]

Non-international armed conflicts

While Additional Protocol II does not include an explicit reference to this rule, more recent treaty law applicable in non-international armed conflicts does so, namely the Second Protocol to the Hague Convention for the Protection of Cultural Property.[33] In addition, the rule is contained in other instruments pertaining also to non-international armed conflicts.[34]

The rule that it is incumbent upon the parties to do everything feasible to verify that targets are military objectives is set forth in military manuals which are applicable in or have been applied in non-international armed conflicts.[35]

The jurisprudence of the International Criminal Tribunal for the Former Yugoslavia in the *Kupreškić case* provides further evidence of the customary nature of this rule in both international and non-international armed conflicts. In its judgement, the Tribunal considered that this rule was customary because it specified and fleshed out general pre-existing norms.[36] It can be argued indeed that the principle of distinction, which is customary in international and non-international armed conflicts, inherently requires respect for this rule. The Tribunal also relied on the fact that this rule had not been contested by any State.[37] This study found no official contrary practice either.

Rule 17. Each party to the conflict must take all feasible precautions in the choice of means and methods of warfare with a view to avoiding, and in any event to minimising, incidental loss of civilian life, injury to civilians and damage to civilian objects.

Practice

Volume II, Chapter 5, Section C.

---

[32] See ICRC, The International Committee's Action in the Middle East (*ibid.*, § 263).
[33] Second Protocol to the Hague Convention for the Protection of Cultural Property, Article 7 (*ibid.*, § 208).
[34] See, e.g., Memorandum of Understanding on the Application of IHL between Croatia and the SFRY, para. 6 (*ibid.*, § 210); Agreement on the Application of IHL between the Parties to the Conflict in Bosnia and Herzegovina, para. 2.5 (*ibid.*, § 211); San Remo Manual, para. 46(b) (*ibid.*, § 212).
[35] See, e.g., the military manuals of Benin (*ibid.*, § 216), Croatia (*ibid.*, §§ 219–220), Ecuador (*ibid.*, § 221), Germany (*ibid.*, § 223), Italy (*ibid.*, § 226), Kenya (*ibid.*, § 227), Madagascar (*ibid.*, § 228), Nigeria (*ibid.*, § 231), Philippines (*ibid.*, § 232), Togo (*ibid.*, § 236) and Yugoslavia (*ibid.*, § 241).
[36] ICTY, *Kupreškić case*, Judgement (*ibid.*, § 260).
[37] ICTY, *Kupreškić case*, Judgement (*ibid.*, § 260).

Summary

State practice establishes this rule as a norm of customary international law applicable in international and non-international armed conflicts. This rule must be applied independently of the simultaneous application of the principle of proportionality (see Rule 14).

International armed conflicts

The duty to take all feasible precautions in the choice of means and methods of warfare is set forth in Article 57(2)(a)(ii) of Additional Protocol I, to which no relevant reservations have been made.[38]

This obligation is included in numerous military manuals.[39] It is also supported by official statements and reported practice.[40] This practice includes that of States not, or not at the time, party to Additional Protocol I.[41] When the ICRC appealed to the parties to the conflict in the Middle East in October 1973, i.e., before the adoption of Additional Protocol I, to take all feasible precautions in the choice of means and methods of warfare, the States concerned (Egypt, Iraq, Israel and Syria) replied favourably.[42]

Non-international armed conflicts

While Additional Protocol II does not include an explicit reference to the obligation to take all feasible precautions in the choice of means and methods of warfare, more recent treaty law applicable in non-international armed conflicts does so, namely the Second Protocol to the Hague Convention for the Protection of Cultural Property.[43] In addition, this rule is contained in other instruments pertaining also to non-international armed conflicts.[44]

---

[38] Additional Protocol I, Article 57(2)(a)(ii) (adopted by 90 votes in favour, none against and 4 abstentions) (*ibid.*, § 265).

[39] See, e.g., the military manuals of Argentina (*ibid.*, § 271), Australia (*ibid.*, § 272), Benin (*ibid.*, § 273), Cameroon (*ibid.*, § 274), Canada (*ibid.*, § 275), Croatia (*ibid.*, §§ 276–277), Ecuador (*ibid.*, § 278), France (*ibid.*, § 279), Germany (*ibid.*, § 280), Hungary (*ibid.*, § 281), Israel (*ibid.*, § 282), Italy (*ibid.*, § 283), Kenya (*ibid.*, § 284), Madagascar (*ibid.*, § 285), Netherlands (*ibid.*, § 286), New Zealand (*ibid.*, § 287), Philippines (*ibid.*, § 288), Spain (*ibid.*, § 289), Sweden (*ibid.*, § 290), Togo (*ibid.*, § 291), United Kingdom (*ibid.*, § 292), United States (*ibid.*, §§ 293–294) and Yugoslavia (*ibid.*, § 295).

[40] See, e.g., the statements of Indonesia (*ibid.*, § 299), Iraq (*ibid.*, § 301), Japan (*ibid.*, § 303), Netherlands (*ibid.*, § 305), United Kingdom (*ibid.*, §§ 307–308) and United States (*ibid.*, §§ 309–311) and the reported practice of Iran (*ibid.*, § 300), Israel (*ibid.*, § 302), Malaysia (*ibid.*, § 304), Syria (*ibid.*, § 306) and Zimbabwe (*ibid.*, § 312).

[41] See, e.g., the practice of Indonesia (*ibid.*, § 299), Iraq (*ibid.*, § 301), Israel (*ibid.*, § 282), Japan (*ibid.*, § 303), Kenya (*ibid.*, § 284), United Kingdom (*ibid.*, §§ 292 and 307–308) and United States (*ibid.*, §§ 293–294 and 309–311) and the reported practice of Iran (*ibid.*, § 300), Israel (*ibid.*, § 302) and Malaysia (*ibid.*, § 304).

[42] See ICRC, The International Committee's Action in the Middle East (*ibid.*, § 263).

[43] Second Protocol to the Hague Convention for the Protection of Cultural Property, Article 7 (*ibid.*, § 208).

[44] See, e.g., Memorandum of Understanding on the Application of IHL between Croatia and the SFRY, para. 6 (*ibid.*, § 268); Agreement on the Application of IHL between the Parties to the

This rule is set forth in military manuals which are applicable in or have been applied in non-international armed conflicts.[45]

The jurisprudence of the International Criminal Tribunal for the Former Yugoslavia and of the European Court of Human Rights provides further evidence of the customary nature of this rule in both international and non-international armed conflicts.[46] In its judgement in the *Kupreškić case*, the International Criminal Tribunal for the Former Yugoslavia considered that this rule was customary because it specified and fleshed out general pre-existing norms.[47] It can be argued indeed that the principle of distinction, which is customary in international and non-international armed conflicts, inherently requires respect for this rule. The Tribunal also relied on the fact that this rule had not been contested by any State.[48] This study found no official contrary practice either.

Examples

Examples of the application of this rule include considerations about the timing of attacks, avoiding combat in populated areas, the selection of means of warfare proportionate to the target, the use of precision weapons and target selection. In addition, Rule 21 sets out a specific requirement with respect to target selection.

Rule 18. Each party to the conflict must do everything feasible to assess whether the attack may be expected to cause incidental loss of civilian life, injury to civilians, damage to civilian objects, or a combination thereof, which would be excessive in relation to the concrete and direct military advantage anticipated.

Practice

Volume II, Chapter 5, Section D.

Summary

State practice establishes this rule as a norm of customary international law applicable in both international and non-international armed conflicts.

Conflict in Bosnia and Herzegovina, para. 2.5 (*ibid.*, § 269); San Remo Manual, para. 46(c) (*ibid.*, § 270).

[45] See, e.g., the military manuals of Benin (*ibid.*, § 273), Croatia (*ibid.*, §§ 276–277), Ecuador (*ibid.*, § 278), Germany (*ibid.*, § 280), Italy (*ibid.*, § 283), Kenya (*ibid.*, § 284), Madagascar (*ibid.*, § 285), Philippines (*ibid.*, § 288), Togo (*ibid.*, § 291) and Yugoslavia (*ibid.*, § 295).

[46] ICTY, *Kupreškić case*, Judgement (*ibid.*, § 260); European Court of Human Rights, *Ergi v. Turkey* (*ibid.*, § 319).

[47] ICTY, *Kupreškić case*, Judgement (*ibid.*, § 260).

[48] ICTY, *Kupreškić case*, Judgement (*ibid.*, § 260).

International armed conflicts

The duty to do everything feasible to assess whether the attack may be expected to cause excessive incidental damage is set forth in Article 57(2)(a)(iii) of Additional Protocol I, to which no relevant reservations have been made.[49]

This obligation is included in numerous military manuals.[50] It is also supported by official statements and reported practice.[51] This practice includes that of States not, or not at the time, party to Additional Protocol I.[52] When the ICRC appealed to the parties to the conflict in the Middle East in October 1973, i.e., before the adoption of Additional Protocol I, to do everything feasible to assess whether the attack may be expected to cause excessive incidental damage, the States concerned (Egypt, Iraq, Israel and Syria) replied favourably.[53]

Non-international armed conflicts

While Additional Protocol II does not include an explicit reference to the obligation to do everything feasible to assess whether the attack may be expected to cause excessive incidental damage, more recent treaty law applicable in non-international armed conflicts does so, namely the Second Protocol to the Hague Convention for the Protection of Cultural Property.[54] In addition, this rule is contained in other instruments pertaining also to non-international armed conflicts.[55]

The rule whereby each party must do everything feasible to assess whether the attack may be expected to cause excessive incidental damage is set forth in military manuals which are applicable in or have been applied in non-international armed conflicts.[56]

---

[49] Additional Protocol I, Article 57(2)(a)(iii) (adopted by 90 votes in favour, none against and 4 abstentions) (*ibid.*, § 325).

[50] See, e.g., the military manuals of Argentina (*ibid.*, § 331), Australia (*ibid.*, § 332), Belgium (*ibid.*, § 333), Benin (*ibid.*, § 334), Cameroon (*ibid.*, § 335), Canada (*ibid.*, § 336), Ecuador (*ibid.*, § 337), France (*ibid.*, § 338), Germany (*ibid.*, § 339), Israel (*ibid.*, § 340), Netherlands (*ibid.*, § 341), New Zealand (*ibid.*, § 342), Nigeria (*ibid.*, § 343), Spain (*ibid.*, § 344), Sweden (*ibid.*, § 345), Togo (*ibid.*, § 346), United States (*ibid.*, §§ 347–348) and Yugoslavia (*ibid.*, § 349).

[51] See, e.g., the statements of Indonesia (*ibid.*, § 353), Iraq (*ibid.*, § 354), Netherlands (*ibid.*, § 355), United Kingdom (*ibid.*, §§ 357–358) and United States (*ibid.*, § 359) and the reported practice of Syria (*ibid.*, § 356) and Zimbabwe (*ibid.*, § 360).

[52] See, e.g., the practice of Indonesia (*ibid.*, § 353), Iraq (*ibid.*, § 354), Israel (*ibid.*, § 340), United Kingdom (*ibid.*, §§ 357–358) and United States (*ibid.*, §§ 347–348 and 359).

[53] See ICRC, The International Committee's Action in the Middle East (*ibid.*, § 365).

[54] Second Protocol to the Hague Convention for the Protection of Cultural Property, Article 7 (*ibid.*, § 326).

[55] See, e.g., Memorandum of Understanding on the Application of IHL between Croatia and the SFRY, para. 6 (*ibid.*, § 328); Agreement on the Application of IHL between the Parties to the Conflict in Bosnia and Herzegovina, para. 2.5 (*ibid.*, § 329); San Remo Manual, para. 46(d) (*ibid.*, § 330).

[56] See, e.g., the military manuals of Benin (*ibid.*, § 334), Ecuador (*ibid.*, § 337), Germany (*ibid.*, § 339), Nigeria (*ibid.*, § 343), Togo (*ibid.*, § 346) and Yugoslavia (*ibid.*, § 349).

The jurisprudence of the International Criminal Tribunal for the Former Yugoslavia in the *Kupreškić case* provides further evidence of the customary nature of this rule in both international and non-international armed conflicts. In its judgement, the Tribunal considered that this rule was customary because it specified and fleshed out general pre-existing norms.[57] It can be argued indeed that the principle of proportionality (see Rule 14), which is customary in international and non-international armed conflicts, inherently requires respect for this rule. The Tribunal also relied on the fact that this rule had not been contested by any State.[58] This study found no official contrary practice either.

Rule 19. Each party to the conflict must do everything feasible to cancel or suspend an attack if it becomes apparent that the target is not a military objective or that the attack may be expected to cause incidental loss of civilian life, injury to civilians, damage to civilian objects, or a combination thereof, which would be excessive in relation to the concrete and direct military advantage anticipated.

Practice

Volume II, Chapter 5, Section E.

Summary

State practice establishes this rule as a norm of customary international law applicable in both international and non-international armed conflicts.

International armed conflicts

The obligation to do everything feasible to cancel or suspend an attack if it becomes apparent that the target is not a military objective or that the attack may be expected to cause excessive incidental damage is set forth in Article 57(2)(b) of Additional Protocol I, to which no relevant reservations have been made.[59] Upon ratification of Additional Protocol I, the United Kingdom stated that this obligation only applied to "those who have the authority and practical possibility to cancel or suspend the attack".[60]

---

[57] ICTY, *Kupreškić case*, Judgement (*ibid.*, § 362).
[58] ICTY, *Kupreškić case*, Judgement (*ibid.*, § 362).
[59] Additional Protocol I, Article 57(2)(b) (adopted by 90 votes in favour, none against and 4 abstentions) (*ibid.*, § 367).
[60] United Kingdom, Reservations and declarations made upon ratification of Additional Protocol I (*ibid.*, § 158).

This obligation is included in numerous military manuals.[61] It is also supported by official statements and reported practice.[62] This practice includes that of States not, or not at the time, party to Additional Protocol I.[63] When the ICRC appealed to the parties to the conflict in the Middle East in October 1973, i.e., before the adoption of Additional Protocol I, to do everything feasible to cancel or suspend an attack if it becomes apparent that the target is not a military objective or that the attack may be expected to cause excessive incidental damage, the States concerned (Egypt, Iraq, Israel and Syria) replied favourably.[64]

Non-international armed conflicts

While Additional Protocol II does not include an explicit reference to this rule, more recent treaty law applicable in non-international armed conflicts does so, namely the Second Protocol to the Hague Convention for the Protection of Cultural Property.[65] In addition, this rule is contained in other instruments pertaining also to non-international armed conflicts.[66]

Military manuals which are applicable in or have been applied in non-international armed conflicts specify the obligation to do everything feasible to cancel or suspend an attack if it becomes apparent that the target is not a military objective or that the attack may be expected to cause excessive incidental damage.[67]

The jurisprudence of the International Criminal Tribunal for the Former Yugoslavia in the *Kupreškić case* provides further evidence of the customary

---

[61] See, e.g., the military manuals of Argentina (*ibid.*, § 373), Australia (*ibid.*, §§ 374–375), Belgium (*ibid.*, § 376), Benin (*ibid.*, § 377), Cameroon (*ibid.*, § 378), Canada (*ibid.*, § 379), Colombia (*ibid.*, § 380), Croatia (*ibid.*, § 381), France (*ibid.*, § 382), Germany (*ibid.*, § 383), Hungary (*ibid.*, § 384), Italy (*ibid.*, § 385), Kenya (*ibid.*, § 386), Madagascar (*ibid.*, § 387), Netherlands (*ibid.*, § 388), New Zealand (*ibid.*, § 389), Spain (*ibid.*, § 390), Sweden (*ibid.*, § 391), Switzerland (*ibid.*, § 392), Togo (*ibid.*, § 393), United Kingdom (*ibid.*, § 394) and United States (*ibid.*, § 395).

[62] See, e.g., the statements of Indonesia (*ibid.*, § 400), Iraq (*ibid.*, § 401), Jordan (*ibid.*, § 403), Netherlands (*ibid.*, § 405), United Kingdom (*ibid.*, § 407) and United States (*ibid.*, §§ 409–411) and the reported practice of Israel (*ibid.*, § 402), Malaysia (*ibid.*, § 404), Syria (*ibid.*, § 406), United States (*ibid.*, § 408) and Zimbabwe (*ibid.*, § 412).

[63] See, e.g., the military manuals of Kenya (*ibid.*, § 386), United Kingdom (*ibid.*, § 394) and United States (*ibid.*, § 395); the statements of Indonesia (*ibid.*, § 400), Iraq (*ibid.*, § 401), United Kingdom (*ibid.*, § 407) and United States (*ibid.*, §§ 409–411) and the reported practice of Israel (*ibid.*, § 402), Malaysia (*ibid.*, § 404) and United States (*ibid.*, § 408).

[64] See ICRC, The International Committee's Action in the Middle East (*ibid.*, § 417).

[65] Second Protocol to the Hague Convention for the Protection of Cultural Property, Article 7 (*ibid.*, § 368).

[66] See, e.g., Memorandum of Understanding on the Application of IHL between Croatia and the SFRY, para. 6 (*ibid.*, § 370); Agreement on the Application of IHL between the Parties to the Conflict in Bosnia and Herzegovina, para. 2.5 (*ibid.*, § 371); San Remo Manual, para. 46(d) (*ibid.*, § 372).

[67] See, e.g., the military manuals of Australia (*ibid.*, § 374), Benin (*ibid.*, § 377), Colombia (*ibid.*, § 380), Croatia (*ibid.*, § 381), Germany (*ibid.*, § 383), Italy (*ibid.*, § 385), Kenya (*ibid.*, § 386), Madagascar (*ibid.*, § 387) and Togo (*ibid.*, § 393).

nature of this rule in both international and non-international armed conflicts. In its judgement, the Tribunal considered that this rule was customary because it specified and fleshed out general pre-existing norms.[68] It can be argued indeed that the principle of distinction (see Rules 1 and 7) and the principle of proportionality (see Rule 14), both of which are customary in international and non-international armed conflicts, inherently require respect for this rule. Disregard for this rule would lead to an attack in violation of the principles of distinction and of proportionality and would be illegal on that basis. The Tribunal also relied on the fact that this rule had not been contested by any State.[69] This study found no official contrary practice either.

Rule 20. Each party to the conflict must give effective advance warning of attacks which may affect the civilian population, unless circumstances do not permit.

Practice

Volume II, Chapter 5, Section F.

Summary

State practice establishes this rule as a norm of customary international law applicable in both international and non-international armed conflicts.

International armed conflicts

The obligation to give effective advance warning prior to an attack which may affect the civilian population is a long-standing rule of customary international law already recognised in the Lieber Code, the Brussels Declaration and the Oxford Manual.[70] It was first codified in the Hague Regulations and is restated in Article 57(2)(c) of Additional Protocol I, to which no relevant reservations have been made.[71]

This obligation is included in a large number of military manuals.[72] Some national legislation incorporates it.[73] The obligation to give advance warning

---

[68] ICTY, *Kupreškić case*, Judgement (*ibid.*, § 416).
[69] ICTY, *Kupreškić case*, Judgement (*ibid.*, § 416).
[70] Lieber Code, Article 19 (*ibid.*, § 424); Brussels Declaration, Article 16 (*ibid.*, § 425); Oxford Manual, Article 33 (*ibid.*, § 426).
[71] Hague Regulations, Article 26 (*ibid.*, §§ 420–421); Additional Protocol I, Article 57(2)(c) (adopted by 90 votes in favour, none against and 4 abstentions) (*ibid.*, § 423).
[72] See, e.g., the military manuals of Argentina (*ibid.*, § 430), Australia (*ibid.*, § 431), Belgium (*ibid.*, § 432), Benin (*ibid.*, § 433), Cameroon (*ibid.*, § 434), Canada (*ibid.*, § 435), Croatia (*ibid.*, § 436), Ecuador (*ibid.*, § 437), France (*ibid.*, § 438), Germany (*ibid.*, § 439), Italy (*ibid.*, §§ 440–441), Kenya (*ibid.*, § 442), Madagascar (*ibid.*, § 443), Netherlands (*ibid.*, §§ 444–445), New Zealand (*ibid.*, § 446), Nigeria (*ibid.*, § 447), South Africa (*ibid.*, § 448), Spain (*ibid.*, § 449), Sweden (*ibid.*, § 450), Switzerland (*ibid.*, § 451), Togo (*ibid.*, § 452), United Kingdom (*ibid.*, §§ 453–454), United States (*ibid.*, §§ 455–457) and Yugoslavia (*ibid.*, § 458).
[73] See, e.g., the legislation of Ireland (*ibid.*, § 460), Italy (*ibid.*, § 461–462) and Norway (*ibid.*, § 463).

is also supported by official statements and other practice, including several accounts of advance warning.[74] Practice includes that of States not, or not at the time, party to Additional Protocol I.[75] When the ICRC appealed to the parties to the conflict in the Middle East in October 1973, i.e., before the adoption of Additional Protocol I, to give effective advance warning prior to an attack which may affect the civilian population, the States concerned (Egypt, Iraq, Israel and Syria) replied favourably.[76]

Non-international armed conflicts

While Additional Protocol II does not include an explicit reference to the obligation to give effective advance warning prior to an attack which may affect the civilian population, more recent treaty law applicable in non-international armed conflicts does so, namely Amended Protocol II to the Convention on Certain Conventional Weapons.[77] While this rule deals with the requirement to give warning of attacks which may affect the civilian population, it is nevertheless relevant to point out that the concept of warnings has also been extended to non-international armed conflicts in the context of the protection of cultural property.[78] In addition, this rule is contained in other instruments pertaining also to non-international armed conflicts.[79]

Military manuals which are applicable in or have been applied in non-international armed conflicts specify this obligation.[80] There are, in addition, several accounts of warnings that were issued in the context of non-international armed conflicts.[81]

The jurisprudence of the International Criminal Tribunal for the Former Yugoslavia in the *Kupreškić case* provides further evidence of the customary

---

[74] See, e.g., the statements of Netherlands (*ibid.*, § 476) and United States (*ibid.*, §§ 482–484), the practice of France (*ibid.*, § 467) and Israel (*ibid.*, §§ 471–472) and the reported practice of Indonesia (*ibid.*, § 468), Iran (*ibid.*, § 469), Iraq (*ibid.*, § 470), Israel (*ibid.*, §§ 473 and 489), Jordan (*ibid.*, § 474), Syria (*ibid.*, § 478), United Kingdom (*ibid.*, § 479), United States (*ibid.*, §§ 480–481 and 485) and Zimbabwe (*ibid.*, § 486).

[75] See, e.g., the military manuals of France (*ibid.*, § 438), Kenya (*ibid.*, § 442), United Kingdom (*ibid.*, §§ 453–454) and United States (*ibid.*, §§ 455–457); the statements of the United States (*ibid.*, §§ 482–484); the practice of France (*ibid.*, § 467) and Israel (*ibid.*, §§ 471–472) and the reported practice of Indonesia (*ibid.*, § 468), Iran (*ibid.*, § 469), Iraq (*ibid.*, § 470), Israel (*ibid.*, §§ 473 and 489), United Kingdom (*ibid.*, § 479) and United States (*ibid.*, §§ 480–481 and 485).

[76] See ICRC, The International Committee's Action in the Middle East (*ibid.*, § 495).

[77] Amended Protocol II to the CCW, Article 3(11).

[78] See Second Protocol to the Hague Convention for the Protection of Cultural Property, Articles 6(d) and 13(2)(c).

[79] See, e.g., Memorandum of Understanding on the Application of IHL between Croatia and the SFRY, para. 6 (cited in Vol. II, Ch. 5, § 428); Agreement on the Application of IHL between the Parties to the Conflict in Bosnia and Herzegovina, para. 2.5 (*ibid.*, § 429).

[80] See, e.g., the military manuals of Benin (*ibid.*, § 433), Croatia (*ibid.*, § 436), Ecuador (*ibid.*, § 437), Germany (*ibid.*, § 439), Italy (*ibid.*, §§ 440–441), Kenya (*ibid.*, § 442), Madagascar (*ibid.*, § 443), Nigeria (*ibid.*, § 447), South Africa (*ibid.*, § 448), Togo (*ibid.*, § 452) and Yugoslavia (*ibid.*, § 458).

[81] See, e.g., the reported practice of China (*ibid.*, § 465), Malaysia (*ibid.*, § 475), Russia (*ibid.*, § 477) and two other States (*ibid.*, §§ 487–488).

nature of this rule in both international and non-international armed conflicts. In its judgement, the Tribunal considered that this rule was customary because it specified and fleshed out general pre-existing norms.[82] It can be argued indeed that respect for the principle of distinction (see Rules 1 and 7) and the principle of proportionality (see Rule 14), both of which are customary in international and non-international armed conflicts, requires respect for this rule by inference. The Tribunal also relied on the fact that this rule had not been contested by any State.[83] This study found no official contrary practice either. Instead, it found accounts of warnings given in the context of both international and non-international armed conflicts.[84]

Interpretation

As the rule indicates, State practice considers that a warning is not required when circumstances do not permit, such as in cases where the element of surprise is essential to the success of an operation or to the security of the attacking forces or that of friendly forces.[85] Necessary speed of response is another consideration cited in practice as relevant to determining the feasibility of warnings.[86]

Furthermore, the rule provides that warnings must only be given of attacks which may affect the civilian population. Hence, the UK Military Manual considers that no warning is required if no civilians are left in the area to be attacked.[87] The US Air Force Pamphlet states that no warning is required if civilians are unlikely to be affected by the attack.[88]

Some practice was found to interpret the requirement that a warning be "effective". The United States, in particular, has stated that a warning need not be specific and may be general in order not to endanger the attacking forces

---

[82] ICTY, *Kupreškić case*, Judgement (*ibid.*, § 492).

[83] ICTY, *Kupreškić case*, Judgement (*ibid.*, § 492).

[84] See, e.g., the practice and reported practice of China (*ibid.*, § 465), Iran (*ibid.*, § 469), Iraq (*ibid.*, § 470), Israel (*ibid.*, §§ 471–473 and 489), Malaysia (*ibid.*, § 475), Russia (*ibid.*, § 477), United Kingdom (*ibid.*, § 479), United States (*ibid.*, §§ 480–481 and 485) and two other States (*ibid.*, §§ 487–488).

[85] See, e.g., Hague Regulations, Article 26 (*ibid.*, §§ 420–421); Additional Protocol I, Article 57(2)(c) (adopted by 90 votes in favour, none against and 4 abstentions) (*ibid.*, § 423); Brussels Declaration, Article 16 (*ibid.*, § 425); Oxford Manual, Article 33 (*ibid.*, § 426); Memorandum of Understanding on the Application of IHL between Croatia and the SFRY, para. 6 (*ibid.*, § 428); Agreement on the Application of IHL between the Parties to the Conflict in Bosnia and Herzegovina, para. 2.5 (*ibid.*, § 429); practice of Australia (*ibid.*, § 431), Belgium (*ibid.*, § 432), Benin (*ibid.*, § 433), Cameroon (*ibid.*, § 434), Canada (*ibid.* § 435), Croatia (*ibid.*, § 436), Ecuador (*ibid.*, § 437), France (*ibid.*, §§ 438 and 467), Germany (*ibid.*, § 439), Italy (*ibid.*, §§ 440–441), Kenya (*ibid.*, § 442), Madagascar (*ibid.*, § 443), Netherlands (*ibid.*, §§ 444–445), New Zealand (*ibid.*, § 446), South Africa (*ibid.*, § 448), Spain (*ibid.*, § 449), Switzerland (*ibid.*, § 451), Togo (*ibid.*, § 452), United Kingdom (*ibid.*, §§ 453–454), United States (*ibid.*, §§ 455–457 and 483–484) and Yugoslavia (*ibid.*, § 458) and the reported practice of Israel (*ibid.*, § 473).

[86] See, e.g., the reported practice of Israel (*ibid.*, § 473).

[87] United Kingdom, *Military Manual* (*ibid.*, § 453).

[88] United States, *Air Force Pamphlet* (*ibid.*, § 456).

or the success of their mission. It has also stated that such a general warning can consist of a blanket alert delivered by broadcast advising the civilian population to stay away from certain military objectives.[89]

State practice indicates that all obligations with respect to the principle of distinction and the conduct of hostilities remain applicable even if civilians remain in the zone of operations after a warning has been issued. Threats that all remaining civilians would be considered liable to attack have been condemned and withdrawn.[90]

Rule 21. When a choice is possible between several military objectives for obtaining a similar military advantage, the objective to be selected must be that the attack on which may be expected to cause the least danger to civilian lives and to civilian objects.

Practice

Volume II, Chapter 5, Section G.

Summary

State practice establishes this rule as a norm of customary international law applicable in international, and arguably also in non-international, armed conflicts.

International armed conflicts

The requirement that, when a choice is possible, the military objective to be selected be that which may be expected to cause the least danger to civilian lives and to civilian objects is set forth in Article 57(3) of Additional Protocol I, to which no relevant reservations have been made.[91]

This obligation is included in numerous military manuals.[92] It is also supported by official statements and reported practice.[93] This practice includes that of States not, or not at the time, party to Additional

---

[89] See the practice of the United States (*ibid.*, §§ 456, 483 and 485); see also the reported practice of Israel (*ibid.*, § 473).

[90] See the practice of Israel (*ibid.*, § 489) and Russia (*ibid.*, § 477).

[91] Additional Protocol I, Article 57(3) (adopted by 90 votes in favour, none against and 4 abstentions) (*ibid.*, § 502).

[92] See, e.g., the military manuals of Australia (*ibid.*, § 506), Benin (*ibid.*, § 507), Canada (*ibid.*, § 508), Croatia (*ibid.*, §§ 509–510), France (*ibid.*, § 511), Germany (*ibid.*, § 512), Hungary (*ibid.*, § 513), Italy (*ibid.*, § 514), Kenya (*ibid.*, § 515), Madagascar (*ibid.*, § 516), Netherlands (*ibid.*, § 517), New Zealand (*ibid.*, § 518), Nigeria (*ibid.*, § 519), Spain (*ibid.*, § 520), Sweden (*ibid.*, § 521), Togo (*ibid.*, § 522), United States (*ibid.*, § 523) and Yugoslavia (*ibid.*, § 524).

[93] See, e.g., the practice of Indonesia (*ibid.*, § 528), Jordan (*ibid.*, § 531), Netherlands (*ibid.*, § 533) and United States (*ibid.*, § 535, but see *ibid.*, § 536) and the reported practice of Iran (*ibid.*, § 529), Israel (*ibid.*, § 530), Malaysia (*ibid.*, § 532), Syria (*ibid.*, § 534) and Zimbabwe (*ibid.*, § 537).

Protocol I.[94] When the ICRC appealed to the parties to the conflict in the Middle East in October 1973, i.e., before the adoption of Additional Protocol I, to respect the requirement that, when a choice is possible, the military objective to be selected be that which may be expected to cause the least danger to civilian lives and to civilian objects, the States concerned (Egypt, Iraq, Israel and Syria) replied favourably.[95]

Non-international armed conflicts

While Additional Protocol II does not contain an explicit reference to the requirement that, when a choice is possible, the military objective to be selected be that which may be expected to cause the least danger to civilian lives and to civilian objects, it has been included in more recent treaty law applicable in non-international armed conflicts, namely the Second Protocol to the Hague Convention for the Protection of Cultural Property.[96] In addition, it is specified in other instruments pertaining also to non-international armed conflicts.[97]

Military manuals which are applicable in or have been applied in non-international armed conflicts specify the requirement that, when a choice is possible, the military objective to be selected be that the attack on which may be expected to cause the least danger to civilian lives and to civilian objects.[98]

The jurisprudence of the International Criminal Tribunal for the Former Yugoslavia in the *Kupreškić case* provides further evidence of the customary nature of this rule in both international and non-international armed conflicts. In its judgement, the Tribunal considered that this rule was customary because it specified and fleshed out general pre-existing norms.[99] It can be argued indeed that the principle of proportionality (see Rule 14) and the obligation to take all feasible precautions to avoid, and in any event to minimise, incidental loss of civilian life, injury to civilians and damage to civilian objects (see Rule 15), which are customary in both international and non-international armed conflicts, inherently require respect for this rule. The Tribunal also relied on the

---

[94] See, e.g., the practice of France (*ibid.*, § 511), Indonesia (*ibid.*, § 528), Kenya (*ibid.*, § 515) and United States (*ibid.*, §§ 523 and 535) and the reported practice of Iran (*ibid.*, § 529), Israel (*ibid.*, § 530) and Malaysia (*ibid.*, § 532).

[95] See ICRC, The International Committee's Action in the Middle East (*ibid.*, § 541).

[96] Second Protocol to the Hague Convention for the Protection of Cultural Property, Article 6 (cited in Vol. II, Ch. 12, § 21).

[97] See, e.g., Memorandum of Understanding on the Application of IHL between Croatia and the SFRY, para. 6 (cited in Vol. II, Ch. 5, § 504); Agreement on the Application of IHL between the Parties to the Conflict in Bosnia and Herzegovina, para. 2.5 (*ibid.*, § 505).

[98] See, e.g., the military manuals of Benin (*ibid.*, § 507), Croatia (*ibid.*, §§ 509–510), Germany (*ibid.*, § 512), Italy (*ibid.*, § 514), Kenya (*ibid.*, § 515), Madagascar (*ibid.*, § 516), Nigeria (*ibid.*, § 519), Togo (*ibid.*, § 522) and Yugoslavia (*ibid.*, § 524).

[99] ICTY, *Kupreškić case*, Judgement (*ibid.*, § 539).

fact that this rule had not been contested by any State.[100] This study found no official contrary practice either.

There is only one instance of apparently contrary practice. In response to an ICRC memorandum on the applicability of international humanitarian law in the Gulf region, the United States denied that this rule was customary but then restated the rule and recognised its validity,[101] consistent with its other practice referred to above.[102]

This rule should also be seen as a further specification of Rule 17 on the precautions to be taken in the choice of means and methods of warfare. Some States indicate that target selection is a means of complying with that requirement, and this rule describes a way in which target selection can operate as a precautionary measure.

Interpretation

The United States has emphasised that the obligation to select an objective the attack on which may be expected to cause the least danger to civilian lives and to civilian objects is not an absolute obligation, as it only applies "when a choice is possible" and thus "an attacker may comply with it if it is possible to do so, subject to mission accomplishment and allowable risk, or he may determine that it is impossible to make such a determination".[103]

---

[100] ICTY, *Kupreškić case*, Judgement (*ibid.*, § 539).
[101] See the practice of the United States (*ibid.*, § 536).
[102] See the practice of the United States (*ibid.*, §§ 523 and 535).
[103] See the practice of the United States (*ibid.*, § 536).

PRECAUTIONS AGAINST THE EFFECTS OF ATTACKS

Rule 22. The parties to the conflict must take all feasible precautions to protect the civilian population and civilian objects under their control against the effects of attacks.

Practice

Volume II, Chapter 6, Section A.

Summary

State practice establishes this rule as a norm of customary international law applicable in both international and non-international armed conflicts. This is a basic rule to which more content is given by the specific obligations contained in Rules 23–24. The practice collected in terms of those specific obligations is also relevant to prove the existence of this rule and *vice versa*.

International armed conflicts

The duty of each party to the conflict to take all feasible precautions to protect the civilian population and civilian objects under its control against the effects of attacks is set forth in Article 58(c) of Additional Protocol I, to which no reservations have been made.[1]

Numerous military manuals restate the duty of parties to the conflict to take all feasible precautions to protect the civilian population and civilian objects under their control against the effects of attacks.[2] This obligation is supported by official statements and reported practice.[3] This practice includes that of States not, or not at the time, party to Additional Protocol I.[4]

---

[1] Additional Protocol I, Article 58(c) (adopted by 80 votes in favour, none against and 8 abstentions) (cited in Vol. II, Ch. 6, § 1).

[2] See, e.g., the military manuals of Argentina (*ibid.*, § 9), Cameroon (*ibid.*, § 11), Canada (*ibid.*, § 12), Croatia (*ibid.*, § 13), Germany (*ibid.*, § 14), Italy (*ibid.*, § 15), Kenya (*ibid.*, § 16), Madagascar (*ibid.*, § 17), Netherlands (*ibid.*, § 18), New Zealand (*ibid.*, § 19), Nigeria (*ibid.*, § 20), Russia (*ibid.*, § 21), Spain (*ibid.*, § 22), Sweden (*ibid.*, § 23) and United States (*ibid.*, § 25).

[3] See, e.g., the statements of Germany (*ibid.*, § 31), Iraq (*ibid.*, § 34) and United States (*ibid.*, § 40) and the reported practice of Iran (*ibid.*, § 33), Malaysia (*ibid.*, § 36), Syria (*ibid.*, § 39) and Zimbabwe (*ibid.*, § 41).

[4] See, e.g., the practice of Iraq (*ibid.*, § 34), Kenya (*ibid.*, § 16) and United States (*ibid.*, §§ 25 and 40) and the reported practice of Iran (*ibid.*, § 33) and Malaysia (*ibid.*, § 36).

Non-international armed conflicts

The obligation to take all feasible precautions to protect the civilian population and civilian objects against the effects of attacks was included in the draft of Additional Protocol II but was dropped at the last moment as part of a package aimed at the adoption of a simplified text.[5] As a result, Additional Protocol II does not explicitly require precautions against the effects of attack. Article 13(1) requires that "the civilian population and individual civilians shall enjoy general protection against the dangers arising from military operations".[6] It would be difficult to comply with this requirement without taking precautions against the effects of attack. The requirement to take precautions against the effects of attacks has, moreover, been included in more recent treaty law applicable in non-international armed conflicts, namely the Second Protocol to the Hague Convention for the Protection of Cultural Property.[7] In addition, this rule is contained in other instruments pertaining also to non-international armed conflicts.[8]

Military manuals which are applicable in or have been applied in non-international armed conflicts specify the requirement to take precautions against the effects of attacks.[9] It is supported by reported practice.[10]

In 1965, the 20th International Conference of the Red Cross adopted a resolution calling on governments and other authorities responsible for action in all armed conflicts to spare the civilian population as much as possible.[11] This was reaffirmed by the UN General Assembly in a resolution on respect for human rights in armed conflict adopted in 1968.[12] In addition, in a resolution adopted in 1970 on basic principles for the protection of civilian populations in armed conflicts, the UN General Assembly required that "in the conduct of military operations, every effort should be made to spare civilian populations from the ravages of war, and all necessary precautions should be taken to avoid injury, loss or damage to civilian populations".[13]

---

[5] Draft Additional Protocol II submitted by the ICRC to the International Conference leading to the adoption of the Additional Protocols, Article 24(2) (*ibid.*, § 3).

[6] Additional Protocol II, Article 13(1) (adopted by consensus) (*ibid.*, § 2).

[7] Second Protocol to the Hague Convention for the Protection of Cultural Property, Article 8 (cited in Vol. II, Ch. 12, § 290).

[8] See, e.g., Memorandum of Understanding on the Application of IHL between Croatia and the SFRY, para. 6 (cited in Vol. II, Ch. 6, § 5); Agreement on the Application of IHL between the Parties to the Conflict in Bosnia and Herzegovina, para. 2.5 (*ibid.*, § 6); CSCE Code of Conduct, para. 36 (*ibid.*, § 7); UN Secretary-General's Bulletin, Section 5.4 (*ibid.*, § 8).

[9] See, e.g., the military manuals of Croatia (*ibid.*, § 13), Germany (*ibid.*, § 14), Italy (*ibid.*, § 15), Kenya (*ibid.*, § 16), Madagascar (*ibid.*, § 17) and Nigeria (*ibid.*, § 20).

[10] See, e.g., the reported practice of Algeria (*ibid.*, § 30) and Malaysia (*ibid.*, § 36).

[11] 20th International Conference of the Red Cross, Res. XXVIII (*ibid.*, § 45).

[12] UN General Assembly, Res. 2444 (XXIII) (adopted by unanimous vote of 111 votes in favour, none against and no abstentions) (*ibid.*, § 42).

[13] UN General Assembly, Res. 2675 (XXV) (adopted by 109 votes in favour, none against and 8 abstentions) (*ibid.*, § 43).

The jurisprudence of the International Criminal Tribunal for the Former Yugoslavia in the *Kupreškić case* provides further evidence of the customary nature of the requirement to take precautions against the effects of attacks in both international and non-international armed conflicts. In its judgement, the Tribunal considered that this rule was customary because it specified and fleshed out general pre-existing norms.[14] It can be argued indeed that the principle of distinction (see Rules 1 and 7), which is customary in international and non-international armed conflicts, inherently requires respect for this rule. The Tribunal also relied on the fact that this rule had not been contested by any State.[15] This study found no official contrary practice either.

This practice should be read together with the extensive practice on the prohibition of the use of human shields (see Rule 97). The deliberate violation of the obligation to take all feasible precautions against the effects of attacks is often related to the use of human shields. In addition, international case-law has confirmed the obligation under international human rights law to take positive steps to protect life (see commentary to Rule 97).

Examples of precautions against the effects of attacks

Specific examples of how the general obligation to take precautions against the effects of attacks has been implemented include first and foremost the two specific obligations identified in Rules 23 and 24 below.

In addition, practice has shown that the construction of shelters, digging of trenches, distribution of information and warnings, withdrawal of the civilian population to safe places, direction of traffic, guarding of civilian property and the mobilisation of civil defence organisations are measures that can be taken to spare the civilian population and civilian objects under the control of a party to the conflict.

Feasibility of precautions against the effects of attack

The obligation to take precautions against the effects of attacks "to the extent feasible" has been interpreted by many States as meaning that the obligation is limited to those precautions which are practicable or practically possible, taking into account all circumstances ruling at the time, including humanitarian and military considerations.[16] The Rapporteur of the Working Group at

---

[14] ICTY, *Kupreškić case*, Judgement (*ibid.*, § 46).
[15] ICTY, *Kupreškić case*, Judgement (*ibid.*, § 46).
[16] See the statements of Algeria (*ibid.*, § 49), Belgium (*ibid.*, § 49), Cameroon (*ibid.*, § 56), Canada (*ibid.*, §§ 49 and 57), France (*ibid.*, § 49), Germany (*ibid.*, §§ 49 and 58), Ireland (*ibid.*, § 49), Italy (*ibid.*, §§ 49 and 59), Netherlands (*ibid.*, §§ 49 and 60), Spain (*ibid.*, § 49), United Kingdom (*ibid.*, §§ 49 and 61) and United States (*ibid.*, § 62).

the Diplomatic Conference leading to the adoption of the Additional Protocols reported that after the phrase "to the maximum extent feasible" had been introduced to qualify all subparagraphs of Article 58, agreement was quickly reached.[17] According to the Rapporteur, this revision reflected the concern of small and densely populated countries which would find it difficult to separate civilians and civilian objects from military objectives and that even large countries would find such separation difficult or impossible to arrange in many cases.[18] Upon ratification of Additional Protocol I, Austria and Switzerland stated that the obligation would be applied subject to the requirements of the defence of the national territory.[19]

State practice indicates that an attacker is not prevented from attacking military objectives if the defender fails to take appropriate precautions or deliberately uses civilians to shield military operations. The attacker remains bound in all circumstances, however, to take appropriate precautions in attack (see Rule 15) and must respect the principle of proportionality (see Rule 14) even though the defender violates international humanitarian law.

Information required for deciding upon precautions against the effects of attack

Numerous States have indicated that military commanders have to reach decisions concerning the taking of precautions against the effects of attack on the basis of their assessment of the information from all sources which is available to them at the relevant time.[20]

Rule 23. Each party to the conflict must, to the extent feasible, avoid locating military objectives within or near densely populated areas.

Practice

Volume II, Chapter 6, Section B.

Summary

State practice establishes this rule as a norm of customary international law applicable in international, and arguably also in non-international, armed

---

[17] Diplomatic Conference leading to the adoption of the Additional Protocols, Report to Committee III on the Work of the Working Group (*ibid.*, § 65).
[18] Diplomatic Conference leading to the adoption of the Additional Protocols, Report to Committee III on the Work of the Working Group (*ibid.*, § 65).
[19] Austria, Reservations made upon ratification of Additional Protocol I (*ibid.*, § 50); Switzerland, Reservations made upon ratification of Additional Protocol I (*ibid.*, § 51).
[20] See Ch. 4, footnote 33.

conflicts. This rule is an application of the principle of distinction (see Rules 1 and 7). It is also related to the prohibition of human shields (see Rule 97), as everything feasible must be done to separate military objectives from the civilian population, but in no event may civilians be used to shield military objectives.

International armed conflicts

The duty of each party to the conflict to avoid locating military objectives within or near densely populated areas is set forth in Article 58(b) of Additional Protocol I, to which no reservations relevant to this rule have been made.[21] It is also contained in the Israel-Lebanon Ceasefire Understanding of 1996.[22]

A large number of military manuals include this obligation.[23] It is also supported by official statements and reported practice.[24] This practice includes that of States not, or not at the time, party to Additional Protocol I.[25]

Non-international armed conflicts

Although Additional Protocol II does not explicitly require precautions against the effects of attacks, Article 13(1) stipulates that "the civilian population and individual civilians shall enjoy general protection against the dangers arising from military operations" and it would be difficult to afford such protection when military objectives are located within or near densely populated areas.[26] The requirement to take this precaution against the effects of attacks has, moreover, been included in more recent treaty law applicable in non-international armed conflicts, namely the Second Protocol to the Hague Convention for the Protection of Cultural Property.[27] In addition, this rule

---

[21] Additional Protocol I, Article 58(b) (adopted by 80 votes in favour, none against and 8 abstentions) (cited in Vol. II, Ch. 6, § 70).

[22] Israel-Lebanon Ceasefire Understanding, Article 3 (ibid., § 71).

[23] See, e.g., the military manuals of Argentina (ibid., § 77), Australia (ibid., § 78), Benin (ibid., § 79), Canada (ibid., § 80), Croatia (ibid., §§ 81–82), Ecuador (ibid., § 83), Hungary (ibid., § 84), Israel (ibid., § 85), Italy (ibid., § 86), Kenya (ibid., § 87), Madagascar (ibid., § 88), Netherlands (ibid., § 89), New Zealand (ibid., § 90), Nigeria (ibid., § 91), Russia (ibid., § 92), Spain (ibid., § 93), Sweden (ibid., § 94), Switzerland (ibid., § 95), Togo (ibid., § 96), United Kingdom (ibid., § 97) and United States (ibid., § 98).

[24] See, e.g., the statements of France (ibid., § 105), Iraq (ibid., § 107), Israel (ibid., §§ 105 and 108), Lebanon (ibid., §§ 105 and 113), Syria (ibid., § 105), United Kingdom (ibid., § 116) and United States (ibid., §§ 105 and 117–123) and the reported practice of Botswana (ibid., § 102), Egypt (ibid., § 104), Israel (ibid., § 109), Jordan (ibid., § 110), Kuwait (ibid., § 112), Malaysia (ibid., § 114), Syria (ibid., § 115), United States (ibid., § 124) and Zimbabwe (ibid., § 125).

[25] See, e.g., the practice of France (ibid., § 105), Iraq (ibid., § 107), Israel (ibid., §§ 71, 85, 105 and 108), Kenya (ibid., § 87), United Kingdom (ibid., §§ 97 and 116) and United States (ibid., §§ 98, 105 and 117–123) and the reported practice of Israel (ibid., § 109), Malaysia (ibid., § 114) and United States (ibid., § 124).

[26] Additional Protocol II, Article 13(1) (adopted by consensus) (ibid., § 2).

[27] Second Protocol to the Hague Convention for the Protection of Cultural Property, Article 8 (cited in Vol. II, Ch. 12, § 292).

is contained in other instruments pertaining also to non-international armed conflicts.[28]

Military manuals which are applicable in or have been applied in non-international armed conflicts specify the duty of each party to the conflict to avoid locating military objectives within or near densely populated areas.[29]

The jurisprudence of the International Criminal Tribunal for the Former Yugoslavia in the *Kupreškić case* provides further evidence of the customary nature of the duty of each party to the conflict to avoid locating military objectives within or near densely populated areas in both international and non-international armed conflicts. In its judgement, the Tribunal considered that this rule was customary because it specified and fleshed out general pre-existing norms.[30] It can be argued indeed that the principle of distinction (see Rules 1 and 7) and the principle of proportionality (see Rule 14), which are both customary in international and non-international armed conflicts, inherently require respect for this rule. The Tribunal also relied on the fact that this rule had not been contested by any State.[31] This study found no official contrary practice either.

In 1979, in the context of the conflict in Rhodesia/Zimbabwe, the ICRC appealed to the Patriotic Front to "clearly separate civilian establishments, particularly refugee camps, from military installations".[32]

The rules which require that persons deprived of their liberty be held in premises which are removed from the combat zone (see Rule 121) and that in case of displacement all possible measures be taken in order that the civilian population may be received under satisfactory conditions of safety (see Rule 131), which are both applicable in international and non-international armed conflicts, are also relevant in establishing the customary nature of this rule.

Interpretation

While some practice refers to the duty to locate military bases and installations outside densely populated areas, practice in general limits this obligation to what is feasible. It is possible, as several reports on State practice point out, that demographic changes cause military bases to be located within or near cities where this was originally not the case.[33] When such objectives involve

---

[28] See, e.g., Memorandum of Understanding on the Application of IHL between Croatia and the SFRY, para. 6 (cited in Vol. II, Ch. 6, § 74); Agreement on the Application of IHL between the Parties to the Conflict in Bosnia and Herzegovina, para. 2.5 (*ibid.*, § 75); UN Secretary-General's Bulletin, Section 5.4 (*ibid.*, § 76).

[29] See, e.g., the military manuals of Benin (*ibid.*, § 79), Croatia (*ibid.*, §§ 81–82), Ecuador (*ibid.*, § 83), Italy (*ibid.*, § 86), Kenya (*ibid.*, § 87), Madagascar (*ibid.*, § 88), Nigeria (*ibid.*, § 91) and Togo (*ibid.*, § 96).

[30] ICTY, *Kupreškić case*, Judgement (*ibid.*, § 46).

[31] ICTY, *Kupreškić case*, Judgement (*ibid.*, § 46).

[32] See ICRC, Conflict in Southern Africa: ICRC appeal (*ibid.*, § 131).

[33] See the Reports on the Practice of Iran (*ibid.*, § 106), Israel (*ibid.*, § 109), Kuwait (*ibid.*, § 112) and Malaysia (*ibid.*, § 114).

immovable property, it is less feasible to move them than in the case of movable property. At the Diplomatic Conference leading to the adoption of the Additional Protocols, South Korea stated that this rule "does not constitute a restriction on a State's military installations on its own territory".[34] Dual use installations, such as railway stations and airports, may even be located near or inside densely populated areas on purpose.

Rule 24. Each party to the conflict must, to the extent feasible, remove civilian persons and objects under its control from the vicinity of military objectives.

Practice

Volume II, Chapter 6, Section C.

Summary

State practice establishes this rule as a norm of customary international law applicable in international, and arguably also in non-international, armed conflicts. This rule is an application of the principle of distinction (see Rules 1 and 7). It is also related to the prohibition on using human shields (see Rule 97), as everything feasible must be done to evacuate the civilian population from the vicinity of military objectives; in no event may civilians be used to shield military objectives.

International armed conflicts

The duty of each party to the conflict, to the extent feasible, to remove civilian persons and objects under its control from the vicinity of military objectives is set forth in Article 58(a) of Additional Protocol I, to which no reservations relevant to this rule have been made.[35]

A large number of military manuals restate this obligation.[36] It is also supported by official statements and reported practice.[37] This practice includes that of States not, or not at the time, party to Additional Protocol I.[38]

---

[34] South Korea, Statement at the Diplomatic Conference leading to the adoption of the Additional Protocols (*ibid.*, § 111).

[35] Additional Protocol I, Article 58(a) (adopted by 80 votes in favour, none against and 8 abstentions) (*ibid.*, § 133).

[36] See, e.g., the military manuals of Argentina (*ibid.*, § 138), Australia (*ibid.*, § 139), Benin (*ibid.*, § 140), Cameroon (*ibid.*, § 141), Canada (*ibid.*, § 142), Croatia (*ibid.*, § 143), Ecuador (*ibid.*, § 144), France (*ibid.*, § 145), Israel (*ibid.*, § 146), Italy (*ibid.*, § 147), Kenya (*ibid.*, § 148), Madagascar (*ibid.*, § 149), Netherlands (*ibid.*, § 150), New Zealand (*ibid.*, § 151), Nigeria (*ibid.*, § 152), Spain (*ibid.*, § 153), Sweden (*ibid.*, § 154), Switzerland (*ibid.*, § 155), Togo (*ibid.*, § 156), United Kingdom (*ibid.*, § 157) and United States (*ibid.*, §§ 158–159).

[37] See, e.g., the statements of Iraq (*ibid.*, § 164) and United States (*ibid.*, §§ 169–172) and the reported practice of Egypt (*ibid.*, § 163), Jordan (*ibid.*, § 165), Kuwait (*ibid.*, § 166), Syria (*ibid.*, § 168), United States (*ibid.*, § 173) and Zimbabwe (*ibid.*, § 174).

[38] See, e.g., the practice of France (*ibid.*, § 145), Iraq (*ibid.*, § 164), Israel (*ibid.*, § 146), Kenya (*ibid.*, § 148), United Kingdom (*ibid.*, § 157) and United States (*ibid.*, §§ 158–159 and 169–172) and the reported practice of the United States (*ibid.*, § 173).

Non-international armed conflicts

Although Additional Protocol II does not explicitly require precautions against the effects of attacks, Article 13(1) stipulates that "the civilian population and individual civilians shall enjoy general protection against the dangers arising from military operations".[39] It would be difficult to afford such protection when civilian persons and objects are not removed from the vicinity of military objectives. The requirement to take this precaution against the effects of attacks has, moreover, been included in more recent treaty law applicable in non-international armed conflicts, namely the Second Protocol to the Hague Convention for the Protection of Cultural Property.[40] In addition, this rule is contained in other instruments pertaining also to non-international armed conflicts.[41]

Military manuals which are applicable in or have been applied in non-international armed conflicts specify the duty of each party to the conflict, to the extent feasible, to remove civilian persons and objects under its control from the vicinity of military objectives.[42]

The jurisprudence of the International Criminal Tribunal for the Former Yugoslavia in the *Kupreškić case* contains further evidence of the customary nature of the duty of each party to the conflict, to the extent feasible, to remove civilian persons and objects under its control from the vicinity of military objectives in both international and non-international armed conflicts. In its judgement, the Tribunal considered that this rule was customary because it specified and fleshed out general pre-existing norms.[43] It can be argued indeed that the principle of distinction (see Rules 1 and 7), which is customary in international and non-international armed conflicts, inherently requires respect for this rule. The Tribunal also relied on the fact that this rule had not been contested by any State.[44] This study found no official contrary practice either.

The ICRC has reminded parties to both international and non-international armed conflicts of the obligation, to the extent feasible, to remove civilian persons and objects under their control from the vicinity of military objectives.[45]

---

[39] Additional Protocol II, Article 13(1) (adopted by consensus) (*ibid.*, § 2).
[40] Second Protocol to the Hague Convention for the Protection of Cultural Property, Article 8.
[41] See, e.g., Memorandum of Understanding on the Application of IHL between Croatia and the SFRY, para. 6 (*ibid.*, § 136); Agreement on the Application of IHL between the Parties to the Conflict in Bosnia and Herzegovina, para. 2.5 (*ibid.*, § 137).
[42] See, e.g., the military manuals of Benin (*ibid.*, § 140), Croatia (*ibid.*, § 143), Ecuador (*ibid.*, § 144), Italy (*ibid.*, § 147), Kenya (*ibid.*, § 148), Madagascar (*ibid.*, § 149), Nigeria (*ibid.*, § 152) and Togo (*ibid.*, § 156).
[43] ICTY, *Kupreškić case*, Judgement (*ibid.*, § 176).
[44] ICTY, *Kupreškić case*, Judgement (*ibid.*, § 176).
[45] See, e.g., ICRC, Memorandum on Respect for International Humanitarian Law in Angola (*ibid.*, § 180) and Memorandum on Compliance with International Humanitarian Law by the Forces Participating in Opération Turquoise (*ibid.*, § 181).

Interpretation

The obligation on each party to the conflict, to the extent feasible, to remove civilian persons and objects under its control from the vicinity of military objectives is particularly relevant where military objectives can not feasibly be separated from densely populated areas according to Rule 23.

This rule is also related to the prohibition of the forcible displacement of a civilian population unless its security demands that it be evacuated (see Rule 129), because it specifies that evacuation must be undertaken to the extent feasible.

According to the US Naval Handbook, "a party to an armed conflict has an affirmative duty to remove civilians under its control as well as the wounded, sick, shipwrecked, and prisoners of war from the vicinity of targets of likely enemy attacks".[46] The extension of this rule to the wounded, sick and shipwrecked and to prisoners of war is consistent with Rules 109–111 concerning the evacuation, care and protection of the wounded sick and shipwrecked and with Rule 121 concerning the holding of persons deprived of their liberty in premises which are removed from the combat zone.

[46] United States, *Naval Handbook* (*ibid.*, § 159).

PART II

SPECIFICALLY PROTECTED PERSONS AND OBJECTS

MEDICAL AND RELIGIOUS PERSONNEL AND OBJECTS

Rule 25. Medical personnel exclusively assigned to medical duties must be respected and protected in all circumstances. They lose their protection if they commit, outside their humanitarian function, acts harmful to the enemy.

Practice

Volume II, Chapter 7, Section A.

Summary

State practice establishes this rule as a norm of customary international law applicable in both international and non-international armed conflicts.

International armed conflicts

This rule goes back to the 1864 Geneva Convention and was repeated in the subsequent Geneva Conventions of 1906 and 1929.[1] It is now set forth in the First, Second and Fourth Geneva Conventions of 1949.[2] Its scope was expanded in Article 15 of Additional Protocol I to cover civilian medical personnel in addition to military medical personnel in all circumstances.[3] This extension is widely supported in State practice, which generally refers to medical personnel without distinguishing between military or civilian medical personnel.[4]

---

[1] 1864 Geneva Convention, Article 2 (cited in Vol. II, Ch. 7, § 1); 1906 Geneva Convention, Articles 9–10 (*ibid.*, §§ 2–3); 1929 Geneva Convention, Articles 9–10 (*ibid.*, §§ 4–5).

[2] First Geneva Convention, Articles 24–26 (*ibid.*, §§ 6–8); Second Geneva Convention, Article 36 (*ibid.*, § 9); Fourth Geneva Convention, Article 20 (*ibid.*, § 10).

[3] Additional Protocol I, Article 15 (adopted by consensus) (*ibid.*, § 12).

[4] See, e.g., the military manuals of Burkina Faso (*ibid.*, § 27), Canada (*ibid.*, § 31), Colombia (*ibid.*, §§ 32–33), Congo (*ibid.*, § 34), Croatia (*ibid.*, § 36), Dominican Republic (*ibid.*, § 37), Ecuador (*ibid.*, § 38), El Salvador (*ibid.*, § 39), France (*ibid.*, § 40), Hungary (*ibid.*, § 44), Lebanon (*ibid.*, § 51), Mali (*ibid.*, § 53), Morocco (*ibid.*, § 54), Netherlands (*ibid.*, § 56), Nicaragua (*ibid.*, § 58), Nigeria (*ibid.*, §§ 59 and 61–62), Romania (*ibid.*, § 63), Russia (*ibid.*, § 64), Senegal (*ibid.*, § 65), Switzerland (*ibid.*, § 69), United Kingdom (*ibid.*, § 72) and United States (*ibid.*, § 76); the legislation of Bosnia and Herzegovina (*ibid.*, § 81), Colombia (*ibid.*, §§ 82–83), Croatia (*ibid.*, § 84), El Salvador (*ibid.*, § 85), Estonia (*ibid.*, § 87), Ethiopia (*ibid.*, § 88), Georgia (*ibid.*, § 89), Nicaragua (*ibid.*, § 93), Poland (*ibid.*, § 96), Slovenia (*ibid.*, § 98), Spain (*ibid.*, §§ 99–100), Tajikistan (*ibid.*, § 101), Ukraine (*ibid.*, § 102), Venezuela (*ibid.*, §§ 103–104) and Yugoslavia (*ibid.*, § 105); see also the draft legislation of Argentina (*ibid.*, § 79), El Salvador (*ibid.*, § 86), Nicaragua (*ibid.*, § 94) and the statements of China (*ibid.*, § 109), Iraq (*ibid.*, § 116), Kuwait (*ibid.*, §§ 118–119), United Kingdom (*ibid.*, § 126), United States (*ibid.*, § 131) and Venezuela (*ibid.*, § 135).

It is also supported by States not, or not at the time, party to Additional Protocol I.[5]

Under the Statute of the International Criminal Court, "intentionally directing attacks against ... personnel using the distinctive emblems of the Geneva Conventions in conformity with international law" constitutes a war crime in international armed conflicts.[6] This war crime is relevant to medical personnel because they are entitled to use the distinctive emblems of the Geneva Conventions.

Numerous military manuals recall the obligation to respect and protect medical personnel.[7] Under the legislation of many States, it is a war crime to violate this rule.[8] Furthermore, the rule is supported by official statements and reported practice.[9]

Non-international armed conflicts

This rule is implicit in common Article 3 of the Geneva Conventions, which requires that the wounded and sick be collected and cared for, because the protection of medical personnel is a subsidiary form of protection granted to ensure that the wounded and sick receive medical care.[10] The rule that medical personnel must be respected and protected is explicitly stated in Additional Protocol II.[11] In addition, under the Statute of the International Criminal Court, "intentionally directing attacks against ... personnel using the distinctive emblems of the Geneva Conventions in conformity with international

---

[5] See, e.g., the military manuals of France (*ibid.*, § 41) and United States (*ibid.*, §§ 75 and 77).

[6] ICC Statute, Article 8(2)(b)(xxiv) (*ibid.*, § 832).

[7] See, e.g., the military manuals of Argentina (*ibid.*, §§ 19–20), Australia (*ibid.*, §§ 21–22), Belgium (*ibid.*, §§ 23–24), Benin (*ibid.*, § 25), Bosnia and Herzegovina (*ibid.*, § 26), Burkina Faso (*ibid.*, § 27), Cameroon (*ibid.*, §§ 28–29), Canada (*ibid.*, §§ 30–31), Colombia (*ibid.*, §§ 32–33), Congo (*ibid.*, § 34), Croatia (*ibid.*, §§ 35–36), Dominican Republic (*ibid.*, § 37), Ecuador (*ibid.*, § 38), El Salvador (*ibid.*, § 39), France (*ibid.*, §§ 40–42), Germany (*ibid.*, § 43), Hungary (*ibid.*, § 44), Indonesia (*ibid.*, §§ 45–46), Israel (*ibid.*, § 47), Italy (*ibid.*, § 48), Kenya (*ibid.*, § 49), South Korea (*ibid.*, § 50), Lebanon (*ibid.*, § 51), Madagascar (*ibid.*, § 52), Mali (*ibid.*, § 53), Morocco (*ibid.*, § 54), Netherlands (*ibid.*, §§ 55–56), New Zealand (*ibid.*, § 57), Nicaragua (*ibid.*, § 58), Nigeria (*ibid.*, §§ 59–62), Romania (*ibid.*, § 63), Russia (*ibid.*, § 64), Senegal (*ibid.*, § 65), South Africa (*ibid.*, § 66), Spain (*ibid.*, § 67), Sweden (*ibid.*, § 68), Switzerland (*ibid.*, § 69), Togo (*ibid.*, § 70), United Kingdom (*ibid.*, §§ 71–72), United States (*ibid.*, §§ 73–77) and Yugoslavia (*ibid.*, § 78).

[8] See, e.g., the legislation of Bangladesh (*ibid.*, § 80), Bosnia and Herzegovina (*ibid.*, § 81), Colombia (*ibid.*, §§ 82–83), Croatia (*ibid.*, § 84), El Salvador (*ibid.*, § 85), Estonia (*ibid.*, § 87), Ethiopia (*ibid.*, § 88), Georgia (*ibid.*, § 89), Ireland (*ibid.*, § 90), Italy (*ibid.*, § 91), Lithuania (*ibid.*, § 92), Nicaragua (*ibid.*, § 93), Norway (*ibid.*, § 95), Poland (*ibid.*, § 96), Romania (*ibid.*, § 97), Slovenia (*ibid.*, § 98), Spain (*ibid.*, §§ 99–100), Tajikistan (*ibid.*, § 101), Ukraine (*ibid.*, § 102), Venezuela (*ibid.*, §§ 103–104) and Yugoslavia (*ibid.*, § 105); see also the draft legislation of Argentina (*ibid.*, § 79), El Salvador (*ibid.*, § 86) and Nicaragua (*ibid.*, § 94).

[9] See, e.g., the statements of China (*ibid.*, § 109), Germany (*ibid.*, § 113), Kuwait (*ibid.*, §§ 118–119), United Kingdom (*ibid.*, § 126), United States (*ibid.*, §§ 129–133), Venezuela (*ibid.*, § 135) and Yugoslavia (*ibid.*, §§ 136–137) and the reported practice of Rwanda (*ibid.*, § 125).

[10] 1949 Geneva Conventions, common Article 3. This reasoning is applied, e.g., in the military manuals of Belgium (*ibid.*, § 24), Colombia (*ibid.*, § 32), El Salvador (*ibid.*, § 39), Israel (*ibid.*, § 47), South Africa (*ibid.*, § 66) and Spain (*ibid.*, § 67).

[11] Additional Protocol II, Article 9(1) (adopted by consensus) (*ibid.*, § 13).

law" constitutes a war crime in non-international armed conflicts.[12] In addition, this rule is contained in other instruments pertaining also to non-international armed conflicts.[13]

Respect for and protection of medical personnel is included in military manuals which are applicable in or have been applied in non-international armed conflicts.[14] It is an offence under the legislation of a large number of States to violate this rule in any armed conflict.[15] The rule has also been invoked in official statements relating to non-international armed conflicts.[16]

No official contrary practice was found with respect to either international or non-international armed conflicts. Alleged attacks against medical personnel have generally been condemned by States.[17] International organisations have also condemned violations of this rule, for example, in the context of the conflicts in Burundi, Chechnya, El Salvador and the former Yugoslavia.[18] The ICRC has called upon parties to both international and non-international armed conflicts to respect this rule.[19]

Definition of medical personnel

The term "medical personnel" refers to personnel assigned, by a party to the conflict, exclusively to the search for, collection, transportation, diagnosis or treatment, including first-aid treatment, of the wounded, sick and shipwrecked, and the prevention of disease, to the administration of medical units or to the operation or administration of medical transports. Such assignments may be either permanent or temporary. The term medical personnel includes:

[12] ICC Statute, Article 8(2)(e)(ii) (*ibid.*, § 832).
[13] See, e.g., Hague Statement on Respect for Humanitarian Principles (*ibid.*, § 17).
[14] See, e.g., the military manuals of Argentina (*ibid.*, § 20), Australia (*ibid.*, §§ 21–22), Benin (*ibid.*, § 25), Bosnia and Herzegovina (*ibid.*, § 26), Cameroon (*ibid.*, § 29), Canada (*ibid.*, §§ 30–31), Colombia (*ibid.*, §§ 32–33), Croatia (*ibid.*, §§ 35–36), Ecuador (*ibid.*, § 38), El Salvador (*ibid.*, § 39), France (*ibid.*, § 42), Germany (*ibid.*, § 43), Hungary (*ibid.*, § 44), Italy (*ibid.*, § 48), Kenya (*ibid.*, § 49), South Korea (*ibid.*, § 50), Lebanon (*ibid.*, § 51), Madagascar (*ibid.*, § 52), Netherlands (*ibid.*, § 55), New Zealand (*ibid.*, § 57), Nigeria (*ibid.*, §§ 60–62), Russia (*ibid.*, § 64), South Africa (*ibid.*, § 66), Spain (*ibid.*, § 67) and Togo (*ibid.*, § 70).
[15] See, e.g., the legislation of Bangladesh (*ibid.*, § 80), Bosnia and Herzegovina (*ibid.*, § 81), Colombia (*ibid.*, §§ 82–83), Croatia (*ibid.*, § 84), El Salvador (*ibid.*, § 85), Estonia (*ibid.*, § 87), Ethiopia (*ibid.*, § 88), Georgia (*ibid.*, § 89), Ireland (*ibid.*, § 90), Lithuania (*ibid.*, § 92), Norway (*ibid.*, § 95), Poland (*ibid.*, § 96), Slovenia (*ibid.*, § 98), Spain (*ibid.*, §§ 99–100), Tajikistan (*ibid.*, § 101), Ukraine (*ibid.*, § 102), Venezuela (*ibid.*, §§ 103–104) and Yugoslavia (*ibid.*, § 105); see also the legislation of Italy (*ibid.*, § 91), Nicaragua (*ibid.*, § 93) and Romania (*ibid.*, § 97), the application of which is not excluded in time of non-international armed conflict, and the draft legislation of Argentina (*ibid.*, § 79), El Salvador (*ibid.*, § 86) and Nicaragua (*ibid.*, § 94).
[16] See, e.g., the practice of the Philippines (*ibid.*, § 123), United States (*ibid.*, § 132), Venezuela (*ibid.*, § 135) and Yugoslavia (*ibid.*, §§ 136 and 137).
[17] See, e.g., the statements of the United States (*ibid.*, § 132), Venezuela (*ibid.*, § 135) and Yugoslavia (*ibid.*, § 137).
[18] See, e.g., UN General Assembly, Res. 39/119 (*ibid.*, § 140), Res. 40/139 (*ibid.*, § 141) and Res. 41/157 (*ibid.*, § 141); UN Commission on Human Rights, Res. 1987/51 (*ibid.*, § 142); OSCE, Chairman in Office, Press Release 86/96 (*ibid.*, § 149).
[19] See, e.g., the practice of the ICRC (*ibid.*, §§ 156–158, 160–164 and 166–172).

(i)   medical personnel of a party to the conflict, whether military or civilian, including those described in the First and Second Geneva Conventions, and those assigned to civil defence organisations;
(ii) medical personnel of National Red Cross or Red Crescent Societies and other voluntary aid societies duly recognised and authorised by a party to the conflict, including the ICRC;
(iii) medical personnel made available to a party to the conflict for humanitarian purposes by a neutral or other State which is not a party to the conflict; by a recognised and authorised aid society of such a State; or by an impartial international humanitarian organisation.

This definition is set out in Article 8(c) of Additional Protocol I and is widely used in State practice.[20] The essence of the definition is that medical personnel have to be *exclusively* assigned to medical duties in order to enjoy the specific protection to which they are entitled. If the medical assignment is permanent, respect and protection are due at all times. If the medical assignment is only temporary, respect and protection are due only during the time of that assignment. Only medical personnel assigned to medical duties by a party to the conflict enjoy protected status. Other persons performing medical duties enjoy protection against attack as civilians, as long as they do not take a direct part in hostilities (see Rule 6). Such persons are not medical personnel and as a result they have no right to display the distinctive emblems. Canada's Code of Conduct thus explains that:

NGOs such as CARE and Médecins Sans Frontières (Doctors Without Borders) might wear other recognizable symbols. The symbols used by CARE, MSF and other NGOs do not benefit from international legal protection, although their work in favour of the victims of armed conflict must be respected. Upon recognition that they are providing care to the sick and wounded, NGOs are also to be respected.[21]

The term "military medical personnel" refers to medical personnel who are members of the armed forces. The term "civilian medical personnel" refers to medical personnel who are not members of the armed forces but who have been assigned by a party to the conflict exclusively to medical tasks.

The same general definition was originally included by consensus in the draft of Additional Protocol II but was dropped at the last moment as part of a package aimed at the adoption of a simplified text.[22] As a result, Additional Protocol II does not contain a definition of medical personnel and the term medical personnel, as used in non-international armed conflicts, may be understood in the same sense as that defined in Additional Protocol I.[23] It can be inferred from

---

[20] Additional Protocol I, Article 8(c) (adopted by consensus) (*ibid.*, § 11).
[21] Canada, *Code of Conduct* (*ibid.*, § 31).
[22] Draft Additional Protocol II submitted by the ICRC to the Diplomatic Conference leading to the adoption of the Additional Protocols, Article 11(f) (*ibid.*, § 14).
[23] See the declaration to this effect by the United States (*ibid.*, § 15) and the practice at the Diplomatic Conference leading to the adoption of the Additional Protocols (*ibid.*, § 150); see also Yves Sandoz, Christophe Swinarski, Bruno Zimmermann (eds.), *Commentary on the Additional Protocols*, ICRC, Geneva, 1987, §§ 4661–4665.

the definition initially put forward in the draft of Additional Protocol II and the negotiations at the Diplomatic Conference leading to the adoption of the Additional Protocols that "medical personnel" means those persons assigned, by a party to the conflict, exclusively to the search for, collection, transportation, diagnosis or treatment, including first-aid treatment, of the wounded, sick and shipwrecked, and the prevention of disease, to the administration of medical units or to the operation or administration of medical transports. Such assignments may be either permanent or temporary. The term medical personnel includes:

(i) medical personnel of a party to the conflict, whether military or civilian, including those assigned to medical tasks of civil defence;
(ii) medical personnel of Red Cross or Red Crescent organisations recognised and authorised by a party to the conflict;
(iii) medical personnel of other aid societies recognised and authorised by a party to the conflict and located within the territory of the State where the armed conflict is taking place.

The negotiations at the Diplomatic Conference leading to the adoption of the Additional Protocols indicate that, owing to the specific nature of non-international armed conflicts, the above examples differ in two respects from those listed for international armed conflicts. First, the term "Red Cross or Red Crescent organisations" was used in order "to cover not only assistance provided on the Government side but also already existing Red Cross groups or branches on the side opposing the Government and even improvised organizations which had come into existence only during the conflict".[24] It should be noted in this respect that the term "Red Cross (Red Crescent, Red Lion and Sun) organizations" is also used in Article 18 of Additional Protocol II.[25] Secondly, the drafting committee had deemed it necessary to specify that aid societies other than Red Cross organisations must be located within the territory of the State where the armed conflict is taking place "in order to avoid the situation of an obscure private group from outside the country establishing itself as an aid society within the territory and being recognized by the rebels".[26]

Respect for and protection of medical personnel

State practice contains the following specifications with respect to the meaning of the term "respect and protection". According to the UK Military Manual and US Field Manual, the term "respect and protection" means that medical

---

[24] CDDH, Official Records, Vol. XI, CDDH/II/SR.40, 20 March 1975, pp. 430–431, § 9; see also Yves Sandoz, Christophe Swinarski, Bruno Zimmermann (eds.), Commentary on the Additional Protocols, ICRC, Geneva, 1987, § 4666.
[25] Additional Protocol II, Article 18(1) (adopted by consensus).
[26] CDDH, Report of the Drafting Committee (cited in Vol. II, Ch. 7, § 150); see also Yves Sandoz, Christophe Swinarski, Bruno Zimmermann (eds.), Commentary on the Additional Protocols, ICRC, Geneva, 1987, § 4667.

personnel "must not knowingly be attacked, fired upon, or unnecessarily prevented from discharging their proper functions".[27] Germany's Military Manual and Switzerland's Basic Military Manual contain a similar understanding.[28] Spain's LOAC Manual states that protection includes the duty to defend, assist and support medical personnel when needed.[29] The military manuals of Benin, Croatia, Madagascar, Nigeria and Togo state that medical personnel may not be attacked, and must be allowed to carry out their tasks as long as the tactical situation permits.[30] Additional Protocol I also requires that "if needed, all available help shall be afforded to civilian medical personnel in an area where civilian medical services are disrupted by reason of combat activity".[31] Additional Protocol II requires that medical personnel "be granted all available help for the performance of their duties".[32]

The principle that medical personnel must not be punished for providing medical assistance is the subject of Rule 26.

Loss of protection of medical personnel

Military manuals and national legislation emphasise that medical personnel who engage in hostile acts lose the specific protection to which they are entitled.[33] This exception is linked to the requirement that such personnel be *exclusively* assigned to medical duties for them to be accorded respect and protection. Also, under the protection regime – which constitutes a corollary of the duty to care for the wounded and sick – specific protection is due because the wounded and sick are being cared for. Spain's LOAC Manual explains that:

It must be underlined that the protection of medical personnel is not a personal privilege but rather a corollary of the respect and protection due to the wounded and sick, who must be treated humanely in all circumstances . . . Medical personnel lose the special protection to which they are entitled if they commit acts of hostility. Such behaviour might even constitute perfidy if in so doing they take advantage of their medical position and the distinctive emblems.[34]

Whereas the First Geneva Convention and Additional Protocol I provide for the loss of protection of medical units and transports in case they are used to commit, "outside their humanitarian function, acts harmful to the enemy",

---

[27] United Kingdom, *Military Manual* (cited in Vol. II, Ch. 7, § 71); United States, *Field Manual* (*ibid.*, § 73).

[28] Germany, *Military Manual* (*ibid.*, § 43); Switzerland, *Basic Military Manual* (*ibid.*, § 69).

[29] Spain, *LOAC Manual* (*ibid.*, § 67).

[30] See the military manuals of Benin (*ibid.*, § 25), Croatia (*ibid.*, § 35), Madagascar (*ibid.*, § 52), Nigeria (*ibid.*, §§ 60 and 62) and Togo (*ibid.*, § 70).

[31] Additional Protocol I, Article 15(2) (adopted by consensus).

[32] Additional Protocol II, Article 9(1) (adopted by consensus) (cited in Vol. II, Ch. 7, § 13).

[33] See, e.g., the military manuals of Australia (*ibid.*, §§ 187–188), Israel (*ibid.*, § 47), Netherlands (*ibid.*, § 200), Spain (*ibid.*, §§ 67 and 203) and United States (*ibid.*, §§ 208 and 210) and the legislation of Italy (*ibid.*, § 91), Nicaragua (*ibid.*, § 93) and Spain (*ibid.*, § 99).

[34] Spain, *LOAC Manual* (*ibid.*, § 67).

Additional Protocol II provides for the loss of protection in case they are used to commit "hostile acts, outside their humanitarian function".[35] According to the Commentary on the Additional Protocols, the meaning of both terms is the same.[36] Although these provisions specifically apply to medical units, the rule on loss of protection contained therein can be applied by analogy to medical personnel.

In general, taking a direct part in hostilities, in violation of the principle of strict neutrality and outside the humanitarian function of medical personnel, is considered an act harmful to the enemy. This means that if medical teams are incorporated into combat units and their medical personnel bear arms and take a direct part in hostilities, they are not entitled to protection. However, neither the mere caring for enemy wounded and sick military personnel nor the sole wearing of enemy military uniforms or bearing of its insignia can be considered a hostile act. As explained below, the equipment of medical personnel with small arms to defend themselves or their patients and the use of such arms for this purpose do not lead to loss of protection. Furthermore, in analogous application of the similar rule applying to medical units, it is not to be considered a hostile act if medical personnel are escorted by military personnel or such personnel are present or if the medical personnel are in possession of small arms and ammunition taken from their patients and not yet handed over to the proper service.

Equipment of medical personnel with light individual weapons

State practice indicates that the protected status of medical personnel does not cease if they are equipped with light individual weapons solely to defend their patients or themselves against acts of violence, for example, against marauders. If they use such weapons in combat against enemy forces acting in conformity with the law of war, notably to resist capture, they forfeit their protection.

This interpretation was first set out in the 1906 Geneva Convention and repeated in the 1929 Geneva Convention.[37] It is now codified in the First Geneva Convention and Additional Protocol I.[38] It was also included by consensus in the draft of Additional Protocol II but dropped at the last moment as part of a package aimed at the adoption of a simplified text.[39] It is clear that in practice protection of medical personnel against violence will be as important

---

[35] First Geneva Convention, Article 21 (*ibid.*, § 586); Additional Protocol I, Article 13 (adopted by consensus) (*ibid.*, § 589); Additional Protocol II, Article 11 (adopted by consensus) (*ibid.*, § 590).

[36] Yves Sandoz, Christophe Swinarski, Bruno Zimmermann (eds.), *Commentary on the Additional Protocols*, ICRC, Geneva, 1987, §§ 4720–4721.

[37] 1906 Geneva Convention, Article 8(1) (cited in Vol. II, Ch. 7, § 180); 1929 Geneva Convention, Article 8(1) (*ibid.*, § 181).

[38] First Geneva Convention, Article 22(1) (*ibid.*, § 182); Additional Protocol I, Article 13(2)(a) (adopted by consensus) (*ibid.*, § 183).

[39] Draft Additional Protocol II submitted by the ICRC to the Diplomatic Conference leading to the adoption of the Additional Protocols, Articles 17(2) and (3)(a) (*ibid.*, § 184).

in situations of non-international armed conflict as in those of international armed conflict. In addition, at the Diplomatic Conference leading to the adoption of the Additional Protocols, the USSR stated that this rule was necessary, even in non-international armed conflicts, for medical personnel who disarmed a wounded soldier would otherwise forfeit their right to protection, unless they threw away the weapon.[40]

Numerous military manuals specify that the carrying of light individual weapons does not deprive medical personnel of their protected status.[41] According to Germany's Military Manual, such "individual weapons" are pistols, submachine guns and rifles.[42] The Military Manual of the Netherlands provides the same interpretation of the term and adds that it excludes machine guns or other weapons that have to be handled by more than one person, weapons intended for use against objects, such as missile launchers and other anti-tank weapons, and fragmentation hand grenades and the like.[43] These understandings are based on the discussions at the Diplomatic Conference leading to the adoption of the Additional Protocols.[44]

At the Diplomatic Conference leading to the adoption of the Additional Protocols, the United States agreed that the carrying of arms by civilian medical personnel should not be considered as an act harmful to the enemy, "but in occupied territories or in areas in which fighting was taking place, the right of the party in control of the area to disarm such personnel should be reserved".[45]

Rule 26. Punishing a person for performing medical duties compatible with medical ethics or compelling a person engaged in medical activities to perform acts contrary to medical ethics is prohibited.

Practice

Volume II, Chapter 7, Section B.

Summary

State practice establishes this rule as a norm of customary international law applicable in both international and non-international armed conflicts.

---

[40] See the statement of the USSR at the Diplomatic Conference leading to the adoption of the Additional Protocols (*ibid.*, § 222).

[41] See, e.g., the military manuals of Argentina (*ibid.*, § 186), Australia (*ibid.*, §§ 187–188), Belgium (*ibid.*, §§ 189–190), Benin (*ibid.*, § 191), Cameroon (*ibid.*, § 192), Canada (*ibid.*, §§ 193–194), Ecuador (*ibid.*, § 195), France (*ibid.*, § 196), Germany (*ibid.*, § 197), Kenya (*ibid.*, § 198), Netherlands (*ibid.*, §§ 199–200), Nigeria (*ibid.*, § 201), South Africa (*ibid.*, § 202), Spain (*ibid.*, § 203), Switzerland (*ibid.*, § 204), Togo (*ibid.*, § 205), United Kingdom (*ibid.*, §§ 206–207), United States (*ibid.*, §§ 208–211) and Yugoslavia (*ibid.*, § 212).

[42] Germany, *Military Manual* (*ibid.*, § 197).   [43] Netherlands, *Military Manual* (*ibid.*, § 199).

[44] See Yves Sandoz, Christophe Swinarski, Bruno Zimmermann (eds.), *Commentary on the Additional Protocols*, ICRC, Geneva, 1987, § 563.

[45] See United States, Statement at the Diplomatic Conference leading to the adoption of the Additional Protocols (cited in Vol. II, Ch. 7, § 224).

Medical ethics

This rule is codified in Article 16 of Additional Protocol I and Article 10 of Additional Protocol II, to which no reservations have been made.[46]

The rule is also set forth in military manuals, including manuals which are applicable in or have been applied in non-international armed conflicts.[47] It is supported by official statements.[48]

Violations of this rule inherently constitute violations of the right of the wounded and sick to protection and care (see Rules 110–111) and also of the obligation to respect and protect medical personnel (see Rule 25).

No official contrary practice was found with respect to either international or non-international armed conflicts. Alleged prosecution of medical personnel has been condemned by States as a violation of humanitarian law.[49] It has also been condemned by the United Nations.[50] This prohibition is further endorsed by the Council of Europe and the World Medical Association.[51]

In addition to acts contrary to "medical ethics", both Article 16 of Additional Protocol I and Article 10 of Additional Protocol II prohibit compelling persons engaged in medical activities to perform acts contrary to "other medical rules designed for the benefit of the wounded and sick".[52] No further specification was found in State practice as to the content of these other rules, over and above the rules of medical ethics. While this wording was added at the Diplomatic Conference leading to the adoption of the Additional Protocols, "no attempt was made to list these various rules".[53] The spirit of this provision seems to be aimed at a prohibition of "compulsion which might be exerted on medical personnel to conduct themselves in a way that is contrary to their patients' interests".[54] In that respect, this rule is a corollary of the fundamental guarantee not to subject anyone to mutilation, medical or scientific experiments or any other medical procedure not indicated by his or her state of health and not consistent with generally accepted medical standards (see Rule 92).

---

[46] Additional Protocol I, Article 16 (adopted by consensus) (*ibid.*, § 232); Additional Protocol II, Article 10 (adopted by consensus) (*ibid.*, § 233).

[47] See, e.g., the military manuals of Argentina (*ibid.*, § 235), Australia (*ibid.*, § 236), Canada (*ibid.*, § 237), Netherlands (*ibid.*, § 238), New Zealand (*ibid.*, § 239), Senegal (*ibid.*, § 240), Spain (*ibid.*, § 241) and Yugoslavia (*ibid.*, § 242).

[48] See, e.g., the statement of the United Kingdom (*ibid.*, § 247).

[49] See, e.g., the statement of the United States (*ibid.*, § 249).

[50] See, e.g., UN General Assembly, Res. 44/165 (*ibid.*, § 250); UN Commission on Human Rights, Res. 1990/77 (*ibid.*, § 251).

[51] Council of Europe, Parliamentary Assembly, Res. 904 (*ibid.*, § 253); World Medical Association, Rules Governing the Care of the Sick and Wounded, Particularly in Time of Conflict (*ibid.*, § 257).

[52] Additional Protocol I, Article 16 (adopted by consensus) (*ibid.*, § 232); Additional Protocol II, Article 10 (adopted by consensus) (*ibid.*, § 233).

[53] Yves Sandoz, Christophe Swinarski, Bruno Zimmermann (eds.), *Commentary on the Additional Protocols*, ICRC, Geneva, 1987, § 669. An example of such a rule could be the prohibition of doctors cooperating in medical procedures undertaken by personnel who are not officially qualified such as, e.g., medical students, *ibid.*, § 4693.

[54] *Ibid.*, § 669.

Medical secrecy

At the Diplomatic Conference leading to the adoption of the Additional Protocols, Cuba, Denmark, France, the Netherlands and Norway opposed the possibility that under national law medical personnel may be obliged to report wounds caused by firearms during armed conflict.[55] In the end, however, neither Additional Protocol I nor Additional Protocol II prohibits this. So, while no one may be punished for providing medical treatment, it remains possible to impose a sanction on persons for withholding information in cases in which they are legally obliged to divulge such information. While some States have adopted a system of complete confidentiality with respect to medical information contained in a medical file, as well as the reporting of particular wounds, there is no rule in international law which prohibits a State from adopting legislation making it compulsory to provide information, including, for example, concerning communicable diseases, and a number of States have done so.[56]

Rule 27. Religious personnel exclusively assigned to religious duties must be respected and protected in all circumstances. They lose their protection if they commit, outside their humanitarian function, acts harmful to the enemy.

Practice

Volume II, Chapter 7, Section C.

Summary

State practice establishes this rule as a norm of customary international law applicable in both international and non-international armed conflicts.

International armed conflicts

The obligation to respect and protect religious personnel goes back to the 1864 Geneva Convention and was repeated in the subsequent Geneva Conventions of 1906 and 1929.[57] It is now set forth in Article 24 of the First Geneva Convention and Article 36 of the Second Geneva Convention.[58] Its scope was expanded in Article 15 of Additional Protocol I to cover civilian religious personnel in

---

[55] See the practice of Cuba (cited in Vol. II, Ch. 7, § 270), Denmark (*ibid.*, §§ 271–272), France (*ibid.*, § 273), Netherlands (*ibid.*, § 274) and Norway (*ibid.*, § 275).

[56] See, e.g., Yugoslavia, *YPA Military Manual*, referring to Yugoslav regulations (*ibid.*, § 266) and Philippines, Executive Order 212 (*ibid.*, § 276).

[57] 1864 Geneva Convention, Article 2 (*ibid.*, § 287); 1906 Geneva Convention, Article 9 (*ibid.*, § 288); 1929 Geneva Convention, Article 9 (*ibid.*, § 289).

[58] First Geneva Convention, Article 24 (*ibid.*, § 290); Second Geneva Convention, Article 36 (*ibid.*, § 291).

addition to military religious personnel in all circumstances.[59] This extension is widely supported in State practice, which generally refers to religious personnel without distinguishing between military or civilian religious personnel.[60] It is also supported by States not, or not at the time, party to Additional Protocol I.[61]

Under the Statute of the International Criminal Court, "intentionally directing attacks against . . . personnel using the distinctive emblems of the Geneva Conventions in conformity with international law" constitutes a war crime in international armed conflicts.[62] This crime is relevant to religious personnel because they are entitled to use the distinctive emblems.

Numerous military manuals require respect for and protection of religious personnel.[63] It is an offence under the legislation of many States to violate this rule.[64] The rule is also supported by official statements.[65]

Non-international armed conflicts

The obligation to respect and protect religious personnel is set forth in Article 9 of Additional Protocol II, to which no reservations have been made.[66] In addition, under the Statute of the International Criminal Court, "intentionally directing attacks against . . . personnel using the distinctive emblems of the Geneva Conventions in conformity with international law" constitutes a war crime in non-international armed conflicts.[67]

---

[59] Additional Protocol I, Article 15 (adopted by consensus) (*ibid.*, § 293).

[60] See, e.g., the military manuals of Argentina (*ibid.*, § 300), Australia (*ibid.*, §§ 301–302), Belgium (*ibid.*, § 303), Benin (*ibid.*, § 305), Cameroon (*ibid.*, § 306), Canada (*ibid.*, § 307), Croatia (*ibid.*, § 308), El Salvador (*ibid.*, § 310), France (*ibid.*, §§ 311–312), Hungary (*ibid.*, § 314), Italy (*ibid.*, § 318), Madagascar (*ibid.*, § 321), Netherlands (*ibid.*, §§ 322–323), South Africa (*ibid.*, § 328), Spain (*ibid.*, § 329), Switzerland (*ibid.*, § 330), Togo (*ibid.*, § 331) and United States (*ibid.*, § 336); the legislation of Croatia (*ibid.*, § 340), Estonia (*ibid.*, § 342), Georgia (*ibid.*, § 343), Ireland (*ibid.*, § 344), Nicaragua (*ibid.*, § 346), Norway (*ibid.*, § 348), Poland (*ibid.*, § 349), Slovenia (*ibid.*, § 350), Spain (*ibid.*, §§ 351–352), Tajikistan (*ibid.*, § 353) and Yugoslavia (*ibid.*, § 354); see also the draft legislation of Argentina (*ibid.*, § 338), El Salvador (*ibid.*, § 341) and Nicaragua (*ibid.*, § 347) and the statements of the United States (*ibid.*, § 361) and Yugoslavia (*ibid.*, § 363).

[61] See, e.g., the military manuals of France (*ibid.*, § 311) and United States (*ibid.*, § 336).

[62] ICC Statute, Article 8(2)(b)(xxiv) (*ibid.*, § 832).

[63] See, e.g., the military manuals of Argentina (*ibid.*, § 300), Australia (*ibid.*, §§ 301–302), Belgium (*ibid.*, §§ 303–304), Benin (*ibid.*, § 305), Cameroon (*ibid.*, § 306), Canada (*ibid.*, § 307), Croatia (*ibid.*, § 308), Ecuador (*ibid.*, § 309), El Salvador (*ibid.*, § 310), France (*ibid.*, §§ 311–312), Germany (*ibid.*, § 313), Hungary (*ibid.*, § 314), Indonesia (*ibid.*, §§ 315–316), Israel (*ibid.*, § 317), Italy (*ibid.*, § 318), Kenya (*ibid.*, § 319), South Korea (*ibid.*, § 320), Madagascar (*ibid.*, § 321), Netherlands (*ibid.*, §§ 322–323), Nicaragua (*ibid.*, § 325), Nigeria (*ibid.*, §§ 326–327), South Africa (*ibid.*, § 328), Spain (*ibid.*, § 329), Switzerland (*ibid.*, § 330), Togo (*ibid.*, § 331), United Kingdom (*ibid.*, §§ 332–333), United States (*ibid.*, §§ 334–336) and Yugoslavia (*ibid.*, § 337).

[64] See, e.g., the legislation of Bangladesh (*ibid.*, § 339), Croatia (*ibid.*, § 340), Estonia (*ibid.*, § 342), Georgia (*ibid.*, § 343), Ireland (*ibid.*, § 344), Nicaragua (*ibid.*, § 346), Norway (*ibid.*, § 348), Poland (*ibid.*, § 349), Slovenia (*ibid.*, § 350), Spain (*ibid.*, §§ 351–352), Tajikistan (*ibid.*, § 353), Yugoslavia (*ibid.*, § 354); see also the draft legislation of Argentina (*ibid.*, § 338), El Salvador (*ibid.*, § 341) and Nicaragua (*ibid.*, § 347).

[65] See, e.g., the statements of the United States (*ibid.*, § 361) and Yugoslavia (*ibid.*, § 363) and the reported practice of Israel (*ibid.*, § 358) and Rwanda (*ibid.*, § 360).

[66] Additional Protocol II, Article 9 (adopted by consensus) (*ibid.*, § 295).

[67] ICC Statute, Article 8(2)(e)(ii) (*ibid.*, § 832).

The protection of religious personnel is also included in military manuals which are applicable in or have been applied in non-international armed conflicts.[68] It is an offence under the legislation of many States to violate this rule in any armed conflict.[69] There is also some other practice supporting the rule specifically in non-international armed conflicts.[70]

The ICRC has called for respect for and protection of religious personnel on several occasions, for example, in 1994 in the context of the conflict in Angola.[71]

No official contrary practice was found with respect to either international or non-international armed conflicts.

Definition of religious personnel

The term "religious personnel" refers to personnel, whether military or civilian, who are exclusively engaged in the work of their ministry and attached to a party to the conflict, to its medical units or transports or to a civil defence organisation. Such assignment may be either permanent or temporary. This definition is based on Article 8(d) of Additional Protocol I.[72] It is widely used in State practice.[73] In the absence of a definition of religious personnel in Additional Protocol II, this term may be understood as applying in the same sense in non-international armed conflicts.[74] The Netherlands has stated that "humanist counsellors" belong to religious personnel.[75] Other persons performing religious functions enjoy the protected status of civilians, as long as

---

[68] See, e.g., the military manuals of Argentina (*ibid.*, § 300), Australia (*ibid.*, §§ 301–302), Benin (*ibid.*, § 305), Cameroon (*ibid.*, § 306), Canada (*ibid.*, § 307), Croatia (*ibid.*, § 308), Ecuador (*ibid.*, § 309), El Salvador (*ibid.*, § 310), France (*ibid.*, § 312), Germany (*ibid.*, § 313), Hungary (*ibid.*, § 314), Italy (*ibid.*, § 318), Kenya (*ibid.*, § 319), South Korea (*ibid.*, § 320), Madagascar (*ibid.*, § 321), Netherlands (*ibid.*, § 322), New Zealand (*ibid.*, § 324), Nigeria (*ibid.*, § 326), South Africa (*ibid.*, § 328), Spain (*ibid.*, § 329), Togo (*ibid.*, § 331) and Yugoslavia (*ibid.*, § 337).

[69] See, e.g., the legislation of Croatia (*ibid.*, § 340), Estonia (*ibid.*, § 342), Georgia (*ibid.*, § 343), Ireland (*ibid.*, § 344), Nicaragua (*ibid.*, § 346), Norway (*ibid.*, § 438), Poland (*ibid.*, § 349), Slovenia (*ibid.*, § 350), Spain (*ibid.*, §§ 351–352), Tajikistan (*ibid.*, § 353) and Yugoslavia (*ibid.*, § 354); see also the legislation of Italy (*ibid.*, § 345), the application of which is not excluded in time of non-international armed conflict, and the draft legislation of Argentina (*ibid.*, § 338), El Salvador (*ibid.*, § 341) and Nicaragua (*ibid.*, § 347).

[70] See, e.g., the practice of Yugoslavia (*ibid.*, § 363) and the reported practice of Rwanda (*ibid.*, § 360).

[71] See ICRC, Memorandum on Respect for International Humanitarian Law in Angola (*ibid.*, § 373).

[72] Additional Protocol I, Article 8(d) (*ibid.*, § 292).

[73] See, e.g., the practice of Australia (*ibid.*, § 302), Croatia (*ibid.*, § 308), France (*ibid.*, §§ 311–312), Italy (*ibid.*, § 318), Madagascar (*ibid.*, § 321), Nicaragua (*ibid.*, § 346), South Africa (*ibid.*, § 328), Spain (*ibid.*, §§ 329 and 351) and Togo (*ibid.*, § 331).

[74] See, e.g., the declaration to this effect by the United States (*ibid.*, § 296); see also Yves Sandoz, Christophe Swinarski, Bruno Zimmermann (eds.), *Commentary on the Additional Protocols*, ICRC, Geneva, 1987, §§ 4662–4663, referring to the discussions at the CDDH, *Official Records*, Vol. XI, CDDH/II/SR.31, 6 March 1975, pp. 317–326.

[75] Netherlands, Lower House of Parliament, Explanatory memorandum on the ratification of the Additional Protocols (cited in Vol. II, Ch. 7, § 294) and *Military Manual* (*ibid.*, § 322).

they do not take a direct part in hostilities. As civilians, they may not, however, display the distinctive emblems.

Respect for and protection of religious personnel

State practice generally indicates that religious personnel enjoy the same privileges as permanent medical personnel.[76] Hence, the meaning of the terms "respect and protection" as interpreted in the context of medical personnel (see commentary to Rule 25) applies *mutatis mutandis* to religious personnel.

Loss of protection of religious personnel

Based on the same reasoning, the interpretation of the exception of loss of protection of medical personnel in case of engagement in acts harmful to the enemy (or hostile acts) (see commentary to Rule 25) applies *mutatis mutandis* to religious personnel. As with medical personnel, only religious personnel *exclusively* assigned to religious duties are protected.

Equipment of religious personnel with light individual weapons

Based on the same reasoning, the principle that medical personnel do not lose their protection if they are equipped with light individual weapons and that they may use these weapons in their own defence or in that of the wounded, sick and shipwrecked in their care (see commentary to Rule 25) would apply *mutatis mutandis* to religious personnel. This is explicitly recognised by Germany's Military Manual, even though it adds that chaplains in the German army are not armed.[77] The UK LOAC Manual, meanwhile, states that chaplains attached to the armed forces may not be armed.[78] No further specifications in practice were found.

Rule 28. Medical units exclusively assigned to medical purposes must be respected and protected in all circumstances. They lose their protection if they are being used, outside their humanitarian function, to commit acts harmful to the enemy.

Practice

Volume II, Chapter 7, Section D.

---

[76] See, e.g., the practice of Australia (*ibid.*, § 302), Belgium (*ibid.*, § 303), Ecuador (*ibid.*, § 309), Hungary (*ibid.*, § 314), Israel (*ibid.*, § 317), Kenya (*ibid.*, § 319), Netherlands (*ibid.*, § 323), Spain (*ibid.*, § 329), United Kingdom (*ibid.*, § 332), Yugoslavia (*ibid.*, § 337), United States (*ibid.*, § 361) and Yugoslavia (*ibid.*, § 363).
[77] Germany, *Military Manual* (*ibid.*, § 313).   [78] United Kingdom, *LOAC Manual* (*ibid.*, § 333).

Summary

State practice establishes this rule as a norm of customary international law applicable in both international and non-international armed conflicts.

International armed conflicts

This rule goes back to the protection of "hospitals and places where the sick and wounded are collected" in the Hague Regulations.[79] It is set forth in the First and Fourth Geneva Conventions.[80] Its scope was expanded in Additional Protocol I to cover civilian medical units in addition to military medical units in all circumstances.[81] This extension is widely supported in State practice, which generally refers to medical units without distinguishing between military or civilian units.[82] It is also supported by States not, or not at the time, party to Additional Protocol I.[83]

Under the Statute of the International Criminal Court, intentionally directing attacks against "hospitals and places where the sick and the wounded are collected, provided they are not military objectives" and against "medical units... using the distinctive emblems of the Geneva Conventions in conformity with international law" constitutes a war crime in international armed conflicts.[84]

---

[79] 1899 and 1907 Hague Regulations, Article 27 (*ibid.*, §§ 377–378).
[80] First Geneva Convention, Article 19 (*ibid.*, § 379); Fourth Geneva Convention, Article 18 (*ibid.*, § 380).
[81] Additional Protocol I, Article 12 (adopted by consensus) (*ibid.*, § 381).
[82] See, e.g., the military manuals of Belgium (*ibid.*, § 396), Burkina Faso (*ibid.*, § 400), Cameroon (*ibid.*, § 401), Canada (*ibid.*, § 403), Colombia (*ibid.*, §§ 404–405), Dominican Republic (*ibid.*, § 409), Ecuador (*ibid.*, § 410), Germany (*ibid.*, §§ 414–415), Hungary (*ibid.*, § 416), Israel (*ibid.*, § 417), Italy (*ibid.*, § 419), Lebanon (*ibid.*, § 424), Netherlands (*ibid.*, §§ 428–429), Nigeria (*ibid.*, § 434), Romania (*ibid.*, § 435), Russia (*ibid.*, § 436), Senegal (*ibid.*, §§ 437–438) and United States (*ibid.*, §§ 448–451); the legislation of Australia (*ibid.*, § 456), Azerbaijan (*ibid.*, § 457), Canada (*ibid.*, § 461), Chile (*ibid.*, § 462), China (*ibid.*, § 463), Colombia (*ibid.*, § 464), Congo (*ibid.*, § 465), Cuba (*ibid.*, § 467), Dominican Republic (*ibid.*, § 468), El Salvador (*ibid.*, § 469), Estonia (*ibid.*, § 471), Ethiopia (*ibid.*, § 472), Georgia (*ibid.*, § 473), Germany (*ibid.*, § 474), Guatemala (*ibid.*, § 475), Iraq (*ibid.*, § 476), Mexico (*ibid.*, § 480), Netherlands (*ibid.*, §§ 481–482), New Zealand (*ibid.*, § 483), Nicaragua (*ibid.*, § 484), Peru (*ibid.*, § 487), Philippines (*ibid.*, § 488), Poland (*ibid.*, § 489), Portugal (*ibid.*, § 490), Romania (*ibid.*, § 491), Spain (*ibid.*, § 493), Tajikistan (*ibid.*, § 495), Ukraine (*ibid.*, § 497), United Kingdom (*ibid.*, § 498), Uruguay (*ibid.*, § 500) and Venezuela (*ibid.*, § 501); see also the draft legislation of Argentina (*ibid.*, § 454), Burundi (*ibid.*, § 460), El Salvador (*ibid.*, § 470), Nicaragua (*ibid.*, § 485), Trinidad and Tobago (*ibid.*, § 496), and the statements of Argentina (*ibid.*, § 505), Canada (*ibid.*, § 506), China (*ibid.*, §§ 507–508), Egypt (*ibid.*, § 511), Finland (*ibid.*, § 512), France (*ibid.*, § 513), Hungary (*ibid.*, § 515), Iraq (*ibid.*, § 517), United States (*ibid.*, § 529) and Venezuela (*ibid.*, § 530)
[83] See, e.g., the practice of France (*ibid.*, § 412), Kenya (*ibid.*, § 421), United Kingdom (*ibid.*, §§ 445 and 524) and United States (*ibid.*, § 527).
[84] ICC Statute, Article 8(2)(b)(ix) (*ibid.*, § 384).

This rule is contained in numerous military manuals.[85] Sweden's IHL Manual identifies the protection of medical units as set out in Article 12 of Additional Protocol I as a codification of a pre-existing rule of customary international law.[86] It is an offence under the legislation of many States to violate this rule.[87] The rule has been invoked in official statements.[88]

Non-international armed conflicts

This rule is implicit in common Article 3 of the Geneva Conventions, which requires that the wounded and sick be collected and cared for, because the protection of medical units is a subsidiary form of protection afforded to ensure that the wounded and sick receive medical care.[89] The rule that medical units must be respected and protected at all times, and must not be the object of attack, is explicitly set forth in Additional Protocol II.[90] In addition, under the Statute of the International Criminal Court, intentionally directing attacks against "hospitals and places where the sick and the wounded are collected, provided

---

[85] See, e.g., the military manuals of Argentina (*ibid.*, §§ 392–393), Australia (*ibid.*, §§ 394–395), Belgium (*ibid.*, §§ 396–397), Benin (*ibid.*, § 398), Bosnia and Herzegovina (*ibid.*, § 399), Burkina Faso (*ibid.*, § 400), Cameroon (*ibid.*, § 401), Canada (*ibid.*, §§ 402–403), Colombia (*ibid.*, §§ 404–405), Congo (*ibid.*, § 406), Croatia (*ibid.*, §§ 407–408), Dominican Republic (*ibid.*, § 409), Ecuador (*ibid.*, § 410), France (*ibid.*, §§ 411–413), Germany (*ibid.*, §§ 414–415), Hungary (*ibid.*, § 416), Israel (*ibid.*, §§ 417–418), Italy (*ibid.*, §§ 419–420), Kenya (*ibid.*, § 421), South Korea (*ibid.*, § 422), Lebanon (*ibid.*, §§ 423–424), Madagascar (*ibid.*, § 425), Mali (*ibid.*, § 426), Morocco (*ibid.*, § 427), Netherlands (*ibid.*, §§ 428–429), New Zealand (*ibid.*, § 430), Nicaragua (*ibid.*, § 431), Nigeria (*ibid.*, §§ 432–434), Romania (*ibid.*, § 435), Russia (*ibid.*, § 436), Senegal (*ibid.*, §§ 437–438), South Africa (*ibid.*, § 439), Spain (*ibid.*, § 440), Sweden (*ibid.*, § 441), Switzerland (*ibid.*, § 442), Togo (*ibid.*, § 443), United Kingdom (*ibid.*, §§ 444–445), United States (*ibid.*, §§ 446–451) and Yugoslavia (*ibid.*, § 452).

[86] Sweden, *IHL Manual* (*ibid.*, § 441).

[87] See, e.g., the legislation of Argentina (*ibid.*, § 453), Australia (*ibid.*, §§ 455–456), Azerbaijan (*ibid.*, § 457), Bangladesh (*ibid.*, § 458), Bosnia and Herzegovina (*ibid.*, § 459), Canada (*ibid.*, § 461), Chile (*ibid.*, § 462), China (*ibid.*, § 463), Colombia (*ibid.*, § 464), Congo (*ibid.*, § 465), Croatia (*ibid.*, § 466), Cuba (*ibid.*, § 467), Dominican Republic (*ibid.*, § 468), El Salvador (*ibid.*, § 469), Estonia (*ibid.*, § 471), Ethiopia (*ibid.*, § 472), Georgia (*ibid.*, § 473), Germany (*ibid.*, § 474), Guatemala (*ibid.*, § 475), Iraq (*ibid.*, § 476), Ireland (*ibid.*, § 477), Italy (*ibid.*, § 478), Lithuania (*ibid.*, § 479), Mexico (*ibid.*, § 480), Netherlands (*ibid.*, §§ 481–482), New Zealand (*ibid.*, § 483), Nicaragua (*ibid.*, § 484), Norway (*ibid.*, § 486), Peru (*ibid.*, § 487), Philippines (*ibid.*, § 488), Poland (*ibid.*, § 489), Portugal (*ibid.*, § 490), Romania (*ibid.*, § 491), Slovenia (*ibid.*, § 492), Spain (*ibid.*, § 493), Sweden (*ibid.*, § 494), Tajikistan (*ibid.*, § 495), Ukraine (*ibid.*, § 497), United Kingdom (*ibid.*, § 498), United States (*ibid.*, § 499), Uruguay (*ibid.*, § 500), Venezuela (*ibid.*, § 501) and Yugoslavia (*ibid.*, § 502); see also the draft legislation of Argentina (*ibid.*, § 454), Burundi (*ibid.*, § 460), El Salvador (*ibid.*, § 470), Nicaragua (*ibid.*, § 485) and Trinidad and Tobago (*ibid.*, § 496).

[88] See, e.g., the statements of Argentina (*ibid.*, § 505), Canada (*ibid.*, § 506), China (*ibid.*, §§ 507–508), Egypt (*ibid.*, §§ 510–511), Finland (*ibid.*, § 512), France (*ibid.*, § 513), Hungary (*ibid.*, § 515), Iraq (*ibid.*, § 517), Norway (*ibid.*, § 521), Rwanda (*ibid.*, § 522), Saudi Arabia (*ibid.*, § 523), United States (*ibid.*, §§ 525–529) and Venezuela (*ibid.*, § 530); see also the reported practice of Israel (*ibid.*, § 518).

[89] This reasoning is put forward, e.g., in the military manuals of Belgium (*ibid.*, § 397), Colombia (*ibid.*, § 404), Israel (*ibid.*, § 418) and Nicaragua (*ibid.*, § 431).

[90] Additional Protocol II, Article 11(1) (adopted by consensus) (*ibid.*, § 382).

they are not military objectives" and against "medical units... using the distinctive emblems of the Geneva Conventions in conformity with international law" constitutes a war crime in non-international armed conflicts.[91] In addition, this rule is contained in other instruments pertaining also to non-international armed conflicts.[92]

The protection of medical units is set forth in military manuals which are applicable in or have been applied in non-international armed conflicts.[93] It is an offence under the legislation of many States to violate this rule.[94] Furthermore, the rule is supported by a number of official statements made in the context of non-international armed conflicts.[95]

No official contrary practice was found with respect to either international or non-international armed conflicts. Alleged attacks against medical units have generally been condemned by States.[96] They have also been condemned by international organisations, for example, in the context of the conflicts in Afghanistan, Burundi, El Salvador, Kampuchea, Korea, Rwanda, Somalia, Vietnam and the former Yugoslavia, between Iran and Iraq and in the Middle East.[97]

---

[91] ICC Statute, Article 8(2)(e)(ii) and (iv) (*ibid.*, §§ 384 and 831).

[92] See, e.g., Agreement on the Application of IHL between the Parties to the Conflict in Bosnia and Herzegovina (*ibid.*, § 389).

[93] See, e.g., the military manuals of Argentina (*ibid.*, § 393), Australia (*ibid.*, §§ 394–395), Benin (*ibid.*, § 398), Bosnia and Herzegovina (*ibid.*, § 399), Canada (*ibid.*, §§ 402–403), Colombia (*ibid.*, §§ 404–405), Croatia (*ibid.*, §§ 407–408), Ecuador (*ibid.*, § 410), Germany (*ibid.*, §§ 414–415), Hungary (*ibid.*, § 416), Italy (*ibid.*, §§ 419–420), Kenya (*ibid.*, § 421), South Korea (*ibid.*, § 422), Lebanon (*ibid.*, §§ 423–424), Madagascar (*ibid.*, § 425), Netherlands (*ibid.*, § 428), New Zealand (*ibid.*, § 430), Nigeria (*ibid.*, §§ 432–433), Russia (*ibid.*, § 436), Senegal (*ibid.*, § 438), South Africa (*ibid.*, § 439), Spain (*ibid.*, § 440), Togo (*ibid.*, § 443) and Yugoslavia (*ibid.*, § 452).

[94] See, e.g., the legislation of Australia (*ibid.*, § 456), Azerbaijan (*ibid.*, § 457), Bosnia and Herzegovina (*ibid.*, § 459), Canada (*ibid.*, § 461), Colombia (*ibid.*, § 464), Congo (*ibid.*, § 465), Croatia (*ibid.*, § 466), Estonia (*ibid.*, § 471), Ethiopia (*ibid.*, § 472), Georgia (*ibid.*, § 473), Germany (*ibid.*, § 474), Ireland (*ibid.*, § 477), Lithuania (*ibid.*, § 479), Netherlands (*ibid.*, § 482), New Zealand (*ibid.*, § 483), Nicaragua (*ibid.*, § 484), Norway (*ibid.*, § 486), Poland (*ibid.*, § 489), Portugal (*ibid.*, § 490), Slovenia (*ibid.*, § 492), Spain (*ibid.*, § 493), Sweden (*ibid.*, § 494), Tajikistan (*ibid.*, § 495), United Kingdom (*ibid.*, § 498), Venezuela (*ibid.*, § 501) and Yugoslavia (*ibid.*, § 502); see also the legislation of Argentina (*ibid.*, § 453), Cuba (*ibid.*, § 467), Guatemala (*ibid.*, § 475), Italy (*ibid.*, § 478), Peru (*ibid.*, § 487), Romania (*ibid.*, § 491) and Uruguay (*ibid.*, § 500), the application of which is not excluded in time of non-international armed conflict, and the draft legislation of Argentina (*ibid.*, § 454), Burundi (*ibid.*, § 460), El Salvador (*ibid.*, § 470), Nicaragua (*ibid.*, § 485) and Trinidad and Tobago (*ibid.*, § 496).

[95] See, e.g., the statements of Argentina (*ibid.*, § 505), Canada (*ibid.*, § 506), Finland (*ibid.*, § 512), France (*ibid.*, § 513), Hungary (*ibid.*, § 515), Rwanda (*ibid.*, § 522) and Venezuela (*ibid.*, § 530).

[96] See, e.g., the statements of Argentina (*ibid.*, § 505), Canada (*ibid.*, § 506), China (*ibid.*, §§ 507–508), Egypt (*ibid.*, § 510), Finland (*ibid.*, § 512), France (*ibid.*, § 513), Hungary (*ibid.*, 515), Iran (*ibid.*, § 516), Iraq (*ibid.*, § 517), Norway (*ibid.*, § 521), Rwanda (*ibid.*, § 522), Saudi Arabia (*ibid.*, § 523), United States (*ibid.*, § 525) and Venezuela (*ibid.*, § 530).

[97] See, e.g., UN Security Council, Res. 467 (*ibid.*, § 533), Res. 771 (*ibid.*, § 534) and Res. 794 (*ibid.*, § 535); UN General Assembly, Res. 39/119 (*ibid.*, § 537), Res. 40/139 (*ibid.*, § 538) and Res. 41/157 (*ibid.*, § 538); UN Commission on Human Rights, Res. 1983/5 (*ibid.*, § 539), Res. 1987/51 (*ibid.*, § 540) and Res. 1992/S-1/1 (*ibid.*, § 542).

The ICRC has called upon parties to both international and non-international armed conflicts to respect this rule.[98]

Definition of medical units

The term "medical units" refers to establishments and other units, whether military or civilian, organised for medical purposes, be they fixed or mobile, permanent or temporary. The term includes, for example, hospitals and other similar units, blood transfusion centres, preventive medicine centres and institutes, medical depots and the medical and pharmaceutical stores of such units.

This definition, which builds upon Article 19 of the First Geneva Convention and Article 18 of the Fourth Geneva Convention, is set out in Article 8(e) of Additional Protocol I.[99] It is widely used in State practice.[100] In the absence of a definition of medical units in Additional Protocol II, this term may be understood as applying in the same sense in non-international armed conflicts.[101]

While a lot of practice does not expressly require medical units to be recognised and authorised by one of the parties, some of it refers to the provisions of Additional Protocol I,[102] or does require such authorisation in another way.[103] Unauthorised medical units must therefore be regarded as being protected according to the rules on the protection of civilian objects (see Chapter 2), but do not have the right to display the distinctive emblems.

Criminal codes often require medical establishments to be properly marked with the distinctive emblems.[104] However, having regard to the principle that means of identification do not, of themselves, confer protected status but only facilitate identification, this can be of importance only for criminal

---

[98] See the practice of the ICRC (*ibid.*, §§ 554–556, 559–564 and 566–573).

[99] Additional Protocol I, Article 8(e) (adopted by consensus).

[100] See, e.g., the practice of Australia (cited in Vol. II, Ch. 7, § 395), Canada (*ibid.*, § 402), Kenya (*ibid.*, § 421), New Zealand (*ibid.*, § 430), South Africa (*ibid.*, § 439), Spain (*ibid.*, § 440), Romania (*ibid.*, § 491) and United States (*ibid.*, § 383).

[101] See the declaration to this effect by the United States (*ibid.*, § 383); see also Yves Sandoz, Christophe Swinarski, Bruno Zimmermann (eds.), *Commentary on the Additional Protocols*, ICRC, Geneva, 1987, §§ 4711–4712.

[102] Article 12(2) of Additional Protocol I requires that civilian medical units be "recognized and authorized by the competent authority of one of the Parties to the conflict" or that they be "recognized in conformity with" Article 9(2) of Additional Protocol I or with Article 27 of the First Geneva Convention, i.e., recognised by a neutral or other State not party to the conflict, by an aid society of such a State, or by an impartial international humanitarian organisation.

[103] See, e.g., the practice of France (cited in Vol. II, Ch. 7, § 413), Ireland (*ibid.*, § 477), Nigeria (*ibid.*, § 433), Norway (*ibid.*, § 486), Sweden (*ibid.*, § 441) and United States (*ibid.*, § 527).

[104] See, e.g., the legislation of Argentina (*ibid.*, § 453), Azerbaijan (*ibid.*, § 457), Chile (*ibid.*, § 462), Colombia (*ibid.*, § 464), Dominican Republic (*ibid.*, § 468), Germany (*ibid.*, § 474), Peru (*ibid.*, § 487) and Romania (*ibid.*, § 491); see also the draft legislation of Argentina (*ibid.*, § 454) and Nicaragua (*ibid.*, § 485).

responsibility in the event of an attack on a medical unit (see commentary to Rule 30).

Respect for and protection of medical units

State practice contains the following specifications with respect to the meaning of the terms "respect and protection". According to Germany's military manuals, the terms "respect and protection" mean that medical units may not be attacked and that their unhampered employment must be ensured.[105] Switzerland's Basic Military Manual contains a similar understanding, specifying that "[medical units] shall not be attacked, nor harmed in any way, nor their functioning be impeded, even if they do not momentarily hold any wounded and sick".[106] Similarly, the US Air Force Commander's Handbook provides that medical units "should not be deliberately attacked, fired upon, or unnecessarily prevented from performing their medical duties".[107]

The military manuals of Benin, Nigeria, Senegal and Togo state that medical units must remain untouched and that armed persons may not enter them, but that their content and actual use may be checked through an inspection.[108]

The First and Fourth Geneva Conventions and Additional Protocol I require that, as far as possible, medical units not be located in the vicinity of military objectives.[109] This requirement is repeated in numerous military manuals.[110] Article 12(4) of Additional Protocol I further provides that medical units may under no circumstances be used in an attempt to shield military objectives from attack.[111] This requirement is explicitly subscribed to in the practice of the Netherlands and the United States.[112] Some military manuals stipulate that medical units may not be used for military purposes or to commit acts harmful to the enemy.[113] Other manuals consider that the improper use of privileged buildings for military purposes is a war crime.[114]

---

[105] See the military manuals of Germany (*ibid.*, §§ 414–415).

[106] Switzerland, *Basic Military Manual* (*ibid.*, § 442).

[107] United States, *Air Force Commander's Handbook* (*ibid.*, § 448).

[108] See the military manuals of Benin (*ibid.*, § 398), Nigeria (*ibid.*, § 433), Senegal (*ibid.*, § 438) and Togo (*ibid.*, § 443).

[109] First Geneva Convention, Article 19 (*ibid.*, § 379); Fourth Geneva Convention, Article 18 (*ibid.*, § 380); Additional Protocol I, Article 12(4) (adopted by consensus) (*ibid.*, § 381).

[110] See, e.g., the military manuals of Argentina (*ibid.*, § 392), Canada (*ibid.*, § 403), Ecuador (*ibid.*, § 410), Germany (*ibid.*, §§ 414–415), Netherlands (*ibid.*, § 428), Nigeria (*ibid.*, § 434), Russia (*ibid.*, § 436), Switzerland (*ibid.*, § 442), United Kingdom (*ibid.*, § 444), United States (*ibid.*, §§ 446 and 451) and Yugoslavia (*ibid.*, § 452).

[111] Additional Protocol I, Article 12(4) (adopted by consensus) (*ibid.*, § 381).

[112] Netherlands, *Military Manual* (*ibid.*, § 428); United States, Department of Defense, Statement (*ibid.*, § 528).

[113] See the military manuals of Ecuador (*ibid.*, § 603), Germany (*ibid.*, §§ 605–606), Kenya (*ibid.*, § 607), Netherlands (*ibid.*, § 609) and United States (*ibid.*, § 622).

[114] See, e.g., the military manuals of Canada (*ibid.*, § 601), New Zealand (*ibid.*, § 610), Nigeria (*ibid.*, § 611), United Kingdom (*ibid.*, §§ 615–616) and United States (*ibid.*, §§ 617–618 and 620).

Loss of protection due to medical units

State practice establishes the exception under customary international law that the protection of medical units ceases when they are being used, outside their humanitarian function, to commit acts harmful to the enemy. This exception is provided for in the First and Fourth Geneva Conventions and in both Additional Protocols.[115] It is contained in numerous military manuals and military orders.[116] It is also supported by other practice.[117]

While the Geneva Conventions and Additional Protocols do not define "acts harmful to the enemy", they do indicate several types of acts which do not constitute "acts harmful to the enemy", for example, when the personnel of the unit is armed, when the unit is guarded, when small arms and ammunition taken from the wounded and sick are found in the unit and when wounded and sick combatants or civilians are inside the unit.[118] According to the Commentary on the First Geneva Convention, examples of acts harmful to the enemy include the use of medical units to shelter able-bodied combatants, to store arms or munitions, as a military observation post or as a shield for military action.[119]

It is further specified in State practice that prior to an attack against a medical unit which is being used to commit acts harmful to the enemy, a warning has to be issued setting, whenever appropriate, a reasonable time-limit and that an attack can only take place after such warning has remained unheeded.[120] These procedural requirements are also laid down in the Geneva Conventions and Additional Protocols.[121]

---

[115] First Geneva Convention, Article 21 (*ibid.*, § 586); Fourth Geneva Convention, Article 19 (*ibid.*, § 588); Additional Protocol I, Article 13 (adopted by consensus) (*ibid.*, § 589); Additional Protocol II, Article 11(2) (adopted by consensus) (*ibid.*, § 590).

[116] See, e.g., the military manuals of Argentina (*ibid.*, §§ 594–595), Australia (*ibid.*, 596–597), Bosnia and Herzegovina (*ibid.*, § 599), Cameroon (*ibid.*, § 600), Canada (*ibid.*, §§ 601–602), Ecuador (*ibid.*, § 603), Germany (*ibid.*, § 605), Kenya (*ibid.*, § 607), Netherlands (*ibid.*, § 608), New Zealand (*ibid.*, § 610), Nigeria (*ibid.*, § 611), South Africa (*ibid.*, § 612), Spain (*ibid.*, § 613), Switzerland (*ibid.*, § 614), United Kingdom (*ibid.*, §§ 615–616), United States (*ibid.*, §§ 617, 619 and 621–622) and Yugoslavia (*ibid.*, § 623).

[117] See, e.g., the practice of Yugoslavia (*ibid.*, § 631) and the reported practice of Bosnia and Herzegovina, Republika Srpska (*ibid.*, § 629) and a State (*ibid.*, § 632).

[118] First Geneva Convention, Article 22 (*ibid.*, § 587); Fourth Geneva Convention, Article 19 (*ibid.*, § 588); Additional Protocol I, Article 13(2) (adopted by consensus) (*ibid.*, § 589).

[119] Jean S. Pictet (ed.), *Commentary on the First Geneva Convention*, ICRC, Geneva, 1952, pp. 200–201; see also the military manuals of South Africa (cited in Vol. II, Ch. 7, § 612), Switzerland (*ibid.*, § 614) and United States (*ibid.*, § 619).

[120] See, e.g., Agreement on the Application of IHL between the Parties to the Conflict in Bosnia and Herzegovina (*ibid.*, § 592) and the military manuals of Argentina (*ibid.*, § 595), Australia (*ibid.*, §§ 596–597), Canada (*ibid.*, §§ 601–602), Ecuador (*ibid.*, § 603), Germany (*ibid.*, § 605), Netherlands (*ibid.*, § 608), New Zealand (*ibid.*, § 610), Nigeria (*ibid.*, § 611), Spain (*ibid.*, § 613), Switzerland (*ibid.*, § 614), United States (*ibid.*, §§ 619 and 621–622) and Yugoslavia (*ibid.*, § 623).

[121] First Geneva Convention, Article 21 (*ibid.*, § 586); Fourth Geneva Convention, Article 19 (*ibid.*, § 588); Additional Protocol I, Article 13(1) (adopted by consensus) (*ibid.*, § 589); Additional Protocol II, Article 11(2) (adopted by consensus) (*ibid.*, § 590).

Rule 29. Medical transports assigned exclusively to medical transportation must be respected and protected in all circumstances. They lose their protection if they are being used, outside their humanitarian function, to commit acts harmful to the enemy.

Practice

Volume II, Chapter 7, Section E.

Summary

State practice establishes this rule as a norm of customary international law applicable in both international and non-international armed conflicts.

International armed conflicts

The obligation to respect and protect medical transports is set forth in Article 35 of the First Geneva Convention and Article 21 of the Fourth Geneva Convention.[122] Its scope was expanded in Article 21 of Additional Protocol I to cover civilian, in addition to military, means of transportation in all circumstances.[123] This extension is widely supported in State practice, which either generally refers to medical transports without distinguishing between military and civilian means of transportation or lists both as being protected.[124] It is also supported by States not, or not at the time, party to Additional Protocol I.[125]

Under the Statute of the International Criminal Court, intentionally directing attacks against "medical units and transports... using the distinctive emblems of the Geneva Conventions in conformity with international law" constitutes a war crime in international armed conflicts.[126]

The rule is contained in numerous military manuals.[127] Sweden's IHL Manual identifies the protection of medical transports as set out in Article 21 of

---

[122] First Geneva Convention, Article 35 (*ibid.*, § 650); Fourth Geneva Convention, Article 21 (*ibid.*, § 651).

[123] Additional Protocol I, Article 21 (adopted by consensus) (*ibid.*, § 652).

[124] See, e.g., the practice of Argentina (*ibid.*, § 661), Australia (*ibid.*, §§ 662–663), Belgium (*ibid.*, §§ 664–665), Benin (*ibid.*, § 666), Burkina Faso (*ibid.*, § 667), Cameroon (*ibid.*, §§ 668–669), Canada (*ibid.*, §§ 670–671), Colombia (*ibid.*, §§ 672–673), Congo (*ibid.*, § 674), Croatia (*ibid.*, §§ 675–676), Dominican Republic (*ibid.*, § 677), Ecuador (*ibid.*, § 678), France (*ibid.*, §§ 679–681), Germany (*ibid.*, §§ 682–683), Hungary (*ibid.*, § 684), Italy (*ibid.*, § 685), Kenya (*ibid.*, § 686), Lebanon (*ibid.*, § 687), Mali (*ibid.*, § 688), Morocco (*ibid.*, § 689), Netherlands (*ibid.*, §§ 690–691), New Zealand (*ibid.*, § 692), Nicaragua (*ibid.*, § 693), Nigeria (*ibid.*, §§ 694–695), Romania (*ibid.*, § 696), Russia (*ibid.*, § 697), Senegal (*ibid.*, §§ 698–699), South Africa (*ibid.*, § 700), Spain (*ibid.*, § 701), Sweden (*ibid.*, § 702), Switzerland (*ibid.*, § 703), Togo (*ibid.*, § 704), United Kingdom (*ibid.*, §§ 705–706), United States (*ibid.*, §§ 708–710) and Yugoslavia (*ibid.*, § 711).

[125] See, e.g., the practice of the United Kingdom (*ibid.*, § 740).

[126] ICC Statute, Article 8(2)(b)(xxiv) (*ibid.*, § 832).

[127] See, e.g., the military manuals of Argentina (*ibid.*, § 661), Australia (*ibid.*, §§ 662–663), Belgium (*ibid.*, §§ 664–665), Benin (*ibid.*, § 666), Burkina Faso (*ibid.*, § 667), Cameroon (*ibid.*, §§ 668–669), Canada (*ibid.*, §§ 670–671), Colombia (*ibid.*, §§ 672–673), Congo (*ibid.*, § 674), Croatia

Additional Protocol I as a codification of a pre-existing rule of customary international law.[128] It is an offence under the legislation of many States to violate this rule.[129] Furthermore, the rule is supported by official statements and reported practice.[130]

Non-international armed conflicts

This rule is implicit in common Article 3 of the Geneva Conventions, which requires that the wounded and sick be collected and cared for, because the protection of medical transports is a subsidiary form of protection granted to ensure that the wounded and sick receive medical care.[131] The rule that medical transports must be respected and protected at all times, and must not be the object of attack, is explicitly set forth in Additional Protocol II.[132] Under the Statute of the International Criminal Court, intentionally directing attacks against "medical units and transports . . . using the distinctive emblems of the Geneva Conventions in conformity with international law" constitutes a war crime in non-international armed conflicts.[133] In addition, this rule is contained in other instruments pertaining also to non-international armed conflicts.[134]

The obligation to respect and protect medical transports is set forth in military manuals which are applicable in or have been applied in non-international armed conflicts.[135] It is an offence under the legislation of many States to violate

---

(*ibid.*, §§ 675–676), Dominican Republic (*ibid.*, § 677), Ecuador (*ibid.*, § 678), France (*ibid.*, §§ 679–681), Germany (*ibid.*, §§ 682–683), Hungary (*ibid.*, § 684), Italy (*ibid.*, § 685), Kenya (*ibid.*, § 686), Lebanon (*ibid.*, § 687), Mali (*ibid.*, § 688), Morocco (*ibid.*, § 689), Netherlands (*ibid.*, §§ 690–691), New Zealand (*ibid.*, § 692), Nicaragua (*ibid.*, § 693), Nigeria (*ibid.*, §§ 694–695), Romania (*ibid.*, § 696), Russia (*ibid.*, § 697), Senegal (*ibid.*, §§ 698–699), South Africa (*ibid.*, § 700), Spain (*ibid.*, § 701), Sweden (*ibid.*, § 702), Switzerland (*ibid.*, § 703), Togo (*ibid.*, § 704), United Kingdom (*ibid.*, §§ 705–706), United States (*ibid.*, §§ 707–710) and Yugoslavia (*ibid.*, § 711).

[128] Sweden, *IHL Manual* (*ibid.*, § 702).

[129] See, e.g., the legislation of Bangladesh (*ibid.*, § 713), Colombia (*ibid.*, § 714), Estonia (*ibid.*, § 716), Georgia (*ibid.*, § 717), Germany (*ibid.*, § 718), Ireland (*ibid.*, § 719), Italy (*ibid.*, § 720), Lithuania (*ibid.*, § 721), Nicaragua (*ibid.*, § 722), Norway (*ibid.*, § 724), Romania (*ibid.*, § 725), Spain (*ibid.*, §§ 726–727), Tajikistan (*ibid.*, § 728) and Venezuela (*ibid.*, § 729); see also the draft legislation of Argentina (*ibid.*, § 712), El Salvador (*ibid.*, § 715) and Nicaragua (*ibid.*, § 723).

[130] See, e.g., the practice of Argentina (*ibid.*, § 731), Egypt (*ibid.*, §§ 732–733), France (*ibid.*, § 734), Germany (*ibid.*, § 735), Hungary (*ibid.*, § 736), Lebanon (*ibid.*, § 738), United Kingdom (*ibid.*, §§ 739–740) and Yugoslavia (*ibid.*, § 742).

[131] This reasoning is put forward in the military manuals of Belgium (*ibid.*, § 665), Colombia (*ibid.*, § 672) and Nicaragua (*ibid.*, § 693).

[132] Additional Protocol II, Article 11(1) (adopted by consensus) (*ibid.*, § 653).

[133] ICC Statute, Article 8(2)(e)(ii) (*ibid.*, § 832).

[134] See, e.g., Agreement on the Application of IHL between the Parties to the Conflict in Bosnia and Herzegovina (*ibid.*, § 657).

[135] See, e.g., the military manuals of Argentina (*ibid.*, § 661), Australia (*ibid.*, §§ 662–663), Benin (*ibid.*, § 666), Cameroon (*ibid.*, § 669), Canada (*ibid.*, §§ 670–671), Colombia (*ibid.*, §§ 672–673), Croatia (*ibid.*, §§ 675–676), Ecuador (*ibid.*, § 678), Germany (*ibid.*, §§ 682–683), Hungary (*ibid.*, § 684), Italy (*ibid.*, § 685), Kenya (*ibid.*, § 686), Lebanon (*ibid.*, § 687), Netherlands (*ibid.*, § 690), New Zealand (*ibid.*, § 692), Nigeria (*ibid.*, § 695), Russia (*ibid.*, § 697), Senegal (*ibid.*, § 699), South Africa (*ibid.*, § 700) and Togo (*ibid.*, § 704).

this rule in any armed conflict.[136] Furthermore, it has been invoked in official statements specifically relating to non-international armed conflicts.[137]

No official contrary practice was found with respect to either international or non-international armed conflicts. Alleged attacks against medical transports have generally been condemned by States.[138] They have also been condemned by the United Nations and other international organisations, for example, in the context of the Iran–Iraq War and the conflicts in the Middle East, Sudan and the former Yugoslavia.[139] The ICRC has called upon parties to both international and non-international armed conflicts to respect this rule.[140]

Definition of medical transports

The term "medical transports" refers to any means of transportation, whether military or civilian, permanent or temporary, assigned exclusively to medical transportation under the control of a competent authority of a party to the conflict. This includes means of transportation by land, water or air, such as ambulances, hospital ships and medical aircraft.[141] These vehicles, ships and aircraft must be exclusively assigned to the conveyance of the wounded, sick and shipwrecked, medical personnel, religious personnel, medical equipment or medical supplies. This definition is based on Article 8(f)–(g) of Additional Protocol I.[142] It is widely used in State practice.[143] In the absence of a definition of medical transports in Additional Protocol II, this term may be understood as applying in the same sense in non-international armed conflicts.[144]

---

[136] See, e.g., the legislation of Bangladesh (ibid., § 713), Colombia (ibid., § 714), Estonia (ibid., § 716), Georgia (ibid., § 717), Germany (ibid., § 718), Ireland (ibid., § 719), Lithuania (ibid., § 721), Nicaragua (ibid., § 722), Norway (ibid., § 724), Spain (ibid., §§ 726–727), Tajikistan (ibid., § 728) and Venezuela (ibid., § 729); see also the legislation of Italy (ibid., § 720) and Romania (ibid., § 725), the application of which is not excluded in time of non-international armed conflict, and the draft legislation of Argentina (ibid., § 712), El Salvador (ibid., § 715) and Nicaragua (ibid., § 723).

[137] See, e.g., the statements of Argentina (ibid., § 731), Hungary (ibid., § 736) and Yugoslavia (ibid., § 742).

[138] See, e.g., the statements of Argentina (ibid., § 731), Egypt (ibid., § 732), Hungary (ibid., § 736), Lebanon (ibid., § 738) and Yugoslavia (ibid., § 742) and the reported practice of Iran (ibid., § 737).

[139] See, e.g., UN Security Council, Res. 771 (ibid., § 743); UN Commission on Human Rights, Res. 1992/S-1/1 (ibid., § 744); UN Commission on Human Rights, Special Rapporteur on the Situation of Human Rights in the Former Yugoslavia, Periodic report (ibid., § 745); Director of MINUGUA, First report (ibid., § 746); UN Commission on Human Rights, Special Rapporteur on the Situation of Human Rights in the Sudan, Report (ibid., § 747).

[140] See the practice of the ICRC (ibid., §§ 752–755 and 757–759).

[141] The protection of hospital ships is governed by the Second Geneva Convention, Articles 22–35, and by Additional Protocol I, Articles 22–23. Medical aircraft are dealt with in the next section.

[142] Additional Protocol I, Article 8(f)–(g).

[143] See, e.g., the practice of Australia (cited in Vol. II, Ch. 7, § 663), Cameroon (ibid., § 669), New Zealand (ibid., § 692), South Africa (ibid., § 700), Spain (ibid., § 701) and Romania (ibid., § 725).

[144] See the declaration to this effect by the United States (ibid., § 654); see also Yves Sandoz, Christophe Swinarski, Bruno Zimmermann (eds.), Commentary on the Additional Protocols, ICRC, Geneva, 1987, § 4712.

Medical aircraft

With respect to medical aircraft, State practice recognises that, in principle, medical aircraft must be respected and protected when performing their humanitarian functions. Under the Geneva Conventions medical aircraft may not be attacked while flying at altitudes, at times and on routes specifically agreed upon and flights over enemy-controlled territory are prohibited, unless otherwise agreed.[145] This is also set forth in several military manuals.[146] Pursuant to Additional Protocol I, attacks on medical aircraft, when they are recognised as such, are prohibited, even when there is no special agreement governing the flight.[147] This prohibition is also set forth in the San Remo Manual on Naval Warfare,[148] as well as in many military manuals.[149] The United States has stated that it supports the principle that "known medical aircraft be respected and protected when performing their humanitarian functions".[150] Some military manuals list "deliberate attack" on medical aircraft as a war crime.[151]

Respect for and protection of medical transports

State practice generally indicates that medical transports enjoy the same protection as mobile medical units. Hence, the meaning of the terms "respect and protection" as interpreted in the context of medical units (see commentary to Rule 28) applies *mutatis mutandis* to medical transports. In practice, this means that medical transports must not be attacked or their passage arbitrarily obstructed. This interpretation is explicitly stated in the military manuals of Germany, South Africa and Switzerland.[152] The military manuals of Benin,

---

[145] First Geneva Convention, Article 36 (cited in Vol. II, Ch. 7, § 768); Fourth Geneva Convention, Article 22 (*ibid.*, § 769).

[146] See, e.g., the military manuals of Belgium (*ibid.*, § 780), Indonesia (*ibid.*, 789), Switzerland (*ibid.*, § 800), United Kingdom (*ibid.*, § 801) and United States (*ibid.*, § 803).

[147] Additional Protocol I, Articles 25–27 (adopted by consensus) (*ibid.*, §§ 770–772).

[148] San Remo Manual, para. 53(a) (*ibid.*, § 776).

[149] See, e.g., the military manuals of Australia (*ibid.*, § 779), Belgium (*ibid.*, § 780), Canada (*ibid.*, § 781), Hungary (*ibid.*, § 788), Netherlands (*ibid.*, § 793), New Zealand (*ibid.*, § 794), South Africa (*ibid.*, § 797), Spain (*ibid.*, § 798), Sweden (*ibid.*, § 799), United States (*ibid.*, §§ 804–805) and Yugoslavia (*ibid.*, § 807); see also the military manuals of Croatia (*ibid.*, § 783), Lebanon (*ibid.*, § 792) and Russia (*ibid.*, § 796) (requiring respect for aircraft displaying the distinctive emblem) and the military manuals of the Dominican Republic (*ibid.*, § 784) (soldiers may not attack military aircraft) and Italy (*ibid.*, § 791) (medical aircraft must be "respected and protected").

[150] United States, Department of State, Remarks of the Deputy Legal Adviser (*ibid.*, § 819).

[151] See, e.g., the military manuals of Ecuador (*ibid.*, § 785) and United States (*ibid.*, §§ 804 and 806).

[152] See the military manuals of Germany (*ibid.*, § 683) ("their unhampered employment shall be ensured at all times"), South Africa (*ibid.*, § 700) ("they may not be attacked or damaged, nor may their passage be obstructed") and Switzerland (*ibid.*, § 703) ("they shall not be attacked, nor harmed in any way, nor their functioning be impeded").

Nigeria, Senegal and Togo state that the mission, content and actual use of medical transports may be checked through inspection.[153]

Loss of protection due to medical transports

State practice generally indicates that medical transports enjoy the same protection as mobile medical units. Hence, the conditions for loss of protection as interpreted in the context of medical units (see commentary to Rule 28) apply *mutatis mutandis* to medical transports.

According to State practice, the transport of healthy troops, arms or munitions and the collection or transmission of military intelligence are examples of uses of medical transports leading to loss of protection.[154] Hence, medical aircraft should not carry any equipment intended for the collection or transmission of intelligence.[155] Upon ratification of Additional Protocol I, France and the United Kingdom made statements with regard to Article 28 in which they recognised the practical need to use non-dedicated aircraft for medical evacuations and therefore interpreted Article 28 as not precluding the presence on board of communications equipment and encryption materials or the use thereof solely to facilitate navigation, identification or communication in support of medical transportation.[156] Article 28 of Additional Protocol I sets out other prohibited acts by medical aircraft.[157] In addition, light arms carried by medical personnel in self-defence or which have just been taken from the wounded and not yet turned over to the proper authority do not constitute prohibited equipment either (see commentary to Rule 25).

Rule 30. Attacks directed against medical and religious personnel and objects displaying the distinctive emblems of the Geneva Conventions in conformity with international law are prohibited.

Practice

Volume II, Chapter 7, Section F.

---

[153] See, e.g., the military manuals of Benin (*ibid.*, § 666), Nigeria (*ibid.*, § 695), Senegal (*ibid.*, § 699) and Togo (*ibid.*, § 704).

[154] See the practice referred to *supra* in footnote 117; see also the practice of Argentina (*ibid.*, § 661), Canada (*ibid.*, §§ 670–671), Croatia (*ibid.*, § 675), France (*ibid.*, § 680), Italy (*ibid.*, § 685), Netherlands (*ibid.*, § 691) and South Africa (*ibid.*, § 700).

[155] Additional Protocol I, Article 28(2) (adopted by consensus) (*ibid.*, § 773); San Remo Manual (*ibid.*, § 777); the military manuals of Australia (*ibid.*, § 779), Canada (*ibid.*, § 781), Croatia (*ibid.*, § 782), France (*ibid.*, § 786), Germany (*ibid.*, § 787), Italy (*ibid.*, § 790), Netherlands (*ibid.*, § 793), Spain (*ibid.*, § 798), Sweden (*ibid.*, § 799) and Yugoslavia (*ibid.*, § 807).

[156] France, Reservations and declarations made upon ratification of Additional Protocol I (*ibid.*, § 774); United Kingdom, Reservations and declarations made upon ratification of Additional Protocol I (*ibid.*, § 775).

[157] Additional Protocol I, Article 28 (adopted by consensus) (*ibid.*, § 773).

Summary

State practice establishes this rule as a norm of customary international law applicable in both international and non-international armed conflicts.

International and non-international armed conflicts

Under the Statute of the International Criminal Court, "intentionally directing attacks against buildings, material, medical units and transport, and personnel using the distinctive emblems of the Geneva Conventions in conformity with international law" constitutes a war crime in both international and non-international armed conflicts.[158]

The prohibition on attacking persons and objects displaying the distinctive emblems is contained in numerous military manuals.[159] It is an offence under the legislation of many States to attack persons and objects displaying the distinctive emblems.[160] Furthermore, the rule is supported by official statements and reported practice.[161]

On numerous occasions, the ICRC has called on parties to both international and non-international armed conflicts to respect persons and objects displaying the distinctive emblems.[162]

No official contrary practice was found with respect to either international or non-international armed conflicts. Attacks directed against persons and objects displaying the distinctive emblems have generally been condemned.[163]

Interpretation

As this rule indicates, respect for the distinctive emblems is conditional on their proper use (see Rule 59). Practice also shows that failure to wear or display the distinctive emblems does not of itself justify an attack on medical or

---

[158] ICC Statute, Article 8(2)(b)(xxiv) and (e)(ii) (*ibid.*, § 832).

[159] See, e.g., the military manuals of Australia (*ibid.*, § 840), Benin (*ibid.*, § 841), Cameroon (*ibid.*, § 842), Canada (*ibid.*, §§ 843–844), Colombia (*ibid.*, § 845), France (*ibid.*, §§ 846–847), Germany (*ibid.*, § 848), Hungary (*ibid.*, § 849), Indonesia (*ibid.*, § 850), Italy (*ibid.*, § 851), Kenya (*ibid.*, § 852), Lebanon (*ibid.*, § 853), Madagascar (*ibid.*, § 854), Nigeria (*ibid.*, § 855), Philippines (*ibid.*, §§ 856–857), Romania (*ibid.*, § 858), Senegal (*ibid.*, § 859), Switzerland (*ibid.*, § 860), Togo (*ibid.*, § 861), United Kingdom (*ibid.*, § 862) and United States (*ibid.*, § 863).

[160] See, e.g., the legislation of Australia (*ibid.*, § 864), Azerbaijan (*ibid.*, § 865), Belarus (*ibid.*, § 866), Canada (*ibid.*, § 868), Colombia (*ibid.*, § 869), Congo (*ibid.*, § 870), Denmark (*ibid.*, § 871), Estonia (*ibid.*, § 873), Germany (*ibid.*, § 874), Netherlands (*ibid.*, § 875), New Zealand (*ibid.*, § 876), Nicaragua (*ibid.*, § 877), Peru (*ibid.*, § 879), Romania (*ibid.*, § 880), Spain (*ibid.*, § 881), Sweden (*ibid.*, § 882), Switzerland (*ibid.*, § 883), United Kingdom (*ibid.*, § 885) and Venezuela (*ibid.*, § 886); see also the draft legislation of Burundi (*ibid.*, § 867), El Salvador (*ibid.*, § 872), Nicaragua (*ibid.*, § 878) and Trinidad and Tobago (*ibid.*, § 884).

[161] See, e.g., the statements of Bosnia and Herzegovina, Republika Srpska (*ibid.*, § 888), Kuwait (*ibid.*, § 890) and Yugoslavia (*ibid.*, § 892).

[162] See the practice of the ICRC (*ibid.*, §§ 906, 908–910, 912–917, 919, 921–925 and 927–928).

[163] See, e.g., the practice of Yugoslavia (*ibid.*, § 891) and the ICRC (*ibid.*, §§ 905 and 926).

religious personnel and objects when they are recognised as such. This is an application of the general principle that the distinctive emblems are intended to facilitate identification and do not, of themselves, confer protected status. In other words, medical and religious personnel and objects are protected because of their function. The display of the emblems is merely the visible manifestation of that function but does not confer protection as such.

The Elements of Crimes for the International Criminal Court stresses that the war crime of "intentionally directing attacks against buildings, material, medical units and transport, and personnel using the distinctive emblems of the Geneva Conventions in conformity with international law" includes attacks against persons and objects displaying a distinctive emblem or other method of identification, such as the distinctive signals, indicating protection under the Geneva Conventions.[164]

---

[164] See Knut Dörmann, *Elements of War Crimes under the Rome Statute of the International Criminal Court, Sources and Commentary*, Cambridge University Press, Cambridge, 2002, p. 350; see also Articles 6–9 of Annex I to Additional Protocol I concerning light signals, radio signals and electronic identification.

HUMANITARIAN RELIEF PERSONNEL AND OBJECTS

Rule 31. Humanitarian relief personnel must be respected and protected.

Practice

Volume II, Chapter 8, Section A.

Summary

State practice establishes this rule as a norm of customary international law applicable in both international and non-international armed conflicts. Respect for and protection of humanitarian relief personnel is a corollary of the prohibition of starvation (see Rule 53), as well as the rule that the wounded and sick must be collected and cared for (see Rules 109–110), which are applicable in both international and non-international armed conflicts. The safety and security of humanitarian relief personnel is an indispensable condition for the delivery of humanitarian relief to civilian populations in need threatened with starvation.

International armed conflicts

The obligation to respect and protect humanitarian relief personnel is set forth in Article 71(2) of Additional Protocol I.[1] Under the Statute of the International Criminal Court, intentionally directing attacks against personnel involved in a humanitarian assistance mission in accordance with the Charter of the United Nations is a war crime in international armed conflicts, as long as such personnel are entitled to the protection given to civilians under international humanitarian law.[2] Hence, members of armed forces delivering humanitarian aid are not covered by this rule. United Nations personnel delivering humanitarian aid, however, enjoy specific protection under the Convention on the Safety of United Nations Personnel.[3]

---

[1] Additional Protocol I, Article 71(2) (adopted by consensus) (cited in Vol. II, Ch. 8, § 3).
[2] ICC Statute, Article 8(2)(b)(iii) (*ibid.*, § 142).
[3] Convention on the Safety of UN Personnel, Article 7(2) (*ibid.*, § 4).

A number of military manuals state the obligation to respect and protect humanitarian relief personnel.[4] Sweden's IHL Manual, in particular, identifies Article 71(2) of Additional Protocol I as codifying pre-existing rules of customary law.[5] It is an offence under the legislation of numerous States to attack humanitarian relief personnel.[6] The rule is also supported by official statements and reported practice.[7] This practice includes that of States not party to Additional Protocol I.[8] The rule has also been invoked by parties to Additional Protocol I against non-parties.[9]

The obligation to respect and protect humanitarian relief personnel is recalled in resolutions of international organisations, the large majority of which deal with non-international armed conflicts (see *infra*).

Non-international armed conflicts

While Article 18(2) of Additional Protocol II requires that relief actions for the civilian population in need be organised, the Protocol does not contain a specific provision on the protection of humanitarian relief personnel. This rule is indispensable, however, if relief actions for civilian populations in need are to succeed. Under the Statutes of the International Criminal Court and of the Special Court for Sierra Leone, intentionally directing attacks against personnel involved in a humanitarian assistance mission in accordance with the Charter of the United Nations is considered a war crime in non-international armed conflicts, as long as such personnel are entitled to the protection given to civilians under international humanitarian law.[10] In addition, this rule is contained in a number of other instruments pertaining also to non-international armed conflicts.[11]

---

[4] See, e.g., the military manuals of Argentina (*ibid.*, § 12), Australia (*ibid.*, § 13), Canada (*ibid.*, § 14), France (*ibid.*, § 15), Netherlands (*ibid.*, § 16), Sweden (*ibid.*, § 17) and Yugoslavia (*ibid.*, § 18).

[5] Sweden, *IHL Manual* (*ibid.*, § 17).

[6] See, e.g., the legislation of Australia (*ibid.*, § 147), Azerbaijan (*ibid.*, § 148), Canada (*ibid.*, § 150), Congo (*ibid.*, § 151), Estonia (*ibid.*, § 152), Ethiopia (*ibid.*, § 153), Germany (*ibid.*, § 154), Ireland (*ibid.*, § 19), New Zealand (*ibid.*, §§ 156–157), Norway (*ibid.*, § 20), Philippines (*ibid.*, §§ 21 and 158), Portugal (*ibid.*, § 159) and United Kingdom (*ibid.*, §§ 161–162); see also the draft legislation of Burundi (*ibid.*, § 149) and Trinidad and Tobago (*ibid.*, § 160).

[7] See, e.g., the statements of Australia (*ibid.*, § 23), Germany (*ibid.*, §§ 25–26), Iraq (*ibid.*, § 28), Slovenia (*ibid.*, § 35), South Africa (*ibid.*, § 36) and Switzerland (*ibid.*, § 37) and the reported practice of Iraq (*ibid.*, § 29), Netherlands (*ibid.*, § 32) and Rwanda (*ibid.*, § 34).

[8] See the practice of Azerbaijan (*ibid.*, § 148), India (*ibid.*, § 170), Iraq (*ibid.*, §§ 28–29), Israel (*ibid.*, § 172), Malaysia (*ibid.*, § 174), Turkey (*ibid.*, § 177) and United Kingdom (*ibid.*, § 38).

[9] See, e.g., the statements of Germany vis-à-vis Afghanistan (*ibid.*, § 25) and vis-à-vis Sudan (*ibid.*, § 169).

[10] ICC Statute, Article 8(2)(e)(iii) (*ibid.*, § 142); Statute of the Special Court for Sierra Leone, Article 4(b) (*ibid.*, § 143).

[11] See, e.g., Agreement No. 2 on the Implementation of the Agreement of 22 May 1992 between the Parties to the Conflict in Bosnia and Herzegovina, para. 2(d) (*ibid.*, § 5); Agreement No. 3 on the ICRC Plan of Action between the Parties to the Conflict in Bosnia and Herzegovina,

The obligation to respect and protect humanitarian relief personnel is laid down in some military manuals which are applicable in or have been applied in non-international armed conflicts.[12] It is also contained in official statements specifically relating to non-international armed conflicts.[13]

In addition, the United Nations and other international organisations have adopted resolutions invoking this rule. The UN Security Council, for example, has on numerous occasions urged the parties to non-international armed conflicts, such as in Afghanistan, Angola, Bosnia and Herzegovina, Burundi, Kosovo, Liberia, Rwanda and Somalia, to respect and protect humanitarian relief personnel.[14]

This rule was reiterated at the World Conference on Human Rights in 1993 and at the 26th and 27th International Conferences of the Red Cross and Red Crescent in 1995 and 1999 respectively.[15]

No official contrary practice was found with respect to either international or non-international armed conflicts. Alleged violations of this rule have generally been condemned by States regardless of whether the conflict was international or non-international in nature.[16] They have also been condemned by international organisations.[17] Following attacks upon a vehicle carrying ICRC

para. II(9) (*ibid.*, § 6); Bahir Dar Agreement, para. 2 (*ibid.*, § 7); Agreement on Ground Rules for Operation Lifeline Sudan (*ibid.*, § 8); UN Secretary-General's Bulletin, Section 9 (*ibid.*, § 9); Agreement on the Protection and Provision of Humanitarian Assistance in the Sudan, para. 1 (*ibid.*, § 10); Cairo Declaration, para. 67 (*ibid.*, § 11).

[12] See, e.g., the military manuals of Canada (*ibid.*, § 14) and Yugoslavia (*ibid.*, § 18).

[13] See, e.g., the statements of Burundi (*ibid.*, § 166), Germany (*ibid.*, § 26), Russia (*ibid.*, § 175), South Africa (*ibid.*, § 36), United Kingdom (*ibid.*, § 178) and United States (*ibid.*, § 180).

[14] See, e.g., UN Security Council, Res. 733 and 814 (*ibid.*, § 41), Res. 746 and 751 (*ibid.*, § 42), Res. 758, 770 and 787 (*ibid.*, § 43), Res. 819 and 824 (*ibid.*, § 44), Res. 851 (*ibid.*, § 45), Res. 897, 923 and 954 (*ibid.*, § 47), Res. 918 and 925 (*ibid.*, § 48), Res. 946 (*ibid.*, § 49), Res. 952 (*ibid.*, § 50), Res. 954 (*ibid.*, § 51), Res. 985, 1001 and 1014 (*ibid.*, § 52), Res. 998 (*ibid.*, § 53), Res. 1040 (*ibid.*, § 54), Res. 1041, 1059 and 1071 (*ibid.*, § 55), Res. 1075 and 1087 (*ibid.*, § 56), Res. 1088 (*ibid.*, § 57), Res. 1127 (*ibid.*, § 58), Res. 1173 (*ibid.*, § 59), Res. 1193 (*ibid.*, § 60), Res. 1195 (*ibid.*, § 61), Res. 1199 and 1203 (*ibid.*, § 62); UN Security Council, Statements by the President (*ibid.*, §§ 67–70, 72–73, 75–76, 81, 87–88, 90–91 and 93).

[15] World Conference on Human Rights, Vienna Declaration and Programme of Action (*ibid.*, § 120); 26th International Conference of the Red Cross and Red Crescent, Res. IV (*ibid.*, § 121); 27th International Conference of the Red Cross and Red Crescent, Plan of Action for the years 2000–2003 (adopted by consensus) (*ibid.*, § 123).

[16] See, e.g., the statements of Germany (*ibid.*, § 169) and United States (*ibid.*, §§ 179–180) and the reported practice of Russia (*ibid.*, § 175).

[17] See, e.g., UN Security Council, Res. 757 (*ibid.*, § 185), Res. 864 (*ibid.*, § 186), Res. 897 and 923 (*ibid.*, § 187), Res. 913 (*ibid.*, § 188), Res. 946 (*ibid.*, § 192), Res. 950 (*ibid.*, § 193), Res. 954 (*ibid.*, § 194), Res. 1049 (*ibid.*, § 195), Res. 1071 and 1083 (*ibid.*, § 196), Res. 1193 (*ibid.*, § 197) and Res. 1265 (*ibid.*, § 198); UN Security Council, Statements by the President (*ibid.*, §§ 199–218); UN General Assembly, Res. 49/196 (*ibid.*, § 219), Res. 49/206 and 50/200 (*ibid.*, § 221), Res. 50/193 (*ibid.*, § 223), Res. 53/87 (*ibid.*, § 227), Res. 54/192 (*ibid.*, § 229) and Res. 55/116 (*ibid.*, § 230); UN Commission on Human Rights, Res. 1994/72 (*ibid.*, § 233), Res. 1995/89 (*ibid.*, § 235), Res. 1995/91 (*ibid.*, § 236), Res. 1996/1 and 1997/77 (*ibid.*, § 237) and Res. 1998/70 (*ibid.*, § 242); OAU, Council of Ministers, Res. 1526 (LX) (*ibid.*, § 255), Res. 1649 (LXIV) (*ibid.*, § 256) and Res. 1662 (LXIV) (*ibid.*, § 257); OSCE, Chairman-in-Office, Press Release No. 86/96 (*ibid.*, § 258).

personnel in Burundi in 1996, the President and the Prime Minister of Burundi both stated that they deplored the incident and that they had requested an independent inquiry to identify the perpetrators.[18] The Russian government reacted similarly when six ICRC aid workers were killed in Chechnya the same year.[19] The ICRC has reminded parties to both international and non-international armed conflicts to respect this rule.[20]

Respect for and protection of humanitarian relief personnel

Civilian humanitarian relief personnel are protected against attack according to the principle of distinction (see Rule 1). In addition to the prohibition of attacks on such personnel, practice indicates that harassment, intimidation and arbitrary detention of humanitarian relief personnel are prohibited under this rule.[21] The collected practice also contains examples in which the following acts against humanitarian aid personnel have been condemned: mistreatment, physical and psychological violence, murder, beating, abduction, hostage-taking, harassment, kidnapping, illegal arrest and detention.[22]

Furthermore, there is a considerable amount of State practice which requires that parties to a conflict ensure the safety of humanitarian relief personnel authorised by them, as invoked in a number of official statements.[23] In addition, the UN Security Council has called on the parties to the conflicts

---

[18] See the practice of Burundi (*ibid.*, § 166).   [19] See the practice of Russia (*ibid.*, § 175).
[20] See the practice of the ICRC (*ibid.*, §§ 125–128 and 130–132).
[21] See the practice of Germany (*ibid.*, § 169) and Philippines (*ibid.*, § 158); UN Security Council, Res. 897 and 923 (*ibid.*, § 187), Res. 918 and 925 (*ibid.*, § 189), Res. 940 (*ibid.*, § 190), Res. 946 (*ibid.*, § 192), Res. 950 (*ibid.*, § 193), Res. 954 (*ibid.*, § 194) and Res. 1071 (*ibid.*, § 196); UN Security Council, Statements by the President (*ibid.*, §§ 199, 202, 204, 212, 216 and 219); UN General Assembly, Res. 51/30 B (*ibid.*, § 222), Res. 53/87 (*ibid.*, § 227), Res. 54/192 (*ibid.*, § 229) and Res. 55/116 (*ibid.*, § 230); UN Commission on Human Rights, Res. 1995/89 (*ibid.*, § 225) and Res. 2001/18 (*ibid.*, § 243); UN Secretary-General, Report on UNOMIL (*ibid.*, § 244); UN Commission on Human Rights, Special Rapporteur on the Situation of Human Rights in the Sudan, Report (*ibid.*, § 248).
[22] See, e.g., the practice of Russia (*ibid.*, § 175) and United States (*ibid.*, §§ 179–180); UN Security Council, Res. 897 and 923 (*ibid.*, § 187), Res. 918 and 925 (*ibid.*, § 189), Res. 940 (*ibid.*, § 190), Res. 945 and 952 (*ibid.*, § 191), Res. 950 (*ibid.*, § 193), Res. 954 (*ibid.*, § 194), Res. 1049 (*ibid.*, § 195), Res. 1193 (*ibid.*, § 197) and Res. 1265 (*ibid.*, § 198); UN Security Council, Statements by the President (*ibid.*, §§ 199, 204–208, 210–213 and 216); UN General Assembly, Res. 52/167 (*ibid.*, § 226), Res. 53/87 (*ibid.*, § 227), Res. 53/164 (*ibid.*, § 228), Res. 54/192 (*ibid.*, § 229) and Res. 55/116 (*ibid.*, § 230); UN Commission on Human Rights, Res. 1994/79 and 1995/77 (*ibid.*, § 234), Res. 1995/91 (*ibid.*, § 236), Res. 1996/1 and 1997/77 (*ibid.*, § 237), 1996/73 (*ibid.*, § 238) and 1997/59 (*ibid.*, § 239); UN Secretary-General, Report on UNOMIL (*ibid.*, § 244); UN Commission on Human Rights, Special Rapporteur on the Situation of Human Rights in Burundi, Second report (*ibid.*, § 247) and Special Rapporteur on the Situation of Human Rights in the Sudan, Report (*ibid.*, § 248); Council of Europe, Parliamentary Assembly, Res. 921 (*ibid.*, § 251); OAU, Council of Ministers, Res. 1526 (LX) (*ibid.*, § 255), Res. 1649 (LXIV) (*ibid.*, § 256) and Res. 1662 (LXIV) (*ibid.*, § 257); OSCE, Chairman-in-Office, Press Release No. 86/96 (*ibid.*, § 258).
[23] See, e.g., the statements of Australia (*ibid.*, § 23), Germany (*ibid.*, § 25), Slovenia (*ibid.*, § 35) and South Africa (*ibid.*, § 36).

in Afghanistan, Angola, Bosnia and Herzegovina, Burundi, Kosovo, Liberia, Rwanda and Somalia to ensure respect for the security and safety of humanitarian relief personnel.[24] In a resolution adopted in 2000 on protection of civilians in armed conflicts, the UN Security Council called upon all parties to an armed conflict, including non-State parties, "to ensure the safety, security and freedom of movement" of humanitarian relief personnel.[25]

While the Additional Protocols provide that the protection of humanitarian relief personnel applies only to "authorised" humanitarian personnel as such, the overwhelming majority of practice does not specify this condition. The notion of authorisation refers to the consent received from the party to the conflict concerned to work in areas under its control.[26] Authorisation may not be withheld for arbitrary reasons to deny access to humanitarian relief personnel (see commentary to Rule 55).

Rule 32. Objects used for humanitarian relief operations must be respected and protected.

Practice

Volume II, Chapter 8, Section B.

Summary

State practice establishes this rule as a norm of customary international law applicable in both international and non-international armed conflicts. This rule is a corollary of the prohibition of starvation (see Rule 53), which is applicable in both international and non-international armed conflicts, because the safety and security of humanitarian relief objects are an indispensable condition for the delivery of humanitarian relief to civilian populations in need threatened with starvation. In that framework, this rule is also a corollary of the prohibition on deliberately impeding the delivery of humanitarian relief (see commentary to Rule 55), because any attack on, destruction or pillage of relief objects inherently amounts to an impediment of humanitarian relief.

---

[24] UN Security Council, Res. 733 and 814 (*ibid.*, § 41), Res. 746 and 751 (*ibid.*, § 42), Res. 758, 770 and 787 (*ibid.*, § 43), Res. 824 (*ibid.*, § 44), Res. 851 (*ibid.*, § 45), Res. 897, 923 and 954 (*ibid.*, § 47), Res. 918 and 925 (*ibid.*, § 48), Res. 946 (*ibid.*, § 49), Res. 952 (*ibid.*, § 50), Res. 954 (*ibid.*, § 51), Res. 985, 1001 and 1014 (*ibid.*, § 52), Res. 998 (*ibid.*, § 53), Res. 1040 (*ibid.*, § 54), Res. 1041, 1059 and 1071 (*ibid.*, § 55), Res. 1075 and 1087 (*ibid.*, § 56), Res. 1193 (*ibid.*, § 60), Res. 1195 (*ibid.*, § 61) and Res. 1199 and 1203 (*ibid.*, § 62).
[25] UN Security Council, Res. 1296 (*ibid.*, § 65).
[26] Additional Protocol I, Article 71(1) (adopted by consensus) (*ibid.*, § 3); Additional Protocol II, Article 18(2) (adopted by consensus) (cited in Vol. II, Ch. 17, § 680).

International armed conflicts

The Fourth Geneva Convention requires that all States guarantee the protection of relief supplies intended for occupied territory.[27] This rule is now more generally set forth in Additional Protocol I.[28] Under the Statute of the International Criminal Court, intentionally directing attacks against installations, material, units or vehicles involved in a humanitarian assistance mission in accordance with the Charter of the United Nations is considered a war crime in international armed conflicts, as long as such objects are entitled to the protection given to civilian objects under the international law of armed conflict.[29]

The protection of objects used for humanitarian relief operations is also contained in the legislation of numerous States, under which it is an offence to attack such objects.[30] This rule is also supported by official statements and other practice.[31] This practice includes that of States not party to Additional Protocol I.[32] It has also been invoked by parties to Additional Protocol I against non-parties.[33]

The rule is also recalled in resolutions of international organisations, the large majority of which, however, deal with non-international conflicts (see *infra*).

Non-international armed conflicts

While Article 18(2) of Additional Protocol II requires relief actions for the civilian population in need to be organised, the Protocol does not contain a specific provision on the protection of objects used in humanitarian relief operations.[34] This rule is indispensable, however, if relief actions for civilian populations in need are to succeed. Under the Statutes of the International Criminal Court and of the Special Court for Sierra Leone, intentionally directing attacks against installations, material, units or vehicles involved in a humanitarian assistance mission in accordance with the Charter of the United Nations is considered a war crime in non-international armed conflicts, as long as such objects are entitled to the protection given to civilian objects under the international law

---

[27] Fourth Geneva Convention, Article 59.

[28] Additional Protocol I, Article 70(4) (adopted by consensus) (cited in Vol. II, Ch. 8, § 282).

[29] ICC Statute, Article 8(2)(b)(iii) (*ibid.*, § 285).

[30] See, e.g., the legislation of Australia (*ibid.*, §§ 294–295), Bosnia and Herzegovina (*ibid.*, § 296), Canada (*ibid.*, § 298), China (*ibid.*, § 299), Colombia (*ibid.*, § 300), Congo (*ibid.*, § 301), Croatia (*ibid.*, § 302), Ethiopia (*ibid.*, § 304), Germany (*ibid.*, § 305), Ireland (*ibid.*, § 306), Netherlands (*ibid.*, §§ 307–308), New Zealand (*ibid.*, § 309), Norway (*ibid.*, § 310), Portugal (*ibid.*, § 311), Slovenia (*ibid.*, § 312), United Kingdom (*ibid.*, § 314) and Yugoslavia (*ibid.*, § 315); see also the draft legislation of Burundi (*ibid.*, § 297), El Salvador (*ibid.*, § 303) and Trinidad and Tobago (*ibid.*, § 313).

[31] See, e.g., the military manual of Kenya (*ibid.*, § 292), the statements of Bosnia and Herzegovina, Republika Srpska (*ibid.*, § 317), Germany (*ibid.*, § 321) and United States (*ibid.*, § 326) and the reported practice of Brazil (*ibid.*, § 318), Nigeria (*ibid.*, § 324) and United Kingdom (*ibid.*, § 325).

[32] See, e.g., the military manual of Kenya (*ibid.*, § 292), the statement of the United States (*ibid.*, § 326) and the reported practice of the United Kingdom (*ibid.*, § 325).

[33] See, e.g., the statement of Germany vis-à-vis Sudan (*ibid.*, § 321).

[34] Additional Protocol II, Article 18(2) (adopted by consensus) (cited in Vol. II, Ch. 17, § 680).

of armed conflict.[35] In addition, this rule is contained in other instruments pertaining also to non-international armed conflicts.[36]

The protection of objects used for humanitarian relief operations is supported by official statements made in the context of non-international armed conflicts and by reported practice.[37]

The rule is recalled in a large number of resolutions adopted by the United Nations and other international organisations. The UN Security Council, for example, has referred to this rule with respect to the conflicts in Angola, Liberia and Rwanda.[38]

No official contrary practice was found with respect to either international or non-international armed conflicts. Alleged violations of this rule have generally been condemned by States, regardless of the nature of the armed conflict.[39] They have also been condemned by the United Nations and other international organisations.[40] The ICRC has reminded parties to both international and non-international armed conflicts to respect this rule.[41]

Respect for and protection of humanitarian relief objects

Objects involved in a humanitarian relief operation are, in principle, civilian objects and as such enjoy protection from attack (see Rule 7). State practice indicates that, in addition to attacks against humanitarian relief objects, destruction, misappropriation and looting of such objects are also prohibited.[42] This is an application of the general rules relating to the destruction and seizure of property (see Chapter 16). There is some practice indicating that each party to the conflict must ensure the safety of humanitarian relief objects. In 1996, for example, the UN Security Council called upon all parties to the conflict in Angola to guarantee the safety of humanitarian supplies throughout the country.[43]

---

[35] ICC Statute, Article 8(2)(e)(iii) (cited in Vol. II, Ch. 8, §§ 142 and 285); Statute of the Special Court for Sierra Leone, Article 4(b) (*ibid.*, §§ 143 and 286).

[36] See, e.g., Bahir Dar Agreement, para. 2 (*ibid.*, § 288); UN Secretary-General's Bulletin, Section 9.9 (*ibid.*, § 290); UNTAET Regulation 2000/15, Section 6(1)(b)(iii) and (e)(iii) (*ibid.*, § 291).

[37] See, e.g., the statements of Germany (*ibid.*, § 321) and United States (*ibid.*, § 326) and the reported practice of Nigeria (*ibid.*, § 324) and United Kingdom (*ibid.*, § 325).

[38] See, e.g., UN Security Council, Res. 918 (*ibid.*, § 329), Res. 925 (*ibid.*, § 329), Res. 950 (*ibid.*, § 330), Res. 1075 (*ibid.*, § 332) and Res. 1087 (*ibid.*, § 332).

[39] See, e.g., the statements of Germany (*ibid.*, § 321) and United States (*ibid.*, § 326).

[40] See, e.g., UN Security Council, Res. 1059 (*ibid.*, § 331), Res. 1071 (*ibid.*, § 331), Res. 1083 (*ibid.*, § 333) and Res. 1265 (*ibid.*, § 334); UN Security Council, Statements by the President (*ibid.*, §§ 336–340); UN General Assembly, Res. 51/30 B (*ibid.*, § 341) and Res. 54/192 (*ibid.*, § 343); UN Commission on Human Rights, Res. 1995/77 (*ibid.*, § 345).

[41] See, e.g., the practice of the ICRC (*ibid.*, §§ 354 and 356–358).

[42] See, e.g., the practice of Australia (*ibid.*, § 294), Ethiopia (*ibid.*, § 304) and Netherlands (*ibid.*, § 307); see also the draft legislation of El Salvador (*ibid.*, § 303); UN Security Council, Res. 950 (*ibid.*, § 330), Res. 1059 (*ibid.*, § 331), Res. 1071 (*ibid.*, § 331) and Res. 1083 (*ibid.*, § 333); UN Security Council, Statements by the President (*ibid.*, §§ 336–340); UN General Assembly, Res. 51/30 B (*ibid.*, § 341), Res. 54/192 (*ibid.*, § 343) and Res. 55/116 (*ibid.*, § 344).

[43] UN Security Council, Res. 1075 and 1087 (*ibid.*, § 332).

PERSONNEL AND OBJECTS INVOLVED IN A PEACEKEEPING MISSION

Rule 33. Directing an attack against personnel and objects involved in a peacekeeping mission in accordance with the Charter of the United Nations, as long as they are entitled to the protection given to civilians and civilian objects under international humanitarian law, is prohibited.

Practice

Volume II, Chapter 9.

Summary

State practice establishes this rule as a norm of customary international law applicable in both international and non-international armed conflicts.

International and non-international armed conflicts

State practice treats peacekeeping forces, which are usually professional soldiers, as civilians because they are not members of a party to the conflict and are deemed to be entitled to the same protection against attack as that accorded to civilians, as long as they are not taking a direct part in hostilities (see Rules 1 and 6). As civilians, peacekeeping forces are entitled to the fundamental guarantees set out in Chapter 32. By the same token, objects involved in a peacekeeping operation are considered to be civilian objects, protected against attack (see Rule 7).

Under the Statute of the International Criminal Court, intentionally directing attacks against personnel and objects involved in a peacekeeping mission in accordance with the Charter of the United Nations constitutes a war crime in both international and non-international armed conflicts, as long as they are entitled to the protection given to civilians and civilian objects under international humanitarian law.[1] The Statute of the Special Court for Sierra Leone also includes the rule.[2]

---

[1] ICC Statute, Article 8(2)(b)(iii) and (e)(iii) (cited in Vol. II, Ch. 9, § 4).
[2] Statute of the Special Court for Sierra Leone, Article 4(b) (*ibid.*, § 5).

The rule is contained in some military manuals.[3] Under the legislation of many States, it is an offence to attack personnel and objects involved in a peacekeeping mission.[4]

No official contrary practice was found. Attacks against peacekeeping personnel and objects have generally been condemned by States.[5] They have also been condemned by the United Nations and other international organisations.[6] Some of these condemnations refer to the attacks as criminal.[7] In addition to direct attacks, the United Nations has condemned other acts perpetrated against peacekeeping personnel which do not amount to attacks as such, including harassment, abuse, intimidation, violence, detention and maltreatment, and has called upon the parties to conflicts to ensure their safety, security and freedom of movement.[8]

In the *Karadžić and Mladić case* before the International Criminal Tribunal for the Former Yugoslavia, the accused have been charged for their role in the "taking of civilians, that is UN peacekeepers, as hostages".[9]

---

[3] See, e.g., the military manuals of Cameroon (*ibid.*, § 10), Germany (*ibid.*, § 11), New Zealand (*ibid.*, § 12) and Spain (*ibid.*, § 14).

[4] See, e.g., the legislation of Australia (*ibid.*, § 15), Azerbaijan (*ibid.*, § 16), Canada (*ibid.*, § 18), Congo (*ibid.*, § 19), Georgia (*ibid.*, § 20), Germany (*ibid.*, § 21), Mali (*ibid.*, § 22), Netherlands (*ibid.*, § 23), New Zealand (*ibid.*, §§ 24–25) and United Kingdom (*ibid.*, §§ 27–28); see also the draft legislation of Burundi (*ibid.*, § 17) and Trinidad and Tobago (*ibid.*, § 26).

[5] See, e.g., the practice of Australia (*ibid.*, § 31), Finland (*ibid.*, § 33), Germany (*ibid.*, § 34), Liberia (*ibid.*, § 35), Russia (*ibid.*, § 37), Ukraine (*ibid.*, § 38), United Kingdom (*ibid.*, §§ 39–40) and United States (*ibid.*, §§ 41–42).

[6] See, e.g., UN Security Council, Res. 757 (*ibid.*, § 46), Res. 788 (*ibid.*, § 47), Res. 794 (*ibid.*, § 48), Res. 802 (*ibid.*, § 49), Res. 804 (*ibid.*, § 50), Res. 897, 923 and 954 (*ibid.*, § 55), Res. 912 (*ibid.*, § 56), Res. 946 (*ibid.*, § 60), Res. 987 (*ibid.*, § 62), Res. 994 (*ibid.*, § 64), Res. 1004 (*ibid.*, § 66), Res. 1009 (*ibid.*, § 67), Res. 1041 (*ibid.*, § 70), Res. 1059, 1071 and 1083 (*ibid.*, § 71), Res. 1099 (*ibid.*, § 73), Res. 1118 (*ibid.*, § 74), Res. 1157 (*ibid.*, § 75), Res. 1164 (*ibid.*, § 76), Res. 1173 and 1180 (*ibid.*, § 77) and Res. 1187 (*ibid.*, § 78); UN General Assembly, Res. 47/121 (*ibid.*, § 98), Res. 49/196 (*ibid.*, § 99) and Res. 50/193 (*ibid.*, § 100); UN Commission on Human Rights, Res. 1993/7 (*ibid.*, § 101), Res. 1994/60 (*ibid.*, § 102), Res. 1994/72 (*ibid.*, § 103) and Res. 1995/89 (*ibid.*, § 104); ECOWAS, First Summit Meeting of the Committee of Nine on the Liberian Crisis, Final Communiqué (*ibid.*, § 118); EU, Statement before the UN Security Council (*ibid.*, § 119); OIC, Conference of Ministers of Foreign Affairs, Res. 1/6-EX (*ibid.*, § 120) and statement before the UN Security Council (*ibid.*, § 121); 88th Inter-Parliamentary Conference, Resolution on support to the recent international initiatives to halt the violence and put an end to the violations of human rights in Bosnia and Herzegovina (*ibid.*, § 122).

[7] See, e.g., UN Security Council, Res. 587 (*ibid.*, § 45), Res. 837 (*ibid.*, § 52), Res. 865 (*ibid.*, § 53) and Res. 1099 (*ibid.*, § 73).

[8] UN Security Council, Res. 467 (*ibid.*, § 44), Res. 788 and 813 (*ibid.*, § 47), Res. 804 (*ibid.*, § 50), Res. 819 (*ibid.*, § 51), Res. 868 (*ibid.*, § 54), Res. 897, 923 and 954 (*ibid.*, § 55), Res. 913 (*ibid.*, § 57), Res. 918 and 925 (*ibid.*, § 58), Res. 940 (*ibid.*, § 59), Res. 946 (*ibid.*, § 60), Res. 950 (*ibid.*, § 61), Res. 987 (*ibid.*, § 62), Res. 993 and 1036 (*ibid.*, § 63), Res. 994 (*ibid.*, § 64), Res. 998 (*ibid.*, § 65), Res. 1004 (*ibid.*, § 66), Res. 1009 (*ibid.*, § 67), Res. 1031 (*ibid.*, § 69), Res. 1099 (*ibid.*, § 73), Res. 1157 (*ibid.*, § 75), Res. 1173 and 1180 (*ibid.*, § 77), Res. 1206 (*ibid.*, § 79) and Res. 1313 (*ibid.*, § 80); UN Commission on Human Rights, Res. 1994/72 (*ibid.*, § 103), Res. 1995/89 (*ibid.*, § 104) and Res. 1995/91 (*ibid.*, § 105).

[9] ICTY, *Karadžić and Mladić case*, First Indictment (*ibid.*, § 125).

Scope of application

This rule applies only to peacekeeping forces, whether established by the United Nations or by a regional organisation, as long as they are entitled to the protection given to civilians and, as a result, excludes forces engaged in peace-enforcement operations who are considered as combatants bound to respect international humanitarian law.[10]

[10] See, e.g., UN Secretary-General's Bulletin, para. 1 (*ibid.*, § 8).

JOURNALISTS

Rule 34. Civilian journalists engaged in professional missions in areas of armed conflict must be respected and protected as long as they are not taking a direct part in hostilities.

Practice

Volume II, Chapter 10.

Summary

State practice establishes this rule as a norm of customary international law applicable in both international and non-international armed conflicts.

International armed conflicts

The protection of civilian journalists is set forth in Article 79 of Additional Protocol I, to which no reservations have been made.[1]

This rule is set forth in numerous military manuals.[2] It is also supported by official statements and reported practice.[3] This practice includes that of States not party to Additional Protocol I.[4]

Non-international armed conflicts

Although Additional Protocol II does not contain any specific provision on civilian journalists, their immunity against attack is based on the prohibition on attacking civilians unless and for such time as they take a direct part in hostilities (see Rule 6). This conclusion is borne out by practice, even before the

---

[1] Additional Protocol I, Article 79 (adopted by consensus) (cited in Vol. II, Ch. 10, § 1).

[2] See, e.g., the military manuals of Argentina (*ibid.*, § 4), Australia (*ibid.*, § 5), Benin (*ibid.*, § 6), Cameroon (*ibid.*, § 7), Canada (*ibid.*, § 8), France (*ibid.*, § 9), Germany (*ibid.*, § 10), Israel (*ibid.*, § 11), Madagascar (*ibid.*, § 12), Netherlands (*ibid.*, § 13), New Zealand (*ibid.*, § 14), Nigeria (*ibid.*, § 15), Spain (*ibid.*, § 16) and Togo (*ibid.*, § 17).

[3] See the statements of Brazil (*ibid.*, § 22), Federal Republic of Germany (*ibid.*, § 23) and United States (*ibid.*, §§ 28–29) and the reported practice of Jordan (*ibid.*, § 24), South Korea (*ibid.*, § 25), Nigeria (*ibid.*, § 26) and Rwanda (*ibid.*, § 27).

[4] See, e.g., the practice of Israel (*ibid.*, § 11) and United States (*ibid.*, §§ 28–29).

adoption of the Additional Protocols. Brazil in 1971 and the Federal Republic of Germany in 1973 stated before the Third Committee of the UN General Assembly that journalists were protected as civilians under the principle of distinction.[5] The UN Commission on the Truth for El Salvador considered the murder of four Dutch journalists, accompanied by members of the FMLN, who were ambushed by a patrol of the Salvadoran armed forces, to be in violation of international humanitarian law, "which stipulates that civilians shall not be the object of attacks".[6] In 1996, the Committee of Ministers of the Council of Europe reaffirmed the importance of Article 79 of Additional Protocol I, "which provides that journalists shall be considered as civilians and shall be protected as such". It considered that "this obligation also applies with respect to non-international armed conflicts".[7]

The obligation to respect and protect civilian journalists is included in other instruments pertaining also to non-international armed conflicts.[8] It is contained in military manuals which are applicable in or have been applied in non-international armed conflicts.[9] It is supported by official statements and reported practice.[10]

No official contrary practice was found with respect to either international or non-international armed conflicts. Deliberate attacks on journalists have generally been condemned, in particular by the United Nations and other international organisations, regardless of whether the conflict was international or non-international. Most of these condemnations concerned non-international armed conflicts such as in Afghanistan, Burundi, Chechnya, Kosovo and Somalia.[11]

Loss of protection

Like other civilians, journalists lose their protection against attack when and for such time as they take a direct part in hostilities (see Rule 6). This principle is also recognised in Article 79(2) of Additional Protocol I, which grants protection

---

[5] See the statements of Brazil (*ibid.*, § 22) and Federal Republic of Germany (*ibid.*, § 23).
[6] UN Commission on the Truth for El Salvador, Report (*ibid.*, § 41).
[7] Council of Europe, Committee of Ministers, Rec. R (96) 4 (*ibid.*, § 42).
[8] See, e.g., Memorandum of Understanding on the Application of IHL between Croatia and the SFRY, para. 4 (*ibid.*, § 2); Agreement on the Application of IHL between the Parties to the Conflict in Bosnia and Herzegovina, para. 2.3 (*ibid.*, § 3).
[9] See, e.g., the military manuals of Benin (*ibid.*, § 6), Germany (*ibid.*, § 10), Madagascar (*ibid.*, § 12), Nigeria (*ibid.*, § 15) and Togo (*ibid.*, § 17).
[10] See, e.g., the statements of Brazil (*ibid.*, § 22), Federal Republic of Germany (*ibid.*, § 23), Nigeria (*ibid.*, § 26) and United States (*ibid.*, §§ 28–29) and the reported practice of Jordan (*ibid.*, § 24), South Korea (*ibid.*, § 25) and Rwanda (*ibid.*, § 27).
[11] See, e.g., UN General Assembly, Res. 2673 (XXV), 2854 (XXVI), 3058 (XXVIII) and 3500 (XXX) (*ibid.*, § 32), Res. 51/108 (*ibid.*, § 33) and Res. 53/164 (*ibid.*, § 34); UN Commission on Human Rights, Res. 1995/56 (*ibid.*, § 36) and Res. 1996/1 (*ibid.*, § 37); European Parliament, Resolution on the situation in Kosovo (*ibid.*, § 45) and Resolution on violations of human rights and humanitarian law in Chechnya (*ibid.*, § 46).

to civilian journalists "provided that they take no action adversely affecting their status".[12] This also implies that journalists, like any other person entering a foreign country, must respect that country's domestic regulations concerning access to its territory. Journalists may lose their right to reside and work in a foreign country if they have entered illegally. In other words, the protection granted to journalists under international humanitarian law in no way changes the rules applicable to access to territory.

Definition

Civilian journalists are not to be confused with "war correspondents". The latter are journalists who accompany the armed forces of a State without being members thereof. As a result, they are civilians and may not be made the object of attack (see Rule 1).[13] Pursuant to Article 4(A)(4) of the Third Geneva Convention, however, war correspondents are entitled to prisoner-of-war status upon capture.[14]

Respect for and protection of journalists

In addition to the prohibition of attacks against journalists, there is also practice which indicates that journalists exercising their professional activities in relation to an armed conflict must be protected.

In 1996, the UN General Assembly called on all parties to the conflict in Afghanistan to "ensure the safety" of representatives of the media.[15] Other practice condemns specific measures taken to dissuade journalists from carrying out their professional activities. In 1998, for example, the UN General Assembly called on parties to the conflict in Kosovo to refrain from any harassment and intimidation of journalists.[16] In 1995, the UN Commission on Human Rights deplored attacks, acts of reprisal, abductions and other acts of violence against representatives of the international media in Somalia.[17] Other acts which have been condemned include: police violence, threats of legal prosecutions and subjection to defamation campaigns and physical violence;[18] threats to treat the media as enemies serving foreign powers and denial of full and unhindered

---

[12] Additional Protocol I, Article 79(2) (adopted by consensus) (*ibid.*, § 1).
[13] See, e.g., Additional Protocol I, Article 50(1) (adopted by consensus) (cited in Vol. II, Ch. 1, § 705).
[14] Third Geneva Convention, Article 4(A)(4) ("persons who accompany the armed forces without actually being members thereof, such as ... war correspondents ... provided that they have received authorization, from the armed forces which they accompany, who shall provide them for that purpose with an identity card similar to the annexed model" are entitled to prisoner-of-war status upon capture).
[15] UN General Assembly, Res. 51/108 (cited in Vol. II, Ch. 10, § 33).
[16] UN General Assembly, Res. 53/164 (*ibid.*, § 34).
[17] UN Commission on Human Rights, Res. 1995/56 (*ibid.*, § 36).
[18] Council of Europe, Parliamentary Assembly, Rec. 1368 (*ibid.*, § 43) and Written Declaration No. 284 (*ibid.*, § 44).

access;[19] assaults upon freedom of the press and crimes against journalists;[20] killing, wounding and abduction;[21] attacks, murder, unjustified imprisonment and intimidation;[22] and harassment, interference, detention and murder.[23]

It should be stressed that, as civilians, journalists are entitled to the fundamental guarantees set out in Chapter 32. If they are accused of spying, for example, they must not be subjected to arbitrary detention (see Rule 99) and must be granted a fair trial (see Rule 100).

---

[19] European Parliament, Resolution on the situation in Kosovo (*ibid.*, § 45) and Resolution on violations of human rights and humanitarian law in Chechnya (*ibid.*, § 46).

[20] OAS General Assembly, Res. 1550 (XXVIII-O/98) (*ibid.*, § 47).

[21] 90th Inter-Parliamentary Conference, Resolution on respect for international humanitarian law and support for humanitarian action in armed conflicts (*ibid.*, § 49).

[22] Committee to Protect Journalists, *Attacks on the Press 2000* (*ibid.*, § 59).

[23] International Federation of Journalists, 22nd World Congress, Resolution on Angola (*ibid.*, § 53).

PROTECTED ZONES

Rule 35. Directing an attack against a zone established to shelter the wounded, the sick and civilians from the effects of hostilities is prohibited.

Practice

Volume II, Chapter 11, Section A.

Summary

State practice establishes this rule as a norm of customary international law applicable in both international and non-international armed conflicts.

International and non-international armed conflicts

The First and Fourth Geneva Conventions provide for the possibility of setting up hospital and safety zones, and a draft agreement for the establishment of such zones is attached thereto.[1] In addition, the Fourth Geneva Convention provides for the possibility of setting up neutralised zones.[2] Both types of zone are intended to shelter the wounded, the sick and civilians from the effects of conflict, but the hospital and safety zones are meant to be far removed from military operations, whereas neutralised zones are intended for areas in which military operations are taking place.

The relevant provisions of the Geneva Conventions are incorporated in many military manuals, which emphasise that these zones must be respected.[3] Under the legislation of several States, it is an offence to attack such zones.[4]

---

[1] First Geneva Convention, Article 23 (cited in Vol. II, Ch. 11, § 1); Fourth Geneva Convention, Article 14, first paragraph (*ibid.*, § 2).

[2] Fourth Geneva Convention, Article 15 (*ibid.*, § 3).

[3] See, e.g., the military manuals of Argentina (*ibid.*, §§ 6–7), Australia (*ibid.*, § 8), Cameroon (*ibid.*, § 9), Canada (*ibid.*, § 10), Ecuador (*ibid.*, § 11), France (*ibid.*, §§ 12–13), Germany (*ibid.*, § 14), Hungary (*ibid.*, § 15), Italy (*ibid.*, §§ 16–17), Kenya (*ibid.*, § 18), Madagascar (*ibid.*, § 19), Netherlands (*ibid.*, § 20), New Zealand (*ibid.*, § 21), Nigeria (*ibid.*, § 22), Senegal (*ibid.*, § 23), Spain (*ibid.*, § 24), Sweden (*ibid.*, § 25), Switzerland (*ibid.*, §§ 26–27), United Kingdom (*ibid.*, §§ 28–29), United States (*ibid.*, §§ 30–33) and Yugoslavia (*ibid.*, § 34).

[4] See, e.g., the legislation of Colombia (*ibid.*, § 36), Italy (*ibid.*, § 37), Poland (*ibid.*, § 40) and Spain (*ibid.*, § 41); see also the draft legislation of Argentina (*ibid.*, § 35), El Salvador (*ibid.*, § 38) and Nicaragua (*ibid.*, § 39).

In a resolution adopted in 1970 on basic principles for the protection of civilian populations in armed conflicts, the UN General Assembly stated that "places or areas designated for the sole protection of civilians, such as hospital zones or similar refuges, should not be the object of military operations".[5]

Zones providing shelter to the wounded, the sick and civilians have been agreed upon in both international and non-international armed conflicts, for example, during Bangladesh's war of independence, the war in the South Atlantic and the conflicts in Cambodia, Chad, Cyprus, Nicaragua, Lebanon, Sri Lanka and the former Yugoslavia.[6] Most of these zones were established on the basis of a written agreement. These agreements were premised on the principle that zones established to shelter the wounded, the sick and civilians must not be attacked. The neutralised zone established at sea during the war in the South Atlantic (the so-called "Red Cross Box") was done without any special agreement in writing. A zone which contains only wounded and sick (see Rule 47), medical and religious personnel (see Rules 25 and 27), humanitarian relief personnel (see Rule 31) and civilians (see Rule 1) may not be attacked by application of the specific rules protecting these categories of persons, applicable in both international and non-international armed conflicts.

Rule 36. Directing an attack against a demilitarised zone agreed upon between the parties to the conflict is prohibited.

Practice

Volume II, Chapter 11, Section B.

Summary

State practice establishes this rule as a norm of customary international law applicable in both international and non-international armed conflicts.

International and non-international armed conflicts

Making a demilitarised zone the object of attack is a grave breach of Additional Protocol I.[7] A demilitarised zone is generally understood to be an area, agreed upon between the parties to the conflict, which cannot be occupied or used

---

[5] UN General Assembly, Res. 2675 (XXV) (adopted by 109 votes in favour, none against and 8 abstentions) (*ibid.*, § 47).

[6] See, e.g., Memorandum of Understanding on the Application of IHL between Croatia and the SFRY (*ibid.*, § 4); Agreement between Croatia and the SFRY on a Protected Zone around the Hospital of Osijek, Articles 1, 2(1) and 4(1) (*ibid.*, § 5); the practice concerning the war in the South Atlantic (*ibid.*, § 45), Bangladesh (*ibid.*, § 53), Cyprus (*ibid.*, § 55), Cambodia (*ibid.*, § 56) and Sri Lanka (*ibid.*, § 57); see also François Bugnion, *The International Committee of the Red Cross and the Protection of War Victims*, ICRC, Geneva, 2003, pp. 756–759 (providing examples from the conflicts in Bangladesh, Cyprus, Cambodia, Nicaragua, Chad and Lebanon among others).

[7] Additional Protocol I, Article 85(3)(d) (adopted by consensus) (cited in Vol. II, Ch. 11, § 106).

for military purposes by any party to the conflict. Such a zone can be established in time of peace as well as in time of armed conflict. Article 60(3) of Additional Protocol I provides a blueprint for the terms of an agreement on a demilitarised zone, but any such agreement can be tailored to each specific situation, as Article 60 recognises.[8] The protection afforded to a demilitarised zone ceases if one of the parties commits a material breach of the agreement establishing the zone.[9] Practice indicates that international supervision is seen as an appropriate method of verifying that the conditions agreed upon are respected.[10] The agreement may authorise the presence of peacekeeping forces or police personnel for the sole purpose of maintaining law and order without the zone losing its demilitarised character.

Numerous military manuals provide for the establishment of demilitarised zones and prohibit their attack.[11] Attacks against demilitarised zones are an offence under the legislation of many States.[12]

Demilitarised zones have been set up in both international and non-international armed conflicts, for example, in the conflicts between India and Pakistan, North and South Korea, Israel and Syria, Israel and Egypt and Iraq and Kuwait, and the conflicts in Bosnia and Herzegovina, Colombia and Nicaragua.[13] Alleged violations of the status of a demilitarised zone have generally been condemned.[14]

---

[8] Additional Protocol I, Article 60(3) (adopted by consensus), provides, *inter alia*, that "the subject of such an agreement shall normally be any zone which fulfils the following conditions: (a) all combatants, as well as mobile weapons and mobile military equipment, must have been evacuated; (b) no hostile use shall be made of fixed military installations or establishments; (c) no acts of hostility shall be committed by the authorities or by the population; and (d) any activity linked to the military effort must have ceased".

[9] Additional Protocol II, Article 60(7) (adopted by consensus) (cited in Vol. II, Ch. 11, § 105).

[10] See, e.g., the Disengagement Agreement between Israel and Syria (*ibid.*, § 64), Agreement on Demilitarisation of Srebrenica and Žepa, Article 3 (*ibid.*, § 67), the statement of Bosnia and Herzegovina (*ibid.*, § 169) and the reported practice of Pakistan (*ibid.*, § 175).

[11] See, e.g., the military manuals of Argentina (*ibid.*, § 108), Australia (*ibid.*, § 109), Benin (*ibid.*, § 110), Cameroon (*ibid.*, § 111), Canada (*ibid.*, § 112), Croatia (*ibid.*, § 113), Ecuador (*ibid.*, § 114), France (*ibid.*, § 115), Germany (*ibid.*, § 116), Hungary (*ibid.*, § 117), Italy (*ibid.*, §§ 118–119), Kenya (*ibid.*, § 120), Netherlands (*ibid.*, § 121), New Zealand (*ibid.*, § 122), Nigeria (*ibid.*, § 123), South Africa (*ibid.*, § 124), Spain (*ibid.*, § 125), Switzerland (*ibid.*, § 126), Togo (*ibid.*, § 127), United States (*ibid.*, §§ 128–130) and Yugoslavia (*ibid.*, § 131).

[12] See, e.g., the legislation of Armenia (*ibid.*, § 133), Australia (*ibid.*, §§ 134–135), Azerbaijan (*ibid.*, § 136), Belarus (*ibid.*, § 137), Belgium (*ibid.*, § 138), Bosnia and Herzegovina (*ibid.*, § 139), Canada (*ibid.*, § 140), Cook Islands (*ibid.*, § 141), Croatia (*ibid.*, § 142), Cyprus (*ibid.*, § 143), Czech Republic (*ibid.*, § 144), Estonia (*ibid.*, § 146), Georgia (*ibid.*, § 147), Germany (*ibid.*, § 148), Hungary (*ibid.*, § 149), Ireland (*ibid.*, § 150), Lithuania (*ibid.*, § 153), Netherlands (*ibid.*, § 154), New Zealand (*ibid.*, § 155), Niger (*ibid.*, § 157), Norway (*ibid.*, § 158), Slovakia (*ibid.*, § 159), Slovenia (*ibid.*, § 160), Spain (*ibid.*, § 161), Tajikistan (*ibid.*, § 162), United Kingdom (*ibid.*, § 163), Yemen (*ibid.*, § 164), Yugoslavia (*ibid.*, § 165) and Zimbabwe (*ibid.*, § 166); see also the draft legislation of Argentina (*ibid.*, § 132), El Salvador (*ibid.*, § 145), Jordan (*ibid.*, § 151), Lebanon (*ibid.*, § 152) and Nicaragua (*ibid.*, § 156).

[13] See the Karachi Agreement, para. D (*ibid.*, § 62); Panmunjom Armistice Agreement, Article I(6) and (10) (*ibid.*, § 63); Disengagement Agreement between Israel and Syria (*ibid.*, § 64); Peace Treaty between Israel and Egypt (*ibid.*, § 66); Agreement on Demilitarisation of Srebrenica and Žepa (*ibid.*, § 67); the practice of Colombia (*ibid.*, § 89), Iraq and Kuwait (*ibid.*, § 90) and Nicaragua (*ibid.*, § 91).

[14] See, e.g., UN Security Council, Statement by the President (*ibid.*, § 94); UN Secretary-General, Report on UNIKOM (*ibid.*, § 96); UN Secretary-General, Report on the UN Observer Mission

Rule 37. Directing an attack against a non-defended locality is prohibited.

Practice

Volume II, Chapter 11, Section C.

Summary

State practice establishes this rule as a norm of customary international law applicable in both international and non-international armed conflicts.

International armed conflicts

The concept of non-defended localities is rooted in the traditional concept of an "open town". The prohibition on attacking undefended places was included in the Brussels Declaration and the Oxford Manual.[15] It was codified in Article 25 of the Hague Regulations, which provides that "the attack or bombardment, by whatever means, of towns, villages, dwellings, or buildings which are undefended is prohibited".[16] The Report of the Commission on Responsibility set up after the First World War identifies "deliberate bombardment of undefended places" as a violation of the laws and customs of war which should be subject to criminal prosecution.[17] Under Additional Protocol I, it is prohibited to making a non-defended locality the object of attack and doing so is a grave breach of the Protocol.[18] Under the Statute of the International Criminal Court, "intentionally attacking towns, villages, dwellings or buildings which are undefended and which are not military objectives" is a war crime in international armed conflicts.[19]

The prohibition on attacking non-defended localities is contained in numerous military manuals.[20] Sweden's IHL Manual identifies the chief rule relating to non-defended localities in Article 59 of Additional Protocol I as a codification of pre-existing customary international law.[21] Under the legislation of

in Prevlaka (*ibid.*, § 97); the practice of Bosnia and Herzegovina (*ibid.*, § 169) and North Korea (*ibid.*, § 173); the reported practice of Iran (*ibid.*, § 172) and Pakistan (*ibid.*, § 175).

[15] Brussels Declaration, Article 15 (*ibid.*, § 233); Oxford Manual, Article 32(c) (*ibid.*, § 234).
[16] 1907 Hague Regulations, Article 25 (*ibid.*, § 228); see also the 1899 Hague Regulations, Article 25 (*ibid.*, § 227).
[17] Report of the Commission on Responsibility (*ibid.*, § 235).
[18] Additional Protocol I, Article 59(1) (*ibid.*, § 230) and Article 85(3)(d) (*ibid.*, § 231).
[19] ICC Statute, Article 8(2)(b)(v) (*ibid.*, § 232).
[20] See, e.g., the military manuals of Argentina (*ibid.*, §§ 241–242), Australia (*ibid.*, § 243), Belgium (*ibid.*, § 244), Bosnia and Herzegovina (*ibid.*, § 245), Canada (*ibid.*, § 246), Croatia (*ibid.*, §§ 247–248), Ecuador (*ibid.*, § 249), France (*ibid.*, §§ 250–251), Germany (*ibid.*, § 252), Hungary (*ibid.*, § 253), Indonesia (*ibid.*, § 254), Italy (*ibid.*, §§ 255–256), Kenya (*ibid.*, § 257), South Korea (*ibid.*, §§ 258–259), Netherlands (*ibid.*, §§ 260–261), New Zealand (*ibid.*, § 262), Nigeria (*ibid.*, § 263), Russia (*ibid.*, § 264), South Africa (*ibid.*, § 265), Spain (*ibid.*, § 266), Sweden (*ibid.*, § 267), Switzerland (*ibid.*, § 268), United Kingdom (*ibid.*, §§ 269–270), United States (*ibid.*, §§ 271–276) and Yugoslavia (*ibid.*, § 277).
[21] Sweden, *IHL Manual* (*ibid.*, § 267).

numerous States, it is an offence to attack non-defended localities.[22] The prohibition is also supported by official statements.[23] This practice includes that of States not, or not at the time, party to Additional Protocol I.[24]

Non-international armed conflicts

The prohibition of attacks against non-defended localities is included in Article 3 of the Statute of the International Criminal Tribunal for the Former Yugoslavia, according to which the Tribunal is competent to prosecute violations of the laws or customs of war, including "attack, or bombardment, by whatever means, of undefended towns, villages, dwellings, or buildings".[25]

This rule is also contained in military manuals which are applicable in or have been applied in non-international armed conflicts.[26] Under the legislation of many States, it is an offence to attack non-defended localities in any armed conflict.[27] In 1997, in the *Perišić and Others case*, in which several persons were convicted of having ordered the shelling of Zadar and its surroundings, Croatia's District Court of Zadar applied Article 25 of the Hague Regulations alongside common Article 3 of the Geneva Conventions and Articles 13–14 of Additional Protocol II.[28]

---

[22] See, e.g., the legislation of Armenia (*ibid.*, § 279), Australia (*ibid.*, §§ 280–282), Azerbaijan (*ibid.*, § 283), Belarus (*ibid.*, § 284), Belgium (*ibid.*, § 285), Bosnia and Herzegovina (*ibid.*, § 286), Canada (*ibid.*, §§ 288–289), China (*ibid.*, § 290), Congo (*ibid.*, § 291), Cook Islands (*ibid.*, § 292), Croatia (*ibid.*, § 293), Cyprus (*ibid.*, § 294), Czech Republic (*ibid.*, § 295), Estonia (*ibid.*, § 297), Georgia (*ibid.*, § 298), Germany (*ibid.*, § 299), Hungary (*ibid.*, § 300), Ireland (*ibid.*, § 301), Lithuania (*ibid.*, § 304), Mali (*ibid.*, § 305), Netherlands (*ibid.*, § 306–307), New Zealand (*ibid.*, §§ 308–309), Niger (*ibid.*, § 311), Norway (*ibid.*, § 312), Poland (*ibid.*, § 313), Slovakia (*ibid.*, § 314), Slovenia (*ibid.*, § 315), Spain (*ibid.*, § 316), Tajikistan (*ibid.*, § 317), United Kingdom (*ibid.*, §§ 319–320), United States (*ibid.*, § 321), Venezuela (*ibid.*, § 322), Yugoslavia (*ibid.*, § 323) and Zimbabwe (*ibid.*, § 324); see also the draft legislation of Argentina (*ibid.*, § 278), Burundi (*ibid.*, § 287), El Salvador (*ibid.*, § 296), Jordan (*ibid.*, § 302), Lebanon (*ibid.*, § 303), Nicaragua (*ibid.*, § 310) and Trinidad and Tobago (*ibid.*, § 318).

[23] See, e.g., the statements of China (*ibid.*, § 330), Egypt (*ibid.*, § 332), Iran (*ibid.*, § 336), Iraq (*ibid.*, § 337) and United States (*ibid.*, § 340).

[24] See, e.g., the practice and reported practice of Azerbaijan (*ibid.*, § 283), China (*ibid.*, §§ 290 and 330), France (*ibid.*, § 250), Indonesia (*ibid.*, § 254), Iran (*ibid.*, § 336), Iraq (*ibid.*, § 337), Netherlands (*ibid.*, § 306), United Kingdom (*ibid.*, §§ 269–270), and United States (*ibid.*, §§ 271–276, 321 and 340).

[25] ICTY Statute, Article 3 (*ibid.*, § 238).

[26] See, e.g., the military manuals of Bosnia and Herzegovina (*ibid.*, § 245), Croatia (*ibid.*, §§ 247–248), Ecuador (*ibid.*, § 249), Germany (*ibid.*, § 252), Italy (*ibid.*, §§ 255–256), Kenya (*ibid.*, § 257), South Korea (*ibid.*, § 259), South Africa (*ibid.*, § 265) and Yugoslavia (*ibid.*, § 277).

[27] See, e.g., the legislation of Armenia (*ibid.*, § 279), Azerbaijan (*ibid.*, § 283), Belarus (*ibid.*, § 284), Belgium (*ibid.*, § 285), Bosnia and Herzegovina (*ibid.*, § 286), Croatia (*ibid.*, § 293), Georgia (*ibid.*, § 298), Germany (*ibid.*, § 299), Lithuania (*ibid.*, § 304), Niger (*ibid.*, § 311), Poland (*ibid.*, § 313), Slovenia (*ibid.*, § 315), Spain (*ibid.*, § 316), Tajikistan (*ibid.*, § 317), Venezuela (*ibid.*, § 322) and Yugoslavia (*ibid.*, § 323); see also the legislation of the Czech Republic (*ibid.*, § 295), Hungary (*ibid.*, § 300) and Slovakia (*ibid.*, § 314), the application of which is not excluded in time of non-international armed conflict, and the draft legislation of Argentina (*ibid.*, § 278), El Salvador (*ibid.*, § 296), Jordan (*ibid.*, § 302) and Nicaragua (*ibid.*, § 310).

[28] Croatia, District Court of Zadar, *Perišić and Others case* (*ibid.*, § 325).

While the concept of non-defended localities was specifically developed for international armed conflicts, it applies to non-international armed conflicts as well. This is especially so since the idea of prohibiting attacks on non-defended localities is based on the more general concept of military necessity: there is no need to attack a town, village, dwelling or building that is open for occupation. This rule is an application of the principle that no more destruction may be wrought upon an adversary than absolutely necessary, a rule which is also applicable in non-international armed conflicts (see Rule 50). As stated in Kenya's LOAC Manual, under customary law "undefended localities that can be occupied, cannot be bombarded".[29]

No official contrary practice was found with respect to either international or non-international armed conflicts.

Definition

The UK Military Manual provides a useful description of an open or undefended town as one

which is so completely undefended from within or without that the enemy may enter and take possession of it without fighting or incurring casualties. It follows that no town behind the immediate front line can be open or undefended for the attacker must fight his way to it. Any town behind the enemy front line is thus a defended town and is open to ground or other bombardment subject to the limitations imposed on all bombardments, namely, that ... the latter must be limited to military objectives ... Thus, the question of whether a town is or is not an open town is distinct from whether it does or does not contain military objectives. A town in the front line with no means of defence, not defended from outside and into which the enemy may enter and of which he may take possession at any time without fighting or incurring casualties, e.g., from crossing unmarked minefields, is undefended even if it contains munitions factories. On the other hand, all defended towns whether situated in the front line or not may be subjected to bombardment.[30]

Article 59(2) of Additional Protocol I defines the concept of a non-defended locality as an "inhabited place near or in a zone where armed forces are in contact which is open for occupation by an adverse Party".[31] This is essentially the same definition as that of an open town or undefended area under traditional customary international law.

---

[29] Kenya, *LOAC Manual* (*ibid.*, § 209).
[30] United Kingdom, *Military Manual* (*ibid.*, § 192).
[31] Additional Protocol I, Article 59(2) (adopted by consensus) (*ibid.*, § 202).

Article 59(2) of Additional Protocol I has clarified the procedure for declaring a locality to be undefended. This procedure is different from that of zones set up by agreement in that a party to the conflict may unilaterally declare a locality to be non-defended provided that: (1) all combatants, mobile weapons and mobile military equipment have been evacuated; (2) no hostile use is made of fixed military installations or establishments; (3) no acts of hostility are committed by the authorities or by the population; and (4) no activities in support of military operations are undertaken.[32] The other party shall acknowledge receipt of such a declaration and shall treat the locality as non-defended unless these conditions are not (or no longer) fulfilled.[33] This procedure is set forth in many military manuals,[34] including those of States not, or not at the time, party to Additional Protocol I.[35]

Article 59(5) of Additional Protocol I nevertheless provides that the parties to the conflict may establish non-defended localities even if the above-mentioned conditions are not fulfilled.[36] It is obvious that the conclusion of an agreement provides greater certainty and allows the parties to establish the conditions as they see fit. Kenya's LOAC Manual explains:

[non-defended localities] can be established through a unilateral declaration and notification given to the enemy Party. However, for greater safety, formal agreements should be passed between the two Parties (under customary law and the Hague regulations undefended localities that can be occupied, cannot be bombarded even if there is no notification).[37]

An attack against an area or locality without it being militarily necessary to do so would constitute a violation of the prohibition on destroying the property of an adversary, unless required by imperative military necessity (see Rule 50).

---

[32] Additional Protocol I, Article 59(2) (adopted by consensus) (*ibid.*, § 202).

[33] Additional Protocol I, Article 59(4) (adopted by consensus), which states that "the declaration made under paragraph 2 shall be addressed to the adverse Party and shall define and describe, as precisely as possible, the limits of the non-defended locality. The Party to the conflict to which the declaration is addressed shall acknowledge its receipt and shall treat the locality as a non-defended locality unless the conditions laid down in paragraph 2 are not in fact fulfilled, in which event it shall immediately so inform the Party making the declaration. Even if the conditions laid down in paragraph 2 are not fulfilled, the locality shall continue to enjoy the protection provided by the other provisions of this Protocol and the other rules of international law applicable in armed conflict".

[34] See, e.g., the military manuals of Argentina (cited in Vol. II, Ch. 11, § 204), Australia (*ibid.*, § 205), Canada (*ibid.*, § 206), France (*ibid.*, § 207), Germany (*ibid.*, § 208), Indonesia (*ibid.*, § 254), Kenya (*ibid.*, § 209), Netherlands (*ibid.*, § 210), New Zealand (*ibid.*, § 211), Sweden (*ibid.*, § 212), Switzerland (*ibid.*, § 213), United States (*ibid.*, § 214) and Yugoslavia (*ibid.*, § 215).

[35] See, e.g., the military manuals of Kenya (*ibid.*, § 209), Indonesia (*ibid.*, § 254) and United States (*ibid.*, § 214).

[36] Additional Protocol I, Article 59(5) (adopted by consensus) (*ibid.*, § 202).

[37] Kenya, *LOAC Manual* (*ibid.*, § 209).

A locality loses its protection from attack when it ceases to fulfil the required conditions. According to Article 59(3) of Additional Protocol I, the presence of persons afforded special protection and of police forces retained for the sole purpose of maintaining law and order is not contrary to these conditions.[38]

---

[38] Additional Protocol I, Article 59(3) (adopted by consensus) (*ibid.*, § 202).

CULTURAL PROPERTY

Rule 38. Each party to the conflict must respect cultural property:

  A. **Special care must be taken in military operations to avoid damage to buildings dedicated to religion, art, science, education or charitable purposes and historic monuments unless they are military objectives.**

  B. **Property of great importance to the cultural heritage of every people must not be the object of attack unless imperatively required by military necessity.**

Practice

Volume II, Chapter 12, Section A.

Summary

State practice establishes this rule as a norm of customary international law applicable in both international and non-international armed conflicts.

Cultural property in general

To the extent that cultural property is civilian, it may not be made the object of attack (see Rule 7). It may only be attacked in case it qualifies as a military objective (see Rule 10). The Statute of the International Criminal Court therefore stresses that intentionally directing attacks against buildings dedicated to religion, education, art, science or charitable purposes or historic monuments is a war crime in both international and non-international armed conflicts, "provided they are not military objectives".[1]

The obligation to take special care to avoid damage to buildings dedicated to religion, art, science, education or charitable purposes and historic monuments, provided they are not used for military purposes, is set forth in many military manuals.[2] It is also restated in the legislation of numerous States, under

---

[1] ICC Statute, Article 8(2)(b)(ix) and (e)(iv) (cited in Vol. II, Ch. 12, § 19).

[2] See, e.g., the military manuals of Argentina (*ibid.*, § 40), Australia (*ibid.*, §§ 41–42), Belgium (*ibid.*, §§ 43–44), Burkina Faso (*ibid.*, § 47), Cameroon (*ibid.*, § 49), Congo (*ibid.*, § 53), Dominican Republic (*ibid.*, § 56), Ecuador (*ibid.*, § 57), France (*ibid.*, § 58), Germany (*ibid.*, § 62), Indonesia (*ibid.*, § 65), Israel (*ibid.*, § 67), South Korea (*ibid.*, § 71), Mali (*ibid.*, § 74),

which it is a punishable offence to attack such objects.[3] Attacks against such objects have been condemned by States, the United Nations and other international organisations, for example, with respect to the conflicts in Afghanistan and Korea, between Iran and Iraq and in the Middle East and the former Yugoslavia.[4]

While in any attack against a military objective, all feasible precautions must be taken to avoid, and in any event, to minimise incidental damage to civilian objects (see Rule 15), special care is required to avoid damage to some of the most precious civilian objects. This requirement was already recognised in the Lieber Code, the Brussels Declaration and the Oxford Manual and was codified in the Hague Regulations.[5] The Report of the Commission on Responsibility set up after the First World War identified the "wanton destruction of religious, charitable, educational and historic buildings and monuments" as a violation of the laws and customs of war subject to criminal prosecution.[6]

The requirement of special care has also been invoked in official statements.[7] The Plan of Action for the years 2000–2003, adopted by the 27th International Conference of the Red Cross and Red Crescent in 1999, called on all parties to an armed conflict to protect cultural property and places of worship, in addition to respecting the total ban on directing attacks against such objects.[8]

Morocco (*ibid.*, § 75), New Zealand (*ibid.*, § 79), Nigeria (*ibid.*, § 81), Russia (*ibid.*, § 84), Senegal (*ibid.*, § 85), Sweden (*ibid.*, § 88), United Kingdom (*ibid.*, §§ 93–94) and United States (*ibid.*, §§ 95–102).

[3] See, e.g., the legislation of Argentina (*ibid.*, § 105), Australia (*ibid.*, § 109), Azerbaijan (*ibid.*, § 110), Bosnia and Herzegovina (*ibid.*, § 113), Bulgaria (*ibid.*, § 114), Canada (*ibid.*, § 117), Chile (*ibid.*, § 118), China (*ibid.*, § 119), Colombia (*ibid.*, § 120), Congo (*ibid.*, § 122), Croatia (*ibid.*, § 124), Dominican Republic (*ibid.*, § 128), Estonia (*ibid.*, § 130), Germany (*ibid.*, § 132), Italy (*ibid.*, § 135), Kyrgyzstan (*ibid.*, § 138), Mali (*ibid.*, § 142), Mexico (*ibid.*, § 143), Netherlands (*ibid.*, §§ 144–145), New Zealand (*ibid.*, § 147), Nicaragua (*ibid.*, § 148), Paraguay (*ibid.*, § 152), Peru (*ibid.*, § 153), Poland (*ibid.*, § 154), Romania (*ibid.*, § 155), Russia (*ibid.*, § 156), Slovenia (*ibid.*, § 158), Spain (*ibid.*, § 160), United Kingdom (*ibid.*, § 167), United States (*ibid.*, § 168), Uruguay (*ibid.*, § 169), Venezuela (*ibid.*, § 170) and Yugoslavia (*ibid.*, § 171); see also the draft legislation of Burundi (*ibid.*, § 115) and Trinidad and Tobago (*ibid.*, § 165).

[4] See, e.g., the practice of Cape Verde (*ibid.*, § 181), China (*ibid.*, § 183), Croatia (*ibid.*, § 185), France (*ibid.*, § 192), Germany (*ibid.*, § 194), Iran (*ibid.*, § 202), Pakistan (*ibid.*, § 215), United Arab Emirates (*ibid.*, § 219) and Yugoslavia (*ibid.*, §§ 237–239); UN Security Council, Res. 1265 (*ibid.*, § 244); UN General Assembly, Res. 47/147, 49/196 and 50/193 (*ibid.*, § 245); UN Commission on Human Rights, Res. 1984/1, 1985/1, 1986/1, 1987/2, 1988/1, 1989/2 and 1986/43 (*ibid.*, § 247), Res. 1994/72 (*ibid.*, § 248) and Res. 1998/70 (*ibid.*, § 249); UNESCO, General Conference, Res. 4.8 (*ibid.*, § 251); OIC, Contact Group on Jammu and Kashmir (*ibid.*, § 260) and Res. 1/5-EX (*ibid.*, § 261); Islamic Summit Conference, Ninth Session, Res. 25/8-C (IS) (*ibid.*, § 266).

[5] Lieber Code, Article 35 (*ibid.*, § 25); Brussels Declaration, Article 17 (*ibid.*, § 26); Oxford Manual, Article 34 (*ibid.*, § 27); Hague Regulations, Article 27 (*ibid.*, §§ 1–2).

[6] Report of the Commission on Responsibility (*ibid.*, § 28).

[7] See, e.g., the statements of Austria (*ibid.*, § 178), Egypt (*ibid.*, § 186), France (*ibid.*, § 189), Israel (*ibid.*, § 205), United Kingdom (*ibid.*, §§ 220 and 222–225), United States (*ibid.*, §§ 226 and 231–233) and Yugoslavia (*ibid.*, § 236).

[8] 27th International Conference of the Red Cross and Red Crescent, Plan of Action for the years 2000–2003 (adopted by consensus) (*ibid.*, § 265).

Property of great importance to the cultural heritage of every people

With respect to property of "great importance to the cultural heritage of every people", the Hague Convention for the Protection of Cultural Property has sought to reinforce its protection by encouraging the marking of such property with a blue-and-white shield,[9] but also by limiting the lawfulness of attacks to very exceptional situations where a waiver can be invoked in case of "imperative military necessity".[10]

At the time of writing, the Hague Convention was ratified by 111 States. The fundamental principles of protecting and preserving cultural property in the Convention are widely regarded as reflecting customary international law, as stated by the UNESCO General Conference and by States which are not party to the Convention.[11] The application of the Hague Convention under customary international law to non-international armed conflicts was recognised by the International Criminal Tribunal for the Former Yugoslavia in the *Tadić case* in 1995.[12]

Many military manuals specify the obligation to respect and protect property of great importance to the cultural heritage of every people.[13] These include manuals of States not, or not at the time, party to the Hague Convention.[14] Under the legislation of numerous States, it is an offence to attack property of great importance to the cultural heritage of every people.[15]

---

[9] Hague Convention for the Protection of Cultural Property, Articles 6 and 16.

[10] Hague Convention for the Protection of Cultural Property, Article 4(2) (cited in Vol. II, Ch. 12, § 7).

[11] UNESCO, General Conference, Res. 3.5 (*ibid.*, § 250); United States, *Annotated Supplement to the US Naval Handbook* (*ibid.*, § 103).

[12] ICTY, *Tadić case*, Interlocutory Appeal (*ibid.*, § 268).

[13] See, e.g., the military manuals of Argentina (*ibid.*, § 40), Australia (*ibid.*, §§ 41–42), Benin (*ibid.*, § 45), Canada (*ibid.*, §§ 50–51), Colombia (*ibid.*, § 52), Croatia (*ibid.*, §§ 54–55), France (*ibid.*, §§ 59–61), Germany (*ibid.*, §§ 62–63), Hungary (*ibid.*, § 64), Israel (*ibid.*, § 67), Italy (*ibid.*, §§ 68–69), Kenya (*ibid.*, § 70), South Korea (*ibid.*, § 72), Madagascar (*ibid.*, § 73), Netherlands (*ibid.*, §§ 76–77), New Zealand (*ibid.*, § 79), Philippines (*ibid.*, §§ 82–83), Russia (*ibid.*, § 84), South African (*ibid.*, § 86), Spain (*ibid.*, § 87), Sweden (*ibid.*, § 89), Switzerland (*ibid.*, §§ 90–91), Togo (*ibid.*, § 92) and United States (*ibid.*, § 103) and the reported practice of Israel (*ibid.*, § 66).

[14] See, e.g., the military manuals of Benin (*ibid.*, § 45), Colombia (*ibid.*, § 52), Croatia (*ibid.*, § 55), Kenya (*ibid.*, § 70), South Korea (*ibid.*, § 72), New Zealand (*ibid.*, § 79), Philippines (*ibid.*, §§ 82–83), Togo (*ibid.*, § 92), United Kingdom (*ibid.*, §§ 93–94) and United States (*ibid.*, § 103).

[15] See, e.g., the legislation of Armenia (*ibid.*, § 107), Australia (*ibid.*, § 108), Belarus (*ibid.*, § 111), Belgium (*ibid.*, § 112), Bosnia and Herzegovina (*ibid.*, § 113), Canada (*ibid.*, § 116), Colombia (*ibid.*, § 121), Cook Islands (*ibid.*, § 123), Croatia (*ibid.*, § 124), Cuba (*ibid.*, § 125), Cyprus (*ibid.*, § 126), Czech Republic (*ibid.*, § 127), Georgia (*ibid.*, § 131), Hungary (*ibid.*, § 133), Ireland (*ibid.*, § 134), Latvia (*ibid.*, § 139), Lithuania (*ibid.*, § 141), Netherlands (*ibid.*, § 145), New Zealand (*ibid.*, § 146), Niger (*ibid.*, § 150), Norway (*ibid.*, § 151), Poland (*ibid.*, § 154), Romania (*ibid.*, § 155), Russia (*ibid.*, § 156), Slovakia (*ibid.*, § 157), Slovenia (*ibid.*, § 158), Spain (*ibid.*, §§ 159–160), Sweden (*ibid.*, § 161), Switzerland (*ibid.*, § 162), Tajikistan (*ibid.*, § 164), United Kingdom (*ibid.*, § 166), Yugoslavia (*ibid.*, § 171) and Zimbabwe (*ibid.*, § 172); see also the draft legislation of Argentina (*ibid.*, § 106), El Salvador (*ibid.*, § 129), Jordan (*ibid.*, § 137), Lebanon (*ibid.*, § 140) and Nicaragua (*ibid.*, § 149).

Waiver in case of imperative military necessity

The Second Protocol to the Hague Convention for the Protection of Cultural Property, adopted by consensus in 1999, brings the Hague Convention up to date in the light of developments in international humanitarian law since 1954. It is significant in this respect that the Second Protocol has maintained the waiver in case of imperative military necessity, as requested by many States during the preparatory meetings, but has sought to clarify its meaning. It provides that a waiver on the basis of imperative military necessity may only be invoked when and for as long as: (1) the cultural property in question has, by its function, been made into a military objective; and (2) there is no feasible alternative to obtain a similar military advantage to that offered by attacking that objective.[16] The Second Protocol further requires that the existence of such necessity be established at a certain level of command and that in case of an attack, an effective advance warning be given whenever circumstances permit.[17] During the negotiation of the Second Protocol, this interpretation of the waiver in case of imperative military necessity was uncontroversial.

This rule should not be confused with the prohibition on attacking cultural property contained in Article 53(1) of Additional Protocol I and Article 16 of Additional Protocol II, which do not provide for a waiver in case of imperative military necessity.[18] As underlined by numerous statements at the Diplomatic Conference leading to the adoption of the Additional Protocols, these articles were meant to cover only a limited amount of very important cultural property, namely that which forms part of the cultural or spiritual heritage of "peoples" (i.e., mankind), while the scope of the Hague Convention is broader and covers property which forms part of the cultural heritage of "every people".[19] The property covered by the Additional Protocols must be of such importance that it will be recognised by everyone, even without being marked. At the Diplomatic Conference leading to the adoption of the Additional Protocols, several States indicated that notwithstanding the absence of a waiver, such highly important cultural property could become the object of attack in case it was used, illegally, for military purposes.[20]

---

[16] Second Protocol to the Hague Convention for the Protection of Cultural Property, Article 6(a) (*ibid.*, § 21).

[17] Second Protocol to the Hague Convention for the Protection of Cultural Property, Article 6(c) and (d) (*ibid.*, § 21).

[18] Additional Protocol I, Article 53(1) (adopted by consensus) (*ibid.*, § 10); Additional Protocol II, Article 16 (adopted by 35 votes in favour, 15 against and 32 abstentions) (*ibid.*, § 18).

[19] See, e.g., the statements of Australia (*ibid.*, § 175), Canada (*ibid.*, § 180), Federal Republic of Germany (*ibid.*, § 193), Netherlands (*ibid.*, §§ 210–211), United Kingdom (*ibid.*, § 220) and United States (*ibid.*, § 227).

[20] See, e.g., the statements of the Federal Republic of Germany (*ibid.*, § 193), Netherlands (*ibid.*, § 210), United Kingdom (*ibid.*, § 220) and United States (*ibid.*, § 227).

Rule 39. The use of property of great importance to the cultural heritage of every people for purposes which are likely to expose it to destruction or damage is prohibited, unless imperatively required by military necessity.

Practice

Volume II, Chapter 12, Section B.

Summary

State practice establishes this rule as a norm of customary international law applicable in both international and non-international armed conflicts.

International and non-international armed conflicts

This rule is contained in Article 4 of the Hague Convention for the Protection of Cultural Property, a provision applicable to both international and non-international armed conflicts.[21] The fundamental principles of protecting and preserving cultural property in the Hague Convention are widely regarded as reflecting customary international law, as stated by the UNESCO General Conference and by States which are not party to the Convention.[22] Its application under customary international law to non-international armed conflicts was recognised by the International Criminal Tribunal for the Former Yugoslavia in the *Tadić case*.[23] In addition, this rule is contained in other instruments pertaining also to non-international armed conflicts.[24]

The prohibition on using property of great importance to the cultural heritage of every people for purposes which are likely to expose it to destruction or damage unless imperatively required by military necessity is set forth in numerous military manuals.[25] These include manuals of States not party to the Hague Convention.[26] In addition, several military manuals state that the use of a privileged building for improper purposes constitutes a war crime.[27]

---

[21] Hague Convention for the Protection of Cultural Property, Article 4 (*ibid.*, § 282) and Article 19 (*ibid.*, § 283).

[22] See, e.g., UNESCO General Conference, Res. 3.5 (*ibid.*, § 347) and United States, *Annotated Supplement to the Naval Handbook* (*ibid.*, § 329).

[23] ICTY, *Tadić case*, Interlocutory Appeal (*ibid.*, § 351).

[24] See, e.g., UN Secretary-General's Bulletin, Section 6.6 (*ibid.*, § 300).

[25] See, e.g., the military manuals of Argentina (*ibid.*, § 301), Australia (*ibid.*, § 302), Canada (*ibid.*, §§ 303–304), Croatia (*ibid.*, § 305), Germany (*ibid.*, §§ 306–307), Israel (*ibid.*, § 308), Italy (*ibid.*, §§ 309–310), Kenya (*ibid.*, § 311), Netherlands (*ibid.*, §§ 312–313), New Zealand (*ibid.*, § 314), Nigeria (*ibid.*, § 316), Russia (*ibid.*, § 317), South Africa (*ibid.*, § 318), Spain (*ibid.*, § 319), Sweden (*ibid.*, § 320), Switzerland (*ibid.*, §§ 321–322) and United States (*ibid.*, §§ 324–329).

[26] See, e.g., the military manuals of Kenya (*ibid.*, § 311), South Africa (*ibid.*, § 318) and United States (*ibid.*, §§ 324–329).

[27] See, e.g., the military manuals of Canada (*ibid.*, § 303), New Zealand (*ibid.*, § 314), Nigeria (*ibid.*, § 315), United Kingdom (*ibid.*, § 323) and United States (*ibid.*, §§ 324–325 and 327).

There are also specific references in State practice to the prohibition on using cultural property in order to shield military operations.[28]

Waiver in case of imperative military necessity

The Second Protocol to the Hague Convention for the Protection of Cultural Property has clarified the meaning of the waiver in case of imperative military necessity with regard to the use of cultural property. It considers that a waiver on the basis of imperative military necessity may only be invoked to use cultural property for purposes which are likely to expose it to destruction or damage "when and for as long as no choice is possible between such use of the cultural property and another feasible method for obtaining a similar military advantage".[29] The Protocol further requires that the existence of such necessity be established at a certain level of command.[30] At the negotiation of the Second Protocol, this interpretation did not give rise to any controversy.

This rule should not be confused with the prohibition on using cultural property contained in Article 53(2) of Additional Protocol I and Article 16 of Additional Protocol II, which do not provide for a waiver in case of imperative military necessity. As underlined by numerous statements at the Diplomatic Conference leading to the adoption of the Additional Protocols, these articles were meant to cover only a limited amount of very important cultural property, namely that which forms part of the cultural or spiritual heritage of "peoples" (i.e., mankind), while the scope of the Hague Convention is broader and covers property which forms part of the cultural heritage of "every people".[31] The property covered by the Additional Protocols must be of such importance that it will be recognised by everyone, even without being marked.

Rule 40. Each party to the conflict must protect cultural property:

A. **All seizure of or destruction or wilful damage done to institutions dedicated to religion, charity, education, the arts and sciences, historic monuments and works of art and science is prohibited.**

B. **Any form of theft, pillage or misappropriation of, and any acts of vandalism directed against, property of great importance to the cultural heritage of every people is prohibited.**

---

[28] See, e.g., the military manual of Israel (*ibid.*, § 308); the statements of the United States (*ibid.*, §§ 345–346); OSCE, Europe Spillover Monitoring Mission to Skopje, Press Release (*ibid.*, § 349).

[29] Second Protocol to the Hague Convention for the Protection of Cultural Property, Article 6(b) (*ibid.*, § 291).

[30] Second Protocol to the Hague Convention for the Protection of Cultural Property, Article 6(c) (*ibid.*, § 21).

[31] See, e.g., the statements of Australia (*ibid.*, § 175), Canada (*ibid.*, § 180), Federal Republic of Germany (*ibid.*, § 193), Netherlands (*ibid.*, §§ 210–211), United Kingdom (*ibid.*, § 220) and United States (*ibid.*, § 227).

Practice

Volume II, Chapter 12, Section C.

Summary

State practice establishes this rule as a norm of customary international law applicable in both international and non-international armed conflicts.

Seizure of or destruction or wilful damage to cultural property

Article 56 of the Hague Regulations prohibits "all seizure of, and destruction, or intentional damage done to" institutions dedicated to religion, charity, education, the arts and sciences, historic monuments and works of art and science.[32] The violation of this provision was included among the violations of the laws and customs of war in the Statute of the International Criminal Tribunal for the Former Yugoslavia over which the Tribunal has jurisdiction.[33] Under the Statute of the International Criminal Court, destruction of buildings dedicated to religion, education, arts, science or charitable purposes and historic monuments and destruction and seizure that is not imperatively demanded by the necessities of the conflict constitute war crimes in both international and non-international armed conflicts.[34]

Many military manuals incorporate this provision.[35] Under the legislation of many States, it is an offence to seize, destroy or wilfully damage cultural property.[36] After the Second World War, France's Permanent Military Tribunal at Metz in the *Lingenfelder case* in 1947 and the US Military Tribunal at Nuremberg in the *Von Leeb (The High Command Trial) case* in 1948 and the *Weizsaecker case* in 1949 convicted the accused of seizure and destruction of cultural property.[37]

---

[32] Hague Regulations, Article 56 (*ibid.*, §§ 355–356).

[33] ICTY Statute, Article 3(d) (*ibid.*, § 366).

[34] ICC Statute, Article 8(2)(b)(ix) (*ibid.*, § 19) and Article 8(2)(b)(xiii) (cited in Vol. II, Ch. 16, § 55), Article 8(2)(e)(iv) (cited in Vol. II, Ch. 12, § 19) and Article 8(2)(e)(xii) (cited in Vol. II, Ch. 16, § 56).

[35] See, e.g., the military manuals of Argentina (cited in Vol. II, Ch. 12, § 371), Australia (*ibid.*, § 372), Canada (*ibid.*, §§ 373–374), Germany (*ibid.*, §§ 375–376), Italy (*ibid.*, § 378), Netherlands (*ibid.*, §§ 379–380), New Zealand (*ibid.*, § 381), Nigeria (*ibid.*, §§ 382–383), Sweden (*ibid.*, § 384), United Kingdom (*ibid.*, § 386) and United States (*ibid.*, §§ 387–388).

[36] See, e.g., the legislation of Bulgaria (*ibid.*, § 389), Estonia (*ibid.*, § 392), Italy (*ibid.*, § 393), Luxembourg (*ibid.*, § 395), Netherlands (*ibid.*, § 396), Nicaragua (*ibid.*, § 397), Poland (*ibid.*, § 399), Portugal (*ibid.*, § 400), Romania (*ibid.*, § 401), Spain (*ibid.*, § 402) and Switzerland (*ibid.*, § 403); see also the draft legislation of El Salvador (*ibid.*, § 391) and Nicaragua (*ibid.*, § 398).

[37] France, Permanent Military Tribunal at Metz, *Lingenfelder case* (*ibid.*, § 405); United States, Military Tribunal at Nuremberg, *Von Leeb (The High Command Trial) case* (*ibid.*, § 406) and *Weizsaecker case* (*ibid.*, § 407).

Theft, pillage, misappropriation and acts of vandalism

Theft, pillage, misappropriation and acts of vandalism are prohibited in Article 4 of the Hague Convention for the Protection of Cultural Property, a provision applicable to both international and non-international armed conflicts.[38] The fundamental principles of protecting and preserving cultural property in the Hague Convention are widely regarded as reflecting customary international law, as stated by the UNESCO General Conference and by States which are not party to the Convention.[39] Its application under customary international law to non-international armed conflicts was recognised by the International Criminal Tribunal for the Former Yugoslavia in the *Tadić case* in 1995.[40] In addition, this rule is contained in other instruments pertaining also to non-international armed conflicts.[41]

The obligation to respect cultural property is set forth in numerous military manuals.[42] Failure to respect cultural property is an offence under the legislation of numerous States.[43] The rule is also supported by official statements made by States not, or not at the time, party to the Hague Convention.[44] The prohibition of pillage of cultural property is a specific application of the general prohibition of pillage (see Rule 52).

No official contrary practice was found. Violations of this rule have generally been denounced by States.[45] The United Nations and other international organisations have also condemned such acts. In 1998, for example, the UN Commission on Human Rights expressed its deep concern over reports of the destruction and looting of the cultural and historical heritage of Afghanistan, a State not party to the Hague Convention for the Protection of Cultural Property, and urged all the Afghan parties to protect and safeguard such heritage.[46] In 2001, there was widespread condemnation, in particular by UNESCO, of the Taliban

---

[38] Hague Convention for the Protection of Cultural Property, Article 4 (*ibid.*, § 357) and Article 19 (*ibid.*, § 358).

[39] See, e.g., UNESCO General Conference Res. 3.5 (*ibid.*, § 419); United States, *Annotated Supplement to the Naval Handbook* (*ibid.*, § 388).

[40] ICTY, *Tadić case*, Interlocutory Appeal (*ibid.*, § 428).

[41] See, e.g., UN Secretary-General's Bulletin, Section 6.6 (*ibid.*, § 370).

[42] See, e.g., the military manuals of Argentina (*ibid.*, § 371), Australia (*ibid.*, § 372), Canada (*ibid.*, §§ 373–374), Germany (*ibid.*, §§ 375–376), Israel (*ibid.*, § 377), Italy (*ibid.*, § 378), Netherlands (*ibid.*, §§ 379–380), New Zealand (*ibid.*, § 381), Nigeria (*ibid.*, §§ 382–383), Sweden (*ibid.*, § 384), Switzerland (*ibid.*, § 385), United Kingdom (*ibid.*, § 386) and United States (*ibid.*, §§ 387–388).

[43] See, e.g., the legislation of Bulgaria (*ibid.*, § 389), China (*ibid.*, § 390), Estonia (*ibid.*, § 392), Italy (*ibid.*, § 393), Lithuania (*ibid.*, § 394), Luxembourg (*ibid.*, § 395), Netherlands (*ibid.*, § 396), Nicaragua (*ibid.*, § 397), Poland (*ibid.*, § 399), Portugal (*ibid.*, § 400), Romania (*ibid.*, § 401), Spain (*ibid.*, § 402), Switzerland (*ibid.*, § 403) and Ukraine (*ibid.*, § 404); see also the draft legislation of El Salvador (*ibid.*, § 391) and Nicaragua (*ibid.*, § 398).

[44] See, e.g., the statements of Azerbaijan (*ibid.*, § 408), China (*ibid.*, §§ 410–411) and United States (*ibid.*, § 414).

[45] See, e.g., the statements of Azerbaijan (*ibid.*, § 408), China (*ibid.*, §§ 410–411), Iran (*ibid.*, § 412) and United States (*ibid.*, § 414).

[46] UN Commission on Human Rights, Res. 1998/70 (*ibid.*, § 418).

regime's decision to destroy a dozen ancient statues belonging to the Afghan National Museum and subsequently to destroy the Buddhas of Bamiyan.[47]

Rule 41. The occupying power must prevent the illicit export of cultural property from occupied territory and must return illicitly exported property to the competent authorities of the occupied territory.

Practice

Volume II, Chapter 12, Section D.

Summary

State practice establishes this rule as a norm of customary international law applicable in international armed conflicts.

Export of cultural property from occupied territory

The obligation to prevent the exportation of cultural property from occupied territory is set forth in paragraph 1 of the First Protocol to the Hague Convention for the Protection of Cultural Property, to which 88 States are party, including States specially affected by occupation.[48] This rule is also contained in Article 2(2) of the Convention on the Illicit Trade in Cultural Property, under which States undertake to oppose the illicit import, export and transfer of ownership of cultural property "with the means at their disposal, and particularly by removing their causes, putting a stop to current practices, and by helping to make the necessary reparations".[49] Article 11 of the Convention states that "the export and transfer of ownership of cultural property under compulsion arising directly or indirectly from the occupation of a country by a foreign power shall be regarded as illicit".[50] The Convention has been ratified by 104 States, 37 of which are not party to the First Protocol to the Hague Convention for the Protection of Cultural Property. Since 88 States are party to the latter, this means that a total of 125 States have adhered to a treaty obligation to respect this rule. In addition, Article 9(1) of the Second Protocol to the Hague Convention requires that an occupying power prohibit and prevent "any illicit export, other removal or transfer of ownership of cultural property", while Article 21 requires States to suppress these violations.[51] The inclusion of these rules in

---

[47] See, e.g., UNESCO, Press Release No. 2001–27 (*ibid.*, § 421) and Press Release No. 2001–38 (*ibid.*, § 422).

[48] First Protocol to the Hague Convention for the Protection of Cultural Property, para. 1 (*ibid.*, § 431).

[49] Convention on the Illicit Trade in Cultural Property, Article 2(2) (*ibid.*, § 455).

[50] Convention on the Illicit Trade in Cultural Property, Article 11 (*ibid.*, § 433).

[51] Second Protocol to the Hague Convention for the Protection of Cultural Property, Article 9(1) (*ibid.*, § 434) and Article 21 (*ibid.*, § 435).

the Second Protocol during the negotiations leading to its adoption was uncontroversial. In the London Declaration in 1943, the Allied governments warned that they would regard any transfer of property rights, including of cultural property, as illegal.[52]

Other practice supporting this rule includes military manuals, national legislation and official statements.[53] While this practice concerns States party to the First Protocol to the Hague Convention for the Protection of Cultural Property, it can nevertheless be concluded that the prohibition on exporting cultural property is customary because, in addition to support for this rule found in the practice mentioned above, this obligation is inherent in the obligation to respect cultural property, and particularly in the prohibition on seizing cultural property (see Rule 40). If cultural property may not be seized, then *a fortiori* it may not be exported.

No official contrary practice was found.

Return of cultural property exported from occupied territory

Several treaties concluded after the Second World War dealt with the restoration of cultural property exported during occupation. Under the Treaty of Peace between the Allied and Associated Powers and Italy concluded in 1947, Italy was obliged to return cultural property to Yugoslavia and Ethiopia.[54] Under the Convention on the Settlement of Matters Arising out of the War and the Occupation adopted in 1952, Germany was to set up an agency to search for, recover and restitute cultural property taken from occupied territory during the Second World War.[55] The obligation to return cultural property which has been illegally exported from occupied territory is set forth in Paragraph 3 of the First Protocol to the Hague Convention for the Protection of Cultural Property, which has been ratified by 88 States.[56]

Paragraph 3 of the First Protocol to the Hague Convention is formulated more generally as applicable to all parties to the Protocol and not only to the occupying power.[57] However, no practice was found on the obligation of third parties to

---

[52] London Declaration (*ibid.*, § 437).
[53] See, e.g., Germany, *Military Manual* (*ibid.*, § 440); Luxembourg, *Law on the Repression of War Crimes* (*ibid.*, § 441); Israel, Military Court of Hebron, judgements under Jordanian law (*ibid.*, § 442); statements of Iraq (*ibid.*, § 443) and Kuwait (*ibid.*, § 468); Islamic Summit Conference, Ninth Session, Res. 25/8-C (IS) (*ibid.*, § 446).
[54] Treaty of Peace between the Allied and Associated Powers and Italy, Article 12 (*ibid.*, § 472) and Article 37 (*ibid.*, § 450).
[55] Convention on the Settlement of Matters Arising out of the War and the Occupation, Chapter Five, Article 1, para. 1 (*ibid.*, § 452).
[56] First Protocol to the Hague Convention for the Protection of Cultural Property, para. 3 (*ibid.*, § 453).
[57] See First Protocol to the Hague Convention for the Protection of Cultural Property, para. 3, which states that "each High Contracting Party undertakes to return, at the close of hostilities, to the competent authorities of the territory previously occupied, cultural property which is in its territory, if such property has been exported in contravention of the principle laid down in the first paragraph. Such property shall never be retained as war reparations." (*ibid.*, § 453).

return cultural property illicitly exported and present on their territory. Hence this rule is formulated more narrowly as applicable, at least, to the occupying power itself, which having failed in its duty to prevent the exportation must remedy this failure by returning the property. According to paragraph 4 of the Protocol, possible holders of the property in good faith must be compensated.[58]

The obligation to return exported cultural property is also recognised in many official statements, including by Germany in relation to its occupation during the Second World War and by Iraq in relation to its occupation of Kuwait.[59] In the context of the Gulf War, the UN Security Council urged Iraq on several occasions to return to Kuwait all property seized.[60] In 2000, the UN Secretary-General noted that a substantial quantity of property had been returned since the end of the Gulf War but that many items remained to be returned. He stressed that "priority should be given to the return by Iraq of the Kuwaiti archives...and museum items".[61] While this practice concerns States party to the First Protocol to the Hague Convention for the Protection of Cultural Property, it can nevertheless be concluded that the obligation to return illicitly exported cultural property is customary because, in addition to support for this rule found in the practice mentioned above, it is also inherent in the obligation to respect cultural property, and particularly in the prohibition on seizing and pillaging cultural property (see Rule 40). If cultural property may not be seized or pillaged, then *a fortiori* it may not be held back in case it has been illegally exported. Restitution of illegally exported property would also constitute an appropriate form of reparation (see Rule 150).

No official contrary practice was found.

Retention of cultural property as war reparations

Paragraph 3 of the First Protocol to the Hague Convention for the Protection of Cultural Property specifies that cultural property shall never be retained as war reparations.[62] In 1997, however, Russia's Law on Removed Cultural Property declared cultural property brought into the USSR by way of exercise of its right to compensatory restitution pursuant to orders of the Soviet authorities to be federal property of the Russian Federation.[63] In 1999, Russia's Constitutional Court upheld the constitutionality of this law insofar as it dealt with "the rights of Russia to cultural property imported into Russia from former enemy states by way of compensatory restitution". In the Court's opinion:

[58] First Protocol to the Hague Convention for the Protection of Cultural Property, para. 4 (*ibid.*, § 453).
[59] See, e.g., the statements of Germany (*ibid.*, § 460) and Iraq (*ibid.*, §§ 464–465).
[60] UN Security Council, Res. 686 and 687 (*ibid.*, § 472) and Res. 1284 (*ibid.*, § 473).
[61] UN Secretary-General, Second report pursuant to paragraph 14 of resolution 1284 (1999) (*ibid.*, § 477).
[62] First Protocol to the Hague Convention for the Protection of Cultural Property, para. 3 (*ibid.*, § 453).
[63] Russia, *Law on Removed Cultural Property* (*ibid.*, § 458).

The obligation of former enemy states to compensate their victims in the form of common restitution and compensatory restitution is based on the well-established principle of international law recognised well before World War II, concerning international legal responsibility of an aggressor state.[64]

Germany has on several occasions objected to this decision and stated that "thefts and destruction of cultural property by the Nazi regime as well as the removal of cultural property by the Soviet Union during and after the Second World War were breaches of international law".[65] It should be stressed, however, that the Russian law applies to acts which occurred before the First Protocol to the Hague Convention for the Protection of Cultural Property entered into force.

---

[64] Russia, Constitutional Court, *Law on Removed Cultural Property case* (*ibid.*, § 459).
[65] See, e.g., the statements of Germany (*ibid.*, §§ 461–462).

WORKS AND INSTALLATIONS CONTAINING DANGEROUS FORCES

Rule 42. Particular care must be taken if works and installations containing dangerous forces, namely dams, dykes and nuclear electrical generating stations, and other installations located at or in their vicinity are attacked, in order to avoid the release of dangerous forces and consequent severe losses among the civilian population.

Practice

Volume II, Chapter 13.

Summary

State practice establishes this rule as a norm of customary international law applicable in both international and non-international armed conflicts.

International and non-international armed conflicts

When works and installations containing dangerous forces are civilian objects, they may not be made the object of attack (see Rule 7). These works and installations may only be attacked in case they qualify as military objectives (see Rule 7). Practice shows that States are conscious of the high risk of severe incidental losses which can result from attacks against such works and installations when they constitute military objectives. Consequently, they recognise that particular care must be taken in case of attack.

The detailed rules contained in Article 56 of Additional Protocol I, as well as in Article 15 of Additional Protocol II, were elaborated on the basis of this recognition.[1] These rules are set forth in numerous military manuals.[2] Attacks against works and installations which result in severe losses are offences under

---

[1] Additional Protocol I, Article 56 (adopted by consensus) (cited in Vol. II, Ch. 13, § 1); Additional Protocol II, Article 15 (adopted by consensus) (*ibid.*, § 5).

[2] See, e.g., the military manuals of Argentina (*ibid.*, § 11), Australia (*ibid.*, § 12), Belgium (*ibid.*, § 14), Benin (*ibid.*, § 15), Cameroon (*ibid.*, § 16), Canada (*ibid.*, § 17), France (*ibid.*, §§ 21–23), Germany (*ibid.*, § 24), Kenya (*ibid.*, § 29), Netherlands (*ibid.*, §§ 32–33), New Zealand (*ibid.*, § 34), South Africa (*ibid.*, § 36), Spain (*ibid.*, § 37), Switzerland (*ibid.*, §§ 38–39), Togo (*ibid.*, § 40), United Kingdom (*ibid.*, § 41) and Yugoslavia (*ibid.*, § 46).

the legislation of a number of States.[3] Military manuals and legislation of a number of other States prohibit attacks against works and installations as such.[4]

Upon ratification of Additional Protocol I, France and the United Kingdom declared that they cannot grant "absolute" protection to works and installations containing dangerous forces which are military objectives. They recognise, however, the special peril inherent in any attack against works and installations containing dangerous forces as they require, respectively, that every "necessary" and every "due" precaution be taken in the exceptional situation where such works and installations are to be attacked, in order to avoid severe incidental losses among the civilian population.[5] The Colombian government similarly expressed the need for restraint and precaution in a statement with respect to an attack by government troops on a dam in order to dislodge guerrillas.[6]

Israel and the United States stress that the proportionality test is important in assessing the legality of an attack against works and installations containing dangerous forces which are military objectives.[7] While an assessment under the principle of proportionality must be made on a case-by-case basis, this position equally reflects sensitivity to the severe losses that may ensue among the civilian population when dangerous forces of such works and installations are released. "Launching an attack against works or installations containing dangerous forces in the knowledge that such attack will cause excessive loss of life, injury to civilians or damage to civilians objects" constitutes a grave breach of Additional Protocol I.[8] Such attacks are also offences under the legislation of many States.[9]

---

[3] See, e.g., the legislation of Azerbaijan (*ibid.*, § 51), Hungary (*ibid.*, § 65) ("which result in heavy damage"), Lithuania (*ibid.*, § 69) ("knowing that it might have extremely grave consequences"), Slovenia (*ibid.*, § 76) ("an attack on which would be particularly dangerous") and Spain (*ibid.*, § 77) ("considerable losses"); see also the draft legislation of Argentina (*ibid.*, § 47), El Salvador (*ibid.*, § 61), Jordan (*ibid.*, § 67) ("widespread loss of life or injury among the civilian population and damage to civilian property") and Nicaragua (*ibid.*, § 72).

[4] See, e.g., the military manuals of Croatia (*ibid.*, § 19), France (*ibid.*, §§ 21–22), Italy (*ibid.*, §§ 27–28), South Korea (*ibid.*, § 30) and Madagascar (*ibid.*, § 31) and the legislation of Belgium (*ibid.*, § 53), Bosnia and Herzegovina (*ibid.*, § 54), Colombia (*ibid.*, § 56) ("without any justification based on imperative military necessity"), Croatia (*ibid.*, § 58), Czech Republic (*ibid.*, § 60) (intentional destruction or damage), Estonia (*ibid.*, § 62), Georgia (*ibid.*, § 63) ("in the knowledge that it will cause loss"), Germany (*ibid.*, § 64), Slovakia (*ibid.*, § 75) (intentional destruction or damage), Tajikistan (*ibid.*, § 79) and Yugoslavia (*ibid.*, § 81).

[5] France, Reservations and declarations made upon ratification of Additional Protocol I (*ibid.*, § 4); United Kingdom, Reservations and declarations made upon ratification of Additional Protocol I (*ibid.*, § 3).

[6] Colombia, Comments of the Office of the Human Rights Adviser of the Presidency (*ibid.*, § 88).

[7] Report on the Practice of Israel (*ibid.*, § 98); United States, *Air Force Pamphlet* (*ibid.*, § 42), *Naval Handbook* (*ibid.*, § 44), *Annotated Supplement to the Naval Handbook* (*ibid.*, § 45) and Remarks of the Deputy Legal Adviser of the Department of State (*ibid.*, § 108).

[8] Additional Protocol I, Article 85(3)(c) (*ibid.*, § 2).

[9] See, e.g., the legislation of Armenia (*ibid.*, § 48), Australia (*ibid.*, §§ 49–50), Belarus (*ibid.*, § 52), Belgium (*ibid.*, § 53), Canada (*ibid.*, § 55), Cook Islands (*ibid.*, § 57), Cyprus (*ibid.*, § 59), Ireland (*ibid.*, § 66), Netherlands (*ibid.*, § 70), New Zealand (*ibid.*, § 71), Niger (*ibid.*, § 73), Norway

States' sensitivity to the possibility of the release of dangerous forces is under-scored by the fact that when attacks against such works and installations have been carried out in recent decades, the attacker stressed they were executed with the greatest care possible.[10] It is further underlined by the condemnations of such attacks, denials of such attacks and generally by the restraint shown by States with respect to attacks against works and installations containing dangerous forces.[11]

It appears, therefore, that attacks could be envisaged in situations where they are indispensable to obtain an important military advantage, which could not be obtained in any other way, and all necessary precautions are taken. The importance of such a decision, given the high risk of severe incidental losses, is illustrated by the position taken by the United Kingdom and the United States that a decision to attack a work or installation containing dangerous forces has to be taken at, respectively, "a high level of command" and "at appropriately high political levels".[12]

State practice does not see this rule as a one-sided requirement. The defender equally has an obligation to preserve or enhance the protection of works and installations containing dangerous forces by taking all feasible precautions against attacks: the works and installations should not be used in direct support of military action; military objectives should not be located at or in the vicinity of such works and installations; and such works and installations should never be used to shield military operations.[13]

Belligerent reprisals against works and installations containing dangerous forces are discussed in Chapter 41.

Scope of application of the rule

The Additional Protocols have limited this rule to dams, dykes and nuclear electrical generating stations.[14] Inclusion of other works and installations con-taining dangerous forces could not be agreed upon at the Diplomatic Con-ference leading to the adoption of the Additional Protocols. However, the

---

(*ibid.*, § 74), Sweden (*ibid.*, § 78), United Kingdom (*ibid.*, § 80) and Zimbabwe (*ibid.*, § 82); see also the draft legislation of Lebanon (*ibid.*, § 68).

[10] See, e.g., United Kingdom, Statement by the Secretary of Defence before the Defence Committee (with respect to the Gulf War) (*ibid.*, § 105) and the practice of the United States with respect to the Vietnam War, reported in W. Hays Parks, "Air War and the Law of War" (*ibid.*, § 107).

[11] See, e.g., the military manuals of the United States (*ibid.*, § 45), the statements of China (*ibid.*, § 87), Iran (*ibid.*, § 95), Iraq (*ibid.*, §§ 96–97) and United Kingdom (*ibid.*, § 104) and the reported practice of Pakistan (*ibid.*, § 101).

[12] United Kingdom, Reservations and declarations made upon ratification of Additional Protocol I (*ibid.*, § 3); United States, *Air Force Pamphlet* (*ibid.*, § 42).

[13] See the practice cited in *ibid.*, §§ 129–153.

[14] Additional Protocol I, Article 56 (adopted by consensus) (*ibid.*, § 1); Additional Protocol II, Article 15 (adopted by consensus) (*ibid.*, § 5).

considerations explained above should equally apply to other installations, such as chemical plants and petroleum refineries. The fact that attacks on such installations may cause severe damage to the civilian population and the natural environment implies that the decision to attack such installations, in case they become military objectives, requires that all necessary precautions be taken when attacking them.

THE NATURAL ENVIRONMENT

Rule 43. The general principles on the conduct of hostilities apply to the natural environment:

A. No part of the natural environment may be attacked, unless it is a military objective.

B. Destruction of any part of the natural environment is prohibited, unless required by imperative military necessity.

C. Launching an attack against a military objective which may be expected to cause incidental damage to the environment which would be excessive in relation to the concrete and direct military advantage anticipated is prohibited.

Practice

Volume II, Chapter 14, Section A.

Summary

State practice establishes this rule as a norm of customary international law applicable in both international and non-international armed conflicts.

Principle of distinction

The rule that it is prohibited to attack any part of the natural environment unless it is a military objective is based on the general requirement that a distinction be made between military objectives and civilian objects (see Rule 7). This rule is reflected in Protocol III to the Convention on Certain Conventional Weapons, which provides that "it is prohibited to make forests or other kinds of plant cover the object of attack by incendiary weapons except when such natural elements are used to cover, conceal or camouflage combatants or other military objectives, or are themselves military objectives".[1] The military manuals and official statements which consider that an area of land may be a military objective if it meets the required conditions also reflect this.[2]

---

[1] Protocol III to the CCW, Article 2(4) (cited in Vol. II, Ch. 30, § 110).

[2] See, e.g., the statements of Belgium (cited in Vol. II, Ch. 2, § 622), Canada (*ibid.*, §§ 597 and 623), Federal Republic of Germany (*ibid.*, §§ 597 and 624), France (*ibid.*, § 598), Italy (*ibid.*, § 597),

The application of the principle of distinction to the natural environment is set forth in the Guidelines on the Protection of the Environment in Times of Armed Conflict.[3] The UN General Assembly has invited all States to disseminate these Guidelines widely and to give due consideration to the possibility of incorporating them into their military manuals and other instructions addressed to their military personnel.[4] The application of the principle of distinction to the natural environment is also supported by military manuals and official statements.[5] The Final Declaration adopted by the International Conference for the Protection of War Victims in 1993 urged States to reaffirm and ensure respect for international humanitarian law protecting the natural environment against "attacks on the environment as such".[6]

The principle of distinction, which is applicable in international and non-international armed conflicts (see Rule 7), applies equally in relation to the environment. The ICRC made such a statement of principle in 1993 in a report submitted to the UN General Assembly on the protection of the environment in time of armed conflict.[7] This assertion was uncontested.

Destruction of property not justified by military necessity

According to State practice, the prohibition on destroying or seizing the property of an adversary, unless required by imperative military necessity, (see Rule 50) applies equally to the natural environment. The applicability of this prohibition to the natural environment is set forth in the Guidelines on the Protection of the Environment in Times of Armed Conflict.[8] This is supported by military manuals, national legislation and official statements.[9]

In its advisory opinion in the *Nuclear Weapons case* in 1996, the International Court of Justice stated that "respect for the environment is one of the

Netherlands (*ibid.*, §§ 597, 599 and 625), New Zealand (*ibid.*, § 597), Pakistan (*ibid.*, § 599), Spain (*ibid.*, § 597), United Kingdom (*ibid.*, §§ 597, 599 and 626) and United States (*ibid.*, §§ 599 and 627–628) and the military manuals of Australia (*ibid.*, § 601), Belgium (*ibid.*, §§ 602–604), Benin (*ibid.*, § 605), Ecuador (*ibid.*, § 608), France (*ibid.*, § 609), Italy (*ibid.*, §§ 610–611), Madagascar (*ibid.*, § 612), Netherlands (*ibid.*, § 613), New Zealand (*ibid.*, § 614), Spain (*ibid.*, § 615), Sweden (*ibid.*, § 616), Togo (*ibid.*, § 617), United Kingdom (*ibid.*, § 618) and United States (*ibid.*, § 619).

[3] Guidelines on the Protection of the Environment in Times of Armed Conflict, para. 4 (cited in Vol. II, Ch. 14, § 5).

[4] UN General Assembly, Res. 49/50 (adopted by consensus) (*ibid.*, § 56); see also Res. 51/157, Annex (*ibid.*, § 57).

[5] See, e.g., Australia, *Defence Force Manual* (*ibid.*, § 8); the statements of Canada (*ibid.*, § 37), Iran (*ibid.*, § 41), Marshall Islands (*ibid.*, § 45), Russia (*ibid.*, § 47) and United States (*ibid.*, §§ 50 and 53).

[6] International Conference for the Protection of War Victims, Final Declaration (*ibid.*, § 61).

[7] ICRC, Report on the protection of the environment in time of armed conflict (*ibid.*, § 67).

[8] Guidelines on the Protection of the Environment in Times of Armed Conflict, paras. 8 and 9 (*ibid.*, § 5).

[9] See, e.g., the military manuals of Australia (*ibid.*, § 8) and United States (*ibid.*, § 11), the legislation of Nicaragua (*ibid.*, § 22) and Spain (*ibid.*, § 25) and the statements of Australia (*ibid.*, § 30), Austria (*ibid.*, § 33), Canada (*ibid.*, § 36), Iran (*ibid.*, §§ 41–42) and United States (*ibid.*, §§ 50 and 52–53); see also Report of an expert meeting on the protection of the environment in time of armed conflict (*ibid.*, § 60).

elements that go to assessing whether an action is in conformity with the principle of necessity".[10] The Committee Established to Review the NATO Bombing Campaign Against the Federal Republic of Yugoslavia was of the view that the environmental impact of that bombing campaign was "best considered from the underlying principles of the law of armed conflicts such as necessity and proportionality".[11]

Furthermore, under the Fourth Geneva Convention, extensive destruction of property "not justified by military necessity and carried out unlawfully and wantonly" constitutes a grave breach.[12] This rule is restated in other instruments with respect to the natural environment.[13] It is also applied to the natural environment in a number of official statements.[14] In a resolution on the protection of the environment in times of armed conflict in 1992, the UN General Assembly stressed that "destruction of the environment, not justified by military necessity and carried out wantonly, is clearly contrary to existing international law".[15] The Final Declaration adopted by the International Conference for the Protection of War Victims in 1993 urged States to reaffirm and ensure respect for international humanitarian law protecting the natural environment against "wanton destruction causing serious environmental damage".[16]

The prohibition of unnecessary destruction of property is applicable in international and non-international armed conflicts (see Rule 50) also in relation to the environment. The ICRC made such a statement of principle in 1993 in a report submitted to the UN General Assembly on the protection of the environment in time of armed conflict.[17] This assertion was uncontested.

Principle of proportionality

Practice shows a general acceptance of the principle that incidental damage affecting the natural environment must not be excessive in relation to the military advantage anticipated from an attack on a military objective. This is set forth in the Guidelines on the Protection of the Environment in Times of Armed Conflict and in the San Remo Manual on Naval Warfare.[18]

---

[10] ICJ, *Nuclear Weapons case*, Advisory Opinion (*ibid.*, § 62).
[11] Committee Established to Review the NATO Bombing Campaign Against the Federal Republic of Yugoslavia, Final Report (*ibid.*, § 63).
[12] Fourth Geneva Convention, Article 147 (cited in Vol. II, Ch. 16, § 53).
[13] See, e.g., Agenda 21, para. 39.6 (cited in Vol. II, Ch. 14, § 3); San Remo Manual, para. 44 (*ibid.*, § 4); Guidelines on the Protection of the Environment in Times of Armed Conflict, para. 8 (*ibid.*, § 5).
[14] See, e.g., the statements of Brazil (*ibid.*, § 35), Iran (*ibid.*, § 41) and United States (*ibid.*, §§ 50 and 52); see also the statements of Japan ("destruction of the environment") (*ibid.*, § 43), Sweden (destruction "on an unprecedented scale") (*ibid.*, § 48) and United Kingdom ("a deliberate crime against the planet") (*ibid.*, § 49).
[15] UN General Assembly, Res. 47/37 (adopted without a vote) (*ibid.*, § 55).
[16] International Conference for the Protection of War Victims, Final Declaration (*ibid.*, § 61).
[17] ICRC, Report on the protection of the environment in time of armed conflict (*ibid.*, § 67).
[18] Guidelines on the Protection of the Environment in Times of Armed Conflict, para. 4 (*ibid.*, § 5); San Remo Manual, para. 13(c) (*ibid.*, § 6).

The applicability of the principle of proportionality to incidental damage to the environment is supported by a number of official statements.[19] During the bombing campaign against the Federal Republic of Yugoslavia, NATO stated that, when making targeting decisions, it took into account "all possible collateral damage, be it environmental, human or to the civilian infrastructure".[20] The Committee Established to Review the NATO Bombing Campaign Against the Federal Republic of Yugoslavia was of the view that the environmental impact of that bombing campaign was "best considered from the underlying principles of the law of armed conflicts such as necessity and proportionality" and stated that "in order to satisfy the requirement of proportionality, attacks against military targets which are known or can reasonably be assumed to cause grave environmental harm may need to confer a very substantial military advantage in order to be considered legitimate".[21]

In its advisory opinion in the *Nuclear Weapons case* in 1996, the International Court of Justice stated that "States must take environmental considerations into account when assessing what is necessary and proportionate in the pursuit of legitimate military objectives".[22]

The principle of proportionality is applicable in both international and non-international armed conflicts (see Rule 14) also in relation to the environment. The ICRC made such a statement of principle in 1993 in a report submitted to the UN General Assembly on the protection of the environment in time of armed conflict.[23] This assertion was uncontested.

Other rules affording protection to the natural environment

A number of other rules of international humanitarian law have the effect of preventing or limiting damage to the environment, even though they were not developed for this purpose, but rather for the purpose of protecting the civilian population. Examples of such rules include the obligation to take particular care when works and installations containing dangerous forces which are military objectives are made the object of an attack (see Rule 42) and the prohibition on attacking objects indispensable to the survival of the civilian population (see Rule 54). Belligerent reprisals against the natural environment are discussed in Chapter 41.

---

[19] See the statements of Australia (*ibid.*, § 30), Austria (*ibid.*, § 34), Canada (*ibid.*, § 37), Colombia (*ibid.*, § 39), Iran (*ibid.*, § 41), Jordan (*ibid.*, § 44), Romania (*ibid.*, § 46) and United States (*ibid.*, §§ 44 and 50); see also Report of an expert meeting on the protection of the environment in time of armed conflict (*ibid.*, § 60).

[20] See the reported practice of NATO (*ibid.*, § 58).

[21] Committee Established to Review the NATO Bombing Campaign Against the Federal Republic of Yugoslavia, Final Report (*ibid.*, § 63).

[22] ICJ, *Nuclear Weapons case*, Advisory Opinion (*ibid.*, § 62).

[23] ICRC, Report on the protection of the environment in time of armed conflict (*ibid.*, § 67).

Rule 44. Methods and means of warfare must be employed with due regard to the protection and preservation of the natural environment. In the conduct of military operations, all feasible precautions must be taken to avoid, and in any event to minimise, incidental damage to the environment. Lack of scientific certainty as to the effects on the environment of certain military operations does not absolve a party to the conflict from taking such precautions.

Practice

Volume II, Chapter 14, Section B.

Summary

State practice establishes this rule as a norm of customary international law applicable in international, and arguably also in non-international, armed conflicts.

International armed conflicts

State practice shows that the protection to be accorded to the environment during armed conflicts stems not only from the application to the environment of the rules protecting civilian objects, but also from a recognition of the need to provide particular protection to the environment as such. The extensive development of international law to protect the environment over the last few decades has been motivated by a recognition of the dangerous degradation of the natural environment caused by mankind. This development has been such that a State's interest in the protection of its natural environment has now been recognised by the International Court of Justice in the *Gabcíkovo-Nagymaros Project case* as an "essential interest" that could justify that State invoking the doctrine of "necessity" to renege from other international obligations.[24]

The importance of the natural environment as such was taken into account by the UN Security Council in a resolution adopted in 1991, in which it affirmed Iraq's responsibility under international law for environmental damage and depletion of natural resources as a result of its unlawful invasion and occupation of Kuwait.[25] Profound concern at the deterioration of the environment during that war was also expressed by the UN General Assembly in resolutions adopted in 1991 and 1992.[26] As a result of this concern, the UN General Assembly declared "6 November each year as the International Day for Preventing the Exploitation of the Environment in War and Armed Conflict".[27] Concern has

---

[24] ICJ, *Gabcíkovo-Nagymaros Project case*, Judgement (*ibid.*, § 121).
[25] UN Security Council, Res. 687 (*ibid.*, § 111).
[26] UN General Assembly, Res. 46/216 (adopted by 135 votes in favour, none against and one abstention) (*ibid.*, § 112) and Res. 47/151 (adopted by 159 votes in favour, none against and two abstentions) (*ibid.*, § 112).
[27] UN General Assembly, Res. 56/4 (*ibid.*, § 115).

also been expressed about the damage to the environment of both Yugoslavia and neighbouring countries by NATO's bombing campaign against Yugoslavia during the Kosovo crisis.[28]

The need to protect the environment during armed conflict is set forth in several international instruments.[29] The general need to protect the environment during armed conflict is also articulated in some military manuals, official statements and reported practice.[30] It is further reflected in condemnations of behaviour in armed conflict that caused severe damage to the environment.[31] In their submissions to the International Court of Justice in the *Nuclear Weapons case* and *Nuclear Weapons (WHO) case,* many States emphasised that international law recognises the importance of the protection of the environment during armed conflict, and they did not limit themselves to the requirements of treaties specifically applicable to armed conflict.[32] There is also evidence that environmental concerns affected military planning during the Gulf War, as the Coalition reportedly desisted from certain attacks out of environmental concerns.[33]

Furthermore, in the *Nuclear Weapons case* in 1996, the International Court of Justice found that States' obligation to ensure that activities within their jurisdiction and control respect the environment of other States or areas beyond national control was part of customary international law.[34]

Non-international armed conflicts

It can be argued that the obligation to pay due regard to the environment also applies in non-international armed conflicts if there are effects in another State. This argument is based on the recognition by the International Court of Justice

---

[28] See, e.g., Council of Europe, Parliamentary Assembly, Committee on the Environment, Regional Planning and Local Authorities, Report on the Environmental Impact of the War in Yugoslavia on South-East Europe (*ibid.,* § 117).

[29] See, e.g., World Charter for Nature, Principle 5 (*ibid.,* § 73) and Principle 20 (*ibid.,* § 74); Rio Declaration, Principle 24 (*ibid.,* § 76); Guidelines on the Protection of the Environment in Times of Armed Conflict, para. 11 (*ibid.,* § 77); San Remo Manual, paras. 35 and 44 (*ibid.,* § 78).

[30] See, e.g., the military manuals of Australia (*ibid.,* § 79), South Korea (*ibid.,* § 80) and United States (*ibid.,* § 81), the statement of Yemen (*ibid.,* § 109) and the reported practice of Lebanon (*ibid.,* § 96).

[31] See, e.g., the statements of China (*ibid.,* § 84), Colombia (*ibid.,* § 85), Germany (*ibid.,* § 91), Iran (*ibid.,* § 93), Netherlands (*ibid.,* § 99) and United Kingdom (*ibid.,* § 105).

[32] See the oral pleadings of or the written statements submitted to the ICJ in the *Nuclear Weapons case* by Egypt (*ibid.,* § 88), Iran (*ibid.,* § 93), Malaysia (*ibid.,* § 97), Qatar (*ibid.,* § 102) and Solomon Islands (*ibid.,* § 103) and the written statements submitted in the *Nuclear Weapons (WHO) case* by Costa Rica (*ibid.,* § 87), Mexico (*ibid.,* § 98) and Sri Lanka (*ibid.,* § 104).

[33] A. P. V. Rogers, *Law on the Battlefield* (*ibid.,* § 68).

[34] ICJ, *Nuclear Weapons case,* Advisory Opinion (*ibid.,* § 120); see also the Convention on Biodiversity, Principle 3 (*ibid.,* § 71); Stockholm Declaration on the Human Environment, Principle 21 (*ibid.,* § 72); Rio Declaration, Principle 2 (*ibid.,* § 75); the statement of Iran (*ibid.,* § 92); American Law Institute, *Restatement of the Foreign Relations Law of the United States* (*ibid.,* § 123).

that safeguarding a State's ecological balance was an "essential interest"[35] and its finding that States' obligation to ensure that activities within their jurisdiction and control respect the environment of other States or areas beyond national control were part of customary international law.[36]

Furthermore, there are indications that this customary rule may also apply to parties' behaviour within the State where the armed conflict is taking place. Some support for drafting a treaty rule for this purpose existed during the negotiation of Additional Protocol II.[37] It was not adopted then, but the general acceptance of the applicability of international humanitarian law to non-international armed conflicts has considerably strengthened since 1977. In addition, many environmental law treaties apply to a State's behaviour within its own territory (see *infra*). There is also a certain amount of State practice indicating the obligation to protect the environment that applies also to non-international armed conflicts, including military manuals, official statements and the many submissions by States to the International Court of Justice in the *Nuclear Weapons case* to the effect that the environment must be protected for the benefit of all.[38]

Obligation to take all feasible precautions to avoid or minimise damage to the environment

Practice indicates that the obligation to take all feasible precautions to avoid, and in any event to minimise, incidental damage to civilian objects (see Rule 15) equally applies to damage to the natural environment. This is set forth in the Guidelines on the Protection of the Environment in Times of Armed Conflict.[39] The principle that precautions must be taken to avoid or minimise damage to the environment is also supported by military manuals and official statements.[40]

---

[35] ICJ, *Gabcíkovo-Nagymaros Project case*, Judgement (*ibid.*, § 121).

[36] ICJ, *Nuclear Weapons case*, Advisory Opinion (*ibid.*, § 120); see also the Convention on Biodiversity, Principle 3 (*ibid.*, § 71); Stockholm Declaration on the Human Environment, Principle 21 (*ibid.*, § 72); Rio Declaration, Principle 2 (*ibid.*, § 75); the statement of Iran (*ibid.*, § 92); American Law Institute, *Restatement of the Foreign Relations Law of the United States* (*ibid.*, § 123).

[37] See State practice in the context of the negotiations at the Diplomatic Conference leading to the adoption of the Additional Protocols (*ibid.*, § 150).

[38] See, e.g., the military manuals of Italy (*ibid.*, § 10) and South Korea (*ibid.*, § 80); the statements of Argentina (*ibid.*, § 29) and Colombia (*ibid.*, § 85); the oral pleadings of and the written statements submitted to the ICJ in the *Nuclear Weapons case* by Egypt (*ibid.*, § 88), Iran (*ibid.*, § 93), Malaysia (*ibid.*, § 97), Qatar (*ibid.*, § 102) and Solomon Islands (*ibid.*, § 103) and the written statements submitted in the *Nuclear Weapons (WHO) case* by Costa Rica (*ibid.*, § 87), Mexico (*ibid.*, § 98), Rwanda (*ibid.*, § 253), Sri Lanka (*ibid.*, § 104) and Ukraine (*ibid.*, § 261).

[39] Guidelines on the Protection of the Environment in Times of Armed Conflict, para. 4 (*ibid.*, § 5); see also World Charter for Nature, Principle 20 (*ibid.*, § 74).

[40] See, e.g., United States, *Naval Handbook* (*ibid.*, § 11); the statements of Argentina (*ibid.*, § 29) and Canada (*ibid.*, §§ 36 and 38); see also Report of an expert meeting on the protection of the environment in time of armed conflict (*ibid.*, § 60).

In 1995, the 26th International Conference of the Red Cross and Red Crescent called on parties to the conflict to "take all feasible precautions to avoid, in their military operations, all acts liable to destroy or damage water sources".[41]

Precautionary principle

There is practice to the effect that lack of scientific certainty as to the effects on the environment of certain military operations does not absolve parties to a conflict from taking proper precautionary measures to prevent undue damage. As the potential effect on the environment will need to be assessed during the planning of an attack, the fact that there is bound to be some uncertainty as to its full impact on the environment means that the "precautionary principle" is of particular relevance to such an attack. The precautionary principle in environmental law has been gaining increasing recognition.[42] There is, furthermore, practice to the effect that this environmental law principle applies to armed conflict. In its advisory opinion in the *Nuclear Weapons case*, the International Court of Justice stated that the basic principles it recognised in the *Nuclear Tests case (Request for an Examination of the Situation)* of 1995 would also apply to the actual use of nuclear weapons in armed conflict.[43] This would include, *inter alia*, the precautionary principle which was central to the arguments in the latter case.[44] The ICRC, in its report submitted in 1993 to the UN General Assembly on the protection of the environment in time of armed conflict, referred to the precautionary principle as "an emerging, but generally recognised principle of international law [whose object it is] to anticipate and prevent damage to the environment and to ensure that, where there are threats of serious or irreversible damage, lack of scientific certainty shall not be used as a reason to postpone any measures to prevent such damage".[45] This assertion was not contested by any State.

---

[41] 26th International Conference of the Red Cross and Red Crescent, Res. II (adopted by consensus) (*ibid.*, § 138).

[42] See, e.g., Convention on Biodiversity, preamble (*ibid.*, § 126); Rio Declaration, Principle 15 (*ibid.*, § 127); the statements of France (*ibid.*, § 131) and New Zealand (*ibid.*, § 132); UN Economic Commission for Europe, Bergen ECE Ministerial Declaration on Sustainable Development, Article 7 (*ibid.*, § 133).

[43] ICJ, *Nuclear Weapons case*, Advisory Opinion, 8 July 1996, § 32.

[44] ICJ, *Nuclear Tests case (Request for an Examination of the Situation)*, Order (cited in Vol. II, Ch. 14, § 139). New Zealand argued that the precautionary principle was a binding rule (*ibid.*, § 132). Although France stated that it was uncertain whether the precautionary principle had become a binding rule of international law, it nevertheless stated that it did in practice carry out precautions that were in keeping with its obligations under international environmental law (*ibid.*, § 131). The ICJ concluded that both France and New Zealand had, in their submissions, reaffirmed their commitment to respect their obligations to respect and protect the natural environment (*ibid.*, § 139).

[45] ICRC, Report on the protection of the environment in time of armed conflict (*ibid.*, § 143).

Continued application of environmental law during armed conflict

There appears to be insufficient uniformity of opinion on whether environmental law treaties continue to be applicable during armed conflict when no reference is made to this in the treaty concerned. The Guidelines on the Protection of the Environment in Times of Armed Conflict states that international environmental law "may continue to be applicable in times of armed conflict to the extent that they are not inconsistent with the applicable law of armed conflict".[46]

In its advisory opinion in the *Nuclear Weapons case*, the International Court of Justice did not address this issue directly, but stated that environmental law "indicates important factors that are properly to be taken into account in the context of the implementation of the principles and rules of the law applicable in armed conflict".[47] The few States that analysed the issue in their submissions to the Court in this case had different views.[48]

Rule 45. The use of methods or means of warfare that are intended, or may be expected, to cause widespread, long-term and severe damage to the natural environment is prohibited. Destruction of the natural environment may not be used as a weapon.

Practice

Volume II, Chapter 14, Section C.

Summary

State practice establishes this rule as a norm of customary international law applicable in international, and arguably also in non-international, armed conflicts. It appears that the United States is a "persistent objector" to the first part of this rule. In addition, France, the United Kingdom and the United States are persistent objectors with regard to the application of the first part of this rule to the use of nuclear weapons.

Causing widespread, long-term and severe damage to the natural environment

Article 35(3) of Additional Protocol I prohibits the use of "methods or means of warfare which are intended, or may be expected to cause, widespread, long-term

---

[46] Guidelines on the Protection of the Environment in Times of Armed Conflict, para. 5 (*ibid.*, § 77).

[47] ICJ, *Nuclear Weapons case*, Advisory Opinion (*ibid.*, § 62).

[48] See the oral pleadings of or the written statements submitted to the ICJ in the *Nuclear Weapons case* by France (*ibid.*, § 89), Solomon Islands (*ibid.*, § 103), United Kingdom (*ibid.*, § 107) and United States (*ibid.*, § 108).

and severe damage to the natural environment".[49] This prohibition is also contained in Article 55(1) of Additional Protocol I.[50] These provisions were clearly new when they were adopted. Upon ratification of Additional Protocol I, France and the United Kingdom stated that the risk of environmental damage falling within the scope of these provisions must be assessed "objectively on the basis of the information available at the time".[51]

However, since then, significant practice has emerged to the effect that this prohibition has become customary. This prohibition is set forth in many military manuals.[52] Causing widespread, long-term and severe damage to the environment is an offence under the legislation of numerous States.[53] This practice includes that of States not, or not at the time, party to Additional Protocol I.[54] Several States indicated in their submissions to the International Court of Justice in the *Nuclear Weapons case* and *Nuclear Weapons (WHO) case* that they considered the rules in Articles 35(3) and 55(1) of Additional Protocol I to be customary.[55] In the same context, other States appeared to be of the view that these rules were customary as they stated that any party to a conflict must observe this rule, or must avoid using methods or means of warfare that would destroy or could have disastrous effects on the environment.[56] The Report on the Practice of Israel, which is not a party to Additional Protocol I, states that the Israeli Defence Forces do not utilise or condone the use of methods or means

---

[49] Additional Protocol I, Article 35(3) (adopted by consensus) (*ibid.*, § 145).
[50] Additional Protocol I, Article 55(1) (adopted by consensus) (*ibid.*, § 146).
[51] France, Reservations and declarations made upon ratification of Additional Protocol I, § 6 (*ibid.*, § 146); United Kingdom, Reservations and declarations made upon ratification of Additional Protocol I, § e (*ibid.*, § 148); see also France, Interpretative declarations made upon ratification of the ICC Statute, § 7 (*ibid.*, § 154).
[52] See, e.g., the military manuals of Argentina (*ibid.*, § 163), Australia (*ibid.*, §§ 164–165), Belgium (*ibid.*, § 166), Benin (*ibid.*, § 167), Canada (*ibid.*, § 168), Colombia (*ibid.*, § 169), France (*ibid.*, § 170), Germany (*ibid.*, §§ 171–173), Italy (*ibid.*, § 174), Kenya (*ibid.*, § 175), Netherlands (*ibid.*, §§ 176–177), New Zealand (*ibid.*, § 178), Russia (*ibid.*, § 179), Spain (*ibid.*, § 180), Sweden (*ibid.*, § 181), Switzerland (*ibid.*, § 182), Togo (*ibid.*, § 183), United Kingdom (*ibid.*, § 184), United States (*ibid.*, §§ 185–186) and Yugoslavia (*ibid.*, § 187).
[53] See, e.g., the legislation of Australia (*ibid.*, § 190), Azerbaijan (*ibid.*, § 191), Belarus (*ibid.*, § 192), Bosnia and Herzegovina (*ibid.*, § 193), Canada (*ibid.*, § 195), Colombia (*ibid.*, § 196), Congo (*ibid.*, § 197), Croatia (*ibid.*, § 198), Georgia (*ibid.*, § 201), Germany (*ibid.*, § 202), Ireland (*ibid.*, § 203), Mali (*ibid.*, § 206), Netherlands (*ibid.*, § 208), New Zealand (*ibid.*, § 209), Norway (*ibid.*, § 211), Slovenia (*ibid.*, § 213), Spain (*ibid.*, § 214), United Kingdom (*ibid.*, § 218) and Yugoslavia (*ibid.*, § 220); see also the draft legislation of Argentina (*ibid.*, § 188), Burundi (*ibid.*, § 194), El Salvador (*ibid.*, § 199), Nicaragua (*ibid.*, § 210) and Trinidad and Tobago (*ibid.*, § 216).
[54] See the military manuals of Belgium (*ibid.*, § 166), United Kingdom (*ibid.*, § 184) and United States ("prolonged damage to the environment") (*ibid.*, § 186) and the legislation of Azerbaijan (*ibid.*, § 191); see also the legislation of Vietnam ("ecocide") (*ibid.*, § 219).
[55] See the oral pleadings and written statements in the *Nuclear Weapons case* of New Zealand (*ibid.*, § 251), Solomon Islands (*ibid.*, § 257), Sweden (*ibid.*, § 259) and Zimbabwe (*ibid.*, § 272) and the written statements, comments or counter memorial in the *Nuclear Weapons (WHO) case* of India (*ibid.*, § 232), Lesotho (*ibid.*, § 247), Marshall Islands (*ibid.*, § 248), Nauru (*ibid.*, § 249) and Samoa (*ibid.*, § 254).
[56] See the oral pleadings and written statements in the *Nuclear Weapons case* of Australia (*ibid.*, § 223), Ecuador (*ibid.*, § 226), New Zealand (*ibid.*, § 251), Sweden (*ibid.*, § 259) and Zimbabwe (*ibid.*, § 272) and the written statements in the *Nuclear Weapons (WHO) case* of Rwanda (*ibid.*, § 253) and Ukraine (*ibid.*, § 261).

of warfare which are intended, or may be expected, to cause widespread, long-term and severe damage to the environment.[57] The United States, in response to an ICRC memorandum on the applicability of IHL in the Gulf region in 1991, stated that "U.S. practice does not involve methods of warfare that would constitute widespread, long-term and severe damage to the environment".[58] Other relevant practice includes condemnations of States not, or not at the time, party to Additional Protocol I for their alleged "ecocide" or "massive destruction of the environment" or for having violated Articles 35(3) and 55(1) of Additional Protocol I.[59]

The prohibition on inflicting widespread, long-term and severe damage to the natural environment is also repeated in the Guidelines on the Protection of the Environment in Times of Armed Conflict and the UN Secretary-General's Bulletin on observance by United Nations forces of international humanitarian law.[60] In its working paper on war crimes submitted in 1997 to the Preparatory Committee for the Establishment of an International Criminal Court, the ICRC considered as a war crime "wilfully causing widespread, long-term and severe damage to the natural environment".[61] The final text agreed for the war crime included in the Statute of the International Criminal Court defines this war crime as "intentionally launching an attack in the knowledge that such attack will cause... widespread, long-term and severe damage to the natural environment which would be clearly excessive in relation to the concrete and direct overall military advantage anticipated".[62] The Statute thus establishes an additional condition with respect to the criminalisation of the prohibition contained in this rule.

There is, however, a certain amount of practice that indicates doubt as to the customary nature of the rule in Additional Protocol I, in particular with respect to the phrase "may be expected to cause". The submissions of the United Kingdom and the United States to the International Court of Justice in the *Nuclear Weapons case* stated that Articles 35(3) and 55(1) of Additional Protocol I were not customary.[63] The Court itself appeared to consider the rule not to be customary as it only referred to the applicability of this provision to "States having

---

[57] Report on the Practice of Israel (*ibid.*, § 241).
[58] United States, Letter from the Department of the Army to the legal adviser of the US Army forces deployed in the Gulf region (*ibid.*, § 264).
[59] See, e.g., the statements of Germany (*ibid.*, § 231), Iran (*ibid.*, § 236) and Kuwait (*ibid.*, § 245) in relation to Iraq in 1991 and the statement of Yugoslavia in relation to the NATO bombing of a petrochemical complex in 1999 (*ibid.*, § 271).
[60] Guidelines on the Protection of the Environment in Times of Armed Conflict, para. 11 (*ibid.*, § 159); UN Secretary-General's Bulletin, Section 6.3 (*ibid.*, § 161).
[61] ICRC, Working paper on war crimes submitted to the Preparatory Committee for the Establishment of an International Criminal Court (*ibid.*, § 287).
[62] ICC Statute, Article 8(2)(b)(iv) (*ibid.*, § 153).
[63] United Kingdom, Written statement submitted to the ICJ in the *Nuclear Weapons case* (*ibid.*, § 262); United States, Written statement submitted to the ICJ in the *Nuclear Weapons case* (*ibid.*, § 269).

subscribed to these provisions".[64] Upon ratification of the Convention on Certain Conventional Weapons, which recalls, in its preamble, the rule in Articles 35(3) and 55(1) of Additional Protocol I, both France and the United States made a statement of interpretation to the effect that this was not a customary rule.[65] Less clear is the Final Report of the Committee Established to Review the NATO Bombing Campaign Against the Federal Republic of Yugoslavia, which stated that Article 55 of Additional Protocol I "may...reflect current customary law".[66]

The problem of the customary law nature of the rule, as articulated in Additional Protocol I, seems to turn on the position of France, the United Kingdom and the United States, which have a certain amount of practice indicating their acceptance of the rule provided that it applies to conventional weapons and not to nuclear weapons. This is made clear by the UK LOAC Manual and the US Air Force Commander's Handbook,[67] and by the reservations made by France and the United Kingdom upon ratifying Additional Protocol I to the effect that the Protocol did not apply to nuclear weapons.[68] This position, combined with the statements of France and the United Kingdom that Articles 35(3) and 55(1) of Additional Protocol I are not customary,[69] means that the *opinio juris* of these three States is that these rules, of themselves, do not prohibit the use of nuclear weapons.

Practice, as far as methods of warfare and use of conventional weapons are concerned, shows a widespread, representative and virtually uniform acceptance of the customary law nature of the rule found in Articles 35(3) and 55(1) of Additional Protocol I. The contrary practice of France, the United Kingdom and the United States in this regard is not totally consistent. Their statements in some contexts that the rules are not customary contradict those made in other contexts (in particular in military manuals) in which the rule is indicated as binding as long as it is not applied to nuclear weapons.[70] As these three States are not "specially affected" States as far the infliction of this type of damage is concerned, this contrary practice is not enough to have prevented the emergence of this customary rule. However, these three States are specially affected as far as possession of nuclear weapons is concerned, and their objection to the

---

[64] ICJ, *Nuclear Weapons case*, Advisory Opinion (*ibid.*, § 282).
[65] France, Reservations made upon ratification of the CCW (*ibid.*, § 152); United States, Statements of understanding made upon ratification of the CCW (*ibid.*, § 153).
[66] Committee Established to Review the NATO Bombing Campaign Against the Federal Republic of Yugoslavia, Final Report (*ibid.*, § 283).
[67] United Kingdom, *LOAC Manual* (*ibid.*, § 184); United States, *Air Force Commander's Handbook* (*ibid.*, § 185).
[68] France, Declaration made upon ratification of Additional Protocol I (*ibid.*, § 147); United Kingdom, Reservations and declarations made upon ratification of Additional Protocol I (*ibid.*, § 149).
[69] France, Reservations made upon ratification of the CCW (*ibid.*, § 152); United Kingdom, Written statement submitted to the ICJ in the *Nuclear Weapons case* (*ibid.*, § 262).
[70] See, e.g., the military manuals of France (*ibid.*, § 169), United Kingdom (*ibid.*, § 183) and United States (*ibid.*, § 184).

application of this specific rule to such weapons has been consistent since the adoption of this rule in treaty form in 1977. Therefore, if the doctrine of "persistent objector" is possible in the context of humanitarian rules, these three States are not bound by this specific rule as far as any use of nuclear weapons is concerned. However, it needs to be noted that this does not prevent any use of nuclear weapons being found unlawful on the basis of other rules, for example the prohibition of indiscriminate attacks (see Rule 11) and the principle of proportionality (see Rule 14).

Use of destruction of the natural environment as a weapon

There is extensive State practice prohibiting the deliberate destruction of the natural environment as a form of weapon. The ENMOD Convention prohibits the deliberate modification of the environment in order to inflict widespread, long-lasting or severe effects as a means of destruction, damage or injury to another State party.[71] The difference between this provision and the one in Additional Protocol I is that the latter refers primarily to the effects, whereas the ENMOD Convention refers to the deliberate use of a technique to modify the environment. Whether the provisions in the ENMOD Convention are now customary is unclear. On the one hand, the military manuals of Israel, South Korea and New Zealand appear to indicate that the treaty only binds parties to it.[72] On the other hand, Indonesia, which is not a party to the ENMOD Convention, states this rule in its military manual.[73] The Guidelines on the Protection of the Environment in Times of Armed Conflict includes this rule.[74] The UN General Assembly, in a resolution on the United Nations Decade of International Law adopted in 1994 without a vote, invites all States to disseminate these Guidelines widely.[75] At the Second ENMOD Review Conference in 1992, the United States stated that the Convention reflected "the international community's consensus that the environment itself should not be used as an instrument of war".[76]

In addition to the specific rules contained in the ENMOD Convention, significant practice exists prohibiting a deliberate attack on the environment as a method of warfare. The legislation of several States criminalises "ecocide".[77]

---

[71] ENMOD Convention, Article I (*ibid.*, § 290).
[72] Israel, *Manual on the Laws of War* (*ibid.*, § 300); South Korea, *Military Law Manual* (*ibid.*, § 301); New Zealand, *Military Manual* (*ibid.*, § 302).
[73] Indonesia, *Military Manual* (*ibid.*, § 299).
[74] Guidelines on the Protection of the Environment in Times of Armed Conflict, para. 12 (*ibid.*, § 294).
[75] UN General Assembly, Res. 49/50 (*ibid.*, § 317).
[76] United States, Statement at the Second ENMOD Review Conference (*ibid.*, § 316).
[77] See, e.g., the legislation of Armenia (*ibid.*, § 189), Belarus (*ibid.*, § 192), Kazakhstan (*ibid.*, § 204), Kyrgyzstan (*ibid.*, § 205), Moldova (*ibid.*, § 207), Russia (*ibid.*, § 212), Tajikistan (*ibid.*, § 215), Ukraine (*ibid.*, § 217) and Vietnam (*ibid.*, § 219).

Estonia's Penal Code prohibits affecting the environment as a method of warfare.[78] Yugoslavia condemned what it called "ecocide" in connection with the NATO attack on a petrochemical plant in 1999.[79] Iraq, in a letter to the UN Secretary-General in 1991, stated that it would not exploit the environment and natural resources "as a weapon".[80] Kuwait, in a letter to the UN Secretary-General the same year, stated that the environment and natural resources must not be used "as a weapon of terrorism".[81] During a debate in the Sixth Committee of the UN General Assembly in 1991, Sweden, referring to the destruction of the environment by Iraqi forces, said that this was an "unacceptable form of warfare in the future".[82] In the same context, Canada stated that "the environment as such should not form the object of direct attack".[83] Also noteworthy is the declaration adopted in 1991 by the OECD Ministers of the Environment condemning Iraq's burning of oil fields and discharging of oil into the Gulf as a violation of international law and urging Iraq to cease resorting to environmental destruction as a weapon.[84]

Therefore, irrespective of whether the provisions of the ENMOD Convention are themselves customary, there is sufficiently widespread, representative and uniform practice to conclude that the destruction of the natural environment may not be used as a weapon.

Non-international armed conflicts

The applicability of both parts of this rule to non-international armed conflicts is less clear than for international armed conflicts. The proposal to include the same rule as Article 35(3) of Additional Protocol I in Additional Protocol II was adopted by Committee III of the Diplomatic Conference leading to the adoption of the Additional Protocols in 1974, but rejected in 1977.[85] The reason for the change of mind is not clear but may have been linked to the simplification process undertaken in the last stages of negotiations in order to ensure the adoption of Additional Protocol II. This rule is contained in other instruments pertaining also to non-international armed conflicts.[86]

---

[78] Estonia, *Penal Code* (*ibid.*, § 200).
[79] Yugoslavia, Appeals and Letter of the Federal Ministry for Development, Science and the Environment (*ibid.*, § 271).
[80] Iraq, Letter to the UN Secretary-General (*ibid.*, § 237).
[81] Kuwait, Letter to the UN Secretary-General (*ibid.*, § 245).
[82] Sweden, Statement before the Sixth Committee of the UN General Assembly (*ibid.*, § 48).
[83] Canada, Statement before the Sixth Committee of the UN General Assembly (*ibid.*, § 37).
[84] OECD, Declaration of the Ministers of Environment (*ibid.*, § 278).
[85] See State practice in the context of the negotiations at the Diplomatic Conference leading to the adoption of the Additional Protocols (*ibid.*, § 150).
[86] See, e.g., Memorandum of Understanding on the Application of IHL between Croatia and the SFRY, para. 6 (*ibid.*, § 157); Agreement on the Application of IHL between the Parties to the Conflict in Bosnia and Herzegovina, para. 2.5 (*ibid.*, § 158).

This rule is included in military manuals which are applicable in or have been applied in non-international armed conflicts.[87] In addition, many States have adopted legislation criminalising "ecocide" or the wilful infliction of "widespread, long-term and severe damage to the natural environment" in any armed conflict.[88] There are a few condemnations in relation to environmental damage caused in non-international armed conflicts.[89] Most official statements condemning environmental damage in armed conflict, however, are of a general nature and do not appear to be limited to international armed conflicts.

However, even if this rule is not yet customary, present trends towards further protection of the environment and towards establishing rules applicable in non-international armed conflicts mean that it is likely to become customary in due course. This is particularly true as major damage to the environment rarely respects international frontiers, and also because the causing of such damage may violate other rules that apply equally in international and non-international armed conflicts, for example the prohibition of indiscriminate attacks (see Rule 11).

Interpretation

The difference between this rule and the rule requiring the application to the environment of the general rules of international humanitarian law applicable to civilian objects (see Rule 43) is that this rule is absolute. If widespread, long-term and severe damage is inflicted, or the natural environment is used as a weapon, it is not relevant to inquire into whether this behaviour or result could be justified on the basis of military necessity or whether incidental damage was excessive. It was for this reason that the expression in Additional Protocol I "widespread, long-term and severe" sets such a high threshold. The three conditions are cumulative and the phrase "long-term" was understood by the adopting States to mean decades. The Committee Established to Review the NATO Bombing Campaign Against the Federal Republic of Yugoslavia stated in its final report in 2000 that the threshold was so high as to make it difficult to find a violation. The report indicated that for this reason there was disagreement as to whether the damage in the Gulf War crossed this threshold.[90] In its

---

[87] See, e.g., the military manuals of Australia (*ibid.*, § 164), Benin (*ibid.*, § 167), Colombia (*ibid.*, § 169), Germany (*ibid.*, §§ 171–173), Italy (*ibid.*, § 174), Kenya (*ibid.*, § 175), South Korea (*ibid.*, § 301), Togo (*ibid.*, § 183) and Yugoslavia (*ibid.*, § 187).

[88] See, e.g., the legislation of Armenia (*ibid.*, § 189), Azerbaijan (*ibid.*, § 191), Belarus (*ibid.*, § 192), Bosnia and Herzegovina (*ibid.*, § 193), Colombia (*ibid.*, § 196), Croatia (*ibid.*, § 198), Kazakhstan (*ibid.*, § 204), Kyrgyzstan (*ibid.*, § 205), Moldova (*ibid.*, § 207), Slovenia (*ibid.*, § 213), Spain (*ibid.*, § 214), Tajikistan (*ibid.*, § 215), Ukraine (*ibid.*, § 217) and Yugoslavia (*ibid.*, § 220); see also the draft legislation of Argentina (*ibid.*, § 188), El Salvador (*ibid.*, § 199) and Nicaragua (*ibid.*, § 210).

[89] See, e.g., the statements of Bosnia and Herzegovina (*ibid.*, § 223) and Colombia (*ibid.*, § 84).

[90] Committee Established to Review the NATO Bombing Campaign Against the Federal Republic of Yugoslavia, Final Report (*ibid.*, § 283).

report to Congress in 1992, the US Department of Defense questioned whether the damage met the threshold of "long-term".[91]

"Ecocide" is defined in the penal codes of the countries of the former Soviet Union as "mass destruction of the flora and fauna and poisoning of the atmosphere or water resources, as well as other acts capable of causing an ecological catastrophe".[92] Vietnam's Penal Code refers to "destroying the natural environment".[93]

As a violation of this rule inevitably presupposes that there can be knowledge or an inference that a certain method or means of warfare will or probably will cause widespread, long-term and severe damage to the environment, there will need to be some understanding of which types of warfare will have such disastrous consequences on which types of environment. If read together with Rule 44, this means that parties to a conflict are obliged to inform themselves as far as possible of the potential results of their planned actions and to refrain from actions that may be expected to cause widespread, long-term and severe damage to the environment. In a report submitted in 1993 to the UN Secretary-General on the protection of the environment in time of armed conflict, the ICRC states that:

It is not easy to know in advance exactly what the scope and duration of some environmentally damaging acts will be; and there is a need to limit as far as possible environmental damage even in cases where it is not certain to meet a strict interpretation of the criteria of "widespread, long-term and severe".[94]

Unlike Additional Protocol I, the ENMOD Convention does not contain a cumulative standard, and the expression "long-lasting" is defined in that Convention as "lasting for a period of months, or approximately a season".[95] The difference was made because ENMOD refers to the deliberate manipulation of the environment, rather than to an intended or expected result on the environment. It is significant that, in 1992, the parties to the ENMOD Convention adopted an interpretation of the Convention that prohibits the use of herbicides if used for environmental modification and having the effect of upsetting the ecological balance of a region.[96] This interpretation was based on a desire by States parties not to limit the Convention to science-fiction-type weapons, and therefore reflects an interest in providing greater protection to the environment during armed conflict.[97]

---

[91] United States, Department of Defense, Final Report to Congress on the Conduct of the Persian Gulf War (ibid., § 267).
[92] See the legislation of Armenia (ibid., § 189), Belarus (ibid., § 192), Kazakhstan, (ibid., § 204), Kyrgyzstan (ibid., § 205), Moldova (ibid., § 207), Russia, (ibid., § 212), Tajikistan, (ibid., § 215) and Ukraine (ibid., § 217).
[93] Vietnam, Penal Code (ibid., § 219).
[94] ICRC, Report on the protection of the environment in time of armed conflict (ibid., § 286).
[95] Conference of the Committee on Disarmament, Understanding relating to Article I of the ENMOD Convention (ibid., § 291).
[96] Second Review Conference of the Parties to the ENMOD Convention, Final Declaration (cited in Vol. II, Ch. 24, § 633).
[97] See, e.g., Canada, Statement at the Second ENMOD Review Conference (ibid., § 616).

PART III

SPECIFIC METHODS OF WARFARE

DENIAL OF QUARTER

Note: *The duty to grant quarter is a basic rule that prohibits attacking a person recognised as* hors de combat *in combat situations on the battlefield. The treatment due to persons* hors de combat *is dealt with in Part V.*

Rule 46. Ordering that no quarter will be given, threatening an adversary therewith or conducting hostilities on this basis is prohibited.

Practice

Volume II, Chapter 15, Section A.

Summary

State practice establishes this rule as a norm of customary international law applicable in both international and non-international armed conflicts. While all those who take a direct part in hostilities must respect this rule, in practice it will be particularly relevant for commanders.

International armed conflicts

The prohibition on declaring that no quarter will be given is a long-standing rule of customary international law already recognised in the Lieber Code, the Brussels Declaration and the Oxford Manual and codified in the Hague Regulations.[1] "Directions to give no quarter" was listed as a war crime in the Report of the Commission on Responsibility set up after the First World War.[2] This rule is now set forth in Additional Protocol I.[3] Under the Statute of the International Criminal Court, "declaring that no quarter will be given" is a war crime in international armed conflicts.[4]

---

[1] Lieber Code, Article 60 (cited in Vol. II, Ch. 15, § 7); Brussels Declaration, Article 13(d) (*ibid.*, § 8); Oxford Manual, Article 9(b) (*ibid.*, § 9); Hague Regulations, Article 23(d) (*ibid.*, § 2).
[2] Report of the Commission on Responsibility (*ibid.*, § 11).
[3] Additional Protocol I, Article 40 (adopted by consensus) (*ibid.*, § 3).
[4] ICC Statute, Article 8(2)(b)(xii) (*ibid.*, § 6).

The prohibition is contained in numerous military manuals.[5] Under the legislation of many States, it is an offence to issue an order that no quarter be given.[6] In several cases after the First and Second World Wars, the accused were charged with violating this rule.[7]

The inclusion in Additional Protocol I of the prohibition of "threats" to order that no quarter shall be given or to conduct hostilities on the basis that no quarter shall be given is uncontested and it is incorporated in numerous military manuals.[8] The legislation of several States also includes it.[9] The prohibition of threats that no quarter shall be given is supported by several States not, or not at the time, party to Additional Protocol I.[10] The prohibition on threatening to carry out a prohibited act is generally recognised in international law. In addition, if it is prohibited to order or threaten that no quarter shall be given then, *a fortiori*, it is prohibited to carry out such an order or threats and to conduct military operations on that basis. To conduct military operations on the basis that no quarter shall be given would constitute multiple violations of the prohibition on attacking persons *hors de combat* (see Rule 47).

Non-international armed conflicts

Article 4 of Additional Protocol II prohibits ordering that there shall be no survivors.[11] In his report on the establishment of the Special Court for Sierra Leone, the UN Secretary-General noted that the provisions of Article 4 had long been

---

5   See, e.g., the military manuals of Argentina (*ibid.*, § 15), Belgium (*ibid.*, § 19), Burkina Faso (*ibid.*, § 22), Cameroon (*ibid.*, § 23), Colombia (*ibid.*, § 27), Congo (*ibid.*, § 28), France (*ibid.*, §§ 29–30), Italy (*ibid.*, § 34), Mali (*ibid.*, § 36), Morocco (*ibid.*, § 37), Nigeria (*ibid.*, §§ 40–42), Senegal (*ibid.*, § 44), South Africa (*ibid.*, § 45), Switzerland (*ibid.*, § 48), United Kingdom (*ibid.*, §§ 50–51) and United States (*ibid.*, § 52).

6   See, e.g., the legislation of Armenia (*ibid.*, § 54), Australia (*ibid.*, § 55), Canada (*ibid.*, § 59), China (*ibid.*, § 60), Congo (*ibid.*, § 61), Ethiopia (*ibid.*, § 63), Georgia (*ibid.*, § 64), Italy (*ibid.*, § 67), Lithuania (*ibid.*, § 68), Mali (*ibid.*, § 69), Netherlands (*ibid.*, §§ 70–71), New Zealand (*ibid.*, § 72), Spain (*ibid.*, § 75), United Kingdom (*ibid.*, § 77) and United States (*ibid.*, § 78); see also the draft legislation of Burundi (*ibid.*, § 58) and Trinidad and Tobago (*ibid.*, § 76).

7   See, e.g., Canada, Military Court at Aurich, *Abbaye Ardenne case* (*ibid.*, § 81); Germany, Leipzig Court, *Stenger and Cruisus case* (*ibid.*, § 85); United Kingdom, Military Court at Hamburg, *Peleus case* (*ibid.*, § 86), *Wickman case* (*ibid.*, § 88) and *Von Ruchteschell case* (*ibid.*, § 89); United Kingdom, Military Court at Brunswick, *Von Falkenhorst case* (*ibid.*, § 87); United Kingdom, Court No. 5 of the Curiohaus, Hamburg-Altona, *Le Paradis case* (*ibid.*, § 90); United States, Military Commission at Augsburg, *Thiele case* (*ibid.*, § 91); United States, Military Tribunal at Nuremberg, *Von Leeb (The High Command Trial) case* (*ibid.*, § 92).

8   See, e.g., the military manuals of Argentina (*ibid.*, § 16), Australia (*ibid.*, §§ 17–18), Belgium (*ibid.*, § 20), Benin (*ibid.*, § 21), Cameroon (*ibid.*, § 24), Canada (*ibid.*, §§ 25–26), France (*ibid.*, §§ 30 and 32), Germany (*ibid.*, § 33), Kenya (*ibid.*, § 35), Netherlands (*ibid.*, § 38), New Zealand (*ibid.*, § 39), Russia (*ibid.*, § 43), Spain (*ibid.*, § 46), Sweden (*ibid.*, § 47), Togo (*ibid.*, § 49) and Yugoslavia (*ibid.*, § 53).

9   See, e.g., the legislation of Australia (*ibid.*, § 56), Bosnia and Herzegovina (*ibid.*, § 57), Croatia (*ibid.*, § 62), Germany (*ibid.*, § 65), Ireland (*ibid.*, § 66), Norway (*ibid.*, § 73), Slovenia (*ibid.*, § 74) and Yugoslavia (*ibid.*, § 79).

10 See the military manuals of France (*ibid.*, § 30) and Kenya (*ibid.*, § 35), the statement of the United States (*ibid.*, § 98) and the reported practice of Israel (*ibid.*, § 95).

11 Additional Protocol II, Article 4(1) (adopted by consensus) (*ibid.*, § 4).

considered part of customary international law.[12] Under the Statute of the International Criminal Court, "declaring that no quarter will be given" is a war crime in non-international armed conflicts.[13]

The prohibition on ordering that there shall be no survivors is also included in military manuals which are applicable in or have been applied in non-international armed conflicts.[14] It is an offence under the legislation of numerous States to order that no quarter shall be given in any armed conflict.[15] Colombia's Constitutional Court ruled that this prohibition met constitutional standards as it sought to protect human life and dignity. It also held that superior orders to cause "death outside combat" must be disobeyed.[16] The prohibition on ordering that there shall be no survivors is also supported by official statements relating to non-international armed conflicts.[17]

In its examination of an incident in which two wounded soldiers were killed by a member of an FMLN patrol, the UN Commission on the Truth for El Salvador found no evidence that the executions were ordered by higher levels of command or that they were carried out in accordance with an FMLN policy of killing prisoners. It reported that the FMLN acknowledged the criminal nature of the incident and tried the accused.[18]

The ICRC has recalled the prohibition on ordering that there shall be no survivors with respect to both international and non-international armed conflicts.[19]

Conducting hostilities on the basis that no quarter will be given would violate common Article 3 of the Geneva Conventions because it would result in the killing of persons *hors de combat*.[20] It would also violate the fundamental guarantee prohibiting murder (see Rule 89).

---

[12] UN Secretary-General, Report on the establishment of a Special Court for Sierra Leone (cited in Vol. II, Ch. 32, § 252).

[13] ICC Statute, Article 8(2)(e)(x) (cited in Vol. II, Ch. 15, § 6).

[14] See, e.g., the military manuals of Argentina (*ibid.*, § 16), Australia (*ibid.*, §§ 17–18), Benin (*ibid.*, § 21), Cameroon (*ibid.*, § 24), Canada (*ibid.*, §§ 25–26), Colombia (*ibid.*, § 27), France (*ibid.*, § 32), Germany (*ibid.*, § 33), Italy (*ibid.*, § 34), Kenya (*ibid.*, § 35), Netherlands (*ibid.*, § 38), New Zealand (*ibid.*, § 39), Nigeria (*ibid.*, §§ 40 and 42), Russia (*ibid.*, § 43), South Africa (*ibid.*, § 45), Spain (*ibid.*, § 46), Togo (*ibid.*, § 49) and Yugoslavia (*ibid.*, § 53).

[15] See, e.g., the legislation of Australia (*ibid.*, § 56), Bosnia and Herzegovina (*ibid.*, § 57), Canada (*ibid.*, § 59), Congo (*ibid.*, § 61), Croatia (*ibid.*, § 62), Ethiopia (*ibid.*, § 63), Georgia (*ibid.*, § 64), Germany (*ibid.*, § 65), Ireland (*ibid.*, § 66), Netherlands (*ibid.*, § 71), New Zealand (*ibid.*, § 72), Norway (*ibid.*, § 73), Slovenia (*ibid.*, § 74), United Kingdom (*ibid.*, § 75) and Yugoslavia (*ibid.*, § 79); see also the legislation of Italy (*ibid.*, § 67), the application of which is not excluded in time of non-international armed conflict, and the draft legislation of Burundi (*ibid.*, § 57) and Trinidad and Tobago (*ibid.*, § 76).

[16] Colombia, Constitutional Court, *Constitutional Case No. T-409* (*ibid.*, § 82), *Constitutional Case No. C-225/95* (*ibid.*, § 83) and *Constitutional Case No. C-578* (*ibid.*, § 84).

[17] See, e.g., China, Announcement of the People's Liberation Army (*ibid.*, § 94).

[18] UN Commission on the Truth for El Salvador, Report (*ibid.*, § 103).

[19] ICRC, Memorandum on Respect for International Humanitarian Law in Angola (*ibid.*, § 110), Memorandum on Compliance with International Humanitarian Law by the Forces Participating in Opération Turquoise (*ibid.*, § 111) and Communication to the Press No. 01/58 (*ibid.*, § 113).

[20] Geneva Conventions, common Article 3 (cited in Vol. II, Ch. 32, § 2).

Rule 47. Attacking persons who are recognised as *hors de combat* is prohibited. A person *hors de combat* is:

(a) **anyone who is in the power of an adverse party;**
(b) **anyone who is defenceless because of unconsciousness, shipwreck, wounds or sickness; or**
(c) **anyone who clearly expresses an intention to surrender;**

provided he or she abstains from any hostile act and does not attempt to escape.

Practice

Volume II, Chapter 15, Section B.

Summary

State practice establishes this rule as a norm of customary international law applicable in both international and non-international armed conflicts.

International armed conflicts

This is a long-standing rule of customary international law already recognised in the Lieber Code, the Brussels Declaration and the Oxford Manual.[21] The Hague Regulations provide that it is especially forbidden "to kill or wound an enemy who, having laid down his arms, or having no longer means of defence, has surrendered at discretion".[22] Additional Protocol I prohibits attacks against persons recognised as *hors de combat* and provides that such attacks constitute grave breaches of the Protocol.[23] Under the Statute of the International Criminal Court, "killing or wounding a combatant who, having laid down his arms or having no longer means of defence, has surrendered at discretion" is a war crime in international armed conflicts.[24]

The prohibition on attacking persons recognised as *hors de combat* is set forth in numerous military manuals.[25] Sweden's IHL Manual identifies the prohibition on attacking persons recognised as *hors de combat* in Article 41 of Additional Protocol I as a codification of customary international law.[26] Violation of this rule is an offence under the legislation of many States.[27] It is also

---

[21] Lieber Code, Article 71 (cited in Vol. II, Ch. 15, § 218); Brussels Declaration, Article 13(c) (*ibid.*, § 219); Oxford Manual, Article 9(b) (*ibid.*, § 220).

[22] Hague Regulations, Article 23(c) (*ibid.*, § 214).

[23] Additional Protocol I, Article 41(1) (adopted by consensus) (*ibid.*, § 119) and Article 85(3)(e) (adopted by consensus) (*ibid.*, § 120).

[24] ICC Statute, Article 8(2)(b)(vi) (*ibid.*, § 217).

[25] See, e.g., the military manuals of Argentina (*ibid.*, § 126), Australia (*ibid.*, §§ 127–128), Belgium (*ibid.*, §§ 129–130), Benin (*ibid.*, § 131), Cameroon (*ibid.*, § 132), Canada (*ibid.*, § 133), Colombia (*ibid.*, §§ 135–136), Croatia (*ibid.*, §§ 137–139), Ecuador (*ibid.*, § 140), France (*ibid.*, §§ 141–143), Hungary (*ibid.*, § 144), Israel (*ibid.*, §§ 145–146), Italy (*ibid.*, §§ 147–148), Kenya (*ibid.*, § 149), Madagascar (*ibid.*, § 150), Netherlands (*ibid.*, § 151), New Zealand (*ibid.*, § 152), Philippines (*ibid.*, § 153), Romania (*ibid.*, § 154), Russia (*ibid.*, § 155), South Africa (*ibid.*, § 156), Spain (*ibid.*, § 157), Sweden (*ibid.*, § 158), Switzerland (*ibid.*, § 159), Togo (*ibid.*, § 160) and United States (*ibid.*, §§ 161–162).

[26] Sweden, *IHL Manual* (*ibid.*, § 158).

[27] See, e.g., the legislation of Armenia (*ibid.*, § 163), Australia (*ibid.*, §§ 164–165), Belarus (*ibid.*, § 166), Belgium (*ibid.*, § 167), Bosnia and Herzegovina (*ibid.*, § 168), Canada (*ibid.*, § 169),

referred to in military communiqués.[28] It is supported by official statements and reported practice.[29] The prohibition on attacking persons *hors de combat* has been upheld in case-law following the First and Second World Wars.[30]

Non-international armed conflicts

The rule is based on common Article 3 of the Geneva Conventions, which prohibits "violence to life and person, in particular murder of all kinds" against persons placed *hors de combat*.[31] This prohibition is repeated in Additional Protocol II, which adds that "it is prohibited to order that there shall be no survivors".[32] In addition, this rule is contained in other instruments pertaining also to non-international armed conflicts.[33]

Military manuals which are applicable in or have been applied in non-international armed conflicts prohibit attacks against persons recognised as *hors de combat*.[34] Such attacks are also defined as a war crime in the legislation of a number of States.[35] The rule has been applied in national case-law.[36] It is supported by official statements and other practice.[37]

Colombia (*ibid.*, § 170), Cook Islands (*ibid.*, § 171), Croatia (*ibid.*, § 172), Cyprus (*ibid.*, § 173), Georgia (*ibid.*, § 175), Germany (*ibid.*, § 176), Ireland (*ibid.*, § 177), Moldova (*ibid.*, § 180), Netherlands (*ibid.*, § 181), New Zealand (*ibid.*, § 182), Niger (*ibid.*, § 184), Norway (*ibid.*, § 185), Slovenia (*ibid.*, § 186), Tajikistan (*ibid.*, § 187), United Kingdom (*ibid.*, § 188), Yemen (*ibid.*, § 189), Yugoslavia (*ibid.*, § 190) and Zimbabwe (*ibid.*, § 191); see also the draft legislation of El Salvador (*ibid.*, § 174), Jordan (*ibid.*, § 178), Lebanon (*ibid.*, § 179) and Nicaragua (*ibid.*, § 183).

[28] See, e.g., Egypt, Military Communiqués Nos. 34 and 46 (*ibid.*, § 196); Iraq, Military Communiqués Nos. 973, 975 and 1902 (*ibid.*, § 199).

[29] See, e.g., the statements of Chile (*ibid.*, § 194) and Syria (*ibid.*, § 201) and the reported practice of Algeria (*ibid.*, § 193), Egypt (*ibid.*, § 195) and Jordan (*ibid.*, § 200).

[30] See, e.g., Germany, Leipzig Court, *Stenger and Cruisus case* (*ibid.*, § 328) and Reichsgericht, *Llandovery Castle case* (*ibid.*, § 329); United Kingdom, Military Court at Hamburg, *Peleus case* (*ibid.*, § 331), Military Court at Elten, *Renoth case* (*ibid.*, § 332) and Military Court at Hamburg, *Von Ruchteschell case* (*ibid.*, § 333); United States, Military Tribunal at Nuremberg, *Von Leeb (The High Command Trial) case* (*ibid.*, § 192) and Military Commission at Rome, *Dostler case* (*ibid.*, § 334).

[31] Geneva Conventions, common Article 3 (cited in Vol. II, Ch. 32, § 2).

[32] Additional Protocol II, Article 4 (adopted by consensus) (cited in Vol. II, Ch. 15, § 4).

[33] See, e.g., Memorandum of Understanding on the Application of IHL between Croatia and the SFRY, para. 6 (*ibid.*, § 123); Agreement on the Application of IHL between the Parties to the Conflict in Bosnia and Herzegovina, para. 2.5 (*ibid.*, § 124).

[34] See, e.g., the military manuals of Australia (*ibid.*, § 127), Benin (*ibid.*, § 131), Canada (*ibid.*, § 134), Colombia (*ibid.*, §§ 135–137), Croatia (*ibid.*, §§ 137–139), Ecuador (*ibid.*, § 140), Italy (*ibid.*, §§ 147–148), Kenya (*ibid.*, § 149), Madagascar (*ibid.*, § 150), Philippines (*ibid.*, § 153), South Africa (*ibid.*, § 156) and Togo (*ibid.*, § 160).

[35] See, e.g., the legislation of Armenia (*ibid.*, § 163), Belarus (*ibid.*, § 166), Belgium (*ibid.*, § 167), Bosnia and Herzegovina (*ibid.*, § 168), Colombia (*ibid.*, § 170), Croatia (*ibid.*, § 172), Georgia (*ibid.*, § 175), Germany (*ibid.*, § 176), Moldova (*ibid.*, § 180), Niger (*ibid.*, § 184), Slovenia (*ibid.*, § 186), Tajikistan (*ibid.*, § 187), Yemen (*ibid.*, § 189) and Yugoslavia (*ibid.*, § 190); see also the draft legislation of El Salvador (*ibid.*, § 174), Jordan (*ibid.*, § 178) and Nicaragua (*ibid.*, § 183).

[36] See, e.g., Argentina, National Court of Appeals, *Military Junta case* (*ibid.*, § 327); Nigeria, *Case of 3 September 1968* (*ibid.*, § 330).

[37] See, e.g., the statement of Chile (*ibid.*, § 194), the practice of Colombia (*ibid.*, § 337) and Yugoslavia (*ibid.*, § 351) and the reported practice of China (*ibid.*, § 365) and Cuba (*ibid.*, § 338).

Contrary practice collected by the Special Rapporteurs of the UN Commission on Human Rights and by the ICRC has been condemned as a violation of the rule.[38] The ICRC has called for respect for the prohibition of attacks on persons *hors de combat* in both international and non-international armed conflicts.[39]

Specific categories of persons hors de combat

A person *hors de combat* is a person who is no longer participating in hostilities, by choice or circumstance. Under customary international law, a person can be placed *hors de combat* in three situations arising in both international and non-international armed conflicts:

(i) Anyone who is in the power of an adverse party. It is uncontested that a person who is in the power of an adverse party is *hors de combat*. This rule is set forth in Additional Protocol I and is implicit in common Article 3 of the Geneva Conventions and in Additional Protocol II.[40] It has been confirmed in numerous military manuals.[41] Respect for and protection of persons who are in the power of an adverse party is a cornerstone of international humanitarian law as reflected in several provisions of the Geneva Conventions and Additional Protocols. Practice, therefore, focuses rather on the treatment to be given to such persons (see in particular Chapters 32 and 37).

(ii) Anyone who is defenceless because of unconsciousness, shipwreck, wounds or sickness. This category is based on the Hague Regulations, common Article 3 of the Geneva Conventions and Additional Protocol I, which prohibit attacks on defenceless persons.[42] It is found in numerous military

---

[38] See, e.g., UN Commission on Human Rights, Reports of the Special Rapporteur on the Situation of Human Rights in Zaire (*ibid.*, § 202), Report of the Independent Expert on the Situation of Human Rights in Guatemala (*ibid.*, § 357) and Report of the Special Rapporteur on Extrajudicial, Summary or Arbitrary Executions (*ibid.*, § 358) and the practice collected in ICRC archive documents (*ibid.*, §§ 383–384, 387, 389 and 393–394).

[39] ICRC, Conflict in Southern Africa: ICRC Appeal (*ibid.*, § 370), Conflict between Iraq and Iran: ICRC Appeal (*ibid.*, § 371), Appeal in behalf of civilians in Yugoslavia (*ibid.*, § 373), Press Release No. 1705 (*ibid.*, § 374), Press Releases Nos. 1712, 1724 and 1726 (*ibid.*, § 375), Press Release, Tajikistan: ICRC urges respect for humanitarian rules (*ibid.*, § 376), Memorandum on Respect for International Humanitarian Law in Angola (*ibid.*, § 377), Memorandum on Compliance with International Humanitarian Law by the Forces Participating in Opération Turquoise (*ibid.*, § 378), Press Release No. 1792 (*ibid.*, § 379), Press Release No. 1793 (*ibid.*, § 380), Communication to the Press No. 00/36 (*ibid.*, § 381) and Communication to the Press No. 01/58 (*ibid.*, § 382).

[40] Geneva Conventions, common Article 3 (cited in Vol. II, Ch. 32, § 2); Additional Protocol I, Article 41(2) (adopted by consensus) (cited in Vol. II, Ch. 15, § 215); Additional Protocol II, Article 4 (adopted by consensus).

[41] See, e.g., the military manuals of Argentina (cited in Vol. II, Ch. 15, § 224), Australia (*ibid.*, §§ 225–226), Burkina Faso (*ibid.*, § 233), Cameroon (*ibid.*, §§ 234–235), Canada (*ibid.*, § 236), Congo (*ibid.*, § 239), Croatia (*ibid.*, § 240), Dominican Republic (*ibid.*, § 243), Ecuador (*ibid.*, § 244), France (*ibid.*, §§ 246 and 248–249), Kenya (*ibid.*, § 256), Lebanon (*ibid.*, § 259), Madagascar (*ibid.*, § 260), Mali (*ibid.*, § 261), Morocco (*ibid.*, § 262), Netherlands (*ibid.*, § 26359), New Zealand (*ibid.*, § 266), Peru (*ibid.*, § 271), Senegal (*ibid.*, § 276), Spain (*ibid.*, § 278), Sweden (*ibid.*, § 279), Switzerland (*ibid.*, § 280), Uganda (*ibid.*, § 282), United Kingdom (*ibid.*, § 283) and United States (*ibid.*, §§ 287 and 291).

[42] Hague Regulations, Article 23(c) (*ibid.*, § 214); Geneva Conventions, common Article 3 (cited in Vol. II, Ch. 32, § 2); Additional Protocol I, Article 41(2) (adopted by consensus) (cited in Vol. II, Ch. 15, § 215).

manuals.[43] It is contained in the legislation of many States.[44] It is also supported by case-law, official statements and other practice, such as instructions to armed forces.[45] In addition, respect for and protection of the wounded, sick and shipwrecked is a cornerstone of international humanitarian law applicable in both international and non-international armed conflicts as reflected in several provisions of the Geneva Conventions and their Additional Protocols. Practice, therefore, focuses rather on the treatment to be given to such persons (see Chapter 34).

(iii) Anyone who clearly indicates an intention to surrender. This category is based on the Hague Regulations, common Article 3 of the Geneva Conventions and Additional Protocol I.[46] It is contained in numerous military manuals.[47] It is included in the national legislation of many States.[48] It is also supported by

---

[43] See, e.g., the military manuals of Argentina (*ibid.*, §§ 223–224), Australia (*ibid.*, §§ 225–226), Belgium (*ibid.*, §§ 228–230), Benin (*ibid.*, § 231), Cameroon (*ibid.*, § 235), Canada (*ibid.*, §§ 236–237), Croatia (*ibid.*, § 241), Dominican Republic (*ibid.*, § 243), Ecuador (*ibid.*, § 244), El Salvador (*ibid.*, § 245), France (*ibid.*, § 249), Germany (*ibid.*, § 250), Indonesia (*ibid.*, § 252), Israel (*ibid.*, § 253), Italy (*ibid.*, §§ 254–255), Kenya (*ibid.*, § 256), South Korea (*ibid.*, § 257), Lebanon (*ibid.*, § 259), Madagascar (*ibid.*, § 260), Netherlands (*ibid.*, §§ 263–264), New Zealand (*ibid.*, § 266), Nigeria (*ibid.*, §§ 268 and 270), Peru (*ibid.*, § 271), Philippines (*ibid.*, § 273), Russia (*ibid.*, § 274), South Africa (*ibid.*, § 277), Spain (*ibid.*, § 278), Sweden (*ibid.*, § 279), Switzerland (*ibid.*, § 280), Togo (*ibid.*, § 281), United Kingdom (*ibid.*, §§ 283–284), United States (*ibid.*, §§ 285–291) and Yugoslavia (*ibid.*, § 292).

[44] See, e.g., the legislation of Azerbaijan (*ibid.*, § 293), Bosnia and Herzegovina (*ibid.*, § 294), Canada (*ibid.*, § 296), Colombia (*ibid.*, § 297), Congo (*ibid.*, § 298), Croatia (*ibid.*, § 299), Egypt (*ibid.*, § 300), Estonia (*ibid.*, § 302), Ethiopia (*ibid.*, § 303), Georgia (*ibid.*, § 304), Ireland (*ibid.*, § 306), Italy (*ibid.*, § 307), Lithuania (*ibid.*, § 308), Mali (*ibid.*, § 309), Netherlands (*ibid.*, § 310), New Zealand (*ibid.*, § 311), Nicaragua (*ibid.*, § 312), Norway (*ibid.*, § 314), Peru (*ibid.*, § 315), Poland (*ibid.*, § 316), Slovenia (*ibid.*, § 317), Spain (*ibid.*, § 319), Sweden (*ibid.*, § 320), Switzerland (*ibid.*, § 321), United Kingdom (*ibid.*, § 323), United States (*ibid.*, § 324) and Yugoslavia (*ibid.*, § 326); see also the draft legislation of Burundi (*ibid.*, § 295), El Salvador (*ibid.*, § 301), Nicaragua (*ibid.*, § 313) and Trinidad and Tobago (*ibid.*, § 322).

[45] See, e.g., the case-law of Argentina (*ibid.*, § 327), Germany (*ibid.*, §§ 328–329) and United Kingdom (*ibid.*, § 331), the statement of the United States (*ibid.*, § 347) and the practice of Egypt (*ibid.*, § 339), Iraq (*ibid.*, § 341), United Kingdom (*ibid.*, § 344) and United States (*ibid.*, § 348).

[46] Hague Regulations, Article 23(c) (*ibid.*, § 214); Geneva Conventions, common Article 3 (cited in Vol. II, Ch. 32, § 2); Additional Protocol I, Article 41(2) (adopted by consensus) (cited in Vol. II, Ch. 15, § 215).

[47] See, e.g., the military manuals of Argentina (*ibid.*, §§ 223–224), Australia (*ibid.*, §§ 225–226), Belgium (*ibid.*, §§ 227–228), Benin (*ibid.*, § 231), Burkina Faso (*ibid.*, § 233), Cameroon (*ibid.*, §§ 234–235), Canada (*ibid.*, §§ 236–237), Colombia (*ibid.*, § 238), Congo (*ibid.*, § 239), Croatia (*ibid.*, §§ 241–242), Dominican Republic (*ibid.*, § 243), Ecuador (*ibid.*, § 244), El Salvador (*ibid.*, § 245), France (*ibid.*, §§ 246–247), Germany (*ibid.*, §§ 250–251), Indonesia (*ibid.*, § 252), Israel (*ibid.*, § 253), Italy (*ibid.*, §§ 254–255), Kenya (*ibid.*, § 257), South Korea (*ibid.*, § 258), Lebanon (*ibid.*, § 259), Madagascar (*ibid.*, § 260), Mali (*ibid.*, § 261), Morocco (*ibid.*, § 262), Netherlands (*ibid.*, §§ 263–265), New Zealand (*ibid.*, § 267), Nigeria (*ibid.*, §§ 267–270), Peru (*ibid.*, § 271), Philippines (*ibid.*, §§ 272–273), Romania (*ibid.*, § 274), Russia (*ibid.*, § 275), Senegal (*ibid.*, § 276), South Africa (*ibid.*, § 277), Spain (*ibid.*, § 278), Sweden (*ibid.*, § 279), Switzerland (*ibid.*, § 280), Togo (*ibid.*, § 281), United Kingdom (*ibid.*, §§ 283–284), United States (*ibid.*, §§ 285–291) and Yugoslavia (*ibid.*, § 292).

[48] See, e.g., the legislation of Azerbaijan (*ibid.*, § 293), Bosnia and Herzegovina (*ibid.*, § 294), Canada (*ibid.*, § 296), Congo (*ibid.*, § 298), Croatia (*ibid.*, § 299), Estonia (*ibid.*, § 302), Ethiopia (*ibid.*, § 303), Georgia (*ibid.*, § 304), Germany (*ibid.*, § 305), Ireland (*ibid.*, § 306), Italy (*ibid.*, § 307), Lithuania (*ibid.*, § 308), Mali (*ibid.*, § 309), Netherlands (*ibid.*, § 310), New Zealand (*ibid.*, § 311), Norway (*ibid.*, § 314), Peru (*ibid.*, § 315), Poland (*ibid.*, § 316), Slovenia (*ibid.*, § 317), Spain (*ibid.*, §§ 318–319), Switzerland (*ibid.*, § 321), United Kingdom (*ibid.*, § 323), United States (*ibid.*, § 324), Venezuela (*ibid.*, § 325) and Yugoslavia (*ibid.*, § 326); see also the draft legislation

official statements and other practice, such as instructions to armed forces.[49] The general tenet that emerges from this practice is that a clear indication of unconditional surrender renders a person *hors de combat*. In land warfare, a clear intention to surrender is generally shown by laying down one's weapons and raising one's hands. Other examples, such as emerging from one's position displaying a white flag, are mentioned in many military manuals.[50] There are specific examples of ways of showing an intent to surrender in air and naval warfare.[51]

The ability to accept surrender under the particular circumstances of combat was discussed by the United Kingdom and the United States in the light of the war in the South Atlantic and the Gulf War respectively.[52] The United Kingdom pointed out that it may not be possible to accept surrender from a unit while under fire from another position. Hence, a party which "takes" surrender is not required to go out to receive surrender; instead, the party offering surrender has to come forward and submit to the control of the enemy forces. The United States took the position that an offer of surrender has to be made at a time when it can be received and properly acted upon and that a last-minute surrender to an onrushing force may be difficult to accept. The question remains, however, as to how to surrender when physical distance may make it difficult to indicate an intention to surrender or may subject one to charges of desertion. The United States also took the position that retreating combatants, if they do not communicate an offer of surrender, whether armed or not, are still subject to attack and that there is no obligation to offer an opportunity to surrender before an attack.

Quarter under unusual circumstances of combat

The prohibition on attacking a person recognised as *hors de combat* applies in all circumstances, even when it is difficult to keep or evacuate prisoners, for example, when a small patrol operating in isolation captures a combatant. Such practical difficulties must be overcome by disarming and releasing the

---

of Burundi (*ibid.*, § 295), El Salvador (*ibid.*, § 301), Nicaragua (*ibid.*, § 313) and Trinidad and Tobago (*ibid.*, § 322).

[49] See, e.g., the statements of Australia (*ibid.*, § 336) and United States (*ibid.*, § 349), the practice of Colombia (*ibid.*, § 337), Egypt (*ibid.*, § 339), United Kingdom (*ibid.*, §§ 345–346), United States (*ibid.*, §§ 348–349) and Yugoslavia (*ibid.*, § 351) and the reported practice of Algeria (*ibid.*, § 335).

[50] See, e.g., the military manuals of Belgium (*ibid.*, § 230), Benin (*ibid.*, § 231), Cameroon (*ibid.*, § 235), Canada (*ibid.*, § 237), Croatia (*ibid.*, § 241), Dominican Republic (*ibid.*, § 243), France (*ibid.*, § 249), Italy (*ibid.*, § 255), Kenya (*ibid.*, § 256), Madagascar (*ibid.*, § 260), Togo (*ibid.*, § 281) and United States (*ibid.*, § 287).

[51] Yves Sandoz, Christophe Swinarski, Bruno Zimmermann (eds.), *Commentary on the Additional Protocols*, ICRC, Geneva, 1987, § 1619; Louise Doswald-Beck (ed.), *San Remo Manual on International Law Applicable to Armed Conflicts at Sea*, Cambridge University Press, 1995, § 47.57, p. 135.

[52] See Report on UK Practice (cited in Vol. II, Ch. 15, § 411); United States, Department of Defense, Final Report to Congress on the Conduct of the Persian Gulf War (*ibid.*, § 349).

persons concerned, according to Additional Protocol I.[53] This is restated in several military manuals.[54] The US Field Manual similarly states that:

A commander may not put his prisoners to death because their presence retards his movements or diminishes his power of resistance by necessitating a large guard, or by reason of their consuming supplies, or because it appears certain that they will regain their liberty through the impending success of their forces. It is likewise unlawful for a commander to kill prisoners on grounds of self-preservation, even in the case of airborne or commando operations.[55]

Israel's Manual on the Laws of War and the UK Military Manual contain similar statements.[56] Additional Protocol I and several military manuals require that all feasible precautions be taken to ensure the safety of released prisoners.[57]

In the context of non-international armed conflicts, some armed opposition groups have raised difficulties in providing for detention, but the duty to give quarter has not been challenged *per se*.[58]

Practice recognises that the duty to give quarter is to the benefit of every person taking a direct part in hostilities, whether entitled to prisoner-of-war status or not. This means that mercenaries, spies and saboteurs also have the right to receive quarter and cannot be summarily executed when captured (see also Rules 107–108).

Loss of protection

According to Additional Protocol I, immunity from attack is conditional on refraining from any hostile act or attempt to escape.[59] This is also set forth in several military manuals.[60] The commission of these acts signifies that the person in question is in fact no longer *hors de combat* and does not qualify for protection under this rule. The Third Geneva Convention specifies that "the use of weapons against prisoners of war, especially against those who are escaping or attempting to escape, shall constitute an extreme measure, which shall always be preceded by warnings appropriate to the circumstances".[61] The

---

[53] Additional Protocol I, Article 41(3) (adopted by consensus) (*ibid.*, § 395).
[54] See, e.g., the military manuals of Canada (*ibid.*, § 399), France (*ibid.*, § 400), Kenya (*ibid.*, § 402), Netherlands (*ibid.*, § 403), Spain (*ibid.*, § 404) and Switzerland (*ibid.*, § 405).
[55] United States, *Field Manual* (*ibid.*, § 407).
[56] Israel, *Manual on the Laws of War* (*ibid.*, § 401); United Kingdom, *Military Manual* (*ibid.*, § 406).
[57] Additional Protocol I, Article 41(3) (adopted by consensus) (*ibid.*, § 395); the military manuals of Canada (*ibid.*, § 399), France (*ibid.*, § 400), Kenya (*ibid.*, § 402), Spain (*ibid.*, § 403) and United Kingdom (*ibid.*, § 406).
[58] See the practice of armed opposition groups in ICRC archive documents (*ibid.*, §§ 418–420).
[59] Additional Protocol I, Article 41 (adopted by consensus) (*ibid.*, § 215).
[60] See, e.g., the military manuals of Argentina (*ibid.*, § 224), Australia (*ibid.*, §§ 225–226), Belgium (*ibid.*, § 230), Canada (*ibid.*, §§ 236–237), France (*ibid.*, § 249), Kenya (*ibid.*, § 256), Netherlands (*ibid.*, § 263), New Zealand (*ibid.*, § 266), Spain (*ibid.*, § 278), Switzerland (*ibid.*, § 280) and United Kingdom (*ibid.*, § 283).
[61] Third Geneva Convention, Article 42 (cited in Vol. II, Ch. 32, § 6).

Convention contains other specific rules applicable to the escape of prisoners of war.[62]

Hostile acts have not been defined, but the Commentary on the Additional Protocols gives examples such as resuming combat if the opportunity arises, attempting to communicate with one's own party and destroying installations of the enemy or one's own military equipment.[63]

Rule 48. Making persons parachuting from an aircraft in distress the object of attack during their descent is prohibited.

Practice

Volume II, Chapter 15, Section C.

Summary

State practice establishes this rule as a norm of customary international law applicable in both international and non-international armed conflicts.

International armed conflicts

The prohibition on attacking persons parachuting from an aircraft in distress during their descent was already recognised in the Hague Rules of Air Warfare, drafted by a commission of jurists in 1922–1923,[64] and was considered to reflect a rule of customary international law.[65] As such, it was codified in Article 42 of Additional Protocol I.[66] Article 42 was not, however, adopted by consensus because some States felt that persons landing in their own territory could not be considered *hors de combat*. But this view was defeated and in the end the issue was resolved in favour of considering such persons as *hors de combat* during their descent, wherever they might land.[67] A parallel can be drawn here with the shipwrecked, who are considered to be *hors de combat* (in both international and non-international armed conflicts) even though they may swim ashore or be collected by a friendly ship and resume fighting. In this respect, it is interesting to note that persons bailing out of an aircraft in distress

---

[62] Third Geneva Convention, Articles 91–94.
[63] Yves Sandoz, Christophe Swinarski, Bruno Zimmermann (eds.), *Commentary on the Additional Protocols*, ICRC, Geneva, 1987, §§ 1621–1622.
[64] Hague Rules of Air Warfare, Article 20 (cited in Vol. II, Ch. 15, § 423).
[65] See United States, *Annotated Supplement to the Naval Handbook* (*ibid.*, § 470).
[66] Additional Protocol I, Article 42 (*ibid.*, § 421). See Yves Sandoz, Christophe Swinarski, Bruno Zimmermann (eds.), *Commentary on the Additional Protocols* (*ibid.*, § 481); Michael Bothe, Karl Joseph Partsch, Waldemar A. Solf (eds.), *New Rules for Victims of Armed Conflicts* (*ibid.*, § 485).
[67] The military and humanitarian reasons for which this decision was taken are explained in Yves Sandoz, Christophe Swinarski, Bruno Zimmermann (eds.), *Commentary on the Additional Protocols*, ICRC, Geneva, 1987, § 1642.

have been called "shipwrecked in the air". This rule is now generally accepted and, as a result, no reservations have been made to Article 42.

In addition, numerous military manuals prohibit attacks against persons parachuting from an aircraft in distress.[68] These include manuals of States not, or not at the time, party to Additional Protocol I.[69] This rule is also supported by official statements, such as military communiqués, and reported practice.[70]

Non-international armed conflicts

The prohibition on attacking persons parachuting from an aircraft in distress is also applicable in non-international armed conflicts on the basis of common Article 3 of the Geneva Conventions, which protects persons placed *hors de combat* by "any" cause.[71] During the negotiation of the elements of war crimes against common Article 3 in the framework of the Statute of the International Criminal Court, the drafters understood that the term *hors de combat* should not be interpreted in a narrow sense, and made reference to Article 42 of Additional Protocol I, in addition to the examples contained in common Article 3.[72] This rule is contained in several military manuals which are applicable in or have been applied in non-international armed conflicts.[73]

As explained above, the main concern about considering persons parachuting from an aircraft in distress as *hors de combat* during their descent was that they might land in their own territory. The international community has resolved this issue in favour of considering such persons as *hors de combat* during the

---

[68] See, e.g., the military manuals of Argentina (cited in Vol. II, Ch. 15, §§ 424–425), Australia (*ibid.*, §§ 426–427), Belgium (*ibid.*, §§ 428–429), Benin (*ibid.*, § 430), Burkina Faso (*ibid.*, § 431), Cameroon (*ibid.*, §§ 432–433), Canada (*ibid.*, § 434), Congo (*ibid.*, § 435), Croatia (*ibid.*, § 436), Dominican Republic (*ibid.*, § 437), Ecuador (*ibid.*, § 438), France (*ibid.*, §§ 439–441), Germany (*ibid.*, § 442), Indonesia (*ibid.*, § 443), Israel (*ibid.*, § 444), Italy (*ibid.*, §§ 446–447), Kenya (*ibid.*, § 448), Lebanon (*ibid.*, § 449), Madagascar (*ibid.*, § 450), Mali (*ibid.*, § 451), Morocco (*ibid.*, § 452), Netherlands (*ibid.*, § 453), New Zealand (*ibid.*, § 454), Nigeria (*ibid.*, § 455), Russia (*ibid.*, § 456), Senegal (*ibid.*, § 457), South Africa (*ibid.*, § 458), Spain (*ibid.*, § 459), Sweden (*ibid.*, § 460), Switzerland (*ibid.*, § 461), Togo (*ibid.*, § 462), United Kingdom (*ibid.*, §§ 463–464), United States (*ibid.*, §§ 465–470) and Yugoslavia (*ibid.*, § 471).

[69] See the military manuals of Cameroon (*ibid.*, § 432), France (*ibid.*, § 439), Indonesia (*ibid.*, § 443), Israel (*ibid.*, § 444), Kenya (*ibid.*, § 448), Lebanon (*ibid.*, § 449), Mali (*ibid.*, § 451), Morocco (*ibid.*, § 452), United Kingdom (*ibid.*, §§ 463–464) and United States (*ibid.*, §§ 465–470).

[70] See, e.g., Egypt, Military Communiqués Nos. 34 and 46 (*ibid.*, § 476); Iran, Military Communiqué of 29 September 1980 (*ibid.*, § 477); Iraq, Military Communiqués Nos. 541, 683, 996 and 1383 and Reply by the Ministry of Defence to a questionnaire (*ibid.*, § 478); United States, Remarks of the Deputy Legal Adviser of the Department of State (*ibid.*, § 480) and Letter from the Department of the Army to the legal adviser of the US Army forces deployed in the Gulf region (*ibid.*, § 481); reported practice of Pakistan (*ibid.*, § 479).

[71] Geneva Conventions, common Article 3 (cited in Vol. II, Ch. 32, § 2).

[72] Knut Dörmann, *Elements of War Crimes under the Rome Statute of the International Criminal Court: Sources and Commentary*, Cambridge University Press, 2003, p. 389.

[73] See, e.g., the military manuals of Australia (cited in Vol. II, Ch. 15, § 426), Benin (*ibid.*, § 430), Croatia (*ibid.*, § 436), Ecuador (*ibid.*, § 438), Germany (*ibid.*, § 442), Italy (*ibid.*, §§ 446–447), Kenya (*ibid.*, § 448), Lebanon (*ibid.*, § 449), Madagascar (*ibid.*, § 450), South Africa (*ibid.*, § 458), Togo (*ibid.*, § 462) and Yugoslavia (*ibid.*, § 471).

time they are in the air, wherever they may land afterwards. Hence, there is no practical impediment to applying this rule in non-international armed conflicts and no opinion has been expressed that it should be so limited.

Interpretation

Practice indicates that upon reaching the ground, persons parachuting from an aircraft in distress are to be given an opportunity to surrender, unless it is apparent that they are engaging in a hostile act. This principle is set forth in Additional Protocol I.[74] It is also contained in many military manuals.[75] The Commentary on the Additional Protocols explains that this rule establishes a presumption that, until they have made the opposite intention known, downed aircrew intend to surrender.[76] The US Air Force Pamphlet specifies, however, that combatants parachuting from an aircraft in distress and landing uninjured behind their own lines may be attacked, since an offer to surrender would be impossible to accept.[77] This is in conformity with the explanation provided concerning the definition of surrender (see commentary to Rule 47).

This rule is to the benefit of all crew of an aircraft in distress, civilians and combatants alike, but does not apply to troops that are airborne as part of a military operation and that are not bailing out in distress.[78]

---

[74] Additional Protocol I, Article 42 (*ibid.*, § 421).

[75] See, e.g., the military manuals of Argentina (*ibid.*, § 425), Australia (*ibid.*, §§ 426–427), Belgium (*ibid.*, §§ 428–429), Cameroon (*ibid.*, § 432), Canada (*ibid.*, § 434), Dominican Republic (*ibid.*, § 437), Ecuador (*ibid.*, § 438), France (*ibid.*, § 441), Indonesia (*ibid.*, § 443), Kenya (*ibid.*, § 448), Netherlands (*ibid.*, § 453), New Zealand (*ibid.*, § 454), Spain (*ibid.*, § 459), Sweden (*ibid.*, § 460), Switzerland (*ibid.*, § 461) and United States (*ibid.*, §§ 466–467 and 469–470).

[76] Yves Sandoz, Christophe Swinarski, Bruno Zimmermann (eds.), *Commentary on the Additional Protocols* (*ibid.*, § 486).

[77] United States, *Air Force Pamphlet* (*ibid.*, § 466).

[78] See, e.g., the military manuals of Argentina (*ibid.*, §§ 424–425), Australia (*ibid.*, §§ 426–427), Belgium (*ibid.*, §§ 428–429), Benin (*ibid.*, § 430), Burkina Faso (*ibid.*, § 431), Cameroon (*ibid.*, §§ 432–433), Canada (*ibid.*, § 434), Congo (*ibid.*, § 435), Dominican Republic (*ibid.*, § 436), Ecuador (*ibid.*, § 438), France (*ibid.*, §§ 439–441), Germany (*ibid.*, § 442), Indonesia (*ibid.*, § 443), Israel (*ibid.*, §§ 444–445), Italy (*ibid.*, § 446), Kenya (*ibid.*, § 448), Lebanon (*ibid.*, § 449), Mali (*ibid.*, § 451), Morocco (*ibid.*, § 452), Netherlands (*ibid.*, § 453), New Zealand (*ibid.*, § 454), Nigeria (*ibid.*, § 455), Russia (*ibid.*, § 456), Senegal (*ibid.*, § 457), South Africa (*ibid.*, § 458), Spain (*ibid.*, § 459), Sweden (*ibid.*, § 460), Switzerland (*ibid.*, § 461), Togo (*ibid.*, § 462), United Kingdom (*ibid.*, §§ 463–464), United States (*ibid.*, §§ 465–467 and 469) and Yugoslavia (*ibid.*, § 471).

DESTRUCTION AND SEIZURE OF PROPERTY

Rule 49. The parties to the conflict may seize military equipment belonging to an adverse party as war booty.

Practice

Volume II, Chapter 16, Section A.

Summary

State practice establishes this rule as a norm of customary international law applicable in international armed conflicts.

International armed conflicts

The rule whereby a party to the conflict may seize military equipment belonging to an adverse party as war booty is set forth in the Lieber Code.[1] It reflects long-standing practice in international armed conflicts. It is also implicit in the Hague Regulations and the Third Geneva Convention, which require that prisoners of war must be allowed to keep all their personal belongings (as well as protective gear).[2]

This rule is also contained in numerous military manuals.[3] As Australia's Defence Force Manual explains, "booty includes all articles captured with prisoners of war and not included under the term 'personal effects'".[4] The rule has also been referred to in case-law.[5]

---

[1] Lieber Code, Article 45 (cited in Vol. II, Ch. 16, § 4).
[2] Hague Regulations, Article 4 (*ibid.*, § 2); Third Geneva Convention, Article 18, first paragraph (*ibid.*, § 3).
[3] See, e.g., the military manuals of Argentina (*ibid.*, § 5), Australia (*ibid.*, §§ 6–7), Belgium (*ibid.*, § 9), Benin (*ibid.*, § 10), Cameroon (*ibid.*, § 12), Canada (*ibid.*, §§ 13–14), Dominican Republic (*ibid.*, § 15), France (*ibid.*, § 16), Germany (*ibid.*, § 17), Hungary (*ibid.*, § 18), Israel (*ibid.*, § 19), Kenya (*ibid.*, § 20), Madagascar (*ibid.*, § 21), Netherlands (*ibid.*, § 22), New Zealand (*ibid.*, § 23), Spain (*ibid.*, § 25), Togo (*ibid.*, § 26), United Kingdom (*ibid.*, § 27) and United States (*ibid.*, §§ 29–31).
[4] Australia, *Defence Force Manual* (*ibid.*, § 7).
[5] See, e.g., Israel, High Court, *Al-Nawar case* (*ibid.*, § 39).

According to the Lieber Code, war booty belongs to the party which seizes it and not to the individual who seizes it.[6] This principle is reflected in numerous military manuals.[7] It is also supported in national case-law.[8] As a result, individual soldiers have no right of ownership over or possession of military equipment thus seized. Some manuals explicitly state that it is prohibited for soldiers to take home "war trophies".[9] It has been reported that in the United Kingdom soldiers have been court-martialled for trying to smuggle out weapons taken from the adversary following the Gulf War.[10]

Practice also indicates that booty may be used without restriction and does not have to be returned to the adversary.[11]

Non-international armed conflicts

With respect to non-international armed conflicts, no rule could be identified which would allow, according to international law, the seizure of military equipment belonging to an adverse party, nor was a rule found which would prohibit such seizure under international law.

Definition

Numerous military manuals define war booty as enemy military objects (or equipment or property) captured or found on the battlefield.[12] Several other manuals specify that it must concern movable "public" property.[13] With respect to private property found on the battlefield, the UK Military Manual and US Field Manual specify that to the extent that they consist of arms, ammunition, military equipment and military papers, they may be taken as booty as well.[14] In the *Al-Nawar case* before Israel's High Court in 1985, Judge Shamgar held that:

---

[6] Lieber Code, Article 45 (*ibid.*, § 4).

[7] See, e.g., the military manuals of Argentina (*ibid.*, § 5), Australia (*ibid.*, §§ 6–7), Benin (*ibid.*, § 10), Bosnia and Herzegovina (*ibid.*, § 11), Canada (*ibid.*, § 13), Germany (*ibid.*, § 17), Hungary (*ibid.*, § 18), Israel (*ibid.*, § 19), Kenya (*ibid.*, § 20), Madagascar (*ibid.*, § 21), Netherlands (*ibid.*, § 22), New Zealand (*ibid.*, § 23), Spain (*ibid.*, § 25), Togo (*ibid.*, § 26), United Kingdom (*ibid.*, § 27) and United States (*ibid.*, § 29).

[8] See, e.g., Israel, High Court, *Al-Nawar case* (*ibid.*, § 39) and United States, Court of Claims, *Morrison case* (*ibid.*, § 41).

[9] See, e.g., the military manuals of Canada (*ibid.*, § 14) and United States (*ibid.*, § 32).

[10] See the Report on UK Practice (*ibid.*, § 40).

[11] See, e.g., the military manuals of Benin (*ibid.*, § 10), Cameroon (*ibid.*, § 12), France (*ibid.*, § 16), Kenya (*ibid.*, § 20), Madagascar (*ibid.*, § 21), Netherlands (*ibid.*, § 22) and Togo (*ibid.*, § 26).

[12] See, e.g., the military manuals of Australia (*ibid.*, §§ 6–7), Benin (*ibid.*, § 10), Cameroon (*ibid.*, § 12), France (*ibid.*, § 16), Hungary (*ibid.*, § 18), Kenya (*ibid.*, § 20), Madagascar (*ibid.*, § 21), Netherlands (*ibid.*, § 22), Spain (*ibid.*, § 25) and Togo (*ibid.*, § 26).

[13] See, e.g., the military manuals of Argentina (*ibid.*, § 5), Canada (*ibid.*, § 13), Germany (*ibid.*, § 17), New Zealand (*ibid.*, § 23), United Kingdom (*ibid.*, § 27) and United States (*ibid.*, § 29).

[14] United Kingdom, *Military Manual* (*ibid.*, § 27); United States, *Field Manual* (*ibid.*, § 29).

All movable State property captured on the battlefield may be appropriated by the capturing belligerent State as booty of war, this includes arms and ammunition, depots of merchandise, machines, instruments and even cash.

All private property actually used for hostile purposes found on the battlefield or in a combat zone may be appropriated by a belligerent State as booty of war.[15]

The definition of booty as used by Judge Shamgar goes beyond military equipment and relies on the wider definition found in Article 53 of the Hague Regulations, which defines the objects that may be seized in occupied territory as including "cash, funds, and realizable securities which are strictly the property of the State, depots of arms, means of transport, stores and supplies, and, generally, all movable property belonging to the State which may be used for military operations".[16] To the extent that these objects may be seized, they are in effect war booty, even though technically they may not be captured or found on the battlefield. This link is also made in the military manuals of France, Germany and the Netherlands.[17] Germany's manual, for example, states that "movable government property which may be used for military purposes shall become spoils of war".

Special rules

The capture of military medical units, both mobile and fixed, and military medical transports is governed by the First Geneva Convention.[18] Mobile medical units must be reserved for the care of the wounded and sick. Fixed medical units may not be diverted from their intended purpose as long as they are required for the care of the wounded and sick.

Additional Protocol I lays down further rules on medical ships and aircraft.[19] The capture of the materiel and buildings of military units permanently assigned to civil defence organisations is also regulated in Additional Protocol I.[20]

Rule 50. The destruction or seizure of the property of an adversary is prohibited, unless required by imperative military necessity.

Practice

Volume II, Chapter 16, Section B.

---

[15] Israel, High Court, *Al-Nawar case* (*ibid.*, § 39).
[16] Hague Regulations, Article 53 (*ibid.*, § 245).
[17] France, *LOAC Manual* (*ibid.*, § 16); Germany, *Military Manual* (*ibid.*, § 17); Netherlands, *Military Manual* (*ibid.*, § 22).
[18] First Geneva Convention, Articles 33 and 35.
[19] Additional Protocol I, Articles 22, 23 and 30.   [20] Additional Protocol I, Article 67.

Summary

State practice establishes this rule as a norm of customary international law applicable in both international and non-international armed conflicts.

International armed conflicts

This is a long-standing rule of customary international law already recognised in the Lieber Code and the Brussels Declaration and codified in the Hague Regulations.[21] The violation of this rule through "extensive destruction and appropriation of property, not justified by military necessity and carried out unlawfully and wantonly," is a grave breach under the Geneva Conventions.[22] Under the Statute of the International Criminal Court, "destroying or seizing the enemy's property unless such destruction or seizure be imperatively demanded by the necessities of war" constitutes a war crime in international armed conflicts.[23] With respect to the requirement that the destruction be extensive for it to constitute a grave breach, the International Criminal Tribunal for the Former Yugoslavia stated in the *Blaškić case* that "the notion of 'extensive' is evaluated according to the facts of the case – a single act, such as the destruction of a hospital, may suffice to characterise an offence under this count".[24]

The rule is contained in numerous military manuals.[25] It is an offence under the legislation of many States to destroy or seize the property of an adversary unless it is required by imperative military necessity.[26] The rule was applied

---

[21] Lieber Code, Articles 15–16 (cited in Vol. II, Ch. 16, §§ 57–58); Brussels Declaration, Article 13(g) (*ibid.*, § 60); Hague Regulations, Article 23(g) (*ibid.*, § 51).

[22] First Geneva Convention, Article 50 (*ibid.*, § 53); Second Geneva Convention, Article 51 (*ibid.*, § 53); Fourth Geneva Convention, Article 147 (*ibid.*, § 53).

[23] ICC Statute, Article 8(2)(b)(xiii) (*ibid.*, § 55).

[24] ICTY, *Blaškić case*, Judgement (*ibid.*, § 239).

[25] See, e.g., the military manuals of Argentina (*ibid.*, §§ 70–71), Australia (*ibid.*, §§ 72–73), Belgium (*ibid.*, §§ 74–75), Benin (*ibid.*, § 76), Cameroon (*ibid.*, § 77), Canada (*ibid.*, §§ 78–79), Colombia (*ibid.*, § 80), Dominican Republic (*ibid.*, § 82), Ecuador (*ibid.*, § 83), France (*ibid.*, §§ 84–87), Germany (*ibid.*, § 88), Israel (*ibid.*, § 90), Italy (*ibid.*, §§ 91–92), Kenya (*ibid.*, § 93), South Korea (*ibid.*, § 94), Lebanon (*ibid.*, § 95), Madagascar (*ibid.*, § 96), Netherlands (*ibid.*, § 97), New Zealand (*ibid.*, § 98), Nigeria (*ibid.*, §§ 100–102), Peru (*ibid.*, § 103), Philippines (*ibid.*, § 104), Romania (*ibid.*, § 105), Russia (*ibid.*, § 106), Senegal (*ibid.*, § 107), South Africa (*ibid.*, § 108), Spain (*ibid.*, § 109), Sweden (*ibid.*, § 110), Switzerland (*ibid.*, § 111), Togo (*ibid.*, § 112), United Kingdom (*ibid.*, §§ 113–114) and United States (*ibid.*, §§ 115–120).

[26] See, e.g., the legislation of Armenia (*ibid.*, § 122), Australia (*ibid.*, §§ 123–125), Azerbaijan (*ibid.*, § 126), Bangladesh (*ibid.*, § 127), Barbados (*ibid.*, § 128), Belarus (*ibid.*, § 129), Belgium (*ibid.*, § 130), Bosnia and Herzegovina (*ibid.*, § 131), Botswana (*ibid.*, § 132), Bulgaria (*ibid.*, § 133), Canada (*ibid.*, §§ 136 and 138), Chile (*ibid.*, § 139), Congo (*ibid.*, § 142), Cook Islands (*ibid.*, § 143), Croatia (*ibid.*, § 144), Cuba (*ibid.*, § 145), Cyprus (*ibid.*, § 146), Czech Republic (*ibid.*, § 147), El Salvador (*ibid.*, §§ 149–150), Estonia (*ibid.*, § 151), Georgia (*ibid.*, § 154), Germany (*ibid.*, § 155), India (*ibid.*, § 157), Iraq (*ibid.*, § 158), Ireland (*ibid.*, § 159), Israel (*ibid.*, § 160), Italy (*ibid.*, §§ 161–162), Kenya (*ibid.*, § 165), Latvia (*ibid.*, § 166), Lithuania (*ibid.*, § 168), Luxembourg (*ibid.*, §§ 169–170), Malawi (*ibid.*, § 171), Malaysia (*ibid.*, § 172), Mali (*ibid.*, § 174), Mauritius (*ibid.*, § 175), Mexico (*ibid.*, § 176), Moldova (*ibid.*, § 177), Mozambique (*ibid.*, § 178), Netherlands (*ibid.*, §§ 179–180), New Zealand (*ibid.*, §§ 181–182), Nicaragua (*ibid.*, §§ 183–184), Niger (*ibid.*, § 185), Nigeria (*ibid.*, § 186), Norway (*ibid.*, § 187), Papua New Guinea

in several cases after the Second World War.[27] Several indictments before the International Criminal Tribunal for the Former Yugoslavia are based on this rule, and in the *Blaškić case* and *Kordić and Čerkez case*, the accused were found guilty of its violation.[28]

Non-international armed conflicts

Under the Statute of the International Criminal Court, "destroying or seizing the property of an adversary unless such destruction or seizure be imperatively demanded by the necessities of the conflict" constitutes a war crime in non-international armed conflicts.[29]

This rule is included in military manuals which are applicable in or have been applied in non-international armed conflicts.[30] Its violation is an offence under the legislation of many States.[31]

No official contrary practice was found with respect to either international or non-international armed conflicts.

(*ibid.*, § 189), Paraguay (*ibid.*, § 190), Peru (*ibid.*, § 181), Philippines (*ibid.*, § 192), Portugal (*ibid.*, § 193), Romania (*ibid.*, § 194), Seychelles (*ibid.*, § 196), Singapore (*ibid.*, § 197), Slovakia (*ibid.*, § 198), Slovenia (*ibid.*, § 199), Spain (*ibid.*, §§ 200–201), Tajikistan (*ibid.*, § 205), Uganda (*ibid.*, § 207), Ukraine (*ibid.*, § 209), United Kingdom (*ibid.*, §§ 210–211), United States (*ibid.*, §§ 212–213), Uzbekistan (*ibid.*, § 215), Vanuatu (*ibid.*, § 216), Vietnam (*ibid.*, § 218), Yugoslavia (*ibid.*, § 219) and Zimbabwe (*ibid.*, § 220); see also the draft legislation of Argentina (*ibid.*, § 121), Burundi (*ibid.*, § 134), Jordan (*ibid.*, § 164), Lebanon (*ibid.*, § 167), Sri Lanka (*ibid.*, § 204) and Trinidad and Tobago (*ibid.*, § 206).

[27] See, in particular, France, Permanent Military Tribunal at Dijon, *Holstein case* (*ibid.*, § 221); Germany, Oberlandsgericht of Dresden, *General Devastation case* (*ibid.*, § 222); Netherlands, Special Court of Cassation, *Wingten case* (*ibid.*, § 224); United States, Military Tribunal at Nuremberg, *List (Hostages Trial) case* (*ibid.*, § 225) and *Von Leeb (The High Command Trial) case* (*ibid.*, § 226).

[28] ICTY, *Nikolić case*, Initial Indictment and Review of the Indictment (*ibid.*, § 236), *Karadžić and Mladić case*, First Indictment and Review of the Indictments (*ibid.*, § 237), *Rajić case*, Initial Indictment and Review of the Indictment (*ibid.*, § 238), *Blaškić case*, Judgement (*ibid.*, § 239), and *Kordić and Čerkez case*, Judgement (*ibid.*, § 240).

[29] ICC Statute, Article 8(2)(e)(xii) (*ibid.*, § 56).

[30] See, e.g., the military manuals of Australia (*ibid.*, § 72), Benin (*ibid.*, § 76), Canada (*ibid.*, § 79), Colombia (*ibid.*, § 80), Ecuador (*ibid.*, § 83), Germany (*ibid.*, § 88), Italy (*ibid.*, §§ 91–92), Kenya (*ibid.*, § 93), Lebanon (*ibid.*, § 95), Madagascar (*ibid.*, § 96), Nigeria (*ibid.*, §§ 100 and 102), Peru (*ibid.*, § 103), Philippines (*ibid.*, § 104), South Africa (*ibid.*, § 108) and Togo (*ibid.*, § 112).

[31] See, e.g., the legislation of Armenia (*ibid.*, § 122), Australia (*ibid.*, § 125), Azerbaijan (*ibid.*, § 126), Belarus (*ibid.*, § 129), Belgium (*ibid.*, § 130), Bosnia and Herzegovina (*ibid.*, § 131), Cambodia (*ibid.*, § 135), Canada (*ibid.*, § 138), Congo (*ibid.*, § 142), Croatia (*ibid.*, § 144), El Salvador (*ibid.*, §§ 149–150), Estonia (*ibid.*, § 151), Georgia (*ibid.*, § 154), Germany (*ibid.*, § 155), Latvia (*ibid.*, § 166), Lithuania (*ibid.*, § 168), Moldova (*ibid.*, § 177), Netherlands (*ibid.*, § 180), New Zealand (*ibid.*, § 182), Nicaragua (*ibid.*, § 184), Niger (*ibid.*, § 185), Portugal (*ibid.*, § 193), Slovenia (*ibid.*, § 199), Spain (*ibid.*, §§ 200–201), Tajikistan (*ibid.*, § 205), United Kingdom (*ibid.*, § 211), Uzbekistan (*ibid.*, § 215) and Yugoslavia (*ibid.*, § 219); see also the legislation of Bulgaria (*ibid.*, § 133), Czech Republic (*ibid.*, § 147), Italy (*ibid.*, §§ 161–162), Mozambique (*ibid.*, § 178), Nicaragua (*ibid.*, § 183), Paraguay (*ibid.*, § 190), Peru (*ibid.*, § 191), Romania (*ibid.*, § 194) and Slovakia (*ibid.*, § 198), the application of which is not excluded in time of non-international armed conflict, and the draft legislation of Argentina (*ibid.*, § 121), Burundi (*ibid.*, § 134), Jordan (*ibid.*, § 164) and Trinidad and Tobago (*ibid.*, § 206).

Rule 51. In occupied territory:

   (a) **movable public property that can be used for military operations may be confiscated;**
   (b) **immovable public property must be administered according to the rule of usufruct; and**
   (c) **private property must be respected and may not be confiscated**

except where destruction or seizure of such property is required by imperative military necessity.

Practice

Volume II, Chapter 16, Section C.

Summary

State practice establishes this rule as a norm of customary international law applicable in international armed conflicts.

Movable public property

The rule that all movable public property that may be used for military operations may be confiscated is a long-standing rule of customary international law already recognised in the Lieber Code, the Brussels Declaration and the Oxford Manual.[32] It is codified in the Hague Regulations, which provides that the following may be confiscated: "cash, funds, and realizable securities which are strictly the property of the State, depots of arms, means of transport, stores and supplies, and, generally, all movable property belonging to the State which may be used for military operations".[33]

This rule is set forth in numerous military manuals.[34] It was applied in several cases after the Second World War.[35]

The military manuals of Australia, Canada and New Zealand define confiscation as "the taking of enemy public movable property without the obligation to compensate the State to which it belongs".[36] Technically, this differs from war booty to the extent that the latter only concerns military equipment captured or found on the battlefield, but both categories have been blurred in practice as

---

[32] Lieber Code, Article 31 (*ibid.*, § 246); Brussels Declaration, Article 6 (*ibid.*, § 247); Oxford Manual, Article 50 (*ibid.*, § 248).

[33] Hague Regulations, Article 53 (*ibid.*, § 245).

[34] See, e.g., the military manuals of Argentina (*ibid.*, § 251), Australia (*ibid.*, § 252), Canada (*ibid.*, § 253), France (*ibid.*, § 254), Germany (*ibid.*, § 255), Italy (*ibid.*, § 256), New Zealand (*ibid.*, § 257), Nigeria (*ibid.*, § 258), United Kingdom (*ibid.*, § 261) and United States (*ibid.*, § 262).

[35] See, in particular, United States, Military Tribunal at Nuremberg, *Flick case* (*ibid.*, § 268), *Krupp case* (*ibid.*, § 269) and *Krauch (I. G. Farben Trial) case* (*ibid.*, § 270).

[36] Australia, *Defence Force Manual* (*ibid.*, § 252); Canada, *LOAC Manual* (*ibid.*, § 253); New Zealand, *Military Manual* (*ibid.*, § 257).

the applicable regime is the same: they may be taken without compensation. Germany's Military Manual, for example, refers to both as "spoils of war".[37]

According to the Hague Regulations the property of municipalities and of institutions dedicated to religion, charity and education, the arts and sciences, even when State property, shall be treated as private property.[38] As a result, it is prohibited to seize or destroy such property, including historic monuments and works of art and science (see Rule 40).

Immovable public property

The rule that immovable public property must be administered according to the rules of usufruct is a long-standing rule of customary international law already recognised in the Lieber Code, the Brussels Declaration and the Oxford Manual.[39] It is codified in the Hague Regulations as follows:

The occupying State shall be regarded only as administrator and usufructuary of public buildings, real estate, forests, and agricultural estates belonging to the hostile State, and situated in the occupied territory. It must safeguard the capital of these properties, and administer them in accordance with the rules of usufruct.[40]

This rule is contained in several military manuals.[41] The manuals of Australia, Canada and New Zealand explain that, as a result, "enemy public immovable property may be administered and used but it may not be confiscated".[42] This rule was applied in several cases after the Second World War.[43]

Several military manuals explicitly apply to immovable public property the principle that property of the adversary may be destroyed in case of imperative military necessity (see Rule 50).[44]

Private property

The protection of private property against confiscation is a long-standing rule of customary international law already recognised in the Lieber Code, the Brussels

---

[37] Germany, *Military Manual* (*ibid.*, § 255).   [38] Hague Regulations, Article 56.
[39] Lieber Code, Article 31 (cited in Vol. II, Ch. 16, § 284); Brussels Declaration, Article 7 (*ibid.*, § 285); Oxford Manual, Article 52 (*ibid.*, § 286).
[40] Hague Regulations, Article 55 (*ibid.*, § 283).
[41] See, e.g., the military manuals of Argentina (*ibid.*, § 288), Australia (*ibid.*, § 289), Canada (*ibid.*, § 290), Germany (*ibid.*, § 291), Italy (*ibid.*, § 292), New Zealand (*ibid.*, § 293), Switzerland (*ibid.*, § 296), United Kingdom (*ibid.*, § 297) and United States (*ibid.*, § 298).
[42] Australia, *Defence Force Manual* (*ibid.*, § 289); Canada, *LOAC Manual* (*ibid.*, § 290); New Zealand, *Military Manual* (*ibid.*, § 293).
[43] See, in particular, Poland, Supreme National Tribunal, *Greiser case* (*ibid.*, § 302); United States, Military Tribunal at Nuremberg, *Flick case* (*ibid.*, § 303), *Krupp case* (*ibid.*, § 304) and *Krauch (I. G. Farben Trial) case* (*ibid.*, § 305).
[44] See, e.g., the military manuals of Canada (*ibid.*, § 290), New Zealand (*ibid.*, § 293), Nigeria (*ibid.*, § 294), United Kingdom (*ibid.*, § 297) and United States (*ibid.*, § 298).

Declaration and the Oxford Manual.[45] The prohibition of confiscation of private property is codified in Article 46 of the Hague Regulations.[46] This prohibition does not mean that no private property may ever be seized because, as stated in Article 53 of the Hague Regulations:

All appliances, whether on land, at sea, or in the air, adapted for the transmission of news, or for the transport of persons or things . . . depots of arms, and, generally, all kinds of munitions of war, may be seized, even if they belong to private individuals, but they must be restored and compensation fixed when peace is made.[47]

This rule is contained in numerous military manuals.[48] As explained in Australia's Defence Force Manual, "these objects may be seized by, but they do not become the property of, the occupying power. The seizure operates merely as a transfer of the possession of the object to the occupying power while ownership remains with the private owner."[49] According to New Zealand's Military Manual, within this category fall:

cables, telegraph and telephone plant; television, telecommunications and radio equipment; horses, motorcars, bicycles, carts and carriages; railways and railway plant, tramways; ships in port, river and canal craft; aircraft of all descriptions, except ambulance aircraft; sporting weapons; and all kinds of property which could serve as war material.[50]

Several military manuals explicitly apply to private property the principle that property of the adversary may be destroyed or seized in case of imperative military necessity (see Rule 50).[51]

The protection of private property against confiscation was confirmed in national case-law after the Second World War and in several other cases.[52] In the

---

[45] Lieber Code, Article 22 (*ibid.*, § 319), Article 37 (*ibid.*, § 320) and Article 38 (*ibid.*, § 321); Brussels Declaration, Article 38 (*ibid.*, § 322); Oxford Manual, Article 54 (*ibid.*, § 323).

[46] Hague Regulations, Article 46 (*ibid.*, § 317).

[47] Hague Regulations, Article 53 (*ibid.*, § 317).

[48] See, e.g., the military manuals of Argentina (*ibid.*, § 327), Australia (*ibid.*, § 329), Benin (*ibid.*, § 330), Canada (*ibid.*, §§ 333–334), Colombia (*ibid.*, §§ 335–337), Germany (*ibid.*, § 342), Hungary (*ibid.*, § 343), Indonesia (*ibid.*, § 344), Israel (*ibid.*, § 345), Italy (*ibid.*, § 346), New Zealand (*ibid.*, § 349), Nigeria (*ibid.*, §§ 350–352), Peru (*ibid.*, § 353), Philippines (*ibid.*, § 354), Romania (*ibid.*, § 356), South Africa (*ibid.*, § 357), Switzerland (*ibid.*, § 358), Togo (*ibid.*, § 359), Uganda (*ibid.*, §§ 360–361), United Kingdom (*ibid.*, § 362) and United States (*ibid.*, §§ 363–364 and 367).

[49] Australia, *Defence Force Manual* (*ibid.*, § 329).

[50] New Zealand, *Military Manual* (*ibid.*, § 349).

[51] See, e.g., the military manuals of Switzerland (*ibid.*, § 358), United Kingdom (*ibid.*, § 362) and United States (*ibid.*, §§ 363 and 365).

[52] See, in particular, Bosnia and Herzegovina, Cantonal Court of Bihac, *Bijelić case* (*ibid.*, § 405); China, War Crimes Military Tribunal of the Ministry of National Defence at Nanking, *Takashi Sakai case* (*ibid.*, § 406); France, Permanent Military Tribunal at Clermont-Ferrand, *Szabados case* (*ibid.*, § 408); France, Permanent Military Tribunal at Metz, *Rust case* (*ibid.*, § 409); France, General Tribunal at Rastadt of the Military Government for the French Zone of Occupation in Germany, *Roechling case* (*ibid.*, § 410); Germany, Higher Regional Court at Düsseldorf and Federal Supreme Court, *Jorgić case* (*ibid.*, § 411); Israel, High Court, *Ayub case* (*ibid.*, § 412) and *Sakhwil case* (*ibid.*, § 413); Japan, District Court of Chiba, *Religious Organisation Hokekyoji case* (*ibid.*, § 415); Japan, District Court of Tokyo, *Takada case* (*ibid.*, § 416) and *Suikosha case* (*ibid.*, § 417); Netherlands, Special Court of Cassation, *Esau case* (*ibid.*, § 418); Netherlands,

Al-Nawar case before the Israeli High Court in 1985, Judge Shamgar considered that Article 46 of the Hague Regulations did not extend to property "actually in use by the hostile army".[53]

The Hague Regulations provides detailed rules with respect to contributions in kind and services, known as requisitions, demanded from the population and authorities of the occupied territory to satisfy the needs of the occupying forces:

Requisitions in kind and services shall not be demanded from municipalities or inhabitants except for the needs of the army of occupation. They shall be in proportion to the resources of the country, and of such a nature as not to involve the inhabitants in the obligation of taking part in military operations against their own country. Such requisitions and services shall only be demanded on the authority of the commander in the locality occupied. Contributions in kind shall as far as possible be paid for in cash; if not, a receipt shall be given and the payment of the amount due shall be made as soon as possible.[54]

These rules are incorporated in many military manuals.[55] Their violation constitutes an offence under the legislation of many States.[56] There exist further detailed rules which restrict the requisitioning of specific types of objects: property of aid societies;[57] civilian hospitals in occupied territory;[58] civil defence materiel and buildings in occupied territories.[59]

The principal rule of respect for private property is explicitly set forth in some manuals which are applicable in non-international armed conflicts.[60] This rule does not, however, establish a specific separate rule outside the prohibition of destruction or seizure except in case of imperative military necessity (see Rule 50) and the prohibition of pillage (see Rule 52). No rule could be identified for non-international armed conflicts which would prohibit, according to international law, the confiscation of private property, nor is there a rule of

---

Special Criminal Court at The Hague, *Fiebig case* (*ibid.*, § 419); Poland, Supreme National Tribunal, *Greiser case* (*ibid.*, § 420); United States, Military Tribunal at Nuremberg, *Flick case* (*ibid.*, § 421), *Krupp case* (*ibid.*, § 422), *Krauch (I. G. Farben Trial) case* (*ibid.*, § 423) and *Von Leeb (The High Command Trial) case* (*ibid.*, § 424).

[53] Israel, High Court, *Al-Nawar case* (*ibid.*, § 414).
[54] Hague Regulations, Article 52 (*ibid.*, § 317).
[55] See, e.g., the military manuals of Argentina (*ibid.*, § 327), Australia (*ibid.*, §§ 328–329), Canada (*ibid.*, §§ 333–334), France (*ibid.*, § 341), Germany (*ibid.*, § 342), Italy (*ibid.*, § 346), New Zealand (*ibid.*, § 349), Nigeria (*ibid.*, § 351), Switzerland (*ibid.*, § 358), United Kingdom (*ibid.*, § 362) and United States (*ibid.*, §§ 363–364).
[56] See, e.g., the legislation of Argentina (*ibid.*, § 368), Bosnia and Herzegovina (*ibid.*, § 373), Bulgaria (*ibid.*, § 374), Chile (*ibid.*, § 376), China (*ibid.*, § 377), Colombia (*ibid.*, § 378), Croatia (*ibid.*, § 379), Estonia (*ibid.*, § 382), Italy (*ibid.*, §§ 387–388), Lithuania (*ibid.*, § 389), Moldova (*ibid.*, § 391), Netherlands (*ibid.*, § 395), Norway (*ibid.*, § 396), Slovenia (*ibid.*, § 398), Spain (*ibid.*, § 399) and Yugoslavia (*ibid.*, § 404); see also the draft legislation of Argentina (*ibid.*, § 370).
[57] First Geneva Convention, Article 34.   [58] Fourth Geneva Convention, Article 57.
[59] Additional Protocol I, Article 63(4)–(6).
[60] See, e.g., the military manuals of Benin (cited in Vol. II, Ch. 16, § 330), Canada (*ibid.*, § 334), Colombia (*ibid.*, §§ 336–337), El Salvador (*ibid.*, § 340), Italy (*ibid.*, § 346), Peru (*ibid.*, § 353), Philippines (*ibid.*, § 354), South Africa (*ibid.*, § 357) and Togo (*ibid.*, § 359).

international law which allows such confiscation. It is expected, however, that this question would be regulated in national legislation.

Rule 52. Pillage is prohibited.

Practice

Volume II, Chapter 16, Section D.

Summary

State practice establishes this rule as a norm of customary international law applicable in both international and non-international armed conflicts.

International armed conflicts

The prohibition of pillage is a long-standing rule of customary international law already recognised in the Lieber Code, the Brussels Declaration and the Oxford Manual.[61] Pillage is prohibited under all circumstances under the Hague Regulations.[62] Pillage is identified as a war crime in the Report of the Commission on Responsibility set up after the First World War, as well as by the Charter of the International Military Tribunal (Nuremberg) established following the Second World War.[63] The Fourth Geneva Convention also prohibits pillage.[64] Under the Statute of the International Criminal Court, "pillaging a town or place, even when taken by assault," constitutes a war crime in international armed conflicts.[65]

The prohibition of pillage is set forth in numerous military manuals.[66] Pillage constitutes an offence under the legislation of a large number of States.[67] This

---

[61] Lieber Code, Article 44 (*ibid.*, § 470); Brussels Declaration, Article 18 (*ibid.*, § 471) and Article 39 (*ibid.*, § 472); Oxford Manual, Article 32 (*ibid.*, § 473).

[62] Hague Regulations, Article 28 (*ibid.*, § 461) and Article 47 (*ibid.*, § 462).

[63] Report of the Commission on Responsibility (*ibid.*, § 475); IMT Charter (Nuremberg), Article 6(b) (punishing "plunder") (*ibid.*, § 465).

[64] Fourth Geneva Convention, Article 33, second paragraph (*ibid.*, § 466).

[65] ICC Statute, Article 8(2)(b)(xvi) (*ibid.*, § 468).

[66] See, e.g., the military manuals of Argentina (*ibid.*, §§ 486–487), Australia (*ibid.*, §§ 488–489), Belgium (*ibid.*, §§ 490–491), Benin (*ibid.*, § 492), Burkina Faso (*ibid.*, § 493), Cameroon (*ibid.*, §§ 494–495), Canada (*ibid.*, §§ 496–497), China (*ibid.*, § 498), Colombia (*ibid.*, §§ 499–500), Congo (*ibid.*, § 501), Croatia (*ibid.*, §§ 502–503), Dominican Republic (*ibid.*, § 504), Ecuador (*ibid.*, § 505), El Salvador (*ibid.*, § 506), France (*ibid.*, §§ 507–510), Germany (*ibid.*, §§ 511–512), Indonesia (*ibid.*, §§ 513–514), Israel (*ibid.*, §§ 515–516), Italy (*ibid.*, §§ 517–518), Kenya (*ibid.*, § 519), South Korea (*ibid.*, §§ 520–521), Madagascar (*ibid.*, § 522), Mali (*ibid.*, § 523), Morocco (*ibid.*, § 524), Netherlands (*ibid.*, §§ 525–526), New Zealand (*ibid.*, § 527), Nigeria (*ibid.*, §§ 528–531), Peru (*ibid.*, § 532), Philippines (*ibid.*, §§ 533–534), Russia (*ibid.*, § 535), Senegal (*ibid.*, §§ 536–537), South Africa (*ibid.*, § 538), Spain (*ibid.*, § 539), Sweden (*ibid.*, § 540), Switzerland (*ibid.*, § 541), Togo (*ibid.*, § 542), Uganda (*ibid.*, §§ 543–544), United Kingdom (*ibid.*, §§ 545–546), United States (*ibid.*, §§ 547–552) and Yugoslavia (*ibid.*, § 553).

[67] See, e.g., the legislation of Albania (*ibid.*, § 554), Algeria (*ibid.*, § 555), Australia (*ibid.*, §§ 557–559), Azerbaijan (*ibid.*, §§ 560–561), Bangladesh (*ibid.*, § 562), Bosnia and Herzegovina

prohibition has been enforced in several cases before national courts after the Second World War,[68] as it has by the International Criminal Tribunal for the Former Yugoslavia.[69] The prohibition of pillage has been supported by official statements and other practice.[70]

Non-international armed conflicts

Pillage is prohibited under Additional Protocol II.[71] Under the Statute of the International Criminal Court, "pillaging a town or place, even when taken by assault," constitutes a war crime in non-international armed conflicts.[72] Pillage is also included as a war crime in the Statutes of the International Criminal Tribunals for the Former Yugoslavia and for Rwanda and of the Special Court for Sierra Leone.[73]

(*ibid.*, § 563), Brazil (*ibid.*, § 564), Bulgaria (*ibid.*, § 565), Burkina Faso (*ibid.*, § 566), Cameroon (*ibid.*, § 568), Canada (*ibid.*, §§ 569–570), Chad (*ibid.*, § 571), Chile (*ibid.*, § 572), China (*ibid.*, §§ 573–574), Colombia (*ibid.*, § 576), Democratic Republic of the Congo (*ibid.*, § 577), Congo (*ibid.*, § 578), Côte d'Ivoire (*ibid.*, § 579), Croatia (*ibid.*, § 580), Czech Republic (*ibid.*, § 581), Ecuador (*ibid.*, § 582), Egypt (*ibid.*, § 583), El Salvador (*ibid.*, §§ 584–585), Estonia (*ibid.*, § 586), Ethiopia (*ibid.*, § 587), France (*ibid.*, § 588), Gambia (*ibid.*, § 589), Georgia (*ibid.*, § 590), Germany (*ibid.*, § 591), Ghana (*ibid.*, § 592), Guinea (*ibid.*, § 593), Hungary (*ibid.*, § 594), India (*ibid.*, § 595), Indonesia (*ibid.*, §§ 596–597), Iraq (*ibid.*, § 598), Ireland (*ibid.*, § 599), Israel (*ibid.*, §§ 600–601), Italy (*ibid.*, §§ 602–603), Jordan (*ibid.*, § 604), Kazakhstan (*ibid.*, § 605), Kenya (*ibid.*, § 606), South Korea (*ibid.*, § 607), Latvia (*ibid.*, § 608), Luxembourg (*ibid.*, § 609), Malaysia (*ibid.*, § 610), Mali (*ibid.*, §§ 611–612), Mexico (*ibid.*, § 613), Moldova (*ibid.*, § 614), Morocco (*ibid.*, § 615), Mozambique (*ibid.*, § 616), Myanmar (*ibid.*, § 617), Netherlands (*ibid.*, §§ 618–620), New Zealand (*ibid.*, §§ 621–622), Nicaragua (*ibid.*, § 623), Nigeria (*ibid.*, § 624), Norway (*ibid.*, § 625), Paraguay (*ibid.*, §§ 626–627), Peru (*ibid.*, § 628), Philippines (*ibid.*, §§ 629–630), Russia (*ibid.*, § 631), Senegal (*ibid.*, § 632), Singapore (*ibid.*, § 633), Slovakia (*ibid.*, § 634), Slovenia (*ibid.*, § 635), Spain (*ibid.*, §§ 636–638), Sri Lanka (*ibid.*, §§ 639–641), Switzerland (*ibid.*, § 642), Tajikistan (*ibid.*, § 643), Togo (*ibid.*, § 644), Trinidad and Tobago (*ibid.*, § 645), Tunisia (*ibid.*, § 647), Uganda (*ibid.*, § 648), Ukraine (*ibid.*, § 649), United Kingdom (*ibid.*, §§ 650–652), United States (*ibid.*, §§ 653–656), Uzbekistan (*ibid.*, § 657), Venezuela (*ibid.*, § 658), Vietnam (*ibid.*, § 659), Yemen (*ibid.*, §§ 660–661), Yugoslavia (*ibid.*, §§ 662–663), Zambia (*ibid.*, § 664) and Zimbabwe (*ibid.*, § 665); see also the draft legislation of Argentina (*ibid.*, § 556), Burundi (*ibid.*, § 567) and Trinidad and Tobago (*ibid.*, § 646).

[68] See, in particular, China, War Crimes Military Tribunal of the Ministry of National Defence at Nanking, *Takashi Sakai case* (*ibid.*, § 667); France, Permanent Military Tribunal at Clermont-Ferrand, *Szabados case* (*ibid.*, § 669); France, Permanent Military Tribunal at Dijon, *Holstein case* (*ibid.*, § 670); France, Permanent Military Tribunal at Metz, *Bauer case* (*ibid.*, § 671); Netherlands, Special Criminal Court at Hertogenbosch and Special Court of Cassation, *Esau case* (*ibid.*, § 675); Netherlands, Special Criminal Court at The Hague, *Fiebig case* (*ibid.*, § 676); United States, Military Tribunal at Nuremberg, *Pohl case* (*ibid.*, § 677) and *Von Leeb (The High Command Trial) case* (*ibid.*, § 678).

[69] ICTY, *Jelisić case*, Judgement (*ibid.*, § 740), *Delalić case*, Judgement (*ibid.*, § 742), *Blaškić case*, Judgement (*ibid.*, § 743) and *Kordić and Čerkez case*, Judgement (*ibid.*, § 744).

[70] See, e.g., the statements of Afghanistan (*ibid.*, § 680), Bahrain (*ibid.*, § 683), China (*ibid.*, § 684), Finland (*ibid.*, § 686), France (*ibid.*, § 687), Germany (*ibid.*, §§ 688–689), Kuwait (*ibid.*, §§ 691–693), Qatar (*ibid.*, § 695), Russia (*ibid.*, § 697), Slovenia (*ibid.*, § 699), Spain (*ibid.*, § 700), United Kingdom (*ibid.*, §§ 701 and 703), United States (*ibid.*, § 704) and Yugoslavia (*ibid.*, § 705), the practice of the United Kingdom (*ibid.*, § 702) and the reported practice of Iran (*ibid.*, § 690).

[71] Additional Protocol II, Article 4(2)(g) (adopted by consensus) (*ibid.*, § 467).

[72] ICC Statute, Article 8(2)(e)(v) (*ibid.*, § 468).

[73] ICTY Statute, Article 3(e) (*ibid.*, § 480); ICTR Statute, Article 4(f) (*ibid.*, § 482); Statute of the Special Court for Sierra Leone, Article 3 (*ibid.*, § 469).

The prohibition of pillage is set forth in military manuals which are applicable in or have been applied in non-international armed conflicts.[74] Pillage is an offence under the legislation of many States.[75] In its judgement in the *Military Junta case* in 1985, Argentina's National Court of Appeals applied the prohibition of pillage in the Hague Regulations to acts committed in the context of internal violence.[76] The prohibition of pillage has been supported by official statements and other practice in the context of non-international armed conflicts.[77]

No official contrary practice was found with respect to either international or non-international armed conflicts. Alleged violations of this rule have generally been condemned by States.[78] They have also been condemned by the United Nations and other international organisations.[79] In most cases, they

---

[74] See, e.g., the military manuals of Argentina (*ibid.*, § 487), Australia (*ibid.*, §§ 488–489), Benin (*ibid.*, § 492), Cameroon (*ibid.*, § 495), Canada (*ibid.*, §§ 496–497), China (*ibid.*, § 498), Colombia (*ibid.*, §§ 499–500), Croatia (*ibid.*, §§ 502–503), Ecuador (*ibid.*, § 505), El Salvador (*ibid.*, § 506), France (*ibid.*, § 510), Germany (*ibid.*, §§ 511–512), Italy (*ibid.*, §§ 517–518), Kenya (*ibid.*, § 519), Madagascar (*ibid.*, § 522), Netherlands (*ibid.*, § 525), New Zealand (*ibid.*, § 527), Nigeria (*ibid.*, §§ 528–529 and 531), Peru (*ibid.*, § 533), Philippines (*ibid.*, §§ 533–534), Russia (*ibid.*, § 535), Senegal (*ibid.*, § 537), South Africa (*ibid.*, § 538), Spain (*ibid.*, § 539), Togo (*ibid.*, § 542), Uganda (*ibid.*, §§ 543–544) and Yugoslavia (*ibid.*, § 553).

[75] See, e.g., the legislation of Australia (*ibid.*, § 559), Azerbaijan (*ibid.*, § 561), Bosnia and Herzegovina (*ibid.*, § 563), Canada (*ibid.*, §§ 569–570), Colombia (*ibid.*, § 576), Democratic Republic of the Congo (*ibid.*, § 577), Congo (*ibid.*, § 578), Croatia (*ibid.*, § 580), Ecuador (*ibid.*, § 582), El Salvador (*ibid.*, §§ 584–585), Estonia (*ibid.*, § 586), Ethiopia (*ibid.*, § 587), Gambia (*ibid.*, § 589), Georgia (*ibid.*, § 590), Germany (*ibid.*, § 591), Ghana (*ibid.*, § 592), Guinea (*ibid.*, § 593), Ireland (*ibid.*, § 599), Kazakhstan (*ibid.*, § 605), Kenya (*ibid.*, § 606), Latvia (*ibid.*, § 608), Moldova (*ibid.*, § 614), Netherlands (*ibid.*, § 620), New Zealand (*ibid.*, §§ 621–622), Nicaragua (*ibid.*, § 623), Nigeria (*ibid.*, § 624), Norway (*ibid.*, § 625), Paraguay (*ibid.*, § 627), Russia (*ibid.*, § 631), Singapore (*ibid.*, § 633), Slovenia (*ibid.*, § 635), Spain (*ibid.*, §§ 637–638), Switzerland (*ibid.*, § 642), Tajikistan (*ibid.*, § 643), Trinidad and Tobago (*ibid.*, § 645), Uganda (*ibid.*, § 648), Ukraine (*ibid.*, § 649), United Kingdom (*ibid.*, § 652), Uzbekistan (*ibid.*, § 657), Venezuela (*ibid.*, § 658), Yemen (*ibid.*, § 661), Yugoslavia (*ibid.*, § 663), Zambia (*ibid.*, § 664) and Zimbabwe (*ibid.*, § 665); see also the legislation of Bulgaria (*ibid.*, § 565), Burkina Faso (*ibid.*, § 566), Czech Republic (*ibid.*, § 581), Hungary (*ibid.*, § 594), Italy (*ibid.*, §§ 602–603), South Korea (*ibid.*, § 607), Mozambique (*ibid.*, § 616), Paraguay (*ibid.*, § 626), Peru (*ibid.*, § 628), Slovakia (*ibid.*, § 634) and Togo (*ibid.*, § 644), the application of which is not excluded in time of non-international armed conflict, and the draft legislation of Argentina (*ibid.*, § 556), Burundi (*ibid.*, § 567) and Trinidad and Tobago (*ibid.*, § 646).

[76] Argentina, National Court of Appeals, *Military Junta case* (*ibid.*, § 666).

[77] See, e.g., the statements of France (*ibid.*, § 687), Germany (*ibid.*, § 688), Russia (*ibid.*, § 696) and Rwanda (*ibid.*, § 698) and the practice of Colombia (*ibid.*, § 685) and Yugoslavia (*ibid.*, § 705).

[78] See, e.g., the statements of Afghanistan (*ibid.*, § 680), Bahrain (*ibid.*, § 683), China (*ibid.*, § 684), Colombia (*ibid.*, § 685), Finland (*ibid.*, § 686), France (*ibid.*, § 687), Germany (*ibid.*, §§ 688–689), Kuwait (*ibid.*, §§ 691–693), Nigeria (*ibid.*, § 694), Qatar (*ibid.*, § 695), Russia (*ibid.*, §§ 696–697), Rwanda (*ibid.*, § 698), Slovenia (*ibid.*, § 699), Spain (*ibid.*, § 700), United Kingdom (*ibid.*, §§ 701–703), United States (*ibid.*, § 704) and Yugoslavia (*ibid.*, § 705).

[79] See, e.g. UN Security Council, Res. 912 (*ibid.*, § 710), Res. 1019 (*ibid.*, § 711) and Res. 1034 (*ibid.*, § 712); UN Security Council, Statements by the President (*ibid.*, §§ 713–715); UN General Assembly, Res. 50/193 (*ibid.*, § 716); UN Commission on Human Rights, Res. 1994/59 (*ibid.*, § 717), Res. 1996/71 (*ibid.*, § 718) and Res. 1997/57 (*ibid.*, § 719); Gulf Cooperation Council, Final Communiqué of the Ministerial Council (*ibid.*, § 736).

have been denied or recognised as unlawful by the parties involved.[80] In another instance the authorities expressed their inability to impose discipline on their troops.[81]

The Plan of Action for the years 2000–2003, adopted by the 27th International Conference of the Red Cross and Red Crescent in 1999, requires that all the parties to an armed conflict ensure that "strict orders are given to prevent all serious violations of international humanitarian law, including... looting".[82]

The specific practice collected with respect to pillage of cultural property (see Rule 40) and of property of the wounded and sick (see Rule 111), the dead (see Rule 113) and persons deprived of their liberty (see Rule 122) should also be considered in the assessment of the customary nature of this rule.

Definition

Pillage (or plunder) is defined in Black's Law Dictionary as "the forcible taking of private property by an invading or conquering army from the enemy's subjects".[83] The Elements of Crimes of the Statute of the International Criminal Court specifies that the appropriation must be done "for private or personal use".[84] As such, the prohibition of pillage is a specific application of the general principle of law prohibiting theft. This prohibition is to be found in national criminal legislation around the world. Pillage is generally punishable under military law or general penal law.

---

[80] See, e.g., the statements of Russia (*ibid.*, § 696) and Rwanda (*ibid.*, § 698) and the reported practice of Bosnia and Herzegovina, Republika Srpska (*ibid.*, § 757).

[81] See, e.g., the reported practice of a State (*ibid.*, § 708).

[82] 27th International Conference of the Red Cross and Red Crescent, Plan of Action for the years 2000–2003 (adopted by consensus) (*ibid.*, § 738).

[83] *Black's Law Dictionary*, Fifth Edition, West Publishing, St. Paul, Minnesota, 1979, p. 1033.

[84] Elements of Crimes for the ICC, Pillage as a war crime (ICC Statute, Article 8(2)(b)(xvi) and (e)(v)).

STARVATION AND ACCESS TO HUMANITARIAN RELIEF

Rule 53. The use of starvation of the civilian population as a method of warfare is prohibited.

Practice

Volume II, Chapter 17, Section A.

Summary

State practice establishes this rule as a norm of customary international law applicable in both international and non-international armed conflicts.

International armed conflicts

While in 1863 the Lieber Code still stated that "it is lawful to starve the hostile belligerent, armed or unarmed, so that it leads to the speedier subjection of the enemy",[1] by 1919 the Report of the Commission on Responsibility set up after the First World War listed "deliberate starvation of civilians" as a violation of the laws and customs of war subject to criminal prosecution.[2] The prohibition of starvation as a method of warfare is codified in Article 54(1) of Additional Protocol I.[3] This provision was generally considered new at the time of the adoption of Additional Protocol I but since then has hardened into a rule of customary international law. Under the Statute of the International Criminal Court, "intentionally using starvation of civilians as a method of warfare" is a war crime in international armed conflicts.[4]

The prohibition of starvation is set forth in numerous military manuals.[5] Starvation of civilians as a method of warfare is an offence under the legislation

---

[1] Lieber Code, Article 17 (cited in Vol. II, Ch. 17, § 4).
[2] Report of the Commission on Responsibility (*ibid.*, § 5).
[3] Additional Protocol I, Article 54(1) (adopted by consensus) (*ibid.*, § 1).
[4] ICC Statute, Article 8(2)(b)(xxv) (*ibid.*, § 3).
[5] See, e.g., the military manuals of Argentina (*ibid.*, § 9), Australia (*ibid.*, §§ 10–11), Belgium (*ibid.*, § 12), Benin (*ibid.*, § 13), Canada (*ibid.*, § 14), Colombia (*ibid.*, § 15), Croatia (*ibid.*, § 16), France (*ibid.*, §§ 17–18), Germany (*ibid.*, § 19), Hungary (*ibid.*, § 20), Indonesia (*ibid.*, § 21), Israel (*ibid.*, § 22), Kenya (*ibid.*, § 23), South Korea (*ibid.*, § 24), Madagascar (*ibid.*, § 25), Netherlands (*ibid.*, § 26), New Zealand (*ibid.*, § 27), Nigeria (*ibid.*, § 28), Russia (*ibid.*, § 29), Spain (*ibid.*, § 30), Sweden (*ibid.*, § 31), Switzerland (*ibid.*, § 32), Togo (*ibid.*, § 33), United Kingdom (*ibid.*, § 34), United States (*ibid.*, § 35) and Yugoslavia (*ibid.*, § 36).

of many States.[6] This rule is also supported by official statements and other practice.[7] This practice includes that of States not, or not at the time, party to Additional Protocol I.[8] Contrary practice has been generally condemned or has been denied by the accused party.[9]

Non-international armed conflicts

The prohibition of starvation as a method of warfare is contained in Additional Protocol II.[10] In addition, this rule is contained in other instruments pertaining also to non-international armed conflicts.[11]

The prohibition of starvation is included in military manuals which are applicable in or have been applied in non-international armed conflicts.[12] Starvation of civilians as a method of warfare constitutes a war crime under the legislation of several States.[13] The prohibition of starvation was applied by the District Court of Zadar in the *Perišić and Others case* in 1997.[14] It is further supported by official statements and reported practice in the context of non-international

---

[6] See, e.g., the legislation of Australia (*ibid.*, §§ 37–38), Azerbaijan (*ibid.*, § 39), Belarus (*ibid.*, § 40), Bosnia and Herzegovina (*ibid.*, § 41), Canada (*ibid.*, § 43), China (*ibid.*, § 44), Congo (*ibid.*, § 45), Côte d'Ivoire (*ibid.*, § 46), Croatia (*ibid.*, § 47), Ethiopia (*ibid.*, § 48), Georgia (*ibid.*, § 49), Germany (*ibid.*, § 50), Ireland (*ibid.*, § 51), Lithuania (*ibid.*, § 52), Mali (*ibid.*, § 53), Netherlands (*ibid.*, §§ 54–55), New Zealand (*ibid.*, § 56), Norway (*ibid.*, § 57), Slovenia (*ibid.*, § 58), United Kingdom (*ibid.*, § 60) and Yugoslavia (*ibid.*, §§ 61–62); see also the draft legislation of Burundi (*ibid.*, § 42) and Trinidad and Tobago (*ibid.*, § 59).

[7] See, e.g., the statements of Belgium (*ibid.*, § 67), China (*ibid.*, § 70), Côte d'Ivoire (*ibid.*, § 74), Cuba (*ibid.*, § 75), Finland (*ibid.*, § 77), Germany (*ibid.*, §§ 81–85), Malaysia (*ibid.*, § 92), United Kingdom (*ibid.*, § 99), United States (*ibid.*, § 101), USSR (*ibid.*, § 106) and Yemen (*ibid.*, § 107), the practice of the United States (*ibid.*, § 103) and the reported practice of Belgium (*ibid.*, § 69) and Israel (*ibid.*, § 88).

[8] See, e.g., the military manuals of France (*ibid.*, § 17), Indonesia (*ibid.*, § 21), Israel (*ibid.*, § 22), Kenya (*ibid.*, § 23), United Kingdom (*ibid.*, § 34) and United States (*ibid.*, § 35), the legislation of Azerbaijan (*ibid.*, § 39), China (*ibid.*, § 44), Ethiopia (*ibid.*, § 48) and Netherlands (*ibid.*, § 54), the statements of Malaysia (*ibid.*, § 92), United Kingdom (*ibid.*, § 99) and United States (*ibid.*, § 101) and the reported practice of Israel (*ibid.*, § 88).

[9] See, e.g., the statements of Austria (*ibid.*, § 66), China (*ibid.*, § 70), Côte d'Ivoire (*ibid.*, § 74), Cuba (*ibid.*, § 75), Egypt (*ibid.*, § 76), Finland (*ibid.*, § 77), Germany (*ibid.*, § 81), Iran (*ibid.*, § 76), Malaysia (*ibid.*, § 92), Pakistan (*ibid.*, § 76), Saudi Arabia (*ibid.*, § 76), Senegal (*ibid.*, § 76), Turkey (*ibid.*, § 76), United Kingdom (*ibid.*, § 99); Yemen (*ibid.*, § 107) and three States (*ibid.*, §§ 108–110).

[10] Additional Protocol II, Article 14 (adopted by consensus) (*ibid.*, § 2).

[11] See, e.g., Memorandum of Understanding on the Application of IHL between Croatia and the SFRY, para. 6 (*ibid.*, § 6); Agreement on the Application of IHL between the Parties to the Conflict in Bosnia and Herzegovina, para. 2.5 (*ibid.*, § 7).

[12] See, e.g., the military manuals of Argentina (*ibid.*, § 9), Australia (*ibid.*, §§ 10–11), Benin (*ibid.*, § 13), Canada (*ibid.*, § 14), Colombia (*ibid.*, § 15), Croatia (*ibid.*, § 16), France (*ibid.*, § 18), Germany (*ibid.*, § 19), Hungary (*ibid.*, § 20), Kenya (*ibid.*, § 23), South Korea (*ibid.*, § 24), Madagascar (*ibid.*, § 25), Netherlands (*ibid.*, § 26), New Zealand (*ibid.*, § 27), Nigeria (*ibid.*, § 28), Russia (*ibid.*, § 29), Spain (*ibid.*, § 30), Togo (*ibid.*, § 33) and Yugoslavia (*ibid.*, § 36).

[13] See, e.g., the legislation of Azerbaijan (*ibid.*, § 39), Belarus (*ibid.*, § 40), Bosnia and Herzegovina (*ibid.*, § 41), Croatia (*ibid.*, § 47), Ethiopia (*ibid.*, § 48), Germany (*ibid.*, § 50), Lithuania (*ibid.*, § 52), Slovenia (*ibid.*, § 57) and Yugoslavia (*ibid.*, § 61).

[14] Croatia, District Court of Zadar, *Perišić and Others case*, Judgement (*ibid.*, § 63).

armed conflicts.[15] States have generally denounced alleged instances of the use of starvation as a method of warfare in non-international armed conflicts, for example, in the civil wars in Nigeria and Sudan.[16]

The 26th International Conference of the Red Cross and Red Crescent in 1995 strongly condemned "attempts to starve civilian populations in armed conflicts" and stressed "the prohibition on using starvation of civilians as a method of warfare".[17] This prohibition was also emphasised in the Plan of Action for the years 2000–2003, adopted by the 27th International Conference of the Red Cross and Red Crescent in 1999.[18]

Rules 54–56 are a corollary to the prohibition of starvation of civilians as a method of warfare. This means that attacking objects indispensable to the survival of the civilian population (see Rule 54) and denying access of humanitarian aid intended for civilians in need, including deliberately impeding humanitarian aid (see Rule 55) or restricting the freedom of movement of humanitarian relief personnel (see Rule 56) may constitute violations of the prohibition of starvation. Practice in respect of Rules 54–56 further reinforces this rule's status as a norm of customary international law.

Sieges that cause starvation

The prohibition of starvation as a method of warfare does not prohibit siege warfare as long as the purpose is to achieve a military objective and not to starve a civilian population. This is stated in the military manuals of France and New Zealand.[19] Israel's Manual on the Laws of War explains that the prohibition of starvation "clearly implies that the city's inhabitants must be allowed to leave the city during a siege".[20] Alternatively, the besieging party must allow the free passage of foodstuffs and other essential supplies, in accordance with Rule 55. States denounced the use of siege warfare in Bosnia and Herzegovina.[21] It was also condemned by international organisations.[22]

---

[15] See, e.g., the statements of Belgium (*ibid.*, § 67), Colombia (*ibid.*, § 72), France (*ibid.*, § 78), Germany (*ibid.*, §§ 79–80), Holy See (*ibid.*, § 86), Iraq (*ibid.*, § 87), Nigeria (*ibid.*, § 94), Philippines (*ibid.*, § 96), Sweden (*ibid.*, § 98), United States (*ibid.*, § 102) and USSR (*ibid.*, § 105) and the reported practice of Belgium (*ibid.*, § 69), Malaysia (*ibid.*, § 93) and Rwanda (*ibid.*, § 97).

[16] See, e.g., the statements of Belgium (*ibid.*, § 67) and Germany (*ibid.*, §§ 79–80).

[17] 26th International Conference of the Red Cross and Red Crescent, Res. II (*ibid.*, § 118).

[18] 27th International Conference of the Red Cross and Red Crescent, Res. I (adopted by consensus) (*ibid.*, § 119).

[19] France, *LOAC Manual* (*ibid.*, § 136); New Zealand, *Military Manual* (*ibid.*, § 138).

[20] Israel, *Manual on the Laws of War* (*ibid.*, § 137).

[21] See, e.g., the statements of Albania (*ibid.*, § 142) and Pakistan (*ibid.*, § 144).

[22] See, e.g., UN Security Council, Res. 761 (*ibid.*, § 145), Res. 764 (*ibid.*, § 146) and Res. 859 (*ibid.*, § 147); UN Security Council, Statement by the President (*ibid.*, § 148); UN General Assembly, Res. 48/88, 49/10 and 49/196 (*ibid.*, § 149); UN Commission on Human Rights, Res. 1994/72 (*ibid.*, § 150); EU, Statement before the UN General Assembly (*ibid.*, § 153); Western European Union, Special Declaration of the Presidential Committee on the situation in the former Yugoslavia (*ibid.*, § 154).

Blockades and embargoes that cause starvation

Likewise, the prohibition of starvation as a method of warfare does not prohibit the imposition of a naval blockade as long as the purpose is to achieve a military objective and not to starve a civilian population. This principle is set forth in the San Remo Manual on Naval Warfare and in several military manuals which further specify that if the civilian population is inadequately provided for, the blockading party must provide for free passage of humanitarian relief supplies.[23] Blockades and embargoes of cities and regions have been condemned by the United Nations and other international organisations, for example, with respect to the conflicts in Afghanistan and the territories occupied by Israel.[24] Embargoes imposed by the United Nations itself must also comply with this rule.

Rule 54. Attacking, destroying, removing or rendering useless objects indispensable to the survival of the civilian population are prohibited.

Practice

Volume II, Chapter 17, Section B.

Summary

State practice establishes this rule as a norm of customary international law applicable in both international and non-international armed conflicts. This rule is a corollary to the prohibition of starvation (see Rule 53).

International armed conflicts

In principle, objects indispensable to the survival of the civilian population are civilian objects and may not be attacked as such (see Rule 7). A specific prohibition on attacking, destroying, removing or rendering useless objects indispensable to the survival of the civilian population is set forth in Article 54(2) of Additional Protocol I.[25] According to the Commentary on the Additional Protocols, "this provision develops the principle formulated in paragraph 1 [of Article 54] of prohibiting starvation of the civilian population; it describes the most usual ways in which this may be applied".[26] Article 54(2) prohibits attacks

---

[23] San Remo Manual, paras. 102–103 (*ibid.*, § 160); military manuals of Australia (*ibid.*, § 162), Canada (*ibid.*, § 163), France (*ibid.*, § 165) and United States (*ibid.*, § 169).

[24] See, e.g., UN Security Council, Statements by the President (*ibid.*, §§ 174–175); UN Commission on Human Rights, Res. 1994/74 (*ibid.*, § 176) and Res. 1995/76 (*ibid.*, § 176); OIC, Conference of Ministers of Foreign Affairs, Res. 1/7-P (IS) (*ibid.*, § 183).

[25] Additional Protocol I, Article 54(2) (adopted by consensus) (*ibid.*, § 188).

[26] Yves Sandoz, Christophe Swinarski, Bruno Zimmermann (eds.), *Commentary on the Additional Protocols*, ICRC, Geneva, 1987, § 2098.

against objects "for the specific purpose of denying them for their sustenance value to the civilian population or to the adverse Party, whatever the motive, whether in order to starve out civilians, to cause them to move away, or for any other motive".[27] Upon ratification of Additional Protocol I, France and the United Kingdom stated that this provision had no application to attacks that were carried out for a specific purpose other than denying sustenance to the civilian population.[28] Under the Statute of the International Criminal Court, "intentionally using starvation of civilians as a method of warfare by depriving them of objects indispensable to their survival" is a war crime in international armed conflicts.[29]

Numerous military manuals state that it is prohibited to attack, destroy, remove or render useless objects indispensable to the survival of the civilian population.[30] These include manuals of States not, or not at the time, party to Additional Protocol I.[31] The Annotated Supplement to the US Naval Handbook provides that this prohibition is part of customary international law.[32] Several military manuals specify that in order to be illegal, the intent of the attack has to be to prevent the civilian population from being supplied.[33] Most military manuals, however, do not indicate such a requirement and prohibit attacks against objects indispensable to the survival of the civilian population as such.[34] This is also the case with much of the national legislation which makes it an offence to violate this rule.[35]

---

[27] Additional Protocol I, Article 54(2) (adopted by consensus) (cited in Vol. II, Ch. 17, § 188).

[28] France, Reservations and declarations made upon ratification of Additional Protocol I (ibid., § 189); United Kingdom, Reservations and declarations made upon ratification of Additional Protocol I (ibid., § 190).

[29] ICC Statute, Article 8(2)(b)(xxiv) (ibid., § 192).

[30] See, e.g., the military manuals of Australia (ibid., §§ 199–200), Belgium (ibid., § 201), Benin (ibid., § 202), Canada (ibid., § 203), Colombia (ibid., § 204), Ecuador (ibid., § 205), France (ibid., §§ 206–208), Germany (ibid., §§ 209–210), Indonesia (ibid., § 212), Israel (ibid., § 213), Kenya (ibid., § 214), Madagascar (ibid., § 215), Netherlands (ibid., §§ 216–217), New Zealand (ibid., § 218), Nigeria (ibid., § 219), South Africa (ibid., § 220), Spain (ibid., § 221), Sweden (ibid., § 222), Switzerland (ibid., § 223), Togo (ibid., § 224), United Kingdom (ibid., § 225), United States (ibid., §§ 226–227) and Yugoslavia (ibid., § 228).

[31] See the military manuals of France (ibid., § 206), Indonesia (ibid., § 212), Israel (ibid., § 213), Kenya (ibid., § 214), United Kingdom (ibid., § 225) and United States (ibid., §§ 226–227).

[32] United States, Annotated Supplement to the Naval Handbook (ibid., § 227).

[33] See, e.g., the military manuals of Australia (ibid., § 200), Ecuador (ibid., § 205), France (ibid., § 208), Germany (ibid., § 210), New Zealand (ibid., § 218), Spain ("with the intent to starve the civilian population") (ibid., § 221), Sweden (ibid., § 222), United States (ibid., §§ 226–227) and Yugoslavia (ibid., § 228).

[34] See, e.g., the military manuals of Belgium (ibid., § 201), Benin (ibid., § 202), Canada ("whatever the motive") (ibid., § 203), Colombia (ibid., § 204), France (ibid., §§ 206–207), Indonesia (ibid., § 212), Israel (ibid., § 213), Kenya (ibid., § 214), Madagascar (ibid., § 215), Netherlands ("whatever the motive") (ibid., §§ 216–217), Nigeria (ibid., § 219), South Africa (ibid., § 220), Switzerland (ibid., § 223), Togo (ibid., § 224) and United Kingdom (ibid., § 225).

[35] See, e.g., the legislation of Colombia (ibid., § 233), Czech Republic (ibid., § 235), Estonia (ibid., § 237), Netherlands (ibid., § 245), Peru (ibid., § 249), Slovakia (ibid., § 250) and Spain (ibid., § 251); see also the draft legislation of Argentina (ibid., § 229), El Salvador (ibid., § 236) and Nicaragua (ibid., § 247).

Non-international armed conflicts

In principle, objects indispensable to the survival of the civilian population are civilian objects and may not be attacked as such (see Rule 7). The prohibition on attacking objects indispensable to the survival of the civilian population is set forth in Additional Protocol II and is defined therein as a corollary to the prohibition of starvation.[36] As stated in the Commentary on the Additional Protocols, this provision "develops the principle prohibiting starvation from being used against civilians by pointing out the most usual ways in which starvation is brought about".[37] In addition, this rule is contained in other instruments pertaining also to non-international armed conflicts.[38]

The prohibition is set forth in military manuals which are applicable in or have been applied in non-international armed conflicts.[39] Attacking objects indispensable to the survival of the civilian population is an offence under the legislation of several States.[40] This rule is also referred to in official statements and other practice relating to non-international armed conflicts.[41]

No official contrary practice was found with respect to either international or non-international armed conflicts. Alleged violations of this rule have generally been condemned, in particular by the United Nations and other international organisations, for example, with respect to the conflicts in Bosnia and Herzegovina and the Democratic Republic of the Congo.[42] The 26th International Conference of the Red Cross and Red Crescent in 1995 underlined in general terms "the prohibition on attacking, destroying, removing or rendering useless any objects indispensable to the survival of the civilian population".[43]

---

[36] Additional Protocol II, Article 14 (adopted by consensus) (*ibid.*, § 191).

[37] Yves Sandoz, Christophe Swinarski, Bruno Zimmermann (eds.), *Commentary on the Additional Protocols*, ICRC, Geneva, 1987, § 4800.

[38] See, e.g., Memorandum of Understanding on the Application of IHL between Croatia and the SFRY, para. 6 (cited in Vol. II, Ch. 17, § 194); Agreement on the Application of IHL between the Parties to the Conflict in Bosnia and Herzegovina, para. 2.5 (*ibid.*, § 195).

[39] See, e.g., the military manuals of Argentina (*ibid.*, § 198), Australia (*ibid.*, §§ 199–200), Benin (*ibid.*, § 202), Canada (*ibid.*, § 203), Colombia (*ibid.*, § 204), Ecuador (*ibid.*, § 205), France (*ibid.*, § 208), Germany (*ibid.*, §§ 209–210), Kenya (*ibid.*, § 214), Madagascar (*ibid.*, § 215), Netherlands (*ibid.*, § 216), New Zealand (*ibid.*, § 218), Nigeria (*ibid.*, § 219), South Africa (*ibid.*, § 220), Spain (*ibid.*, § 221), Togo (*ibid.*, § 224) and Yugoslavia (*ibid.*, § 228).

[40] See, e.g., the legislation of Colombia (*ibid.*, § 233), Estonia (*ibid.*, § 237), Germany (*ibid.*, § 239), Ireland (*ibid.*, § 241), Norway (*ibid.*, § 248) and Spain (*ibid.*, § 251); see also the legislation of Czech Republic (*ibid.*, § 235), Peru (*ibid.*, § 249) and Slovakia (*ibid.*, § 250), the application of which is not excluded in time of non-international armed conflict, and the draft legislation of Argentina (*ibid.*, § 229), El Salvador (*ibid.*, § 236) and Nicaragua (*ibid.*, § 247).

[41] See, e.g., the statement of Colombia (*ibid.*, § 259) and Philippines (*ibid.*, § 267) and the reported practice of Malaysia (*ibid.*, § 266) and Rwanda (*ibid.*, § 268).

[42] See, e.g., UN Security Council, Statements by the President (*ibid.*, §§ 274–275); UN High Commissioner for Human Rights and UN Under-Secretary-General for Humanitarian Affairs, Press release on the situation in the Democratic Republic of the Congo (*ibid.*, § 281); EU, Press Statement by the Presidency on the situation in the Democratic Republic of the Congo (*ibid.*, § 283).

[43] 26th International Conference of the Red Cross and Red Crescent, Res. II (*ibid.*, § 286).

The prohibition was also stressed in the Plan of Action for the years 2000–2003, adopted by the 27th International Conference of the Red Cross and Red Crescent in 1999.[44] The ICRC has called on parties to both international and non-international armed conflicts to respect this rule.[45]

Exceptions

There are two exceptions to the prohibition on attacking objects indispensable to the survival of the civilian population. The first exception is based on the consideration that these objects can be attacked if they qualify as military objectives. Additional Protocol I provides that this may be the case if the objects are used as sustenance solely for combatants or otherwise in direct support of military action.[46] This exception is set forth in several military manuals, some legislation and official statements.[47] This practice recognises, however, that when such objects are not used as sustenance solely for combatants but nevertheless in direct support of military action, the prohibition of starvation prohibits the attack of such objects if the attack may be expected to cause starvation among the civilian population. This practice includes that of States not party to Additional Protocol I.[48] It is doubtful, however, whether this exception also applies to non-international armed conflicts, because Article 14 of Additional Protocol II does not provide for it and there is no practice supporting it.

The second exception consists of the so-called "scorched earth policy" applied in defence of national territory against invasion. Additional Protocol I allows for this exception "in recognition of the vital requirements of any Party to the conflict in the defence of its national territory against invasion ... where required by imperative military necessity".[49] This exception is recognised in several military manuals and official statements.[50] This practice includes that

---

44 27th International Conference of the Red Cross and Red Crescent, Res. I (adopted by consensus) (*ibid.*, § 287).
45 See, e.g., ICRC, Conflict in Southern Africa: ICRC appeal (*ibid.*, § 290), Memorandum on the Applicability of International Humanitarian Law (*ibid.*, § 291), Appeal in behalf of civilians in Yugoslavia (*ibid.*, § 293), Press Release No. 1705 (*ibid.*, § 296), Press Release No. 1712 (*ibid.*, § 297), Press Release No. 1726 (*ibid.*, § 297), Memorandum on Respect for International Humanitarian Law in Angola (*ibid.*, § 298) and Memorandum on Compliance with International Humanitarian Law by the Forces Participating in Opération Turquoise (*ibid.*, § 299).
46 Additional Protocol I, Article 54(3) (adopted by consensus) (*ibid.*, § 308).
47 See, e.g., the military manuals of Australia (*ibid.*, § 313), Belgium (*ibid.*, § 314), Canada (*ibid.*, § 315), Israel (*ibid.*, § 316), Netherlands (*ibid.*, § 317), New Zealand (*ibid.*, § 318), Spain (*ibid.*, § 319), Sweden (*ibid.*, § 320) and Yugoslavia (*ibid.*, § 321) and the legislation of Spain (*ibid.*, § 323); see also the draft legislation of Argentina (*ibid.*, § 322) and the statements of Colombia (*ibid.*, § 325) and United States (*ibid.*, § 327).
48 See Israel, *Manual on the Laws of War* (*ibid.*, § 316); United States, Address by the Deputy Legal Adviser of the Department of State (*ibid.*, § 327).
49 Additional Protocol I, Article 54(5) (adopted by consensus) (*ibid.*, § 333).
50 See, e.g., the military manuals of Australia (*ibid.*, §§ 336–337), Canada (*ibid.*, § 338), Germany (*ibid.*, § 340), Israel (*ibid.*, § 341), Netherlands (*ibid.*, § 342), New Zealand (*ibid.*, § 343), Spain (*ibid.*, § 344), Sweden (*ibid.*, § 345) and Yugoslavia (*ibid.*, § 347); the statements of Sweden (*ibid.*, § 350) and United States (*ibid.*, § 351).

of States not party to Additional Protocol I.[51] It is doubtful, however, whether the exception of scorched earth policy applies to non-international armed conflicts because Article 14 of Additional Protocol II does not contain it. Colombia's Basic Military Manual states that "in all armed conflicts" it is prohibited to order a scorched earth policy as a method of combat.[52]

Belligerent reprisals against objects indispensable to the survival of the civilian population are discussed in Chapter 41.

Definition of objects indispensable to the survival of the civilian population

Additional Protocols I and II provide the following examples of objects indispensable to the survival of the civilian population: foodstuffs, agricultural areas for the production of foodstuffs, crops, livestock, drinking water installations and supplies, and irrigation works.[53] This list of examples is not exhaustive as indicated by the words "such as" in the relevant provisions. During the negotiation of the Elements of Crimes for the International Criminal Court, it was recognised that the ordinary meaning of the word "starvation" covered not only the more restrictive meaning of starving as killing by deprivation of water and food, but also the more general meaning of deprivation or insufficient supply of some essential commodity, of something necessary to survival. As a result, other examples that were mentioned during those negotiations included indispensable non-food items such as medicines and, in some cases, blankets.[54] It is important to point out in this respect that both Additional Protocols I and II consider food and medical supplies as essential to the survival of the civilian population, while Additional Protocol I also mentions clothing, bedding and means of shelter.[55]

Rule 55. The parties to the conflict must allow and facilitate rapid and unimpeded passage of humanitarian relief for civilians in need, which is impartial in character and conducted without any adverse distinction, subject to their right of control.

Practice

Volume II, Chapter 17, Section C.

---

[51] See, e.g., the military manual of Israel (*ibid.*, § 341) and the statement of the United States (*ibid.*, § 351).
[52] Colombia, *Basic Military Manual* (*ibid.*, § 339).
[53] Additional Protocol I, Article 54(2) (adopted by consensus) (*ibid.*, § 188); Additional Protocol II, Article 14 (adopted by consensus) (*ibid.*, § 191).
[54] Knut Dörmann, "Preparatory Commission for the International Criminal Court: The Elements of War Crimes – Part II: Other Serious Violations of the Laws and Customs Applicable in International and Non-International Armed Conflicts", *International Review of the Red Cross*, Vol. 83, 2001, pp. 475–476.
[55] Additional Protocol I, Article 69(1); Additional Protocol II, Article 18(2).

Summary

State practice establishes this rule as a norm of customary international law applicable in both international and non-international armed conflicts.

International armed conflicts

The Fourth Geneva Convention requires States to "allow the free passage of all consignments of medical and hospital stores" intended only for civilians and "the free passage of all consignments of essential foodstuffs, clothing and tonics intended for children under fifteen, expectant mothers and maternity cases".[56] Additional Protocol I broadens this obligation to cover "rapid and unimpeded passage of all relief consignments, equipment and personnel".[57] This broadening is generally accepted, including by States not, or not at the time, party to Additional Protocol I.[58]

Many military manuals contain the obligation to allow and facilitate access of humanitarian relief to civilians in need.[59] The obligation to allow and facilitate access of humanitarian relief to civilians in need is also supported by official statements and reported practice.[60] The United Nations, in particular, has on many occasions called for respect for the rule. The UN Security Council, for example, has called for unimpeded access for humanitarian relief efforts in Iraq and in all areas affected by the conflict between Armenia and Azerbaijan.[61]

Non-international armed conflicts

The requirement to allow and facilitate access for humanitarian relief to civilians in need was included in the draft of Additional Protocol II adopted by Committee II of the Diplomatic Conference leading to the adoption of the Additional Protocols but was deleted at the last moment as part of a package aimed at the adoption of a simplified text.[62] As a result, Additional Protocol II requires that relief actions for the civilian population in need be organised but does not contain a specific provision on access of humanitarian relief even

---

[56] Fourth Geneva Convention, Article 23 (cited in Vol. II, Ch. 17, § 361).
[57] Additional Protocol I, Article 70(2) (adopted by consensus) (*ibid.*, § 362).
[58] See, e.g., the military manual of Kenya (*ibid.*, § 388) and the statement of the United States (*ibid.*, § 435).
[59] See, e.g., the military manuals of Argentina ("allow") (*ibid.*, §§ 380–381), Australia ("allow") (*ibid.*, § 383), Canada ("allow" and "facilitate" in case of siege warfare) (*ibid.*, § 384), Colombia ("allow") (*ibid.*, § 385), Germany ("permit") (*ibid.*, § 386), Italy ("accept") (*ibid.*, § 387), Kenya ("allow and facilitate") (*ibid.*, § 388), Netherlands ("have to give" and "facilitate") (*ibid.*, § 389), New Zealand ("allow") (*ibid.*, § 390), Russia ("give all facilities") (*ibid.*, § 391), Switzerland ("all necessary facilities") (*ibid.*, § 393), United Kingdom ("allow", "all necessary facilities" and "guarantee") (*ibid.*, §§ 394–395) and United States ("agree" and "facilitate") (*ibid.*, § 396).
[60] See, e.g., the statements of Norway (*ibid.*, § 430) and United States (*ibid.*, § 435) and the reported practice of Kuwait (*ibid.*, § 426).
[61] UN Security Council, Res. 688 (*ibid.*, § 440), Res. 706 (*ibid.*, § 441), Res. 822 (*ibid.*, § 445), Res. 853 (*ibid.*, § 448) and Res. 874 (*ibid.*, § 449).
[62] Draft Additional Protocol II, Article 33 (*ibid.*, § 363).

though such access is clearly a *conditio sine qua non* for relief actions.[63] In addition, this rule is contained in other instruments pertaining also to non-international armed conflicts.[64]

The obligation to allow the free passage of relief supplies is also set forth in military manuals which are applicable in non-international armed conflicts.[65] The obligation to allow the free passage of relief supplies is also supported by many official statements and other practice relating to non-international armed conflicts.[66]

It is also relevant that under the Statute of the International Criminal Court, extermination, defined as including "the intentional infliction of conditions of life, *inter alia*, the deprivation of access to food and medicine, calculated to bring about the destruction of part of a population", constitutes a crime against humanity when committed as part of a widespread or systematic attack directed against any civilian population, with knowledge of the attack.[67] The legislation of numerous States provides for the crime of extermination.[68]

Contrary practice has generally been condemned with respect to both international and non-international armed conflicts. For example, the Mengistu regime in Ethiopia reportedly used the denial of access to food as a weapon against armed opposition groups, including by banning the movement of relief supplies after a famine emerged in late 1989. It is reported, however, that "after an international outcry against his policy, Mengistu reversed his decision".[69] The United Nations in particular has called for respect for this rule. The UN Security Council, for example, has called on the parties to numerous conflicts, such as those in Afghanistan, Angola, between Armenia and Azerbaijan, Bosnia and Herzegovina, Burundi, Democratic Republic of the Congo, Georgia, Kosovo, Liberia, Somalia and Yemen, to provide unimpeded access for humanitarian assistance.[70] In a resolution adopted in 1999 on children in

---

[63] Additional Protocol II, Article 18(2) (adopted by consensus) (*ibid.*, § 680).

[64] See, e.g., Memorandum of Understanding on the Application of IHL between Croatia and the SFRY, para. 9 (*ibid.*, § 368); Agreement on the Application of IHL between the Parties to the Conflict in Bosnia and Herzegovina, para. 2.6 (*ibid.*, § 369); Bahir Dar Agreement, para. 2 (*ibid.*, § 370); Agreement on a Cease-fire in the Republic of Yemen, para. 3 (*ibid.*, § 373); Guiding Principles on Internal Displacement, Principle 25 (*ibid.*, § 375); UN Secretary-General's Bulletin, Section 9.9 (*ibid.*, § 376); Agreement on the Protection and Provision of Humanitarian Assistance in Sudan, para. 1 (*ibid.*, § 377).

[65] See, e.g., the military manuals of Colombia (*ibid.*, § 385), Germany (*ibid.*, § 386), Italy (*ibid.*, § 387) and Kenya (*ibid.*, § 388).

[66] See, e.g., the statements of Germany (*ibid.*, § 423), Nigeria (*ibid.*, § 429), United States (*ibid.*, § 434) and Yugoslavia (*ibid.*, § 437), the practice of Jordan (*ibid.*, § 425), Philippines (*ibid.*, §§ 431–432) and Yugoslavia (*ibid.*, § 438) and the reported practice of Rwanda (*ibid.*, § 433).

[67] ICC Statute, Article 7 (*ibid.*, § 365).

[68] See, e.g., the legislation of Australia (*ibid.*, § 397), Azerbaijan (*ibid.*, § 398), Belgium (*ibid.*, § 400), Cambodia (*ibid.*, § 402), Canada (*ibid.*, § 403), Congo (*ibid.*, § 404), Germany (*ibid.*, § 407), Israel (*ibid.*, § 409), Mali (*ibid.*, § 410), New Zealand (*ibid.*, § 411), United Kingdom (*ibid.*, § 415), United States (*ibid.*, §§ 416–417) and Vietnam (*ibid.*, § 418); see also the draft legislation of Burundi (*ibid.*, § 401) and Trinidad and Tobago (*ibid.*, § 414).

[69] See Thomas P. Ofcansky and LaVerle Berry (eds.), *Ethiopia: A Country Study* (*ibid.*, § 422).

[70] UN Security Council, Res. 752 (*ibid.*, § 442), Res. 757 (*ibid.*, § 443), Res. 794 (*ibid.*, § 444), Res. 822 (*ibid.*, § 445), Res. 824 (*ibid.*, § 446), Res. 851 (*ibid.*, § 447), Res. 853 (*ibid.*, § 448),

armed conflicts, the UN Security Council called on all parties to armed conflicts "to ensure the full, safe and unhindered access of humanitarian personnel and the delivery of humanitarian assistance to all children affected by armed conflicts".[71] In another resolution adopted in 1999 on protection of civilians in armed conflicts, the UN Security Council expressed its concern at "the denial of safe and unimpeded access to people in need" and underlined "the importance of safe and unhindered access of humanitarian personnel to civilians in armed conflicts".[72] These statements were repeated in resolutions adopted in 2000.[73]

The 26th International Conference of the Red Cross and Red Crescent in 1995 emphasised "the importance for humanitarian organisations to have unimpeded access in times of armed conflict to civilian populations in need, in accordance with the applicable rules of international humanitarian law".[74] The Plan of Action for the years 2000–2003, adopted by the 27th International Conference of the Red Cross and Red Crescent in 1999, requires that all the parties to an armed conflict ensure that "rapid and unimpeded access to the civilian population is given to impartial humanitarian organizations in accordance with international humanitarian law in order that they can provide assistance and protection to the population".[75] The ICRC has called on parties to both international and non-international armed conflicts to respect this rule.[76]

Consent

Both Additional Protocols I and II require the consent of the parties concerned for relief actions to take place.[77] Most of the practice collected does not mention this requirement. It is nonetheless self-evident that a humanitarian

---

Res. 874 (*ibid.*, § 449), Res. 876 (*ibid.*, § 450), Res. 908 (*ibid.*, § 451), Res. 931 (*ibid.*, § 452), Res. 998 (*ibid.*, § 453), Res. 1004 (*ibid.*, § 454), Res. 1019 (*ibid.*, § 456), Res. 1059 and 1071 (*ibid.*, § 457), Res. 1083 (*ibid.*, § 459), Res. 1160 (*ibid.*, § 460), Res. 1199 (*ibid.*, § 461), Res. 1213 (*ibid.*, § 462), Res. 1239 (*ibid.*, § 463), Res. 1291 (*ibid.*, § 468), Res. 1333 (*ibid.*, § 471) and Statements by the President (*ibid.*, §§ 472–479 and 483).

[71] UN Security Council, Res. 1261 (*ibid.*, § 464).
[72] UN Security Council, Res. 1265 (*ibid.*, § 466).
[73] UN Security Council, Res. 1296 (*ibid.*, § 469) and Res. 1314 (*ibid.*, § 470).
[74] 26th International Conference of the Red Cross and Red Crescent, Res. II (*ibid.*, § 533).
[75] 27th International Conference of the Red Cross and Red Crescent, Res. I (adopted by consensus) (*ibid.*, § 536).
[76] See, e.g., ICRC, Conflict in Southern Africa: ICRC appeal (*ibid.*, § 540), Press Release No. 1488 (*ibid.*, § 541), *Annual Report 1986* (*ibid.*, § 542), Press Release, ICRC denies allegations (*ibid.*, § 545), Press Release, Tajikistan: ICRC urges respect for humanitarian rules (*ibid.*, § 546), Press Release No. 1744 (*ibid.*, § 547), Press Release, ICRC Appeal for respect for international humanitarian law in central Bosnia (*ibid.*, § 548), Communication to the Press No. 93/17 (*ibid.*, § 549), Communication to the Press No. 93/22 (*ibid.*, § 550), Memorandum on Respect for International Humanitarian Law in Angola (*ibid.*, § 553), Memorandum on Compliance with International Humanitarian Law by the Forces Participating in Opération Turquoise (*ibid.*, § 554), Communication to the Press No. 97/08 (*ibid.*, § 556) and Communication to the Press No. 01/47 (*ibid.*, § 557).
[77] Additional Protocol I, Article 70(1) (adopted by consensus) (*ibid.*, § 679); Additional Protocol II, Article 18(2) (adopted by consensus) (*ibid.*, § 680).

organisation cannot operate without the consent of the party concerned. However, such consent must not be refused on arbitrary grounds. If it is established that a civilian population is threatened with starvation and a humanitarian organisation which provides relief on an impartial and non-discriminatory basis is able to remedy the situation, a party is obliged to give consent.[78] The 26th International Conference of the Red Cross and Red Crescent in 1995 stressed the obligation of all parties to a conflict "to accept, under the conditions prescribed by international humanitarian law, impartial humanitarian relief operations for the civilian population when it lacks supplies essential to its survival".[79] While consent may not be withheld for arbitrary reasons, practice recognises that the party concerned may exercise control over the relief action.[80] In addition, humanitarian relief personnel must respect domestic law on access to territory and must respect the security requirements in force.[81]

Practice further indicates that a party that imposes a siege, blockade or embargo which has the effect of starving the civilian population has an obligation to provide access for humanitarian aid for the civilian population in need (see commentary to Rule 53).

With respect to occupied territories, the Fourth Geneva Convention imposes an obligation on the occupying power to ensure food and medical supplies for the population.[82] It would make sense, although practice does not yet clarify this, to require all parties to a conflict to ensure their populations have access to the basic necessities, and if sufficient supplies are unavailable, to appeal for international assistance and not wait until such assistance is offered.

Impediment of humanitarian relief

Practice indicates that each party to the conflict must refrain from deliberately impeding the delivery of relief supplies to civilians in need in areas under its control. Under the Statute of the International Criminal Court, "wilfully impeding relief supplies" as part of the use of starvation of civilians as a method of warfare is a war crime in international armed conflicts.[83] Such impediment

---

[78] See Yves Sandoz, Christophe Swinarski, Bruno Zimmermann (eds.), *Commentary on the Additional Protocols* (*ibid.*, § 539); see also § 2805 of the *Commentary*.

[79] 26th International Conference of the Red Cross and Red Crescent, Res. II (cited in Vol. II, Ch. 17, § 533).

[80] See, e.g., Fourth Geneva Convention, Article 23 (*ibid.*, § 361); Additional Protocol I, Article 70(3) (adopted by consensus) (*ibid.*, § 362); the military manuals of Argentina (*ibid.*, § 380), Australia (*ibid.*, § 383), Canada (*ibid.*, § 384), Germany (*ibid.*, § 386), Kenya (*ibid.*, § 388), Netherlands (*ibid.*, § 389), New Zealand (*ibid.*, § 390), United Kingdom (*ibid.*, § 394) and United States (*ibid.*, § 396).

[81] Additional Protocol I, Article 71(4) (adopted by consensus) (*ibid.*, § 725).

[82] Fourth Geneva Convention, Article 55.

[83] ICC Statute, Article 8(2)(b)(xxv) (cited in Vol. II, Ch. 17, § 564).

is also an offence under the legislation of numerous States,[84] some of which applies to both international and non-international armed conflicts.[85]

The impediment of relief actions in Bosnia and Herzegovina was widely condemned.[86] Numerous resolutions of the UN Security Council, UN General Assembly and UN Commission on Human Rights condemn such impediment.[87] Some of these resolutions are explicitly addressed to governmental armed forces, while others are explicitly addressed to armed opposition groups.

While some resolutions do not qualify the prohibition on impeding humanitarian relief, others only prohibit the "deliberate" or "wilful" impediment. Both treaty law and practice indicate that the parties to the conflict can take a number of measures to control the content and delivery of humanitarian aid but cannot "deliberately" impede its delivery as such. Such measures of control may include the search of relief consignments and their delivery under supervision.[88]

Access for humanitarian relief via third States

Additional Protocol I requires unimpeded passage of humanitarian relief, not only by the parties to the conflict but by each State party to the Protocol.[89] Such a provision was also included in the draft of Additional Protocol II by Committee II at the Diplomatic Conference leading to the adoption of the Additional Protocols, but it was deleted at the last moment as part of a package aimed at the adoption of a simplified text.[90] In a resolution adopted in 2000 on protection of civilians in armed conflicts, the UN Security Council called upon "all parties concerned, including neighbouring states, to cooperate fully" in providing access for humanitarian personnel.[91] Earlier, in 1994, the Security

---

[84] See, e.g., the legislation of Australia (*ibid.*, § 569), Canada (*ibid.*, § 572), Colombia (*ibid.*, § 573), Congo (*ibid.*, § 574), Georgia (*ibid.*, § 576), Germany (*ibid.*, § 577), Ireland (*ibid.*, § 578), Mali (*ibid.*, § 579), Netherlands (*ibid.*, § 580), New Zealand (*ibid.*, § 581), Norway (*ibid.*, § 583), Philippines (*ibid.*, § 584) and United Kingdom (*ibid.*, § 586); see also the draft legislation of Burundi (*ibid.*, § 571), El Salvador (*ibid.*, § 575), Nicaragua (*ibid.*, § 582) and Trinidad and Tobago (*ibid.*, § 585).

[85] See, e.g., the legislation of Colombia (*ibid.*, § 573) and Germany (*ibid.*, § 577); see also the draft legislation of El Salvador (*ibid.*, § 575) and Nicaragua (*ibid.*, § 582).

[86] See the statements of China (*ibid.*, § 589), Egypt (*ibid.*, § 590), Iran (*ibid.*, § 590), Pakistan (*ibid.*, § 590), Saudi Arabia (*ibid.*, § 590), Senegal (*ibid.*, § 590), Turkey (*ibid.*, § 590) and United Kingdom (*ibid.*, § 593); see also the statements of Germany vis-à-vis Sudan and Afghanistan (*ibid.*, §§ 591–592).

[87] See, e.g., UN Security Council, Res. 758 (*ibid.*, § 594), Res. 761 (*ibid.*, § 595), Res. 770 (*ibid.*, § 596), Res. 771 (*ibid.*, § 597), Res. 787 (*ibid.*, § 598), Res. 794 (*ibid.*, § 599), Res. 836 (*ibid.*, § 600), Res. 945 and 952 (*ibid.*, § 601), Res. 998 (*ibid.*, § 602), Res. 1132 (*ibid.*, § 603) and Res. 1193 (*ibid.*, § 604); UN General Assembly, Res. 46/242 (*ibid.*, § 622), Res. 49/196 and 50/193 (*ibid.*, § 623), Res. 52/140 (*ibid.*, § 624) and Res. 52/145 (*ibid.*, § 625); UN Commission on Human Rights, Res. 1983/29 (*ibid.*, § 626), Res. 1994/72 (*ibid.*, § 627), Res. 1994/75 (*ibid.*, § 628), Res. 1995/77 (*ibid.*, § 629), Res. 1995/89 (*ibid.*, § 630), Res. 1996/73 (*ibid.*, § 631) and Res. 1998/67 (*ibid.*, § 632).

[88] See Additional Protocol I, Article 70(3) (adopted by consensus) (*ibid.*, § 362).

[89] Additional Protocol I, Article 70(2) (adopted by consensus) (*ibid.*, § 656).

[90] Draft Additional Protocol II, Article 33(2) (*ibid.*, § 657).

[91] UN Security Council, Res. 1296 (*ibid.*, § 666).

Council had called upon "States bordering Rwanda...to facilitate transfer of goods and supplies to meet the needs of the displaced persons within Rwanda".[92] The Guiding Principles on Humanitarian Assistance adopted by the UN General Assembly in 1991 emphasise that "States in proximity to emergencies are urged to participate closely with the affected countries in international efforts, with a view to facilitating, to the extent possible, the transit of humanitarian assistance".[93]

Right of the civilian population in need to receive humanitarian relief

There is practice which recognises that a civilian population in need is entitled to receive humanitarian relief essential to its survival, in accordance with international humanitarian law. The Fourth Geneva Convention recognises the right of protected persons to make application to the protecting powers, the ICRC or a National Red Cross or Red Crescent Society, as well as to any organisation that might assist them.[94] The Additional Protocols implicitly recognise the entitlement of a civilian population in need to receive humanitarian relief as they require that relief actions "shall be undertaken" whenever a population is in need.[95]

Other State practice explicitly recognises this right. Nicaragua's Military Manual, for example, states that "the civilian population has the right to receive the relief they need".[96] This right is also recognised in practice pertaining to non-international armed conflicts.[97]

The UN Security Council, UN General Assembly and UN Commission on Human Rights have on several occasions underlined the obligation to grant civilians access to relief supplies.[98] In a report on emergency assistance to Sudan in 1996, the UN Secretary-General stated that:

Any attempt to diminish the capacity of the international community to respond to conditions of suffering and hardship among the civilian population in the Sudan can only give rise to the most adamant expressions of concern as a violation of recognized humanitarian principles, most importantly, the right of civilian populations to receive humanitarian assistance in times of war.[99]

The 26th International Conference of the Red Cross and Red Crescent in 1995 reasserted "the right of a civilian population in need to benefit from impartial humanitarian relief actions in accordance with international humanitarian

---

[92] UN Security Council, Statement by the President (*ibid.*, § 667).
[93] UN General Assembly, Res. 46/182 (*ibid.*, § 668).
[94] Fourth Geneva Convention, Article 30, first paragraph (*ibid.*, § 678).
[95] Additional Protocol I, Article 70(1) (adopted by consensus) (*ibid.*, § 679); Additional Protocol II, Article 18(2) (adopted by consensus) (*ibid.*, § 680).
[96] Nicaragua, *Military Manual* (*ibid.*, § 688).
[97] See, e.g., the practice of Colombia (*ibid.*, § 696).
[98] See, e.g., UN Security Council, Res. 824 (*ibid.*, § 701); UN General Assembly, Res. 55/2 (*ibid.*, § 704); UN Commission on Human Rights, Res. 1995/77 (*ibid.*, § 705).
[99] UN Secretary-General, Report on emergency assistance to Sudan (*ibid.*, § 706); see also Report on protection for humanitarian assistance to refugees and others in conflict situations (*ibid.*, § 707) and Reports on the protection of civilians in armed conflict (*ibid.*, §§ 708–709).

law".[100] In a communication to the press in 1997 concerning the conflict in Zaire, the ICRC appealed to all concerned to "respect the victims' right to assistance and protection".[101]

Rule 56. The parties to the conflict must ensure the freedom of movement of authorised humanitarian relief personnel essential to the exercise of their functions. Only in case of imperative military necessity may their movements be temporarily restricted.

Practice

Volume II, Chapter 17, Section D.

Summary

State practice establishes this rule as a norm of customary international law applicable in both international and non-international armed conflicts. The obligation to ensure freedom of movement is a corollary to the obligation to provide access to civilians in need and the prohibition on deliberately impeding the delivery of humanitarian assistance (see Rule 55).

International and non-international armed conflicts

The obligation to accord freedom of movement to authorised humanitarian personnel is set forth in Additional Protocol I.[102] Additional Protocol II requires that relief actions for the civilian population in need be organised, but does not contain a specific provision on the freedom of movement of humanitarian aid personnel, which is essential to the provision of humanitarian aid.[103]

Amended Protocol II to the Convention on Certain Conventional Weapons implements the freedom of movement, as well as the need for rapid and unimpeded passage, of humanitarian relief personnel by imposing a duty on each party to a conflict to take "such measures as are necessary to protect the force or mission from the effects of mines, booby-traps and other devices in any area under its control". It provides, in particular, that each high contracting party or party to a conflict shall:

if access to or through any place under its control is necessary for the performance of the mission's functions and in order to provide the personnel of the mission with safe passage to or through that place:

---

[100] 26th International Conference of the Red Cross and Red Crescent, Res. II (*ibid.*, § 713).
[101] ICRC, Communication to the Press No. 97/08 (*ibid.*, § 721).
[102] Additional Protocol I, Article 71(3) (adopted by consensus) (*ibid.*, § 725).
[103] Additional Protocol II, Article 18(2) (adopted by consensus) (*ibid.*, § 680).

(aa) unless on-going hostilities prevent, inform the head of the mission of a safe route to that place if such information is available; or

(bb) if information identifying a safe route is not provided in accordance with subparagraph (aa), so far as is necessary and feasible, clear a lane through minefields.[104]

The need for humanitarian relief personnel to enjoy freedom of movement essential for the exercise of their functions has been claimed in practice with respect to both international and non-international armed conflicts. Violations of this rule have been condemned, regardless of whether the conflict was international or non-international. The United Nations, in particular, has issued numerous statements and adopted numerous resolutions in this respect, many of them with regard to non-international armed conflicts. The UN Security Council, for example, has called upon all parties to the conflicts in Afghanistan, Angola, Bosnia and Herzegovina, Georgia, Liberia, Somalia, Tajikistan and the Great Lakes region to ensure the freedom of movement of humanitarian relief personnel.[105] In a resolution adopted in 1999 on protection of civilians in armed conflicts, the Security Council emphasised "the need for combatants to ensure the... freedom of movement of... personnel of international humanitarian organizations".[106] In a resolution on the same subject adopted in 2000, the Security Council reiterated "its call to all parties concerned, including non-State parties, to ensure the... freedom of movement of... personnel of humanitarian organizations".[107]

The ICRC has called upon parties to both international and non-international armed conflicts to respect this rule.[108]

No official contrary practice was found.

Interpretation

Most practice does not mention the requirement that the rule concern authorised humanitarian personnel, but it is self-evident that a party to the conflict cannot be required to ensure the freedom of movement of an organisation it has not authorised. It must be stressed, however, that such authorisation

---

[104] Amended Protocol II to the CCW, Article 12 (cited in Vol. II, Ch. 29, § 352).

[105] UN Security Council, Res. 746 (cited in Vol. II, Ch. 17, § 734), Res. 751 (*ibid.*, § 735), Res. 819 (*ibid.*, § 736), Res. 998 (*ibid.*, § 737), Res. 1075 (*ibid.*, § 738), Res. 1078 (*ibid.*, § 739), Res. 1080 (*ibid.*, § 740), Res. 1083 (*ibid.*, § 741), Res. 1088 (*ibid.*, § 742), Res. 1173 and 1180 (*ibid.*, § 743), Res. 1193 (*ibid.*, § 744), Res. 1202 (*ibid.*, § 745), Res. 1213 (*ibid.*, § 746), Res. 1333 (*ibid.*, § 750) and Statements by the President (*ibid.*, §§ 752–762).

[106] UN Security Council, Res. 1265 (*ibid.*, § 748).

[107] UN Security Council, Res. 1296 (*ibid.*, § 749).

[108] See, e.g., ICRC, Conflict in Southern Africa: ICRC appeal (*ibid.*, § 772), Appeal in behalf of the civilians in Yugoslavia (*ibid.*, § 773), Press Release No. 1705 (*ibid.*, § 774), Press Release No. 1712 (*ibid.*, § 775), Press Release No. 1726 (*ibid.*, § 775), Memorandum on Respect for International Humanitarian Law in Angola (*ibid.*, § 776) and Memorandum on Compliance with International Humanitarian Law by the Forces Participating in Opération Turquoise (*ibid.*, § 777).

cannot be refused arbitrarily (see commentary to Rule 55). In addition, the right of each party to the conflict to make sure that the personnel concerned are actually involved in humanitarian aid work is recognised in practice.[109] Pursuant to the Third and Fourth Geneva Conventions, "the special position of the International Committee of the Red Cross in this field shall be recognised and respected at all times".[110]

Exception

Additional Protocol I provides that "only in case of imperative military necessity may the activities of the relief personnel be limited or their movements temporarily restricted".[111] The exception of imperative military necessity is justified on the basis that relief operations must not be allowed to interfere with military operations, lest the safety of humanitarian relief personnel be endangered. These restrictions can only be limited and temporary, however. In no case may they involve violations of the preceding rules (see Rules 53–55).

[109] See also Additional Protocol I, Article 71(4) (adopted by consensus) (*ibid.*, § 725).
[110] Third Geneva Convention, Article 125, third paragraph; Fourth Geneva Convention, Article 142, third paragraph.
[111] Additional Protocol I, Article 71(3) (adopted by consensus) (*ibid.*, § 725).

DECEPTION

Rule 57. Ruses of war are not prohibited as long as they do not infringe a rule of international humanitarian law.

Practice

Volume II, Chapter 18, Section A.

Summary

State practice establishes this rule as a norm of customary international law applicable in both international and non-international armed conflicts.

International armed conflicts

This is a long-standing rule of customary international law already recognised in the Lieber Code and the Brussels Declaration, and codified in the Hague Regulations.[1] It is also set forth in Additional Protocol I.[2]

The rule permitting ruses of war is stated in numerous military manuals.[3] It is supported by several official statements and other practice.[4]

Non-international armed conflicts

This rule was included in the draft of Additional Protocol II by Committee III of the Diplomatic Conference leading to the adoption of the Additional Protocols,

---

[1] Lieber Code, Articles 15–16 and 101 (cited in Vol. II, Ch. 18, § 5); Brussels Declaration, Article 14 (*ibid.*, § 6); Hague Regulations, Article 24 (*ibid.*, § 2).

[2] Additional Protocol I, Article 37(2) (adopted by consensus) (*ibid.*, § 3).

[3] See, e.g., the military manuals of Argentina (*ibid.*, §§ 11–12), Australia (*ibid.*, §§ 13–14), Belgium (*ibid.*, §§ 15–16), Benin (*ibid.*, § 17), Cameroon (*ibid.*, § 18), Canada (*ibid.*, §§ 19–21), Croatia (*ibid.*, § 22), Ecuador (*ibid.*, § 23), France (*ibid.*, §§ 24–25), Germany (*ibid.*, § 26), Indonesia (*ibid.*, § 28), Israel (*ibid.*, § 29), Italy (*ibid.*, §§ 30–31), Kenya (*ibid.*, § 32), South Korea (*ibid.*, § 33), Madagascar (*ibid.*, § 34), Netherlands (*ibid.*, §§ 35–36), New Zealand (*ibid.*, § 37), Nigeria (*ibid.*, §§ 38–39), South Africa (*ibid.*, § 40), Spain (*ibid.*, §§ 41–42), Sweden (*ibid.*, § 43), Switzerland (*ibid.*, § 44), Togo (*ibid.*, § 45), United Kingdom (*ibid.*, §§ 46–47), United States (*ibid.*, §§ 48–50) and Yugoslavia (*ibid.*, § 51).

[4] See, e.g., the statement of the United States (*ibid.*, § 59); the practice of Iraq (*ibid.*, § 55) and United States (*ibid.*, § 59) and the reported practice of Algeria (*ibid.*, § 54), Malaysia (*ibid.*, § 56) and United Kingdom (*ibid.*, § 57).

but was deleted at the last moment as part of a package aimed at the adoption of a simplified text.[5] In addition, it is contained in other instruments pertaining also to non-international armed conflicts.[6]

The rule permitting ruses of war provided they do not infringe a rule of international humanitarian law is set forth in military manuals which are applicable in or have been applied in non-international armed conflicts.[7] Colombia's Constitutional Court ruled in 1997 that the use of military tactics and stratagems must be in conformity with constitutional standards, implicitly recognising that they may be applied in non-international armed conflicts.[8]

The practice collected gives examples in both international and non-international armed conflicts, while no practice was found suggesting ruses were prohibited in either type of conflict.

Definition

Ruses are acts intended to confuse the enemy. It is often stated that ruses are common in armed conflict. The UK Military Manual mentions the following examples of lawful ruses: surprises; ambushes; feigning attacks, retreats or flights; simulating quiet and inactivity; giving large strongpoints to a small force; constructing works, bridges, etc. which are not intended to be used; transmitting bogus signal messages, and sending bogus despatches and newspapers with a view to their being intercepted by the enemy; making use of the enemy's signals, watchwords, wireless code signs and tuning calls, and words of command; conducting a false military exercise on the wireless on a frequency easily interrupted while substantial troop movements are taking place on the ground; pretending to communicate with troops or reinforcements which do not exist; moving landmarks; constructing dummy airfields and aircraft; putting up dummy guns or dummy tanks; laying dummy mines; removing badges from uniforms; clothing the men of a single unit in the uniforms of several different units so that prisoners and dead may give the idea of a large force; and giving false ground signals to enable airborne personnel or

---

5 Draft Additional Protocol II, Article 21(2) (ibid., § 4).
6 See, e.g., Memorandum of Understanding on the Application of IHL between Croatia and the SFRY, para. 6 (ibid., § 8); Agreement on the Application of IHL between the Parties to the Conflict in Bosnia and Herzegovina, para. 2.5 (ibid., § 9); San Remo Manual, para. 110 (ibid., § 10).
7 See, e.g., the military manuals of Australia (ibid., § 13), Benin (ibid., § 17), Canada (ibid., § 21), Croatia (ibid., § 22), Ecuador (ibid., § 23), Germany (ibid., § 26), Italy (ibid., §§ 30–31), Kenya (ibid., § 32), Madagascar (ibid., § 34), Nigeria (ibid., § 38), South Africa (ibid., § 40), Togo (ibid., § 45) and Yugoslavia (ibid., § 51).
8 Colombia, Constitutional Court, Constitutional Case No. T-303 (ibid., § 53).

supplies to be dropped in a hostile area, or to induce aircraft to land in a hostile area.[9]

Rule 58. The improper use of the white flag of truce is prohibited.

Practice

Volume II, Chapter 18, Section B.

Summary

State practice establishes this rule as a norm of customary international law applicable in both international and non-international armed conflicts.

International armed conflicts

This is a long-standing rule of customary international law already recognised in the Lieber Code, the Brussels Declaration and the Oxford Manual.[10] It is codified in the Hague Regulations.[11] The Report of the Commission on Responsibility set up after the First World War identified the "misuse of flags" as a violation of the laws and customs of war subject to criminal prosecution.[12] This rule is contained in Additional Protocol I.[13] Under the Statute of the International Criminal Court, "making improper use of a flag of truce" constitutes a war crime in international armed conflicts when it results in death or serious personal injury.[14]

The prohibition of improper use of the white flag of truce is contained in numerous military manuals.[15] Violations of this rule constitute an offence

---

[9] United Kingdom, *Military Manual* (*ibid.*, § 46); see also the military manuals of Argentina (*ibid.*, § 12), Australia (*ibid.*, §§ 13–14), Belgium (*ibid.*, § 15), Canada (*ibid.*, § 20), Croatia (*ibid.*, § 22), Ecuador (*ibid.*, § 23), France (*ibid.*, § 25), Germany (*ibid.*, § 26), Hungary (*ibid.*, § 27), Indonesia (*ibid.*, § 28), Israel (*ibid.*, § 29), Italy (*ibid.*, § 31), Kenya (*ibid.*, § 32), South Korea (*ibid.*, § 33), Madagascar (*ibid.*, § 34), Netherlands (*ibid.*, §§ 35–36), New Zealand (*ibid.*, § 37), Nigeria (*ibid.*, §§ 38–39), South Africa (*ibid.*, § 40), Spain (*ibid.*, §§ 41–42), Sweden (*ibid.*, § 43), Switzerland (*ibid.*, § 44), United Kingdom (*ibid.*, § 47), United States (*ibid.*, §§ 48–50) and Yugoslavia (*ibid.*, § 51).

[10] Lieber Code, Article 114 (*ibid.*, § 72) and Article 117 (*ibid.*, § 73); Brussels Declaration, Article 13(f) (*ibid.*, § 74); Oxford Manual, Article 8(d) (*ibid.*, § 75).

[11] Hague Regulations, Article 23(f) (*ibid.*, § 68).

[12] Report of the Commission on Responsibility (*ibid.*, § 76).

[13] Additional Protocol I, Article 38(1) (adopted by consensus) (*ibid.*, § 69).

[14] ICC Statute, Article 8(2)(b)(vii) (*ibid.*, § 71).

[15] See, e.g., the military manuals of Argentina (*ibid.*, §§ 80–81), Australia (*ibid.*, §§ 82–83), Belgium (*ibid.*, § 84), Burkina Faso (*ibid.*, § 85), Cameroon (*ibid.*, §§ 86–87), Canada (*ibid.*, § 88), Congo (*ibid.*, § 89), Ecuador (*ibid.*, § 90), France (*ibid.*, §§ 91–92), Germany (*ibid.*, § 93), Italy (*ibid.*, § 94), South Korea (*ibid.*, § 95), Lebanon (*ibid.*, § 96), Madagascar (*ibid.*, § 97), Mali (*ibid.*, § 98), Morocco (*ibid.*, § 99), Netherlands (*ibid.*, §§ 100–101), New Zealand (*ibid.*, § 102), Nigeria (*ibid.*, §§ 103–105), Russia (*ibid.*, § 106), Senegal (*ibid.*, § 107), South Africa (*ibid.*, § 108), Spain (*ibid.*, § 109), Sweden (*ibid.*, § 110), United Kingdom (*ibid.*, §§ 111–112), United States (*ibid.*, §§ 113–116) and Yugoslavia (*ibid.*, § 117).

under the legislation of many States.[16] This rule is also supported by official statements and other practice.[17]

Non-international armed conflicts

The prohibition of improper use of the flag of truce was included in the draft of Additional Protocol II by Committee III of the Diplomatic Conference leading to the adoption of the Additional Protocols but was deleted at the last moment as part of a package aimed at the adoption of a simplified text.[18] The prohibition is contained in other instruments pertaining also to non-international armed conflicts.[19]

This rule is set forth in military manuals which are applicable in or have been applied in non-international armed conflicts.[20] Violations of this rule constitute an offence under the legislation of many States.[21]

No official contrary practice was found. There is no practice either to indicate that it would be lawful to use improperly the protection of a white flag of truce in non-international armed conflicts. Such improper use would undermine the protection to which persons advancing in good faith under a white flag are entitled (see commentary to Rule 67). It can be concluded that the general abstention from improperly using the white flag of truce in practice is based on a legitimate expectation to that effect.

---

[16] See, e.g., the legislation of Algeria (*ibid.*, § 118), Australia (*ibid.*, §§ 120–122), Azerbaijan (*ibid.*, § 123), Belarus (*ibid.*, § 124), Bosnia and Herzegovina (*ibid.*, § 125), Burkina Faso (*ibid.*, § 126), Canada (*ibid.*, § 128), China (*ibid.*, § 129), Congo (*ibid.*, § 130), Democratic Republic of the Congo (*ibid.*, § 131), Côte d'Ivoire (*ibid.*, § 132), Croatia (*ibid.*, § 133), Estonia (*ibid.*, § 134), France (*ibid.*, § 135), Georgia (*ibid.*, § 136), Germany (*ibid.*, § 137), Guinea (*ibid.*, § 138), Ireland (*ibid.*, § 139), Italy (*ibid.*, §§ 140–141), Mali (*ibid.*, § 142), Netherlands (*ibid.*, §§ 144–145), New Zealand (*ibid.*, § 146), Nicaragua (*ibid.*, § 147), Norway (*ibid.*, § 148), Poland (*ibid.*, § 149), Slovenia (*ibid.*, § 150), Spain (*ibid.*, §§ 151–152), Sweden (*ibid.*, § 153), United Kingdom (*ibid.*, § 155), United States (*ibid.*, § 156) and Yugoslavia (*ibid.*, § 157); see also the draft legislation of Argentina (*ibid.*, § 119), Burundi (*ibid.*, § 127) and Trinidad and Tobago (*ibid.*, § 154).

[17] See, e.g., the statement of the United States (*ibid.*, § 160) and the practice of the United Kingdom (*ibid.*, § 159).

[18] Draft Additional Protocol II, Article 23(2) (*ibid.*, § 70).

[19] See, e.g., Memorandum of Understanding on the Application of IHL between Croatia and the SFRY, para. 6 (*ibid.*, § 77); Agreement on the Application of IHL between the Parties to the Conflict in Bosnia and Herzegovina, para. 2.5 (*ibid.*, § 78).

[20] See, e.g., the military manuals of Australia (*ibid.*, § 82), Ecuador (*ibid.*, § 90), Germany (*ibid.*, § 93), Italy (*ibid.*, § 94), Lebanon (*ibid.*, § 96), Madagascar (*ibid.*, § 97), Nigeria (*ibid.*, §§ 103 and 105), South Africa (*ibid.*, § 108) and Yugoslavia (*ibid.*, § 117).

[21] See, e.g., the legislation of Azerbaijan (*ibid.*, § 123), Belarus (*ibid.*, § 124), Bosnia and Herzegovina (*ibid.*, § 125), Democratic Republic of the Congo (*ibid.*, § 131), Croatia (*ibid.*, § 133), Estonia (*ibid.*, § 134), Germany (*ibid.*, § 137), Guinea (*ibid.*, § 138), Nicaragua (*ibid.*, § 147), Poland (*ibid.*, § 149), Slovenia (*ibid.*, § 150), Spain (*ibid.*, § 152), Sweden (*ibid.*, § 153) and Yugoslavia (*ibid.*, § 157); see also the legislation of Burkina Faso (*ibid.*, § 126) and Italy (*ibid.*, §§ 140–141), the application of which is not excluded in time of non-international armed conflict, and the draft legislation of Argentina (*ibid.*, § 119).

Definition

Improper use refers to any use other than that for which the flag of truce was intended, namely a request to communicate, for example, in order to negotiate a cease-fire or to surrender.[22] Any other use, for example, to gain a military advantage over the enemy, is improper and unlawful.

Rule 59. The improper use of the distinctive emblems of the Geneva Conventions is prohibited.

Practice

Volume II, Chapter 18, Section C.

Summary

State practice establishes this rule as a norm of customary international law applicable in both international and non-international armed conflicts.

International armed conflicts

This is a long-standing rule of customary international law already recognised in the Lieber Code, the Brussels Declaration and the Oxford Manual.[23] It was codified in the 1899 and 1907 Hague Regulations and the Geneva Conventions of 1906, 1929 and 1949.[24] It is set forth in Additional Protocol I.[25] Under the Statute of the International Criminal Court, "making improper use of the distinctive emblems of the Geneva Conventions" constitutes a war crime in international armed conflicts when it results in death or serious personal injury.[26]

The prohibition of improper use of the distinctive emblems has been stated in numerous military manuals.[27] Violation of this rule is an offence under the

---

[22] See Vol. II, Ch. 19, §§ 49–92.

[23] Lieber Code, Article 117 (cited in Vol. II, Ch. 18, § 186); Brussels Declaration, Article 13(f) (*ibid.*, § 187); Oxford Manual, Article 8(d) (*ibid.*, § 188).

[24] 1899 Hague Regulations, Article 23(f) (*ibid.*, § 168); 1907 Hague Regulations, Article 23(f) (*ibid.*, § 170); 1906 Geneva Convention, Articles 27–28 (*ibid.*, § 169); 1929 Geneva Convention, Article 24 (*ibid.*, § 171) and Article 28 (*ibid.*, § 172); First Geneva Convention, Article 39 (*ibid.*, § 173), Article 44 (*ibid.*, § 174), Article 53 (*ibid.*, § 175) and Article 54 (*ibid.*, § 176); Second Geneva Convention, Article 41, first paragraph (*ibid.*, § 177), Article 44 (*ibid.*, § 178) and Article 45 (*ibid.*, § 179).

[25] Additional Protocol I, Article 38(1) (adopted by consensus) (*ibid.*, § 182).

[26] ICC Statute, Article 8(2)(b)(vii) (*ibid.*, § 185).

[27] See, e.g., the military manuals of Argentina (*ibid.*, §§ 196–197), Australia (*ibid.*, §§ 198–199), Belgium (*ibid.*, §§ 200–201), Burkina Faso (*ibid.*, § 202), Cameroon (*ibid.*, §§ 203–204), Canada (*ibid.*, §§ 205–206), Colombia (*ibid.*, § 207), Congo (*ibid.*, § 208), Dominican Republic (*ibid.*, § 209), Ecuador (*ibid.*, § 210), France (*ibid.*, §§ 211–212), Germany (*ibid.*, § 213), Indonesia (*ibid.*, § 214), Italy (*ibid.*, § 215), Japan (*ibid.*, § 216), South Korea (*ibid.*, §§ 217–218), Lebanon

legislation of many States.[28] This rule is also supported by national case-law,[29] official statements and other practice.[30] In its judgement in the *Emblem case* in 1994, Germany's Federal Supreme Court stated that there was an essential common interest in the protection of the emblems against unauthorised use.[31]

Non-international armed conflicts

Additional Protocol II provides for the prohibition of improper use of the distinctive emblems.[32] In addition, this prohibition is contained in other instruments pertaining also to non-international armed conflicts.[33]

The prohibition of improper use of the distinctive emblems is set forth in military manuals which are applicable in or have been applied in non-international armed conflicts.[34] Violation of this rule is an offence under the legislation of many States.[35] This rule is supported by national

---

(*ibid.*, § 219), Madagascar (*ibid.*, § 220), Mali (*ibid.*, § 221), Morocco (*ibid.*, § 222), Netherlands (*ibid.*, §§ 223–224), New Zealand (*ibid.*, § 225), Nigeria (*ibid.*, § 226), Russia (*ibid.*, § 227), Senegal (*ibid.*, § 228), Spain (*ibid.*, §§ 229–230), Sweden (*ibid.*, § 231), Switzerland (*ibid.*, § 232), United Kingdom (*ibid.*, §§ 233–234), United States (*ibid.*, §§ 235–238) and Yugoslavia (*ibid.*, § 239).

[28] See, e.g., legislation (*ibid.*, §§ 240–412).

[29] See, e.g., Colombia, Council of State, *Administrative Case No. 11369* (*ibid.*, § 413); Germany, Federal Supreme Court, *Emblem case* (*ibid.*, § 414); Netherlands, Supreme Court, *Red Cross Emblem case* (*ibid.*, § 415).

[30] See, e.g., the statement of the United States (*ibid.*, § 425), the practice of France (*ibid.*, § 421), Iraq (*ibid.*, § 423) and United Kingdom (*ibid.*, § 424) and the reported practice of Germany (*ibid.*, § 422).

[31] Germany, Federal Supreme Court, *Emblem case* (*ibid.*, § 414).

[32] Additional Protocol II, Article 12 (adopted by consensus) (*ibid.*, § 184).

[33] See, e.g., Hague Statement on Respect for Humanitarian Principles (*ibid.*, § 189); Memorandum of Understanding on the Application of IHL between Croatia and the SFRY, para. 6 (*ibid.*, § 190); Agreement on the Application of IHL between the Parties to the Conflict in Bosnia and Herzegovina, paras. 2.5 and 3 (*ibid.*, § 191).

[34] See, e.g., the military manuals of Argentina (*ibid.*, § 197), Australia (*ibid.*, §§ 198–199), Cameroon (*ibid.*, § 204), Canada (*ibid.*, §§ 205–206), Colombia (*ibid.*, § 207), Ecuador (*ibid.*, § 210), France (*ibid.*, § 212), Germany (*ibid.*, § 213), Italy (*ibid.*, § 215), Lebanon (*ibid.*, § 219), Madagascar (*ibid.*, § 220), New Zealand (*ibid.*, § 225), Russia (*ibid.*, § 227), Spain (*ibid.*, § 230) and Yugoslavia (*ibid.*, § 239).

[35] See, e.g., the legislation of Antigua and Barbuda (*ibid.*, § 242), Armenia (*ibid.*, §§ 245–246), Azerbaijan (*ibid.*, § 251), Belarus (*ibid.*, §§ 256–257), Belgium (*ibid.*, § 258), Belize (*ibid.*, § 259), Bolivia (*ibid.*, § 260), Bosnia and Herzegovina (*ibid.*, §§ 261–262), Bulgaria (*ibid.*, § 266), Cameroon (*ibid.*, § 270), Chile (*ibid.*, § 274), China (*ibid.*, § 275), Democratic Republic of the Congo (*ibid.*, § 279), Costa Rica (*ibid.*, § 282), Croatia (*ibid.*, §§ 284–285), Czech Republic (*ibid.*, § 291), El Salvador (*ibid.*, § 296), Estonia (*ibid.*, § 297), Ethiopia (*ibid.*, § 298), Finland (*ibid.*, §§ 299–300), Germany (*ibid.*, § 306), Guatemala (*ibid.*, § 311), Guinea (*ibid.*, § 313), Hungary (*ibid.*, § 317), Ireland (*ibid.*, § 321), Kazakhstan (*ibid.*, § 329), Kyrgyzstan (*ibid.*, § 331), Malta (*ibid.*, § 342), Moldova (*ibid.*, §§ 345–346), Netherlands (*ibid.*, § 350), Nicaragua (*ibid.*, §§ 355–356), Norway (*ibid.*, §§ 359–360), Panama (*ibid.*, § 361), Poland (*ibid.*, §§ 365–366), Saint Kitts and Nevis (*ibid.*, § 370), Slovakia (*ibid.*, § 376), Slovenia (*ibid.*, §§ 377–378), Spain (*ibid.*, §§ 380–381), Sweden (*ibid.*, § 384), Tajikistan (*ibid.*, §§ 386–387), Togo (*ibid.*, § 391), Ukraine (*ibid.*, § 398 and 400), Uruguay (*ibid.*, § 405), Yemen (*ibid.*, § 408) and Yugoslavia (*ibid.*, §§ 409–410); see also the legislation of Bulgaria (*ibid.*, § 265), Burkina Faso (*ibid.*, § 267), Czech Republic (*ibid.*, § 290), Hungary (*ibid.*, § 316), Italy (*ibid.*, §§ 323 and 325), Nicaragua (*ibid.*, § 354), Romania (*ibid.*, § 367), Slovakia (*ibid.*, § 375) and Togo (*ibid.*, § 390), the application of which is not excluded in time of non-international armed conflict, and the draft legislation of Argentina (*ibid.*, § 244) and Latvia (*ibid.*, § 332).

case-law.[36] It is also supported by official statements made in the context of non-international armed conflicts.[37]

In 1977, the 23rd International Conference of the Red Cross requested that States parties to the Geneva Conventions "enforce effectively the existing national legislation repressing the abuses of the emblem of the red cross, red crescent, red lion and sun, to enact such legislation wherever it does not exist at present and to provide for punishment by way of adequate sentences for offenders".[38] The ICRC has appealed to parties to both international and non-international armed conflicts to refrain from the misuse of the distinctive emblems.[39]

While several instances of improper use of the distinctive emblems have been reported, they have been denounced, principally by the ICRC but also by third States and the Inter-American Commission on Human Rights.[40] Some of the parties involved in those incidents recognised that such acts were unlawful and stated that they would take measures to prevent future occurrences.[41] It can be concluded that the general abstention from improperly using the distinctive emblems in practice is based on a legitimate expectation to that effect.

Definition

Improper use refers to any use other than that for which the distinctive emblems were intended, namely the identification of medical and religious personnel, medical units and medical transports, as well as personnel and property of the components of the International Movement of the Red Cross and Red Crescent. These uses are defined in the Geneva Conventions and in Additional Protocols I and II.[42] This definition of improper use is also used in numerous military manuals and in the legislation of a large number of States.[43]

---

[36] See, e.g., Colombia, Council of State, *Administrative Case No. 11369* (*ibid.*, § 413).

[37] See, e.g., the statements of Bosnia and Herzegovina (*ibid.*, § 417) and Colombia (*ibid.*, §§ 419–420).

[38] 23rd International Conference of the Red Cross, Res. XI (*ibid.*, § 434).

[39] See, e.g., ICRC, Communication to the Press No. 87/19/MMR (*ibid.*, § 443), Press Release No. 1673 (*ibid.*, § 444) Press Release, ICRC denies allegations (*ibid.*, § 448), Communication to the Press No. 93/17 (*ibid.*, § 450), Memorandum on Respect for International Humanitarian Law in Angola (*ibid.*, § 452), Memorandum on Compliance with International Humanitarian Law by the Forces Participating in Opération Turquoise (*ibid.*, § 453), Information to the Press (*ibid.*, § 458), Communication to the Press No. 00/42 (*ibid.*, § 460) and the practice reported in ICRC archive documents (*ibid.*, §§ 439, 441–442, 445, 449, 451 and 454).

[40] See, e.g., ICRC, Communication to the Press No. 87/19/MMR (*ibid.*, § 443); the practice reported in ICRC archive documents (*ibid.*, §§ 429, 441–442, 449, 454 and 458) and Inter-American Commission on Human Rights, Report on the situation of human rights in Nicaragua (*ibid.*, § 436).

[41] See, e.g., the practice reported in ICRC archive documents (*ibid.*, §§ 441 and 454).

[42] See First Geneva Convention, Articles 24–27 and 38–44 (*ibid.*, §§ 173–174 and 180); Second Geneva Convention, Articles 22, 24–25, 27, 36–39 and 41–44 (*ibid.*, §§ 177–178 and 180); Fourth Geneva Convention, Articles 18–22 (*ibid.*, § 180); Additional Protocol I, Articles 8, 18 and 22–23 (*ibid.*, § 183); Additional Protocol II, Article 12 (adopted by consensus) (*ibid.*, § 184).

[43] See, e.g., the military manuals of Argentina (*ibid.*, §§ 196–197), Belgium (*ibid.*, §§ 200–201), Dominican Republic (*ibid.*, § 209), Ecuador (*ibid.*, § 210), Spain (*ibid.*, §§ 229–230), Sweden

Rule 60. The use of the United Nations emblem and uniform is prohibited, except as authorised by the organisation.

Practice

Volume II, Chapter 18, Section D.

Summary

State practice establishes this rule as a norm of customary international law applicable in both international and non-international armed conflicts.

International armed conflicts

The prohibition of unauthorised use of the United Nations emblem and uniform is included in Additional Protocol I.[44] Under the Statute of the International Criminal Court, making improper, i.e., unauthorised, use of the flag or the military insignia or uniforms of the United Nations constitutes a war crime in international armed conflicts when it results in death or serious personal injury.[45]

The prohibition of the unauthorised use of the United Nations emblem and uniform is recognised in many military manuals.[46] Violation of this rule is an offence under the legislation of numerous States.[47] This practice includes that of States not, or not at the time, party to Additional Protocol I.[48]

(*ibid.*, § 231), Switzerland (*ibid.*, § 232), United Kingdom (*ibid.*, § 233) and United States (*ibid.*, §§ 235–238) and legislation (*ibid.*, §§ 240–412).

[44] Additional Protocol I, Article 38(2) (adopted by consensus) (*ibid.*, § 465).

[45] ICC Statute, Article 8(2)(b)(vii) (*ibid.*, § 468).

[46] See, e.g., the military manuals of Argentina (*ibid.*, § 473), Australia (*ibid.*, §§ 474–475), Belgium (*ibid.*, § 476), Burkina Faso (*ibid.*, § 477), Cameroon (*ibid.*, §§ 478–479), Canada (*ibid.*, § 480), Colombia (*ibid.*, § 481), Congo (*ibid.*, § 482), Ecuador (*ibid.*, § 483), France (*ibid.*, §§ 484–485), Germany (*ibid.*, § 486), Italy (*ibid.*, § 487), Mali (*ibid.*, § 488), Morocco (*ibid.*, § 489), Netherlands (*ibid.*, § 490), New Zealand (*ibid.*, § 491), Russia (*ibid.*, § 492), Senegal (*ibid.*, § 493), Spain (*ibid.*, § 494), Sweden (*ibid.*, § 495), United States (*ibid.*, §§ 496–497) and Yugoslavia (*ibid.*, § 498).

[47] See, e.g., the legislation of Algeria (*ibid.*, § 499), Armenia (*ibid.*, § 501), Australia (*ibid.*, §§ 502–503), Azerbaijan (*ibid.*, § 504), Belarus (*ibid.*, § 505), Bosnia and Herzegovina (*ibid.*, § 506), Burkina Faso (*ibid.*, § 507), Canada (*ibid.*, § 509), Democratic Republic of the Congo (*ibid.*, § 510), Congo (*ibid.*, § 511), Côte d'Ivoire (*ibid.*, § 512), Croatia (*ibid.*, § 513), Czech Republic (*ibid.*, § 514), Denmark (*ibid.*, § 515), France (*ibid.*, § 516), Georgia (*ibid.*, § 517), Germany (*ibid.*, § 518), Guinea (*ibid.*, § 519), Ireland (*ibid.*, § 520), Italy (*ibid.*, § 521), Lithuania (*ibid.*, § 522), Mali (*ibid.*, §§ 523–524), Netherlands (*ibid.*, § 525), New Zealand (*ibid.*, § 526), Norway (*ibid.*, §§ 527–528), Poland (*ibid.*, § 529), Slovakia (*ibid.*, § 530), Slovenia (*ibid.*, § 531), Spain (*ibid.*, § 532), Sweden (*ibid.*, § 533), Switzerland (*ibid.*, § 534), United Kingdom (*ibid.*, § 536) and Yugoslavia (*ibid.*, § 537); see also the draft legislation of Argentina (*ibid.*, § 500), Burundi (*ibid.*, § 508) and Trinidad and Tobago (*ibid.*, § 535).

[48] See the military manuals of Mali (*ibid.*, § 488) and United States (*ibid.*, § 497), the legislation of Azerbaijan (*ibid.*, § 504), the statement of the United States (*ibid.*, § 541), the practice of United Kingdom (*ibid.*, § 540), and the reported practice of Indonesia (*ibid.*, § 539).

Non-international armed conflicts

This rule was included in the draft of Additional Protocol II by Committee III of the Diplomatic Conference leading to the adoption of the Additional Protocols but was deleted at the last moment as part of a package aimed at the adoption of a simplified text.[49] It is contained in other instruments pertaining also to non-international armed conflicts.[50]

The prohibition of the unauthorised use of the United Nations emblem and uniform is set forth in military manuals which are applicable in or have been applied in non-international armed conflicts.[51] Violation of this rule is an offence under the legislation of numerous States.[52]

No official contrary practice was found with respect to either international or non-international armed conflicts. Alleged violations of this rule have generally been condemned, in particular in the context of the conflict in Bosnia and Herzegovina.[53] No party to a conflict has denied the applicability of this rule or claimed that it would be lawful to use United Nations emblems and uniforms without being so authorised.

Rule 61. The improper use of other internationally recognised emblems is prohibited.

Practice

Volume II, Chapter 18, Section E.

Summary

State practice establishes this rule as a norm of customary international law applicable in both international and non-international armed conflicts.

---

[49] Draft Additional Protocol II, Article 23(2) (*ibid.*, § 466).

[50] See, e.g., Memorandum of Understanding on the Application of IHL between Croatia and the SFRY, para. 6 (*ibid.*, § 470); Agreement on the Application of IHL between the Parties to the Conflict in Bosnia and Herzegovina, para. 2.5 (*ibid.*, § 471).

[51] See, e.g., the military manuals of Australia (*ibid.*, § 474), Colombia (*ibid.*, § 481), Ecuador (*ibid.*, § 483), Germany (*ibid.*, § 486), Italy (*ibid.*, § 487) and Yugoslavia (*ibid.*, § 498).

[52] See, e.g., the legislation of Armenia (*ibid.*, § 501), Azerbaijan (*ibid.*, § 504), Belarus (*ibid.*, § 505), Bosnia and Herzegovina (*ibid.*, § 506), Democratic Republic of the Congo (*ibid.*, § 510), Croatia (*ibid.*, § 513), Germany (*ibid.*, § 518), Guinea (*ibid.*, § 519), Poland (*ibid.*, § 529), Slovenia (*ibid.*, § 531), Spain (*ibid.*, § 532), Sweden (*ibid.*, § 533) and Yugoslavia (*ibid.*, § 537); see also the legislation of Burkina Faso (*ibid.*, § 507), Czech Republic (*ibid.*, § 514), Italy (*ibid.*, § 521) and Slovakia (*ibid.*, § 530), the application of which is not excluded in time of non-international armed conflict, and the draft legislation of Argentina (*ibid.*, § 500).

[53] See, e.g., UN Secretary-General, Report submitted pursuant to Security Council Resolution 1010 (1995) (*ibid.*, § 543).

International armed conflicts

With respect to the distinctive emblem for cultural property, this rule is contained in the Hague Convention for the Protection of Cultural Property.[54] It is also contained in Article 38(1) of Additional Protocol I with respect to internationally recognised emblems in general, including the protective emblem of cultural property.[55] Article 66(8) of Additional Protocol I requires States party to take measures to prevent and repress any misuse of the international distinctive sign of civil defence.[56]

The prohibition of the improper use of other internationally recognised emblems is stated in numerous military manuals.[57] Violation of this rule is an offence under the legislation of numerous States.[58] This rule is also supported by the practice of States not, or not at the time, party to Additional Protocol I or to the Hague Convention for the Protection of Cultural Property.[59]

Non-international armed conflicts

With respect to the distinctive emblem for cultural property, this rule is contained in the Hague Convention for the Protection of Cultural Property.[60] The rule that it is "forbidden to misuse deliberately in armed conflict other internationally recognized protective emblems", including the protective emblem of cultural property, was included by consensus in the draft of Additional Protocol II by Committee III of the Diplomatic Conference leading to the adoption of the Additional Protocols but was deleted at the last moment as part of a package aimed at the adoption of a simplified text.[61]

---

[54] Hague Convention for the Protection of Cultural Property, Article 17 (ibid., § 550).

[55] Additional Protocol I, Article 38(1) (adopted by consensus) (ibid., § 551).

[56] Additional Protocol I, Article 66(8) (adopted by consensus) (ibid., § 552).

[57] See, e.g., the military manuals of Argentina (ibid., § 556), Australia (ibid., §§ 557–558), Belgium (ibid., § 559), Burkina Faso (ibid., § 560), Cameroon (ibid., §§ 561–562), Canada (ibid., § 563), Colombia (ibid., § 564), Congo (ibid., § 565), Ecuador (ibid., § 566), France (ibid., §§ 567–568), Germany (ibid., § 569), Italy (ibid., § 570), Lebanon (ibid., § 571), Mali (ibid., § 572), Morocco (ibid., § 573), Netherlands (ibid., § 574), New Zealand (ibid., § 575), Russia (ibid., § 576), Senegal (ibid., § 577), Spain (ibid., § 578), Sweden (ibid., § 579), United States (ibid., §§ 580–581) and Yugoslavia (ibid., § 582).

[58] See, e.g., the legislation of Algeria (ibid., § 583), Argentina (ibid., § 585), Armenia (ibid., § 586), Australia (ibid., § 587), Belarus (ibid., § 589), Bosnia and Herzegovina (ibid., § 590), Burkina Faso (ibid., § 591), Democratic Republic of the Congo (ibid., § 592), Cook Islands (ibid., § 593), Côte d'Ivoire (ibid., § 594), Croatia (ibid., § 595), Denmark (ibid., § 596), Estonia (ibid., § 597), Finland (ibid., § 598), France (ibid., § 599), Guinea (ibid., § 600), Ireland (ibid., § 601), Italy (ibid., § 602), Mali (ibid., § 603), Norway (ibid., §§ 604–605), Poland (ibid., § 606), Slovenia (ibid., § 607), Spain (ibid., § 608), Sweden (ibid., §§ 609–610), Switzerland (ibid., §§ 611–612), United Kingdom (ibid., § 613), Yugoslavia (ibid., § 614) and Zimbabwe (ibid., § 615); see also the draft legislation of Argentina (ibid., § 584) and Bangladesh (ibid., § 588).

[59] See the military manuals of the United States (ibid., §§ 580–581), the statements of Israel (ibid., § 617) and United States (ibid., § 619) and the practice of the United Kingdom (ibid., § 618).

[60] Hague Convention for the Protection of Cultural Property, Article 17 (ibid., § 550).

[61] Draft Additional Protocol II, Article 23 (ibid., § 554).

The prohibition of the improper use of other internationally recognised emblems is stated in military manuals which are applicable in or have been applied in non-international armed conflicts.[62] Violation of this rule is an offence under the legislation of numerous States.[63]

No official contrary practice was found with respect to either international or non-international armed conflicts. No party has denied the applicability of this rule or claimed that it would be lawful to use improperly internationally recognised emblems. Improper use would also undermine the protection due to persons and objects identified by such emblems.

Definitions

The term "other internationally recognised emblems" includes the protective emblem of cultural property, the international distinctive sign of civil defence and the international special sign for works and installations containing dangerous forces. It also includes the protective emblem for hospital zones and localities,[64] the protective emblem for hospital and safety zones and localities,[65] the letters "PW" or "PG" used to mark prisoner-of-war camps[66] and the letters "IC" used to mark civilian internment camps.[67]

The phrase "improper use" refers to any use other than that for which these emblems were intended, namely the identification of the respective objects, zones, localities and camps.

Rule 62. Improper use of the flags or military emblems, insignia or uniforms of the adversary is prohibited.

Practice

Volume II, Chapter 18, Section F.

---

[62] See, e.g., the military manuals of Australia (*ibid.*, § 557), Colombia (*ibid.*, § 564), Ecuador (*ibid.*, § 566), Germany (*ibid.*, § 569), Italy (*ibid.*, § 570), Lebanon (*ibid.*, § 571) and Yugoslavia (*ibid.*, § 582).

[63] See, e.g., the legislation of Argentina (*ibid.*, § 585), Armenia (*ibid.*, § 586), Belarus (*ibid.*, § 589), Bosnia and Herzegovina (*ibid.*, § 590), Democratic Republic of the Congo (*ibid.*, § 592), Croatia (*ibid.*, § 595), Denmark (*ibid.*, § 596), Estonia (*ibid.*, § 597), Guinea (*ibid.*, § 600), Norway (*ibid.*, §§ 604–605), Poland (*ibid.*, § 606), Slovenia (*ibid.*, § 607), Spain (*ibid.*, § 608), Sweden (*ibid.*, § 610), Switzerland (*ibid.*, § 612) and Yugoslavia (*ibid.*, § 614); see also the legislation of Burkina Faso (*ibid.*, § 591) and Italy (*ibid.*, § 602), the application of which is not excluded in time of non-international armed conflict, and the draft legislation of Argentina (*ibid.*, § 584) and Bangladesh (*ibid.*, § 588).

[64] First Geneva Convention, Article 23 and Annex I, Article 6.

[65] Fourth Geneva Convention, Article 14 and Annex I, Article 6.

[66] Third Geneva Convention, Article 23, third paragraph.

[67] Fourth Geneva Convention, Article 83, third paragraph.

Summary

State practice establishes the customary nature of this rule in international armed conflicts. It can be argued that it should also apply in non-international armed conflicts when the parties to the conflict do in fact wear uniforms.

International armed conflicts

This is a long-standing rule of customary international law already recognised in the Lieber Code, the Brussels Declaration and the Oxford Manual.[68] It was codified in the Hague Regulations.[69] Additional Protocol I prohibits the use of enemy flags, military emblems, insignia or uniforms "while engaging in attacks or in order to shield, favour, protect or impede military operations".[70] Under the Statute of the International Criminal Court, "making improper use . . . of the flag or of the military insignia and uniform of the enemy" constitutes a war crime in international armed conflicts when it results in death or serious personal injury.[71]

This rule is set forth in numerous military manuals.[72] Sweden's IHL Manual considers that the prohibition of improper use of emblems of nationality in Article 39 of Additional Protocol I is a codification of customary international law.[73] Violation of this rule is an offence under the legislation of many States.[74] The rule is also supported by official statements and other practice.[75]

Some practice was found that considers the wearing of enemy uniforms as perfidious.[76] This does not square entirely, however, with the definition of

[68] Lieber Code, Articles 63 and 65 (cited in Vol. II, Ch. 18, § 634); Brussels Declaration, Article 13(f) (*ibid.*, § 635); Oxford Manual, Article 8(d) (*ibid.*, § 636).

[69] Hague Regulations, Article 23(f) (*ibid.*, § 627).

[70] Additional Protocol I, Article 39(2) (adopted by consensus) (*ibid.*, § 630).

[71] ICC Statute, Article 8(2)(b)(vii) (*ibid.*, § 633).

[72] See, e.g., military manuals of Argentina (*ibid.*, §§ 641–642), Australia (*ibid.*, §§ 643–644), Belgium (*ibid.*, §§ 645–646), Burkina Faso (*ibid.*, § 647), Cameroon (*ibid.*, §§ 648–649), Canada (*ibid.*, § 650), Congo (*ibid.*, § 651), Croatia (*ibid.*, § 652), Ecuador (*ibid.*, § 653), France (*ibid.*, §§ 654 and 657), Germany (*ibid.*, § 658), Hungary (*ibid.*, § 659), Israel (*ibid.*, §§ 661–662), Italy (*ibid.*, § 664), South Korea (*ibid.*, § 665), Lebanon (*ibid.*, § 666), Mali (*ibid.*, § 668), Morocco (*ibid.*, § 669), New Zealand (*ibid.*, § 672), Nigeria (*ibid.*, §§ 673–674), Russia (*ibid.*, § 676), Senegal (*ibid.*, § 677), South Africa (*ibid.*, § 678), Spain (*ibid.*, § 679), Sweden (*ibid.*, § 680), Switzerland (*ibid.*, § 681), United Kingdom (*ibid.*, §§ 682–683), United States (*ibid.*, §§ 684–686) and Yugoslavia (*ibid.*, § 687).

[73] Sweden, *IHL Manual* (*ibid.*, § 680).

[74] See, e.g., the legislation of Algeria (*ibid.*, § 688), Armenia (*ibid.*, § 690), Australia (*ibid.*, § 691), Belarus (*ibid.*, § 692), Canada (*ibid.*, § 694), Colombia (*ibid.*, § 695), Congo (*ibid.*, § 696), Egypt (*ibid.*, § 697), Georgia (*ibid.*, § 698), Germany (*ibid.*, § 699), Greece (*ibid.*, § 700), Ireland (*ibid.*, § 701), Italy (*ibid.*, §§ 702–703), Mali (*ibid.*, § 704), Netherlands (*ibid.*, § 705), New Zealand (*ibid.*, § 706), Nicaragua (*ibid.*, § 707), Norway (*ibid.*, § 708), Poland (*ibid.*, § 710), Spain (*ibid.*, §§ 711–712), Syria (*ibid.*, § 714), United Kingdom (*ibid.*, § 716), United States (*ibid.*, § 717) and Yugoslavia (*ibid.*, § 718); see also the draft legislation of Argentina (*ibid.*, § 689), Burundi (*ibid.*, § 693) and Trinidad and Tobago (*ibid.*, § 715).

[75] See, e.g., the reported practice of Germany (*ibid.*, § 721), Iraq (*ibid.*, § 723) and South Korea (*ibid.*, § 725).

[76] See, e.g., the military manuals of France (*ibid.*, §§ 655–656), Hungary (*ibid.*, § 659), Israel (*ibid.*, § 662), Romania (*ibid.*, § 675) and Switzerland (*ibid.*, § 681).

perfidy inasmuch as enemy uniforms are not entitled to specific protection under humanitarian law, even though the wearing of such uniforms may invite the confidence of the enemy (for a definition of perfidy, see commentary to Rule 65). Other practice considers it a violation of the principle of good faith.[77]

Definition of improper use

The Brussels Declaration, the Oxford Manual and the Hague Regulations prohibit the "improper" use of enemy flags, military insignia and uniforms without specifying what is improper and what is not.[78] The Elements of Crimes of the Statute of the International Criminal Court specifies that it is a war crime to use enemy uniforms "in a manner prohibited under the international law of armed conflict while engaged in an attack".[79]

Many military manuals prohibit "improper" use without further explanation.[80] The UK Military Manual specifies that:

The employment of the national flag, military insignia or uniform of the enemy for the purpose of ruse is not forbidden, but the [Hague Regulations] prohibit their improper use, leaving unsettled what use is proper and what use is not. However, their employment is forbidden during a combat, that is, the opening of fire whilst in the guise of the enemy. But there is no unanimity as to whether the uniform of the enemy may be worn and his flag displayed for the purpose of approach or withdrawal. Use of enemy uniform for the purpose of and in connection with sabotage is in the same category as spying.[81]

Belgium's Law of War Manual provides the following examples of improper use: opening fire or participating in an attack while wearing enemy uniform and opening fire from a captured enemy combat vehicle with its insignia. The manual states that "infiltrating enemy lines in order to create panic to the point that the adversary starts firing on its own soldiers believing that they are disguised enemies or operating behind enemy lines wearing enemy uniform in order to collect information or commit acts of sabotage" is not considered an improper use,[82] although these acts may lead to loss of the right to prisoner-of-war status (see Rule 106). Sweden's IHL Manual explains that:

The prohibition of improper use has been interpreted to mean that enemy uniform may not be used in connection with or during combat, and this has led to great

---

[77] See, e.g., Argentina, *Law of War Manual* (*ibid.*, § 641).
[78] Brussels Declaration, Article 13(f) (*ibid.*, § 635); Oxford Manual, Article 8(d) (*ibid.*, § 636); Hague Regulations, Article 23(f) (*ibid.*, § 628).
[79] Elements of Crimes for the ICC, Improper use of uniforms of the enemy as a war crime (ICC Statute, Article 8(2)(b)(xii)).
[80] See, e.g., the military manuals of Burkina Faso (cited in Vol. II, Ch. 18, § 647), Cameroon (*ibid.*, § 648), Congo (*ibid.*, § 651), France (*ibid.*, § 654), Germany (*ibid.*, § 658), Israel (*ibid.*, § 661), South Korea (*ibid.*, § 665), Lebanon (*ibid.*, § 666), Mali (*ibid.*, § 668), Morocco (*ibid.*, § 669), Nigeria (*ibid.*, § 674), Russia (*ibid.*, § 676) and Senegal (*ibid.*, § 677).
[81] United Kingdom, *Military Manual* (*ibid.*, § 682).
[82] Belgium, *Law of War Manual* (*ibid.*, § 645).

uncertainty in application. During the 1974–1977 diplomatic conference, certain of the great powers wished to retain the possibility of appearing in enemy uniforms, while most of the smaller States claimed that this possibility should be excluded or minimised. The Conference accepted the view of the smaller States here. The rule in Article 39(2) [of Additional Protocol I that the use of enemy uniforms is improper "when engaging in attacks or in order to shield, favour, protect or impede military operations"] can be interpreted to mean that enemy uniform may be used only as personal protection, for example under extreme weather conditions, and may never be used in connection with any type of military operation. Where prisoners of war make use of enemy uniforms in connection with escape attempts, this may not be seen as an infringement of Article 39.[83]

A number of military manuals restate the definition of "improper use" of enemy uniform contained in Additional Protocol I, namely "while engaging in attacks or in order to shield, favour, protect or impede military operations".[84] Upon ratification of Additional Protocol I, Canada made a reservation to the effect that it would only be bound by the prohibition on using enemy uniforms while engaging in attacks but not in order to shield, favour, protect or impede military operations.[85] Its LOAC Manual restates this point.[86] Several manuals similarly limit the prohibition to combat operations.[87] It should also be pointed out that several manuals prohibit the use as such of enemy uniforms.[88]

In the *Skorzeny case* in 1947, the US General Military Court of the US Zone of Germany acquitted the accused of charges of improper use by entering into combat disguised in enemy uniforms. The Court did not consider it improper for German officers to wear enemy uniforms while trying to occupy enemy military objectives and there was no evidence that they had used their weapons while so disguised.[89] The United States has stated that it does "not support the prohibition in article 39 [of Additional Protocol I] of the use of enemy emblems and uniforms during military operations".[90] There are several examples of conflicts since the Second World War in which the wearing of enemy uniforms was practised, including in non-international armed conflicts.[91] It cannot be concluded that the wearing of enemy uniforms outside combat would be improper.

Several manuals indicate that naval forces may fly enemy colours to deceive the enemy but must display their true colours prior to an actual armed

[83] Sweden, *IHL Manual* (ibid., § 680).
[84] See, e.g., the military manuals of Australia (ibid., §§ 643–644), Belgium (ibid., § 646), New Zealand (ibid., § 672), South Africa (ibid., § 678) and Spain (ibid., § 679).
[85] Canada, Reservations and statements of understanding made upon ratification of Additional Protocol I (ibid., § 631).
[86] Canada, *LOAC Manual* (ibid., § 650).
[87] See, e.g., the military manuals of Argentina (ibid., §§ 641–642), Ecuador (ibid., § 653), France ("in combat with a view to dissimulate, favour or impede military operations") (ibid., § 657), Nigeria (ibid., § 673), United Kingdom (ibid., § 683), United States (ibid., §§ 685–686) and Yugoslavia (ibid., § 687).
[88] See the military manuals of France (ibid., §§ 655–656), Indonesia (ibid., § 660), Italy (ibid., § 663), Madagascar (ibid., § 667), Netherlands (ibid., §§ 670–671) and Romania (ibid., § 675).
[89] United States, General Military Court of the US Zone of Germany, *Skorzeny case* (ibid., § 719).
[90] United States, Remarks of the Deputy Legal Adviser of the Department of State (ibid., § 729).
[91] See W. Hays Parks, "Air War and the Law of War" (ibid., § 740).

engagement.[92] However, there appears to be agreement that military aircraft may not use enemy markings. While Ecuador's Naval Manual and the US Naval Handbook restrict this prohibition to combat, Germany's Military Manual, New Zealand's Military Manual and the US Air Force Pamphlet state that military aircraft may not bear enemy markings.[93] Canada's LOAC Manual considers it an act of perfidy in air warfare if a hostile act is committed while "using false markings on military aircraft such as the markings of ... enemy aircraft".[94] The different treatment between ships and aircraft is explained by the fact that it is practically possible to change the flag under which a ship is sailing before engaging in combat, while an aircraft cannot change its marking whilst in the air.

Non-international armed conflicts

The draft of Additional Protocol II submitted by the ICRC to the Diplomatic Conference leading to the adoption of the Additional Protocols provided that "when carried out in order to commit or resume hostilities ... the use in combat of the enemy's distinctive military emblems" constitutes perfidy. This provision was deleted from the draft during the negotiations in Committee III of the Diplomatic Conference.[95] The prohibition on making use of the flags or military emblems, insignia or uniforms of adverse parties while engaging in attacks or in order to shield, favour, protect or impede military operations is contained in other instruments pertaining also to non-international armed conflicts.[96]

The prohibition of improper use of enemy uniforms and insignia is contained in military manuals which are applicable in or have been applied in non-international armed conflicts.[97] Violation of this rule in any armed conflict is an offence under the legislation of numerous States.[98] The application of this rule in non-international armed conflicts is also supported by official

---

[92] See, e.g., the military manuals of Australia (*ibid.*, §§ 643–644), Belgium (*ibid.*, § 645), Canada (*ibid.*, § 650), Ecuador (*ibid.*, § 653), France (*ibid.*, § 657), Germany (*ibid.*, § 658), New Zealand (*ibid.*, § 672) and United States (*ibid.*, § 686).

[93] Ecuador, *Naval Manual* (*ibid.*, § 653); Germany, *Military Manual* (*ibid.*, § 658); New Zealand, *Military Manual* (*ibid.*, § 672); United States, *Air Force Pamphlet* (*ibid.*, § 685) and *Naval Handbook* (*ibid.*, § 686).

[94] Canada, *LOAC Manual* (*ibid.*, § 650).

[95] Draft Additional Protocol II, Article 21(1) (*ibid.*, § 632).

[96] See, e.g., Memorandum of Understanding on the Application of IHL between Croatia and the SFRY, para. 6 (*ibid.*, § 637); Agreement on the Application of IHL between the Parties to the Conflict in Bosnia and Herzegovina, para. 2.5 (*ibid.*, § 638).

[97] See, e.g., military manuals of Australia (*ibid.*, § 643), Croatia (*ibid.*, § 652), Ecuador (*ibid.*, § 653), Germany (*ibid.*, § 658), Italy (*ibid.*, § 664), Lebanon (*ibid.*, § 666), Nigeria (*ibid.*, § 674), South Africa (*ibid.*, § 678) and Yugoslavia (*ibid.*, § 687).

[98] See, e.g., the legislation of Armenia (*ibid.*, § 690), Belarus (*ibid.*, § 692), Colombia (*ibid.*, § 695), Germany (*ibid.*, § 699), Nicaragua (*ibid.*, § 707), Poland (*ibid.*, § 710), Spain (*ibid.*, § 713) and Yugoslavia (*ibid.*, § 718); see also the legislation of Italy (*ibid.*, §§ 702–703), the application of which is not excluded in time of non-international armed conflict, and the draft legislation of Argentina (*ibid.*, § 689).

statements and other national practice.[99] During the Chinese civil war, for example, the Chinese Communist Party denounced the use of Red Army uniforms by Nationalist soldiers alleging they were used while committing acts designed to discredit the Red Army.[100]

Rule 63. Use of the flags or military emblems, insignia or uniforms of neutral or other States not party to the conflict is prohibited.

Practice

Volume II, Chapter 18, Section G.

Summary

State practice establishes this rule as a norm of customary international law applicable in international armed conflicts and, arguably, also in non-international armed conflicts.

International armed conflicts

This rule is set forth in Additional Protocol I.[101] It is restated in other instruments, in particular the San Remo Manual on Naval Warfare.[102]

The prohibition is contained in numerous military manuals.[103] Violation of this rule is an offence under the legislation of many States.[104] This includes the practice of States not party to Additional Protocol I.[105]

No official contrary practice was found. No party has claimed the right to use the uniforms of neutral or other States not party to the conflict.

---

[99] See, e.g., the statement of Turkey (*ibid.*, § 727) and the reported practice of China (*ibid.*, § 720) and Rwanda (*ibid.*, § 726).
[100] Report on the Practice of China (*ibid.*, § 720).
[101] Additional Protocol I, Article 39(1) (adopted by consensus) (*ibid.*, § 742).
[102] San Remo Manual, para. 109 (*ibid.*, § 743).
[103] See, e.g., the military manuals of Australia (*ibid.*, §§ 744–745), Belgium (*ibid.*, § 746), Cameroon (*ibid.*, § 747), Canada (*ibid.*, § 748), Ecuador (*ibid.*, § 749), France (*ibid.*, § 750), Germany (*ibid.*, § 751), Indonesia (*ibid.*, § 752), Italy (*ibid.*, § 753), Netherlands (*ibid.*, §§ 754–755), New Zealand (*ibid.*, § 756), Russia (*ibid.*, § 757), Spain (*ibid.*, § 758), Sweden (*ibid.*, § 759) and United States (*ibid.*, §§ 760–761).
[104] See, e.g., the legislation of Algeria (*ibid.*, § 762), Armenia (*ibid.*, § 764), Australia (*ibid.*, § 765), Belarus (*ibid.*, § 766), Czech Republic (*ibid.*, § 767), Ireland (*ibid.*, § 768), Italy (*ibid.*, §§ 769–770), Nicaragua (*ibid.*, § 771), Norway (*ibid.*, § 772), Philippines (*ibid.*, § 773), Poland (*ibid.*, § 774), Slovakia (*ibid.*, § 775), Spain (*ibid.*, §§ 776–777) and Syria (*ibid.*, § 778); see also the draft legislation of Argentina (*ibid.*, § 763).
[105] See the military manuals of Indonesia (*ibid.*, § 752) and United States (*ibid.*, §§ 760–761) and the legislation of the Philippines (*ibid.*, § 773).

Non-international armed conflicts

Military manuals which are applicable in or have been applied in non-international armed conflicts include this prohibition.[106] Violation of this rule is an offence in any armed conflict under the legislation of several States.[107]

While no particular other practice was found with regard to non-international armed conflicts, no contrary practice was found either. No party to a non-international armed conflict was reported to have claimed the right to use the emblems or uniform of a neutral or other State not party to the conflict. It is very likely that the fact of implying involvement of a third State in a non-international armed conflict by wearing its uniform, for example, would be denounced by that State, as well as by the adverse party, as unlawful conduct. It can be argued therefore that there is a legitimate expectation that parties to a non-international armed conflict abide by this rule and that this rule is part of customary international law.

Rule 64. Concluding an agreement to suspend combat with the intention of attacking by surprise the enemy relying on that agreement is prohibited.

Practice

Volume II, Chapter 18, Section H.

Summary

State practice establishes this rule as a norm of customary international law applicable in both international and non-international armed conflicts. The rule is based on respect for good faith (see Rule 66). Violations would involve violations of those rules that are implemented via agreements to suspend combat, such as the evacuation of the wounded and sick or civilians (see Rules 109 and 129).

International armed conflicts

A breach of an agreement to suspend combat constitutes a breach of trust and is a violation of the principle of good faith. The fact that this rule finds its basis in the principle of good faith is expressed in the Lieber Code, which states

---

[106] See, e.g., the military manuals of Australia (*ibid.*, § 744), Ecuador (*ibid.*, § 749), Germany (*ibid.*, § 751) and Italy (*ibid.*, § 753).

[107] See, e.g., the legislation of Armenia (*ibid.*, § 764), Belarus (*ibid.*, § 766), Nicaragua (*ibid.*, § 771), Philippines (*ibid.*, § 773), Poland (*ibid.*, § 774) and Spain (*ibid.*, § 777); see also the legislation of Czech Republic (*ibid.*, § 767), Italy (*ibid.*, §§ 769–770) and Slovakia (*ibid.*, § 775), the application of which is not excluded in time of non-international armed conflict, and the draft legislation of Argentina (*ibid.*, § 763).

that "military necessity admits . . . of such deception as does not involve the breaking of good faith either positively pledged, regarding agreements entered into during the war, or supposed by the modern law of war to exist".[108] The UK Military Manual emphasises that "good faith, as expressed in the observance of promises, is essential in war".[109]

This rule is set forth in numerous military manuals.[110] Some of these manuals consider the feigning of a cease-fire "perfidious".[111] The US Field Manual and Naval Handbook, for example, state that a false broadcast to the enemy that an armistice has been agreed upon has been widely recognised to be "treacherous".[112]

The violation of any agreement to suspend combat, whether a truce, armistice, capitulation or other agreement to that effect, is an offence under the legislation of many States.[113] This rule is also supported by official statements, for example, by Iraq in the context of the Iran–Iraq War.[114]

Non-international armed conflicts

The draft of Additional Protocol II submitted by the ICRC to the Diplomatic Conference leading to the adoption of the Additional Protocols provided that "when carried out in order to commit or resume hostilities . . . the feigning of a cease-fire" constitutes perfidy.[115] This provision was deleted from the draft during the negotiations in Committee III of the Diplomatic Conference. This does not mean, however, that such acts would be lawful in non-international armed conflicts. The principle of good faith in the implementation of agreements applies equally in international and non-international armed conflicts (see Rule 66).

Military manuals which are applicable in or have been applied in non-international armed conflicts include this prohibition.[116] Violation of the rule

---

[108] Lieber Code, Article 15 (*ibid.*, § 786).

[109] United Kingdom, *Military Manual* (*ibid.*, § 803).

[110] See, e.g., the military manuals of Belgium (*ibid.*, § 787), Burkina Faso (*ibid.*, § 788), Cameroon (*ibid.*, § 789), Canada (*ibid.*, § 790), Congo (*ibid.*, § 791), France (*ibid.*, § 792), Germany (*ibid.*, § 793), South Korea (*ibid.*, § 795), Mali (*ibid.*, § 796), Morocco (*ibid.*, § 797), Netherlands (*ibid.*, § 798), New Zealand (*ibid.*, § 799), Nigeria (*ibid.*, § 800), Senegal (*ibid.*, § 801), Switzerland (*ibid.*, § 802), United Kingdom (*ibid.*, § 803) and United States (*ibid.*, §§ 804–806).

[111] See the military manuals of Belgium (*ibid.*, § 787), Germany (*ibid.*, § 793), United Kingdom (*ibid.*, § 803) and United States (*ibid.*, §§ 804–805).

[112] United States, *Field Manual* (*ibid.*, § 804) and *Air Force Pamphlet* (*ibid.*, § 805).

[113] See, e.g., the legislation of Argentina (*ibid.*, §§ 807–808), Azerbaijan (*ibid.*, § 810), Belarus (*ibid.*, § 811), Bolivia (*ibid.*, § 812), Chile (*ibid.*, § 813), Costa Rica (*ibid.*, § 814), Ecuador (*ibid.*, §§ 815–816), El Salvador (*ibid.*, § 817), Ethiopia (*ibid.*, § 818), Guatemala (*ibid.*, § 819), Hungary (*ibid.*, § 820), Italy (*ibid.*, §§ 821–822), Mexico (*ibid.*, § 823), Netherlands (*ibid.*, § 824), Nicaragua (*ibid.*, § 825), Peru (*ibid.*, §§ 826–827), Spain (*ibid.*, §§ 828–829), Switzerland (*ibid.*, § 830) and Venezuela (*ibid.*, §§ 831–832); see also the draft legislation of Argentina (*ibid.*, § 809).

[114] Iraq, Letter to the UN Secretary-General (*ibid.*, § 835) and Military communiqué of 1 March 1987 (*ibid.*, § 836).

[115] Draft Additional Protocol II, Article 21(1) (*ibid.*, § 785).

[116] See, e.g., Germany, *Military Manual* (*ibid.*, § 793).

is an offence in any armed conflict under the legislation of many States.[117] This rule is also supported by official statements and reported practice in the context of non-international armed conflicts.[118]

No official contrary practice was found. Violations of this rule have generally been condemned. No party to a non-international armed conflict was reported to have claimed the right to conclude an agreement to suspend combat with the intention of attacking by surprise the enemy relying on that agreement.

Rule 65. Killing, injuring or capturing an adversary by resort to perfidy is prohibited.

Practice

Volume II, Chapter 18, Section I.

Summary

State practice establishes this rule as a norm of customary international law applicable in both international and non-international armed conflicts.

International armed conflicts

This is a long-standing rule of customary international law already recognised in the Lieber Code, the Brussels Declaration and the Oxford Manual, and codified in the Hague Regulations.[119] It is also set forth in Additional Protocol I.[120] Under the Statute of the International Criminal Court, "killing or wounding treacherously individuals belonging to the hostile nation or army" constitutes a war crime in international armed conflicts.[121]

The prohibition of perfidy is set forth in a large number of military manuals.[122] Sweden's IHL Manual considers that the prohibition of perfidy in

---

[117] See, e.g., the legislation of Azerbaijan (*ibid.*, § 810), Belarus (*ibid.*, § 811), Costa Rica (*ibid.*, § 814), Ecuador (*ibid.*, § 815), El Salvador (*ibid.*, § 817), Ethiopia (*ibid.*, § 818), Nicaragua (*ibid.*, § 825), Spain (*ibid.*, § 829), Switzerland (*ibid.*, § 830) and Venezuela (*ibid.*, § 831); see also the legislation of Argentina (*ibid.*, § 808), Hungary (*ibid.*, § 820) and Italy (*ibid.*, §§ 821–822), the application of which is not excluded in time of non-international armed conflict, and the draft legislation of Argentina (*ibid.*, § 809).

[118] See, e.g., the statements of China (*ibid.*, § 834) and Yugoslavia (*ibid.*, § 837) and the reported practice of Yugoslavia (*ibid.*, § 839) and a State (*ibid.*, § 840).

[119] Lieber Code, Article 101 (*ibid.*, § 930); Brussels Declaration, Article 13(b) (*ibid.*, § 931); Oxford Manual, Article 8(b) (*ibid.*, § 932); Hague Regulations, Article 23(b) (*ibid.*, § 926).

[120] Additional Protocol I, Article 37(1) (adopted by consensus) (*ibid.*, § 927).

[121] ICC Statute, Article 8(2)(b)(xi) (*ibid.*, § 929).

[122] See, e.g., the military manuals of Argentina (*ibid.*, §§ 856–857 and 937), Australia (*ibid.*, §§ 858–859 and 938–939), Belgium (*ibid.*, §§ 861 and 940), Benin (*ibid.*, § 863), Cameroon (*ibid.*, §§ 864 and 941), Canada (*ibid.*, §§ 866 and 942), Colombia (*ibid.*, § 867), Croatia (*ibid.*, §§ 868–869), Ecuador (*ibid.*, § 870), France (*ibid.*, §§ 871–873 and 943), Germany (*ibid.*, § 875), Hungary (*ibid.*, § 876), Indonesia (*ibid.*, § 944), Israel (*ibid.*, § 945), Italy (*ibid.*, § 947), Kenya (*ibid.*, § 948), South

Article 37 of Additional Protocol I is a codification of customary international law.[123] Violation of this rule is an offence under the legislation of numerous States.[124] The prohibition is also supported by official statements and other national practice.[125]

Non-international armed conflicts

The prohibition of perfidy was included in the draft of Additional Protocol II by Committee III of the Diplomatic Conference leading to the adoption of the Additional Protocols but was deleted at the last moment as part of a package aimed at the adoption of a simplified text.[126] Under the Statute of the International Criminal Court, "killing or wounding treacherously a combatant adversary" constitutes a war crime in non-international armed conflicts.[127] In addition, this rule is contained in other instruments pertaining also to non-international armed conflicts.[128]

Military manuals which are applicable in or have been applied in non-international armed conflicts prohibit resort to perfidy.[129] Violations of the rule are an offence in any armed conflict under the legislation of numerous States.[130]

Korea (*ibid.*, §§ 880–881), Netherlands (*ibid.*, §§ 883–885 and 949–950), New Zealand (*ibid.*, § 951), Nigeria (*ibid.*, §§ 886–887 and 952–953), Romania (*ibid.*, § 954), Russia (*ibid.*, §§ 888 and 955), South Africa (*ibid.*, §§ 889–890), Spain (*ibid.*, §§ 891 and 956), Sweden (*ibid.*, §§ 893 and 957), Switzerland (*ibid.*, §§ 894 and 958), Togo (*ibid.*, § 895), United Kingdom (*ibid.*, §§ 896 and 959–960), United States (*ibid.*, §§ 898, 900–901 and 961–962) and Yugoslavia (*ibid.*, §§ 902 and 963).

[123] Sweden, *IHL Manual* (*ibid.*, § 893).

[124] See, e.g., the legislation of Australia (*ibid.*, § 964), Bosnia and Herzegovina (*ibid.*, § 965), Canada (*ibid.*, § 967), Congo (*ibid.*, § 968), Croatia (*ibid.*, § 969), Georgia (*ibid.*, § 970), Germany (*ibid.*, § 971), Ireland (*ibid.*, § 972), Italy (*ibid.*, § 973), Mali (*ibid.*, § 974), Netherlands (*ibid.*, § 975), New Zealand (*ibid.*, § 976), Norway (*ibid.*, § 977), Slovenia (*ibid.*, § 978), Sweden (*ibid.*, § 979), United Kingdom (*ibid.*, § 981), United States (*ibid.*, § 982) and Yugoslavia (*ibid.*, § 983); see also the draft legislation of Burundi (*ibid.*, § 966), El Salvador (*ibid.*, § 903) and Trinidad and Tobago (*ibid.*, § 980).

[125] See, e.g., the statements of the United States (*ibid.*, §§ 917 and 988), the practice of the United States (*ibid.*, §§ 916 and 990) and the reported practice of Iraq (*ibid.*, §§ 912 and 985).

[126] Draft Additional Protocol II, Article 21(1) (*ibid.*, § 928).

[127] ICC Statute, Article 8(2)(e)(ix) (*ibid.*, § 929).

[128] See, e.g., Memorandum of Understanding on the Application of IHL between Croatia and the SFRY, para. 6 (*ibid.*, §§ 853 and 934); Agreement on the Application of IHL between the Parties to the Conflict in Bosnia and Herzegovina, para. 2.5 (*ibid.*, §§ 854 and 935); San Remo Manual, para. 111 (*ibid.*, § 855); UNTAET Regulation 2000/15, Section 6(1)(e)(ix) (*ibid.*, § 936).

[129] See, e.g., the military manuals of Australia (*ibid.*, §§ 858 and 939), Benin (*ibid.*, § 863), Canada (*ibid.*, § 866), Colombia (*ibid.*, § 867), Croatia (*ibid.*, §§ 868–869), Ecuador (*ibid.*, § 870), Germany (*ibid.*, § 875), Italy (*ibid.*, § 947), Kenya (*ibid.*, § 948), South Korea (*ibid.*, § 881), Nigeria (*ibid.*, §§ 886 and 952–953), South Africa (*ibid.*, §§ 889–890), Sweden (*ibid.*, § 893), Togo (*ibid.*, § 895) and Yugoslavia (*ibid.*, §§ 902 and 963).

[130] See, e.g., the legislation of Australia (*ibid.*, § 964), Bosnia and Herzegovina (*ibid.*, § 965), Canada (*ibid.*, § 967), Congo (*ibid.*, § 968), Croatia (*ibid.*, § 969), Georgia (*ibid.*, § 970), Germany (*ibid.*, § 971), Netherlands (*ibid.*, § 975), New Zealand (*ibid.*, § 976), Slovenia (*ibid.*, § 978), Sweden (*ibid.*, § 979), United Kingdom (*ibid.*, § 981) and Yugoslavia (*ibid.*, § 983); see also the legislation of Italy (*ibid.*, § 973), the application of which is not excluded in time of non-international armed conflict, and the draft legislation of Burundi (*ibid.*, § 966), El Salvador (*ibid.*, § 903) and Trinidad and Tobago (*ibid.*, § 980).

The rule is supported by official statements and other practice pertaining to non-international armed conflicts.[131]

No official contrary practice was found with respect to either international or non-international armed conflicts. No party has claimed the right to resort to perfidy.

Definition of perfidy

Additional Protocol I defines perfidy as "acts inviting the confidence of an adversary to lead him to believe that he is entitled to, or obliged to accord, protection under the rules of international law applicable in armed conflict, with intent to betray that confidence".[132] This definition is restated in the Elements of Crimes for the International Criminal Court.[133] It is also contained in numerous military manuals.[134] It is supported by other practice.[135] This practice includes that of States not, or not at the time, party to Additional Protocol I.[136] New Zealand's Military Manual and Sweden's IHL Manual point out that the definition of perfidy contained in Article 37 codifies customary international law.[137] The essence of perfidy is thus the invitation to obtain and then breach the adversary's confidence, i.e., an abuse of good faith. This requirement of a specific intent to breach the adversary's confidence sets perfidy apart from an improper use, making perfidy a more serious violation of international humanitarian law. Some military manuals translate this rule as follows: it is prohibited to commit a hostile act under the cover of a legal protection.[138]

The above definition of perfidy was also included in the draft of Additional Protocol II submitted by the ICRC to the Diplomatic Conference leading to

---

[131] See, e.g., the statements of Chile (*ibid.*, § 910), Peru (*ibid.*, § 913) and Yugoslavia (*ibid.*, § 918) and the reported practice of Colombia (*ibid.*, § 911) and the Philippines (*ibid.*, § 914).

[132] Additional Protocol I, Article 37(1) (adopted by consensus) (*ibid.*, § 847).

[133] Elements of Crimes for the ICC, Definition of killing or wounding treacherously individuals belonging to the hostile nation or army/a combatant adversary as a war crime (ICC Statute, Article 8(2)(b)(xi) and (e)(ix)).

[134] See, e.g., the military manuals of Argentina (cited in Vol. II, Ch. 18, § 857), Australia (*ibid.*, §§ 858–859), Belgium (*ibid.*, §§ 860–862), Cameroon (*ibid.*, § 864), Canada (*ibid.*, § 865), Croatia (*ibid.*, § 869), Ecuador (*ibid.*, § 870), France (*ibid.*, §§ 871 and 873), Germany (*ibid.*, §§ 874–875), Hungary (*ibid.*, § 876), Israel (*ibid.*, § 877), Kenya (*ibid.*, § 879), Netherlands (*ibid.*, § 883), New Zealand (*ibid.*, § 885), Spain (*ibid.*, § 892), Sweden (*ibid.*, § 893), United Kingdom (*ibid.*, § 897) and United States (*ibid.*, §§ 899 and 901).

[135] See, e.g., the statements of United States (*ibid.*, §§ 916–917) and the reported practice of Iraq (*ibid.*, § 912).

[136] See, e.g., the military manuals of France (*ibid.*, § 871), Israel (*ibid.*, § 877), Kenya (*ibid.*, § 879), United Kingdom (*ibid.*, § 897) and United States (*ibid.*, §§ 899 and 901), the statements of the United States (*ibid.*, §§ 916–917) and the reported practice of Iraq (*ibid.*, § 912).

[137] New Zealand, *Military Manual* (*ibid.*, § 885); Sweden, *IHL Manual* (*ibid.*, § 893).

[138] See, e.g., the military manuals of Benin (*ibid.*, § 863), Canada (*ibid.*, § 865) and Togo (*ibid.*, § 895).

the adoption of the Additional Protocols but was deleted by Committee III.[139] However, the Preparatory Committee for the Elements of Crimes for the International Criminal Court concluded that the elements of the crime of treacherously killing or wounding were identical in international and non-international armed conflicts.[140]

Given that the definition of perfidy provides that the confidence of an adversary be based on a situation which requires protection under international humanitarian law, the following acts are considered perfidious if committed with the intent to betray the confidence of the adversary:

- simulation of being disabled by injuries or sickness because an enemy who is thus disabled is considered *hors de combat* and may not be attacked but must be collected and cared for (see Rules 47 and 109–110);[141]
- simulation of surrender because an adversary who surrenders is considered *hors de combat* and may not be attacked but must be captured or released (see Rule 47);[142]
- simulation of an intent to negotiate under a flag of truce because a person advancing under a flag of truce must be respected (see Rule 67);[143]
- simulation of protected status by using the red cross or red crescent emblem because medical and religious personnel, units and transports displaying the distinctive emblems must be respected and protected (see Chapter 7);[144]
- simulation of protected status by using United Nations emblems, signs or uniforms because peacekeeping personnel and humanitarian relief personnel using United Nations emblems, signs or uniforms must be respected, as long as they are entitled to the protection given to civilians, and those emblems, signs or uniforms may not be used without authorisation (see Rules 31, 33 and 60);[145]
- simulation of protected status by using other protective emblems because the personnel using other protective emblems, including the distinctive emblem of cultural property, must be respected and such emblems may not be used improperly (see Rule 61);[146]
- simulation of civilian status because civilians not taking a direct part in hostilities must be respected and may not be the object of attack (see Rules 1 and 6);[147]
- the wearing of uniforms or the use of emblems of neutral States or other States not party to the conflict because uniforms or emblems of neutral States or of other States not party to the conflict may not be used (see Rule 63).[148]

This definition is supported by the practice collected for each particular category and by the fact that the rules on which the protection is based apply to both international and non-international armed conflicts.

---

[139] Draft Additional Protocol II, Article 21(1) (*ibid.*, § 848).
[140] Knut Dörmann, *Elements of War Crimes under the Rome Statute of the International Criminal Court: Sources and Commentary*, Cambridge University Press, 2003, p. 476.
[141] See, e.g., the practice (cited in Vol. II, Ch. 18, §§ 1000–1044).
[142] See, e.g., the practice (*ibid.*, §§ 1045–1129).   [143] See, e.g., the practice (*ibid.*, §§ 1130–1218).
[144] See, e.g., the practice (*ibid.*, §§ 1219–1324).   [145] See, e.g., the practice (*ibid.*, §§ 1325–1397).
[146] See, e.g., the practice (*ibid.*, §§ 1398–1451).   [147] See, e.g., the practice (*ibid.*, §§ 1452–1505).
[148] See, e.g., the practice (*ibid.*, §§ 1506–1545).

While the Hague Regulations prohibit "to kill or wound treacherously", Additional Protocol I prohibits "to kill, injure or capture an adversary by resort to perfidy".[149] The Statute of the International Criminal Court uses the language of the Hague Regulations.[150] Similarly, some military manuals prohibit killing or injuring by resort to perfidy, while others prohibit killing, injuring or capturing by resort to perfidy.[151] The military manuals of States not party to Additional Protocol I generally do not mention capturing, with the exception of a manual used by Israel.[152] Almost all national legislation making it an offence to violate this rule refers to killing or injuring only.[153] The United States has asserted that it supports "the principle that individual combatants not kill, injure, or capture enemy personnel by resort to perfidy".[154] On the basis of this practice, it can be argued that killing, injuring or capturing by resort to perfidy is illegal under customary international law but that only acts that result in serious bodily injury, namely killing or injuring, would constitute a war crime. This argument is also based on the consideration that the capture of an adversary by resort to perfidy nevertheless undermines a protection provided under international humanitarian law even though the consequences may not be grave enough for it to constitute a war crime. It should also be stressed that the capture of an adversary is often accompanied by a threat to kill or injure and that a threat to commit an illegal act is generally considered to be illegal as well.

Treacherous attempt upon the life of an enemy

The Lieber Code provides that "the common law of war allows even capital punishment for clandestine or treacherous attempts to injure an enemy, because

---

[149] Hague Regulations, Article 23(b) (*ibid.*, § 926); Additional Protocol I, Article 37(1) (adopted by consensus) (*ibid.*, § 927).

[150] ICC Statute, Article 8(2)(b)(xi) and (e)(ix) (*ibid.*, § 929).

[151] The military manuals of Argentina (*ibid.*, § 937), Cameroon (*ibid.*, § 941), Canada (*ibid.*, § 942), France (*ibid.*, § 943), Israel (*ibid.*, § 945), Netherlands (*ibid.*, §§ 949–950), New Zealand (*ibid.*, § 951), Romania (*ibid.*, § 954) and Spain (*ibid.*, § 956) prohibit killing, injuring and capturing by resort to perfidy, whereas the military manuals of Belgium (*ibid.*, § 940), Indonesia (*ibid.*, § 944), Italy (*ibid.*, § 947), Kenya (*ibid.*, § 948), Nigeria (*ibid.*, § 952–953), Russia (*ibid.*, § 955), Sweden (*ibid.*, § 957), Switzerland (*ibid.*, § 958), United Kingdom (*ibid.*, §§ 959–960), United States (*ibid.*, §§ 961–962) and Yugoslavia (*ibid.*, § 963) limit this prohibition to killing or injuring. The military manuals of Benin (*ibid.*, § 863), Canada (*ibid.*, § 865) and Togo (*ibid.*, § 895) formulate the prohibition as applicable to "hostile acts committed under the cover of a legal protection" and this would cover killing and injuring but also capturing and possibly other acts.

[152] See Israel, *Law of War Booklet* (*ibid.*, § 946).

[153] See, e.g., the legislation of Australia (*ibid.*, § 964), Bosnia and Herzegovina (*ibid.*, § 965), Canada (*ibid.*, § 967), Congo (*ibid.*, § 968), Croatia (*ibid.*, § 969), Georgia (*ibid.*, § 970), Germany (*ibid.*, § 971), Italy (*ibid.*, § 973), Mali (*ibid.*, § 974), New Zealand (*ibid.*, § 976), Slovenia (*ibid.*, § 978), Sweden (*ibid.*, § 979), United Kingdom (*ibid.*, § 981), United States (*ibid.*, § 982) and Yugoslavia (*ibid.*, § 983); see also the draft legislation of Burundi (*ibid.*, § 966) and Trinidad and Tobago (*ibid.*, § 980). The only exceptions are the legislation of Ireland (*ibid.*, § 972) and Norway (*ibid.*, § 977), which punish any breach of Additional Protocol I.

[154] United States, Remarks of the Deputy Legal Adviser of the Department of State (*ibid.*, § 988).

they are so dangerous, and it is difficult to guard against them".[155] The Brussels Declaration prohibits "murder by treachery of individuals belonging to the hostile nation or army" and the Oxford Manual prohibits the making of "treacherous attempts upon the life of an enemy; as for example by keeping assassins in pay".[156] Under the Hague Regulations, it is prohibited "to kill or wound treacherously individuals belonging to the hostile nation or army".[157] The use of the term "individuals belonging to the hostile nation or army" clearly covers civilians as well as combatants.

The US Air Force Pamphlet states that Article 23(b) of the Hague Regulations has been construed as prohibiting "assassination, proscription, or outlawry of an enemy, or putting a price upon an enemy's head, as well as offering a reward for an enemy 'dead or alive'", but it specifies that "obviously, it does not preclude lawful attacks by lawful combatants on individual soldiers or officers of the enemy".[158] Several other military manuals also prohibit assassination and the putting of a price on the head of an enemy.[159] New Zealand's Military Manual defines assassination as "the killing or wounding of a selected individual behind the line of battle by enemy agents or unlawful combatants".[160] The prohibition of assassination is also supported by official statements.[161]

---

[155] Lieber Code, Article 101 (*ibid.*, § 930).
[156] Brussels Declaration, Article 13(b) (*ibid.*, § 931); Oxford Manual (*ibid.*, § 932).
[157] Hague Regulations, Article 23(b) (*ibid.*, § 926).
[158] United States, *Air Force Pamphlet* (*ibid.*, § 962).
[159] See, e.g., the military manuals of Australia (*ibid.*, § 938) (assassination of non-combatants, putting a price on the head of an enemy individual, any offer for an enemy "dead or alive"), Australia (*ibid.*, § 939) (assassination of a selected individual, proscription, outlawing, putting a price on the head of an enemy individual, any offer for an enemy "dead or alive"), Canada (*ibid.*, § 942) (assassination of selected non-combatants, putting a price on the head of an enemy individual or offering a bounty for an enemy "dead or alive"), Israel (*ibid.*, § 946) (attempt on the lives of enemy leaders (civilian or military), requesting the death of a specific person by dispatching an assassin or by offering an award for his liquidation), New Zealand (*ibid.*, § 951) (assassination, proscription, outlawing, putting a price on the head of an enemy individual, any offer for an enemy "dead or alive"), Switzerland (*ibid.*, § 958) (place a price on the head of an enemy military or civil leader), United Kingdom (*ibid.*, § 959) (assassination, proscription, outlawing, putting a price on the head of an enemy individual, any offer for an enemy "dead or alive") and Yugoslavia (*ibid.*, § 963) (putting a price on someone's head, whether State or military commander or any other person).
[160] New Zealand, *Military Manual* (*ibid.*, § 951).
[161] See, e.g., United States, Presidential Executive Order 12333 (*ibid.*, § 987) and Memorandum of Law of the Department of the Army: Executive Order 12333 and Assassination (*ibid.*, § 989).

COMMUNICATION WITH THE ENEMY

Note: *This chapter addresses communication related to warfare and not political negotiations undertaken with a view to resolving an armed conflict.*

Rule 66. Commanders may enter into non-hostile contact through any means of communication. Such contact must be based on good faith.

Practice

Volume II, Chapter 19, Section A.

Summary

State practice establishes this rule as a norm of customary international law applicable in both international and non-international armed conflicts.

International and non-international armed conflicts

Most military manuals stress that the need may arise, for humanitarian or military reasons, for commanders to enter into contact with the adverse party, in particular to conclude local arrangements dealing with such issues as the search for the wounded, sick and dead, the disposal of the dead, exchange of prisoners, evacuation of persons from a besieged area, passage of medical and religious personnel and flights of medical aircraft. At higher levels, agreements may be concluded to establish a hospital or safety zone, a neutralised zone or a demilitarised zone.[1]

Some military manuals specify that combatants themselves may not enter into contact with the enemy.[2] The Military Handbook of the Netherlands,

---

[1] See, e.g., the military manuals of Belgium (cited in Vol. II, Ch. 19, § 5), Canada (*ibid.*, § 8), Croatia (*ibid.*, § 10), Germany (*ibid.*, § 12), Hungary (*ibid.*, § 13), Italy (*ibid.*, § 15), Kenya (*ibid.*, § 16), South Korea (*ibid.*, § 17), Madagascar (*ibid.*, § 19), Netherlands (*ibid.*, § 20), New Zealand (*ibid.*, § 21), Nigeria (*ibid.*, § 22), Spain (*ibid.*, § 23), Switzerland (*ibid.*, § 24), United Kingdom (*ibid.*, §§ 25–26) and United States (*ibid.*, § 27).

[2] See, e.g., the military manuals of Belgium (*ibid.*, § 4), Burkina Faso (*ibid.*, § 6), Cameroon (*ibid.*, § 7), Congo (*ibid.*, § 9), France (*ibid.*, § 11), Lebanon (*ibid.*, § 18) and Netherlands (*ibid.*, § 20).

for example, states that "only a commander may decide to negotiate with the adverse party".[3]

Practice indicates that communication may be carried out by various means, via intermediaries known as *parlementaires* but also by telephone and radio.[4] A *parlementaire* is a person belonging to a party to the conflict who has been authorised to enter into communication with another party to the conflict. The traditional method of making oneself known as a *parlementaire* is by advancing bearing a white flag.[5] This traditional method has been found to be still valid, as attested by various military manuals.[6] In addition, practice recognises that the parties may appeal to a third party to facilitate communication, in particular protecting powers or an impartial and neutral humanitarian organisation acting as a substitute, in particular the ICRC, but also international organisations and members of peacekeeping forces. Collected practice shows that various institutions and organisations have acted as intermediaries in negotiations both in international and non-international armed conflicts, and that this is generally accepted.[7]

Several military manuals emphasise that in any communication with the adversary good faith must be scrupulously observed.[8] This implies that negotiators accepted as such by both sides must be respected and that negotiated agreements must be respected or else they constitute unlawful deception. Without good faith, negotiation on the battlefield is both dangerous and of little use. The parties have to be able to rely on the assurance given by the other side concerning the safety of their negotiators and compliance with what was agreed (*pacta sunt servanda* as an application of the general principle of good faith). The principle of good faith applies by definition in both international and non-international armed conflicts and implies that the white flag, which

---

[3] Netherlands, *Military Handbook* (*ibid.*, § 20).

[4] See, e.g., the military manuals of Belgium (*ibid.*, § 4), Canada (*ibid.*, § 8), Croatia (*ibid.*, § 10), Germany (*ibid.*, § 12), Hungary (*ibid.*, § 13), Italy (*ibid.*, §§ 14–15), South Korea (*ibid.*, § 17), Madagascar (*ibid.*, § 19), New Zealand (*ibid.*, § 21), Spain (*ibid.*, § 23), United Kingdom (*ibid.*, § 25) and United States (*ibid.*, § 27) and the reported practice of Colombia (*ibid.*, § 31), Rwanda (*ibid.*, § 36) and Zimbabwe (*ibid.*, § 41).

[5] For a definition of a *parlementaire*, see, e.g., Brussels Declaration, Article 43 (*ibid.*, § 95), Oxford Manual, Article 27 (*ibid.*, § 96) and Hague Regulations, Article 32 (*ibid.*, § 94) and the military manuals of Argentina (*ibid.*, § 98), Belgium (*ibid.*, §§ 99–101), Canada (*ibid.*, § 103), Germany (*ibid.*, § 104), Italy (*ibid.*, § 105), Netherlands (*ibid.*, § 106), New Zealand (*ibid.*, § 107), Nigeria (*ibid.*, § 108), Spain (*ibid.*, §§ 109–110), Switzerland (*ibid.*, § 111), United Kingdom (*ibid.*, § 112), United States (*ibid.*, § 113) and Yugoslavia (*ibid.*, § 114).

[6] See, e.g., the military manuals of Argentina (*ibid.*, § 98), Belgium (*ibid.*, §§ 99–101), Cameroon (*ibid.*, § 102), Italy (*ibid.*, § 105), Netherlands (*ibid.*, § 106), New Zealand (*ibid.*, § 107), Nigeria (*ibid.*, § 108), Spain (*ibid.*, § 110), Switzerland (*ibid.*, § 111), United Kingdom (*ibid.*, § 112), United States (*ibid.*, § 113) and Yugoslavia (*ibid.*, § 114).

[7] See, e.g., the military manuals of Germany (*ibid.*, § 12), Madagascar (*ibid.*, § 19), Spain (*ibid.*, § 23) and United States (*ibid.*, § 27) and the reported practice of Colombia (*ibid.*, § 31), Georgia (*ibid.*, § 33), Philippines (*ibid.*, § 35), Rwanda (*ibid.*, § 36) and two States (*ibid.*, §§ 42 and 44).

[8] See, e.g., the military manuals of Argentina (*ibid.*, § 3), Belgium (*ibid.*, § 5), Kenya (*ibid.*, § 16), New Zealand (*ibid.*, § 21), United Kingdom (*ibid.*, §§ 25–26) and United States (*ibid.*, § 27).

indicates a desire to communicate,[9] must be respected in both types of conflict. The detailed rules applicable to the sending and receiving of *parlementaires* are a specific application of the principle of good faith (see Rules 67–69).

Refusal to receive parlementaires

It is a long-established rule of customary international law that commanders are not obliged to receive *parlementaires*, but it is prohibited to declare beforehand that no *parlementaire* will be received. This is stated in the Brussels Declaration, the Oxford Manual and the Hague Regulations.[10] It has been restated in many military manuals.[11] Some of these manuals are applicable in, or have been applied in, non-international armed conflicts.[12] No official contrary practice was found.

Rule 67. *Parlementaires* are inviolable.

Practice

Volume II, Chapter 19, Section B.

Summary

State practice establishes this rule as a norm of customary international law applicable in both international and non-international armed conflicts.

International and non-international armed conflicts

This is a long-standing rule of customary international law already recognised in the Brussels Declaration and the Oxford Manual, and codified in the Hague

---

[9] See, e.g., the military manuals of Australia (*ibid.*, §§ 50–51), Belgium (*ibid.*, § 53), Benin (*ibid.*, § 54), Canada (*ibid.*, §§ 56–57), Colombia (*ibid.*, § 58), Dominican Republic (*ibid.*, § 59), Ecuador (*ibid.*, § 60), Italy (*ibid.*, § 65), Kenya (*ibid.*, § 66), South Korea (*ibid.*, § 67), Madagascar (*ibid.*, § 68), Netherlands (*ibid.*, §§ 69–70), New Zealand (*ibid.*, § 71), Nigeria (*ibid.*, § 72), South Africa (*ibid.*, § 74), Togo (*ibid.*, § 75), United Kingdom (*ibid.*, §§ 76–77), United States (*ibid.*, §§ 78–80) and Yugoslavia (*ibid.*, § 81); the practice of the United Kingdom (*ibid.*, § 88); the reported practice of China (*ibid.*, § 85) and Rwanda (*ibid.*, § 87).

[10] Brussels Declaration, Article 44 (*ibid.*, § 125); Oxford Manual, Article 29 (*ibid.*, § 126); Hague Regulations, Article 33 (*ibid.*, § 124).

[11] See, e.g., the military manuals of Argentina (*ibid.*, § 128), Belgium (*ibid.*, §§ 129–130), Canada (*ibid.*, § 131), Germany (*ibid.*, § 132), Italy (*ibid.*, § 133), Kenya (*ibid.*, § 134), Netherlands (*ibid.*, § 135), New Zealand (*ibid.*, § 136), Nigeria (*ibid.*, § 137), Spain (*ibid.*, §§ 138–139), Switzerland (*ibid.*, § 140), United Kingdom (*ibid.*, §§ 141–142), United States (*ibid.*, § 143) and Yugoslavia (*ibid.*, § 144).

[12] See, e.g., the military manuals of Germany (*ibid.*, § 132), Italy (*ibid.*, § 133), Kenya (*ibid.*, § 134) and Yugoslavia (*ibid.*, § 144).

Regulations.[13] The inviolability of *parlementaires* is restated in numerous military manuals.[14] Some of these manuals are applicable in, or have been applied in, non-international armed conflicts.[15] Several manuals consider that attacks against a *parlementaire* displaying the white flag of truce constitutes a war crime.[16] Breach of the inviolability of *parlementaires* is an offence under the legislation of many States.[17] This rule is also supported by other national practice.[18] This includes practice in the context of non-international armed conflicts.[19]

No official contrary practice was found. No party has claimed the right to breach the inviolability of *parlementaires*.

Interpretation

According to the Brussels Declaration, the Oxford Manual and the Hague Regulations, inviolability extends to the persons accompanying the *parlementaire*.[20] This point is also stated in many military manuals.[21] The UK Military Manual and LOAC Manual explain that the persons accompanying a *parlementaire*

---

[13] Brussels Declaration, Article 43 (*ibid.*, § 156); Oxford Manual, Article 27 (*ibid.*, § 157); Hague Regulations, Article 32 (*ibid.*, § 155).

[14] See, e.g., the military manuals of Argentina (*ibid.*, § 160), Australia (*ibid.*, §§ 161–162), Belgium (*ibid.*, §§ 163–164), Burkina Faso (*ibid.*, § 165), Cameroon (*ibid.*, § 166), Canada (*ibid.*, § 167), Congo (*ibid.*, § 168), Ecuador (*ibid.*, § 169), France (*ibid.*, §§ 170–171), Germany (*ibid.*, § 172), Italy (*ibid.*, § 173), Kenya (*ibid.*, § 174), South Korea (*ibid.*, § 175), Mali (*ibid.*, § 176), Netherlands (*ibid.*, §§ 177–178), New Zealand (*ibid.*, § 179), Nigeria (*ibid.*, § 180), Philippines (*ibid.*, §§ 181–182), Russia (*ibid.*, § 183), Senegal (*ibid.*, § 184), South Africa (*ibid.*, § 185), Spain (*ibid.*, §§ 186–187), Switzerland (*ibid.*, §§ 188–189), United Kingdom (*ibid.*, §§ 190–191), United States (*ibid.*, §§ 192–195) and Yugoslavia (*ibid.*, § 196).

[15] See, e.g., the military manuals of Australia (*ibid.*, § 161), Ecuador (*ibid.*, § 169), Germany (*ibid.*, § 172), Italy (*ibid.*, § 173), Kenya (*ibid.*, § 174), Philippines (*ibid.*, §§ 181–182), South Africa (*ibid.*, § 185) and Yugoslavia (*ibid.*, § 196).

[16] See, e.g., the military manuals of Australia (*ibid.*, §§ 161–162), Canada (*ibid.*, § 167), Ecuador (*ibid.*, § 169), South Korea (*ibid.*, § 175), New Zealand (*ibid.*, § 179), Nigeria (*ibid.*, § 180), South Africa (*ibid.*, § 185), Switzerland (*ibid.*, § 189), United Kingdom (*ibid.*, § 190) and United States (*ibid.*, §§ 192–195).

[17] See, e.g., the legislation of Argentina (*ibid.*, § 197), Bosnia and Herzegovina (*ibid.*, § 199), Chile (*ibid.*, § 200), Croatia (*ibid.*, § 201), Dominican Republic (*ibid.*, § 202), Ecuador (*ibid.*, § 203), El Salvador (*ibid.*, § 204), Estonia (*ibid.*, § 205), Ethiopia (*ibid.*, § 206), Hungary (*ibid.*, § 207), Italy (*ibid.*, § 208), Mexico (*ibid.*, §§ 209–210), Nicaragua (*ibid.*, § 211), Peru (*ibid.*, § 212), Slovenia (*ibid.*, § 213), Spain (*ibid.*, §§ 214–216), Switzerland (*ibid.*, § 217), Venezuela (*ibid.*, §§ 218–219) and Yugoslavia (*ibid.*, § 220); see also the draft legislation of Argentina (*ibid.*, § 198).

[18] See, e.g., the practice of the United Kingdom (*ibid.*, § 225) and the reported practice of China (*ibid.*, § 222), Colombia (*ibid.*, § 223), Philippines (*ibid.*, § 224) and United States (*ibid.*, § 227).

[19] See, e.g., the reported practice of China (*ibid.*, § 222), Colombia (*ibid.*, § 223) and Philippines (*ibid.*, § 224).

[20] Brussels Declaration, Article 43 (*ibid.*, § 156); Oxford Manual, Article 28 (*ibid.*, § 157); Hague Regulations, Article 32 (*ibid.*, § 155).

[21] See, e.g., the military manuals of Argentina (*ibid.*, § 160), Belgium (*ibid.*, § 163), Canada (*ibid.*, § 167), Germany (*ibid.*, § 172), Italy (*ibid.*, § 173), Netherlands (*ibid.*, §§ 177–178), New Zealand (*ibid.*, § 179), Nigeria (*ibid.*, § 180), Russia (*ibid.*, § 183), Spain (*ibid.*, § 187), Switzerland (*ibid.*, §§ 188–189), United Kingdom (*ibid.*, §§ 190–191), United States (*ibid.*, § 192) and Yugoslavia (*ibid.*, § 196).

were traditionally a trumpeter, bugler or drummer, a flagbearer and an interpreter, but that these days a *parlementaire* may advance in an armoured vehicle
flying a white flag, accompanied by a driver, wireless and loudspeaker operator
and interpreter.[22]

Several military manuals stress that it is not required that there be a complete cease-fire in the entire sector in which the *parlementaire* arrives, but that
the party advancing with the white flag may not be fired upon.[23] In addition, a
number of military manuals emphasise that it is the duty of the *parlementaire*
to choose a propitious moment to display the white flag of truce and to avoid
dangerous zones.[24] Lastly, a number of military manuals specify that the inviolability of *parlementaires* and of the persons accompanying them lasts until
they have safely returned to friendly territory.[25]

Practice indicates that a *parlementaire* bearing the white flag of truce has
to advance towards the other party. The party with which the *parlementaire*
wishes to communicate need not advance. This has also been discussed in
relation to the particular circumstances of surrender in connection with an
incident that took place during the war in the South Atlantic (see commentary
to Rule 47).

**Rule 68. Commanders may take the necessary precautions to prevent the
presence of a *parlementaire* from being prejudicial.**

Practice

Volume II, Chapter 19, Section C.

Summary

State practice establishes this rule as a norm of customary international law
applicable in both international and non-international armed conflicts.

International and non-international armed conflicts

This is a long-standing rule of customary international law already recognised
in the Brussels Declaration and the Oxford Manual, and codified in the Hague

---

[22] United Kingdom, *Military Manual* (*ibid.*, § 190) and *LOAC Manual* (*ibid.*, § 191).

[23] See, e.g., the military manuals of Canada (*ibid.*, § 167), Germany (*ibid.*, § 172), Italy (*ibid.*,
§ 173), Netherlands (*ibid.*, §§ 177–178), New Zealand (*ibid.*, § 179), United Kingdom (*ibid.*,
§ 190), United States (*ibid.*, § 192) and Yugoslavia (*ibid.*, § 196).

[24] See, e.g., the military manuals of New Zealand (*ibid.*, § 179), Nigeria (*ibid.*, § 180), United
Kingdom (*ibid.*, § 190) and United States (*ibid.*, § 192).

[25] See, e.g., the military manuals of Canada (*ibid.*, § 167), Germany (*ibid.*, § 172), Italy (*ibid.*, § 173),
Kenya (*ibid.*, § 174), New Zealand (*ibid.*, § 179) and United Kingdom (*ibid.*, §§ 190–191).

Regulations.[26] It has been restated in several military manuals.[27] Some of these manuals are applicable in, or have been applied in, non-international armed conflicts.[28] No official contrary practice was found.

Detention of parlementaires

Practice indicates that *parlementaires* may be temporarily detained if they have accidentally acquired information the disclosure of which to the adversary would have adverse consequences on the success of a current or impending operation. The permissibility of temporary detention is provided for in the Brussels Declaration and the Oxford Manual and codified in the Hague Regulations.[29] The rule is restated in a number of military manuals.[30] Some of these manuals are applicable in, or have been applied in, non-international armed conflicts.[31] No official contrary practice was found.

Rule 69. *Parlementaires* taking advantage of their privileged position to commit an act contrary to international law and detrimental to the adversary lose their inviolability.

Practice

Volume II, Chapter 19, Section D.

Summary

State practice establishes this rule as a norm of customary international law applicable in both international and non-international armed conflicts.

---

[26] Brussels Declaration, Article 44 (*ibid.*, § 236); Oxford Manual, Article 30 (*ibid.*, § 237); Hague Regulations, Article 33 (*ibid.*, § 235).

[27] See, e.g., the military manuals of Argentina (*ibid.*, § 239), Belgium (*ibid.*, §§ 240–241), Canada (*ibid.*, § 242), Germany (*ibid.*, § 243), Italy (*ibid.*, § 244), New Zealand (*ibid.*, § 245), Nigeria (*ibid.*, § 246), Spain (*ibid.*, § 247), Switzerland (*ibid.*, § 248), United Kingdom (*ibid.*, § 249), United States (*ibid.*, § 250) and Yugoslavia (*ibid.*, § 251).

[28] See, e.g., the military manuals of Germany (*ibid.*, § 243), Italy (*ibid.*, § 244) and Yugoslavia (*ibid.*, § 251).

[29] Brussels Declaration, Article 44 (*ibid.*, § 263); Oxford Manual, Article 31 (*ibid.*, § 264); Hague Regulations, Article 33 (*ibid.*, § 262).

[30] See, e.g., the military manuals of Argentina (*ibid.*, § 266), Belgium (*ibid.*, §§ 267–268), Canada (*ibid.*, § 269), Germany (*ibid.*, § 270), Italy (*ibid.*, § 271), New Zealand (*ibid.*, § 272), Nigeria (*ibid.*, § 273), Spain (*ibid.*, § 274), Switzerland (*ibid.*, § 275), United Kingdom (*ibid.*, § 276), United States (*ibid.*, § 277) and Yugoslavia (*ibid.*, § 278).

[31] See, e.g., the military manuals of Germany (*ibid.*, § 270), Italy (*ibid.*, § 271) and Yugoslavia (*ibid.*, § 278).

International and non-international armed conflicts

This is a long-standing rule of customary international law already recognised in the Brussels Declaration and the Oxford Manual, and codified in the Hague Regulations.[32] It has been restated in several military manuals.[33] Some of these manuals are applicable in, or have been applied in, non-international armed conflicts.[34] No official contrary practice was found.

Examples of taking advantage of the *parlementaire*'s privileged position cited in practice include: collecting information; carrying out acts of sabotage; inducing soldiers to collaborate in collecting intelligence; instigating soldiers to refuse to do their duty; encouraging soldiers to desert; and organising espionage in the territory of the adverse party.[35]

Loss of inviolability means that the *parlementaire* can be held prisoner and tried in accordance with national legislation. The fundamental guarantees provided for in Chapter 32, in particular fair trial guarantees (see Rule 100), would apply in such a case.

---

[32] Brussels Declaration, Article 45 (*ibid.*, § 290); Oxford Manual, Article 31 (*ibid.*, § 291); Hague Regulations, Article 34 (*ibid.*, § 289).

[33] See, e.g., the military manuals of Argentina (*ibid.*, § 294), Belgium (*ibid.*, § 295), Canada (*ibid.*, § 296), Germany (*ibid.*, § 297), Italy (*ibid.*, § 298), New Zealand (*ibid.*, § 299), Spain (*ibid.*, §§ 300–301), Switzerland (*ibid.*, § 302), United Kingdom (*ibid.*, § 303), United States (*ibid.*, § 304) and Yugoslavia (*ibid.*, § 305).

[34] See, e.g., the military manuals of Germany (*ibid.*, § 297), Italy (*ibid.*, § 298) and Yugoslavia (*ibid.*, § 305).

[35] See, e.g., the military manuals of Belgium (*ibid.*, § 295), Canada (*ibid.*, § 296), Germany (*ibid.*, § 297), Spain (*ibid.*, §§ 300–301) and Yugoslavia (*ibid.*, § 305) and the legislation of Yugoslavia (*ibid.*, § 308).

PART IV

WEAPONS

GENERAL PRINCIPLES ON THE USE OF WEAPONS

Rule 70. The use of means and methods of warfare which are of a nature to cause superfluous injury or unnecessary suffering is prohibited.

Practice

Volume II, Chapter 20, Section A.

Summary

State practice establishes this rule as a norm of customary international law applicable in both international and non-international armed conflicts.

International armed conflicts

The prohibition of the use of means and methods of warfare which are of a nature to cause superfluous injury or unnecessary suffering is set forth in a large number of treaties, including early instruments such as the St. Petersburg Declaration and the Hague Declarations and Regulations.[1] The prohibition on the use of chemical and biological weapons in the Geneva Gas Protocol was originally motivated by this rule.[2] Its reaffirmation in recent treaties, in particular Additional Protocol I, the Convention on Certain Conventional Weapons and its Protocol II and Amended Protocol II, the Ottawa Convention banning anti-personnel landmines and the Statute of the International Criminal Court, indicates that it remains valid.[3] The rule is also included in other instruments.[4]

---

[1] St. Petersburg Declaration (cited in Vol. II, Ch. 20, § 1); Hague Declaration concerning Asphyxiating Gases (*ibid.*, § 2); Hague Declaration concerning Expanding Bullets (*ibid.*, § 3); 1899 Hague Regulations, Article 23(e) (*ibid.*, § 4); 1907 Hague Regulations, Article 23(e) (*ibid.*, § 5).

[2] See, e.g., the military manuals of Australia (*ibid.*, §§ 34–35), France (*ibid.*, §§ 55–56) and Germany (*ibid.*, § 59).

[3] Additional Protocol I, Article 35(2) (adopted by consensus) (*ibid.*, § 6); CCW, preamble (*ibid.*, § 8); Protocol II to the CCW, Article 6(2) (*ibid.*, § 13); Amended Protocol II to the CCW, Article 3(3) (*ibid.*, § 15); Ottawa Convention, preamble (*ibid.*, § 16); ICC Statute, Article 8(2)(b)(xx) (*ibid.*, § 17).

[4] See, e.g., Oxford Manual of Naval War, Article 16(2) (*ibid.*, § 21); ICTY Statute, Article 3(a) (*ibid.*, § 27); San Remo Manual, para. 42(a) (*ibid.*, § 28); UN Secretary-General's Bulletin, Section 6.4 (*ibid.*, § 30); UNTAET Regulation No. 2000/15, Section 6(1)(b)(xx) (*ibid.*, § 31).

Numerous military manuals include the rule.[5] Sweden's IHL Manual, in particular, identifies the prohibition of means and methods of warfare which cause superfluous injury or unnecessary suffering, as set forth in Article 35(2) of Additional Protocol I, as a rule of customary international law.[6] Violations of this rule constitute an offence under the legislation of many States.[7] It has been relied upon in national case-law.[8]

Numerous resolutions of the UN General Assembly, as well as some resolutions of the OAS General Assembly, recall this rule.[9] The rule has also been recalled by several international conferences.[10]

In their submissions to the International Court of Justice in the *Nuclear Weapons case*, numerous States referred to the rule.[11] In its advisory opinion, the Court affirmed that the prohibition of means and methods of warfare which

---

[5] See, e.g., the military manuals of Argentina (*ibid.*, §§ 32–33), Australia (*ibid.*, §§ 34–35), Belgium (*ibid.*, §§ 36–38), Benin (*ibid.*, § 39), Bosnia and Herzegovina (*ibid.*, § 40), Burkina Faso (*ibid.*, § 41), Cameroon (*ibid.*, §§ 42–43), Canada (*ibid.*, §§ 44–45), Colombia (*ibid.*, §§ 46–47), Congo (*ibid.*, § 48), Croatia (*ibid.*, §§ 49–50), Dominican Republic (*ibid.*, § 51), Ecuador (*ibid.*, § 52), France (*ibid.*, §§ 53–56), Germany (*ibid.*, §§ 57–59), Hungary (*ibid.*, § 60), Indonesia (*ibid.*, § 61), Israel (*ibid.*, §§ 62–63), Italy (*ibid.*, §§ 64–65), Kenya (*ibid.*, § 66), South Korea (*ibid.*, § 67), Madagascar (*ibid.*, § 68), Mali (*ibid.*, § 69), Morocco (*ibid.*, § 70), Netherlands (*ibid.*, §§ 71–72), New Zealand (*ibid.*, § 73), Nigeria (*ibid.*, §§ 74–76), Romania (*ibid.*, § 77), Russia (*ibid.*, § 78), Senegal (*ibid.*, § 79), South Africa (*ibid.*, § 80), Spain (*ibid.*, § 81), Sweden (*ibid.*, § 82), Switzerland (*ibid.*, § 83), Togo (*ibid.*, § 84), United Kingdom (*ibid.*, §§ 85–86), United States (*ibid.*, §§ 87–93) and Yugoslavia (*ibid.*, § 94).

[6] Sweden, *IHL Manual* (*ibid.*, § 82).

[7] See, e.g., the legislation of Azerbaijan (*ibid.*, § 96), Belarus (*ibid.*, § 97), Canada (*ibid.*, § 99), Colombia (*ibid.*, § 102), Congo (*ibid.*, § 103), Georgia (*ibid.*, § 104), Ireland (*ibid.*, § 105), Italy (*ibid.*, § 106), Mali (*ibid.*, § 107), New Zealand (*ibid.*, § 109), Nicaragua (*ibid.*, § 110), Norway (*ibid.*, § 111), Spain (*ibid.*, §§ 112–113), United Kingdom (*ibid.*, § 115), United States (*ibid.*, § 116), Venezuela (*ibid.*, § 117) and Yugoslavia (*ibid.*, § 118); see also the draft legislation of Argentina (*ibid.*, § 95), Burundi (*ibid.*, § 98) and Trinidad and Tobago (*ibid.*, § 114).

[8] See, e.g., Japan, District Court of Tokyo, *Shimoda case*, Judgement (*ibid.*, § 120).

[9] UN General Assembly, Res. 3076 (XXVIII) (*ibid.*, §§ 214 and 217), Res. 3102 (XXVIII) (*ibid.*, § 215), Res. 3255 (XXIX) (*ibid.*, §§ 217–218), Res. 31/64 (*ibid.*, §§ 217 and 219), Res. 32/152 (*ibid.*, §§ 217 and 220), Res. 33/70 (*ibid.*, § 217), Res. 34/82 (*ibid.*, §§ 217 and 222), Res. 35/153 (*ibid.*, §§ 217 and 223), Res. 36/93 and 37/79 (*ibid.*, §§ 217 and 224), Res. 38/66, 39/56, 40/84, 41/50, 45/64, 46/40, 47/56, 48/79, 49/79, 50/74, 51/49, 52/42, 53/81 and 54/58 (*ibid.*, § 224); OAS, General Assembly, Res. 1270 (XXIV-O/94) (*ibid.*, § 229) and Res. 1565 (XXVIII-O/98) (*ibid.*, § 230).

[10] See, e.g., 22nd International Conference of the Red Cross, Res. XIV (*ibid.*, § 231); 26th International Conference of the Red Cross and Red Crescent, Res. II (*ibid.*, § 234); Second Review Conference of States Parties to the CCW, Final Declaration (*ibid.*, § 236); African Parliamentary Conference on International Humanitarian Law for the Protection of Civilians during Armed Conflict, Final Declaration (*ibid.*, § 237).

[11] See, e.g., the oral pleadings and written statements in the *Nuclear Weapons case* of Australia (*ibid.*, § 123), Ecuador (*ibid.*, § 133), Egypt (*ibid.*, § 135), France (implicitly) (*ibid.*, § 136), India (*ibid.*, § 144), Indonesia (*ibid.*, § 147), Iran (*ibid.*, § 147), Italy (*ibid.*, § 149), Japan (*ibid.*, § 151), Lesotho (*ibid.*, § 153), Marshall Islands (*ibid.*, § 155), Mexico (*ibid.*, § 159), Netherlands (*ibid.*, § 162), New Zealand (*ibid.*, § 165), Russia (*ibid.*, §§ 171–172), Samoa (*ibid.*, § 175), Solomon Islands (*ibid.*, § 178), Sweden (*ibid.*, § 182), United Kingdom (*ibid.*, §§ 191–192) and United States (*ibid.*, §§ 202–203); see also the written statements in the *Nuclear Weapons (WHO) case* of Nauru (*ibid.*, § 161), Rwanda (*ibid.*, § 173), Samoa (*ibid.*, § 174), Solomon Islands (*ibid.*, § 177) and Sri Lanka (*ibid.*, § 179).

are of a nature to cause superfluous injury or unnecessary suffering was one of the "cardinal principles" of international humanitarian law.[12]

Non-international armed conflicts

The prohibition of the use of means and methods of warfare which are of a nature to cause superfluous injury or unnecessary suffering was included by consensus in the draft of Additional Protocol II but was dropped at the last moment without debate as part of a package aimed at the adoption of a simplified text.[13] There was no indication, however, of any objection to the rule as such in this context.

When adopting the Ottawa Convention banning anti-personnel landmines and the Convention on Certain Conventional Weapons, applicable to non-international armed conflict pursuant to an amendment to Article 1 in 2001, States declared that they were basing themselves, *inter alia*, on the prohibition of means and methods of warfare which are of a nature to cause superfluous injury or unnecessary suffering.[14] Amended Protocol II to the Convention on Certain Conventional Weapons, also applicable to non-international armed conflicts, prohibits "the use of any mine, booby-trap or other device designed or of a nature to cause superfluous injury or unnecessary suffering".[15]

Military manuals which are applicable in or have been applied in non-international armed conflicts also include the rule.[16] It is also contained in the legislation of several States.[17] It has been relied upon in national case-law.[18]

During the conflicts in the former Yugoslavia, the prohibition of means and methods of warfare which are of a nature to cause superfluous injury or unnecessary suffering was included in the agreements relating to what were then regarded as non-international armed conflicts.[19] In addition, in 1991, Yugoslavia denounced Slovenia's alleged use of "soft-nosed bullets" because they caused "disproportionate and needless injury".[20]

---

[12] ICJ, *Nuclear Weapons case*, Advisory Opinion (*ibid.*, § 238).
[13] Draft Additional Protocol II, Article 20(2) (*ibid.*, § 7).
[14] Ottawa Convention, preamble (*ibid.*, § 16); CCW, preamble (*ibid.*, § 8).
[15] Amended Protocol II to the CCW, Article 3(3) (*ibid.*, § 15).
[16] See, e.g., the military manuals of Australia (*ibid.*, § 34), Benin (*ibid.*, § 39), Bosnia and Herzegovina (*ibid.*, § 40), Canada (*ibid.*, § 45), Colombia (*ibid.*, §§ 46–47), Croatia (*ibid.*, §§ 49–50), Ecuador (*ibid.*, § 52), Germany (*ibid.*, §§ 57–59), Italy (*ibid.*, §§ 64–65), Kenya (*ibid.*, § 66), South Korea (*ibid.*, § 67), Madagascar (*ibid.*, § 68), Nigeria (*ibid.*, §§ 74 and 76), South Africa (*ibid.*, § 80), Togo (*ibid.*, § 84) and Yugoslavia (*ibid.*, § 94).
[17] See, e.g., the legislation of Azerbaijan (*ibid.*, § 96), Belarus (*ibid.*, § 97), Colombia (*ibid.*, § 102), Nicaragua (*ibid.*, § 110), Spain (*ibid.*, § 113), Venezuela (*ibid.*, § 117) and Yugoslavia (*ibid.*, § 118); see also the legislation of Italy (*ibid.*, § 106), the application of which is not excluded in time of non-international armed conflict, and the draft legislation of Argentina (*ibid.*, § 95).
[18] See, e.g., Argentina, National Court of Appeals, *Military Junta case*, Judgement (*ibid.*, § 119).
[19] Memorandum of Understanding on the Application of International Humanitarian Law between Croatia and the SFRY, para. 6 (*ibid.*, § 25); Agreement on the Application of International Humanitarian Law between the Parties to the Conflict in Bosnia and Herzegovina, para. 2.5 (*ibid.*, § 26).
[20] Yugoslavia, Ministry of Defence, Examples of violations of the rules of international law committed by the so-called armed forces of Slovenia (*ibid.*, § 209).

Practice is in conformity with the rule's applicability in both international and non-international conflicts, as States generally do not have a different set of military weapons for international and non-international armed conflicts.[21]

No official contrary practice was found with respect to either international or non-international armed conflict. No State has indicated that it may use means or methods of warfare causing unnecessary suffering in any type of armed conflict. Practice shows that parties to a conflict abstain from using in non-international armed conflicts weapons prohibited in international armed conflicts. In the *Tadić case* in 1996, the International Criminal Tribunal for the Former Yugoslavia stated that:

Indeed, elementary considerations of humanity and common sense make it preposterous that the use by States of weapons prohibited in armed conflicts between themselves be allowed when States try to put down rebellion by their own nationals on their own territory. What is inhumane, and consequently proscribed, in international wars cannot but be inhumane and inadmissible in civil strife.[22]

Definition of means of warfare which are of a nature to cause superfluous injury or unnecessary suffering

The prohibition of means of warfare which are of a nature to cause superfluous injury or unnecessary suffering refers to the effect of a weapon on combatants. Although there is general agreement on the existence of the rule, views differ on how it can actually be determined that a weapon causes superfluous injury or unnecessary suffering. States generally agree that suffering that has no military purpose violates this rule. Many States point out that the rule requires that a balance be struck between military necessity, on the one hand, and the expected injury or suffering inflicted on a person, on the other hand, and that excessive injury or suffering, i.e., that which is out of proportion to the military advantage sought, therefore violates the rule.[23] Some States also refer to the availability of alternative means as an element that has to go into the assessment of whether a weapon causes unnecessary suffering or superfluous injury.[24]

---

[21] The use of riot-control agents and expanding bullets by police forces outside situations of armed conflict is addressed in the commentary to Rules 75 and 77.

[22] ICTY, *The Prosecutor v. Duško Tadić aka "Dule"*, Decision on the Defence Motion for Interlocutory Appeal on Jurisdiction, Appeals Chamber, 2 October 1995, Case No. IT-94-1-AR72, § 119.

[23] See, e.g., the military manuals of Australia (cited in Vol. II, Ch. 20, § 35), Canada (*ibid.*, §§ 44–45), Ecuador (*ibid.*, § 52), France (*ibid.*, §§ 54–56), Germany (*ibid.*, § 58), New Zealand (*ibid.*, § 73), South Africa (*ibid.*, § 80), United States (*ibid.*, §§ 88–89 and 93) and Yugoslavia (*ibid.*, § 94); the legislation of Belarus (*ibid.*, § 97); the statements of India (*ibid.*, § 144), Netherlands (*ibid.*, § 162), United Kingdom (*ibid.*, §§ 191–192) and United States (*ibid.*, §§ 194, 202 and 206).

[24] See the military manual of the United States (*ibid.*, § 88) and the statement of the United Kingdom (*ibid.*, § 191).

In its advisory opinion in the *Nuclear Weapons case*, the International Court of Justice defined unnecessary suffering as "a harm greater than that unavoidable to achieve legitimate military objectives".[25]

A relevant factor in establishing whether a weapon would cause superfluous injury or unnecessary suffering is the inevitability of serious permanent disability. The US Air Force Pamphlet, for example, lists as one of the bases for the prohibition of poison the "inevitability of... permanent disability".[26] The rule prohibiting the targeting of the eyes of soldiers with lasers, as laid down in Protocol IV to the Convention on Certain Conventional Weapons (see Rule 86), was inspired by the consideration that deliberately causing permanent blindness in this fashion amounted to the infliction of superfluous injury or unnecessary suffering.[27] When adopting the Ottawa Convention banning anti-personnel landmines, States were basing themselves, in part, on the prohibition of means of warfare which are of a nature to cause superfluous injury or unnecessary suffering.[28] The serious disabilities that are frequently the result of the use of incendiary weapons prompted many States to propose a ban on their use against personnel (see commentary to Rule 85).

A related issue is the use of weapons that render death inevitable. The preamble to the St. Petersburg Declaration states that the use of such weapons "would be contrary to the laws of humanity", and it was this consideration that led to the prohibition of exploding bullets by the Declaration.[29] The US Air Force Pamphlet, for example, states that "the long-standing customary prohibition against poison" is based, in part, on "the inevitability of death" and that international law has condemned "dum-dum" bullets because of "types of injuries and inevitability of death".[30] Several military manuals and official statements state that weapons that render death inevitable are prohibited.[31]

Definition of methods of warfare which are of a nature to cause superfluous injury or unnecessary suffering

The prohibition of methods of warfare which are of a nature to cause superfluous injury or unnecessary suffering was first introduced in Additional

---

[25] ICJ, *Nuclear Weapons case*, Advisory Opinion (*ibid.*, § 238).
[26] United States, *Air Force Pamphlet* (*ibid.*, § 88).
[27] See, e.g., Sweden, Declaration made upon acceptance of Protocol IV to the CCW (*ibid.*, § 14) and the military manuals of France (*ibid.*, §§ 55–56).
[28] Ottawa Convention, preamble (*ibid.*, § 16).
[29] St. Petersburg Declaration, preamble (*ibid.*, § 1).
[30] United States, *Air Force Pamphlet* (*ibid.*, § 88); see also Ecuador, *Naval Manual* (*ibid.*, § 52) and United States, *Air Force Commander's Handbook* (*ibid.*, § 89) and *Naval Handbook* (*ibid.*, § 93).
[31] See, e.g., the military manual of Belgium (*ibid.*, § 36), Ecuador (*ibid.*, § 52) and United States (*ibid.*, § 93) and the statements of Egypt (*ibid.*, § 135), India (*ibid.*, § 144), Russia (*ibid.*, §§ 171–172) and Solomon Islands (*ibid.*, § 178); see also the statements of Australia (*ibid.*, § 121) and New Zealand (*ibid.*, § 164).

Protocol I.[32] When adopting the Convention on Certain Conventional Weapons and the Ottawa Convention banning anti-personnel landmines, States were basing themselves on the prohibition of "weapons, projectiles and material and *methods* of warfare of a nature to cause superfluous injury or unnecessary suffering" (emphasis added).[33] The Statute of the International Criminal Court also includes the use of "*methods* of warfare which are of nature to cause superfluous injury or unnecessary suffering" (emphasis added) as a war crime.[34]

Numerous States have included the prohibition of methods of warfare that cause superfluous injury or unnecessary suffering in their military manuals and legislation.[35] It is also referred to in official statements and other practice.[36] This practice includes that of States not, or not at the time, party to Additional Protocol I.[37] However, States articulating this rule do not give any examples of methods of warfare that would be prohibited by virtue of this rule.

Interpretation

Although the existence of the prohibition of means and methods of warfare which are of a nature to cause superfluous injury or unnecessary suffering is not contested, views differ as to whether the rule itself renders a weapon illegal or whether a weapon is illegal only if a specific treaty or customary rule prohibits its use.

While most military manuals prohibit weapons that cause unnecessary suffering as such,[38] some indicate that the weapons covered by this prohibition

---

[32] Additional Protocol I, Article 35(2) (adopted by consensus) (*ibid.*, § 6).
[33] CCW, preamble (*ibid.*, § 8); Ottawa Convention, preamble (*ibid.*, § 16).
[34] ICC Statute, Article 8(2)(b)(xx) (*ibid.*, § 17).
[35] See, e.g., the military manuals of Argentina (*ibid.*, § 33), Australia (*ibid.*, §§ 34–35), Belgium (*ibid.*, § 36), Benin (*ibid.*, § 39), Colombia (*ibid.*, § 46), Croatia (*ibid.*, § 49), Dominican Republic (*ibid.*, § 51), Ecuador (*ibid.*, § 52), Germany (*ibid.*, §§ 57–59), Hungary (*ibid.*, § 60), Italy (*ibid.*, § 64), Kenya (*ibid.*, § 66), Netherlands (*ibid.*, § 71), Spain (*ibid.*, § 81), Sweden (*ibid.*, § 82), Togo (*ibid.*, § 84) and United States (*ibid.*, §§ 88 and 93) and the legislation of Azerbaijan (*ibid.*, § 96), Belarus (*ibid.*, § 97), Canada (*ibid.*, § 99), Colombia (*ibid.*, § 102), Congo (*ibid.*, § 103), Georgia (*ibid.*, § 104), Ireland (*ibid.*, § 105), Mali (*ibid.*, § 107), New Zealand (*ibid.*, § 109), Nicaragua (*ibid.*, § 110), Norway (*ibid.*, § 111), Spain (*ibid.*, §§ 112–113), United Kingdom (*ibid.*, § 115) and Yugoslavia (*ibid.*, § 118)); see also the draft legislation of Argentina (*ibid.*, § 95), Burundi (*ibid.*, § 98) and Trinidad and Tobago (*ibid.*, § 114).
[36] See, e.g., the statements of Australia (*ibid.*, § 123), Egypt (*ibid.*, § 135), France (*ibid.*, § 139), Federal Republic of Germany (*ibid.*, § 140), Iran (*ibid.*, § 147), Mexico (*ibid.*, § 159), Netherlands (*ibid.*, § 162), New Zealand (*ibid.*, § 165), Sri Lanka (*ibid.*, § 179), United Kingdom (*ibid.*, § 192), United States (*ibid.*, §§ 196 and 198), Yugoslavia (*ibid.*, § 208) and Zimbabwe (*ibid.*, § 210) and the practice of France (*ibid.*, § 138).
[37] See, e.g., the military manuals of the United States (*ibid.*, §§ 88 and 93), the legislation of Azerbaijan (*ibid.*, § 96), the statements of Iran (*ibid.*, § 147), Sri Lanka (*ibid.*, § 179), United Kingdom (*ibid.*, § 192) and United States (*ibid.*, § 196) and the practice of France (*ibid.*, § 138).
[38] See, e.g., the military manuals of Argentina (*ibid.*, § 33), Australia (*ibid.*, §§ 34–35), Belgium (*ibid.*, §§ 36–38), Benin (*ibid.*, § 39), Bosnia and Herzegovina (*ibid.*, § 40), Burkina Faso (*ibid.*, § 41), Cameroon (*ibid.*, §§ 42–43), Canada (*ibid.*, §§ 44–45), Colombia (*ibid.*, §§ 46–47), Congo (*ibid.*, § 48), Croatia (*ibid.*, §§ 49–50), Dominican Republic (*ibid.*, § 51), Ecuador (*ibid.*, § 52), France (*ibid.*, §§ 53–56), Germany (*ibid.*, §§ 57–59), Hungary (*ibid.*, § 60), Indonesia (*ibid.*, § 61), Israel (*ibid.*, §§ 62–63), Italy (*ibid.*, §§ 64–65),

must be determined by the practice of States to refrain from using certain weapons in recognition that they cause unnecessary suffering.[39]

In their submissions to the International Court of Justice in the *Nuclear Weapons case,* France and Russia stated that a weapon can only be prohibited by virtue of this rule if States choose to prohibit the weapon by treaty.[40] Most other States, however, did not express such a requirement and assessed the legality of the effects of nuclear weapons on the basis of the rule itself.[41]

In its advisory opinion in the *Nuclear Weapons case,* the International Court of Justice analysed the legality of the effects of nuclear weapons on the basis of the rule itself and independent of treaty law, as did the judges in their individual opinions.[42]

Examples

The following weapons have been cited in practice as causing unnecessary suffering if used in certain or all contexts: lances or spears with a barbed head;[43] serrated-edged bayonets;[44] expanding bullets;[45] explosive bullets;[46]

Kenya (*ibid.*, § 66), South Korea (*ibid.*, § 67), Madagascar (*ibid.*, § 68), Mali (*ibid.*, § 69), Morocco (*ibid.*, § 70), Netherlands (*ibid.*, §§ 71–72), New Zealand (*ibid.*, § 73), Nigeria (*ibid.*, §§ 74–76), Romania (*ibid.*, § 77), Russia (*ibid.*, § 78), Senegal (*ibid.*, § 79), South Africa (*ibid.*, § 80), Spain (*ibid.*, § 81), Sweden (*ibid.*, § 82), Switzerland (*ibid.*, § 83), Togo (*ibid.*, § 84), United Kingdom (*ibid.*, §§ 85–86), United States (*ibid.*, §§ 89–90 and 92–93) and Yugoslavia (*ibid.*, § 94).

[39] See, e.g., the military manuals of Argentina (*ibid.*, § 32) and the United States (*ibid.*, §§ 87–88 and 91).

[40] See the oral pleadings and written statements in the *Nuclear Weapons case* of France (*ibid.*, § 136) and Russia (*ibid.*, §§ 171–172).

[41] See, e.g., the oral pleadings and written statements in the *Nuclear Weapons case* of Ecuador (*ibid.*, § 133), Iran (*ibid.*, § 147), Japan (*ibid.*, § 151), Lesotho (*ibid.*, § 153), Marshall Islands (*ibid.*, § 155), Mexico (*ibid.*, § 159), Nauru (*ibid.*, § 161), Netherlands (*ibid.*, § 162), New Zealand (*ibid.*, § 165), Samoa (*ibid.*, § 175), Sweden (*ibid.*, § 182), United Kingdom (*ibid.*, §§ 191–192) and United States (*ibid.*, § 202); see also the written statements submitted in the *Nuclear Weapons (WHO) case* by Samoa (*ibid.*, § 174) and Sri Lanka (*ibid.*, § 179).

[42] ICJ, *Nuclear Weapons case,* Advisory Opinion (*ibid.*, § 238), including the judges' individual opinions (*ibid.*, §§ 239–245).

[43] See, e.g., the military manuals of New Zealand (*ibid.*, § 73), South Africa (*ibid.*, § 80), United Kingdom (*ibid.*, § 85) and United States (*ibid.*, § 87); see also UN Secretariat, Existing rules of international law concerning the prohibition or restriction of use of specific weapons, Survey (*ibid.*, § 227).

[44] See, e.g., the military manuals of the Netherlands (*ibid.*, §§ 71–72).

[45] See, e.g., the military manuals of Australia (*ibid.*, § 34) ("hollow point weapons"), Ecuador (*ibid.*, § 52), France (*ibid.*, §§ 55–56), Germany (*ibid.*, §§ 57–59), Netherlands (*ibid.*, §§ 71–72), Russia (*ibid.*, § 78), South Africa (*ibid.*, 80), United States (*ibid.*, § 91) and Yugoslavia (*ibid.*, § 94); see also the military manuals of New Zealand (*ibid.*, § 73), United Kingdom (*ibid.*, 85) and United States (*ibid.*, § 87), which prohibit "irregularly shaped bullets"; see also UN Secretariat, Existing rules of international law concerning the prohibition or restriction of use of specific weapons, Survey (*ibid.*, § 227).

[46] See, e.g., the military manuals of Germany (*ibid.*, § 58) and Russia (*ibid.*, § 78); see also UN Secretariat, Existing rules of international law concerning the prohibition or restriction of use of specific weapons, Survey (*ibid.*, § 227).

poison and poisoned weapons, including projectiles smeared with substances that inflame wounds;[47] biological and chemical weapons;[48] weapons that primarily injure by fragments not detectable by X-ray, including projectiles filled with broken glass;[49] certain booby-traps;[50] anti-personnel landmines;[51] torpedoes without self-destruction mechanisms;[52] incendiary weapons;[53] blinding laser weapons;[54] and nuclear weapons.[55] There is insufficient consensus concerning all of these examples to conclude that, under customary international law, they all violate the rule prohibiting unnecessary suffering. However, there is agreement that some of them are prohibited and they are discussed in subsequent chapters.

Rule 71. The use of weapons which are by nature indiscriminate is prohibited.

Practice

Volume II, Chapter 20, Section B.

Summary

State practice establishes this rule as a norm of customary international law applicable in both international and non-international armed conflicts. Weapons that are by nature indiscriminate are those that cannot be directed at a military objective or whose effects cannot be limited as required by international humanitarian law. The prohibition of such weapons is also supported by the general prohibition of indiscriminate attacks (see Rules 11–12).

---

[47] See, e.g., the military manuals of Ecuador (*ibid.*, § 52), Netherlands (*ibid.*, § 72), New Zealand (*ibid.*, § 73), South Africa (*ibid.*, § 80), United Kingdom (*ibid.*, § 85) and United States (*ibid.*, §§ 87, 89, 91 and 93); see also UN Secretariat, Existing rules of international law concerning the prohibition or restriction of use of specific weapons, Survey (*ibid.*, § 227).

[48] See, e.g., the military manuals of Australia (*ibid.*, §§ 34–35), France (*ibid.*, §§ 55–56) and Germany (*ibid.*, § 59).

[49] See, e.g., the military manuals of Australia (*ibid.*, § 34), Ecuador (*ibid.*, § 52), France (*ibid.*, §§ 55–56), Germany (*ibid.*, § 59), Netherlands (*ibid.*, §§ 71–72), New Zealand (*ibid.*, § 73), South Africa (*ibid.*, § 80), United Kingdom (*ibid.*, § 85) and United States (*ibid.*, §§ 87, 89, 91 and 93); see also UN Secretariat, Existing rules of international law concerning the prohibition or restriction of use of specific weapons, Survey (*ibid.*, § 227).

[50] See, e.g., the military manuals of Germany (*ibid.*, § 59) and Netherlands (*ibid.*, § 72).

[51] See, e.g., the military manuals of France (*ibid.*, §§ 55–56).

[52] See, e.g., the military manuals of France (*ibid.*, §§ 55–56).

[53] See, e.g., the statements of Colombia (*ibid.*, §§ 130–131), Mauritania (*ibid.*, § 156), Mexico (*ibid.*, §§ 157–158) and Norway (*ibid.*, § 166) and the reported practice of Zimbabwe (*ibid.*, § 211); see also UN Secretariat, Existing rules of international law concerning the prohibition or restriction of use of specific weapons, Survey (*ibid.*, § 227).

[54] See, e.g., Sweden, Declaration made upon acceptance of Protocol IV to the CCW (*ibid.*, § 14) and the military manuals of France (*ibid.*, §§ 55–56).

[55] See, e.g., the oral pleadings and written statements in the *Nuclear Weapons case* of Ecuador (*ibid.*, § 133), Egypt (*ibid.*, § 135), India (*ibid.*, § 144), Iran (*ibid.*, § 147), Japan (*ibid.*, § 151), Lesotho (*ibid.*, § 153), Marshall Islands (*ibid.*, § 155), Sweden (*ibid.*, § 182) and Zimbabwe (*ibid.*, § 210) and the written statements in the *Nuclear Weapons (WHO) case* of Samoa (*ibid.*, § 174) and Solomon Islands (*ibid.*, § 177).

International armed conflicts

Additional Protocol I prohibits the use of weapons which are "of a nature to strike military objectives and civilians or civilian objects without distinction".[56] This prohibition was reaffirmed in the Statute of the International Criminal Court.[57] It has also been included in other instruments.[58]

This rule is set forth in many military manuals.[59] Violations of this rule constitute an offence under the legislation of several States.[60] This rule is also supported by official statements and reported practice.[61] This practice includes that of States not, or not at the time, party to Additional Protocol I.[62]

The prohibition of weapons which are by nature indiscriminate is also recalled in numerous resolutions adopted by the UN General Assembly, as well as in some resolutions adopted by the OAS General Assembly.[63] The rule has also been recalled by several international conferences.[64]

---

[56] Additional Protocol I, Article 51(4) (cited in Vol. II, Ch. 3, §§ 206 and 251).

[57] ICC Statute, Article 8(2)(b)(xx) (cited in Vol. II, Ch. 20, § 265).

[58] See, e.g., San Remo Manual, para. 42(b) (*ibid.*, § 268); UNTAET Regulation No. 200/15, Section 6(1)(b)(xx) (*ibid.*, § 269).

[59] See, e.g., the military manuals of Australia (*ibid.*, §§ 270–271), Belgium (*ibid.*, § 272), Canada (*ibid.*, § 273), Colombia (*ibid.*, § 274), Ecuador (*ibid.*, § 275), France (*ibid.*, §§ 276–277), Germany (*ibid.*, §§ 278–279), Israel (*ibid.*, § 280), South Korea (*ibid.*, § 281), New Zealand (*ibid.*, § 282), Nigeria (*ibid.*, § 283), Russia (*ibid.*, § 284), Sweden (*ibid.*, § 285), Switzerland (*ibid.*, § 286), United States (*ibid.*, §§ 287–289) and Yugoslavia (*ibid.*, § 290).

[60] See, e.g., the legislation of Canada (*ibid.*, § 292), Congo (*ibid.*, § 293), Georgia (*ibid.*, § 294), Mali (*ibid.*, § 295), New Zealand (*ibid.*, § 296) and United Kingdom (*ibid.*, § 298); see also the draft legislation of Burundi (*ibid.*, § 291) and Trinidad and Tobago (*ibid.*, § 297).

[61] See, e.g., the statements of Australia (*ibid.*, §§ 300–301), Canada (*ibid.*, §§ 302–304), China (*ibid.*, § 305), Cyprus (*ibid.*, § 306), Ecuador (*ibid.*, §§ 307–308), Egypt (*ibid.*, §§ 309–311), France (*ibid.*, §§ 312–313), Federal Republic of Germany (*ibid.*, § 314), Holy See (*ibid.*, § 315), Iran (*ibid.*, §§ 317–318), Israel (*ibid.*, § 320), Italy (*ibid.*, § 322), Japan (*ibid.*, § 323), Lesotho (*ibid.*, § 327), Malaysia (*ibid.*, § 328), Marshall Islands (*ibid.*, §§ 329–330), Mexico (*ibid.*, § 331), Nauru (*ibid.*, § 332), Netherlands (*ibid.*, §§ 333–335), New Zealand (*ibid.*, § 336), Nigeria (*ibid.*, § 337), Peru (*ibid.*, § 339), Poland (*ibid.*, § 340), Romania (*ibid.*, § 341), Russia (*ibid.*, §§ 342–344), Rwanda (*ibid.*, § 345), Solomon Islands (*ibid.*, §§ 347–348), Sri Lanka (*ibid.*, § 349), Sweden (*ibid.*, § 350), Switzerland (*ibid.*, § 351), South Africa (*ibid.*, § 352), Turkey (*ibid.*, § 353), USSR (*ibid.*, § 354), United Kingdom (*ibid.*, §§ 355–358), United States (*ibid.*, §§ 359–365), Vietnam (*ibid.*, § 367) and Zimbabwe (*ibid.*, § 368) and the reported practice of India (*ibid.*, § 316), Iran (*ibid.*, § 319), Israel (*ibid.*, § 321), Jordan (*ibid.*, § 324), South Korea (*ibid.*, § 325), Kuwait (*ibid.*, § 326), Pakistan (*ibid.*, § 338), Rwanda (*ibid.*, § 346) and United States (*ibid.*, § 366).

[62] See, e.g., the military manuals of France (*ibid.*, § 276) and Israel (*ibid.*, § 280), the statements of Cyprus (*ibid.*, § 306), Egypt (*ibid.*, § 309), Holy See (*ibid.*, § 315), Israel (*ibid.*, § 320), Poland (*ibid.*, § 340), Romania (*ibid.*, § 341), Turkey (*ibid.*, § 353), USSR (*ibid.*, § 354), United Kingdom (*ibid.*, §§ 355–357), United States (*ibid.*, §§ 359–364) and Vietnam (*ibid.*, § 367), the practice of the United States (*ibid.*, § 366) and the reported practice of India (*ibid.*, § 316), Iran (*ibid.*, § 319), Israel (*ibid.*, § 321) and Pakistan (*ibid.*, § 338).

[63] See UN General Assembly, Res. 1653 (XVI) (*ibid.*, § 369), Res. 3032 (XXVII) (*ibid.*, § 370), Res. 3076 (XXVIII) (*ibid.*, §§ 371–373), Res. 3255 A (XXIX) (*ibid.*, §§ 371–372), Res. 31/64 (*ibid.*, §§ 371 and 374), Res. 32/15 and 33/70 (*ibid.*, § 371), Res. 34/82 (*ibid.*, §§ 371 and 375), Res. 35/153 and 36/93 (*ibid.*, §§ 371 and 376–377), Res. 37/79 (*ibid.*, §§ 371 and 376–377) and Res. 38/66, 39/56, 40/84, 41/50, 42/30, 43/67, 45/64, 46/40, 47/56, 48/79, 49/79, 50/74, 51/49, 52/42, 53/81 and 54/58 (*ibid.*, §§ 376–377); OAS, General Assembly, Res. 1270 (XXIV-O/94) and 1335 (XXV-O/95) (*ibid.*, § 381) and Res. 1565 (XXVIII-O/98) (*ibid.*, § 382).

[64] See, e.g., 22nd International Conference of the Red Cross, Res. XIV (*ibid.*, § 383); 24th International Conference of the Red Cross, Res. XIII (*ibid.*, § 383); 26th International Conference of the

In their submissions to the International Court of Justice in the *Nuclear Weapons case*, several States not at the time party to Additional Protocol I referred to the prohibition of indiscriminate weapons.[65] In its advisory opinion, the Court affirmed that this prohibition was one of the "cardinal principles" of international humanitarian law.[66]

Non-international armed conflicts

By virtue of the customary rule that civilians must not be made the object of attack (see Rule 1), weapons that are by nature indiscriminate are also prohibited in non-international armed conflicts. This was the reasoning behind the prohibition of certain types of mines and booby-traps in Amended Protocol II to the Convention on Certain Conventional Weapons, which is applicable in non-international armed conflicts.[67] Similarly, the Ottawa Convention, which prohibits the use of anti-personnel landmines in all armed conflicts, is based, in part, on the principle that a distinction must be made between civilians and combatants.[68]

The prohibition of weapons which are by nature indiscriminate is also set forth in several military manuals which are applicable in or have been applied in non-international armed conflicts.[69] It is also supported by a number of official statements and reported practice.[70] Practice is in conformity with the rule's applicability in both international and non-international conflicts, as States generally do not have a different set of military weapons for international and non-international armed conflicts.

In their submissions to the International Court of Justice in the *Nuclear Weapons case*, many States considered that the prohibition of indiscriminate weapons was based on the principle that a distinction must be made between

---

Red Cross and Red Crescent, Res. II (*ibid.*, § 386); Second Review Conference of States Parties to the CCW, Final Declaration (*ibid.*, § 387); African Parliamentary Conference on International Humanitarian Law for the Protection of Civilians during Armed Conflict, Final Declaration (*ibid.*, § 388).

[65] See, e.g., the oral pleadings and written statements in the *Nuclear Weapons case* of Iran (*ibid.*, §§ 317–318), Japan (*ibid.*, § 323), Marshall Islands (*ibid.*, §§ 329–330), Nauru (*ibid.*, § 332), United Kingdom (*ibid.*, § 358) and United States (*ibid.*, § 364); see also the written statements in the *Nuclear Weapons (WHO) case* of Malaysia (*ibid.*, § 328) and Sri Lanka (*ibid.*, § 349).

[66] ICJ, *Nuclear Weapons case*, Advisory Opinion (*ibid.*, § 389).

[67] Amended Protocol II to the CCW, Article 1(2).

[68] Ottawa Convention, preamble (cited in Vol. II, Ch. 20, § 264).

[69] See, e.g., the military manuals of Australia (*ibid.*, § 270), Colombia (*ibid.*, § 274), Ecuador (*ibid.*, § 275), Germany (*ibid.*, §§ 278–279), South Korea (*ibid.*, § 281), Nigeria (*ibid.*, § 283) and Yugoslavia (*ibid.*, § 290).

[70] See, e.g., the statements of Ecuador (*ibid.*, § 307), Egypt (*ibid.*, §§ 309–310), Holy See (*ibid.*, § 315), Israel (*ibid.*, § 320), Lesotho (*ibid.*, § 327), Marshall Islands (*ibid.*, § 329), Netherlands (*ibid.*, §§ 333–335), Romania (*ibid.*, § 341), Russia (*ibid.*, §§ 342–343), Rwanda (*ibid.*, § 345), South Africa (*ibid.*, § 352), United Kingdom (*ibid.*, § 358) and United States (*ibid.*, § 365) and the reported practice of India (*ibid.*, § 316), Iran (*ibid.*, § 317), Kuwait (*ibid.*, § 326) and United States (*ibid.*, § 366).

civilians and combatants and between civilian objects and military objectives.[71] While the Court noted that it would not consider the issue of non-international armed conflicts, it did state, however, that "States must never make civilians the object of attack and must consequently never use weapons that are incapable of distinguishing between civilian and military targets".[72]

No official contrary practice was found with respect to either international or non-international armed conflicts. No State has indicated that it may use indiscriminate weapons in any type of armed conflict.

Definition of indiscriminate weapons

Several military manuals and official statements mention weapons that "have indiscriminate effects", "strike military objectives and civilians indiscriminately" or "cannot distinguish between military objectives and civilians", without further detail.[73] Beyond such general statements, the two criteria that are most frequently referred to are whether the weapon is capable of being targeted at a military objective and whether the effects of the weapon can be limited as required by international law. These criteria are both laid out in Additional Protocol I: Article 51(4)(b) prohibits weapons which cannot be directed at a specific military objective and Article 51(4)(c) prohibits weapons the effects of which cannot be limited as required by the Protocol.[74] These criteria are part of the definition of indiscriminate attacks under customary international law (see Rule 12).

The criterion whereby a weapon cannot be directed at a specific military objective is referred to in several military manuals, official statements and reported practice.[75] Judge Higgins, in her dissenting opinion in the *Nuclear Weapons case*, stated that a weapon is indiscriminate in nature if it is incapable of being targeted at a military objective.[76] In the *Martić case* in 1996, the

---

[71] See, e.g., the oral pleadings and written statements in the *Nuclear Weapons case* of Ecuador (*ibid.*, § 308), Egypt (*ibid.*, § 310), Iran (*ibid.*, §§ 317–318), Japan (*ibid.*, § 323), Nauru (*ibid.*, § 332), New Zealand (*ibid.*, § 336), Solomon Islands (*ibid.*, § 348), United Kingdom (*ibid.*, § 358) and United States (*ibid.*, § 364); see also the written statements in the *Nuclear Weapons (WHO) case* of Malaysia (*ibid.*, § 328), Mexico (*ibid.*, § 331), Solomon Islands (*ibid.*, § 347) and Sri Lanka (*ibid.*, § 349).

[72] ICJ, *Nuclear Weapons case*, Advisory Opinion (*ibid.*, § 389).

[73] See, e.g., the military manuals of Colombia (*ibid.*, § 274), France (*ibid.*, §§ 276–277), Germany (*ibid.*, §§ 278–279), Sweden (*ibid.*, § 285) and Switzerland (*ibid.*, § 286) and the statements of China (*ibid.*, § 305), Iran (*ibid.*, § 317), Marshall Islands (*ibid.*, § 330), Mexico (*ibid.*, § 331), Nauru (*ibid.*, § 332), New Zealand (*ibid.*, § 336), Romania (*ibid.*, § 341) and Solomon Islands (*ibid.*, § 347).

[74] Additional Protocol I, Article 51(4)(b) (cited in Vol. II, Ch. 3, § 206) and Article 51(4)(c) (*ibid.*, § 251).

[75] See, e.g., the military manuals of Australia (cited in Vol. II, Ch. 20, § 270), Canada (*ibid.*, § 273), Ecuador (*ibid.*, § 275), Israel (*ibid.*, § 280), New Zealand (*ibid.*, § 282) and United States (*ibid.*, §§ 287–289), the statements of Israel (*ibid.*, § 320) and United Kingdom (*ibid.*, § 357) and the reported practice of Israel (*ibid.*, § 321).

[76] ICJ, *Nuclear Weapons case*, Dissenting Opinion of Judge Higgins (*ibid.*, § 392).

International Criminal Tribunal for the Former Yugoslavia also referred to this criterion.[77]

The criterion whereby the effects of a weapon cannot be limited as required by international humanitarian law is also referred to in several military manuals and official statements.[78] In their submissions to the International Court of Justice in the *Nuclear Weapons case*, several States argued that a weapon is indiscriminate if it has uncontrollable effects or if the damage would be extensive and may be expected to cause incidental civilian losses which would be excessive in relation to the military advantage anticipated.[79]

In their individual opinions in the *Nuclear Weapons case*, those judges of the International Court of Justice who believed that nuclear weapons are indiscriminate in nature seem to have based their analysis on the criterion of a weapon whose effects cannot be limited, as they supported their opinions by referring to the widespread destruction caused by the weapon both in time and in space.[80] These judges did not, however, attempt a specific definition.

In the preamble to a resolution adopted in 1969, the UN General Assembly stated that biological and chemical weapons "are inherently reprehensible because their effects are often uncontrollable and unpredictable".[81] The prohibition of weapons that have "indiscriminate effects" was also recalled in a resolution adopted by the Organization of American States in 1998.[82]

Interpretation

Although the existence of the rule prohibiting indiscriminate weapons is not contested, there are differing views on whether the rule itself renders a weapon illegal or whether a weapon is illegal only if a specific treaty or customary rule prohibits its use. In their submissions to the International Court of Justice in the *Nuclear Weapons case*, the majority of States used the rule prohibiting indiscriminate weapons itself to argue their case on the lawfulness or otherwise of nuclear weapons.[83] France, however, stated that it believed the existence of a

---

[77] ICTY, *Martić case*, Review of the Indictment (*ibid.*, § 397).

[78] See, e.g., the military manuals of Australia (*ibid.*, § 270), Canada (*ibid.*, § 273), Colombia (*ibid.*, § 274), Ecuador (*ibid.*, § 275), Israel (*ibid.*, § 280), New Zealand (*ibid.*, § 282), Switzerland (*ibid.*, § 286), United States (*ibid.*, §§ 287–289) and Yugoslavia (*ibid.*, § 290) and the statements of China (*ibid.*, § 305), Romania (*ibid.*, § 341) and Sweden (*ibid.*, § 350).

[79] See, e.g., the oral pleadings and written statements in the *Nuclear Weapons case* of Ecuador (*ibid.*, § 308), Egypt (*ibid.*, §§ 310–311), Iran (*ibid.*, § 317), Japan (*ibid.*, § 323), Marshall Islands (*ibid.*, § 330) and Zimbabwe (*ibid.*, § 368); see also the written statements in the *Nuclear Weapons (WHO) case* of Malaysia (*ibid.*, § 328) and Solomon Islands (*ibid.*, § 347).

[80] See, e.g., ICJ, *Nuclear Weapons case*, Separate Opinion of Judge Fleischhauer (*ibid.*, § 394), Declaration of Judge Herczegh (*ibid.*, § 395) and Declaration of President Bedjaoui (*ibid.*, § 396); see also the individual opinions of Judges Ferrari-Bravo, Koroma, Ranjeva, Shahabuddeen and Weeramantry.

[81] UN General Assembly, Res. 2603 A (XXIV). Although three States voted against this resolution and 36 abstained, the disagreement was primarily in relation to herbicides and not the general principles.

[82] OAS General Assembly, Res. 1565 (XXVIII-O/98) (cited in Vol. II, Ch. 20, § 382).

[83] See, e.g., the oral pleadings and written statements in the *Nuclear Weapons case* of Ecuador (*ibid.*, § 308), Egypt (*ibid.*, §§ 310–311), Iran (*ibid.*, §§ 317–318), Marshall Islands (*ibid.*,

specific rule to be necessary before a particular weapon could be considered by nature indiscriminate and thus illegal.[84] In their individual opinions, the judges of the Court assessed the legality of the effects of nuclear weapons on the basis of the rule itself and independent of treaty law.[85] The discussions leading to the adoption of various UN General Assembly resolutions and the Convention on Certain Conventional Weapons are ambiguous, with some statements giving the impression that certain weapons are already prohibited by virtue of this rule and others arguing the need for a specific prohibition.[86]

Examples

The following weapons have been cited in practice as being indiscriminate in certain or all contexts: chemical,[87] biological[88] and nuclear weapons;[89] anti-personnel landmines;[90] mines;[91] poison;[92] explosives discharged from

---

§§ 329–330), Nauru (*ibid.*, § 332), Netherlands (*ibid.*, § 335), New Zealand (*ibid.*, § 336), Solomon Islands (*ibid.*, § 348), United Kingdom (*ibid.*, § 358), United States (*ibid.*, § 364) and Zimbabwe (*ibid.*, § 368); see also the written statements in the *Nuclear Weapons (WHO) case* of Mexico (*ibid.*, § 331), Rwanda (*ibid.*, § 345), Solomon Islands (*ibid.*, § 347) and Sri Lanka (*ibid.*, § 349).

[84] France, Written statement submitted to the ICJ in the *Nuclear Weapons (WHO) case* (*ibid.*, § 313); see also Italy, Statement at the Diplomatic Conference leading to the adoption of the Additional Protocols (*ibid.*, § 322).

[85] See ICJ, *Nuclear Weapons case*, Judges' individual opinions (*ibid.*, §§ 390–396).

[86] See, e.g., the statements of Canada (*ibid.*, §§ 303–304), Cyprus (*ibid.*, § 306), Ecuador (*ibid.*, § 307), Egypt (*ibid.*, § 309), France (*ibid.*, § 312), Federal Republic of Germany (*ibid.*, § 314), Holy See (*ibid.*, § 315), Israel (*ibid.*, § 320), Italy (*ibid.*, § 322), Netherlands (*ibid.*, § 334), Nigeria (*ibid.*, § 337), Poland (*ibid.*, § 340), Romania (*ibid.*, § 341), Russia (*ibid.*, § 343), Sweden (*ibid.*, § 350), Switzerland (*ibid.*, § 351), Turkey (*ibid.*, § 353), United Kingdom (*ibid.*, § 355) and Vietnam (*ibid.*, § 367).

[87] See, e.g., the military manuals of Australia (*ibid.*, §§ 270–271), France (*ibid.*, §§ 276–277) and Russia (*ibid.*, § 284) and the statements of Romania (*ibid.*, § 341) and United States (*ibid.*, § 360); see also the UN Sub-Commission on Human Rights, Res. 1989/39 (*ibid.*, § 378) and Res. 1996/16 (*ibid.*, § 379) and UN Secretariat, Existing rules of international law concerning the prohibition or restriction of use of specific weapons, Survey (*ibid.*, § 380).

[88] See, e.g., the military manuals of Australia (*ibid.*, §§ 270–271), France (*ibid.*, §§ 276–277), Russia (*ibid.*, § 284) and United States (*ibid.*, § 287) and the statements of Romania (*ibid.*, § 341) and Sweden (*ibid.*, § 350); see also the UN Sub-Commission on Human Rights, Res. 1996/16 (*ibid.*, § 379) and UN Secretariat, Existing rules of international law concerning the prohibition or restriction of use of specific weapons, Survey (*ibid.*, § 380).

[89] See, e.g., the military manual of Switzerland (*ibid.*, § 286) and the statements of Australia (*ibid.*, § 301), Ecuador (*ibid.*, § 308), Egypt (*ibid.*, § 311), Iran (*ibid.*, §§ 317–318), Japan (*ibid.*, § 323), Lesotho (*ibid.*, § 327), Malaysia (*ibid.*, § 328), Marshall Islands (*ibid.*, §§ 329–330), Solomon Islands (*ibid.*, § 347) and Zimbabwe (*ibid.*, § 368); see also UN Sub-Commission on Human Rights, Res. 1996/16 (*ibid.*, § 379) and UN Secretariat, Existing rules of international law concerning the prohibition or restriction of use of specific weapons, Survey (*ibid.*, § 380).

[90] See, e.g., the military manuals of France (*ibid.*, §§ 276–277) and the reported practice of Peru (*ibid.*, § 339).

[91] See, e.g., the military manuals of Ecuador (*ibid.*, § 275) and United States (*ibid.*, § 289), the statement of Australia (*ibid.*, § 300) and the reported practice of Jordan (*ibid.*, § 324) and Rwanda (*ibid.*, § 346); see also UN Secretariat, Existing rules of international law concerning the prohibition or restriction of use of specific weapons, Survey (*ibid.*, § 380).

[92] See, e.g., the military manuals of Australia (*ibid.*, §§ 270–271), Canada (*ibid.*, § 273), France (*ibid.*, §§ 276–277) and Russia (*ibid.*, § 284).

balloons;[93] V-1 and V-2 rockets;[94] cluster bombs;[95] booby-traps;[96] Scud missiles;[97] Katyusha rockets;[98] incendiary weapons;[99] and environmental modification techniques.[100] There is insufficient consensus concerning all of these examples to conclude that, under customary international law, they all violate the rule prohibiting the use of indiscriminate weapons. However, there is agreement that some of them are prohibited and they are discussed in subsequent chapters.

* * * *

N.B. In order to ensure that the use of a means or method of warfare complies with international humanitarian law, Additional Protocol I requires States to adopt a national mechanism or procedure to that effect.[101] Several States, including States not party to Additional Protocol I, have implemented this requirement.[102]

---

[93] See, e.g., the military manuals of Ecuador (*ibid.*, § 275) and United States (*ibid.*, §§ 287 and 289).

[94] See, e.g., the military manuals of Ecuador (*ibid.*, § 275) and United States (*ibid.*, §§ 287 and 289) and the reported practice of Jordan (*ibid.*, § 324).

[95] See, e.g., the statement of Switzerland (*ibid.*, § 351); see also the UN Sub-Commission on Human Rights, Res. 1996/16 (*ibid.*, § 379) and UN Secretariat, Existing rules of international law concerning the prohibition or restriction of use of specific weapons, Survey (*ibid.*, § 380).

[96] See, e.g., the statements of Australia (*ibid.*, § 300) and Russia (*ibid.*, § 342); see also UN Secretariat, Existing rules of international law concerning the prohibition or restriction of use of specific weapons, Survey (*ibid.*, § 380).

[97] See, e.g., the military manual of Canada (*ibid.*, § 273), the statements of Israel (*ibid.*, § 320), United Kingdom (*ibid.*, § 356) and United States (*ibid.*, §§ 361 and 363) and the reported practice of Israel (*ibid.*, § 321).

[98] See, e.g., the reported practice of Israel (*ibid.*, § 321).

[99] See, e.g., the statements of Australia (*ibid.*, § 300), Russia (*ibid.*, § 342), Sweden (*ibid.*, § 350), Switzerland (*ibid.*, § 351) and Turkey (*ibid.*, § 353); see also UN Secretariat, Existing rules of international law concerning the prohibition or restriction of use of specific weapons, Survey (*ibid.*, § 380).

[100] See, e.g., the military manual of Russia (*ibid.*, § 284).

[101] Additional Protocol I, Article 36.

[102] In particular, Australia, Belgium, Canada, Denmark, Germany, Netherlands, Norway, Sweden, United Kingdom and United States. See Isabelle Daoust, Robin Coupland and Rikke Ishoey, "New wars, new weapons? The obligation of States to assess the legality of means and methods of warfare", *International Review of the Red Cross*, No. 846, 2002, p. 345; Justin McClelland, "The review of weapons in accordance with Article 36 of Additional Protocol I", *International Review of the Red Cross*, No. 850, 2003, p. 397.

POISON

Rule 72. The use of poison or poisoned weapons is prohibited.

Practice

Volume II, Chapter 21.

Summary

State practice establishes this rule as a norm of customary international law applicable in both international and non-international armed conflicts. This prohibition exists independently of the prohibition of chemical weapons (see Rule 74). Although the Geneva Gas Protocol was inspired by the existing prohibition of the use of poison, there is sufficient separate practice establishing a specific rule on poison and poisoned weapons.

International armed conflicts

The prohibition of poison or poisoned weapons is a long-standing rule of customary international law already recognised in the Lieber Code and the Hague Regulations.[1] "Employing poison or poisoned weapons" constitutes a war crime in international armed conflicts under the Statute of the International Criminal Court.[2]

The prohibition of poison or poisoned weapons is set forth in numerous military manuals.[3] The use of poison or poisoned weapons is an offence under the legislation of many States.[4] This prohibition is also supported by official

---

[1] Lieber Code, Article 70 (cited in Vol. II, Ch. 21, § 4); Hague Regulations, Article 23(a) (*ibid.*, § 2).
[2] ICC Statute, Article 8(2)(b)(xvii) (*ibid.*, § 3).
[3] See, e.g., the military manuals of Argentina (*ibid.*, § 12), Australia (*ibid.*, §§ 13–14), Belgium (*ibid.*, § 15), Bosnia and Herzegovina (*ibid.*, § 16), Canada (*ibid.*, §§ 17–18), Colombia (*ibid.*, § 19), Dominican Republic (*ibid.*, § 20), Ecuador (*ibid.*, § 21), France (*ibid.*, §§ 22–24), Germany (*ibid.*, § 25), Indonesia (*ibid.*, § 26), Israel (*ibid.*, §§ 27–28), Italy (*ibid.*, § 29), Kenya (*ibid.*, § 30), South Korea (*ibid.*, § 31), Netherlands (*ibid.*, §§ 32–33), New Zealand (*ibid.*, § 34), Nigeria (*ibid.*, §§ 35–37), Russia (*ibid.*, § 38), South Africa (*ibid.*, § 39), Spain (*ibid.*, § 40), Switzerland (*ibid.*, §§ 41–43), United Kingdom (*ibid.*, §§ 44–45), United States (*ibid.*, §§ 46–51) and Yugoslavia (*ibid.*, § 52).
[4] See, e.g., the legislation of Australia (*ibid.*, §§ 54–55), Brazil (*ibid.*, § 56), Canada (*ibid.*, § 58), China (*ibid.*, § 59), Democratic Republic of the Congo (*ibid.*, § 61), Congo (*ibid.*, § 60), Estonia

statements and reported practice.[5] There is national case-law to the effect that the rule is part of customary international law.[6]

In their submissions to the International Court of Justice in the *Nuclear Weapons case*, several States recalled the prohibition of poison and poisoned weapons.[7] In its advisory opinion, the Court reaffirmed the customary character of the prohibition of the use of poison or poisoned weapons.[8]

Non-international armed conflicts

The Statute of the International Criminal Court does not include the use of poison or poisoned weapons as a war crime in the sections dealing with non-international armed conflicts, and this issue was not openly debated during the Rome diplomatic conference. As a result, some implementing legislation of the Statute of the International Criminal Court limits to international armed conflicts the rule that the use of poison or poisoned weapons is a war crime.[9] However, the legislation of some States criminalising the use of poison or poisoned weapons does apply to non-international armed conflicts.[10] Germany's legislation states explicitly that the rule applies to both international and non-international armed conflicts.[11] The rule is also included in some military manuals which are applicable in or have been applied in non-international armed conflicts.[12] Several military manuals explain the prohibition of poison or poisoned weapons in armed conflicts on the grounds that they are "inhuman"

(*ibid.*, § 62), Georgia (*ibid.*, § 63), Germany (*ibid.*, § 64), Italy (*ibid.*, § 65), Mali (*ibid.*, § 66), Netherlands (*ibid.*, §§ 67–68), New Zealand (*ibid.*, § 69), Switzerland (*ibid.*, § 70), United Kingdom (*ibid.*, § 72), United States (*ibid.*, § 73) and Yugoslavia (*ibid.*, § 74); see also the draft legislation of Burundi (*ibid.*, § 57) and Trinidad and Tobago (*ibid.*, § 71).

5   See, e.g., the statements of Iraq (*ibid.*, § 80), Pakistan (*ibid.*, § 91) and United States (*ibid.*, §§ 98–99) and the reported practice of Bosnia and Herzegovina, Republika Srpska (*ibid.*, § 77), India (*ibid.*, § 79), Jordan (*ibid.*, § 82), Kuwait (*ibid.*, § 83), Malaysia (*ibid.*, § 85), Norway (*ibid.*, § 90), Philippines (*ibid.*, § 92) and Rwanda (*ibid.*, § 93).

6   See, e.g., Japan, District Court of Tokyo, *Shimoda case* (*ibid.*, § 75).

7   See, e.g., the oral pleadings and written statements in the *Nuclear Weapons case* of Egypt (*ibid.*, § 78), Marshall Islands (*ibid.*, § 86), Mexico (*ibid.*, § 87), New Zealand (*ibid.*, § 89), Solomon Islands (*ibid.*, §§ 94–95), Sweden (*ibid.*, § 96), United Kingdom (*ibid.*, § 97), United States (*ibid.*, § 100) and Zimbabwe (*ibid.*, § 101); see also the oral pleadings and written statements in the *Nuclear Weapons (WHO) case* of Malaysia (*ibid.*, § 84) and Nauru (*ibid.*, § 88).

8   ICJ, *Nuclear Weapons case*, Advisory Opinion, §§ 80–82.

9   See, e.g., the legislation of Australia (cited in Vol. II, Ch. 21, § 55), Canada (*ibid.*, § 58), Congo (*ibid.*, § 60), Mali (*ibid.*, § 66), Netherlands (*ibid.*, § 68), New Zealand (*ibid.*, § 69) and United Kingdom (*ibid.*, § 72); see also the draft legislation of Burundi (*ibid.*, § 57) and Trinidad and Tobago (*ibid.*, § 71).

10   See, e.g., the legislation of the Democratic Republic of the Congo (*ibid.*, § 61), Estonia (*ibid.*, § 62), Germany (*ibid.*, § 64), Switzerland (*ibid.*, § 70) and Yugoslavia (*ibid.*, § 74); see also the legislation of Italy (*ibid.*, § 65), the application of which is not excluded in time of non-international armed conflict.

11   Germany, *Law Introducing the International Crimes Code* (*ibid.*, § 64).

12   See, e.g., the military manuals of Australia (*ibid.*, § 13), Bosnia and Herzegovina (*ibid.*, § 16), Canada (*ibid.*, § 18), Colombia (*ibid.*, § 19), Ecuador (*ibid.*, § 21), Germany (*ibid.*, § 25), Italy (*ibid.*, § 29), Kenya (*ibid.*, § 30), Nigeria (*ibid.*, §§ 35 and 37), South Africa (*ibid.*, § 39) and Yugoslavia (*ibid.*, § 52).

and/or "indiscriminate", an argument that is equally valid in non-international armed conflicts.[13] There is also reported practice from a number of States that supports the application of this rule in non-international armed conflicts.[14]

Practice is in conformity with the rule's applicability in both international and non-international armed conflicts, as States generally do not have a different set of military weapons for international and non-international armed conflicts. There have been no confirmed reports of the use of poison or poisoned weapons in either international or non-international armed conflicts.[15] Allegations of such use have been rare.

No State has claimed that poison may lawfully be used in either international or non-international armed conflicts. The one example of limited contrary practice – a manual asserting that poisoning of drinking water and food is not forbidden if it is announced or marked – is not sufficient to deny the customary law character of this rule.[16]

Definition of poison or poisoned weapons

Most States indicate that poison or poisoned weapons are prohibited without further detail. In its advisory opinion in the *Nuclear Weapons case*, the International Court of Justice stated that the terms "poison" and "poisoned weapons" "have been understood, in the practice of States, in their ordinary sense as covering weapons whose primary, or even exclusive, effect is to poison or asphyxiate".[17] In their submissions to the International Court of Justice in the *Nuclear Weapons case*, the United Kingdom and the United States stated that the prohibition did not apply to weapons which could incidentally poison, but only to weapons that were designed to kill or injure by the effect of such poison.[18] This interpretation does not indicate that poison must be the primary or exclusive injury mechanism but that it must be an "intended" injury mechanism and is in keeping with the origin of the rule, namely, to prohibit the smearing of arrows with poison which would prevent recovery from the injury caused by the arrow.

---

[13] See, e.g., the military manuals of Australia (*ibid.*, §§ 13–14), Canada (*ibid.*, § 17), France (*ibid.*, §§ 23–24), Israel (*ibid.*, § 28) and United States (*ibid.*, § 47) and the military manuals of Ecuador (cited in Vol. II, Ch. 20, § 52), Netherlands (*ibid.*, § 72), New Zealand (*ibid.*, § 73), South Africa (*ibid.*, § 80), United Kingdom (*ibid.*, § 85) and United States (*ibid.*, §§ 87, 89, 91 and 93).

[14] See, e.g., the reported practice of Bosnia and Herzegovina, Republika Srpska (cited in Vol. II, Ch. 21, § 77), India (*ibid.*, § 79) Philippines (*ibid.*, § 92) and Rwanda (*ibid.*, § 93).

[15] Reports of the use of chemical weapons and riot-control agents are addressed in Chapter 24.

[16] See Yugoslavia, *YPA Military Manual* (cited in Vol. II, Ch. 21, § 52).

[17] ICJ, *Nuclear Weapons case*, Advisory Opinion (*ibid.*, § 111).

[18] Written statements in the *Nuclear Weapons case* of the United Kingdom (*ibid.*, § 97) and United States (*ibid.*, § 100).

Examples

The prohibition of the use of poison or poisoned weapons is understood as outlawing such practices as the smearing of bullets with poison or poisoning the food and drink of the adverse party. In their explanation of the application of this rule, several military manuals specify that the prohibition of poison extends to poisoning wells and other water supplies.[19]

---

[19] See, e.g., the military manuals of Australia (*ibid.*, § 14) (even if notice is given), Belgium (*ibid.*, § 15) (even if notice is given), Canada (*ibid.*, § 17) (even if notice is given), Colombia (*ibid.*, § 19), Dominican Republic (*ibid.*, § 20), Germany (*ibid.*, § 25), Israel (*ibid.*, § 28), South Korea (*ibid.*, § 31), Netherlands (*ibid.*, § 32), Nigeria (*ibid.*, § 36), South Africa (*ibid.*, § 39), Spain (*ibid.*, § 40), Switzerland (*ibid.*, § 43), United Kingdom (*ibid.*, § 44) (even if notice is given), United States (*ibid.*, §§ 46 and 48–49) and Yugoslavia (*ibid.*, § 52) (unless notice is given).

CHAPTER 22

NUCLEAR WEAPONS

The present study was mandated by the 26th International Conference of the Red Cross and Red Crescent in December 1995. A year earlier, the UN General Assembly had asked the International Court of Justice for an advisory opinion on the following question: "Is the threat or use of nuclear weapons in any circumstance permitted under international law?"[1] All States wishing to do so had the opportunity to express their opinion on this question, in written statements and the oral pleadings before the Court. In an advisory opinion of 8 July 1996, the International Court of Justice stated in relation to customary international law and the applicability of international humanitarian law to nuclear weapons that:

There is in neither customary nor conventional international law any specific authorization of the threat or use of nuclear weapons;

There is in neither customary nor conventional international law any comprehensive and universal prohibition of the threat or use of nuclear weapons as such;
. . .

A threat or use of nuclear weapons should also be compatible with the requirements of the international law applicable in armed conflict, particularly those of the principles and rules of international humanitarian law, as well as with specific obligations under treaties and other undertakings which expressly deal with nuclear weapons;

It follows from the above-mentioned requirements that the threat or use of nuclear weapons would generally be contrary to the rules of international law applicable in armed conflict, and in particular the principles and rules of humanitarian law;

However, in view of the current state of international law, and of the elements of fact at its disposal, the Court cannot conclude definitively whether the threat or use of nuclear weapons would be lawful or unlawful in an extreme circumstance of self-defence, in which the very survival of a State would be at stake.[2]

As mentioned above, this opinion took into account a wide range of legal analysis and scientific evidence presented by States. As a result, the Court being the principal judicial organ of the United Nations, the ICRC had to take due note of the Court's opinion and deemed it not appropriate to engage in a similar exercise at virtually the same time.

---

[1] UN General Assembly, Res. 49/75 K on request for an advisory opinion from the International Court of Justice on the legality of the threat or use of nuclear weapons, 15 December 1994, preamble, tenth paragraph.
[2] ICJ, *Nuclear Weapons case*, Advisory Opinion, 8 July 1996, *ICJ Reports 1996*, p. 226.

BIOLOGICAL WEAPONS

Rule 73. The use of biological weapons is prohibited.

Practice

Volume II, Chapter 23.

Summary

State practice establishes this rule as a norm of customary international law applicable in both international and non-international armed conflicts. This rule applies to biological weapons that are meant to affect humans. Whether it is intended to apply to herbicides is discussed under Rule 76.

International and non-international armed conflicts

The prohibition of the use of biological weapons in international armed conflicts is based on the Geneva Gas Protocol and the Biological Weapons Convention.[1] When they became party to the Geneva Gas Protocol, 37 States entered a reservation to the effect that they retained the right to retaliate if an adverse party (and in some cases that party's ally) violated the terms of the Protocol. Because 17 of these "no first use" reservations have been withdrawn,[2] only 20 such reservations remain.[3] However, 18 of the remaining 20 States that have kept their reservations are party to the Biological Weapons Convention, which prohibits any possession of biological weapons, thereby making it unlawful for them to retaliate using such weapons.[4] Thus, at present, Angola and Israel are the only States that have maintained their "no first use" reservation to the Geneva Gas Protocol and are not party to the Biological Weapons Convention.

---

[1] Geneva Gas Protocol (cited in Vol. II, Ch. 23, § 1); Biological Weapons Convention, preamble (*ibid.*, § 4) and Article 1 (*ibid.*, § 5).

[2] Australia, Belgium, Bulgaria, Canada, Chile, Estonia, France, Ireland, South Korea, Netherlands, New Zealand, Romania, Russia, Slovakia, South Africa, Spain and United Kingdom (*ibid.*, § 1).

[3] Algeria, Angola, Bahrain, Bangladesh, China, Fiji, India, Iraq, Israel, Jordan, North Korea, Kuwait, Libya, Nigeria, Pakistan, Papua New Guinea, Portugal, Solomon Islands, Vietnam and Yugoslavia (*ibid.*, § 1).

[4] Biological Weapons Convention, Article 1 (*ibid.*, § 5).

It can be concluded from the drive to eliminate biological weapons over the last three decades that States believe that these weapons should not exist and therefore must not be used in any circumstances, including in non-international armed conflicts.

Virtually all allegations of possession by States have been denied. When Russia admitted in 1992 that it continued to have a biological weapons programme, it stated that it would definitely halt the programme. Since then, it has vigorously denied allegations that it continued to manufacture biological weapons.[5] Reports of Iraq's biological weapons programmes attracted the condemnation of the international community.[6] Statements and other practice of States, both parties and non-parties to the Biological Weapons Convention, indicate that the prohibition on using biological weapons in any circumstances is not purely treaty-based.[7]

There is widespread State practice in the form of military manuals and legislation to the effect that the use of biological weapons is prohibited irrespective of whether the State concerned is a party to the Biological Weapons Convention or whether it has made a "no first use" reservation to the Geneva Gas Protocol.[8] The US Naval Handbook states that the prohibition of biological weapons is part of customary law and binds all States, whether or not they are party to the Geneva Gas Protocol or the Biological Weapons Convention.[9] Three States not party to the Biological Weapons Convention have criminalised the production, acquisition, sale or use of biological weapons.[10] There is also national case-law to the effect that biological weapons are prohibited, including in non-international armed conflicts.[11]

---

[5] See the practice of Russia (and formerly the USSR) (*ibid.*, §§ 210–213).

[6] See, e.g., the statements of Cuba (*ibid.*, § 106), Ecuador (*ibid.*, § 115), France (*ibid.*, § 121), USSR (*ibid.*, § 209), United Kingdom (*ibid.*, §§ 219–220 and 222), United States (*ibid.*, § 233) and Yemen (*ibid.*, § 237); UN Secretary-General, Reports on the work of the Special Commission established pursuant to Security Council resolution 687 (1991) (*ibid.*, § 257); UNSCOM, Final report of the Panel on disarmament and current and future ongoing monitoring and verification issues (*ibid.*, § 258).

[7] See, e.g., the statements, practice and reported practice (*ibid.*, §§ 76–241).

[8] See, e.g., the military manuals of Australia (*ibid.*, §§ 12–13), Belgium (*ibid.*, § 14), Bosnia and Herzegovina (*ibid.*, § 15), Cameroon (*ibid.*, § 16), Canada (*ibid.*, § 17), Colombia (*ibid.*, § 18), Ecuador (*ibid.*, § 19), France (*ibid.*, §§ 20–22), Germany (*ibid.*, §§ 23–25), Italy (*ibid.*, § 26), Kenya (*ibid.*, § 27), Netherlands (*ibid.*, §§ 28–29), New Zealand (*ibid.*, § 30), Nigeria (*ibid.*, § 31), Russia (*ibid.*, § 32), South Africa (*ibid.*, § 33), Spain (*ibid.*, § 34), Switzerland (*ibid.*, §§ 35–36), United Kingdom (*ibid.*, §§ 37–38), United States (*ibid.*, §§ 39–43) and Yugoslavia (*ibid.*, §§ 39–43) and the legislation of Armenia (*ibid.*, § 45), Belarus (*ibid.*, § 47), Brazil (*ibid.*, § 48), China (*ibid.*, § 49), Colombia (*ibid.*, § 50), Croatia (*ibid.*, § 51), Estonia (*ibid.*, § 52), Georgia (*ibid.*, § 54), Germany (*ibid.*, § 55), Hungary (*ibid.*, § 57), Italy (*ibid.*, § 58), Moldova (*ibid.*, § 61), Poland (*ibid.*, § 64), Switzerland (*ibid.*, § 66), Tajikistan (*ibid.*, § 68), Ukraine (*ibid.*, § 69) and Yugoslavia (*ibid.*, § 73).

[9] United States, *Naval Handbook* (*ibid.*, § 43); see also France, *LOAC Teaching Note* (*ibid.*, § 22).

[10] See the legislation of Kazakhstan ("production, acquisition or sale") (*ibid.*, § 60), Moldova (draft legislation adopted in 2003) ("use") (*ibid.*, § 61) and Tajikistan ("production, acquisition" or "sale" and "use") (*ibid.*, § 68).

[11] Japan, District Court of Tokyo, *Shimoda case* (*ibid.*, § 75); Colombia, Constitutional Court, *Constitutional Case No. 225/95* (*ibid.*, § 74).

The prohibition of the use of biological weapons is also supported by a number of official statements. For example, in January 1991, the United Kingdom and the United States informed Iraq that they expected it not to use biological weapons, although at that time Iraq had a "no first use" reservation to the Geneva Gas Protocol and was not yet party to the Biological Weapons Convention.[12] In 2001, the United States accused Syria of violating the terms of the Biological Weapons Convention, although Syria was not a party to the Convention.[13] In its submission to the International Court of Justice in the *Nuclear Weapons case*, Australia stated that the use of biological weapons would be contrary to "fundamental general principles of humanity".[14]

Several UN General Assembly resolutions called for States to adhere to the Geneva Gas Protocol and/or the Biological Weapons Convention and for strict observance by all States of the principles and objectives contained therein.[15]

In 1990 and 1991, the ICRC reminded all parties to the Gulf War that the use of biological weapons was prohibited under international humanitarian law.[16] In 1994, it recalled the prohibition in the context of the conflict in Angola, although Angola had a "no first use" reservation to the Geneva Gas Protocol and was not party to the Biological Weapons Convention.[17] In neither instance was the ICRC's assertion contested.

Practice is in conformity with the rule's applicability in both international and non-international armed conflicts, as States generally do not have a different set of military weapons for international and non-international armed conflicts. All allegations of use of biological weapons by States have been denied and in most cases disproved.[18]

---

[12] United Kingdom, Letter to the President of the UN Security Council (*ibid.*, § 220); United States, Department of State, Diplomatic Note to Iraq (*ibid.*, § 233).

[13] United States, Statement at the Fifth Review Conference of States Parties to the Biological Weapons Convention (*ibid.*, § 236).

[14] Australia, Oral pleadings before the ICJ in the *Nuclear Weapons case* (*ibid.*, § 79).

[15] See, e.g., UN General Assembly, Res. 3256 (XXIX) (*ibid.*, §§ 245–247) and Res. 32/77 and 33/59 A (*ibid.*, §§ 245–246 and 253), all of which were adopted without a vote.

[16] ICRC, Memorandum on the Applicability of International Humanitarian Law (*ibid.*, § 272) and Press Release No. 1658 (*ibid.*, § 273).

[17] ICRC, Memorandum on Respect for International Humanitarian Law in Angola (*ibid.*, § 274).

[18] See, e.g., the practice of Russia (and formerly USSR) (*ibid.*, §§ 212, 231 and 277) and United States (*ibid.*, § 108).

CHEMICAL WEAPONS

Rule 74. The use of chemical weapons is prohibited.

Practice

Volume II, Chapter 24, Section A.

Summary

State practice establishes this rule as a norm of customary international law applicable in both international and non-international armed conflicts.

International armed conflicts

The use of chemical weapons is prohibited in international armed conflicts in a series of treaties, including the Hague Declaration concerning Asphyxiating Gases, the Geneva Gas Protocol, the Chemical Weapons Convention and the Statute of the International Criminal Court.[1] At present, only 13 States are not party to either the Geneva Gas Protocol or the Chemical Weapons Convention.[2] Of these, at least three have made statements to the effect that the use of chemical weapons is unlawful, or have indicated that they do not possess or use them or that they are committed to their elimination.[3] The prohibition is also contained in a number of other instruments.[4]

---

[1] Hague Declaration concerning Asphyxiating Gases (cited in Vol. II, Ch. 24, § 1); Geneva Gas Protocol (*ibid.*, § 4); Chemical Weapons Convention, Article I (*ibid.*, § 13); ICC Statute, Article 8(2)(b)(xviii) (*ibid.*, § 15).

[2] Bahamas, Chad, Comoros, Democratic Republic of the Congo, Congo, Djibouti, Haiti, Honduras, Marshall Islands, Myanmar, Niue, Somalia and Vanuatu.

[3] See the statements of the Democratic Republic of the Congo (*ibid.*, § 187), Haiti (*ibid.*, § 240) and Honduras (*ibid.*, § 242).

[4] See, e.g., Oxford Manual of Naval War, Article 16(1) (*ibid.*, § 16); Report of the Commission on Responsibility (*ibid.*, § 17); Mendoza Declaration on Chemical and Biological Weapons (*ibid.*, § 20); Cartagena Declaration on Weapons of Mass Destruction (*ibid.*, § 21); India-Pakistan Declaration on Prohibition of Chemical Weapons (*ibid.*, § 22); UN Secretary-General's Bulletin, Section 6.2 (*ibid.*, § 24); UNTAET Regulation No. 2000/15, Section 6(1)(b)(xviii) (*ibid.*, § 25).

Numerous military manuals restate the prohibition of the use of chemical weapons.[5] This prohibition is also contained in the legislation of many States.[6] There are numerous statements and other practice by States from all parts of the world to the effect that the use of chemical weapons is prohibited under customary international law.[7] Most allegations of use since the 1930s either are unsubstantiated or have been denied; the few confirmed cases have been widely denounced by other States.[8] There is also national case-law to the effect that the use of chemical weapons is prohibited under customary international law.[9]

There is increasing evidence that it may now be unlawful to retaliate in kind to another State's use of chemical weapons. There are still 21 reservations to the Geneva Gas Protocol stating that if an adverse party (and in some cases that party's ally) does not respect the Protocol, the ratifying State will no longer consider itself bound by it.[10] However, 16 of these States are party to the Chemical Weapons Convention, which prohibits all use and to which no reservations are allowed. This leaves only five States (Angola, Iraq, Israel, North Korea and Libya) which, under treaty law, could avail themselves of their reserved right to retaliate in kind to the first use of chemical weapons. Of these, three (Israel, North Korea and Libya) have asserted that they will

---

[5] See, e.g., the military manuals of Australia (*ibid.*, §§ 26–27), Belgium (*ibid.*, § 28), Bosnia and Herzegovina (*ibid.*, § 29), Cameroon (*ibid.*, § 30), Canada (*ibid.*, §§ 31–32), Colombia (*ibid.*, § 33), Ecuador (*ibid.*, § 34), France (*ibid.*, §§ 35–37), Germany (*ibid.*, §§ 38–40), Israel (*ibid.*, § 41), Italy (*ibid.*, § 42), Kenya (*ibid.*, § 43), Netherlands (*ibid.*, §§ 44–45), New Zealand (*ibid.*, § 46), Nigeria (*ibid.*, § 47), Russia (*ibid.*, § 48), South Africa (*ibid.*, § 49), Spain (*ibid.*, § 50), Switzerland (*ibid.*, §§ 51–52), United Kingdom (*ibid.*, §§ 53–54), United States (*ibid.*, §§ 55–59) and Yugoslavia (*ibid.*, § 60).

[6] See, e.g., the legislation (*ibid.*, §§ 61–117).

[7] See, e.g., the military manuals of Israel (*ibid.*, § 41), Netherlands (*ibid.*, § 44), New Zealand (*ibid.*, § 46) and United States (*ibid.*, § 59) (prohibition of first use), the statements of Belarus (*ibid.*, § 144), Belgium (*ibid.*, § 150), Bulgaria (*ibid.*, § 160), Czechoslovakia (*ibid.*, § 196), Hungary (*ibid.*, § 243), Italy (*ibid.*, § 266), Democratic Kampuchea (*ibid.*, § 279), Lesotho (*ibid.*, § 295), Netherlands (*ibid.*, § 320), New Zealand (*ibid.*, § 324), Poland (*ibid.*, § 343), Romania (*ibid.*, § 347), Saudi Arabia (*ibid.*, § 353), Sweden (*ibid.*, § 371), Switzerland (*ibid.*, § 375), Tanzania (*ibid.*, § 379), Ukraine (*ibid.*, § 389), USSR (*ibid.*, § 395), United Kingdom (*ibid.*, § 414) and United States (*ibid.*, § 420) (prohibition of first use) and the reported practice of Iran (*ibid.*, § 255), South Korea (*ibid.*, § 288), South Africa (*ibid.*, § 361) and Zimbabwe (*ibid.*, § 443).

[8] See, e.g., the statements of Belgium (*ibid.*, §§ 151–152), Canada (*ibid.*, § 173), China (*ibid.*, § 177), Denmark (*ibid.*, § 203), Egypt (*ibid.*, § 208), France (*ibid.*, § 222), Germany (*ibid.*, §§ 230 and 233), Hungary (*ibid.*, § 243), Iran (*ibid.*, § 250), Israel (*ibid.*, § 260), Cambodia (and formerly Kampuchea) (*ibid.*, §§ 278–279), Luxembourg (*ibid.*, § 301), Mongolia (*ibid.*, § 313), Netherlands (*ibid.*, § 319), Norway (*ibid.*, § 328), Peru (*ibid.*, § 338), Portugal (*ibid.*, § 344), Russia (*ibid.*, § 350), Sweden (*ibid.*, §§ 371–372), Syria (*ibid.*, § 378), Turkey (*ibid.*, § 388), USSR (*ibid.*, § 397), United Kingdom (*ibid.*, §§ 406–407 and 409–412), United States (*ibid.*, §§ 397, 416, 418, 424 and 430) and Vietnam (*ibid.*, § 434) and the reported practice of China (*ibid.*, § 269), India (*ibid.*, § 332), Iran (*ibid.*, § 255), Italy (*ibid.*, § 264), Japan (*ibid.*, § 269), Pakistan (*ibid.*, § 333), Sudan (*ibid.*, § 366) and Yugoslavia (*ibid.*, §§ 439–440).

[9] See, e.g., Colombia, Constitutional Court, *Constitutional Case No. C-225/95* (*ibid.*, § 119); Japan, District Court of Tokyo, *Shimoda case* (*ibid.*, § 120).

[10] Algeria, Angola, Bahrain, Bangladesh, China, Fiji, India, Iraq, Israel, Jordan, North Korea, Kuwait, Libya, Nigeria, Pakistan, Papua New Guinea, Portugal, Solomon Islands, United States, Vietnam and Yugoslavia.

never use chemical weapons or are strongly committed to their elimination.[11] It is significant that "employing asphyxiating, poisonous or other gases, and all analogous liquids, materials or devices" is listed in the Statute of the International Criminal Court as a war crime over which the Court has jurisdiction, and that the crime is not limited to first use of such weapons.[12]

The US Naval Handbook implies that, for non-parties to the Chemical Weapons Convention, retaliation in kind is lawful, but that it must stop once the use that prompted the retaliation has terminated.[13] However, in January 1991, both the United States and the United Kingdom stated that they expected Iraq to abide by its obligations under the Geneva Gas Protocol and not use chemical weapons, even though Iraq had made a "no first use" reservation.[14] Iran stated in 1987 that it had never retaliated against Iraq's use of chemical weapons, although its position at the time was that the Geneva Gas Protocol only prohibited first use.[15]

In several resolutions between 1986 and 1988, the UN Security Council condemned the use of chemical weapons in the Iran–Iraq War without any regard to whether the use was a first use or in retaliation.[16]

In 1990 and 1991, the ICRC reminded the parties to the Gulf War that the use of chemical weapons was prohibited.[17] The parties concerned had "no first use" reservations to the Geneva Gas Protocol, and the Chemical Weapons Convention did not yet exist.

Non-international armed conflicts

The prohibition of the use of chemical weapons contained in the Chemical Weapons Convention applies in all circumstances, including in non-international armed conflicts.[18] In addition, the prohibition is contained in several other instruments pertaining also to non-international armed conflicts.[19]

---

[11] See the statements of Israel (*ibid.*, §§ 260–263), North Korea (*ibid.*, §§ 283–284) and Libya (*ibid.*, §§ 297–299).

[12] ICC Statute, Article 8(2)(b)(xviii) (*ibid.*, § 15).

[13] United States, *Naval Handbook* (*ibid.*, § 59).

[14] United Kingdom, Letter to the President of the UN Security Council (*ibid.*, § 410) and Statement by the Minister of State, Foreign and Commonwealth Office (*ibid.*, § 411); United States, Department of State, Diplomatic Note to Iraq (*ibid.*, § 424).

[15] Iran, Statement before the First Committee of the UN General Assembly (*ibid.*, § 250).

[16] UN Security Council, Res. 582 (*ibid.*, § 448), Res. 598 (*ibid.*, § 449), Res. 612 (*ibid.*, § 450) and Res. 620 (*ibid.*, § 451).

[17] ICRC, Memorandum on the Applicability of International Humanitarian Law (*ibid.*, § 505) and Press Release No. 1658 (*ibid.*, § 506).

[18] Chemical Weapons Convention, Article I (*ibid.*, § 13).

[19] See, e.g., Mendoza Declaration on Chemical and Biological Weapons (*ibid.*, § 20); Cartagena Declaration on Weapons of Mass Destruction (*ibid.*, § 21); Comprehensive Agreement on Respect for Human Rights and IHL in the Philippines, Part IV, Article 4(4) (*ibid.*, § 23); UN Secretary-General's Bulletin, Section 6.2 (*ibid.*, § 24).

Several military manuals which apply or have been applied in non-international armed conflicts restate the prohibition on using chemical weapons.[20] This prohibition is also contained in the legislation of numerous States.[21] Colombia's Constitutional Court has held that the prohibition of the use of chemical weapons in non-international armed conflicts is part of customary international law.[22]

Allegations of use of chemical weapons by Russia in Chechnya, Sudan against armed opposition groups and Turkey in south-eastern Turkey were denied by the governments concerned.[23] Furthermore, as the International Criminal Tribunal for the Former Yugoslavia recalled in the *Tadić case* in 1995, the international community condemned Iraq's use of chemical weapons against the Kurds.[24] The United Kingdom, for example, stated that this use was a violation of the Geneva Gas Protocol and international humanitarian law.[25]

In the *Tadić case* referred to above, the International Criminal Tribunal for the Former Yugoslavia held that "there undisputedly emerged a general consensus in the international community on the principle that the use of [chemical] weapons is also prohibited in internal armed conflicts".[26]

In a Memorandum on Respect for International Humanitarian Law in Angola in 1994, the ICRC reminded the parties to the conflict that the use of chemical weapons was prohibited, although Angola had not ratified the Chemical Weapons Convention.[27]

Practice is in conformity with the rule's applicability in both international and non-international armed conflicts, as States generally do not have a different set of military weapons for international and non-international armed conflicts.

[20] See, e.g., the military manuals of Australia (*ibid.*, § 26), Bosnia and Herzegovina (*ibid.*, § 29), Canada (*ibid.*, § 32), Colombia (*ibid.*, § 33), Ecuador (*ibid.*, § 34), Germany (*ibid.*, §§ 38–40), Italy (*ibid.*, § 42), Kenya (*ibid.*, § 43), South Africa (*ibid.*, § 49), Spain (*ibid.*, § 50) and Yugoslavia (*ibid.*, § 60).

[21] See, e.g., the legislation of Armenia (*ibid.*, § 61), Australia (*ibid.*, § 63), Belarus (*ibid.*, § 65), Canada (*ibid.*, § 68), Croatia (*ibid.*, § 74), Czech Republic (*ibid.*, § 75), Ecuador (*ibid.*, § 77), Estonia (*ibid.*, § 78), Finland (*ibid.*, § 79), France (*ibid.*, § 80), Georgia (*ibid.*, § 81), Germany (*ibid.*, § 82), India (*ibid.*, § 84), Ireland (*ibid.*, § 85), Italy (*ibid.*, § 87), Japan (*ibid.*, §§ 88–89), Kazakhstan (*ibid.*, § 90), South Korea (*ibid.*, § 91), Luxembourg (*ibid.*, § 92), Netherlands (*ibid.*, § 96), New Zealand (*ibid.*, § 97), Norway (*ibid.*, § 98), Panama (*ibid.*, § 99), Peru (*ibid.*, § 100), Poland (*ibid.*, § 102), Romania (*ibid.*, § 103), Russia (*ibid.*, § 104), Singapore (*ibid.*, § 105), Slovenia (*ibid.*, § 106), South Africa (*ibid.*, § 107), Sweden (*ibid.*, § 108), Switzerland (*ibid.*, §§ 109–110), Tajikistan (*ibid.*, § 111), Ukraine (*ibid.*, § 113), United Kingdom (*ibid.*, § 114), United States (*ibid.*, § 116), Yugoslavia (*ibid.*, § 117) and Zimbabwe (*ibid.*, § 118); see also the legislation of Bulgaria (*ibid.*, § 66), Hungary (*ibid.*, § 83) and Italy (*ibid.*, § 86), the application of which is not excluded in time of non-international armed conflict.

[22] Colombia, Constitutional Court, *Constitutional Case No. C-225/95* (*ibid.*, § 119).

[23] See the statements of Russia (*ibid.*, § 350), Sudan (*ibid.*, § 366) and Turkey (*ibid.*, § 388).

[24] ICTY, *Tadić case*, Interlocutory Appeal (*ibid.*, § 499).

[25] United Kingdom, Statement by the FCO Spokesperson at a Press Conference (*ibid.*, § 406) and Draft resolution submitted at the UN Commission on Human Rights (*ibid.*, § 407).

[26] ICTY, *Tadić case*, Interlocutory Appeal (*ibid.*, § 499).

[27] ICRC, Memorandum on Respect for International Humanitarian Law in Angola (*ibid.*, § 512).

No official contrary practice was found. No State has claimed that chemical weapons may lawfully be used in either international or non-international armed conflicts. On the contrary, there are numerous statements to the effect that chemical weapons must never be used and must be eliminated.[28]

Rule 75. The use of riot-control agents as a method of warfare is prohibited.

Practice

Volume II, Chapter 24, Section B.

Summary

State practice establishes this rule as a norm of customary international law applicable in situations constituting military hostilities during international and non-international armed conflicts, as opposed to domestic riot control.

International armed conflicts

Before the adoption of the Chemical Weapons Convention, there was disagreement as to whether riot-control agents are prohibited under the Geneva Gas Protocol. The vast majority of States are of the opinion that the Geneva Gas Protocol prohibits the use of all asphyxiating and poisonous gases and analogous materials, including riot-control agents, and apply it as such.[29] In the late

---

[28] See, e.g., the statements of Afghanistan (*ibid.*, §§ 121–122), Albania (*ibid.*, § 124), Algeria (*ibid.*, §§ 125–126), Armenia (*ibid.*, § 132), Australia (*ibid.*, § 136), Austria (*ibid.*, §§ 139–140), Bahrain (*ibid.*, § 141), Bangladesh (*ibid.*, § 143), Belarus (*ibid.*, §§ 146–147), Belgium (*ibid.*, § 153), Benin (*ibid.*, § 154), Brazil (*ibid.*, § 158), Bulgaria (*ibid.*, § 162), Burkina Faso (*ibid.*, § 166), Burma (*ibid.*, § 167), Cameroon (*ibid.*, § 169), Canada (*ibid.*, §§ 172 and 174), Chile (*ibid.*, § 176), China (*ibid.*, §§ 178–181 and 183), Colombia (*ibid.*, § 184), Cuba (*ibid.*, §§ 190–191 and 194), Czech Republic (*ibid.*, § 200), Ecuador (*ibid.*, §§ 206–207), El Salvador (*ibid.*, § 212), Ethiopia (*ibid.*, §§ 213–215), Finland (*ibid.*, § 218), France (*ibid.*, §§ 221–222 and 224), Federal Republic of Germany (*ibid.*, §§ 228–229), German Democratic Republic (*ibid.*, § 231), Germany (*ibid.*, § 233), Ghana (*ibid.*, § 234), Greece (*ibid.*, § 238), Guinea (*ibid.*, § 239), Haiti (*ibid.*, §§ 240–241), Honduras (*ibid.*, § 242), India (*ibid.*, §§ 244 and 246), Iran (*ibid.*, § 253), Israel (*ibid.*, §§ 261–263), Italy (*ibid.*, § 268), Japan (*ibid.*, §§ 271–272 and 275), Democratic Kampuchea (*ibid.*, § 279), South Korea (*ibid.*, § 286), Libya (*ibid.*, §§ 298–299), Liechtenstein (*ibid.*, § 300), Malaysia (*ibid.*, §§ 303 and 305), Mexico (*ibid.*, §§ 311–312), Mongolia (*ibid.*, § 314), Nepal (*ibid.*, § 316), Netherlands (*ibid.*, §§ 317 and 320), Nigeria (*ibid.*, § 327), Norway (*ibid.*, § 329), Pakistan (*ibid.*, § 332), Peru (*ibid.*, § 335), Qatar (*ibid.*, § 346), Romania (*ibid.*, § 349), Saudi Arabia (*ibid.*, §§ 354 and 356), South Africa (*ibid.*, § 360), Sri Lanka (*ibid.*, §§ 362–363), Sweden (*ibid.*, §§ 367–369 and 371), Switzerland (*ibid.*, § 376), Syria (*ibid.*, § 377), Thailand (*ibid.*, §§ 381 and 383), Tunisia (*ibid.*, § 385), Turkey (*ibid.*, § 386), Ukraine (*ibid.*, §§ 390–391 and 393), USSR (*ibid.*, § 398), United Kingdom (*ibid.*, §§ 403, 405–406 and 412), United States (*ibid.*, §§ 427–428), Venezuela (*ibid.*, § 433), Vietnam (*ibid.*, § 435), Yemen (*ibid.*, § 437), Yugoslavia (*ibid.*, § 438) and Zaire (*ibid.*, § 441); see also the practice of Belarus (*ibid.*, § 149), Belgium (*ibid.*, § 153), Indonesia (*ibid.*, § 248), North Korea (*ibid.*, § 283) and the reported practice of Jordan (*ibid.*, § 277).

[29] See, e.g., the statements of Canada (*ibid.*, § 568), China (*ibid.*, § 568), Czechoslovakia (*ibid.*, § 568), France (*ibid.*, § 560), Italy (*ibid.*, § 561), Japan (*ibid.*, § 568), Romania (*ibid.*, § 568), Spain (*ibid.*, § 568), Turkey (*ibid.*, § 564), USSR (*ibid.*, § 565), United Kingdom (*ibid.*, § 568) and Yugoslavia (*ibid.*, § 568).

1960s and early 1970s, Australia, Portugal and the United Kingdom changed their earlier positions, stating that the Geneva Gas Protocol did not apply to certain riot-control agents.[30] A consistent exception to the majority view is that of the United States, which maintains that the customary prohibition of chemical weapons does not apply to agents with temporary effects.[31] During the Vietnam War, when it was not yet a party to the Geneva Gas Protocol, the United States declared that it had applied the Protocol's provisions, which did not stop it from using riot-control agents.[32] However, the United States is now a party to the Chemical Weapons Convention, which prohibits the use of riot-control agents as a method of warfare and which allows no reservations. The United States has therefore renounced "first use of riot control agents in war except in defensive military modes to save lives" because, according to the United States, use in such modes would not constitute a "method of warfare".[33]

During the negotiations leading to the adoption of the Chemical Weapons Convention, the vast majority of States, including Australia and the United Kingdom, were of the view that riot-control agents must not be used in hostilities. The final wording of the treaty makes a distinction between use during hostilities as a method of warfare, which is prohibited, and use for purposes of law-enforcement, which is permitted.[34] This distinction has been confirmed by State practice since then. In particular, the prohibition of the use of riot control agents as a method of warfare is set forth in several military manuals.[35] It is also included in the legislation of several States.[36]

---

[30] Australia, Statement before the First Committee of the UN General Assembly (*ibid.*, § 557) and *Protection of the Civil Population Against the Effects of Certain Weapons* (*ibid.*, § 558); Portugal, Vote against Resolution 2603 A (XXIV) of the UN General Assembly (*ibid.*, § 586); United Kingdom, Reply by the Secretary of State for Foreign and Commonwealth Affairs in the House of Commons (*ibid.*, § 569); see also New Zealand, *Military Manual* (*ibid.*, § 541).

[31] See, e.g., United States, Statement before the First Committee of the UN General Assembly (*ibid.*, § 577), Statement at the Diplomatic Conference leading to the adoption of the Additional Protocols (*ibid.*, § 580) and Memorandum of law of the Department of State on the "Reported Use of Chemical Agents in Afghanistan, Laos, and Kampuchea" (*ibid.*, § 581).

[32] See, e.g., United States, Department of the Navy, Legal Review of Oleoresin Capsicum (OC) Pepper Spray (*ibid.*, § 584) and Department of Defense, Review of Allegations Concerning "Operation Tailwind" (*ibid.*, § 585).

[33] United States, *Naval Handbook* (*ibid.*, § 548), Executive Order No. 11850 (*ibid.*, § 578) and Message from the US President transmitting the report on the chemical weapons convention (*ibid.*, § 582). When the US Senate gave its advice and consent for ratification of the Convention on Chemical Weapons it required that "the President shall take no measure, and prescribe no rule or regulation, which would alter or eliminate Executive Order 11850 of April 8, 1975". US Senate, Executive Resolution 75, 24 April 1997.

[34] Chemical Weapons Convention, Article I(5) (cited in Vol. II, Ch. 24, § 528) and Article II(9)(d) (*ibid.*, § 532).

[35] See, e.g., the military manuals of Australia (*ibid.*, §§ 534–535), Canada (*ibid.*, §§ 537–538), Germany (*ibid.*, § 539), Netherlands (*ibid.*, § 540), New Zealand (*ibid.*, § 541), Spain (*ibid.*, § 542) and United States (*ibid.*, § 548).

[36] See, e.g., the legislation of Australia (*ibid.*, § 549), Hungary (*ibid.*, § 550), India (*ibid.*, § 551), New Zealand (*ibid.*, § 552), Romania (*ibid.*, § 553), Singapore (*ibid.*, § 554) and Sweden (*ibid.*, § 555).

Non-international armed conflicts

Although the use of riot control agents has been reported in the Greek and Spanish civil wars and by South Vietnam in the Vietnam War,[37] the trend has been towards a prohibition of their use in all armed conflicts. This is reflected in the fact that the prohibition of the use of riot-control agents as a method of warfare contained in the Chemical Weapons Convention applies to all conflicts. It is significant that States did not consider making a general exception in the Convention allowing for the use of riot-control agents in non-international armed conflicts.

The prohibition of the use of riot control agents as a method of warfare in non-international armed conflicts is also set forth in several military manuals.[38] The United States has stated that the prohibition of the use of riot control agents as a method of warfare "applies in international as well as internal armed conflict".[39]

No official contrary practice was found with respect to either international or non-international armed conflicts. No State has claimed the right to use riot control agents as a method of warfare in military hostilities. As explained in the military manual of the Netherlands, the prohibition of the use of riot control agents as a method of warfare is inspired by the fact that use of tear gas, for example, in armed conflict "runs the danger of provoking the use of other more dangerous chemicals".[40] A party which is being attacked by riot control agents may think it is being attacked by deadly chemical weapons and resort to the use of chemical weapons. It is this danger of escalation that States sought to avert by agreeing to prohibit the use of riot control agents as a method of warfare in armed conflict. This motivation is equally valid in international and non-international armed conflicts.

Rule 76. The use of herbicides as a method of warfare is prohibited if they:

(a) are of a nature to be prohibited chemical weapons;
(b) are of a nature to be prohibited biological weapons;
(c) are aimed at vegetation that is not a military objective;
(d) would cause incidental loss of civilian life, injury to civilians, damage to civilian objects, or a combination thereof, which may be expected to be excessive in relation to the concrete and direct military advantage anticipated; or
(e) would cause widespread, long-term and severe damage to the natural environment.

---

[37] See the reported practice in the context of the Spanish Civil War (*ibid.*, § 592), Greek Civil War (*ibid.*, § 593) and Vietnam War (*ibid.*, § 594).
[38] See, e.g., the military manuals of Australia (*ibid.*, § 534), Canada (*ibid.*, § 537), Germany (*ibid.*, § 539), Spain (*ibid.*, § 542) and United States (*ibid.*, § 548).
[39] United States, *Naval Handbook* (*ibid.*, § 548).
[40] Netherlands, *Military Manual* (*ibid.*, § 540).

Practice

Volume II, Chapter 24, Section C.

Summary

State practice establishes this rule as a norm of customary international law applicable in both international and non-international armed conflicts.

International armed conflicts

Before the adoption of the Chemical Weapons Convention, there was disagreement as to whether herbicides were prohibited under the Geneva Gas Protocol. In 1969, for example, 80 States voted in favour of a UN General Assembly resolution indicating that the use of herbicides would be contrary to "generally recognized rules of international law, as embodied in the Geneva Gas Protocol", although the 3 negative votes and 36 abstentions show that this was not a universally held view.[41] In particular, several States considered that the use of herbicides and defoliants was not prohibited under the Geneva Gas Protocol.[42]

The experience of the Vietnam War, however, revealed the potentially long-term serious effects of herbicides on human health. This use was condemned by other States.[43] Developments in international law since then have attached increased importance to the protection of the environment. It is clear that any use of herbicides in warfare would be controversial, in particular in the light of the clear trend in favour of protecting the environment against deliberate damage. Environmental considerations reportedly led the United States to end its herbicidal programme.[44]

It is relevant in this respect that the Final Declaration of the Second Review Conference of the Parties to the ENMOD Convention reaffirmed that the military and any other hostile use of herbicides as an environmental modification technique is a prohibited method of warfare "if such a use of herbicides upsets the ecological balance of a region, thus causing widespread, long-lasting or severe effects as the means of destruction, damage or injury to another State Party".[45] In a resolution adopted without a vote, the UN General Assembly noted with satisfaction this reaffirmation.[46] Some States welcomed it as a

---

[41] UN General Assembly, Res. 2603 A (XXIV) (*ibid.*, § 630).

[42] See, e.g., the statements of Australia (*ibid.*, § 615), United Kingdom (*ibid.*, § 624) and United States (*ibid.*, §§ 625–626).

[43] See, e.g., the statements of China (*ibid.*, § 617) and Hungary (*ibid.*, § 619); see also the statement of China (*ibid.*, § 618).

[44] See William A. Buckingham, *Operation Ranch Hand: The Air Force and Herbicides in Southeast Asia, 1961–1971* (*ibid.*, § 628).

[45] Second Review Conference of the Parties to the ENMOD Convention, Final Declaration (*ibid.*, § 633).

[46] UN General Assembly, Res. 47/52 E (*ibid.*, § 631).

confirmation of the ban on the use of herbicides as a method of warfare.[47] These and other considerations led the negotiators of the Chemical Weapons Convention to recognise "the prohibition, embodied in pertinent agreements and relevant principles of international law, of the use of herbicides as a method of warfare".[48]

The Chemical Weapons Convention does not, however, define what use would qualify as a method of warfare. The United States, for example, has stated that it reserves the right to use herbicides "for control of vegetation within U.S. bases and installations or around their immediate defensive perimeters".[49]

It is clear, however, that the use of herbicides in armed conflict as a method of warfare would violate the general prohibition of the use of chemical weapons if they are of a nature to harm humans or animals (see Rule 74). In addition, the use of herbicides consisting of, or containing, biological agents would violate the Biological Weapons Convention in that it prohibits the use of all biological agents that are not for prophylactic, protective or other peaceful purposes (see Rule 73).

In addition, attacks on vegetation by herbicides would violate the general rules on the conduct of hostilities if the vegetation is not a military objective (see Rule 7), if the attack causes excessive incidental civilian losses or damage to civilian objects (see Rule 14) or if the attack may be expected to cause widespread, long-term and severe damage to the natural environment (see Rule 45).

Other rules of international humanitarian law that may be relevant to the use of herbicides are the prohibition of starvation as a method of warfare (see Rule 53) and the prohibition on attacking objects indispensable to the survival of the civilian population (see Rule 54), in case herbicides would be used against crops.

Non-international armed conflicts

Although there is less specific practice concerning the use of herbicides in non-international armed conflicts, the specific limitations on or prohibitions of the use of herbicides contained in this rule are general rules that apply also to non-international armed conflicts.

In addition, recent allegations of possible use in Chechnya were denied by the Russian government.[50] This shows that there is a legitimate expectation on the part of States that herbicides must not be used in a way that would violate other rules applicable in any type of armed conflict.

---

[47] See the statements of Argentina (*ibid.*, § 614) and Sweden (*ibid.*, § 614); see also the statement of the Netherlands (*ibid.*, § 620).
[48] Chemical Weapons Convention, preamble (*ibid.*, § 599).
[49] United States, Executive Order No. 11850 (*ibid.*, § 627).
[50] See "Russian army not to use defoliants in Chechnya", ITAR-TASS, Moscow, 17 April 2000 (*ibid.*, § 622).

EXPANDING BULLETS

Rule 77. The use of bullets which expand or flatten easily in the human body is prohibited.

Practice

Volume II, Chapter 25.

Summary

State practice establishes this rule as a norm of customary international law applicable in both international and non-international armed conflicts.

International armed conflicts

The prohibition in respect of international armed conflicts was introduced in 1899 by the Hague Declaration concerning Expanding Bullets in reaction to the development of the so-called "dum-dum" bullet for use in military rifles.[1] The Declaration was ratified or acceded to by 28 States in the early years of the 20th century and 6 States succeeded to the Declaration in the second half of the 20th century.[2] The use of expanding bullets is listed as a war crime in the Statute of the International Criminal Court.[3] The prohibition has also been included in other instruments.[4]

---

[1] Hague Declaration concerning Expanding Bullets (cited in Vol. II, Ch. 25, § 1).

[2] The following states ratified or acceded to the Declaration: Austria-Hungary (4 September 1900), Belgium (4 September 1900), Bulgaria (4 September 1900), China (21 November 1904), Denmark (4 September 1900), Ethiopia (9 August 1935), France (4 September 1900), Germany (4 September 1900), Great Britain and Ireland (13 August 1907), Greece (4 April 1901), Italy (4 September 1900), Japan (6 October 1900), Luxembourg (12 July 1901), Mexico (17 April 1901), Montenegro (16 October 1900), Netherlands (4 September 1900), Nicaragua (11 October 1907), Norway (4 September 1900), Persia (4 September 1900), Portugal (29 August 1907), Romania (4 September 1900), Russia (4 September 1900), Serbia (11 May 1901), Siam (4 September 1900), Spain (4 September 1900), Sweden (4 September 1900), Switzerland (29 December 1900) and Turkey (12 June 1907). The following States succeeded to the Declaration: Byelorussian Socialist Soviet Republic (4 June 1962), Fiji (2 April 1973), German Democratic Republic (9 February 1959), South Africa (10 March 1978), USSR (7 March 1955) and Yugoslavia (8 April 1969).

[3] ICC Statute, Article 8(2)(b)(xix) (cited in Vol. II, Ch. 25, § 2).

[4] See, e.g., Oxford Manual of Naval War, Article 16(2) (*ibid.*, § 3); Report of the Commission on Responsibility (*ibid.*, § 4); UN Secretary-General's Bulletin, Section 6.2 (*ibid.*, § 5); UNTAET Regulation No. 2000/15, Section 6(1)(b)(xix) (*ibid.*, § 6).

The prohibition of expanding bullets is set forth in numerous military manuals.[5] The use of expanding bullets in armed conflict is an offence under the legislation of many States.[6] The prohibition is also supported by official statements and other practice.[7] This practice includes that of many States which are not party to the Hague Declaration.[8]

Practice is in conformity with the prohibition and no State has asserted that it would be lawful to use such ammunition. The only exception to a complete prohibition of the use of expanding bullets is possibly the practice of the United States, although it is ambiguous. While several of its military manuals prohibit the use of expanding bullets,[9] three legal reviews of ammunition and weapons by the US Department of the Army state that the United States will adhere to the Hague Declaration to the extent that the rule is consistent with Article 23(e) of the 1907 Hague Regulations, i.e. the prohibition of weapons causing unnecessary suffering.[10] Hence, the use of expanding ammunition is lawful according to the United States if there is "a clear showing of military necessity for its use".[11] However, during the negotiation of the Statute of the International Criminal Court in 1998, the United States did not contest the criminality of the use of expanding ammunition.

---

[5] See, e.g., the military manuals of Australia (*ibid.*, §§ 7–8), Belgium (*ibid.*, § 9), Cameroon (*ibid.*, § 10), Canada (*ibid.*, §§ 11–12), Dominican Republic (*ibid.*, § 13), Ecuador (*ibid.*, § 14), France (*ibid.*, §§ 15–17), Germany (*ibid.*, §§ 18–20), Israel (*ibid.*, § 21), Italy (*ibid.*, § 22), Kenya (*ibid.*, § 23), Netherlands (*ibid.*, §§ 24–25), New Zealand (*ibid.*, § 26), Nigeria (*ibid.*, § 27), Russia (*ibid.*, § 28), South Africa (*ibid.*, § 29), Spain (*ibid.*, § 30), United Kingdom (*ibid.*, § 31) and United States (*ibid.*, §§ 33–35).

[6] See, e.g., the legislation of Andorra (*ibid.*, § 36), Australia (*ibid.*, §§ 37–38), Canada (*ibid.*, § 40), Congo (*ibid.*, § 41), Ecuador (*ibid.*, § 42), Estonia (*ibid.*, § 43), Georgia (*ibid.*, § 44), Germany (*ibid.*, § 45), Italy (*ibid.*, § 46), Mali (*ibid.*, § 47), Netherlands (*ibid.*, § 48), New Zealand (*ibid.*, § 50), United Kingdom (*ibid.*, § 52) and Yugoslavia (*ibid.*, § 53); see also the draft legislation of Burundi (*ibid.*, § 39) and Trinidad and Tobago (*ibid.*, § 51).

[7] See, e.g., the statements of Algeria (*ibid.*, § 55), Canada (*ibid.*, § 56), Colombia (*ibid.*, § 57), Egypt (*ibid.*, § 58), Finland (*ibid.*, § 60), Iraq (*ibid.*, § 64), Italy (*ibid.*, § 65), Philippines (*ibid.*, § 67), Sweden (*ibid.*, §§ 68–69), Switzerland (*ibid.*, § 70), United States (*ibid.*, §§ 71 and 73–77) and Yugoslavia (*ibid.*, §§ 78–79), the practice of Indonesia (*ibid.*, § 63) and the reported practice of India (*ibid.*, § 62) and Jordan (*ibid.*, § 66).

[8] See, e.g., the military manuals of Australia (*ibid.*, §§ 7–8), Cameroon (*ibid.*, § 10), Canada (*ibid.*, §§ 11–12), Dominican Republic (*ibid.*, § 13), Ecuador (*ibid.*, § 14), Israel (*ibid.*, § 21), Kenya (*ibid.*, § 23), New Zealand (*ibid.*, § 26), Nigeria (*ibid.*, § 27) and United States (*ibid.*, §§ 33–35), the legislation of Andorra (*ibid.*, § 36), Australia (*ibid.*, §§ 37–38), Canada (*ibid.*, § 40), Congo (*ibid.*, § 41), Ecuador (*ibid.*, § 42), Estonia (*ibid.*, § 43), Georgia (*ibid.*, § 44), Mali (*ibid.*, § 47) and New Zealand (*ibid.*, § 50), the draft legislation of Burundi (*ibid.*, § 39) and Trinidad and Tobago (*ibid.*, § 51), the statements of Algeria (*ibid.*, § 55), Canada (*ibid.*, § 56), Colombia (*ibid.*, § 57), Egypt (*ibid.*, § 58), Finland (*ibid.*, § 60), Iraq (*ibid.*, § 64), Philippines (*ibid.*, § 67) and United States (*ibid.*, §§ 71 and 73–77), the practice of Indonesia (*ibid.*, § 63) and the reported practice of India (*ibid.*, § 62) and Jordan (*ibid.*, § 66).

[9] United States, *Field Manual* (*ibid.*, § 33), *Air Force Pamphlet* (*ibid.*, § 34) and *Instructor's Guide* (*ibid.*, § 35).

[10] United States, Department of the Army, Memorandum of Law on Sniper Use of Open-Tip Ammunition (*ibid.*, §§ 74–75), Legal Review of USSOCOM Special Operations Offensive Handgun (*ibid.*, § 76) and Legal Review of the Fabrique Nationale 5.7 × 28mm Weapon System (*ibid.*, § 77).

[11] United States, Department of the Army, Legal Review of USSOCOM Special Operations Offensive Handgun (*ibid.*, § 76).

Non-international armed conflicts

The prohibition of expanding bullets in any armed conflict is set forth in several military manuals.[12] The use of expanding bullets is an offence under the legislation of several States.[13] Colombia's Constitutional Court has held that the prohibition of "dum-dum" bullets in non-international armed conflicts is part of customary international law.[14]

Practice is in conformity with the rule's applicability in both international and non-international armed conflicts, as the same ammunition is used in non-international conflicts as in international conflicts, and bullets which expand or flatten easily in the human body are not employed in either case. That this general abstention is not purely coincidental can be deduced also from the fact that weapons which cause unnecessary suffering are prohibited in both international and non-international armed conflicts (see Rule 70) and that there is general agreement that such bullets would cause unnecessary suffering.[15]

No official contrary practice was found with respect to either international or non-international armed conflicts. With the possible exception of the United States, no State has claimed that it has the right to use expanding bullets. However, several States have decided that for domestic law-enforcement purposes, outside armed conflict, in particular where it is necessary to confront an armed person in an urban environment or crowd of people, expanding bullets may be used by police to ensure that the bullets used do not pass through the body of a suspect into another person and to increase the chance that once hit, the suspect is instantly prevented from firing back. It should be noted that expanding bullets commonly used by police in situations other than armed conflict are fired from a pistol and therefore deposit much less energy than a normal rifle bullet or a rifle bullet which expands or flattens easily. Police forces therefore do not normally use the type of expanding bullet that is prohibited for military rifles.

The introduction of expanding bullets for police use indicates that States consider such bullets necessary for certain law-enforcement purposes. However, the use of expanding bullets has not been introduced for hostilities in armed conflicts.

---

[12] See, e.g., the military manuals of Australia (*ibid.*, § 7), Canada (*ibid.*, § 12), Ecuador (*ibid.*, § 14), France (*ibid.*, §§ 16–17) ("totally prohibited"), Germany (*ibid.*, §§ 18–20), Italy (*ibid.*, § 22), Kenya (*ibid.*, § 23), South Africa (*ibid.*, § 29) and Spain (*ibid.*, § 30) ("absolute prohibition").

[13] See, e.g., the legislation of Andorra (*ibid.*, § 36), Ecuador (*ibid.*, § 42), Estonia (*ibid.*, § 43), Germany (*ibid.*, § 45) and Yugoslavia (*ibid.*, § 53); see also the legislation of Italy (*ibid.*, § 46), the application of which is not excluded in time of non-international armed conflict.

[14] Colombia, Constitutional Court, *Constitutional Case No. C-225/95* (*ibid.*, § 54).

[15] See, e.g., Hague Declaration concerning Expanding Bullets (cited in Vol. II, Ch. 20, § 3); the military manual of Australia (*ibid.*, § 34) ("hollow point weapons"), Ecuador (*ibid.*, § 52), France (*ibid.*, §§ 55–56), Germany (*ibid.*, §§ 57–59), Netherlands (*ibid.*, §§ 71–72), Russia (*ibid.*, § 78), South Africa (*ibid.*, 80), United States (*ibid.*, § 91) and Yugoslavia (*ibid.*, § 94).

Interpretation

As far as the design of the bullets is concerned, a number of military manuals refer to the wording of the Hague Declaration or specify that "dum-dum" bullets (i.e., "soft-nosed" or "hollow-point" bullets) are prohibited.[16] However, most manuals specifically refer to the fact that the bullet expands or flattens easily, rather than to whether it has a hollow point, soft nose or incisions, as indicated by way of example in the Hague Declaration.[17] Germany's Military Manual adds examples of other types of projectiles that create large wounds similar to those caused by "dum-dum" bullets: projectiles of a nature to burst or deform while penetrating the human body, to tumble early in the human body or to cause shock waves leading to extensive tissue damage or even lethal shock.[18] A memorandum of law on sniper use of open-tip ammunition prepared by the US Department of the Army in 1990 found that a certain type of hollow-point bullet was not unlawful because it did not expand or flatten easily, and the particular circumstances of intended use, namely by army snipers, was justified because of the accuracy at long range that the design allowed.[19]

[16] See, e.g., the military manuals of Australia (cited in Vol. II, Ch. 25, §§ 7–8), Dominican Republic (*ibid.*, § 13), Germany (*ibid.*, § 18), Israel (*ibid.*, § 21), Netherlands (*ibid.*, § 25), New Zealand (*ibid.*, § 26), South Africa (*ibid.*, § 29), United Kingdom (*ibid.*, §§ 31–32) and United States (*ibid.*, §§ 33 and 35).

[17] See, e.g., the military manuals of Belgium (*ibid.*, § 9), Cameroon (*ibid.*, § 10), Canada (*ibid.*, §§ 11–12), Ecuador (*ibid.*, § 14), France (*ibid.*, §§ 15–17), Germany (*ibid.*, §§ 19–20), Italy (*ibid.*, § 22), Kenya (*ibid.*, § 23), Netherlands (*ibid.*, § 24), Nigeria (*ibid.*, § 27), Russia (*ibid.*, § 28), Spain (*ibid.*, § 30) and United States (*ibid.*, § 34).

[18] Germany, *Military Manual* (*ibid.*, § 19).

[19] United States, Department of the Army, Memorandum of Law on Sniper Use of Open-Tip Ammunition (*ibid.*, § 75).

EXPLODING BULLETS

Rule 78. The anti-personnel use of bullets which explode within the human body is prohibited.

Practice

Volume II, Chapter 26.

Summary

State practice establishes this rule as a norm of customary international law applicable in both international and non-international armed conflicts.

International armed conflicts

The prohibition of exploding bullets originated in 1868 with the adoption of the St. Petersburg Declaration, which was motivated by the desire to avoid inflicting suffering which exceeded that needed to render a combatant *hors de combat*. To this end, the Declaration specifically prohibits the use of "any projectile of a weight below 400 grammes, which is either explosive or charged with fulminating or inflammable substances", 400 grams being the weight of the smallest artillery shell at the time.[1] Nineteen States adhered to the St. Petersburg Declaration in 1868 or 1869, i.e., most of the States in existence at that time.[2] The prohibition contained in the St. Petersburg Declaration was repeated in the Brussels Declaration, the Oxford Manual and the Oxford Manual of Naval War.[3] The Report of the Commission on Responsibility set up after the First World War identified the use of "explosive bullets" as a war crime under customary international law.[4]

Practice since the adoption of the St. Petersburg Declaration has modified this prohibition, as exploding anti-aircraft bullets were introduced in the First

---

[1] St. Petersburg Declaration (cited in Vol. II, Ch. 26, § 1).
[2] Austria-Hungary, Baden, Bavaria, Belgium, Brazil, Denmark, France, Greece, Italy, Netherlands, Persia, Portugal, Prussia and the North German Confederation, Russia, Sweden and Norway, Switzerland, Turkey, United Kingdom and Würtemberg. Estonia adhered in 1991.
[3] Brussels Declaration, Article 13(e) (*ibid.*, § 2); Oxford Manual, Article 9(a) (*ibid.*, § 3); Oxford Manual of Naval War, Article 16(2) (*ibid.*, § 4).
[4] Report of the Commission on Responsibility (*ibid.*, § 5).

World War.[5] Furthermore, lighter grenades and exploding anti-materiel bullets have been introduced since. These developments have occurred without any objection. The military manuals or statements of several States consider only the anti-personnel use of such projectiles to be prohibited or only if they are designed to explode upon impact with the human body.[6] Some military manuals and legislation, nevertheless, continue to refer back to the wording of the prohibition contained in the St. Petersburg Declaration, even though practice has since modified this prohibition.[7]

Further to concerns that arose following tests which showed that certain 12.7 mm bullets exploded in human tissue simulant, the ICRC convened, in 1999, a group of military, legal and ballistics experts from four States that manufactured or stocked the 12.7 mm exploding bullet (and therefore "specially affected" States). The governmental experts, who participated in their personal capacity, agreed that the targeting of combatants with bullets the foreseeable effect of which was to explode on impact with the human body would be contrary to the object and purpose of the St. Petersburg Declaration.[8]

Non-international armed conflicts

The prohibition of exploding bullets in any armed conflict is contained in several military manuals and in the legislation of several States.[9] It is also supported by other practice.[10] In addition, the UN Secretary-General's Bulletin on observance by United Nations forces of international humanitarian law, which is not limited to international armed conflicts, prohibits the use of bullets which explode in the human body.[11]

---

[5] This development is reflected in Article 18 of the Hague Rules of Air Warfare (*ibid.*, § 6), which states that "the use of tracer, incendiary or explosive projectiles by or against aircraft is not prohibited. This provision applies equally to states which are parties to the Declaration of St. Petersburg, 1868, and to those which are not."

[6] See, e.g., the military manuals of Germany (*ibid.*, § 13), Italy (*ibid.*, § 14) and United Kingdom (*ibid.*, §§ 18–19) and the statements of Brazil (*ibid.*, § 28) and United States (*ibid.*, §§ 35–36).

[7] See, e.g., the military manuals of Australia (*ibid.*, §§ 8–9), Canada (*ibid.*, § 11), New Zealand (*ibid.*, § 15), Spain (*ibid.*, § 17), United States (*ibid.*, § 20), the legislation of Andorra (*ibid.*, § 21), Australia (*ibid.*, § 22), Ecuador (*ibid.*, § 23) and Yugoslavia (*ibid.*, § 26) and the statements of Brazil (*ibid.*, § 28), Colombia (*ibid.*, § 29), and Yugoslavia (*ibid.*, § 37); see also the reported practice of Indonesia (*ibid.*, § 30) and Jordan (*ibid.*, § 31).

[8] See ICRC, Statement before the First Committee of the UN General Assembly (*ibid.*, § 46) and Ensuring respect for the 1868 St. Petersburg Declaration: Prohibiting the use of certain explosive projectiles, Report submitted to the Third Preparatory Committee for the Second Review Conference of the States Parties to the CCW (*ibid.*, § 47).

[9] See, e.g., the military manuals of Australia (*ibid.*, § 8), Germany (*ibid.*, § 13), Italy (*ibid.*, § 14) and Spain (*ibid.*, § 17) ("total prohibition") and the legislation of Andorra (*ibid.*, § 21), Ecuador (*ibid.*, § 23) and Yugoslavia (*ibid.*, § 26); see also the legislation of Italy (*ibid.*, § 24), the application of which is not excluded in time of non-international armed conflict.

[10] See, e.g., the statement of Yugoslavia (*ibid.*, § 37) and the reported practice of Indonesia (*ibid.*, 30) and Jordan (*ibid.*, § 31).

[11] UN Secretary-General's Bulletin, Section 6.2 (*ibid.*, § 7).

Practice shows no evidence of the anti-personnel use of bullets which explode within the human body in non-international armed conflicts. In particular, States have indicated that the anti-personnel use of exploding bullets would cause unnecessary suffering.[12] The rule prohibiting means of warfare which cause unnecessary suffering is applicable in both international and non-international armed conflicts (see Rule 70).

No official contrary practice was found with respect to either international or non-international armed conflicts. No State has claimed the right to use against personnel bullets which explode within the human body. The effect of bullets which explode within the human body are much worse than that of expanding bullets, which are also prohibited (see Rule 77).

---

[12] See, e.g., St. Petersburg Declaration (*ibid.*, § 1) and the military manuals of Germany (cited in Vol. II, Ch. 20, § 58) and Russia (*ibid.*, § 78).

WEAPONS PRIMARILY INJURING BY NON-DETECTABLE FRAGMENTS

Rule 79. The use of weapons the primary effect of which is to injure by fragments which are not detectable by X-rays in the human body is prohibited.

Practice

Volume II, Chapter 27.

Summary

State practice establishes this rule as a norm of customary international law applicable in both international and non-international armed conflicts.

International armed conflicts

Protocol I to the Convention on Certain Conventional Weapons prohibits the use of weapons the primary effect of which is to injure by fragments not detectable by X-rays.[1] It was adopted without any controversy.

The prohibition is contained in numerous military manuals.[2] The use of weapons injuring by fragments not detectable by X-rays is a war crime under the legislation of some States.[3] It is also supported by official statements and reported practice.[4] This practice includes that of

---

[1] Protocol I to the CCW (cited in Vol. II, Ch. 27, § 1).
[2] See, e.g., the military manuals of Argentina (*ibid.*, § 8), Australia (*ibid.*, §§ 9–10), Belgium (*ibid.*, § 11), Canada (*ibid.*, § 12), Ecuador (*ibid.*, § 13), France (*ibid.*, §§ 14–15), Germany (*ibid.*, §§ 16–17), Israel (*ibid.*, § 18), Italy (*ibid.*, § 19), Kenya (*ibid.*, § 20), Netherlands (*ibid.*, § 21), New Zealand (*ibid.*, § 22), Nigeria (*ibid.*, § 23), Russia (*ibid.*, § 24), South Africa (*ibid.*, § 25), Spain (*ibid.*, § 26), Sweden (*ibid.*, § 27), Switzerland (*ibid.*, § 28), United Kingdom (*ibid.*, §§ 29–30) and United States (*ibid.*, §§ 31–34).
[3] See, e.g., the legislation of Estonia (*ibid.*, § 35) and Hungary (*ibid.*, § 36).
[4] See, e.g., the statements of Australia (*ibid.*, §§ 39–40), Austria (*ibid.*, §§ 38–39), Belarus (*ibid.*, § 39), Belgium (*ibid.*, § 39), Bulgaria (*ibid.*, § 39), Canada (*ibid.*, § 39), Colombia (*ibid.*, § 38), Cuba (*ibid.*, § 39), Denmark (*ibid.*, §§ 38–39), Finland (*ibid.*, § 39), France (*ibid.*, § 39), Federal Republic of Germany (*ibid.*, §§ 38–39), German Democratic Republic (*ibid.*, § 39), Greece (*ibid.*, § 39), Hungary (*ibid.*, § 39), India (*ibid.*, § 41), Ireland (*ibid.*, § 39), Italy (*ibid.*, § 39), Jamaica (*ibid.*, § 39), Mexico (*ibid.*, §§ 38–39), Morocco (*ibid.*, § 39), Netherlands (*ibid.*, §§ 39 and 45), New Zealand (*ibid.*, § 39), Norway (*ibid.*, §§ 38–39), Panama (*ibid.*, § 39), Philippines (*ibid.*, § 39), Poland (*ibid.*, § 39), Portugal (*ibid.*, § 39), Romania (*ibid.*, § 39), Spain (*ibid.*, §§ 38–39), Sudan (*ibid.*, § 39), Sweden (*ibid.*, §§ 38–39), Switzerland (*ibid.*, §§ 38–39), Syria (*ibid.*, § 39), Togo (*ibid.*, § 39), Ukraine (*ibid.*, § 39), USSR (*ibid.*, § 39), United Kingdom (*ibid.*, § 39), United States

States not at the time party to the Convention on Certain Conventional Weapons.[5]

Non-international armed conflicts

When adopted, Protocol I to the Convention on Certain Conventional Weapons only applied to international armed conflicts. However, on ratification of the Convention, France, Israel and the United States stated that they would apply the Protocol to non-international armed conflicts as well.[6] At the Second Review Conference of the Convention on Certain Conventional Weapons in 2001, the Convention was amended to extend application of the Protocol also to non-international armed conflicts.[7] The amendment was not controversial during the negotiations and has meanwhile entered into force.[8] In addition, the UN Secretary-General's Bulletin on observance by United Nations forces of international humanitarian law, which is not limited to international armed conflicts, prohibits the use of weapons primarily injuring by non-detectable fragments.[9]

The prohibition in any armed conflict is contained in several military manuals.[10] The use of weapons injuring by fragments not detectable by X-rays is a war crime under the legislation of some States.[11] It is also supported by official statements and reported practice.[12]

Practice is in conformity with the rule's applicability in both international and non-international armed conflicts, as States generally do not have a different set of military weapons for international and non-international armed conflicts. No weapons the primary effect of which is to injure by non-detectable fragments appear to exist, although the ability to produce them has been widely available

---

(*ibid.*, §§ 38–39 and 46), Venezuela (*ibid.*, §§ 38–39), Yugoslavia (*ibid.*, §§ 38–39) and Zaire (*ibid.*, § 39) and the reported practice of India (*ibid.*, § 42), Indonesia (*ibid.*, § 43) and Jordan (*ibid.*, § 44).

[5] See, e.g., the military manuals of Argentina (*ibid.*, § 8), Belgium (*ibid.*, § 11), Italy (*ibid.*, § 19), Kenya (*ibid.*, § 20) and New Zealand (*ibid.*, § 22) and the reported practice of Indonesia (*ibid.*, § 43).

[6] France, Reservations made upon ratification of the CCW (*ibid.*, § 3); Israel, Declarations and understandings made upon accession to the CCW (*ibid.*, § 4); United States, Declaration made upon ratification of the CCW (*ibid.*, § 5).

[7] CCW, amended Article 1 (*ibid.*, § 6).

[8] The amendment entered into force on 18 May 2004. To date, 29 States have ratified the amended CCW: Argentina, Australia, Austria, Belgium, Bulgaria, Burkina Faso, Canada, China, Croatia, Estonia, Finland, France, Holy See, Hungary, Japan, Latvia, Liechtenstein, Lithuania, Mexico, Netherlands, Norway, Republic of Korea, Romania, Serbia and Montenegro, Slovakia, Spain, Sweden, Switzerland and United Kingdom.

[9] UN Secretary-General's Bulletin, Section 6.2 (cited in Vol. II, Ch. 27, § 7).

[10] See, e.g., the military manuals of Australia (*ibid.*, § 9), Ecuador (*ibid.*, § 13), France (*ibid.*, §§ 14–15) ("totally prohibited"), Germany (*ibid.*, §§ 16–17), Italy (*ibid.*, § 19), Kenya (*ibid.*, § 20), South Africa (*ibid.*, § 25) and Spain (*ibid.*, § 26) ("absolute prohibition").

[11] See, e.g., the legislation of Estonia (*ibid.*, § 35); see also the legislation of Hungary (*ibid.*, § 36), the application of which is not excluded in time of non-international armed conflict.

[12] See, e.g., the statement of India (*ibid.*, § 41) and the reported practice of India (*ibid.*, § 42), Indonesia (*ibid.*, § 43) and Jordan (*ibid.*, § 44).

for a very long time. That this general abstention is not purely coincidental can be deduced also from the fact that weapons which cause unnecessary suffering are prohibited in both international and non-international armed conflicts (see Rule 70) and that there is general agreement that such weapons would cause unnecessary suffering.[13]

No official contrary practice was found with respect to either international or non-international armed conflicts. No State has claimed that it may use weapons the primary effect of which is to injure by non-detectable fragments in any type of armed conflict.

Interpretation

The reasoning behind the adoption of Protocol I to the Convention on Certain Conventional Weapons was that weapons injuring by non-detectable fragments would make it very difficult to treat the resulting wounds, that the extra suffering caused by this difficulty has no military utility and that they would therefore cause unnecessary suffering. This view is supported by the assertion made in the UK Military Manual, drafted well before the adoption of Protocol I to the Convention on Certain Conventional Weapons, that the prohibition on causing unnecessary suffering included "projectiles filled with broken glass".[14] It is for this reason that Protocol I to the Convention on Certain Conventional Weapons specifies that prohibited weapons are those whose "primary effect" is to injure by non-detectable fragments. Weapons which contain plastic, for example, as part of their design, are therefore not illegal if the plastic is not part of the primary injuring mechanism.[15]

---

[13] See, e.g., the military manuals of Australia (cited in Vol. II, Ch. 20, § 34), Ecuador (*ibid.*, § 52), France (*ibid.*, §§ 55–56), Germany (*ibid.*, § 59), Netherlands (*ibid.*, §§ 71–72), New Zealand (*ibid.*, § 73), South Africa (*ibid.*, § 80), United Kingdom (*ibid.*, § 85) and United States (*ibid.*, §§ 87, 89, 91 and 93).

[14] United Kingdom, *Military Manual* (cited in Vol. II, Ch. 27, § 29); see also the military manuals of Nigeria (*ibid.*, § 23) and United States (*ibid.*, §§ 31–33).

[15] See, e.g., United States, Legal Review of Maverick Alternate Warhead (*ibid.*, § 46).

BOOBY-TRAPS

Rule 80. The use of booby-traps which are in any way attached to or associated with objects or persons entitled to special protection under international humanitarian law or with objects that are likely to attract civilians is prohibited.

Practice

Volume II, Chapter 28.

Summary

State practice establishes this rule as a norm of customary international law applicable in both international and non-international armed conflicts.

International armed conflicts

Both treaty practice and other State practice support the premise that booby-traps are prohibited if, by their nature or employment, their use violates the legal protection accorded to a protected person or object by another customary rule of international humanitarian law. This is the reasoning behind the list of booby-traps prohibited in Protocol II and Amended Protocol II to the Convention on Certain Conventional Weapons.[1]

The list of booby-traps prohibited by Protocol II and Amended Protocol II to the Convention on Certain Conventional Weapons is found in the military manuals and legislation of some States party to these treaties.[2] Other military manuals are more general in their description and stress that booby-traps associated with objects in normal civilian daily use are prohibited, and that booby-traps must not be used in association with protected persons, protected objects (such as medical supplies, gravesites and cultural or religious property) or internationally recognised protective emblems or signs (such as the red cross

---

[1] Protocol II to the CCW, Article 6(1) (cited in Vol. II, Ch. 28, § 5); Amended Protocol II to the CCW, Article 7(1) (*ibid.*, § 5).

[2] See, e.g., the military manuals of Australia (*ibid.*, §§ 30–31), Canada (*ibid.*, § 36), France (*ibid.*, § 41), Germany (*ibid.*, § 42), Israel (*ibid.*, § 44), Kenya (*ibid.*, § 45), Netherlands (*ibid.*, § 46) and New Zealand (*ibid.*, § 47) and the legislation of South Korea (*ibid.*, § 61).

and red crescent).[3] Several manuals further specify that booby-traps must not be used in connection with certain objects likely to attract civilians, such as children's toys.[4] These prohibitions are also to be found in the military manuals and statements of States not, or not at the time, party to Protocol II or Amended Protocol II to the Convention on Certain Conventional Weapons.[5]

Non-international armed conflicts

The premise behind the prohibitions of the use of certain kinds of booby-traps or the use of booby-traps in certain situations during international armed conflicts is equally valid for non-international armed conflicts. Furthermore, during the discussions on the extension of the applicability of Amended Protocol II to the Convention on Certain Conventional Weapons to non-international armed conflicts, the application of the Protocol's provisions on booby-traps to such conflicts was uncontested. Although the discussions took place in the context of treaty negotiations, they indicate that States considered it pertinent that civilians and objects protected by the rules of international humanitarian law applicable in non-international armed conflicts should equally be protected against booby-traps that would have the effect of violating those rules.

In addition, the regulation of booby-traps is also contained in military manuals and national legislation applicable in non-international armed conflicts.[6] Colombia's Constitutional Court has held that the prohibition of certain booby-traps in non-international armed conflicts is part of customary international law.[7]

Use of other booby-traps

Booby-traps which are used in a way not prohibited by the current rule are still subject to the general rules on the conduct of hostilities, in particular the principle of distinction (see Rules 1 and 7) and the principle of proportionality (see Rule 14). In addition, the rule that all feasible precautions must be taken to avoid, and in any event to minimise, incidental loss of civilian life, injury to civilians and damage to civilian objects (see Rule 15) must also be respected.

---

[3] See, e.g., the military manuals of Cameroon (*ibid.*, § 34), Ecuador (*ibid.*, § 38), Switzerland (*ibid.*, §§ 52–54) and United States (*ibid.*, §§ 56 and 58).

[4] See, e.g., the military manuals of Belgium (*ibid.*, § 32), France (*ibid.*, § 39) and Germany (*ibid.*, § 43).

[5] See the military manuals of Argentina (*ibid.*, § 29), Belgium (*ibid.*, § 32), Cameroon (*ibid.*, § 34), Kenya (*ibid.*, § 45) and United States (*ibid.*, §§ 56–58) and the statement of Egypt (*ibid.*, § 66).

[6] See, e.g., the military manuals of Australia (*ibid.*, § 30), Canada (*ibid.*, § 37), Ecuador (*ibid.*, § 38), Germany (*ibid.*, §§ 42–43), Kenya (*ibid.*, § 45) and South Africa (*ibid.*, § 49) and the legislation of Estonia (*ibid.*, § 59); see also the legislation of Hungary (*ibid.*, § 60), the application of which is not excluded in time of non-international armed conflict.

[7] Colombia, Constitutional Court, *Constitutional Case No. C-225/95* (*ibid.*, § 62).

LANDMINES

Rule 81. When landmines are used, particular care must be taken to minimise their indiscriminate effects.

Practice

Volume II, Chapter 29, Section B.

Summary

State practice establishes this rule as a norm of customary international law applicable in both international and non-international armed conflicts. This rule applies to the use of anti-vehicle mines. It also applies in relation to anti-personnel landmines for States which have not yet adopted a total ban on their use.

International armed conflicts

Many of the rules in both the original and amended versions of Protocol II to the Convention on Certain Conventional Weapons, as well as other State practice, are aimed at obviating the indiscriminate effects of mines.[1] The provisions of these treaties, which include the prohibitions of certain types of mines as well as further limitations, are specifically aimed at limiting the potentially indiscriminate damage caused by these weapons. Furthermore, practice shows that the customary rules applying to the conduct of hostilities, such as the principle of distinction (see Rules 1 and 7), the principle of proportionality (see Rule 14) and the obligation to take all feasible precautions in attack (see Rule 15), are equally applicable to the use of landmines.

The obligation to take particular care when using landmines is based on a number of rules that have been codified in Protocol II to the Convention on

---

[1] In particular, the prohibitions of certain types of mines contained in Amended Protocol II to the CCW, Article 3(5) (cited in Vol. II, Ch. 29, § 2), Article 3(6) (*ibid.*, § 3), Article 4 (*ibid.*, § 4), Article 6(2) (*ibid.*, § 5) and Article 6(3) (*ibid.*, § 6) and the further limitations contained in Protocol II to the CCW, Articles 4–5 (*ibid.*, § 194) and Amended Protocol II, Articles 5–6 (*ibid.*, § 203).

Certain Conventional Weapons. This Protocol sets out general rules on the emplacement of all landmines.[2] It also outlines specific restrictions on the use of remotely delivered landmines and non-remotely delivered landmines used in populated areas.[3] In addition, the Protocol requires that all feasible precautions be taken to protect civilians from the effects of these weapons.[4] The Protocol also refers to special precautionary measures such as marking and signposting of minefields, recording minefields, monitoring minefields and procedures to protect UN forces and missions.[5] Protocol II to the Convention on Certain Conventional Weapons was adopted by consensus and was not controversial at the time.

Many military manuals set forth special precautionary measures to be taken when using landmines.[6] There are also indications that the provisions of Protocol II to the Convention on Certain Conventional Weapons are considered to constitute an authoritative minimum standard in relation to the use of landmines which are not specifically prohibited under treaty obligations, as are anti-personnel landmines under the Ottawa Convention.[7] As a result, these precautionary measures as a whole provide an indication of the types of measures States believe must be taken to minimise the indiscriminate effects of landmines.

Amended Protocol II to the Convention on Certain Conventional Weapons reaffirms and develops the precautionary measures to be taken when using landmines.[8]

Non-international armed conflicts

The original Protocol II to the Convention on Certain Conventional Weapons was only applicable in international armed conflicts, and physical practice in internal conflicts has for the most part not been consistent with these rules. However, the concern shown by the UN Security Council, UN General

---

[2] Protocol II to the CCW, Article 7 (*ibid.*, § 341).
[3] Protocol II to the CCW, Articles 4–5 (*ibid.*, § 194).
[4] Protocol II to the CCW, Article 3(4) (*ibid.*, § 192).
[5] Protocol II to the CCW, Article 4(2) (*ibid.*, § 194), Article 7 (*ibid.*, § 341) and Article 8 (*ibid.*, § 342).
[6] See, e.g., the military manuals of Argentina (*ibid.*, § 221), Australia (*ibid.*, §§ 222–223), Belgium (*ibid.*, § 224), Cameroon (*ibid.*, § 225), Canada (*ibid.*, § 226), France (*ibid.*, §§ 227–228), Germany (*ibid.*, § 229), Israel (*ibid.*, § 230), Kenya (*ibid.*, § 231), Netherlands (*ibid.*, § 232), New Zealand (*ibid.*, § 233), Spain (*ibid.*, § 234), Sweden (*ibid.*, § 235) and United States (*ibid.*, §§ 236–238).
[7] See, e.g., the statement of Canada (*ibid.*, § 245) and UN General Assembly, Res. 49/75 D (*ibid.*, § 283) and Res. 50/70 O (*ibid.*, § 283).
[8] See, e.g., Amended Protocol II to the CCW, Article 3(10) (*ibid.*, § 192), Article 3(11) (*ibid.*, § 202), Articles 5–6 (*ibid.*, § 203), Article 9 (*ibid.*, § 350), Article 10 (*ibid.*, § 351) and Article 12 (*ibid.*, § 352).

Assembly and individual States about the effects of landmines on civilians in non-international armed conflicts is an indication of the international community's view that civilians must be protected from mines in such situations.[9] The extension of the scope of application of Amended Protocol II to the Convention on Certain Conventional Weapons to non-international armed conflicts reflects this view.[10] Since then, the Convention on Certain Conventional Weapons itself has been amended so that the original Protocol II is also applicable in non-international armed conflicts for States adhering to the amended Convention.[11] The amendment, adopted at the Second Review Conference in 2001, was not controversial. Hence, there is a strong case for the existence of a customary rule in non-international armed conflicts that mines must not be used in ways that amount to indiscriminate attacks and that particular care must therefore be taken to minimise their indiscriminate effects.

Anti-personnel landmines

With over 140 ratifications of the Ottawa Convention, and others on the way, the majority of States are treaty-bound no longer to use, produce, stockpile and transfer anti-personnel landmines. However, several States, including China, Finland, India, South Korea, Pakistan, Russia and the United States, have not ratified the Ottawa Convention and maintain that they are still entitled to use anti-personnel landmines.[12] About a dozen non-party States have used anti-personnel mines in recent conflicts.[13] This practice means that it cannot be said at this stage that the use of anti-personnel landmines is prohibited under customary international law.

However, almost all States, including those that are not party to the Ottawa Convention and are not in favour of their immediate ban, have agreed that they need to work towards the eventual elimination of anti-personnel landmines. Particularly noteworthy is the Final Declaration adopted by consensus by States party to the Convention on Certain Conventional Weapons at the Second Review Conference in 2001, including by a number of States not party to

---

[9] See, e.g., UN Security Council, Res. 965 (ibid., § 277), Res. 1005 (ibid., § 278), Res. 1076 (ibid., § 279), Res. 1089 (ibid., § 280) and Res. 1096 (ibid., § 281); UN General Assembly, Res. 49/198 (ibid., § 285), Res. 49/199 (ibid., § 284), Res. 50/178 (ibid., § 284), Res. 50/197 (ibid., § 285), Res. 51/98 (ibid., § 284), Res. 51/112 (ibid., § 285) and Res. 55/116 (ibid., § 289) and the statements of Australia (ibid., § 242), Canada (ibid., §§ 244–245) and United Kingdom (ibid., § 272).

[10] Amended Protocol II to the CCW, Article 1(2) (ibid., § 200).

[11] CCW, amended Article 1 (ibid., § 218).

[12] See, e.g., the statements of China (ibid., § 54), Finland (ibid., § 62), India (ibid., § 66), South Korea (ibid., § 72), Pakistan (ibid., §§ 83–84 and 262), Russia (ibid., § 88) and United States (ibid., § 101).

[13] See the practice reported in International Campaign to Ban Landmines, *Landmine Monitor Report 1999* (ibid., § 187) and *Landmine Monitor Report 2000* (ibid., §§ 188 and 190).

the Ottawa Convention.[14] In the Declaration, the States parties "solemnly declare...their conviction that all States should strive towards the goal of the eventual elimination of anti-personnel mines globally".[15] In addition, a number of UN General Assembly resolutions have urged States to contribute to the elimination of anti-personnel landmines.[16] Although there were some abstentions to these resolutions, the majority of abstaining States have since joined the Declaration adopted at the Second Review Conference or have made statements recognising the goal of the eventual elimination of anti-personnel mines, in particular Ethiopia in 1995 and Turkey in 2002 (which has now also ratified the Ottawa Convention).[17] Resolutions adopted by the OIC Conference of Ministers of Foreign Affairs in 1995 and 1996 and by the 26th International Conference of the Red Cross and Red Crescent in 1995 also support the eventual elimination of landmines.[18] It is particularly noteworthy that, at their First Meeting in Maputo in 1999, States party to the Ottawa Convention adopted a Declaration calling upon States still using or possessing anti-personnel landmines to "cease now" from so doing.[19] Such a statement to non-party States is a significant indication of the belief that all States should work towards the elimination of anti-personnel mines. All the practice cited above appears to indicate that an obligation to eliminate anti-personnel landmines is emerging.

Rule 82. A party to the conflict using landmines must record their placement, as far as possible.

Practice

Volume II, Chapter 29, Section C.

Summary

State practice establishes this rule as a norm of customary international law applicable in international, and arguably also in non-international, armed conflicts. This rule applies to the use of anti-vehicle mines. It also applies in relation to anti-personnel mines to States which have not yet adopted a total ban on their use.

---

[14] States not party to the Ottawa Convention which participated in this Declaration were: Belarus, China, Cuba, Estonia, Finland, Greece, India, Israel, South Korea, Latvia, Lithuania, Mongolia, Pakistan, Poland, Russia, Ukraine, United States and Yugoslavia.

[15] Second Review Conference of States Parties to the CCW, Final Declaration (cited in Vol. II, Ch. 29, § 163).

[16] See, e.g., UN General Assembly, Res. 49/75 D (*ibid.*, § 108), Res. 49/199 (*ibid.*, § 109), Res. 50/70 O (*ibid.*, § 108), Res. 50/178 (*ibid.*, § 109), Res. 51/45 S (*ibid.*, § 110), Res. 51/98 (*ibid.*, § 109) and Res. 52/38 H (*ibid.*, § 112).

[17] Ethiopia, Statement before the First Committee of the UN General Assembly (*ibid.*, § 61) and Turkey, Press Release of the Minister of Foreign Affairs (*ibid.*, § 96).

[18] OIC Conference of Ministers of Foreign Affairs, Res. 36/23-P and 27/24-P (*ibid.*, § 152); 26th International Conference of the Red Cross and Red Crescent, Res. II (*ibid.*, § 156).

[19] First Meeting of States Parties to the Ottawa Convention, Declaration (*ibid.*, § 160).

International armed conflicts

The original Protocol II to the Convention on Certain Conventional Weapons specifies the requirement to record pre-planned minefields and, to the degree possible, record other minefields.[20] Amended Protocol II to the Convention on Certain Conventional Weapons specifies that information relating to all landmines and mined areas must be recorded.[21]

Many military manuals specify the requirements contained in the original Protocol II to the Convention on Certain Conventional Weapons or state more generally that the placement of minefields should be recorded.[22] Some of these manuals simply reproduce the rules of the Protocol to which the State is party.[23] The manuals of Canada, France, Germany, Israel, Switzerland and the United States, however, state that there is a requirement to record all minefields (in the case of Switzerland "large-scale minefields") and are thus not limited to pre-planned minefields.[24] These States were not party to Amended Protocol II to the Convention on Certain Conventional Weapons at the time of publication of their respective manuals, or their publication pre-dated the adoption of Amended Protocol II.

Several resolutions adopted by consensus by the UN General Assembly in 1994, 1995 and 1998 emphasise the importance of recording the location of landmines.[25] It is interesting to note that in the earlier resolutions adopted in 1994 and 1995, the term "where appropriate" was used in relation to the recording of the location of mines, whereas it was dropped in the 1998 resolution. The wording of the later resolution reflects the growing concern of States about the devastating effects of landmines and a consensus that the rules concerning their use needed to be stricter.

Non-international armed conflicts

The original Protocol II to the Convention on Certain Conventional Weapons only applied to international armed conflicts. It is not clear whether the more extensive recording requirements of Amended Protocol II, which apply to

---

[20] Protocol II to the CCW, Article 7 (*ibid.*, § 341).
[21] Amended Protocol II to the CCW, Article 9 (*ibid.*, § 350).
[22] See, e.g., the military manuals of Argentina (*ibid.*, § 360), Australia (*ibid.*, §§ 361–362), Belgium (*ibid.*, § 363), Cameroon (*ibid.*, § 364), Canada (*ibid.*, § 365), France (*ibid.*, §§ 366–367), Germany (*ibid.*, § 368), Israel (*ibid.*, § 369), Kenya (*ibid.*, § 370), Netherlands (*ibid.*, § 371), New Zealand (*ibid.*, § 372), Spain (*ibid.*, § 373), Sweden (*ibid.*, § 374), Switzerland (*ibid.*, § 375) and United States (*ibid.*, §§ 377–378).
[23] See, e.g., the military manuals of Argentina (*ibid.*, § 360), Cameroon (*ibid.*, § 364), Netherlands (*ibid.*, § 371), New Zealand (*ibid.*, § 372), Spain (*ibid.*, § 373) and Sweden (*ibid.*, § 374).
[24] Canada, *LOAC Manual* (*ibid.*, § 365); France, *LOAC Teaching Note* (*ibid.*, § 366) and *LOAC Manual* (*ibid.*, § 367); Germany, *Military Manual* (*ibid.*, § 368); Israel, *Manual on the Laws of War* (*ibid.*, § 369); Switzerland, *Basic Military Manual* (*ibid.*, § 375); United States, *Air Force Commander's Handbook* (*ibid.*, § 377) and *Naval Handbook* (*ibid.*, § 378).
[25] UN General Assembly, Res. 49/215 and 50/82 (*ibid.*, § 405) and Res. 53/26 (*ibid.*, § 408).

non-international armed conflicts,[26] are part of customary international law. Although in many cases parties to non-international armed conflicts (especially non-State parties) did not record the emplacement of mines, recent developments show that the international community now agrees that the use of landmines is to be recorded in all circumstances, if at all possible. In particular, UN General Assembly resolutions deliberately make no distinction between international and non-international armed conflicts in respect of landmines.[27]

Rule 83. At the end of active hostilities, a party to the conflict which has used landmines must remove or otherwise render them harmless to civilians, or facilitate their removal.

Practice

Volume II, Chapter 29, Section C.

Summary

State practice establishes this rule as a norm of customary international law applicable in both international and non-international armed conflicts. This rule applies to the use of anti-vehicle mines. It also applies in relation to anti-personnel mines for States which have not yet adopted a total ban on their use, with the proviso that the Ottawa Convention contains special provisions on the destruction of anti-personnel landmines in mined areas.[28]

International and non-international armed conflicts

Until the 1990s, there was little practice indicating a requirement that those laying mines have to remove them, and generally speaking the expectation was that it was up to the State with mines on its territory to decide what to do. The original Protocol II to the Convention on Certain Conventional Weapons merely encourages cooperation to remove or render minefields ineffective.[29] However, the attitude of the international community has changed in this regard. The wording of Article 3(2) of Amended Protocol II, incorporating the principle that States laying mines are responsible for them,

---

[26] Amended Protocol II to the CCW, Article 1(2) (*ibid.*, § 347) and Article 9 (*ibid.*, § 350).

[27] With respect to the recording of landmines in particular, see UN General Assembly, Res. 49/215 and 50/82 (*ibid.*, § 405) and Res. 53/26 (*ibid.*, § 408). With respect to the issue of landmines in general, see UN General Assembly, Res. 48/75 K (*ibid.*, § 403), Res. 49/79 (*ibid.*, § 404), Res. 49/199 (*ibid.*, § 406), Res. 49/215 (*ibid.*, § 405), Res. 50/82 (*ibid.*, § 405), Res. 50/178 (*ibid.*, § 406), Res. 51/49 (*ibid.*, § 407), Res. 51/98 (*ibid.*, § 406), Res. 53/26 (*ibid.*, § 408) and Res. 53/164 (*ibid.*, § 409).

[28] Ottawa Convention, Article 5.

[29] Protocol II to the CCW, Article 9 (*ibid.*, § 346).

reflects this change of attitude.[30] Amended Protocol II provides detailed rules on the removal of mines or otherwise rendering them harmless at the end of hostilities.[31]

A large number of UN Security Council and UN General Assembly resolutions have been adopted since 1993 deploring the danger to civilians of mines remaining on or in the ground and specifying the need to ensure their removal.[32] These resolutions were deliberately not limited to international armed conflicts, as the worst problems relating to uncleared mines are frequently associated with non-international armed conflicts. Several of these resolutions specifically refer to the need to clear mines laid in a non-international armed conflict, including in Angola, Cambodia, Rwanda and Kosovo.[33]

This practice indicates that it is no longer permissible for a party to a conflict to simply abandon mines they have laid. The UN Secretary-General's Report on Assistance in Mine Clearance also supports this view.[34] The actual method to be adopted to remove the mines or otherwise render them harmless is, however, couched in relatively general terms. Military manuals and the various UN resolutions refer to removal by the mine-layer, or the requirement to aid third parties, including international bodies, to undertake such removal through the provision of information or other appropriate resources.[35]

---

[30] Amended Protocol II to the CCW, Article 3(2) (ibid., § 348).
[31] Amended Protocol II to the CCW, Article 10 (ibid., § 351).
[32] See, e.g., UN Security Council, Res. 1005 (ibid., § 399), Res. 1055 (ibid., § 401), Res. 1062 (ibid., § 400), Res. 1064 (ibid., § 401), Res. 1074 (ibid., § 401), Res. 1087 (ibid., § 401), Res. 1093 (ibid., § 402) and Res. 1119 (ibid., § 402); UN General Assembly, Res. 48/75 K (ibid., § 403), Res. 49/79 (ibid., § 404), Res. 49/199 (ibid., § 406), Res. 49/215 (ibid., § 405), Res. 50/82 (ibid., § 405), Res. 50/178 (ibid., § 406), Res. 51/49 (ibid., § 407), Res. 51/98 (ibid., § 406), Res. 53/26 (ibid., § 408) and Res. 53/164 (ibid., § 409).
[33] UN Security Council, Res. 1005 (ibid., § 399), Res. 1055 (ibid., § 401), Res. 1064 (ibid., § 401), Res. 1075 (ibid., § 401), Res. 1087 (ibid., § 401); UN General Assembly, Res. 49/199 (ibid., § 406), Res. 50/178 (ibid., § 406), Res. 51/98 (ibid., § 406) and Res. 53/164 (ibid., § 409).
[34] UN Secretary-General, Report on Assistance in Mine Clearance (ibid., § 411).
[35] See, e.g., the military manuals of Canada (ibid., § 365), France (ibid., §§ 366–367), Germany (ibid., § 368), Switzerland (ibid., § 375) and United States (ibid., § 378); UN Security Council, Res. 1005 (ibid., § 399), Res. 1055 (ibid., § 401), Res. 1062 (ibid., § 400), Res. 1064 (ibid., § 401), Res. 1075 (ibid., § 401), Res. 1087 (ibid., § 401), Res. 1093 (ibid., § 402) and Res. 1119 (ibid., § 402); UN General Assembly, Res. 49/79 (ibid., § 404), Res. 49/199 (ibid., § 406), Res. 49/215 (ibid., § 405), Res. 50/82 (ibid., § 405), Res. 50/178 (ibid., § 406), Res. 51/49 (ibid., § 407), Res. 51/98 (ibid., § 406), Res. 53/26 (ibid., § 408) and Res. 53/164 (ibid., § 409); UN Commission on Human Rights, Res. 1996/54 (ibid., § 410).

INCENDIARY WEAPONS

Rule 84. If incendiary weapons are used, particular care must be taken to avoid, and in any event to minimise, incidental loss of civilian life, injury to civilians and damage to civilian objects.

Practice

Volume II, Chapter 30, Section A.

Summary

State practice establishes this rule as a norm of customary international law applicable in both international and non-international armed conflicts.

International armed conflicts

The discussions in the 1970s at the UN General Assembly and during the diplomatic conferences that led to the adoption of the Additional Protocols and the Convention on Certain Conventional Weapons show that the use of incendiary weapons is a sensitive issue. The controversy was occasioned in particular by the effects of these weapons during the Vietnam War, and a large number of States advocated a total prohibition of their use.[1] The majority of those that did not subscribe to a total ban did urge strict restrictions in order to avoid civilian casualties.[2]

The treaty provisions finally adopted by consensus in Protocol III to the Convention on Certain Conventional Weapons reflect the latter trend, not only by repeating the principle of distinction applicable to the use of all weapons, but also by prohibiting the use of air-delivered incendiary weapons against military objectives located within a concentration of civilians and by restricting

---

[1] See, e.g., the statements (cited in Vol. II, Ch. 30, §§ 9–73).
[2] See, e.g., the statements of Austria (*ibid.*, § 146), Australia (*ibid.*, §§ 141 and 143–144), Denmark (*ibid.*, §§ 148–149), Egypt (*ibid.*, § 146), Ghana (*ibid.*, § 146), Indonesia (*ibid.*, § 154), Jamaica (*ibid.*, § 146), Japan (*ibid.*, §§ 155–156), Mexico (*ibid.*, § 146), Netherlands (*ibid.*, §§ 142–144 and 158), New Zealand (*ibid.*, § 159), Norway (*ibid.*, §§ 149 and 160), Romania (*ibid.*, § 146), Sweden (*ibid.*, § 146), Syria (*ibid.*, § 162), USSR (*ibid.*, § 163), United Kingdom (*ibid.*, § 164), United States (*ibid.*, §§ 165–166), Venezuela (*ibid.*, § 146) and Yugoslavia (*ibid.*, § 146); see also the reported practice of the United States (*ibid.*, § 167).

the use of other incendiary weapons within such a concentration.[3] Fewer than half of all States are party to this treaty. However, many States do not stock incendiary weapons, and such weapons have rarely been used since the adoption of the Protocol.

Furthermore, most military manuals either refer to the rules in Protocol III to the Convention on Certain Conventional Weapons or state the requirement to avoid, or at least to minimise, civilian casualties.[4] This includes manuals of several States not, or not at the time, party to the Protocol.[5]

While the rule in Article 2(1) of Protocol III, which is a mere application of the principle of distinction (see Rules 1 and 7), is undoubtedly part of customary international law, it is more difficult to conclude that the detailed rules in Article 2(2)–(4) of Protocol III are also customary international law, but they may be seen as guidelines for the implementation of the customary rule that particular care must be taken to avoid civilian casualties.[6] Furthermore, military manuals, official statements and other practice stress that incendiary weapons may only be used for certain legitimate purposes.[7] Combined with the fact that incendiary weapons are far less frequently used than other conventional weapons, this indicates that the general opinion of States is that their use should be avoided, if militarily feasible (see also Rule 85).

Non-international armed conflicts

Protocol III to the Convention on Certain Conventional Weapons, until the amendment of the Convention in December 2001,[8] applied only to international armed conflicts. Most developments in relation to the application of international humanitarian law in non-international armed conflicts have

---

[3] Protocol III to the CCW, Article 2 (*ibid.*, § 110).
[4] See, e.g., the military manuals of Argentina (*ibid.*, § 117), Australia (*ibid.*, §§ 118–119), Belgium (*ibid.*, § 120), Cameroon (*ibid.*, § 121), Canada (*ibid.*, § 122), Ecuador (*ibid.*, § 123), France (*ibid.*, §§ 124–125), Germany (*ibid.*, § 126), Israel (*ibid.*, § 127), Kenya (*ibid.*, § 128), Netherlands (*ibid.*, § 129), New Zealand (*ibid.*, § 130), Russia (*ibid.*, § 131), Spain (*ibid.*, § 132), Sweden (*ibid.*, § 133), Switzerland (*ibid.*, § 134) and United States (*ibid.*, §§ 136–137).
[5] See the military manuals of Argentina (*ibid.*, § 117), Belgium (*ibid.*, § 120), Cameroon (*ibid.*, § 121), Israel (*ibid.*, § 127), Kenya (*ibid.*, § 128) and United States (*ibid.*, § 136).
[6] Protocol III to the CCW, Article 2(2)-(4) (*ibid.*, § 110).
[7] See, e.g., the military manuals of Argentina (*ibid.*, § 117), Australia (*ibid.*, §§ 118–119), Belgium (*ibid.*, § 120), Cameroon (*ibid.*, § 121), Canada (*ibid.*, § 122), Ecuador (*ibid.*, § 123), France (*ibid.*, §§ 124–125), Germany (*ibid.*, § 126), Israel (*ibid.*, § 127), Kenya (*ibid.*, § 128), Netherlands (*ibid.*, § 129), New Zealand (*ibid.*, § 130), Russia (*ibid.*, § 131), Spain (*ibid.*, § 132), Sweden (*ibid.*, § 133), Switzerland (*ibid.*, § 134) and United States (*ibid.*, §§ 136–137), the statements of Austria (*ibid.*, § 146), Australia (*ibid.*, §§ 141 and 143–144), Denmark (*ibid.*, §§ 148–149), Egypt (*ibid.*, § 146), Ghana (*ibid.*, § 146), Indonesia (*ibid.*, § 154), Jamaica (*ibid.*, § 146), Japan (*ibid.*, §§ 155–156), Mexico (*ibid.*, § 146), Netherlands (*ibid.*, §§ 142–144 and 158), New Zealand (*ibid.*, § 159), Norway (*ibid.*, §§ 149 and 160), Romania (*ibid.*, § 146), Sweden (*ibid.*, § 146), Syria (*ibid.*, § 162), USSR (*ibid.*, § 163), United Kingdom (*ibid.*, § 164), United States (*ibid.*, §§ 165–166 and 168), Venezuela (*ibid.*, § 146) and Yugoslavia (*ibid.*, § 146) and the reported practice of the United States (*ibid.*, § 167).
[8] See CCW, amended Article 1 (*ibid.*, § 115).

occurred over the last two decades, and the fact that incendiary weapons have generally not been used during this period means that there has been no reason for the international community to address the issue. However, given the controversy that the use of incendiary weapons occasioned in the 1970s and the clear opinion that has developed since then in the international community that civilians need to be protected with particular care against the effects of armed conflict, it can be concluded that this rule is equally valid for non-international armed conflicts. The fact that the extension of the scope of application of Protocol III to non-international armed conflicts in 2001 was not controversial during the negotiations and has meanwhile entered into force further supports this conclusion.[9]

Rule 85. The anti-personnel use of incendiary weapons is prohibited, unless it is not feasible to use a less harmful weapon to render a person *hors de combat*.

Practice

Volume II, Chapter 30, Section B.

Summary

State practice establishes this rule as a norm of customary international law applicable in both international and non-international armed conflicts.

International armed conflicts

During the discussions in the 1970s, many States were in favour of a total prohibition of the use of incendiary weapons, including against combatants.[10] Official statements supporting a total ban were also made by a number of States.[11]

---

[9] The amendment entered into force on 18 May 2004. To date, 29 States have ratified the amended CCW: Argentina, Australia, Austria, Belgium, Bulgaria, Burkina Faso, Canada, China, Croatia, Estonia, Finland, France, Holy See, Hungary, Japan, Latvia, Liechtenstein, Lithuania, Mexico, Netherlands, Norway, Republic of Korea, Romania, Serbia and Montenegro, Slovakia, Spain, Sweden, Switzerland and United Kingdom.

[10] Formal proposals to this effect were submitted to the Ad Hoc Committee on Conventional Weapons of the Diplomatic Conference leading to the adoption of the Additional Protocols by Afghanistan, Algeria, Austria, Colombia, Côte d'Ivoire, Egypt, Iran, Kuwait, Lebanon, Lesotho, Mali, Mauritania, Mexico, Norway, Romania, Sudan, Sweden, Switzerland, Tanzania, Tunisia, Venezuela, Yugoslavia and Zaire (*ibid.*, § 9). However, it seems that in 1975 Kuwait had slightly changed its position in support of a prohibition of the indiscriminate use of incendiary weapons against combatants and civilians and the prohibition of the use of such weapons against civilian objects (see *ibid.*, § 36).

[11] See, e.g., the statements of Barbados (*ibid.*, § 12), China (*ibid.*, § 16), Cyprus (*ibid.*, § 19), Czechoslovakia (*ibid.*, § 20), Ecuador (*ibid.*, § 21), Iraq (*ibid.*, §§ 30–31), Madagascar (*ibid.*, § 37), Mongolia (*ibid.*, § 42), New Zealand (*ibid.*, §§ 45–46), Peru (*ibid.*, § 50), Poland (*ibid.*, §§ 53–55), Syria (*ibid.*, § 63), Togo (*ibid.*, § 64), USSR (*ibid.*, §§ 66–67) and United Arab Emirates (*ibid.*, § 68).

The legislation of several States prohibits the use of incendiary weapons altogether.[12] In 1972, the UN General Assembly adopted a resolution on general and complete disarmament in which it deplored the use of napalm and other incendiary weapons in all armed conflicts.[13]

When it became clear, however, that a total prohibition would not command consensus at the Preparatory Conference for the Convention on Certain Conventional Weapons, a number of States tried, as a fall-back position, to achieve a prohibition of their use against combatants with limited exceptions, such as when they were under armoured protection or in field fortifications.[14] However, this was still opposed by a few States, in particular the United States and to some degree the United Kingdom.[15] Since Protocol III to the Convention on Certain Conventional Weapons was to be adopted by consensus, this prohibition was not included in the Protocol. The fact that this prohibition was not included in the Protocol does not mean, however, that the use of incendiary weapons against combatants is lawful in all circumstances.

Several States have specified the few restricted situations in which incendiary weapons may be used, namely when combatants are under armoured protection or in field fortifications.[16] Others have stated that incendiary weapons may not be used in a way that would cause unnecessary suffering.[17] Several military manuals and a number of official statements make the point that the use of incendiary weapons against combatants is prohibited because it causes unnecessary suffering.[18]

There are very few reports of use of napalm and similar incendiary weapons against combatants since the adoption of the Convention on Certain Conventional Weapons. What reports there are have been in the form of accusations condemning their use and are unconfirmed.[19] It can be concluded from this

[12] See, e.g., Colombia, *Basic Military Manual* (*ibid.*, § 4) and the legislation of Andorra (*ibid.*, § 5), Hungary (*ibid.*, § 6) and Yugoslavia (*ibid.*, § 7).
[13] UN General Assembly, Res. 2932 A (XXVII) (adopted by 99 votes in favour, none against and 15 abstentions) (*ibid.*, § 74).
[14] See the proposals submitted to the Preparatory Conference for the CCW by Austria (*ibid.*, § 146), Egypt (*ibid.*, § 146), Ghana (*ibid.*, § 146), Indonesia (*ibid.*, § 154), Jamaica (*ibid.*, § 146), Mexico (*ibid.*, § 146), Romania (*ibid.*, § 146), Sweden (*ibid.*, § 146), Venezuela (*ibid.*, § 146), Yugoslavia (*ibid.*, § 146) and Zaire (*ibid.*, § 146).
[15] See the statements made at the Preparatory Conference for the CCW by the United States (*ibid.*, §§ 166 and 206) and United Kingdom (*ibid.*, § 164).
[16] See the proposals submitted to the Preparatory Conference for the CCW by Austria (*ibid.*, § 198), Denmark (*ibid.*, § 199), Egypt (*ibid.*, § 198), Ghana (*ibid.*, § 198), Indonesia (*ibid.*, § 200), Jamaica (*ibid.*, § 198), Mexico (*ibid.*, § 198), Norway (*ibid.*, § 199), Romania (*ibid.*, § 198), Sweden (*ibid.*, § 198), Venezuela (*ibid.*, § 198), Yugoslavia (*ibid.*, § 198) and Zaire (*ibid.*, § 198).
[17] See, e.g., the military manuals of Australia (*ibid.*, § 187), Canada (*ibid.*, § 189), New Zealand (*ibid.*, § 191), United Kingdom (*ibid.*, § 193) and United States (*ibid.*, §§ 194–195) and the statements of Poland (*ibid.*, § 203) and United Kingdom (*ibid.*, § 205).
[18] See, e.g., the military manuals of Belgium (*ibid.*, § 188), Colombia (*ibid.*, § 190) and Sweden (*ibid.*, § 192) and the statements of Norway (*ibid.*, § 202) and USSR (*ibid.*, § 204).
[19] See the condemnations by Jordan (*ibid.*, § 201) and USSR (*ibid.*, § 204) and the reported practice of Angola (*ibid.*, § 214) and Ethiopia (*ibid.*, § 215).

practice that incendiary weapons may not be used against combatants if such use would cause unnecessary suffering, i.e., if it is feasible to use a less harmful weapon to render a combatant *hors de combat*.

Non-international armed conflicts

The situation with respect to non-international armed conflicts is similar to that described under the previous rule, namely that there has been no particular need for the international community to address the issue in the last 20 years. It is nevertheless reasonable to conclude that the rule is applicable in non-international armed conflicts. As it is prohibited in non-international armed conflicts to use means and methods of warfare of a nature to cause unnecessary suffering (see Rule 70), the anti-personnel use of incendiary weapons in situations where such use is not required by military necessity would constitute a violation of that rule.

BLINDING LASER WEAPONS

Rule 86. The use of laser weapons that are specifically designed, as their sole combat function or as one of their combat functions, to cause permanent blindness to unenhanced vision is prohibited.

Practice

Volume II, Chapter 31.

Summary

State practice establishes this rule as a norm of customary international law applicable in both international and non-international armed conflicts. Blindness to unenhanced vision refers to blindness caused to the naked eye or to the eye with corrective eyesight devices.[1]

International armed conflicts

Although the adoption of Protocol IV to the Convention on Certain Conventional Weapons governing the use of blinding laser weapons in 1995 is only recent, the circumstances of that adoption and developments since then indicate that this is an instance of customary international law developing as a result of the negotiation and adoption of a treaty. In its judgement in the *North Sea Continental Shelf cases*, the International Court of Justice stated that customary international law can develop in this way:

Although the passage of only a short period of time is not necessarily, or of itself, a bar to the formation of a new rule of customary international law on the basis of what was originally a purely conventional rule, an indispensable requirement would be that within the period in question, short though it might be, State practice, including that of States whose interests are specially affected, should have been both extensive and virtually uniform in the sense of the provision invoked; and should moreover have occurred in such a way as to show a general recognition that a rule of law or legal obligation is involved.[2]

---

[1] Protocol IV to the CCW, Article 1 (cited in Vol. II, Ch. 31, § 1).
[2] ICJ, *North Sea Continental Shelf cases*, Judgement, 20 February 1969, *ICJ Reports 1969*, p. 44, § 74; see also *supra*, Introduction.

Prior to the negotiation of Protocol IV to the Convention on Certain Conventional Weapons, several States had laser weapons programmes that allegedly included the development of blinding anti-personnel laser weapons or dual-use laser weapons. According to a report by Human Rights Watch, China, France, Germany, Israel, Russia, Ukraine, the United Kingdom and the United States had such programmes.[3] However, apart from the systems developed by China and the United States, it is not clear to what extent this report is accurate and, if so, which of the proposed systems would have fallen within the prohibition of Protocol IV. Nonetheless, it is clear that, with the exception of Sweden, States did not consider that such programmes were prohibited before the First Review Conference of the Convention on Certain Conventional Weapons.[4] They began to consider the issue because of concerns raised by some States, the ICRC and non-governmental organisations which objected to deliberate blinding as a method of warfare.[5]

Protocol IV to the Convention on Certain Conventional Weapons was adopted by consensus, with every State said to have been involved in the development of anti-personnel laser systems present at the conference. All the States mentioned in the Human Rights Watch report, with the exception of the United States, have become party to the Protocol. In the case of the United States, the Protocol mirrors the Pentagon's policy, which was announced a few weeks before the adoption of the Protocol.[6] The United States withdrew the anti-personnel lasers it was about to deploy, even though it was not party to Protocol IV.[7] All major weapons-exporting States, with the exception of the United States, and the vast majority of other States capable of producing such weapons, have acceded to it. The fact that the Protocol also prohibits transfers means that non-party States will not be able to acquire the weapon unless they produce it themselves.[8] At present, there is no indication that this is occurring.

Although the United States is not yet a party to Protocol IV, its Secretary of Defense stated in relation to blinding lasers that "the Department has no intent to spend money developing weapons we are prohibited from using".[9] China stated at the adoption of the Protocol that "this is the first time in human history that a kind of inhumane weapon is declared illegal and prohibited before it is actually used".[10]

---

[3] Human Rights Watch Arms Project, *Blinding Laser Weapons: The Need to Ban a Cruel and Inhumane Weapon* (cited in Vol. II, Ch. 31, § 83).

[4] See the statements of Sweden (*ibid.*, §§ 39–45).

[5] See, e.g., the statements of France (*ibid.*, § 30), Germany (*ibid.*, §§ 31–32), Ireland (*ibid.*, § 35), Netherlands (*ibid.*, § 38), Sweden (*ibid.*, §§ 39–45), Switzerland (*ibid.*, § 40) and USSR (*ibid.*, § 46), the statements and practice of the ICRC (*ibid.*, §§ 76–78) and the statements of several non-governmental organisations (*ibid.*, §§ 85–90).

[6] United States, Announcement by the Secretary of Defense (*ibid.*, § 48).

[7] See the practice of the United States (*ibid.*, §§ 48–50).

[8] Protocol IV to the CCW, Article 1 (*ibid.*, § 1).

[9] United States, Letter from the Secretary of Defense to Senator Patrick Leahy (*ibid.*, § 49).

[10] China, Statement at the First Review Conference of States Parties to the CCW (*ibid.*, § 29).

Subsequent practice is universally consistent with the prohibition of using laser weapons contained in Protocol IV. There have been no reports that such weapons have been deployed or used by any State since the adoption of the Protocol. Government statements are consistent with this prohibition and none have expressed the belief that they are entitled to use such weapons.[11]

Non-international armed conflicts

At the negotiations of Protocol IV to the Convention on Certain Conventional Weapons in 1995, all States were in favour of making the Protocol applicable to non-international armed conflicts, with the exception of one State. The objecting State was not in the process of developing or acquiring this weapon and the State's representative indicated orally that while his government was in favour of totally banning such weapons, it would resist the adoption of a treaty on international humanitarian law applicable to non-international armed conflicts as a matter of principle, irrespective of the subject matter.[12] Since then, however, this State agreed to the amendment of the Convention on Certain Conventional Weapons in 2001 to extend application of the Protocol also to non-international armed conflicts and the amendment has meanwhile entered into force.[13] It is also noteworthy that the Protocol prohibits transfers to both States and non-State entities.[14]

Practice is in conformity with the rule's applicability in both international and non-international armed conflicts, as States generally do not have a different set of military weapons for international and non-international armed conflicts. There have been no reports of use or deployment in either international or non-international armed conflict. No State has claimed that it is entitled to use such systems in either international or non-international armed conflicts.

The Final Declaration adopted by consensus at the First Review Conference of the Convention on Certain Conventional Weapons in 1996 noted "the need for achieving the total prohibition of blinding laser weapons, the use and transfer of which are prohibited in Protocol IV", thus reflecting the wish to achieve the elimination of such systems and not to limit the law to a prohibition of use and transfer.[15] In the Final Declaration adopted at the Second Review Conference in 2001, States parties to the Convention solemnly declared "their

---

[11] See, e.g., the statements of Australia (ibid., § 26), Burkina Faso (ibid., § 27), China (ibid., § 29), United Kingdom (ibid., § 47) and United States (ibid., §§ 49 and 51–53).

[12] See the practice (ibid., § 71).

[13] CCW, amended Article 1 (ibid., § 12). The amendment entered into force on 18 May 2004. To date, 29 States have ratified the amended CCW: Argentina, Australia, Austria, Belgium, Bulgaria, Burkina Faso, Canada, China, Croatia, Estonia, Finland, France, Holy See, Hungary, Japan, Latvia, Liechtenstein, Lithuania, Mexico, Netherlands, Norway, Republic of Korea, Romania, Serbia and Montenegro, Slovakia, Spain, Sweden, Switzerland and United Kingdom.

[14] Protocol IV to the CCW, Article 1 (ibid., § 1).

[15] First Review Conference of States Parties to the CCW, Final Declaration (ibid., § 73).

reaffirmation of the recognition by the First Review Conference of the need for the total prohibition of blinding laser weapons, the use or transfer of which are prohibited in Protocol IV".[16]

The United States has indicated that it intends to apply the terms of Protocol IV in all circumstances, and a number of States specified, on declaring their intention to be bound by it, that they would not limit the Protocol's application to situations of international armed conflict.[17] It is not clear whether those States which adhered to the Protocol without making a statement as to its scope intended that scope to be limited or whether they simply did not consider it important to make such a statement. States have in practice totally abstained from the use of such weapons since the adoption of the Protocol, and it can reasonably be inferred that this is a reaction to the international community's expectation that such weapons must not be used.

Some States consider that the use of blinding laser weapons would cause unnecessary suffering,[18] an argument equally valid in international and non-international armed conflicts (see Rule 70).

Deliberate blinding by other laser systems

In addition to prohibiting the use and transfer of a certain type of laser weapon, Protocol IV to the Convention on Certain Conventional Weapons has the effect of prohibiting the deliberate use of other laser systems (for example, range-finders) to blind combatants.[19] The deliberate use of laser systems, other than those prohibited by Protocol IV, to blind combatants would frustrate the aim and purpose of the prohibition of laser weapons that are specifically designed to cause permanent blindness. There is no evidence of deliberate use of other laser systems to blind combatants and no State has claimed the right to do so since the adoption of Protocol IV.

It is noteworthy that during the negotiations leading to the adoption of Protocol IV in 1995, a number of States, including some not yet party to Protocol IV, stated that they would have preferred a stronger text that included a prohibition of blinding as a method of warfare.[20] This was resisted by a few States

---

[16] Second Review Conference of States Parties to the CCW, Final Declaration (*ibid.*, § 74).

[17] United States, Statement at the First Review Conference of States Parties to the CCW (*ibid.*, § 51) and Message from the President transmitting the Protocols to the Convention on Certain Conventional Weapons to the Senate for consent to ratification (*ibid.*, § 53); Declarations made upon acceptance of Protocol IV by Australia (*ibid.*, § 5), Austria (*ibid.*, § 4), Belgium (*ibid.*, § 4), Canada (*ibid.*, § 4), Germany (*ibid.*, § 6), Greece (*ibid.*, § 4), Ireland (*ibid.*, § 4), Israel (*ibid.*, § 7), Italy (*ibid.*, § 4), Liechtenstein (*ibid.*, § 4), Netherlands (*ibid.*, § 8), South Africa (*ibid.*, § 4), Sweden (*ibid.*, § 9), Switzerland (*ibid.*, § 10) and United Kingdom (*ibid.*, § 11).

[18] See, e.g., Sweden, Declaration made upon acceptance of Protocol IV to the CCW (cited in Vol. II, Ch. 20, § 14) and the military manuals of France (*ibid.*, §§ 55–56).

[19] Protocol IV to the CCW, Article 2 (cited in Vol. II, Ch. 31, § 91).

[20] See the statements of Australia, Austria, Belgium, Denmark, Ecuador, Finland, France, Germany, Iran, Mexico, Netherlands, Norway, Poland, Romania, Russia and Sweden (*ibid.*, § 3). Iran and Poland are not party to Protocol IV.

during the negotiations on the basis that weapons which are not laser weapons can sometimes have the effect of blinding, for example, bomb fragments, and that laser target designators may also have this effect although this would be unintended. However, these States did not suggest that the deliberate use of a weapon to blind would therefore be lawful, but, on the contrary, accepted the inclusion of the requirement to take feasible precautions in the employment of laser systems to avoid permanent blindness contained in Article 2 of Protocol IV.[21] This requirement is set forth in military manuals and official statements, including those of States not, or not at the time, party to Protocol IV.[22]

---

[21] Protocol IV to the CCW, Article 2 (*ibid.*, § 91).
[22] See Israel, *Manual on the Laws of War* (*ibid.*, § 94); United Kingdom, Letter from the Secretary of Defence to the ICRC President (*ibid.*, § 99); United States, *Annotated Supplement to the Naval Handbook* (*ibid.*, § 95); Defenselink News Release (*ibid.*, § 100).

PART V

TREATMENT OF CIVILIANS AND PERSONS HORS DE COMBAT

CHAPTER 32

FUNDAMENTAL GUARANTEES

Introduction

The fundamental guarantees identified in this chapter apply to all civilians in the power of a party to the conflict and who do not take a direct part in hostilities, as well as to all persons who are *hors de combat*. Because these fundamental guarantees are overarching rules that apply to all persons, they are not sub-divided into specific rules relating to different types of persons. The rules applicable to specific categories of persons are to be found in Chapters 33–39.

The fundamental guarantees listed in this chapter all have a firm basis in international humanitarian law applicable in both international and non-international armed conflicts. Most of the rules set out in this chapter are couched in traditional humanitarian law language, because this best reflects the substance of the corresponding customary rule. Some rules, however, are drafted so as to capture the essence of a range of detailed provisions relating to a specific subject, in particular the rules relating to detention (see Rule 99), forced labour (see Rule 95) and family life (see Rule 105). In addition, references to human rights law instruments, documents and case-law have been included. This was done, not for the purpose of providing an assessment of customary human rights law, but in order to support, strengthen and clarify analogous principles of humanitarian law. While it is the majority view that international human rights law only binds governments and not armed opposition groups,[1] it is accepted that international humanitarian law binds both.

It is beyond the scope of this study to determine whether these guarantees apply equally outside armed conflict although collected practice appears to indicate that they do.

Continued applicability of human rights law during armed conflict

Human rights law applies at all times although some human rights treaties allow for certain derogations in a "state of emergency".[2] As stated by the

---

[1] But see, e.g., Christian Tomuschat, "The Applicability of Human Rights Law to Insurgent Movements", in Horst Fischer *et al.*, *Crisis Management and Humanitarian Protection*, Berliner Wissenschafts-Verlag, Berlin, 2004.

[2] International Covenant on Civil and Political Rights, Article 4; European Convention on Human Rights, Article 15; American Convention on Human Rights, Article 27 (which also expressly

International Court of Justice in its advisory opinion in the *Nuclear Weapons case*:

The protection of the International Covenant of Civil and Political Rights does not cease in times of war, except by operation of Article 4 of the Covenant whereby certain provisions may be derogated from in a time of national emergency.[3]

Having recognised the continued applicability of human rights law during armed conflict, the Court analysed the interplay between the application of international humanitarian law and international human rights law in a situation of armed conflict with respect to the non-derogable human right not to be arbitrarily deprived of life. The Court stated that "the test of what is an arbitrary deprivation of life, however, then falls to be determined by the applicable *lex specialis*, namely, the law applicable in armed conflict which is designed to regulate the conduct of hostilities".[4]

In its General Comment on Article 4 of the International Covenant on Civil and Political Rights, the UN Human Rights Committee stated that:

During armed conflict, whether international or non-international, rules of international humanitarian law become applicable and help, in addition to the provisions in article 4 and article 5, paragraph 1, of the Covenant, to prevent the abuse of a State's emergency powers. The Covenant requires that even during an armed conflict measures derogating from the Covenant are allowed only if, and to the extent that, the situation constitutes a threat to the life of the nation.[5]

If an armed conflict occurs, a State will need to consider whether the situation is one that amounts to an emergency "threatening the life of the nation". According to international case-law, this phrase does not require that the whole nation be involved in the emergency but that the essence of the emergency consist of the fact that the normal application of human rights law – taking into account limitations that are allowed in relation to a number of rights for public safety and order – cannot be ensured in view of the nature of the emergency. If that is the case, a State party to a human rights treaty is entitled to declare a state of emergency and inform the appropriate organs, as required by the treaty concerned – or else the State continues to be bound by the whole treaty.[6]

refers to the period of time strictly required). The African Charter on Human and Peoples' Rights contains no derogation clause, but limitations are possible on the basis of Article 27(2), which states that "the rights and freedoms of each individual shall be exercised with due regard to the rights of others, collective security, morality and common interest". In practice, this has been strictly interpreted by the African Commission on Human and Peoples' Rights.

[3] ICJ, *Nuclear Weapons case*, Advisory Opinion, § 25.
[4] ICJ, *Nuclear Weapons case*, Advisory Opinion (cited in Vol. II, Ch. 32, § 926).
[5] UN Human Rights Committee, General Comment No. 29 (Article 4 of the International Covenant on Civil and Political Rights), 24 July 2001, § 3.
[6] For a more complete description of the interpretation of these treaties by the treaty bodies in relation to detention, judicial guarantees and states of emergency, see Louise Doswald-Beck and

Most of the human rights provisions cited in this chapter are listed in the major human rights treaties as rights that may not be derogated from in any circumstance, and these treaties are widely ratified.[7] However, this chapter also cites some rights that are not listed as "non-derogable" as such in those treaties, not only because these rights are seen as particularly important to both international humanitarian law and human rights law, but also because human rights case-law has in practice treated them as largely non-derogable.

It should be noted that it is the consistent practice of human rights treaty bodies to insist on a strict interpretation of the provision that any derogation measures during a state of emergency be limited "to the extent strictly required by the exigencies of the situation". The UN Human Rights Committee stressed that:

This requirement relates to the duration, geographical coverage and material scope of the state of emergency and any measures of derogation resorted to because of the emergency... The mere fact that a permissible derogation from a specific provision may, of itself, be justified by the exigencies of the situation does not obviate the requirement that specific measures taken pursuant to the derogation must also be shown to be required by the exigencies of the situation. In practice this will ensure that no provision of the Covenant, however validly derogated from, will be entirely inapplicable to the behaviour of a State party.[8]

The European and Inter-American Courts of Human Rights have taken the same approach when examining derogation measures from specific rights, stressing the need for safeguards so that the essence of the right is not totally eliminated, as well as the need for proportionality so that the measures are only those strictly required and not more.[9] The African Commission on Human and Peoples' Rights, in a case concerning killings and disappearances during a civil

Robert Kolb, *Judicial Process and Human Rights: United Nations, European, American and African Systems, Texts and Summaries of International Case-law*, International Commission of Jurists, N.P. Engel Publisher, Kehl, 2004.

[7] The International Covenant on Civil and Political Rights has been ratified by 152 States, the European Convention on Human Rights by 45 States (i.e., all members of the Council of Europe), the African Charter on Human and Peoples' Rights by 53 States (i.e., all members of the African Union) and the American Convention on Human Rights by 25 States (i.e., all States party to the Organization of American States except Antigua and Barbuda, Bahamas, Belize, Canada, Guyana, St. Kitts and Nevis, Santa Lucia, St. Vincent and the Grenadines and the United States; Belize, Canada, Guyana, St. Vincent and the Grenadines and the United States have, however, ratified the International Covenant on Civil and Political Rights). This means that 34 States are not party to either the Covenant nor one of the regional human rights conventions (Antigua and Barbuda, Bahamas, Bahrain, Bhutan, Brunei, China, Cook Islands, Cuba, Indonesia, Kazakhstan, Kiribati, Laos, Malaysia, Maldives, Marshall Islands, Micronesia, Myanmar, Nauru, Niue, Oman, Pakistan, Palau, Papua New Guinea, Qatar, Saint Kitts and Nevis, Saint Lucia, Samoa, Saudi Arabia, Singapore, Solomon Islands, Tonga, Tuvalu, United Arab Emirates and Vanuatu).

[8] UN Human Rights Committee, General Comment No. 29 (Article 4 of the International Covenant on Civil and Political Rights), 24 July 2001, § 4.

[9] See, e.g., European Court of Human Rights, *Fox, Campbell and Hartley*, Judgement, 30 August 1990, § 32; *Lawless case*, Judgement, 1 July 1961, § 37; *Brannigan and McBride v. UK*, Judgement, 25 May 1993, §§ 43 and 61–65; *Aksoy v. Turkey*, Judgement, 18 December 1996, §§ 83–84; Inter-American Court of Human Rights, *Castillo Petruzzi and Others case*, Judgement, 30 May 1999, § 109.

war, confirmed that no derogation was possible under the African Charter on Human and Peoples' Rights, and that the government remained responsible for securing the safety and liberty of its citizens and for conducting investigations into murders.[10] In another case, the Commission confirmed that no derogations were possible and referred to Article 27(2) of the African Charter on Human and Peoples' Rights, which states that the rights "shall be exercised with due regard to the rights of others, collective security, morality and common interest". The Commission added that this provision must be interpreted as meaning that "limitations must be strictly proportionate with and absolutely necessary for the advantages which follow. Most important, a limitation may not erode a right such that the right itself becomes illusory."[11]

The UN Human Rights Committee also relied on crimes against humanity and international humanitarian law to establish the impermissibility of derogations, even if the rights concerned were not listed as "non-derogable". With respect to crimes against humanity, the Human Rights Committee stated that:

If action conducted under the authority of a State constitutes a basis for individual criminal responsibility for a crime against humanity by the persons involved in that action, article 4 of the Covenant cannot be used as a justification that a state of emergency exempted the State in question from its responsibility in relation to the same conduct. Therefore, the recent codification of crimes against humanity ... in the Rome Statute of the International Criminal Court is of relevance in the interpretation of Article 4 of the Covenant.[12]

In relation to international humanitarian law, the Human Rights Committee stated that:

Safeguards related to derogation, as embodied in article 4 of the Covenant, are based on the principles of legality and the rule of law inherent in the Covenant as a whole. As certain elements of the right to a fair trial are explicitly guaranteed under international humanitarian law during armed conflict, the Committee finds no justification for derogation from these guarantees during other emergency situations. The Committee is of the opinion that the principles of legality and the rule of law require that fundamental requirements of fair trial must be respected during a state of emergency. Only a court of law may try and convict a person for a criminal offence.[13]

The above comments show how international humanitarian law and human rights law reinforce each other, not only to reaffirm rules applicable in times of armed conflict, but in all situations.

---

[10] African Commission on Human and Peoples' Rights, *Civil Liberties Organisation v. Chad*, Communication No. 74/92, 18th Ordinary Session, Praia, 11 October 1995, *9th Annual Activity Report*, §§ 21–22.

[11] African Commission on Human and Peoples' Rights, *Constitutional Rights Project v. Nigeria*, Communication Nos. 140/94, 141/94 and 145/95, 26th Ordinary Session, Kigali, 1–15 November 1999, *13th Annual Activity Report 1999–2000*, Doc. AHG/222 (XXVI), Annex V, §§ 41–42.

[12] UN Human Rights Committee, General Comment No. 29 (Article 4 of the International Covenant on Civil and Political Rights), 24 July 2001, § 12.

[13] UN Human Rights Committee, General Comment No. 29 (Article 4 of the International Covenant on Civil and Political Rights), 24 July 2001, § 16.

State practice requiring respect for human rights during armed conflicts

There is extensive State practice to the effect that human rights law must be applied during armed conflicts. The resolutions adopted at the International Conference on Human Rights in Teheran in 1968 and by the UN General Assembly the same year referred to "human rights in armed conflict", whereas the content of the resolutions related primarily to international humanitarian law.[14] However, shortly afterwards the approach changed. UN General Assembly Resolution 2675 (XXV) on basic principles for the protection of civilian populations in armed conflicts, adopted in 1970, referred in its preamble to the four Geneva Conventions and also specifically to the Fourth Geneva Convention, as well as to "the progressive development of the international law of armed conflict". In its first operative paragraph, the resolution stated that "fundamental human rights, as accepted in international law and laid down in international instruments, continue to apply fully in situations of armed conflict".[15] Since then, the understanding that both human rights law and international humanitarian law apply in armed conflicts has been confirmed by numerous resolutions condemning violations of both these areas of law in specific armed conflicts and by United Nations investigations into violations of both areas of law in armed conflict situations.

Human rights violations have been condemned, for example, in the context of armed conflicts or military occupations in Afghanistan,[16] Iraq,[17] Sudan,[18] Russia,[19] the former Yugoslavia[20] and Uganda.[21] The United Nations has also conducted investigations into violations of human rights, for example,

---

[14] International Conference on Human Rights, Teheran, 12 May 1968, Res. XXIII; UN General Assembly, Res. 2444 (XXIII), 19 December 1968.

[15] UN General Assembly, Res. 2675 (XXV), 9 December 1970 (adopted by 109 in favour, none against and 8 abstentions), preamble and § 1.

[16] UN General Assembly, Res. 52/145, 12 December 1997 (adopted by consensus), § 2 ("notes with deep concern the intensification of armed hostilities in Afghanistan") and § 3 ("condemns the violations and abuses of human rights and humanitarian law, including the rights to life, liberty and security of person, freedom from torture and from other forms of cruel, inhuman or degrading treatment or punishment, freedom of opinion, expression, religion, association and movement").

[17] UN Commission on Human Rights, Res. 1992/60, 3 March 1992, preamble (§§ 3, 6 and 8) indicating respectively that the resolution is guided by, *inter alia*, the international covenants on human rights and the Geneva Conventions of 1949, that it expresses "deep concern at the grave violations of human rights and fundamental freedoms during the occupation of Kuwait" and notes "with grave concern the information to the effect that the treatment of prisoners of war and detained civilians does not conform to the internationally recognised principles of humanitarian law". There are similar statements in UN General Assembly, Res. 46/135, 17 December 1991.

[18] UN Commission on Human Rights, Res. 1996/73, 23 April 1996.

[19] UN Commission on Human Rights, Res. 2000/58, 25 April 2000, preamble (§ 10) ("the need to ... observe international human rights and humanitarian law in situations of conflict") and § 4 (calling on Russia to "investigate promptly alleged violations of human rights and breaches of international humanitarian law committed in the Republic of Chechnya").

[20] UN Security Council, Res. 1019, 9 November 1995; UN Security Council, Res. 1034, 21 December 1995; UN General Assembly, Res. 50/193, 22 December 1995; UN Commission on Human Rights, Res. 1996/71, 23 April 1996.

[21] UN Commission on Human Rights, Res. 1998/75, 22 April 1998.

in connection with the conflicts in Liberia[22] and Sierra Leone,[23] Israel's military occupation of the Palestinian territories,[24] Iraq's military occupation of Kuwait,[25] and the situation in Afghanistan during and after the Soviet occupation.[26] The UN High Commissioner for Human Rights also has national offices that monitor and promote respect for both human rights and humanitarian law in non-international armed conflicts.[27]

The reports of the investigations into the situation in Afghanistan from 1985 onwards and into the situation in Kuwait during the Iraqi occupation, as well as States' reaction to them, are examples of the acceptance of the simultaneous applicability of both areas of international law.

The various reports of the UN Special Rapporteurs for Afghanistan referred to aspects of both human rights and humanitarian law, for example, in the report submitted to the UN Commission on Human Rights in 1987.[28] This report was commended in a resolution adopted by consensus by the UN Commission on Human Rights, in which it expressed concern that "the Afghan authorities, with heavy support from foreign troops, are acting...without any respect for the international human rights obligations which they have assumed", voiced "its deep concern about the number of persons detained for seeking to exercise their fundamental human rights and freedoms, and their detention contrary to internationally recognized standards", noted "with concern that such widespread violations of human rights...are still giving rise to large flows of refugees" and called on "the parties to the conflict to apply fully the principles and rules of international humanitarian law".[29]

---

[22] UN Secretary-General, Progress report on UNOMIL, UN Doc. S/1996/47, 23 January 1996.

[23] UN Secretary-General, Progress report on UNOMSIL, UN Doc. S/1998/750, 12 August 1998.

[24] UN Commission on Human Rights, Res. S-5/1, 19 October 2000, § 6 (decided "to establish ...a human rights inquiry commission...to gather and compile information on violations of human rights and acts which constitute grave breaches of international humanitarian law by the Israeli occupying Power in the occupied Palestinian territories"). Its first and last preambular paragraphs refer specifically to human rights treaties and to humanitarian law treaties respectively.

[25] UN Commission on Human Rights, Res. 1991/67, 6 March 1991, § 9 (mandated a Special Rapporteur "to examine the human rights violations committed in occupied Kuwait by the invading and occupying forces of Iraq").

[26] UN Economic and Social Council, Decision 1985/147, 30 May 1985, approving UN Commission on Human Rights Res. 1985/38 of 13 May 1985 "to extend for one year the mandate of the Special Rapporteur on the question of human rights and fundamental freedoms in Afghanistan and to request him to report to the General Assembly...and to the Commission [on Human Rights]...on the situation of human rights in that country", reprinted in UN Doc. E/1985/85, 1985. The mandate was renewed on many occasions. See UN Doc. A/52/493, 16 October 1997, the introduction to which lists the reports submitted by Special Rapporteurs for Afghanistan between 1985 and 1997.

[27] For example, the field office in Santafé de Bogotá, Colombia, established by agreement in November 1996, which has the mandate to monitor the situation and to "promote respect for and observance of human rights and international humanitarian law in Colombia" (see www.unhchr.ch/html/menu2/5/colombia.htm).

[28] UN Commission on Human Rights, Special Rapporteur on the Situation of Human Rights in Afghanistan, Report, UN Doc. E/CN.4/1987/22, 19 February 1987.

[29] UN Commission on Human Rights, Res. 1987/58, 11 March 1987, §§ 2, 7, 9 and 10.

The report on the Iraqi occupation of Kuwait examined issues such as arbitrary arrest, disappearances, right to life, right to food, right to health in the light of the provisions of the International Covenant on Civil and Political Rights and the International Covenant on Economic, Social and Cultural Rights, but also of international humanitarian law. In particular, the report states that "there is consensus within the international community that the fundamental human rights of all persons are to be respected and protected both in times of peace and during periods of armed conflict".[30] Resolutions adopted by the UN General Assembly and by the UN Commission on Human Rights on the situation of human rights in Kuwait under Iraqi occupation in 1991 expressed these bodies' appreciation of the Special Rapporteur's report.[31]

Territorial scope of application of human rights law

Most human rights treaties specify that they are to be applied by States parties wherever they have jurisdiction. However, it should be noted that treaty bodies, and significant State practice, have interpreted this as meaning wherever State organs have effective control.

Article 2 of the International Covenant on Civil and Political Rights specifies that States parties are to "respect and ensure to all individuals within its territory and subject to its jurisdiction the rights recognised in the present Covenant". State practice has interpreted this widely. In particular, the UN Special Rapporteur for Iraqi-occupied Kuwait was instructed by States to report on respect for or the violation of human rights by Iraq in Kuwait, even though Kuwait could not be considered to be its "territory" and recognition of any formal jurisdiction did not occur. As mentioned above, the Special Rapporteur analysed the implementation of the provisions of the Covenant by Iraq in Kuwait and his report was welcomed by States.

Article 1 of the European and American Conventions on Human Rights specify that the Conventions are to be applied by States parties to persons within their jurisdiction. This has been interpreted by their treaty bodies as meaning "effective control". In *Loizidou v. Turkey* in 1995 concerning the situation in northern Cyprus, the European Court of Human Rights held that a State party is bound to respect the Convention when, as a consequence of military action, it exercises effective control over an area outside its national territory.[32]

---

[30] UN Commission on Human Rights, UN Doc. E/CN.4/1992/26, 16 January 1992, § 33; see also the introduction to this report by Walter Kälin and Larisa Gabriel, which catalogues and analyses the bases for the applicability of both human rights law and humanitarian law during armed conflicts and occupation, reprinted in Walter Kälin (ed.), *Human Rights in Times of Occupation: The Case of Kuwait*, Law Books in Europe, Berne, 1994.

[31] UN General Assembly, Res. 46/135, 17 December 1991 (adopted by consensus), § 2; UN Commission on Human Rights, Res. 1991/67, 6 March 1991 (adopted by 41 votes in favour, I against and no abstentions), § 1.

[32] European Court of Human Rights, *Loizidou v. Turkey*, Preliminary Objections, Judgement, 23 March 1995, § 62.

In the case of *Banković* against seventeen NATO States, the European Court confirmed that it applied the European Convention extra-territorially when a "State, through the effective control of the relevant territory and its inhabitants abroad as a consequence of military occupation or through the consent, invitation or acquiescence of the Government of that territory, exercises all or some of the public powers normally to be exercised by that Government".[33] The same yardstick of effective control to evaluate the applicability of the Inter-American Convention on Human Rights was made by the Inter-American Commission on Human Rights in *Alejandre and Others v. Cuba*, in which the Commission cited the *Loizidou v. Turkey* case with approval.[34]

Rule 87. Civilians and persons *hors de combat* must be treated humanely.

Practice

Volume II, Chapter 32, Section A.

Summary

State practice establishes this rule as a norm of customary international law applicable in both international and non-international armed conflicts.

International and non-international armed conflicts

The obligation to treat prisoners of war humanely was already recognised in the Lieber Code, the Brussels Declaration and the Oxford Manual and was codified in the Hague Regulations.[35] The requirement of humane treatment for civilians and persons *hors de combat* is set forth in common Article 3 of the Geneva Conventions, as well as in specific provisions of all four Conventions.[36] This requirement is recognised as a fundamental guarantee by both Additional Protocols I and II.[37]

---

[33] European Court of Human Rights, *Banković v. Belgium, the Czech Republic, Denmark, France, Germany, Greece, Hungary, Iceland, Italy, Luxembourg, the Netherlands, Norway, Poland, Portugal, Spain, Turkey and the United Kingdom*, Decision as to Admissibility, 12 December 2001, § 71.

[34] Inter-American Commission on Human Rights, Case 11.589, *Alejandre and Others v. Cuba*, Report No. 86/99, 29 September 1999, §§ 24–25.

[35] Lieber Code, Article 76 (cited in Vol. II, Ch. 32, § 215); Brussels Declaration, Article 23(2) (*ibid.*, § 216); Oxford Manual, Article 63 (*ibid.*, § 217); Hague Regulations, Article 4, second paragraph (*ibid.*, § 206).

[36] Geneva Conventions, common Article 3 (*ibid.*, § 1); First Geneva Convention, Article 12, first paragraph (*ibid.*, § 143); Second Geneva Convention, Article 12, first paragraph (*ibid.*, § 144); Third Geneva Convention, Article 13 (*ibid.*, § 208); Fourth Geneva Convention, Articles 5 and 27, first paragraph (*ibid.*, §§ 82–83).

[37] Additional Protocol I, Article 75(1) (adopted by consensus) (*ibid.*, § 2); Additional Protocol II, Article 4(1) (adopted by consensus) (*ibid.*, § 3).

The requirement of humane treatment is set forth in numerous military manuals.[38] It has been reaffirmed in national and international case-law.[39]

Human rights law is similarly based on the principle of humane treatment of persons. In particular, human rights instruments stress the requirement of humane treatment and respect for human dignity of persons deprived of their liberty.[40] In its General Comment on Article 4 of the International Covenant on Civil and Political Rights, the UN Human Rights Committee declared Article 10, which requires that persons deprived of their liberty be treated with humanity and with respect for the inherent dignity of the human person, to be non-derogable and therefore applicable at all times.[41]

Definition of humane treatment

The actual meaning of "humane treatment" is not spelled out, although some texts refer to respect for the "dignity" of a person or the prohibition of "ill-treatment" in this context.[42] The requirement of humane treatment is an

---

[38] See, e.g., the military manuals of Argentina (*ibid.*, §§ 9–10 and 90–91), Australia (*ibid.*, §§ 11 and 92–93), Belgium (*ibid.*, §§ 12 and 94), Benin (*ibid.*, §§ 13 and 95), Burkina Faso (*ibid.*, § 14), Cameroon (*ibid.*, §§ 15–16), Canada (*ibid.*, § 17), Colombia (*ibid.*, §§ 18–20), Congo (*ibid.*, § 21), Croatia (*ibid.*, § 22), Dominican Republic (*ibid.*, § 23), France (*ibid.*, §§ 24–26), Germany (*ibid.*, § 27), India (*ibid.*, § 28), Kenya (*ibid.*, § 30), Madagascar (*ibid.*, § 31), Mali (*ibid.*, § 32), Morocco (*ibid.*, § 33), Netherlands (*ibid.*, §§ 34–35), New Zealand (*ibid.*, § 36), Nicaragua (*ibid.*, § 37), Peru (*ibid.*, § 38), Philippines (*ibid.*, § 39), Romania (*ibid.*, § 40), Russia (*ibid.*, § 41), Senegal (*ibid.*, §§ 42–43), Sweden (*ibid.*, § 44), Switzerland (*ibid.*, § 45), Togo (*ibid.*, § 46), United Kingdom (*ibid.*, § 47) and United States (*ibid.*, §§ 48–51) and the reported practice of Israel (*ibid.*, § 29).

[39] See, e.g., Chile, Appeal Court of Santiago, *Videla case* (*ibid.*, § 57); Russia, Constitutional Court, *Situation in Chechnya case* (*ibid.*, § 58); ICJ, *Nicaragua case (Merits)*, Judgement (*ibid.*, § 69); ICTY, *Aleksovski case*, Judgement (*ibid.*, § 70); Inter-American Commission on Human Rights, *Case 10.559 (Peru)* (*ibid.*, § 71).

[40] See American Declaration on the Rights and Duties of Man, Article XXV (*ibid.*, § 218); International Covenant on Civil and Political Rights, Article 10(1) (*ibid.*, § 211); American Convention on Human Rights, Article 5(1) (*ibid.*, § 212); European Prison Rules, Rule 1 (*ibid.*, § 219); Body of Principles for the Protection of All Persons under Any Form of Detention or Imprisonment, Principle 1 (*ibid.*, § 220); Basic Principles for the Treatment of Prisoners, para. 1 (*ibid.*, § 221).

[41] UN Human Rights Committee, General Comment No. 29 (Article 4 of the International Covenant on Civil and Political Rights) (*ibid.*, § 321).

[42] Texts which use the term "dignity" include, e.g., International Covenant on Civil and Political Rights, Article 10(1) (*ibid.*, § 211); American Convention on Human Rights, Article 5 (*ibid.*, § 212); African Charter on Human and Peoples' Rights, Article 5; Body of Principles for the Protection of All Persons under Any Form of Detention or Imprisonment, Principle 1 (*ibid.*, § 220); Basic Principles for the Treatment of Prisoners, para. 1 (*ibid.*, § 221); UN Secretary-General's Bulletin, Section 8 (*ibid.*, § 224); the military manuals of France (*ibid.*, § 246), Germany (*ibid.*, § 248) Peru (*ibid.*, § 38) and United States (*ibid.*, §§ 122 and 284); the legislation of Paraguay (*ibid.*, § 55) and Uruguay (*ibid.*, § 294); UN Human Rights Committee, General Comment No. 21 (Article 10 of the International Covenant on Civil and Political Rights) (*ibid.*, § 320) and General Comment No. 29 (Article 4 of the International Covenant on Civil and Political Rights) (*ibid.*, § 321); ICTY, *Aleksovski case* (*ibid.*, § 70); ICRC, Communication to the Press No. 01/47 (*ibid.*, § 80). Texts which refer to the prohibition of "ill-treatment" include, e.g., IMT Charter (Nuremberg), Article 6 (*ibid.*, § 982); the military manual of Romania (*ibid.*, § 111); UN Commission on Human Rights, Res. 1989/67, 1990/53, 1991/78 and 1992/68 (*ibid.*, § 311) and Res. 1991/67 and 1992/60 (*ibid.*, § 312); ICRC, Memorandum on Respect for International Humanitarian Law in Angola (*ibid.*, § 343) and Memorandum on Compliance

overarching concept. It is generally understood that the detailed rules found in international humanitarian law and human rights law give expression to the meaning of "humane treatment". The rules in Chapters 33–39 contain specific applications of the requirement of humane treatment for certain categories of persons: the wounded, sick and shipwrecked, persons deprived of their liberty, displaced persons, women, children, the elderly, the disabled and infirm. However, these rules do not necessarily express the full meaning of what is meant by humane treatment, as this notion develops over time under the influence of changes in society. This is shown, for example, by the fact that the requirement of humane treatment has been mentioned in international instruments since the mid-19th century, but the detailed rules which stem from this requirement have developed since then, and may do so still further.

Rule 88. Adverse distinction in the application of international humanitarian law based on race, colour, sex, language, religion or belief, political or other opinion, national or social origin, wealth, birth or other status, or on any other similar criteria is prohibited.

Practice

Volume II, Chapter 32, Section B.

Summary

State practice establishes this rule as a norm of customary international law applicable in both international and non-international armed conflicts.

International and non-international armed conflicts

The prohibition of adverse distinction in the treatment of civilians and persons *hors de combat* is stated in common Article 3 of the Geneva Conventions, as well in the Third and Fourth Geneva Conventions.[43] It is recognised as a fundamental guarantee by Additional Protocols I and II.[44] It is contained in

---

with International Humanitarian Law by the Forces Participating in Opération Turquoise (*ibid.*, § 344).

[43] Geneva Conventions, common Article 3 (*ibid.*, § 356); Third Geneva Convention, Article 16; Fourth Geneva Convention, Article 13.

[44] Additional Protocol I, Article 75(1) (adopted by consensus) (cited in Vol. II, Ch. 32, § 368); Additional Protocol II, Article 4(1) (adopted by consensus) (*ibid.*, § 370); see also Additional Protocol I, preamble (*ibid.*, § 366), Article 9(1) (adopted by consensus) (*ibid.*, § 367), Article 69(1) (adopted by consensus) (*ibid.*, § 462) and Article 70(1) (adopted by consensus) (*ibid.*, § 463); Additional Protocol II, Article 2(1) (adopted by consensus) (*ibid.*, § 369) and Article 18(2) (adopted by consensus) (*ibid.*, § 464).

numerous military manuals.[45] It is also supported by official statements and other practice.[46]

The notion of "adverse distinction" implies that while discrimination between persons is prohibited, a distinction may be made to give priority to those in most urgent need of care. In application of this principle, no distinction may be made among the wounded, sick and shipwrecked on any grounds other than medical (see Rule 110). Another application can be found in Article 16 of the Third Geneva Convention, which provides that all prisoners of war must be treated alike, "taking into consideration the provisions of the present Convention relating to rank and sex, and subject to any privileged treatment which may be accorded to them by reason of their state of health, age or professional qualifications".[47] There is no indication that adverse distinction is lawful in relation to some rules, and no State has asserted that any such exception exists.

The human rights law equivalent of the prohibition of adverse distinction is the principle of non-discrimination. The prohibition of discrimination in the application of human rights law is included in the Charter of the United Nations and in the major human rights treaties.[48] With respect to the derogability of the right to non-discrimination, the UN Human Rights Committee stated in its General Comment on Article 4 of the International Covenant on Civil and Political Rights that:

Even though article 26 or the other Covenant provisions related to non-discrimination... have not been listed among the non-derogable provisions in article 4, paragraph 2, there are elements or dimensions of the right to non-discrimination that cannot be derogated from in any circumstances. In particular,

---

[45] See, e.g., the military manuals of Argentina (*ibid.*, §§ 385–386, 469, 499 and 554–555), Australia (*ibid.*, §§ 387, 500–501 and 556), Belgium (*ibid.*, §§ 388 and 502–503), Benin (*ibid.*, §§ 389, 504 and 557), Bosnia and Herzegovina (*ibid.*, §§ 390 and 505), Burkina Faso (*ibid.*, § 391), Cameroon (*ibid.*, § 392), Canada (*ibid.*, §§ 393, 470–471, 506 and 558–559), Colombia (*ibid.*, §§ 394–395), Congo (*ibid.*, § 396), Croatia (*ibid.*, § 507), Dominican Republic (*ibid.*, § 508), Ecuador (*ibid.*, §§ 509 and 560), El Salvador (*ibid.*, § 397), France (*ibid.*, §§ 398–399 and 510), Germany (*ibid.*, §§ 472, 511 and 561–562), Israel (*ibid.*, §§ 400 and 512), Italy (*ibid.*, §§ 473 and 513), Kenya (*ibid.*, § 401), Madagascar (*ibid.*, § 402), Mali (*ibid.*, § 403), Morocco (*ibid.*, §§ 404 and 514), Netherlands (*ibid.*, §§ 405–406, 515–516 and 563), New Zealand (*ibid.*, §§ 407, 474 and 564), Nicaragua (*ibid.*, §§ 408, 475 and 517), Nigeria (*ibid.*, §§ 518–519 and 565), Peru (*ibid.*, § 409), Senegal (*ibid.*, §§ 410–411), Spain (*ibid.*, §§ 520 and 566), Sweden (*ibid.*, §§ 412 and 476), Switzerland (*ibid.*, §§ 477, 521 and 567), Togo (*ibid.*, §§ 413, 522 and 508), United Kingdom (*ibid.*, §§ 414, 478–479, 523–524 and 569), United States (*ibid.*, §§ 415–417, 480–481, 525–527 and 570–572) and Yugoslavia (*ibid.*, § 528).

[46] See, e.g., the statements of Bosnia and Herzegovina (*ibid.*, § 534) and United States (*ibid.*, § 440), the practice of Iraq (*ibid.*, § 438) and the reported practice of China (*ibid.*, § 487) and United States (*ibid.*, § 441).

[47] Third Geneva Convention, Article 16.

[48] UN Charter, Article 1(3) (cited in Vol. II, Ch. 32, § 355); International Covenant on Civil and Political Rights, Article 2(1) (*ibid.*, § 359); International Covenant on Economic, Social and Cultural Rights, Articles 2(2) and 3 (*ibid.*, §§ 362–363); European Convention on Human Rights, Article 14 (*ibid.*, § 357); American Convention on Human Rights, Article 1(1) (*ibid.*, § 364); African Charter on Human and Peoples' Rights, Article 2 (*ibid.*, § 372); Convention on the Elimination of Racial Discrimination, Article 2 (*ibid.*, § 358); Convention on the Elimination of Discrimination against Women, Article 2 (*ibid.*, § 371); Convention on the Rights of the Child, Article 2(1) (*ibid.*, § 373).

the provision of article 4, paragraph 1, must be complied with if any distinctions between persons are made when resorting to measures that derogate from the Covenant.[49]

Article 4(1) of the Covenant provides that measures that derogate from it may not involve "discrimination solely on the ground of race, colour, sex, language, religion or social origin".[50] While discrimination on grounds of political or other opinion, national origin, property, birth or other status is prohibited under Article 2(1) of the Covenant, these grounds are not listed in Article 4(1) dealing with derogations.[51] It is significant, however, that the Additional Protocols prohibit discrimination on grounds of political or other opinion, national origin, wealth, birth or other status and thus recognise that the prohibition of discrimination on such grounds cannot be dispensed with, even during armed conflict.[52] This is also the approach of the African Charter on Human and Peoples' Rights and the Convention on the Rights of the Child, which prohibit discrimination on grounds of political or other opinion, national origin, property, birth or other status and do not allow for any derogation.[53]

Apartheid

According to Additional Protocol I, "practices of apartheid and other inhuman or degrading practices involving outrages upon personal dignity, based on racial discrimination" constitute grave breaches.[54] This rule is set forth in several military manuals.[55] The legislation of many States also contains this rule.[56] In addition, apartheid constitutes a crime against humanity under several

---

[49] UN Human Rights Committee, General Comment No. 29 (Article 4 of the International Covenant on Civil and Political Rights) (*ibid.*, § 450).

[50] International Covenant on Civil and Political Rights, Article 4(1) (*ibid.*, § 360); see also American Convention on Human Rights, Article 27(1), which contains a similar provision (*ibid.*, § 365).

[51] International Covenant on Civil and Political Rights, Article 2(1) (*ibid.*, § 359) and Article 4(1) (*ibid.*, § 360).

[52] Additional Protocol I, preamble (*ibid.*, § 366), Article 9(1) (adopted by consensus) (*ibid.*, § 367) and Article 75(1) (adopted by consensus) (*ibid.*, § 368); Additional Protocol II, Article 2(1) (adopted by consensus) (*ibid.*, § 369) and Article 4(1) (adopted by consensus) (*ibid.*, § 370).

[53] African Charter on Human and Peoples' Rights, Article 2 (*ibid.*, § 372); Convention on the Rights of the Child, Article 2(1) (*ibid.*, § 373).

[54] Additional Protocol I, Article 85(4)(c) (adopted by consensus) (*ibid.*, § 584).

[55] See, e.g., the military manuals of Argentina (*ibid.*, § 589), Canada (*ibid.*, § 590), Germany (*ibid.*, § 592), Italy (*ibid.*, § 593), Netherlands (*ibid.*, § 594), New Zealand (*ibid.*, § 595), South Africa (*ibid.*, § 597), Spain (*ibid.*, § 598) and Switzerland (*ibid.*, § 599).

[56] See, e.g., the legislation of Armenia (*ibid.*, § 600), Australia (*ibid.*, §§ 601–602), Azerbaijan (*ibid.*, § 603), Belgium (*ibid.*, § 604), Bulgaria (*ibid.*, § 605), Canada (*ibid.*, § 607), Colombia (*ibid.*, § 609), Cook Islands (*ibid.*, § 611), Cyprus (*ibid.*, § 612), Czech Republic (*ibid.*, § 613), Georgia (*ibid.*, § 615), Hungary (*ibid.*, § 616), Ireland (*ibid.*, § 617), Moldova (*ibid.*, § 621), Netherlands (*ibid.*, § 622), New Zealand (*ibid.*, § 623), Niger (*ibid.*, § 626), Norway (*ibid.*, § 627), Peru (*ibid.*, § 628), Slovakia (*ibid.*, § 629), Spain (*ibid.*, § 630), Tajikistan (*ibid.*, § 631), United Kingdom (*ibid.*, § 633) and Zimbabwe (*ibid.*, § 635); see also the draft legislation of El Salvador (*ibid.*, § 614), Jordan (*ibid.*, § 618), Lebanon (*ibid.*, § 619) and Nicaragua (*ibid.*, § 625).

international treaties and other international instruments.[57] The legislation of several States also prohibits apartheid as a crime against humanity.[58]

Rule 89. Murder is prohibited.

Practice

Volume II, Chapter 32, Section C.

Summary

State practice establishes this rule as a norm of customary international law applicable in both international and non-international armed conflicts.

International and non-international armed conflicts

The prohibition of murder of civilians was already recognised in the Lieber Code.[59] Murder of civilians and prisoners of war was included as a war crime in the Charter of the International Military Tribunal at Nuremberg.[60] Common Article 3 of the Geneva Conventions prohibits "violence to life and person, in particular murder of all kinds" of civilians and persons *hors de combat*.[61] All four Geneva Conventions list "wilful killing" of protected persons as a grave breach.[62] The prohibition of murder is recognised as a fundamental guarantee by Additional Protocols I and II.[63] Murder is also specified as a war crime under the Statute of the International Criminal Court with respect to both international and non-international armed conflicts and under the Statutes of the International Criminal Tribunals for the Former Yugoslavia and for Rwanda and of the Special Court for Sierra Leone.[64]

---

[57] International Convention on the Suppression and Punishment of the Crime of Apartheid, Article I (*ibid.*, § 583); ICC Statute, Article 7(1)(j) (*ibid.*, § 585); UNTAET Regulation 2000/15, Section 6(1)(j) (*ibid.*, § 588).

[58] See, e.g., the legislation of Australia (*ibid.*, § 602), Canada (*ibid.*, § 608), Congo (*ibid.*, § 610), Mali (*ibid.*, § 620), New Zealand (*ibid.*, § 624) and United Kingdom (*ibid.*, § 634); see also the draft legislation of Burundi (*ibid.*, § 606) and Trinidad and Tobago (*ibid.*, § 632).

[59] Lieber Code, Articles 23 and 44 (*ibid.*, §§ 678–679).

[60] IMT Charter (Nuremberg), Article 6(b) (*ibid.*, § 654).

[61] Geneva Conventions, common Article 3 (*ibid.*, § 655).

[62] First Geneva Convention, Article 50 (*ibid.*, § 662); Second Geneva Convention, Article 51 (*ibid.*, § 662); Third Geneva Convention, Article 130 (*ibid.*, § 662); Fourth Geneva Convention, Article 147 (*ibid.*, § 662).

[63] Additional Protocol I, Article 75(2)(a) (adopted by consensus) (*ibid.*, § 669); Additional Protocol II, Article 4(2)(a) (adopted by consensus) (*ibid.*, § 670).

[64] ICC Statute, Article 8(2)(a)(i) and (c)(i) (*ibid.*, §§ 675–676); ICTY Statute, Article 2(a) (*ibid.*, § 695); ICTR Statute, Article 4(a) (*ibid.*, § 696); Statute of the Special Court for Sierra Leone, Article 3(a) (*ibid.*, § 677).

The prohibition on killing civilians and persons *hors de combat* is set forth in numerous military manuals.[65] It is also contained in the legislation of a large number of States.[66] This prohibition has been upheld extensively in national and international case-law.[67] Furthermore, it is supported by official statements and other practice.[68]

---

[65] See, e.g., the military manuals of Argentina (*ibid.*, §§ 702–703), Australia (*ibid.*, §§ 704–705), Belgium (*ibid.*, § 706), Benin (*ibid.*, § 707), Bosnia and Herzegovina (*ibid.*, § 708), Burkina Faso (*ibid.*, § 709), Cameroon (*ibid.*, §§ 710–711), Canada (*ibid.*, § 712), Colombia (*ibid.*, §§ 713–715), Congo (*ibid.*, § 716), Croatia (*ibid.*, §§ 717–718), Ecuador (*ibid.*, § 719), El Salvador (*ibid.*, § 720), France (*ibid.*, §§ 721–724), Germany (*ibid.*, §§ 725–726), Hungary (*ibid.*, § 727), Israel (*ibid.*, § 728), Italy (*ibid.*, § 729), Kenya (*ibid.*, § 730), South Korea (*ibid.*, § 731), Madagascar (*ibid.*, § 732), Mali (*ibid.*, § 733), Morocco (*ibid.*, § 734), Netherlands (*ibid.*, § 735), New Zealand (*ibid.*, § 736), Nicaragua (*ibid.*, § 737), Nigeria (*ibid.*, §§ 738–740), Peru (*ibid.*, §§ 741–742), Philippines (*ibid.*, § 743), Romania (*ibid.*, § 744), Russia (*ibid.*, § 745), Senegal (*ibid.*, §§ 746–747), South Africa (*ibid.*, § 748), Spain (*ibid.*, § 749), Switzerland (*ibid.*, §§ 750–751), Togo (*ibid.*, § 752), Uganda (*ibid.*, § 753), United Kingdom (*ibid.*, §§ 755–756) and United States (*ibid.*, §§ 757–761).

[66] See, e.g., the legislation (*ibid.*, §§ 762–853).

[67] See, e.g., Australia, Military Court at Rabaul, *Ohashi case* and *Baba Masao case* (*ibid.*, § 854); Belgium, Court-Martial of Brussels, *Sergeant W. case*, (*ibid.*, § 855); Chile, Appeal Court of Santiago, *Videla case* (*ibid.*, § 856); China, War Crimes Military Tribunal of the Ministry of National Defence at Nanking, *Takashi Sakai case* (*ibid.*, § 854); Colombia, Constitutional Court, *Constitutional Case No. C-225/95* (*ibid.*, § 857); Israel, District Court of Jerusalem and Supreme Court, *Eichmann case* (*ibid.*, § 854); Netherlands, Temporary Court-Martial at Makassar, *Motomura case* (*ibid.*, § 854); Netherlands, Temporary Court-Martial at Makassar, *Notomi Sueo case* (*ibid.*, § 854); Netherlands, Temporary Court-Martial at Amboina, *Motosuke case* (*ibid.*, § 854); Netherlands, Special Court of Cassation, *Silbertanne murders case* (*ibid.*, § 854) and *Burghof case* (*ibid.*, § 854); Netherlands, Special Court (War Criminals) at Arnhem, *Enkelstroth case* (*ibid.*, § 854); Norway, Court of Appeal, *Bruns case* (*ibid.*, § 854) and *Hans case* (*ibid.*, § 854); United Kingdom, Military Court at Almelo, *Sandrock case* (*ibid.*, § 854); United States, Military Commission at Rome, *Dostler case* (*ibid.*, § 854); United States, Military Tribunal at Nuremberg, *List (Hostages Trial) case* (*ibid.*, § 854); United States, Military Commission in the Far East, *Jaluit Atoll case* (*ibid.*, § 858); United States, Court of Military Appeals, *Schultz case* (*ibid.*, § 859); ICJ, *Nicaragua case (Merits)*, Judgement (*ibid.*, § 925); ICJ, *Nuclear Weapons case*, Advisory Opinion (*ibid.*, § 926); ICTR, *Ntakirutimana case*, Amended Indictment (*ibid.*, § 927); ICTY, *Tadić case*, Interlocutory Appeal, Second Amended Indictment and Judgement (*ibid.*, §§ 928–930), *Mrkšić case*, Initial Indictment and Review of the Indictment (*ibid.*, § 931), *Erdemović case*, Sentencing Judgement, Judgement on Appeal and Sentencing Judgement *bis* (*ibid.*, § 932), *Delalić case*, Judgement (*ibid.*, § 933), *Jelisić case*, Judgement (*ibid.*, § 934), *Kupreškić case*, Judgement (*ibid.*, § 935), *Blaškić case*, Judgement (*ibid.*, § 936) and *Kordić and Čerkez case*, First Amended Indictment and Judgement (*ibid.*, § 937); UN Human Rights Committee, General Comment No. 6 (Article 6 of the International Covenant on Civil and Political Rights) (*ibid.*, § 938); UN Human Rights Committee, *Camargo v. Colombia* (*ibid.*, § 939); African Commission on Human and Peoples' Rights, *Civil Liberties Organisation v. Chad* (*ibid.*, § 940); European Commission of Human Rights, *Dujardin and Others v. France* (*ibid.*, § 941); European Court of Human Rights, *McCann and Others v. UK* (*ibid.*, § 942), *Ergi v. Turkey* (*ibid.*, § 943), *Yasa v. Turkey* (*ibid.*, § 943), *Kurt v. Turkey* (*ibid.*, § 944), *Kaya v. Turkey* (*ibid.*, § 945), *Avsar v. Turkey* (*ibid.*, § 946) and *K.-H. W. v. Germany* (*ibid.*, § 947); Inter-American Commission on Human Rights, Resolution adopted at the 1968 Session (*ibid.*, § 948), *Case 10.559 (Peru)* (*ibid.*, § 949), *Case 6724 (El Salvador)*, *Case 10.190 (El Salvador)* and *Case 10.284 (El Salvador)* (*ibid.*, § 950), *Case 10.287 (El Salvador)* (*ibid.*, § 951), Report on the situation of human rights in Peru (*ibid.*, § 952), *Case 11.137 (Argentina)* (*ibid.*, § 953) and *Case of the Ríofrío massacre (Colombia)* (*ibid.*, § 954); Inter-American Court of Human Rights, *Velásquez Rodríguez case* (*ibid.*, § 955) and *Neira Alegría and Others case* (*ibid.*, § 956).

[68] See, e.g., the statements of Botswana (*ibid.*, § 860), Brazil (*ibid.*, § 861), China (*ibid.*, § 863), Colombia (*ibid.*, §§ 864–865), Costa Rica (*ibid.*, § 866), Egypt (*ibid.*, § 867), Indonesia (*ibid.*, § 870), Israel (*ibid.*, § 871), Malaysia (*ibid.*, § 872), Mexico (*ibid.*, § 873), Nauru (*ibid.*, § 874), Netherlands (*ibid.*, § 875), Nigeria (*ibid.*, § 877), Oman (*ibid.*, § 878), Qatar (*ibid.*, § 879),

Alleged violations of this rule have consistently been condemned by States and international organisations, for example, by the UN Security Council, UN General Assembly and UN Commission on Human Rights with respect to the conflicts in Afghanistan, Burundi and the former Yugoslavia.[69] Allegations of such violations have also been denied by the States concerned, for example, during the Iran–Iraq War.[70]

The ICRC has on numerous occasions condemned the killing of civilians and persons *hors de combat*, stating that such behaviour is prohibited under international humanitarian law.[71]

Murder of civilians and persons *hors de combat* is also prohibited under international human rights law, albeit in different terms. Human rights treaties prohibit the "arbitrary deprivation of the right to life".[72] This prohibition is non-derogable under these treaties and therefore applicable at all times.[73] In their statements before the International Court of Justice in the *Nuclear Weapons case* and *Nuclear Weapons (WHO) case*, several States which were not at the time party to the main human rights treaties stressed the elementary and non-derogable character of the right to life.[74]

The prohibition of "arbitrary deprivation of the right to life" under human rights law, however, also encompasses unlawful killing in the conduct of hostilities, i.e., the killing of civilians and persons *hors de combat not* in the

---

Russia (*ibid.*, § 880), Rwanda (*ibid.*, § 882), South Africa (*ibid.*, § 884) and United States (*ibid.*, §§ 886–887 and 889), the practice of China (*ibid.*, § 862), France (*ibid.*, § 869) and Rwanda (*ibid.*, § 883) and the reported practice of Nigeria (*ibid.*, § 876) and United States (*ibid.*, § 890).

[69] See, e.g., UN Security Council, Res. 827 (*ibid.*, § 896), Res. 1019 (*ibid.*, § 897) and Res. 1072 (*ibid.*, § 898); UN General Assembly, Res. 50/193 (*ibid.*, § 902); UN Commission on Human Rights, Res. 1989/67, 1990/53, 1991/78 and 1992/68 (*ibid.*, § 904).

[70] See the reported practice of Iran and Iraq (*ibid.*, § 916).

[71] See, e.g., ICRC, *Annual Report 1982* (*ibid.*, § 958), Conflict between Iraq and Iran: ICRC Appeal (*ibid.*, § 959), Memorandum on the Applicability of International Humanitarian Law (*ibid.*, § 961), Appeal in behalf of civilians in Yugoslavia (*ibid.*, § 962), Communication to the Press No. 94/16 (*ibid.*, § 964), Memorandum on Respect for International Humanitarian Law in Angola (*ibid.*, § 965), Memorandum on Compliance with International Humanitarian Law by the Forces Participating in Opération Turquoise (*ibid.*, § 966) and Communication to the Press No. 01/47 (*ibid.*, § 969).

[72] See International Covenant on Civil and Political Rights, Article 6(1) (*ibid.*, § 666); American Convention on Human Rights, Article 4 (*ibid.*, § 667); African Charter on Human and Peoples' Rights, Article 4 (*ibid.*, § 671). The European Convention on Human Rights, Article 2 (*ibid.*, § 664), does not use the term "arbitrary" but specifies a general right to life and gives an exhaustive list of when a deprivation of the right to life may be lawful.

[73] See International Covenant on Civil and Political Rights, Article 4(2) (*ibid.*, § 666); American Convention on Human Rights, Article 27(2) (*ibid.*, § 667); European Convention on Human Rights, Article 15(2) (*ibid.*, § 664). The African Charter on Human and Peoples' Rights does not provide for any derogation of its provisions in a state of emergency and Article 15 of the European Convention states that the right to life is non-derogable, except for "lawful acts of war" in a situation which amounts to armed conflict.

[74] See the statements before the ICJ in the *Nuclear Weapons case* and *Nuclear Weapons (WHO) case* of Indonesia (cited in Vol. II, Ch. 32, § 870), Malaysia (*ibid.*, § 872), Mexico (*ibid.*, § 873), Nauru (*ibid.*, § 874) and Qatar (*ibid.*, § 879).

power of a party to the conflict not justified under the rules on the conduct of hostilities. In its advisory opinion in the *Nuclear Weapons case*, the International Court of Justice stated that "the test of what is an arbitrary deprivation of life, however, then falls to be determined by the applicable *lex specialis*, namely, the law applicable in armed conflict which is designed to regulate the conduct of hostilities".[75] As discussed in the chapters that deal with the conduct of hostilities, unlawful killings can result, for example, from a direct attack against a civilian (see Rule 1), from an indiscriminate attack (see Rule 11) or from an attack against military objectives causing excessive loss of civilian life (see Rule 14), all of which are prohibited by the rules on the conduct of hostilities.

The Inter-American Commission on Human Rights has also used international humanitarian law as a method of interpreting the right to life during hostilities in situations amounting to armed conflict.[76] However, in other cases, human rights bodies have directly applied human rights law, without reference to international humanitarian law, in assessing whether there has been a violation of the right to life during hostilities.[77] In a number of cases relating to non-international armed conflicts or serious internal disturbances (including those involving the use of military force), the UN Human Rights Committee, the African Commission on Human and Peoples' Rights, the European Court of Human Rights, the Inter-American Commission on Human Rights and the Inter-American Court of Human Rights have stressed the need for proper precautions to be taken, for limitation of the use of force to the degree strictly necessary and for investigations to be undertaken in the case of suspicious deaths in order to ensure that a loss of life is not "arbitrary".[78]

---

[75] ICJ, *Nuclear Weapons case*, Advisory Opinion (*ibid.*, § 926).

[76] See Inter-American Commission on Human Rights, *Case 11.137 (Argentina)* (*ibid.*, § 953) and *Case of the Ríofrío massacre (Colombia)* (*ibid.*, § 954).

[77] See, e.g., African Commission on Human and Peoples' Rights, *Civil Liberties Organisation v. Chad* (*ibid.*, § 940); Inter-American Commission on Human Rights, *Case 6724 (El Salvador)* (*ibid.*, § 950), *Case 10.190 (El Salvador)* (*ibid.*, § 950) and *Case 10.284 (El Salvador)* (*ibid.*, § 950).

[78] See UN Human Rights Committee, General Comment No. 6 (Article 6 of the International Covenant on Civil and Political Rights (*ibid.*, § 938) and *Camargo v. Colombia* (*ibid.*, § 939); African Commission on Human and Peoples' Rights, *Civil Liberties Organisation v. Chad* (*ibid.*, § 940); European Court of Human Rights, *McCann and Others v. UK* (*ibid.*, § 942), *Ergi v. Turkey* (*ibid.*, § 943) and *Yasa v. Turkey* (*ibid.*, § 943); Inter-American Commission on Human Rights, Report on the situation of human rights in Peru (*ibid.*, § 952); Inter-American Court of Human Rights, *Neira Alegría and Others case* (*ibid.*, § 956). Judicial or quasi-judicial practice confirming the need to investigate suspicious deaths, including in armed conflict situations, includes: UN Human Rights Committee, General Comment No. 6 (Article 6 of the International Covenant on Civil and Political Rights) (*ibid.*, § 938); African Commission on Human and Peoples' Rights, *Civil Liberties Organisation v. Chad* (*ibid.*, § 940); European Court of Human Rights, *Kaya v. Turkey* (*ibid.*, § 945) and *Avsar v. Turkey* (*ibid.*, § 946); Inter-American Commission on Human Rights, *Case 10.559 (Peru)* (*ibid.*, § 949); Inter-American Court of Human Rights, *Velásquez Rodríguez case* (*ibid.*, § 955).

Rule 90. Torture, cruel or inhuman treatment and outrages upon personal dignity, in particular humiliating and degrading treatment, are prohibited.

Practice

Volume II, Chapter 32, Section D.

Summary

State practice establishes this rule as a norm of customary international law applicable in both international and non-international armed conflicts.

International and non-international armed conflicts

The prohibition of torture was already recognised in the Lieber Code.[79] The Charter of the International Military Tribunal at Nuremberg included "ill-treatment" of civilians and prisoners of war as a war crime.[80] Common Article 3 of the Geneva Conventions prohibits "cruel treatment and torture" and "outrages upon personal dignity, in particular humiliating and degrading treatment" of civilians and persons *hors de combat*.[81] Torture and cruel treatment are also prohibited by specific provisions of the four Geneva Conventions.[82] In addition, "torture or inhuman treatment" and "wilfully causing great suffering or serious injury to body or health" constitute grave breaches of the Geneva Conventions and are war crimes under the Statute of the International Criminal Court.[83]

The prohibition of torture and outrages upon personal dignity, in particular humiliating and degrading treatment, is recognised as a fundamental guarantee for civilians and persons *hors de combat* by Additional Protocols I and II.[84] Torture, cruel treatment and outrages upon personal dignity, in particular humiliating and degrading treatment, constitute war crimes in non-international armed conflicts under the Statutes of the International Criminal

---

[79] Lieber Code, Article 16 (*ibid.*, § 1010).
[80] IMT Charter (Nuremberg), Article 6(b) (*ibid.*, § 982).
[81] Geneva Conventions, common Article 3 (*ibid.*, § 984).
[82] First Geneva Convention, Article 12, second paragraph ("torture") (*ibid.*, § 985); Second Geneva Convention, Article 12, second paragraph ("torture") (*ibid.*, § 986); Third Geneva Convention, Article 17, fourth paragraph ("physical or mental torture") (*ibid.*, § 987), Article 87, third paragraph ("torture or cruelty") (*ibid.*, § 988) and Article 89 ("inhuman, brutal or dangerous" disciplinary punishment) (*ibid.*, § 989); Fourth Geneva Convention, Article 32 ("torture" and "other measures of brutality") (*ibid.*, § 990).
[83] First Geneva Convention, Article 50 (*ibid.*, § 991); Second Geneva Convention, Article 51 (*ibid.*, § 991); Third Geneva Convention, Article 130 (*ibid.*, § 991); Fourth Geneva Convention, Article 147 (*ibid.*, § 991); ICC Statute, Article 8(2)(a)(ii) and (iii) and (c)(i) (*ibid.*, §§ 1006–1007).
[84] Additional Protocol I, Article 75(2) (adopted by consensus) (*ibid.*, § 996); Additional Protocol II, Article 4(2) (adopted by consensus) (*ibid.*, § 997).

Court, of the International Criminal Tribunal for Rwanda and of the Special Court for Sierra Leone.[85]

The prohibition of torture, cruel or inhuman treatment and outrages upon personal dignity is contained in numerous military manuals.[86] This prohibition is also set forth in the legislation of a large number of States.[87] It has been upheld in national case-law,[88] as well as in international case-law.[89] It is also supported by official statements and other practice.[90] The case-law of the International Criminal Tribunal for the Former Yugoslavia in the *Furundžija case* and *Kunarac case* provides further evidence of the customary nature of the prohibition of torture in both international and non-international armed conflicts.[91]

Allegations of torture, cruel or inhuman treatment, whether in international or non-international armed conflicts, have invariably been condemned by the UN Security Council, UN General Assembly and UN Commission on Human Rights, as well as by regional organisations and International Conferences of

---

[85] ICC Statute, Article 8(2)(c)(i) and (ii) (*ibid.*, §§ 1007–1008); ICTR Statute, Article 4(a) and (e) (*ibid.*, § 1028); Statute of the Special Court for Sierra Leone, Article 3(a) and (e) (*ibid.*, § 1009).

[86] See, e.g., the military manuals of Argentina (*ibid.*, §§ 1039–1040), Australia (*ibid.*, §§ 1041–1042), Belgium (*ibid.*, §§ 1043–1044), Benin (*ibid.*, § 1045), Bosnia and Herzegovina (*ibid.*, § 1046), Burkina Faso (*ibid.*, § 1047), Canada (*ibid.*, §§ 1048–1049), China (*ibid.*, § 1050), Colombia (*ibid.*, §§ 1051–1052), Congo (*ibid.*, § 1053), Croatia (*ibid.*, §§ 1054–1055), Dominican Republic (*ibid.*, § 1056), Ecuador (*ibid.*, § 1057), El Salvador (*ibid.*, §§ 1058–1059), France (*ibid.*, §§ 1060–1063), Germany (*ibid.*, § 1064), Hungary (*ibid.*, § 1065), India (*ibid.*, § 1066), Indonesia (*ibid.*, §§ 1067–1068), Israel (*ibid.*, § 1069), Italy (*ibid.*, § 1070), Kenya (*ibid.*, § 1071), Madagascar (*ibid.*, § 1072), Mali (*ibid.*, § 1073), Morocco (*ibid.*, § 1074), Netherlands (*ibid.*, § 1075), New Zealand (*ibid.*, § 1076), Nicaragua (*ibid.*, § 1077), Nigeria (*ibid.*, §§ 1078–1079), Peru (*ibid.*, § 1080), Philippines (*ibid.*, §§ 1081–1082), Romania (*ibid.*, § 1083), Russia (*ibid.*, § 1084), Senegal (*ibid.*, §§ 1085–1086), South Africa (*ibid.*, § 1087), Spain (*ibid.*, § 1088), Sweden (*ibid.*, §§ 1089–1090), Switzerland (*ibid.*, § 1091), Togo (*ibid.*, § 1092), Uganda (*ibid.*, § 1093), United Kingdom (*ibid.*, §§ 1094–1095) and United States (*ibid.*, §§ 1096–1100).

[87] See, e.g., the legislation (*ibid.*, §§ 1101–1215).

[88] See, e.g., Australia, Military Court at Rabaul, *Baba Masao case* (*ibid.*, § 1216); Australia, Military Court at Rabaul, *Tanaka Chuichi case* (*ibid.*, § 1217); Bosnia and Herzegovina, Cantonal Court in Tuzla, *Drago case* (*ibid.*, § 1218); Canada, Court Martial Appeal Court, *Brocklebank case* (*ibid.*, § 1219); Chile, Appeal Court of Santiago, *Benado Medwinsky case* (*ibid.*, § 1220); Chile, Appeal Court of Santiago, *Videla case* (*ibid.*, § 1221); China, War Crimes Military Tribunal of the Ministry of National Defence at Nanking, *Takashi Sakai case* (*ibid.*, § 1216); Colombia, Constitutional Court, *Constitutional Case No. C-225/95* (*ibid.*, § 1222); Israel, District Court of Jerusalem, *Eichmann case* (*ibid.*, § 1216); Israel, Supreme Court, *Eichmann case* (*ibid.*, § 1223); Israel, High Court, *General Security Service case* (*ibid.*, § 1224); Netherlands, Temporary Court-Martial at Makassar, *Motomura case* (*ibid.*, § 1216) and *Notomi Sueo case* (*ibid.*, § 1216); Norway, Court of Appeal, *Bruns case* (*ibid.*, § 1216); United Kingdom, Military Court at Hanover, *Heering case* (*ibid.*, § 1225); United States, Military Tribunal at Nuremberg, *List (Hostages Trial) case* (*ibid.*, § 1216); United States, District Court of the Eastern District of New York, *Filartiga case* (*ibid.*, § 1226).

[89] See, e.g., ICJ, *Nicaragua case (Merits)*, Judgement (*ibid.*, § 1278); ICTY, *Tadić case*, Second Amended Indictment and Judgement (*ibid.*, § 1279), *Mrkšić case*, Initial Indictment (*ibid.*, § 1280), *Delalić case*, Judgement (*ibid.*, § 1281), *Furundžija case*, Judgement (*ibid.*, § 1282), *Jelisić case*, Judgement (*ibid.*, § 1283), *Kupreškić case*, Judgement (*ibid.*, § 1284), *Blaškić case*, Judgement (*ibid.*, § 1285), *Kunarac case*, Judgement (*ibid.*, § 1286) and *Kordić and Čerkez case*, Judgement (*ibid.*, § 1287).

[90] See, e.g., the statements of Egypt (*ibid.*, § 1230), Netherlands (*ibid.*, § 1233) and United States (*ibid.*, §§ 1234–1238) and the practice of Azerbaijan (*ibid.*, § 1228), China (*ibid.*, § 1229), France (*ibid.*, § 1231) and Yugoslavia (*ibid.*, § 1241).

[91] ICTY, *Furundžija case*, Judgement (*ibid.*, § 1282) and *Kunarac case*, Judgement (*ibid.*, § 1286).

the Red Cross and Red Crescent.[92] Such allegations have generally been denied by the authorities concerned.[93]

The prohibition of torture and cruel, inhuman or degrading treatment or punishment is to be found in general human rights treaties,[94] as well as in specific treaties that seek to prevent and punish these practices.[95] This prohibition is non-derogable under these instruments.

Definition of torture

The Elements of Crimes for the International Criminal Court provides that the war crime of torture consists of the infliction of "severe physical or mental pain or suffering" for purposes such as "obtaining information or a confession, punishment, intimidation or coercion or for any reason based on discrimination of any kind".[96] Contrary to human rights law, e.g. Article 1 of the Convention against Torture, the Elements of Crimes does not require that such pain or suffering be inflicted "by or at the instigation of or with the consent or acquiescence of a public official or other person acting in an official capacity".

In its early case-law in the *Delalić case* and *Furundžija case* in 1998, the International Criminal Tribunal for the Former Yugoslavia considered the definition contained in Article 1 of the Convention against Torture to be part of customary international law applicable in armed conflict.[97] In its subsequent case-law in the *Kunarac case* in 2001, however, the Tribunal concluded that "the definition of torture under international humanitarian law does not comprise the same elements as the definition of torture generally applied under human rights law". In particular, the Tribunal held that "the presence of a state official or of any other authority-wielding person in the torture process

---

[92] See, e.g., UN Security Council, Res. 674 (*ibid.*, § 1248), Res. 770 (*ibid.*, § 1249), Res. 771 (*ibid.*, § 1250) and Res. 1072 (*ibid.*, § 1251); UN General Assembly, Res. 2547 (XXIV) (*ibid.*, § 1253), Res. 3103 (XXVIII) (*ibid.*, § 1253), Res. 3318 (XXIX) (*ibid.*, § 1254), Res. 34/93 H (*ibid.*, § 1253), Res. 41/35 (*ibid.*, § 1253), Res. 50/193 (*ibid.*, § 1255) and Res. 53/164 (*ibid.*, § 1256); UN Commission on Human Rights, Res. 1989/67 (*ibid.*, § 1257), Res. 1990/53 (*ibid.*, § 1257), Res. 1991/67 (*ibid.*, § 1258), Res. 1991/78 (*ibid.*, § 1257), Res. 1992/60 (*ibid.*, § 1258), Res. 1992/68 (*ibid.*, § 1257), Res. 1994/72 (*ibid.*, § 1259), Res. 1996/71 (*ibid.*, § 1260) and Res. 1996/73 (*ibid.*, § 1261); 21st International Conference of the Red Cross, Res. XI (*ibid.*, § 1270); 23rd International Conference of the Red Cross, Res. XIV (*ibid.*, § 1271); 24th International Conference of the Red Cross, Res. XIV (*ibid.*, § 1272); 25th International Conference of the Red Cross, Res. X (*ibid.*, § 1273).

[93] See, e.g., the practice reported in ICRC archive documents (*ibid.*, §§ 1243–1244 and 1246–1247).

[94] See International Covenant on Civil and Political Rights, Article 7 (*ibid.*, § 993); European Convention on Human Rights, Article 3 (*ibid.*, § 992); American Convention on Human Rights, Article 5(2) (*ibid.*, § 994); African Charter on Human and Peoples' Rights, Article 5 (*ibid.*, § 998); Convention on the Rights of the Child, Article 37(a) (*ibid.*, § 1002).

[95] See Convention against Torture (*ibid.*, § 999), Inter-American Convention to Prevent and Punish Torture (*ibid.*, § 1000) and European Convention for the Prevention of Torture (*ibid.*, § 1001).

[96] Elements of Crimes for the ICC, Definition of torture as a war crime (ICC Statute, Article 8(2)(a)(ii) and (c)(i)).

[97] ICTY, *Delalić case*, Judgement (cited in Vol. II, Ch. 32, § 1329) and *Furundžija case*, Judgement (*ibid.*, § 1330).

is not necessary for the offence to be regarded as torture under international humanitarian law". It defined torture as the intentional infliction, by act or omission, of severe pain or suffering, whether physical or mental, in order to obtain information or a confession, or to punish, intimidate or coerce the victim or a third person, or to discriminate on any ground, against the victim or a third person.[98]

The International Criminal Tribunal for the Former Yugoslavia, as well as regional human rights bodies, have held that rape can constitute torture.[99] On the prohibition of rape and other forms of sexual violence, see Rule 93.

Definition of inhuman treatment

The term "inhuman treatment" is defined in the Elements of Crimes for the International Criminal Court as the infliction of "severe physical or mental pain or suffering".[100] The element that distinguishes inhuman treatment from torture is the absence of the requirement that the treatment be inflicted for a specific purpose. The International Criminal Tribunal for the Former Yugoslavia has used a wider definition determining that inhuman treatment is that which "causes serious mental or physical suffering or injury or constitutes a serious attack on human dignity".[101] The element of "a serious attack on human dignity" was not included in the definition of inhuman treatment under the Elements of Crimes for the International Criminal Court because the war crime of "outrages upon personal dignity" covers such attacks.[102]

In their case-law, human rights bodies apply a definition which is similar to the one used in the Elements of Crimes for the International Criminal Court, stressing the severity of the physical or mental pain or suffering. They have found violations of the prohibition of inhuman treatment in cases of active maltreatment but also in cases of very poor conditions of detention,[103] as well as in cases of solitary confinement.[104] Lack of adequate food, water or medical

---

[98] ICTY, *Kunarac case*, Judgement (*ibid.*, § 1333).

[99] See, e.g., ICTY, *Delalić case*, Judgement (*ibid.*, §§ 1329 and 1733); European Court of Human Rights, *Aydin v. Turkey* (*ibid.*, §§ 1346 and 1743); Inter-American Commission on Human Rights, *Case 10.970 (Peru)* (*ibid.*, §§ 1351 and 1745).

[100] Elements of Crimes for the ICC, Definition of inhuman treatment as a war crime (ICC Statute, Article 8(2)(a)(ii)).

[101] See ICTY, *Delalić case*, Judgement (cited in Vol. II, Ch. 32, § 1329) and *Kordić and Čerkez case*, Judgement (*ibid.*, § 1331).

[102] Knut Dörmann, *Elements of War Crimes under the Rome Statute of the International Criminal Court: Sources and Commentary*, Cambridge University Press, 2003, pp. 63–64.

[103] See, e.g., UN Human Rights Committee, *Améndola Massiotti and Baritussio v. Uruguay* (cited in Vol. II, Ch. 32, § 1335) and *Deidrick v. Jamaica* (*ibid.*, § 1336); African Commission on Human and Peoples' Rights, *Civil Liberties Organisation v. Nigeria (151/96)* (*ibid.*, § 1339); European Commission of Human Rights, *Greek case* (*ibid.*, § 1341).

[104] See, e.g., UN Human Rights Committee, General Comment No. 20 (Article 7 of the International Covenant on Civil and Political Rights) (*ibid.*, § 1334), *Gómez de Voituret v. Uruguay* (*ibid.*, § 1334) and *Espinoza de Polay v. Peru* (*ibid.*, § 1334); European Committee for the Prevention of Torture, Second General Report (*ibid.*, § 1348); Inter-American Court of Human Rights,

treatment for detained persons has also been found to amount to inhuman treatment.[105]

Definition of outrages upon personal dignity, in particular humiliating and degrading treatment

The notion of "outrages upon personal dignity" is defined in the Elements of Crimes for the International Criminal Court as acts which humiliate, degrade or otherwise violate the dignity of a person to such a degree "as to be generally recognized as an outrage upon personal dignity". The Elements of Crimes further specifies that degrading treatment can apply to dead persons and that the victim need not be personally aware of the humiliation.[106] The last point was made in order to cover the deliberate humiliation of unconscious or mentally handicapped persons. The Elements of Crimes adds that the cultural background of the person needs to be taken into account, thereby covering treatment that is humiliating to someone of a particular nationality or religion, for example.

The notion of "degrading treatment" has been defined by the European Commission of Human Rights as treatment or punishment that "grossly humiliates the victim before others or drives the detainee to act against his/her will or conscience".[107]

Rule 91. Corporal punishment is prohibited.

Practice

Volume II, Chapter 32, Section E.

Summary

State practice establishes this rule as a norm of customary international law applicable in both international and non-international armed conflicts.

International and non-international armed conflicts

The prohibition of corporal punishment is set forth in the Third and Fourth Geneva Conventions.[108] The prohibition is recognised by Additional Protocols I

Velásquez Rodríguez case (ibid., § 1349); Inter-American Court of Human Rights, *Castillo Petruzzi and Others case (ibid.*, § 1353).

[105] UN Human Rights Committee, *Essono Mika Miha v. Equatorial Guinea.* Communication No. 414/1990, 8 July 1994, § 6.4; UN Human Rights Committee, *Williams v. Jamaica.* Communication No. 609/1995, § 6.5; European Court of Human Rights, *Keenan v. United Kingdom*, Judgement, 3 April 2001, § 115; African Commission on Human and Peoples' Rights, *Civil Liberties Organisation v. Nigeria*, Communication No. 151/96, 15 November 1999, § 27.

[106] Elements of Crimes for the ICC, Definition of outrages upon personal dignity, in particular humiliating and degrading treatment, as a war crime (ICC Statute, Article 8(2)(b)(xxi) and (c)(ii)).

[107] European Commission of Human Rights, *Greek case* (cited in Vol. II, Ch. 32, § 1340).

[108] Third Geneva Convention, Article 87, third paragraph *(ibid.*, § 1355); Fourth Geneva Convention, Article 32 *(ibid.*, § 1356).

and II as a fundamental guarantee for civilians and persons *hors de combat*.[109]
Corporal punishment constitutes a war crime in non-international armed conflicts under the Statutes of the International Criminal Tribunal for Rwanda
and of the Special Court for Sierra Leone.[110] The prohibition of corporal punishment is contained in numerous military manuals.[111] It is also provided for
in the legislation of some States.[112]

The prohibition of corporal punishment is not explicitly spelled out in international human rights treaties. However, human rights case-law has held that
corporal punishment is prohibited when it amounts to inhuman or degrading treatment or punishment.[113] In its General Comment on Article 7 of the
International Covenant on Civil and Political Rights, the UN Human Rights
Committee stated that the prohibition of torture and cruel, inhuman or degrading treatment or punishment "must extend to corporal punishment, including
excessive chastisement ordered as punishment for a crime or as an educative or
disciplinary measure".[114] The prohibition of inhuman or degrading treatment
or punishment is non-derogable under human rights law.

**Rule 92. Mutilation, medical or scientific experiments or any other medical
procedure not indicated by the state of health of the person concerned and not
consistent with generally accepted medical standards are prohibited.**

Practice

Volume II, Chapter 32, Section F.

Summary

State practice establishes this rule as a norm of customary international law
applicable in both international and non-international armed conflicts.

---

[109] Additional Protocol I, Article 75(2)(iii) (adopted by consensus) (*ibid.*, § 1358); Additional Protocol II, Article 4(2)(a) (adopted by consensus) (*ibid.*, § 1359).
[110] ICTR Statute, Article 4(a) (*ibid.*, § 1363); Statute of the Special Court for Sierra Leone, Article 3
(*ibid.*, § 1360).
[111] See, e.g., the military manuals of Argentina (*ibid.*, § 1367), Australia (*ibid.*, § 1368), Benin (*ibid.*,
§ 1369), Canada (*ibid.*, § 1370), Colombia (*ibid.*, § 1371), Croatia (*ibid.*, § 1372), France (*ibid.*,
§§ 1373–1374), Israel (*ibid.*, § 1375), Italy (*ibid.*, § 1376), Madagascar (*ibid.*, § 1377), Netherlands
(*ibid.*, § 1378), New Zealand (*ibid.*, § 1379), Nicaragua (*ibid.*, § 1380), Romania (*ibid.*, § 1381),
Spain (*ibid.*, § 1382), Sweden (*ibid.*, § 1383), Switzerland (*ibid.*, § 1384), Togo (*ibid.*, § 1385),
United Kingdom (*ibid.*, §§ 1386–1387) and United States (*ibid.*, § 1388).
[112] See, e.g., the legislation of Azerbaijan (*ibid.*, § 1389), Bangladesh (*ibid.*, § 1390), Ireland (*ibid.*,
§ 1391), Mozambique (*ibid.*, § 1392), Norway (*ibid.*, § 1393) and Poland (*ibid.*, § 1394).
[113] See, e.g., European Court of Human Rights, *Tyrer case* (*ibid.*, § 1403) and *A. v. UK case* (*ibid.*,
§ 1404).
[114] UN Human Rights Committee, General Comment No. 20 (Article 7 of the International
Covenant on Civil and Political Rights) (*ibid.*, § 1402).

International and non-international armed conflicts

The prohibition of mutilation was already recognised in the Lieber Code.[115] Common Article 3 of the Geneva Conventions prohibits "mutilation" of civilians and persons *hors de combat*.[116] Mutilation is also prohibited by specific provisions of the Third and Fourth Geneva Conventions.[117] In addition, the prohibition of mutilation is recognised as a fundamental guarantee for civilians and persons *hors de combat* by Additional Protocols I and II.[118] Mutilation constitutes a war crime in both international and non-international armed conflicts under the Statute of the International Criminal Court.[119] It is also recognised as a war crime in non-international armed conflicts under the Statutes of the International Criminal Tribunal for Rwanda and of the Special Court for Sierra Leone.[120]

"Biological experiments" are prohibited by the First and Second Geneva Conventions, while the Third and Fourth Geneva Conventions prohibit "medical or scientific experiments" not justified by the medical treatment of the person concerned.[121] Conducting "biological experiments" on persons protected under the Geneva Conventions is a grave breach and a war crime under the Statutes of the International Criminal Court and of the International Criminal Tribunal for the Former Yugoslavia.[122] Additional Protocol I prohibits "medical or scientific experiments".[123] In the *Brandt (The Medical Trial) case* in 1947, the US Military Tribunal at Nuremberg convicted 16 persons of carrying out medical experiments on prisoners of war and civilians.[124]

Additional Protocol I also prohibits "any medical procedure which is not indicated by the state of health of the person concerned and which is not consistent with generally accepted medical standards" and makes it a grave breach of the Protocol if the medical procedure undertaken seriously endangers the physical or mental health or integrity of the person concerned.[125] Additional

---

[115] Lieber Code, Article 56 (*ibid.*, § 1425).
[116] Geneva Conventions, common Article 3 (*ibid.*, § 1409).
[117] Third Geneva Convention, Article 13 (*ibid.*, § 1412); Fourth Geneva Convention, Article 32 (*ibid.*, § 1414).
[118] Additional Protocol I, Article 75(2) (adopted by consensus) (*ibid.*, § 1416); Additional Protocol II, Article 4(2) (adopted by consensus) (*ibid.*, § 1420).
[119] ICC Statute, Article 8(2)(b)(x) and (e)(xi) (*ibid.*, § 1423).
[120] ICTR Statute, Article 4(a) (*ibid.*, § 1429); Statute of the Special Court for Sierra Leone, Article 3 (*ibid.*, § 1424).
[121] First Geneva Convention, Article 12 (*ibid.*, § 1410); Second Geneva Convention, Article 12 (*ibid.*, § 1411); Third Geneva Convention, Article 13 (*ibid.*, § 1412); Fourth Geneva Convention, Article 32 (*ibid.*, § 1413).
[122] ICC Statute, Article 8(2)(a)(ii) (*ibid.*, § 1422); ICTY Statute, Article 2(b) (*ibid.*, § 1428).
[123] Additional Protocol I, Article 11(2) (adopted by consensus) (*ibid.*, § 1415).
[124] United States, Military Tribunal at Nuremberg, *In re Brandt and Others (The Medical Trial)*(*ibid.*, § 1540).
[125] Additional Protocol I, Article 11(1) and (4) (adopted by consensus) (*ibid.*, § 1415).

Protocol II contains the same prohibition with respect to persons deprived of their liberty for reasons related to the armed conflict.[126]

Under the Statute of the International Criminal Court, subjecting persons who are in the power of another party to the conflict to "medical or scientific experiments of any kind which are neither justified by the medical, dental or hospital treatment of the person concerned nor carried out in his or her interest, and which cause death or seriously endanger the health of such person or persons" constitutes a war crime in both international and non-international armed conflicts.[127]

Numerous military manuals specify the prohibition of physical mutilation, medical or scientific experiments or any other medical procedure not indicated by the state of health of the patient and not consistent with generally accepted medical standards.[128] The prohibition is also found extensively in national legislation.[129]

Most international instruments, official statements and case-law relating to war crimes refer to this prohibition without making any specific mention of a possible exception if the detained person consented to the procedure.[130] The issue was discussed during the negotiation of the Elements of Crimes for the International Criminal Court. The conference came to the conclusion that the prohibition was absolute, as a detained person cannot validly give consent.[131]

The prohibition of mutilation is not expressed in such terms in human rights treaties but would be covered by the prohibition of torture and cruel, inhuman or degrading treatment or punishment, from which no derogation is permissible. As regards the prohibition of medical or scientific experiments, the International Covenant on Civil and Political Rights expressly includes this in its

---

[126] Additional Protocol II, Article 5(2)(e) (adopted by consensus) (*ibid.*, § 1421).

[127] ICC Statute, Article 8(2)(b)(x) and (e)(xi) (*ibid.*, § 1423).

[128] See, e.g., the military manuals of Argentina (*ibid.*, §§ 1434–1435), Australia (*ibid.*, §§ 1436–1437), Belgium (*ibid.*, § 1438), Bosnia and Herzegovina (*ibid.*, § 1439), Burkina Faso (*ibid.*, § 1440), Canada (*ibid.*, § 1441), Ecuador (*ibid.*, § 1442), France (*ibid.*, §§ 1443–1445), Germany (*ibid.*, § 1446), Israel (*ibid.*, § 1447), Italy (*ibid.*, § 1448), Morocco (*ibid.*, § 1449), Netherlands (*ibid.*, § 1450), New Zealand (*ibid.*, § 1451), Nigeria (*ibid.*, §§ 1452–1453), Russia (*ibid.*, § 1454), Senegal (*ibid.*, §§ 1455–1456), South Africa (*ibid.*, § 1457), Spain (*ibid.*, § 1458), Sweden, (*ibid.*, § 1459), Switzerland (*ibid.*, § 1460), United Kingdom (*ibid.*, §§ 1461–1462) and United States (*ibid.*, §§ 1463–1466).

[129] See, e.g., the legislation (*ibid.*, §§ 1467–1535).

[130] See First Geneva Convention, Article 50 (*ibid.*, § 1410); Second Geneva Convention, Article 51 (*ibid.*, § 1411); Third Geneva Convention, Article 130 (*ibid.*, § 1412); Fourth Geneva Convention, Article 147 (*ibid.*, § 1413); Additional Protocol I, Articles 11 and 85 (adopted by consensus) (*ibid.*, §§ 1415 and 1417); ICC Statute, Article 8(2)(a)(ii), (b)(x) and (e)(xi) (*ibid.*, §§ 1422–1423); Statute of the Special Court for Sierra Leone, Article 3 (*ibid.*, § 1424); United States, Concurrent resolution of the Congress (*ibid.*, § 1545); Chile, Appeal Court of Santiago, *Videla Case* (*ibid.*, § 1536); Poland, Supreme National Tribunal at Poznan, *Hoess trial* (*ibid.*, § 1538); United States, Military Tribunal at Nuremberg, *Milch case* (*ibid.*, § 1539) and *Brandt (The Medical Trial) case* (*ibid.*, § 1540); United States, Court of Military Appeals, *Schultz case* (*ibid.*, § 1541).

[131] Elements of Crimes for the ICC, Definition of physical mutilation or medical or scientific experiments of any kind which are neither justified by the medical, dental or hospital treatment of the person concerned nor carried out in his or her interest, as war crimes (Footnote 46 relating to Article 8(2)(b)(x) and Footnote 68 relating to Article 8(2)(e)(xi) of the ICC Statute).

non-derogable Article 7, which prohibits torture and cruel, inhuman or degrading treatment or punishment.[132] The UN Human Rights Committee, in its General Comment on Article 7, specifies that special protection against such experiments is necessary in the case of persons not capable of giving valid consent, in particular those under any form of detention or imprisonment.[133] The Body of Principles for the Protection of All Persons under Any Form of Detention or Imprisonment, adopted by consensus by the UN General Assembly, prohibits medical or scientific experimentation which may be detrimental to health, even with the detainee's consent.[134] The European Court of Human Rights has held that those medical measures taken in relation to a detainee that are dictated by therapeutic necessity cannot be regarded as inhuman or degrading.[135]

Rule 93. Rape and other forms of sexual violence are prohibited.

Practice

Volume II, Chapter 32, Section G.

Summary

State practice establishes this rule as a norm of customary international law applicable in both international and non-international armed conflicts.

International and non-international armed conflicts

The prohibition of rape was already recognised in the Lieber Code.[136] While common Article 3 of the Geneva Conventions does not explicitly mention rape or other forms of sexual violence, it prohibits "violence to life and person" including cruel treatment and torture and "outrages upon personal dignity".[137] The Third Geneva Convention provides that prisoners of war are in all circumstances entitled to "respect for their persons and their honour".[138] The prohibition of "outrages upon personal dignity" is recognised in Additional Protocols I and II as a fundamental guarantee for civilians and persons

---

[132] International Covenant on Civil and Political Rights, Article 7 (cited in Vol. II, Ch. 32, § 1414).
[133] UN Human Rights Committee, General Comment No. 20 (Article 7 of the International Covenant on Civil and Political Rights) (*ibid.*, § 1551).
[134] Body of Principles for the Protection of All Persons under Any Form of Detention or Imprisonment, Principle 22 (*ibid.*, § 1426).
[135] European Court of Human Rights, *Herczegfalvy v. Austria* (*ibid.*, § 1552). The Court held that forcible administration of food and drugs to a violent and mentally ill patient on hunger strike was not a breach of Article 3 of the European Convention on Human Rights.
[136] Lieber Code, Article 44 (*ibid.*, § 1572).
[137] Geneva Conventions, common Article 3 (*ibid.*, § 1557).
[138] Third Geneva Convention, Article 14, first paragraph.

hors de combat.[139] Article 75 of Additional Protocol I specifies that this prohibition covers in particular "humiliating and degrading treatment, enforced prostitution and any form of indecent assault", while Article 4 of Additional Protocol II specifically adds "rape" to this list.[140] The Fourth Geneva Convention and Additional Protocol I require protection for women and children against rape, enforced prostitution or any other form of indecent assault.[141] Rape, enforced prostitution and any form of indecent assault are war crimes under the Statutes of the International Criminal Tribunal for Rwanda and of the Special Court for Sierra Leone.[142] The expressions "outrages upon personal dignity" and "any form of indecent assault" refer to any form of sexual violence. Under the Statute of the International Criminal Court, "committing rape, sexual slavery, enforced prostitution, forced pregnancy . . . enforced sterilization, or any other form of sexual violence" also constituting a grave breach of the Geneva Conventions or also constituting a serious violation of common Article 3 of the Geneva Conventions constitutes a war crime in international and non-international armed conflicts respectively.[143] Furthermore, "rape, sexual slavery, enforced prostitution, forced pregnancy, enforced sterilization, or any other form of sexual violence of comparable gravity" constitutes a crime against humanity under the Statute of the International Criminal Court and "rape" constitutes a crime against humanity under the Statutes of the International Criminal Tribunals for the Former Yugoslavia and Rwanda.[144]

Numerous military manuals state that rape, enforced prostitution and indecent assault are prohibited and many of them specify that these acts are war crimes.[145] The legislation of many States provides that rape and other forms of sexual violence are war crimes.[146] National case-law has confirmed that rape

---

[139] Additional Protocol I, Article 75(2) (adopted by consensus) (cited in Vol. II, Ch. 32, § 996); Additional Protocol II, Article 4(2) (adopted by consensus) (*ibid.*, § 997).

[140] Additional Protocol I, Article 75(2) (adopted by consensus) (*ibid.*, § 1560); Additional Protocol II, Article 4(2) (adopted by consensus) (*ibid.*, § 1561).

[141] Fourth Geneva Convention, Article 27, second paragraph (*ibid.*, § 1558); Additional Protocol I, Articles 76–77 (adopted by consensus) (*ibid.*, §§ 1562–1563).

[142] ICTR Statute, Article 4(e) (*ibid.*, § 1579); Statute of the Special Court for Sierra Leone, Article 3(e) (*ibid.*, § 1571).

[143] ICC Statute, Article 8(2)(b)(xxii) and (e)(vi) (*ibid.*, § 1567).

[144] ICC Statute, Article 7(1)(g) (*ibid.*, § 1566); ICTY Statute, Article 5(g) (*ibid.*, § 1578); ICTR Statute, Article 3(g) (*ibid.*, § 1579).

[145] See, e.g., the military manuals of Argentina (*ibid.*, §§ 1586–1587), Australia (*ibid.*, §§ 1588–1589), Canada (*ibid.*, § 1590–1591), China (*ibid.*, § 1592), Dominican Republic (*ibid.*, § 1593), El Salvador (*ibid.*, § 1594), France (*ibid.*, §§ 1596–1597), Germany (*ibid.*, § 1598), Israel (*ibid.*, § 1599), Madagascar (*ibid.*, § 1600), Netherlands (*ibid.*, § 1601), New Zealand (*ibid.*, § 1602), Nicaragua (*ibid.*, § 1603), Nigeria (*ibid.*, § 1604), Peru (*ibid.*, § 1605), Senegal (*ibid.*, § 1606), Spain (*ibid.*, § 1607), Sweden (*ibid.*, § 1608), Switzerland (*ibid.*, § 1609), Uganda (*ibid.*, § 1610), United Kingdom (*ibid.*, §§ 1611–1612), United States (*ibid.*, §§ 1613–1617) and Yugoslavia (*ibid.*, § 1618).

[146] See, e.g., the legislation of Armenia (*ibid.*, § 1620), Australia (*ibid.*, §§ 1621–1623), Azerbaijan (*ibid.*, § 1625), Bangladesh (*ibid.*, § 1626), Belgium (*ibid.*, § 1627), Bosnia and Herzegovina (*ibid.*, § 1628), Canada (*ibid.*, § 1630), China (*ibid.*, § 1631), Colombia (*ibid.*, § 1632), Congo (*ibid.*, § 1633), Croatia (*ibid.*, § 1634), Estonia (*ibid.*, § 1636), Ethiopia (*ibid.*, § 1637), Georgia (*ibid.*, § 1638), Germany (*ibid.*, § 1639), South Korea (*ibid.*, § 1643), Lithuania (*ibid.*, § 1644), Mali

constitutes a war crime, as early as 1946 in the *Takashi Sakai case* before the War Crimes Military Tribunal of the Chinese Ministry of National Defence.[147] In the *John Schultz case* in 1952, the US Court of Military Appeals held that rape was a "crime universally recognized as properly punishable under the law of war".[148]

Violations of the prohibition of rape and other forms of sexual violence have been widely condemned by States and international organisations.[149] For example, the UN Security Council, UN General Assembly and UN Commission on Human Rights condemned the sexual violence that occurred during the conflicts in Rwanda, Sierra Leone, Uganda and the former Yugoslavia.[150] The European Parliament, Council of Europe and Gulf Cooperation Council have condemned rape in the former Yugoslavia as a war crime.[151] It is significant that in 1993 Yugoslavia acknowledged in its report to the Committee on the Elimination of Discrimination Against Women that abuses of women in war zones were crimes contrary to international humanitarian law and apologised for an earlier statement giving the false impression that rape was considered normal behaviour in times of war.[152]

Sexual violence is prohibited under human rights law primarily through the prohibition of torture and cruel, inhuman or degrading treatment or punishment. Thus, both the European Court of Human Rights and the Inter-American Commission on Human Rights have, in their case-law, found instances of rape of detainees to amount to torture.[153] The European Court of Human Rights has also found the strip-searching of a male prisoner in the presence of a female prison officer to be degrading treatment.[154] The Committee on the Elimination of Discrimination Against Women stated in a General Recommendation that

---

(*ibid.*, § 1645), Mozambique (*ibid.*, § 1646), Netherlands (*ibid.*, §§ 1648–1649), New Zealand (*ibid.*, § 1650), Paraguay (*ibid.*, § 1653), Slovenia (*ibid.*, § 1654), Spain (*ibid.*, § 1656), United Kingdom (*ibid.*, § 1658) and Yugoslavia (*ibid.*, §§ 1659–1660); see also the draft legislation of Argentina (*ibid.*, § 1619), Burundi (*ibid.*, § 1629) and Trinidad and Tobago (*ibid.*, § 1657).

[147] China, War Crimes Military Tribunal of the Ministry of National Defence, *Takashi Sakai case* (*ibid.*, § 1661).

[148] United States, Court of Military Appeals, *John Schultz case* (*ibid.*, § 1663).

[149] See, e.g., the statements of Germany (*ibid.*, §§ 1667–1668), Netherlands (*ibid.*, § 1669) and United States (*ibid.*, §§ 1674–1675).

[150] See, e.g., UN Security Council, Res. 798 (*ibid.*, § 1680), Res. 820 (*ibid.*, § 1681), Res. 827 (*ibid.*, § 1682), Res. 1019 (*ibid.*, § 1683) and Res. 1034 (*ibid.*, § 1684); UN Security Council, Statement by the President (*ibid.*, § 1687); UN General Assembly, Res. 48/143 (*ibid.*, § 1690), Res. 49/196 (*ibid.*, § 1691), Res. 50/192 (*ibid.*, § 1692), Res. 50/193 (*ibid.*, §§ 1692–1693), Res. 51/114 (*ibid.*, § 1694) and Res. 51/115 (*ibid.*, § 1692); UN Commission on Human Rights, Res. 1994/72 (*ibid.*, § 1696), Res. 1996/71 (*ibid.*, § 1697) and Res. 1998/75 (*ibid.*, § 1698).

[151] See European Parliament, Resolution on the rape of women in the former Yugoslavia (*ibid.*, § 1714); Council of Europe, Committee of Ministers, Declaration on the Rape of Women and Children in the Territory of Former Yugoslavia (*ibid.*, § 1711); Gulf Cooperation Council, Supreme Council, Final Communiqué of the 13th Session (*ibid.*, § 1717).

[152] Yugoslavia, Statement before the Committee on the Elimination of Discrimination Against Women (*ibid.*, § 1680).

[153] See, e.g., European Court of Human Rights, *Aydin v. Turkey* (*ibid.*, § 1743); Inter-American Commission on Human Rights, *Case 10.970 (Peru)* (*ibid.*, § 1745).

[154] European Court of Human Rights, *Valasinas v. Lithuania* (*ibid.*, § 1744).

discrimination includes gender-based violence.[155] There is also an increasing number of treaties and other international instruments which state that trafficking in women and children for the purpose of prostitution is a criminal offence,[156] as well as an increased recognition of the need to punish all persons responsible for sexual violence.[157] The prohibition of using sexual violence as an official punishment is clear; not only is such a punishment not officially provided for by States, but also any confirmed reports of such an incident have either been denied or the relevant persons prosecuted.[158]

Definition of rape

With respect to the definition of rape, the International Criminal Tribunal for the Former Yugoslavia considered in its judgement in the *Furundžija case* in 1998 that rape required "coercion or force or threat of force against the victim or a third person".[159] In its later case-law in the *Kunarac case* in 2001, however, the Tribunal considered that there might be other factors "which would render an act of sexual penetration non-consensual or non-voluntary on the part of the victim" and that this consideration defined the accurate scope of the definition of rape under international law.[160] The International Criminal Tribunal for Rwanda in the *Akayesu case* in 1998 held that "rape is a form of aggression" and that "the central elements of the crime of rape cannot be captured in a mechanical description of objects and body parts". It defined rape as "a physical invasion of a sexual nature, committed on a person under circumstances which are coercive".[161]

---

[155] Committee on the Elimination of Discrimination Against Women, General Recommendation 19 (Violence against Women) (*ibid.*, § 1737).

[156] See, e.g., Convention for the Suppression of the Traffic in Persons and of the Exploitation of the Prostitution of Others, Article 1 (*ibid.*, § 1559); Protocol on Trafficking in Persons, Article 1 (*ibid.*, § 1569); SAARC Convention on Preventing and Combating Trafficking in Women and Children for Prostitution (not yet in force), Article 3 (*ibid.*, § 1570); UN High Commissioner for Human Rights, Recommended Principles and Guidelines on Human Rights and Human Trafficking (*ibid.*, §§ 1709–1710); ECOWAS, Declaration on the Fight against Trafficking in Persons (*ibid.*, § 1716); OAS Inter-American Commission of Women, Res. CIM/RES 225 (XXXI-0/02) (*ibid.*, § 1718).

[157] See, e.g., UN General Assembly, Res. 48/104 proclaiming the UN Declaration on the Elimination of Violence against Women (*ibid.*, § 1689); Committee on the Elimination of Discrimination Against Women, General Recommendation No. 19 (Violence against Women) (*ibid.*, § 1728); European Court of Human Rights, *S. W. v. UK* (*ibid.*, § 1742).

[158] For example, when a Pakistani tribal council ordered the rape of a girl as a punishment, widespread outrage resulted in the Chief Justice of Pakistan ordering the prosecution of the persons concerned and resulting in conviction and a severe punishment. See news.bbc.co.uk/1/world/south_asia/2089624.stm, 3 July 2002 and the official reply of Pakistan dated 7 January 2003 to the letter of the International Commission of Jurists protesting this event and pointing out the government's international responsibility (on file with the authors); see also Committee on the Elimination of Discrimination Against Women, General Recommendation 19 (Violence against Women), 29 January 1992, § 8.

[159] ICTY, *Furundžija case*, Judgement (cited in Vol. II, Ch. 32, § 1734).

[160] ICTY, *Kunarac case*, Judgement (*ibid.*, § 1736).

[161] ICTR, *Akayesu case*, Judgement (*ibid.*, § 1728).

Rape and sexual violence can also be constituent elements of other crimes under international law. The International Criminal Tribunal for the Former Yugoslavia in the *Delalić case* held that rape could constitute torture when the specific conditions of torture were fulfilled.[162] The International Criminal Tribunal for Rwanda in the *Akayesu case* and *Musema case* held that rape and sexual violence could constitute genocide when the specific conditions of genocide were fulfilled.[163]

It has been specified in practice that the prohibition of sexual violence is non-discriminatory, i.e., that men and women, as well as adults and children, are equally protected by this prohibition. Except for forced pregnancy, the crimes of sexual violence in the Statute of the International Criminal Court are prohibited when committed against "any person", not only women. In addition, in the Elements of Crimes for the International Criminal Court, the concept of "invasion" used to define rape is "intended to be broad enough to be gender-neutral".[164]

Rule 94. Slavery and the slave trade in all their forms are prohibited.

Practice

Volume II, Chapter 32, Section H.

Summary

State practice establishes this rule as a norm of customary international law applicable in both international and non-international armed conflicts.

International and non-international armed conflicts

The prohibition of slavery was specified as early as the Lieber Code.[165] Although not actually spelled out in the Hague and Geneva Conventions, nor in Additional Protocol I, it is clear that enslaving persons in an international armed conflict is prohibited. The various rules in the Geneva Conventions relating to the labour of prisoners of war and civilians, concerning their release and return, as well as the prohibition in the Hague Regulations of the forced allegiance of persons in occupied territory, presuppose the prohibition of slavery.[166]

---

[162] ICTY, *Delalić case*, Judgement (*ibid.*, § 1733).
[163] ICTR, *Akayesu case*, Judgement (*ibid.*, § 1728) and *Musema case*, Judgement (*ibid.*, § 1730).
[164] Elements of Crimes for the ICC, Definition of rape as a war crime (Footnote 50 relating to Article 8(2)(b)(xxii) and Footnote 62 relating to Article 8(2)(e)(vi) of the ICC Statute).
[165] Lieber Code, Article 23 (cited in Vol. II, Ch. 32, § 1784), Article 42 (*ibid.*, § 1785) and Article 58 (*ibid.*, § 1786).
[166] Third Geneva Convention, Articles 49–68 (*ibid.*, §§ 1762–1764) and Articles 109–119 (cited in Vol. II, Ch. 37, §§ 606–607); Fourth Geneva Convention, Article 40 (cited in Vol. II, Ch. 32,

The prohibition of "slavery and the slave trade in all their forms" has been recognised in Additional Protocol II as a fundamental guarantee for civilians and persons *hors de combat*.[167]

"Enslavement" was considered a crime against humanity in the Charters of the International Military Tribunals at Nuremberg and Tokyo.[168] "Enslavement" is also listed as a crime against humanity under the Statutes of the International Criminal Court and of the International Criminal Tribunals for the Former Yugoslavia and for Rwanda.[169]

The military manuals and the legislation of many States prohibit slavery and the slave trade, or "enslavement", which is often, but not always, referred to as a crime against humanity.[170] In the *Krnojelac case*, the International Criminal Tribunal for the Former Yugoslavia found the defendants guilty of "enslavement as a crime against humanity" and of "slavery as a violation of the laws or customs of war".[171]

Slavery and the slave trade are equally prohibited in international human rights law. The first universal treaty outlawing slavery and the slave trade was the Slavery Convention in 1926.[172] This was supplemented in 1956 by the Supplementary Convention on the Abolition of Slavery, the Slave Trade, and Institutions and Practices similar to Slavery, outlawing debt bondage, serfdom and inheritance or transfer of women or children.[173] The prohibition of slavery, servitude and the slave trade is a non-derogable right under the International Covenant on Civil and Political Rights and the regional human rights conventions.[174] A series of recent treaties criminalise trafficking in persons, such as

---

§ 1765), Articles 51–52 (*ibid.*, § 1766), Articles 95–96 (*ibid.*, § 1767) and Articles 132–135 (cited in Vol. II, Ch. 37, §§ 608–610); Hague Regulations, Article 45.

[167] Additional Protocol II, Article 4(2)(f) (adopted by consensus) (cited in Vol. II, Ch. 32, § 1774).

[168] IMT Charter (Nuremberg), Article 6 (*ibid.*, § 1761); IMT Charter (Tokyo), Article 5(c) (*ibid.*, § 1789).

[169] ICTY Statute, Article 5(c) (*ibid.*, § 1795); ICTR Statute, Article 3(c) (*ibid.*, § 1796); ICC Statute, Article 7(1)(c) (*ibid.*, § 1779).

[170] See, e.g., the military manuals of Canada (*ibid.*, § 1802), France (*ibid.*, § 1804), Israel (*ibid.*, § 1805), Netherlands (*ibid.*, § 1806), New Zealand (*ibid.*, § 1807), Senegal (*ibid.*, § 1809) and United States (*ibid.*, § 1815) and the legislation of Armenia (*ibid.*, § 1817), Australia (*ibid.*, § 1820), Belgium (*ibid.*, § 1825), Canada (*ibid.*, § 1828), China (*ibid.*, § 1829), Congo (*ibid.*, § 1831), Croatia (*ibid.*, § 1833), France (*ibid.*, § 1835), Ireland (*ibid.*, § 1836), Kenya (*ibid.*, § 18390), Mali (*ibid.*, § 1843), Netherlands (*ibid.*, § 1844), New Zealand (*ibid.*, § 1846), Niger (*ibid.*, § 1848), Norway (*ibid.*, § 1849), Philippines (*ibid.*, § 1851), United Kingdom (*ibid.*, § 1855) and United States (*ibid.*, §§ 1856–1857); see also the draft legislation of Burundi (*ibid.*, § 1827) and Trinidad and Tobago (*ibid.*, § 1853).

[171] ICTY, *Krnojelac case*, Judgement (*ibid.*, § 1897).

[172] Slavery Convention, Article 2 (*ibid.*, § 1758).

[173] Supplementary Convention on the Abolition of Slavery, the Slave Trade and Institutions similar to Slavery, Article 1 (*ibid.*, § 1769).

[174] International Covenant on Civil and Political Rights, Article 8 (slavery, slave-trade and servitude) (*ibid.*, § 1772); European Convention on Human Rights, Article 4(1) (slavery and servitude) (*ibid.*, § 1768); American Convention on Human Rights, Article 6(1) (slavery, involuntary servitude and slave trade) (*ibid.*, § 1773); African Charter on Human and Peoples' Rights, Article 5 (slavery and slave trade) (*ibid.*, § 1776).

the Protocol on the Trafficking in Persons adopted in 2000.[175] Slavery and the slave trade are also prohibited in other international instruments.[176]

Definition of slavery and slave trade

The Slavery Convention defines slavery as "the status or condition of a person over whom any or all of the powers attaching to the right of ownership are exercised". It defines slave trade as including:

all acts involved in the capture, acquisition or disposal of a person with intent to reduce him to slavery; all acts involved in the acquisition of a slave with a view to selling or exchanging him; all acts of disposal by sale or exchange of a slave acquired with a view to being sold or exchanged, and, in general, every act of trade or transport in slaves.[177]

These definitions have served as the basis for the definition of "enslavement" in the Statute of the International Criminal Court as "the exercise of any or all of the powers attaching to the right of ownership over a person and includes the exercise of such power in the course of trafficking in persons, in particular women and children".[178]

The Supplementary Convention on the Abolition of Slavery, the Slave Trade, and Institutions and Practices similar to Slavery defines serfdom as "the condition or status of a tenant who is by law, custom or agreement bound to live and labour on land belonging to another person and to render some determinate service to such other person, whether for reward or not, and is not free to change his status".[179] In the *Pohl case* in 1947, the US Military Tribunal at Nuremberg held that "involuntary servitude, even if tempered by humane treatment, is still slavery".[180]

Sexual slavery

Under the Statute of the International Criminal Court, sexual slavery is a war crime in both international and non-international armed conflicts.[181] The elements of crimes for this offence were deliberately drafted to avoid too narrow an interpretation of "sexual slavery", defining it as the exercise of "any or all of the powers attaching to the right of ownership over one or more persons,

---

[175] Protocol on Trafficking in Persons, Articles 1, 3 and 5 (*ibid.*, § 1783).
[176] See, e.g., Universal Declaration on Human Rights, Article 4 (*ibid.*, § 1790); Cairo Declaration on Human Rights in Islam, Article 11(a) (*ibid.*, § 1793); EU Charter of Fundamental Rights, Article 5 (*ibid.*, § 1800).
[177] Slavery Convention, Article 1 (*ibid.*, § 1758).
[178] ICC Statute, Article 7(2)(c) (*ibid.*, § 1779).
[179] Supplementary Convention on the Abolition of Slavery, the Slave Trade and Institutions similar to Slavery, Article 1(b). For an application of this definition, see European Commission of Human Rights, *Van Droogenbroeck v. Belgium* (*ibid.*, § 1900).
[180] United States, Military Tribunal at Nuremberg, *Pohl case* (*ibid.*, § 1869).
[181] ICC Statute, Article 8(2)(b)(xxii) and (e)(vi) (*ibid.*, § 1780).

such as by purchasing, selling, lending or bartering such a person or persons, or by imposing on them a similar deprivation of liberty" combined with the causing of such person or persons "to engage in one or more acts of a sexual nature". In relation to the first element of this war crime, the Elements of Crimes specifies that "it is understood that such deprivation of liberty may, in some circumstances, include exacting forced labour or otherwise reducing a person to servile status" as defined in the Supplementary Convention on the Abolition of Slavery, the Slave Trade, and Institutions and Practices similar to Slavery and that "it is also understood that the conduct described in this element includes trafficking in persons, in particular women and children".[182]

In a report submitted in 1998 to the UN Sub-Commission on Human Rights, the Special Rapporteur on the Situation of Systematic Rape, Sexual Slavery and Slavery-like Practices during Wartime stated that "sexual slavery is slavery and its prohibition is a *jus cogens* norm".[183] In the ongoing debate surrounding the so-called "comfort women" during the Second World War, both the Special Rapporteur on the Situation of Systematic Rape, Sexual Slavery and Slavery-like Practices during Wartime and the Special Rapporteur on Violence against Women, its Causes and Consequences have stated that they consider the practice of "comfort women" to be a case of sexual slavery. Japan, on the other hand, maintains that the definition of slavery does not apply to the treatment of the women in question.[184]

Rule 95. Uncompensated or abusive forced labour is prohibited.

Practice

Volume II, Chapter 32, Section H.

Summary

State practice establishes this rule as a norm of customary international law applicable in both international and non-international armed conflicts.

International and non-international armed conflicts

In the context of international armed conflicts, the Third Geneva Convention provides that "the Detaining Power may utilize the labour of prisoners of war

---

[182] Elements of Crimes for the ICC, Definition of sexual slavery (ICC Statute, Article 8(2)(b)(xxii), including Footnote 53, and Article 8(2)(e)(vi), including Footnote 65).

[183] UN Sub-Commission on Human Rights, Special Rapporteur on the Situation of Systematic Rape, Sexual Slavery and Slavery-like Practices during Wartime, Final report (cited in Vol. II, Ch. 32, § 1887).

[184] UN Commission on Human Rights, Special Rapporteur on Violence against Women, its Causes and Consequences, Report (*ibid.*, § 1885); UN Sub-Commission on Human Rights, Special Rapporteur on the Situation of Systematic Rape, Sexual Slavery and Slavery-like Practices during Wartime, Final report (*ibid.*, § 1887).

who are physically fit, taking into account their age, sex, rank and physical aptitude, and with a view particularly to maintaining them in a good state of physical and mental health".[185]

The Convention lists in detail the types of work a prisoner of war may be compelled to perform, "besides work connected with camp administration, installation or maintenance".[186] This list builds upon the general prohibition found in the 1929 Geneva Convention Relative to the Treatment of Prisoners of War that "work done by prisoners of war shall have no direct connection with the operations of the war".[187] In addition, the Third Geneva Convention provides that "unless he be a volunteer, no prisoner of war may be employed on labour which is of an unhealthy or dangerous nature. No prisoner of war shall be assigned to labour which would be looked upon as humiliating for a member of the Detaining Power's own forces. The removal of mines or similar devices shall be considered as dangerous labour."[188] The Convention contains further detailed provisions concerning working conditions, duration of labour, working pay, occupational accidents and medical supervision.[189]

The Fourth Geneva Convention provides that protected civilians may be compelled to work, but only under strict conditions, excluding work which is "directly related to the conduct of military operations" or which would involve them "in the obligation of taking part in military operations", and payment of a wage is required.[190] Lastly, the Fourth Geneva Convention provides that civilian internees shall not be employed "unless they so desire", in which case they must also receive a salary.[191]

The military manuals and the legislation of many States state that imposing forced labour on prisoners of war or civilians,[192] as well as compelling prisoners of war or civilians to perform prohibited work, are criminal offences.[193] In several national war crimes trials, the accused were found guilty of

---

[185] Third Geneva Convention, Article 49.
[186] Third Geneva Convention, Article 50 (cited in Vol. II, Ch. 32, § 1763).
[187] 1929 Geneva Convention Relative to the Treatment of Prisoners of War, Article 31 (*ibid.*, § 1759).
[188] Third Geneva Convention, Article 52 (*ibid.*, § 1764).
[189] See Third Geneva Convention, Articles 51 and 53–55.
[190] Fourth Geneva Convention, Article 40 (cited in Vol. II, Ch. 32, § 1765) and Article 51 (*ibid.*, § 1766).
[191] Fourth Geneva Convention, Article 95 (*ibid.*, § 1767).
[192] See, e.g., the military manuals of Ecuador (*ibid.*, § 1803) and United States (*ibid.*, § 1815) and the legislation of Australia (*ibid.*, §§ 1818–1819), Azerbaijan (*ibid.*, § 1822), Bosnia and Herzegovina (*ibid.*, § 1826), Democratic Republic of the Congo (*ibid.*, § 1830), Côte d'Ivoire (*ibid.*, § 1832), Croatia (*ibid.*, § 1833), Ethiopia (*ibid.*, § 1834), Latvia (*ibid.*, § 1840), Lithuania (*ibid.*, § 1841), Paraguay (*ibid.*, § 1850), Slovenia (*ibid.*, § 1852), Uzbekistan (*ibid.*, § 1858) and Yugoslavia (*ibid.*, §§ 1859–1860).
[193] See, e.g., the military manuals of Netherlands (*ibid.*, § 1806), Nigeria (*ibid.*, § 1808), South Africa (*ibid.*, § 1810), United Kingdom (*ibid.*, § 1811) and United States (*ibid.*, §§ 1812–1815); the legislation of Bangladesh (*ibid.*, § 1823), China (*ibid.*, § 1829), Ireland (*ibid.*, § 1836), Italy (*ibid.*, § 1838), Luxembourg (*ibid.*, § 1842), Nicaragua (*ibid.*, § 1847) and Norway (*ibid.*, § 1849).

having forced prisoners of war or civilians to engage in work related to the war.[194]

In the context of non-international armed conflicts, Additional Protocol II provides that persons who are deprived of their liberty for reasons related to the armed conflict "shall, if made to work, have the benefit of working conditions and safeguards similar to those enjoyed by the local civilian population".[195]

The Forced Labour Convention and Convention concerning the Abolition of Forced Labour, as well as the International Covenant on Civil and Political Rights and the regional human rights conventions, prohibit "forced or compulsory labour".[196] The Forced Labour Convention defines this as "all work or service which is exacted from any person under the menace of any penalty and for which the said person has not offered himself voluntarily".[197] But human rights law provides for exceptions to the general rule in that certain types of labour would not amount to unlawful forced labour, for example, labour by prisoners within prison establishments, labour required for the community to overcome calamity situations or normal civic obligations.[198] In addition, contrary to the prohibition of slavery and the slave trade, the prohibition of forced or compulsory labour may be derogated from, for example, in case of armed conflict where the above-mentioned specific rules of international humanitarian law become applicable.[199]

Deportation to slave labour

Deportation to slave labour violates the prohibition of deportation (see Rule 129) but has also been specified as a separate war crime in international armed

---

[194] See, e.g., Canada, Federal Court of Appeal, *Rudolph and Minister of Employment and Immigration case* (use of civilians in the production of V2 rockets) (*ibid.*, § 1861); France, General Tribunal at Rastadt of the Military Government for the French Zone of Occupation in Germany, *Roechling case* (prisoners of war working in the metallurgical industry) (*ibid.*, § 1863); Netherlands, Temporary Court-Martial of Makassar, *Koshiro case* (prisoners of war building and filling up ammunition depots) (*ibid.*, § 1865); Netherlands, Special Court of Cassation, *Rohrig and Others case* (civilians constructing fortifications) (*ibid.*, § 1866); United Kingdom, Military Court at Lüneberg, *Student case* (prisoners of war unloading arms, ammunition and warlike stores from aircraft) (*ibid.*, § 1868); United States, Military Tribunal at Nuremberg, *Krauch (I. G. Farben Trial) case* (prisoners of war working in coal mines) (*ibid.*, § 1872) and *Von Leeb (High Command) case* (civilians constructing fortifications) (*ibid.*, § 1874).

[195] Additional Protocol II, Article 5(1)(e) (adopted by consensus) (*ibid.*, § 1775).

[196] Forced Labour Convention, Article 1 (*ibid.*, § 1760); Convention concerning the Abolition of Forced Labour, Articles 1 and 2 (*ibid.*, §§ 1770–1771); International Covenant on Civil and Political Rights, Article 8(3) (*ibid.*, § 1772); European Convention on Human Rights, Article 4(2) (*ibid.*, § 1768); American Convention on Human Rights, Article 6(2); African Charter on Human and Peoples' Rights, Article 15 (right to work under equitable and satisfactory conditions).

[197] Forced Labour Convention, Article 2 (cited in Vol. II, Ch. 32, § 1760); see the further interpretation provided by the European Court of Human Rights, *Van der Mussele v. Belgium* (*ibid.*, § 1901).

[198] See International Covenant on Civil and Political Rights, Article 8(3)(b) and (c); European Convention on Human Rights, Article 4(3); American Convention on Human Rights, Article 6(3).

[199] See, e.g., International Covenant on Civil and Political Rights, Articles 4(2) and 8(3) (cited in Vol. II, Ch. 32, § 1772) and European Convention on Human Rights, Articles 4(2) and 15(2) (*ibid.*, § 1768).

conflicts. The Charter of the International Military Tribunal at Nuremberg included "deportation to slave labour or for any other purpose of civilian population of or in occupied territory" as a war crime.[200] Several defendants before the Tribunal were charged with and convicted of deporting thousands of civilians for slave labour, i.e., performing compulsory uncompensated labour.[201] Deportation to slave labour is also prohibited by the military manuals and legislation of several States.[202] Several national courts have found persons guilty of this crime, including in the *List (Hostages Trial) case*, in which the accused was found guilty of "deportation to slave labour of prisoners of war and members of the civilian populations in territories occupied by the German Armed Forces".[203]

Compelling persons to serve in the forces of a hostile power

Compelling persons to serve in the forces of a hostile power is a specific type of forced labour that is prohibited in international armed conflicts. The Hague Regulations specify that it is forbidden to compel nationals of the hostile party to take part in operations of war directed against their own country, even if they were in the belligerent's service before the war.[204] The Third and Fourth Geneva Conventions state that so compelling a prisoner of war or a protected civilian is a grave breach.[205] The prohibition is repeated in the list of war crimes in the Statute of the International Criminal Court.[206]

The prohibition on compelling persons to serve in the forces of a hostile power is contained in numerous military manuals.[207] It is also set forth in the legislation of a large number of States.[208] The reasoning behind the rule is

[200] IMT Charter (Nuremberg), Article 6 (*ibid.*, § 1761).
[201] See International Military Tribunal at Nuremberg, *Case of the Major War Criminals* (*ibid.*, § 1892).
[202] See, e.g., the military manuals of Nigeria (*ibid.*, § 1808) and United Kingdom (*ibid.*, § 1811) and the legislation of Australia (*ibid.*, § 1819), Bangladesh (*ibid.*, § 1823), Belarus (*ibid.*, § 1824), Ethiopia (*ibid.*, § 1834), Israel (*ibid.*, § 1837) and Ukraine (*ibid.*, § 1854).
[203] See, e.g., Canada, Federal Court of Appeal, *Rudolph and Minister of Employment and Immigration case* (*ibid.*, § 1861); Netherlands, Special Court of Cassation, *Rohrig and Others case* (*ibid.*, § 1866); Poland, Supreme National Tribunal of Poland at Poznan, *Greiser case* (*ibid.*, § 1867); United States, Military Tribunal at Nuremberg, *List (Hostages Trial) case* (*ibid.*, § 1870), *Milch case* (*ibid.*, § 1871), *Krauch (I. G. Farben Trial) case* (*ibid.*, § 1872) and *Krupp case* (*ibid.*, § 1873).
[204] Hague Regulations, Article 23(h) (*ibid.*, § 1909).
[205] Third Geneva Convention, Article 130 (*ibid.*, § 1912); Fourth Geneva Convention, Article 147 (*ibid.*, § 1912).
[206] ICC Statute, Article 8(2)(a)(v) and (b)(xv) (*ibid.*, § 1914).
[207] See, e.g., the military manuals of Argentina (*ibid.*, § 1920), Australia (*ibid.*, §§ 1921–1922), Belgium (*ibid.*, § 1923), Benin (*ibid.*, § 1924), Burkina Faso (*ibid.*, § 1925), Cameroon (*ibid.*, § 1926), Canada (*ibid.*, § 1927), France (*ibid.*, §§ 1928–1930), Germany (*ibid.*, § 1931), Israel (*ibid.*, § 1932), Italy (*ibid.*, § 1933), Kenya (*ibid.*, § 1934), South Korea (*ibid.*, § 1935), Mali (*ibid.*, § 1936), Morocco (*ibid.*, § 1937), Netherlands (*ibid.*, § 1938), New Zealand (*ibid.*, § 1939), Nigeria (*ibid.*, §§ 1940–1941), Russia (*ibid.*, § 1942), Senegal (*ibid.*, § 1943), South Africa (*ibid.*, § 1944), Sweden (*ibid.*, § 1945), Switzerland (*ibid.*, § 1946), Togo (*ibid.*, § 1947), United Kingdom (*ibid.*, §§ 1948–1949) and United States (*ibid.*, §§ 1950–1952).
[208] See, e.g., the legislation (*ibid.*, §§ 1953–2034).

the distressing and dishonourable nature of making persons participate in military operations against their own country – whether or not they are remunerated.

Rule 96. The taking of hostages is prohibited.

Practice

Volume II, Chapter 32, Section I.

Summary

State practice establishes this rule as a norm of customary international law applicable in both international and non-international armed conflicts.

International and non-international armed conflicts

Common Article 3 of the Geneva Conventions prohibits the taking of hostages.[209] It is also prohibited by the Fourth Geneva Convention and is considered a grave breach thereof.[210] These provisions were to some extent a departure from international law as it stood at that time, articulated in the *List (Hostages Trial) case* in 1948, in which the US Military Tribunal at Nuremberg did not rule out the possibility of an occupying power taking hostages as a measure of last resort and under certain strict conditions.[211] However, in addition to the provisions in the Geneva Conventions, practice since then shows that the prohibition of hostage-taking is now firmly entrenched in customary international law and is considered a war crime.

The prohibition of hostage-taking is recognised as a fundamental guarantee for civilians and persons *hors de combat* in Additional Protocols I and II.[212] Under the Statute of the International Criminal Court, the "taking of hostages" constitutes a war crime in both international and non-international armed conflicts.[213] Hostage-taking is also listed as a war crime under the Statutes of the International Criminal Tribunals for the Former Yugoslavia and for Rwanda and of the Special Court for Sierra Leone.[214] Numerous military manuals prohibit

---

[209] Geneva Conventions, common Article 3 (*ibid.*, § 2048).
[210] Fourth Geneva Convention, Article 34 (*ibid.*, § 2049) and Article 147 (*ibid.*, § 2050).
[211] United States, Military Tribunal at Nuremberg, *List (Hostages Trial) case* (*ibid.*, § 2197).
[212] Additional Protocol I, Article 75(2)(c) (adopted by consensus) (*ibid.*, § 2052); Additional Protocol II, Article 4(2)(c) (adopted by consensus) (*ibid.*, § 2053).
[213] ICC Statute, Article 8(2)(a)(viii) and (c)(iii) (*ibid.*, § 2056).
[214] ICTY Statute, Article 2(h) (*ibid.*, § 2064); ICTR Statute, Article 4(c) (*ibid.*, § 2065); Statute of the Special Court for Sierra Leone, Article 3(c) (*ibid.*, § 2057).

the taking of hostages.[215] This prohibition is also set forth in the legislation of numerous States.[216]

Instances of hostage-taking, whether in international or non-international armed conflicts, have been condemned by States.[217] International organisations, in particular the United Nations, have also condemned such instances with respect to the Gulf War and the conflicts in Cambodia, Chechnya, El Salvador, Kosovo, Middle East, Sierra Leone, Tajikistan and the former Yugoslavia.[218]

In the *Karadžić and Mladić case* in 1995 before the International Criminal Tribunal for the Former Yugoslavia, the accused were charged with grave breaches for taking UN peacekeepers as hostages. In its review of the indictments, the Tribunal confirmed this charge.[219] In the *Blaškić case* in 2000, the Tribunal found the accused guilty of the taking of hostages as a violation of the laws and customs of war and the taking of civilians as hostages as a grave breach of the Fourth Geneva Convention.[220] In the *Kordić and Čerkez case* before the Tribunal in 2001, the accused were found guilty of the grave breach of taking civilians hostage.[221]

The ICRC has called on parties to both international and non-international armed conflicts to refrain from taking hostages.[222]

---

[215] See, e.g., the military manuals of Argentina (*ibid.*, § 2070), Australia (*ibid.*, §§ 2071–2072), Belgium (*ibid.*, §§ 2073–2074), Benin (*ibid.*, § 2075), Burkina Faso (*ibid.*, § 2076), Cameroon (*ibid.*, §§ 2077–2078), Canada (*ibid.*, § 2079), Colombia (*ibid.*, § 2080), Congo (*ibid.*, § 2081), Croatia (*ibid.*, §§ 2082–2083), Dominican Republic (*ibid.*, § 2084), Ecuador (*ibid.*, § 2085), France (*ibid.*, §§ 2086–2089), Germany (*ibid.*, § 2090), Hungary (*ibid.*, § 2091), Italy (*ibid.*, §§ 2092–2093), Kenya (*ibid.*, § 2094), South Korea (*ibid.*, § 2095), Madagascar (*ibid.*, § 2096), Mali (*ibid.*, § 2097), Morocco (*ibid.*, § 2098), Netherlands (*ibid.*, § 2099), New Zealand (*ibid.*, § 2100), Nicaragua (*ibid.*, § 2101), Nigeria (*ibid.*, § 2102), Philippines (*ibid.*, § 2103), Romania (*ibid.*, § 2104), Russia (*ibid.*, § 2105), Senegal (*ibid.*, § 2106), South Africa (*ibid.*, § 2107), Spain (*ibid.*, § 2108), Sweden (*ibid.*, § 2109), Switzerland (*ibid.*, § 2110), Togo (*ibid.*, § 2111), United Kingdom (*ibid.*, §§ 2112–2113), United States (*ibid.*, §§ 2114–2117) and Yugoslavia (*ibid.*, § 2118).

[216] See, e.g., the legislation (*ibid.*, §§ 2119–2194).

[217] See, e.g., the statements of Germany (in the context of the conflict in Nagorno-Karabakh) (*ibid.*, § 2200), Italy (*ibid.*, § 2201), Pakistan (in the context of the conflict in Kashmir) (*ibid.*, § 2204), United States (in relation to the Gulf War) (*ibid.*, §§ 2206–2207) and Yugoslavia (*ibid.*, § 2209).

[218] See, e.g., UN Security Council, Res. 664 (*ibid.*, § 2212), Res. 674 (*ibid.*, § 2212), Res. 686 (*ibid.*, § 2212) and Res. 706 (*ibid.*, § 2212); UN Security Council, Statements by the President (*ibid.*, §§ 2213–2214); UN General Assembly, Res. 53/164 (*ibid.*, § 2215); UN Commission on Human Rights, Res. 1992/71 (*ibid.*, § 2216), Res. 1992/S-1/1 (*ibid.*, § 2217), Res. 1995/55 (*ibid.*, § 2218), Res. 1998/60 (*ibid.*, § 2219) and Res. 1998/62 (*ibid.*, § 2220); Council of Europe, Parliamentary Assembly, Res. 950 (*ibid.*, § 2226); European Parliament, Resolution on violations of human rights and humanitarian law in Chechnya (*ibid.*, § 2227); OAS, Permanent Council, Resolution on Hostages in El Salvador (*ibid.*, § 2228).

[219] ICTY, *Karadžić and Mladić case*, Initial Indictment and Review of the Indictments (*ibid.*, § 2233).

[220] ICTY, *Blaškić case*, Judgement (*ibid.*, § 2234).

[221] ICTY, *Kordić and Čerkez case*, Judgement (*ibid.*, § 2235).

[222] See, e.g., ICRC, Memorandum on the Applicability of International Humanitarian Law (*ibid.*, § 2238), Press Release, Tajikistan: ICRC urges respect for humanitarian rules (*ibid.*, § 2240), Communication to the Press No. 93/25 (*ibid.*, § 2242), Memorandum on Respect for International Humanitarian Law in Angola (*ibid.*, § 2243), Memorandum on Compliance with International Humanitarian Law by the Forces Participating in Opération Turquoise (*ibid.*, § 2244),

International human rights law does not specifically prohibit "hostage-taking", but the practice is prohibited by virtue of non-derogable human rights law because it amounts to an arbitrary deprivation of liberty (see Rule 99). The UN Commission on Human Rights has stated that hostage-taking, wherever and by whoever committed, is an illegal act aimed at the destruction of human rights and is never justifiable.[223] In its General Comment on Article 4 of the International Covenant on Civil and Political Rights (concerning states of emergency), the UN Human Rights Committee stated that States parties may "in no circumstances" invoke a state of emergency "as justification for acting in violation of humanitarian law or peremptory norms of international law, for instance by taking hostages".[224]

Definition of hostage-taking

The International Convention against the Taking of Hostages defines the offence as the seizure or detention of a person (the hostage), combined with threatening to kill, to injure or to continue to detain the hostage, in order to compel a third party to do or to abstain from doing any act as an explicit or implicit condition for the release of the hostage.[225] The Elements of Crimes for the International Criminal Court uses the same definition but adds that the required behaviour of the third party could be a condition not only for the release of the hostage but also for the safety of the hostage.[226] It is the specific intent that characterises hostage-taking and distinguishes it from the deprivation of someone's liberty as an administrative or judicial measure.

Although the prohibition of hostage-taking is specified in the Fourth Geneva Convention and is typically associated with the holding of civilians as hostages, there is no indication that the offence is limited to taking civilians hostage. Common Article 3 of the Geneva Conventions, the Statute of the International Criminal Court and the International Convention against the Taking of Hostages do not limit the offence to the taking of civilians, but apply it to the taking of any person. Indeed, in the Elements of Crimes for the International Criminal Court, the definition applies to the taking of any person protected by the Geneva Conventions.[227]

Press Release No. 1793 (*ibid.*, § 2245) and Communication to the Press of ICRC Moscow (*ibid.*, § 2246).

[223] UN Commission on Human Rights, Res. 1998/73 (*ibid.*, § 2221) and Res. 2001/38 (*ibid.*, § 2222).

[224] UN Human Rights Committee, General Comment No. 29 (Article 4 of the International Covenant on Civil and Political Rights) (*ibid.*, § 2236).

[225] International Convention against the Taking of Hostages, Article 1 (*ibid.*, § 2054).

[226] Elements of Crimes for the ICC, Definition of the taking of hostages as a war crime (ICC Statute, Article 8(2)(a)(viii) and (c)(iii)).

[227] Elements of Crimes for the ICC, Definition of the taking of hostages as a war crime (ICC Statute, Article 8(2)(a)(viii)).

Rule 97. The use of human shields is prohibited.

Practice

Volume II, Chapter 32, Section J.

Summary

State practice establishes this rule as a norm of customary international law applicable in both international and non-international armed conflicts.

International and non-international armed conflicts

In the context of international armed conflicts, this rule is set forth in the Third Geneva Convention (with respect to prisoners of war), the Fourth Geneva Convention (with respect to protected civilians) and Additional Protocol I (with respect to civilians in general).[228] Under the Statute of the International Criminal Court, "utilizing the presence of a civilian or other protected person to render certain points, areas or military forces immune from military operations" constitutes a war crime in international armed conflicts.[229]

The prohibition of using human shields is contained in numerous military manuals, many of which extend the prohibition to all civilians.[230] Using human shields constitutes a criminal offence under the legislation of many States.[231] This practice includes that of States not, or not at the time, party to Additional Protocol I or to the Statute of the International Criminal Court.[232] In 1990 and 1991, there was extensive condemnation by States of the use of prisoners of

---

[228] Third Geneva Convention, Article 23, second paragraph (cited in Vol. II, Ch. 32, § 2253); Fourth Geneva Convention, Article 28 (*ibid.*, § 2254); Additional Protocol I, Article 51(7) (adopted by consensus) (*ibid.*, § 2256).

[229] ICC Statute, Article 8(2)(b)(xxiii) (*ibid.*, § 2257).

[230] See, e.g., the military manuals of Argentina (*ibid.*, § 2261), Australia (*ibid.*, §§ 2262–2263), Belgium (*ibid.*, § 2264), Cameroon (*ibid.*, § 2265), Canada (*ibid.*, § 2266), Colombia (*ibid.*, § 2267), Croatia (*ibid.*, § 2268), Dominican Republic (*ibid.*, § 2269), Ecuador (*ibid.*, § 2270), France (*ibid.*, §§ 2271–2273), Germany (*ibid.*, § 2274), Israel (*ibid.*, § 2275), Italy (*ibid.*, § 2276), Kenya (*ibid.*, § 2277), Netherlands (*ibid.*, § 2278), New Zealand (*ibid.*, § 2279), Spain (*ibid.*, § 2280), Switzerland (*ibid.*, § 2281), United Kingdom (*ibid.*, §§ 2282–2283) and United States (*ibid.*, §§ 2284 and 2286).

[231] See, e.g., the legislation of Australia (*ibid.*, § 2287), Azerbaijan (*ibid.*, §§ 2288–2289), Bangladesh (*ibid.*, § 2290), Belarus (*ibid.*, § 2291), Canada (*ibid.*, § 2293), Democratic Republic of the Congo (*ibid.*, § 2294), Congo (*ibid.*, § 2295), Germany (*ibid.*, § 2296), Georgia (*ibid.*, § 2297), Ireland (*ibid.*, § 2298), Lithuania (*ibid.*, § 2299), Mali (*ibid.*, § 2300), Netherlands (*ibid.*, § 2301), New Zealand (*ibid.*, § 2302), Norway (*ibid.*, § 2303), Peru (*ibid.*, § 2304), Poland (*ibid.*, § 2305), Tajikistan (*ibid.*, § 2306), United Kingdom (*ibid.*, § 2308) and Yemen (*ibid.*, § 2309); see also the draft legislation of Burundi (*ibid.*, § 2292) and Trinidad and Tobago (*ibid.*, § 2307).

[232] See, e.g., the military manuals of France (*ibid.*, § 2271), Kenya (*ibid.*, § 2277), United Kingdom (*ibid.*, § 2283) and United States (*ibid.*, §§ 2284 and 2286) and the legislation of Azerbaijan (*ibid.*, §§ 2288–2289), Bangladesh (*ibid.*, § 2290), Belarus (*ibid.*, § 2291), Democratic Republic of the Congo (*ibid.*, § 2294), Georgia (*ibid.*, § 2297), Lithuania (*ibid.*, § 2299), Peru (*ibid.*, § 2304), Poland (*ibid.*, § 2305), Tajikistan (*ibid.*, § 2306) and Yemen (*ibid.*, § 2309); see also the draft legislation of Burundi (*ibid.*, § 2292).

war and civilians by Iraq as human shields, and the United States declared that such use amounted to a war crime.[233] The use of prisoners of war as human shields during the Second World War was the subject of war crimes trials by the UK Military Court at Lüneberg in the *Student case* in 1946 and by the US Military Tribunal at Nuremberg in the *Von Leeb (The High Command Trial) case* in 1948.[234] In the *Karadžić and Mladić case* in 1995 before the International Criminal Tribunal for the Former Yugoslavia, the accused were charged with war crimes for using UN peacekeepers as human shields. In its review of the indictments, the Tribunal upheld this charge.[235]

With respect to non-international armed conflicts, Additional Protocol II does not explicitly mention the use of human shields, but such practice would be prohibited by the requirement that "the civilian population and individual civilians shall enjoy general protection against the dangers arising from military operations".[236] It is significant, furthermore, that the use of human shields has often been equated with the taking of hostages,[237] which is prohibited by Additional Protocol II,[238] and by customary international law (see Rule 96). In addition, deliberately using civilians to shield military operations is contrary to the principle of distinction and violates the obligation to take feasible precautions to separate civilians and military objectives (see Rules 23–24).

Several military manuals which apply in non-international armed conflicts prohibit the use of human shields.[239] The legislation of several States criminalizes the use of human shields in non-international armed conflicts.[240] The use of human shields in non-international armed conflicts has been condemned by States and by the United Nations, for example, with respect to the conflicts in Liberia, Rwanda, Sierra Leone, Somalia, Tajikistan and the former Yugoslavia.[241]

---

[233] See, e.g., the statements of El Salvador (*ibid.*, § 2314), Germany (*ibid.*, § 2316), Italy (*ibid.*, § 2319), Kuwait (*ibid.*, § 2321), Senegal (*ibid.*, § 2326), United Kingdom (*ibid.*, §§ 2329–2330) and United States (*ibid.*, §§ 2337–2345) and the reported practice of Spain (*ibid.*, § 2327).

[234] United Kingdom, Military Court at Lüneberg, *Student case* (*ibid.*, § 2310); United States, Military Tribunal at Nuremberg, *Von Leeb (The High Command Trial) case* (*ibid.*, § 2311).

[235] ICTY, *Karadžić and Mladić case*, First Indictment and Review of the Indictments (*ibid.*, § 2366).

[236] Additional Protocol II, Article 13(1) (adopted by consensus) (cited in Vol. II, Ch. 5, § 2).

[237] See, e.g., the practice of El Salvador (cited in Vol. II, Ch. 32, § 2314) and the European Community (*ibid.*, § 2361).

[238] Additional Protocol II, Article 4(2)(c) (adopted by consensus) (*ibid.*, § 2053).

[239] See, e.g., the military manuals of Australia (*ibid.*, § 2262), Canada (*ibid.*, § 2266), Colombia (*ibid.*, § 2267), Croatia (*ibid.*, § 2268), Ecuador (*ibid.*, § 2270), Germany (*ibid.*, § 2274), Italy (*ibid.*, § 2276) and Kenya (*ibid.*, § 2277).

[240] See, e.g., the legislation of Azerbaijan (*ibid.*, §§ 2288–2289), Belarus (*ibid.*, § 2291), Democratic Republic of the Congo (*ibid.*, § 2294), Germany (*ibid.*, § 2296), Georgia (*ibid.*, § 2297), Lithuania (*ibid.*, § 2299), Poland (*ibid.*, § 2305) and Tajikistan (*ibid.*, § 2306); see also the legislation of Peru (*ibid.*, § 2304) and Yemen (*ibid.*, § 2309), the application of which is not excluded in time of non-international armed conflict, and the draft legislation of Burundi (*ibid.*, § 2292).

[241] See, e.g., the statements of Chile (*ibid.*, § 2312), Tajikistan (*ibid.*, § 2328) and Yugoslavia (*ibid.*, § 2348); the reported practice of Rwanda (*ibid.*, § 2325); UN Commission on Human Rights, Res. 1995/89 (*ibid.*, § 2350); UN Secretary-General, Progress report on UNOMIL (*ibid.*, § 2351), Progress report on UNOMSIL (*ibid.*, § 2352) and Report pursuant to paragraph 5 of Security Council resolution 837 (1993) on the investigation into the 5 June 1993 attack on the UN forces in Somalia conducted on behalf of the UN Security Council (*ibid.*, § 2353).

No official contrary practice was found in the context of either international or non-international armed conflicts.

The ICRC has reminded parties to both international and non-international armed conflicts of the prohibition of using human shields.[242]

International human rights law does not prohibit the use of human shields as such, but this practice would constitute, among other things, a violation of the non-derogable right not to be arbitrarily deprived of the right to life (see commentary to Rule 89). The UN Human Rights Committee and regional human rights bodies have indicated that this right involves not only the right not to be killed, but also the duty of States to take measures to protect life.[243] In *Demiray v. Turkey*, in which the applicant submitted that her husband had been used as a human shield, the European Court of Human Rights stated that "Article 2 may . . . imply in certain well-defined circumstances a positive obligation on the authorities to take preventive operational measures to protect an individual for which they are responsible".[244]

Definition of human shields

The prohibition of using human shields in the Geneva Conventions, Additional Protocol I and the Statute of the International Criminal Court are couched in terms of using the presence (or movements) of civilians or other protected persons to render certain points or areas (or military forces) immune from military operations.[245] Most examples given in military manuals, or which have been the object of condemnations, have been cases where persons were actually taken to military objectives in order to shield those objectives from attacks. The military manuals of New Zealand and the United Kingdom give as examples the placing of persons in or next to ammunition trains.[246] There were many condemnations of the threat by Iraq to round up and place prisoners of war and civilians in strategic sites and around military defence points.[247] Other condemnations on the basis of this prohibition related to rounding up civilians

---

[242] See, e.g., ICRC, Communication to the Press No. 93/17 (*ibid.*, § 2369) and archive document (*ibid.*, § 2370).

[243] UN Human Rights Committee, General Comment No. 6 (Article 6 of the International Covenant on Civil and Political Rights) (*ibid.*, § 2367); African Commission on Human and Peoples' Rights, *Civil Liberties Organisation v. Chad* (*ibid.*, § 940); European Court of Human Rights, *Demiray v. Turkey* (*ibid.*, § 2368).

[244] European Court of Human Rights, *Demiray v. Turkey* (*ibid.*, § 2368).

[245] Third Geneva Convention, Article 23, second paragraph (*ibid.*, § 2253); Fourth Geneva Convention, Article 28 (*ibid.*, § 2254); Additional Protocol I, Article 12(4) (adopted by consensus) (*ibid.*, § 2255) and Article 51(7) (*ibid.*, § 2256); ICC Statute, Article 8(2)(b)(xxiii) (*ibid.*, § 2257).

[246] See the military manuals of New Zealand (*ibid.*, § 2279) and United Kingdom (*ibid.*, § 2282).

[247] See, e.g., the statements of Germany (*ibid.*, § 2316), Italy (*ibid.*, § 2319), Kuwait (*ibid.*, § 2321), Senegal (*ibid.*, § 2326), United Kingdom (*ibid.*, §§ 2329–2334) and United States (*ibid.*, §§ 2337–2342 and 2344–2345); UN Commission on Human Rights, Res. 1992/71 (*ibid.*, § 2349); EC, Declaration on the situation of foreigners in Iraq and Kuwait (*ibid.*, § 2358), Statement before the Third Committee of the UN General Assembly (*ibid.*, § 2359), Statement on the situation of prisoners of war (*ibid.*, § 2360) and Declaration on the Gulf crisis (*ibid.*, § 2361).

and putting them in front of military units in the conflicts in the former Yugoslavia and Liberia.[248]

In the Review of the Indictments in the *Karadžić and Mladić case*, the International Criminal Tribunal for the Former Yugoslavia qualified physically securing or otherwise holding peacekeeping forces against their will at potential NATO air targets, including ammunition bunkers, a radar site and a communications centre, as using "human shields".[249]

It can be concluded that the use of human shields requires an intentional co-location of military objectives and civilians or persons *hors de combat* with the specific intent of trying to prevent the targeting of those military objectives.

Rule 98. Enforced disappearance is prohibited.

Practice

Volume II, Chapter 32, Section K.

Summary

State practice establishes this rule as a norm of customary international law applicable in both international and non-international armed conflicts.

International and non-international armed conflicts

International humanitarian law treaties do not refer to the term "enforced disappearance" as such. However, enforced disappearance violates, or threatens to violate, a range of customary rules of international humanitarian law, most notably the prohibition of arbitrary deprivation of liberty (see Rule 99), the prohibition of torture and other cruel or inhuman treatment (see Rule 90) and the prohibition of murder (see Rule 89). In addition, in international armed conflicts, the extensive requirements concerning registration, visits and transmission of information with respect to persons deprived of their liberty are aimed, *inter alia*, at preventing enforced disappearances (see Chapter 37). In non-international armed conflicts, parties are also required to take steps to prevent disappearances, including through the registration of persons deprived of their liberty (see Rule 123). This prohibition should also be viewed in the light of the rule requiring respect for family life (see Rule 105) and the rule that each party to the conflict must take all feasible measures to account for persons reported missing as a result of armed conflict and to provide their family members with information it has on their fate (see Rule 117). The cumulative

---

[248] See, e.g., the statement of Yugoslavia (*ibid.*, § 2348); UN Commission on Human Rights, Res. 1995/89 (*ibid.*, § 2350); UN Secretary-General, Progress report on UNOMIL (*ibid.*, § 2351).
[249] ICTY, *Karadžić and Mladić case*, Review of the Indictments (*ibid.*, § 2366).

effect of these rules is that the phenomenon of "enforced disappearance" is prohibited by international humanitarian law.

Although the articulation of the prohibition of enforced disappearance in military manuals and national legislation is in its early stages, the prohibition is expressly provided for in the military manuals of Colombia, El Salvador, Indonesia and Peru.[250] The legislation of many States also specifically prohibits this practice.[251]

The 24th International Conference of the Red Cross in 1981 considered that enforced disappearances "imply violations of fundamental human rights such as the right to life, freedom and personal safety, the right not to be subjected to torture or cruel, inhuman or degrading treatment, the right not to be arbitrarily arrested or detained, and the right to a just and public trial".[252] The 25th International Conference of the Red Cross in 1986 condemned "any act leading to the forced or involuntary disappearance of individuals or groups of individuals".[253] The Plan of Action for the years 2000–2003, adopted by the 27th International Conference of the Red Cross and Red Crescent in 1999, requested all parties to an armed conflict to take effective measures to ensure that "strict orders are given to prevent all serious violations of international humanitarian law, including... enforced disappearances".[254] All these resolutions were adopted by consensus.

No official contrary practice was found in the sense that no State has claimed the right to enforce the disappearance of persons. In addition, alleged instances of enforced disappearances have generally been condemned by States and the United Nations. Disappearances during the conflict in the former Yugoslavia, for example, were condemned in UN Security Council debates in 1995 by Botswana, Honduras and Indonesia.[255] They were condemned in resolutions adopted by consensus by the UN Security Council and UN Commission on Human Rights.[256] The UN General Assembly also condemned enforced disappearances in the former Yugoslavia in a resolution adopted in 1995.[257] The

---

[250] Colombia, *Basic Military Manual* (*ibid.*, § 2386); El Salvador, *Human Rights Charter of the Armed Forces* (*ibid.*, § 2387); Indonesia, *Directive on Human Rights in Irian Jaya and Maluku* (*ibid.*, § 2388); Peru, *Human Rights Charter of the Security Forces* (*ibid.*, § 2389).

[251] See, e.g., the legislation of Armenia (*ibid.*, § 2390), Australia (*ibid.*, § 2391), Azerbaijan (*ibid.*, § 2392), Belarus (*ibid.*, § 2393), Canada (*ibid.*, § 2395), Congo (*ibid.*, § 2396), El Salvador (*ibid.*, § 2397), France (*ibid.*, § 2398), Germany (*ibid.*, § 2399), Mali (*ibid.*, § 2400), Netherlands (*ibid.*, § 2401), New Zealand (*ibid.*, § 2403), Niger (*ibid.*, § 2402), Paraguay (*ibid.*, § 2405), Peru (*ibid.*, § 2406) and United Kingdom (*ibid.*, § 2408); see also the draft legislation of Burundi (*ibid.*, § 2394), Nicaragua (*ibid.*, § 2404) and Trinidad and Tobago (*ibid.*, § 2407).

[252] 24th International Conference of the Red Cross, Res. II (*ibid.*, § 2434).

[253] 25th International Conference of the Red Cross, Res. XIII (*ibid.*, § 2435).

[254] 27th International Conference of the Red Cross and Red Crescent, Res. I (adopted by consensus) (*ibid.*, § 2437).

[255] See the statements of Botswana (*ibid.*, § 2411), Honduras (*ibid.*, § 2413) and Indonesia (*ibid.*, § 2414).

[256] UN Security Council, Res. 1034 (*ibid.*, § 2416); UN Commission on Human Rights, Res. 1994/72 (*ibid.*, § 2421) and Res. 1996/71 (*ibid.*, § 2422).

[257] UN General Assembly, Res. 50/193 (*ibid.*, § 2417). The resolution was adopted by 114 votes in favour, one against and 20 abstentions. However, the explanation of vote of Russia, which

General Assembly again condemned enforced disappearances in a resolution on Sudan adopted in 2000.[258]

Under the Statute of the International Criminal Court, the systematic practice of enforced disappearance constitutes a crime against humanity.[259] The Inter-American Convention on the Forced Disappearance of Persons also prohibits enforced disappearance as "a grave and abominable offence against the inherent dignity of the human being" and states that it "violates numerous non-derogable and essential human rights".[260] The UN Declaration on Enforced Disappearance, adopted by consensus, specifies that enforced disappearance constitutes a violation of the right to recognition as a person before the law, the right to liberty and security of the person and the right not to be subjected to torture and other cruel, inhuman or degrading treatment or punishment and that it violates or constitutes a grave threat to the right to life.[261]

It is significant that in the *Kupreškić case* in 2000, the International Criminal Tribunal for the Former Yugoslavia found that enforced disappearance could be characterised as a crime against humanity, although it was not listed as such in the Tribunal's Statute. The Tribunal took into account the fact that enforced disappearances consisted of the violation of several human rights and were prohibited under the UN Declaration on Enforced Disappearance and the Inter-American Convention on the Forced Disappearance of Persons. It therefore decided that it fell into the category of "other inhumane acts" provided for in Article 5(i) of its Statute.[262]

In addition, regional human rights bodies found in several cases that enforced disappearances violate several rights. For example, the Inter-American Commission and Court of Human Rights have found that enforced disappearances

---

voted against the resolution, shows that it did not object to the principle of condemning forced disappearance but thought that the resolution was too one-sided. See the statement of Russia in the Third Committee of the UN General Assembly, UN Doc. A/C.3/50/SR.58, 14 December 1995, § 17.

258 UN General Assembly, Res. 55/116 (cited in Vol. II, Ch. 32, § 2418). The resolution was adopted by 85 votes in favour, 32 against and 49 abstentions. However, in explanations of vote given by Canada, Bangladesh, Libya, Thailand and the United States, there is no indication that there was a disagreement on the principle which is under discussion here; see the explanations of vote of these States given in the Third Committee of the UN General Assembly, 10 October 2000, UN Doc. A/C.3/55/SR.55, 29 November 2000, § 138 (Canada), § 139 (United States), § 146 (Bangladesh), § 147 (Thailand) and § 148 (Libya).

259 ICC Statute, Article 7(1)(i) (cited in Vol. II, Ch. 32, § 2373). Article 7(2)(i) (*ibid.*, § 2374) defines enforced disappearance as "the arrest, detention or abduction of persons by, or with the authorization, support or acquiescence of, a State or a political organization, followed by a refusal to acknowledge that deprivation of freedom or to give information on the fate or whereabouts of those persons, with the intention of removing them from the protection of the law for a prolonged period of time".

260 Inter-American Convention on the Forced Disappearance of Persons, preamble (*ibid.*, § 2372); see also UN Commission on Human Rights, Res. 2001/46 (*ibid.*, § 2423); World Conference on Human Rights, Vienna Declaration and Programme of Action (*ibid.*, § 2436).

261 UN Declaration on Enforced Disappearance, Article 1 (*ibid.*, § 2380).

262 ICTY, *Kupreškić case*, Judgement (*ibid.*, § 2438).

violate the right to liberty and security of person, the right to fair trial and the right to life.[263] In addition, as stated in the UN Declaration on Enforced Disappearance, enforced disappearances inflict severe suffering, not only on the victims but also on their families.[264] The UN Human Rights Committee and the European Court of Human Rights have similarly found that the enforced disappearance of a close family member constitutes inhuman treatment of the next-of-kin.[265] The UN Human Rights Committee also stressed in its General Comment on Article 4 of the International Covenant on Civil and Political Rights that the prohibition of abductions and unacknowledged detention were not subject to derogation and stated that "the absolute nature of these prohibitions, even in times of emergency, is justified by their status as norms of general international law".[266] It should therefore be noted that, although it is the widespread or systematic practice of enforced disappearance that constitutes a crime against humanity, any enforced disappearance is a violation of international humanitarian law and human rights law.

There is extensive practice indicating that the prohibition of enforced disappearance encompasses a duty to investigate cases of alleged enforced disappearance.[267] The duty to prevent enforced disappearances is further supported by the requirement to record the details of persons deprived of their liberty (see Rule 123).

---

[263] See, e.g., Inter-American Commission on Human Rights, *Case 9466 (Peru)* (*ibid.*, § 2447), *Case 9786 (Peru)* (*ibid.*, § 2449) and Third report on the human rights situation in Colombia (*ibid.*, § 2450) and Inter-American Court of Human Rights, *Velásquez Rodríguez case* (*ibid.*, § 2451); see also African Commission on Human and Peoples' Rights, *Mouvement Burkinabé des Droits de l'Homme et des Peuples v. Burkina Faso* (*ibid.*, § 2442) (violation of the right to recognition before the law, right to freedom and security of person).

[264] UN Declaration on Enforced Disappearance, Article 1(2) (*ibid.*, § 2380).

[265] UN Human Rights Committee, *Quinteros v. Uruguay* (*ibid.*, § 2440), *Lyashkevich v. Belarus* (*ibid.*, § 2441); European Court of Human Rights, *Kurt v. Turkey* (*ibid.*, § 2443), *Timurtas v. Turkey* (*ibid.*, § 2444) and *Cyprus case* (*ibid.*, § 2445).

[266] UN Human Rights Committee, General Comment No. 29 (Article 4 of the International Covenant on Civil and Political Rights) (*ibid.*, § 2439).

[267] See, e.g., UN Declaration on Enforced Disappearance, Article 13 (*ibid.*, § 2485); Inter-American Convention on the Enforced Disappearance of Persons, Article 12 (*ibid.*, § 2482); the practice of Argentina (National Commission concerning Missing Persons) (*ibid.*, § 2490), Chile (Special Panel) (*ibid.*, § 2412), Croatia (Commission for Tracing Persons Missing in War Activities in the Republic of Croatia) (*ibid.*, § 2491), Philippines (Task Force on Involuntary Disappearances) (*ibid.*, § 2493), Sri Lanka (Commission of Inquiry into Involuntary Removal or Disappearances of Persons in certain provinces) (*ibid.*, § 2415), former Yugoslavia (Joint Commission to Trace Missing Persons and Mortal Remains) (*ibid.*, § 2486) and Iraq, on the one hand, France, Kuwait, Saudi Arabia, United Kingdom and United States, on the other hand (Tripartite Commission set up under the auspices of the ICRC) (*ibid.*, § 2515); UN Human Rights Committee, General Comment No. 6 (Article 6 of the International Covenant on Civil and Political Rights) (*ibid.*, § 2505) and *Quinteros v. Uruguay* (*ibid.*, § 2506); UN General Assembly, Res. 40/140 (*ibid.*, § 2494); UN Commission on Human Rights, Res. 2001/46 (*ibid.*, § 2496); 24th International Conference of the Red Cross, Res. II (*ibid.*, § 2503); World Conference on Human Rights, Vienna Declaration and Programme of Action (*ibid.*, § 2504); European Court of Human Rights, *Kurt v. Turkey* (*ibid.*, § 2507), *Timurtas v. Turkey* (*ibid.*, § 2505) and *Cyprus case* (*ibid.*, § 2506); Inter-American Court of Human Rights, *Velásquez Rodríguez case* (*ibid.*, § 2513).

Rule 99. Arbitrary deprivation of liberty is prohibited.

Practice

Volume II, Chapter 32, Section L.

Summary

State practice establishes this rule as a norm of customary international law applicable in both international and non-international armed conflicts. It should be noted that common Article 3 of the Geneva Conventions, as well as both Additional Protocols I and II, require that all civilians and persons *hors de combat* be treated humanely (see Rule 87), whereas arbitrary deprivation of liberty is not compatible with this requirement.

The concept that detention must not be arbitrary is part of both international humanitarian law and human rights law. Although there are differences between these branches of international law, both international humanitarian law and human rights law aim to prevent arbitrary detention by specifying the grounds for detention based on needs, in particular security needs, and by providing for certain conditions and procedures to prevent disappearance and to supervise the continued need for detention.

International armed conflicts

Grounds for detention
Rules on the reasons for which persons may be deprived of their liberty by a party to an international armed conflict are to be found in all four Geneva Conventions:[268]

- The First Geneva Convention regulates the detention or retention of medical and religious personnel.[269]
- The Second Geneva Convention regulates the detention or retention of medical and religious personnel of hospital ships.[270]
- The Third Geneva Convention is based on the long-standing custom that prisoners of war may be interned for the duration of active hostilities.[271] There are additional conditions in the Third Geneva Convention with respect to disciplinary punishments, judicial investigations and repatriation of seriously wounded or sick prisoners of war.[272]
- The Fourth Geneva Convention specifies that a civilian may only be interned or placed in assigned residence if "the security of the Detaining Power makes

---

[268] Deprivation of liberty by neutral States is governed by Hague Conventions (V) and (XIII). Articles 11, 13 and 14 of Hague Convention (V) state the grounds for detention of belligerent persons by neutral States. Article 24 of Hague Convention (XIII) states the grounds for the detention of belligerent ships, their officers and crew by neutral States.
[269] First Geneva Convention, Articles 28, 30 and 32.
[270] Second Geneva Convention, Articles 36 and 37.
[271] Third Geneva Convention, Articles 21 and 118.
[272] Third Geneva Convention, Articles 90, 95, 103 and 109.

it absolutely necessary" (Article 42) or, in occupied territory, for "imperative reasons of security" (Article 78).[273] In the *Delalić case*, the International Criminal Tribunal for the Former Yugoslavia interpreted Article 42 as permitting internment only if there are "serious and legitimate reasons" to think that the interned persons may seriously prejudice the security of the detaining power by means such as sabotage or espionage.[274]

The grounds for initial or continued detention have been limited to valid needs, as evidenced by the list above. For example, the detention of "enemy aliens" has been restricted in the Fourth Geneva Convention to those "absolutely necessary" for security purposes, and the Third Geneva Convention requires the repatriation of seriously wounded and sick prisoners of war because they are no longer likely to take part in hostilities against the Detaining Power.

Procedural requirements

In addition to valid grounds, certain procedures must be followed in order for a deprivation of liberty to be lawful. Article 43 of the Fourth Geneva Convention provides that any person interned or placed in assigned residence is entitled to have such decision reconsidered as soon as possible by an appropriate court or administrative board and if the decision is maintained to have it reviewed periodically, and a least twice yearly.[275] Article 78 of the Fourth Geneva Convention provides that decisions regarding assigned residence or internment in occupied territory must be made according to a regular procedure to be prescribed by the occupying power in accordance with the provisions of the Convention. It also provides that such decision is subject to an appeal to be decided with the least possible delay. If the appeal is upheld it must be subject to periodical review, if possible every six months, by a competent body set up by the occupying power.[276] These procedures are also set forth in a number of military manuals.[277] In addition, the Third Geneva Convention requires the examination of sick or wounded prisoners of war by a Mixed Medical Commission in order to establish whether they should be repatriated or accommodated in neutral countries.[278]

Apart from the specific provisions of Articles 43 and 78 of the Fourth Geneva Convention, the Geneva Conventions provide for the appointment of Protecting Powers to try and prevent arbitrary detention and the ill-treatment that

---

[273] Fourth Geneva Convention, Article 42 (cited in Vol. II, Ch. 32, § 2517) and Article 78 (*ibid.*, § 2664).
[274] ICTY, *Delalić case*, Judgement (*ibid.*, § 2644).
[275] Fourth Geneva Convention, Article 43, first paragraph (*ibid.*, § 2747).
[276] Fourth Geneva Convention, Article 78 (*ibid.*, §§ 2664 and 2748).
[277] See, e.g., the military manuals of Argentina (*ibid.*, §§ 2756–2757), Canada (*ibid.*, § 2758), Germany (*ibid.*, § 2760), New Zealand (*ibid.*, § 2761), United Kingdom (*ibid.*, § 2762) and United States (*ibid.*, §§ 2763–2764).
[278] Third Geneva Convention, Articles 110 and 112.

often accompanies such detention. The Protecting Powers must be impartial supervisors who scrutinise the implementation of the Conventions in order to safeguard the interests of the parties to the conflict.[279] In particular, a Detaining Power must immediately inform the Protecting Powers, as well as the Information Bureau and Central Information Agency, of the capture of prisoners of war or the internment of civilians.[280]

Furthermore, Additional Protocol I provides that "any person arrested, detained or interned for actions related to the armed conflict shall be informed promptly, in a language he understands, of the reasons why these measures have been taken".[281] This rule is set forth in a number of military manuals.[282]

Detention that is not in conformity with the various rules provided by the Geneva Conventions is referred to as "unlawful confinement". "Unlawful confinement" of civilians is a grave breach of the Fourth Geneva Convention.[283] "Unlawful confinement" of a person protected under the Geneva Conventions is a grave breach under the Statute of the International Criminal Court, the Statute of the International Criminal Tribunal for the Former Yugoslavia and UNTAET Regulation 2000/15 for East Timor.[284] The Elements of Crimes for the International Criminal Court states that unlawful confinement may be in relation to any person protected under one of the Geneva Conventions and not only in relation to civilians.[285]

The military manuals of many States prohibit unlawful confinement.[286] This prohibition is also contained in the legislation of numerous States.[287] The terminology used in these manuals and legislation varies: unlawful/illegal confinement, unlawful/illegal detention, arbitrary detention, unnecessary detention, arrest or deprivation of liberty contrary to international law, unjustified restriction of liberty and indiscriminate mass arrests. The prohibition of unlawful detention was also upheld in several cases after the Second World War.[288]

---

[279] First Geneva Convention, Articles 8 and 10; Second Geneva Convention, Articles 8 and 10; Third Geneva Convention, Articles 8 and 10; Fourth Geneva Convention, Articles 9 and 11.

[280] Third Geneva Convention, Articles 69 and 122–123; Fourth Geneva Convention, Articles 43, 105 and 136–137.

[281] Additional Protocol I, Article 75(3) (adopted by consensus) (cited in Vol. II, Ch. 32, § 2694).

[282] See, e.g., the military manuals of Canada (*ibid.*, § 2698), New Zealand (*ibid.*, § 2700), Sweden (*ibid.*, § 2701) and Switzerland (*ibid.*, § 2702).

[283] Fourth Geneva Convention, Article 147 (*ibid.*, § 2518).

[284] ICC Statute, Article 8(2)(a)(vii) (*ibid.*, § 2524); ICTY Statute, Article 2(g) (*ibid.*, § 2530); UNTAET Regulation 2000/15, Section 6(1)(a)(vii) (*ibid.*, § 2535).

[285] Elements of Crimes for the ICC, Definition of unlawful confinement as a war crime (ICC Statute, Article 8(2)(a)(vii)).

[286] See, e.g., the military manuals of Argentina (cited in Vol. II, Ch. 32, § 2536), Australia (*ibid.*, § 2537), Canada (*ibid.*, § 2538), Croatia (*ibid.*, § 2540), France (*ibid.*, §§ 2542–2543), Germany (*ibid.*, § 2544), Hungary (*ibid.*, § 2545), Netherlands (*ibid.*, § 2546), New Zealand (*ibid.*, § 2547), Nigeria (*ibid.*, § 2549), South Africa (*ibid.*, § 2550), Switzerland (*ibid.*, § 2551), Uganda (*ibid.*, § 2552), United Kingdom (*ibid.*, § 2553) and United States (*ibid.*, § 2554).

[287] See, e.g., the legislation (*ibid.*, §§ 2555–2626).

[288] See, e.g., Netherlands, Temporary Court-Martial at Makassar, *Motomura case* and *Notomi Sueo case* (*ibid.*, § 2627); Netherlands, Special Court (War Criminals) at The Hague and Special Court of Cassation, *Rauter case* (*ibid.*, § 2627); Netherlands Special Court in Amsterdam and Special

Non-international armed conflicts

Grounds for detention

The prohibition of arbitrary deprivation of liberty in non-international armed conflicts is established by State practice in the form of military manuals, national legislation and official statements, as well as on the basis of international human rights law (see *infra*). While all States have legislation specifying the grounds on which a person may be detained, more than 70 of them were found to criminalise unlawful deprivation of liberty during armed conflict.[289] Most of this legislation applies the prohibition of unlawful deprivation of liberty to both international and non-international armed conflicts.[290] Several military manuals which are applicable in or have been applied in non-international armed conflicts also prohibit unlawful deprivation of liberty.[291] As indicated above, the terminology used in these manuals and legislation varies from unlawful/illegal confinement and unlawful/illegal detention to arbitrary or unnecessary detention.

No official contrary practice was found with respect to either international or non-international armed conflicts. Alleged cases of unlawful deprivation of liberty have been condemned. The UN Security Council, for example, has condemned "arbitrary detention" in the conflicts in Bosnia and Herzegovina and Burundi.[292] Similarly, the UN General Assembly has expressed its deep concern over serious violations of international humanitarian law and of human rights in the former Yugoslavia and Sudan, including "unlawful detention" and "arbitrary detention".[293] The UN Commission on Human Rights has also

---

Court of Cassation, *Zühlke case* (*ibid.*, § 2627); United Kingdom, Military Court at Lüneberg, *Auschwitz and Belsen case* (*ibid.*, § 2627); United States, Military Tribunal at Nuremberg, *Pohl case* (*ibid.*, § 2627).

[289] See, e.g., the legislation (*ibid.*, §§ 2555–2626).

[290] See, e.g., the legislation of Armenia (*ibid.*, § 2556), Australia (*ibid.*, § 2557), Azerbaijan (*ibid.*, § 2560), Belgium (*ibid.*, § 2563), Bosnia and Herzegovina (*ibid.*, § 2564), Cambodia (*ibid.*, § 2568), Democratic Republic of the Congo (*ibid.*, § 2573), Croatia (*ibid.*, § 2577), Ethiopia (*ibid.*, § 2580), Georgia (*ibid.*, § 2581), Moldova (*ibid.*, § 2594), Nicaragua (*ibid.*, § 2599), Niger (*ibid.*, § 2601), Paraguay (*ibid.*, § 2606), Poland (*ibid.*, § 2607), Portugal (*ibid.*, § 2608), Slovenia (*ibid.*, § 2612), Spain (*ibid.*, § 2614), Sweden (*ibid.*, § 2616), Tajikistan (*ibid.*, § 2617) and Yugoslavia (*ibid.*, § 2625); see also the legislation of Bulgaria (*ibid.*, § 2566) and Romania (*ibid.*, § 2609), the application of which is not excluded in time of non-international armed conflict, and the draft legislation of Argentina (*ibid.*, § 2555), Burundi (*ibid.*, § 2567), El Salvador (*ibid.*, § 2579), Jordan (*ibid.*, § 2585) and Nicaragua (*ibid.*, § 2600).

[291] See, e.g., the military manuals of Australia (*ibid.*, § 2537), Croatia (*ibid.*, § 2540), Germany (*ibid.*, § 2544) and South Africa (*ibid.*, § 2550).

[292] UN Security Council, Res. 1019 and 1034 (*ibid.*, § 2630) and Res. 1072 (*ibid.*, § 2631).

[293] UN General Assembly, Res. 50/193 (*ibid.*, § 2634) and Res. 55/116 (*ibid.*, § 2635). Resolution 50/193 was adopted by 114 votes in favour, one against and 20 abstentions. However, the explanation of Russia, which voted against the resolution, shows that it did not object to the principle of condemning unlawful detention but thought that the resolution was too one-sided; see the statement by Russia in the Third Committee of the UN General Assembly, UN Doc. A/C.3/50/SR.58, 14 December 1995, § 17. Resolution 55/116 was adopted by 85 votes in favour, 32 against and 49 abstentions. In explanations given by Canada, Bangladesh, Libya, Thailand and the United States, there is no indication that there was a disagreement on the principle which is under discussion here; see the explanations of vote of these States given in

condemned "detentions" in the former Yugoslavia and "arbitrary detention" in Sudan in resolutions adopted without a vote.[294]

The International Covenant on Civil and Political Rights, the Convention on the Rights of the Child and the regional human rights treaties recognise the right to liberty and security of person and/or provide that no one may be deprived of his or her liberty except for reasons and under conditions previously provided by law.[295] These principles are also provided for in other international instruments.[296]

The International Covenant on Civil and Political Rights, the Convention on the Rights of the Child and the European and American Conventions on Human Rights provide that no one may be subjected to arbitrary arrest or detention.[297] The European Convention on Human Rights spells out the grounds on which a person may be deprived of his or her liberty.[298] In its General Comment on Article 4 of the International Covenant on Civil and Political Rights (concerning states of emergency), the UN Human Rights Committee stated that States parties may "in no circumstances" invoke a state of emergency "as justification for acting in violation of humanitarian law or peremptory norms of international law, for instance ... through arbitrary deprivations of liberty".[299] The prohibition of arbitrary arrest or detention is also set forth in other international instruments.[300]

The need for a valid reason for the deprivation of liberty concerns both the initial reason for such deprivation and the continuation of such deprivation. Detention which continues beyond that provided for by law is a violation of the principle of legality and amounts to arbitrary detention. This point was

the Third Committee of the UN General Assembly, 10 October 2000, UN Doc. A/C.3/55/SR.55, 29 November 2000, § 138 (Canada), § 139 (United States), § 146 (Bangladesh), § 147 (Thailand) and § 148 (Libya).

[294] UN Commission on Human Rights, Res. 1996/71 (cited in Vol. II, Ch. 32, § 2636) and Res. 1996/73 (ibid., § 2637).

[295] International Covenant on Civil and Political Rights, Article 9(1) (ibid., §§ 2520 and 2666); Convention on the Rights of the Child, Article 37(b) (ibid., §§ 2523 and 2669) (no general reference to liberty and security of person; limited to requirement of arrest, detention or imprisonment in conformity with law); European Convention on Human Rights, Article 5(1) (ibid., §§ 2519 and 2665); American Convention on Human Rights, Article 7 (ibid., §§ 2521 and 2667); African Charter on Human and Peoples' Rights, Article 6 (ibid., §§ 2522 and 2668).

[296] See, e.g., Universal Declaration on Human Rights, Article 3 (ibid., § 2527); American Declaration on the Rights and Duties of Man, Articles I and XXV (ibid., §§ 2528 and 2673); Body of Principles for the Protection of All Persons under Any Form of Detention or Imprisonment, Principle 2 (ibid., § 2674); Cairo Declaration on Human Rights in Islam, Article 20 (ibid., § 2529); EU Charter of Fundamental Rights, Article 6 (ibid., § 2534).

[297] International Covenant on Civil and Political Rights, Article 9(1) (ibid., § 2520); Convention on the Rights of the Child, Article 37(b) (ibid., § 2523); American Convention on Human Rights, Article 7(3) (ibid., § 2521); African Charter on Human and Peoples' Rights, Article 6 (ibid., § 2522).

[298] European Convention on Human Rights, Article 5(1); see also UN Human Rights Committee, General Comment No. 8 (Article 9 of the International Covenant on Civil and Political Rights) (ibid., § 2645) (the prohibition of arbitrary deprivation of liberty applies to all such deprivations, "whether in criminal cases or in other cases such as, e.g., mental illness, vagrancy, drug addiction, educational purposes, immigration control, etc.").

[299] UN Human Rights Committee, General Comment No. 29 (Article 4 of the International Covenant on Civil and Political Rights) (ibid., § 2646).

[300] See, e.g., Universal Declaration on Human Rights, Article 9 (ibid., § 2527).

made by the UN Human Rights Committee and the African Commission on Human and Peoples' Rights in cases concerning persons who continued to be detained after their prison term was completed,[301] or despite an acquittal,[302] or despite an order for their release.[303]

Procedural requirements

Since the adoption of the Geneva Conventions, there has been a significant development in international human rights law relating to the procedures required to prevent arbitrary deprivation of liberty. Human rights law establishes (i) an obligation to inform a person who is arrested of the reasons for arrest, (ii) an obligation to bring a person arrested on a criminal charge promptly before a judge, and (iii) an obligation to provide a person deprived of liberty with an opportunity to challenge the lawfulness of detention (so-called writ of *habeas corpus*). Although obligations (i) and (ii) are not listed as non-derogable in the relevant human rights treaties, human rights case-law has held that they may never be dispensed with altogether.[304]

(i) *Obligation to inform a person who is arrested of the reasons for arrest.* The requirement that persons who are arrested be informed promptly of the reasons therefor is contained in the International Covenant on Civil and Political Rights and the European and American Conventions on Human Rights.[305] While the African Charter on Human and Peoples' Rights does not explicitly provide for this right, the African Commission on Human and Peoples' Rights has specified that it is part and parcel of the right to fair trial.[306] This requirement is also provided for in the Body of Principles for the Protection of All Persons under Any Form of Detention or Imprisonment, adopted by the UN General Assembly without a vote.[307] In its General Comment on Article 9 of the International Covenant on Civil and Political Rights, the UN Human Rights Committee held that "if so-called preventive detention is used, for reasons of public security, it must be controlled by these

---

[301] UN Human Rights Committee, *García Lanza de Netto v. Uruguay* (*ibid.*, § 2647); African Commission on Human and Peoples' Rights, *Pagnoulle v. Cameroon* (*ibid.*, § 2650).

[302] African Commission on Human and Peoples' Rights, *Constitutional Rights Project v. Nigeria (148/96)* (*ibid.*, § 2652).

[303] UN Human Rights Committee, *Torres Ramírez v. Uruguay* (*ibid.*, § 2648).

[304] With respect to the obligation to inform a person who is arrested of the reasons for arrest, see e.g., Inter-American Commission on Human Rights, Report on Terrorism and Human Rights (*ibid.*, § 3020), Doctrine concerning judicial guarantees and the right to personal liberty and security, reprinted in *Ten years of activities (1971–1981)*, Washington, D.C., 1982, p. 337. With respect to the obligation to bring a person arrested on a criminal charge promptly before a judge, see, e.g., Human Rights Committee, General Comment No. 8 (*ibid.*, § 2736); European Court of Human Rights, *Aksoy v. Turkey*, (*ibid.*, 2743) and *Brogan and Others case* (*ibid.*, § 2741); Inter-American Court of Human Rights, *Castillo Petruzzi and Others case*, (*ibid.*, § 2744).

[305] International Covenant on Civil and Political Rights, Article 9(2) (*ibid.*, § 2692); European Convention on Human Rights, Article 5(2) (*ibid.*, § 2691); American Convention on Human Rights, Article 7(4) (*ibid.*, § 2693).

[306] African Commission on Human and Peoples' Rights, Resolution on the Right to Recourse and Fair Trial (*ibid.*, § 2713).

[307] Body of Principles for the Protection of All Persons under Any Form of Detention or Imprisonment, Principle 10 (*ibid.*, § 2695).

same provisions, i.e. ... information of the reasons must be given".[308] This rule is part of the domestic law of most, if not all, States in the world.[309] It was included in the agreements concluded between the parties to the conflicts in the former Yugoslavia.[310]

(ii) *Obligation to bring a person arrested on a criminal charge promptly before a judge.* The International Covenant on Civil and Political Rights and the European and American Conventions on Human Rights require the prompt appearance of a person who is arrested or detained before a judge or other officer authorised to exercise judicial power.[311] While the African Charter on Human and Peoples' Rights does not explicitly provide for this right, the African Commission on Human and Peoples' Rights has specified that it is part and parcel of the right to fair trial.[312] This requirement is also provided for in the Body of Principles for the Protection of All Persons under Any Form of Detention or Imprisonment and the UN Declaration on Enforced Disappearance, both adopted by the UN General Assembly without a vote.[313] This rule is part of the domestic law of most, if not all, States in the world.[314] In its General Comment on Article 9 of the International Covenant on Civil and Political Rights, the UN Human Rights Committee stated that a prompt appearance means that "delays must not exceed a few days".[315] There is now also significant case-law by regional human rights courts on the application of this principle during states of emergency.[316]

(iii) *Obligation to provide a person deprived of liberty with an opportunity to challenge the lawfulness of detention.* The International Covenant on Civil and

---

[308] UN Human Rights Committee, General Comment No. 8 (Article 9 of the International Covenant on Civil and Political Rights) (*ibid.*, § 2711).

[309] See, e.g., the legislation of India (*ibid.*, § 2703), Spain (*ibid.*, § 2706) and Zimbabwe (*ibid.*, § 2707).

[310] Memorandum of Understanding on the Application of International Humanitarian Law between Croatia and the SFRY, para. 4 (*ibid.*, § 2696); Agreement on the Application of International Humanitarian Law between the Parties to the Conflict in Bosnia and Herzegovina, para. 2.3 (*ibid.*, § 2697).

[311] International Covenant on Civil and Political Rights, Article 9(3) (*ibid.*, § 2721); European Convention on Human Rights, Article 5(3) (*ibid.*, § 2720); American Convention on Human Rights, Article 7(5) (*ibid.*, § 2722).

[312] African Commission on Human and Peoples' Rights, Resolution on the Right to Recourse and Fair Trial (*ibid.*, § 2738).

[313] Body of Principles for the Protection of All Persons under Any Form of Detention or Imprisonment, Principles 11 and 37 (*ibid.*, §§ 2725–2726); UN Declaration on Enforced Disappearance, Article 10 (*ibid.*, § 2727).

[314] See, e.g., the legislation of India (*ibid.*, § 2730), Myanmar (*ibid.*, § 2731) and Uganda (*ibid.*, § 2732).

[315] UN Human Rights Committee, General Comment No. 8 (Article 9 of the International Covenant on Civil and Political Rights) (*ibid.*, § 2736).

[316] See European Court of Human Rights, *Brogan and Others case* (*ibid.*, § 2741) (delay must not exceed three days), *Brannigan and McBride v. UK* (*ibid.*, § 2742) (delay of up to seven days not found to be excessive because the detainees were allowed to consult a lawyer, contact a family member or friend and to be examined by a doctor within 48 hours) and *Aksoy v. Turkey* (*ibid.*, § 2743) (delay of 14 days incommunicado detention found to be excessive); Inter-American Court of Human Rights, *Castillo Petruzzi and Others case* (*ibid.*, § 2744) (delay of 36 days found to be excessive).

Political Rights and European and American Conventions on Human Rights provide for the right to have the lawfulness of detention reviewed by a court and the release ordered in case it is not lawful (so-called writ of *habeas corpus*).[317] This right is also provided for in the American Declaration on the Rights and Duties of Man and the Body of Principles for the Protection of All Persons under Any Form of Detention or Imprisonment, adopted by the UN General Assembly without a vote.[318] This rule is part of the domestic law of most, if not all, States in the world.[319] It was included in the Comprehensive Agreement on Respect for Human Rights and International Humanitarian Law in the Philippines.[320]

In its General Comment on Article 4 of the International Covenant on Civil and Political Rights (states of emergency), the UN Human Rights Committee stated that "in order to protect non-derogable rights, the right to take proceedings before a court to enable the court to decide without delay on the lawfulness of detention, must not be diminished by a State party's decision to derogate from the Covenant".[321] In its advisory opinions in the *Habeas Corpus case* and the *Judicial Guarantees case* in 1987, the Inter-American Court of Human Rights concluded that the writ of *habeas corpus* is among those judicial remedies that are "essential" for the protection of various rights whose derogation is prohibited under the American Convention on Human Rights and which is non-derogable in itself as a result.[322]

The African Commission on Human and Peoples' Rights has held that proceedings to decide on the lawfulness of detention must be brought before a court that is independent of the executive authority that ordered the detention, in particular in emergency-type situations where administrative detention is practiced.[323] The European Court of Human Rights has similarly stressed the requirement that the review of the legality of detention be undertaken by a body which is independent of the executive.[324]

---

[317] International Covenant on Civil and Political Rights, Article 9(4) (*ibid.*, § 2750); European Convention on Human Rights, Article 5(4) (*ibid.*, § 2749); American Convention on Human Rights, Article 7(6) (*ibid.*, § 2751).

[318] American Declaration on the Rights and Duties of Man, Article XXV (*ibid.*, § 2753); Body of Principles for the Protection of All Persons under Any Form of Detention or Imprisonment, Principle 32 (*ibid.*, § 2754).

[319] See, e.g., the legislation of Russia (*ibid.*, § 2765).

[320] Comprehensive Agreement on Respect for Human Rights and IHL in the Philippines, Part II, Article 5 (*ibid.*, § 2755).

[321] UN Human Rights Committee, General Comment No. 29 (Article 4 of the International Covenant on Civil and Political Rights) (*ibid.*, § 2777).

[322] Inter-American Court of Human Rights, *Habeas Corpus case* (*ibid.*, § 2782) and *Judicial Guarantees case* (*ibid.*, § 2783); see also *Neira Alegría and Others case* (*ibid.*, § 2784).

[323] African Commission on Human and Peoples' Rights, Communication Nos. 48/90, 50/91, 52/91 and 89/93, *Amnesty International and Others v. Sudan*, Decision, 26th Session, Kigali, 1–15 November 1999, § 60; Communication Nos. 143/95 and 159/96, *Constitutional Rights Project and Civil Liberties Organisation v. Nigeria*, 26th Session, Kigali, 1–15 November 1999, §§ 31 and 34.

[324] European Court of Human Rights, *Lawless case*, Judgement (Merits), 1 July 1961, § 14; *Ireland v. UK*, Judgement (Merits and just satisfaction), 18 January 1978, §§ 199–200.

There is, in addition, extensive practice to the effect that persons deprived of their liberty must have access to a lawyer.[325] The Body of Principles for the Protection of All Persons under Any Form of Detention or Imprisonment, adopted by the UN General Assembly without a vote, also specifies that "a detained person shall be entitled to have the assistance of a legal counsel".[326] In particular, the opportunity to challenge the lawfulness of one's detention requires the assistance of a lawyer, in order to be effective.

It should be noted, however, that all persons deprived of their liberty for reasons related to a non-international armed conflict must be given the opportunity to challenge the legality of the detention unless the government of the State affected by the non-international armed conflict claimed for itself belligerent rights, in which case captured enemy "combatants" should benefit from the same treatment as granted to prisoners of war in international armed conflicts and detained civilians should benefit from the same treatment as granted to civilian persons protected by the Fourth Geneva Convention in international armed conflicts.

Rule 100. No one may be convicted or sentenced, except pursuant to a fair trial affording all essential judicial guarantees.

Practice

Volume II, Chapter 32, Section M.

Summary

State practice establishes this rule as a norm of customary international law applicable in both international and non-international armed conflicts.

International and non-international armed conflicts

Several trials held after the Second World War, but before the adoption of the Geneva Conventions in 1949, found the defendants guilty of denying fair trial to prisoners of war or civilians.[327] The right to fair trial is provided for in all

---

[325] See, e.g., UN Human Rights Committee, Concluding observations on the report of Senegal (cited in Vol. II, Ch. 32, § 3277); UN Committee against Torture, Report of the Committee against Torture on the Situation in Turkey, UN Doc. A/48/44/Add.1, 15 November 1993, § 48; European Court of Human Rights, *Aksoy v. Turkey*, Judgement, 18 December 1996, Reports of Judgements and Decisions 1996-VI, § 83.

[326] Body of Principles for the Protection of All Persons under Any Form of Detention or Imprisonment, Principle 17 (*ibid.*, § 3230).

[327] See, e.g., Australia, Military Court at Rabaul, *Ohashi case* (*ibid.*, § 2958); United Kingdom, Military Court at Almelo, *Almelo case* (*ibid.*, § 2960); United States, Military Commission at Rome, *Dostler case* (*ibid.*, § 2961); United States, Military Commission at Shanghai, *Sawada*

four Geneva Conventions and in Additional Protocols I and II.[328] Depriving a protected person of a fair and regular trial is a grave breach under the Third and Fourth Geneva Conventions and under Additional Protocol I.[329] Common Article 3 of the Geneva Conventions prohibits the sentencing of persons or the carrying out of executions without previous judgement pronounced by a regularly constituted court.[330] Depriving a person of the right to a fair trial is listed as a war crime in the Statutes of the International Criminal Court, of the International Criminal Tribunals for the Former Yugoslavia and for Rwanda and of the Special Court for Sierra Leone.[331]

The right to fair trial is set forth in numerous military manuals.[332] The denial of fair trial is a criminal offence under the legislation of a very large number of States, most being applicable in both international and non-international armed conflicts.[333] The right to fair trial is also supported by official statements and

---

case (*ibid.*, § 2962) and *Isayama case* (*ibid.*, § 2963); United States, Military Court at Wuppertal, *Rhode case* (*ibid.*, § 2964); United States, Military Tribunal at Nuremberg, *Altstötter case* (*ibid.*, § 2965).

[328] First Geneva Convention, Article 49, fourth paragraph (*ibid.*, § 2789); Second Geneva Convention, Article 50, fourth paragraph (*ibid.*, § 2789); Third Geneva Convention, Articles 102–108 (*ibid.*, § 2790); Fourth Geneva Convention, Articles 5 and 66–75 (*ibid.*, §§ 2792–2793); Additional Protocol I, Articles 71(1) (*ibid.*, § 2799) and 75(4) (adopted by consensus) (*ibid.*, § 2800); Additional Protocol II, Article 6(2) (adopted by consensus) (*ibid.*, § 3046). The principle of the right to fair trial is also provided for in Article 17(2) of the Second Protocol to the Hague Convention for the Protection of Cultural Property (*ibid.*, § 2808).

[329] Third Geneva Convention, Article 130 (*ibid.*, § 2791); Fourth Geneva Convention, Article 147 (*ibid.*, § 2795); Additional Protocol I, Article 85(4)(e) (adopted by consensus) (*ibid.*, § 2801).

[330] Geneva Conventions, common Article 3 (*ibid.*, § 2788).

[331] ICC Statute, Article 8(2)(a)(vi) and (c)(iv) (*ibid.*, § 2804); ICTY Statute, Article 2(f) (*ibid.*, § 2823); ICTR Statute, Article 4(g) (*ibid.*, § 2826); Statute of the Special Court for Sierra Leone, Article 3(g) (*ibid.*, § 2809).

[332] See, e.g., the military manuals of Argentina (*ibid.*, §§ 2837–2838), Australia (*ibid.*, §§ 2839–2840), Belgium (*ibid.*, § 2841), Benin (*ibid.*, § 2842), Burkina Faso (*ibid.*, § 2843), Cameroon (*ibid.*, § 2844), Canada (*ibid.*, § 2845), Colombia (*ibid.*, §§ 2846–2849), Congo (*ibid.*, § 2850), Ecuador (*ibid.*, § 2851), El Salvador (*ibid.*, § 2853), France (*ibid.*, §§ 2854–2857), Germany (*ibid.*, § 2858), Indonesia (*ibid.*, § 2859), Italy (*ibid.*, § 2860), Kenya (*ibid.*, § 2861), South Korea (*ibid.*, § 2862), Madagascar (*ibid.*, § 2863), Mali (*ibid.*, § 2864), Morocco (*ibid.*, § 2865), Netherlands (*ibid.*, § 2866), New Zealand (*ibid.*, § 2867), Nigeria (*ibid.*, § 2869), Peru (*ibid.*, §§ 2870–2871), Russia (*ibid.*, § 2872), Senegal (*ibid.*, §§ 2873–2874), South Africa (*ibid.*, § 2875), Spain (*ibid.*, § 2876), Sweden (*ibid.*, §§ 2877–2878), Switzerland (*ibid.*, § 2879), Togo (*ibid.*, § 2880), United Kingdom (*ibid.*, §§ 2881–2882) and United States (*ibid.*, §§ 2883–2888).

[333] See in general the legislation (*ibid.*, §§ 2889–2957) and in particular the legislation of Armenia (*ibid.*, § 2890), Australia (*ibid.*, § 2892), Azerbaijan (*ibid.*, § 2893), Bangladesh (*ibid.*, § 2894), Belarus (*ibid.*, § 2896), Belgium (*ibid.*, § 2897), Bosnia and Herzegovina (*ibid.*, § 2898), Cambodia (*ibid.*, § 2902), Canada (*ibid.*, § 2904), Colombia (*ibid.*, § 2905), Congo (*ibid.*, § 2906), Croatia (*ibid.*, § 2908), Estonia (*ibid.*, § 2912), Ethiopia (*ibid.*, § 2913), Georgia (*ibid.*, § 2914), Germany (*ibid.*, § 2915), Ireland (*ibid.*, § 2918), Lithuania (*ibid.*, § 2924), Moldova (*ibid.*, § 2930), Netherlands (*ibid.*, § 2931), New Zealand (*ibid.*, § 2933), Nicaragua (*ibid.*, § 2934), Niger (*ibid.*, § 2936), Norway (*ibid.*, § 2938), Poland (*ibid.*, § 2940), Slovenia (*ibid.*, § 2944), Spain (*ibid.*, §§ 2945–2946), Tajikistan (*ibid.*, § 2948), Thailand (*ibid.*, § 2949), United Kingdom (*ibid.*, § 2953), United States (*ibid.*, § 2954) and Yugoslavia (*ibid.*, § 2956); see also the legislation of Bulgaria (*ibid.*, § 2900), Hungary (*ibid.*, § 2916), Italy (*ibid.*, § 2919) and Romania (*ibid.*, § 2941), the application of which is not excluded in time of non-international armed conflict, and the draft legislation of Argentina (*ibid.*, § 2889), Burundi (*ibid.*, § 2901), El Salvador (*ibid.*, § 2911), Jordan (*ibid.*, § 2920), Nicaragua (*ibid.*, § 2935) and Trinidad and Tobago (*ibid.*, § 2950).

other practice in relation to non-international armed conflicts.[334] There is also national case-law to the effect that a violation of this rule in non-international armed conflicts amounts to a war crime.[335]

The right to fair trial is also included in the Statutes of the International Criminal Court, of the International Criminal Tribunals for the Former Yugoslavia and for Rwanda and of the Special Court for Sierra Leone for accused persons appearing before them.[336]

The International Covenant on Civil and Political Rights, the Convention on the Rights of the Child and the regional human rights conventions provide for the right to fair trial.[337] This right is also set forth in other international instruments.[338] In its General Comment on Article 4 of the International Covenant on Civil and Political Rights, the UN Human Rights Committee stated that "fundamental principles of fair trial" may never be derogated from.[339] This conclusion is supported by the practice of regional human rights bodies.[340]

Definition of a fair trial affording all essential judicial guarantees

Both international humanitarian law and human rights law incorporate a series of judicial guarantees aimed at ensuring that accused persons receive a fair trial.

Trial by an independent, impartial and regularly constituted court
Pursuant to common Article 3 of the Geneva Conventions, only a "regularly constituted court" may pass judgement on an accused person.[341] The Third Geneva Convention requires that courts judging prisoners of war offer the essential guarantees of "independence" and "impartiality".[342] This

---

[334] See, e.g., the statements of Belgium (*ibid.*, § 2967) and United States (*ibid.*, § 2972) and the practice of China (*ibid.*, § 2968).

[335] See, e.g., Chile, Appeal Court of Santiago, *Videla case* (*ibid.*, § 2959).

[336] ICC Statute, Article 67(1) (*ibid.*, § 2806); ICTY Statute, Article 21(2) (*ibid.*, § 2825); ICTR Statute, Article 20(2) (*ibid.*, § 2828); Statute of the Special Court for Sierra Leone, Article 17(2) (*ibid.*, § 2810).

[337] International Covenant on Civil and Political Rights, Article 14(1) (*ibid.*, § 2797); Convention on the Rights of the Child, Article 40(2)(b)(iii) (*ibid.*, § 2803); European Convention on Human Rights, Article 6(1) (*ibid.*, § 2796); American Convention on Human Rights, Article 8(1) (*ibid.*, § 2798); African Charter on Human and Peoples' Rights, Article 7 (*ibid.*, § 2802).

[338] See, e.g., Universal Declaration on Human Rights, Article 10 (*ibid.*, § 2813); American Declaration on the Rights and Duties of Man, Article XVIII (*ibid.*, § 2814); Cairo Declaration on Human Rights in Islam, Article 19(e) (*ibid.*, § 2819); EU Charter on Fundamental Rights, Article 47 (*ibid.*, § 2834).

[339] UN Human Rights Committee, General Comment No. 29 (Article 4 of the International Covenant on Civil and Political Rights) (*ibid.*, § 2999).

[340] See, e.g., African Commission on Human and Peoples' Rights, *Civil Liberties Organisation and Others v. Nigeria* (*ibid.*, § 3008); Inter-American Commission on Human Rights, Resolution concerning the law applicable to emergency situations (*ibid.*, § 3017) and Report on Terrorism and Human Rights (*ibid.*, § 3020); Inter-American Court of Human Rights, *Judicial Guarantees case* (*ibid.*, § 3021).

[341] Geneva Conventions, common Article 3 (*ibid.*, § 3039).

[342] Third Geneva Convention, Article 84, second paragraph (*ibid.*, § 3040).

requirement is also set forth in Additional Protocol II.[343] Additional Protocol I requires an "impartial and regularly constituted court".[344]

The requirements that courts be independent, impartial and regularly constituted are set forth in a number of military manuals.[345] These requirements are also contained in national legislation and are supported by official statements and reported practice.[346] Several of these sources stress that these requirements may not be suspended during emergencies.[347]

Whereas common Article 3 of the Geneva Conventions and Article 75 of Additional Protocol I require a "regularly constituted" court, human rights treaties require a "competent" tribunal,[348] and/or a tribunal "established by law".[349] A court is regularly constituted if it has been established and organised in accordance with the laws and procedures already in force in a country.

The International Covenant on Civil and Political Rights, the Convention on the Rights of the Child and the regional human rights conventions specify that for a trial to be fair it must be conducted by a court that is "independent" and "impartial".[350] The requirements of independence and impartiality are also to be found in a number of other international instruments.[351] Both the UN Human Rights Committee and the Inter-American Commission on Human Rights have indicated that the requirement for courts to be independent and impartial can never be dispensed with.[352]

---

[343] Additional Protocol II, Article 6(2) (adopted by consensus) (*ibid.*, § 3046).

[344] Additional Protocol I, Article 75(4) (adopted by consensus) (*ibid.*, § 3045).

[345] See, e.g., the military manuals of Argentina (*ibid.*, §§ 3059–3060), Belgium (*ibid.*, § 3061), Canada (*ibid.*, § 3062), Croatia (*ibid.*, § 3063), Netherlands (*ibid.*, § 3064), New Zealand (*ibid.*, § 3065), Spain (*ibid.*, § 3066), Sweden (*ibid.*, § 3067), Switzerland (*ibid.*, § 3068), United Kingdom (*ibid.*, § 3069) and United States (*ibid.*, §§ 3070–3071).

[346] See, e.g., the legislation of Bangladesh (*ibid.*, § 3072), Czech republic (*ibid.*, § 3073), Georgia (*ibid.*, § 3074), Germany (*ibid.*, § 3075), Ireland (*ibid.*, § 3076), Kenya (*ibid.*, § 3077), Kuwait (*ibid.*, § 3078), Kyrgyzstan (*ibid.*, § 3079), Lithuania (*ibid.*, § 3080), Norway (*ibid.*, § 3082), Netherlands (*ibid.*, § 3081) and Slovakia (*ibid.*, § 3083), the statements of the United States (*ibid.*, §§ 3086–3087) and the reported practice of Nicaragua (*ibid.*, § 3086) and Cambodia (*ibid.*, § 3086).

[347] See, e.g., the military manual of Croatia (*ibid.*, § 3063) and the legislation of Georgia (*ibid.*, § 3074), Kuwait (*ibid.*, § 3078) and Kyrgyzstan (*ibid.*, § 3079).

[348] International Covenant on Civil and Political Rights, Article 14(1) (*ibid.*, § 3043); American Convention on Human Rights, Article 8(1) (*ibid.*, § 3044); Convention on the Rights of the Child, Article 40(2)(b)(iii) (*ibid.*, § 3049).

[349] International Covenant on Civil and Political Rights, Article 14(1) (*ibid.*, § 2797); European Convention on Human Rights, Article 6(1) (*ibid.*, § 2796); American Convention on Human Rights, Article 8(1) (*ibid.*, § 2798).

[350] International Covenant on Civil and Political Rights, Article 14(1) (*ibid.*, § 3043); Convention on the Rights of the Child, Article 40(2)(b)(iii) (*ibid.*, § 3049); European Convention on Human Rights, Article 6(1) (*ibid.*, § 3042); American Convention on Human Rights, Article 8(1) (*ibid.*, § 3044); African Charter on Human and Peoples' Rights, Article 7(1)(d) (*ibid.*, § 3047) and Article 26 (*ibid.*, § 3048).

[351] See, e.g., Universal Declaration on Human Rights, Article 10 (*ibid.*, § 3051); American Declaration on the Rights and Duties of Man, Article XXVI (*ibid.*, § 3052); Basic Principles on the Independence of the Judiciary, paras. 1 and 2 (*ibid.*, § 3053); EU Charter of Fundamental Rights, Article 47 (*ibid.*, § 3058).

[352] UN Human Rights Committee, General Comment No. 29 (Article 4 of the International Covenant on Civil and Political Rights) (*ibid.*, § 2999); Inter-American Commission on Human Rights, Report on Terrorism and Human Rights (*ibid.*, § 3020).

The meaning of an independent and impartial tribunal has been considered in case-law. In order to be independent, a court must be able to perform its functions independently of any other branch of the government, especially the executive.[353] In order to be impartial, the judges composing the court must not harbour preconceptions about the matter before them, nor act in a way that promotes the interests of one side.[354] In addition to this requirement of subjective impartiality, regional human rights bodies have pointed out that a court must also be impartial from an objective viewpoint, i.e., it must offer sufficient guarantees to exclude any legitimate doubt about its impartiality.[355]

The need for independence of the judiciary from the executive, as well as subjective and objective impartiality, has meant that in a number of cases, military tribunals and special security courts have been found not to be independent and impartial. While none of these cases concluded that military tribunals inherently violate these requirements, they all stressed that military tribunals and special security courts must respect the same requirements of independence and impartiality as civilian tribunals.[356]

In this context, it should also be noted that the Third Geneva Convention provides that prisoners of war are to be tried by a military court, unless the laws of the detaining power would allow civilian courts to try its own soldiers for the same type of offence. However, this provision is conditioned by the requirement that "in no circumstances whatever shall a prisoner of war be tried by a court of any kind which does not offer the essential guarantees of independence and impartiality".[357]

Furthermore, the Fourth Geneva Convention provides that the occupying power may hand over persons who violate penal provisions promulgated by it to "its properly constituted, non-political military courts, on condition that the said courts sit in the occupied territory. Courts of appeal shall preferably sit in the occupied territory."[358] Regional human rights bodies have found, however,

---

[353] UN Human Rights Committee, *Bahamonde v. Equatorial Guinea* (*ibid.*, § 3092); African Commission on Human and Peoples' Rights, *Centre For Free Speech v. Nigeria (206/97)* (*ibid.*, § 3095); European Court of Human Rights, *Belilos case* (*ibid.*, § 3099) and *Findlay v. UK* (*ibid.*, § 3101). The Inter-American Commission on Human Rights underlined the need for freedom from interference from the executive and security of tenure of the judges in its *Annual Report 1992–1993* (*ibid.*, § 3105) and *Case 11.006 (Peru)* (*ibid.*, § 3107).

[354] See Australia, Military Court at Rabaul, *Ohashi case* (*ibid.*, § 3084); UN Human Rights Committee, *Karttunen v. Finland* (*ibid.*, § 3091).

[355] See African Commission on Human and Peoples' Rights, *Constitutional Rights Project v. Nigeria (60/91)* (*ibid.*, § 3094) and *Malawi African Association and Others v. Mauritania* (*ibid.*, § 3096); European Court of Human Rights, *Piersack case* (*ibid.*, § 3098) and *Findlay case* (*ibid.*, § 3101); Inter-American Commission on Human Rights, *Case 10.970 (Peru)* (*ibid.*, § 3108).

[356] See African Commission on Human and Peoples' Rights, *Constitutional Rights Project v. Nigeria (60/91)* (*ibid.*, § 3094) and *Civil Liberties Organisation and Others v. Nigeria* (*ibid.*, § 3097); European Court of Human Rights, *Findlay v. UK* (*ibid.*, § 3101), *Ciraklar v. Turkey* (*ibid.*, § 3102) and *Sahiner v. Turkey* (*ibid.*, § 3104); Inter-American Commission on Human Rights, *Case 11.084 (Peru)* (*ibid.*, § 3106).

[357] Third Geneva Convention, Article 84 (*ibid.*, § 3040).

[358] Fourth Geneva Convention, Article 66 (*ibid.*, § 3041).

that the trial of civilians by military courts constitutes a violation of the right to be tried by an independent and impartial tribunal.[359]

Presumption of innocence

The presumption of innocence is provided for in Additional Protocols I and II.[360] It is also included in the Statutes of the International Criminal Court, of the International Criminal Tribunals for the Former Yugoslavia and for Rwanda and of the Special Court for Sierra Leone for accused persons appearing before these tribunals.[361]

The presumption of innocence is included in several military manuals and is part of most, if not all, national legal systems.[362] In the *Ohashi case*, a war crimes trial in 1946, the judge advocate stressed the need for no preconceived notions on the part of the judges and that the court must satisfy itself that the accused was guilty.[363]

The presumption of innocence is set forth in the International Covenant on Civil and Political Rights, the Convention on the Rights of the Child and the regional human rights conventions.[364] It is also contained in several other international instruments.[365] Both the UN Human Rights Committee and the Inter-American Commission on Human Rights have indicated that the presumption of innocence can never be dispensed with.[366]

[359] African Commission on Human and Peoples' Rights, *Media Rights Agenda v. Nigeria (224/98)* (*ibid.*, § 3004) (trial of a civilian "by a Special Military Tribunal, presided over by serving military officers, who are still subject to military commands, without more, [is] prejudicial to the basic principles of fair hearing") and *Civil Liberties Organisation and Others v. Nigeria* (*ibid.*, § 3097) ("the military tribunal fails the independence test"); European Court of Human Rights, *Cyprus case* (*ibid.*, § 3103) (because of "the close structural links between the executive power and the military officers serving on the 'TRNC' military courts"); Inter-American Commission on Human Rights, Doctrine concerning judicial guarantees and the right to personal liberty and security (*ibid.*, § 3020).
[360] Additional Protocol I, Article 75(4)(d) (adopted by consensus) (*ibid.*, § 3116); Additional Protocol II, Article 6(2)(d) (adopted by consensus) (*ibid.*, § 3117).
[361] ICC Statute, Article 66 (*ibid.*, § 3120); ICTY Statute, Article 21(3) (*ibid.*, § 3129); ICTR Statute, Article 20(3) (*ibid.*, § 3130); Statute of the Special Court for Sierra Leone, Article 17(3) (*ibid.*, § 3121).
[362] See, e.g., the military manuals of Argentina (*ibid.*, § 3134), Canada (*ibid.*, § 3135), Colombia (*ibid.*, §§ 3136–3137), New Zealand (*ibid.*, § 3138) and Sweden (*ibid.*, § 3139) and the legislation of Bangladesh (*ibid.*, § 3141), Ethiopia (*ibid.*, § 3140), Georgia (*ibid.*, § 3140), Ireland (*ibid.*, § 3142), Kenya (*ibid.*, § 3140), Kyrgyzstan (*ibid.*, § 3140), Norway (*ibid.*, § 3143) and Russia (*ibid.*, § 3140).
[363] Australia, Military Court at Rabaul, *Ohashi case* (*ibid.*, § 3144).
[364] International Covenant on Civil and Political Rights, Article 14(2) (*ibid.*, § 3114); Convention on the Rights of the Child, Article 40(2)(b)(i) (*ibid.*, § 3119); European Convention on Human Rights, Article 6(2) (*ibid.*, § 3113); American Convention on Human Rights, Article 8(2) (*ibid.*, § 3115); African Charter on Human and Peoples' Rights, Article 7(1) (*ibid.*, § 3118).
[365] See, e.g., Universal Declaration on Human Rights, Article 11 (*ibid.*, § 3122); American Declaration on the Rights and Duties of Man, Article XXVI (*ibid.*, § 3123); Body of Principles for the Protection of All Persons under Any Form of Detention or Imprisonment, Principle 36 (*ibid.*, § 3124); Cairo Declaration on Human Rights in Islam, Article 19 (*ibid.*, § 3125); EU Charter of Fundamental Rights, Article 48(1) (*ibid.*, § 3133).
[366] UN Human Rights Committee, General Comment No. 29 (Article 4 of the International Covenant on Civil and Political Rights) (*ibid.*, § 2999); Inter-American Commission on Human Rights, Report on Terrorism and Human Rights (*ibid.*, § 3020).

The presumption of innocence means that any person subject to penal proceedings must be presumed to be not guilty of the act he or she is charged with until proven otherwise. This means that the burden of proof lies on the prosecution, while the defendant has the benefit of the doubt.[367] It also means that guilt must be proven according to a determined standard: "beyond a reasonable doubt" (in common law countries) or "to the intimate conviction of the trier of fact" (in civil law countries). It is, moreover, the duty of all officials involved in a case, as well as of public authorities, to refrain from prejudging the outcome of a trial.[368] The African Commission on Human and Peoples' Rights found a violation of the presumption of innocence in a case where a court presumed the guilt of the defendants because they refused to defend themselves.[369]

Information on the nature and cause of the accusation
The obligation to inform the accused of the nature and cause of the accusation is provided for in the Third and Fourth Geneva Conventions, as well as in Additional Protocols I and II.[370] This obligation is also included in the Statutes of the International Criminal Court, of the International Criminal Tribunals for the Former Yugoslavia and for Rwanda and of the Special Court for Sierra Leone for accused persons appearing before these tribunals.[371]

The obligation to inform the accused of the nature and cause of the accusation is set forth in several military manuals and is part of most, if not all, national legal systems.[372] This obligation was recalled in war crimes trials after the Second World War.[373]

The obligation to inform the accused of the nature and cause of the charges is also contained in the International Covenant on Civil and Political Rights, the Convention on the Rights of the Child and the European and American

---

[367] See, e.g., UN Human Rights Committee, General Comment No. 13 (Article 14 of the International Covenant on Civil and Political Rights) (ibid., § 3148).
[368] See, e.g., UN Human Rights Committee, General Comment No. 13 (Article 14 of the International Covenant on Civil and Political Rights) (ibid., § 3148) and Gridin v. Russia (ibid., § 3149); European Court of Human Rights, Allenet de Ribemont v. France (ibid., § 3154).
[369] African Commission on Human and Peoples' Rights, Malawi African Association and Others v. Mauritania (54/91) (ibid., § 3152).
[370] Third Geneva Convention, Article 96, fourth paragraph (ibid., § 3162) and Article 105, fourth paragraph (ibid., § 3163); Fourth Geneva Convention, Article 71, second paragraph (ibid., § 3164) and Article 123, second paragraph (ibid., § 3165); Additional Protocol I, Article 75(4)(a) (adopted by consensus) (ibid., § 3169); Additional Protocol II, Article 6(2)(a) (adopted by consensus) (ibid., § 3170).
[371] ICC Statute, Article 67(1)(a) (ibid., § 3174); ICTY Statute, Article 21(4)(a) (ibid., § 3181); ICTR Statute, Article 20(4)(a) (ibid., § 3182); Statute of the Special Court for Sierra Leone, Article 17(4)(a) (ibid., § 3175).
[372] See, e.g., the military manuals of Argentina (ibid., §§ 3184–3185), Australia (ibid., § 3186), Canada (ibid., § 3187), Indonesia (ibid., § 3188), Netherlands (ibid., § 3189), New Zealand (ibid., § 3190), Spain (ibid., § 3191), Sweden (ibid., § 3192), Switzerland (ibid., § 3193), United Kingdom (ibid., § 3194) and United States (ibid., §§ 3195–3197) and the legislation of Bangladesh (ibid., § 3199), Ethiopia (ibid., § 3198), Georgia (ibid., § 3198), India (ibid., § 3198), Ireland (ibid., § 3200), Kenya (ibid., § 3198), Kyrgyzstan (ibid., § 3198), Mexico (ibid., § 3198) and Norway (ibid., § 3201).
[373] See, e.g., Australia, Military Court at Rabaul, Ohashi case (ibid., § 3202); United States, Military Tribunal at Nuremberg, Altstötter (The Justice Trial) case (ibid., § 2965).

Conventions on Human Rights.[374] The African Commission on Human and Peoples' Rights held that compliance with this obligation was indispensable for the enjoyment of the right to fair trial.[375] This obligation is also set forth in other international instruments.[376] Both the UN Human Rights Committee and the Inter-American Commission on Human Rights have indicated that the obligation to inform the accused of the nature and cause of the charges can never be dispensed with.[377]

Most of the treaty provisions specify that information on the nature and cause of the charge must be given to the accused "without delay" or "promptly" and that the information must be provided in a language the accused understands.[378]

Necessary rights and means of defence

The requirement that an accused must have the necessary rights and means of defence is contained in all four Geneva Conventions, as well as in Additional Protocols I and II.[379]

This requirement is provided for in a number of military manuals and is part of most, if not all, national legal systems.[380]

The right to defence is also set forth in the International Covenant on Civil and Political Rights and the regional human rights conventions.[381] It is also

---

[374] International Covenant on Civil and Political Rights, Article 14(3)(a) (*ibid.*, § 3167); Convention on the Rights of the Child, Article 40(2)(b)(ii) (*ibid.*, § 3171); European Convention on Human Rights, Article 6(3)(a) (*ibid.*, § 3166); American Convention on Human Rights, Article 8(2)(b) (*ibid.*, § 3168).

[375] African Commission on Human and Peoples' Rights, *Malawi African Association and Others v. Mauritania*, Communications 54/91, 61/91, 98/93, 164/97–196/97 and 210/98, Decision, 27ᵗʰ Session, Algiers, 11 May 2000, § 97.

[376] See, e.g., Body of Principles for the Protection of All Persons under Any Form of Detention or Imprisonment, Principle 10 (*ibid.*, § 3177).

[377] UN Human Rights Committee, General Comment No. 29 (Article 4 of the International Covenant on Civil and Political Rights) (*ibid.*, § 2999); Inter-American Commission on Human Rights, Report on Terrorism and Human Rights (*ibid.*, § 3020).

[378] See Third Geneva Convention, Article 105, fourth paragraph (*ibid.*, § 3163); Fourth Geneva Convention, Article 71, second paragraph (*ibid.*, § 3164); Additional Protocol I, Article 75(4)(a) (adopted by consensus) (*ibid.*, § 3169); Additional Protocol II, Article 6(2)(a) (adopted by consensus) (*ibid.*, § 3170).

[379] First Geneva Convention, Article 49, fourth paragraph (*ibid.*, § 3210); Second Geneva Convention, Article 50, fourth paragraph (*ibid.*, § 3211); Third Geneva Convention, Article 84, second paragraph (*ibid.*, § 3212) and Article 96, fourth paragraph (*ibid.*, § 3213); Fourth Geneva Convention, Article 72, first paragraph (*ibid.*, § 3216) and Article 123, first paragraph (*ibid.*, § 3217); Additional Protocol I, Article 75(4)(a) (adopted by consensus) (*ibid.*, § 3221); Additional Protocol II, Article 6(2)(a) (adopted by consensus) (*ibid.*, § 3222).

[380] See, e.g., the military manuals of Argentina (*ibid.*, §§ 3245–3246), Australia (*ibid.*, § 3247), Canada (*ibid.*, § 3248), Colombia (*ibid.*, § 3249), Ecuador (*ibid.*, § 3250), Germany (*ibid.*, § 3251), Hungary (*ibid.*, § 3252), Netherlands (*ibid.*, § 3253), New Zealand (*ibid.*, § 3254), Spain (*ibid.*, § 3256), Sweden (*ibid.*, § 3257), Switzerland (*ibid.*, § 3258), United Kingdom (*ibid.*, § 3259) and United States (*ibid.*, §§ 3260–3263) and the legislation of Argentina (*ibid.*, § 3265), Bangladesh (*ibid.*, § 3266), Ethiopia (*ibid.*, § 3264), Georgia (*ibid.*, § 3264), India (*ibid.*, § 3264), Ireland (*ibid.*, § 3267), Kenya (*ibid.*, § 3264), Kuwait (*ibid.*, § 3264), Kyrgyzstan (*ibid.*, § 3264), Mexico (*ibid.*, § 3264), Norway (*ibid.*, § 3268) and Russia (*ibid.*, § 3264).

[381] International Covenant on Civil and Political Rights, Article 14(3) (*ibid.*, § 3219); European Convention on Human Rights, Article 6(3) (*ibid.*, § 3218); American Convention on Human Rights, Article 8(2) (*ibid.*, § 3220); African Charter on Human and Peoples' Rights, Article 7(1) (*ibid.*, § 3223). Article 14(3) of the International Covenant on Civil and Political Rights and

contained in other international instruments.[382] The UN Human Rights Committee has indicated that the right of an accused to necessary rights and means of defence can never be dispensed with.[383]

These sources specify that the necessary rights and means of defence include the following:

(i) Right to defend oneself or to be assisted by a lawyer of one's own choice. The right to have the assistance of counsel was set forth in the Charters of the International Military Tribunals at Nuremberg and at Tokyo.[384] This right is also set forth in the Third and Fourth Geneva Conventions.[385] The Statutes of the International Criminal Court, of the International Criminal Tribunals for the Former Yugoslavia and for Rwanda and of the Special Court for Sierra Leone provide that accused persons appearing before the tribunals are entitled to defend themselves or to be assisted by counsel of their own choice and to be informed of this right if they have no legal assistance.[386]

Denial of the right to counsel of one's own choice or to counsel altogether was one of the bases for the finding of a violation of the right to fair trial in several war crimes trials after the Second World War.[387] In a resolution on the human rights situation in the former Yugoslavia adopted in 1996, the UN Commission on Human Rights called upon Croatia "to pursue vigorously prosecutions against those suspected of past violations of international humanitarian law and human rights, while ensuring that the rights . . . to legal representation are afforded to all persons suspected of such crimes".[388]

The right to defence, including the right to be defended by a lawyer of one's own choice is also contained in the International Covenant on Civil and Political Rights and the regional human rights conventions.[389] The Inter-American

---

Article 8(2) of the American Convention on Human Rights state that during the proceedings the defendant must benefit with "full equality" from the judicial guarantees listed in these articles.

[382] See, e.g., Universal Declaration on Human Rights, Article 11 (*ibid.*, § 3229); Cairo Declaration on Human Rights in Islam, Article 19(e) (*ibid.*, § 3233); EU Charter of Fundamental Rights, Article 48(2) (*ibid.*, § 3222).

[383] UN Human Rights Committee, General Comment No. 29 (Article 4 of the International Covenant on Civil and Political Rights) (*ibid.*, § 2999).

[384] IMT Charter (Nuremberg), Article 16(d) (*ibid.*, § 3209); IMT Charter (Tokyo), Article 9(c) (*ibid.*, § 3228).

[385] Third Geneva Convention, Article 99, third paragraph ("assistance of a qualified advocate or counsel") (*ibid.*, § 3214) and Article 105, first paragraph ("defence by a qualified advocate or counsel of his own choice") (*ibid.*, § 3215); Fourth Geneva Convention, Article 72, first paragraph ("right to be assisted by a qualified advocate or counsel of their own choice") (*ibid.*, § 3216).

[386] ICC Statute, Article 67(1) (*ibid.*, § 3226); ICTY Statute, Article 21(4) (*ibid.*, § 3238); ICTR Statute, Article 20(4) (*ibid.*, § 3240); Statute of the Special Court for Sierra Leone, Article 17(4) (*ibid.*, § 3227).

[387] See United States, Military Commission at Shanghai, *Isayama case* (*ibid.*, § 2963), Military Tribunal at Nuremberg, *Altstötter (The Justice Trial) case* (*ibid.*, § 2965) and Supreme Court, *Ward case* (*ibid.*, § 3269).

[388] UN Commission on Human Rights, Res. 1996/71 (*ibid.*, § 3273).

[389] International Covenant on Civil and Political Rights, Article 14(3)(d) (*ibid.*, § 3219); European Convention on Human Rights, Article 6(3)(c) (*ibid.*, § 3218); American Convention on Human

Commission on Human Rights has indicated that the right to be defended by a lawyer of one's own choice can never be dispensed with.[390] Human rights case-law has held that this requirement means that an accused cannot be forced to accept a government's choice of lawyer.[391]

The Geneva Conventions do not indicate how soon a person has the right to a lawyer except to specify that a lawyer must be had, not only during the trial, but before it as well.[392] The Body of Principles for the Protection of All Persons under Any Form of Detention or Imprisonment, adopted by the UN General Assembly without a vote, specifies that communication with counsel may not be denied for more than "a matter of days".[393] The Basic Principles on the Role of Lawyers specifies that this must be the case "not later than forty-eight hours from the time of arrest or detention".[394] The need for early access to a lawyer before the trial, as well as at all important stages of the trial, has been stated in the case-law of the UN Human Rights Committee and regional human rights bodies.[395]

(ii) Right to free legal assistance if the interests of justice so require. This right is implicitly recognised in the Third and Fourth Geneva Conventions.[396] It is also provided for in the Statutes of the International Criminal Court, of the International Criminal Tribunals for the Former Yugoslavia and for Rwanda and of the Special Court for Sierra Leone.[397]

Rights, Article 8(2)(d) (*ibid.*, § 3220); African Charter on Human and Peoples' Rights, Article 7(1)(c) (*ibid.*, § 3223). With the exception of the European Convention, these treaties also provide that the accused must be informed of the right to counsel if they do not have legal assistance.

[390] Inter-American Commission on Human Rights, Report on Terrorism and Human Rights (*ibid.*, § 3020).

[391] See, e.g., UN Human Rights Committee, *Saldías López v. Uruguay* (*ibid.*, § 3281); African Commission on Human and Peoples' Rights, *Civil Liberties Organisation and Others v. Nigeria (218/98)* (*ibid.*, § 3285).

[392] Third Geneva Convention, Article 105, third paragraph (counsel must have at least two weeks to prepare before the opening of the trial) (*ibid.*, § 3215); Fourth Geneva Convention, Article 72, first paragraph (counsel must enjoy the necessary facilities for preparing the defence) (*ibid.*, § 3216).

[393] Body of Principles for the Protection of All Persons under Any Form of Detention or Imprisonment, Principle 15 (*ibid.*, § 3230).

[394] Basic Principles on the Role of Lawyers, Principle 7 (*ibid.*, § 3242).

[395] See, e.g., UN Human Rights Committee, *Sala de Tourón v. Uruguay, Pietraroia v. Uruguay, Wight v. Madagascar, Lafuente Peñarrieta and Others v. Bolivia* (*ibid.*, § 3278) and *Little v. Jamaica* (*ibid.*, § 3280); African Commission on Human and Peoples' Rights, *Avocats Sans Frontières v. Burundi (231/99)* (*ibid.*, § 3284); European Court of Human Rights, *Campbell and Fell case* (*ibid.*, § 3288), *Can case* (*ibid.*, § 3289), *Imbrioscia v. Switzerland* (*ibid.*, § 3291) and *Averill v. UK* (*ibid.*, § 3292); Inter-American Commission on Human Rights, *Case 10.198 (Nicaragua)* (*ibid.*, § 3293).

[396] Third Geneva Convention, Article 105, second paragraph ("failing a choice by the prisoner of war, the Protecting Power shall find him an advocate or counsel" or if that fails "the Detaining Power shall appoint a competent advocate or counsel to conduct the defence"); Fourth Geneva Convention, Article 72, second paragraph ("failing a choice by the accused, the Protecting Power may provide him with an advocate or counsel" or if that fails "the Occupying Power, subject to the consent of the accused, shall provide an advocate or counsel").

[397] ICC Statute, Article 67(1)(d) (cited in Vol. II, Ch. 32, § 3226); ICTY Statute, Article 21(4)(d) (*ibid.*, § 3238); ICTR Statute, Article 20(4)(d) (*ibid.*, § 3240); Statute of the Special Court for Sierra Leone, Article 17(4)(d) (*ibid.*, § 3227).

The right to the services of a lawyer free of charge if the interests of justice so require is also set forth in the International Covenant on Civil and Political Rights and the European and American Conventions on Human Rights.[398] This right is also contained in other international instruments.[399] The Inter-American Commission on Human Rights has indicated that the right to free legal assistance if the interests of justice so require can never be dispensed with.[400] A number of criteria have been identified in human rights case-law on the basis of which it must be determined whether the interests of justice require the free services of a lawyer, in particular the complexity of the case, the seriousness of the offence and the severity of the sentence the accused risks.[401]

(iii) Right to sufficient time and facilities to prepare the defence. The Third and Fourth Geneva Conventions specify that the necessary means of defence include sufficient time and facilities before the trial to prepare the defence.[402] This requirement is also set forth in the Statutes of the International Criminal Court, of the International Criminal Tribunals for the Former Yugoslavia and for Rwanda and of the Special Court for Sierra Leone.[403]

The right to sufficient time and facilities to prepare the defence is contained in the International Covenant on Civil and Political Rights and the European and American Conventions on Human Rights.[404] It is also included in other international instruments.[405] The Inter-American Commission on Human Rights has indicated that the right to sufficient time and facilities to prepare the defence can never be dispensed with.[406]

---

[398] International Covenant on Civil and Political Rights, Article 14(3)(d) (*ibid.*, § 3219); European Convention on Human Rights, Article 6(3)(c) (*ibid.*, § 3218); American Convention on Human Rights, Article 8(2)(e) (*ibid.*, § 3220). The American Convention actually refers to payment depending on the requirement of domestic law, but the Inter-American Court of Human Rights has interpreted this as requiring the free services of a lawyer if the accused cannot afford one and if the fairness of the hearing would be affected by the lack of such a lawyer; see Inter-American Court of Human Rights, *Exceptions to the Exhaustion of Domestic Remedies case* (*ibid.*, § 3294).

[399] See, e.g., Body of Principles for the Protection of All Persons under Any Form of Detention or Imprisonment, Principle 17 (*ibid.*, § 3231); Basic Principles on the Role of Lawyers, Principle 6 (*ibid.*, § 3242).

[400] Inter-American Commission on Human Rights, Report on Terrorism and Human Rights (*ibid.*, § 3020).

[401] See, e.g., UN Human Rights Committee, *Currie v. Jamaica* and *Thomas v. Jamaica* (*ibid.*, § 3279); African Commission on Human and Peoples' Rights, *Avocats Sans Frontières v. Burundi (231/99)* (*ibid.*, § 3284); European Court of Human Rights, *Pakelli case* (*ibid.*, § 3287) and *Quaranta v. Switzerland* (*ibid.*, § 3290).

[402] Third Geneva Convention, Article 105, third paragraph (*ibid.*, § 3215); Fourth Geneva Convention, Article 72, first paragraph (*ibid.*, § 3216).

[403] ICC Statute, Article 67(1)(b) (*ibid.*, § 3226); ICTY Statute, Article 21(4)(b) (*ibid.*, § 3238); ICTR Statute, Article 20(4)(b) (*ibid.*, § 3240); Statute of the Special Court for Sierra Leone, Article 17(4)(b) (*ibid.*, § 3227).

[404] International Covenant on Civil and Political Rights, Article 14(3)(b) (*ibid.*, § 3219); European Convention on Human Rights, Article 6(3)(b) (*ibid.*, § 3218); American Convention on Human Rights, Article 8(2)(c) (*ibid.*, § 3220).

[405] See, e.g., Body of Principles for the Protection of All Persons under Any Form of Detention or Imprisonment, Principles 17–18 (*ibid.*, §§ 3231–3232); Basic Principles on the Role of Lawyers, Principle 8 (*ibid.*, § 3242).

[406] Inter-American Commission on Human Rights, Report on Terrorism and Human Rights (*ibid.*, § 3020).

As specified in the Body of Principles for the Protection of All Persons under Any Form of Detention or Imprisonment, adopted by the UN General Assembly without a vote, this right requires that "a detained person shall be allowed adequate time and facilities for consultation with his legal counsel".[407]

(iv) Right of the accused to communicate freely with counsel. The right of counsel to visit the accused freely is provided for in the Third and Fourth Geneva Conventions.[408] The right of the accused to communicate freely with counsel is also provided for in the Statutes of the International Criminal Court, of the International Criminal Tribunals for the Former Yugoslavia and for Rwanda and of the Special Court for Sierra Leone.[409]

The right of the accused to communicate freely with counsel is provided for in the American Convention on Human Rights and in other international instruments.[410] The UN Human Rights Committee and regional human rights bodies have stressed the importance of the right of the accused to communicate freely with counsel in order to have a fair trial.[411]

The Body of Principles for the Protection of All Persons under Any Form of Detention or Imprisonment, adopted by the UN General Assembly without a vote, specifies that "interviews between a detained or imprisoned person and his legal counsel may be within sight, but not within hearing, of a law enforcement official".[412]

Trial without undue delay

The right to a trial without undue delay is provided for in the Third and Fourth Geneva Conventions.[413] This right is also set forth in the Statutes of the International Criminal Court, of the International Criminal Tribunals for the Former Yugoslavia and for Rwanda and of the Special Court for Sierra Leone.[414]

---

[407] Body of Principles for the Protection of All Persons under Any Form of Detention or Imprisonment, Principle 18(2) (*ibid.*, § 3232).

[408] Third Geneva Convention, Article 105, third paragraph (*ibid.*, § 3215); Fourth Geneva Convention, Article 72, first paragraph (*ibid.*, § 3216).

[409] ICC Statute, Article 67(1)(b) (*ibid.*, § 3226); ICTY Statute, Article 21(4)(b) (*ibid.*, § 3238); ICTR Statute, Article 20(4)(b) (*ibid.*, § 3240); Statute of the Special Court for Sierra Leone, Article 17(4)(b) (*ibid.*, § 3227).

[410] American Convention on Human Rights, Article 8(2)(d) (*ibid.*, § 3220); Body of Principles for the Protection of All Persons under Any Form of Detention or Imprisonment, Principle 18 (*ibid.*, § 3232); Basic Principles on the Role of Lawyers, Principle 8 (*ibid.*, § 3242).

[411] See, e.g., UN Human Rights Committee, General Comment No. 13 (Article 14 of the International Covenant on Civil and Political Rights) (*ibid.*, § 3276); African Commission on Human and Peoples' Rights, Resolution on the Right to Recourse and Fair Trial (*ibid.*, § 3282) and *Civil Liberties Organisation and Others v. Nigeria (218/98)* (*ibid.*, § 3285); European Court of Human Rights, *Can case* (*ibid.*, § 3289).

[412] Body of Principles for the Protection of All Persons under Any Form of Detention or Imprisonment, Principle 18(4) (*ibid.*, § 3232).

[413] Third Geneva Convention, Article 103, first paragraph (*ibid.*, § 3297) ("as soon as possible"); Fourth Geneva Convention, Article 71, second paragraph (*ibid.*, § 3298) ("as rapidly as possible").

[414] ICC Statute, Article 64(2) and (3) ("expeditious") (*ibid.*, § 3306) and Article 67(1)(c) ("without undue delay") (*ibid.*, § 3307); ICTY Statute, Article 20(1) ("expeditious") (*ibid.*, § 3311) and Article 21(4)(c) ("without undue delay") (*ibid.*, § 3312); ICTR Statute, Article 19(1) ("expeditious") (*ibid.*, § 3313) and Article 20(4)(c) ("without undue delay") (*ibid.*, § 3314);

The right to trial without delay is set forth in several military manuals and is part of most, if not all, national legal systems.[415]

The right to a trial without undue delay (or within a reasonable time) is provided for in the International Covenant on Civil and Political Rights, the Convention on the Rights of the Child and the regional human rights conventions.[416] It is also provided for in other international instruments.[417]

The actual length of time is not specified in any instrument and must be judged on a case-by-case basis taking into account factors such as the complexity of the case, the behaviour of the accused and the diligence of the authorities.[418] The proceedings subject to this requirement are those from the time of the charge to the final trial on the merits, including appeal.[419]

Examination of witnesses

The right of the accused to examine and to have examined witnesses is provided for by the Third and Fourth Geneva Conventions and Additional Protocol I.[420] This right is also set forth in the Statutes of the International Criminal Court, of the International Criminal Tribunals for the Former Yugoslavia and for Rwanda and of the Special Court for Sierra Leone.[421]

Several military manuals specify this right, and it is part of most, if not all, national legal systems.[422] The inability to examine and to have examined

---

Statute of the Special Court for Sierra Leone, Article 17(4)(c) ("without undue delay") (ibid., § 3308).

[415] See, e.g., the military manuals of Argentina (ibid., § 3317), Australia (ibid., § 3318), Canada (ibid., § 3319), Colombia (ibid., § 3320), New Zealand (ibid., § 3321), Spain (ibid., § 3322), United Kingdom (ibid., § 3323) and United States (ibid., § 3324) and the legislation of Bangladesh (ibid., § 3326), Ireland (ibid., § 3327), Kenya (ibid., § 3325) and Norway (ibid., § 3328).

[416] International Covenant on Civil and Political Rights, Article 9(3) ("within a reasonable time") (ibid., § 3301) and Article 14(3)(c) ("without undue delay") (ibid., § 3302); Convention on the Rights of the Child, Article 40(2)(b)(iii) ("without delay") (ibid., § 3306); European Convention on Human Rights, Article 5(3) (ibid., § 3299) and Article 6(1) ("within a reasonable time") (ibid., § 3300); American Convention on Human Rights, Article 8(1) ("within a reasonable time") (ibid., § 3303); African Charter on Human and Peoples' Rights, Article 7(1)(d) ("within a reasonable time") (ibid., § 3304).

[417] See, e.g., Body of Principles for the Protection of All Persons under Any Form of Detention or Imprisonment, Principle 38 (ibid., § 3309); EU Charter of Fundamental Rights, Article 47 (ibid., § 3316).

[418] See European Court of Human Rights, Wemhoff case, Matznetter v. Austria, Stögmüller case, König v. Germany, Letellier v. France, Kemmache v. France, Tomasi v. France, Olsson v. Sweden and Scopelliti v. Italy (ibid., § 3339); Inter-American Commission on Human Rights, Case 11.245 (Argentina) (ibid., § 3342).

[419] See UN Human Rights Committee, General Comment No. 13 (Article 14 of the International Covenant on Civil and Political Rights) (ibid., § 3335).

[420] Third Geneva Convention, Article 96, third paragraph (ibid., § 3346) and Article 105, first paragraph (ibid., § 3347); Fourth Geneva Convention, Article 72, first paragraph (ibid., § 3348) and Article 123, second paragraph (ibid., § 3349); Additional Protocol I, Article 75(4)(g) (adopted by consensus) (ibid., § 3353).

[421] ICC Statute, Article 67(1)(e) (ibid., § 3355); ICTY Statute, Article 21(4)(e) (ibid., § 3361); ICTR Statute, Article 20(4)(e) (ibid., § 3362); Statute of the Special Court for Sierra Leone, Article 17(4)(e) (ibid., § 3356).

[422] See, e.g., the military manuals of Argentina (ibid., §§ 3364–3365), Canada (ibid., § 3366), New Zealand (ibid., § 3367), Spain (ibid., § 3368), Sweden (ibid., § 3369), United Kingdom (ibid.,

witnesses for the prosecution was one of the bases of the finding of a violation of the right to fair trial in war crimes trials after the Second World War.[423]

The right to examine and to have examined witnesses is provided for by the International Covenant on Civil and Political Rights, the Convention on the Rights of the Child and the European and American Conventions on Human Rights.[424] While the African Charter on Human and Peoples' Rights does not explicitly provide for this right, the African Commission on Human and Peoples' Rights has specified that it is part and parcel of the right to fair trial.[425] Both the UN Human Rights Committee and the Inter-American Commission on Human Rights have indicated that the right to examine and to have examined witnesses can never be dispensed with.[426]

Assistance of an interpreter

The right to the assistance of an interpreter, if the accused cannot understand the language used in the proceedings, is provided for in the Third and Fourth Geneva Conventions.[427] It is included in the Statutes of the International Criminal Court, of the International Criminal Tribunals for the Former Yugoslavia and for Rwanda and of the Special Court for Sierra Leone for accused persons appearing before these tribunals.[428]

The right to the assistance of an interpreter, if the accused cannot understand the language used in the proceedings, is set forth in the International Covenant on Civil and Political Rights, the Convention on the Rights of the Child and the European and American Conventions on Human Rights.[429] While the African Charter on Human and Peoples' Rights does not explicitly provide for this right, the African Commission on Human and Peoples' Rights has specified that it

---

§ 3370) and United States (*ibid.*, §§ 3371–3373) and the legislation of Bangladesh (*ibid.*, § 3375), Ethiopia (*ibid.*, § 3374), Georgia (*ibid.*, § 3374), Ireland (*ibid.*, § 3376), Kenya (*ibid.*, § 3374), Mexico (*ibid.*, § 3374) and Norway (*ibid.*, § 3377).

[423] See, e.g., United States, Military Commission at Shanghai, *Isayama case* (*ibid.*, § 2963) and Military Tribunal at Nuremberg, *Altstötter (The Justice Trial) case* (*ibid.*, § 2965).

[424] International Covenant on Civil and Political Rights, Article 14(3)(e) (*ibid.*, § 3351); European Convention on Human Rights, Article 6(3)(d) (*ibid.*, § 3350); American Convention on Human Rights, Article 8(2)(f) (*ibid.*, § 3352).

[425] African Commission on Human and Peoples' Rights, Resolution on the Right to Recourse and Fair Trial (*ibid.*, § 3383).

[426] UN Human Rights Committee, General Comment No. 29 (Article 4 of the International Covenant on Civil and Political Rights) (*ibid.*, § 2999); Inter-American Commission on Human Rights, Report on Terrorism and Human Rights (*ibid.*, § 3020).

[427] Third Geneva Convention, Article 96, fourth paragraph (*ibid.*, § 3389) and Article 105, first paragraph (*ibid.*, § 3390); Fourth Geneva Convention, Article 72, third paragraph (*ibid.*, § 3391) and Article 123, second paragraph (*ibid.*, § 3392).

[428] ICC Statute, Article 67(1)(f) (*ibid.*, § 3398); ICTY Statute, Article 21(4)(f) (*ibid.*, § 3401); ICTR Statute, Article 20(4)(f) (*ibid.*, § 3402); Statute of the Special Court for Sierra Leone, Article 17(4)(f) (*ibid.*, § 3399).

[429] International Covenant on Civil and Political Rights, Article 14(3)(f) (*ibid.*, § 3395); Convention on the Rights of the Child, Article 40(2)(b)(vi) (*ibid.*, § 3396); European Convention on Human Rights, Article 6(3)(e) (*ibid.*, § 3393); American Convention on Human Rights, Article 8(2)(a) (*ibid.*, § 3395).

is part and parcel of the right to fair trial.[430] The European Court of Human Rights has held that this right includes the obligation of the authorities to have translated or interpreted not only oral statements, but also documents used as evidence.[431]

Presence of the accused at the trial
Additional Protocols I and II provide that accused persons have the right to be tried in their presence.[432] Upon ratification of the Additional Protocols, several States made a reservation to this right to the effect that this provision is subject to the power of a judge to exclude the accused from the courtroom, in exceptional circumstances, when the accused causes a disturbance and thereby impedes the progress of the trial.[433] The right of an accused to be present at his or her trial is provided for in the Statutes of the International Criminal Court, of the International Criminal Tribunals for the Former Yugoslavia and for Rwanda and of the Special Court for Sierra Leone.[434]

The right of the accused to be present at the trial is contained in several military manuals and is part of most, if not all, national legal systems.[435]

The International Covenant on Civil and Political Rights and the European and American Conventions on Human Rights provide that an accused has the right to be present at the trial.[436] The UN Human Rights Committee and the European Court of Human Rights have stated that a hearing *in absentia* is possible if the State has given effective notice of the hearing and the accused chooses not to appear.[437] Both have also stated that the right to be present in person is also required in appeal proceedings if the appeal hears questions of both fact and law, and not only of law.[438] There is clearly a trend, however, against trials

---

[430] African Commission on Human and Peoples' Rights, Resolution on the Right to Recourse and Fair Trial (*ibid.*, § 3423).

[431] See, e.g., European Court of Human Rights, *Luedicke, Belkacem and Koç case* (*ibid.*, § 3364) and *Kamasinski case* (*ibid.*, § 3426).

[432] Additional Protocol I, Article 75(4)(e) (adopted by consensus) (*ibid.*, § 3434); Additional Protocol II, Article 6(2)(e) (adopted by consensus) (*ibid.*, § 3440).

[433] See the reservations made upon ratification of the Additional Protocols by Austria (*ibid.*, §§ 3435 and 3441), Germany (*ibid.*, §§ 3436 and 3442), Ireland (*ibid.*, §§ 3437 and 3443), Liechtenstein (*ibid.*, §§ 3438 and 3444) and Malta (*ibid.*, §§ 3439 and 3445).

[434] ICC Statute, Article 63(1) (*ibid.*, § 3446) and Article 67(1)(d) (*ibid.*, § 3447); ICTY Statute, Article 21(4)(d) (*ibid.*, § 3453); ICTR Statute, Article 20(4)(d) (*ibid.*, § 3454); Statute of the Special Court for Sierra Leone, Article 17(4)(d) (*ibid.*, § 3448).

[435] See, e.g., the military manuals of Argentina (*ibid.*, § 3456), Canada (*ibid.*, § 3457), New Zealand (*ibid.*, § 3458) and Sweden (*ibid.*, § 3459) and the legislation of Bangladesh (*ibid.*, § 3461), Georgia (*ibid.*, § 3460), Ireland (*ibid.*, § 3462), Kenya (*ibid.*, § 3460), Kyrgyzstan (*ibid.*, § 3460), Norway (*ibid.*, § 3463) and Russia (*ibid.*, § 3460).

[436] International Covenant on Civil and Political Rights, Article 14(3)(d) (*ibid.*, § 3432); European Convention on Human Rights, Article 6(3)(c) (*ibid.*, § 3431); American Convention on Human Rights, Article 8(2)(d) (*ibid.*, § 3433). The last two Articles in fact provide for the right to defend oneself, which implies the right to be present at the trial.

[437] UN Human Rights Committee, *Daniel Monguya Mbenge v. Zaire* (*ibid.*, § 3470); European Court of Human Rights, *Colozza case* (*ibid.*, § 3472).

[438] UN Human Rights Committee, *Karttunen v. Finland* (*ibid.*, § 3471); European Court of Human Rights, *Ekbatani v. Sweden* (*ibid.*, § 3473) and *Kremzow v. Austria* (*ibid.*, § 3473).

in absentia, as evidenced by the Statutes of the International Criminal Court, of the International Criminal Tribunals for the Former Yugoslavia and for Rwanda and of the Special Court for Sierra Leone, which do not allow such trials.[439]

Compelling accused persons to testify against
themselves or to confess guilt

The prohibition on compelling accused persons to testify against themselves or to confess guilt is set forth in the Third Geneva Convention, as well as in Additional Protocols I and II.[440] This prohibition is provided for in the Statutes of the International Criminal Court, of the International Criminal Tribunals for the Former Yugoslavia and for Rwanda and of the Special Court for Sierra Leone.[441]

This prohibition is contained in several military manuals and is part of most, if not all, national legal systems.[442] In the *Ward case* in 1942, the US Supreme Court held that the use of a confession obtained under compulsion constituted a denial of due process.[443]

The International Covenant on Civil and Political Rights, the Convention on the Rights of the Child and the American Convention on Human Rights prohibit compelling accused persons to testify against themselves or to confess guilt.[444] This prohibition is also to be found in several other international instruments.[445] Both the UN Human Rights Committee and the Inter-American Commission on Human Rights have indicated that the prohibition against compelling accused persons to testify against themselves or to confess guilt can never be dispensed with.[446]

The UN Human Rights Committee has underlined that "the law should require that evidence provided by means of such methods or any other form of

---

[439] ICC Statute, Article 63(1) (*ibid.*, § 3446) and Article 67(1)(d) (*ibid.*, § 3447); ICTY Statute, Article 21(4)(d) (*ibid.*, § 3453); ICTR Statute, Article 20(4)(d) (*ibid.*, § 3454); Statute of the Special Court for Sierra Leone, Article 17(4)(d) (*ibid.*, § 3448).

[440] Third Geneva Convention, Article 99, second paragraph (*ibid.*, § 3477); Additional Protocol I, Article 75(4)(f) (adopted by consensus) (*ibid.*, § 3480); Additional Protocol II, Article 6(2)(f) (adopted by consensus) (*ibid.*, § 3481).

[441] ICC Statute, Article 55(1)(a) (*ibid.*, § 3483) and Article 67(1)(g) (*ibid.*, § 3484); ICTY Statute, Article 21(4)(g) (*ibid.*, § 3490); ICTR Statute, Article 20(4)(g) (*ibid.*, § 3491); Statute of the Special Court for Sierra Leone, Article 17(4)(g) (*ibid.*, § 3485).

[442] See, e.g., the military manuals of Argentina (*ibid.*, §§ 3494–3495), Canada (*ibid.*, § 3496), Colombia (*ibid.*, § 3497), New Zealand (*ibid.*, § 3498), Sweden (*ibid.*, § 3499), Switzerland (*ibid.*, § 3500) and United States (*ibid.*, § 3501) and the legislation of Bangladesh (*ibid.*, § 3503), Georgia (*ibid.*, § 3502), India (*ibid.*, § 3502), Ireland (*ibid.*, § 3504), Kenya (*ibid.*, § 3502), Mexico (*ibid.*, § 3502), Norway (*ibid.*, § 3505) and Russia (*ibid.*, § 3502).

[443] United States, Supreme Court, *Ward case* (*ibid.*, § 3506).

[444] International Covenant on Civil and Political Rights, Article 14(3)(g) (*ibid.*, § 3478); Convention on the Rights of the Child, Article 40(2)(b)(iv) (*ibid.*, § 3482); American Convention on Human Rights, Article 8(2)(g) (*ibid.*, § 3479).

[445] See, e.g., Body of Principles for the Protection of All Persons under Any Form of Detention or Imprisonment, Principle 21 (*ibid.*, § 3486).

[446] UN Human Rights Committee, General Comment No. 29 (Article 4 of the International Covenant on Civil and Political Rights) (*ibid.*, § 2999); Inter-American Commission on Human Rights, Report on Terrorism and Human Rights (*ibid.*, § 3020).

compulsion is wholly unacceptable".[447] The UN Convention against Torture provides that statements which have been made as a result of torture may not be invoked as evidence in any proceedings.[448] This view is confirmed in national and international case-law.[449]

Public proceedings

The Third and Fourth Geneva Conventions provide that representatives of the protecting power are entitled to attend the trial, unless, exceptionally, it is held *in camera* in the interests of security, whereas Additional Protocol I states that the judgement must be pronounced publicly.[450] The Statutes of the International Criminal Court, of the International Criminal Tribunals for the Former Yugoslavia and for Rwanda and of the Special Court for Sierra Leone similarly lay down the principle of a public hearing, subject to narrow exceptions, and the requirement of a public pronouncement of the judgement.[451]

The requirement of public proceedings is set forth in several military manuals and is part of most, if not all, national legal systems.[452] In the war crimes trial of *Altstötter (The Justice Trial) case* in 1947, the US Military Tribunal at Nuremberg found a violation of the right to fair trial because proceedings were held in secret and no public record was kept.[453]

The requirement that the trial be held in public and judgement pronounced publicly, unless this would prejudice the interests of justice, is set forth in the International Covenant on Civil and Political Rights and the European and American Conventions on Human Rights.[454] Although the right to public proceedings is not mentioned in the African Charter on Human and Peoples' Rights, the African Commission on Human and Peoples' Rights has stated that

---

[447] UN Human Rights Committee, General Comment No. 13 (Article 14 of the International Covenant on Civil and Political Rights) (*ibid.*, § 3510).

[448] UN Convention against Torture, Article 15.

[449] See, e.g., United States, Supreme Court, *Ward case* (cited in Vol. II, Ch. 32, § 3506); European Court of Human Rights, *Coëme and Others v. Belgium* (*ibid.*, § 3512).

[450] Third Geneva Convention, Article 105, fifth paragraph (*ibid.*, § 3518); Fourth Geneva Convention, Article 74, first paragraph (*ibid.*, § 3519); Additional Protocol I, Article 75(4)(i) (adopted by consensus) (*ibid.*, § 3523).

[451] ICC Statute, Article 64(7) (*ibid.*, § 3526), Article 67(1) (*ibid.*, § 3527), Article 68(2) (*ibid.*, § 3528) and Article 76(4) (*ibid.*, § 3529); ICTY Statute, Article 20(4) (*ibid.*, § 3538) and Article 23(2) (*ibid.*, § 3539); ICTR Statute, Article 19(4) (*ibid.*, § 3540) and Article 22(2) (*ibid.*, § 3541); Statute of the Special Court for Sierra Leone, Article 17(2) (*ibid.*, § 3530) and Article 18 (*ibid.*, § 3531).

[452] See, e.g., the military manuals of Argentina (*ibid.*, § 3544), Colombia (*ibid.*, § 3545), New Zealand (*ibid.*, § 3546) and Sweden (*ibid.*, § 3547) and the legislation of Bangladesh (*ibid.*, § 3550), Ethiopia (*ibid.*, § 3549), Ireland (*ibid.*, § 3551), Kenya (*ibid.*, § 3549), Kuwait (*ibid.*, § 3549), Mexico (*ibid.*, § 3549), Norway (*ibid.*, § 3552) and Russia (*ibid.*, § 3549).

[453] United States, Military Tribunal at Nuremberg, *Altstötter (The Justice Trial) case* (*ibid.*, § 3553).

[454] International Covenant on Civil and Political Rights, Article 14(1) (*ibid.*, § 3521); European Convention on Human Rights, Article 6(1) (*ibid.*, § 3520); American Convention on Human Rights, Article 8(5) (*ibid.*, § 3522).

this is required for a trial to be fair.[455] The principle of a public trial is to be found in several other international instruments.[456]

Advising convicted persons of available remedies and of their time-limits

The Third and Fourth Geneva Conventions and both Additional Protocols provide that convicted persons are to be advised of their judicial or other remedies and the time-limits within which they may be exercised.[457] Article 106 of the Third Geneva Convention states that convicted persons shall have a right to appeal in the same manner as members of the armed forces of the detaining power.[458] Article 73 of the Fourth Geneva Convention states that a convicted person shall have the right to appeal provided for by the law applied by the court.[459]

The ICRC Commentary on the Additional Protocols states that at the time of the adoption of the Protocols in 1977 not enough national legislation provided for the right to appeal in order to make this an absolute requirement – even though no one should be denied the right to appeal where it exists.[460] However, there have been significant developments since that time in both national and international law. The majority of States now have constitutions or legislation providing for the right to appeal, especially those adopted or amended since the adoption of the Additional Protocols.[461] In addition, the International Covenant on Civil and Political Rights, the Convention on the Rights of the Child and the regional human rights conventions all provide for the right to appeal to a higher tribunal.[462] The Inter-American Commission on Human Rights has stated that the right of appeal can never be dispensed with and must be provided in situations of non-international armed conflict.[463]

In conclusion, the influence of human rights law on this issue is such that it can be argued that the right of appeal proper – and not only the right to be

---

[455] African Commission on Human and Peoples' Rights, *Civil Liberties Organisation and Others v. Nigeria (218/98)* (*ibid.*, § 3558).

[456] See, e.g., Universal Declaration on Human Rights, Articles 10–11 (*ibid.*, §§ 3532–3533); American Declaration on the Rights and Duties of Man, Article XXVI (*ibid.*, § 3534); EU Charter of Fundamental Rights, Article 47(2) (*ibid.*, § 3543).

[457] Third Geneva Convention, Article 106 (*ibid.*, § 3563); Fourth Geneva Convention, Article 73, first paragraph (*ibid.*, § 3564); Additional Protocol I, Article 75(4)(j) (adopted by consensus) (*ibid.*, § 3565); Additional Protocol II, Article 6(3) (adopted by consensus) (*ibid.*, § 3566).

[458] Third Geneva Convention, Article 106 (*ibid.*, § 3563).

[459] Fourth Geneva Convention, Article 73, first paragraph (*ibid.*, § 3564).

[460] Yves Sandoz, Christophe Swinarski, Bruno Zimmermann (eds.), *Commentary on the Additional Protocols* (*ibid.*, § 3588).

[461] See, e.g., the legislation of Colombia (*ibid.*, § 3606), Estonia (*ibid.*, § 3607), Ethiopia (*ibid.*, § 3605), Georgia (*ibid.*, § 3605), Hungary (*ibid.*, § 3608), Kuwait (*ibid.*, § 3605) and Russia (*ibid.*, § 3605).

[462] International Covenant on Civil and Political Rights, Article 14(5) (*ibid.*, § 3592); Convention on the Rights of the Child, Article 40(2)(b)(v) (*ibid.*, § 3595); Protocol 7 to the European Convention on Human Rights, Article 2(1) (*ibid.*, § 3596); American Convention on Human Rights, Article 8(2)(h) (*ibid.*, § 3593); African Charter on Human and Peoples' Rights, Article 7(1)(a) (*ibid.*, § 3594).

[463] Inter-American Commission on Human Rights, *Case 11.137* (Argentina) (*ibid.*, § 3622) and *Report on Terrorism and Human Rights* (*ibid.*, § 3623).

informed whether appeal is available – has become a basic component of fair trial rights in the context of armed conflict.

Non bis in idem

The Third and Fourth Geneva Conventions provide that a prisoner of war and civilian internee, respectively, must not be punished more than once for the same act or on the same charge.[464] Additional Protocol I provides that no one shall be prosecuted or punished by the same party for an offence in respect of which a final judgement has been pronounced.[465] The same rule is set forth in the Statutes of the International Criminal Court, of the International Criminal Tribunals for the Former Yugoslavia and for Rwanda and of the Special Court for Sierra Leone.[466]

The principle of *non bis in idem* is set forth in several military manuals and is part of most, if not all, national legal systems.[467]

The International Covenant on Civil and Political Rights, the American Convention on Human Rights and Protocol 7 to the European Convention on Human Rights include the principle of *non bis in idem*.[468] This principle is also included in other international instruments.[469]

It should be noted that the principle of *non bis in idem* does not prohibit the reopening of a trial in exceptional circumstances, and several States made a reservation to this effect upon ratification of Additional Protocol I.[470] The UN Human Rights Committee has stated that most States make a clear distinction between a resumption of a trial justified by exceptional circumstances and a re-trial prohibited pursuant to the principle of *non bis in idem* and has held that the principle of *non bis in idem* does not exclude prosecutions for the same offence in different States.[471] Protocol 7 to the European Convention on Human Rights provides that a case may be reopened if there is evidence of

---

[464] Third Geneva Convention, Article 86 (*ibid.*, § 3626); Fourth Geneva Convention, Article 117, third paragraph (*ibid.*, § 3627).

[465] Additional Protocol I, Article 75(4)(h) (adopted by consensus) (*ibid.*, § 3630).

[466] ICC Statute, Article 20(2) (*ibid.*, § 3640); ICTY Statute, Article 10(1) (*ibid.*, § 3645); ICTR Statute, Article 9(1) (*ibid.*, § 3646); Statute of the Special Court for Sierra Leone, Article 9(1) (*ibid.*, § 3641).

[467] See, e.g., the military manuals of Argentina (*ibid.*, §§ 3649–3650), Canada (*ibid.*, § 3651), Colombia (*ibid.*, § 3652), Germany (*ibid.*, § 3653), New Zealand (*ibid.*, § 3654), Spain (*ibid.*, § 3655), Sweden (*ibid.*, § 3656), Switzerland (*ibid.*, § 3657), United Kingdom (*ibid.*, § 3658) and United States (*ibid.*, §§ 3659–3660) and the legislation of Bangladesh (*ibid.*, § 3662), Ethiopia (*ibid.*, § 3661), Georgia (*ibid.*, § 3661), India (*ibid.*, § 3661), Ireland (*ibid.*, § 3663), Kenya (*ibid.*, § 3661), Kyrgyzstan (*ibid.*, § 3661), Mexico (*ibid.*, § 3661), Norway (*ibid.*, § 3664) and Russia (*ibid.*, § 3661).

[468] International Covenant on Civil and Political Rights, Article 14(7) (*ibid.*, § 3628); American Convention on Human Rights, Article 8(4) (*ibid.*, § 3629); Protocol 7 to the European Convention on Human Rights, Article 4 (*ibid.*, § 3639).

[469] See, e.g., EU Charter of Fundamental Rights, Article 50 (*ibid.*, § 3648).

[470] See the reservations made upon ratification of the Additional Protocols by Austria (*ibid.*, § 3631), Denmark (*ibid.*, § 3632), Finland (*ibid.*, § 3633), Germany (*ibid.*, § 3634), Iceland (*ibid.*, § 3635), Liechtenstein (*ibid.*, § 3636), Malta (*ibid.*, § 3637) and Sweden (*ibid.*, § 3638).

[471] UN Human Rights Committee, General Comment No. 13 (Article 14 of the International Covenant on Civil and Political Rights) (*ibid.*, § 3669) and A. P. v. Italy (*ibid.*, § 3670).

new facts or if there has been a fundamental defect in the previous proceedings which could affect the outcome of the case.[472]

Rule 101. No one may be accused or convicted of a criminal offence on account of any act or omission which did not constitute a criminal offence under national or international law at the time it was committed; nor may a heavier penalty be imposed than that which was applicable at the time the criminal offence was committed.

Practice

Volume II, Chapter 32, Section N.

Summary

State practice establishes this rule as a norm of customary international law applicable in both international and non-international armed conflicts.

International and non-international armed conflicts

The Third and Fourth Geneva Conventions provide that prisoners of war and civilians respectively may not be tried for acts that were not criminal offences, provided for by law, prior to the commission of those acts.[473] Additional Protocols I and II repeat the same principle and add that a heavier penalty may not be imposed than that applicable at the time the act was committed but that if, subsequent to the commission of the offence, provision is made by law for the imposition of a lighter penalty, the offender shall benefit from this.[474] This principle of legality is also set forth in the Statute of the International Criminal Court.[475]

The principle of legality is set forth in several military manuals and is part of most, if not all, national legal systems.[476]

The principle of legality, including the prohibition on imposing a heavier penalty than that applicable at the time of the commission of the offence, is set forth in the International Covenant on Civil and Political Rights, the Convention on the Rights of the Child and the regional human rights

---

[472] Protocol 7 to the European Convention on Human Rights, Article 4 (*ibid.*, § 3639).
[473] Third Geneva Convention, Article 99, first paragraph (*ibid.*, § 3674); Fourth Geneva Convention, Article 67 (*ibid.*, § 3676).
[474] Additional Protocol I, Article 75(4)(c) (adopted by consensus) (*ibid.*, § 3680); Additional Protocol II, Article 6(2)(c) (adopted by consensus) (*ibid.*, § 3681).
[475] ICC Statute, Article 22(1) (*ibid.*, § 3684) and Article 24(1)–(2) (*ibid.*, § 3685).
[476] See, e.g., the military manuals of Argentina (*ibid.*, §§ 3692–3693), Canada (*ibid.*, § 3694), Colombia (*ibid.*, § 3695), Netherlands (*ibid.*, § 3696), New Zealand (*ibid.*, § 3697), Spain (*ibid.*, § 3698), Sweden (*ibid.*, § 3699), United Kingdom (*ibid.*, §§ 3700–3701) and United States (*ibid.*, §§ 3702–3703) and the legislation of Bangladesh (*ibid.*, § 3705), India (*ibid.*, § 3704), Ireland (*ibid.*, § 3706), Kenya (*ibid.*, § 3704), Kuwait (*ibid.*, § 3704), Kyrgyzstan (*ibid.*, § 3704) and Norway (*ibid.*, § 3707).

conventions.[477] It is specifically listed as non-derogable in the International Covenant on Civil and Political Rights and the European and American Conventions on Human Rights,[478] while the Convention on the Rights of the Child and the African Charter on Human and Peoples' Rights do not allow for the possibility of derogations. In addition, the International Covenant on Civil and Political Rights and the American Convention on Human Rights specify that if, subsequent to the commission of the offence, provision is made by law for the imposition of a lighter penalty, the offender shall benefit from this.[479] The principle of legality is also contained in other international instruments.[480]

Interpretation

The principle of legality has been interpreted by the European Court of Human Rights as embodying the principle that only the law can define a crime and prescribe a penalty and the principle that criminal law must not be extensively construed to an accused's detriment, for instance by analogy. This requires that the offence be clearly defined in law, so that "the individual can know from the wording of the relevant provision and, if need be, with the assistance of the court's interpretation of it, what acts and omissions will make him liable".[481] The European Court of Human Rights has stated that the principle of legality allows courts to gradually clarify the rules of criminal liability through judicial interpretation from case to case, "provided that the resultant development is consistent with the essence of the offence and could reasonably be foreseen".[482] The Inter-American Court of Human Rights has also stressed that the principle of legality requires that crimes be classified and described in "precise and unambiguous language that narrowly defines the punishable offence".[483]

Rule 102. No one may be convicted of an offence except on the basis of individual criminal responsibility.

Practice

Volume II, Chapter 32, Section O.

---

[477] International Covenant on Civil and Political Rights, Article 15(1) (*ibid.*, § 3678); Convention on the Rights of the Child, Article 40(2)(a) (*ibid.*, § 3683); European Convention on Human Rights, Article 7(1) (*ibid.*, § 3677); American Convention on Human Rights, Article 9 (*ibid.*, § 3679); African Charter on Human and Peoples' Rights, Article 7(2) (*ibid.*, § 3682).

[478] International Covenant on Civil and Political Rights, Article 4 (*ibid.*, § 3678); European Convention on Human Rights, Article 15(2) (*ibid.*, § 3677); American Convention on Human Rights, Article 27 (*ibid.*, § 3679).

[479] International Covenant on Civil and Political Rights, Article 15(1) (*ibid.*, § 3678); American Convention on Human Rights, Article 9 (*ibid.*, § 3679).

[480] See, e.g., Universal Declaration on Human Rights, Article 11 (*ibid.*, § 3686); EU Charter of Fundamental Rights, Article 49 (*ibid.*, § 3691).

[481] European Court of Human Rights, *Kokkinakis v. Greece* (*ibid.*, § 3713).

[482] European Court of Human Rights, *S. W. v. UK* (*ibid.*, § 3714).

[483] Inter-American Court of Human Rights, *Castillo Petruzzi and Others case* (*ibid.*, § 3715).

Summary

State practice establishes this rule as a norm of customary international law applicable in both international and non-international armed conflicts.

International and non-international armed conflicts

The Hague Regulations specify that no penalty can be inflicted on persons for acts for which they are not responsible.[484] The Fourth Geneva Convention provides that "no protected person may be punished for an offence he or she has not personally committed".[485] The requirement of individual criminal responsibility is recognised as a fundamental rule of criminal procedure in Additional Protocols I and II.[486]

The requirement of individual criminal responsibility is explicitly provided for in several military manuals.[487] It is a basic rule of most, if not all, national legal systems.[488]

The requirement of individual criminal responsibility is included in the American Convention on Human Rights (as a non-derogable right), the African Charter on Human and Peoples' Rights and the Cairo Declaration on Human Rights in Islam.[489] The European Convention on Human Rights does not spell out this rule, but the European Court of Human Rights has stated that "it is a fundamental rule of criminal law that criminal liability does not survive the person who has committed the criminal act".[490]

Interpretation

It is a basic principle of criminal law that individual criminal responsibility for a crime includes attempting to commit such crime, as well as assisting in, facilitating, aiding or abetting, the commission of a crime. It also includes planning or instigating the commission of a crime. This is confirmed, for example, in the Statute of the International Criminal Court.[491] Article 28 of the Statute also confirms the principle of command responsibility for crimes under

---

[484] Hague Regulations, Article 50 (*ibid.*, § 3719).
[485] Fourth Geneva Convention, Article 33, first paragraph (*ibid.*, § 3722).
[486] Additional Protocol I, Article 75(4)(b) (adopted by consensus) (*ibid.*, § 3724); Additional Protocol II, Article 6(2)(b) (adopted by consensus) (*ibid.*, § 3726).
[487] See, e.g., the military manuals of Argentina (*ibid.*, § 3740), Canada (*ibid.*, § 3746), Colombia (*ibid.*, § 3747), France (*ibid.*, § 3752), Netherlands (*ibid.*, § 3761), New Zealand (*ibid.*, § 3762), Romania (*ibid.*, § 3764), Sweden (*ibid.*, § 3768), Switzerland (*ibid.*, § 3769) and United States (*ibid.*, §§ 3773–3774).
[488] See, e.g., the legislation of Kyrgyzstan (*ibid.*, § 3788).
[489] American Convention on Human Rights, Article 5(3) (*ibid.*, § 3723); African Charter on Human and Peoples' Rights, Article 7(2) (*ibid.*, § 3727); Cairo Declaration on Human Rights in Islam, Article 19(c) (*ibid.*, § 3732).
[490] European Court of Human Rights, *A. P., M. P. and T. P. v. Switzerland* (*ibid.*, § 3811).
[491] ICC Statute, Article 25 (cited in Vol. II, Ch. 43, § 20).

international law.[492] The principles of individual responsibility and command responsibility for war crimes are dealt with in Chapter 43.

Rule 103. Collective punishments are prohibited.

Practice

Volume II, Chapter 32, Section O.

Summary

State practice establishes this rule as a norm of customary international law applicable in both international and non-international armed conflicts. This prohibition is an application, in part, of Rule 102 that no one may be convicted of an offence except on the basis of individual criminal responsibility. However, the prohibition of collective punishments is wider in scope because it does not only apply to criminal sanctions but also to "sanctions and harassment of any sort, administrative, by police action or otherwise".[493]

International and non-international armed conflicts

The prohibition of collective punishments is stated in the Hague Regulations and the Third and Fourth Geneva Conventions.[494] The prohibition is recognised in Additional Protocols I and II as a fundamental guarantee for all civilians and persons *hors de combat*.[495]

The imposition of "collective penalties" was considered a war crime in the Report of the Commission on Responsibility set up after the First World War.[496] The customary nature of this rule, already applicable during the Second World War, was affirmed by the Military Tribunal of Rome in the *Priebke case* in 1997.[497] The specification that the imposition of collective punishments is a war crime is also to be found in the Statutes of the International Criminal Tribunal for Rwanda and of the Special Court for Sierra Leone.[498]

---

[492] ICC Statute, Article 28 (*ibid.*, § 574).
[493] Yves Sandoz, Christophe Swinarski, Bruno Zimmermann (eds.), *Commentary on the Additional Protocols*, ICRC, Geneva, 1987, § 3055, see also § 4536.
[494] Hague Regulations, Article 50 (cited in Vol. II, Ch. 32, § 3719); Third Geneva Convention, Article 87, third paragraph (*ibid.*, § 3721); Fourth Geneva Convention, Article 33, first paragraph (*ibid.*, § 3722).
[495] Additional Protocol I, Article 75(2)(d) (adopted by consensus) (*ibid.*, § 3724); Additional Protocol II, Article 4(2)(b) (adopted by consensus) (*ibid.*, § 3725).
[496] Report of the Commission on Responsibility (*ibid.*, § 3730).
[497] Italy, Military Tribunal of Rome, *Priebke case* (*ibid.*, § 3796).
[498] ICTR Statute, Article 4(b) (*ibid.*, § 3736); Statute of the Special Court for Sierra Leone, Article 3(b) (*ibid.*, § 3729).

The prohibition of collective punishments is contained in numerous military manuals.[499] This prohibition is also set forth in the legislation of many States.[500] It is further supported by official statements.[501]

In the *Delalić case*, the International Criminal Tribunal for the Former Yugoslavia stated that internment or assigned residence under Article 78 of the Fourth Geneva Convention is an exceptional measure that may never be taken on a collective basis.[502]

While human rights law does not explicitly prohibit "collective punishments" as such, such acts would constitute a violation of specific human rights, in particular the right to liberty and security of person and the right to a fair trial. In its General Comment on Article 4 of the International Covenant on Civil and Political Rights (concerning states of emergency), the UN Human Rights Committee stated that States parties may "in no circumstances" invoke a state of emergency "as justification for acting in violation of humanitarian law or peremptory norms of international law, for instance . . . by imposing collective punishments".[503]

Rule 104. The convictions and religious practices of civilians and persons *hors de combat* must be respected.

Practice

Volume II, Chapter 32, Section P.

Summary

State practice establishes this rule as a norm of customary international law applicable in both international and non-international armed conflicts. A specific application of this rule for persons deprived of their liberty is contained in

---

[499] See, e.g., the military manuals of Argentina (*ibid.*, §§ 3739–3740), Australia (*ibid.*, § 3741), Belgium (*ibid.*, § 3742), Benin (*ibid.*, § 3743), Burkina Faso (*ibid.*, § 3744), Cameroon (*ibid.*, § 3745), Canada (*ibid.*, § 3746), Congo (*ibid.*, § 3748), Ecuador (*ibid.*, § 3749), France (*ibid.*, §§ 3750 and 3752), Germany (*ibid.*, §§ 3753–3755), Israel (*ibid.*, § 3756), Italy (*ibid.*, § 3757), Mali (*ibid.*, § 3758), Morocco (*ibid.*, § 3760), Netherlands (*ibid.*, § 3761), New Zealand (*ibid.*, § 3762), Nicaragua (*ibid.*, § 3763), Romania (*ibid.*, § 3764), Russia (*ibid.*, § 3765), Senegal (*ibid.*, § 3766), Spain (*ibid.*, § 3767), Sweden (*ibid.*, § 3768), Switzerland (*ibid.*, § 3769), Togo (*ibid.*, § 3770), United Kingdom (*ibid.*, §§ 3771–3772), United States (*ibid.*, §§ 3773–3775) and Yugoslavia (*ibid.*, § 3776).

[500] See, e.g., the legislation of Australia (*ibid.*, § 3778), Bangladesh (*ibid.*, § 3779), Bosnia and Herzegovina (*ibid.*, § 3780), Democratic Republic of the Congo (*ibid.*, § 3782), Côte d'Ivoire (*ibid.*, § 3783), Croatia (*ibid.*, § 3784), Ethiopia (*ibid.*, § 3785), Ireland (*ibid.*, § 3786), Italy (*ibid.*, § 3787), Lithuania (*ibid.*, § 3789), Norway (*ibid.*, § 3790), Romania (*ibid.*, § 3791), Slovenia (*ibid.*, § 3792), Spain (*ibid.*, § 3793) and Yugoslavia (*ibid.*, § 3794); see also the draft legislation of Argentina (*ibid.*, § 3777).

[501] See, e.g., the statements of the United States (*ibid.*, §§ 3799–3800).

[502] ICTY, *Delalić case*, Judgement (*ibid.*, § 3809).

[503] UN Human Rights Committee, General Comment No. 29 (Article 4 of the International Covenant on Civil and Political Rights) (*ibid.*, § 3810).

Rule 127 on respect for the convictions and religious practices of persons deprived of their liberty.

International and non-international armed conflicts

The obligation to respect the religious convictions and practices of persons in occupied territory was already recognised in the Lieber Code, the Brussels Declaration and the Oxford Manual.[504] It was codified in the Hague Regulations.[505] This obligation is extended to all protected persons under the Fourth Geneva Convention.[506] The Geneva Conventions require respect for religion and religious practices in a series of detailed rules concerning burial rites and cremation of the dead, religious activities of prisoners of war and interned persons, and the education of orphaned children or children separated from their parents.[507] Respect for convictions and religious practices is recognised in Additional Protocols I and II as a fundamental guarantee for civilians and persons *hors de combat*.[508]

The requirement to respect a person's convictions and religious practices is set forth in numerous military manuals.[509] Violation of the right to respect for a person's convictions and religious practices, in particular forcible conversion to another faith, is a punishable offence under the legislation of several States.[510] This practice includes that of States not, or not at the time, party to

---

[504] Lieber Code, Article 37 (*ibid.*, § 3831); Brussels Declaration, Article 38 (*ibid.*, § 3832); Oxford Manual, Article 49 (*ibid.*, § 3833).

[505] Hague Regulations, Article 46 (*ibid.*, § 3819).

[506] Fourth Geneva Convention, Article 27, first paragraph (*ibid.*, § 3820), Article 38, third paragraph (*ibid.*, § 3821) and Article 58 (*ibid.*, § 3822).

[507] First Geneva Convention, Article 17, third paragraph (burial of the dead according to the rites of the religion to which they belong if possible); Third Geneva Convention, Articles 34–36 (religious activities of prisoners of war), Article 120, fourth paragraph (burial of prisoners of war deceased in captivity according to the rites of the religion to which they belonged if possible) and fifth paragraph (cremation of deceased prisoners of war on account of the religion of the deceased); Fourth Geneva Convention, Article 50, third paragraph (education of children who are orphaned or separated from their parents as a result of the war by persons of their own religion if possible), Article 76, third paragraph (spiritual assistance for persons detained in occupied territory), Article 86 (religious services for interned persons), Article 93 (religious activities of interned persons) and Article 130, first paragraph (burial of deceased internees according to the rites of the religion to which they belonged if possible) and second paragraph (cremation of deceased internees on account of the religion of the deceased).

[508] Additional Protocol I, Article 75(1) (adopted by consensus) (cited in Vol. II, Ch. 32, § 3826); Additional Protocol II, Article 4(1) (adopted by consensus) (*ibid.*, § 3827).

[509] See the military manuals of Argentina (*ibid.*, §§ 3841–3842), Australia (*ibid.*, § 3843), Canada (*ibid.*, §§ 3844–3845), Colombia (*ibid.*, §§ 3846–3847), Dominican Republic (*ibid.*, § 3848), Ecuador (*ibid.*, § 3849), France (*ibid.*, §§ 3850–3852), Germany (*ibid.*, § 3853), Hungary (*ibid.*, § 3854), Indonesia (*ibid.*, § 3855), Italy (*ibid.*, § 3856), Kenya (*ibid.*, § 3857), Madagascar (*ibid.*, § 3858), New Zealand (*ibid.*, § 3859), Nicaragua (*ibid.*, § 3860), Romania (*ibid.*, § 3861), Spain (*ibid.*, § 3862), Sweden (*ibid.*, § 3863), Switzerland (*ibid.*, § 3864), United Kingdom (*ibid.*, §§ 3865–3866) and United States (*ibid.*, §§ 3868–3870).

[510] See, e.g., the legislation of Bangladesh (*ibid.*, § 3872), Bosnia and Herzegovina (*ibid.*, § 3873), Croatia (*ibid.*, § 3874), Ethiopia (*ibid.*, § 3875), Ireland (*ibid.*, § 3876), Lithuania (*ibid.*, § 3877), Myanmar (*ibid.*, § 3878), Norway (*ibid.*, § 3879), Slovenia (*ibid.*, § 3880) and Yugoslavia (*ibid.*, §§ 3881–3882).

the Additional Protocols.[511] This rule was upheld in several war crimes trials after the Second World War. In the *Zühlke case*, the Special Court of Cassation of the Netherlands found that the refusal to admit a clergyman or priest to a person awaiting execution of the death sentence constituted a war crime.[512] In the *Tanaka Chuichi case*, the Australian Military Court at Rabaul found that forcing Sikh prisoners of war to cut their hair and beards and to smoke cigarettes, acts forbidden by their religion, amounted to a war crime.[513] It should also be noted that the Elements of Crimes for the International Criminal Court, in the context of the war crime of "outrages upon personal dignity", specifies that this crime takes into account relevant aspects of the cultural background of the victim.[514] This was inserted in order to include, as a war crime, forcing persons to act against their religious beliefs.[515]

The International Covenant on Civil and Political Rights, the Convention on the Rights of the Child and the regional human rights treaties provide that everyone has the right to freedom of "thought, conscience and religion" or, alternatively, "conscience and religion".[516] These treaties also provide for the right to manifest one's religion and beliefs, subject only to limitations prescribed by law which are necessary to protect public safety, order, health, morals or the rights and freedoms of others.[517] The above-mentioned rights are specifically listed as non-derogable in the International Covenant on Civil and Political Rights and the American Convention on Human Rights,[518] while the Convention on the Rights of the Child and the African Charter on Human and Peoples' Rights do not allow for the possibility of derogations. The right to freedom of thought, conscience and religion, to manifest one's religion or

---

[511] See, e.g., the military manuals of France (*ibid.*, § 3850), Indonesia (*ibid.*, § 3855), Kenya (*ibid.*, § 3857) and United Kingdom (*ibid.*, § 3866) and the legislation of Myanmar (*ibid.*, § 3878).

[512] Netherlands, Special Court of Cassation, *Zühlke case* (*ibid.*, § 3883).

[513] Australia, Military Court at Rabaul, *Tanaka Chuichi case* (*ibid.*, § 3884).

[514] See Elements of Crimes for the ICC, Definition of outrages upon personal dignity as a war crime (ICC Statute, Footnote 49 relating to Article 8(2)(b)(xxi) and Footnote 57 relating to Article 8(2)(c)(ii)).

[515] See Knut Dörmann, *Elements of War Crimes under the Rome Statute of the International Criminal Court: Sources and Commentary*, Cambridge University Press, 2003, Commentary on Article 8(2)(b)(xxii) of the ICC Statute, p. 315.

[516] International Covenant on Civil and Political Rights, Article 18(1) (cited in Vol. II, Ch. 32, § 3824); Convention on the Rights of the Child, Article 14(1) (*ibid.*, § 3829); European Convention on Human Rights, Article 9(1) (*ibid.*, § 3823); American Convention on Human Rights, Article 12(1) (*ibid.*, § 3825); African Charter on Human and Peoples' Rights, Article 8 (*ibid.*, § 3828).

[517] International Covenant on Civil and Political Rights, Article 18(3) (*ibid.*, § 3824); Convention on the Rights of the Child, Article 14(3) (*ibid.*, § 3829); European Convention on Human Rights, Article 9(2) (*ibid.*, § 3823); American Convention on Human Rights, Article 12(3) (*ibid.*, § 3825); African Charter on Human and Peoples' Rights, Article 8 (*ibid.*, § 3828).

[518] International Covenant on Civil and Political Rights, Article 4(2) (*ibid.*, § 3824); American Convention on Human Rights, Article 27(2) (*ibid.*, § 3825); see also UN Human Rights Committee, General Comment No. 22 (Article 18 of the International Covenant on Civil and Political Rights) (*ibid.*, § 3893); Inter-American Commission on Human Rights, Resolution concerning the law applicable to emergency situations (*ibid.*, § 3897).

beliefs and to change religion or belief is also set forth in other international instruments.[519]

Interpretation

The right to respect for religious or other personal convictions of persons is not subject to limitations, unlike their manifestation as explained further below. Humanitarian law treaties stress the requirement to respect the religion of protected persons. The International Covenant on Civil and Political Rights and the European and American Conventions on Human Rights specifically provide that the right to freedom of thought, conscience and religion includes the right of free choice of a religion or belief.[520] Subjecting a person to coercion which would impair this right is explicitly prohibited under the International Covenant on Civil and Political Rights and the American Convention on Human Rights.[521] In its General Comment on Article 18 of the International Covenant on Civil and Political Rights, the UN Human Rights Committee stated that the prohibition of coercion protects the right to change one's belief, to maintain the same belief or to adopt atheistic views. It added that policies or practices having the same intention or effect, such as, for example, those restricting access to medical care, education or employment, would violate this rule.[522] The same point was made by the European Court of Human Rights and by the African Commission on Human and Peoples' Rights, which also stressed the importance of respecting secular views.[523]

Any form of persecution, harassment or discrimination because of a person's convictions, religious or non-religious, would violate this rule. The Inter-American Commission on Human Rights, in its report on terrorism and human rights, stated that laws, methods of investigation and prosecution must not be purposefully designed or implemented in a way that distinguishes to their detriment members of a group based on, *inter alia*, their religion.[524]

The manifestation of personal convictions or the practice of one's religion must also be respected. This includes, for example, access to places of worship

---

[519] See, e.g., Universal Declaration on Human Rights, Article 18 (*ibid.*, § 3834); American Declaration on the Rights and Duties of Man, Article III (limited to freedom of religion) (*ibid.*, § 3835); Declaration on the Elimination of All Forms of Intolerance and of Discrimination based on Religion or Belief, Article 1 (*ibid.*, § 3836); EU Charter of Fundamental Rights, Article 10 (*ibid.*, § 3840).

[520] International Covenant on Civil and Political Rights, Article 18(1) (*ibid.*, § 3824); European Convention on Human Rights, Article 9(1) (freedom to change religion or belief) (*ibid.*, § 3823); American Convention on Human Rights, Article 12(1) (*ibid.*, § 3825).

[521] International Covenant on Civil and Political Rights, Article 18(2) (*ibid.*, § 3824); American Convention on Human Rights, Article 12(2) (*ibid.*, § 3825).

[522] UN Human Rights Committee, General Comment No. 22 (Article 18 of the International Covenant on Civil and Political Rights), 30 July 1993, § 5.

[523] European Court of Human Rights, *Kokkinakis v. Greece* (*ibid.*, § 3833); African Commission on Human and Peoples' Rights, *Association of Members of the Episcopal Conference of East Africa v. Sudan* (*ibid.*, § 3832).

[524] Inter-American Commission on Human Rights, Report on Terrorism and Human Rights, October 2002, § 363.

and access to religious personnel.[525] Limitations are only permitted if needed for order, security or the rights and freedoms of others. As stated in the commentary to Rule 127, the practice of detainees' religion may be subject to military regulations. However, the limitations on such practice may only be those that are reasonable and necessary in the specific context. In its General Comment on Article 18 of the International Covenant on Civil and Political Rights, the UN Human Rights Committee stated that limitations must be directly related and proportionate to the specific need, and that limitations applied for the protection of morals must not derive exclusively from a single tradition. It added that persons under legal constraints, such as prisoners, continue to enjoy their right to manifest their religion or belief "to the fullest extent compatible with the specific nature of the constraint".[526]

Rule 105. Family life must be respected as far as possible.

Practice

Volume II, Chapter 32, Section Q.

Summary

State practice establishes this rule as a norm of customary international law applicable in both international and non-international armed conflicts.

International and non-international armed conflicts

The obligation to respect the family rights of persons in occupied territory was already recognised in the Lieber Code, the Brussels Declaration and the Oxford Manual.[527] It was codified in the Hague Regulations.[528] This obligation is extended to all protected civilians in the Fourth Geneva Convention.[529] The Fourth Geneva also provides that, as far as possible, interned families must be given "facilities for leading a proper family life".[530] Although not articulated in these general terms in treaty rules relating to non-international armed conflicts, this rule is the basis of the more specific rules relating to family unity in treaty provisions governing such conflicts.[531]

---

[525] See, e.g., European Court of Human Rights, *Cyprus case* (cited in Vol. II, Ch. 32, § 3896); Netherlands, Special Court of Cassation, *Zühlke case* (*ibid.*, § 3883); ICRC Press release (*ibid.*, § 3900); see also practice referred to in the commentary to Rule 127.

[526] UN Human Rights Committee, General Comment No. 22 (Article 18 of the International Covenant on Civil and Political Rights), 30 July 1993, § 8.

[527] Lieber Code, Article 37 (cited in Vol. II, Ch. 32, § 3924); Brussels Declaration, Article 38 (*ibid.*, § 3925); Oxford Manual, Article 48 (*ibid.*, § 3926).

[528] Hague Regulations, Article 46 (*ibid.*, § 3906).

[529] Fourth Geneva Convention, Article 27, first paragraph (*ibid.*, § 3908).

[530] Fourth Geneva Convention, Article 82, third paragraph.

[531] See Additional Protocol II, Article 4(3)(b) (adopted by consensus) (reunion of families temporarily separated) (cited in Vol. II, Ch. 32, § 3916); Additional Protocol II, Article 5(2)(a) (adopted

Several military manuals refer in general terms to the duty to respect family rights, often without specific reference to the Fourth Geneva Convention.[532] There is also extensive practice in the form of post-conflict agreements and resolutions of the United Nations and other international organisations that stresses the need to respect family life.[533]

The protection of the family as the "natural and fundamental group unit of society" or, alternatively, "natural unit and basis of society" is provided for in the International Covenant on Civil and Political Rights, the International Covenant on Economic, Social and Cultural Rights and in the three regional human rights conventions.[534] Under the American Convention on Human Rights, the protection due to the family cannot be dispensed with.[535] Such protection is also required under other international instruments.[536]

Interpretation

Collected practice shows that respect for family life requires, to the degree possible, the maintenance of family unity, contact between family members and the provision of information on the whereabouts of family members.

(i) Maintenance of family unity. The duty to avoid, as far as possible, separation of members of a family is provided for in the Fourth Geneva Convention in the context of transfers or evacuations of civilians by an occupying power.[537] The commentary to Rule 131 on the treatment of displaced persons includes practice requiring respect for family unity in general terms not limited to displacement.

In addition, there is significant practice relating to the obligation to facilitate the reunion of dispersed families. The Fourth Geneva Convention provides that "each Party to the conflict shall facilitate enquiries made by members of families dispersed owing to the war, with the object of renewing contact with

by consensus) (accommodation of men and women of the same family in detention or internment) (cited in Vol. II, Ch. 37, § 106); Convention on the Rights of the Child, Article 37(c) (accommodation of children with their parents during deprivation of liberty) (*ibid.*, § 149).

[532] See, e.g., the military manuals of Australia (cited in Vol. II, Ch. 32, § 3936), Canada (*ibid.*, § 3937), Dominican Republic (*ibid.*, § 3938), El Salvador (*ibid.*, § 3939), Germany (*ibid.*, § 3940), Kenya (*ibid.*, § 3942), Nicaragua (*ibid.*, § 3944), Spain (*ibid.*, § 3946) and United Kingdom (*ibid.*, § 3949).

[533] See commentary below and also the practice referred to in the commentaries to Rules 117, 119–120, 125–126 and 131.

[534] International Covenant on Civil and Political Rights, Article 23(1) (*ibid.*, § 3911); International Covenant on Economic, Social and Cultural Rights, Article 10(1) (*ibid.*, § 3912); American Convention on Human Rights, Article 17(1) (*ibid.*, § 3914); Protocol of San Salvador, Article 15(1) (*ibid.*, § 3918); African Charter on Human and Peoples' Rights, Article 18 (*ibid.*, § 3917); see also UNHCR, Executive Committee, Conclusion No. 84 (XLVIII): Refugee Children and Adolescents (*ibid.*, § 3969).

[535] American Convention on Human Rights, Article 17 (*ibid.*, § 3914) and Article 27(2).

[536] See, e.g., Universal Declaration on Human Rights, Article 16(3) (cited in Vol. II, Ch. 32, § 3928); American Declaration on the Rights and Duties of Man, Article VI (*ibid.*, § 3930); Cairo Declaration on Human Rights in Islam, Article 5(b) (*ibid.*, § 3931).

[537] Fourth Geneva Convention, Article 49, third paragraph (cited in Vol. II, Ch. 38, § 541).

one another and of meeting, if possible".[538] Additional Protocols I and II provide
that parties to a conflict must facilitate the reunion of families dispersed as
a result of armed conflict.[539] This obligation is set forth in several military
manuals and in the legislation of several States.[540] It is supported by official
statements, including a statement of the United States which is not party to the
Additional Protocols.[541] A number of agreements, laws and policies have been
adopted by States involved in armed conflict and facing the problem of dispersed
families, which seek to implement the principle of family reunification.[542] The
obligation to facilitate the reunification of dispersed families is also supported
by several resolutions adopted by consensus by International Conferences of
the Red Cross and Red Crescent.[543] The importance of family reunification
in human rights law, in particular in relation to reuniting children with their
parents, is reflected in treaties and other international instruments, case-law
and resolutions.[544]

There is also practice relating to the maintenance of family unity during
deprivation of liberty. The Fourth Geneva Convention requires that "whenever
possible, interned members of the same family shall be housed together in the
same premises and given separate accommodation from other internees".[545]
Further practice is referred to in the commentaries to Rules 119 and 120, which
require that members of the same family be accommodated together during
deprivation of liberty.

(ii) Contact between family members. The Fourth Geneva Convention provides that "all persons in the territory of a Party to the conflict, or in territory occupied by it, shall be enabled to give news of a strictly personal
nature to members of their families, wherever they may be, and to receive

---

[538] Fourth Geneva Convention, Article 26 (cited in Vol. II, Ch. 32, § 3907).
[539] Additional Protocol I, Article 74 (adopted by consensus) ("in every possible way") (*ibid.*, § 3915);
Additional Protocol II, Article 4(3)(b) (adopted by consensus) ("all appropriate steps") (*ibid.*,
§ 3916).
[540] See, e.g., the military manuals of Argentina (*ibid.*, §§ 3934–3935), New Zealand (*ibid.*, § 3943),
Spain (*ibid.*, § 3946) and United States (*ibid.*, § 3953) and the legislation of Angola (*ibid.*,
§ 3954), Colombia (*ibid.*, § 3956) and Philippines (*ibid.*, § 3960).
[541] See, e.g., the statements of South Korea (*ibid.*, § 3962) and United States (*ibid.*, § 3963).
[542] See, e.g., the Quadripartite Agreement on Georgian Refugees and Internally Displaced Persons
(*ibid.*, § 3923), the legislation of Angola (*ibid.*, § 3954), Colombia (*ibid.*, § 3956) and Philippines
(*ibid.*, § 3960) and the practice of South Korea (*ibid.*, § 3962).
[543] 19th International Conference of the Red Cross, Res. XX; 25th International Conference of the
Red Cross, Res. IX (*ibid.*, § 3971); 26th International Conference of the Red Cross and Red
Crescent, Res. II (*ibid.*, § 3972).
[544] See, e.g., Convention on the Rights of the Child, Article 10 (*ibid.*, § 3920) and Article 22(2)
(*ibid.*, § 3922); Guiding Principles on Internal Displacement, Principle 17(3) (*ibid.*, § 3932); UN
General Assembly, Res. 51/77 (*ibid.*, § 3965), Res. 52/107 (*ibid.*, § 3965) and Res. 53/128 (*ibid.*,
§ 3965); UN Commission on Human Rights, Res. 1997/78 (*ibid.*, § 3966) and Res. 1998/76 (*ibid.*,
§ 3966); UNHCR Executive Committee, Conclusion No. 24 (XXXII) (*ibid.*, § 3968); Committee
on the Rights of the Child, Concluding observations on the report of Myanmar (*ibid.*, § 3974);
European Court of Human Rights, *Eriksson case, Andersson v. Sweden, Rieme v. Sweden,
Olsson v. Sweden, Hokkanen v. Finland* and *Gül v. Switzerland* (*ibid.*, § 3975).
[545] Fourth Geneva Convention, Article 82, third paragraph.

news from them".[546] Rule 125 requires that persons deprived of their liberty be allowed to correspond with their families, subject to reasonable conditions relating to frequency and the need for censorship by authorities. Rule 126 requires that persons deprived of their liberty must be allowed to receive visitors to the degree practicable. In addition to the practice cited in the commentaries to Rules 125 and 126, human rights case-law confirms that the right to family life includes the right of detainees to communicate with their families through correspondence and receiving visits, subject to reasonable restrictions concerning timing and censorship of mail.[547]

(iii) Provision of information on the whereabouts of family members. There is extensive practice on the measures to be taken by authorities to account for missing persons and on the duty to inform families of the whereabouts of persons when such information is available. Deliberately withholding such information has been found to amount to inhuman treatment in human rights case-law. This practice is to be found in the commentary to Rule 117 which provides that each party to a conflict must take all feasible measures to account for persons reported missing as a result of armed conflict and to provide their family members with any information it has on their fate.

In addition, the International Covenant on Civil and Political Rights, the Convention on the Rights of the Child and the American Convention on Human Rights guarantee the right to be free from arbitrary, unlawful or abusive interference with one's family life.[548] This is also provided for in other international instruments.[549] The European Convention on Human Rights, meanwhile, contains a general right to respect for "private and family life" which may not be interfered with by a public authority

except such as is in accordance with the law and is necessary in a democratic society in the interests of national security, public safety or the economic well-being of the country, for the prevention of disorder or crime, for the protection of health or morals, or for the protection of the rights and freedoms of others.[550]

---

[546] Fourth Geneva Convention, Article 25, first paragraph (cited in Vol. II, Ch. 37, § 468).

[547] See, e.g., African Commission on Human and Peoples' Rights, *Constitutional Rights Project and Civil Liberties Organisation v. Nigeria*, Communication Nos. 143/95 and 150/96, 15 November 1999, § 29; Inter-American Commission on Human Rights, Report on the situation of human rights in Peru, 12 March 1993, p. 29; European Court of Human Rights, *Branningan and McBride v. UK*, Judgement, 26 May 1993, § 64.

[548] International Covenant on Civil and Political Rights, Article 17(1) ("arbitrary or unlawful interference") (cited in Vol. II, Ch. 32, § 3910); Convention on the Rights of the Child, Article 16(1) ("arbitrary or unlawful interference") (*ibid.*, § 3921); American Convention on Human Rights, Article 11 ("arbitrary or abusive interference") (*ibid.*, § 3913).

[549] See, e.g., Universal Declaration on Human Rights, Article 12 ("arbitrary interference") (*ibid.*, § 3927); American Declaration on the Rights and Duties of Man, Article V ("abusive attacks") (*ibid.*, § 3929); EU Charter of Fundamental Rights, Article 7 ("respect for his or her private and family life") (*ibid.*, § 3933).

[550] European Convention on Human Rights, Article 8(2) (*ibid.*, § 3909).

The UN Human Rights Committee's General Comment on Article 17 of the International Covenant on Civil and Political Rights states that interference with family life will be "arbitrary" if the interference is not in accordance with the provisions, aims and objectives of the Covenant and if it is not "reasonable in the particular circumstances".[551]

Definition of the term "family"

In its General Comment on Article 17 of the International Covenant on Civil and Political Rights, the UN Human Rights Committee stated that, for the purposes of the Article, the term family should be interpreted as including "all those comprising the family as understood in the society of the State party concerned".[552] The European Court of Human Rights includes the relationship between husband and wife and the children dependent on them within the notion of family.[553] It has also, depending on the circumstances and in particular when children are involved, included brothers and sisters, persons living together outside marriage and grandparents.[554]

---

[551] UN Human Rights Committee, General Comment No. 16 (Article 17 of the International Covenant on Civil and Political Rights) (*ibid.*, § 3973); see also Inter-American Commission on Human Rights, Report on Terrorism and Human Rights, Doc. OEA/Ser.L/V/I.116, Doc. 5 rev. 1 corr., 22 October 2002, § 55.

[552] UN Human Rights Committee, General Comment No. 16 (Article 17 of the International Covenant on Civil and Political Rights) (cited in Vol. II, Ch. 32, § 3973).

[553] European Court of Human Rights, *B. v. UK* (*ibid.*, § 3977) (the Court stated that "the mutual enjoyment by parent and child of each other's company constitutes a fundamental element of family life").

[554] European Court of Human Rights, *Johnston and Others v. Ireland* (*ibid.*, § 3976), *Moustaquim v. Belgium*, (*ibid.*, § 3978) and *Vermeire v. Belgium* (*ibid.*, § 3979).

CHAPTER 33

COMBATANTS AND PRISONER-OF-WAR STATUS

Note: *The implications of being recognised as a combatant in an international armed conflict are significant, as only combatants have the right to participate directly in hostilities (for a definition of combatants, see Rule 3). Upon capture, combatants entitled to prisoner-of-war status may neither be tried for their participation in the hostilities nor for acts that do not violate international humanitarian law. This is a long-standing rule of customary international humanitarian law. Treatment due to prisoners of war is spelled out in detail in the Third Geneva Convention.*

Rule 106. Combatants must distinguish themselves from the civilian population while they are engaged in an attack or in a military operation preparatory to an attack. If they fail to do so, they do not have the right to prisoner-of-war status.

Practice

Volume II, Chapter 33, Section A.

Summary

State practice establishes this rule as a norm of customary international law applicable in international armed conflicts.

International armed conflicts

The requirement that combatants distinguish themselves from the civilian population is a long-standing rule of customary international law already recognised in the Brussels Declaration, the Oxford Manual and the Hague Regulations.[1] It was subsequently codified in the Third Geneva Convention and Additional Protocol I.[2]

---

[1] Brussels Declaration, Article 9 (cited in Vol. II, Ch. 1, § 634); Oxford Manual, Article 2 (*ibid.*, § 635); Hague Regulations, Article 1 (*ibid.*, § 627).

[2] Third Geneva Convention, Article 4(A) (*ibid.*, § 629); Additional Protocol I, Article 44(3) (cited in Vol. II, Ch. 33, § 1).

Numerous military manuals specify that combatants must distinguish themselves from the civilian population.[3] This includes the manuals of States not, or not at the time, party to Additional Protocol I.[4] This obligation is also supported by a number of official statements and other practice.[5]

The Hague Regulations and the Third Geneva Convention state that members of regular armed forces are entitled to prisoner-of-war status, whereas members of militias and volunteer corps are required to comply with four conditions in order to benefit from such status.[6] Additional Protocol I imposes the obligation to distinguish oneself from the civilian population on all members of armed forces, whether regular or irregular.[7] Although it is not specifically stated in the Hague Regulations or the Third Geneva Convention, it is clear that regular armed forces have to distinguish themselves from the civilian population during a military operation. Additional Protocol I recognises "the generally accepted practice of States with respect to the wearing of the uniform by combatants assigned to the regular, uniformed armed units of a Party to the conflict",[8] although the Protocol, like the Hague Regulations and the Third Geneva Convention, does not explicitly make this a condition for prisoner-of-war status.

Several military manuals remark that the obligation to distinguish oneself does not pose a problem for the regular armed forces because it is "customary" or "usual" for members of the regular armed forces to wear a uniform as a distinctive sign.[9]

If members of regular armed forces do not wear a uniform, they risk being charged as spies or saboteurs.[10] In the *Swarka case* in 1974, an Israeli Military Court found that members of the Egyptian armed forces who had infiltrated Israeli territory and launched an attack in civilian attire were not entitled to prisoner-of-war status and could be prosecuted as saboteurs. The Court considered that it would have been illogical to regard the duty to distinguish oneself

---

[3] See, e.g., the military manuals of Argentina (*ibid.*, § 5), Australia (*ibid.*, § 6), Belgium (*ibid.*, § 7), Benin (*ibid.*, § 8), Cameroon (*ibid.*, § 9), Canada (*ibid.*, § 10), Colombia (*ibid.*, § 11), Croatia (*ibid.*, §§ 12–13), France (*ibid.*, § 15), Germany (*ibid.*, § 16), Hungary (*ibid.*, § 17), Israel (*ibid.*, § 18), Italy (*ibid.*, §§ 19–20), Kenya (*ibid.*, § 21), Madagascar (*ibid.*, § 22), Netherlands (*ibid.*, § 23), New Zealand (*ibid.*, § 24), South Africa (*ibid.*, § 25), Sweden (*ibid.*, § 26), Switzerland (*ibid.*, § 27), Togo (*ibid.*, § 28), United Kingdom (*ibid.*, § 29) and United States (*ibid.*, §§ 30–31).

[4] See, e.g., the military manuals of France (*ibid.*, § 15), Israel (*ibid.*, § 18), Kenya (*ibid.*, § 21), United Kingdom (*ibid.*, § 29) and United States (*ibid.*, §§ 30–31).

[5] See, e.g., the statements of the Federal Republic of Germany (*ibid.*, § 37), Italy (*ibid.*, § 39), Netherlands (*ibid.*, § 40) and United States (*ibid.*, §§ 41–43) and the practice of Botswana (*ibid.*, § 36) and Indonesia (*ibid.*, § 38).

[6] Hague Regulations, Articles 1 and 3; Third Geneva Convention, Article 4(A) (cited in Vol. II, Ch. 1, § 629).

[7] Additional Protocol I, Article 44(3) (cited in Vol. II, Ch. 33, § 1).

[8] Additional Protocol I, Article 44(7) (*ibid.*, § 1).

[9] See the military manuals of Australia (*ibid.*, § 6), Belgium (*ibid.*, § 7), Colombia (*ibid.*, § 11), Germany (*ibid.*, § 16), Kenya (*ibid.*, § 21), Madagascar (*ibid.*, § 22), Netherlands (*ibid.*, § 23), New Zealand (*ibid.*, § 24), South Africa (*ibid.*, § 25), Sweden (*ibid.*, § 26), Switzerland (*ibid.*, § 27) and United Kingdom (*ibid.*, § 29).

[10] See, e.g., United Kingdom, *Military Manual* (1958), §§ 96 and 331.

as applicable to irregular armed forces but not to regular armed forces, as the defendants had claimed.[11]

Interpretation

State practice indicates that in order to distinguish themselves from the civilian population, combatants are expected to wear a uniform or a distinctive sign and must carry arms openly. Germany's Military Manual states, for example, that:

In accordance with the generally agreed practice of States, members of regular armed forces shall wear their uniform. Combatants who are not members of uniformed armed forces nevertheless wear a permanent distinctive sign visible from a distance and carry their arms openly.[12]

The US Air Force Pamphlet states that a uniform ensures that combatants are clearly distinguishable but that "less than a complete uniform will suffice provided it serves to distinguish clearly combatants from civilians".[13] In the *Kassem case* in 1969, the Israeli Military Court at Ramallah held that the defendants sufficiently fulfilled the requirement of distinguishing themselves by wearing mottled caps and green clothes, as this was not the usual attire of the inhabitants of the area in which they were captured.[14]

With respect to carrying arms openly, the US Air Force Pamphlet states that this requirement is not fulfilled "by carrying arms concealed about the person or if the individuals hide their weapons on the approach of the enemy".[15] In the *Kassem case*, the Court held that the condition of carrying arms openly was neither fulfilled in a case where the person carried the arms openly in places where they could not be seen nor by the mere fact of bearing the arms during a hostile engagement. The fact that the defendants used their weapons during the encounter with the Israeli army was not determinative, since no weapons were known to be in their possession until they started firing at Israeli soldiers.[16]

Levée en masse

Participants in a *levée en masse*, namely the inhabitants of a country which has not yet been occupied who, on the approach of the enemy, spontaneously take up arms to resist the invading troops without having time to form themselves

---

[11] Israel, Military Court, *Swarka case* (cited in Vol. II, Ch. 33, § 35).
[12] Germany, *Military Manual* (ibid., § 16).
[13] United States, *Air Force Pamphlet* (ibid., § 30).
[14] Israel, Military Court at Ramallah, *Kassem case* (ibid., § 34).
[15] United States, *Air Force Pamphlet* (ibid., § 30).
[16] Israel, Military Court at Ramallah, *Kassem case* (ibid., § 113).

into an armed force, are considered combatants entitled to prisoner-of-war status if they carry arms openly and respect international humanitarian law. This is a long-standing rule of customary international law already recognised in the Lieber Code, the Brussels Declaration and the Hague Regulations.[17] It is also set forth in the Third Geneva Convention.[18]

While this exception may be considered of limited current application, it is still repeated in many military manuals, including very recent ones, and it therefore continues to be regarded as a valid possibility.[19]

Resistance and liberation movements

According to Additional Protocol I, in situations of armed conflict where "owing to the nature of the hostilities an armed combatant cannot... distinguish himself" from the civilian population while he is engaged in an attack or in a military operation preparatory to an attack, he shall retain his status as a combatant, provided he carries his arms openly:

(a) during each military engagement, and
(b) during such time as he is visible to the adversary while he is engaged in a military deployment preceding the launching of an attack in which he is to participate.[20]

This rule was subject to much debate at the Diplomatic Conference leading to the adoption of the Additional Protocols, and Article 44 was, as a result, accepted by 73 votes in favour, one against and 21 abstentions.[21] The abstaining States generally expressed concern that this provision might have a negative impact on the civilian population. The United Kingdom, for example, stated that "any failure to distinguish between combatants and civilians could only put the latter at risk. That risk might well become unacceptable unless a satisfactory interpretation could be given to certain provisions."[22] All but two

---

[17] Lieber Code, Article 51 (*ibid.*, § 52); Brussels Declaration, Article 10 (*ibid.*, § 53); Hague Regulations, Article 2 (*ibid.*, § 50).

[18] Third Geneva Convention, Article 4(A)(6) (*ibid.*, § 51).

[19] See, e.g., the military manuals of Argentina (*ibid.*, § 55), Australia (*ibid.*, § 56), Belgium (*ibid.*, § 57), Cameroon (*ibid.*, § 58), Canada (*ibid.*, § 59), Germany (*ibid.*, § 60), Italy (*ibid.*, § 61), Kenya (*ibid.*, § 62), Madagascar (*ibid.*, § 63), Netherlands (*ibid.*, § 64), New Zealand (*ibid.*, § 65), Nigeria (*ibid.*, § 66), Russia (*ibid.*, § 67), South Africa (*ibid.*, § 68), Spain (*ibid.*, § 69), Switzerland (*ibid.*, § 70), United Kingdom (*ibid.*, § 71), United States (*ibid.*, § 72) and Yugoslavia (*ibid.*, § 73).

[20] Additional Protocol I, Article 44(3) (*ibid.*, § 81).

[21] See the practice of the Diplomatic Conference leading to the adoption of the Additional Protocols (*ibid.*, § 81).

[22] United Kingdom, Statement at the Diplomatic Conference leading to the adoption of the Additional Protocols (*ibid.*, § 133); see also the statements of Argentina (*ibid.*, § 114), Brazil (*ibid.*, § 115), Canada (*ibid.*, § 116), Colombia (*ibid.*, § 117), Ireland (*ibid.*, § 123), Italy (*ibid.*, § 126), Japan (*ibid.*, § 127), Portugal (*ibid.*, § 129), Spain (*ibid.*, § 130), Switzerland (*ibid.*, § 131) and Uruguay (*ibid.*, § 134). Canada and Italy abstained in the vote and stated that the text might be acceptable if its terms could be better defined.

of the abstaining States have in the meantime ratified Additional Protocol I without any reservation in this respect.[23]

In line with the need to arrive at a satisfactory interpretation, many States have tried to clarify the meaning of this exception and to clearly set out its limits. These limits are threefold. First, many States have indicated that the exception is limited to situations where armed resistance movements are organised, namely in occupied territories or in wars of national liberation.[24] Secondly, many States have indicated that the term "deployment" refers to any movement towards a place from which an attack is to be launched.[25] Thirdly, Australia, Belgium and New Zealand have further indicated that the term "visible" includes being visible with the aid of technical means and not just visible with the naked eye.[26] Egypt, supported by the United Arab Emirates, however, stated at the Diplomatic Conference leading to the adoption of the Additional Protocols that the term military deployment meant "the last step when the combatants were taking their firing positions just before the commencement of hostilities; a guerrilla should carry his arms openly only when within range of the natural vision of his adversary".[27] The United States, which voted in favour of Article 44 of Additional Protocol I at the Diplomatic Conference, explained that the exception was clearly designed:

to ensure that combatants, while engaged in military operations preparatory to an attack, could not use their failure to distinguish themselves from civilians as an element of surprise in the attack. Combatants using their appearance as civilians in such circumstances in order to aid in the attack would forfeit their status as combatants.[28]

---

[23] The Philippines and Thailand abstained in the vote and have not yet ratified Additional Protocol I.

[24] See the statements made at the Diplomatic Conference leading to the adoption of the Additional Protocols by Canada (*ibid.*, § 116), Egypt (*ibid.*, § 118), Germany (*ibid.*, § 119), Greece (*ibid.*, § 121), Iran (*ibid.*, § 122), Italy (*ibid.*, § 126), Japan (*ibid.*, § 127), United Kingdom (*ibid.*, § 133) and United States (*ibid.*, § 135) and the statements made upon ratification/signature of Additional Protocol I by Australia (*ibid.*, § 83), Belgium (*ibid.*, § 83), Canada (*ibid.*, § 83), France (*ibid.*, § 83), Germany (*ibid.*, § 83), Ireland (*ibid.*, § 83), Italy (*ibid.*, § 84), South Korea (*ibid.*, § 83), Spain (*ibid.*, § 84) and United Kingdom (*ibid.*, § 83); the military manuals of Belgium (*ibid.*, § 102), France (*ibid.*, § 93), Germany (*ibid.*, § 103), Italy (*ibid.*, § 104), Netherlands (*ibid.*, § 106), New Zealand (*ibid.*, § 107), Spain (*ibid.*, § 97), Sweden (*ibid.*, § 109) and United Kingdom (*ibid.*, § 110).

[25] See the statements made at the Diplomatic Conference leading to the adoption of the Additional Protocols by Canada (*ibid.*, § 116), Germany (*ibid.*, § 119), Japan (*ibid.*, § 127), Netherlands (*ibid.*, § 128), United Kingdom (*ibid.*, § 133) and United States (*ibid.*, § 135), the statements made upon ratification/signature of Additional Protocol I by Australia (*ibid.*, § 85), Belgium (*ibid.*, § 85), Canada (*ibid.*, § 85), France (*ibid.*, § 85), Germany (*ibid.*, § 85), Ireland (*ibid.*, § 85), Italy (*ibid.*, § 85), South Korea (*ibid.*, § 85), Netherlands (*ibid.*, § 85), New Zealand (*ibid.*, § 85), Spain (*ibid.*, § 85), United Kingdom (*ibid.*, § 85) and United States (*ibid.*, § 85) and the military manuals of Belgium (*ibid.*, § 102), Germany (*ibid.*, § 103), Italy (*ibid.*, § 104), Kenya (*ibid.*, § 105), Netherlands (*ibid.*, § 106), New Zealand (*ibid.*, § 107), South Africa (*ibid.*, § 108), Spain (*ibid.*, § 97) and United Kingdom (*ibid.*, § 110).

[26] See the statements made upon ratification of Additional Protocol I by Australia (*ibid.*, § 86) and New Zealand (*ibid.*, § 87) and the military manuals of Belgium (*ibid.*, § 102) and New Zealand (*ibid.*, § 107).

[27] Egypt, Statement at the Diplomatic Conference leading to the adoption of the Additional Protocols (*ibid.*, § 118); see also the statement of the United Arab Emirates (*ibid.*, § 132).

[28] United States, Statement at the Diplomatic Conference leading to the adoption of the Additional Protocols (*ibid.*, § 135).

In the meantime, the United States has changed its position and voiced its opposition to this rule.[29] Israel voted against Article 44 of Additional Protocol I because paragraph 3 "could be interpreted as allowing the combatant not to distinguish himself from the civilian population, which would expose the latter to serious risks and was contrary to the spirit and to a fundamental principle of humanitarian law".[30]

As stated in Additional Protocol I, combatants who fail to distinguish themselves and are not, as a result, entitled to prisoner-of-war status (and who do not benefit from more favourable treatment in accordance with the Fourth Geneva Convention) are, as a minimum, entitled to the fundamental guarantees set out in Chapter 32, including the right to a fair trial (see Rule 100).[31]

Rule 107. Combatants who are captured while engaged in espionage do not have the right to prisoner-of-war status. They may not be convicted or sentenced without previous trial.

Practice

Volume II, Chapter 33, Section B.

Summary

State practice establishes this rule as a norm of customary international law applicable in international armed conflicts.

International armed conflicts

The rule that combatants engaged in espionage have no right to prisoner-of-war status and may be tried is a long-standing rule of customary international law already recognised in the Lieber Code, the Brussels Declaration and the Hague Regulations.[32] It is also set forth in Additional Protocol I.[33]

Numerous military manuals specify that combatants engaged in espionage have no right to prisoner-of-war status and that they may be regarded as spies.[34]

No official contrary practice was found.

---

[29] See the statements of the United States (*ibid.*, §§ 136–137).
[30] Israel, Statement at the Diplomatic Conference leading to the adoption of the Additional Protocols (*ibid.*, § 124).
[31] Additional Protocol I, Article 45(3) (adopted by consensus) (*ibid.*, § 82).
[32] Lieber Code, Article 88 (*ibid.*, § 181); Brussels Declaration, Articles 20–21 (*ibid.*, § 182); Hague Regulations, Articles 30–31 (*ibid.*, § 178).
[33] Additional Protocol I, Article 46(1) (adopted by consensus) (*ibid.*, § 179).
[34] See, e.g., the military manuals of Argentina (*ibid.*, § 186), Australia (*ibid.*, § 187), Belgium (*ibid.*, § 188), Cameroon (*ibid.*, §§ 189–190), Canada (*ibid.*, § 191), Croatia (*ibid.*, §§ 192–193), Ecuador (*ibid.*, § 194), France (*ibid.*, §§ 195–196), Germany (*ibid.*, § 197), Hungary (*ibid.*, § 198), Israel (*ibid.*, § 199), Italy (*ibid.*, § 200), Kenya (*ibid.*, § 201), Madagascar (*ibid.*, § 202), Netherlands (*ibid.*, § 203), New Zealand (*ibid.*, § 204), Nigeria (*ibid.*, §§ 205–206), South Africa (*ibid.*, § 207), Spain (*ibid.*, § 208), Sweden (*ibid.*, § 209), Switzerland (*ibid.*, § 210), United Kingdom (*ibid.*, §§ 211–212), United States (*ibid.*, § 213) and Yugoslavia (*ibid.*, § 214).

Definition of spies

It is also long-standing practice already recognised in the Lieber Code, the Brussels Declaration and the Hague Regulations that espionage is defined as gathering or attempting to gather information in territory controlled by an adverse party through an act undertaken on false pretences or deliberately in a clandestine manner.[35] The definition includes combatants who wear civilian attire or who wear the uniform of the adversary but excludes combatants who are gathering information while wearing their own uniform. This definition is now codified in Additional Protocol I.[36] It is set forth in numerous military manuals.[37]

In addition, this rule applies only to a spy captured in the act whilst in enemy-controlled territory. The Brussels Declaration and the Hague Regulations recognise that a spy who rejoins his or her armed forces and who is subsequently captured must be treated as a prisoner of war and incurs no responsibility for previous acts of espionage.[38] This rule is also set forth in Additional Protocol I.[39] It is recognised in a number of military manuals.[40]

Right to fair trial

A spy taken in the act may not be punished without previous trial. This requirement was already recognised in the Brussels Declaration and the Hague Regulations.[41] It is also set forth in a number of military manuals.[42] Captured spies are entitled to the fundamental guarantees set out in Chapter 32, including the right to a fair trial (see Rule 100). This is emphasised in the military manuals of Canada, Germany, New Zealand and Nigeria.[43] It is also laid down in Additional Protocol I, which states that anyone who is not entitled to

---

[35] Lieber Code, Article 88 (*ibid.*, § 145); Brussels Declaration, Article 19 (*ibid.*, § 146); Hague Regulations, Article 29 (*ibid.*, § 143).

[36] Additional Protocol I, Article 46(2) (adopted by consensus) (*ibid.*, § 144).

[37] See, e.g., the military manuals of Argentina (*ibid.*, § 149), Australia (*ibid.*, §§ 150–151), Belgium (*ibid.*, § 152), Cameroon (*ibid.*, § 153), Canada (*ibid.*, § 154), Ecuador (*ibid.*, § 155), France (*ibid.*, § 156), Germany (*ibid.*, § 157), Kenya (*ibid.*, § 158), Netherlands (*ibid.*, § 159), New Zealand (*ibid.*, § 160), Nigeria (*ibid.*, § 161), South Africa (*ibid.*, § 162), Spain (*ibid.*, § 163), Switzerland (*ibid.*, § 164), United Kingdom (*ibid.*, § 165), United States (*ibid.*, § 166) and Yugoslavia (*ibid.*, § 167).

[38] Brussels Declaration, Article 21 (*ibid.*, § 182); Hague Regulations, Article 31 (*ibid.*, § 178).

[39] Additional Protocol I, Article 46(4) (adopted by consensus).

[40] See, e.g., the military manuals of Argentina (cited in Vol. II, Ch. 33, § 186), Canada (*ibid.*, § 191), Ecuador (*ibid.*, § 194), Israel (*ibid.*, § 199), Kenya (*ibid.*, § 201), Netherlands (*ibid.*, § 203), New Zealand (*ibid.*, § 204), Nigeria (*ibid.*, § 206), United Kingdom (*ibid.*, § 212), United States (*ibid.*, § 213) and Yugoslavia (*ibid.*, § 214).

[41] Brussels Declaration, Article 20 (*ibid.*, § 182); Hague Regulations, Article 30 (*ibid.*, § 178).

[42] See, e.g., the military manuals of Argentina (*ibid.*, § 186), Belgium (*ibid.*, § 188), Canada (*ibid.*, § 191), Germany (*ibid.*, § 197), Kenya (*ibid.*, § 201), Netherlands (*ibid.*, § 203), New Zealand (*ibid.*, § 204), Nigeria (*ibid.*, § 206), Switzerland (*ibid.*, § 210), United Kingdom (*ibid.*, §§ 211–212), United States (*ibid.*, § 213) and Yugoslavia (*ibid.*, § 214).

[43] See Canada, *LOAC Manual* (*ibid.*, § 191); Germany, *Military Manual* (*ibid.*, § 197), New Zealand, *Military Manual* (*ibid.*, § 204) and Nigeria, *Manual on the Laws of War* (*ibid.*, § 206).

prisoner-of-war status, and does not benefit from more favourable treatment in accordance with the Fourth Geneva Convention, still enjoys the fundamental guarantees of Article 75 contained in Additional Protocol I.[44] Consequently, the summary execution of spies is prohibited.

Rule 108. Mercenaries, as defined in Additional Protocol I, do not have the right to combatant or prisoner-of-war status. They may not be convicted or sentenced without previous trial.

Practice

Volume II, Chapter 33, Section C.

Summary

State practice establishes this rule as a norm of customary international law applicable in international armed conflicts.

International armed conflicts

The rule that mercenaries do not have the right to combatant or prisoner-of-war status is set forth in Additional Protocol I.[45] It is also contained in a few other treaties.[46]

Numerous military manuals specify that mercenaries are not entitled to combatant or prisoner-of-war status.[47] A manual used for instruction in the Israeli army states that this rule is part of customary international law.[48] The participation of a mercenary in an armed conflict is punishable under the legislation of a number of States.[49] This rule is also supported by official statements and reported practice.[50] This practice includes that of States not, or not at the time,

---

[44] Additional Protocol, Article 45(3) (adopted by consensus) (*ibid.*, § 180).

[45] Additional Protocol I, Article 47(1) (adopted by consensus) (*ibid.*, § 270).

[46] OAU Convention against Mercenarism, Article 3 (*ibid.*, § 274) (the Convention is ratified by 24 of the 53 member States); UN Mercenary Convention, Articles 3 and 16 (under the UN Convention, ratified by 25 States, it is an offence for a mercenary to participate directly in hostilities, but the Convention applies without prejudice to the provisions of the law of armed conflict relating to the status of combatant or of prisoner of war).

[47] See, e.g., the military manuals of Argentina (*ibid.*, § 277), Australia (*ibid.*, § 277), Belgium (*ibid.*, § 277), Cameroon (*ibid.*, § 277), Canada (*ibid.*, § 278), France (*ibid.*, § 277), Germany (*ibid.*, § 279), Israel (*ibid.*, § 280), Italy (*ibid.*, § 277), Kenya (*ibid.*, § 281), Netherlands (*ibid.*, § 277), New Zealand (*ibid.*, §§ 277 and 282), Nigeria (*ibid.*, §§ 277 and 284), Spain (*ibid.*, §§ 277 and 285), Sweden (*ibid.*, § 277), Switzerland (*ibid.*, §§ 277 and 286), United Kingdom (*ibid.*, § 277), United States (*ibid.*, § 287) and Yugoslavia (*ibid.*, § 277).

[48] Israel, *Manual on the Laws of War* (*ibid.*, § 280).

[49] See, e.g., the legislation of Armenia (*ibid.*, § 288), Azerbaijan (*ibid.*, § 288), Belarus (*ibid.*, § 288), Georgia (*ibid.*, § 288), Kazakhstan (*ibid.*, § 288), Moldova (*ibid.*, § 288), Russia (*ibid.*, § 288), Tajikistan (*ibid.*, § 288), Ukraine (*ibid.*, § 288), Uzbekistan (*ibid.*, § 288) and Vietnam (*ibid.*, § 288).

[50] See, e.g., the statements of China (*ibid.*, § 295), Iraq (*ibid.*, § 301), Italy (*ibid.*, § 302), Nigeria (*ibid.*, § 307) and Yugoslavia (*ibid.*, § 316) and the reported practice of Iran (*ibid.*, § 319).

party to Additional Protocol I.[51] The United States, however, has stated that it does not consider the provisions of Article 47 of Additional Protocol I to be customary.[52]

This rule may have lost much of its meaning because the definition of mercenaries that was agreed upon in Additional Protocol I is very restrictive (see *infra*). This point was recognised by the United States and may explain why it did not object to Article 47 at the Diplomatic Conference leading to the adoption of the Additional Protocols.[53]

In addition, because the opposition from African countries against mercenary activity was mainly related to their involvement in wars of national liberation where mercenaries were fighting against a people wishing to exercise their right to self-determination, this issue has been less vigorously pursued in recent years, and mercenaries have been less stigmatised.

Definition of mercenaries

Additional Protocol I defines a mercenary as a person who:

a) is specially recruited locally or abroad in order to fight in an armed conflict;
b) does, in fact, take a direct part in the hostilities;
c) is motivated to take part in the hostilities essentially by the desire for private gain and, in fact, is promised, by or on behalf of a Party to the conflict, material compensation substantially in excess of that promised or paid to combatants of similar ranks and functions in the armed forces of that Party;
d) is neither a national of a Party to the conflict nor a resident of territory controlled by a Party to the conflict;
e) is not a member of the armed forces of a Party to the conflict; and
f) has not been sent by a State which is not a Party to the conflict on official duty as a member of its armed forces.[54]

This definition is very restrictive because it requires that all six conditions be cumulatively fulfilled. In addition, the definition requires evidence that a person accused of being a mercenary is "motivated to take part in the hostilities essentially by the desire for private gain" and is promised "material compensation substantially in excess of that promised or paid to combatants of similar ranks and functions in the armed forces". At the Diplomatic Conference leading to the adoption of the Additional Protocols, Afghanistan, Cameroon, Cuba,

---

[51] See, e.g., the military manuals of Israel (*ibid.*, § 280), Kenya (*ibid.*, § 281), Nigeria (*ibid.*, § 283) and United Kingdom (*ibid.*, § 277), the legislation of Azerbaijan (*ibid.*, § 288), the statements of Iraq (*ibid.*, § 301) and Yugoslavia (*ibid.*, § 316) and the reported practice of Iran (*ibid.*, § 319).

[52] See United States, Remarks of the Deputy Legal Adviser of the Department of State (*ibid.*, § 314).

[53] See United States, *Air Force Commander's Handbook* (*ibid.*, § 242).

[54] Additional Protocol I, Article 47(2) (adopted by consensus) (*ibid.*, § 232).

Mauritania, Nigeria and Zaire expressed their opposition to this formulation.[55] Cameroon, for example, stated that "it would be very difficult to prove that a mercenary received exorbitant pay".[56] The Netherlands was against any reference to the motivation of a mercenary altogether.[57] The OAU Convention against Mercenarism dropped the requirement of material compensation "substantially in excess of that promised or paid to combatants of similar ranks and functions".[58] The UN Mercenary Convention, however, does contain this requirement.[59]

Among those military manuals collected for this study that contain a definition of a mercenary, nine follow the definition in Additional Protocol I,[60] while four others simply refer to the desire for private gain.[61] The legislation of 11 States of the former Soviet Union define mercenaries with respect to their desire for private gain without further qualification.[62]

In the light of the foregoing, it can be concluded that the customary rule that mercenaries do not have the right to combatant or prisoner-of-war status applies only to those persons fulfilling the conditions set forth in the definition of a mercenary in Article 47 of Additional Protocol I.

Lastly, it should be recalled that members of the armed forces of a party to the conflict who are not nationals of that party and who do not fulfil all six conditions of the definition of a mercenary in Article 47 of Additional Protocol I are entitled to prisoner-of-war status.[63] It is important to note in this respect that nationality is not a condition for prisoner-of-war status according to long-standing practice and to Article 4 of the Third Geneva Convention.[64]

Right to fair trial

A person accused of being a mercenary may not be punished without previous trial. At the Diplomatic Conference leading to the adoption of the Additional Protocols, several States stressed that mercenaries enjoy the protection of

---

[55] See the statements made at the Diplomatic Conference leading to the adoption of the Additional Protocols by Afghanistan (*ibid.*, § 255), Cameroon (*ibid.*, § 256), Cuba (*ibid.*, § 257), Mauritania (*ibid.*, § 258), Nigeria (*ibid.*, § 260) and Zaire (*ibid.*, § 263).

[56] Cameroon, Statement at the Diplomatic Conference leading to the adoption of the Additional Protocols (*ibid.*, § 256).

[57] Netherlands, Statement at the Diplomatic Conference leading to the adoption of the Additional Protocols (*ibid.*, § 259).

[58] See the definition of mercenary contained in the OAU Convention against Mercenarism, Article 1 (*ibid.*, § 234).

[59] UN Mercenary Convention, Article 1 (*ibid.*, § 235).

[60] See the military manuals of Argentina, Australia, Belgium, Canada, France, Netherlands, New Zealand, Spain and Yugoslavia (*ibid.*, § 237).

[61] See the military manuals of Cameroon (*ibid.*, § 238), Germany (*ibid.*, § 239), Kenya (*ibid.*, § 240) and United Kingdom (*ibid.*, § 241).

[62] See the legislation of Armenia (*ibid.*, § 243), Azerbaijan (*ibid.*, § 244), Belarus (*ibid.*, § 245), Georgia (*ibid.*, § 246), Kazakhstan (*ibid.*, § 247), Kyrgyzstan (*ibid.*, § 248), Moldova (*ibid.*, § 249), Russia (*ibid.*, § 250), Tajikistan (*ibid.*, § 251), Ukraine (*ibid.*, § 252) and Uzbekistan (*ibid.*, § 253).

[63] See 1907 Hague Convention (V), Article 17.

[64] See Third Geneva Convention, Article 4.

Article 75 of Additional Protocol I and some specified that they would have wished to see an explicit reference to Article 75 in the provision on mercenaries.[65] The Rapporteur of Committee III of the Diplomatic Conference reported that although there was no such explicit reference in Article 47 of Additional Protocol I, it was understood that mercenaries would be one of the groups who would be entitled to the fundamental guarantees provided for in Article 75.[66] This point was reiterated by Ireland and the Netherlands upon ratification of Additional Protocol I.[67]

The military manuals of Canada, Germany, Kenya and New Zealand emphasise that mercenaries are entitled to a fair trial.[68] This is consistent with the fundamental guarantees set out in Chapter 32, including the right to a fair trial (see Rule 100). This is also laid down in Additional Protocol I, which states that anyone who is not entitled to prisoner-of-war status, and does not benefit from more favourable treatment in accordance with the Fourth Geneva Convention, still enjoys the fundamental guarantees provided for in Article 75 of Additional Protocol I.[69] Consequently, the summary execution of mercenaries is prohibited.

According to this rule, States are free to grant prisoner-of-war status to a mercenary or withhold it, but the mercenary has no right to claim such status as a defence against prosecution. As the UN Secretary-General reported in 1988, Iran claimed to have captured nationals from other countries whom it alleged were mercenaries, but it asserted that, rather than punish them, it chose to treat them like other prisoners of war.[70] Similarly, the US Air Force Commander's Handbook asserts that the United States has regarded mercenaries as combatants entitled to prisoner-of-war status upon capture.[71] This shows that a State is free to grant such status. The Handbook also states, however, that "the US government has always vigorously protested against any attempt by other nations to punish American citizens as mercenaries".[72] This statement does not undermine the current rule to the extent that these protests were made with respect to persons who did not fulfil the stringent conditions of the

---

[65] See the statements made at the Diplomatic Conference leading to the adoption of the Additional Protocols by Australia (*ibid.*, § 292), Canada (*ibid.*, § 294), Colombia (*ibid.*, § 296), Cyprus (*ibid.*, § 297), Holy See (*ibid.*, § 299), India (*ibid.*, § 300), Italy (*ibid.*, § 302), Mexico (*ibid.*, § 304), Netherlands (*ibid.*, § 305), Nigeria (*ibid.*, § 307), Portugal (*ibid.*, § 308), Sweden (*ibid.*, § 311) and Switzerland (*ibid.*, § 312).

[66] Diplomatic Conference leading to the adoption of the Additional Protocols, Statement of the Rapporteur of Committee III (*ibid.*, § 321).

[67] Ireland, Declarations and reservations made upon ratification of Additional Protocol I (*ibid.*, § 272); Netherlands, Declarations made upon ratification of Additional Protocol I (*ibid.*, § 273).

[68] Canada, *LOAC Manual* (*ibid.*, § 278), Germany, *Military Manual* (*ibid.*, § 279), Kenya, *LOAC Manual* (*ibid.*, § 281) and New Zealand, *Military Manual* (*ibid.*, § 282).

[69] Additional Protocol I, Article 45(3) (adopted by consensus) (*ibid.*, § 271).

[70] See UN Secretary-General, Report of the mission dispatched by the Secretary-General on the situation of prisoners of war in the Islamic Republic of Iran and Iraq (*ibid.*, § 319).

[71] United States, *Air Force Commander's Handbook* (*ibid.*, § 287).

[72] United States, *Air Force Commander's Handbook* (*ibid.*, § 287).

definition of mercenaries contained in Article 47 of Additional Protocol I, which was adopted by consensus.

Non-international armed conflicts

Mercenaries participating in a non-international armed conflict are not entitled to prisoner-of-war status as no right to that status exists in such situations.[73]

---

[73] See, e.g., United States, Memorandum on International Legal Rights of Captured Mercenaries (*ibid.*, § 313).

THE WOUNDED, SICK AND SHIPWRECKED

Rule 109. Whenever circumstances permit, and particularly after an engagement, each party to the conflict must, without delay, take all possible measures to search for, collect and evacuate the wounded, sick and shipwrecked without adverse distinction.

Practice

Volume II, Chapter 34, Section A.

Summary

State practice establishes this rule as a norm of customary international law applicable in both international and non-international armed conflicts.

International armed conflicts

The duty to collect wounded and sick combatants without distinction in international armed conflicts was first codified in the 1864 Geneva Convention.[1] This subject is dealt with in more detail in the 1949 Geneva Conventions.[2] This duty is now codified in Article 10 of Additional Protocol I,[3] albeit in more general terms of "protecting" the wounded, sick and shipwrecked, which means "coming to their defence, lending help and support".[4]

The numerous military manuals which contain this rule are phrased in general terms covering all wounded, sick and shipwrecked, whether military or civilian.[5] Sweden's IHL Manual, in particular, identifies Article 10 of

---

[1] 1864 Geneva Convention, Article 6 (cited in Vol. II, Ch. 34, § 1).
[2] First Geneva Convention, Article 15, first paragraph (*ibid.*, § 5); Second Geneva Convention, Article 18, first paragraph (*ibid.*, § 7); Fourth Geneva Convention, Article 16, second paragraph (*ibid.*, § 10).
[3] Additional Protocol I, Article 10 (adopted by consensus) (*ibid.*, § 199).
[4] Yves Sandoz, Christophe Swinarski, Bruno Zimmermann (eds.), *Commentary on the Additional Protocols*, ICRC, Geneva, 1987, § 446.
[5] See, e.g., the military manuals of Argentina (cited in Vol. II, Ch. 34, §§ 21–22 and 127), Australia (*ibid.*, §§ 23 and 128–129), Belgium (*ibid.*, §§ 24–25 and 130), Benin (*ibid.*, §§ 26 and 131), Burkina Faso (*ibid.*, § 27), Cameroon (*ibid.*, §§ 28–29 and 134), Canada (*ibid.*, §§ 30–31 and 132–133), Colombia (*ibid.*, §§ 32–35), Congo (*ibid.*, § 36), Croatia (*ibid.*, §§ 37–40 and 135), Dominican Republic (*ibid.*, § 136), Ecuador (*ibid.*, §§ 41 and 137), France (*ibid.*, §§ 42–43 and 138), Germany

Additional Protocol I as a codification of customary international law.[6] The legislation of many States provides for the punishment of persons who abandon the wounded, sick and shipwrecked.[7]

Non-international armed conflicts

In the context of non-international armed conflicts, this rule is based on common Article 3 of the Geneva Conventions, which provides that "the wounded and sick shall be collected".[8] It is codified in a more detailed manner in Additional Protocol II.[9] In addition, it is set forth in a number of other instruments pertaining also to non-international armed conflicts.[10]

The duty to search for, collect and evacuate the wounded, sick and shipwrecked is contained in a number of military manuals which are applicable in or have been applied in non-international armed conflicts.[11] It is an offence under the legislation of several States to abandon the wounded and sick.[12]

(*ibid.*, § 44), Hungary (*ibid.*, §§ 45 and 139), India (*ibid.*, § 140), Indonesia (*ibid.*, § 46), Italy (*ibid.*, §§ 47 and 141), Kenya (*ibid.*, §§ 48 and 142), Lebanon (*ibid.*, § 49), Madagascar (*ibid.*, §§ 50 and 143), Mali (*ibid.*, § 51), Morocco (*ibid.*, § 52), Netherlands (*ibid.*, §§ 53–55 and 144), New Zealand (*ibid.*, §§ 56 and 145), Nigeria (*ibid.*, §§ 58–60 and 146), Philippines (*ibid.*, §§ 61 and 147–149), Romania (*ibid.*, §§ 62 and 150), Rwanda (*ibid.*, § 151), Senegal (*ibid.*, § 64), Spain (*ibid.*, §§ 66 and 153), Switzerland (*ibid.*, §§ 68 and 154), Togo (*ibid.*, §§ 69 and 155), United Kingdom (*ibid.*, §§ 70–71 and 156–157), United States (*ibid.*, §§ 72–74 and 158–161) and Yugoslavia (*ibid.*, §§ 75 and 162).

6 Sweden, *IHL Manual* (1991), Section 2.2.3, p. 18.
7 See, e.g., the legislation of China (cited in Vol. II, Ch. 34, § 80), Colombia (*ibid.*, § 81), Democratic Republic of the Congo (*ibid.*, § 82), Iraq (*ibid.*, § 84), Italy (*ibid.*, § 86), Nicaragua (*ibid.*, § 87), Spain (*ibid.*, § 90), Uruguay (*ibid.*, § 93), Venezuela (*ibid.*, § 94) and Vietnam (*ibid.*, § 95); see also the draft legislation of Argentina (*ibid.*, § 76), El Salvador (*ibid.*, § 83) and Nicaragua (*ibid.*, § 88).
8 Geneva Conventions, common Article 3 (*ibid.*, § 3).
9 Additional Protocol II, Article 8 (adopted by consensus) (*ibid.*, § 13).
10 See, e.g., Memorandum of Understanding on the Application of IHL between Croatia and the SFRY, para. 1 (*ibid.*, § 16); Agreement on the Application of IHL between the Parties to the Conflict in Bosnia and Herzegovina, para. 2.1 (*ibid.*, § 18); Hague Statement on Respect for Humanitarian Principles (*ibid.*, § 17); Comprehensive Agreement on Respect for Human Rights and International Humanitarian Law in the Philippines, Part IV, Article 4(2) and (9) (*ibid.*, § 19).
11 See, e.g., the military manuals of Argentina (*ibid.*, § 22), Australia (*ibid.*, §§ 23 and 128), Belgium (*ibid.*, § 24), Benin (*ibid.*, §§ 26 and 131), Cameroon (*ibid.*, § 29), Canada (*ibid.*, §§ 30–31 and 133), Colombia (*ibid.*, §§ 32–35), Croatia (*ibid.*, §§ 37–40 and 135), Ecuador (*ibid.*, §§ 41 and 137), Germany (*ibid.*, § 44), Hungary (*ibid.*, § 45), India (*ibid.*, § 140), Italy (*ibid.*, §§ 47 and 141), Kenya (*ibid.*, §§ 48 and 142), Lebanon (*ibid.*, § 49), Madagascar (*ibid.*, §§ 50 and 143), Netherlands (*ibid.*, §§ 53–54), New Zealand (*ibid.*, § 56), Nicaragua (*ibid.*, § 57), Nigeria (*ibid.*, §§ 58 and 60), Philippines (*ibid.*, §§ 61 and 147–149), Rwanda (*ibid.*, § 151), Senegal (*ibid.*, § 65), Spain (*ibid.*, § 66), Togo (*ibid.*, §§ 69 and 155), United Kingdom (*ibid.*, §§ 70–71), United States (*ibid.*, §§ 72–73) and Yugoslavia (*ibid.*, §§ 75 and 162).
12 See, e.g., the legislation of Colombia (*ibid.*, § 81), Democratic Republic of the Congo (*ibid.*, § 82), Nicaragua (*ibid.*, § 87), Venezuela (*ibid.*, § 94) and Vietnam (*ibid.*, § 95); see also the legislation of Italy (*ibid.*, § 86) and Uruguay (*ibid.*, § 93), the application of which is not excluded in time of non-international armed conflict, and the draft legislation of Argentina (*ibid.*, § 76), El Salvador (*ibid.*, § 83) and Nicaragua (*ibid.*, § 88).

No official contrary practice was found with respect to either international or non-international armed conflicts. The ICRC has called on parties to both international and non-international armed conflicts to respect this rule.[13]

Interpretation

The obligation to search for, collect and evacuate the wounded, sick and shipwrecked is an obligation of means. Each party to the conflict has to take *all possible measures* to search for, collect and evacuate the wounded, sick and shipwrecked. This includes permitting humanitarian organisations to assist in their search and collection. Practice shows that the ICRC in particular has engaged in the evacuation of the wounded and sick.[14] It is clear that in practice humanitarian organisations will need permission from the party in control of a certain area to carry out such activities, but such permission must not be denied arbitrarily (see also commentary to Rule 55). The UN Security Council, UN General Assembly and UN Commission on Human Rights have called upon the parties to the conflicts in El Salvador and Lebanon to permit the ICRC to evacuate the wounded and sick.[15]

In addition, the possibility of calling upon the civilian population to assist in the search, collection and evacuation of the wounded, sick and shipwrecked is recognised in the Geneva Conventions and their Additional Protocols.[16] It is also provided for in several military manuals.[17] Article 18 of the First Geneva Convention provides that "no one may ever be molested or convicted for having nursed the wounded or sick".[18] This principle is also set forth in Article 17(1) of Additional Protocol I, to which no reservations have been made.[19]

The Geneva Conventions and other instruments, such as the UN Secretary-General's Bulletin on observance by United Nations forces of international

---

[13] See, e.g., ICRC, Conflict between Iraq and Iran: ICRC Appeal (*ibid.*, § 110), Memorandum on the Applicability of International Humanitarian Law (*ibid.*, § 111), Communication to the Press No. 93/17 (*ibid.*, § 112), Memorandum on Respect for International Humanitarian Law in Angola (*ibid.*, § 113), Memorandum on Compliance with International Humanitarian Law by the Forces Participating in Opération Turquoise (*ibid.*, § 114) and Communication to the Press No. 00/42 (*ibid.*, § 115).

[14] See, e.g., the practice of the ICRC (*ibid.*, § 185) and Communication to the Press No. 96/25 (*ibid.*, § 189).

[15] UN Security Council, Res. 436 (*ibid.*, § 173); UN General Assembly, Res. 40/139 (*ibid.*, § 174); UN Commission on Human Rights, Res. 1986/39 (*ibid.*, § 175).

[16] First Geneva Convention, Article 18 (*ibid.*, § 6); Second Geneva Convention, Article 21, first paragraph (*ibid.*, § 8); Additional Protocol I, Article 17(2) (adopted by consensus) (*ibid.*, § 11); Additional Protocol II, Article 18(1) (adopted by consensus) (*ibid.*, § 14).

[17] See, e.g., the military manuals of Argentina (*ibid.*, § 21), Cameroon (*ibid.*, § 29), Canada (*ibid.*, §§ 30–31), Germany (*ibid.*, § 44), Kenya (*ibid.*, § 48), New Zealand (*ibid.*, § 56), Russia (*ibid.*, § 63), Switzerland (*ibid.*, § 68), United Kingdom (*ibid.*, §§ 70–71), United States (*ibid.*, § 72) and Yugoslavia (*ibid.*, § 75).

[18] First Geneva Convention, Article 18 (cited in Vol. II, Ch. 7, § 231).

[19] Additional Protocol I, Article 17(1) (adopted by consensus).

humanitarian law, state that cease-fires and other local arrangements are seen as appropriate ways to create the conditions in which the wounded and sick can be evacuated and require the parties to the conflict to conclude such agreements, whenever circumstances permit, to remove, exchange and transport the wounded from the battlefield.[20] Many military manuals make the same point.[21]

Scope of application

This rule applies to all wounded, sick and shipwrecked, without adverse distinction (see Rule 88). This means that it applies to the wounded, sick and shipwrecked regardless to which party they belong, but also regardless of whether or not they have taken a direct part in hostilities. The application of this rule to civilians was already the case pursuant to Article 16 of the Fourth Geneva Convention, which applies to the whole of the populations of the countries in conflict, and is repeated in Article 10 of Additional Protocol I.[22] With respect to non-international armed conflicts, common Article 3 of the Geneva Conventions applies to all persons taking no active part in the hostilities, which includes civilians.[23] In addition, Article 8 of Additional Protocol II does not indicate any distinction (see also Article 2(1) of Additional Protocol II on non-discrimination).[24] Most military manuals state this rule in general terms.[25]

---

[20] First Geneva Convention, Article 15, second and third paragraphs (cited in Vol. II, Ch. 34, § 118); Second Geneva Convention, Article 18, second paragraph (*ibid.*, § 119); Fourth Geneva Convention, Article 17 (*ibid.*, § 120); UN Secretary-General's Bulletin, Section 9.2 (*ibid.*, § 126).

[21] See, e.g., the military manuals of Argentina (*ibid.*, § 127), Australia (*ibid.*, §§ 128–129), Cameroon (*ibid.*, § 134), Canada (*ibid.*, §§ 132–133), Ecuador (*ibid.*, § 137), France (*ibid.*, § 138), India (*ibid.*, § 140), Kenya (*ibid.*, § 142), Madagascar (*ibid.*, § 143), Netherlands (*ibid.*, § 144), New Zealand (*ibid.*, § 145), Nigeria (*ibid.*, § 146), Senegal (*ibid.*, § 152), Spain (*ibid.*, § 153), Switzerland (*ibid.*, § 154), United Kingdom (*ibid.*, §§ 156–157), United States (*ibid.*, §§ 158–159 and 161) and Yugoslavia (*ibid.*, § 162).

[22] Fourth Geneva Convention, Article 16 (*ibid.*, §§ 10 and 198); Additional Protocol I, Article 10 (adopted by consensus) (*ibid.*, §§ 199 and 346).

[23] Geneva Conventions, common Article 3 (*ibid.*, § 3).

[24] Additional Protocol II, Article 8 (adopted by consensus) (*ibid.*, § 13) and Article 2(1) (adopted by consensus) (cited in Vol. II, Ch. 32, § 369).

[25] See, e.g., the military manuals of Argentina (cited in Vol. II, Ch. 34, §§ 21–22 and 127), Australia (*ibid.*, §§ 23 and 128–129), Belgium (*ibid.*, §§ 24–25 and 130), Benin (*ibid.*, §§ 26 and 131), Burkina Faso (*ibid.*, § 27), Cameroon (*ibid.*, §§ 28–29 and 134), Canada (*ibid.*, §§ 30–31 and 132–133), Colombia (*ibid.*, §§ 32–35), Congo (*ibid.*, § 36), Croatia (*ibid.*, §§ 37–40 and 135), Dominican Republic (*ibid.*, § 136), Ecuador (*ibid.*, §§ 41 and 137), France (*ibid.*, §§ 42–43 and 138), Germany (*ibid.*, § 44), Hungary (*ibid.*, §§ 45 and 139), India (*ibid.*, § 140), Indonesia (*ibid.*, § 46), Italy (*ibid.*, §§ 47 and 141), Kenya (*ibid.*, §§ 48 and 142), Lebanon (*ibid.*, § 49), Madagascar (*ibid.*, §§ 50 and 143), Mali (*ibid.*, § 51), Morocco (*ibid.*, § 52), Netherlands (*ibid.*, §§ 53–55 and 144), New Zealand (*ibid.*, §§ 56 and 145), Nigeria (*ibid.*, §§ 58–60 and 146), Philippines (*ibid.*, §§ 61 and 147–149), Romania (*ibid.*, §§ 62 and 150), Rwanda (*ibid.*, § 151), Senegal (*ibid.*, § 64), Spain (*ibid.*, §§ 66 and 153), Switzerland (*ibid.*, §§ 68 and 154), Togo (*ibid.*, §§ 69 and 155), United Kingdom (*ibid.*, §§ 70–71 and 156–157), United States (*ibid.*, §§ 72–74 and 158–161) and Yugoslavia (*ibid.*, §§ 75 and 162).

Rule 110. The wounded, sick and shipwrecked must receive, to the fullest extent practicable and with the least possible delay, the medical care and attention required by their condition. No distinction may be made among them founded on any grounds other than medical ones.

Practice

Volume II, Chapter 34, Section B.

Summary

State practice establishes this rule as a norm of customary international law applicable in both international and non-international armed conflicts.

International armed conflicts

The duty to care for wounded and sick combatants without distinction is a long-standing rule of customary international law already recognised in the Lieber Code and codified in the 1864 Geneva Convention.[26] This subject is dealt with in more detail by the 1949 Geneva Conventions.[27] It is codified in Article 10 of Additional Protocol I.[28]

The numerous military manuals which contain this rule are phrased in general terms covering all wounded, sick and shipwrecked.[29] Sweden's IHL Manual, in particular, identifies Article 10 of Additional Protocol I as a codification of customary international law.[30] To deny medical care to the wounded, sick and shipwrecked is an offence under the legislation of many States.[31]

---

[26] Lieber Code, Article 79 (*ibid.*, § 205); 1864 Geneva Convention, Article 6 (*ibid.*, § 191).

[27] First Geneva Convention, Article 12, second paragraph, and Article 15, first paragraph (*ibid.*, §§ 193–194); Second Geneva Convention, Article 12, second paragraph, and Article 18, first paragraph (*ibid.*, §§ 193 and 196); Fourth Geneva Convention, Article 16, first paragraph (*ibid.*, § 198).

[28] Additional Protocol I, Article 10 (adopted by consensus) (*ibid.*, §§ 199 and 346).

[29] See, e.g., the military manuals of Argentina (*ibid.*, §§ 215 and 355), Australia (*ibid.*, §§ 216–217 and 357), Belgium (*ibid.*, §§ 218–219), Benin (*ibid.*, §§ 220 and 359), Bosnia and Herzegovina (*ibid.*, § 221), Burkina Faso (*ibid.*, § 222), Cameroon (*ibid.*, §§ 223–224), Canada (*ibid.*, §§ 225–226), Colombia (*ibid.*, §§ 227–229), Congo (*ibid.*, § 230), Croatia (*ibid.*, §§ 231 and 233), Ecuador (*ibid.*, § 234), El Salvador (*ibid.*, § 235), France (*ibid.*, §§ 236–238), Germany (*ibid.*, §§ 239–240), Hungary (*ibid.*, § 241), India (*ibid.*, § 243), Indonesia (*ibid.*, § 244), Israel (*ibid.*, § 245), Italy (*ibid.*, § 246), Kenya (*ibid.*, §§ 247 and 367), Lebanon (*ibid.*, § 248), Madagascar (*ibid.*, §§ 249 and 368), Mali (*ibid.*, § 250), Morocco (*ibid.*, § 251), Netherlands (*ibid.*, §§ 252–254 and 370), New Zealand (*ibid.*, §§ 255 and 371), Nicaragua (*ibid.*, § 256), Nigeria (*ibid.*, §§ 257–260), Philippines (*ibid.*, §§ 261–264 and 374), Romania (*ibid.*, § 375), Rwanda (*ibid.*, § 267), Senegal (*ibid.*, § 268), South Africa (*ibid.*, § 269), Spain (*ibid.*, § 270), Sweden (*ibid.*, §§ 271–272), Switzerland (*ibid.*, §§ 273 and 379), Togo (*ibid.*, §§ 274 and 380), Uganda (*ibid.*, § 275), United Kingdom (*ibid.*, §§ 276–277) and United States (*ibid.*, §§ 278–281).

[30] Sweden, *IHL Manual* (*ibid.*, § 272).

[31] See, e.g., the legislation of Azerbaijan (*ibid.*, § 283), Bangladesh (*ibid.*, § 284), China (*ibid.*, § 285), Colombia (*ibid.*, § 286), Cuba (*ibid.*, § 287), Czech Republic (*ibid.*, § 288), Estonia (*ibid.*, § 290), Ireland (*ibid.*, § 291), Norway (*ibid.*, § 292), Slovakia (*ibid.*, § 293), Spain (*ibid.*, § 294), Ukraine (*ibid.*, § 295), Uruguay (*ibid.*, § 296), Venezuela (*ibid.*, § 297) and Vietnam (*ibid.*, § 298); see also the draft legislation of Argentina (*ibid.*, § 282) and El Salvador (*ibid.*, § 289).

Non-international armed conflicts

In the context of a non-international armed conflict, this rule is based on common Article 3 of the Geneva Conventions, which provides that "the wounded and sick shall be collected and cared for".[32] It is codified in a more detailed manner in Additional Protocol II.[33] In addition, it is set forth in a number of other instruments pertaining also to non-international armed conflicts.[34]

The duty to care for wounded and sick combatants without distinction is set forth in a number of military manuals which are applicable in or have been applied in non-international armed conflicts.[35] Under the legislation of many States, it is an offence to deny medical care to the wounded, sick and shipwrecked.[36] Respect for this rule was required by Argentina's National Court of Appeals in the *Military Junta case* in 1985.[37] Furthermore, there are official statements and other practice supporting this rule in the context of non-international armed conflicts.[38]

No official contrary practice was found with respect to either international or non-international armed conflicts. States and international organisations have generally condemned violations of this rule.[39] The ICRC has called on

---

[32] Geneva Conventions, common Article 3 (*ibid.*, § 192).

[33] Additional Protocol II, Articles 7–8 (adopted by consensus) (*ibid.*, §§ 201–202).

[34] Cairo Declaration on Human Rights in Islam, Article 3(a) (*ibid.*, § 208); Hague Statement on Respect for Humanitarian Principles, paras. 1 and 2 (*ibid.*, § 209); Memorandum of Understanding on the Application of International Humanitarian Law between Croatia and the SFRY, para. 1 (*ibid.*, §§ 210 and 351); Agreement on the Application of International Humanitarian Law between the Parties to the Conflict in Bosnia and Herzegovina, para. 2.1 (*ibid.*, §§ 211 and 352); Comprehensive Agreement on Respect for Human Rights and International Humanitarian Law in the Philippines, Part IV, Article 4(2) and (9) (*ibid.*, § 212).

[35] See, e.g., the military manuals of Argentina (*ibid.*, §§ 215 and 355), Australia (*ibid.*, §§ 216–217 and 357), Belgium (*ibid.*, § 218), Benin (*ibid.*, §§ 220 and 359), Bosnia and Herzegovina (*ibid.*, § 221), Cameroon (*ibid.*, § 224), Canada (*ibid.*, §§ 225–226), Colombia (*ibid.*, §§ 227–229), Croatia (*ibid.*, §§ 231 and 233), Ecuador (*ibid.*, § 234), El Salvador (*ibid.*, § 235), Germany (*ibid.*, §§ 239–240), India (*ibid.*, §§ 242–243), Italy (*ibid.*, § 246), Kenya (*ibid.*, §§ 247 and 367), Lebanon (*ibid.*, § 248), Madagascar (*ibid.*, §§ 249 and 368), Netherlands (*ibid.*, §§ 252–253 and 369), New Zealand (*ibid.*, § 255), Nicaragua (*ibid.*, § 256), Nigeria (*ibid.*, §§ 257–258 and 260), Philippines (*ibid.*, §§ 261–264 and 374), Rwanda (*ibid.*, § 267), South Africa (*ibid.*, § 269), Spain (*ibid.*, § 270), Sweden (*ibid.*, § 271), Togo (*ibid.*, §§ 274 and 380), Uganda (*ibid.*, § 275), United Kingdom (*ibid.*, § 277) and United States (*ibid.*, § 278).

[36] See, e.g., the legislation of Azerbaijan (*ibid.*, § 283), Bangladesh (*ibid.*, § 284), Colombia (*ibid.*, § 286), Estonia (*ibid.*, § 290), Ireland (*ibid.*, § 291), Norway (*ibid.*, § 292), Spain (*ibid.*, § 294), Ukraine (*ibid.*, § 295), Venezuela (*ibid.*, § 297) and Vietnam (*ibid.*, § 298); see also the legislation of the Czech Republic (*ibid.*, § 288), Slovakia (*ibid.*, § 293) and Uruguay (*ibid.*, § 296), the application of which is not excluded in time of non-international armed conflict, and the draft legislation of Argentina (*ibid.*, § 282) and El Salvador (*ibid.*, § 289).

[37] Argentina, National Court of Appeals, *Military Junta case* (*ibid.*, § 299).

[38] See, e.g., the statements of Australia (*ibid.*, § 300), Rwanda (*ibid.*, § 311), Uruguay (*ibid.*, § 314) and Yugoslavia (*ibid.*, § 315), the practice of Honduras (*ibid.*, § 304) and the reported practice of Jordan (*ibid.*, § 307), Malaysia (*ibid.*, § 308) and Philippines (*ibid.*, § 309).

[39] See, e.g., the statements of South Africa (*ibid.*, § 312) and Yugoslavia (*ibid.*, § 315); UN Commission on Human Rights, Report of the Special Rapporteur on the Situation of Human Rights in Burundi (*ibid.*, § 320); ONUSAL, Report of the Director of the Human Rights Division (*ibid.*, § 322).

parties to both international and non-international armed conflicts to respect this rule.[40]

Interpretation

The obligation to protect and care for the wounded, sick and shipwrecked is an obligation of means. Each party to the conflict must use its best efforts to provide protection and care for the wounded, sick and shipwrecked, including permitting humanitarian organisations to provide for their protection and care. Practice shows that humanitarian organisations, including the ICRC, have engaged in the protection and care of the wounded, sick and shipwrecked. It is clear that in practice these organisations need permission from the party in control of a certain area to provide protection and care, but such permission must not be denied arbitrarily (see also commentary to Rule 55).

In addition, the possibility of calling on the civilian population to assist in the care of the wounded, sick and shipwrecked is recognised in practice. Aid offered by the civilian population is recognised by the 1864 Geneva Convention, the First Geneva Convention and Additional Protocols I and II.[41] This possibility is also recognised in a number of military manuals.[42]

The rule that no distinction may be made among the wounded, sick and shipwrecked except on medical grounds is often expressed in international humanitarian law as a prohibition of "adverse distinction" (see also Rule 88). This means that a distinction may be made which is beneficial, in particular by treating persons requiring urgent medical attention first, without this being discriminatory treatment between those treated first and those treated afterwards. This principle is set forth in many military manuals.[43] It is also supported by

---

[40] See, e.g., ICRC, Memorandum on the Applicability of International Humanitarian Law (*ibid.*, §§ 329 and 397), Press Releases Nos. 1658 and 1659 (*ibid.*, § 330), Press Release, Tajikistan: ICRC urges respect for humanitarian rules (*ibid.*, § 331), Press Release No. 1670 (*ibid.*, §§ 332 and 398), Communication to the Press No. 93/17 (*ibid.*, § 333), Press Release No. 1764 (*ibid.*, § 334), Memorandum on Respect for International Humanitarian Law in Angola (*ibid.*, §§ 336 and 399), Memorandum on Compliance with International Humanitarian Law by the Forces Participating in Opération Turquoise (*ibid.*, §§ 337 and 400), Press Release No. 1793 (*ibid.*, § 338), Press Release No. 1797 (*ibid.*, § 339) and Communication to the Press No. 00/42 (*ibid.*, § 340).

[41] 1864 Geneva Convention, Article 5; First Geneva Convention, Article 18 (*ibid.*, § 195); Additional Protocol I, Article 17(2) (adopted by consensus) (*ibid.*, § 200); Additional Protocol II, Article 18(1) (adopted by consensus) (*ibid.*, § 203).

[42] See, e.g., the military manuals of Argentina (*ibid.*, § 214), Cameroon (*ibid.*, § 224), Canada (*ibid.*, §§ 225–226), Croatia (*ibid.*, § 232), Germany (*ibid.*, § 240), Kenya (*ibid.*, § 247), New Zealand (*ibid.*, § 255), Russia (*ibid.*, § 266), Sweden (*ibid.*, § 272), Switzerland (*ibid.*, § 273), United Kingdom (*ibid.*, §§ 276–277) and United States (*ibid.*, §§ 278–279).

[43] See, e.g., the military manuals of Argentina (*ibid.*, §§ 354–355), Australia (*ibid.*, §§ 356–357), Belgium (*ibid.*, § 358), Canada (*ibid.*, §§ 360–361), Colombia (*ibid.*, § 362), Ecuador (*ibid.*, § 363), France (*ibid.*, § 364), Germany (*ibid.*, § 365), Hungary (*ibid.*, § 366), Netherlands (*ibid.*, §§ 369–370), New Zealand (*ibid.*, § 371), Nigeria (*ibid.*, §§ 372–373), Senegal (*ibid.*, § 377), Spain (*ibid.*, § 378), Switzerland (*ibid.*, § 379), United Kingdom (*ibid.*, § 381), United States (*ibid.*, §§ 382–384) and Yugoslavia (*ibid.*, § 385).

the requirement of respect for medical ethics, as set forth in Additional Protocols I and II (see also Rule 26), to the effect that medical personnel may not be required to give priority to any person, except on medical grounds.[44]

Rule 111. Each party to the conflict must take all possible measures to protect the wounded, sick and shipwrecked against ill-treatment and against pillage of their personal property.

Practice

Volume II, Chapter 34, Section C.

Summary

State practice establishes this rule as a norm of customary international law applicable in both international and non-international armed conflicts. The acts against which the wounded, sick and shipwrecked have to be protected according to this rule, namely pillage and ill-treatment, are prohibited pursuant to Rules 52 and 87.

International armed conflicts

The obligation to take all possible measures to protect the wounded, sick and shipwrecked from pillage and ill-treatment in the context of international armed conflicts was first codified in the 1906 Geneva Convention and 1907 Hague Convention (X).[45] It is now set forth in the 1949 Geneva Conventions.[46]

Numerous military manuals refer to the duty to take all possible measures to protect the wounded, sick and shipwrecked against ill-treatment and pillage.[47] In particular, many manuals prohibit pillage of the wounded, sick and shipwrecked, sometimes referred to as "marauding", or specify that it constitutes a war crime.[48] For a definition of pillage, see Rule 52.

---

[44] Additional Protocol I, Article 15(3) (adopted by consensus) (*ibid.*, § 347); Additional Protocol II, Article 9(2) (adopted by consensus) (*ibid.*, § 349).

[45] 1906 Geneva Convention, Article 28 (*ibid.*, § 403); Hague Convention (X), Article 16 (*ibid.*, § 404).

[46] First Geneva Convention, Article 15, first paragraph (*ibid.*, § 405); Second Geneva Convention, Article 18, first paragraph (*ibid.*, § 406); Fourth Geneva Convention, Article 16, second paragraph (*ibid.*, § 407).

[47] See, e.g., the military manuals of Argentina (*ibid.*, § 415), Australia (*ibid.*, § 416), Canada (*ibid.*, §§ 419–420), Colombia (*ibid.*, § 421), Germany (*ibid.*, § 424), Indonesia (*ibid.*, § 427), New Zealand (*ibid.*, § 432), Nigeria (*ibid.*, § 433), United Kingdom (*ibid.*, §§ 438–439) and United States (*ibid.*, §§ 440–441).

[48] See, e.g., the military manuals of Burkina Faso (*ibid.*, § 417), Cameroon (*ibid.*, § 418), Canada (*ibid.*, § 420), Congo (*ibid.*, § 422), France (*ibid.*, § 423), Israel (*ibid.*, § 425), Italy (*ibid.*, § 426), Lebanon (*ibid.*, § 428), Mali (*ibid.*, § 429), Morocco (*ibid.*, § 430), Philippines ("mistreat") (*ibid.*, § 434), Romania (*ibid.*, § 435), Senegal (*ibid.*, § 436), Switzerland (*ibid.*, § 437), United Kingdom (*ibid.*, § 438) and United States ("mistreating") (*ibid.*, § 442).

Non-international armed conflicts

The obligation to take all possible measures to protect the wounded, sick and shipwrecked from pillage and ill-treatment in non-international armed conflicts is set forth in Additional Protocol II.[49] In addition, it is contained in a number of other instruments pertaining also to non-international armed conflicts.[50]

A number of military manuals which are applicable in or have been applied in non-international armed conflicts prohibit pillage and ill-treatment of the wounded, sick and shipwrecked or specify the obligation to take all possible measures to protect them from pillage and ill-treatment.[51] In 1991, the Chief of Staff of the Yugoslav People's Army ordered troops to prevent the pillage and mistreatment of the wounded and sick.[52]

No official contrary practice was found with respect to either international or non-international armed conflicts.

Respect by civilians for the wounded, sick and shipwrecked

Practice further indicates that civilians have a duty to respect the wounded, sick and shipwrecked. With respect to international armed conflicts, this principle is set forth in Article 18 of the First Geneva Convention and in Article 17 of Additional Protocol I.[53] It is also stated in a number of military manuals.[54] Sweden's IHL Manual, in particular, identifies Article 17 of Additional Protocol I as a codification of customary international law.[55] The Commentary on the Additional Protocols notes with respect to Article 17 of Additional Protocol I that:

The duty imposed here upon the civilian population is only to respect the wounded, sick and shipwrecked, and not to protect them. Thus it is above all an obligation to refrain from action, i.e., to commit no act of violence against the wounded or take advantage of their condition. There is no positive obligation to assist a wounded

---

[49] Additional Protocol II, Article 8 (adopted by consensus) (*ibid.*, § 409).

[50] See, e.g., Memorandum of Understanding on the Application of International Humanitarian Law between Croatia and the SFRY, para. 1 (*ibid.*, § 412); Agreement on the Application of International Humanitarian Law between the Parties to the Conflict in Bosnia and Herzegovina, para. 2.1 (*ibid.*, § 413).

[51] See, e.g., the military manuals of Australia (*ibid.*, § 416), Canada (*ibid.*, §§ 419–420), Colombia (*ibid.*, § 421), Germany (*ibid.*, § 424), Italy (*ibid.*, § 426), Lebanon (*ibid.*, § 428), Netherlands (*ibid.*, § 431), New Zealand (*ibid.*, § 432) and Philippines ("mistreat") (*ibid.*, § 434).

[52] Yugoslavia, *Order No. 579 of the Chief of General Staff of the Yugoslav People's Army* (*ibid.*, § 519).

[53] First Geneva Convention, Article 18, second paragraph (*ibid.*, § 524); Additional Protocol I, Article 17(1) (adopted by consensus) (*ibid.*, § 525).

[54] See, e.g., the military manuals of Argentina (*ibid.*, § 527), Australia (*ibid.*, § 528), Germany (*ibid.*, § 529), Spain (*ibid.*, § 530), Switzerland (*ibid.*, § 532), United Kingdom (*ibid.*, § 533) and United States (*ibid.*, §§ 534–535).

[55] Sweden, *IHL Manual* (*ibid.*, § 531).

person, though obviously the possibility of imposing such an obligation remains open for national legislation, and in several countries the law has indeed provided for the obligation to assist persons who are in danger, on pain of penal sanctions.[56]

The duty of civilians to respect the wounded, sick and shipwrecked also applies in non-international armed conflicts, because non-respect would be a violation of the fundamental guarantees accorded to all persons *hors de combat* (see Chapter 32). Under the Statute of the International Criminal Court, it is a war crime for anyone to kill or wound a person *hors de combat* whether in international or non-international armed conflicts.[57]

---

[56] Yves Sandoz, Christophe Swinarski, Bruno Zimmermann (eds.), *Commentary on the Additional Protocols*, ICRC, Geneva, 1987, § 701.
[57] ICC Statute, Article 8(2)(a)(i) and (c)(i) (cited in Vol. II, Ch. 32, §§ 675–676) and Article 8(2)(b)(VI) (cited in Vol. II, Ch. 15, § 217).

THE DEAD

Rule 112. Whenever circumstances permit, and particularly after an engagement, each party to the conflict must, without delay, take all possible measures to search for, collect and evacuate the dead without adverse distinction.

Practice

Volume II, Chapter 35, Section A.

Summary

State practice establishes this rule as a norm of customary international law applicable in both international and non-international armed conflicts.

International armed conflicts

The duty to search for the dead in international armed conflicts was first codified in the 1929 Geneva Convention for the Amelioration of the Condition of the Wounded and Sick in Armies in the Field.[1] This rule is now codified in the 1949 Geneva Conventions.[2]

Numerous military manuals specify the duty to search for and collect the dead.[3] In the *Jenin (Mortal Remains) case* in 2002, Israel's High Court of Justice stated that locating the dead was a "highly important humanitarian deed".[4]

---

[1] 1929 Geneva Convention for the Amelioration of the Condition of the Wounded and Sick in Armies in the Field, Article 3 (cited in Vol. II, Ch. 35, § 1).

[2] First Geneva Convention, Article 15, first paragraph (*ibid.*, § 2); Second Geneva Convention, Article 18, first paragraph (*ibid.*, § 3); Fourth Geneva Convention, Article 16, second paragraph (*ibid.*, § 5).

[3] See, e.g., the military manuals of Argentina (*ibid.*, § 11), Australia (*ibid.*, § 12), Belgium (*ibid.*, § 13), Benin (*ibid.*, § 14), Cameroon (*ibid.*, § 15), Canada (*ibid.*, §§ 16–17), Croatia (*ibid.*, § 18), France (*ibid.*, § 19), Germany (*ibid.*, § 20), Italy (*ibid.*, § 22), Kenya (*ibid.*, § 23), Madagascar (*ibid.*, § 24), Netherlands (*ibid.*, § 26), New Zealand (*ibid.*, § 27), Nigeria (*ibid.*, §§ 28–29), Philippines (*ibid.*, § 30), Spain (*ibid.*, § 31), Switzerland (*ibid.*, § 32), Togo (*ibid.*, § 33), United Kingdom (*ibid.*, §§ 34–35) and United States (*ibid.*, §§ 36–39).

[4] Israel, High Court of Justice, *Jenin (Mortal Remains) case* (*ibid.*, § 46).

Non-international armed conflicts

In the context of a non-international armed conflict, the duty to search for the dead is set forth in Additional Protocol II.[5] In addition, this rule is contained in other instruments pertaining also to non-international armed conflicts.[6]

A number of military manuals which are applicable in or have been applied in non-international armed conflicts specify the duty to search for and collect the dead.[7]

Respect for this rule is a *conditio sine qua non* of respect for the subsequent rules in this chapter requiring return of remains, decent burial and identification of the dead. In addition, much of the practice relating to the search for and collection of the wounded, sick and shipwrecked (see practice relating to Rule 109) is also relevant to this rule as, in a first phase after combat, the dead will be searched for and collected together with the wounded and sick. The Annotated Supplement to the US Naval Handbook, for example, recognises that the obligation to search for and collect the wounded, sick and shipwrecked "also extends to the dead".[8]

No official contrary practice was found with respect to either international or non-international armed conflicts.

Interpretation

The obligation to search for and collect the dead is an obligation of means. Each party to the conflict has to take *all possible measures* to search for and collect the dead. This includes permitting the search for and collection of the dead by humanitarian organisations. Practice shows that humanitarian organisations, including the ICRC, have engaged in the search for and collection of the dead.[9] It is clear that in practice these organisations need permission from the party in control of a certain area to carry out search and collection activities, but such permission must not be denied arbitrarily (see also commentary to Rule 55).

In addition, the possibility of calling on the civilian population to assist in the search for and collection of the dead is recognised in Additional Protocol I.[10] A number of military manuals also provide for this possibility.[11]

---

[5] Additional Protocol II, Article 8 (adopted by consensus) (*ibid.*, § 8).

[6] See, e.g., Comprehensive Agreement on Respect for Human Rights and International Humanitarian Law in the Philippines, Part IV, Article 4(9) (*ibid.*, § 10).

[7] See, e.g., the military manuals of Argentina (*ibid.*, § 11), Australia (*ibid.*, § 12), Benin (*ibid.*, § 14), Cameroon (*ibid.*, § 15), Canada (*ibid.*, §§ 16–17), Croatia (*ibid.*, § 18), Germany (*ibid.*, § 20), India (*ibid.*, § 21), Italy (*ibid.*, § 22), Kenya (*ibid.*, § 23), Madagascar (*ibid.*, § 24), Netherlands (*ibid.*, § 25), New Zealand (*ibid.*, § 27), Nigeria (*ibid.*, § 28), Philippines (*ibid.*, § 30), Spain (*ibid.*, § 31) and Togo (*ibid.*, § 33).

[8] United States, *Annotated Supplement to the Naval Handbook* (*ibid.*, § 39).

[9] See, e.g., the practice of the ICRC reported by the UN Secretary-General (*ibid.*, § 51).

[10] Additional Protocol I, Article 17(2) (adopted by consensus) (*ibid.*, § 6).

[11] See, e.g., the military manuals of Benin (*ibid.*, § 14), Cameroon (*ibid.*, § 15), Kenya (*ibid.*, § 23), Nigeria (*ibid.*, § 28), Togo (*ibid.*, § 33), United States (*ibid.*, § 36) and Yugoslavia (*ibid.*, § 40).

As noted in the commentary to Rule 109, the Geneva Conventions require parties to arrange a suspension of fire, whenever circumstances permit, to remove, exchange and transport the wounded from the battlefield, but this provision does not explicitly mention the dead. In practice, however, the dead are in many cases collected at the same time. In cases of extreme urgency, however, it may be that only the wounded are collected for immediate care and that the dead are left behind for collection at a later time. Additional Protocol I has therefore introduced the rule that parties shall endeavour to agree on arrangements for teams to search for and recover the dead from the battlefield areas.[12] This rule is also set forth in several military manuals.[13] The United States has expressed its support for this provision in Additional Protocol I.[14]

Scope of application

This rule applies to all the dead, without adverse distinction (see Rule 88). This means that it applies to the dead regardless to which party they belong, but also regardless of whether or not they have taken a direct part in hostilities. The application of this rule to civilians was already the case pursuant to Article 16 of the Fourth Geneva Convention, which applies to the whole of the populations of the countries in conflict, and to Article 8 of Additional Protocol II, which does not specify any distinction.[15]

Most military manuals state this rule in general terms.[16] The military manuals of Cameroon and Kenya state that in case of civilian losses, civil defence units shall participate in the search for the victims.[17] In its judgement in the *Jenin (Mortal Remains) case*, Israel's High Court of Justice stated that the obligation to search for and collect the dead derived from "respect for every dead".[18]

---

[12]   Additional Protocol I, Article 33(4) (adopted by consensus) (*ibid.*, § 7).

[13]   See, e.g., the military manuals of Australia (*ibid.*, § 12), Canada (*ibid.*, § 16), India (*ibid.*, § 21), Kenya (*ibid.*, § 23) and New Zealand (*ibid.*, § 27).

[14]   United States, Remarks of the Deputy Legal Adviser of the Department of State (*ibid.*, § 49).

[15]   Fourth Geneva Convention, Article 16 (*ibid.*, § 5); Additional Protocol II, Article 8 (adopted by consensus) (*ibid.*, § 8); see also Additional Protocol II, Article 2(1) on non-discrimination (adopted by consensus) (cited in Vol. II, Ch. 32, § 369).

[16]   See, e.g., the military manuals of Argentina (cited in Vol. II, Ch. 35, § 11), Australia (*ibid.*, § 12), Belgium (*ibid.*, § 13), Benin (*ibid.*, § 14), Cameroon (*ibid.*, § 15), Canada (*ibid.*, §§ 16–17), Croatia (*ibid.*, § 18), France (*ibid.*, § 19), Germany (*ibid.*, § 20), India (*ibid.*, § 21), Italy (*ibid.*, § 22), Kenya (*ibid.*, § 23), Madagascar (*ibid.*, § 24), Netherlands (*ibid.*, §§ 25–26), New Zealand (*ibid.*, § 27), Nigeria (*ibid.*, §§ 28–29), Philippines (*ibid.*, § 30), Spain (*ibid.*, § 31), Switzerland (*ibid.*, § 32), Togo (*ibid.*, § 33), United Kingdom (*ibid.*, §§ 34–35) and United States (*ibid.*, §§ 36–39).

[17]   Cameroon, *Instructors' Manual* (*ibid.*, § 15); Kenya, *LOAC Manual* (*ibid.*, § 23).

[18]   Israel, High Court of Justice, *Jenin (Mortal Remains) case* (*ibid.*, § 46).

Rule 113. Each party to the conflict must take all possible measures to prevent the dead from being despoiled. Mutilation of dead bodies is prohibited.

Practice

Volume II, Chapter 35, Section B.

Summary

State practice establishes this rule as a norm of customary international law applicable in both international and non-international armed conflicts.

International armed conflicts

The obligation to take all possible measures to prevent the dead from being despoiled (or pillaged) was first codified in the 1907 Hague Convention (X).[19] It is now also codified in the Geneva Conventions.[20] It is also contained in Additional Protocol I,[21] albeit in more general terms of "respecting" the dead, which includes the notion of preventing the remains from being despoiled.[22]

The obligation to take all possible measures to prevent the dead from being despoiled or the prohibition of the despoliation of the dead is set forth in numerous military manuals.[23] The despoliation of dead bodies is an offence under the legislation of many States.[24] In the *Pohl case* in 1947, the US Military Tribunal at Nuremberg stated that robbing the dead "is and always has been a crime".[25] In addition, the prohibition of despoliation of dead bodies is an application of the general prohibition of pillage (see Rule 52).

The prohibition of mutilating dead bodies in international armed conflicts is covered by the crime of "committing outrages upon personal dignity" under the Statute of the International Criminal Court, which according to the Elements of Crimes also applies to dead persons (see commentary to Rule 90).[26]

---

[19] Hague Convention (X), Article 16 (*ibid.*, § 125).

[20] First Geneva Convention, Article 15, first paragraph (*ibid.*, § 126); Second Geneva Convention, Article 18, first paragraph (*ibid.*, § 127); Fourth Geneva Convention, Article 16, second paragraph (*ibid.*, § 128).

[21] Additional Protocol I, Article 34(1) (adopted by consensus) (*ibid.*, § 59).

[22] Yves Sandoz, Christophe Swinarski, Bruno Zimmermann (eds.), *Commentary on the Additional Protocols*, ICRC, Geneva, 1987, § 446.

[23] See, e.g., the military manuals of Argentina (cited in Vol. II, Ch. 35, § 134), Australia (*ibid.*, § 135), Belgium (*ibid.*, § 136), Benin (*ibid.*, § 137), Burkina Faso (*ibid.*, § 138), Cameroon (*ibid.*, § 139), Canada (*ibid.*, §§ 140–141), Congo (*ibid.*, § 142), France (*ibid.*, § 143), Germany (*ibid.*, § 144), Kenya (*ibid.*, § 145), Lebanon (*ibid.*, § 146), Madagascar (*ibid.*, § 147), Mali (*ibid.*, § 148), Morocco (*ibid.*, § 149), Netherlands (*ibid.*, § 150), New Zealand (*ibid.*, § 151), Nigeria (*ibid.*, § 152), Romania (*ibid.*, § 153), Senegal (*ibid.*, § 154), Spain (*ibid.*, § 155), Switzerland (*ibid.*, § 156), Togo (*ibid.*, § 157), United Kingdom (*ibid.*, §§ 158–159) and United States (*ibid.*, §§ 160–164).

[24] See, e.g., the legislation (*ibid.*, §§ 165–234).

[25] United States, Military Tribunal at Nuremberg, *Pohl case* (*ibid.*, § 235).

[26] Elements of Crimes for the ICC, Definition of committing outrages upon personal dignity as a war crime (ICC Statute, Footnote 49 relating to Article 8(2)(b)(xxi)).

Many military manuals prohibit the mutilation or other maltreatment of the dead.[27] Mutilation of the dead is an offence under the legislation of many States.[28] In several trials after the Second World War, the accused were convicted on charges of mutilation of dead bodies and cannibalism.[29] The prohibition on mutilating the dead is further supported by official statements and other practice.[30]

Non-international armed conflicts

The obligation to take all possible measures to prevent the dead from being despoiled in non-international armed conflicts is set forth in Additional Protocol II.[31] In addition, this obligation is contained in other instruments pertaining also to non-international armed conflicts.[32]

The obligation to take all possible measures to prevent the dead from being despoiled or the prohibition of the despoliation of the dead is set forth in a number of military manuals which are applicable in or have been applied in non-international armed conflicts.[33] It is also an offence in any armed conflict under the legislation of many States.[34] In addition, the prohibition of despoliation of dead bodies is an application of the general prohibition of pillage (see Rule 52).

[27] See, e.g., the military manuals of Australia (ibid., § 67), Bosnia and Herzegovina (ibid., § 68), Canada (ibid., §§ 69–70), Ecuador (ibid., § 71), Israel (ibid., § 72), South Korea (ibid., §§ 73–74), Netherlands (ibid., §§ 75–76), New Zealand (ibid., § 77), Nigeria (ibid., § 78), Philippines (ibid., § 79), South Africa (ibid., § 80), Spain (ibid., § 81), Switzerland (ibid., § 82), United Kingdom (ibid., §§ 83–84) and United States (ibid., §§ 85–87).

[28] See, e.g., the legislation of Australia (ibid., §§ 88–89), Bangladesh (ibid., § 90), Canada (ibid., § 91), Congo (ibid., § 92), Ethiopia (ibid., § 93), Ireland (ibid., § 94), Italy (ibid., §§ 95–96), Lithuania (ibid., § 97), Netherlands (ibid., § 98), New Zealand (ibid., § 99), Norway (ibid., § 100), Spain (ibid., § 101), Switzerland (ibid., § 102), United Kingdom (ibid., § 104) and Venezuela (ibid., § 105); see also the draft legislation of Trinidad and Tobago (ibid., § 103).

[29] Australia, Military Court at Wewak, Takehiko case (ibid., § 106); Australia, Military Court at Rabaul, Tisato case (ibid., § 107); United States, Military Commission at Yokohama, Kikuchi and Mahuchi case (ibid., § 109); United States, Military Commission at the Mariana Islands, Yochio and Others case (ibid., § 110); United States, General Military Court at Dachau, Schmid case (ibid., § 111).

[30] See, e.g., the statement of the United States (ibid., § 115) and the practice of Azerbaijan (ibid., § 112).

[31] Additional Protocol II, Article 8 (adopted by consensus) (ibid., § 130).

[32] See, e.g., Comprehensive Agreement on Respect for Human Rights and International Humanitarian Law in the Philippines, Part IV, Article 4(9) (ibid., § 133).

[33] See, e.g., the military manuals of Australia (ibid., § 135), Benin (ibid., § 137), Canada (ibid., §§ 140–141), Germany (ibid., § 144), Kenya (ibid., § 145), Lebanon (ibid., § 146), Madagascar (ibid., § 147), Spain (ibid., § 155) and Togo (ibid., § 157).

[34] See, e.g., the legislation of Armenia (ibid., § 168), Azerbaijan (ibid., § 170), Bosnia and Herzegovina (ibid., § 172), Canada (ibid., § 176), Colombia (ibid., § 179), Croatia (ibid., § 181), Ethiopia (ibid., § 188), Gambia (ibid., § 190), Georgia (ibid., § 191), Ghana (ibid., § 192), Guinea (ibid., § 193), Ireland (ibid., § 197), Kazakhstan (ibid., § 199), Kenya (ibid., § 200), Latvia (ibid., § 202), Moldova (ibid., § 207), New Zealand (ibid., § 209), Nicaragua (ibid., § 211), Nigeria (ibid., § 212), Norway (ibid., § 213), Singapore (ibid., § 215), Slovenia (ibid., § 217), Spain (ibid., §§ 218–219), Switzerland (ibid., § 220), Tajikistan (ibid., § 221), Trinidad and Tobago (ibid., § 223), Uganda (ibid., § 224), Ukraine (ibid., § 225), Venezuela (ibid., § 229), Yemen (ibid., § 231), Yugoslavia (ibid., § 232), Zambia (ibid., § 233) and Zimbabwe (ibid., § 234); see also the legislation of Bulgaria (ibid., § 174), Burkina Faso (ibid., § 175), Czech Republic (ibid., § 183), Hungary (ibid., § 194), Italy (ibid., § 198), South Korea (ibid., § 201), Nicaragua (ibid., § 210),

It has been argued by the Prosecutor before Colombia's Council of State that the obligation to respect the dead is inherent in common Article 3 of the Geneva Conventions.[35] The prohibition of mutilation is set forth in Additional Protocol II.[36] The prohibition of mutilating dead bodies in non-international armed conflicts is covered by the crime of "committing outrages upon personal dignity" under the Statute of the International Criminal Court, which according to the Elements of Crimes also applies to dead persons (see commentary to Rule 90).[37] This prohibition is set forth in other instruments pertaining also to non-international armed conflicts.[38]

Many military manuals which are applicable in or have been applied in non-international armed conflicts prohibit the mutilation or other maltreatment of the dead.[39] Under the legislation of many States, it is an offence to mutilate or otherwise maltreat dead bodies.[40]

No official contrary practice was found with respect to either international or non-international armed conflicts.

Rule 114. Parties to the conflict must endeavour to facilitate the return of the remains of the deceased upon request of the party to which they belong or upon the request of their next of kin. They must return their personal effects to them.

Practice

Volume II, Chapter 35, Section C.

Summary

State practice establishes the customary nature of this rule in international armed conflicts. In the context of non-international armed conflicts, there is

---

Romania (*ibid.*, § 214), Slovakia (*ibid.*, § 216), Togo (*ibid.*, § 222) and Uruguay (*ibid.*, § 228), the application of which is not excluded in time of non-international armed conflict, and the draft legislation of Argentina (*ibid.*, § 167).

[35] Colombia, Council of State, *Case No. 9276*, Statement of the Prosecutor (*ibid.*, § 113).

[36] Additional Protocol II, Article 4(2)(a) (adopted by consensus) (cited in Vol. II, Ch. 32, § 1420).

[37] Elements of Crimes for the ICC, Definition of committing outrages upon personal dignity as a war crime (ICC Statute, Footnote 57 relating to Article 8(2)(c)(ii)) (cited in Vol. II, Ch. 35, § 65).

[38] Cairo Declaration on Human Rights in Islam, Article 3(a) (*ibid.*, § 63); Comprehensive Agreement on Respect for Human Rights and International Humanitarian Law in the Philippines, Part IV, Article 3(4) (*ibid.*, § 64); UNTAET Regulation 2000/15, Section 6(1)(c)(ii) (*ibid.*, § 66).

[39] See, e.g., the military manuals of Australia (*ibid.*, § 67), Bosnia and Herzegovina (*ibid.*, § 68), Canada (*ibid.*, § 70), Ecuador (*ibid.*, § 71), South Korea (*ibid.*, § 73), New Zealand (*ibid.*, § 77), Philippines (*ibid.*, § 79), South Africa (*ibid.*, § 80) and Spain (*ibid.*, § 81).

[40] See, e.g., the legislation of Australia (*ibid.*, § 89), Canada (*ibid.*, § 91), Congo (*ibid.*, § 92), Ethiopia (*ibid.*, § 93), Ireland (*ibid.*, § 94), New Zealand (*ibid.*, § 99), Norway (*ibid.*, § 100), Switzerland (*ibid.*, § 102), United Kingdom (*ibid.*, § 104) and Venezuela (*ibid.*, § 105); see also the legislation of Italy (*ibid.*, §§ 95–96), the application of which is not excluded in time of non-international armed conflict, and the draft legislation of Trinidad and Tobago (*ibid.*, § 103).

a growing trend towards recognition of the obligation of parties to a conflict to facilitate the return of the remains of the dead to their families upon their request. The fact that this obligation is in keeping with the requirement of respect for family life (see Rule 105) implies that it should apply equally in both international and non-international armed conflicts.

International armed conflicts

The rule with respect to the return of the remains of the deceased is based on the Geneva Conventions.[41] The relevant provisions in the Conventions, however, are rather general and require agreement between parties for the remains to be returned. Additional Protocol I also recognises the need for such agreement, but sets out the procedure to be followed in the absence of an agreement.[42] A few examples of such agreements were found.[43] There are other examples of practice, such as the exchange of mortal remains between Egypt and Israel in 1975 and 1976 and the return of the ashes of 3,500 Japanese soldiers killed during the Second World War in Irian Jaya and handed over by Indonesia to the Japanese ambassador in Jakarta in 1991.[44]

The obligation to facilitate the return of the remains of the deceased is provided for in a number of military manuals.[45] These manuals include that of the United States, which is not party to Additional Protocol I.[46] This obligation is also set forth in the legislation of Azerbaijan, which is not party to Additional Protocol I.[47] In the *Abu-Rijwa case* before Israel's High Court in 2000, the Israel Defence Forces carried out DNA identification tests when asked by family members to repatriate remains. According to the Report on the Practice of Israel, this means that when remains can be identified correctly, they will be returned.[48] The United States has declared that it supports the rules in Additional Protocol I that are aimed at facilitating the return of remains when requested.[49]

---

[41] First Geneva Convention, Article 17, third paragraph (*ibid.*, § 244); Third Geneva Convention, Article 120, sixth paragraph (*ibid.*, § 245); Fourth Geneva Convention, Article 130, second paragraph (*ibid.*, § 246).

[42] Additional Protocol I, Article 34(2) and (3) (adopted by consensus) (*ibid.*, § 249).

[43] Panmunjon Armistice Agreement, Article II(13)(f) (*ibid.*, § 247); Agreement on Ending the War and Restoring Peace in Viet-Nam, Article 8(b) (*ibid.*, § 248); Finnish-Russian Agreement on War Dead (*ibid.*, § 250); Estonian-Finnish Agreement on War Dead (*ibid.*, § 251).

[44] See the reported practice of Egypt (*ibid.*, § 271), Indonesia (*ibid.*, § 275) and Israel (*ibid.*, § 271).

[45] See, e.g., the military manuals of Argentina (*ibid.*, § 254), Australia (*ibid.*, § 255), Croatia (*ibid.*, § 256), France (*ibid.*, § 257), Hungary (*ibid.*, § 258), Netherlands (*ibid.*, § 259), Spain (*ibid.*, § 260), Switzerland (*ibid.*, § 261), United Kingdom (*ibid.*, § 262) and United States (*ibid.*, §§ 263–264).

[46] United States, *Field Manual* (*ibid.*, § 263) and *Annotated Supplement to the Naval Handbook* (*ibid.*, § 264).

[47] Azerbaijan, *Law concerning the Protection of Civilian Persons and the Rights of Prisoners of War* (*ibid.*, § 265).

[48] Report on the Practice of Israel, referring to High Court, *Abu-Rijwa case* (*ibid.*, § 270).

[49] United States, Remarks of the Deputy Legal Adviser of the Department of State (*ibid.*, § 276).

The obligation to return the personal effects of the dead was first codified in the 1929 Geneva Convention for the Amelioration of the Condition of the Wounded and Sick in Armies in the Field.[50] It is now set forth in the 1949 Geneva Conventions.[51] These provisions oblige parties to return the personal effects of the dead through the Information Bureaux. Additional Protocol I encourages parties to conclude agreements to facilitate such return.[52]

Several military manuals specify the obligation to collect and return the personal effects of the dead.[53] It is also set forth in the legislation of some States.[54] This practice indicates that the objects in question are last wills, other documents of importance to the next of kin, money and all articles of an intrinsic or sentimental value. Weapons and other material which may be used in military operations may be kept as war booty (see Rule 49).

Non-international armed conflicts

There is no treaty provision requiring measures to transfer the remains of the dead to their families in the context of non-international armed conflicts. Nevertheless, a few agreements dealing with this issue were found.[55] There are also other examples of practice, such as the exchange under ICRC auspices of the mortal remains of more than 1,000 soldiers and LTTE fighters in Sri Lanka in 1998.[56]

Furthermore, in 1985, Colombia's Administrative Court in Cundinamarca held that families must not be denied their legitimate right to claim the bodies of their relatives, transfer them to wherever they see fit and bury them.[57] It is likely that such rights are also recognised in the legislation and/or case-law of other countries. There is a statement by a government involved in a non-international armed conflict that it would repatriate mortal remains.[58] There is also a case, however, where the military did not allow family members to collect the remains of the dead killed by government forces.[59]

---

[50] 1929 Geneva Convention for the Amelioration of the Condition of the Wounded and Sick in Armies in the Field, Article 4, third paragraph (*ibid.*, § 290).

[51] First Geneva Convention, Article 16, fourth paragraph (*ibid.*, § 291); Second Geneva Convention, Article 19, third paragraph (*ibid.*, § 291); Third Geneva Convention, Article 122, ninth paragraph (*ibid.*, § 292); Fourth Geneva Convention, Article 139 (*ibid.*, § 292).

[52] Additional Protocol I, Article 34(2) (adopted by consensus) (*ibid.*, § 293).

[53] See, e.g., the military manuals of Argentina (*ibid.*, § 296), Croatia (*ibid.*, § 299), France (*ibid.*, § 302), Hungary (*ibid.*, § 303), Israel (*ibid.*, § 304), Netherlands (*ibid.*, §§ 307 and 308), Nigeria (*ibid.*, § 309), Spain (*ibid.*, § 311), United Kingdom (*ibid.*, § 313) and United States (*ibid.*, § 314).

[54] See, e.g., the legislation of Azerbaijan (*ibid.*, § 315).

[55] Plan of Operation for the Joint Commission to Trace Missing Persons and Mortal Remains, Proposal 2.1 (*ibid.*, § 252); Comprehensive Agreement on Respect for Human Rights and International Humanitarian Law in the Philippines, Part IV, Article 3(4) (*ibid.*, § 253).

[56] See ICRC, *Annual Report 1998* (*ibid.*, § 287).

[57] Colombia, Administrative Court in Cundinamarca, *Case No. 4010* (*ibid.*, § 269).

[58] See statement (*ibid.*, § 277).

[59] See Inter-American Commission on Human Rights, *Case 10.124 (Suriname)* (*ibid.*, § 284).

This practice shows an equal concern for this issue in non-international armed conflicts, but it is not clear whether this arises from a sense of legal obligation. Three resolutions adopted at the international level, which received very wide support and no negative vote, called upon parties to armed conflicts to facilitate the return of the dead. In 1973, the 22nd International Conference of the Red Cross adopted a resolution by consensus in which it called upon parties to armed conflicts "during hostilities and after cessation of hostilities ... to facilitate the disinterment and return of remains".[60] In a resolution adopted in 1974, the UN General Assembly called upon parties to armed conflicts, regardless of their character, "to take such action as may be within their power ... to facilitate the disinterment and the return of remains, if requested by their families".[61] More recently, the Plan of Action for the years 2000–2003, adopted by the 27th International Conference of the Red Cross and Red Crescent in 1999, requires that all parties to an armed conflict take effective measures to ensure that "every effort is made ... to identify dead persons, inform their families and return their bodies to them".[62]

Furthermore, the practice mentioned above states the right of the families of the deceased to have the bodies returned to them.[63] This is an expression of the respect due to family life (see Rule 105) and is in line with the right of families to know the fate of their relatives (see Rule 117).

The obligation to return the personal effects of the dead in non-international armed conflicts is not provided for in treaty law, but it is likely that this issue is regulated under domestic law.

Rule 115. The dead must be disposed of in a respectful manner and their graves respected and properly maintained.

Practice

Volume II, Chapter 35, Section D.

Summary

State practice establishes this rule as a norm of customary international law applicable in both international and non-international armed conflicts.

---

[60] 22nd International Conference of the Red Cross, Res. V (*ibid.*, § 282).
[61] UN General Assembly, Res. 3220 (XXIX) (adopted by 95 votes in favour, none against and 32 abstentions) (*ibid.*, § 279).
[62] 27th International Conference of the Red Cross and Red Crescent, Res. I (adopted by consensus) (*ibid.*, § 283).
[63] Colombia, Administrative Court in Cundinamarca, *Case No. 4010* (*ibid.*, § 269); UN General Assembly, Res. 3220 (XXIX) (adopted by 95 votes in favour, none against and 32 abstentions) (*ibid.*, § 279); 27th International Conference of the Red Cross and Red Crescent, Res. I (adopted by consensus) (*ibid.*, § 283).

International armed conflicts

The obligation to dispose of the dead respectfully was first codified in the 1929 Geneva Conventions.[64] It is now dealt with in detail in the 1949 Geneva Conventions.[65]

Many military manuals specify that the dead must be disposed of decently.[66] This obligation is set forth in the legislation of most, if not all, States.[67] It was upheld in 2002 by Israel's High Court in the *Jenin (Mortal Remains) case*.[68]

The above-mentioned treaty provisions also require that graves be respected and properly maintained. Additional Protocol I adds that the parties must conclude agreements to protect and maintain gravesites permanently.[69] The requirement to respect and maintain gravesites is also laid down in numerous military manuals.[70]

Non-international armed conflicts

The obligation to dispose of the dead decently in non-international armed conflicts is set forth in Additional Protocol II.[71] In addition, this rule is contained in other instruments pertaining also to non-international armed conflicts.[72]

A number of military manuals which are applicable in or have been applied in non-international armed conflicts specify that the dead must be disposed of decently.[73] The legislation of most, if not all, States requires respect for this

---

[64] 1929 Geneva Convention for the Amelioration of the Condition of the Wounded and Sick in Armies in the Field, Article 4, fifth paragraph (*ibid.*, § 328); 1929 Geneva Convention Relative to the Treatment of Prisoners of War, Article 76, third paragraph (*ibid.*, § 329).

[65] First Geneva Convention, Article 17 (*ibid.*, § 330); Second Geneva Convention, Article 20 (*ibid.*, § 330); Third Geneva Convention, Article 120 (*ibid.*, § 330); Fourth Geneva Convention, Article 130 (*ibid.*, § 330).

[66] See, e.g., the military manuals of Argentina (*ibid.*, § 333), Australia (*ibid.*, § 334), Belgium (*ibid.*, § 335), Canada (*ibid.*, §§ 336–337), Croatia (*ibid.*, § 338), France (*ibid.*, § 340), Hungary (*ibid.*, § 341), Israel (*ibid.*, § 342), Italy (*ibid.*, § 343), Kenya (*ibid.*, § 344), Madagascar (*ibid.*, § 345), New Zealand (*ibid.*, § 346), Philippines (*ibid.*, § 347), Spain (*ibid.*, § 349), Switzerland (*ibid.*, § 350), Togo (*ibid.*, § 351), United Kingdom (*ibid.*, § 352) and United States (*ibid.*, §§ 353–354).

[67] See, e.g., the legislation of Azerbaijan (*ibid.*, § 355), Italy (*ibid.*, § 358) and Venezuela (*ibid.*, § 360).

[68] Israel, High Court of Justice, *Jenin (Mortal Remains) case* (*ibid.*, § 361).

[69] Additional Protocol I, Article 34(2) (adopted by consensus) (*ibid.*, § 488).

[70] See, e.g., the military manuals of Argentina (*ibid.*, § 491), Australia (*ibid.*, § 492), Canada (*ibid.*, § 493), Croatia (*ibid.*, § 494), France (*ibid.*, § 495), Hungary (*ibid.*, § 496), Israel (*ibid.*, § 497), Netherlands (*ibid.*, § 498), New Zealand (*ibid.*, § 499), Spain (*ibid.*, § 500), Switzerland (*ibid.*, § 501), United Kingdom (*ibid.*, § 502), United States (*ibid.*, §§ 503–504) and Yugoslavia (*ibid.*, § 505).

[71] Additional Protocol II, Article 8 (adopted by consensus) (*ibid.*, § 331).

[72] See, e.g., Comprehensive Agreement on Respect for Human Rights and International Humanitarian Law in the Philippines, Part IV, Article 4(9) (*ibid.*, § 332).

[73] See, e.g., the military manuals of Australia (*ibid.*, § 334), Canada (*ibid.*, §§ 336–337), Croatia (*ibid.*, § 338), Hungary (*ibid.*, § 341), Italy (*ibid.*, § 343), Kenya (*ibid.*, § 344), Madagascar (*ibid.*,

rule.[74] It may be said that this rule reflects a general principle of law requiring respect for the dead and their graves.

No official contrary practice was found with respect to either international or non-international armed conflicts. A reported case of the disrespectful disposal of dead civilians in Papua New Guinea was condemned by the UN Special Rapporteur on Extrajudicial, Summary or Arbitrary Executions.[75]

It is also likely that further detailed rules supporting the requirement of decent disposal of the dead and respect and proper maintenance of their gravesites are contained in domestic legislation.

Interpretation

The Geneva Conventions specify that the dead must be buried, if possible, according to the rites of the religion to which they belonged and that they may only be cremated in exceptional circumstances, namely because of imperative reasons of hygiene, on account of the religion of the deceased or in accordance with the express wish of the deceased.[76] The Geneva Conventions furthermore require that, in principle, burial should be in individual graves. Collective graves may only be used when circumstances do not permit the use of individual graves or, in case of burial of prisoners of war or civilian internees, because unavoidable circumstances require the use of collective graves.[77] Lastly, the Geneva Conventions require that graves be grouped according to nationality if possible.[78] These requirements are also set forth in numerous military manuals.[79]

§ 345), New Zealand (*ibid.*, § 346), Philippines (*ibid.*, § 347), Spain (*ibid.*, § 349) and Togo (*ibid.*, § 351).

[74] See, e.g., the legislation of Azerbaijan (*ibid.*, § 355) and Venezuela (*ibid.*, § 360).

[75] UN Commission on Human Rights, Special Rapporteur on Extrajudicial, Summary or Arbitrary Executions, Report (*ibid.*, § 365).

[76] First Geneva Convention, Article 17 (*ibid.*, §§ 372 and 398); Third Geneva Convention, Article 120 (*ibid.*, §§ 372 and 399); Fourth Geneva Convention, Article 130 (*ibid.*, §§ 372 and 400).

[77] First Geneva Convention, Article 17, first paragraph (*ibid.*, § 430); Second Geneva Convention, Article 20, first paragraph (*ibid.*, § 431); Third Geneva Convention, Article 120, fifth paragraph (*ibid.*, § 432); Fourth Geneva Convention, Article 130, second paragraph (*ibid.*, § 433).

[78] First Geneva Convention, Article 17, third paragraph (*ibid.*, § 464); Third Geneva Convention, Article 120, fourth paragraph (*ibid.*, § 465).

[79] Concerning respect for the religious beliefs of the dead, see, e.g., the military manuals of Argentina (*ibid.*, § 375), Australia (*ibid.*, § 376), Benin (*ibid.*, § 377), Cameroon (*ibid.*, § 378), Canada (*ibid.*, §§ 379–380), Israel (*ibid.*, § 381), Philippines (*ibid.*, § 382), Switzerland (*ibid.*, § 383), Togo (*ibid.*, § 384), United Kingdom (*ibid.*, § 385) and United States (*ibid.*, § 386). Concerning the cremation of bodies, see, e.g., the military manuals of Argentina (*ibid.*, § 402), Australia (*ibid.*, § 403), Benin (*ibid.*, § 404), Canada (*ibid.*, §§ 405–406), France (*ibid.*, § 407), Israel (*ibid.*, § 408), Kenya (*ibid.*, § 409), Netherlands (*ibid.*, § 410), Spain (*ibid.*, § 411), Switzerland (*ibid.*, § 412), Togo (*ibid.*, § 413), United Kingdom (*ibid.*, §§ 414–415) and United States (*ibid.*, §§ 416–418). Concerning the burial in individual or collective graves, see, e.g., the military manuals Argentina (*ibid.*, § 436), Australia (*ibid.*, § 437), Benin (*ibid.*, § 438), Canada (*ibid.*, §§ 439–440), Croatia (*ibid.*, § 441), France (*ibid.*, § 442), Italy (*ibid.*, § 443), Kenya (*ibid.*, § 444), Madagascar (*ibid.*, § 445), Netherlands (*ibid.*, § 446), Spain (*ibid.*, § 447), Switzer-

It is likely that some of these requirements also apply in non-international armed conflicts on the basis of national law. In 1995, for example, Colombia's Council of State held that the deceased must be buried individually subject to all the requirements of the law, and not in mass graves.[80]

Rule 116. With a view to the identification of the dead, each party to the conflict must record all available information prior to disposal and mark the location of the graves.

Practice

Volume II, Chapter 35, Section E.

Summary

State practice establishes this rule as a norm of customary international law applicable in both international and non-international armed conflicts. This rule is reinforced by the requirement of respect for family life (see Rule 105) and the right of families to know the fate of their relatives (see Rule 117).

International armed conflicts

The obligation to identify the dead prior to their disposal was first codified in the 1929 Geneva Convention for the Amelioration of the Condition of the Wounded and Sick in Armies in the Field.[81] This obligation, together with the details to be recorded and the obligation to transmit the information to the other party and the Central Tracing Agency, is now set forth in the 1949 Geneva Conventions.[82]

Numerous military manuals set forth the obligation to identify the dead prior to disposal.[83] Some of them specify what details are to be recorded with regard to

---

(*ibid.*, § 448), Togo (*ibid.*, § 449), United Kingdom (*ibid.*, § 450), United States (*ibid.*, § 451) and Yugoslavia (*ibid.*, § 452). Concerning the grouping of graves according to nationality, see, e.g., the military manuals of Argentina (*ibid.*, § 468), Australia (*ibid.*, § 469), Cameroon (*ibid.*, § 470), Netherlands (*ibid.*, § 471), United States (*ibid.*, § 472) and Yugoslavia (*ibid.*, § 473).

[80] Colombia, Council of State, *Administrative Case No. 10941* (*ibid.*, § 456).

[81] 1929 Geneva Convention for the Amelioration of the Condition of the Wounded and Sick in Armies in the Field, Article 4 (*ibid.*, § 518).

[82] First Geneva Convention, Articles 16–17 (*ibid.*, §§ 519–520, 589 and 670); Second Geneva Convention, Articles 19–20 (*ibid.*, §§ 519–520); Third Geneva Convention, Articles 120–122 (*ibid.*, §§ 521, 589 and 670); Fourth Geneva Convention, Articles 129–131 (*ibid.*, §§ 522–523, 589 and 670) and Articles 136–139.

[83] See, e.g., the military manuals of Argentina (cited in Vol. II, Ch. 35, § 529), Australia (*ibid.*, § 530), Belgium (*ibid.*, § 531), Benin (*ibid.*, § 532), Cameroon (*ibid.*, § 533), Canada (*ibid.*, §§ 534–535), Croatia (*ibid.*, §§ 536–537), France (*ibid.*, §§ 538–539), Germany (*ibid.*, § 540), Hungary (*ibid.*, § 541), Israel (*ibid.*, § 543), Italy (*ibid.*, § 544), Kenya (*ibid.*, § 545), Madagascar (*ibid.*, § 546), Netherlands (*ibid.*, §§ 547–548), New Zealand (*ibid.*, § 549), Nigeria (*ibid.*, § 550), Spain (*ibid.*, § 552), Switzerland (*ibid.*, § 553), Togo (*ibid.*, § 554), United Kingdom (*ibid.*, § 555) and United States (*ibid.*, §§ 556–557).

the deceased.[84] In addition, several military manuals include the requirement to record the location of the place of burial.[85] In the *Jenin (Mortal Remains) case*, Israel's High Court of Justice stated that the identification of the dead was a "highly important humanitarian deed".[86]

Non-international armed conflicts

There is no treaty provision explicitly requiring measures to identify the dead prior to their disposal in the context of a non-international armed conflict. There is consistent practice which indicates, nevertheless, that this obligation is also incumbent upon parties to non-international armed conflicts. This practice includes military manuals which are applicable in or have been applied in non-international armed conflicts.[87] In addition, the case-law of Argentina and Colombia has required that prior to their disposal the dead must be examined so that they can be identified and the circumstances of death established.[88] It is likely that such requirements are part of the legislation of numerous States.[89]

Measures to identify the dead and investigate the cause of death are also required by international human rights law, in particular in order to protect the right to life. The European Court of Human Rights and the Inter-American Commission and Court of Human Rights have required that effective measures be taken to this effect in a timely fashion, even in situations of armed violence.[90] Other instances have called for such measures in the context of the conflicts in Chechnya, El Salvador and the former Yugoslavia.[91] In addition, on two occasions, the Inter-American Court of Human Rights ruled that the State was obliged to do all it could to inform the relatives of the location of the remains of persons killed as a result of enforced disappearances.[92]

---

[84] See, e.g., the military manuals of Australia (*ibid.*, § 530) and United States (*ibid.*, § 556).
[85] See, e.g., the military manuals of Argentina (*ibid.*, § 592), Australia (*ibid.*, § 593), Canada (*ibid.*, § 594), Kenya (*ibid.*, § 595), Netherlands (*ibid.*, § 596), Spain (*ibid.*, § 597), United Kingdom (*ibid.*, § 598) and United States (*ibid.*, §§ 599–600).
[86] Israel, High Court of Justice, *Jenin (Mortal Remains) case* (*ibid.*, § 566).
[87] See, e.g., the military manuals of Benin (*ibid.*, § 532), Canada (*ibid.*, § 535), Croatia (*ibid.*, §§ 536–537), Germany (*ibid.*, § 540), India (*ibid.*, § 542), Italy (*ibid.*, § 544), Kenya (*ibid.*, § 545), Madagascar (*ibid.*, § 546), Senegal (*ibid.*, 551) and Togo (*ibid.*, § 554).
[88] Argentina, Court of Appeal, *Military Junta case* (*ibid.*, § 563); Colombia, Council of State, *Case No. 10941* (*ibid.*, § 564).
[89] See, e.g., the legislation of Azerbaijan (*ibid.*, § 558).
[90] European Court of Human Rights, *Kaya v. Turkey* (*ibid.*, § 580), *Ergi v. Turkey* (*ibid.*, § 581) and *Yasa v. Turkey* (*ibid.*, § 582); Inter-American Commission on Human Rights, *Case 11.137 (Argentina)* (*ibid.*, § 583); Inter-American Court of Human Rights, *Neira Alegría and Others case* (*ibid.*, § 584).
[91] See UN Commission on Human Rights, Report of the Special Rapporteur on the Situation of Human Rights in the Former Yugoslavia (*ibid.*, § 570); ONUSAL, Report of the Director of the Human Rights Division (*ibid.*, § 571); UN Commission of Experts Established pursuant to Security Council Resolution 780 (1992), Final Report (*ibid.*, § 572); EU, Statement before the Permanent Council of the OSCE (*ibid.*, § 576).
[92] Inter-American Court of Human Rights, *Velásquez Rodríguez case* (*ibid.*, § 709) and *Godínez Cruz case* (*ibid.*, § 710).

In December 1991, when the conflict in the former Yugoslavia was charac-terised as non-international, the parties to the conflict reached an agreement with respect to the exchange of information regarding the identification of the deceased.[93] Other practice found includes that of the Philippine government, which collects information on dead insurgents after clashes,[94] and that of the Salvadoran army photographing the bodies of the dead after a clash between FMLN troops and a military patrol.[95]

Three resolutions adopted at the international level, which received very wide support and no negative vote, called upon parties to armed conflicts to account for the dead (identify and provide information about the dead). In 1973, the 22nd International Conference of the Red Cross called upon parties to armed conflicts "during hostilities and after cessation of hostilities . . . to accomplish the humanitarian mission of accounting for the dead".[96] In a resolution adopted in 1974, the UN General Assembly called upon parties to armed conflicts, regardless of their character, to cooperate "in providing information on the missing and dead in armed conflicts".[97] More recently, the Plan of Action for the years 2000–2003, adopted by the 27th International Conference of the Red Cross and Red Crescent in 1999, required that all parties to an armed conflict take effective measures to ensure that "every effort is made . . . to identify dead persons".[98]

Furthermore, one of the main purposes of this rule is to prevent the enforced disappearance of persons (see Rule 98) and to ensure that they do not otherwise go missing (see Rule 117), two obligations which apply equally to international and non-international armed conflicts.

No official contrary practice was found with respect to either international or non-international armed conflicts.

Interpretation

The obligation to identify the dead is an obligation of means, and parties have to use their best efforts and all means at their disposal in this respect. According to the practice collected, the measures envisaged here include collecting one half of the double identity disk, autopsies, the recording of autopsies, the estab-lishment of death certificates, the recording of the disposal of the dead, burial

---

[93] See Plan of Operation for the Joint Commission to Trace Missing Persons and Mortal Remains, Proposal 1.1 (*ibid.*, § 673).
[94] See Report on the Practice of the Philippines (*ibid.*, § 700).
[95] See UN Commission on the Truth for El Salvador, Report (*ibid.*, § 573).
[96] 22nd International Conference of the Red Cross, Res. V (*ibid.*, § 706).
[97] UN General Assembly, Res. 3220 (XXIX) (adopted by 95 votes in favour, none against and 32 abstentions) (*ibid.*, §§ 569 and 701).
[98] 27th International Conference of the Red Cross and Red Crescent, Res. I (adopted by consensus) (*ibid.*, § 579).

in individual graves, prohibition of collective graves without prior identification, and the proper marking of graves. Practice also suggests that exhumation combined with the application of forensic methods, including DNA testing, may be an appropriate method of identifying the dead after burial.

In general, this obligation also requires effective cooperation between all parties concerned. The Plan of Action for the years 2000–2003, adopted by the 27th International Conference of the Red Cross and Red Crescent in 1999, requires that in order to comply with this rule, "appropriate procedures be put into place at the latest from the beginning of an armed conflict".[99]

---

[99] 27th International Conference of the Red Cross and Red Crescent, Geneva, 31 October–6 November 1999, Res. I, Annex 2, Plan of Action for the years 2000–2003, Actions proposed for final goal 1.1, § 1(e).

MISSING PERSONS

Rule 117. Each party to the conflict must take all feasible measures to account for persons reported missing as a result of armed conflict and must provide their family members with any information it has on their fate.

Practice

Volume II, Chapter 36, Section A.

Summary

State practice establishes this rule as a norm of customary international law applicable in both international and non-international armed conflicts. The obligation to account for missing persons is consistent with the prohibition of enforced disappearances (see Rule 98) and the requirement to respect family life (see Rule 105). This rule is also supported by the obligation to record all available information prior to disposal of the dead (see Rule 116). The rules cross-referred to here all apply in both international and non-international armed conflicts.

International and non-international armed conflicts

The Geneva Conventions provide for the setting up of Information Bureaux whose role it is to centralise information on prisoners of war and civilians belonging to an adverse party, to transmit such information to that party and to open inquiries in order to elucidate the fate of missing persons.[1] The Fourth Geneva Convention requires that parties to the conflict facilitate enquiries by persons looking for family members dispersed by the conflict.[2] Additional Protocol I requires each party to the conflict to search for persons who have been reported missing by the adverse party.[3] The obligation to account for

---

[1] Third Geneva Convention, Article 122 (cited in Vol. II, Ch. 36, § 53); Fourth Geneva Convention, Article 136 (*ibid.*, § 53). Articles 16 and 17 of the First Geneva Convention and Article 19 of the Second Geneva Convention refer to the information bureaux established according to Article 122 of the Third Geneva Convention.

[2] Fourth Geneva Convention, Article 26 (*ibid.*, § 143).

[3] Additional Protocol I, Article 33 (adopted by consensus) (*ibid.*, § 2).

missing persons is recognised in numerous agreements between parties to both international and non-international armed conflicts.[4]

The rule requiring parties to the conflict to search for missing persons is set forth in a number of military manuals.[5] It is contained in some national legislation.[6] It is supported by official statements.[7] There are also reports of physical practice supporting this rule.[8] This practice includes that of States not, or not at the time, party to Additional Protocol I.[9]

States and international organisations have on many occasions requested that persons missing as a result of the conflicts in Bosnia and Herzegovina, Cyprus, East Timor, Guatemala, Kosovo and the former Yugoslavia be accounted for.[10] The creation of the position of Expert for the Special Process on Missing Persons in the Territory of the Former Yugoslavia is further evidence of the international community's expectation that the fate of missing persons be clarified.[11]

In addition to country-specific resolutions, several resolutions adopted at the international level, which received very wide support and no negative vote, state the general duty to clarify the fate of missing persons. For example, in a resolution on assistance and cooperation in accounting for persons who are

---

[4] See, e.g., Joint Declaration on Soviet-Japanese Relations, para. 5 (*ibid.*, § 1); Israel-PLO Agreement on the Gaza Strip, Article XIX (*ibid.*, §§ 3 and 57); Comprehensive Agreement on Respect for Human Rights and International Humanitarian Law in the Philippines, Part IV, Article 4(9), (*ibid.*, § 4); Agreement on Refugees and Displaced Persons annexed to the Dayton Accords, Article 5 (*ibid.*, § 55); Agreement on the Normalization of Relations between Croatia and the FRY, Article 6 (*ibid.*, § 56); Protocol to the Moscow Agreement on a Cease-fire in Chechnya to Locate Missing Persons and to Free Forcibly Detained Persons, paras. 5–6 (*ibid.*, § 58); Agreement on Ending the War and Restoring Peace in Viet-Nam, Chapter III (*ibid.*, § 96); Memorandum of Understanding on the Application of International Humanitarian Law between Croatia and the SFRY, para. 8 (*ibid.*, § 98); Plan of Operation for the 1991 Joint Commission to Trace Missing Persons and Mortal Remains, para. 2.1.1 and 2.2.2 (*ibid.*, § 100); Joint Declaration by the Presidents of the FRY and Croatia (October 1992), para. 3 (*ibid.*, § 101).

[5] See, e.g., the military manuals of Argentina (*ibid.*, § 5), Australia (*ibid.*, § 6), Canada (*ibid.*, § 7), Croatia (*ibid.*, § 8), Hungary (*ibid.*, § 9), Indonesia (*ibid.*, § 10), Israel (*ibid.*, § 11), Kenya (*ibid.*, § 12), Madagascar (*ibid.*, § 13), Netherlands (*ibid.*, § 14), New Zealand (*ibid.*, § 15) and Spain (*ibid.*, § 16).

[6] See, e.g., the legislation of Azerbaijan (*ibid.*, § 17) and Zimbabwe (*ibid.*, § 20).

[7] See, e.g., the statements of the Federal Republic of Germany (*ibid.*, § 24), Germany (*ibid.*, § 25) and United States (*ibid.*, §§ 33–34).

[8] See, e.g., the practice of Croatia (*ibid.*, § 23) and Netherlands (*ibid.*, § 30) and the reported practice of Australia (*ibid.*, § 108), Israel (*ibid.*, § 26), Japan (*ibid.*, § 32), Malaysia (*ibid.*, § 29), Peru (*ibid.*, § 31), Philippines (*ibid.*, § 74), USSR (*ibid.*, § 32) and Vietnam (*ibid.*, § 108).

[9] See, e.g., the military manuals of Indonesia (*ibid.*, § 10), Israel (*ibid.*, § 11) and Kenya (*ibid.*, § 12), the legislation of Azerbaijan (*ibid.*, § 17), the statements of the United States (*ibid.*, §§ 33–34) and the reported practice of Israel (*ibid.*, § 26), Japan (*ibid.*, § 32) and Malaysia (*ibid.*, § 29); see also the statements of Indonesia (*ibid.*, § 112) and United Kingdom (*ibid.*, § 114).

[10] See, e.g., the statements of Germany (*ibid.*, §§ 25 and 109–110) and United States (*ibid.*, § 34); UN Security Council, Statement by the President (*ibid.*, § 35); UN General Assembly, Res. 54/183 (*ibid.*, § 77), Res. 49/196 (*ibid.*, § 117) and Res. 50/193 (*ibid.*, § 118); UN Commission on Human Rights, Res. 1987/50 (*ibid.*, § 36), Res. 1994/72 (*ibid.*, §§ 78 and 120), Res. 1995/35 (*ibid.*, §§ 79 and 121) and Res. 1998/79 (*ibid.*, § 80); UN Commission on Human Rights, Statement by the Chairman (*ibid.*, § 38); Council of Europe, Parliamentary Assembly, Rec. 974 (*ibid.*, § 42), Rec. 1056 (*ibid.*, § 43), Res. 1066 (*ibid.*, § 83) and Rec. 1385 (*ibid.*, § 84); European Parliament, Resolution on the violation of human rights in Cyprus (*ibid.*, § 85).

[11] See the practice (*ibid.*, §§ 41 and 127).

missing or dead in armed conflicts, adopted in 1974, the UN General Assembly called on parties to armed conflicts, regardless of their character, "to take such action as may be within their power . . . to provide information about those who are missing in action".[12] In a resolution on missing persons in 2002, the UN Commission on Human Rights reaffirmed that each party to an armed conflict "shall search for the persons who have been reported missing by an adverse party".[13] When this resolution was adopted, India, Indonesia, Japan, Malaysia, Pakistan, Sudan and Thailand were members of the Commission but had not ratified the Additional Protocols. The 26th International Conference of the Red Cross and Red Crescent in 1995 strongly urged all parties to an armed conflict "to provide families with information on the fate of their missing relatives".[14] The Plan of Action for the years 2000–2003, adopted by the 27th International Conference of the Red Cross and Red Crescent in 1999, requires that all parties to an armed conflict ensure that "every effort is made to clarify the fate of all persons unaccounted for and to inform the families accordingly".[15]

The SPLM/A Penal and Disciplinary Laws show that non-State actors also consider it necessary to keep records of military personnel in order to facilitate the search for missing persons.[16]

Interpretation

Practice indicates that this rule is motivated by the right of families to know the fate of their missing relatives. This is implicit in Article 26 of the Fourth Geneva Convention, whereby States must facilitate enquiries made by members of families dispersed as a result of armed conflict.[17] Additional Protocol I states explicitly that in the implementation of the section on missing and dead persons, including the obligation to search for persons reported missing, the activities of States, parties to the conflict and international humanitarian organisations must be "prompted mainly by the right of families to know the fate of their relatives".[18] An interpretation of this sentence in the light of the ordinary meaning of the words and the context suggests that the right of families to know the fate of their relatives pre-existed the adoption of Additional Protocol I and that the obligations the Protocol sets out with regard to missing persons (Article 33) and the treatment of the remains of the dead (Article 34)

---

[12] UN General Assembly, Res. 3220 (XXIX) (adopted by 95 votes in favour, none against and 32 abstentions) (*ibid.*, § 76).

[13] UN Commission on Human Rights, Res. 2002/60 (adopted without a vote) (*ibid.*, § 37).

[14] 26th International Conference of the Red Cross and Red Crescent, Res. II (*ibid.*, §§ 87 and 184).

[15] 27th International Conference of the Red Cross and Red Crescent, Res. I (adopted by consensus) (*ibid.*, §§ 45, 88 and 185).

[16] SPLM/A, *Penal and Disciplinary Laws* (*ibid.*, § 195).

[17] Fourth Geneva Convention, Article 26 (*ibid.*, § 143).

[18] Additional Protocol I, Article 32 (adopted by consensus) (*ibid.*, § 144). For the *travaux préparatoires* leading to the adoption of this provision see the statements at the CDDH (*ibid.*, §§ 165–168 and 171–173).

are based on this right.[19] The right of families to know the fate of their relatives is also set forth in other international instruments.[20]

A number of military manuals, official statements and other practice emphasise the right of families to know the fate of their relatives.[21] This practice includes that of States not, or not at the time, party to Additional Protocol I.[22] An explanatory memorandum submitted by the German government to parliament in the process of the ratification procedure of the Additional Protocols remarks that Article 32 of Additional Protocol I does not confer a subjective right on the relatives of a missing person to gain information, but this is the only State to have made such a statement.[23]

It is interesting to note that the SPLM/A publishes the names and other particulars of persons who fall into its hands during military operations and that it claims to do this for the benefit of the families of the captives.[24]

The right of families to know the fate of their relatives is also supported by a number of resolutions adopted by international organisations and conferences. For example, in a resolution adopted in 1974, the UN General Assembly stated that "the desire to know the fate of loved ones lost in armed conflicts is a basic human need which should be satisfied to the greatest extent possible".[25] In a resolution adopted in 2002, the UN Commission on Human Rights reaffirmed "the right of families to know the fate of their relatives reported missing in connection with armed conflict".[26] The right of families to know the fate of their relatives is also supported by a resolution of the European Parliament and by recommendations of the Parliamentary Assembly of the Council of Europe.[27]

The International Conference of the Red Cross and Red Crescent adopted resolutions in 1986, 1995 and 1999 stressing the right of families to be informed of

---

[19] Yves Sandoz, Christophe Swinarski, Bruno Zimmermann (eds.), *Commentary on the Additional Protocols*, ICRC, Geneva, 1987, §§ 1217–1218.

[20] See, e.g., Guiding Principles on Internal Displacement, Principles 16(1) and 17(4) (cited in Vol. II, Ch. 36, § 147); UN Secretary-General's Bulletin, Section 9.8 (*ibid.*, § 148).

[21] See, e.g., the military manuals of Argentina (*ibid.*, § 149), Australia (*ibid.*, § 150), Cameroon (*ibid.*, § 151), Canada (*ibid.*, § 152), Kenya (*ibid.*, § 153), Israel (*ibid.*, § 154), Madagascar (*ibid.*, § 155), New Zealand (*ibid.*, § 156), Spain (*ibid.*, § 157), United Kingdom (*ibid.*, § 158) and United States (*ibid.*, §§ 159–161), the statements of Austria (*ibid.*, § 166), Cyprus (*ibid.*, §§ 165–166), France (*ibid.*, §§ 165–166), Germany (*ibid.*, § 167), Greece (*ibid.*, §§ 165–166), Holy See (*ibid.*, §§ 165–166 and 168), Nicaragua (*ibid.*, § 166), Spain (*ibid.*, § 166) and United States (*ibid.*, §§ 172–174) and the practice of South Korea (*ibid.*, § 170).

[22] See, e.g., the military manuals of Kenya (*ibid.*, § 153), Israel (*ibid.*, § 154) and United States (*ibid.*, § 161) and the statement of the United States (*ibid.*, § 174).

[23] Germany, Explanatory memorandum on the Additional Protocols to the Geneva Conventions (*ibid.*, § 169).

[24] Report on the Practice of the SPLM/A (*ibid.*, § 195).

[25] UN General Assembly, Res. 3220 (XXIX) (adopted by 95 votes in favour, none against and 32 abstentions) (*ibid.*, § 175).

[26] UN Commission on Human Rights, Res. 2002/60 (*ibid.*, § 176).

[27] European Parliament, Resolution on the problem of missing persons in Cyprus (*ibid.*, § 181); Council of Europe, Parliamentary Assembly, Rec. 868 (*ibid.*, § 178) and Rec. 1056 (*ibid.*, § 180).

the fate of their relatives.[28] The Final Declaration adopted by the International Conference for the Protection of War Victims in 1993 insisted that families of missing persons must not be denied information about the fate of their relatives.[29] These four resolutions were adopted with the support of States not party to Additional Protocol I and were couched in general terms, deliberately not limited to international armed conflicts.

Case-law of the UN Human Rights Committee and regional human rights bodies confirms that it is prohibited to withhold deliberately from families information on missing relatives. The Committee stated that disappearances gravely violated the rights of the disappeared person's family, who suffered severe and often prolonged periods of mental anguish owing to uncertainty about the fate of their loved one.[30] The European Court of Human Rights found in several cases that withholding information from the families of persons detained by security forces, or silence in the case of persons missing during armed conflict, attained a degree of severity that amounted to inhuman treatment.[31] The Inter-American Court of Human Rights expressed the same view when it held that the State is obliged to use the means at its disposal to inform the relatives of the fate of disappeared persons.[32] It also stated that, in the event of the death of a victim, the State is obliged to give information to the relatives on where the remains of the deceased person are located.[33] The African Commission on Human and Peoples' Rights has similarly held that "holding an individual without permitting him or her to have any contact with his or her family, and refusing to inform the family whether the individual is being held and his or her whereabouts is an inhuman treatment of both the detainee and the family concerned".[34]

The African Charter on the Rights and Welfare of the Child provides that if families are separated as a result of State action, the State must provide the children with essential information concerning the whereabouts of their family members.[35] The Charter also provides that if separation is caused by internal

---

[28] 25th International Conference of the Red Cross, Res. XIII (ibid., § 182); 26th International Conference of the Red Cross and Red Crescent, Res. II (ibid., § 184); 27th International Conference of the Red Cross and Red Crescent, Res. I (adopted by consensus) (ibid., § 185).

[29] International Conference for the Protection of War Victims, Final Declaration (adopted by consensus) (ibid., § 183).

[30] See, e.g., UN Human Rights Committee, Quinteros v. Uruguay (ibid., § 186). The views of the Committee were based, inter alia, on Article 7 of the American Convention on Human Rights.

[31] European Court of Human Rights, Kurt v. Turkey (ibid., § 188), Timurtas v. Turkey (ibid., § 188) and Cyprus case (ibid., § 189).

[32] Inter-American Court of Human Rights, Velásquez Rodríguez case (ibid., § 191). In this case, the Court found that there was a violation of Articles 4, 5 and 7 of the American Convention on Human Rights.

[33] See, e.g., Inter-American Court of Human Rights, Bámaca Velásquez case (ibid., § 192) and Bámaca Velásquez case (Reparations) (ibid., § 193). In this case, the Court found that there was a violation of Article 5(1) and (2) of the American Convention on Human Rights.

[34] African Commission on Human and Peoples' Rights, Amnesty International and Others v. Sudan (ibid., § 187).

[35] African Charter on the Rights and Welfare of the Child, Article 19(3) (ibid., § 145).

or external displacement arising from an armed conflict, States must take all necessary measures to trace the parents or relatives of children.[36]

The obligation to account for missing persons is an obligation of means. Each party to the conflict must use its best efforts in this respect. This includes searching for, but also facilitating the search for, persons reported missing as a result of the conflict. As part of that obligation, each party to the conflict has a duty to keep records of deceased persons and of persons deprived of their liberty (see Rules 116 and 123). The obligation to provide that information which is available, however, is an obligation of result.

Practice suggests that exhumation may be an appropriate method of establishing the fate of missing persons.[37] Practice also indicates that possible ways of seeking to account for missing persons include the setting up of special commissions or other tracing mechanisms. Croatia's Commission for Tracing Persons Missing in War Activities in the Republic of Croatia set up in 1991 and re-established in 1993 is one example.[38] Where such commissions are created, the parties have an obligation to cooperate in good faith with each other and with such commissions, for it is clear that cooperation is essential for their success. These commissions may include the ICRC or other organisations. The UN Secretary-General's Bulletin on observance by United Nations forces of international humanitarian law provides that the UN force shall facilitate the work of the ICRC's Central Tracing Agency.[39] Additional specifications for international armed conflict are to be found in the Fourth Geneva Convention and Additional Protocol I.[40]

Practice indicates that the obligation to account for missing persons arises at the latest after an adverse party provides notification of those who are missing. The military manuals of Kenya, Netherlands and New Zealand provide that this duty arises "as soon as circumstances permit" or "as soon as possible".[41] In an official statement in 1987, the United States supported the rule that the search for missing persons should be carried out "when circumstances permit, and at the latest from the end of hostilities".[42] Azerbaijan's Law concerning the Protection of Civilian Persons and the Rights of Prisoners of War requires

---

[36] African Charter on the Rights and Welfare of the Child, Article 25(2)(b) (*ibid.*, § 146).
[37] See, e.g., Office of the UN High Commissioner for Human Rights, Statement of the Expert for the Special Process on Missing Persons in the Territory of the Former Yugoslavia (*ibid.*, § 41) and Briefing on Progress Reached in Investigation of Violations of International Law in certain areas of Bosnia and Herzegovina (*ibid.*, § 126) and High Representative for the Implementation of the Peace Agreement on Bosnia and Herzegovina, Reports (*ibid.*, § 127).
[38] See the practice of Croatia (*ibid.*, § 23).
[39] UN Secretary-General's Bulletin, Section 9.8 (*ibid.*, § 102).
[40] Fourth Geneva Convention, Articles 136–141 (*ibid.*, §§ 53 and 95); Additional Protocol I, Article 33 (adopted by consensus) (*ibid.*, § 54).
[41] Kenya, *LOAC Manual* (*ibid.*, § 12); Netherlands, *Military Manual* (*ibid.*, § 14); New Zealand, *Military Manual* (*ibid.*, § 15).
[42] United States, Remarks of the Deputy Legal Adviser of the Department of State (*ibid.*, § 33).

that tracing begin "at the first opportunity and at the latest as soon as active military operations are over".[43]

In a resolution adopted in 1974, the UN General Assembly called upon parties to armed conflicts, "regardless of their character or location, during and after the end of hostilities", to provide information about those who are missing in action.[44] In a resolution on missing persons adopted in 2002, the UN Commission on Human Rights reaffirmed that "each party to an armed conflict, as soon as circumstances permit and at the latest from the end of active hostilities, shall search for the persons who have been reported missing by an adverse party".[45]

---

[43] Azerbaijan, *Law concerning the Protection of Civilian Persons and the Rights of Prisoners of War* (*ibid.*, § 17).

[44] UN General Assembly, Res. 3220 (XXIX) (adopted by 95 votes in favour, none against and 32 abstentions) (*ibid.*, § 76).

[45] UN Commission on Human Rights, Res. 2002/60 (adopted without a vote) (*ibid.*, § 37).

CHAPTER 37

PERSONS DEPRIVED OF THEIR LIBERTY

Note: *This chapter addresses the treatment of persons deprived of their liberty for reasons related to armed conflict, whether international or non-international. With regard to international armed conflicts, this term includes combatants who have fallen into the hands of the adverse party, civilian internees and security detainees. With regard to non-international armed conflicts, it includes persons who have taken a direct part in hostilities and who have fallen into the power of the adverse party, as well as those detained on criminal charges or for security reasons, provided that a link exists between the situation of armed conflict and the deprivation of liberty. The term "detainees" as used in this chapter covers all persons thus deprived of their liberty.*

Rule 118. Persons deprived of their liberty must be provided with adequate food, water, clothing, shelter and medical attention.

Practice

Volume II, Chapter 37, Section A.

Summary

State practice establishes this rule as a norm of customary international law applicable in both international and non-international armed conflicts.

International armed conflicts

The rule according to which prisoners of war must be provided with adequate food and clothing is a long-standing rule of customary international law already recognised in the Lieber Code, the Brussels Declaration and the Oxford Manual.[1] It was codified in the Hague Regulations and is now dealt

---

[1] Lieber Code, Article 76 (cited in Vol. II, Ch. 37, § 9); Brussels Declaration, Article 27 (*ibid.*, § 10); Oxford Manual, Article 69 (*ibid.*, § 11).

with in detail by the Third Geneva Convention.[2] Under the Fourth Geneva Convention, this rule is also applicable to civilians deprived of their liberty in connection with an international armed conflict.[3]

The rule requiring provision for the basic needs of persons deprived of their liberty is set forth in numerous military manuals.[4] Violation of this rule is an offence under the legislation of many States.[5] This rule is also supported by official statements and other practice.[6]

In a resolution on the protection of prisoners of war adopted in 1969, the 21st International Conference of the Red Cross recognised that, irrespective of the Third Geneva Convention, "the international community has consistently demanded humane treatment for prisoners of war, including... provision of an adequate diet and medical care".[7]

Non-international armed conflicts

Specific treaty practice with respect to the provision of detainees' basic needs in non-international armed conflicts is contained in Additional Protocol II.[8] In addition, this rule is contained in other instruments pertaining also to non-international armed conflicts.[9] The Standard Minimum Rules for the Treatment of Prisoners provides detailed provisions concerning accommodation, hygiene, clothing, bedding and food.[10]

Several military manuals which are applicable in or have been applied in non-international armed conflicts contain this rule.[11] Violation of this rule is an

---

[2] Hague Regulations, Article 7 (*ibid.*, § 1); Third Geneva Convention, Articles 25–32 (*ibid.*, § 3) and Article 125 (*ibid.*, § 5).

[3] Fourth Geneva Convention, Articles 76, 85, 87 and 89–92 (*ibid.*, § 4) and Article 142 (*ibid.*, § 5).

[4] See, e.g., the military manuals of Argentina (*ibid.*, §§ 19–20), Australia (*ibid.*, §§ 21–22), Benin (*ibid.*, § 23), Cameroon (*ibid.*, § 24), Canada (*ibid.*, §§ 26–27), Colombia (*ibid.*, §§ 28–29), Dominican Republic (*ibid.*, § 31), Ecuador (*ibid.*, § 32), France (*ibid.*, §§ 34–35), Germany (*ibid.*, § 36), Hungary (*ibid.*, § 37), Israel (*ibid.*, § 38), Italy (*ibid.*, § 39), Kenya (*ibid.*, § 40), Madagascar (*ibid.*, § 41), Mali (*ibid.*, § 42), Netherlands (*ibid.*, §§ 43–44), New Zealand (*ibid.*, § 45), Nicaragua (*ibid.*, § 46), Nigeria (*ibid.*, § 47), Philippines (*ibid.*, § 48), Romania (*ibid.*, § 49), Senegal (*ibid.*, § 50), Spain (*ibid.*, § 51), Switzerland (*ibid.*, § 52), Togo (*ibid.*, § 53), United Kingdom (*ibid.*, §§ 54–55) and United States (*ibid.*, §§ 56–59).

[5] See, e.g., the legislation of Australia (*ibid.*, § 61), Azerbaijan (*ibid.*, § 62), Bangladesh (*ibid.*, § 63), Chile (*ibid.*, § 64), Dominican Republic (*ibid.*, § 65), Ireland (*ibid.*, § 66), Mexico (*ibid.*, § 67), Nicaragua (*ibid.*, § 68), Norway (*ibid.*, § 69), Peru (*ibid.*, § 70), Rwanda (*ibid.*, § 71), Spain (*ibid.*, § 72) and Uruguay (*ibid.*, § 73); see also the draft legislation of Argentina (*ibid.*, § 60).

[6] See, e.g., the statement of the United States (*ibid.*, § 79) and the practice of Azerbaijan (*ibid.*, § 76) and United States (*ibid.*, § 79).

[7] 21st International Conference of the Red Cross, Res. XI (*ibid.*, § 88).

[8] Additional Protocol II, Article 5(1) (adopted by consensus) (*ibid.*, § 8).

[9] See, e.g., Comprehensive Agreement on Respect for Human Rights and International Humanitarian Law in the Philippines, Part IV, Article 4(6) (*ibid.*, § 17); UN Secretary-General's Bulletin, Section 8(c) (*ibid.*, § 18).

[10] Standard Minimum Rules for the Treatment of Prisoners, Rules 9–20 (*ibid.*, § 12).

[11] See, e.g., the military manuals of Australia (*ibid.*, § 22), Benin (*ibid.*, § 23), Cameroon (*ibid.*, § 24), Canada (*ibid.*, §§ 26–27), Colombia (*ibid.*, §§ 28–29), Ecuador (*ibid.*, § 32), Germany (*ibid.*, § 36), Hungary (*ibid.*, § 37), Italy (*ibid.*, § 39), Kenya (*ibid.*, § 40), Madagascar (*ibid.*, § 41), New

offence under the legislation of a number of States.[12] This rule is also supported by official statements and other practice in the context of non-international armed conflicts.[13]

The rule that persons deprived of their liberty must be provided with their basic needs is supported by practice of the United Nations. For example, in 1992, the UN Security Council demanded that all detainees in camps, prisons and detention centres in Bosnia and Herzegovina "receive humane treatment, including adequate food, shelter and medical care".[14] In addition, the Code of Conduct for Law Enforcement Officials and the Basic Principles for the Treatment of Prisoners, adopted by the UN General Assembly without a vote in 1979 and 1990 respectively, require, in particular, that prisoners' health be protected.[15] It should be noted that lack of adequate food, water or medical treatment for detained persons amounts to inhuman treatment (see commentary to Rule 90). In the *Aleksovski case* in 1999, the International Criminal Tribunal for the Former Yugoslavia took into consideration the quality of the shelter, food and medical care allotted to each detainee in determining whether the accused had treated detainees inhumanely.[16]

No official contrary practice was found with respect to either international or non-international armed conflicts.

Interpretation

Practice indicates that provision for the basic needs of persons deprived of their liberty has to be adequate, taking into account the means available and the local conditions. Additional Protocol II states that provision for basic needs is required "to the same extent as the local civilian population".[17]

In the *Aleksovski case*, the International Criminal Tribunal for the Former Yugoslavia considered that the relative lack of food was the result of shortages caused by the war and affected everyone and that the medical care would probably have been considered insufficient in ordinary times, but that the detainees in question did receive available medical care.[18]

Zealand (*ibid.*, § 45), Nicaragua (*ibid.*, § 46), Philippines (*ibid.*, § 48), Senegal (*ibid.*, § 50) and Togo (*ibid.*, § 53).

[12] See, e.g., the legislation of Azerbaijan (*ibid.*, § 62), Nicaragua (*ibid.*, § 68) and Spain (*ibid.*, § 72); see also the legislation of Peru (*ibid.*, § 70) and Uruguay (*ibid.*, § 73), the application of which is not excluded in time of non-international armed conflict, and the draft legislation of Argentina (*ibid.*, § 60).

[13] See, e.g., the statement of Yugoslavia (*ibid.*, § 82), the practice of the Philippines (*ibid.*, § 78) and the reported practice of Malaysia (*ibid.*, § 77) and United States (*ibid.*, § 81).

[14] UN Security Council, Res. 770 (*ibid.*, § 86).

[15] Code of Conduct for Law Enforcement Officials, Article 6 (*ibid.*, § 14); Basic Principles for the Treatment of Prisoners, para. 9 (*ibid.*, § 16).

[16] ICTY, *Aleksovski case*, Judgement (*ibid.*, § 90).

[17] Additional Protocol II, Article 5(1)(b) (adopted by consensus).

[18] ICTY, *Aleksovski case*, Judgement (cited in Vol. II, Ch. 37, § 90).

According to practice, if the detaining power is unable to provide for the basic needs of detainees, it must allow humanitarian agencies to provide assistance in their stead and that detainees have a right to receive individual or collective relief in such a context. The right to receive relief shipments is recognised in the Third and Fourth Geneva Conventions and in Additional Protocol II.[19] This interpretation is also supported by military manuals, national legislation and a report by the Inter-American Commission on Human Rights.[20] This practice is further supported by the practice cited in the commentaries to Rules 53 and 55 on starvation and access to humanitarian relief.

Rule 119. Women who are deprived of their liberty must be held in quarters separate from those of men, except where families are accommodated as family units, and must be under the immediate supervision of women.

Practice

Volume II, Chapter 37, Section B.

Summary

State practice establishes this rule as a norm of customary international law applicable in both international and non-international armed conflicts.

International armed conflicts

The Third and Fourth Geneva Conventions require that women who are deprived of their liberty be accommodated in separate quarters from those of men.[21] They also require women deprived of their liberty to be under the immediate supervision of women.[22] This rule is set forth in Article 75 of Additional

---

[19] Third Geneva Convention, Articles 72–73 (*ibid.*, § 4); Fourth Geneva Convention, Articles 76 and 108–109 (*ibid.*, § 4); Additional Protocol II, Article 5(1)(c) (adopted by consensus) (*ibid.*, § 8).

[20] See, e.g., the military manuals of Benin (*ibid.*, § 23), Cameroon (*ibid.*, § 24), Croatia (*ibid.*, § 30), Israel (*ibid.*, § 38), Netherlands (*ibid.*, § 43), New Zealand (*ibid.*, § 45), Nigeria (*ibid.*, § 47), Senegal (*ibid.*, § 50), Spain (*ibid.*, § 51), Switzerland (*ibid.*, § 52), Togo (*ibid.*, § 53), United Kingdom (*ibid.*, § 54) and United States (*ibid.*, §§ 56 and 58); the legislation of Azerbaijan (*ibid.*, § 62), Bangladesh (*ibid.*, § 63), Ireland (*ibid.*, § 66) and Norway (*ibid.*, § 69); Inter-American Commission on Human Rights, Report on the Situation of Human Rights in Peru (*ibid.*, § 93).

[21] Third Geneva Convention, Article 25, fourth paragraph (*ibid.*, § 99), Article 29, second paragraph (*ibid.*, § 99), Article 97, fourth paragraph (*ibid.*, § 100) and Article 108, second paragraph (*ibid.*, § 100); Fourth Geneva Convention, Article 76, fourth paragraph (*ibid.*, § 101), Article 82, third paragraph (*ibid.*, § 102), Article 85, fourth paragraph (*ibid.*, § 103) and Article 124, third paragraph (*ibid.*, § 104).

[22] Third Geneva Convention, Article 97, fourth paragraph (*ibid.*, § 100) and Article 108, second paragraph (*ibid.*, § 100); Fourth Geneva Convention, Article 76, fourth paragraph (*ibid.*, § 101) and Article 124, third paragraph (*ibid.*, § 104).

Protocol I as a fundamental guarantee applicable to all women deprived of their liberty for reasons related to the armed conflict.[23]

Many military manuals specify that female detainees must be accommodated in separate quarters from those of men.[24] Sweden's IHL Manual, in particular, identifies Article 75 of Additional Protocol I as a codification of customary international law.[25] The legislation of several States requires that female and male detainees be housed separately.[26]

Non-international armed conflicts

Additional Protocol II provides that, "except when men and women of a family are accommodated together, women shall be held in quarters separated from those of men and shall be under the immediate supervision of women".[27] Separate accommodation for male and female detainees is required by other instruments pertaining also to non-international armed conflicts.[28]

This rule is contained in several military manuals which are applicable in or have been applied in non-international armed conflicts.[29] The legislation of several States and other regulations require that female and male detainees be housed separately.[30]

The practice collected in respect of this rule is supported by the requirement to take the specific needs of women affected by armed conflict into account (see Rule 134), and in particular to prevent women becoming victims of sexual violence (see Rule 93). In fact, the purpose of this rule is to implement the specific protection accorded to women. The rule that members of the same family must be housed together is supported by the requirement to respect family life (see Rule 105).

No official contrary practice was found with respect to either international or non-international armed conflicts. It is the ICRC's experience that separation

---

[23] Additional Protocol I, Article 75(5) (adopted by consensus) (*ibid.*, § 105).

[24] See, e.g., the military manuals of Argentina (*ibid.*, § 112), Australia (*ibid.*, § 113), Cameroon (*ibid.*, § 114), Canada (*ibid.*, § 115), Italy (*ibid.*, § 116), Netherlands (*ibid.*, § 117), New Zealand (*ibid.*, § 118), Senegal (*ibid.*, § 119), Spain (*ibid.*, § 120), Sweden (*ibid.*, § 121), Switzerland (*ibid.*, § 122), United Kingdom (*ibid.*, § 123), and United States (*ibid.*, §§ 124–125).

[25] Sweden, *IHL Manual* (*ibid.*, § 121).

[26] See, e.g., the legislation of Bangladesh (*ibid.*, § 127), Ireland (*ibid.*, § 128), Norway (*ibid.*, § 129), Pakistan (*ibid.*, § 130) and Rwanda (*ibid.*, § 131); see also the draft legislation of Argentina (*ibid.*, § 126).

[27] Additional Protocol II, Article 5(2)(a) (adopted by consensus) (*ibid.*, § 106).

[28] See, e.g., Memorandum of Understanding on the Application of International Humanitarian Law between Croatia and the SFRY, para. 4 (*ibid.*, § 109); Agreement on the Application of International Humanitarian Law between the Parties to the Conflict in Bosnia and Herzegovina, para. 2.3 (*ibid.*, § 110); UN Secretary-General's Bulletin, Section 8(e) (*ibid.*, § 111).

[29] See, e.g., the military manuals of Argentina (*ibid.*, § 112), Australia (*ibid.*, § 113), Cameroon (*ibid.*, § 114), Canada (*ibid.*, § 115), Italy (*ibid.*, § 116), Netherlands (*ibid.*, § 117), New Zealand (*ibid.*, § 118), Senegal (*ibid.*, § 119) and Spain (*ibid.*, § 120).

[30] See, e.g., the legislation of Pakistan (*ibid.*, § 130) and Rwanda (*ibid.*, § 131) and the practice of India (*ibid.*, §§ 133–134) and Malaysia (*ibid.*, § 136).

of men and women in detention generally occurs. If sometimes only minimal separation is provided, this is not because of a lack of acceptance of this rule but rather a result of limited resources available to the detaining authorities. Additional Protocol II, in particular, provides that this rule must be respected by those who are responsible for the internment or detention "within the limits of their capabilities".[31]

Rule 120. Children who are deprived of their liberty must be held in quarters separate from those of adults, except where families are accommodated as family units.

Practice

Volume II, Chapter 37, Section C.

Summary

State practice establishes this rule as a norm of customary international law applicable in both international and non-international armed conflicts.

International armed conflicts

The Fourth Geneva Convention provides that interned children must be lodged together with their parents, except when separation of a temporary nature is necessitated for reasons of employment or health or for the purpose of enforcement of penal or disciplinary sanctions.[32] This rule is contained in Additional Protocol I.[33] The Convention on the Rights of the Child, which has been almost universally ratified, specifies this requirement.[34] In addition, the International Covenant on Civil and Political Rights requires that juveniles in detention be separated from adults.[35]

Several military manuals set forth the requirement to separate children from adults while in detention, unless they are accommodated with their families.[36] This requirement is also contained in the legislation of a number of States.[37]

---

[31] Additional Protocol II, Article 5(2) (chapeau).
[32] Fourth Geneva Convention, Article 82, second paragraph (cited in Vol. II, Ch. 37, § 146).
[33] Additional Protocol I, Article 77(4) (adopted by consensus) (*ibid.*, § 148).
[34] Convention on the Rights of the Child, Article 37(c) (*ibid.*, § 149).
[35] International Covenant on Civil and Political Rights, Article 10 (*ibid.*, § 147).
[36] See, e.g., the military manuals of Argentina (*ibid.*, §§ 164–165), Australia (*ibid.*, § 166), Cameroon (*ibid.*, § 167), Canada (*ibid.*, § 168), Germany (*ibid.*, § 169), Spain (*ibid.*, § 170), United Kingdom (*ibid.*, § 171) and United States (*ibid.*, § 172).
[37] See, e.g., the legislation of Bangladesh (*ibid.*, § 173), Ireland (*ibid.*, § 174), Nicaragua (*ibid.*, § 175), Norway (*ibid.*, § 176), Pakistan (*ibid.*, § 177), Philippines (*ibid.*, § 178) and Rwanda (*ibid.*, §§ 179).

Non-international armed conflicts

The requirement to house child and adult detainees separately is set forth in the International Covenant on Civil and Political Rights and in the Convention on the Rights of the Child, the latter ratified almost universally.[38] In addition, it is provided for in many other instruments pertaining also to non-international armed conflicts.[39]

This rule is contained in some military manuals which are applicable in non-international armed conflicts.[40] The legislation and other regulations of several States require respect for this rule.[41] In 1993, Peru and the Philippines informed the UN Committee on the Rights of the Child that they required that detained children be separated from adults.[42]

No official contrary practice was found with respect to either international or non-international armed conflicts.

Interpretation

As the rule indicates, children must only be separated from adults to the extent that this does not involve a violation of the right of families to be housed together. Additional Protocol I, the UN Secretary-General's Bulletin on observance by United Nations forces of international humanitarian law and the Rules for the Protection of Juveniles Deprived of their Liberty formulate the exception in terms of keeping members of the same family together.[43] The Convention on the Rights of the Child, meanwhile, formulates the exception in terms of what is required by the "best interests of the child".[44]

Upon ratification of the Convention on the Rights of the Child, Australia reserved the right not to detain children separately where this would be inconsistent with "the obligation that children be able to maintain contact with

---

[38] International Covenant on Civil and Political Rights, Article 10 (*ibid.*, § 147); Convention on the Rights of the Child, Article 37(c) (*ibid.*, § 149).

[39] See, e.g., Standard Minimum Rules for the Treatment of Prisoners, Rule 8(d) (*ibid.*, § 156); Standard Minimum Rules for the Administration of Juvenile Justice, Rule 13.4 (*ibid.*, § 158); Rules for the Protection of Juveniles Deprived of their Liberty, Rule 29 (*ibid.*, § 159); Memorandum of Understanding on the Application of International Humanitarian Law between Croatia and the SFRY, para. 4 (*ibid.*, § 160); Agreement on the Application of International Humanitarian Law between the Parties to the Conflict in Bosnia and Herzegovina, para. 2.3 (*ibid.*, § 161); UN Secretary-General's Bulletin, Section 8(f) (*ibid.*, § 163).

[40] See, e.g., the military manuals of Argentina (*ibid.*, § 165), Canada (*ibid.*, § 168) and Germany (*ibid.*, § 169).

[41] See, e.g., the legislation of Nicaragua (*ibid.*, § 175), Pakistan (*ibid.*, § 177), Philippines (*ibid.*, § 178) and Rwanda (*ibid.*, § 179) and the practice of Malaysia (*ibid.*, § 182).

[42] Peru, Statement before the UN Committee on the Rights of the Child (*ibid.*, § 183); Philippines, Initial Report to the UN Committee on the Rights of the Child (*ibid.*, § 184).

[43] Additional Protocol I, Article 77(4) (adopted by consensus) (*ibid.*, § 148); UN Secretary-General's Bulletin, Section 8(f) (*ibid.*, § 163); Rules for the Protection of Juveniles Deprived of their Liberty, Rule 29 (*ibid.*, § 159).

[44] Convention on the Rights of the Child, Article 37(c) (*ibid.*, § 149).

their families".[45] Canada, New Zealand and the United Kingdom made similar statements upon ratification of the Convention (providing for an exception where separation would not be "appropriate" or mixing would be "mutually beneficial").[46]

The rule that members of the same family must be housed together is supported by the requirement to respect family life (see Rule 105).

Collected practice does not uniformly point to an age limit to determine what constitutes a child under this rule. Additional Protocol I leaves the issue open but suggests that 15 is the absolute minimum.[47] The Convention on the Rights of the Child defines a child as "every human being below the age of eighteen years unless, under the law applicable to the child, majority is attained earlier".[48] This divergence is also reflected in national legislation, for example, Rwanda's Prison Order requires that prisoners under the age of 18 be held separately, while Pakistan's Prisons Act requires such a measure for prisoners under the age of 21.[49]

Rule 121. Persons deprived of their liberty must be held in premises which are removed from the combat zone and which safeguard their health and hygiene.

Practice

Volume II, Chapter 37, Section D.

Summary

State practice establishes this rule as a norm of customary international law applicable in both international and non-international armed conflicts. This rule is reinforced by the fundamental guarantee that civilians and persons *hors de combat* must be treated humanely (see Rule 87).

International armed conflicts

The rule according to which persons deprived of their liberty must be held in premises which are removed from the combat zone and which safeguard

---

[45] Australia, Reservation made upon ratification of the Convention on the Rights of the Child (*ibid.*, § 150).

[46] Canada, Reservation made upon ratification of the Convention on the Rights of the Child (*ibid.*, § 151); New Zealand, Reservations and declarations made upon ratification of the Convention on the Rights of the Child (*ibid.*, § 154); United Kingdom, Reservations and declarations made upon ratification of the Convention on the Rights of the Child (*ibid.*, § 155).

[47] Additional Protocol I, Article 77(2) (adopted by consensus) (cited in Vol. II, Ch. 39, § 379).

[48] Convention on the Rights of the Child, Article 1.

[49] Rwanda, *Prison Order* (cited in Vol. II, Ch. 37, § 179); Pakistan, *Prisons Act* (*ibid.*, § 177).

their health and hygiene is provided for by the Third and Fourth Geneva Conventions.[50]

Safe, healthy and hygienic conditions of detention are required by numerous military manuals.[51] These requirements are also included in the legislation of several States.[52] In a diplomatic note in 1991, the United States assured Iraq that it would not expose Iraqi prisoners of war to danger but would safeguard them against harm during combat operations.[53] In a report to the UN Security Council on operations in the Gulf War, the United States alleged that Iraq had exposed coalition prisoners of war to the dangers resulting from combat "in blatant disregard for international law".[54]

Non-international armed conflicts

Additional Protocol II requires that detainees be held in healthy and hygienic conditions and that places of internment and detention not be located close to the combat zone.[55] In addition, this rule is contained in other instruments pertaining also to non-international armed conflicts.[56]

This rule is contained in several military manuals which are applicable in or have been applied in non-international armed conflicts.[57] The legislation of a number of States requires that safe, healthy and hygienic conditions of detention be provided.[58]

The ICRC has called on parties to both international and non-international armed conflicts to respect the rule that detainees be held in safe, healthy and hygienic conditions.[59]

---

[50] Third Geneva Convention, Article 22, first paragraph (*ibid.*, § 191) and Article 23, first paragraph (*ibid.*, § 192); Fourth Geneva Convention, Article 83, first paragraph (*ibid.*, § 193) and Article 85, first paragraph (*ibid.*, § 194).

[51] See, e.g., the military manuals of Argentina (*ibid.*, §§ 198–199), Australia (*ibid.*, § 200), Belgium (*ibid.*, §§ 201–202), Cameroon (*ibid.*, § 203), Canada (*ibid.*, § 204), Colombia (*ibid.*, § 205), Croatia (*ibid.*, § 206), France (*ibid.*, §§ 207–209), Germany (*ibid.*, § 210), Israel (*ibid.*, § 211), Italy (*ibid.*, § 212), Madagascar (*ibid.*, § 213), Mali (*ibid.*, § 214), Netherlands (*ibid.*, § 215), New Zealand (*ibid.*, § 216), Senegal (*ibid.*, § 217), Spain (*ibid.*, § 218), Switzerland (*ibid.*, § 219), United Kingdom (*ibid.*, §§ 220–221) and United States (*ibid.*, §§ 222–223).

[52] See, e.g., the legislation of Azerbaijan (*ibid.*, § 224), Bangladesh (*ibid.*, § 225), Ireland (*ibid.*, § 226) and Norway (*ibid.*, § 227).

[53] United States, Department of State, Diplomatic Note to Iraq (*ibid.*, § 229).

[54] United States, Letter to the President of the UN Security Council (*ibid.*, § 230).

[55] Additional Protocol II, Article 5(1)(b) and (2)(c) (adopted by consensus) (*ibid.*, § 195).

[56] See, e.g., Comprehensive Agreement on Respect for Human Rights and International Humanitarian Law in the Philippines, Part IV, Article 4(6) (*ibid.*, § 196); UN Secretary-General's Bulletin, Section 8(b) (*ibid.*, § 197).

[57] See, e.g., the military manuals of Argentina (*ibid.*, § 199), Cameroon (*ibid.*, § 203), Canada (*ibid.*, § 204), Colombia (*ibid.*, § 205), Croatia (*ibid.*, § 206), Germany (*ibid.*, § 210), Italy (*ibid.*, § 212), Madagascar (*ibid.*, § 213), Netherlands (*ibid.*, § 215), New Zealand (*ibid.*, § 216), Senegal (*ibid.*, § 217) and Spain (*ibid.*, § 218).

[58] See, e.g., the legislation of Azerbaijan (*ibid.*, § 224).

[59] See, e.g., ICRC, Press Release No. 1504 (*ibid.*, § 236), practice in the context of a non-international armed conflict (*ibid.*, § 237), Memorandum on Respect for International Humanitarian Law in Angola (*ibid.*, § 238) and Memorandum on Compliance with International Humanitarian Law by the Forces Participating in Opération Turquoise (*ibid.*, § 239).

It should be noted that poor conditions of detention may amount to inhuman treatment (see commentary to Rule 90).

No official contrary practice was found with respect to either international or non-international armed conflicts.

Rule 122. Pillage of the personal belongings of persons deprived of their liberty is prohibited.

Practice

Volume II, Chapter 37, Section E.

Summary

State practice establishes this rule as a norm of customary international law applicable in both international and non-international armed conflicts. This rule is an application of the general prohibition of pillage (see Rule 52).

International armed conflicts

The prohibition of pillage is a long-standing rule of customary international law already recognised in the Lieber Code, the Brussels Declaration and the Oxford Manual.[60] The prohibition of pillage was first codified in the Hague Regulations.[61] Pillage (or plunder) is identified as a war crime in the Report of the Commission on Responsibility set up after the First World War, as well as in the Charter of the International Military Tribunal (Nuremberg) established following the Second World War.[62] The Third Geneva Convention provides that all effects and articles of personal use belonging to a prisoner of war, including for personal protection, shall remain in his or her possession, and the Fourth Geneva Convention permits internees to retain articles of personal use.[63] The Fourth Geneva Convention also prohibits pillage.[64]

The prohibition of pillage of detainees is contained in some military manuals.[65] The pillage of detainees is an offence under the legislation of numerous States.[66]

---

[60] Lieber Code, Article 44 (cited in Vol. II, Ch. 16, § 470); Brussels Declaration, Articles 18 and 39 (*ibid.*, §§ 471–472); Oxford Manual, Article 32(a) (*ibid.*, § 473).

[61] Hague Regulations, Article 47 (*ibid.*, § 460).

[62] Report of the Commission on Responsibility (*ibid.*, § 475); IMT Charter (Nuremberg), Article 6(b) (*ibid.*, § 465).

[63] Third Geneva Convention, Article 18 (cited in Vol. II, Ch. 37, § 241); Fourth Geneva Convention, Article 97 (*ibid.*, § 242).

[64] Fourth Geneva Convention, Article 33, second paragraph (cited in Vol. II, Ch. 16, § 466).

[65] See, e.g., the military manuals of Canada (cited in Vol. II, Ch. 37, § 245), Netherlands (*ibid.*, § 246) and United States (*ibid.*, § 247).

[66] See, e.g., the legislation of Australia (*ibid.*, § 249), Bulgaria (*ibid.*, § 250), Chad (*ibid.*, § 251), Chile (*ibid.*, § 252), Colombia (*ibid.*, § 253), Cuba (*ibid.*, § 254), El Salvador (*ibid.*, § 255), Greece (*ibid.*, § 256), Iraq (*ibid.*, § 257), Ireland (*ibid.*, § 258), Italy (*ibid.*, § 259), New Zealand (*ibid.*,

Pillage is a war crime under the Statute of the International Criminal Tribunal for the Former Yugoslavia.[67] In the *Tadić case* before the International Criminal Tribunal for the Former Yugoslavia in 1995, the accused was charged with plundering the personal property of captured persons but was acquitted on this charge in 1997 because of lack of evidence.[68] In the *Delalić case* before the International Criminal Tribunal for the Former Yugoslavia in 1998, two of the accused were charged with the plunder of money, watches and other valuable property belonging to persons detained in the Čelebići prison-camp. However, the Trial Chamber dismissed the charge, finding that it lacked evidence that the property taken was "of sufficient monetary value for its unlawful appropriation to involve grave consequences for the victims"; therefore, it could not find that the violation of international humanitarian law was "serious".[69]

Non-international armed conflicts

Article 4 of Additional Protocol II prohibits the pillage of persons whose liberty has been restricted.[70] Such pillage is a war crime under the Statutes of the International Criminal Tribunals for the Former Yugoslavia and for Rwanda and of the Special Court for Sierra Leone.[71] In his report on the establishment of a Special Court for Sierra Leone, the UN Secretary-General qualified violations of Article 4 of Additional Protocol II as crimes under customary international law.[72] The UN Secretary-General's Bulletin on observance by United Nations forces of international humanitarian law prohibits pillage of any person not, or no longer, participating in military operations.[73]

The pillage of detainees is an offence under the legislation of numerous States.[74]

In the *Jelisić case* before the International Criminal Tribunal for the Former Yugoslavia, the accused was charged under Article 3(e) of the Tribunal's Statute with the plunder of private property in violation of the laws and customs of

---

§ 260), Nicaragua (*ibid.*, §§ 261–262), Nigeria (*ibid.*, § 263), Norway (*ibid.*, § 264), Paraguay (*ibid.*, § 265), Peru (*ibid.*, § 266), Singapore (*ibid.*, § 267), Spain (*ibid.*, §§ 268–269), United Kingdom (*ibid.*, §§ 270–271), Venezuela (*ibid.*, § 272) and Yemen (*ibid.*, § 273); see also the draft legislation of Argentina (*ibid.*, § 248).

[67] ICTY Statute, Article 3(e) (cited in Vol. II, Ch. 16, § 480).
[68] ICTY, *Tadić case*, Second Amended Indictment and Judgement (cited in Vol. II, Ch. 37, § 279).
[69] ICTY, *Delalić case*, Initial Indictment and Judgement (*ibid.*, § 281).
[70] Additional Protocol II, Article 4(2)(g) (adopted by consensus) (*ibid.*, § 243).
[71] ICTY Statute, Article 3(e) (cited in Vol. II, Ch. 16, § 480); ICTR Statute, Article 4(f) (*ibid.*, § 482); Statute of the Special Court for Sierra Leone, Article 3(f) (*ibid*, § 469).
[72] UN Secretary-General, Report on the establishment of a Special Court for Sierra Leone (cited in Vol. II, Ch. 37, § 276).
[73] UN Secretary-General's Bulletin, Section 7.2 (*ibid.*, § 244).
[74] See, e.g., the legislation of Colombia (*ibid.*, § 253), New Zealand (*ibid.*, § 260), Nicaragua (*ibid.*, § 262), Nigeria (*ibid.*, § 263), Singapore (*ibid.*, § 267), Spain (*ibid.*, §§ 268–269), Venezuela (*ibid.*, § 272) and Yemen (*ibid.*, § 273); see also the legislation of Bulgaria (*ibid.*, § 250), Italy (*ibid.*, § 259), Nicaragua (*ibid.*, § 261) Paraguay (*ibid.*, § 265) and Peru (*ibid.*, § 266), the application of which is not excluded in time of non-international armed conflict, and the draft legislation of Argentina (*ibid.*, § 248).

war and the defendant pleaded guilty to the offence of having stolen money, watches, jewellery and other valuables from detainees upon their arrival at Luka camp in Bosnia and Herzegovina.[75]

No official contrary practice was found with respect to either international or non-international armed conflicts.

Interpretation

Practice contained in military manuals shows that this rule prohibits the taking of the personal belongings of detainees with the intent of unlawful appropriation. It does not prohibit the taking as war booty of objects which could be used in military operations, such as weapons and other military equipment, in international armed conflicts (see Rule 49).

The Third Geneva Convention provides that prisoners of war must remain in possession of their helmets, gas masks and like articles issued for personal protection. It sets out a specific procedure for the taking and deposit of sums of money carried by prisoners of war and for the withdrawal of articles of value for security reasons.[76] A similar procedure for the taking and deposit of monies, cheques, bonds and other valuables in the possession of civilian internees is set out in the Fourth Geneva Convention.[77]

Rule 123. The personal details of persons deprived of their liberty must be recorded.

Practice

Volume II, Chapter 37, Section F.

Summary

State practice establishes this rule as a norm of customary international law applicable in both international and non-international armed conflicts. This rule overlaps with both the prohibition of enforced disappearances (see Rule 98) and the obligation to account for persons reported missing (see Rule 117). The practice collected under those rules supports this rule and permits the conclusion that the requirement to record detainees' details constitutes customary law in both international and non-international armed conflicts.

[75] ICTY, *Jelisić case*, Initial Indictment and Judgement (*ibid.*, § 280).
[76] Third Geneva Convention, Article 18 (*ibid.*, § 241).
[77] Fourth Geneva Convention, Article 97 (*ibid.*, § 242).

International armed conflicts

This rule was first codified in the Hague Regulations, which provides for the establishment of national information bureaux to receive and give information on each prisoner of war.[78] The creation of such bureaux is also required by the Third Geneva Convention (with respect to prisoners of war) and the Fourth Geneva Convention (with respect to enemy aliens and civilian internees).[79] These last two Conventions also make provision for the establishment of the Central Tracing Agency at the ICRC to ensure the exchange of information between the national information bureaux.[80] In addition, in international armed conflicts, there is an obligation under the Third and Fourth Geneva Conventions to grant the ICRC access to detainees and provide it with their personal details (see Rule 124).[81]

Numerous military manuals specify the obligation to record the details of persons deprived of their liberty.[82] It is also stated in the legislation of several States.[83] This rule is further supported by official statements and reported practice.[84]

In a resolution on the protection of prisoners of war, the 21st International Conference of the Red Cross in 1969 recognised that, irrespective of the Third Geneva Convention, "the international community has consistently demanded humane treatment for prisoners of war, including identification and accounting for all prisoners".[85]

No official contrary practice was found.

Interpretation

As to the extent of the information to be recorded, the duty of the State cannot exceed the level of information available from detainees or from documents they may carry. According to the Third Geneva Convention, prisoners of war, when questioned, are bound to give only their surname, first names, date of

---

[78] Hague Regulations, Article 14, first paragraph (*ibid.*, § 284).
[79] Third Geneva Convention, Article 122 (*ibid.*, § 286); Fourth Geneva Convention, Article 136 (*ibid.*, § 288).
[80] Third Geneva Convention, Article 123 (*ibid.*, § 287); Fourth Geneva Convention, Article 140 (*ibid.*, § 288).
[81] Third Geneva Convention, Article 125 (*ibid.*, § 353) and Article 126 (*ibid.*, § 351); Fourth Geneva Convention, Article 142 (*ibid.*, § 353) and Article 143 (*ibid.*, § 351).
[82] See, e.g., the military manuals of Argentina (*ibid.*, § 301), Australia (*ibid.*, § 302), Burkina Faso (*ibid.*, § 303), Cameroon (*ibid.*, §§ 304–305), Canada (*ibid.*, § 306), Congo (*ibid.*, § 307), El Salvador (*ibid.*, § 308), France (*ibid.*, §§ 309–310), Germany (*ibid.*, § 311), India (*ibid.*, § 312), Indonesia (*ibid.*, § 313), Madagascar (*ibid.*, § 315), Mali (*ibid.*, § 316), Morocco (*ibid.*, § 317), Netherlands (*ibid.*, § 318), New Zealand (*ibid.*, § 319), Spain (*ibid.*, § 321), Switzerland (*ibid.*, § 322), United Kingdom (*ibid.*, § 323) and United States (*ibid.*, § 324).
[83] See, e.g., the legislation of Azerbaijan (*ibid.*, § 326), Bangladesh (*ibid.*, § 327), China (*ibid.*, § 328), Ireland (*ibid.*, § 329) and Norway (*ibid.*, § 330).
[84] See, e.g., the statement of the United Kingdom (*ibid.*, § 334) and the reported practice of Israel (*ibid.*, § 333).
[85] 21st International Conference of the Red Cross, Res. XI (*ibid.*, § 340).

birth, rank and army, regimental, personal or serial number or equivalent information.[86]

In international armed conflicts, the details recorded pursuant to this rule must be forwarded to the other party and to the Central Tracing Agency at the ICRC.

Non-international armed conflicts

The obligation to record the personal details of persons deprived of their liberty is set forth in the Inter-American Convention on the Forced Disappearance of Persons and in the Agreement on the Military Aspects of the Peace Settlement annexed to the Dayton Accords.[87] In addition, it is contained in various agreements concluded between the parties to the conflicts in the former Yugoslavia and in the Philippines.[88]

Some military manuals which are applicable in or have been applied in non-international armed conflicts require that detainees' personal details be recorded.[89] Official statements and reported practice further support this rule.[90]

In a resolution on the situation of human rights in Kosovo adopted in 1999, the UN General Assembly demanded that the representatives of Yugoslavia "provide an updated list of all persons detained and transferred from Kosovo to other parts of the FRY, specifying the charge, if any, under which each individual is detained".[91] The requirement to record the personal details of detainees is also contained in a number of international instruments pertaining also to non-international armed conflicts.[92]

If, as stated above, the purpose of this rule is to ensure that no one goes missing or forcibly disappears, this rule must equally be respected in non-international armed conflicts. In this respect, the European Commission and

---

[86] Third Geneva Convention, Article 17.
[87] Inter-American Convention on the Forced Disappearance of Persons, Article XI (*ibid.*, § 289); Agreement on the Military Aspects of the Peace Settlement annexed to the Dayton Accords, Article IX (*ibid.*, § 290).
[88] See, e.g., Agreement between Croatia and the SFRY on the Exchange of Prisoners, para. 3 (*ibid.*, § 294); Agreement No. 2 on the Implementation of the Agreement of 22 May 1992 between the Parties to the Conflict in Bosnia and Herzegovina, para. 2 (*ibid.*, § 295); Agreement No. 3 on the ICRC Plan of Action between the Parties to the Conflict in Bosnia and Herzegovina, Section IV (*ibid.*, § 296); Agreement between the Parties to the Conflict in Bosnia and Herzegovina on the Release and Transfer of Prisoners, Article 6(2) (*ibid.*, § 297); Comprehensive Agreement on Respect for Human Rights and International Humanitarian Law in the Philippines, Part IV, Article 3 (*ibid.*, § 298).
[89] See, e.g., the military manuals of Australia (*ibid.*, § 302), El Salvador (*ibid.*, § 308), Germany (*ibid.*, § 311), India (*ibid.*, § 312), Madagascar (*ibid.*, § 315) and Senegal (*ibid.*, § 320).
[90] See, e.g., the statement of Botswana (*ibid.*, § 332) and the practice of two States (*ibid.*, §§ 335–336).
[91] UN General Assembly, Res. 54/183 (*ibid.*, § 337).
[92] Standard Minimum Rules for the Treatment of Prisoners, Rule 7 (*ibid.*, § 291); European Prison Rules, Rule 8 (*ibid.*, § 292); Body of Principles for the Protection of All Persons under Any Form of Detention or Imprisonment, Principle 16 (*ibid.*, § 293); UN Secretary-General's Bulletin, Section 8(a) (*ibid.*, § 300).

Court of Human Rights have found that "the absence of holding data recording such matters as the date, time and location of detention, the name of the detainee as well as the reasons for the detention" is incompatible with the very purpose of the right to liberty and security.[93] The Inter-American Commission on Human Rights has recommended to various countries that they establish central records "to account for all persons who have been detained, so that their relatives and other interested persons may promptly learn of any arrests".[94]

The ICRC has consistently called for respect for this rule, for example, in the context of the conflict in Bosnia and Herzegovina in 1992.[95]

No official contrary practice was found with respect to either international or non-international armed conflicts.

Rule 124.

    A. In international armed conflicts, the ICRC must be granted regular access to all persons deprived of their liberty in order to verify the conditions of their detention and to restore contacts between those persons and their families.

    B. In non-international armed conflicts, the ICRC may offer its services to the parties to the conflict with a view to visiting all persons deprived of their liberty for reasons related to the conflict in order to verify the conditions of their detention and to restore contacts between those persons and their families.

Practice

Volume II, Chapter 37, Section G.

Summary

State practice establishes these rules as norms of customary international law applicable in international and non-international armed conflicts respectively.

International armed conflicts

The right of the ICRC to visit detainees in international armed conflicts is provided for in the Third and Fourth Geneva Conventions.[96] According to these provisions, the ICRC has full liberty to select the places it wishes to visit and must be able to interview the detainees without witnesses. The duration and frequency of such visits may not be restricted. However, according to the Third

---

[93] European Commission and Court of Human Rights, *Kurt v. Turkey* (*ibid.*, § 341).
[94] Inter-American Commission on Human Rights, *Annual Report 1980–1981* and Reports on the situation of human rights in Argentina, Chile and Peru (*ibid.*, § 342).
[95] ICRC, Solemn Appeal to All Parties to the Conflict in Bosnia and Herzegovina (*ibid.*, § 346).
[96] Third Geneva Convention, Article 126 (*ibid.*, § 351); Fourth Geneva Convention, Article 76, sixth paragraph, and Article 143 (*ibid.*, § 351).

Geneva Convention, visits may be refused for reasons of imperative military necessity, but only as an exceptional and temporary measure.[97] The right of the ICRC to visit persons deprived of their liberty is also recognised in other treaties and instruments.[98]

Numerous military manuals recognise the right of the ICRC to visit detainees.[99] This right is supported by official statements and other practice.[100] It is also confirmed by the numerous visits to prisoners of war, civilian internees and security detainees carried out regularly by the ICRC in countries affected by international armed conflict all over the world.

In 1981, in a resolution on humanitarian activities of the ICRC for the benefit of victims of armed conflicts, the 24th International Conference of the Red Cross deplored the fact that "the ICRC is refused access to the captured combatants and detained civilians in the armed conflicts of Western Sahara, Ogaden and later on Afghanistan".[101]

Non-international armed conflicts

There is no specific treaty provision requiring access by the ICRC to detainees in non-international armed conflicts. However, on the basis of common Article 3 of the Geneva Conventions, the ICRC may "offer its services" to the parties to the conflict.[102] According to the Statutes of the International Red Cross and Red Crescent Movement, adopted by consensus in 1986 by the 25th International Conference of the Red Cross, it is the role of the ICRC

to endeavour at all times – as a neutral institution whose humanitarian work is carried out particularly in time of international and other armed conflicts or internal strife – to ensure the protection of and assistance to military and civilian victims of such events and of their direct results.[103]

On this basis, the ICRC systematically requests access to persons deprived of their liberty in connection with non-international armed conflicts, and such

---

[97] Third Geneva Convention, Article 126 (*ibid.*, § 351).
[98] Agreement on the Military Aspects of the Peace Settlement annexed to the Dayton Accords, Article IX (*ibid.*, § 356); UN Secretary-General's Bulletin, Section 8(g) (*ibid.*, § 365).
[99] See, e.g., the military manuals of Argentina (*ibid.*, § 366), Belgium (*ibid.*, § 367), Benin (*ibid.*, § 368), Canada (*ibid.*, § 369), Ecuador (*ibid.*, § 370), El Salvador (*ibid.*, § 371), Israel (*ibid.*, § 372), Madagascar (*ibid.*, § 373), New Zealand (*ibid.*, § 374), Spain (*ibid.*, § 375), Sweden (*ibid.*, § 376), Switzerland (*ibid.*, § 377), Togo (*ibid.*, § 378), United Kingdom (*ibid.*, §§ 379 and 381) and United States (*ibid.*, §§ 380 and 382–383).
[100] See, e.g., the statements of United Kingdom (*ibid.*, § 397) and United States (*ibid.*, §§ 399–401), the practice of the United Kingdom (*ibid.*, §§ 397–398) and United States (*ibid.*, §§ 400–401) and the reported practice of Lebanon (*ibid.*, § 393).
[101] 24th International Conference of the Red Cross, Res. IV (*ibid.*, § 435); see also 21st International Conference of the Red Cross, Res. IX and 22nd International Conference of the Red Cross, Res. I.
[102] Geneva Conventions, common Article 3 (cited in Vol. II, Ch. 37, § 354).
[103] Statutes of the International Red Cross and Red Crescent Movement, Article 5(2) (*ibid.*, § 358).

access is generally granted, for example, in relation to the conflicts in Algeria, Afghanistan, Chechnya, El Salvador, Nicaragua, Nigeria, Rwanda and Yemen.[104] Conditions are often laid down in formal agreements, such as the agreements concluded in the context of the conflicts in the former Yugoslavia and the Ashgabat Protocol on Prisoner Exchange in Tajikistan.[105] There are also numerous examples of armed opposition groups and separatist entities according the ICRC access to persons held in detention.[106]

The UN Security Council, UN General Assembly and UN Commission on Human Rights, as well as the European Parliament and the Organization for Security and Cooperation in Europe, have requested ICRC access to detainees in the context of several non-international armed conflicts, in particular in Afghanistan, Chechnya, Rwanda, Tajikistan and the former Yugoslavia.[107] In 1995, the UN Security Council condemned "in the strongest possible terms" the failure of the Bosnian Serb party to comply with its commitment in respect of access to detainees.[108]

In a resolution adopted in 1986, the 25th International Conference of the Red Cross appealed to the parties involved in armed conflicts "to grant regular access to the ICRC to all prisoners in armed conflicts covered by international humanitarian law".[109]

The purpose of ICRC visits is to implement other existing rules of customary international law, including the prevention of enforced disappearances, extrajudicial executions, torture and other cruel, inhuman or degrading treatment or punishment, monitoring the standard of detention conditions and the restoration of family links through the exchange of Red Cross messages.

---

[104] See, e.g., the practice of El Salvador (*ibid.*, § 390), Russia (*ibid.*, § 395) and Rwanda (*ibid.*, § 396) and the reported practice of Afghanistan (*ibid.*, § 388) and Yemen (*ibid.*, § 403); see also François Bugnion, *The International Committee of the Red Cross and the Protection of War Victims*, ICRC, Geneva, 2003, pp. 632–759 (describing examples from the conflicts in Algeria, El Salvador, Nicaragua and Nigeria, among others).

[105] Agreement between the Government of Greece and the ICRC (cited in Vol. II, Ch. 37, § 357); Agreement between Croatia and the SFRY on the Exchange of Prisoners, para. 4 (*ibid.*, § 360); Agreement No. 3 on the ICRC Plan of Action between the Parties to the Conflict in Bosnia and Herzegovina, Section IV (*ibid.*, § 361); Agreement between the Parties to the Conflict in Bosnia and Herzegovina on the Release and Transfer of Prisoners, Article 8 (*ibid.*, § 362); Agreement on the Application of International Humanitarian Law between the Parties to the Conflict in Bosnia and Herzegovina, para. 2.4 (*ibid.*, § 363); Ashgabat Protocol on Prisoner Exchange in Tajikistan, para. 5 (*ibid.*, § 364).

[106] See, e.g., the reported practice of armed opposition groups and separatist entities (*ibid.*, §§ 452–465).

[107] See, e.g., UN Security Council, Res. 770 and 771 (*ibid.*, § 411), Res. 968 (*ibid.*, § 412), Res. 1009 (*ibid.*, § 413), Res. 1010 (*ibid.*, § 414) and Res. 1019 and 1034 (*ibid.*, § 415); UN Security Council, Statement by the President (*ibid.*, § 416); UN General Assembly, Res. 46/242 (*ibid.*, § 418); UN Commission on Human Rights, Res. 1998/70 (*ibid.*, § 419); UN Commission on Human Rights, Statement by the Chairman (*ibid.*, § 420); European Parliament, Resolution on violations of human rights and humanitarian law in Chechnya (*ibid.*, § 428); OSCE, Permanent Council, Resolution on Chechnya (*ibid.*, § 431).

[108] UN Security Council, Res. 1019 (*ibid.*, § 415).

[109] 25th International Conference of the Red Cross, Res. I (*ibid.*, § 436).

It can therefore be concluded that an ICRC offer to visit persons deprived of their liberty in the context of a non-international armed conflict must be examined in good faith and may not be refused arbitrarily.[110]

Conditions

When granted access to detainees, the ICRC visits them in accordance with a number of established operational principles. The standard terms and conditions under which the ICRC conducts visits include:

- access to all persons deprived of their liberty for reasons related to armed conflict, at all stages of their detention and in all places where they are held;
- the possibility of talking freely and in private with the detainees of its choice;
- the possibility of registering the identity of the persons deprived of their liberty;
- the possibility of repeating its visits on a regular basis;
- authorisation to inform the family of the detention of a relative and to ensure the exchange of news between persons deprived of their liberty and their families, whenever necessary.[111]

These operational principles are the result of the ICRC's long-standing practice in this field and aim to attain the humanitarian objectives of those visits. The ICRC considers these principles as essential conditions for its visits both in international armed conflicts (where some of these conditions are explicitly set forth in the Geneva Conventions) and in non-international armed conflicts.

Rule 125. Persons deprived of their liberty must be allowed to correspond with their families, subject to reasonable conditions relating to frequency and the need for censorship by the authorities.

Practice

Volume II, Chapter 37, Section H.

Summary

State practice establishes this rule as a norm of customary international law applicable in both international and non-international armed conflicts. Correspondence is to be of a strictly personal nature, i.e., not connected with political or military issues in any way.

---

[110] See also Yves Sandoz, "Le droit d'initiative du Comité international de la Croix-Rouge", *German Yearbook of International Law*, Vol. 22, 1979, pp. 352–373.
[111] See the practice of the ICRC (cited in Vol. II, Ch. 37, § 441).

International armed conflicts

The rule that persons deprived of their liberty must be allowed to correspond with their families is laid down in the Third and Fourth Geneva Conventions.[112] With respect to civilians, derogation from this right is possible in accordance with Article 5 of the Fourth Geneva Convention.[113] This right is also recognised in other treaties, including in a protocol to the Agreement on Ending the War and Restoring Peace in Viet-Nam and in the Convention on the Rights of the Child.[114]

Numerous military manuals provide for the right of persons deprived of their freedom to correspond with their families.[115] This right is set forth in the legislation of several States.[116] It is also recognised in official statements and other practice.[117]

The 20th and 21st International Conferences of the Red Cross adopted resolutions recognising the right of detainees to correspond with their families.[118]

In the context of the Iran–Iraq War, the ICRC reported that by 1 March 1983 it had registered 6,800 Iranian prisoners of war and that these prisoners had been able "to correspond with their families in a satisfactory manner".[119] During the Gulf War, the United States condemned Iraq's refusal to accord prisoners of war the rights afforded them by the Third Geneva Convention, "such as the right of correspondence authorised by Article 70".[120]

It should also be noted that it is the regular practice of the ICRC to facilitate, with the cooperation of the authorities, correspondence between detainees and their families, in the form of "Red Cross messages", in both international and non-international armed conflicts. For example, after the conflict of December 1971 between India and Pakistan, the ICRC facilitated the exchange

---

[112] Third Geneva Convention, Article 70 (*ibid.*, § 466) and Article 71 (*ibid.*, § 467); Fourth Geneva Convention, Article 106 (*ibid.*, § 466) and Article 107 (*ibid.*, § 467).

[113] Fourth Geneva Convention, Article 5.

[114] Protocol to the Agreement on Ending the War and Restoring Peace in Viet-Nam concerning the Return of Captured Military Personnel and Foreign Civilians and Captured and Detained Vietnamese Civilian Personnel, Article 8 (cited in Vol. II, Ch. 37, § 469); Convention on the Rights of the Child, Article 37 (*ibid.*, § 471).

[115] See, e.g., the military manuals of Argentina (*ibid.*, §§ 475–476), Australia (*ibid.*, § 477), Belgium (*ibid.*, § 478), Benin (*ibid.*, § 479), Cameroon (*ibid.*, §§ 480–481), Canada (*ibid.*, § 482), Colombia (*ibid.*, §§ 483–484), Croatia (*ibid.*, § 485), France (*ibid.*, §§ 486–487), Germany (*ibid.*, § 488), Israel (*ibid.*, § 489), Madagascar (*ibid.*, § 490), Netherlands (*ibid.*, §§ 491–492), New Zealand (*ibid.*, § 493), Nicaragua (*ibid.*, § 494), Nigeria (*ibid.*, § 495), Romania (*ibid.*, § 496), Senegal (*ibid.*, § 497), Spain (*ibid.*, § 498), Switzerland (*ibid.*, § 499), Togo (*ibid.*, § 500), United Kingdom (*ibid.*, §§ 501–502) and United States (*ibid.*, §§ 503–505).

[116] See, e.g., the legislation of Azerbaijan (*ibid.*, § 506), Bangladesh (*ibid.*, § 507), Ireland (*ibid.*, § 508), Norway (*ibid.*, § 509) and Rwanda (*ibid.*, § 510).

[117] See, e.g., the statement of the United States (*ibid.*, § 515) and the practice of France (*ibid.*, § 513).

[118] 20th International Conference of the Red Cross, Res. XXIV (*ibid.*, § 519); 21st International Conference of the Red Cross, Res. XI (*ibid.*, § 520).

[119] ICRC, Conflict between Iraq and Iran: ICRC Appeal (*ibid.*, § 523).

[120] United States, Final Report of the Department of Defense on the Conduct of the Persian Gulf War (*ibid.*, § 515).

of 15 million messages between prisoners of war and their families.[121] More recently, during the Gulf War in 1991, the ICRC recorded 683 Red Cross messages sent by detainees and 12,738 received by them. From 1998 to 2002, during the conflict between Ethiopia and Eritrea, detainees sent 64,620 Red Cross messages and received 55,025, including those sent after the Peace Agreement between Eritrea and Ethiopia of 12 December 2000.

Non-international armed conflicts

Additional Protocol II provides that internees and detainees "shall be allowed to send and receive letters and cards, the number of which may be limited by competent authority if it deems it necessary".[122] The right to correspondence is also set forth in other instruments pertaining to non-international armed conflicts.[123]

Several military manuals which are applicable in or have been applied in non-international armed conflicts specify the right of persons deprived of their liberty to correspond with their families.[124] National legislation and reported practice further support this rule in the context of non-international armed conflicts.[125]

The conclusion that this rule is also customary in non-international armed conflicts is further supported by the practice of exchange of Red Cross messages, which the ICRC requires as one of the conditions of its visits irrespective of the nature of the armed conflict. For example, between 1996 and 2002, 18,341 Red Cross messages were sent and 10,632 messages received by detainees during the conflict in Sri Lanka. During the same period, 2,179 Red Cross messages were sent and 2,726 received by detainees in the conflict in Liberia. In Colombia, also during the same period, 2,928 Red Cross messages were sent and 3,436 messages were received by detainees.

Furthermore, the obligation to allow persons deprived of their liberty to correspond with their families is consistent with the requirement to respect family life (see Rule 105), which implies that this obligation must be respected in both international and non-international armed conflicts.

No official contrary practice was found with respect to either international or non-international armed conflicts.

[121] François Bugnion, *The International Committee of the Red Cross and the Protection of War Victims*, ICRC, Geneva, 2003, p. 565.

[122] Additional Protocol II, Article 5(2)(b) (adopted by consensus) (cited in Vol. II, Ch. 37, § 470).

[123] Standard Minimum Rules for the Treatment of Prisoners, Rule 37 (*ibid.*, § 472); European Prison Rules, Rule 43(1) (*ibid.*, § 473); Body of Principles for the Protection of All Persons under Any Form of Detention or Imprisonment, Principle 15 (*ibid.*, § 474).

[124] See, e.g., the military manuals of Australia (*ibid.*, § 477), Benin (*ibid.*, § 479), Canada (*ibid.*, § 482), Colombia (*ibid.*, §§ 483–484), Croatia (*ibid.*, § 485), Germany (*ibid.*, § 488), Madagascar (*ibid.*, § 490), New Zealand (*ibid.*, § 493), Nicaragua (*ibid.*, § 494), Senegal (*ibid.*, § 497) and Togo (*ibid.*, § 500).

[125] See, e.g., the legislation of Azerbaijan (*ibid.*, § 506) and Rwanda (*ibid.*, § 510) and the reported practice of Malaysia (*ibid.*, § 514) and United States (*ibid.*, § 516).

Rule 126. Civilian internees and persons deprived of their liberty in connection with a non-international armed conflict must be allowed to receive visitors, especially near relatives, to the degree practicable.

Practice

Volume II, Chapter 37, Section I.

Summary

State practice establishes this rule as a norm of customary international law. This rule does not address visits by ICRC delegates (see Rule 124), visits by counsel as part of fair trial guarantees (see Rule 100) and visits by religious personnel as part of access to spiritual assistance (see commentary to Rule 127).

International armed conflicts

The right of civilian internees held in connection with an international armed conflict "to receive visitors, especially near relatives, at regular intervals and as frequently as possible" is recognised in the Fourth Geneva Convention.[126] Under the Convention, derogation from this provision is possible.[127]

A number of military manuals specify the right of civilian internees to receive visitors, especially near relatives.[128]

Non-international armed conflicts

Practice with respect to non-international armed conflicts shows that persons deprived of their liberty must be allowed to receive visits from family members to the degree practicable. This practice consists of the Convention on the Rights of the Child, which provides that every child deprived of liberty "shall have the right to maintain contact with his or her family through … visits, save in exceptional circumstances".[129] The Joint Circular on Adherence to International Humanitarian Law and Human Rights of the Philippines and the legislation of some States, for example, Rwanda's Prison Order, provide for the right of persons deprived of their liberty to receive visitors.[130]

---

[126] Fourth Geneva Convention, Article 116, first paragraph (*ibid.*, § 525).
[127] Fourth Geneva Convention, Article 5.
[128] See, e.g., the military manuals of Argentina (cited in Vol. II, Ch. 37, §§ 531–532), Philippines (*ibid.*, § 533), United Kingdom (*ibid.*, § 534) and United States (*ibid.*, § 535).
[129] Convention on the Rights of the Child, Article 37 (*ibid.*, § 526).
[130] Philippines, *Joint Circular on Adherence to International Humanitarian Law and Human Rights* (*ibid.*, § 533); Rwanda, *Prison Order* (*ibid.*, § 536).

In a resolution adopted in 1999, the UN General Assembly demanded that Yugoslavia respect the requirement to allow detainees to receive family visits in the context of the conflict in Kosovo.[131] In the *Greek case* in 1969, the European Court of Human Rights condemned the severe limitations on family visits to detainees.[132] In 1993, the Inter-American Commission on Human Rights recommended that Peru allow relatives to visit prisoners belonging to the Tupac Amaru Revolutionary Movement.[133]

Allowing family visits is required under a number of instruments pertaining also to non-international armed conflicts.[134] The Body of Principles for the Protection of All Persons under Any Form of Detention or Imprisonment provides that the right of detainees to receive visitors is "subject to reasonable conditions and restrictions as specified by law or lawful regulations".[135]

The ICRC facilitates visits by families of detainees in both international and non-international armed conflicts. In 2002, for example, the ICRC facilitated the visits of a total of 52,268 family members to 4,654 detainees held in connection with various armed conflicts, most of them of a non-international character (e.g., in Colombia, Georgia, Kosovo and Sri Lanka). The governments concerned generally accepted the principle that such visits should be able to occur where practicable. However, efforts by the ICRC to facilitate family visits are sometimes obstructed by military operations which endanger the safety and dignity of family members.[136]

To the extent that visits by family members are supported by the requirement to respect family life (see Rule 105), such visits would also be required in non-international armed conflicts.

No official contrary practice was found with respect to either international or non-international armed conflicts.

Rule 127. The personal convictions and religious practices of persons deprived of their liberty must be respected.

Practice

Volume II, Chapter 37, Section J.

---

[131] UN General Assembly, Res. 54/183 (*ibid.*, § 542).
[132] European Court of Human Rights, *Greek case* (*ibid.*, § 545).
[133] Inter-American Commission on Human Rights, Report on the situation of human rights in Peru (*ibid.*, § 547).
[134] See, e.g., Standard Minimum Rules for the Treatment of Prisoners, Rule 37 (*ibid.*, § 527); European Prison Rules, Rule 43(1) (*ibid.*, § 528); Body of Principles for the Protection of All Persons under Any Form of Detention or Imprisonment, Principle 19 (*ibid.*, § 529); Cairo Declaration on Human Rights in Islam, Article 3(a) (*ibid.*, § 530).
[135] Body of Principles for the Protection of All Persons under Any Form of Detention or Imprisonment, Principle 19 (*ibid.*, § 529).
[136] See, e.g., ICRC, *Annual Report 2002*, Geneva, 2003, p. 305.

Summary

State practice establishes this rule as a norm of customary international law applicable in both international and non-international armed conflicts. This rule is an application of the fundamental guarantee of respect for convictions and religious practices (see Rule 104).

International armed conflicts

The recognition of the freedom of prisoners of war to exercise their religion was first codified in the Hague Regulations.[137] The Third Geneva Convention governing prisoners of war and the Fourth Geneva Convention governing civilians now regulate this subject in detail.[138] Additional Protocol I also requires respect for the convictions and religious practices of detainees.[139]

The right of detainees to respect for their religious convictions and practices is set forth in numerous military manuals.[140] It is also contained in the legislation of several States.[141]

In the *Aleksovski case*, the International Criminal Tribunal for the Former Yugoslavia found the accused not guilty of prohibiting detainees from practising their faith because "it was not established that the difficulties encountered by the detainees in respect of the observance of religious rites resulted from any deliberate policy of the accused".[142]

Non-international armed conflicts

Article 5 of Additional Protocol II requires that persons whose liberty has been restricted be allowed to practise their religion and, if requested and appropriate, to receive spiritual assistance.[143] Article 4 of Additional Protocol II also requires respect for detainees' convictions and religious practices.[144] In his report on the establishment of a Special Court for Sierra Leone, the UN Secretary-General

---

[137] Hague Regulations, Article 18 (cited in Vol. II, Ch. 37, § 550).
[138] Third Geneva Convention, Article 34 (*ibid.*, §§ 552–553) and Article 35 (*ibid.*, § 554); Fourth Geneva Convention, Article 76 (*ibid.*, § 555), Article 86 (*ibid.*, § 553) and Article 93 (*ibid.*, §§ 552–554).
[139] Additional Protocol I, Article 75(1) (adopted by consensus) (cited in Vol. II, Ch. 32, § 368).
[140] See, e.g., the military manuals of Argentina (cited in Vol. II, Ch. 37, §§ 561–562), Australia (*ibid.*, § 563), Benin (*ibid.*, § 564), Canada (*ibid.*, § 565), Colombia (*ibid.*, § 566), Ecuador (*ibid.*, § 567), Germany (*ibid.*, § 568), Israel (*ibid.*, § 569), Italy (*ibid.*, § 570), Madagascar (*ibid.*, § 571), Netherlands (*ibid.*, § 572), New Zealand (*ibid.*, § 573), Nicaragua (*ibid.*, § 574), Nigeria (*ibid.*, § 575), Romania (*ibid.*, § 576), Senegal (*ibid.*, § 577), Spain (*ibid.*, § 578), Switzerland (*ibid.*, § 579), Togo (*ibid.*, § 580), United Kingdom (*ibid.*, §§ 581–582) and United States (*ibid.*, §§ 583–586).
[141] See, e.g., the legislation of Azerbaijan (*ibid.*, § 587), Bangladesh (*ibid.*, § 588), Ireland (*ibid.*, § 589), Italy (*ibid.*, § 590) and Norway (*ibid.*, § 591).
[142] ICTY, *Aleksovski case*, Judgement (*ibid.*, § 599).
[143] Additional Protocol II, Article 5(1)(d) (adopted by consensus) (*ibid.*, § 557).
[144] Additional Protocol II, Article 4(1) (adopted by consensus) (*ibid.*, § 556).

qualified violations of Article 4 of Additional Protocol II as crimes under customary international law.[145]

Several military manuals which are applicable in or have been applied in non-international armed conflicts specify the right of detainees to practise their religion and to receive spiritual assistance.[146] This right is also set forth in the legislation of some States.[147]

No official contrary practice was found with respect to either international or non-international armed conflicts.

Interpretation

Practice indicates that the manifestation of personal convictions, the practice of one's religion and access to spiritual assistance may be subject to reasonable regulation. Article 18 of the Hague Regulations and Article 34 of the Third Geneva Convention provide that prisoners of war are entitled to practise their religion provided that they comply with military regulations for order and discipline.[148] Similarly, with respect to civilian internees, the Fourth Geneva Convention provides that they shall enjoy complete latitude in the exercise of their religion "on condition that they comply with the disciplinary routine prescribed by the detaining authorities".[149] Furthermore, the Third and Fourth Geneva Conventions require that religious personnel who are retained or interned be allowed to correspond, subject to censorship, on matters concerning their religious duties.[150]

Rule 128.

A. Prisoners of war must be released and repatriated without delay after the cessation of active hostilities.

B. Civilian internees must be released as soon as the reasons which necessitated internment no longer exist, but at the latest as soon as possible after the close of active hostilities.

C. Persons deprived of their liberty in relation to a non-international armed conflict must be released as soon as the reasons for the deprivation of their liberty cease to exist.

---

[145] UN Secretary-General, Report on the establishment of a Special Court for Sierra Leone (*ibid.*, § 596).

[146] See, e.g., the military manuals of Benin (*ibid.*, § 564), Canada (*ibid.*, § 565), Colombia (*ibid.*, § 566), Ecuador (*ibid.*, § 567), Germany (*ibid.*, § 568), Italy (*ibid.*, § 570), Madagascar (*ibid.*, § 571), Netherlands (*ibid.*, § 572), New Zealand (*ibid.*, § 573), Nicaragua (*ibid.*, § 574), Senegal (*ibid.*, § 577) and Togo (*ibid.*, § 580).

[147] See, e.g., the legislation of Azerbaijan (*ibid.*, § 587).

[148] Hague Regulations, Article 18 (*ibid.*, § 551); Third Geneva Convention, Article 34 (*ibid.*, § 552).

[149] Fourth Geneva Convention, Article 93 (*ibid.*, § 552).

[150] Third Geneva Convention, Article 35 (*ibid.*, §554); Fourth Geneva Convention, Article 93 (*ibid.*, § 554).

The persons referred to may continue to be deprived of their liberty if penal proceedings are pending against them or if they are serving a sentence lawfully imposed.

Practice

Volume II, Chapter 37, Section K.

Summary

State practice establishes these rules as norms of customary international law applicable in international (A and B) and non-international (C) armed conflicts respectively. Refusal to release detainees when the reason for their detention has ceased to exist would violate the prohibition of arbitrary deprivation of liberty (see Rule 99) and may also constitute hostage-taking (see Rule 96).

International armed conflicts

The Hague Regulations provide for the obligation to repatriate prisoners of war as soon as possible after the conclusion of peace.[151] The Third Geneva Convention requires the release and repatriation of prisoners of war without delay after the cessation of active hostilities.[152]

According to Article 132 of the Fourth Geneva Convention, each interned person must be released as soon as the reasons for internment end, while Article 133 provides that, in any event, internment must cease as soon as possible after the close of hostilities. Article 132 encourages the parties to the conflict to conclude, during the course of hostilities, agreements for the release, repatriation, return to places of residence or the accommodation in a neutral country of certain classes of internees with special needs (children, pregnant women and mothers with infants and young children, wounded and sick, and internees who have been detained for a long time).[153]

An "unjustifiable delay in the repatriation of prisoners of war or civilians" constitutes a grave breach of Additional Protocol I.[154]

The basic obligation to repatriate prisoners without delay upon the close of active hostilities is recognised in a number of other treaties.[155]

---

[151] Hague Regulations, Article 20 (*ibid.*, § 604).
[152] Third Geneva Convention, Articles 118 (*ibid.*, § 607).
[153] Fourth Geneva Convention, Article 132 (*ibid.*, § 608) and Article 133 (*ibid.*, § 609).
[154] Additional Protocol I, Article 85(4)(b) (adopted by consensus) (*ibid.*, § 615).
[155] Panmunjon Armistice Agreement, Article III(51)(a) (*ibid.*, § 611); Protocol to the Agreement on Ending the War and Restoring Peace in Viet-Nam concerning the Return of Captured Military Personnel and Foreign Civilians and Captured and Detained Vietnamese Civilian Personnel, Articles 4 and 6 (*ibid.*, § 613); Agreement on Repatriation of Detainees between Bangladesh, India and Pakistan (*ibid.*, § 614); CIS Agreement on the Protection of Victims of Armed

Numerous military manuals specify the obligation to repatriate prisoners after the end of (active) hostilities.[156] The unjustifiable delay in the repatriation of prisoners is an offence under the legislation of numerous States.[157] The rule is further supported by reported practice.[158] It has been reaffirmed on many occasions by the United Nations and other international organisations.[159]

On several occasions, the International Conference of the Red Cross and Red Crescent has called for respect for this rule. For example, the Plan of Action for the years 2000–2003, adopted by the 27th International Conference in 1999, called on all the parties to an armed conflict to ensure that:

prisoners of war are released and repatriated without delay after the cessation of active hostilities, unless subject to due judicial process; the prohibition of taking hostages is strictly respected; the detention of prisoners and internees is not prolonged for bargaining purposes which practice is prohibited by the Geneva Conventions.[160]

Non-international armed conflicts

The practice establishing the customary nature of this rule in non-international armed conflicts consists of numerous agreements concluded, for example, in

Conflicts, Article 4 (*ibid.*, § 618); Agreement on the Military Aspects of the Peace Settlement annexed to the Dayton Accords, Article IX (*ibid.*, § 619); Peace Agreement between Ethiopia and Eritrea, Article 2(1) and (2) (*ibid.*, § 620).

[156] See, e.g., the military manuals of Argentina (*ibid.*, §§ 638–639), Australia (*ibid.*, § 640), Cameroon (*ibid.*, § 642), Canada (*ibid.*, § 641), Colombia (*ibid.*, § 643), Croatia (*ibid.*, § 644), France (*ibid.*, § 645), Germany (*ibid.*, § 646), Hungary (*ibid.*, § 647), Israel (*ibid.*, § 648), Italy (*ibid.*, § 649), Madagascar (*ibid.*, § 650), Netherlands (*ibid.*, § 651), New Zealand (*ibid.*, § 653), Nigeria (*ibid.*, § 654), South Africa (*ibid.*, § 655), Spain (*ibid.*, § 656), Switzerland (*ibid.*, § 657), United Kingdom (*ibid.*, §§ 658–659) and United States (*ibid.*, §§ 660–661).

[157] See, e.g., the legislation of Armenia (*ibid.*, § 663), Australia (*ibid.*, §§ 664–665), Azerbaijan (*ibid.*, § 666), Bangladesh (*ibid.*, § 667), Belarus (*ibid.*, § 668), Belgium (*ibid.*, § 669), Bosnia and Herzegovina (*ibid.*, § 670), Canada (*ibid.*, § 671), Cook Islands (*ibid.*, § 672), Croatia (*ibid.*, § 673), Cyprus (*ibid.*, § 674), Czech Republic (*ibid.*, § 675), Estonia (*ibid.*, § 677), Georgia (*ibid.*, § 678), Germany (*ibid.*, § 679), Hungary (*ibid.*, § 680), Ireland (*ibid.*, § 681), Lithuania (*ibid.*, § 684), Moldova (*ibid.*, § 685), Netherlands (*ibid.*, § 686), New Zealand (*ibid.*, § 687), Niger (*ibid.*, § 689), Norway (*ibid.*, § 690), Slovakia (*ibid.*, § 691), Slovenia (*ibid.*, § 692); Spain (*ibid.*, § 693), Tajikistan (*ibid.*, § 694), United Kingdom (*ibid.*, § 695), Yugoslavia (*ibid.*, § 696) and Zimbabwe (*ibid.*, § 697); see also the draft legislation of Argentina (*ibid.*, § 662), El Salvador (*ibid.*, § 676), Jordan (*ibid.*, § 682), Lebanon (*ibid.*, § 683) and Nicaragua (*ibid.*, § 688).

[158] See, e.g., the reported practice of Botswana (*ibid.*, § 701), Egypt (*ibid.*, § 703) and Kuwait (*ibid.*, § 709).

[159] See, e.g., UN Security Council, Res. 968 (*ibid.*, § 719); UN General Assembly, Res. 50/193 (*ibid.*, § 722); UN Commission on Human Rights, Res. 1996/71 (*ibid.*, § 725) and Res. 1998/79 (*ibid.*, § 727); Council of Europe, Parliamentary Assembly, Rec. 1287 (*ibid.*, § 736); Gulf Cooperation Council, Supreme Council, Final Communiqués of the 12th, 13th, 14th, 15th and 16th sessions (*ibid.*, §§ 740–744); League of Arab States, Council, Res. 4938 (*ibid.*, § 745), Res. 5169 (*ibid.*, § 747), Res. 5231 (*ibid.*, § 746), Res. 5324 (*ibid.*, § 747), Res. 5414 (*ibid.*, § 748) and Res. 5635 (*ibid.*, § 749); OIC, Conference of Foreign Ministers, Res. 1/6-EX (*ibid.*, § 751); OSCE, Ministerial Council, Decision on the Minsk Process (*ibid.*, § 752).

[160] 27th International Conference of the Red Cross and Red Crescent, Res. I (adopted by consensus) (*ibid.*, § 756).

the context of the conflicts in Afghanistan, Angola, Bosnia and Herzegovina, Cambodia, Chechnya, El Salvador, Liberia, Mozambique and Rwanda.[161] The Esquipulas II Accords provide for the release by the "irregular forces of the country concerned" of all persons in their power simultaneously with the issuance of amnesty decrees.[162]

Unjustifiable delay in the return home of detainees held in connection with a non-international armed conflict is an offence under the legislation of some States.[163] There are also accounts of the release of persons detained in connection with non-international armed conflicts, for example, in Colombia, Nigeria and Rwanda.[164]

This rule is supported by official statements and other practice, which praise the releases of detainees when they occur, demand (further) releases or condemn parties failing to cooperate in such releases.[165]

The United Nations and other international organisations have on various occasions highlighted the importance of the release of detainees held in connection with non-international armed conflicts, for example, in Afghanistan, Angola, Bosnia and Herzegovina, Chechnya and Tajikistan.[166] Armed opposition groups have also indicated that they wish to comply with this rule, sometimes prompted by their inability to detain prisoners in safety.[167]

Interpretation

As is evident from its formulation, this rule does not apply to persons against whom criminal proceedings are pending nor to persons lawfully convicted and serving a sentence in connection with the armed conflict. This is reflected

---

[161] Afghan Peace Accord, Article 5 (*ibid.*, § 635); Peace Accords between the Government of Angola and UNITA, para. II.3 (*ibid.*, § 627); Agreement between the Parties to the Conflict in Bosnia and Herzegovina on the Release and Transfer of Prisoners, Article 3(1) (*ibid.*, § 631); Final Act of the Paris Conference on Cambodia, Articles 21–22 (*ibid.*, § 626); N'Sele Cease-fire Agreement, Article 4 (*ibid.*, § 633); Government of El Salvador-FMLN Agreement on Human Rights, para. 3 (*ibid.*, § 624); Cotonou Agreement on Liberia, Article 10 (*ibid.*, § 634); General Peace Agreement for Mozambique, Part III (*ibid.*, § 632); Moscow Agreement on a Cease-fire in Chechnya, Article 2 (*ibid.*, § 637).

[162] Esquipulas II Accords (*ibid.*, § 617).

[163] See, e.g., the legislation of Georgia (*ibid.*, § 678), Germany (*ibid.*, § 679) and Tajikistan (*ibid.*, § 694).

[164] See the practice of Colombia (*ibid.*, § 702) and the reported practice of Nigeria (*ibid.*, § 710) and Rwanda (*ibid.*, § 712).

[165] See, e.g., the statements of Bangladesh (*ibid.*, § 700) and France (*ibid.*, § 704), the practice of the Philippines (*ibid.*, § 711) and the reported practice of India (*ibid.*, § 707) and United States (*ibid.*, § 713).

[166] See, e.g., UN Security Council, Res. 968 (*ibid.*, § 719) and Statements by the President (*ibid.*, §§ 720–721); UN General Assembly, Res. 50/193 (*ibid.*, § 722), UN Commission on Human Rights, Res. 1994/72 and 1995/89 (*ibid.*, § 724), Res. 1996/71 (*ibid.*, § 725), Res. 1998/79 (*ibid.*, § 727) and Statement by the Chairman (*ibid.*, § 728); European Parliament, Resolution on the situation in Chechnya (*ibid.*, § 739); League of Arab States, Council, Res. 5231 (*ibid.*, § 746); OAU, Report of the Secretary-General on the situation in Angola (*ibid.*, § 750).

[167] See, e.g., the statement of FARC-EP (*ibid.*, § 765) and the reported practice of the SPLM/A (*ibid.*, § 766) and armed opposition groups (*ibid.*, §§ 762–764).

in a number of agreements.[168] Hence, those lawfully convicted and serving a sentence for reasons related to the armed conflict may remain in detention following the end of hostilities but should be considered for an amnesty, unless they are serving a sentence for a war crime (see Rule 159).

According to the Fourth Geneva Convention, no protected person may be transferred to a country "where he or she may have reason to fear persecution for his or her political opinions or religious beliefs".[169] While the Third Geneva Convention does not contain a similar clause, practice since 1949 has developed to the effect that in every repatriation in which the ICRC has played the role of neutral intermediary, the parties to the conflict, whether international or non-international, have accepted the ICRC's conditions for participation, including that the ICRC be able to check prior to repatriation (or release in case of a non-international armed conflict), through an interview in private with the persons involved, whether they wish to be repatriated (or released).[170]

Practice indicates that release often occurs under an agreement at the end of a conflict based on bilateral exchange.[171] Each phase of the release process almost invariably involves the participation of a neutral intermediary, usually the ICRC, from negotiation of the release of persons to supervision of the release itself or even receipt of the former prisoners following their release. Practice stresses that the parties involved in such an exchange must cooperate in good faith with the ICRC or other intermediaries.[172] Similar practice is also reported with regard to Angola,[173]

---

[168] See, e.g., Agreement between the Parties to the Conflict in Bosnia and Herzegovina on the Release and Transfer of Prisoners, Article 3(1); General Peace Agreement for Mozambique, Part III (*ibid.*, § 631).

[169] Fourth Geneva Convention, Article 45, fourth paragraph (*ibid.*, § 835).

[170] See, e.g., Agreement on the Military Aspects of the Peace Settlement annexed to the Dayton Accords (*ibid.*, § 823); Agreement between Croatia and the SFRY on the Exchange of Prisoners, para. 6 (*ibid.*, § 840); Agreement between Croatia and the FRY on the Exchange of Prisoners (July 1992), para. 3 (*ibid.*, § 841); Agreement between Croatia and the FRY on the Release and Repatriation of Prisoners, Article 1(4) (*ibid.*, § 842); Agreement between the Parties to the Conflict in Bosnia and Herzegovina on the Release and Transfer of Prisoners, Article 3(6) (*ibid.*, § 843).

[171] See, e.g., Agreement on the Military Aspects of the Peace Settlement annexed to the Dayton Accords, Article IX (*ibid.*, § 787); Agreement between Croatia and the SFRY on the Exchange of Prisoners, paras. 1–2 (*ibid.*, § 792); Protocol to the Moscow Agreement on a Cease-fire in Chechnya, Article 2 (*ibid.*, § 793); Ashgabat Protocol on Prisoner Exchange in Tajikistan, para. 1 (*ibid.*, § 794).

[172] See, e.g., Peace Accords between the Government of Angola and UNITA, Cease-fire Agreement, Section II(3) (*ibid.*, § 913); Agreement between Croatia and the SFRY on the Exchange of Prisoners, paras. 3–6 and 11 (*ibid.*, § 915); Agreement No. 3 on the ICRC Plan of Action between the Parties to the Conflict in Bosnia and Herzegovina, Section IV (*ibid.*, § 916); Agreement between Croatia and the FRY on the Release and Repatriation of Prisoners, Article 1(1) (*ibid.*, § 917); London Programme of Action on Humanitarian Issues, Article 2(f) (*ibid.*, § 918); Agreement between the Parties to the Conflict in Bosnia and Herzegovina on the Release and Transfer of Prisoners, Article 3 (*ibid.*, § 919); Agreement among the Parties to Halt the Conflict in Bosnia and Herzegovina, Article II (*ibid.*, § 921); General Peace Agreement for Mozambique, Protocol VI, Section III(2) (*ibid.*, § 920); Cotonou Agreement on Liberia, Article 10 (*ibid.*, § 922); Ashgabat Protocol on Prisoner Exchange in Tajikistan, para. 2 (*ibid.*, § 923).

[173] See UN Secretary-General, Further report on the UN Angola Verification Mission (UNAVEM II) (*ibid.*, § 937).

Colombia,[174] El Salvador,[175] Rwanda,[176] Somalia[177] and Sudan.[178] The UN Security Council and UN Commission on Human Rights, as well as the Parliamentary Assembly of the Council of Europe, have called upon parties to cooperate with the ICRC in the release of detainees.[179]

Practice indicates that the responsibility of the former detaining power does not end at the moment of release, but continues in the sense of ensuring the safety of persons during return and providing subsistence for the duration of the journey. The Third Geneva Convention requires that the repatriation of prisoners of war take place under the same humane conditions as transfers of prisoners.[180] Additional Protocol II provides that "if it is decided to release persons deprived of their liberty, necessary measures to ensure their safety shall be taken by those so deciding".[181] This last requirement is set forth in the Agreement between Croatia and the SFRY on the Exchange of Prisoners (March 1992),[182] a number of military manuals which are applicable in or have been applied in non-international armed conflicts,[183] national legislation providing for the punishment of violations of Additional Protocol II,[184] and in a statement by the President of the UN Security Council.[185]

With respect to the meaning of the expression "end of active hostilities" in Article 118 of the Third Geneva Convention, Germany's Military Manual states that this requires neither a formal armistice agreement nor the conclusion of a peace treaty.[186]

N.B. The direct repatriation and accommodation in neutral countries of prisoners of war with special needs are governed by Articles 109–117 of the Third Geneva Convention.[187] The obligations set forth in these provisions are independent of the rule requiring release and repatriation at the end of active hostilities.

---

[174] Report on the Practice of Colombia (ibid., § 928).
[175] See UN Commission on the Truth for El Salvador, Report (ibid., § 939).
[176] See Association rwandaise pour la défense des droits de la personne et des libertés publiques, Rapport sur les droits de l'homme au Rwanda – Année 1992 (ibid., § 929).
[177] UN Secretary-General, Progress report on the situation in Somalia (ibid., § 938).
[178] See ICRC, Annual Report 1986 (ibid., § 945).
[179] See, e.g., UN Security Council, Res. 1089 (ibid., § 932) and Res. 1284 (ibid., § 933); UN Commission on Human Rights, Res. 1996/71 (ibid., § 934); Council of Europe, Parliamentary Assembly, Rec. 1287 (ibid., § 940).
[180] Third Geneva Convention, Article 119, first paragraph (the provision refers to the conditions for transfers set forth in Articles 46–48 of the Convention).
[181] Additional Protocol II, Article 5(4) (adopted by consensus) (cited in Vol. II, Ch. 37, § 891).
[182] Agreement between Croatia and the SFRY on the Exchange of Prisoners (March 1992), Article VII (ibid., § 892).
[183] See, e.g., the military manuals of Canada (ibid., § 895) and New Zealand (ibid., § 897).
[184] See, e.g., the legislation of Ireland (ibid., § 900) and Norway (ibid., § 901).
[185] UN Security Council, Statement by the President (ibid., § 905).
[186] Germany, Military Manual (ibid., § 646).
[187] Third Geneva Convention, Articles 109–117 (ibid., § 606).

CHAPTER 38

DISPLACEMENT AND DISPLACED PERSONS

Note: *This chapter addresses forced displacement of civilians for reasons related to an armed conflict, whether within or outside the bounds of national territory. It thus covers the treatment of both internally displaced persons and persons who have crossed an international border (refugees). The only exception to this is Rule 130, which covers both forcible and non-forcible transfer of populations into occupied territory.*

Rule 129.

   A. Parties to an international armed conflict may not deport or forcibly transfer the civilian population of an occupied territory, in whole or in part, unless the security of the civilians involved or imperative military reasons so demand.

   B. Parties to a non-international armed conflict may not order the displacement of the civilian population, in whole or in part, for reasons related to the conflict, unless the security of the civilians involved or imperative military reasons so demand.

Practice

Volume II, Chapter 38, Section A.

Summary

State practice establishes these rules as norms of customary international law applicable in international (A) and non-international (B) armed conflicts respectively.

International armed conflicts

The prohibition of the deportation or transfer of civilians goes back to the Lieber Code, which provides that "private citizens are no longer . . . carried off to distant parts".[1] Under the Charter of the International Military Tribunal (Nuremberg), "deportation to slave labour or for any other purpose of civilian

---

[1] Lieber Code, Article 23 (cited in Vol. II, Ch. 38, § 20).

population of or in occupied territory" constitutes a war crime.[2] The prohibition of the transfer or deportation of civilians is set forth in the Fourth Geneva Convention.[3] In addition, according to the Fourth Geneva Convention and Additional Protocol I, it is a grave breach of these instruments to deport or transfer the civilian population of an occupied territory, unless the security of the civilians involved or imperative military reasons so demand.[4] Under the Statute of the International Criminal Court, "the deportation or transfer [by the Occupying Power] of all or parts of the population of the occupied territory within or outside this territory" constitutes a war crime in international armed conflicts.[5]

Numerous military manuals specify the prohibition of unlawful deportation or transfer of civilians in occupied territory.[6] It is an offence under the legislation of many States to carry out such deportations or transfers.[7] There is case-law relating to the Second World War supporting the prohibition.[8] It is also supported by official statements and by many resolutions adopted by international organisations and international conferences, including condemnations of alleged cases of deportation and transfer.[9]

The Supreme Court of Israel has stated on several occasions, however, that Article 49 of the Fourth Geneva Convention was not meant to apply to the deportation of selected individuals for reasons of public order and security,[10] or that Article 49 did not form part of customary international law and that

---

[2] IMT Charter (Nuremberg), Article 6(b) (*ibid.*, § 1).

[3] Fourth Geneva Convention, Article 49, first paragraph (*ibid.*, § 3).

[4] Fourth Geneva Convention, Article 147 (*ibid.*, § 4); Additional Protocol I, Article 85(4)(a) (adopted by consensus) (*ibid.*, § 9).

[5] ICC Statute, Article 8(2)(b)(viii) (*ibid.*, § 18).

[6] See, e.g., the military manuals of Argentina (*ibid.*, §§ 39–40), Australia (*ibid.*, §§ 41–42), Canada (*ibid.*, § 43), Colombia (*ibid.*, § 44), Croatia (*ibid.*, § 45), Ecuador (*ibid.*, § 46), France (*ibid.*, §§ 47–49), Germany (*ibid.*, § 50), Hungary (*ibid.*, § 51), Italy (*ibid.*, § 52), Netherlands (*ibid.*, § 53), New Zealand (*ibid.*, § 54), Nigeria (*ibid.*, § 55), Philippines (*ibid.*, § 56), South Africa (*ibid.*, § 57), Spain (*ibid.*, § 58), Sweden (*ibid.*, § 59), Switzerland (*ibid.*, § 60), United Kingdom (*ibid.*, § 61) and United States (*ibid.*, §§ 62–64).

[7] See, e.g., the legislation (*ibid.*, §§ 65–156).

[8] See, e.g., China, War Crimes Military Tribunal of the Ministry of National Defence, *Takashi Sakai case* (*ibid.*, § 159); France, General Tribunal at Rastadt of the Military Government for the French Zone of Occupation in Germany, *Roechling case* (*ibid.*, § 157); Israel, District Court of Jerusalem, *Eichmann case* (*ibid.*, § 161); Netherlands, Special Court of Cassation, *Zimmermann case* (*ibid.*, § 166); Poland, Supreme National Tribunal at Poznan, *Greiser case* (*ibid.*, § 157); United States, Military Tribunal at Nuremberg, *Krauch (I.G. Farben Trial) case, Krupp case, Milch case, List (Hostages Trial) case* (*ibid.*, § 157) and *Von Leeb (The High Command Trial) case* (*ibid.*, § 157).

[9] See, e.g., the statements of Switzerland (*ibid.*, § 186) and United States (*ibid.*, §§ 188–190); UN General Assembly, Res. 2675 (XXV) (*ibid.*, § 204), Res. 3318 (XXIX) (*ibid.*, § 205), Res. 36/147 D, 37/88 D, 38/79 E, 39/95 E and 40/161 E (*ibid.*, § 206), Res. 36/147 C, 37/88 C, 38/79 D, 39/95 D and 40/161 D (*ibid.*, § 207); League of Arab States, Council, Res. 4430 (*ibid.*, § 223), Res. 5169 (*ibid.*, § 224) and Res. 5324 (*ibid.*, § 225); 25th International Conference of the Red Cross, Res. I (*ibid.*, § 226).

[10] See, e.g., Israel, High Court, *Abu-Awad case* (*ibid.*, § 162) and *Affo and Others case* (*ibid.*, § 165).

therefore deportation orders against individual citizens did not contravene the domestic law of Israel.[11]

Non-international armed conflicts

The prohibition of displacing the civilian population in non-international armed conflicts is set forth in Additional Protocol II.[12] Under the Statute of the International Criminal Court, "ordering the displacement of the civilian population for reasons related to the conflict, unless the security of the civilians involved or imperative military reasons so demand," constitutes a war crime in non-international armed conflicts.[13] This rule is contained in other instruments pertaining also to non-international armed conflicts.[14] It should also be noted that, under the Statutes of the International Criminal Tribunals for the Former Yugoslavia and for Rwanda and of the International Criminal Court, deportation or transfer of the civilian population constitutes a crime against humanity.[15]

The rule prohibiting the forcible displacement of the civilian population is also specified in a number of military manuals which are applicable in or have been applied in non-international armed conflicts.[16] The legislation of many States makes it an offence to violate this rule.[17] The prohibition is also

---

[11] See, e.g., Israel, High Court, *Kawasme and Others case* (*ibid.*, § 163) and *Nazal and Others case* (*ibid.*, § 164); see also Yoram Dinstein, "The Israeli Supreme Court and the Law of Belligerent Occupation: Deportations", *Israel Yearbook on Human Rights*, Vol. 23, 1993, pp. 1–26.

[12] Additional Protocol II, Article 17 (adopted by consensus) (cited in Vol. II, Ch. 38, § 10).

[13] ICC Statute, Article 8(2)(e)(viii) (*ibid.*, § 19).

[14] See, e.g., Agreement on the Application of International Humanitarian Law between the Parties to the Conflict in Bosnia and Herzegovina, para. 2.3 (*ibid.*, § 28); Comprehensive Agreement on Respect for Human Rights and International Humanitarian Law in the Philippines, Part IV, Article 3(7) (*ibid.*, § 35).

[15] ICTY Statute, Article 5(d) (*ibid.*, § 31); ICTR Statute, Article 3(d) (*ibid.*, § 32); ICC Statute, Article 7(1)(d) (*ibid.*, § 16).

[16] See, e.g., the military manuals of Australia (*ibid.*, §§ 41–42), Canada (*ibid.*, § 43), Colombia (*ibid.*, § 44), Croatia (*ibid.*, § 45), Ecuador (*ibid.*, § 46), France (*ibid.*, § 49), Germany (*ibid.*, § 50), Hungary (*ibid.*, § 51), Italy (*ibid.*, § 52), Netherlands (*ibid.*, § 53), New Zealand (*ibid.*, § 54), Philippines (*ibid.*, § 56), South Africa (*ibid.*, § 57) and Spain (*ibid.*, § 58).

[17] See, e.g., the legislation of Armenia (*ibid.*, § 66), Australia (*ibid.*, §§ 67 and 69), Azerbaijan (*ibid.*, § 70), Belarus (*ibid.*, § 73), Belgium (*ibid.*, § 74), Bosnia and Herzegovina (*ibid.*, § 75), Cambodia (*ibid.*, § 79), Canada (*ibid.*, § 81), Colombia (*ibid.*, §§ 83–84), Congo (*ibid.*, § 86), Croatia (*ibid.*, § 89), El Salvador (*ibid.*, § 93), Estonia (*ibid.*, § 95), Ethiopia (*ibid.*, § 96), Finland (*ibid.*, § 97), Georgia (*ibid.*, § 99), Germany (*ibid.*, § 100), Kazakhstan (*ibid.*, § 108), Latvia (*ibid.*, § 110), Moldova (*ibid.*, § 120), Netherlands (*ibid.*, § 121), New Zealand (*ibid.*, § 123), Nicaragua (*ibid.*, § 125), Niger (*ibid.*, § 127), Paraguay (*ibid.*, § 131), Poland (*ibid.*, § 133), Portugal (*ibid.*, § 134), Russia (*ibid.*, § 136), Slovenia (*ibid.*, § 140), Spain (*ibid.*, § 141), Tajikistan (*ibid.*, § 143), Ukraine (*ibid.*, § 146), United Kingdom (*ibid.*, § 148), Uzbekistan (*ibid.*, § 152) and Yugoslavia (*ibid.*, § 154); see also the legislation of Bulgaria (*ibid.*, § 77), Czech Republic (*ibid.*, § 92), Hungary (*ibid.*, § 101), Romania (*ibid.*, § 135) and Slovakia (*ibid.*, § 139), the application of which is not excluded in time of non-international armed conflict, and the draft legislation of Argentina (*ibid.*, § 65), Burundi (*ibid.*, § 78), El Salvador (*ibid.*, § 93), Jordan (*ibid.*, § 107), Nicaragua (*ibid.*, § 126) and Trinidad and Tobago (*ibid.*, § 144).

supported by official statements and reported practice in the context of non-international armed conflicts.[18]

In a resolution on basic principles for the protection of civilian populations in armed conflicts, adopted in 1970, the UN General Assembly affirmed that "civilian populations, or individual members thereof, should not be the object of... forcible transfers".[19] In a resolution on the protection of women and children in emergency and armed conflict, adopted in 1974, the UN General Assembly declared that "forcible eviction, committed by belligerents in the course of military operations or in occupied territories, shall be considered criminal".[20] The UN Security Council, UN General Assembly and UN Commission on Human Rights have condemned instances of forced displacement in international armed conflicts but also in non-international armed conflicts, for example, in the context of the conflicts in Bosnia and Herzegovina, Burundi and Sudan.[21]

The 26th International Conference of the Red Cross and Red Crescent adopted two resolutions stressing the prohibition of forced displacement of the civilian population.[22] The ICRC has called on parties to both international and non-international armed conflicts to respect this rule.[23]

Evacuation of the civilian population

In both international and non-international armed conflicts, State practice establishes an exception to the prohibition of displacement in cases where the security of the civilians involved or imperative military reasons (such as clearing a combat zone) require the evacuation for as long as the conditions warranting it exist. This exception is contained in the Fourth Geneva Convention and Additional Protocol II.[24] The possibility of evacuation is also provided

---

[18] See, e.g., the statements of Afghanistan (*ibid.*, § 168), Botswana (*ibid.*, § 169) Japan (*ibid.*, § 175), Netherlands (*ibid.*, §§ 177–178), New Zealand (*ibid.*, § 180), Nigeria (*ibid.*, § 181), Russia (*ibid.*, § 183), Spain (*ibid.*, § 185), United Kingdom (*ibid.*, § 187) and United States (*ibid.*, § 190), and the reported practice of Jordan (*ibid.*, § 176) and United States (*ibid.*, § 191).

[19] UN General Assembly, Res. 2675 (XXV) (adopted by 109 votes in favour, none against and 8 abstentions) (*ibid.*, § 204).

[20] UN General Assembly, Res. 3318 (XXIX) (adopted by 110 votes in favour, none against and 14 abstentions) (*ibid.*, § 205).

[21] See, e.g., UN Security Council, Res. 752 (*ibid.*, § 193) and Res. 819 (*ibid.*, § 194); UN Security Council, Statement by the President (*ibid.*, § 201); UN General Assembly, Res. 55/116 (*ibid.*, § 212); UN Commission on Human Rights, Res. 1995/77 (*ibid.*, § 212) and Res. 1996/73 (*ibid.*, § 213).

[22] 26th International Conference of the Red Cross and Red Crescent, Res. II (*ibid.*, § 228) and Res. IV (*ibid.*, § 229).

[23] See, e.g., ICRC, Memorandum on the Applicability of International Humanitarian Law (*ibid.*, § 237) and Memorandum on Respect for International Humanitarian Law in Angola (*ibid.*, § 240).

[24] Fourth Geneva Convention, Article 49, second paragraph (*ibid.*, § 245); Additional Protocol II, Article 17(1) (adopted by consensus) (*ibid.*, § 246).

for in numerous military manuals.[25] It is contained in the legislation of many States.[26]

The Guiding Principles on Internal Displacement prohibits the "arbitrary" displacement of persons, which is defined as including displacement in situations of armed conflict, "unless the security of civilians involved or imperative military reasons so demand".[27]

The exception of "imperative military reasons" can never cover cases of removal of the civilian population in order to persecute it.[28]

The Fourth Geneva Convention further specifies that evacuations may not involve displacement outside the bounds of the occupied territory "except where for material reasons it is impossible to avoid such displacement".[29] With respect to non-international armed conflicts, Additional Protocol II specifies that evacuations may never involve displacement outside the national territory.[30]

Prevention of displacement

State practice also underlines the duty of parties to a conflict to prevent displacement caused by their own acts, at least those acts which are prohibited in and of themselves (e.g., terrorising the civilian population or carrying out indiscriminate attacks). As stated in the Guiding Principles on Internal Displacement:

All authorities and international actors shall respect and ensure respect for their obligations under international law, including human rights and humanitarian law, in all circumstances, so as to prevent and avoid conditions that might lead to displacement of persons.[31]

Ethnic cleansing

"Ethnic cleansing" aims to change the demographic composition of a territory. In addition to displacement of the civilian population of a territory, this can be

---

[25] See, e.g., the military manuals of Argentina (*ibid.*, §§ 250–251), Cameroon (*ibid.*, § 253), Canada (*ibid.*, § 254), Croatia (*ibid.*, § 255), Dominican Republic (*ibid.*, § 256), France (*ibid.*, § 257), Germany (*ibid.*, § 258), Hungary (*ibid.*, § 259), Israel (*ibid.*, § 260), Italy (*ibid.*, § 261), Kenya (*ibid.*, § 262), Netherlands (*ibid.*, § 264), New Zealand (*ibid.*, § 265), Philippines (*ibid.*, § 266), Spain (*ibid.*, § 267), Sweden (*ibid.*, § 268), Switzerland (*ibid.*, § 269), United Kingdom (*ibid.*, §§ 270–271) and United States (*ibid.*, §§ 272–274).

[26] See, e.g., the legislation of Argentina (*ibid.*, § 275), Australia (*ibid.*, § 276), Azerbaijan (*ibid.*, § 277), Canada (*ibid.*, § 278), Congo (*ibid.*, § 279), Cuba (*ibid.*, § 280), Ireland (*ibid.*, § 281), Netherlands (*ibid.*, § 282), New Zealand (*ibid.*, § 283), Norway (*ibid.*, § 284), Rwanda (*ibid.*, § 286) and United Kingdom (*ibid.*, § 288); see also the draft legislation of Trinidad and Tobago (*ibid.*, § 287).

[27] Guiding Principles on Internal Displacement, Principle 6(2) (*ibid.*, § 248).

[28] See, e.g., Fourth Geneva Convention, Article 45, fourth paragraph (*ibid.*, § 2).

[29] Fourth Geneva Convention, Article 49.

[30] Additional Protocol II, Article 17(2) (adopted by consensus).

[31] Guiding Principles on Internal Displacement, Principle 5 (cited in Vol. II, Ch. 38, § 34).

achieved through other acts which are prohibited in and of themselves such as attacks against civilians (see Rule 1), murder (see Rule 89) and rape and other forms of sexual violence (see Rule 93). These acts are prohibited regardless of the nature of the conflict and have been widely condemned.

Rule 130. States may not deport or transfer parts of their own civilian population into a territory they occupy.

Practice

Volume II, Chapter 38, Section B.

Summary

State practice establishes this rule as a norm of customary international law applicable in international armed conflicts.

International armed conflicts

The prohibition on deporting or transferring parts of a State's own civilian population into the territory it occupies is set forth in the Fourth Geneva Convention.[32] It is a grave breach of Additional Protocol I.[33] Under the Statute of the International Criminal Court, "the transfer, directly or indirectly, by the Occupying Power of parts of its own civilian population into the territory it occupies" constitutes a war crime in international armed conflicts.[34]

Many military manuals prohibit the deportation or transfer by a party to the conflict of parts of its civilian population into the territory it occupies.[35] This rule is included in the legislation of numerous States.[36] Official statements and reported practice also support the prohibition on transferring one's own civilian population into occupied territory.[37]

---

[32] Fourth Geneva Convention, Article 49, sixth paragraph (*ibid.*, § 334).
[33] Additional Protocol I, Article 85(4)(a) (adopted by consensus) (*ibid.*, § 335).
[34] ICC Statute, Article 8(2)(b)(VIII) (*ibid.*, § 336).
[35] See, e.g., the military manuals of Argentina (*ibid.*, §§ 346–347), Australia (*ibid.*, § 348), Canada (*ibid.*, § 349), Croatia (*ibid.*, § 350), Hungary (*ibid.*, § 351), Italy (*ibid.*, § 352), Netherlands (*ibid.*, § 353), New Zealand (*ibid.*, § 354), Spain (*ibid.*, § 355), Sweden (*ibid.*, § 357), Switzerland (*ibid.*, § 357), United Kingdom (*ibid.*, § 358) and United States (*ibid.*, § 359).
[36] See, e.g., the legislation of Armenia (*ibid.*, § 361), Australia (*ibid.*, §§ 362–363), Azerbaijan (*ibid.*, §§ 364–365), Bangladesh (*ibid.*, § 366), Belarus (*ibid.*, § 367), Belgium (*ibid.*, § 368), Bosnia and Herzegovina (*ibid.*, § 369), Canada (*ibid.*, §§ 371–372), Congo (*ibid.*, § 373), Cook Islands (*ibid.*, § 374), Croatia (*ibid.*, § 375), Cyprus (*ibid.*, § 376), Czech Republic (*ibid.*, § 377), Germany (*ibid.*, § 379), Georgia (*ibid.*, § 380), Ireland (*ibid.*, § 381), Mali (*ibid.*, § 384), Moldova (*ibid.*, § 385), Netherlands (*ibid.*, § 386), New Zealand (*ibid.*, §§ 387–388), Niger (*ibid.*, § 390), Norway (*ibid.*, § 391), Slovakia (*ibid.*, § 392), Slovenia (*ibid.*, § 393), Spain (*ibid.*, § 394), Tajikistan (*ibid.*, § 395), United Kingdom (*ibid.*, §§ 397–398), Yugoslavia (*ibid.*, § 399) and Zimbabwe (*ibid.*, § 400); see also the draft legislation of Argentina (*ibid.*, § 360), Burundi (*ibid.*, § 370), Jordan (*ibid.*, § 382), Lebanon (*ibid.*, § 383) and Trinidad and Tobago (*ibid.*, § 396).
[37] See, e.g., the statements of Kuwait (*ibid.*, § 405) and United States (*ibid.*, §§ 406–407) and the reported practice of Egypt (*ibid.*, § 402) and France (*ibid.*, § 403).

Attempts to alter the demographic composition of an occupied territory have been condemned by the UN Security Council.[38] In 1992, it called for the cessation of attempts to change the ethnic composition of the population, anywhere in the former Yugoslavia.[39] Similarly, the UN General Assembly and UN Commission on Human Rights have condemned settlement practices.[40] According to the final report of the UN Special Rapporteur on the Human Rights Dimensions of Population Transfer, including the Implantation of Settlers and Settlements, "the implantation of settlers" is unlawful and engages State responsibility and the criminal responsibility of individuals.[41]

In 1981, the 24th International Conference of the Red Cross reaffirmed that "settlements in occupied territory are incompatible with articles 27 and 49 of the Fourth Geneva Convention".[42]

In the *Case of the Major War Criminals* in 1946, the International Military Tribunal at Nuremberg found two of the accused guilty of attempting the "Germanization" of occupied territories.[43]

Rule 131. In case of displacement, all possible measures must be taken in order that the civilians concerned are received under satisfactory conditions of shelter, hygiene, health, safety and nutrition and that members of the same family are not separated.

Practice

Volume II, Chapter 38, Section C.

Summary

State practice establishes this rule as a norm of customary international law applicable in both international and non-international armed conflicts. This rule is additional to the right of displaced civilians to the same protection as other civilians, including the fundamental guarantees provided for in Chapter 32.

---

[38] See, e.g., UN Security Council, Res. 446 , 452 and 476 (*ibid.*, § 408), Res. 465 (*ibid.*, § 409) and Res. 677 (*ibid.*, § 410).

[39] UN Security Council, Res. 752 (*ibid.*, § 411).

[40] See, e.g., UN General Assembly, Res. 36/147 C, 37/88 C, 38/79 D, 39/95 D and 40/161 D (*ibid.*, § 412) and Res. 54/78 (*ibid.*, § 405); UN Commission on Human Rights, Res. 2001/7 (*ibid.*, § 413).

[41] UN Sub-Commission on Human Rights, Final report of the Special Rapporteur on the Human Rights Dimensions of Population Transfer, including the Implantation of Settlers and Settlements (*ibid.*, § 415).

[42] 24th International Conference of the Red Cross, Res. III (*ibid.*, § 419).

[43] International Military Tribunal at Nuremberg, *Case of the Major War Criminals*, Judgement (*ibid.*, § 421).

International armed conflicts

The Fourth Geneva Convention provides that an occupying power undertaking an evacuation for the security of the civilian population or for imperative military reasons, "shall ensure, to the greatest practicable extent, that proper accommodation is provided to receive the protected persons, that the removals are effected in satisfactory conditions of hygiene, health, safety and nutrition, and that members of the same family are not separated".[44]

The rule is repeated in many military manuals.[45] In the *Krupp case* in 1948, the United States Military Tribunal at Nuremberg adopted the statement by Judge Phillips in his concurring opinion of 1947 in the *Milch case*, according to which one of the conditions under which deportation becomes illegal

occurs whenever generally recognized standards of decency and humanity are disregarded...A close study of the pertinent parts of Control Council Law No. 10 strengthens the conclusions of the foregoing statements that deportation is criminal...whenever the deportation is characterized by inhumane or illegal methods.[46]

Non-international armed conflicts

Additional Protocol II provides that should displacements of the civilian population be ordered for the security of the civilians involved or for imperative military reasons, "all possible measures shall be taken in order that the civilian population may be received under satisfactory conditions of shelter, hygiene, health, safety and nutrition".[47] Furthermore, Additional Protocol II requires that "all appropriate steps shall be taken to facilitate the reunion of families temporarily separated".[48]

The rule requiring measures to be taken to safeguard the civilian population in case of displacement is also set forth in agreements concluded between the parties to the armed conflicts in Bosnia and Herzegovina, Mozambique and Sudan.[49]

---

[44] Fourth Geneva Convention, Article 49, third paragraph (*ibid.*, §§ 427, 492 and 541).

[45] Concerning the provision of basic necessities, see, e.g., the military manuals of Argentina (*ibid.*, § 436), Croatia (*ibid.*, § 439), Dominican Republic (*ibid.*, § 440), Germany (*ibid.*, § 441), Hungary (*ibid.*, § 442), Spain (*ibid.*, § 444), Switzerland (*ibid.*, § 445), United Kingdom (*ibid.*, § 446) and United States (*ibid.*, § 447). Concerning the security of displaced persons, see, e.g., the military manuals of Argentina (*ibid.*, § 495), Croatia (*ibid.*, § 497), Dominican Republic (*ibid.*, § 498), Hungary (*ibid.*, § 499), Spain (*ibid.*, § 501), Switzerland (*ibid.*, § 502), United Kingdom (*ibid.*, § 503) and United States (*ibid.*, §§ 504–505). Concerning respect for family unity, see, e.g., the military manuals of Argentina (*ibid.*, §§ 547–548), Colombia (*ibid.*, § 550), Croatia (*ibid.*, § 551), Germany (*ibid.*, § 552), Hungary (*ibid.*, § 553), Spain (*ibid.*, § 554), Switzerland (*ibid.*, § 555), United Kingdom (*ibid.*, § 556) and United States (*ibid.*, § 557).

[46] United States, Military Tribunal at Nuremberg, *Krupp case*, adopting the concurring opinion by Judge Phillips in the *Milch case* (*ibid.*, § 455).

[47] Additional Protocol II, Article 17(1) (adopted by consensus) (*ibid.*, §§ 428 and 493).

[48] Additional Protocol II, Article 4(3)(b) (adopted by consensus) (cited in Vol. II, Ch. 32, § 3916).

[49] Agreement on the Application of International Humanitarian Law between the Parties to the Conflict in Bosnia and Herzegovina, para. 2.3 (cited in Vol. II, Ch. 38, § 430); Recommendation on

Several military manuals which are applicable in or have been applied in non-international armed conflicts contain this rule.[50] This rule is also provided for in national legislation, in particular that of Colombia, Croatia and Georgia concerning displaced persons.[51] In 1996, Colombia's Constitutional Court held that displaced persons had the right to receive humanitarian assistance and to be accorded protection by the State.[52] Official statements and other practice relating to non-international armed conflicts also support this rule.[53]

No official contrary practice was found with respect to either international or non-international armed conflicts. The UN Security Council has called for respect for this rule in both international and non-international armed conflicts.[54] The Guiding Principles on Internal Displacement requires that competent authorities must provide internally displaced persons with and ensure safe access to essential food and potable water, basic shelter and housing, appropriate clothing and essential medical services and sanitation.[55]

The International Conferences of the Red Cross and Red Crescent have adopted several resolutions stressing the importance of this rule.[56] The Plan of Action for the years 2000–2003, adopted by the 27th International Conference of the Red Cross and Red Crescent in 1999, requires that all parties to an armed conflict take effective measures to ensure that if displacement occurs, "appropriate assistance" is provided to persons thus displaced.[57]

Respect for family unity

The duty to avoid, as far as possible, the separation of family members during the transfer or evacuation of civilians by an occupying power is provided for

---

the Tragic Situation of Civilians in Bosnia and Herzegovina, para. 3 (*ibid.*, § 494); General Peace Agreement for Mozambique, para. III, Protocol III (*ibid.*, § 429); Agreement on the Protection and Provision of Humanitarian Assistance in Sudan, para. 5 (*ibid.*, § 434).

[50] Concerning the provision of basic necessities, see, e.g., the military manuals of Argentina (*ibid.*, § 437), Canada (*ibid.*, § 438), Croatia (*ibid.*, § 439), Germany (*ibid.*, § 441), Hungary (*ibid.*, § 442), New Zealand (*ibid.*, § 443) and Spain (*ibid.*, § 444). Concerning the security of displaced persons, see, e.g., the military manuals of Canada (*ibid.*, § 496), Croatia (*ibid.*, § 497), Hungary (*ibid.*, § 499), New Zealand (*ibid.*, § 500) and Spain (*ibid.*, § 501). Concerning respect for family unity, see, e.g., the military manuals of Canada (*ibid.*, § 549), Colombia (*ibid.*, § 550), Croatia (*ibid.*, § 551), Germany (*ibid.*, § 552), Hungary (*ibid.*, § 553) and Spain (*ibid.*, § 554).

[51] Colombia, *Law on Internally Displaced Persons* (*ibid.*, § 449); Croatia, *Law on Displaced Persons* (*ibid.*, § 450); Georgia, *Law on Displaced Persons* (*ibid.*, § 451).

[52] Colombia, Constitutional Court, *Constitutional Case No. C-092* (*ibid.*, § 454).

[53] See, e.g., the statements of Mexico (*ibid.*, § 459), Oman (*ibid.*, § 460) and Russia (*ibid.*, § 515) and the practice of Bosnia and Herzegovina (*ibid.*, § 456), Lebanon (*ibid.*, § 458), Philippines (*ibid.*, §§ 461, 514 and 565), United Kingdom (*ibid.*, § 517) and United States (*ibid.*, § 463).

[54] See, e.g., UN Security Council, Res. 361 (*ibid.*, § 464), Res. 752 (*ibid.*, § 466), Res. 1004 (*ibid.*, § 467), Res. 1040 (*ibid.*, § 469) and Res. 1078 (*ibid.*, § 470).

[55] Guiding Principles on Internal Displacement, Principle 18(2) (*ibid.*, § 432).

[56] 24th International Conference of the Red Cross, Res. XXI (*ibid.*, § 480); 25th International Conference of the Red Cross, Res. XVII (*ibid.*, § 481); 26th International Conference of the Red Cross and Red Crescent, Res. IV (*ibid.*, § 483).

[57] 27th International Conference of the Red Cross and Red Crescent, Res. I (adopted by consensus) (*ibid.*, § 484).

in the Fourth Geneva Convention.[58] The principle of preserving the family unity of refugees and displaced persons is also set forth in some other treaties.[59] This duty is also set forth in a number of military manuals.[60] It should be noted, furthermore, that respect for family unity during displacement is an element of the requirement to respect family life (see Rule 105).

With respect to separation of children from their parents, the Convention on the Rights of the Child provides that "States Parties shall ensure that a child shall not be separated from his or her parents against their will".[61] The UNHCR Executive Committee urged States to take all possible measures to prevent separation of children and adolescent refugees from their families.[62] In his report on unaccompanied refugee minors in 1998, the UN Secretary-General stated that in situations such as Sierra Leone, Guinea-Bissau and Kosovo, children fleeing from war zones were involuntarily separated from their families, and he urged States to support measures that would avoid such occurrences.[63]

The same point was made in two resolutions adopted by consensus by International Conferences of the Red Cross and Red Crescent. In a resolution on protection of children in armed conflict, the 25th International Conference referred to the Geneva Conventions and the two Additional Protocols and recommended that "all necessary measures be taken to preserve the unity of the family".[64] In a resolution on protection of the civilian population in period of armed conflict, the 26th International Conference demanded that "all parties to armed conflict avoid any action aimed at, or having the effect of, causing the separation of families in a manner contrary to international humanitarian law".[65]

Specific needs of displaced women, children, disabled or elderly

Several treaties and other instruments indicate that in providing protection and assistance to displaced persons, the parties to the conflict must consider the condition of each person. As a result, the specific needs of children, and in particular unaccompanied children, expectant and nursing mothers, persons with

---

[58] Fourth Geneva Convention, Article 49, third paragraph (*ibid.*, § 541).
[59] See, e.g., Quadripartite Agreement on Georgian Refugees and Internally Displaced Persons, para. 3(i) ("fundamental principle of preserving family unity") (*ibid.*, § 544); Agreement on Refugees and Displaced Persons annexed to the Dayton Accords, Article 1 ("the principle of the unity of the family shall be preserved") (*ibid.*, § 545).
[60] See, e.g., the military manuals of Argentina (*ibid.*, §§ 547–548), Canada (*ibid.*, § 549), Colombia (*ibid.*, § 550), Croatia (*ibid.*, § 551), Germany (*ibid.*, § 552), Hungary (*ibid.*, § 553), Spain (*ibid.*, § 554), Switzerland (*ibid.*, § 555), United Kingdom (*ibid.*, § 556) and United States (*ibid.*, § 557).
[61] Convention on the Rights of the Child, Article 9(1) (*ibid.*, § 542).
[62] UNHCR Executive Committee, Conclusion No. 84 (XLVIII): Refugee Children and Adolescents (*ibid.*, § 569).
[63] UN Secretary-General, Report on unaccompanied refugee minors (*ibid.*, § 570).
[64] 25th International Conference of the Red Cross, Res. IX (*ibid.*, § 576).
[65] 26th International Conference of the Red Cross and Red Crescent, Res. II (*ibid.*, § 577).

disabilities and the elderly must be taken into account.[66] This is also recognised in military manuals, legislation and official statements.[67] Furthermore, it is supported by the practice of international organisations and international conferences.[68]

International assistance to displaced persons

It is stressed in practice that the primary responsibility for caring for internally displaced persons rests with the government concerned.[69] However, as the government is often not in control of zones where people are displaced, this responsibility includes an obligation to permit the free passage of humanitarian assistance to internally displaced persons (see also Rule 55). The

[66] See, e.g. Additional Protocol I, Article 78 (adopted by consensus) (*ibid.*, § 581); Convention on the Rights of the Child, Article 22 (*ibid.*, § 582); African Charter on the Rights and Welfare of the Child, Article 23 (*ibid.*, § 583); Inter-American Convention on Violence against Women, Article 9 (*ibid.*, § 584); Memorandum of Understanding on the Application of IHL between Croatia and the SFRY, para. 4 (*ibid.*, § 585); Sarajevo Declaration on Humanitarian Treatment of Displaced Persons (*ibid.*, § 586); Agreement on the Application of IHL between the Parties to the Conflict in Bosnia and Herzegovina, para. 2.3 (*ibid.*, § 587); UN Declaration on the Elimination of Violence against Women, preamble (*ibid.*, § 588); Guiding Principles on Internal Displacement, Principles 4(2) and 19(2) (*ibid.*, §§ 589–590).

[67] See, e.g., the military manuals of Argentina (*ibid.*, § 591), Australia (*ibid.*, § 592), Indonesia (*ibid.*, § 593); the legislation of Angola (*ibid.*, § 594), Belarus (*ibid.*, § 595), Colombia (*ibid.*, § 596), Croatia (*ibid.*, § 597), Ireland (*ibid.*, § 598), Norway (*ibid.*, § 599) and Philippines (*ibid.*, § 600), the statements of El Salvador (*ibid.*, § 602), Ghana (*ibid.*, § 603), Oman (*ibid.*, § 605), Peru (*ibid.*, § 606), Philippines (*ibid.*, § 607), Sri Lanka (*ibid.*, § 608) and Yugoslavia (*ibid.*, § 609) and the reported practice of Jordan (*ibid.*, § 604).

[68] See, e.g. UN Security Council, Res. 819 (*ibid.*, § 610), Res. 1261 (*ibid.*, § 611), Res. 1314 ((*ibid.*, § 612), Res. 1325 (*ibid.*, § 613); UN Security Council, Statement by the President (*ibid.*, § 614); UN General Assembly, Res. 48/116 (*ibid.*, § 615) and Res. 49/198 (*ibid.*, § 616); ECOSOC, Res. 1982/25 (*ibid.*, § 617) and Res. 1991/23 (*ibid.*, § 618); UN Commission on Human Rights, Res. 1995/77 (*ibid.*, § 619) and Res. 1998/76 (*ibid.*, § 620); UNHCR Executive Committee Conclusion No. 39 (XXXVI) (*ibid.*, § 622), Conclusion No. 64 (XLI) (*ibid.*, § 623) and Conclusion No. 84 (XLVIII) (*ibid.*, § 624); UN Secretary-General, Report on human rights and mass exoduses (*ibid.*, § 625); Representative of the UN Secretary-General on Internally Displaced Persons, Report on the Representative's visit to Mozambique (*ibid.*, § 626); UN Expert on the Impact of Armed Conflict on Children, Report (*ibid.*, § 627); UN High Commissioner for Human Rights, Report on human rights and mass exoduses (*ibid.*, § 628); UN Commission on Human Rights, Special Rapporteur on Extrajudicial, Summary or Arbitrary Executions, Report on the Special Rapporteur's mission to Burundi (*ibid.*, § 629); UN Commission on Human Rights, Special Rapporteur on the Situation of Human Rights in Zaire, Report on the Special Rapporteur's visit to Rwanda (*ibid.*, § 630); UN Commission on Human Rights, Special Rapporteur on Violence against Women, Its Causes and Consequences, Report on violence against women perpetrated and/or condoned by the State during times of armed conflict (*ibid.*, § 631); UNHCR, Executive Committee, Standing Committee update on regional development in the former Yugoslavia (*ibid.*, § 632); OAS, General Assembly, Res. 1602 (XXVIII-O/98) (*ibid.*, § 633); OAU, Council of Ministers, Res. 1448 (LVIII) (*ibid.*, § 634); 25th International Conference of the Red Cross, Geneva, Res. XVII, § 8 (*ibid.*, § 635); CEDAW, Consideration of the report of Peru (*ibid.*, § 636); CEDAW, Report of the Committee, 20th Session (*ibid.*, § 637); CRC, Preliminary observations on the report of Sudan (*ibid.*, § 638); CRC, Concluding observations on the report of Sudan (*ibid.*, § 638); CRC, Concluding observations on the report of Uganda (*ibid.*, § 639); CRC, Concluding observations on the report of Myanmar (*ibid.*, § 640).

[69] See, e.g., Guiding Principles on Internal Displacement, Principle 25(1) (*ibid.*, §§ 432 and 649); UNHCR Executive Committee, Conclusion No. 75 (XLV): Internally Displaced Persons (*ibid.*, § 473).

evidence suggesting that the assistance of the international community, particularly UNHCR and the ICRC, may be sought includes practice in the context of both international and non-international armed conflicts, in particular that of the UN Security Council.[70] This practice indicates that it is not unlawful for the international community to provide assistance even if the displacement was illegal. This view is also supported by the Guiding Principles on Internal Displacement.[71]

Rule 132. Displaced persons have a right to voluntary return in safety to their homes or places of habitual residence as soon as the reasons for their displacement cease to exist.

Practice

Volume II, Chapter 38, Section D.

Summary

State practice establishes this rule as a norm of customary international law applicable in both international and non-international armed conflicts. The right to return applies to those who have been displaced, voluntarily or involuntarily, on account of the conflict and not to non-nationals who have been lawfully expelled.

International and non-international armed conflicts

The Fourth Geneva Convention provides that persons who have been evacuated must be transferred back to their homes as soon as hostilities in the area in question have ceased.[72] The right to voluntary return in general is recognised in some other treaties, such as the Panmunjon Armistice Agreement and the Convention Governing Refugee Problems in Africa.[73] The Universal Declaration on Human Rights recognises that "everybody has the right . . . to return to his country".[74] According to the International Covenant on Civil and Political

---

[70] See UN Security Council, Res. 688 (*ibid.*, § 660), Res. 999 (*ibid.*, § 661), Res. 1010, 1019 and 1034 (*ibid.*, § 662), Res. 1078 (*ibid.*, § 663), Res. 1097 (*ibid.*, § 664) and Res. 1120 (*ibid.*, § 665); UN Security Council, Statements by the President (*ibid.*, §§ 666–669).

[71] Guiding Principles on Internal Displacement, Principle 25 (*ibid.*, § 649).

[72] Fourth Geneva Convention, Article 49, second paragraph (*ibid.*, § 682).

[73] Panmunjon Armistice Agreement (*ibid.*, § 683), Article III(59)(a) and (b); Convention Governing Refugee Problems in Africa, Article 5(1) (*ibid.*, § 686).

[74] Universal Declaration on Human Rights, Article 13(2) (*ibid.*, § 692).

Rights, "no one shall be arbitrarily deprived of the right to enter his own country".[75] The regional human rights treaties contain a similar rule.[76]

Several military manuals underline that displacement must be limited in time and that displaced persons must be allowed to return to their homes or places of habitual residence.[77]

The right of refugees and displaced persons to return is also supported by numerous official statements, mostly relating to non-international armed conflicts, such as in Abkhazia (Georgia), Bosnia and Herzegovina, the Philippines and Tajikistan, and by other practice.[78] This right is also recognised in several peace agreements and agreements on refugees and displaced persons, for example, with respect to the conflicts in Abkhazia (Georgia), Afghanistan, Bosnia and Herzegovina, Croatia, Korea, Liberia, Sudan and Tajikistan.[79]

The UN Security Council, UN General Assembly and UN Commission on Human Rights have on numerous occasions recalled the right of refugees and displaced persons to return freely to their homes in safety.[80] The Guiding Principles on Internal Displacement provide that "displacement shall last no longer than required by the circumstances".[81] In addition to the option of returning to their places of origin or of habitual residence, the Guiding Principles also

---

[75] International Covenant on Civil and Political Rights, Article 12(4) (*ibid.*, § 685).

[76] See Protocol 4 to the European Convention on Human Rights, Article 3 (*ibid.*, § 684); American Convention on Human Rights, Article 22(5) (*ibid.*, § 687); African Charter on Human and Peoples' Rights, Article 12(2) (*ibid.*, § 688).

[77] See, e.g., the military manuals of Argentina (*ibid.*, § 699), Croatia (*ibid.*, § 700), Hungary (*ibid.*, § 701), Kenya (*ibid.*, § 702), Madagascar (*ibid.*, § 703), Philippines (*ibid.*, § 704), Spain (*ibid.*, § 705), United Kingdom (*ibid.*, § 706) and United States (*ibid.*, § 707).

[78] See, e.g., the statements of Angola (*ibid.*, § 716), Brazil (*ibid.*, § 717), Czech Republic (*ibid.*, § 719), Egypt (*ibid.*, § 720), France (*ibid.*, § 721), Georgia (*ibid.*, § 723), Honduras (*ibid.*, § 724), Indonesia (*ibid.*, § 725), Italy (*ibid.*, § 726), New Zealand (*ibid.*, § 727), Nigeria (*ibid.*, § 728), Russia (*ibid.*, § 730), Tunisia (*ibid.*, § 731), United Kingdom (*ibid.*, § 732) and United States (*ibid.*, § 733), the practice of the Philippines (*ibid.*, § 729) and the reported practice of France (*ibid.*, § 722).

[79] See Quadripartite Agreement on Georgian Refugees and Internally Displaced Persons, para. 5 (*ibid.*, § 788); Afghan Peace Accords, para. 6 (*ibid.*, § 798); Agreement on Refugees and Displaced Persons annexed to the Dayton Accords, Article 1 (*ibid.*, § 789); Agreement on the Normalisation of Relations between Croatia and the FRY, Article 7 (*ibid.*, § 790); Panmunjon Armistice Agreement, Article III(59)(a) and (b) (*ibid.*, § 786); Cotonou Agreement on Liberia, Article 18(1) (*ibid.*, § 796); Sudan Peace Agreement, Chapter 4, para. 3(a), and Chapter 5, para. 2, (*ibid.*, § 696); Protocol on Tajik Refugees, para. 1 (*ibid.*, § 695).

[80] See UN Security Council, Res. 361 (*ibid.*, § 734), Res. 726 (*ibid.*, § 735), Res. 779 and 820 A (*ibid.*, § 736), Res. 859 (*ibid.*, § 737), Res. 874 (*ibid.*, § 738), Res. 896 and 906 (*ibid.*, § 739), Res. 947 (*ibid.*, § 740), Res. 993 (*ibid.*, § 739), Res. 999 (*ibid.*, § 741), Res. 1036 (*ibid.*, § 739), Res. 1078 (*ibid.*, § 742), Res. 1096 (*ibid.*, § 739), Res. 1124 (*ibid.*, § 739), Res. 1187 (*ibid.*, § 743), Res. 1199 and 1203 (*ibid.*, § 744), Res. 1225 (*ibid.*, § 739), Res. 1239 and 1244 (*ibid.*, § 744), Res. 1272 (*ibid.*, § 745); UN Security Council, Statements by the President (*ibid.*, §§ 746–750); UN General Assembly, Res. 48/116 (*ibid.*, § 751), Res. 49/10 and 50/193 (*ibid.*, § 752), Res. 53/164 and 54/183 (*ibid.*, § 753); UN Commission on Human Rights, Res. 1992/S-2/1 (*ibid.*, § 756), Res. 1994/59 (*ibid.*, § 754), Res. 1994/75, 1995/89 and 1996/71 (*ibid.*, § 756), Res. 1997/2 (*ibid.*, § 755), Res. 1998/79 (*ibid.*, § 756) and Res. 1999/S-4/1 (*ibid.*, § 757).

[81] Guiding Principles on Internal Displacement, Principle 6(3) (*ibid.*, § 697).

provide for the right of displaced persons to resettle voluntarily in another part of the country.[82]

No official contrary practice was found.

Measures to facilitate return and integration

The duty of the competent authorities to take measures to facilitate the voluntary and safe return and reintegration of displaced persons is provided for in the Convention Governing Refugee Problems in Africa and the Guiding Principles on Internal Displacement.[83] It is also contained in peace accords and other agreements,[84] national legislation,[85] official statements and other practice,[86] resolutions of the United Nations and other international organisations,[87] and resolutions and other documents adopted by international conferences.[88] The UN Security Council and UN General Assembly, in particular, have on numerous occasions called upon parties to both international and non-international armed conflicts to facilitate the voluntary and safe return and reintegration of displaced persons.[89] The UN Secretary-General and his Special Representative on Internally Displaced Persons have reported on measures taken or to be

---

[82] Guiding Principles on Internal Displacement, Principle 28(1) (*ibid.*, § 800).

[83] Convention Governing Refugee Problems in Africa, Article V (*ibid.*, § 787); Guiding Principles on Internal Displacement, Principle 28 (*ibid.*, § 800).

[84] See, e.g., Panmunjon Armistice Agreement, Article III(59)(d)(1) (*ibid.*, § 786); Quadripartite Agreement on Georgian Refugees and IDPs, para. 5 (*ibid.*, § 788); Agreement on Refugees and Displaced Persons annexed to the Dayton Accords, Articles I and II (*ibid.*, § 789); Agreement on the Normalisation of Relations between Croatia and the FRY, Article 7 (*ibid.*, § 790); Agreement of the Joint Working Group on Operational Procedures of Return (*ibid.*, § 791); Memorandum of Understanding between Iraq and the UN, paras. 2 and 3 (*ibid.*, § 793); Joint Declaration by the Presidents of the FRY and Croatia (September 1992), para. 2 (*ibid.*, § 794); Joint Declaration by the Presidents of the FRY and Croatia (October 1992), para. 3 (*ibid.*, § 795); Cotonou Agreement on Liberia, Article 18(1) (*ibid.*, § 796); Arusha Peace Accords, Article 23(D) (*ibid.*, § 797); Arusha Protocol on Displaced Persons, Articles 36 and 42 (*ibid.*, § 797); Afghan Peace Accord, para. 6 (*ibid.*, § 798); Sudan Peace Agreement, Chapter 4, para. 6(iii)(1) (*ibid.*, § 799); Cairo Plan of Action, para. 70 (*ibid.*, § 801).

[85] See, e.g., the legislation of Angola (*ibid.*, § 803), Colombia (*ibid.*, § 804) and Ethiopia (*ibid.*, § 805).

[86] See, e.g., the statements of Afghanistan (*ibid.*, § 807), Rwanda (*ibid.*, § 811) and the practice of Peru (*ibid.*, § 809), Philippines (*ibid.*, § 810) and Turkey (*ibid.*, § 812).

[87] See, e.g., UN Commission on Human Rights, Res. 1996/71 (*ibid.*, § 835), Res. 1999/10 (*ibid.*, § 836) and Res. 2001/18 (*ibid.*, § 837); Council of Europe, Parliamentary Assembly, Rec. 1376, 1384 and 1385 (*ibid.*, § 853); OAU, Council of Ministers, Res. 1589 and 1653 (LXIV) and Decision 362 (*ibid.*, § 854); OSCE, Final Declaration of the Kosovo International Human Rights Conference (*ibid.*, § 855).

[88] See, e.g., 21st International Conference of the Red Cross, Res. X (*ibid.*, § 856); 22nd International Conference of the Red Cross, Res. III (*ibid.*, § 857); International Conference on Central American Refugees (CIREFCA), Declaration and Concerted Plan of Action (*ibid.*, § 858); 88th Inter-Parliamentary Conference, Resolution on support to the recent international initiatives to halt the violence and put an end to the violations of human rights in Bosnia and Herzegovina (*ibid.*, § 859); 89th Inter-Parliamentary Conference, Resolution on the need for urgent action in the former Yugoslavia (*ibid.*, § 860); Peace Implementation Conference for Bosnia and Herzegovina, Chairman's Conclusions (*ibid.*, § 861); 27th International Conference of the Red Cross and Red Crescent, Res. I (adopted by consensus) (*ibid.*, § 862).

[89] See, e.g., UN Security Council, Res. 876 (*ibid.*, § 814), Res. 882 and 898 (*ibid.*, § 815), Res. 1009 (*ibid.*, § 816), Res. 1034 (*ibid.*, § 817), Res. 1075 (*ibid.*, § 818), Res. 1088 (*ibid.*, § 819), Res. 1120

taken in the context of a number of conflicts to comply with the obligation to facilitate the voluntary and safe return and reintegration of displaced persons.[90]

Examples of measures taken to facilitate the voluntary and safe return and reintegration of displaced persons include: measures to ensure a safe return, in particular mine clearance; provision of assistance to cover basic needs (shelter, food, water and medical care); provision of construction tools, household items and agricultural tools, seeds and fertilizer; and rehabilitation of schools, skills training programmes and education. A number of cases were found where displaced persons (or their representatives) were allowed to visit the areas of return prior to return to assess the situation with respect to safety and material conditions.[91] Practice also indicates that amnesties are a proper measure to facilitate return as they can guarantee that no criminal proceedings will be brought against returnees for acts such as draft evasion or desertion, while excluding the commission of war crimes and crimes against humanity (see Rule 159).[92]

While the prohibition of adverse distinction applies to displaced persons in all circumstances (see Rule 88), there is also specific practice which underlines the importance that returnees not be discriminated against. Hence, all rules of international humanitarian law protecting civilians apply equally to displaced civilians who have returned.[93] This principle has also been recognised in a number of treaties and other instruments,[94] national legislation and official

---

(*ibid.*, § 820), Res. 1124 (*ibid.*, § 821), Res. 1199 and 1203 (*ibid.*, § 822) and Res. 1272 (*ibid.*, § 823); UN Security Council, Statements by the President (*ibid.*, §§ 824–827); UN General Assembly, Res. 46/136 (*ibid.*, § 828), Res. 48/116 (*ibid.*, § 829), Res. 49/206 (*ibid.*, § 830), Res. 50/193 (*ibid.*, § 831), Res. 53/164 (*ibid.*, § 832), Res. 54/183 (*ibid.*, § 833) and Res. 55/116 (*ibid.*, § 834).

[90] See, e.g., UN Secretary-General, Report on Cambodia (*ibid.*, § 842), Report on the situation in Tajikistan (*ibid.*, § 843) and Report concerning the situation in Abkhazia, Georgia (*ibid.*, § 844); Special Representative of the UN Secretary-General on Internally Displaced Persons, Report on visit to Mozambique (*ibid.*, § 845).

[91] See, e.g., Quadripartite Agreement on Georgian Refugees and Internally Displaced Persons, para. 10 (*ibid.*, § 867); UNHCR Executive Committee, Conclusion No. 18 (XXXI): Voluntary Repatriation (*ibid.*, § 870); UN Secretary-General, Further reports pursuant to Security Council resolutions 743 and 762 (*ibid.*, § 871); UN Commission on Human Rights, Report of the Special Rapporteur on the Situation of Human Rights in the Former Yugoslavia (*ibid.*, § 873); Special Representative of the UN Secretary-General on Internally Displaced Persons, Report on visit to Mozambique (*ibid.*, § 874); Peace Implementation Conference for Bosnia and Herzegovina, Chairman's Conclusions (*ibid.*, § 876).

[92] See, e.g., Quadripartite Agreement on Georgian Refugees and Internally Displaced Persons, para. 3(c) (*ibid.*, § 880); Agreement on Refugees and Displaced Persons annexed to the Dayton Accords (*ibid.*, § 881); Protocol on Tajik Refugees, para. 2 (*ibid.*, § 882); UN Secretary-General, Further report on the situation of human rights in Croatia pursuant to Security Council Resolution 1019 (1995) (*ibid.*, § 884); UN High Commissioner for Human Rights, Statement before the UN Commission on Human Rights (*ibid.*, § 885); UN Commission on Human Rights, Periodic report of the Special Rapporteur on the Situation of Human Rights in the Former Yugoslavia (*ibid.*, § 886); Council of Europe, Parliamentary Assembly, Rec. 1385 (*ibid.*, §§ 887).

[93] Convention Governing Refugee Problems in Africa, Article 5 (*ibid.*, § 892); Guiding Principles on Internal Displacement, Principle 29(1) (*ibid.*, § 899); UNHCR Executive Committee, Conclusion No. 18 (XXXI): Voluntary Repatriation (*ibid.*, § 906).

[94] See, e.g., Quadripartite Agreement on Georgian Refugees and Internally Displaced Persons, para. 3(a) (*ibid.*, § 893); Cotonou Agreement on Liberia, Article 18(2) (*ibid.*, § 898); General Peace Agreement for Mozambique (*ibid.*, § 897); Agreement on Refugees and Displaced Persons annexed to the Dayton Accords, Articles I and II (*ibid.*, § 894); Agreement on the Joint Working

statements,[95] and practice of the United Nations and international conferences,[96] with respect to the conflicts in Central America, Afghanistan, Colombia, Georgia, Liberia, Mozambique and the former Yugoslavia.

Rule 133. The property rights of displaced persons must be respected.

Practice

Volume II, Chapter 38, Section E.

Summary

State practice establishes this rule as a norm of customary international law applicable in both international and non-international armed conflicts.

International and non-international armed conflicts

Special attention has been paid to the issue of the property rights of displaced persons in recent conflicts, first and foremost in the context of the conflicts in the former Yugoslavia, but also in Afghanistan, Colombia, Cyprus, Georgia and Mozambique. In all cases, this rule has been reaffirmed and its violation has been condemned.

Respect for the property rights of displaced persons with regard to property left behind is supported by a number of agreements.[97] The Guiding Principles on Internal Displacement states that "property and possessions left behind by internally displaced persons should be protected against destruction and arbitrary and illegal appropriation, occupation or use".[98]

The three regional human rights treaties guarantee the right to property, subject to restrictions imposed by law in the public interest.[99] The arbitrary deprivation of displaced persons of their property would violate this right. For

---

Group on Operational Procedures of Return (*ibid.*, § 895); Sarajevo Declaration on Humanitarian Treatment of Displaced Persons (*ibid.*, § 896).

[95] See, e.g., Colombia, *Law on Internally Displaced Persons* (*ibid.*, § 901); Afghanistan, Letters addressed to the UN Secretary-General and to the President of the UN Security Council (*ibid.*, § 903).

[96] See, e.g., UN Security Council, Statement by the President (*ibid.*, § 905); UN Secretary-General, Further report on the situation of human rights in Croatia (*ibid.*, § 907); International Conference on Central American Refugees (CIREFCA), Concerted Plan of Action (*ibid.*, § 910).

[97] General Peace Agreement for Mozambique, Article IV(e) (*ibid.*, § 961); Afghan Peace Accord, para. 6 (*ibid.*, § 962); Quadripartite Agreement on Georgian Refugees and Internally Displaced Persons, para. 3(g) (*ibid.*, § 957); Agreement on Refugees and Displaced Persons annexed to the Dayton Accords, Article I(1) (*ibid.*, § 958); Agreement on the Normalisation of Relations between Croatia and the FRY, Article 7 (*ibid.*, § 963).

[98] Guiding Principles on Internal Displacement, Principle 21(3) (*ibid.*, § 918).

[99] First Protocol to the European Convention on Human Rights, Article 1 (*ibid.*, § 914); American Convention on Human Rights, Article 21(1) (*ibid.*, § 915); African Charter on Human and Peoples' Rights, Article 14 (*ibid.*, § 906).

example, a violation of the right to respect for the peaceful enjoyment of property of displaced persons was found by the European Court of Human Rights in *Loizidou v. Turkey* in 1996 and by the Human Rights Chamber of the Commission on Human Rights of Bosnia and Herzegovina in the *Turundžić case* in 2001.[100]

In the context of the conflicts in the former Yugoslavia, it has been stated in treaties and other instruments that statements and commitments regarding property rights made under duress are null and void.[101] This has also been affirmed in resolutions adopted by the UN Security Council, UN General Assembly and UN Commission on Human Rights.[102] The Agreement on Refugees and Displaced Persons annexed to the Dayton Accords provides that "all refugees and displaced persons...shall have the right to have restored to them property of which they were deprived in the course of hostilities since 1991 and to be compensated for any property that cannot be restored to them".[103] Following condemnation for failing to implement this provision, in particular by the UN Commission on Human Rights in 1996, the Federation of Bosnia and Herzegovina and the Republika Srpska adopted new laws safeguarding the property rights of displaced persons.[104]

Under the Agreement on Refugees and Displaced Persons annexed to the Dayton Accords, an independent Commission for Real Property Claims of Displaced Persons and Refugees was established "to receive and decide any claims for real property in Bosnia and Herzegovina, where the property has not voluntarily been sold or otherwise transferred since April 1, 1992, and where the claimant does not now enjoy possession of that property".[105] A similar commission was set up after the conflict in Kosovo. There was also criticism with respect to Croatia's implementation of the Agreement on Refugees and Displaced Persons annexed to the Dayton Accords. In particular, in a resolution

---

[100] European Court of Human Rights, *Loizidou v. Turkey*, Judgement (Merits), 18 December 1996, § 64; Bosnia and Herzegovina, Commission on Human Rights (Human Rights Chamber), *Turundžić case* (cited in Vol. II, Ch. 38, § 967).

[101] See, e.g., Agreement on Refugees and Displaced Persons annexed to the Dayton Accords, Article 12(3) (*ibid.*, § 936); Recommendation on the Tragic Situation of Civilians in Bosnia and Herzegovina, para. 4(c) (*ibid.*, § 937); Joint Declaration by the Presidents of the FRY and Croatia (September 1992), para. 6 (*ibid.*, § 938).

[102] See, e.g., UN Security Council, Res. 779 and 820 (*ibid.*, § 943), Res. 941 and Res. 947 (*ibid.*, § 944); UN General Assembly, Res. 48/153 and 49/196 (*ibid.*, § 945), Res. 49/10 (*ibid.*, § 946), Res. 50/193 (*ibid.*, § 947) and Res. 55/24 (*ibid.*, § 948); UN Commission on Human Rights, Res. 1992/S-2/1, 1994/72, 1994/75 and 1995/89 (*ibid.*, § 949).

[103] Agreement on Refugees and Displaced Persons annexed to the Dayton Accords, Article I(1) (*ibid.*, § 958).

[104] See UN Commission on Human Rights, Res. 1996/71 (*ibid.*, § 979); Bosnia and Herzegovina, Federation, *Law on Sale of Apartments with Occupancy Rights* (*ibid.*, § 920), *Law on Cessation of the Application of the Law on Temporary Abandoned Real Property Owned by Citizens* (*ibid.*, § 920) and *Law on the Cessation of the Application of the Law on Abandoned Apartments* (*ibid.*, § 920); Bosnia and Herzegovina, Republika Srpska, *Law on the Cessation of the Application of the Law on the Use of Abandoned Property* (*ibid.*, § 921).

[105] Agreement on Refugees and Displaced Persons annexed to the Dayton Accords, Articles VII and XI (*ibid.*, § 959).

adopted in 1995, the UN Security Council urged Croatia "to lift any time-limits placed on the return of refugees to Croatia to reclaim their property".[106] In a subsequent letter, Croatia informed the Chairman of the UN Commission on Human Rights that legislation governing the property rights of refugees and internally displaced persons had been amended and the time limit for the return of persons who had abandoned their property had been lifted.[107]

Colombia's Law on Internally Displaced Persons recognises that displaced persons have the right to retain ownership and possession of abandoned property.[108] Its Constitutional Court ruled to this effect in 1996.[109]

Beyond specific laws and procedures to ensure respect for the property rights of displaced persons, it should also be noted that the legislation of most, if not all, countries in the world guarantees a form of protection against arbitrary or illegal seizure of property which can be said to constitute a general principle of law. As a result, the protection of property rights must usually be enforced through the existing domestic court system, based on domestic law.

Alleged violations of this rule have been condemned, in particular by the UN Security Council with respect to Croatia and by the UN Commission on Human Rights with respect to Bosnia and Herzegovina.[110] The Commission on Human Rights condemned violations of the property rights of displaced persons because they "undermine the principle of the right to return".[111] This point was also made by the UN Sub-Commission on Human Rights in a resolution adopted in 1998 on housing and property restitution in the context of the return of refugees and internally displaced persons.[112] The fact that violations of property rights may impede implementation of the right to return (see Rule 132) further supports the customary nature of this rule.

---

[106] UN Security Council, Res. 1019 (ibid., § 972).
[107] Croatia, Letter to the Chairman of the UN Commission on Human Rights (ibid., § 969).
[108] Colombia, Law on Internally Displaced Persons (ibid., § 922).
[109] Colombia, Constitutional Court, Constitutional Case No. C-092 (ibid., § 923).
[110] UN Security Council, Statement by the President (ibid., § 925); UN Commission on Human Rights, Res. 1996/71 (ibid., § 926) and Res. 1998/26 (ibid., § 927).
[111] UN Commission on Human Rights, Res. 1996/71 (ibid., § 926).
[112] UN Sub-Commission on Human Rights, Res. 1998/26 (ibid., § 927).

OTHER PERSONS AFFORDED SPECIFIC PROTECTION

Rule 134. The specific protection, health and assistance needs of women affected by armed conflict must be respected.

Note: *International humanitarian law affords women the same protection as men – be they combatants, civilians or persons hors de combat. All the rules set out in the present study therefore apply equally to men and women without discrimination. However, recognising their specific needs and vulnerabilities, international humanitarian law grants women a number of further specific protections and rights. The present rule identifies certain of these additional protections and rights.*[1]

Practice

Volume II, Chapter 39, Section A.

Summary

State practice establishes this rule as a norm of customary international law applicable in both international and non-international armed conflicts. The practice collected with regard to the specific needs of women is reinforced by and should be viewed in the light of the specific practice relating to the prohibition of sexual violence (see Rule 93) and the obligation to separate women deprived of their liberty from men (see Rule 119), as well as the prominent place of women's rights in human rights law.

International armed conflicts

The rule that the specific needs of women affected by armed conflict must be respected flows from provisions found in each of the four Geneva Conventions.[2] The Fourth Geneva Convention, for example, requires that "women shall be

---

[1] For an exhaustive study of the impact of armed conflict on women, see Charlotte Lindsey, *Women Facing War*, ICRC, Geneva, 2001.

[2] First Geneva Convention, Article 12, fourth paragraph (cited in Vol. II, Ch. 39, § 1); Second Geneva Convention, Article 12, fourth paragraph (*ibid.*, § 1); Third Geneva Convention, Article 14, second paragraph (*ibid.*, § 2); Fourth Geneva Convention, Article 27, second paragraph (*ibid.*, § 3).

treated with all consideration due to their sex". Additional Protocol I provides that "women shall be the object of special respect".[3]

Numerous military manuals refer to the obligation to respect the specific needs of women affected by armed conflict.[4] Violation of this obligation is an offence under the legislation of some States.[5] This obligation is also supported by official statements.[6] Inspired by the terminology used in the Geneva Conventions and Additional Protocol I, this practice is often phrased in terms of special protection or special respect to be granted to women, or in terms of treatment to be accorded "with due regard to their sex" or "with all consideration due to their sex" or other similar expressions. The formulation used in the present rule, namely that the specific needs of women must be respected, is based on the meaning of these phrases.

Non-international armed conflicts

While common Article 3 of the Geneva Conventions and Additional Protocol II do not contain a general rule stating that the specific needs of women must be respected, they refer to specific aspects of this rule by requiring respect for the person and honour of each, prohibiting violence to life, health and physical and mental well-being, prohibiting outrages upon personal dignity, including humiliating and degrading treatment, rape, enforced prostitution and any form of indecent assault, and requiring the separation of women and men in detention.[7] These specific rules indicate a similar concern for the fate of women in non-international armed conflicts.

The requirement to respect the specific needs of women is included in several military manuals which are applicable in or have been applied in non-international armed conflicts.[8] Violation of this obligation in any armed conflict is an offence under the legislation of some States.[9] In addition, the requirement of special respect for women is contained in other instruments pertaining also to non-international armed conflicts.[10]

---

[3] Additional Protocol I, Article 76(1) (adopted by consensus) (*ibid.*, § 5).

[4] See, e.g., the military manuals of Argentina (*ibid.*, § 15), Australia (*ibid.*, §§ 16–17), Benin (*ibid.*, § 18), Canada (*ibid.*, § 20), Ecuador (*ibid.*, § 21), El Salvador (*ibid.*, §§ 22–23), France (*ibid.*, § 24), India (*ibid.*, § 25), Indonesia (*ibid.*, § 26), Madagascar (*ibid.*, § 27), Morocco (*ibid.*, § 28), Netherlands (*ibid.*, § 29), New Zealand (*ibid.*, § 30), Nigeria (*ibid.*, § 31), Philippines (*ibid.*, § 32), Spain (*ibid.*, § 33), Sweden (*ibid.*, § 34), Switzerland (*ibid.*, § 35), Togo (*ibid.*, § 36), United Kingdom (*ibid.*, § 37), United States (*ibid.*, §§ 38–40) and Yugoslavia (*ibid.*, § 41).

[5] See, e.g., the legislation of Azerbaijan (*ibid.*, § 43), Bangladesh (*ibid.*, § 44), Ireland (*ibid.*, § 45), Norway (*ibid.*, § 46) and Venezuela (*ibid.*, § 47); see also the draft legislation of Argentina (*ibid.*, § 42).

[6] See, e.g., the statement of the United States (*ibid.*, § 50).

[7] Geneva Conventions, common Article 3; Additional Protocol II, Articles 4–5 (adopted by consensus).

[8] See, e.g., the military manuals of Australia (cited in Vol. II, Ch. 39, § 16), Benin (*ibid.*, § 18), Ecuador (*ibid.*, § 21), El Salvador (*ibid.*, §§ 22–23), India (*ibid.*, § 25), Madagascar (*ibid.*, § 27), Philippines (*ibid.*, § 32), Togo (*ibid.*, § 36) and Yugoslavia (*ibid.*, § 41).

[9] See, e.g., the legislation of Azerbaijan (*ibid.*, § 43) and Venezuela (*ibid.*, § 47); see also the draft legislation of Argentina (*ibid.*, § 42).

[10] See, e.g., Memorandum of Understanding on the Application of International Humanitarian Law between Croatia and the SFRY, para. 4 (*ibid.*, § 12); Agreement on the Application of

The UN Security Council, ECOSOC and the UN Commission on Human Rights do not distinguish between international and non-international armed conflicts with respect to the protection of women in armed conflicts.[11] The UN Security Council, for example, has called for respect for the specific needs of women in the context of particular conflicts, such as in Afghanistan, but also in general.[12] In a resolution adopted in 2000 on protection of civilians in armed conflicts, the UN Security Council expressed its grave concern at the "particular impact that armed conflict has on women" and reaffirmed "the importance of fully addressing their special protection and assistance needs".[13] The UN Secretary-General's Bulletin on observance by United Nations forces of international humanitarian law provides that "women shall be especially protected against any attack".[14] The UN Special Rapporteur on Violence against Women, its Causes and Consequences and the Committee on the Elimination of Discrimination against Women have expressed concern at the violation of women's rights in international and non-international armed conflicts.[15] In 1992, the Committee stated that gender-based violence impairs or nullifies "the right to equal protection according to humanitarian norms in time of international or internal armed conflict".[16]

The Plan of Action for the years 2000–2003, adopted by the 27th International Conference of the Red Cross and Red Crescent in 1999, called for "particular protective measures for women and girls".[17]

Interpretation

The specific needs of women may differ according to the situation in which they find themselves – at home, in detention or displaced as a result of the conflict – but they must be respected in all situations. Practice contains numerous references to the specific need of women to be protected against all forms of sexual violence, including through separation from men while deprived of liberty (see Rule 119). While the prohibition of sexual violence applies equally to men and women, in practice women are much more affected by sexual violence during armed conflicts (see also commentary to Rule 93).

International Humanitarian Law between the Parties to the Conflict in Bosnia and Herzegovina, para. 2.3(2) (*ibid.*, § 13).

[11] See, e.g., UN Security Council, Res. 1325 (*ibid.*, § 55); ECOSOC, Res. 1998/9 (*ibid.*, § 58); UN Commission on Human Rights, Res. 1998/70 (*ibid.*, § 60).

[12] See, e.g., UN Security Council, Res. 1076 (*ibid.*, § 51), Res. 1193 and 1214 (*ibid.*, § 52), Res. 1261 (*ibid.*, § 53), Res. 1333 (*ibid.*, § 56) and Statement by the President (*ibid.*, § 57).

[13] UN Security Council, Res. 1296 (*ibid.*, § 54).

[14] UN Secretary-General's Bulletin, Section 7.3 (*ibid.*, § 14).

[15] See, e.g., UN Commission on Human Rights, Reports of the Special Rapporteur on Violence against Women, its Causes and Consequences (*ibid.*, §§ 61–62); Committee on the Elimination of Discrimination against Women, Reports to the UN General Assembly (*ibid.*, §§ 70–72).

[16] Committee on the Elimination of Discrimination against Women, General Recommendation No. 19 (Violence against women) (*ibid.*, § 68).

[17] 27th International Conference of the Red Cross and Red Crescent, Res. I (adopted by consensus) (*ibid.*, § 67).

The 26th International Conference of the Red Cross and Red Crescent indicated other specific needs when it called for measures "to ensure that women victims of conflict receive medical, psychological and social assistance".[18] Similarly, in 1999, in a report to the UN General Assembly, the Committee on the Elimination of Discrimination against Women required States to ensure that "adequate protection and health services, including trauma treatment and counselling, are provided for women in especially difficult circumstances, such as those trapped in situations of armed conflict".[19]

Particular care for pregnant women and mothers of young children

One specific example of respect for the specific needs of women is the requirement that pregnant women and mothers of young children, in particular nursing mothers, be treated with particular care. This requirement is found throughout the Fourth Geneva Convention, as well as in Additional Protocol I.[20] These provisions require special care for pregnant women and mothers of young children with regard to the provision of food, clothing, medical assistance, evacuation and transportation. Such requirements are set forth in many military manuals.[21] They are also found in the legislation of some States.[22]

Additional Protocol I provides that the protection and care due to the wounded and sick is also due to maternity cases and "other persons who may be in need of immediate medical assistance or care, such as . . . expectant mothers".[23] Such persons are thus entitled to the rights identified in Chapter 34, including adequate medical care and priority in treatment based on medical grounds (see Rule 110).

Death penalty on pregnant women and mothers of young children

Additional Protocol I requires that parties to a conflict endeavour, to the maximum extent feasible, to avoid the pronouncement of the death penalty on pregnant women or mothers having dependent infants for an offence related to the armed conflict. Furthermore, the death penalty for such offences may

---

[18] 26th International Conference of the Red Cross and Red Crescent, Res. II (ibid., § 66).

[19] Committee on the Elimination of Discrimination against Women, Report to the UN General Assembly (ibid., § 71).

[20] See Fourth Geneva Convention, Articles 16–18, 21–23, 38, 50, 89, 91 and 127 (ibid., §§ 76–80); Additional Protocol I, Article 70(1) (adopted by consensus) (ibid., § 81) and Article 76(2) (adopted by consensus) (ibid., § 82).

[21] See, e.g., the military manuals of Argentina (ibid., §§ 86–87), Australia (ibid., § 88), Canada (ibid., § 90), Colombia (ibid., § 91), France (ibid., §§ 92–93), Germany (ibid., § 94), Kenya (ibid., § 95), Madagascar (ibid., § 96), Netherlands (ibid., § 97), New Zealand (ibid., § 98), Nigeria (ibid., §§ 99–100), Spain (ibid., § 101), Switzerland (ibid., § 102), United Kingdom (ibid., §§ 103–104) and United States (ibid., §§ 105–106).

[22] See, e.g., the legislation of Azerbaijan (ibid., § 107), Bangladesh (ibid., § 108), Ireland (ibid., § 109), Norway (ibid., § 110) and Philippines (ibid., § 111).

[23] Additional Protocol I, Article 8(a) (adopted by consensus) (ibid., § 83).

not be executed on such women.[24] Additional Protocol II prohibits altogether the imposition of the death penalty on pregnant women or mothers of young children.[25] These rules are also set forth in some military manuals.[26]

The prohibition on carrying out the death penalty on pregnant women is also set forth in the International Covenant on Civil and Political Rights and the American Convention on Human Rights.[27]

Rule 135. Children affected by armed conflict are entitled to special respect and protection.

Practice

Volume II, Chapter 39, Section B.

Summary

State practice establishes this rule as a norm of customary international law applicable in both international and non-international armed conflicts.

International armed conflicts

The requirement of special protection for children can be found throughout the Fourth Geneva Convention and in Additional Protocol I.[28] These articles relate to the provision of food, clothing and tonics, care of children who are orphaned or separated from their families, treatment during deprivation of liberty and the distribution of relief consignments. Additional Protocol I also provides more generally that "children shall be the object of special respect".[29] Relevant rules in the Convention on the Rights of the Child and the African Charter on the Rights and Welfare of the Child are mentioned below.

Numerous military manuals require special respect and protection for children.[30] This rule is also set forth in the legislation of several States.[31] It is further

---

[24] Additional Protocol I, Article 76(3) (adopted by consensus) (*ibid.*, § 120).
[25] Additional Protocol II, Article 6(4) (adopted by consensus) (*ibid.*, § 121).
[26] See, e.g., the military manuals of Argentina (*ibid.*, § 124), Canada (*ibid.*, § 125), New Zealand (*ibid.*, § 126), Nigeria (*ibid.*, § 127) and Spain (*ibid.*, § 128).
[27] International Covenant on Civil and Political Rights, Article 6(5) (*ibid.*, § 118); American Convention on Human Rights, Article 4(5) (*ibid.*, § 119).
[28] Fourth Geneva Convention, Articles 23–24, 38, 50, 76 and 89 (*ibid.*, §§ 139–144); Additional Protocol I, Article 70(1) (adopted by consensus) (*ibid.*, § 146).
[29] Additional Protocol I, Article 77(1) (adopted by consensus) (*ibid.*, § 147).
[30] See, e.g., the military manuals of Argentina (*ibid.*, §§ 162–163), Australia (*ibid.*, § 165), Benin (*ibid.*, § 166), Canada (*ibid.*, § 167), Colombia (*ibid.*, § 168), Ecuador (*ibid.*, § 169), El Salvador (*ibid.*, §§ 170–171), France (*ibid.*, §§ 172–173), Germany (*ibid.*, § 174), India (*ibid.*, §§ 175–176), Indonesia (*ibid.*, § 177), Italy (*ibid.*, § 178) Kenya (*ibid.*, § 179), Madagascar (*ibid.*, § 180), Morocco (*ibid.*, § 181), Netherlands (*ibid.*, § 182), New Zealand (*ibid.*, § 183), Nicaragua (*ibid.*, § 184), Nigeria (*ibid.*, § 185), Philippines (*ibid.*, § 186) Spain (*ibid.*, § 187), Sweden (*ibid.*, § 188), Switzerland (*ibid.*, § 189), Togo (*ibid.*, § 190), United Kingdom (*ibid.*, §§ 191–192) and United States (*ibid.*, §§ 193–195).
[31] See, e.g., the legislation of Azerbaijan (*ibid.*, § 197), Bangladesh (*ibid.*, § 198), Belarus (*ibid.*, § 199), Ireland (*ibid.*, § 200), Norway (*ibid.*, § 201) and Venezuela (*ibid.*, § 202); see also the draft legislation of Argentina (*ibid.*, § 196).

supported by official statements and other practice.[32] This practice includes references to the general requirement of special respect and protection made by States not, or not at the time, party to Additional Protocol I.[33]

Non-international armed conflicts

Additional Protocol II states that "children shall be provided with the care and aid they require".[34] Pursuant to the Convention on the Rights of the Child, States must respect and ensure respect for rules of international humanitarian law relevant to the child and they must take "all feasible measures to ensure protection and care of children who are affected by armed conflict".[35] Similar language can be found in the African Charter on the Rights and Welfare of the Child.[36] The requirement of special respect and protection for children is contained in other instruments pertaining also to non-international armed conflicts.[37]

The requirement to respect and protect children in armed conflict is set forth in many military manuals which are applicable in or have been applied in non-international armed conflicts.[38] It is also supported by other practice in the context of non-international armed conflicts.[39]

The rule has also been invoked in several resolutions of the UN Security Council and UN General Assembly in the context of specific conflicts such as Sierra Leone and Sudan but also in general.[40] In a resolution on children in armed conflicts, adopted in 1999, the UN Security Council called upon parties to

---

[32] See, e.g., the statements of France (*ibid.*, § 205) and United States (*ibid.*, §214) and the practice of Indonesia (*ibid.*, § 207).

[33] See, e.g., the military manuals of India (*ibid.*, § 175), Nigeria (*ibid.*, § 185), Philippines (*ibid.*, § 186) and United States (*ibid.*, § 195) and the statements of Indonesia (*ibid.*, § 207) and United States (*ibid.*, § 214).

[34] Additional Protocol II, Article 4(3) (adopted by consensus) (*ibid.*, § 148).

[35] Convention on the Rights of the Child, Article 38 (*ibid.*, § 149).

[36] African Charter on the Rights and Welfare of the Child, Article 22 (*ibid.*, § 151).

[37] Memorandum of Understanding on the Application of International Humanitarian Law between Croatia and the SFRY, para. 4 (*ibid.*, § 156); Agreement on the Application of International Humanitarian Law between the Parties to the Conflict in Bosnia and Herzegovina, para. 2.3 (*ibid.*, § 157); Comprehensive Agreement on Respect for Human Rights and International Humanitarian Law in the Philippines, Part III, Article 2(24) (*ibid.*, § 158); UN Secretary-General's Bulletin, Section 7.4 (*ibid.*, § 159); UN Millennium Declaration, para. 26 (*ibid.*, § 160); EU Charter of Fundamental Rights, Article 24 (*ibid.*, § 161).

[38] See, e.g., the military manuals of Argentina (*ibid.*, § 163), Australia (*ibid.*, § 165), Benin (*ibid.*, § 166), Canada (*ibid.*, § 167), Colombia (*ibid.*, § 168), Ecuador (*ibid.*, § 169), El Salvador (*ibid.*, §§ 170–171), France (*ibid.*, § 173), Germany (*ibid.*, § 174), India (*ibid.*, §§ 175–176), Italy (*ibid.*, § 178) Kenya (*ibid.*, § 179), Madagascar (*ibid.*, § 180), New Zealand (*ibid.*, § 183), Nicaragua (*ibid.*, § 184), Nigeria (*ibid.*, § 185), Philippines (*ibid.*, § 186) Spain (*ibid.*, § 187) and Togo (*ibid.*, § 190).

[39] See, e.g., the practice of Colombia (*ibid.*, § 204), Ghana (*ibid.*, § 206) Philippines (*ibid.*, § 209), Sri Lanka (*ibid.*, § 210) and Sudan (*ibid.*, §§ 211–212).

[40] See, e.g., UN Security Council, Res. 1181 (*ibid.*, § 216), Res. 1296 (*ibid.*, § 218) and Res. 1314 (*ibid.*, § 219); UN General Assembly, Res. 48/157 (*ibid.*, § 223) and Res. 55/116 (*ibid.*, § 224).

armed conflicts "to undertake such feasible measures during armed conflicts to minimize the harm suffered by children".[41]

The International Conferences of the Red Cross and Red Crescent in 1986 and 1995 adopted resolutions stressing the importance of respect for and protection of children in armed conflict.[42] The Plan of Action for the years 2000–2003, adopted by the 27th International Conference of the Red Cross and Red Crescent in 1999, requires that all parties to an armed conflict take effective measures to ensure that "children receive the special protection, care and assistance" to which they are entitled.[43]

Interpretation

Practice indicates that the special respect and protection due to children affected by armed conflict includes, in particular:

- protection against all forms of sexual violence (see also Rule 93);
- separation from adults while deprived of liberty, unless they are members of the same family (see also Rule 120);
- access to education, food and health care (see also Rules 55, 118 and 131);
- evacuation from areas of combat for safety reasons (see also Rule 129);
- reunification of unaccompanied children with their families (see also Rules 105 and 131).

The UN Committee on the Rights of the Child recalled that provisions essential for the realisation of the rights of children affected by armed conflict include: protection of children within the family environment; ensuring the provision of essential care and assistance; access to food, health care and education; prohibition of torture, abuse or neglect; prohibition of the death penalty; and the preservation of the child's cultural environment; protection in situations of deprivation of liberty; and ensuring humanitarian assistance and relief and humanitarian access to children in armed conflict.[44]

Definition of children

Pursuant to the Convention on the Rights of the Child, "a child means every human being below the age of eighteen years unless, under the law applicable to the child, majority is attained earlier".[45] The Geneva Conventions and

---

[41] UN Security Council, Res. 1261 (*ibid.*, § 217).

[42] 25th International Conference of the Red Cross, Res. IX (*ibid.*, § 237); 26th International Conference of the Red Cross and Red Crescent, Res. II (*ibid.*, § 238).

[43] 27th International Conference of the Red Cross and Red Crescent, Res. I (adopted by consensus) (*ibid.*, § 239).

[44] Committee on the Rights of the Child, Report on the Second Session, UN Doc. CRC/C/10, 19 October 1992, § 73.

[45] Convention on the Rights of the Child, Article 1.

Additional Protocols use different age-limits with respect to different protective measures for children, although 15 is the most common.[46]

Death penalty on children

The Fourth Geneva Convention provides that "the death penalty may not be pronounced against a protected person who was under eighteen years of age at the time of the offence".[47] Additional Protocol I provides that "the death penalty for an offence related to the armed conflict shall not be executed on persons who had not attained the age of eighteen years at the time the offence was committed".[48] Additional Protocol II prohibits the imposition of the death penalty on children under 18 years of age.[49] These rules are also set forth in a number of military manuals.[50]

The prohibition on imposing the death penalty on children under 18 years of age is also set forth in the International Covenant on Civil and Political Rights, the American Convention on Human Rights and the Convention on the Rights of the Child.[51]

Rule 136. Children must not be recruited into armed forces or armed groups.

Practice

Volume II, Chapter 39, Section C.

Summary

State practice establishes this rule as a norm of customary international law applicable in both international and non-international armed conflicts.

[46] 18 years of age: compulsion to work in occupied territory (Fourth Geneva Convention, Article 51), pronouncement of the death penalty (Fourth Geneva Convention, Article 68) (cited in Vol. II, Ch. 39, § 347), execution of the death penalty (Additional Protocol I, Article 77 (adopted by consensus)) (*ibid.*, § 350), pronouncement of the death penalty (Additional Protocol II, Article 6 (adopted by consensus)) (*ibid.*, § 351); 15 years of age: measures to ensure that orphans and children separated from their families are not left on their own (Fourth Geneva Convention, Article 24) (*ibid.*, § 140), same preferential treatment for aliens as for nationals (Fourth Geneva Convention, Article 38) (*ibid.*, § 141), preferential measures in regard to food, medical care and protection adopted prior to occupation (Fourth Geneva Convention, Article 50) (*ibid.*, § 142), additional food for interned children in proportion with their physiological needs (Fourth Geneva Convention, Article 89) (*ibid.*, § 144), participation in hostilities and recruitment (Additional Protocol I, Article 77 (adopted by consensus), and Additional Protocol II, Article 4 (adopted by consensus)) (*ibid.*, §§ 379–380); 12 years of age: arrangement for all children to be identified by the wearing of identity discs, or by some other means (Fourth Geneva Convention, Article 24).
[47] Fourth Geneva Convention, Article 68, fourth paragraph (cited in Vol. II, Ch. 39, § 347).
[48] Additional Protocol I, Article 77(5) (adopted by consensus) (*ibid.*, § 350).
[49] Additional Protocol II, Article 6(4) (adopted by consensus) (*ibid.*, § 351).
[50] See, e.g., the military manuals of Argentina (*ibid.*, §§ 355–356), Australia (*ibid.*, § 357), Canada (*ibid.*, § 358), Netherlands (*ibid.*, § 360), New Zealand (*ibid.*, § 361), Switzerland (*ibid.*, § 362), United Kingdom (*ibid.*, § 363) and United States (*ibid.*, § 364).
[51] International Covenant on Civil and Political Rights, Article 6(5) (*ibid.*, § 348); American Convention on Human Rights, Article 4(5) (*ibid.*, § 349); Convention on the Rights of the Child, Article 37(a) (*ibid.*, § 352).

International and non-international armed conflicts

Additional Protocols I and II prohibit the recruitment of children.[52] This prohibition is also found in the Convention on the Rights of the Child, the African Charter on the Rights and Welfare of the Child and the Convention on the Worst Forms of Child Labour.[53] Under the Statute of the International Criminal Court, "conscripting or enlisting children" into armed forces or groups constitutes a war crime in both international and non-international armed conflicts.[54] This war crime is also included in the Statute of the Special Court for Sierra Leone.[55] In his report on the establishment of a Special Court for Sierra Leone, the UN Secretary-General stated that the provisions of Article 4 of Additional Protocol II have long been regarded as part of customary international law.[56]

The recruitment of children is prohibited in numerous military manuals,[57] including those which are applicable in non-international armed conflicts.[58] It is also prohibited under the legislation of many States.[59]

No official contrary practice was found. Alleged practices of recruiting children have generally been condemned by States and international organisations, for example, in Burundi, the Democratic Republic of the Congo, Liberia, Myanmar and Uganda.[60] In a resolution on children in armed conflicts adopted in 1999, the UN Security Council strongly condemned the recruitment of children in violation of international law.[61] In a resolution adopted in 1996 on the plight of African children in situation of armed conflicts, the OAU Council of Ministers exhorted all African countries, in particular the warring

---

[52] Additional Protocol I, Article 77(2) (adopted by consensus) (*ibid.*, § 379); Additional Protocol II, Article 4(3)(c) (adopted by consensus) (*ibid.*, § 380).

[53] Convention on the Rights of the Child, Article 38(3) (*ibid.*, § 381); African Charter on the Rights and Welfare of the Child, Article 22(2) (*ibid.*, § 386); Convention on the Worst Forms of Child Labour, Articles 1 and 3 (*ibid.*, § 388).

[54] ICC Statute, Article 8(2)(b)(XXVI) and (e)(VII) (*ibid.*, § 387).

[55] Statute of the Special Court for Sierra Leone, Article 4 (*ibid.*, § 390).

[56] UN Secretary-General, Report on the establishment of a Special Court for Sierra Leone (*ibid.*, § 582).

[57] See, e.g., the military manuals of Cameroon (*ibid.*, § 395), France (*ibid.*, § 398), Germany (*ibid.*, § 399), Kenya (*ibid.*, § 400), Netherlands (*ibid.*, § 401), Nigeria (*ibid.*, § 403), Spain (*ibid.*, § 404) and United States (*ibid.*, § 405).

[58] See, e.g., the military manuals of Argentina (*ibid.*, § 394), Cameroon (*ibid.*, § 395), Canada (*ibid.*, § 396), Colombia (*ibid.*, § 397), France (*ibid.*, § 398), Germany (*ibid.*, § 399), Kenya (*ibid.*, § 400), New Zealand (*ibid.*, § 402), Nigeria (*ibid.*, § 403) and Spain (*ibid.*, § 404).

[59] See, e.g., the legislation of Australia (*ibid.*, § 407), Azerbaijan (*ibid.*, § 408), Bangladesh (*ibid.*, § 409), Belarus (*ibid.*, §§ 410–411), Canada (*ibid.*, § 413), Colombia (*ibid.*, §§ 414–415), Congo (*ibid.*, § 416), Georgia (*ibid.*, § 418), Germany (*ibid.*, § 419), Ireland (*ibid.*, § 420), Jordan (*ibid.*, § 421), Malawi (*ibid.*, § 422), Malaysia (*ibid.*, § 423), Netherlands (*ibid.*, § 425), New Zealand (*ibid.*, § 426), Norway (*ibid.*, § 427), Philippines (*ibid.*, § 428), Spain (*ibid.*, § 429), Ukraine (*ibid.*, § 431) and United Kingdom (*ibid.*, § 432); see also the draft legislation of Argentina (*ibid.*, § 406), Burundi (*ibid.*, § 412) and Trinidad and Tobago (*ibid.*, § 430).

[60] See, e.g., the statements of Italy (*ibid.*, § 441) and United States (*ibid.*, § 451); UN Security Council, Res. 1071 (*ibid.*, § 454) and Res. 1083 (*ibid.*, § 454); UN Security Council, Statement by the President (*ibid.*, § 458); UN Commission on Human Rights, Res. 1998/63 (*ibid.*, § 460), Res. 1998/75 (*ibid.*, § 465) and Res. 1998/82 (*ibid.*, § 467).

[61] UN Security Council, Res. 1261 (*ibid.*, § 455).

parties in those countries embroiled in civil wars, "to refrain from recruiting children".[62]

The International Conferences of the Red Cross and Red Crescent in 1986 and 1995 adopted resolutions stressing the prohibition of recruitment of children.[63] The Plan of Action for the years 2000–2003, adopted by the 27th International Conference of the Red Cross and Red Crescent in 1999, requires that all parties to an armed conflict ensure that all measures, including penal measures, be taken to stop the recruitment of children into armed forces or armed groups.[64]

Age-limit for the recruitment of children

Additional Protocols I and II, the Statute of the International Criminal Court and of the Special Court for Sierra Leone put the minimum age for recruitment in armed forces or armed groups at 15, as does the Convention on the Rights of the Child.[65] Upon ratification of the Convention on the Rights of the Child, Colombia, Netherlands, Spain and Uruguay expressed their disagreement with the age-limit (15) for the recruitment of children set by the Convention, favouring 18 years instead.[66] At the 27th International Conference of the Red Cross and Red Crescent in 1999, Canada, Denmark, Finland, Guinea, Iceland, Mexico, Mozambique, Norway, South Africa, Sweden, Switzerland, Thailand and Uruguay pledged support to raise the age-limit for recruitment to 18 years.[67] At the same conference, the International Red Cross and Red Crescent Movement stated that it would continue its efforts pursuant to the Plan of Action for Children Affected by Armed Conflict (CABAC) to promote the principle of non-recruitment of children under 18 years of age.[68] Eighteen is the age-limit set by the Convention on the Worst Forms of Child Labour.[69] It is also the

---

[62] OAU, Council of Ministers, Res. 1659 (LXIV) (ibid., § 477).

[63] 25th International Conference of the Red Cross, Res. IX (ibid., § 481); 26th International Conference of the Red Cross and Red Crescent, Res. II (ibid., § 482).

[64] 27th International Conference of the Red Cross and Red Crescent, Res. I (adopted by consensus) (ibid., § 485).

[65] Additional Protocol I, Article 77(2) (adopted by consensus) (ibid., § 502); Additional Protocol II, Article 4(3)(c) (adopted by consensus) (ibid., § 503); ICC Statute, Article 8(2)(b)(XXVI) and (e)(VII) (ibid., § 513); Statute of the Special Court for Sierra Leone, Article 4 (ibid., § 515); Convention on the Rights of the Child, Article 38(3) (ibid., § 381).

[66] Declarations and reservations made upon ratification of the Convention on the Rights of the Child by Colombia (ibid., § 382), Netherlands (ibid., § 383), Spain (ibid., § 384) and Uruguay (ibid., § 385).

[67] Pledges made at the 27th International Conference of the Red Cross and Red Crescent by Canada (ibid., § 435), Denmark (ibid., § 437), Finland (ibid., § 438), Guinea (ibid., § 439), Iceland (ibid., § 440), Mexico (ibid., § 442), Mozambique (ibid., § 443), Norway (ibid., § 444), South Africa (ibid., § 446), Sweden (ibid., § 447), Switzerland (ibid., § 448), Thailand (ibid., § 450) and Uruguay (ibid., § 453).

[68] 27th International Conference of the Red Cross and Red Crescent, Res. I (adopted by consensus) (ibid., § 485).

[69] Convention on the Worst Forms of Child Labour, Articles 2 and 3(a) (ibid., § 388).

age-limit used in the African Charter on the Rights and Welfare of the Child and was supported by the OAU Council of Ministers in a resolution adopted in 1996.[70]

Under the Optional Protocol to the Convention on the Rights of the Child on the Involvement of Children in Armed Conflict, States must ensure that persons who have not attained the age of 18 years are not *compulsorily* recruited into their armed forces, while armed groups that are distinct from the armed forces of a State should not, under any circumstances, recruit persons under the age of 18 years.[71] The UN Secretary-General has announced a minimum age requirement for soldiers involved in UN peacekeeping missions and has asked States to send in their national contingents soldiers preferably not younger than 21 years of age, and in no case less than 18.[72]

Although there is not, as yet, a uniform practice with respect to the minimum age for recruitment, there is agreement that it should not be below 15 years of age. In addition, Additional Protocol I and the Convention on the Rights of the Child require that, in recruiting persons between 15 and 18, priority be given to the older ones.[73]

Rule 137. Children must not be allowed to take part in hostilities.

Practice

Volume II, Chapter 39, Section D.

Summary

State practice establishes this rule as a norm of customary international law applicable in both international and non-international armed conflicts.

International and non-international armed conflicts

Additional Protocols I and II prohibit the participation of children in hostilities.[74] The Convention on the Rights of the Child and the African Charter on the Rights and Welfare of the Child also contain this rule.[75] Under the Statute

---

[70] African Charter on the Rights and Welfare of the Child, Article 2; OAU, Council of Ministers, Res. 1659 (LXIV) (*ibid.*, § 477).
[71] Optional Protocol to the Convention on the Rights of the Child on the Involvement of Children in Armed Conflict, Articles 2 and 4 (*ibid.*, § 389).
[72] UN Secretary-General, Report on the protection of civilians in armed conflict (*ibid.*, § 472).
[73] Additional Protocol I, Article 77(2) (adopted by consensus) (*ibid.*, § 379); Convention on the Rights of the Child, Article 38(3) (*ibid.*, § 381).
[74] Additional Protocol I, Article 77(2) (adopted by consensus) (*ibid.*, § 502); Additional Protocol II, Article 4(3)(c) (adopted by consensus) (*ibid.*, § 503).
[75] Convention on the Rights of the Child, Article 38(2) (*ibid.*, § 504); African Charter on the Rights and Welfare of the Child, Article 22(2) (*ibid.*, § 386).

of the International Criminal Court, using children to "participate actively in hostilities" constitutes a war crime in both international and non-international armed conflicts.[76] It is also included as a war crime in the Statute of the Special Court for Sierra Leone.[77] In his report on the establishment of the Special Court for Sierra Leone, the UN Secretary-General stated that the provisions of Article 4 of Additional Protocol II have long been regarded as part of customary international law.[78]

The participation of children in hostilities is prohibited in many military manuals,[79] including those which are applicable in non-international armed conflicts.[80] It is also prohibited under the legislation of numerous States.[81]

No official contrary practice was found. Alleged practices of using children to take part in hostilities have generally been condemned by States and international organisations, for example, with respect to conflicts in the Democratic Republic of the Congo, Liberia and Sudan.[82] In a resolution adopted in 1999 on children in armed conflicts, the UN Security Council strongly condemned the "use of children in armed conflict in violation of international law".[83] In a resolution adopted in 1996 on the plight of African children in situations of armed conflict, the OAU Council of Ministers reaffirmed that "the use of children in armed conflicts constitutes a violation of their rights and should be considered as war crimes".[84]

The International Conferences of the Red Cross and Red Crescent in 1986 and 1995 adopted resolutions stressing the prohibition of the participation of children in hostilities.[85] The Plan of Action for the years 2000–2003, adopted by the 27th International Conference of the Red Cross and Red Crescent in 1999, requires that all parties to an armed conflict ensure that "all measures,

---

[76] ICC Statute, Article 8(2)(b)(XXVI) and (e)(VII) (*ibid.*, § 387).
[77] Statute of the Special Court for Sierra Leone, Article 4(c) (*ibid.*, § 515).
[78] UN Secretary-General, Report on the establishment of a Special Court for Sierra Leone (*ibid.*, § 341).
[79] See, e.g., the military manuals of Argentina (*ibid.*, § 520), Australia (*ibid.*, § 521), France (*ibid.*, § 524), Germany (*ibid.*, § 525), Netherlands (*ibid.*, § 526) and Nigeria (*ibid.*, § 528).
[80] See, e.g., the military manuals of Argentina (*ibid.*, § 520), Australia (*ibid.*, § 521), Canada (*ibid.*, § 522), Colombia (*ibid.*, § 523), France (*ibid.*, § 524), Germany (*ibid.*, § 525), New Zealand (*ibid.*, § 527) and Nigeria (*ibid.*, § 528).
[81] See, e.g., the legislation of Australia (*ibid.*, § 529), Belarus (*ibid.*, §§ 530–531), Canada (*ibid.*, § 533), Colombia (*ibid.*, §§ 534–535), Congo (*ibid.*, § 536), Germany (*ibid.*, § 537), Georgia (*ibid.*, § 538), Ireland (*ibid.*, § 539), Jordan (*ibid.*, § 540), Malaysia (*ibid.*, § 541), Mali (*ibid.*, § 542), Netherlands (*ibid.*, § 543), New Zealand (*ibid.*, § 544), Norway (*ibid.*, § 545), Philippines (*ibid.*, § 546) and United Kingdom (*ibid.*, § 548); see also the draft legislation of Burundi (*ibid.*, § 532) and Trinidad and Tobago (*ibid.*, § 547).
[82] See, e.g., the statements of Italy (*ibid.*, § 559) and United States (*ibid.*, § 569); UN Security Council, Res. 1071 (*ibid.*, § 572) and Res. 1083 (*ibid.*, § 572); UN Security Council, Statement by the President (*ibid.*, § 575); UN General Assembly, Res. 51/112 (*ibid.*, § 576).
[83] UN Security Council, Res. 1261 (*ibid.*, § 573).
[84] OAU, Council of Ministers, Res. 1659 (LXIV) (*ibid.*, § 584).
[85] 25th International Conference of the Red Cross, Res. IX (*ibid.*, § 585); 26th International Conference of the Red Cross and Red Crescent, Res. II (*ibid.*, § 586).

including penal measures, are taken to stop the participation of children . . . in armed hostilities".[86]

In addition, the UN Security Council, UN General Assembly and UN Commission on Human Rights frequently require the rehabilitation and reintegration of children who have taken part in armed conflict.[87] The Optional Protocol to the Convention on the Rights of the Child on the Involvement of Children in Armed Conflict specifically requires governments to take measures to demobilise and rehabilitate former child soldiers and to reintegrate them into society.[88]

Lastly, it should be noted that Additional Protocol I provides that children who do take a direct part in hostilities and fall into the power of an adverse party shall continue to benefit from the special protection to which they are entitled, whether they are prisoners of war or not.[89] None of the rules which identify such special protection, such as the prohibition of sexual violence (see Rule 93) and the obligation to separate children from adults in detention (see Rule 120) provide for an exception in the event that children have taken part in hostilities. In addition, none of the practice supporting the prohibition of the participation of children in hostilities provides that they should be deprived of their special protection if they do participate in hostilities.

Definition of participation in hostilities

In the framework of the war crime of "using children to participate actively in hostilities" contained in the Statute of the International Criminal Court, the words "using" and "participate" have been adopted in order to:

> cover both direct participation in combat and also active participation in military activities linked to combat such as scouting, spying, sabotage and the use of children as decoys, couriers or at military checkpoints. It would not cover activities clearly unrelated to the hostilities such as food deliveries to an airbase or the use of domestic staff in an officer's married accommodation. However, use of children in a direct support function such as acting as bearers to take supplies to the front line, or activities at the front line itself, would be included within the terminology.[90]

---

[86] 27th International Conference of the Red Cross and Red Crescent, Res. I (adopted by consensus) (*ibid.*, § 589).

[87] See, e.g., UN Security Council, Statement by the President (*ibid.*, § 574); UN General Assembly, Res. 55/116 (*ibid.*, § 459); UN Commission on Human Rights, Res. 1998/76 (*ibid.*, § 227).

[88] Optional Protocol to the Convention on the Rights of the Child on the Involvement of Children in Armed Conflict, Articles 6(3) and 7(1) (*ibid.*, § 389).

[89] Additional Protocol I, Article 77(3) (adopted by consensus).

[90] Draft Statute of the International Criminal Court, Report of the Preparatory Committee on the Establishment of an International Criminal Court, Addendum, Part One, UN Doc. A/CONF.183/2/Add.1, 14 April 1998, p. 2 (cited in Vol. II, Ch. 39, § 513).

The Act on Child Protection of the Philippines provides that children shall not "take part in the fighting, or be used as guides, couriers or spies".[91] Upon ratification of the Convention on the Rights of the Child, the Netherlands stated that "States should not be allowed to involve children directly or indirectly in hostilities".[92]

Age-limit for participation in hostilities

Additional Protocols I and II, the Statute of the International Criminal Court and the Statute of the Special Court for Sierra Leone put the minimum age for participation in hostilities at 15, as does the Convention on the Rights of the Child.[93] Upon ratification of the Convention on the Rights of the Child, Austria and Germany stated that the age-limit of 15 years was incompatible with the best interests of the child.[94] Colombia, Spain and Uruguay also expressed disagreement with this age-limit.[95] At the 27th International Conference of the Red Cross and Red Crescent in 1999, Belgium, Canada, Denmark, Finland, Guinea, Iceland, Mexico, Mozambique, Norway, South Africa, Sweden, Switzerland and Uruguay pledged support to raise the age-limit for participation in hostilities to 18 years.[96] Under the African Charter on the Rights and Welfare of the Child, the age-limit for participation in hostilities is 18 years.[97] Under the Optional Protocol to the Convention on the Rights of the Child on the Involvement of Children in Armed Conflict, States must take all feasible measures to ensure that members of their armed forces who have not attained the age of 18 years do not take a direct part in hostilities, while armed groups that are distinct from the armed forces of a State may not, under any circumstances, use persons under the age of 18 in hostilities.[98]

Although there is not, as yet, a uniform practice regarding the minimum age for participation in hostilities, there is agreement that it should not be below 15 years of age.

[91] Philippines, *Act on Child Protection* (*ibid.*, § 546).
[92] Netherlands, Reservations and declarations made upon ratification of the Convention on the Rights of the Child (*ibid.*, § 509).
[93] Additional Protocol I, Article 77(2) (adopted by consensus) (*ibid.*, § 379); Additional Protocol II, Article 4(3)(c) (adopted by consensus) (*ibid.*, § 380); ICC Statute, Article 8(2)(b)(XXVI) and (e)(VII) (*ibid.*, § 387); Statute of the Special Court for Sierra Leone, Article 4(c) (*ibid.*, § 515); Convention on the Rights of the Child, Article 38(2) (*ibid.*, § 504).
[94] Reservations and declarations made upon ratification of the Convention on the Rights of the Child by Austria (*ibid.*, § 506) and Germany (*ibid.*, § 508).
[95] Declarations made upon ratification of the Convention on the Rights of the Child by Colombia (*ibid.*, § 507), Spain (*ibid.*, § 510) and Uruguay (*ibid.*, § 511).
[96] Pledges made at the 27th International Conference of the Red Cross and Red Crescent by Belgium (*ibid.*, § 550), Canada (*ibid.*, § 551), Denmark (*ibid.*, § 553), Finland (*ibid.*, § 554), Guinea (*ibid.*, § 555), Iceland (*ibid.*, § 556), Mexico (*ibid.*, § 560), Mozambique (*ibid.*, § 561), Norway (*ibid.*, § 562), South Africa (*ibid.*, § 564), Sweden (*ibid.*, § 565), Switzerland (*ibid.*, § 566) and Uruguay (*ibid.*, § 571).
[97] African Charter on the Rights and Welfare of the Child, Article 2.
[98] Optional Protocol to the Convention on the Rights of the Child on the Involvement of Children in Armed Conflict, Articles 1 and 4 (cited in Vol. II, Ch. 39, § 514).

Rule 138. The elderly, disabled and infirm affected by armed conflict are entitled to special respect and protection.

Practice

Volume II, Chapter 39, Section E.

Summary

State practice establishes this rule as a norm of customary international law applicable in both international and non-international armed conflicts.

The elderly

The recognition of the special respect and protection due to the elderly is contained in various provisions of the Third and Fourth Geneva Conventions relating to their evacuation and the treatment of persons deprived of their liberty.[99] These provisions are set forth in numerous military manuals,[100] including those which apply to non-international armed conflicts.[101] They are also included in the legislation of some States.[102]

The Plan of Action for the years 2000–2003, adopted by the 27th International Conference of the Red Cross and Red Crescent in 1999, requires that all parties to an armed conflict take effective measures to ensure that in the conduct of hostilities, every effort is made to spare the lives of and protect and respect the civilian population, with particular protective measures for groups with special vulnerabilities such as the elderly.[103] The Vienna Declaration and Programme of Action adopted by the World Conference on Human Rights in 1993 called upon States and parties to armed conflicts strictly to observe international humanitarian law out of concern for the violations that affected the civilian population, in particular the elderly.[104]

No official contrary practice was found with respect to either international or non-international armed conflicts.

---

[99] Third Geneva Convention, Articles 16, 44–45 and 49 (*ibid.*, § 604); Fourth Geneva Convention, Articles 17, 27, 85 and 119 (*ibid.*, §§ 603–604).

[100] See, e.g., the military manuals of Argentina (*ibid.*, § 606), Australia (*ibid.*, § 607), Canada (*ibid.*, § 608), Colombia (*ibid.*, § 609), El Salvador (*ibid.*, §§ 610–611), France (*ibid.*, §§ 612–613), Kenya (*ibid.*, § 614), Morocco (*ibid.*, § 615), New Zealand (*ibid.*, § 616), Philippines (*ibid.*, § 617), Spain (*ibid.*, § 618), Sweden (*ibid.*, § 619), Switzerland (*ibid.*, § 620), United Kingdom (*ibid.*, §§ 621–622) and United States (*ibid.*, §§ 623–624).

[101] See, e.g., the military manuals of Australia (*ibid.*, § 607), Colombia (*ibid.*, § 609), El Salvador (*ibid.*, §§ 610–611), Kenya (*ibid.*, § 614) and Philippines (*ibid.*, § 617).

[102] See, e.g., the legislation of Azerbaijan (*ibid.*, § 625), Bangladesh (*ibid.*, § 626), Ireland (*ibid.*, § 627), Norway (*ibid.*, § 628) and Venezuela (*ibid.*, § 629).

[103] 27th International Conference of the Red Cross and Red Crescent, Res. I (adopted by consensus) (*ibid.*, § 635).

[104] World Conference on Human Rights, Vienna Declaration and Programme of Action (*ibid.*, § 634).

The disabled and infirm

The recognition of the special respect and protection due to the disabled and infirm is contained in various provisions of the Third and Fourth Geneva Conventions relating to their evacuation and the treatment of persons deprived of their liberty.[105] The Fourth Geneva Convention provides that the infirm "shall be the object of particular protection and respect".[106] The right of the disabled to protection and care is also recognised in instruments pertaining to non-international armed conflicts.[107]

Many military manuals require special respect and protection for the disabled and infirm,[108] including those which apply to non-international armed conflicts.[109] This requirement is also set forth in the legislation of some States.[110]

The Plan of Action for the years 2000–2003, adopted by the 27th International Conference of the Red Cross and Red Crescent in 1999, requires that all parties to an armed conflict take effective measures to ensure that in the conduct of hostilities, every effort is made to spare the lives of, protect and respect the civilian population, with particular protective measures for groups with special vulnerabilities such as persons with disabilities.[111] The Vienna Declaration and Programme of Action adopted by the World Conference on Human Rights called upon States and parties to armed conflicts strictly to observe international humanitarian law out of concern for the violations that affected the civilian population, in particular the disabled.[112]

No official contrary practice was found with respect to either international or non-international armed conflicts.

Interpretation

The protection due to the elderly and disabled may differ according to the circumstances in which they find themselves. For example, the Fourth Geneva

---

[105] Third Geneva Convention, Articles 16, 30, 44–45, 49 and 110 (*ibid.*, §§ 639–640 and 644); Fourth Geneva Convention, Articles 16–17, 21–22, 27, 85, 119 and 127 (*ibid.*, §§ 641–644).

[106] Fourth Geneva Convention, Article 16, first paragraph (*ibid.*, § 638).

[107] See, e.g., Comprehensive Agreement on Respect for Human Rights and International Humanitarian Law in the Philippines, Part III, Article 2(24) (*ibid.*, § 646).

[108] See, e.g., the military manuals of Argentina (*ibid.*, §§ 647–648), Australia (*ibid.*, §§ 648–649), Canada (*ibid.*, § 651), Colombia (*ibid.*, § 652), El Salvador (*ibid.*, § 653), France (*ibid.*, §§ 654–655), Madagascar (*ibid.*, § 656), New Zealand (*ibid.*, § 657), Nigeria (*ibid.*, § 658), Spain (*ibid.*, § 659), Switzerland (*ibid.*, § 660), United Kingdom (*ibid.*, § 661) and United States (*ibid.*, §§ 662–663).

[109] See, e.g., the military manuals of Australia (*ibid.*, § 648), Colombia (*ibid.*, § 652), El Salvador (*ibid.*, § 653), Madagascar (*ibid.*, § 656) and Nigeria (*ibid.*, § 658).

[110] See, e.g., the legislation of Azerbaijan (*ibid.*, § 664), Bangladesh (*ibid.*, § 665), Ireland (*ibid.*, § 666) and Norway (*ibid.*, § 667).

[111] 27th International Conference of the Red Cross and Red Crescent, Res. I (adopted by consensus) (*ibid.*, § 673).

[112] World Conference on Human Rights, Vienna Declaration and Programme of Action (*ibid.*, § 672).

Convention indicates as possibilities of honouring this obligation the establishment of safety zones and agreements for the evacuation from besieged or encircled areas of the elderly, disabled and infirm.[113] Priority in the release and repatriation of wounded and sick detainees is another way of honouring this obligation.[114] With respect to the disabled, Additional Protocol I considers that the protection and care due to the wounded and sick is also due to persons with a disability and to "other persons who may be in need of immediate medical assistance or care, such as the infirm . . . and who refrain from any act of hostility".[115] They are thus entitled to the rights identified in Chapter 34, including adequate medical care and priority in treatment based on medical grounds (see Rule 110).

[113] Fourth Geneva Convention, Articles 14 and 17 (*ibid.*, §§ 603 and 642).
[114] Third Geneva Convention, Articles 109–117; Fourth Geneva Convention, Article 132.
[115] Additional Protocol I, Article 8(a) (adopted by consensus) (cited in Vol. II, Ch. 39, § 645).

PART VI

IMPLEMENTATION

PART VI

IMPLEMENTATION

COMPLIANCE WITH INTERNATIONAL HUMANITARIAN LAW

Rule 139. Each party to the conflict must respect and ensure respect for international humanitarian law by its armed forces and other persons or groups acting in fact on its instructions, or under its direction or control.

Practice

Volume II, Chapter 40, Section A.

Summary

State practice establishes this rule as a norm of customary international law applicable in both international and non-international armed conflicts. The term armed forces, as used in the formulation of this rule, must be understood in its generic meaning.

States

The obligation of States to respect international humanitarian law is part of their general obligation to respect international law. This obligation is spelled out in the 1929 and 1949 Geneva Conventions.[1] Common Article 1 of the 1949 Geneva Conventions, however, has enlarged the formulation of this requirement to incorporate an obligation to *ensure* respect for international humanitarian law.[2] This obligation to respect and ensure respect is also found in Additional Protocol I.[3]

The obligation to respect and ensure respect for international humanitarian law is found in numerous military manuals.[4] It is supported by the practice

---

[1] 1929 Geneva Convention for the Protection of the Wounded and Sick, Article 25 (cited in Vol. II, Ch. 40, § 1); 1929 Geneva Convention Relative to the Treatment of Prisoners of War, Article 82 (*ibid.*, § 2); 1949 Geneva Conventions, common Article 1 (*ibid.*, § 3).

[2] Geneva Conventions, common Article 1 (*ibid.*, § 3).

[3] Additional Protocol I, Article 1(1) (adopted by 87 votes in favour, one against and 11 abstentions) (*ibid.*, § 4).

[4] See the military manuals of Argentina (*ibid.*, § 15), Australia (*ibid.*, §§ 16–17), Belgium (*ibid.*, §§ 18–20), Benin (*ibid.*, § 21), Cameroon (*ibid.*, §§ 22–23), Canada (*ibid.*, §§ 24–25), Colombia (*ibid.*, §§ 26–27), Congo (*ibid.*, § 28), Croatia (*ibid.*, § 29), Ecuador (*ibid.*, § 30), El Salvador (*ibid.*, §§ 31–32), France (*ibid.*, §§ 33–34) Germany (*ibid.*, § 35), Israel (*ibid.*, § 36), Italy (*ibid.*, § 37),

of international organisations[5] and international conferences.[6] There is also international case-law in support of this rule.[7]

A State's obligation pursuant to this rule is not limited to ensuring respect for international humanitarian law by its own armed forces but extends to ensuring respect by other persons or groups acting in fact on its instructions, or under its direction or control. This is a corollary of Rule 149, according to which States incur responsibility for the acts of such persons or groups, and is supported by international case-law to this effect.[8]

In addition, some military manuals and national legislation affirm that States are under an obligation to ensure that civilians do not violate international humanitarian law.[9] This obligation is also recalled in a resolution of the UN Security Council.[10] It was already recognised in case-law after the Second World War.[11]

Orders and instructions to ensure respect for international humanitarian law

The obligation of States to issue orders and instructions to their armed forces which ensure respect for international humanitarian law was first codified in

Kenya (*ibid.*, § 38), Madagascar (*ibid.*, § 39), Netherlands (*ibid.*, § 40), New Zealand (*ibid.*, § 41), Nigeria (*ibid.*, § 42), Philippines (*ibid.*, §§ 43–44), Russia (*ibid.*, § 45), Spain (*ibid.*, § 46), Switzerland (*ibid.*, § 47), Togo (*ibid.*, § 48), United Kingdom (*ibid.*, § 49) and United States (*ibid.*, §§ 50–52).

5   See, e.g., UN Security Council, Res. 822 (*ibid.*, § 70) and Res. 853 (*ibid.*, § 73); UN General Assembly, Res. 2674 (XXV) (*ibid.*, § 90), Res. 2677 (XXV) (*ibid.*, § 91), Res. 2852 (XXVI) (*ibid.*, § 92), Res. 2853 (XXVI) (*ibid.*, § 93), Res. 3032 (XXVII) (*ibid.*, § 94), Res. 3102 (XXVIII) (*ibid.*, § 95), Res. 3319 (XXIX) (*ibid.*, § 96), Res. 3500 (XXX) (*ibid.*, § 97), Res. 32/44 (*ibid.*, § 98), Res. 47/37 (*ibid.*, § 100) and Res. 48/30 (*ibid.*, § 101); UN Commission on Human Rights, Res. 1994/85 (*ibid.*, § 104), Res. 1995/72 (*ibid.*, § 105) and Res. 1996/80 (*ibid.*, § 105); Council of Europe, Parliamentary Assembly, Res. 1085 (*ibid.*, § 114); OAS, General Assembly, Res. 1408 (*ibid.*, § 116).

6   See, e.g., 24th International Conference of the Red Cross, Res. VI (*ibid.*, § 119); 25th International Conference of the Red Cross, Res. I (*ibid.*, § 120); CSCE, Budapest Summit of Heads of State or Government, Budapest Document (*ibid.*, § 123); International Conference for the Protection of War Victims, Final Declaration (*ibid.*, § 122); 93rd Inter-Parliamentary Conference, Resolution on the International Community in the Face of the Challenges posed by Calamities Arising from Armed Conflicts and by Natural or Man-made Disasters: The Need for a Coherent and Effective Response through Political and Humanitarian Assistance Means and Mechanisms Adapted to the Situation (*ibid.*, § 124); 102nd Inter-Parliamentary Conference, Resolution on the contribution of parliaments to ensuring respect for and promoting international humanitarian law on the occasion of the 50th anniversary of the Geneva Conventions (*ibid.*, § 126); African Conference on the Use of Children as Soldiers, Maputo Declaration on the Use of Children as Soldiers (*ibid.*, § 125); Conference of High Contracting Parties to the Fourth Geneva Convention, Declaration (*ibid.*, § 127); African Parliamentary Conference on International Humanitarian Law for the Protection of Civilians during Armed Conflict, Final Declaration (*ibid.*, § 128).

7   See, e.g., ICJ, *Armed Activities on the Territory of the DRC case (Provisional Measures)* (*ibid.*, § 131).

8   ICJ, *Application of the Genocide Convention case (Provisional Measures)* (*ibid.*, § 130).

9   See, e.g., the military manuals of Kenya (*ibid.*, § 38), Russia (*ibid.*, § 45) and Switzerland (*ibid.*, § 47) and the legislation of Azerbaijan (*ibid.*, § 174).

10 UN Security Council, Res. 904 (*ibid.*, § 75).

11 See, e.g., United Kingdom, Military Court at Essen, *The Essen Lynching case*, Judgement, 21–22 December 1945, published in *WCR*, Vol. I, 1946, p. 88.

the Hague Conventions of 1899 and 1907 and is reiterated in the Hague Convention for the Protection of Cultural Property, Additional Protocol I and Amended Protocol II to the Convention on Certain Conventional Weapons.[12] This obligation is also set forth in many military manuals.[13] While most military manuals instruct each soldier to comply with international humanitarian law, many contain specific provisions requiring commanders to ensure that troops under their command respect the law and that orders and instructions to that effect are issued. Compliance with this obligation may be achieved in a number of ways, for example, through military manuals, orders, regulations, instructions and rules of engagement.

Armed opposition groups

The requirement that armed opposition groups respect, as a minimum, certain rules of international humanitarian law applicable in non-international armed conflicts is set forth in common Article 3 of the Geneva Conventions.[14] This requirement is also set forth in the Hague Convention for the Protection of Cultural Property and its Second Protocol and in Amended Protocol II to the Convention on Certain Conventional Weapons.[15] While Additional Protocol II is less clear in spelling out the requirement that all parties to the conflict are bound by its rules, in particular because all references to "parties to the conflict" were removed, the Protocol develops and supplements common Article 3 of the Geneva Conventions and is binding upon both government forces and armed opposition groups.[16]

The United Nations and other international organisations have on numerous occasions recalled the duty of all parties to non-international conflicts to respect international humanitarian law. The UN Security Council, for example, has stressed this obligation with respect to the conflicts in Afghanistan, Angola, Bosnia and Herzegovina, the Democratic Republic of the Congo and Liberia.[17]

---

[12] Hague Convention (II), Article 1; Hague Convention (IV), Article 1; Hague Convention for the Protection of Cultural Property, Article 7(1); Additional Protocol I, Article 80(2); Amended Protocol II to the Convention on Certain Conventional Weapons, Article 14(3).

[13] See, e.g., the military manuals of Argentina (cited in Vol. II, Ch. 40, § 15), Benin (*ibid.*, § 21), Cameroon (*ibid.*, § 23), Ecuador (*ibid.*, § 30), Germany (*ibid.*, §§ 164–165), Hungary (*ibid.*, § 166), Russia (*ibid.*, § 45), Sweden (*ibid.*, § 171), Switzerland (*ibid.*, § 47), Togo (*ibid.*, § 48) and United States (*ibid.*, §§ 51–52).

[14] 1949 Geneva Conventions, common Article 3, which states, *inter alia*, that "in the case of armed conflict not of an international character occurring in the territory of one of the High Contracting Parties, each Party to the conflict shall be bound to apply, as a minimum, the following provisions".

[15] Hague Convention for the Protection of Cultural Property, Article 19(1); Second Protocol to the Hague Convention for the Protection of Cultural Property, Article 22; Amended Protocol II to the Convention on Certain Conventional Weapons, Article 1(3).

[16] Additional Protocol II, Article 1(1); see also Yves Sandoz, Christophe Swinarski, Bruno Zimmermann (eds.), *Commentary on the Additional Protocols*, ICRC, Geneva, 1987, § 4442.

[17] See, e.g., UN Security Council, Res. 788 (cited in Vol. II, Ch. 40, § 69), Res. 834 (*ibid.*, § 71), Res. 851 (*ibid.*, § 72), Res. 864 (*ibid.*, § 74), Res. 985 and 1001 (*ibid.*, § 76), Res. 1041 and 1059

Similarly, the UN General Assembly has on numerous occasions affirmed the principle that all parties to any armed conflict are bound to respect international humanitarian law.[18] The UN Commission on Human Rights made similar assertions in resolutions on Afghanistan and El Salvador.[19]

The obligation to *ensure* respect for international humanitarian law is set forth in a number of instruments also pertaining to non-international armed conflicts.[20] The UN Security Council has also recalled this obligation in relation to the conflicts in Angola and Liberia.[21]

The ICRC has called on numerous occasions upon all parties to non-international armed conflicts to respect and *ensure* respect for international humanitarian law, for example, with respect to the conflicts in Afghanistan, Angola, Bosnia and Herzegovina, Somalia and the former Yugoslavia.[22]

Rule 140. The obligation to respect and ensure respect for international humanitarian law does not depend on reciprocity.

Practice

Volume II, Chapter 40, Section B.

Summary

State practice establishes this rule as a norm of customary international law applicable in both international and non-international armed conflicts. This rule must be distinguished from the concept of reprisals, which is addressed in Chapter 41.

International and non-international armed conflicts

The Geneva Conventions emphasise in common Article 1 that the High Contracting Parties undertake to respect and ensure respect for the Conventions

---

[18] (*ibid.*, § 78), Res. 1071 (*ibid.*, § 79), Res. 1083 (*ibid.*, § 80), Res. 1193 (*ibid.*, § 81) and Res. 1213 (*ibid.*, § 82); UN Security Council, Statements by the President (*ibid.*, §§ 84, 85, 87, 88 and 89).
[18] See, e.g., UN General Assembly, Res. 2677 (XXV) (*ibid.*, § 91), Res. 2852 (XXVI) (*ibid.*, § 92), Res. 2853 (XXVI) (*ibid.*, § 93), Res. 3032 (XXVII) (*ibid.*, § 94), Res. 3102 (XXVIII) (*ibid.*, § 95), Res. 3319 (XXIX) (*ibid.*, § 96), Res. 3500 (XXX) (*ibid.*, § 97), Res. 32/44 (*ibid.*, § 98), Res. 40/137 (*ibid.*, § 99) and Res. 50/193 (*ibid.*, § 102).
[19] See, e.g., UN Commission on Human Rights, Res. 1991/75 (*ibid.*, § 103) and Res. 1998/70 (*ibid.*, § 106).
[20] Hague Statement on Respect for Humanitarian Principles (*ibid.*, § 7); Memorandum of Understanding on the Application of IHL between Croatia and SFRY, para. 14 (*ibid.*, § 8); Agreement on the Application of IHL between the Parties to the Conflict in Bosnia and Herzegovina, para. 1 (*ibid.*, § 9).
[21] UN Security Council, Statements by the President (*ibid.*, §§ 84 and 85).
[22] See, e.g., the practice of the ICRC with respect to the conflicts in Afghanistan (*ibid.*, § 138), Angola (*ibid.*, § 141), Bosnia and Herzegovina (*ibid.*, § 137), Somalia (*ibid.*, § 139) and the former Yugoslavia (*ibid.*, § 135).

"in all circumstances".[23] The rules in common Article 3 must also be observed "in all circumstances".[24] General recognition that respect for treaties of a "humanitarian nature" cannot be dependent on respect by other States parties is found in the Vienna Convention on the Law of Treaties.[25]

The rule that international humanitarian law must be respected even if the adversary does not do so is set forth in many military manuals, some of which are applicable in non-international armed conflicts.[26] Some military manuals explain that the practical utility of respecting the law is that it encourages respect by the adversary, but they do not thereby imply that respect is subject to reciprocity.[27] The Special Court of Cassation in the Netherlands in the *Rauter case* in 1948 and the US Military Tribunal at Nuremberg in the *Von Leeb (The High Command Trial) case* in 1947–1948 rejected the argument by the defendants that they were released from their obligation to respect international humanitarian law because the adversary had violated it.[28] This rule is also supported by official statements.[29]

The International Court of Justice, in the *Namibia case* in 1971, and the International Criminal Tribunal for the Former Yugoslavia, in its review of the indictment in the *Martić case* in 1996 and in its judgement in the *Kupreškić case* in 2000, stated that it was a general principle of law that legal obligations of a humanitarian nature could not be dependent on reciprocity.[30] These statements and the context in which they were made make it clear that this principle is valid for any obligation of a humanitarian nature, whether in international or non-international armed conflicts.

---

[23] Geneva Conventions, common Article 1 (*ibid.*, § 3).

[24] Geneva Conventions, common Article 3, which states, *inter alia*, that "in the case of armed conflict not of an international character occurring in the territory of one of the High Contracting Parties, each Party to the conflict shall be bound to apply, as a minimum, the following provisions: (1) Persons taking no active part in the hostilities, including members of armed forces who have laid down their arms and those placed *hors de combat* by sickness, wounds, detention, or any other cause, shall in all circumstances be treated humanely, without any adverse distinction founded on race, colour, religion or faith, sex, birth or wealth, or any other similar criteria".

[25] Vienna Convention on the Law of Treaties, Article 60(5) (cited in Vol. II, Ch. 40, § 197).

[26] See, e.g., the military manuals of Australia (*ibid.*, § 200), Belgium (*ibid.*, § 201), Canada (*ibid.*, §§ 202–203), Colombia (*ibid.*, § 204), Ecuador (*ibid.*, § 205), Germany (*ibid.*, §§ 206–207), France (*ibid.*, §§ 208–209), Israel (*ibid.*, § 210), Netherlands (*ibid.*, § 211), New Zealand (*ibid.*, § 212), Spain (*ibid.*, § 213), United Kingdom (*ibid.*, § 214) and United States (*ibid.*, §§ 215–216).

[27] See, e.g., the military manuals of Canada (*ibid.*, § 202), Germany (*ibid.*, §§ 206–207), Israel (*ibid.*, § 210) and United States (*ibid.*, §§ 215–216).

[28] Netherlands, Special Court of Cassation, *Rauter case* (*ibid.*, § 218); United States, Military Tribunal at Nuremberg, *Von Leeb (High Command Trial) case* (*ibid.*, § 219).

[29] See, e.g., the statements of Belgium (*ibid.*, § 220), India (*ibid.*, § 221), Iraq (*ibid.*, § 222), Mexico (*ibid.*, § 223), Solomon Islands (*ibid.*, § 224), United Kingdom (*ibid.*, § 225) and United States (*ibid.*, § 226).

[30] ICJ, *Namibia case*, Advisory Opinion (*ibid.*, § 231); ICTY, *Martić case*, Review of the Indictment (*ibid.*, § 232) and *Kupreškić case*, Judgement (*ibid.*, § 233).

Rule 141. Each State must make legal advisers available, when necessary, to advise military commanders at the appropriate level on the application of international humanitarian law.

Practice

Volume II, Chapter 40, Section C.

Summary

State practice establishes this rule as a norm of customary international law for State armed forces. The practice collected does not indicate that any distinction is made between advice on international humanitarian law applicable in international armed conflicts and that applicable in non-international armed conflicts.

Legal advisers for State armed forces

A specific requirement to provide legal advisers to commanders was first introduced in Article 82 of Additional Protocol I with a view to helping ensure that decisions taken by commanders are in conformity with international humanitarian law and that appropriate instruction is provided to armed forces.[31] No reservations or statements of interpretation were made to Article 82 by States adhering to the Protocol.

This rule is contained in many military manuals.[32] It is also supported by official statements and reported practice.[33] Practice indicates that many States which are not party to Additional Protocol I have legal advisers available to their armed forces.[34] The United States, which is not a party to Additional Protocol I, has specifically stated that it supports this rule.[35]

No official contrary practice was found.[36]

---

[31] Additional Protocol I, Article 82 (adopted by consensus) (*ibid.*, § 238).

[32] See, e.g., the military manuals of Australia (*ibid.*, §§ 240–242), Belgium (*ibid.*, § 243), Cameroon (*ibid.*, § 244), Canada (*ibid.*, § 245), France (*ibid.*, § 246), Germany (*ibid.*, § 247), Hungary (*ibid.*, § 248), Italy (*ibid.*, § 249), Netherlands (*ibid.*, § 250), New Zealand (*ibid.*, § 251), Nigeria (*ibid.*, § 252), Russia (*ibid.*, § 253), Spain (*ibid.*, § 254), Sweden (*ibid.*, § 255) and United States (*ibid.*, §§ 256–257).

[33] See, e.g., the statements of Austria (*ibid.*, § 262), Burkina Faso (*ibid.*, § 264), Niger (*ibid.*, § 271), United States (*ibid.*, §§ 273–274) and Trinidad and Tobago (*ibid.*, § 276) and the reported practice of India (*ibid.*, § 266), Israel (*ibid.*, § 267) and Netherlands (*ibid.*, § 270).

[34] See the practice of the United States (*ibid.*, §§ 272–275), the reported practice of India (*ibid.*, § 266) and Israel (*ibid.*, § 267) and the practice of Afghanistan, Azerbaijan, Fiji, Indonesia, Japan, Malaysia, Nepal, Pakistan, Papua New Guinea, Philippines, Singapore, Sri Lanka, Sudan, Thailand and Turkey (on file with the authors).

[35] See the practice of the United States (cited in Vol. II, Ch. 40, § 273).

[36] The four States that indicated that they did not have legal advisers available to the armed forces did not deny that they were under an obligation to do so. At any rate, as parties to Additional Protocol I, these States are treaty-bound to have legal advisers to the armed forces, and two of the States pledged at the 27th International Conference of the Red Cross and Red Crescent to introduce such advisers. See the practice of Burkina Faso (*ibid.*, §§ 263–264), Gambia (*ibid.*, § 265), Malawi (*ibid.*, § 269) and Niger (*ibid.*, § 271).

This rule is a corollary to the obligation to respect and ensure respect for international humanitarian law (see Rule 139), in particular as commanders have important responsibilities in the system of ensuring respect for international humanitarian law: they are responsible for providing instruction in international humanitarian law to the armed forces under their command (see commentary to Rule 142); they must give orders and instructions which ensure respect for international humanitarian law (see commentary to Rule 139); and they are criminally responsible for war crimes committed in accordance with their orders (see Rule 152), as well as for war crimes committed by their subordinates which they failed to prevent or punish when under an obligation to do so (see Rule 153).

Legal advisers for armed opposition groups

While armed opposition groups must equally respect and ensure respect for international humanitarian law (see Rule 139), no practice was found requiring such groups to have legal advisers. The absence of legal advisers can never be an excuse, however, for any violation of international humanitarian law by any party to any armed conflict.

Rule 142. States and parties to the conflict must provide instruction in international humanitarian law to their armed forces.

Practice

Volume II, Chapter 40, Section D.

Summary

State practice establishes this rule as a norm of customary international law applicable to States in time of peace, as well as to parties to international or non-international armed conflicts. The term armed forces, as used in the formulation of this rule, must be understood in its generic meaning. The practice collected does not indicate that any distinction is made between instruction in international humanitarian law applicable in international armed conflicts or that applicable in non-international armed conflicts.

Instruction within State armed forces

The duty of States to teach international humanitarian law to their armed forces was first codified in the 1906 and 1929 Geneva Conventions.[37] It was subsequently restated in the 1949 Geneva Conventions and their Additional

---

[37] 1906 Geneva Convention for the Protection of the Wounded and Sick, Article 26; 1929 Geneva Convention for the Protection of the Wounded and Sick, Article 27.

Protocols, in the Hague Convention for the Protection of Cultural Property and its Second Protocol, and in the Convention on Certain Conventional Weapons, all of which specify that the obligation to teach international humanitarian law to armed forces applies in time of peace as in time of armed conflict.[38]

Several military manuals lay down the obligation to teach international humanitarian law, some of which state that this obligation applies even in peacetime.[39] The legislation of several States provides that combatants must receive instruction in their duties under international humanitarian law or includes provisions that directly aim to fulfil this requirement by introducing such training programmes.[40] Most of the practice with respect to this rule consists of actual instruction in international humanitarian law provided by many States to their armed forces and of numerous official statements stressing the duty to provide such instruction or pledging to do so.[41] This practice shows that it is not required that all members of the armed forces be totally familiar with every detail of international humanitarian law, but rather that they should know the essential rules of the law that are relevant to their actual functions.[42]

---

[38] First Geneva Convention, Article 47; Second Geneva Convention, Article 48; Third Geneva Convention, Article 127; Fourth Geneva Convention, Article 144; Additional Protocol I, Article 83 (adopted by consensus); Additional Protocol II, Article 19 (adopted by consensus); Hague Convention for the Protection of Cultural Property, Article 25; Second Protocol to the Hague Convention on the Protection of Cultural Property, Article 30; Convention on Certain Conventional Weapons, Article 6.

[39] See, e.g., the military manuals of Argentina (cited in Vol. II, Ch. 40, § 318), Cameroon (ibid., § 316), Canada (ibid., § 319), Colombia (ibid., §§ 322–323), Kenya (ibid., § 334), Netherlands (ibid., § 337), Russia (ibid., § 342) and United Kingdom (ibid., § 350).

[40] See, e.g., the legislation of Argentina (ibid., § 357), Azerbaijan (ibid., § 358), Belarus (ibid., § 359), Côte d'Ivoire (ibid., § 360), Croatia (ibid., § 361), Germany (ibid., § 362), Peru (ibid., § 363), Russia (ibid., § 364), Sweden (ibid., § 366) and Uruguay (ibid., § 367).

[41] See, e.g., the practice of Argentina (ibid., §§ 371–373), Australia (ibid., §§ 374–376), Austria (ibid., § 377), Belarus (ibid., § 378), Belgium (ibid., § 379), Benin (ibid., §§ 380–381), Bolivia (ibid., § 382), Bosnia and Herzegovina (ibid., § 383), Burkina Faso (ibid., §§ 386–388), Cameroon (ibid., § 389), Canada (ibid., §§ 390–391), Chile (ibid., §§ 392–394), Colombia (ibid., § 396), Congo (ibid., § 397), Croatia (ibid., § 398), Egypt (ibid., § 401), El Salvador (ibid., § 403), Estonia (ibid., § 405), Ethiopia (ibid., § 406), France (ibid., §§ 407–408), Gambia (ibid., § 409), Federal Republic of Germany (ibid., §§ 410–411), Germany (ibid., §§ 412–413), Greece (ibid., §§ 414–415), Guatemala (ibid., § 416), Honduras (ibid., § 418), Indonesia (ibid., § 419), Israel (ibid., § 422), Italy (ibid., § 424), South Korea (ibid., § 426), Laos (ibid., § 429), Lebanon (ibid., § 430), Madagascar (ibid., § 431), Malawi (ibid., § 432), Malaysia (ibid., § 433), Mali (ibid., § 434), Mozambique (ibid., § 435), Netherlands (ibid., §§ 436–437), New Zealand (ibid., § 438), Niger (ibid., §§ 439–440), Nigeria (ibid., §§ 441–442), Norway (ibid., § 443), Peru (ibid., § 445), Philippines (ibid., §§ 447–449), Poland (ibid., § 450), Russia (ibid. § 451), Slovenia (ibid., §§ 453–454), South Africa (ibid., §§ 455–460), Spain (ibid., § 461), Sweden (ibid., § 463), Switzerland (ibid., § 464), Thailand (ibid., § 466), Trinidad and Tobago (ibid., § 467), Turkey (ibid., § 468), United Kingdom (ibid., § 469), Uruguay (ibid., § 470), United States (ibid., §§ 471–474), Yugoslavia (ibid., § 475) and Zimbabwe (ibid., § 477) and the reported practice of Algeria (ibid., § 370), Brazil (ibid., § 385), China (ibid., § 395), Croatia (ibid., § 399), Cuba (ibid., § 400), Egypt (ibid., § 402), El Salvador (ibid. § 404), India (ibid., § 418), Indonesia (ibid., § 420), Iraq (ibid., § 421), Israel (ibid., § 423), Jordan (ibid., § 425), Kuwait (ibid., § 428), Pakistan (ibid., § 444), Peru (ibid., § 446), Rwanda (ibid., § 452), Spain (ibid., § 462), Syria (ibid., § 465) and Zaire (ibid., § 476).

[42] See, e.g., Canada, Code of Conduct (ibid., § 320).

The obligation of States to provide instruction on international humanitarian law to their armed forces has been recalled on numerous occasions by the UN Security Council, UN General Assembly and UN Commission on Human Rights.[43] In addition, States have adopted resolutions reaffirming this obligation at numerous international conferences.[44]

The practice collected seems to show that much of the teaching is primarily or exclusively in the form of written instruction or classroom teaching, which may not be sufficient to ensure effective compliance during the stress of combat. As explained by South Africa's LOAC Manual, "in the circumstances of combat, soldiers may often not have time to consider the principles of the LOAC before acting. Soldiers must therefore not only know these principles but must be trained so that the proper response to specific situations is second nature".[45]

Increasing use of international peacekeeping and peace-enforcement troops has given rise to a particular concern that such forces be trained in the application of international humanitarian law before being deployed. Some States have an official policy to this effect.[46] A number of other States have stated that they will undertake such training.[47] As early as 1965, the 20th International Conference of the Red Cross emphasised that it was of "paramount importance" that governments provide adequate instruction in the Geneva Conventions to contingents made available to the United Nations before they leave the country.[48] Pursuant to the UN Secretary-General's Bulletin on observance by United Nations forces of international humanitarian law issued in 1999, the United Nations undertakes to ensure that the military personnel of such forces are "fully acquainted" with the principles and rules of international

---

[43] See, e.g., UN Security Council, Res. 1265 (*ibid.*, § 485) and Res. 1296 (*ibid.*, § 486); UN General Assembly, Res. 2852 (XXVI) (*ibid.*, § 487), Res. 3032 (XXVII) (*ibid.*, § 488), Res. 3102 (XXVIII) (*ibid.*, § 489) and Res. 47/37 (*ibid.*, § 492); UN Commission on Human Rights, Res. 1994/85, 1995/72 and 1996/80 (*ibid.*, § 496), Res. 1995/73 (*ibid.*, § 497) and Res. 2000/58 (*ibid.*, § 498).

[44] See, e.g., 4th International Conference of the Red Cross, Res. VIII (*ibid.*, § 521); 20th International Conference of the Red Cross, Res. XXI and XXV (*ibid.*, §§ 522–523); 22nd International Conference of the Red Cross, Res. XII (*ibid.*, § 525); Diplomatic Conference leading to the adoption of the Additional Protocols, Res. 21 (*ibid.*, § 526); CSCE, Helsinki Summit of Heads of State or Government, Helsinki Document 1992 (*ibid.*, § 528); International Conference for the Protection of War Victims, Final Declaration (*ibid.*, § 529); 90th Inter-Parliamentary Conference, Canberra, Resolution on Respect for International Humanitarian Law and Support for Humanitarian Action in Armed Conflicts (*ibid.*, § 530); CSCE, Budapest Summit of Heads of State or Government, Budapest Document 1994 (*ibid.*, § 531); 26th International Conference of the Red Cross and Red Crescent, Res. I (*ibid.*, § 532); 27th International Conference of the Red Cross and Red Crescent, Res. I (*ibid.*, § 534); Conference of High Contracting Parties to the Fourth Geneva Convention, Declaration (*ibid.*, § 535); Second Review Conference of States Parties to the CCW, Final Declaration (*ibid.*, § 536).

[45] South Africa, *LOAC Manual* (*ibid.*, § 343).

[46] See, e.g., the practice of Germany (*ibid.*, § 413), Italy (*ibid.*, § 424), Jordan (*ibid.*, § 425), Malaysia (*ibid.*, § 433) and Spain (*ibid.*, § 346).

[47] See the statements of Austria (*ibid.*, § 377), Belgium (*ibid.*, § 379), Greece (*ibid.*, § 414), South Korea (*ibid.*, § 426), Niger (*ibid.*, § 439), Russia (*ibid.*, § 451) and Trinidad and Tobago (*ibid.*, § 467).

[48] 20th International Conference of the Red Cross, Res. XXV (*ibid.*, § 523).

humanitarian law.[49] Similarly, in a resolution on the protection of civilians in armed conflicts adopted in 2000, the UN Security Council reiterated the importance of providing appropriate training in international humanitarian law for personnel involved in peacemaking, peacekeeping and peacebuilding activities.[50]

Obligation of commanders to instruct the armed forces under their command

The obligation of commanders to ensure that members of the armed forces under their command are aware of their obligations under international humanitarian law is set forth in Article 87(2) of Additional Protocol I.[51] This provision seems to be based on the reasoning that the most effective way to ensure compliance with the States' obligation to instruct their armed forces is by making commanders responsible for the instruction of the armed forces under their command.

The obligation of commanders to ensure that members of the armed forces under their command are aware of their obligations under international humanitarian law is set forth in numerous military manuals.[52] These include the manuals of States not, or not at the time, party to Additional Protocol I.[53] Some of these mention this obligation in the same breath as commanders' responsibility to ensure that their troops respect international humanitarian law.[54] The obligation of commanders to ensure instruction in international humanitarian law is also supported by official statements.[55] Canada's Commission of Inquiry into the serious violations of international humanitarian law by Canadian peacekeeping troops in Somalia blamed a number of officers for the violations committed by their subordinates because they had not adequately trained the latter in their legal obligations.[56]

---

[49] UN Secretary-General's Bulletin, Section 3 (*ibid.*, § 304).
[50] See UN Security Council, Res. 1296 (*ibid.*, § 486).
[51] Additional Protocol I, Article 87(2) (adopted by consensus) (*ibid.*, § 558).
[52] See, e.g., the military manuals of Australia (*ibid.*, §§ 560–562), Belgium (*ibid.*, §§ 563–564), Benin (*ibid.*, § 565), Cameroon (*ibid.*, §§ 566–567), Canada (*ibid.*, §§ 568–569), Colombia (*ibid.*, §§ 570–571), Croatia (*ibid.*, § 572), France (*ibid.*, §§ 573–575), Germany (*ibid.*, § 576), Hungary (*ibid.*, § 577), Italy (*ibid.*, § 578), South Korea (*ibid.*, § 579), Madagascar (*ibid.*, § 580), Netherlands (*ibid.*, §§ 581–582), New Zealand (*ibid.*, § 583), Nigeria (*ibid.*, § 584), Philippines (*ibid.*, § 585), Spain (*ibid.*, § 586), Sweden (*ibid.*, § 587), Switzerland (*ibid.*, § 588), Togo (*ibid.*, § 589) and United States (*ibid.*, § 590).
[53] See, e.g., the military manuals of France (*ibid.*, § 573), Philippines (*ibid.*, § 585) and United States (*ibid.*, § 590).
[54] See the military manuals of Benin (*ibid.*, § 565), Cameroon (*ibid.*, § 567), Canada (*ibid.*, § 568), Croatia (*ibid.*, § 572), France (*ibid.*, §§ 573 and 575), Italy (*ibid.*, § 578), Madagascar (*ibid.*, § 580), New Zealand (*ibid.*, § 583), Spain (*ibid.*, § 586), Togo (*ibid.*, § 589) and United States (*ibid.*, § 590).
[55] See the practice of Canada (*ibid.*, § 596), Netherlands (*ibid.*, § 599), United States (*ibid.*, § 601) and Zimbabwe (*ibid.*, § 603).
[56] Canada, Commission of Inquiry into the Deployment of Canadian Forces to Somalia, Report (*ibid.*, § 596).

Instruction within armed opposition groups

Article 19 of Additional Protocol II states that the Protocol "shall be disseminated as widely as possible",[57] and this provision binds armed opposition groups.[58] In the agreements on the application of international humanitarian law concluded in 1991 and 1992, the parties to the conflicts in the former Yugoslavia undertook to spread knowledge thereof, especially among combatants, to facilitate dissemination of ICRC appeals urging respect and to distribute ICRC publications.[59]

Colombia's Basic Military Manual states that the obligation to instruct armed forces also binds armed opposition groups.[60] A resolution on respect for human rights in armed conflicts adopted by the UN General Assembly in 1972 calls upon all parties to armed conflicts "to provide instruction concerning [the international humanitarian rules which are applicable to] their armed forces".[61]

Armed opposition groups must respect and ensure respect for international humanitarian law (see Rule 139), and dissemination is generally seen as an indispensable tool in this respect. In practice, armed opposition groups have frequently allowed the ICRC to disseminate international humanitarian law among their members. The ICRC itself has called upon parties to non-international armed conflicts to ensure dissemination of international humanitarian law to their troops, or to allow or facilitate ICRC efforts to do so.[62]

Rule 143. States must encourage the teaching of international humanitarian law to the civilian population.

Practice

Volume II, Chapter 40, Section E.

Summary

State practice establishes this rule as a norm of customary international law. The practice collected does not indicate that any distinction is made between teaching international humanitarian law applicable in international armed conflicts and that applicable in non-international armed conflicts.

---

[57] Additional Protocol II, Article 19 (adopted by consensus) (*ibid.*, § 287).
[58] Yves Sandoz, Christophe Swinarski, Bruno Zimmermann (eds.), *Commentary on the Additional Protocols*, ICRC, Geneva, 1987, § 4909.
[59] Memorandum of Understanding on the Application of IHL between Croatia and the SFRY, para. 13 (cited in Vol. II, Ch. 40, § 296); Agreement on the Application of IHL between the Parties to the Conflict in Bosnia and Herzegovina, para. 4 (*ibid.*, § 297).
[60] See Colombia, *Basic Military Manual* (*ibid.*, § 322).
[61] UN General Assembly, Res. 3032 (XXVII) (adopted by 103 votes in favour, none against and 25 abstentions) (*ibid.*, § 488).
[62] See, e.g., ICRC, Memorandum on Respect for International Humanitarian Law in Angola (*ibid.*, § 549), Press Release No. 1705 (*ibid.*, § 543), Conflict in Southern Africa: ICRC appeal (*ibid.*, § 539) and Appeal in behalf of civilians in Yugoslavia (*ibid.*, § 542).

State authorities

The 1906 and 1929 Geneva Conventions required States to take the steps necessary to make the conventions known to the population at large.[63] The 1949 Geneva Conventions and the Hague Convention for the Protection of Cultural Property require States to include the study of international humanitarian law in their programmes of civilian training "if possible".[64] The qualifier "if possible" was not included to make civilian instruction optional but was added to take into account the possibility in federal countries that the central government has no authority in educational matters.[65]

Additional Protocol I requires States to disseminate international humanitarian law as widely as possible and, in particular, to "encourage the study thereof by the civilian population".[66]

States' obligation to encourage the study of international humanitarian law by the civilian population or to disseminate international humanitarian law as widely as possible so that it becomes known to the civilian population is stated in many military manuals.[67] In addition, the legislation of several States provides that the civilian population must receive instruction in international humanitarian law or includes provisions that directly aim to fulfil this requirement by introducing such training programmes.[68]

In practice, many States facilitate courses in international humanitarian law, often through the provision of funds to organisations such as the National Red Cross or Red Crescent Society. According to the Statutes of the International Red Cross and Red Crescent Movement, National Societies "disseminate and assist their governments in disseminating international humanitarian law; they take initiatives in this respect".[69] In addition, more than 60 States have created national committees on international humanitarian law whose tasks usually include dissemination and promotion.[70] An increasing number of institutions

---

[63] 1906 Geneva Convention for the Protection of the Wounded and Sick, Article 26 (*ibid.*, § 611); 1929 Geneva Convention for the Protection of the Wounded and Sick, Article 27 (*ibid.*, § 612).

[64] First Geneva Convention, Article 47 (*ibid.*, § 613); Second Geneva Convention, Article 48 (*ibid.*, § 613); Third Geneva Convention, Article 127 (*ibid.*, § 613); Fourth Geneva Convention, Article 144 (*ibid.*, § 613); Hague Convention for the Protection of Cultural Property, Article 25 (*ibid.*, § 614).

[65] See United Kingdom, *Military Manual* (*ibid.*, § 636); Jean. S. Pictet (ed.), *Commentary on the First Geneva Convention* (*ibid.*, § 708).

[66] Additional Protocol I, Article 83 (adopted by consensus) (*ibid.*, § 615).

[67] See, e.g., the military manuals of Australia (*ibid.*, § 622), Belgium (*ibid.*, § 623), Canada (*ibid.*, § 624), Cameroon (*ibid.*, § 625), Colombia (*ibid.*, § 626), Germany (*ibid.*, § 627), Hungary (*ibid.*, § 628), New Zealand (*ibid.*, § 629), Nigeria (*ibid.*, § 630), Sweden (*ibid.*, § 631), Spain (*ibid.*, § 632), Tajikistan (*ibid.*, §§ 633–634) and United States (*ibid.*, §§ 636–637).

[68] See, e.g., the legislation of Azerbaijan (*ibid.*, § 639), Croatia (*ibid.*, § 640), Peru (*ibid.*, § 641), Russia (*ibid.*, §§ 642–643) and Slovakia (*ibid.*, § 645).

[69] Statutes of the International Red Cross and Red Crescent Movement, Article 3(2) (*ibid.*, § 617).

[70] ICRC, Advisory Service, Table of National Committees on International Humanitarian Law, 30 June 2002.

of higher education have started to offer courses in international humanitarian law in recent years.[71]

In addition, the UN Security Council, UN General Assembly and UN Commission on Human Rights, as well as the Council of Europe and the Organization of African Unity, have called on or invited States to disseminate international humanitarian law or to promote the teaching thereof to the civilian population.[72]

The International Conference of the Red Cross and Red Crescent has adopted several resolutions by consensus requiring States to encourage the teaching of international humanitarian law to the civilian population.[73] Similarly, the International Conference for the Protection of War Victims in 1993 urged all States to "disseminate international humanitarian law in a systematic way by teaching its rules to the general population".[74]

No official contrary practice was found. At the 27th International Conference of the Red Cross and Red Crescent in 1999, a large number of States from different parts of the world pledged to review the curricula of educational and training establishments with a view to integrating international humanitarian law into their courses or to intensifying dissemination to the population in general.[75]

Additional Protocol I further introduced the obligation of civilian authorities who, in time of armed conflict, assume responsibilities in respect of the application of international humanitarian law, to be fully acquainted therewith.[76] While States are required to encourage the teaching of international humanitarian law to the entire civilian population, many governments emphasise training for civil servants, in particular law enforcement personnel (judiciary, police, prison personnel).[77] Several resolutions of the UN Security Council and

---

[71] See, e.g., the reported practice of Algeria (*ibid.*, § 647), Argentina (*ibid.*, § 650), Belgium (*ibid.*, § 656), Democratic Republic of the Congo (*ibid.*, § 660), Cuba (*ibid.*, § 662), Egypt (*ibid.*, § 663), India (*ibid.*, § 669), Indonesia (*ibid.*, § 671), Iraq (*ibid.*, § 672), Kuwait (*ibid.*, § 674), Malaysia (*ibid.*, § 675), Peru (*ibid.*, § 680) and Uruguay (*ibid.*, § 683).

[72] See, e.g., UN Security Council, Res. 1265 (*ibid.*, § 688); UN General Assembly, Res. 3032 (XXVII) (*ibid.*, § 689) and Res. 3102 (XXVIII) (*ibid.*, § 690); UN Commission on Human Rights, Res. 1995/73 (*ibid.*, § 497); Council of Europe, Parliamentary Assembly, Rec. 945 (*ibid.*, § 691); OAU, Council of Ministers, Res. 1526 (LX) (*ibid.*, § 692).

[73] See, e.g., 19th International Conference of the Red Cross, Res. XXX (*ibid.*, § 697); 22nd International Conference of the Red Cross, Res. XII (*ibid.*, § 699); 23rd International Conference of the Red Cross, Res. VII (*ibid.*, § 701); 25th International Conference of the Red Cross, Res. VIII (*ibid.*, § 702).

[74] See International Conference for the Protection of War Victims, Final Declaration (*ibid.*, § 703).

[75] See the pledges made at the 27th International Conference of the Red Cross and Red Crescent by Argentina (*ibid.*, § 648), Belarus (*ibid.*, § 654, Belgium (*ibid.*, § 655), Chile (*ibid.*, § 657), China (*ibid.*, § 658), Colombia (*ibid.*, § 659), Cuba (*ibid.*, § 661), Greece (*ibid.*, § 665), Holy See (*ibid.*, § 667), Iceland (*ibid.*, § 668), Indonesia (*ibid.*, § 670), Mozambique (*ibid.*, § 677) and Slovenia (*ibid.*, § 681).

[76] Additional Protocol I, Article 83 (adopted by consensus) (*ibid.*, § 615).

[77] See the practice of Belgium (*ibid.*, § 655), Colombia (*ibid.*, §§ 321–322 and 396), Germany (*ibid.*, §§ 627 and 664), Greece (*ibid.*, §§ 665–666), Iceland (*ibid.*, § 668), Malawi (*ibid.*, §§ 432 and 676), Mozambique (*ibid.*, § 435), Nigeria (*ibid.*, § 630), Peru (*ibid.*, § 363), Philippines (*ibid.*, § 341) and Sweden (*ibid.*, § 631).

UN Commission on Human Rights support this requirement.[78] It was also recalled in resolutions of the International Conference of the Red Cross and Red Crescent.[79] Other States emphasise the importance of teaching international humanitarian law to youth, including in secondary education.[80] Resolutions adopted by the International Conference of the Red Cross and the Diplomatic Conference leading to the adoption of the Additional Protocols have similarly emphasised this aspect of dissemination.[81]

Armed opposition groups

Article 19 of Additional Protocol II states that the Protocol "shall be disseminated as widely as possible",[82] and this provision binds armed opposition groups.[83] This rule is contained in other instruments pertaining also to non-international armed conflicts.[84]

In a resolution on respect for human rights in armed conflicts adopted in 1972, the UN General Assembly called upon all parties to armed conflicts "to provide . . . instruction concerning [the international humanitarian rules which are applicable] to the civilian population".[85]

Although practice with respect to the obligation of armed opposition groups to encourage the teaching of international humanitarian law to the civilian population under their control is limited, it is important that "information concerning [rules of international humanitarian law] be given to civilians everywhere, with a view to securing their strict observance".[86] In practice, armed opposition groups have frequently allowed the ICRC to disseminate international humanitarian law to civilians living in areas they controlled.

---

[78] See, e.g., UN Security Council, Res. 1265 (ibid., § 688); UN Commission on Human Rights, Res. 1994/85, 1995/72 and 1996/80 (ibid., § 496) and Res. 1995/73 (ibid., § 497).

[79] See, e.g., 22nd International Conference of the Red Cross, Res. XII (ibid., § 699); 27th International Conference of the Red Cross and Red Crescent, Res. I (adopted by consensus) (ibid., § 705).

[80] See, e.g., the statements of Argentina (ibid., § 648) and Greece (ibid., § 665) and the reported practice of Argentina (ibid., § 650).

[81] See, e.g., 15th International Conference of the Red Cross, Res. IX (ibid., § 695); 19th International Conference of the Red Cross, Res. XIX and XXX (ibid., §§ 696–697); 23rd International Conference of the Red Cross, Res. VII (ibid., § 701); Diplomatic Conference leading to the adoption of the Additional Protocols, Res. 21 (adopted by 63 votes in favour, 2 against and 21 abstentions) (ibid., § 700).

[82] Additional Protocol II, Article 19 (adopted by consensus) (ibid., § 287).

[83] Yves Sandoz, Christophe Swinarski, Bruno Zimmermann (eds.), Commentary on the Additional Protocols, ICRC, Geneva, 1987, § 4909.

[84] Memorandum of Understanding on the Application of IHL between Croatia and the SFRY, para. 13 (cited in Vol. II, Ch. 40, § 618); Agreement on the Application of IHL between the Parties to the Conflict in Bosnia and Herzegovina, para. 4 (ibid., § 619).

[85] UN General Assembly, Res. 3032 (XXVII) (adopted by 103 votes in favour, none against and 25 abstentions) (ibid., § 689).

[86] UN General Assembly, Res. 3102 (XXVIII) (adopted by 107 votes in favour, none against and 6 abstentions) (ibid., § 690).

ENFORCEMENT OF INTERNATIONAL HUMANITARIAN LAW

Rule 144. States may not encourage violations of international humanitarian law by parties to an armed conflict. They must exert their influence, to the degree possible, to stop violations of international humanitarian law.

Practice

Volume II, Chapter 41, Section A.

Summary

State practice establishes this rule as a norm of customary international law applicable in both international and non-international armed conflicts.

International and non-international armed conflicts

Common Article 1 of the Geneva Conventions provides that States parties undertake to "ensure respect for the present Convention".[1] The same provision is repeated in Additional Protocol I in relation to respect for the provisions of that Protocol.[2] Additional Protocol I further provides that in the event of serious violations of the Protocol, States parties undertake to act, jointly or individually, in cooperation with the United Nations and in conformity with the Charter of the United Nations.[3] A similar provision is included in the Second Protocol to the Hague Convention for the Protection of Cultural Property.[4]

Beginning with its commentary on common Article 1 of the Geneva Conventions, the ICRC has repeatedly stated that the obligation to "ensure respect" is not limited to behaviour by parties to a conflict, but includes

---

[1] Geneva Conventions, common Article 1 (cited in Vol. II, Ch. 41, § 1).
[2] Additional Protocol I, Article 1(1) (adopted by 87 votes in favour, one against and 11 abstentions) (*ibid.*, § 2).
[3] Additional Protocol I, Article 89 (adopted by 50 votes in favour, 3 against and 40 abstentions) (*ibid.*, § 3).
[4] Second Protocol to the Hague Convention for the Protection of Cultural Property, Article 31, which states that "in situations of serious violations of this Protocol, the Parties undertake to act, jointly through the Committee, or individually, in cooperation with UNESCO and the United Nations and in conformity with the Charter of the United Nations".

the requirement that States do all in their power to ensure that international humanitarian law is respected universally.[5]

The interpretation that common Article 1 involves obligations beyond those of the parties to the conflict was supported by the UN Security Council in a resolution adopted in 1990 calling on States parties to the Fourth Geneva Convention to ensure respect by Israel for its obligations, in accordance with Article 1 of the Convention.[6] The UN General Assembly has adopted several resolutions to the same effect and in relation to the same conflict.[7] Other international organisations have likewise called on their member States to respect and ensure respect for international humanitarian law, in particular the Council of Europe, NATO, the Organization of African Unity and the Organization of American States.[8]

International conferences have similarly appealed to States to ensure respect for international humanitarian law. In 1968, the International Conference on Human Rights in Teheran adopted a resolution noting that States parties to the Geneva Conventions sometimes failed "to appreciate their responsibility to take steps to ensure the respect of these humanitarian rules in all circumstances by other States, even if they are not themselves directly involved in an armed conflict".[9] In the Final Declaration adopted by the International Conference for the Protection of War Victims in 1993, the participants undertook "to act in cooperation with the UN and in conformity with the UN Charter to ensure full compliance with international humanitarian law in the event of genocide and other serious violations of this law" and affirmed their responsibility, "in accordance with Article 1 common to the Geneva Conventions, to respect and ensure respect for international humanitarian law in order to protect the victims of war". They further urged all States to make every effort to "ensure the effectiveness of international humanitarian law and take resolute action, in accordance with that law, against States bearing responsibility for violations of international humanitarian law with a view to terminating such violations".[10] More recently, the Conference of High Contracting Parties to the Fourth Geneva Convention in 2001 welcomed and encouraged initiatives

---

[5] Jean S. Pictet (ed.), *Commentary on the Third Geneva Convention*, ICRC, Geneva, 1960, p. 18; Yves Sandoz, Christophe Swinarski, Bruno Zimmermann (eds.), *Commentary on the Additional Protocols*, ICRC, Geneva, 1987, § 45.

[6] UN Security Council, Res. 681 (cited in Vol. II, Ch. 41, § 21).

[7] See UN General Assembly, Res. 32/91 A (*ibid.*, § 22), Res. 37/123 A (*ibid.*, § 23), Res. 38/180 A (*ibid.*, § 24) and Res. 43/21 (*ibid.*, § 25).

[8] See, e.g., Council of Europe, Parliamentary Assembly, Res. 823 (*ibid.*, § 30), Res. 881 (*ibid.*, § 31), Res. 921 (*ibid.*, § 32) and Res. 948 (*ibid.*, § 33); Council of Europe, Committee of Ministers, Declaration on the rape of women and children in the territory of former Yugoslavia (*ibid.*, § 34); NATO, Parliamentary Assembly, Resolution of the Civilian Affairs Committee (*ibid.*, § 35); OAU, Conference of African Ministers of Health, Res. 14 (V) (*ibid.*, § 36); OAS, General Assembly, Res. 1408 (XXVI-O/96) (*ibid.*, § 37).

[9] International Conference on Human Rights, Res. XXIII (*ibid.*, § 38).

[10] International Conference for the Protection of War Victims, Final Declaration (*ibid.*, § 43).

by States, both individually and collectively, aimed at ensuring respect for the Convention.[11]

Practice shows that the obligation of third States to ensure respect for international humanitarian law is not limited to implementing the treaty provision contained in common Article 1 of the Geneva Conventions and Article 1(1) of Additional Protocol I. For example, the ICRC's appeals in relation to the conflict in Rhodesia/Zimbabwe in 1979 and to the Iran–Iraq War in 1983 and 1984 involved calls to ensure respect for rules not found in the Geneva Conventions but in the Additional Protocols (bombardment of civilian zones and indiscriminate attacks) and the countries alleged to be committing these violations were not party to the Protocols.[12] It is significant that these appeals were addressed to the international community, that no State objected to them and that several States not party to the Additional Protocols supported them.[13]

In the *Nicaragua case (Merits)* in 1986, the International Court of Justice held that the duty to respect and ensure respect did not derive only from the Geneva Conventions, but "from the general principles of humanitarian law to which the Conventions merely give specific expression". The Court concluded, therefore, that the United States was "under an obligation not to encourage persons or groups engaged in the conflict in Nicaragua to act in violation of the provisions of Article 3 common to the four 1949 Geneva Conventions".[14] Similarly, according to the Draft Articles on State Responsibility, "a State which aids or assists another State in the commission of an internationally wrongful act by the latter is internationally responsible for doing so".[15] In several cases, national courts have rejected claims that this rule would prevent States from deporting persons to countries where violations of common Article 3 of the Geneva Conventions were allegedly occurring.[16]

With respect to any positive obligations imposed by the duty to ensure respect for international humanitarian law, there is agreement that all States have a right to require respect for international humanitarian law by parties

---

[11] Conference of High Contracting Parties to the Fourth Geneva Convention, Declaration (*ibid.*, § 45).

[12] See ICRC, Conflict in Southern Africa: ICRC appeal (*ibid.*, § 52), Conflict between Iraq and Iran: ICRC appeal (*ibid.*, § 53), Conflict between Iran and Iraq: Second ICRC appeal (*ibid.*, § 54) and Press Release No. 1498 (*ibid.*, § 55).

[13] See, e.g., the statements of the United Kingdom (*ibid.*, § 19) and United States (*ibid.*, § 20).

[14] ICJ, *Nicaragua case (Merits)* (*ibid.*, § 46).

[15] Draft Articles on State Responsibility, Article 16 (*ibid.*, § 10).

[16] See, e.g., United States, Executive Office for Immigration Review and Board of Immigration Appeals, *Medina case* (*ibid.*, § 14), in which the Board of Immigration Appeals found that it was unclear "what obligations, if any" common Article 1 was intended to impose with respect to violations of international humanitarian law by other States; United States, District Court for the Northern District of California, *Baptist Churches case* (*ibid.*, § 15), in which the Court considered that common Article 1 was not a self-executing treaty provision because it did not "provide any intelligible guidelines for judicial enforcement" and did not prevent the United States from deporting persons to El Salvador and Guatemala; Canada, Federal Court Trial Division, *Sinnappu case* (*ibid.*, § 13), in which the Court held that common Article 1 did not prevent Canada from returning unsuccessful refugee claimants to Sri Lanka.

to any conflict. The Trial Chamber of the International Criminal Tribunal for the Former Yugoslavia stated in its judgements in the *Furundžija case* in 1998 and *Kupreškić case* in 2000 that the norms of international humanitarian law were norms *erga omnes* and therefore all States had a "legal interest" in their observance and consequently a legal entitlement to demand their respect.[17] State practice shows an overwhelming use of (i) diplomatic protest and (ii) collective measures through which States exert their influence, to the degree possible, to try and stop violations of international humanitarian law.[18]

(i) Diplomatic protest. There is extensive practice, especially over the last two decades, of States objecting to violations of international humanitarian law by other States. These objections concern both international and non-international armed conflicts. They are not limited to violations of the Geneva Conventions and are often in relation to conflicts with which the protesting States have no specific connection. These objections have been made through bilateral diplomatic protests, in international fora or by means of resolutions of international organisations. They are usually directly aimed at the violating parties. Such protests have, on occasion, referred specifically to the duty of States, under common Article 1 of the Geneva Conventions, to ensure respect for international humanitarian law. The practice in this regard is catalogued in the context of the various rules covered by this study.

(ii) Collective measures. Apart from resolutions by international bodies, collective measures by States to try to "ensure respect" have taken the form, *inter alia*, of holding international conferences on specific situations, investigating possible violations, creating *ad hoc* criminal tribunals and courts, creating the International Criminal Court, imposing international sanctions and sending of peacekeeping or peace-enforcement troops. This practice is catalogued throughout this study in connection with each rule.

It should also be noted that States' obligation to establish universal jurisdiction over grave breaches (see commentary to Rule 157) and their obligation to investigate war crimes falling within their jurisdiction and to prosecute the suspects if appropriate (see Rule 158) illustrate how respect for international humanitarian law can be enforced through the action of third States.

Lastly, it should be noted that neither the intention of the drafters of common Article 1 of the Geneva Conventions, nor practice since then, justifies the obligation to ensure respect for international humanitarian law being used as the sole basis for resort to the use of force. It is therefore expected that measures aimed at ensuring respect, beyond those decided by the UN Security Council, be peaceful ones. Additional Protocol I provides that in the event of serious violations of the Protocol, States parties undertake to act, jointly or individually, in cooperation with the United Nations and in conformity with the

---

[17] ICTY, *Furundžija case*, Judgement (*ibid.*, § 47) and *Kupreškić case*, Judgement (*ibid.*, § 48).
[18] For an overview of measures available to States to fulfil their obligation to ensure respect for international humanitarian law, see *International Review of the Red Cross*, No. 298, 1994, p. 9.

Charter of the United Nations.[19] By referring to measures in conformity with the Charter of the United Nations, the Protocol makes it clear that States cannot use force in a manner unauthorised by the Charter to ensure respect for international humanitarian law. The same reasoning applies to Article 31 of the Second Protocol to the Hague Convention for the Protection of Cultural Property, which contains a similar provision.

Rule 145. Where not prohibited by international law, belligerent reprisals are subject to stringent conditions.

Practice

Volume II, Chapter 41, Section B.

Summary

State practice establishes this rule as a norm of customary international law applicable in international armed conflicts. A belligerent reprisal consists of an action that would otherwise be unlawful but that in exceptional cases is considered lawful under international law when used as an enforcement measure in reaction to unlawful acts of an adversary. In international humanitarian law there is a trend to outlaw belligerent reprisals altogether. Those that may still be lawful are subject to the stringent conditions set forth below.

International armed conflicts

As stated in several military manuals, reprisals have been a traditional method of enforcement of international humanitarian law, albeit subject to the stringent conditions mentioned below.[20] During the past century the categories of persons and objects that can be subjected to reprisal action have been reduced, and reprisal action against certain persons and objects is now prohibited under customary international law (see Rules 146–147).

In the course of the many armed conflicts that have marked the past two decades, belligerent reprisals have not been resorted to as a measure of enforcing international humanitarian law, the main exception being the Iran–Iraq War, where such measures were severely criticised by the UN Security Council and UN Secretary-General (see *infra*). The trend towards outlawing reprisals, beyond those already prohibited by the Geneva Conventions, can be seen in a UN General Assembly resolution on basic principles for the protection of civilian populations in armed conflicts adopted in 1970, which stated that

---

[19] Additional Protocol I, Article 89 (adopted by 50 votes in favour, 3 against and 40 abstentions) (cited in Vol. II, Ch. 41, § 3).

[20] See the military manuals of Benin (*ibid.*, § 70), Kenya (*ibid.*, § 82), Netherlands (*ibid.*, § 85), Togo (*ibid.*, § 93) and United Kingdom (*ibid.*, §§ 94–95).

"civilian populations, or individual members thereof, should not be the object of reprisals".[21]

The reticence of States to resort to reprisals can be explained by the fact that they are ineffective as a means of enforcement, in particular because reprisals risk leading to an escalation of violations. As stated by Kenya's LOAC Manual, "reprisals are an unsatisfactory way of enforcing the law. They tend to be used as an excuse for illegal methods of warfare and carry a danger of escalation through repeated reprisals and counter reprisals."[22] Several other military manuals, as well as other practice, similarly warn of the risk of escalation.[23] Still others underline the limited military advantage gained by using reprisals.[24]

During the negotiation of Additional Protocol I, a number of States asserted that resort to reprisals ought not to be allowed at all.[25] Others stated that they were a very questionable means of securing enforcement.[26] Several States prohibit reprisals altogether.[27] Others state that they may only be taken against combatants and military objectives.[28] There is also national case-law, as well as official statements, to the effect that reprisals must not be inhumane.[29] This requirement was already set forth in the Oxford Manual and recently restated, albeit in different terms, in the Draft Articles on State Responsibility.[30]

The reticence to approve of the resort to belligerent reprisals, together with the stringent conditions found in official practice, indicates that the international community is increasingly opposed to the use of violations of international humanitarian law as a method of trying to enforce the law. It is also relevant that there is much more support these days for the notion of ensuring respect for international humanitarian law through diplomatic channels than there was in the 19th and early 20th centuries, when the doctrine of belligerent reprisals as a method of enforcement was developed. In interpreting

---

[21] See UN General Assembly, Res. 2675 (XXV) (adopted by 109 votes in favour, none against and 8 abstentions) (ibid., § 840).

[22] See Kenya, LOAC Manual (ibid., § 82).

[23] See, e.g., the military manuals of Australia (ibid., §§ 67–68), Sweden (ibid., § 91), United Kingdom (ibid., §§ 94–95) and United States (ibid., §§ 97–99) and the practice of Argentina (ibid., § 115), Canada (ibid., § 119), Hungary (ibid., § 129), Mexico (ibid., § 134), Netherlands (ibid., § 136), Norway (ibid., § 137), Poland (ibid., § 139) and Venezuela (ibid., § 148).

[24] See, e.g., United States, Annotated Supplement to the Naval Handbook (ibid., § 100) (with respect to orders that no quarter will be given or that no prisoners will be taken); Canada, Ministry of Defence, Memorandum on Ratification of Additional Protocol I (ibid., § 120).

[25] See the practice of Belarus (ibid., § 118), Colombia (ibid., § 121), Czechoslovakia (ibid., § 122), Mexico (ibid., § 134), Poland (ibid., § 139) and USSR (ibid., § 142).

[26] See the practice of Canada (ibid., § 119), Federal Republic of Germany (ibid., § 126), Hungary (ibid., § 129), Netherlands (ibid., § 135) and Norway (ibid., § 137).

[27] See the military manuals of Burkina Faso (ibid., § 802), Cameroon (ibid., § 803), Congo (ibid., § 805) and Morocco (ibid., § 818).

[28] See the military manuals of Benin (ibid., § 801) and Togo (ibid., § 824).

[29] See, e.g., Italy, Military Tribunal of Rome, Kappler case (ibid., § 345), Priebke case (ibid., § 346) and Hass and Priebke case (ibid., § 347) and the official statements of Finland (ibid., § 348), India (ibid., § 349) and Malaysia (ibid., § 352).

[30] Oxford Manual, Article 86 (ibid., § 337); Draft Articles on State Responsibility, Article 50(1) (ibid., § 338).

the condition that reprisal action may only be taken as a measure of last resort, when no other possibility is available, States must take into account the possibility of appealing to other States and international organisations to help put a stop to the violations (see also commentary to Rule 144).

Conditions

Five conditions must be met in order for belligerent reprisals against permitted categories of persons and objects not to be unlawful. Most of these conditions are laid down in military manuals and are supported by official statements. These conditions are:

(i) Purpose of reprisals. Reprisals may only be taken in reaction to a prior serious violation of international humanitarian law, and only for the purpose of inducing the adversary to comply with the law. This condition is set forth in numerous military manuals, as well as in the legislation of some States.[31] It is also confirmed in national case-law.[32]

Because reprisals are a reaction to a prior serious violation of international humanitarian law, "anticipatory" reprisals or "counter-reprisals" are not permissible, nor can belligerent reprisals be a reaction to a violation of another type of law. In addition, as reprisals are aimed at inducing the adversary to comply with the law, they may not be carried out for the purpose of revenge or punishment.

There is limited practice allowing reprisals against allies of the violating State but it dates back to the arbitration in the *Cysne case* in 1930 and to the Second World War.[33] Practice since then appears to indicate that resort to such reprisals is no longer valid. According to the Draft Articles on State Responsibility, countermeasures are legitimate only "against a State which is responsible for an internationally wrongful act".[34] This element of responsibility is also reflected in some military manuals.[35] However, whereas most military manuals remain

---

[31] See, e.g., the military manuals of Australia (*ibid.*, §§ 67–68), Belgium (*ibid.*, § 69), Benin (*ibid.*, § 70), Canada (*ibid.*, § 71), Croatia (*ibid.*, § 73), Ecuador (*ibid.*, § 74), France (*ibid.*, § 75), Germany (*ibid.*, §§ 76–78), Hungary (*ibid.*, § 79), Indonesia (*ibid.*, § 80), Italy (*ibid.*, § 81), Kenya (*ibid.*, § 82), Netherlands (*ibid.*, § 85), New Zealand (*ibid.*, § 86), Nigeria (*ibid.*, § 87), South Africa (*ibid.*, § 89), Spain (*ibid.*, § 90), Sweden (*ibid.*, § 91), Switzerland (*ibid.*, § 92), Togo (*ibid.*, § 93), United Kingdom (*ibid.*, §§ 94–95), United States (*ibid.*, §§ 96–100) and Yugoslavia (*ibid.*, § 101) and the legislation of Italy (*ibid.*, § 103).

[32] See Italy, Military Tribunal of Rome, *Priebke case* (*ibid.*, § 108); Italy, Military Tribunal of Rome (confirmed by the Military Appeals Court and the Supreme Court of Cassation), *Hass and Priebke case* (*ibid.*, § 109); Netherlands, Special Court (War Criminals) at The Hague and Special Court of Cassation, *Rauter case* (*ibid.*, § 110); Norway, Eidsivating Court of Appeal and Supreme Court, *Bruns case* (*ibid.*, § 111); Norway, Frostating Court of Appeal and Supreme Court, *Flesch case* (*ibid.*, § 112); United States, Military Tribunal at Nuremberg, *List (Hostages Trial) case* (*ibid.*, § 113).

[33] See Special Arbitral Tribunal, *Cysne case* (*ibid.*, § 156) and the reported practice of the United Kingdom during the Second World War (*ibid.*, § 159).

[34] Draft Articles on State Responsibility, Article 49 (*ibid.*, § 66).

[35] See the military manuals of Canada (*ibid.*, § 71), Ecuador (*ibid.*, § 74), New Zealand (*ibid.*, § 86) and United States (*ibid.*, §§ 97 and 99).

silent on the question of reprisals against allies of the violating State, Italy's IHL Manual expressly states that a reprisal can, "as a general rule, only be directed against the belligerent that violated the laws of war".[36] Other military manuals explain that reprisals are used against another State in order *to induce that State* to stop the violation of international law.[37]

Some military manuals specify that in the light of their specific purpose, reprisals must be announced as such and publicised so that the adversary is aware of its obligation to comply with the law.[38]

(ii) Measure of last resort. Reprisals may only be carried out as a measure of last resort, when no other lawful measures are available to induce the adversary to respect the law. This condition is set forth in many military manuals.[39] It is confirmed by national case-law.[40] It is also repeated in the statements and proposals made by States at the Diplomatic Conference leading to the adoption of the Additional Protocols, before the International Court of Justice in the *Nuclear Weapons case* and on other occasions, when it was sometimes mentioned that prior warning must be given and/or that other measures must have failed before resorting to reprisals.[41] In its reservation concerning reprisals made upon ratification of Additional Protocol I, the United Kingdom reserved the right to take reprisal action "only after formal warning to the adverse party requiring cessation of the violations has been disregarded".[42]

According to the Draft Articles on State Responsibility, before taking countermeasures an injured State must call on the responsible State to fulfil its obligations, notify the responsible State of any decision to take countermeasures and offer to negotiate with that State.[43] In its judgement in the *Kupreškić*

---

[36] Italy, *IHL Manual* (*ibid.*, § 81).

[37] See, e.g., the military manuals of Germany (*ibid.*, §§ 76 and 78); United States, *Field Manual* (reprisals are "resorted to by one belligerent against enemy personnel or property for acts of warfare committed by the other belligerent") (*ibid.*, § 96) and *Air Force Pamphlet* ("they are directed against an adversary in order to induce him to refrain from further violations of the law") (*ibid.*, § 97); see also the practice of Canada ("after that belligerent has violated the laws of war") (*ibid.*, § 120) and Netherlands ("to compel another State to cease a violation which that other State is committing") (*ibid.*, § 136).

[38] See the military manuals of Canada (*ibid.*, § 71), Ecuador (*ibid.*, § 74), New Zealand (*ibid.*, § 86) and United States (*ibid.*, §§ 97 and 99–100).

[39] See the military manuals of Australia (*ibid.*, § 162), Belgium (*ibid.*, § 163), Canada (*ibid.*, § 165), Croatia (*ibid.*, § 166), Ecuador (*ibid.*, § 167), Germany (*ibid.*, § 169), Hungary (*ibid.*, § 170), Netherlands (*ibid.*, § 173), Spain (*ibid.*, § 176), United Kingdom (*ibid.*, § 178), United States (*ibid.*, §§ 180–183) and Yugoslavia (*ibid.*, § 184). Other military manuals require that prior warning be given: see the military manuals of Benin (*ibid.*, § 164), France (*ibid.*, § 168), Hungary (*ibid.*, § 170), Indonesia (*ibid.*, § 171), Kenya (*ibid.*, § 172), Togo (*ibid.*, § 177) and United Kingdom (*ibid.*, § 179).

[40] See Italy, Military Tribunal of Rome (confirmed by Military Appeals Court and Supreme Court of Cassation), *Hass and Priebke case* (*ibid.*, § 186); Netherlands, Special Court (War Criminals), *Rauter case* (*ibid.*, § 187); United States, Military Tribunal at Nuremberg, *List (Hostages Trial) case* (*ibid.*, § 188).

[41] See, e.g., the practice of France (*ibid.*, §§ 190–191), Netherlands (*ibid.*, §§ 192–194), United Kingdom (*ibid.*, § 195) and United States (*ibid.*, §§ 196–197).

[42] United Kingdom, Reservation made upon ratification of Additional Protocol I (*ibid.*, § 160).

[43] Draft Articles on State Responsibility, Article 52 (*ibid.*, § 161).

case in 2000, the International Criminal Tribunal for the Former Yugoslavia confirmed what had already been stated by the Special Arbitral Tribunal in the *Naulilaa case* in 1928, namely that reprisals may only be carried out after a warning to the adverse party requiring cessation of the violations has remained unheeded.[44]

(iii) Proportionality. Reprisal action must be proportionate to the violation it aims to stop. This condition was already laid down in 1880 in the Oxford Manual and was recently reaffirmed in the Draft Articles on State Responsibility.[45] It is also contained in many military manuals.[46] Furthermore, there is case-law concerning violations committed in the Second World War in which the accused's claims that their acts had been committed as lawful reprisals were rejected because, *inter alia*, they were found to be disproportionate to the original violation.[47]

The requirement that reprisal measures be proportionate to the original wrong is repeated in various statements and proposals made by States at the Diplomatic Conference leading to the adoption of the Additional Protocols, before the International Court of Justice in the *Nuclear Weapons case* and on other occasions.[48] In its reservation concerning reprisals made upon ratification of Additional Protocol I, the United Kingdom stated that "any measures thus taken by the United Kingdom will not be disproportionate to the violations giving rise thereto".[49]

The International Court of Justice in its advisory opinion in the *Nuclear Weapons case* in 1996 and the International Criminal Tribunal for the Former Yugoslavia in its judgement in the *Kupreškić case* in 2000 confirmed what the Special Arbitral Tribunal had already stated in the *Naulilaa case* in 1928, namely that belligerent reprisals are subject to the principle of proportionality.[50]

---

[44] See ICTY, *Kupreškić case*, Judgement (*ibid.*, § 202); Special Arbitral Tribunal, *Naulilaa case* (*ibid.*, § 203).

[45] Oxford Manual, Article 86 (*ibid.*, § 208); Draft Articles on State Responsibility, Article 51 (*ibid.*, § 209).

[46] See the military manuals of Australia (*ibid.*, § 210), Belgium (*ibid.*, § 211), Benin (*ibid.*, § 212), Canada (*ibid.*, § 213), Croatia (*ibid.*, § 214), Ecuador (*ibid.*, § 215), Germany (*ibid.*, § 216), Hungary (*ibid.*, § 217), Italy (*ibid.*, § 218), Kenya (*ibid.*, § 219), Netherlands (*ibid.*, § 220), New Zealand (*ibid.*, § 221), Spain (*ibid.*, § 223), Togo (*ibid.*, § 224), United Kingdom (*ibid.*, §§ 225–226), United States (*ibid.*, §§ 227–230) and Yugoslavia (*ibid.*, § 231).

[47] See Italy, Military Tribunal of Rome, *Kappler case* (*ibid.*, § 233), *Priebke case* (*ibid.*, § 234), (confirmed by Military Appeals Court and Supreme Court of Cassation) *Hass and Priebke case* (*ibid.*, § 235); Netherlands, Special Court (War Criminals) and Special Court of Cassation, *Rauter case* (*ibid.*, § 236); United States, Military Tribunal at Nuremberg, *List (Hostages Trial) case* (*ibid.*, § 237).

[48] See, e.g., the statements of Canada (*ibid.*, § 239), India (*ibid.*, § 244), Mexico (*ibid.*, § 245), Netherlands (*ibid.*, §§ 246–247), United Kingdom (*ibid.*, § 248) and United States (*ibid.*, §§ 249–250) and the reported practice of China (*ibid.*, § 240), France (*ibid.*, §§ 241–242) and Germany (*ibid.*, § 243).

[49] United Kingdom, Reservation made upon ratification of Additional Protocol I (*ibid.*, § 207).

[50] ICJ, *Nuclear Weapons case*, Advisory Opinion (*ibid.*, § 255); ICTY, *Kupreškić case*, Judgement (*ibid.*, § 256); Special Arbitral Tribunal, *Naulilaa case* (*ibid.*, § 257).

Most of the practice collected requires that acts taken in reprisal be proportionate to the original violation. Only a few pieces of practice specify that proportionality must be observed with regard to the damage suffered.[51]

(iv) Decision at the highest level of government. The decision to resort to reprisals must be taken at the highest level of government. Whereas the Oxford Manual states that only a commander in chief is entitled to authorise reprisals,[52] more recent practice indicates that such a decision must be taken at the highest political level.[53] State practice confirming this condition is found in military manuals, as well as in some national legislation and official statements.[54] In its reservation concerning reprisals made upon ratification of Additional Protocol I, the United Kingdom stated that reprisals would be taken "only after a decision taken at the highest level of government".[55]

In its judgement in the Kupreškić case in 2000, the International Criminal Tribunal for the Former Yugoslavia held that the decision to resort to a reprisal must be taken at the highest political or military level and may not be decided by local commanders.[56]

(v) Termination. Reprisal action must cease as soon as the adversary complies with the law. This condition, formulated as a formal prohibition in the event that the original wrong had been repaired, was already laid down in 1880 in the Oxford Manual and was recently restated in the Draft Articles on State Responsibility.[57] It is also contained in several military manuals, official statements and reported practice.[58] In its reservation concerning reprisals made upon ratification of Additional Protocol I, the United Kingdom stated that reprisals would not be continued "after the violations have ceased".[59]

In its judgement in the Kupreškić case in 2000, the International Criminal Tribunal for the Former Yugoslavia confirmed that reprisal action must stop as soon as the unlawful act has been discontinued.[60]

---

[51] See, e.g., the military manuals of Belgium (ibid., § 211), Netherlands (ibid., § 220) and Yugoslavia (ibid., § 231) and the statement of India (ibid., § 244).

[52] Oxford Manual, Article 86 (ibid., § 262).

[53] See the military manuals of Australia (ibid., § 264), Croatia (ibid., § 271), Ecuador (ibid., § 272), Germany (ibid., §§ 274–275), Hungary (ibid., § 276), Italy (ibid., § 277), Netherlands (ibid., § 280), New Zealand (ibid., § 281), Spain (ibid., § 283), Sweden (ibid., § 284), Switzerland (ibid., § 285), United Kingdom (for reprisals taken against the enemy civilian population or civilian objects) (ibid., § 288) and United States (ibid., §§ 290–294).

[54] See, e.g., the military manuals of Australia (ibid., § 263), Belgium (ibid., § 265), Benin (ibid., § 266), Canada (ibid., § 269), Kenya (ibid., § 278), South Africa (ibid., § 282), Togo (ibid., § 286), United Kingdom (ibid., § 287) and United States (ibid., § 289), the legislation of Argentina (ibid., § 296) and Italy (ibid., § 297) and the practice of France (ibid., §§ 299–300).

[55] United Kingdom, Reservation made upon ratification of Additional Protocol I (ibid., § 261).

[56] ICTY, Kupreškić case, Judgement (ibid., § 302).

[57] Oxford Manual, Article 85 (ibid., § 306); Draft Articles on State Responsibility, Article 53 (ibid., § 307).

[58] See, e.g., the military manuals of Benin (ibid., § 308), Canada (ibid., § 309), Croatia (ibid., § 310), Ecuador (ibid., § 311), Hungary (ibid., § 312), Italy (ibid., § 313), Kenya (ibid., § 314), New Zealand (ibid., § 315), Spain (ibid., § 317), Togo (ibid., § 318), United Kingdom (ibid., §§ 319–320), United States (ibid., §§ 321–322) and Yugoslavia (ibid., § 323) and the official statements of France (ibid., § 327) and Netherlands (ibid., § 328); the reported practice of Iran (ibid., § 326).

[59] United Kingdom, Reservation made upon ratification of Additional Protocol I (ibid., § 305).

[60] ICTY, Kupreškić case, Judgement (ibid., § 333).

Rule 146. Belligerent reprisals against persons protected by the Geneva Conventions are prohibited.

Practice

Volume II, Chapter 41, Section C.

Summary

State practice establishes this rule as a norm of customary international law applicable in international armed conflicts.

Reprisals against persons protected by the Geneva Conventions

The Geneva Conventions prohibit the taking of belligerent reprisals against persons in the power of a party to the conflict, including the wounded, sick and shipwrecked, medical and religious personnel, captured combatants, civilians in occupied territory and other categories of civilians in the power of an adverse party to the conflict.[61] This prohibition is also contained in numerous military manuals.[62] It is also set forth in the legislation of several

---

[61] First Geneva Convention, Article 46 (*ibid.*, § 448); Second Geneva Convention, Article 47 (*ibid.*, § 449); Third Geneva Convention, Article 13, third paragraph (*ibid.*, § 360); Fourth Geneva Convention, Article 33, third paragraph (*ibid.*, § 590).

[62] Concerning captured combatants and prisoners of war, see, e.g., the military manuals of Argentina, (*ibid.*, §§ 364–365), Australia (*ibid.*, §§ 366–367), Belgium (*ibid.*, § 368), Benin (*ibid.*, § 369), Burkina Faso (*ibid.*, § 370), Cameroon (*ibid.*, § 371), Canada (*ibid.*, §§ 372–373), Colombia (*ibid.*, § 374), Congo (*ibid.*, § 375), Croatia (*ibid.*, §§ 376–377), Dominican Republic (*ibid.*, § 378), Ecuador (*ibid.*, § 379), France (*ibid.*, §§ 380–382), Germany (*ibid.*, §§ 383–385), Hungary (*ibid.*, § 386), Indonesia (*ibid.*, § 387), Italy (*ibid.*, § 388), Kenya (*ibid.*, § 389), Madagascar (*ibid.*, § 390), Morocco (*ibid.*, § 391), Netherlands (*ibid.*, §§ 392–393), New Zealand (*ibid.*, § 394), Nicaragua (*ibid.*, § 395), Nigeria (*ibid.*, §§ 396–397), South Africa (*ibid.*, § 398), Spain (*ibid.*, § 399), Sweden (*ibid.*, § 400), Switzerland (*ibid.*, § 401), Togo (*ibid.*, § 402), United Kingdom (*ibid.*, §§ 403–404), United States (*ibid.*, §§ 405–411) and Yugoslavia (*ibid.*, § 412). Concerning the wounded, sick and shipwrecked, see, e.g., the military manuals of Australia (*ibid.*, §§ 458–459), Belgium (*ibid.*, § 460), Benin (*ibid.*, § 461), Burkina Faso (*ibid.*, § 462), Cameroon (*ibid.*, § 463), Canada (*ibid.*, § 464), Congo (*ibid.*, § 465), Croatia (*ibid.*, § 466), Ecuador (*ibid.*, § 467), France (*ibid.*, §§ 468–469), Germany (*ibid.*, §§ 470–472), Hungary (*ibid.*, § 473), Indonesia (*ibid.*, § 474), Italy (*ibid.*, § 475), Kenya (*ibid.*, § 476), Madagascar (*ibid.*, § 477), Morocco (*ibid.*, § 478), Netherlands (*ibid.*, §§ 479–480), New Zealand (*ibid.*, § 481), Nigeria (*ibid.*, § 482), South Africa (*ibid.*, § 483), Spain (*ibid.*, § 484), Sweden (*ibid.*, § 485), Switzerland (*ibid.*, § 486), Togo (*ibid.*, § 487), United Kingdom (*ibid.*, §§ 488–489), United States (*ibid.*, §§ 490–494) and Yugoslavia (*ibid.*, § 495). Concerning medical and religious personnel, see, e.g., the military manuals of Australia (*ibid.*, §§ 527–528), Belgium (*ibid.*, § 529), Benin (*ibid.*, § 530), Burkina Faso (*ibid.*, § 531), Cameroon (*ibid.*, § 532), Canada (*ibid.*, § 533), Congo (*ibid.*, § 534), Croatia (*ibid.*, § 535), Ecuador (*ibid.*, § 536), France (*ibid.*, §§ 537–538), Germany (*ibid.*, §§ 539–540), Hungary (*ibid.*, § 541), Indonesia (*ibid.*, § 542), Italy (*ibid.*, § 543), Kenya (*ibid.*, § 544), Madagascar (*ibid.*, § 545), Morocco (*ibid.*, § 546), Netherlands (*ibid.*, §§ 547–548), New Zealand (*ibid.* § 549), Nigeria (*ibid.*, §§ 550–551), Spain (*ibid.*, § 552), Sweden (*ibid.*, § 553), Switzerland (*ibid.*, § 554), Togo (*ibid.*, § 555), United Kingdom (*ibid.*, §§ 556–557), United States (*ibid.*, §§ 558–561) and Yugoslavia (*ibid.*, § 562). Concerning civilians in occupied territory and other categories of civilians in the power of an adverse party to the conflict, see, e.g., the military manuals of Argentina (*ibid.*, §§ 594–596), Australia (*ibid.*, §§ 597–598), Belgium (*ibid.*, § 599), Benin (*ibid.*, § 600), Burkina Faso (*ibid.*, § 601), Cameroon (*ibid.*, § 602), Canada (*ibid.*, § 603), Colombia (*ibid.*, § 604), Congo (*ibid.*, § 605), Dominican Republic (*ibid.*, § 606), Ecuador (*ibid.*, §§ 607–608), France (*ibid.*, §§ 609–611),

States.[63] Official statements and reported practice further support this prohibition.[64]

Reprisals against civilians during the conduct of hostilities

The trend to ban reprisals against civilians during the conduct of hostilities was introduced in a UN General Assembly resolution adopted in 1970, which affirmed the principle that "civilian populations, or individual members thereof, should not be the object of reprisals" as a basic principle for the protection of civilian populations in armed conflict.[65]

The prohibition on taking reprisals against civilians during the conduct of hostilities is codified in Article 51(6) of Additional Protocol I.[66] It is also found in both the original and amended versions of Protocol II to the Convention on Certain Conventional Weapons regulating the use of landmines, booby-traps and other devices.[67] At the time of the adoption of the Additional Protocols, the prohibition of reprisals introduced in Article 51(6) of Additional Protocol I was a new rule. In the vote on Article 51 as a whole, France voted against and 16 States abstained.[68] Of the 16 abstaining States, 10 have since become party to Additional Protocol I without entering a reservation.[69] Three States which have not ratified Additional Protocol I, namely Indonesia, Malaysia and Morocco, nevertheless support the prohibition of reprisals against civilians in general.[70]

Germany (*ibid.*, § 612), Hungary (*ibid.*, § 613), India (*ibid.*, § 614), Indonesia (*ibid.*, § 615), Italy (*ibid.*, § 616), Kenya (*ibid.*, § 617), Madagascar (*ibid.*, § 618), Morocco (*ibid.*, § 619), Netherlands (*ibid.*, § 620), New Zealand (*ibid.*, § 621), South Africa (*ibid.*, § 622), Spain (*ibid.*, § 623), Sweden (*ibid.*, § 624), Switzerland (*ibid.*, § 625), Togo (*ibid.*, § 626), United Kingdom (*ibid.*, §§ 627–628), United States (*ibid.*, §§ 629–634) and Yugoslavia (*ibid.*, § 635).

63 See, e.g., the legislation of Azerbaijan (*ibid.*, §§ 563 and 636), Colombia (*ibid.*, §§ 413, 496, 564 and 637), and Italy (*ibid.*, §§ 414, 497, 565 and 638).

64 See, e.g., the statements of Australia (*ibid.*, § 567), Canada (*ibid.*, §§ 418 and 568), Colombia (*ibid.*, §§ 419, 499, 569 and 642), Egypt (*ibid.*, §§ 420–421, 500–501, 570–571 and 643), France (*ibid.*, §§ 422, 502, 573 and 644), Federal Republic of Germany (*ibid.*, §§ 423 and 645), Iraq (*ibid.*, §§ 424, 503 and 574), Lebanon (*ibid.*, § 427), Poland (*ibid.*, §§ 429, 507, 578 and 649), Solomon Islands (*ibid.*, §§ 508 and 579), United Kingdom (*ibid.*, §§ 430, 509, 580 and 650) and United States (*ibid.*, §§ 431–433, 510, 581 and 651–652) and the reported practice of Israel (*ibid.*, §§ 425, 504, 575 and 646) and Jordan (*ibid.*, §§ 426, 505, 576 and 647).

65 UN General Assembly, Res. 2675 (XXV) (adopted by 109 votes in favour, none against and 8 abstentions) (*ibid.*, § 766). Because this resolution was not adopted by a roll-call vote, it cannot be verified which States voted in favour and which ones abstained.

66 Additional Protocol I, Article 51(6) (adopted by 77 votes in favour, 1 against and 16 abstentions) (*ibid.*, § 662).

67 Protocol II to the Convention on Certain Conventional Weapons, Article 3(2) (*ibid.*, § 670); Amended Protocol II to the Convention on Certain Conventional Weapons, Article 3(7) (*ibid.*, § 671).

68 The abstaining States were: Afghanistan, Algeria, Cameroon, Colombia, Federal Republic of Germany, Italy, Kenya, South Korea, Madagascar, Mali, Monaco, Morocco, Senegal, Thailand, Turkey and Zaire (see CDDH, *Official Records*, Vol. VI, CDDH/SR.41, 26 May 1977, p. 163).

69 Algeria, Cameroon, Colombia, Democratic Republic of the Congo, Kenya, South Korea, Madagascar, Mali, Monaco and Senegal.

70 See, e.g., the military manuals of Indonesia (cited in Vol. II, Ch. 41, § 695) and Morocco (*ibid.*, § 619) and the statement of Malaysia (*ibid.*, § 747).

The vast majority of States have, as a result, committed themselves not to make civilians the object of reprisals. Although practice in favour of a specific ban on the use of reprisals against all civilians is widespread and representative, it is not yet uniform. The United States, which is not a party to Additional Protocol I, has indicated on several occasions that it does not accept such a total ban, even though it voted in favour of Article 51 of Additional Protocol I and ratified Protocol II to the Convention on Certain Conventional Weapons without making a reservation to the prohibition on reprisals against civilians contained therein.[71] The United Kingdom also voted in favour of Article 51, but on becoming a party to Additional Protocol I, made a reservation to Article 51 which reproduces a list of stringent conditions for resorting to reprisals against an adversary's civilians.[72] It has also ratified Protocol II to the Convention on Certain Conventional Weapons without making a reservation to the prohibition on reprisals against civilians contained therein. Egypt, France, Germany and Italy also made a declaration upon ratification of Additional Protocol I in relation to the articles providing protection to the civilian population, but these are ambiguous in that they indicate that these States will react to serious and repeated violations with means admissible under international law to prevent further violations.[73] In referring back to what is lawful under international law, these declarations beg the question as to whether reprisals against civilians are lawful or not. Subsequent practice of these States helps to assess their current position on the issue of reprisals against civilians.

At the adoption of Additional Protocol I, Egypt strongly supported the prohibition of reprisals against civilians and, more recently, in its submissions before the International Court of Justice in the *Nuclear Weapons case*, it stated that it considered this prohibition to be customary.[74] The recent military manuals of France and Germany prohibit reprisals against civilians, citing Article 51(6) of Additional Protocol I.[75] Italy's IHL Manual, however, supports a narrow possibility of reprisals against civilians in very general terms by stating that "reprisals cannot be directed against the civilian population, except in case of absolute necessity".[76]

The other practice of note is the series of reprisals that Iran and Iraq, both not party to Additional Protocol I, directed at each other's cities. In press releases in 1983 and 1984, the ICRC stated that civilians must not be the object of reprisals and appealed to Iran and Iraq to cease the bombardment of civilians.[77] In 1984, the UN Secretary-General, in a message addressed to the Presidents of

---

[71] See the practice of the United States (*ibid.*, §§ 709, 711 and 757–760).
[72] United Kingdom, Reservation made upon ratification of Additional Protocol I (*ibid.*, § 669).
[73] See the reservations or declarations made upon ratification of Additional Protocol I by Egypt (*ibid.*, § 664), France (*ibid.*, § 665), Germany (*ibid.*, § 666) and Italy (*ibid.*, § 667).
[74] See the practice of Egypt (*ibid.*, §§ 729–730 and 748).
[75] See the military manuals of France (*ibid.*, § 689) and Germany (*ibid.*, §§ 690–692).
[76] Italy, *IHL Manual* (*ibid.*, § 696).
[77] See ICRC, Press Release No. 1479 (*ibid.*, § 778) and Press Release No. 1489 (*ibid.*, § 779).

Iran and Iraq, stated that "deliberate attacks on civilian areas cannot be condoned by the international community". He went on to state that reprisals and counter-reprisals resulted in loss of life and suffering to the civilian population and that "it is imperative that this immediately cease".[78] In a statement by its President in 1986, the UN Security Council deplored "the violation of international humanitarian law and other laws of armed conflict" and expressed its "deepening concern over the widening of the conflict through the escalation of attacks on purely civilian targets".[79] In 1987, both Iran and Iraq, in letters to the UN Secretary-General, justified their attacks on the other's cities as limited retaliatory measures to stop such attacks by the adversary.[80] In 1988, in another statement by its President, the UN Security Council strongly deplored "the escalation of hostilities . . . particularly the attacks against civilian targets and cities" and stated that "the members of the Security Council insist that Iran and Iraq immediately cease all such attacks and desist forthwith from all acts that lead to the escalation of the conflict".[81] Although the two UN Security Council statements do not explicitly use the term "reprisals", it is significant that they condemn the escalation of attacks on civilians. The second statement was made after Iran and Iraq had sent the letters justifying the basis of the reprisals taken, which would suggest that the UN Security Council did not accept both parties' arguments.

Historically, reprisal action has tended to have the effect of escalating attacks on civilians, rather than stopping them, a fact commented on in several military manuals.[82] As explained by the US Naval Handbook, for example, "there is always a risk that [reprisal] will trigger retaliatory escalation (counter-reprisals) by the enemy. The United States has historically been reluctant to resort to reprisal for just this reason."[83]

Enforcement action based on attacking civilians not taking a direct part in hostilities does not fit well either with the development of human rights law and the importance given to the right to life. In addition, since the Second World War, both human rights law and international humanitarian law have recognised that civilians not taking a direct part in hostilities cannot be held responsible for their governments' violations of international law and therefore cannot be subject to attack (see Rule 1) nor to collective punishment (see Rule 103).

---

[78] UN Secretary-General, Message dated 9 June 1984 to the Presidents of the Islamic Republic of Iran and the Republic of Iraq (*ibid.*, § 769).

[79] UN Security Council, Statement by the President (*ibid.*, § 765). The United States held the Presidency. Other members of the Security Council were: Australia, Bulgaria, China, Congo, Denmark, France, Ghana, Madagascar, Thailand, Trinidad and Tobago, USSR, United Arab Emirates, United Kingdom and Venezuela.

[80] See the practice of Iran (*ibid.*, §§ 737–740) and Iraq (*ibid.*, § 743).

[81] UN Security Council, Statement by the President (*ibid.*, § 766). The Presidency was held by Yugoslavia. Other members of the Security Council were: Algeria, Argentina, Brazil, China, France, Germany, Italy, Japan, Nepal, Senegal, USSR, United Kingdom, United States and Zambia.

[82] See the military manuals of Australia (*ibid.*, §§ 67–68), Sweden (*ibid.*, § 91), United Kingdom (*ibid.*, §§ 94–95) and United States (*ibid.*, §§ 97–99).

[83] United States, *Naval Handbook* (*ibid.*, § 99).

Because of existing contrary practice, albeit very limited, it is difficult to conclude that there has yet crystallised a customary rule specifically prohibiting reprisals against civilians during the conduct of hostilities. Nevertheless, it is also difficult to assert that a right to resort to such reprisals continues to exist on the strength of the practice of only a limited number of States, some of which is also ambiguous. Hence, there appears, at a minimum, to exist a trend in favour of prohibiting such reprisals. The International Criminal Tribunal for the Former Yugoslavia, in its review of the indictment in the *Martić case* in 1996 and in its judgement in the *Kupreškić case* in 2000, found that there was such a prohibition already in existence, based largely on the imperatives of humanity or public conscience.[84] These are important indications, consistent with a substantial body of practice now condemning or outlawing such reprisals.

Rule 147. Reprisals against objects protected under the Geneva Conventions and Hague Convention for the Protection of Cultural Property are prohibited.

Practice

Volume II, Chapter 41, Section D.

Summary

State practice establishes this rule as a norm of customary international law applicable in international armed conflicts.

Reprisals against property of persons protected by the Geneva Conventions

The Fourth Geneva Convention provides that reprisals are prohibited against the property of protected persons, i.e., civilians in the power of the adverse party.[85] A number of military manuals prohibit reprisals against the property of persons protected by the Fourth Geneva Convention,[86] whereas several other manuals prohibit reprisals against the property of protected persons in general.[87] The US Field Manual and Operational Law Handbook extend this

---

[84] ICTY, *Martić case*, Review of the Indictment (*ibid.*, § 776) and *Kupreškić case*, Judgement (*ibid.*, § 777).
[85] Fourth Geneva Convention, Article 33 (*ibid.*, § 783).
[86] See, e.g., the military manuals of Argentina (*ibid.*, §§ 794–796), Belgium (*ibid.*, § 799), Benin (*ibid.*, § 801), Canada (*ibid.*, § 804), Dominican Republic (*ibid.*, § 807), Ecuador (*ibid.*, § 808), Germany (*ibid.*, §§ 811–812), Kenya (*ibid.*, § 816), New Zealand (*ibid.*, § 820), Spain (*ibid.*, § 822), United Kingdom (*ibid.*, §§ 825–826) and United States (*ibid.*, §§ 827–833).
[87] See, e.g., the military manuals of Benin (*ibid.*, § 801), Croatia (*ibid.*, § 806), Hungary (*ibid.*, § 813), Indonesia (*ibid.*, § 814), Italy (*ibid.*, § 815), Kenya (*ibid.*, § 816), South Africa (*ibid.*, § 821), Togo (*ibid.*, § 824) and United Kingdom (*ibid.*, § 826); see also the legislation of Colombia (*ibid.*, § 837).

prohibition to the property of all persons protected by the Geneva Conventions, including the property of the wounded, sick and shipwrecked and that of prisoners of war.[88]

Reprisals against medical objects

The First and Second Geneva Conventions prohibit reprisals against medical buildings, vessels and equipment protected thereunder.[89] These prohibitions are also stated in numerous military manuals.[90]

Reprisals against cultural property

The Hague Convention for the Protection of Cultural Property prohibits "any act directed by way of reprisals against cultural property" of great importance to the cultural heritage of a people.[91] The Convention has been ratified by 105 States. As stated in Chapter 12 on cultural property, the fundamental principles of protecting and preserving cultural property in the Convention are widely regarded as reflecting customary international law, as affirmed by the UNESCO General Conference,[92] and by States which are not party to the Convention.[93] Article 53(c) of Additional Protocol I prohibits reprisals against historic monuments, works of art or places of worship which constitute the cultural or spiritual heritage of peoples.[94]

The prohibition of reprisals against cultural property is also found in numerous military manuals and national legislation, including of States not party to the Hague Convention.[95] According to the Report on the Practice of Iran, during the Iran–Iraq War, Iran specifically excluded Iraq's holy cities from its

---

[88] United States, *Field Manual* (*ibid.*, § 827) and *Operational Law Handbook* (*ibid.*, § 831).

[89] First Geneva Convention, Article 46 (*ibid.*, § 880); Second Geneva Convention, Article 47 (*ibid.*, § 881).

[90] See, e.g., the military manuals of Australia (*ibid.*, §§ 891–892), Benin (*ibid.*, § 893), Burkina Faso (*ibid.*, § 894), Cameroon (*ibid.*, § 895), Canada (*ibid.*, § 896), Congo (*ibid.*, § 898), Croatia (*ibid.*, § 897), Ecuador (*ibid.*, § 899), France (*ibid.*, §§ 900–901), Germany (*ibid.*, §§ 902–903), Hungary (*ibid.*, § 904), Indonesia (*ibid.*, § 905), Italy (*ibid.*, § 906), Kenya (*ibid.*, § 907), Madagascar (*ibid.*, § 908), Morocco (*ibid.*, § 909), Netherlands (*ibid.*, § 910), New Zealand (*ibid.*, § 911), Nigeria (*ibid.*, § 912), Spain (*ibid.*, § 913), Sweden (*ibid.*, § 914), Togo (*ibid.*, § 915), United Kingdom (*ibid.*, §§ 916–917), United States (*ibid.*, §§ 918–922) and Yugoslavia (*ibid.*, § 923).

[91] Hague Convention for the Protection of Cultural Property, Article 4(4) (*ibid.*, § 950).

[92] See UNESCO, General Conference, Res. 3.5 (cited in Vol. II, Ch. 12, § 419).

[93] See, e.g., United States, *Annotated Supplement to the Naval Handbook* (*ibid.*, § 103).

[94] Additional Protocol I, Article 53(c) (adopted by consensus) (cited in Vol. II, Ch. 41, § 951).

[95] See the practice of Argentina (*ibid.*, §§ 960 and 991), Australia (*ibid.*, §§ 961–962), Azerbaijan (*ibid.*, § 992), Belgium (*ibid.*, § 963), Benin (*ibid.*, § 964), Burkina Faso (*ibid.*, § 965), Cameroon (*ibid.*, § 966), Canada (*ibid.*, § 967), Colombia (*ibid.*, § 993), Congo (*ibid.*, § 968), Croatia (*ibid.*, § 969), France (*ibid.*, §§ 970–971), Germany (*ibid.*, §§ 972–974), Hungary (*ibid.*, § 975), Indonesia (*ibid.*, § 976), Italy (*ibid.*, §§ 977 and 994), Kenya (*ibid.*, § 978), Netherlands (*ibid.*, §§ 979–980), New Zealand (*ibid.*, § 981), Spain (*ibid.*, §§ 982 and 995), Sweden (*ibid.*, § 983), Switzerland (*ibid.*, §§ 984 and 996), Togo (*ibid.*, § 985), United States (*ibid.*, §§ 987 and 989) and Yugoslavia (*ibid.*, § 990). Benin, Kenya, Togo and the United States are not party to the Hague Convention.

reprisal actions.[96] There is some contrary practice in that the United Kingdom's reservation to Additional Protocol I relating to reprisals covers Article 53 on cultural property.[97] This contrary practice appears too limited to prevent the formation of this rule of customary international law prohibiting the attack of cultural objects in reprisal.

Reprisals against civilian objects during the conduct of hostilities

In addition to the provisions in the Geneva Conventions and Hague Convention for the Protection of Cultural Property, Additional Protocol I has introduced prohibitions on attacking the following objects by way of reprisal during the conduct of hostilities: civilian objects in general (Article 52); historic monuments, works of art or places of worship which constitute the cultural or spiritual heritage of peoples (Article 53); objects indispensable to the survival of the civilian population (Article 54); the natural environment (Article 55); and works and installations containing dangerous forces, namely dams, dykes and nuclear electrical generating stations (Article 56).[98]

Practice with respect to reprisals against these civilian objects, to the extent that they are not the property of civilians protected by Article 33 of the Fourth Geneva Convention, is similar, but not as extensive, as that relating to reprisals against civilians during the conduct of hostilities. While the vast majority of States have now specifically committed themselves not to take reprisal action against such objects, because of existing contrary practice,[99] albeit very limited, it is difficult to conclude that there has yet crystallised a customary rule specifically prohibiting reprisals against these civilian objects in all situations. Nevertheless, it is also difficult to assert that a right to resort to such reprisals continues to exist on the strength of the practice of only a limited number of States, some of which is also ambiguous.

---

[96] See the Report on the Practice of Iran (*ibid.*, § 1004).

[97] United Kingdom, Reservation made upon ratification of Additional Protocol I (*ibid.*, § 955).

[98] Additional Protocol I, Article 52 (adopted by 79 votes in favour, none against and 7 abstentions) (*ibid.*, § 784), Article 53 (adopted by consensus) (*ibid.*, § 951), Article 54 (adopted by consensus) (*ibid.*, § 1020), Article 55 (adopted by consensus) (*ibid.*, § 1075) and Article 56 (adopted by consensus) (*ibid.*, § 1136).

[99] With respect to reprisals against cultural property, see the practice of Egypt (*ibid.*, § 952), Germany (*ibid.*, § 953), Italy (*ibid.*, § 954), United Kingdom (*ibid.*, §§ 955 and 1009) and United States (*ibid.*, §§ 988 and 1010–1012), but see the practice of the United States prohibiting reprisals against "religious or cultural edifices" (*ibid.*, § 989, see also *ibid.*, § 987). With respect to reprisals against objects indispensable to the survival of the civilian population, see the practice of Egypt (*ibid.*, § 1021), Germany (*ibid.*, § 1022), Italy (*ibid.*, § 1023), United Kingdom (*ibid.*, §§ 1024 and 1064) and United States (*ibid.*, §§ 1065–1067), but see the practice of the United States prohibiting reprisals against such objects (*ibid.*, § 1052). With respect to reprisals against the natural environment, see the practice of Egypt (*ibid.*, § 1076), Germany (*ibid.*, § 1077), Italy (*ibid.*, § 1078), United Kingdom (*ibid.*, §§ 1079 and 1123) and United States (*ibid.*, §§ 1106 and 1124–1126). With respect to reprisals against works and installations containing dangerous forces, see the practice of Egypt (*ibid.*, § 1137), Germany (*ibid.*, § 1139), Italy (*ibid.*, § 1140), United Kingdom (*ibid.*, § 1183) and United States (*ibid.*, §§ 1184–1186).

No specific instances of reprisals against the above-mentioned objects have been recorded. It is likely that any such reprisals would attract condemnation, in particular as they are likely to affect both these objects and the civilian population.

Rule 148. Parties to non-international armed conflicts do not have the right to resort to belligerent reprisals. Other countermeasures against persons who do not or who have ceased to take a direct part in hostilities are prohibited.

Practice

Volume II, Chapter 41, Section E.

Summary

State practice establishes this rule as a norm of customary international law applicable in non-international armed conflicts.

Non-international armed conflicts

Common Article 3 of the Geneva Conventions prohibits violence to life and person, the taking of hostages, outrages upon personal dignity, in particular humiliating and degrading treatment, and the denial of fair trial. These prohibitions apply and remain applicable "at any time and in any place whatsoever".[100] Consequently, any reprisal which entails one of these acts is prohibited.[101] In addition, common Article 3 provides that all persons who do not or no longer take a direct part in hostilities must be treated humanely "in all circumstances".[102] Any reprisal which is incompatible with this requirement of humane treatment is, therefore, also prohibited.[103] In addition, the rules contained in common Article 3 constitute, as confirmed by the International Court of Justice, a "minimum yardstick" for all armed conflicts and reflect "elementary considerations of humanity".[104] Article 4 of Additional Protocol II similarly allows no room for reprisals against persons who do not or no longer take a direct part in hostilities.[105]

---

[100] Geneva Conventions, common Article 3.
[101] See Jean S. Pictet (ed.), *Commentary on the First Geneva Convention*, ICRC, Geneva, 1952, p. 55.
[102] Geneva Conventions, common Article 3.
[103] See Jean S. Pictet (ed.), *Commentary on the First Geneva Convention*, ICRC, Geneva, 1952, p. 55.
[104] Geneva Conventions, common Article 3; ICJ, *Case concerning Military and Paramilitary Activities in and against Nicaragua (Nicaragua v. United States)*, Merits, Judgement, 27 June 1986, *ICJ Reports 1986*, p. 114, § 218.
[105] See Yves Sandoz, Christophe Swinarski, Bruno Zimmermann (eds.), *Commentary on the Additional Protocols*, ICRC, Geneva, 1987, § 4530; see also Michael Bothe, Karl Joseph Partsch,

Acts of reprisal in non-international armed conflicts have, in practice, been condemned. For example, in resolutions adopted in the context of the conflict in Afghanistan, the UN General Assembly and UN Commission on Human Rights condemned measures of reprisal against civilians.[106] Various Special Rapporteurs of the UN Commission on Human Rights have also condemned "reprisal" killings and detention with respect to the conflicts in Chad, Colombia, Democratic Republic of the Congo, Mali, Rwanda and Turkey.[107]

In a resolution adopted in 1970, the UN General Assembly reaffirmed the principle that "civilian populations, or individual members thereof, should not be the object of reprisals" as a basic principle for the protection of the civilian population in armed conflict.[108] In the *Tadić case* in 1995, the International Criminal Tribunal for the Former Yugoslavia considered that this resolution was "declaratory of the principles of customary international law regarding the protection of civilian populations and property in armed conflicts of any kind".[109]

In the *Martić case* in 1996, the Tribunal inferred a prohibition of reprisals against civilians in non-international armed conflicts on the basis of Article 4(2) of Additional Protocol II because they are contrary to "the absolute and non-derogable prohibitions enumerated in this provision" and because prohibited behaviour must remain so "at any time and in any place whatsoever". The Tribunal also considered that the prohibition of reprisals against civilians in non-international armed conflicts is strengthened by the inclusion of the prohibition of "collective punishments" in Article 4(2)(b) of Additional Protocol II.[110] Collective punishments are also prohibited under customary international law (see Rule 103). Several military manuals further emphasise that all acts of vengeance are prohibited.[111]

There is insufficient evidence that the very concept of lawful reprisal in non-international armed conflict has ever materialised in international law. All practice describing the purpose of reprisals and conditions for resort to them refers to inter-State relations and originates from practice in the 19th and early 20th centuries. Recent practice relating to non-international armed

---

Waldemar A. Solf (eds.), *New Rules for Victims of Armed Conflicts*, Martinus Nijhoff, The Hague, 1982, p. 637.

[106] See, e.g., UN General Assembly, Res. 48/152 and 49/207 (*ibid.*, § 1248); UN Commission on Human Rights, Res. 1993/66 and 1994/84 (*ibid.*, § 1249) and Res. 1995/74 (*ibid.*, § 1250).

[107] See, e.g., UN Commission on Human Rights, Special Rapporteur on Extrajudicial, Summary or Arbitrary Executions, Reports (*ibid.*, §§ 1251–1253), Special Rapporteur on the Situation of Human Rights in Rwanda, Reports (*ibid.*, §§ 1254–1255), Special Rapporteur on Torture and Special Rapporteur on Extrajudicial, Summary or Arbitrary Executions, Joint Report (*ibid.*, § 1256), Special Rapporteur on the Situation of Human Rights in Zaire, Report (*ibid.*, § 1257); see also UN Verification Mission in Guatemala, Director, First–Fourth Reports (*ibid.*, § 1258).

[108] UN General Assembly, Res. 2675 (XXV) (adopted by 109 votes in favour, none against and 8 abstentions) (*ibid.*, § 766).

[109] ICTY, *Tadić case*, Interlocutory Appeal (*ibid.*, § 1263).

[110] ICTY, *Martić case*, Review of the Indictment (*ibid.*, § 1264).

[111] See, e.g., the military manuals of Benin (*ibid.*, § 70), France (*ibid.*, § 75), Philippines (*ibid.*, § 88) and Togo (*ibid.*, § 93).

conflicts has in no way supported the idea of enforcing the law in such conflicts through reprisals or similar countermeasures, but, on the contrary, has stressed the importance of the protection of civilians and persons *hors de combat*, of respect for human rights law and of diplomatic means to stop violations. Several military manuals define belligerent reprisals as a measure of enforcement by one State against another.[112]

A suggestion to include specific prohibitions of reprisals in non-international armed conflicts made during the Diplomatic Conference leading to the adoption of the Additional Protocols was rejected. The reasons given during the Conference for this rejection are significant in this respect. Only four States said they thought the concept of reprisals in non-international armed conflicts was possible in international law, namely Cameroon, Finland, Germany and Yugoslavia. Cameroon, however, was of the opinion that such reprisals should be "limited to certain well-defined cases, restrictively enumerated".[113] Finland could accept the idea but stated that they should "never in any circumstances be used against the civilian populations" because "there was universal agreement that reprisals of an inhumane character were inadmissible".[114] According to Yugoslavia, it went without saying that reprisals against persons and objects in the power of the adversary were prohibited; "this rule of customary international law . . . was codified in 1949 in the Geneva Conventions". Beyond this prohibition, it considered that reprisals should never be exercised against "non-combatants, women and children".[115] Germany thought that there was no objection from a legal point of view to use of the term "reprisal", but from a political point of view it could be inferred that the use of this term "gave the Parties to a conflict a status under international law which they had no right to claim" and suggested that the formulation "measures of retaliation comparable to reprisals" might not meet the same objections.[116]

Several States voted against the proposal because they felt that the very concept of reprisals had no place in non-international armed conflicts.[117] Some expressed the fear that the introduction of the term, even by way of a prohibition, could give the impression a *contrario* that the concept was possible.[118]

In order to avoid introducing the concept of reprisals (as this would erroneously give the impression that there was, in international law, such a possibility in non-international armed conflict), Canada, Iran, Italy, Pakistan and the

---

[112] See, e.g., the military manuals of Australia (*ibid.*, §§ 67–68), Canada (*ibid.*, § 71), Ecuador (*ibid.*, § 74), Germany (*ibid.*, §§ 76 and 78), Netherlands (*ibid.*, § 85), New Zealand (*ibid.*, § 86), United Kingdom (*ibid.*, § 94) and United States (*ibid.*, §§ 97 and 99).

[113] See the statement of Cameroon (*ibid.*, § 1208).

[114] See the statement of Finland (*ibid.*, § 1215); see also the statement of New Zealand (*ibid.*, § 1233).

[115] See the statement of Yugoslavia (*ibid.*, § 1244).

[116] See the statement of the Federal Republic of Germany (*ibid.*, § 1219).

[117] See the statements of Canada (*ibid.*, § 1212), Iran (*ibid.*, §§ 1226–1227), Iraq (*ibid.*, § 1228), Mexico (*ibid.*, § 1231), Nigeria (*ibid.*, § 1234) and United States (*ibid.*, § 1242).

[118] See the statements of Mexico (*ibid.*, § 1221), Poland (*ibid.*, § 1238) and Syria (*ibid.*, § 1240).

Philippines submitted various proposals avoiding the use of the term "reprisal" to get across the idea that parties were prohibited from any countermeasure or act of retaliation in response to a violation of the adverse party.[119]

The Belgian delegation at the Diplomatic Conference expressed the view that, as to the fundamental guarantees in Article 4 of Additional Protocol II, "the question of reprisals could not arise, since under the terms of that article, persons who did not take a direct part or who had ceased to take part in hostilities, were in all circumstances to be treated humanely".[120] A similar position was taken by Italy, Sweden and the United Kingdom.[121]

---

[119] See the proposals submitted to the CDDH by Canada (*ibid.*, §§ 1210–1211) ("acts of retaliation comparable to reprisals" and "measures which are in breach of the Protocol"), Iran (*ibid.*, § 1225) ("acts of vengeance"), Italy (*ibid.*, § 1229) ("the provisions of the present Part must be observed at all times and in all circumstances, even if the other Party to the conflict is guilty of violating the provisions of the present Protocol"), Pakistan (*ibid.*, § 1236) ("isolated cases of disrespect...by one party shall not in any circumstances authorize non-compliance by the other party...even for purposes of inducing the adverse party to comply with its obligations") and Philippines (*ibid.*, § 1237) ("countermeasures"); see also the statement of Nigeria (*ibid.*, § 1234) ("retaliation" or "vengeance").

[120] See the statement of Belgium (*ibid.*, § 1207).

[121] See the statement of Italy (*ibid.*, § 1230), Sweden (*ibid.*, § 1239) and United Kingdom (*ibid.*, § 1241); see also the statement of Yugoslavia (*ibid.*, § 1244).

RESPONSIBILITY AND REPARATION

Rule 149. A State is responsible for violations of international humanitarian law attributable to it, including:

  (a) **violations committed by its organs, including its armed forces;**
  (b) **violations committed by persons or entities it empowered to exercise elements of governmental authority;**
  (c) **violations committed by persons or groups acting in fact on its instructions, or under its direction or control; and**
  (d) **violations committed by private persons or groups which it acknowledges and adopts as its own conduct.**

Practice

Volume II, Chapter 42, Section A.

Summary

State practice establishes this rule as a norm of customary international law applicable to violations committed in both international and non-international armed conflicts.

State responsibility for violations committed by the organs of a State, including its armed forces

It is a long-standing rule of customary international law, set forth in Article 3 of the 1907 Hague Convention (IV) and repeated in Article 91 of Additional Protocol I, that a State is responsible for "all acts committed by persons forming part of its armed forces".[1] This rule is an application of the general rule of State responsibility for internationally wrongful acts, whereby a State is responsible for the behaviour of its organs.[2] The armed forces are considered to be a State

---

[1] Hague Convention (IV), Article 3 (cited in Vol. II. Ch. 42, § 1); Additional Protocol I, Article 91 (adopted by consensus) (*ibid.*, § 3).

[2] See Article 4 of the Draft Articles on State Responsibility, adopted in 2001 after more than 40 years of work (*ibid.*, § 8). These Draft Articles "seek to formulate...the basic rules of international law concerning the responsibility of States for their internationally wrongful acts" (ILC, Commentaries to the Draft Articles on State Responsibility, Report of the International

organ, like any other entity of the executive, legislative or judicial branch of government. The application of this general rule of attribution of responsibility to international humanitarian law is reflected in the four Geneva Conventions, which specify that State responsibility exists in addition to the requirement to prosecute individuals for grave breaches.[3] The principle that State responsibility exists in addition to individual criminal responsibility is also reaffirmed in the Second Protocol to the Hague Convention for the Protection of Cultural Property.[4]

A number of military manuals specify that a State is responsible for violations of international humanitarian law. Some of these manuals expressly refer to acts committed by members of the armed forces of a State, while others more generally deal with responsibility for grave breaches or war crimes, not specifying by whom such acts must be committed in order to be attributable to the State.[5] However, it is clear from the above-mentioned general principle of international law that the acts of all State organs are attributable to the State, be they military or civilian.

There is also national case-law supporting this rule. In its judgement in the *Eichmann case* in 1961, Israel's District Court of Jerusalem attributed the wrongful acts committed by the accused to Germany as its own "acts of State".[6] Furthermore, in the *Reparation Payments case* in 1963, Germany's Federal Supreme Court referred to the "principle of public international law according to which a State party to a conflict is also responsible for acts committed by its nationals in relation to the conduct of hostilities which are *not* in line with public international law" (emphasis in original).[7] In the *Distomo case* in 2003, the same German court affirmed that the responsibility of States for internationally wrongful acts committed during hostilities "comprises liability for the acts of all persons belonging to the armed forces".[8] The *J. T. case* before the District Court of The Hague in the Netherlands in 1949 involved a claim for reimbursement of money that had disappeared during the arrest of an individual by the Dutch resistance movement during the Second World

---

Law Commission on the work of its Fifty-third session, UN Doc. A/56/10, New York, 2001, p. 59). They were taken note of in UN General Assembly Resolution 56/83 on the responsibility of States for internationally wrongful acts (cited in Vol. II. Ch. 42, § 51), which commended them to the attention of governments.

[3] First Geneva Convention, Article 51 (*ibid.*, § 2); Second Geneva Convention, Article 52 (*ibid.*, § 2); Third Geneva Convention, Article 131 (*ibid.*, § 2); Fourth Geneva Convention, Article 148 (*ibid.*, § 2).

[4] Second Protocol to the Hague Convention for the Protection of Cultural Property, Article 38 (*ibid.*, § 4).

[5] See, e.g., the military manuals of Argentina (*ibid.*, § 9), Canada (*ibid.*, § 10), Colombia (*ibid.*, § 11), Germany (*ibid.*, § 12), Netherlands (*ibid.*, § 13), New Zealand (*ibid.*, § 14), Nigeria (*ibid.*, § 15), Russia (*ibid.*, § 16), Spain (*ibid.*, § 17), Switzerland (*ibid.*, § 18), United Kingdom (*ibid.*, § 19), United States (*ibid.*, §§ 20–21) and Yugoslavia (*ibid.*, § 22).

[6] Israel, District Court of Jerusalem, *Eichmann case* (*ibid.*, § 26).

[7] Germany, Federal Supreme Court, *Reparation Payments case* (*ibid.*, § 24).

[8] Germany, Federal Supreme Court, *Distomo case* (*ibid.*, § 25).

War and was later found to have been taken by the police.[9] The case is further evidence of the rule that States are responsible for violations of international humanitarian law committed by State organs. Official statements and reported practice further support this conclusion.[10]

The International Criminal Tribunal for the Former Yugoslavia, in its judgement in the *Furundžija case* in 1998 and in its judgement on appeal in the *Tadić case* in 1999, held that a State is responsible for the behaviour of its armed forces.[11]

Omissions

A State is also responsible for the omissions of its organs when they are under a duty to act, such as in the case of commanders and other superiors who are responsible for preventing and punishing war crimes (see Rule 153). This principle is reflected in Article 2 of the Draft Articles on State Responsibility, which states that an internationally wrongful act can consist of "an act or omission".[12] In the *British Claims in the Spanish Zone of Morocco case* in 1925, the arbitrator Max Huber stated that a State that failed to exercise due diligence in preventing or punishing the unlawful actions of armed groups could be held responsible for such failure.[13] In the *Essen Lynching case* before the UK Military Court at Essen, the members of a German military escort were convicted because they failed to protect allied prisoners of war from being aggressed by a crowd.[14] In the *Velásquez Rodríguez case*, the Inter-American Court of Human Rights stated that a State would be responsible for the actions of armed groups if it did not seriously investigate acts that violated an individual's rights.[15] The same point was made by the African Commission on Human and Peoples' Rights in relation to killings and ill-treatment during the armed conflict in Chad.[16]

---

[9] Netherlands, District Court of The Hague, *J. T. case* (*ibid.*, § 28).

[10] See, e.g., the statements of Argentina (*ibid.*, § 29), Austria (*ibid.*, § 30), China (*ibid.*, § 31), Indonesia (*ibid.*, § 32), Iran (*ibid.*, § 33), Israel (*ibid.*, § 34), Mexico (*ibid.*, § 36), Norway (*ibid.*, § 37), Pakistan (*ibid.*, § 38), Peru (*ibid.*, § 39), Solomon Islands (*ibid.*, § 40), Turkey (*ibid.*, § 42), United Kingdom (*ibid.*, § 43), United States (*ibid.*, § 44) and Yugoslavia (*ibid.*, § 46) and the reported practice of Israel (*ibid.*, § 35) and Spain (*ibid.*, § 41).

[11] ICTY, *Furundžija case*, Judgement (*ibid.*, § 63) and *Tadić case*, Judgement on Appeal (*ibid.*, § 64).

[12] Draft Articles on State Responsibility, Article 2 (*ibid.*, § 8).

[13] Arbitral Tribunal, *British Claims in the Spanish Zone of Morocco case* (*Affaire des biens britanniques au Maroc espagnol*), Arbitral Award, 1 May 1925, reprinted in *Reports of International Arbitral Awards*, Vol. II, United Nations, New York, 1949, Section III(II), pp. 642–646, §§ 3–6.

[14] United Kingdom, Military Court at Essen, *The Essen Lynching case*, Judgement, 21–22 December 1945, *WCR*, Vol. I, 1946, p. 88.

[15] Inter-American Court of Human Rights, *Velásquez Rodríguez case* (cited in Vol. II, Ch. 42, § 70).

[16] African Commission on Human and Peoples' Rights, *Civil Liberties Organisation v. Chad* (*ibid.*, § 68).

State responsibility for violations committed by persons or entities
empowered to exercise elements of governmental authority

States are also responsible for acts committed by other persons or entities
which they have empowered, under their internal law, to exercise elements
of governmental authority.[17] This rule is based on the consideration that
States can have recourse to para-statal entities in carrying out certain activities instead of letting State organs carry them out, but do not thereby avoid
responsibility.

States are responsible for the acts of private firms or individuals that are used
by the armed forces to accomplish tasks that are typically those of the armed
forces. Examples of such individuals or entities are mercenaries or private
military companies.

State responsibility for acts committed in excess of authority or
contrary to instructions

A State is responsible for all acts committed by its organs and other persons or
entities empowered to act on its behalf, even if such organs or persons exceed
their authority or contravene instructions.[18]

With regard to the armed forces of a State, this principle is contained in
Article 3 of the 1907 Hague Convention (IV) and in Article 91 of Additional
Protocol I, which provide that a party to the conflict is responsible for "all acts"
committed by persons forming part of its armed forces.[19] In the *Distomo case*
in 2003, Germany's Federal Supreme Court stated that the responsibility of a
State "comprises liability for the acts of all persons belonging to the armed
forces, and this not only in case these persons commit acts falling within their
sphere of competence, but also in case they act without or against orders".[20]

The Report on US Practice, however, states that it is the *opinio juris* of the
United States that a State is not responsible for "private" acts of its armed
forces.[21] The US Air Force Pamphlet states that no obligation of the State arises
for violations by individuals of the law of armed conflicts committed outside
their general area of responsibility unless some fault can be shown such as

---

[17] See Draft Articles on State Responsibility, Article 5 (*ibid.*, § 8) (State responsibility for such
persons or entities is limited to their conduct whilst acting in the capacity vested in them).
[18] See Draft Articles on State Responsibility, Article 7 (*ibid.*, § 8).
[19] 1907 Hague Convention (IV), Article 3 (*ibid.*, § 1); Additional Protocol I, Article 91 (adopted by
consensus) (*ibid.*, § 3).
[20] Germany, Federal Supreme Court, *Distomo case* (*ibid.*, § 25). Apparent contrary practice can
be found in the *Khamzaev case* in 2001, in which the Russian government asserted that it was
not liable to provide compensation because a pilot having caused destruction of a house had
"exceeded the limits of the order". Russia, Basmanny District Court, *Khamzaev case* (*ibid.*,
§ 202). This case does not, however, deal with Russia's responsibility under international law
vis-à-vis another State but with its responsibility under domestic law for damage caused by a
State employee to a private person.
[21] Report on US Practice (*ibid.*, § 45).

inadequate supervision or training.[22] The commentary on the Draft Articles on State Responsibility similarly distinguishes between "cases where officials acted in their capacity as such, albeit unlawfully or contrary to instructions", which are attributable to the State, and "cases where the conduct is so removed from the scope of their official functions that it should be assimilated to that of private individuals", which are not attributable to the State.[23]

State responsibility for violations committed by persons or groups acting in fact on the instructions of, or under the direction or control of, a State

A State can also be held responsible for the actions of persons or groups which are neither its organs nor entitled, under national law, to exercise governmental authority, if these persons or groups act in fact on the instructions of, or under the direction or control of, that State.[24]

The International Court of Justice stated in the *Nicaragua case (Merits)* in 1986 that to be responsible for violations of international human rights and humanitarian law committed by the *Contras* in Nicaragua, the United States would have to have had "effective control over the military or paramilitary operations in the course of which the violations occurred".[25] In the judgement on appeal in the *Tadić case* in 1999, the International Criminal Tribunal for the Former Yugoslavia stated that "the extent of the requisite State control varies". According to the Tribunal, the conduct of a single private individual or a group that is not militarily organised is attributable to the State only if specific instructions concerning that conduct were given. However, conduct of subordinate armed forces, militias or paramilitary units is attributable to a State which has control of an "overall character".[26] Such control would exist, according to the Tribunal, where a State "has a role in organising, coordinating or planning the military actions of the military group, in addition to financing, training and equipping or providing operational support to that group". But the requirement of "overall control" does not go so far as to include "the issuing of specific orders by the State, or its direction of each individual operation". In cases where the armed groups operate in the territory of another State, the Tribunal considered that "more extensive and compelling evidence is required to show that the State is genuinely in control of the units or groups not merely

---

22 United States, *Air Force Pamphlet* (*ibid.*, § 21).
23 ILC, Commentary on Article 7 of the Draft Articles on State Responsibility (*ibid.*, § 59). The commentary concludes that conduct attributable to the State in this context "comprises only the actions and omissions of organs purportedly or apparently carrying out their official functions, and not the private actions or omissions of individuals who happen to be organs or agents of the State. In short, the question is whether they were acting with apparent authority."
24 See Draft Articles on State Responsibility, Article 8 (*ibid.*, § 8).
25 ICJ, *Nicaragua case (Merits)* (*ibid.*, § 62).
26 ICTY, *Tadić case*, Judgement on Appeal (*ibid.*, § 64); see also *Blaškić case*, Judgement (*ibid.*, § 65), *Aleksovski case*, Judgement on Appeal (*ibid.*, § 66) and *Delalić case*, Judgement on Appeal (*ibid.*, § 67).

by financing and equipping them, but also by generally directing or helping plan their actions".[27]

As stated in the commentary on the Draft Articles on State Responsibility, "the legal issues and the factual situation" in the above-mentioned cases before the International Court of Justice and the International Criminal Tribunal for the Former Yugoslavia were different and "it is a matter for appreciation in each case whether particular conduct was or was not carried out under the control of a State, to such an extent that the conduct controlled should be attributed to it".[28]

In 2001, in a report on the alleged killings in 1991 in Riofrío in Colombia, the Inter-American Commission on Human Rights established that the State was responsible for the actions of the paramilitary forces because there was evidence to show that agents of the State (namely branches of the army) helped coordinate the massacre, carry it out and then cover it up.[29]

As to private individuals or groups which are not militarily organised, the International Criminal Tribunal for the Former Yugoslavia, in the *Tadić case* in 1999, stated that they could be considered a *de facto* organ of a State, and thus responsibility for their acts could be attributed to that State, if specific instructions concerning the commission of those acts had been issued to the individual or group.[30]

State responsibility for violations committed by private persons or groups which are acknowledged and adopted by a State as its own conduct

State practice also indicates that State responsibility for acts committed by private individuals or groups can arise through subsequent acknowledgement and adoption of the acts of these persons or groups.[31] Such acts then become acts of the State, regardless of the fact that the acting person or entity was not, at the time of the commission of the acts, an organ of the State and was not mandated to act on behalf of the State. For example, in the *Priebke case* in 1996, the Military Tribunal of Rome attributed responsibility to Italy for the behaviour of Italian partisans during the Second World War on the basis that it had encouraged their actions and had officially recognised them after the conflict.[32] In the *J. T. case* in 1949, the District Court of The Hague also raised the question of how far a State whose territory had been occupied could be held liable, after liberation, for acts committed by the resistance movement organised

---

[27] ICTY, *Tadić case*, Judgement on Appeal (*ibid.*, § 64).
[28] ILC, Commentary on Article 8 of the Draft Articles on State Responsibility (*ibid.*, § 57).
[29] Inter-American Commission on Human Rights, *Case of the Riofrío massacre (Colombia)* (*ibid.*, § 71).
[30] ICTY, *Tadić case*, Judgement on Appeal (*ibid.*, § 64).
[31] See Draft Articles on State Responsibility, Article 11 (*ibid.*, § 8).
[32] Italy, Military Tribunal of Rome, *Priebke case* (*ibid.*, § 27).

with the consent of the government-in-exile.[33] The International Criminal Tribunal for the Former Yugoslavia made the same point in its judgement on appeal in the *Tadić case* in 1999, when it held that a State was responsible for the acts of individuals or groups that were not militarily organised and that could be regarded as *de facto* State organs if the unlawful act had been publicly endorsed or approved *ex post facto* by the State.[34]

Responsibility of armed opposition groups

Armed opposition groups must respect international humanitarian law (see Rule 139) and they must operate under a "responsible command".[35] It can therefore be argued that they incur responsibility for acts committed by persons forming part of such groups, but the consequences of such responsibility are not clear.

Article 14(3) of the Draft Articles on State Responsibility, as provisionally adopted on first reading in 1996, stated that the fact that the conduct of an organ of an insurrectional movement was not to be considered an act of State "is without prejudice to the attribution of the conduct of the organ of the insurrectional movement to that movement in any case in which such attribution may be made under international law".[36] While this Article was subsequently deleted because it was deemed to fall outside the scope of the subject matter under discussion, the Special Rapporteur noted that "the responsibility of such movements, for example for breaches of international humanitarian law, can certainly be envisaged".[37] As a result of the exclusion of this subject from the Draft Articles, Article 10 states only that the conduct of an insurrectional movement which becomes the new government must be considered an act of that State under international law.[38]

In addition to practice indicating the obligation of armed opposition groups to respect international humanitarian law (see commentary to Rule 139), there are some examples of attribution of responsibility to armed opposition groups. For example, in a report on the situation of human rights in Sudan, the Special Rapporteur of the UN Commission on Human Rights stated that the Sudanese People's Liberation Army was responsible for the killing and abduction of civilians, looting and hostage-taking of relief workers committed by "local commanders from its own ranks".[39]

---

[33] Netherlands, District Court of The Hague, *J. T. case* (*ibid.*, § 28).
[34] ICTY, *Tadić case*, Judgement on Appeal (*ibid.*, § 64).   [35] Additional Protocol II, Article 1(1).
[36] 1996 version of the Draft Articles on State Responsibility, Article 14(3), provisionally adopted on first reading (cited in Vol. II, Ch. 42, § 58).
[37] ILC, First report on State responsibility by the Special Rapporteur, Addendum (*ibid.*, § 58).
[38] Draft Articles on State Responsibility, Article 10 (*ibid.*, § 8).
[39] UN Commission on Human Rights, Special Rapporteur on the Situation of Human Rights in the Sudan, Interim Report (*ibid.*, § 53).

Rule 150. A State responsible for violations of international humanitarian law is required to make full reparation for the loss or injury caused.

Practice

Volume II, Chapter 42, Section B.

Summary

State practice establishes this rule as a norm of customary international law applicable in both international and non-international armed conflicts.

International armed conflicts

It is a basic rule of international law that reparation is to be made for violations of international law. In the *Chorzów Factory case (Merits)* in 1928, the Permanent Court of International Justice stated that:

It is a principle of international law, and even a general conception of the law, that any breach of an engagement involves an obligation to make reparation . . . Reparation is the indispensable complement of a failure to apply a convention, and there is no necessity for this to be stated in the convention itself.[40]

The Draft Articles on State Responsibility provide that "the responsible State is under an obligation to make full reparation for the injury caused by the internationally wrongful act".[41]

The duty to make reparation for violations of international humanitarian law is explicitly referred to in the Second Protocol to the Hague Convention for the Protection of Cultural Property.[42] It is also implied in the rule contained in the Geneva Conventions, according to which States cannot absolve themselves or another High Contracting Party of any liability incurred in respect of grave breaches.[43]

Reparation sought by States
There exist numerous examples of reparation sought by States for violations of international humanitarian law. With respect to the form of reparation, the

---

[40] PCIJ, *Chorzów Factory case (Merits)* (*ibid.*, § 103); see also PCIJ Statute, Article 36, which states that "the States Parties to the present Statute may at any time declare that they recognize as compulsory *ipso facto* and without special agreement, in relation to any other state accepting the same obligation, the jurisdiction of the Court in all legal disputes concerning: . . . (d) the nature of the reparation to be made for the breach of an international obligation". Article 36(2) of the ICJ Statute contains similar wording.
[41] Draft Articles on State Responsibility, Article 31 (cited in Vol. II. Ch. 42, § 87).
[42] Second Protocol to the Hague Convention for the Protection of Cultural Property, Article 38 (*ibid.*, § 81).
[43] First Geneva Convention, Article 51 (*ibid.*, § 2); Second Geneva Convention, Article 52 (*ibid.*, § 2); Third Geneva Convention, Article 131 (*ibid.*, § 2); Fourth Geneva Convention, Article 148 (*ibid.*, § 2).

Draft Articles on State Responsibility provide that "full reparation for the injury caused by the internationally wrongful act shall take the form of restitution, compensation or satisfaction, either singly or in combination".[44]

(i) Restitution. As explained in Article 35 of the Draft Articles on State Responsibility, the purpose of restitution is to re-establish the situation that existed before the wrongful act was committed. The Article provides that a State responsible for an internationally wrongful act is under an obligation to make restitution provided that this "is not materially impossible" and "does not involve a burden out of all proportion to the benefit deriving from restitution instead of compensation". The commentary on the Draft Articles explains that restitution can, in its simplest form, involve such conduct as the release of persons wrongly detained or the return of property wrongly seized, but can also be a more complex act, and that restitution comes first among the forms of reparation.[45]

Paragraph 1 of the First Protocol to the Hague Convention for the Protection of Cultural Property provides that States must prevent the exportation of cultural property from occupied territory. Paragraph 3 obliges the occupying State (as well as other States) to return cultural property exported in violation of Paragraph 1 at the close of hostilities to the territory previously occupied (see Rule 41).[46]

A number of agreements relating to the Second World War provided for the restitution of property that had been stolen, seized or confiscated.[47] In 1970, during a debate in the Special Political Committee of the UN General Assembly on measures carried out by Israel in the occupied territories, Poland stated that Israel was liable for the restitution of Palestinian property.[48] Hungary's Military Manual provides that, after a conflict, civilian, cultural and requisitioned objects have to be returned.[49]

In 1991, Germany declared its acceptance of the rule that cultural property has to be returned after the end of hostilities and also stated that it had returned cultural property in all cases in which the cultural goods were found and could be identified. In other cases, Germany has paid compensation to the State of the original owner.[50]

In 1999, during a debate in the UN General Assembly, the United Arab Emirates called upon Iraq to return Kuwaiti cultural property.[51] Kuwait also insisted

---

[44] Draft Articles on State Responsibility, Article 34 (*ibid.*, § 87).

[45] ILC, Commentary on Article 35 of the Draft Articles on State Responsibility (*ibid.*, § 352).

[46] First Protocol to the Hague Convention for the Protection of Cultural Property, paras. 1 and 3 (*ibid.*, § 311).

[47] Paris Agreement on Reparation from Germany (*ibid.*, §§ 302–303); Convention on the Settlement of Matters Arising out of the War and the Occupation (*ibid.*, §§ 305–310).

[48] Poland, Statement before the Special Political Committee of the UN General Assembly (*ibid.*, § 231).

[49] Hungary, *Military Manual* (*ibid.*, § 327).

[50] See the statement of Germany (cited in Vol. II, Ch. 12, § 460).

[51] See the statement of the United Arab Emirates (*ibid.*, § 471).

on the restitution by Iraq of cultural property, and Iraq explained its readiness to do so.[52] Similarly, the UN Security Council urged Iraq on several occasions to return to Kuwait all property seized.[53] The UN Secretary-General reported on compliance by Iraq with obligations placed upon it by several UN Security Council resolutions and noted, in 2000, that a substantial amount of property had been returned since the end of the Gulf War, but that many items remained unreturned. He stressed that "priority should be given to the return by Iraq of the Kuwaiti archives . . . and museum items".[54]

In 2001, Russia and Belgium reached an agreement on the return to Belgium of the military archives stolen by the Nazis during the Second World War and then taken to Moscow by Soviet forces. Russia accepted to return these archives provided it was reimbursed the cost of having maintained them.[55]

(ii) Compensation. It is a long-standing rule of customary international law, set forth in the 1907 Hague Convention (IV) and repeated in Additional Protocol I, that a State which violates international humanitarian law must pay compensation, if the case demands.[56] This obligation has been put into practice through numerous post-conflict settlements.[57] It is also spelled out in the Draft Articles on State Responsibility, which oblige a State "to compensate for the damage caused . . . insofar as such damage is not made good by restitution".[58]

---

[52] See the practice of Iraq (cited in Vol. II, Ch. 12, §§ 463–464 and 466) and Kuwait (*ibid.*, §§ 467–468) and the reported practice of Kuwait (cited in Vol. II, Ch. 42, § 336).

[53] UN Security Council, Res. 686 (*ibid.*, § 472) and Res. 1284 (*ibid.*, § 473); see also Res. 687 (cited in Vol. II, Ch. 42, § 346).

[54] See UN Secretary-General, Further report on the status of compliance by Iraq with the obligations placed upon it under certain of the Security Council resolutions relating to the situation between Iraq and Kuwait (cited in Vol. II, Ch. 12, § 476) and Second report pursuant to paragraph 14 of resolution 1284 (1999) (*ibid.*, § 477).

[55] See the reported practice of Belgium (*ibid.*, § 470) and Russia (*ibid.*, § 470).

[56] 1907 Hague Convention (IV), Article 3 (*ibid.*, § 111); Additional Protocol I, Article 91 (adopted by consensus) (*ibid.*, § 126).

[57] See, e.g., Peace Treaty for Japan (cited in Vol. II, Ch. 42, §§ 114–115); Yoshida-Stikker Protocol between Japan and the Netherlands (*ibid.*, § 116); Convention on the Settlement of Matters Arising out of the War and the Occupation (*ibid.*, §§ 117–119); Luxembourg Agreement between Germany and Israel (*ibid.*, §§ 120–121); Protocols Nos. 1 and 2 of the Luxembourg Agreement between Germany and the Conference on Jewish Material Claims against Germany (*ibid.*, §§ 149–150); Austrian State Treaty (*ibid.*, § 122); Agreement concerning Payments on behalf of Norwegian Nationals Victimized by National Socialist Persecution (*ibid.*, § 124); Implementation Agreement to the German Unification Treaty (*ibid.*, § 128); US-Germany Agreement concerning Final Benefits to Certain US Nationals Who Were Victims of National Socialist Measures of Persecution (also known as the "Princz Agreement") (*ibid.*, §§ 129–130); Agreement on Refugees and Displaced Persons annexed to the Dayton Accords (*ibid.*, §§ 131–133); US-Chinese Agreement on the Settlement of Chinese Claims resulting from the Bombardment of the Chinese Embassy in Belgrade and US-Chinese Memorandum of Understanding on the Settlement of US Claims resulting from the Bombardment of the Chinese Embassy in Belgrade (*ibid.*, §§ 134–135); Agreement on the Foundation "Remembrance, Responsibility and the Future" concluded between Germany and the United States (*ibid.*, §§ 136–138); Austrian-US Executive Agreement concerning the Austrian Reconciliation Fund (*ibid.*, § 139); Bilateral agreements between Austria and six Central and Eastern European States (*ibid.*, § 140); Peace Agreement between Eritrea and Ethiopia (*ibid.*, § 141); Washington Agreement between France and the United States (*ibid.*, §§ 142–143); Annex A to the Austrian-US Agreement concerning the Austrian General Settlement Fund (*ibid.*, §§ 144–145).

[58] Draft Articles on State Responsibility, Article 36 (*ibid.*, § 159).

The commentary on the Draft Articles explains that "restitution, despite its primacy as a legal principle, is frequently unavailable or inadequate . . . The role of compensation is to fill gaps so as to ensure full reparation for damage suffered."[59]

The obligation to compensate for damage caused by violations of international humanitarian law is confirmed by a number of official statements.[60] It has also been recalled in a number of resolutions adopted by the UN Security Council and UN General Assembly.[61]

(iii) Satisfaction. Article 37 of the Draft Articles on State Responsibility provides that:

1. The State responsible for an internationally wrongful act is under an obligation to give satisfaction for the injury caused by the act insofar as its obligation cannot be made good by restitution or compensation.
2. Satisfaction may consist in an acknowledgement of the breach, an expression of regret, a formal apology or another appropriate modality.
3. Satisfaction shall not be out of proportion to the injury and may not take a form humiliating to the responsible State.[62]

The requirement to establish the truth through investigation and to bring perpetrators to justice is mentioned in the commentary on Article 37 of the Draft Articles on State Responsibility, which lists "inquiry into the causes of an accident resulting in harm or injury" and "disciplinary or penal action against the individuals whose conduct caused the internationally wrongful act" among the possible ways of giving satisfaction.[63] The US Field Manual includes, as types of remedies for violations of international humanitarian law, publication of the facts and punishment of captured offenders as war criminals.[64] It should be noted that, independent of the duty to provide appropriate reparation, States are

---

59 ILC, Commentary on Article 36 of the Draft Articles on State Responsibility (*ibid.*, § 264). As to whether the damage is financially assessable in order to be compensated, the commentary states that "compensable personal injury encompasses not only associated material losses, such as loss of earnings and earning capacity, medical expenses and the like, but also non-material damage suffered by the individual (sometimes, though not universally, referred to as 'moral damage' in national legal systems). Non-material damage is generally understood to encompass loss of loved ones, pain and suffering as well as the affront to sensibilities associated with an intrusion on the person, home or private life."

60 See, e.g., the practice of Canada (*ibid.*, § 212), China (*ibid.*, § 215), Iraq (*ibid.*, § 221), Kuwait (*ibid.*, § 225), Lebanon, speaking on behalf of the Group of Arab States (*ibid.*, § 227), Mexico (*ibid.*, § 228), Syria (*ibid.*, § 236), United Kingdom (*ibid.*, § 238) and United States (*ibid.*, § 239).

61 See, e.g., UN Security Council, Res. 387 (*ibid.*, § 243), Res. 455 (*ibid.*, § 244), Res. 471 (*ibid.*, § 245), Res. 527 (*ibid.*, § 246), Res. 571 (*ibid.*, § 247), Res. 687 (*ibid.*, § 248), Res. 692 (*ibid.*, § 249) and Res. 827 (*ibid.*, § 250); UN General Assembly, Res. 50/22 C (*ibid.*, § 251), Res. 51/233 (*ibid.*, § 252) and Res. 56/83 (*ibid.*, § 253).

62 ILC, Draft Articles on State Responsibility, Article 37 (*ibid.*, § 326). The commentary on Article 36 of the Draft Articles on State Responsibility (*ibid.*, § 264) explains that satisfaction "is concerned with non-material injury, specifically non-material injury to the State, on which a monetary value can be put only in a highly approximate and notional way" and that "satisfaction . . . is the remedy for those injuries, not financially assessable, which amount to an affront [to the State]" (*ibid.*, § 353).

63 ILC, Commentary on Article 37 of the Draft Articles on State Responsibility (*ibid.*, § 354).

64 United States, *Field Manual* (*ibid.*, § 329).

under an obligation to investigate war crimes over which they have jurisdiction and to prosecute the suspects if necessary (see Rule 158).

Guarantees of non-repetition are a possible form of satisfaction referred to in the Draft Articles on State Responsibility, which require a State responsible for an internationally wrongful act to cease the violation, and to offer appropriate assurances and guarantees of non-repetition, if circumstances so demand.[65]

Reparation sought directly by individuals
There is an increasing trend in favour of enabling individual victims of violations of international humanitarian law to seek reparation directly from the responsible State. Article 33(2) of the Draft Articles on State Responsibility states that Part II of the Draft Articles ("Content of the international responsibility of a State") "is without prejudice to any right, arising from the international responsibility of a State, which may accrue directly to any person or entity other than a State".[66] The commentary on Article 33 furthermore states that:

When an obligation of reparation exists towards a State, reparation does not necessarily accrue to that State's benefit. For instance, a State's responsibility for the breach of an obligation under a treaty concerning the protection of human rights may exist towards all the other parties to the treaty, but the individuals concerned should be regarded as the ultimate beneficiaries and in that sense as the holders of the relevant rights.[67]

Croatia, in its views and comments on the 1997 version of the Draft Principles and Guidelines on the Right to Reparation for Victims of [Gross] Violations of Human Rights and International Humanitarian Law, as they were then called, and the United States, in a Concurrent Resolution of the House of Representatives in 2001 with regard to violations committed by Japan against so-called "comfort women", have referred to the right of victims to receive reparation directly.[68] In two resolutions on the former Yugoslavia, the UN General Assembly recognised "the right of victims of 'ethnic cleansing' to receive just reparation for their losses" and urged all parties "to fulfil their agreements to this end".[69]

Reparation has been provided directly to individuals via different procedures, in particular via mechanisms set up by inter-State agreements, via unilateral State acts such as national legislation or reparation sought by individuals directly before national courts.

---

[65] Draft Articles on State Responsibility, Article 30.
[66] Draft Articles on State Responsibility, Article 33(2).
[67] ILC, Commentary on Article 33 of the Draft Articles on State Responsibility (cited in Vol. II. Ch. 42, § 351).
[68] See the practice of Croatia (*ibid.*, § 91) and United States (*ibid.*, § 94).
[69] UN General Assembly, Res. 48/153 (*ibid.*, § 95) and Res. 49/196 (*ibid.*, § 96); see also UN Commission on Human Rights, Res. 1998/70 (*ibid.*, § 99).

(i) Reparation provided on the basis of inter-State and other agreements.
Under a number of agreements concluded in the aftermath of the Second World
War, Germany was obliged to restitute to victims stolen property such as jewellery, precious household goods and other household effects, and cultural property.[70]

A more recent example of restitution to individuals on the basis of an inter-
State agreement is the Agreement on Refugees and Displaced Persons annexed
to the Dayton Accords which establishes the Commission for Real Property
Claims of Displaced Persons and Refugees in Bosnia and Herzegovina and which
mandates the Commission to decide on, *inter alia,* claims for return of real
property,[71] as well as for compensation for the deprivation of property in the
course of hostilities since 1991, which cannot be restored to them.[72]

The Agreement between the Government of Canada and the National Association of Japanese Canadians (Japanese-Canadian Redress Agreement) adopted
in 1988 provides for apology for and acknowledgement of violations of international humanitarian law.[73]

Another example is the United Nations Compensation Commission (UNCC)
established by a UN Security Council resolution, which reviews claims for
compensation for direct loss and damage arising "as a result of [Iraq's] unlawful
invasion and occupation of Kuwait" suffered by States, international organisations, corporations and individuals. Although the UNCC deals principally with
losses arising from Iraq's unlawful use of force, awards have also covered violations of international humanitarian law suffered by individuals.[74] For example,
the UNCC has awarded compensation to former prisoners of war held by Iraq
who had been subjected to ill-treatment in violation of the Third Geneva Convention.[75]

A further example is the Eritrea-Ethiopia Claims Commission established
by the 2000 Peace Agreement between Eritrea and Ethiopia, which has the
mandate "to decide through binding arbitration all claims for loss, damage or
injury by ... nationals (including both natural and juridical persons) of one party
against the Government of the other party or entities owned or controlled by
the other party".[76]

---

[70] See Convention on the Settlement of Matters Arising out of the War and the Occupation,
Chapter 3, Article 2 (*ibid.,* § 305); Protocol No. 1 of the Luxembourg Agreement between
Germany and the Conference on Jewish Material Claims against Germany (*ibid.,* § 316); see
also the legislation of Germany (*ibid.,* § 331).

[71] See Agreement on Refugees and Displaced Persons annexed to the Dayton Accords, Articles VII
and XI (*ibid.,* § 318).

[72] See Agreement on Refugees and Displaced Persons annexed to the Dayton Accords, Articles I
and XII(2) (*ibid.,* §§ 131–133).

[73] See the practice of Canada (*ibid.,* § 334).

[74] See, e.g., UNCC, Governing Council, Decision 3 (*ibid.,* §§ 249 and 273) and Decision 11 (*ibid.,*
§§ 249 and 275).

[75] UNCC, Report and Recommendations made by the Panel of Commissioners concerning Part
One of the Second Instalment of Claims for Serious Personal Injury or Death (*ibid.,* § 277).

[76] To date, the Commission, ruling on claims brought by Eritrea and Ethiopia on behalf of their
nationals respectively, has awarded compensation related to the treatment of former prisoners

Various specific funds have been created in the recent past with a mandate to award compensation to individuals. Examples include the Austrian Reconciliation Fund and the German Foundation "Remembrance, Responsibility and the Future", both established by national legislation on the basis of agreements concluded by Austria and Germany with the United States. The Austrian Reconciliation Fund was created "to make a contribution toward reconciliation, peace, and cooperation through a voluntary gesture of the Republic of Austria to natural persons who were coerced into slave labour or forced labour by the National Socialist regime on the territory of the present day Republic of Austria". The German Foundation was set up in order to "make financial compensation available... to former forced labourers and those affected by other injustices from the National Socialist period".[77]

Another example is the Victims Trust Fund established pursuant to Article 79 of the Statute of the International Criminal Court. The fund will include money and other property collected through fines and forfeitures imposed by the Court on perpetrators. However, it is expected that funds will also come from voluntary contributions from States, corporations, organisations and individuals.[78]

(ii) Reparation provided on the basis of a unilateral State act. There are reports of direct compensation by Germany to inmates of concentration camps and to victims of medical experiments and by Norway to persons suffering from anti-Jewish measures during the Second World War.[79] Japan has provided an apology for the treatment of "comfort women" and Norway for anti-Jewish measures during the Second World War.[80]

Austria and Germany have adopted laws related to the restitution of objects to victims, as has the United States in the form of its Law on Restitution for WWII Internment of Japanese-Americans and Aleuts.[81]

The creation in 1997 by France of the Study Mission on the Spoliation of Jews in France (also known as the "Mattéoli Mission") with the task of conducting a study of the various forms of spoliation visited upon the Jews of France during the Second World War, and of the scope and effect of post-war restitution efforts, points in the same direction.[82]

---

of war by the two States, see Eritrea-Ethiopia Claims Commission, *Prisoners of War, Eritrea's and Ethiopia's Claims, Partial Awards* (*ibid.*, § 282).

[77] See the legislation of Austria (*ibid.*, § 180) and Germany (*ibid.*, § 184).

[78] ICC Statute, Article 79, which states that "(1) A Trust Fund shall be established by decision of the Assembly of States Parties for the benefit of victims of crimes within the jurisdiction of the Court, and of the families of such victims. (2) The Court may order money and other property collected through fines or forfeiture to be transferred, by order of the Court, to the Trust Fund. (3) The Trust Fund shall be managed according to criteria to be determined by the Assembly of States Parties."

[79] See the practice of Germany (cited in Vol. II. Ch. 42, § 220) and Norway (*ibid.*, § 230); "On behalf of victims of pseudo-medical experiments: Red Cross action", *International Review of the Red Cross*, No. 142, 1973, pp. 3–21.

[80] See the practice of Japan (cited in Vol. II, Ch. 42, §§ 337–340) and Norway (*ibid.*, § 230).

[81] See the legislation of Austria (*ibid.*, § 330), Germany (*ibid.*, § 331) and United States (*ibid.*, § 332).

[82] See the practice of France (*ibid.*, § 335).

(iii) Reparation sought in national courts. The Hague Convention (IV) and Additional Protocol I require that compensation be paid but do not indicate whether only States are recipients or also individuals, nor do they specify the mechanism for reviewing claims for compensation.[83]

Individual claimants before national courts have encountered a number of obstacles in trying to obtain compensation on the basis of Article 3 of Hague Convention (IV), although no court has explicitly ruled out such a possibility under contemporary international law.[84] In the *Shimoda case* in 1963, for example, the Tokyo District Court held that individuals did not have a direct right to compensation under international law, and considerations of sovereign immunity precluded proceedings against another State before Japanese courts.[85]

Until the 1990s, German courts generally considered that the 1953 London Agreement on German External Debts had postponed the question of indemnification of individuals, though it did not exclude the possibility of granting compensation once the issue of reparations to States had been settled.[86] As a result, after the coming into force of the 1990 Treaty on the Final Settlement with Respect to Germany ("Two-Plus-Four-Treaty"),[87] the German courts held that, in general, they were no longer prevented from dealing with the question of compensation to individuals.[88] As a consequence, Germany's Constitutional Court in the *Forced Labour case* in 1996 stated that there did not exist a rule of general international law preventing the payment of compensation to individuals for violations of international law.[89] However, in the *Distomo case* in 2003, Germany's Federal Supreme Court stated that, owing to a concept of war as a "relationship from State to State" as it existed during the Second World War, a State which was responsible for crimes committed at that time was only liable

---

[83] Hague Convention (IV), Article 3 (*ibid.*, § 111); Additional Protocol I, Article 91 (*ibid.*, § 126).

[84] See, e.g., Germany, Administrative Court of Appeal of Münster, *Personal Injuries case* (*ibid.*, § 191); Germany, Federal Supreme Court, *Reparation Payments case* (*ibid.*, § 192); Germany, Second Chamber of the Constitutional Court, *Forced Labour case* (*ibid.*, § 193); Germany, Federal Supreme Court, *Distomo case*, (*ibid.*, 194); Greece, Court of First Instance of Leivadia, *Prefecture of Voiotia case* (*ibid.*, § 195); Japan, Tokyo District Court, *Shimoda case* (*ibid.*, § 196); Japan, Tokyo High Court and Supreme Court, *Siberian Detainees case* (*ibid.*, § 197); Japan, Tokyo District Court and Tokyo High Court, *Apology for the Kamishisuka Slaughter of Koreans case* (*ibid.*, § 198); Japan, Tokyo District Court, *Ex-Allied Nationals Claims case, Dutch Nationals Claims case* and *Filippino "Comfort Women" Claims case* (*ibid.*, § 199); Japan, Fukuoka District Court, *Zhang Baoheng and Others case* (*ibid.*, § 200); Japan, Yamaguchi Lower Court and Hiroshima High Court, *Ko Otsu Hei Incidents case* (*ibid.*, § 201); United States, Court of Appeals (Fourth Circuit), *Goldstar case* (*ibid.*, § 204); United States, District Court for the District of Columbia and Court of Appeals for the District of Columbia, *Princz case* (*ibid.*, § 205); United States, District Court of Columbia, *Comfort Women case* (*ibid.*, § 210).

[85] Japan, Tokyo District Court, *Shimoda case* (*ibid.*, §196).

[86] See Germany, Federal Supreme Court, *Reparation Payments case* (*ibid.*, § 192).

[87] Treaty on the Final Settlement with Respect to Germany ("Two-Plus-Four-Treaty") between the Federal Republic of Germany, the German Democratic Republic, France, the USSR, the United Kingdom and the United States, 12 September 1990.

[88] See, e.g., Germany, Constitutional Court, *Forced Labour case* (cited in Vol. II. Ch. 42, § 193); Germany, Federal Supreme Court, *Distomo case* (*ibid.*, § 194).

[89] Germany, Constitutional Court, *Forced Labour case* (*ibid.*, § 193).

to pay compensation vis-à-vis another State but not vis-à-vis the individual victims. According to the Court, international law conferred upon States the right to exercise diplomatic protection of their nationals, and the right to claim compensation was the right of the State "at least for the period in question", i.e., during the Second World War.[90]

In the *Goldstar case* in 1992 relating to the intervention by the United States in Panama, a US Court of Appeals found that Article 3 of the 1907 Hague Convention (IV) was not self-executing because there was no evidence of an intent to provide a private right of action.[91] In the *Princz case* in 1992, another US Court of Appeals dismissed a claim for damages against Germany for treatment inflicted during the Second World War because it lacked jurisdiction for reasons of State immunity.[92]

An example of compensation granted to individual claimants for injury suffered during the Second World War is the decision by Greece's Court of First Instance of Leivadia in the *Prefecture of Voiotia case* in 1997, which was upheld in 2000 by the Supreme Court. In this case, the courts applied Article 3 of the 1907 Hague Convention (IV) and Article 46 of the Hague Regulations and ruled that the victims of the Distomo killings could directly bring a claim against Germany for compensation and that sovereign immunity could not be invoked in connection with violations of a rule of *jus cogens* (*inter alia* wilful killing). However, with regard to the same case, Greece refused to give its consent necessary for the execution of the judgement against Germany for reasons of State immunity.[93]

Non-international armed conflicts

There is an increasing amount of State practice from all parts of the world that shows that this rule applies to violations of international humanitarian law committed in non-international armed conflicts and attributable to a State. It flows directly from the basic legal principle that a breach of law involves an obligation to make reparation,[94] as well as from the responsibility of a State for violations which are attributable to it (see Rule 149). Practice varies in that it sometimes refers to the duty to make reparations in general terms, and at other

---

[90] Germany, Federal Supreme Court, *Distomo case* (*ibid.*, § 194).
[91] United States, Court of Appeals, *Goldstar case* (*ibid.*, § 204).
[92] United States, Court of Appeals for the District of Columbia, *Princz case* (*ibid.*, § 205).
[93] Greece, Court of First Instance of Leivadia and Supreme Court, *Prefecture of Voiotia case* (*ibid.*, § 195); Greece, Statement before the European Court of Human Rights in the *Kalogeropoulou and Others case* (*ibid.*, § 195).
[94] See, e.g., PCIJ, *Chorzów Factory case (Merits)* (*ibid.*, § 103); see also PCIJ Statute, Article 36, which states that "the States Parties to the present Statute may at any time declare that they recognize as compulsory *ipso facto* and without special agreement, in relation to any other state accepting the same obligation, the jurisdiction of the Court in all legal disputes concerning: ... (d) the nature of the reparation to be made for the breach of an international obligation". Article 36(2) of the Statute of the International Court of Justice contains similar wording.

times to specific forms of reparation, including restitution, compensation and satisfaction (see *infra*).[95] Some reparation was provided on the basis of a recognition by the government of its responsibility to provide such reparation and sometimes on the basis of its recognition that it ought to make such reparation.

It lies in the nature of non-international armed conflicts, however, that the procedures which have been made available to provide reparation in international armed conflict are not necessarily relevant in non-international armed conflict. In particular, in non-international armed conflicts, victims suffer violations in their own State and generally have access to domestic courts to claim reparation in accordance with domestic law.[96] It is noteworthy in this respect that the International Covenant on Civil and Political Rights, as well as the three regional human rights treaties, require that States must provide a remedy for violations.[97] The UN Human Rights Committee and the Inter-American Court of Human Rights have stated that this obligation is non-derogable.[98]

Reparation sought from a State

The possibility for an individual victim of a violation of international humanitarian law to seek reparation from a State can be inferred from Article 75(6) of the Statute of the International Criminal Court, which states that "nothing in this article shall be interpreted as prejudicing the rights of victims under national or international law".[99] Article 38 of the Second Protocol to the Hague Convention for the Protection of Cultural Property, which expressly refers to the duty of States to provide reparation and applies in any armed conflict.[100]

An example from practice is the Joint Circular on Adherence to International Humanitarian Law and Human Rights of the Philippines, which provides that in the case of damage to private property in the course of legitimate security or police operations, "measures shall be undertaken whenever practicable . . . to

---

[95] Article 34 of the Draft Articles on State Responsibility provides that "full reparation for the injury caused by the internationally wrongful act shall take the form of restitution, compensation or satisfaction, either singly or in combination" (*ibid.*, §§ 158 and 324). In addition, it should be noted that Article 75(2) of the ICC Statute (*ibid.*, § 314) concerning "Reparations to victims" gives the Court the power to "make an order directly against a convicted person specifying appropriate reparations to, or in respect of, victims, including restitution, compensation and rehabilitation".

[96] See, e.g., Colombia, *Basic Military Manual* (cited in Vol. II. Ch. 42, § 163); American Law Institute, Restatement (Third) of the Foreign Relations Law of the United States (*ibid.*, §§ 108, 293 and 363). It should be noted that diplomatic protection would still be possible in a situation where foreign residents or visitors are injured by the armed forces of a State in the context of a non-international armed conflict.

[97] International Covenant on Civil and Political Rights, Article 2(3); European Convention on Human Rights, Article 13; American Convention on Human Rights, Articles 10 and 25; African Charter on Human and Peoples' Rights, Article 7(1)(a) (implicit).

[98] See, e.g., UN Human Rights Committee, General Comment No. 29, § 14; Inter-American Court of Human Rights, *Judicial Guarantees case*, Advisory Opinion, §§ 24–26.

[99] ICC Statute, Article 75(6) (cited in Vol. II, Ch. 42, § 80).

[100] Second Protocol to the Hague Convention for the Protection of Cultural Property, Article 38 (*ibid.*, § 81).

repair the damage caused".[101] Also, in a resolution adopted in 1996, the UN General Assembly urged the Afghan authorities to provide "efficient and effective remedies" to victims of serious violations of international humanitarian law.[102]

Other examples from practice relate to specific forms of reparation, including restitution, compensation and satisfaction:

(i) *Restitution.* In the case of *Akdivar and Others v. Turkey*, the European Court of Human Rights stated that there was a legal obligation for a violating State to put an end to the breach and to "make reparation for its consequences in such a way as to restore as far as possible the situation existing before the breach (restitutio in integrum)". However, it also stated that if this was in practice impossible, the State that ought to make reparation was to choose another means in order to comply with the judgement.[103]

Another example is the Agreement on Refugees and Displaced Persons annexed to the Dayton Accords, which established the Commission for Real Property Claims of Displaced Persons and Refugees in Bosnia and Herzegovina, stating that refugees and displaced persons shall have the right to restitution of property of which they were deprived during the hostilities since 1991.[104]

Similarly, the Housing and Property Claims Commission in Kosovo is given the power to decide on claims for restitution, repossession and return of the property brought by certain categories of persons, including those who lost their property rights as a result of discrimination, as well as refugees and displaced persons.[105]

Another example is the 1998 Comprehensive Agreement on Respect for Human Rights and International Humanitarian Law in the Philippines which provides for restitution as a possible form of reparation.[106]

(ii) *Compensation.* There is widespread and representative practice in which States have made efforts to compensate victims of violations of international humanitarian law committed in non-international armed conflicts. Examples

---

[101] Philippines, Joint Circular on Adherence to IHL and Human Rights (*ibid.*, § 88).

[102] UN General Assembly, Res. 51/108 (*ibid.*, § 97).

[103] European Court of Human Rights, *Akdivar and Others v. Turkey* (*ibid.*, § 357). The Court's powers to provide "just satisfaction" are based on the European Convention for the Protection of Human Rights and Fundamental Freedoms, Article 41 (*ibid.*, § 304). The Inter-American Court of Human Rights has similar powers to provide "fair compensation" on the basis of the American Convention on Human Rights, Article 63(1) (*ibid.*, § 313). The African Court of Human and Peoples' Rights will have powers to order "the payment of fair compensation or reparation" on the basis of the Protocol to the African Charter on Human and Peoples' Rights on the Establishment of an African Court of Human and Peoples' Rights, Article 27 (*ibid.*, § 315).

[104] Agreement on Refugees and Displaced Persons annexed to the Dayton Accords, Article I(1) (*ibid.*, § 317).

[105] UNMIK Regulation No. 2000/60, Section 2(2), (5) and (6) (*ibid.*, § 157). The Housing and Property Claims Commission was established by UNMIK Regulation No. 1999/23 (*ibid.*, § 320).

[106] Comprehensive Agreement on Respect for Human Rights and IHL in the Philippines, Part III, Article 2(3) (*ibid.*, § 319).

include: the Comprehensive Agreement on Human Rights in Guatemala by which the parties "recognize that it is a humanitarian duty to compensate and/or assist victims of human rights violations"; the Comprehensive Agreement on Respect for Human Rights and International Humanitarian Law in the Philippines, by which the parties recognise the right of the victims and their families to seek justice for violations of human rights, including "adequate compensation or indemnification"; and Russia's Resolution on Compensation for Destruction of Property for Citizens Having Suffered from the Settling of the Crisis in Chechnya and Having Left Chechnya Irrevocably.[107] Also, Chile's National Commission for Truth and Reconciliation, El Salvador's special committee investigating the whereabouts of missing persons and Sri Lanka's Commission of Inquiry into Voluntary Removal or Disappearance of Persons in certain provinces made recommendations that compensation should be paid to victims or their relatives.[108] In its views and comments on the 1997 version of the Draft Principles and Guidelines on the Right to Reparation for Victims of [Gross] Violations of Human Rights and International Humanitarian Law, as they were then called, Chile called for inclusion of a specific provision establishing "the State's immediate, direct liability for compensation".[109] Rwanda, in 1996, and Zimbabwe, in 1999, also announced their willingness to compensate victims of, respectively, acts of genocide and crimes against humanity committed in Rwanda and of killings committed during the armed conflict in the early 1980s in Zimbabwe.[110]

Another instrument implementing the right of victims to compensation is the Agreement on Refugees and Displaced Persons annexed to the Dayton Accords, which establishes the Commission for Real Property Claims of Displaced Persons and Refugees in Bosnia and Herzegovina and which states that refugees and displaced persons who were deprived of their property in the course of hostilities since 1991 must be compensated if the property cannot be restored to them.[111] UNMIK Regulation No. 2000/60, containing the Rules of Procedure and Evidence of the Housing and Property Claims Commission in Kosovo, provides for compensation to persons whose property rights were lost as a result of discrimination.[112]

There has also been practice by international organisations calling for or recommending compensation to victims of violations of international humanitarian law in non-international armed conflicts.[113]

---

[107] See Comprehensive Agreement on Human Rights in Guatemala, Article VIII (*ibid.*, § 153); Comprehensive Agreement on Respect for Human Rights and IHL in the Philippines, Part III, Article 2(3) (*ibid.*, § 155); the legislation of Russia (*ibid.*, § 185).

[108] See the practice of Chile (*ibid.*, § 213), El Salvador (*ibid.*, § 216) and Sri Lanka (*ibid.*, §§ 234–235).

[109] See the practice of Chile (*ibid.*, § 213).

[110] See the practice of Rwanda (*ibid.*, § 233) and Zimbabwe (*ibid.*, § 242).

[111] Agreement on Refugees and Displaced Persons annexed to the Dayton Accords, Article XI (*ibid.*, § 154).

[112] UNMIK Regulation No. 2000/60, Section 2(2) (*ibid.*, § 157).

[113] UN Commission on Human Rights, Res. 1995/77 (*ibid.*, § 254); UN Sub-Commission on Human Rights, Res. 1993/23 (*ibid.*, § 255) and Res. 1995/5 (*ibid.*, § 256); UN Secretary-General,

(iii) Satisfaction. There are examples of practice where satisfaction has been provided as a form of reparation, including in the form of rehabilitation, apology, guarantees of non-repetition and establishing the truth. For example, as early as the Spanish Civil War, apologies, guarantees of non-repetition and a promise of punishing persons responsible for certain violations were made.[114]

More recently, the Comprehensive Agreement on Respect for Human Rights and International Humanitarian Law in the Philippines provides for "rehabilitation" as a possible form of reparation.[115] The requirement to establish the truth through investigation and to bring perpetrators to justice was stressed by the Inter-American Commission on Human Rights in a case concerning the murder of Archbishop Romero by death squads in El Salvador in 1980. The Commission established, *inter alia*, that El Salvador was responsible for

failing to carry out its duty to investigate seriously and in good faith the violation of rights recognized by the [American Convention on Human Rights]; to identify the persons responsible for that violation, place them on trial, punish them, and make reparations for the human rights violations.

Referring to decisions by the UN Human Rights Committee, it furthermore stated that "the duty to make reparations for damage is not satisfied merely by offering a sum of money to the victim's next-of-kin. First, an end must be brought to their uncertainty and ignorance, i.e. they must be given the complete and public knowledge of the truth." It stated that this right to know the full, complete and public truth "is part of the right to reparation for human rights violations, with respect to satisfaction and guarantees of non-repetition".[116] The principle that reparation includes the right to the truth, as well as the investigation and prosecution of the persons responsible for human rights violations, was confirmed by the Inter-American Court of Human Rights in the case of *Street Children v. Guatemala* in 2001.[117]

Reparation sought from armed opposition groups

There is some practice to the effect that armed opposition groups are required to provide appropriate reparation for the damage resulting from violations of international humanitarian law. An example is the Comprehensive Agreement on Respect for Human Rights and International Humanitarian Law in the Philippines, which states that "the Parties to the armed conflict shall adhere to and be bound by the generally accepted principles and standards of international

---

Report on the causes of conflict and the promotion of durable peace and sustainable development in Africa (*ibid.*, § 259); UN Commission on the Truth for El Salvador, Report (*ibid.*, § 263).

[114] Spain, Note from the President of the Spanish Junta de Defensa Nacional (*ibid.*, § 361).

[115] Comprehensive Agreement on Respect for Human Rights and IHL in the Philippines, Part III, Article 2(3) (*ibid.*, § 155).

[116] Inter-American Commission on Human Rights, *Monsignor Oscar Arnulfo Romero y Galdámez (El Salvador)* (*ibid.*, § 358).

[117] Inter-American Court of Human Rights, *Street Children v. Guatemala* (*ibid.*, § 359).

humanitarian law" and which provides for indemnification of the victims of violations of international humanitarian law.[118] It is also significant that in 2001 a provincial arm of the ELN in Colombia publicly apologised for the death of three children resulting from an armed attack and the destruction of civilian houses during "an action of war" and expressed its willingness to collaborate in the recuperation of remaining objects.[119]

There is also some practice of the United Nations supporting the obligation of armed opposition groups to provide appropriate reparation. In a resolution on Liberia adopted in 1996, the UN Security Council called upon "the leaders of the factions" to ensure the return of looted property.[120] In a resolution on Afghanistan adopted in 1998, the UN Commission on Human Rights urged "all the Afghan parties" to provide effective remedies to the victims of violations of human rights and humanitarian law.[121] In 1998, in his report on the causes of conflict and the promotion of durable peace and sustainable development in Africa, the UN Secretary-General recommended that "in order to make warring parties more accountable for their actions . . . international legal machinery be developed to facilitate efforts to find, attach and seize the assets of transgressing parties and their leaders".[122]

Even if it can be argued that armed opposition groups incur responsibility for acts committed by persons forming part of such groups (see commentary to Rule 149), the consequences of such responsibility are not clear. In particular, it is unclear to what extent armed opposition groups are under an obligation to make full reparation, even though in many countries victims can bring a civil suit for damages against the offenders (see commentary to Rule 151).

---

[118] Comprehensive Agreement on Respect for Human Rights and IHL in the Philippines, Part III, Article 2(3) and Part IV, Articles 1 and 6 (*ibid.*, § 319).
[119] See the practice of the National Liberation Army (Colombia) (*ibid.*, § 366).
[120] UN Security Council, Res. 1071 (*ibid.*, § 347).
[121] UN Commission on Human Rights, Res. 1998/70 (*ibid.*, § 349).
[122] UN Secretary-General, Report on the causes of conflict and the promotion of durable peace and sustainable development in Africa (*ibid.*, § 259).

INDIVIDUAL RESPONSIBILITY

Rule 151. Individuals are criminally responsible for war crimes they commit.

Practice

Volume II, Chapter 43, Section A.

Summary

State practice establishes this rule as a norm of customary international law applicable in both international and non-international armed conflicts.

International armed conflicts

The principle of individual criminal responsibility for war crimes is a long-standing rule of customary international law already recognised in the Lieber Code and the Oxford Manual and repeated in many treaties of international humanitarian law since then.[1] Individual criminal responsibility for war crimes committed in international armed conflicts was the basis for prosecutions under the Charters of the International Military Tribunals at Nuremberg and at Tokyo, as it is under the Statute of the International Criminal Tribunal for the Former Yugoslavia and the Statute of the International Criminal Court.[2]

Numerous military manuals specify that individuals are criminally responsible for war crimes.[3] The principle of individual criminal responsibility for war

---

[1] See Lieber Code, Articles 44 and 47 (cited in Vol. II, Ch. 43, *ibid.*, §§ 27–28); Oxford Manual, Article 84 (*ibid.*, § 29); First Geneva Convention, Article 49 (*ibid.*, § 7); Second Geneva Convention, Article 50 (*ibid.*, § 7); Third Geneva Convention, Article 129 (*ibid.*, § 7); Fourth Geneva Convention, Article 146 (*ibid.*, § 7); Hague Convention for the Protection of Cultural Property, Article 28 (*ibid.*, § 8); Second Protocol to the Hague Convention for the Protection of Cultural Property, Article 15 (*ibid.*, § 22); Additional Protocol I, Article 85 (adopted by consensus) (*ibid.*, § 10); Amended Protocol II to the Convention on Certain Conventional Weapons, Article 14 (*ibid.*, § 14); Ottawa Convention, Article 9 (*ibid.*, § 15); Optional Protocol to the Convention on the Rights of the Child on the Involvement of Children in Armed Conflict, Article 4 (*ibid.*, § 23).

[2] IMT Charter (Nuremberg), Article 6 (*ibid.*, § 4); IMT Charter (Tokyo), Article 5 (*ibid.*, § 33); ICTY Statute, Articles 2–3 (*ibid.*, § 46); ICC Statute, Articles 5 and 25 (*ibid.*, §§ 18 and 20).

[3] See, e.g., the military manuals of Argentina (*ibid.*, § 64), Australia (*ibid.*, §§ 65–66), Benin (*ibid.*, § 67), Cameroon (*ibid.*, § 68), Canada (*ibid.*, § 69), Colombia (*ibid.*, § 70), Dominican Republic (*ibid.*, § 71), Ecuador (*ibid.*, § 72), El Salvador (*ibid.*, § 73), France (*ibid.*, § 74), Germany (*ibid.*, § 75), Italy (*ibid.*, § 76), Netherlands (*ibid.*, § 77), Peru (*ibid.*, § 78), South Africa (*ibid.*, § 79), Spain

crimes is implemented in the legislation of numerous States.[4] Many suspected war criminals have been tried on the basis of this principle.[5] This rule is also supported by official statements and reported practice.[6]

The principle has also been recalled in numerous resolutions of the UN Security Council, UN General Assembly and UN Commission on Human Rights.[7] It has also been recalled on many occasions by other international organisations.[8]

Non-international armed conflicts

With respect to non-international armed conflicts, significant developments took place from the early 1990s onwards. Individual criminal responsibility for war crimes committed in non-international armed conflicts has been explicitly included in three recent international humanitarian law treaties, namely Amended Protocol II to the Convention on Certain Conventional Weapons, the Statute of the International Criminal Court and the Second Protocol to

---

(*ibid.*, § 80), Sweden (*ibid.*, § 81), Switzerland (*ibid.*, § 82), Togo (*ibid.*, § 83), United Kingdom (*ibid.*, § 84), United States (*ibid.*, §§ 85–88) and Yugoslavia (*ibid.*, § 89).

4 See, e.g., the legislation (*ibid.*, §§ 90–217).

5 See, e.g., Denmark, High Court and Supreme Court, *Sarić case* (*ibid.*, § 221); Germany, Supreme Court of Bavaria, *Djajić case* (*ibid.*, § 224); Germany, Higher Regional Court at Düsseldorf, Federal Supreme Court and Federal Constitutional Court, *Jorgić case* (*ibid.*, § 225); Germany Supreme Court of Bavaria and Federal Supreme Court, *Kusljić case* (*ibid.*, § 226); Germany, Higher Regional Court at Düsseldorf and Federal Supreme Court, *Sokolović case* (*ibid.*, § 227); Israel, District Court of Jerusalem and Supreme Court, *Eichmann case* (*ibid.*, §§ 228–229); Italy, Military Appeals Court and Supreme Court of Cassation, *Hass and Priebke case* (*ibid.*, § 231); Switzerland, Military Tribunal at Lausanne, *Grabež case* (*ibid.*, § 233); see also the cases based on Control Council Law No. 10, including, e.g., United Kingdom, Military Court at Lüneberg, *Auschwitz and Belsen case* (*ibid.*, § 235); United Kingdom, Military Court at Essen, *Essen Lynching case* (*ibid.*, § 236); United States, Military Tribunal at Nuremberg, *Alstötter (The Justice Trial) case* (*ibid.*, § 239), *Flick case* (*ibid.*, § 240), *Krauch (I. G. Farben Trial) case* and *Von Leeb case (The High Command Trial)* (*ibid.*, § 241).

6 See, e.g., the statements of Afghanistan (*ibid.*, § 246), Australia (*ibid.*, §§ 247–248), Austria (*ibid.*, § 249), Chile (*ibid.*, § 250), China (*ibid.*, § 252), Ethiopia (*ibid.*, §§ 253–255), France (*ibid.*, §§ 256–258), Germany (*ibid.*, §§ 259–260), Hungary (*ibid.*, §§ 261–262), Indonesia (*ibid.*, § 263), Israel (*ibid.*, § 264), Netherlands (*ibid.*, § 265), New Zealand (*ibid.*, § 266), Pakistan (*ibid.*, § 268), Rwanda (*ibid.*, § 269), South Africa (*ibid.*, § 270), United Kingdom (*ibid.*, §§ 271–281), United States (*ibid.*, §§ 282–286) and Yugoslavia (*ibid.*, §§ 287–288) and the reported practice of China (*ibid.*, § 251).

7 See, e.g., UN Security Council, Res. 670 (*ibid.*, § 290), Res. 771 (*ibid.*, § 291), Res. 780 (*ibid.*, § 292) and Res. 808 (*ibid.*, § 294); UN General Assembly, Res. 3074 (XXVIII) (*ibid.*, § 333), Res. 47/121 (*ibid.*, § 335), Res. 48/143 (*ibid.*, § 336), Res. 48/153 (*ibid.*, § 337), Res. 49/10 (*ibid.*, § 338), Res. 49/196 (*ibid.*, § 339), Res. 49/205 (*ibid.*, § 340), Res. 50/192 (*ibid.*, § 342), Res. 50/193 (*ibid.*, § 343) and Res. 51/115 (*ibid.*, § 345); UN Commission on Human Rights, Res. 1993/7 (*ibid.*, § 347), Res. 1993/8 (*ibid.*, § 348); 1994/72 (*ibid.*, § 349), Res. 1994/77 (*ibid.*, § 350), Res. 1995/89 (*ibid.*, § 351), Res. 1996/71 (*ibid.*, § 352) and Res. 2002/79 (*ibid.*, § 356).

8 See, e.g., Council of Europe, Parliamentary Assembly, Res. 954 (*ibid.*, § 373), Rec. 1189 (*ibid.*, § 374), Rec. 1218 and Res. 1066 (*ibid.*, § 375); EC, Declaration on Yugoslavia (*ibid.*, § 376); EU, Council, Decision 94/697/CFSP (*ibid.*, § 377); Gulf Cooperation Council, Supreme Council, 13th Session, Final Communiqué (*ibid.*, § 378); League of Arab States, Council, Res. No. 4238 (*ibid.*, § 379); OAU, Council of Ministers, Res. 1650 (LXIV) (*ibid.*, § 380).

the Hague Convention for the Protection of Cultural Property.[9] It is implicitly recognised in two other recent treaties, namely the Ottawa Convention banning anti-personnel landmines and the Optional Protocol to the Convention on the Rights of the Child on the Involvement of Children in Armed Conflict, which require States to criminalise prohibited behaviour, including in non-international armed conflicts.[10] The Statutes of the International Criminal Tribunal for Rwanda and of the Special Court for Sierra Leone explicitly provide that individuals are criminally responsible for war crimes committed in non-international armed conflicts.[11]

Numerous States have adopted legislation criminalising war crimes committed in non-international armed conflicts, most of it in the past decade.[12] It is likely that more will follow, in particular States adopting implementing legislation for ratification of the Statute of the International Criminal Court and wishing to take advantage of its complementarity principle. Several individuals have been tried by national courts for war crimes committed during non-international armed conflicts.[13] There have also been many official statements since the early 1990s in national and international fora regarding individual criminal responsibility in non-international armed conflicts.[14]

---

[9] Amended Protocol II to the Convention on Certain Conventional Weapons, Article 14 (*ibid.*, § 14); ICC Statute, Articles 8 and 25 (*ibid.*, §§ 19–20); Second Protocol to the Hague Convention for the Protection of Cultural Property, Articles 15 and 22 (*ibid.*, § 22).

[10] Ottawa Convention, Article 9 (*ibid.*, § 15); Optional Protocol to the Convention on the Rights of the Child on the Involvement of Children in Armed Conflict, Article 4 (*ibid.*, § 23).

[11] ICTR Statute, Articles 4–5 (*ibid.*, §§ 51–52); Statute of the Special Court for Sierra Leone, Article 1 (*ibid.*, § 24).

[12] See, e.g., the legislation of Armenia (*ibid.*, § 93), Australia (*ibid.*, §§ 94 and 96), Azerbaijan (*ibid.*, §§ 98–99), Bangladesh (*ibid.*, § 100), Belarus (*ibid.*, § 102), Belgium (*ibid.*, § 103), Bosnia and Herzegovina (*ibid.*, § 104), Cambodia (*ibid.*, § 108), Canada (*ibid.*, § 110), Colombia (*ibid.*, § 113), Democratic Republic of the Congo (*ibid.*, § 114), Congo (*ibid.*, § 115), Costa Rica (*ibid.*, § 117), Croatia (*ibid.*, § 119), Cuba (*ibid.*, § 120), El Salvador (*ibid.*, §§ 125–126), Estonia (*ibid.*, § 128), Ethiopia (*ibid.*, § 129), Finland (*ibid.*, § 131), France (*ibid.*, § 135), Georgia (*ibid.*, § 136), Germany (*ibid.*, § 137), Guinea (*ibid.*, § 139), Ireland (*ibid.*, § 142), Italy (*ibid.*, § 144), Kazakhstan (*ibid.*, § 146), Kyrgyzstan (*ibid.*, § 148), Latvia (*ibid.*, § 149), Lithuania (*ibid.*, § 151), Moldova (*ibid.*, § 161), Netherlands (*ibid.*, §§ 163–164), New Zealand (*ibid.*, § 166), Nicaragua (*ibid.*, §§ 168–169), Niger (*ibid.*, § 171), Norway (*ibid.*, § 173), Paraguay (*ibid.*, § 176), Poland (*ibid.*, § 179), Portugal (*ibid.*, § 180), Russia (*ibid.*, § 184), Rwanda (*ibid.*, § 185), Slovenia (*ibid.*, § 189), Spain (*ibid.*, §§ 191–192), Sweden (*ibid.*, § 194), Switzerland (*ibid.*, § 195), Tajikistan (*ibid.*, § 196), Thailand (*ibid.*, § 197), Ukraine (*ibid.*, § 200), United Kingdom (*ibid.*, §§ 202 and 204), United States (*ibid.*, § 207), Uzbekistan (*ibid.*, § 209), Venezuela (*ibid.*, §§ 211–212), Vietnam (*ibid.*, § 213), Yemen (*ibid.*, § 214) and Yugoslavia (*ibid.*, § 216); see also the draft legislation of Argentina (*ibid.*, § 92), Burundi (*ibid.*, § 107), El Salvador (*ibid.*, § 127), Jordan (*ibid.*, § 145), Nicaragua (*ibid.*, § 170), Sri Lanka (*ibid.*, § 193) and Trinidad and Tobago (*ibid.*, § 198); see also the legislation of Austria (*ibid.*, § 97), Bulgaria (*ibid.*, § 106), Czech Republic (*ibid.*, § 123), Guatemala (*ibid.*, § 138), Hungary (*ibid.*, § 140), Italy (*ibid.*, § 144), Mozambique (*ibid.*, § 162), Nicaragua (*ibid.*, § 167), Paraguay (*ibid.*, § 175), Peru (*ibid.*, § 177), Romania (*ibid.*, § 182), Slovakia (*ibid.*, § 188) and Uruguay (*ibid.*, § 208), the application of which is not excluded in time of non-international armed conflict.

[13] See, e.g., Belgium, Cour d'Assises de Bruxelles and Court of Cassation, *The Four from Butare case* (*ibid.*, § 219); Switzerland, Military Tribunal at Lausanne, *Grabež case* (*ibid.*, § 233); Switzerland, Military Tribunal at Lausanne, *Niyonteze case* (*ibid.*, § 234); Yugoslavia, Communal Court of Mitrovica, *Ademi case* (*ibid.*, § 243).

[14] See, e.g., the practice of China (*ibid.*, § 251), Ethiopia (*ibid.*, §§ 254–255), France (*ibid.*, §§ 256–257), Hungary (*ibid.*, § 261), Indonesia (*ibid.*, § 263), Rwanda (*ibid.*, § 269), South

Practice of international organisations has also, since the early 1990s, confirmed the criminality of serious violations of international humanitarian law committed in non-international armed conflicts. The UN Security Council, UN General Assembly and UN Commission on Human Rights have recalled the principle of individual criminal responsibility for war crimes committed in non-international armed conflicts, for example, in Afghanistan, Angola, Bosnia and Herzegovina, Burundi, Rwanda, Sierra Leone, Somalia and the former Yugoslavia.[15] Similar statements were also made by the European Union in relation to Rwanda in 1994 and by the Organization of African Unity in relation to Liberia in 1996.[16]

The trials by the International Criminal Tribunals for the Former Yugoslavia and for Rwanda of persons accused of war crimes committed in non-international armed conflicts confirm that persons are criminally responsible for those crimes. Of particular interest in this regard is the analysis of the Appeals Chamber of the International Criminal Tribunal for the Former Yugoslavia in the *Tadić case* in 1995, in which it concluded that there was individual criminal responsibility for war crimes committed in non-international armed conflicts.[17]

Forms of individual criminal responsibility

Individuals are not only criminally responsible for committing a war crime, but also for attempting to commit a war crime, as well as for assisting in, facilitating, aiding or abetting the commission of a war crime. They are also responsible for planning or instigating the commission of a war crime.[18]

Individual civil liability

It should be noted that recent practice favours the award of reparations to victims of war crimes. This is most noticeable in Article 75(2) of the Statute of

Africa (*ibid.*, § 270), United Kingdom (*ibid.*, §§ 278–281), United States (*ibid.*, §§ 284–285) and Yugoslavia (*ibid.*, § 288).

[15] See, e.g., UN Security Council, Res. 771 (*ibid.*, § 291), Res. 780 (*ibid.*, § 292), Res. 794 (*ibid.*, § 293), Res. 808 (*ibid.*, § 294), Res. 814 (*ibid.*, § 295), Res. 820 (*ibid.*, § 296), Res. 827 (*ibid.*, § 297), Res. 859 (*ibid.*, § 298), Res. 913 (*ibid.*, § 299), Res. 935 (*ibid.*, § 300), Res. 955 (*ibid.*, § 301), Res. 1009 (*ibid.*, § 302), Res. 1012 (*ibid.*, § 303), Res. 1034 (*ibid.*, § 304), Res. 1072 (*ibid.*, § 305) and Res. 1087 (*ibid.*, § 306), Res. 1193 (*ibid.*, § 307) and Res. 1315 (*ibid.*, § 310); UN General Assembly, Res. 47/121 (*ibid.* § 335), Res. 48/143 (*ibid.*, § 336), Res. 48/153 (*ibid.*, § 337), Res. 49/10 (*ibid.*, § 338), Res. 49/196 (*ibid.*, § 339), Res. 49/205 (*ibid.*, § 340), Res. 49/206 (*ibid.*, § 341), Res. 50/192 (*ibid.*, § 342), Res. 50/193 (*ibid.*, § 343), Res. 51/108 (*ibid.*, § 344) and Res. 51/115 (*ibid.*, § 345); UN Commission on Human Rights, Res. 1993/7 (*ibid.*, § 347), Res. 1993/8 (*ibid.*, § 348), Res. 1994/72 (*ibid.*, § 349), Res. 1994/77 (*ibid.*, § 350), Res. 1995/89 (*ibid.*, § 351), Res. 1996/71 (*ibid.*, § 352), Res. 1995/91 (*ibid.*, § 353) and Res. 1999/1 (*ibid.*, § 355).

[16] EU, Council, Decision 94/697/CFSP (*ibid.*, § 377); OAU, Council of Ministers, Res. 1650 (LXIV) (*ibid.*, § 380).

[17] ICTY, *Tadić case*, Interlocutory Appeal (*ibid.*, § 391).

[18] See, e.g., ICC Statute, Article 25 (*ibid.*, § 20); ICTY Statute, Article 7 (*ibid.*, § 48); ICTR Statute, Article 6 (*ibid.*, 53); Statute of the Special Court for Sierra Leone, Article 6 (*ibid.*, § 26); UNTAET Regulation No. 2000/15, Section 14 (*ibid.*, § 62).

the International Criminal Court concerning "Reparations to victims", which gives the Court the power to "make an order directly against a convicted person specifying appropriate reparations to, or in respect of, victims, including restitution, compensation and rehabilitation".[19] UNTAET Regulation No. 2000/30 for East Timor gives the Court, i.e., the competent panels within the District Court in Dili and the Court of Appeal in Dili, the power "to include in its disposition an order that requires the accused to pay compensation or reparations to the victim".[20] This goes further than the powers of the International Criminal Tribunals for the Former Yugoslavia and for Rwanda whose Statutes only give them the power to "order the return of any property and proceeds acquired by criminal conduct, including by means of duress, to their rightful owner".[21] The Rules of Procedure and Evidence of the Tribunals state, however, that "pursuant to the relevant national legislation, a victim or persons claiming through the victim may bring an action in a national court or other competent body to obtain compensation".[22]

In a report on the causes of conflict and the promotion of durable peace and sustainable development in Africa, the UN Secretary-General recommended that "combatants be held financially liable to their victims under international law where civilians are made the deliberate target of aggression" in order to make warring parties more accountable for their actions.[23] In a report on human rights in Rwanda, the Special Representative of the UN Commission on Human Rights for Rwanda noted that "those convicted of crimes against property will be expected to pay restitution for the damage they caused" during the *gacaca* trials instituted in Rwanda to try genocide suspects.[24]

Under the domestic legislation of many States, victims can also bring claims before civil courts, and there are some examples of such suits being successfully brought.[25] In addition, some States provide in their national law for the possibility for courts in criminal matters to order reparation, including restoration or restitution of property, for victims of war crimes.[26]

---

[19] ICC Statute, Article 75(2) (*ibid.*, § 416).
[20] UNTAET Regulation No. 2000/30, Section 49(2) (*ibid.*, § 417).
[21] ICTY Statute, Article 24(3) (*ibid.*, § 411); ICTR Statute, Article 23(3) (*ibid.*, § 412); see also Rules of Procedure and Evidence of the International Criminal Tribunals for the Former Yugoslavia and for Rwanda, Rule 105 (*ibid.*, §§ 413 and 418).
[22] Rules of Procedure and Evidence of the International Criminal Tribunals for the Former Yugoslavia and for Rwanda, Rule 106(B) (*ibid.*, §§ 414 and 419).
[23] UN Secretary-General, Report on the causes of conflict and the promotion of durable peace and sustainable development in Africa (*ibid.*, § 450).
[24] UN Commission on Human Rights, Report of the Special Representative for Rwanda (*ibid.*, § 451).
[25] See, e.g., Italy, Tribunal at Livorno and Court of Appeals at Florence, *Ercole case* (*ibid.*, § 437); United States, Court of Appeals for the Second Circuit and District Court, Southern District of New York, *Karadžić case* (*ibid.*, §§ 438–439).
[26] See, e.g., the legislation of France (*ibid.*, §§ 423 and 426), Germany (*ibid.*, § 427), Luxembourg (*ibid.*, § 428) (restitution of seized objects and exhibits), United Kingdom (*ibid.*, § 431) (restitution of money or property), United States (*ibid.*, § 432) and Yemen (*ibid.*, § 436) (restitution); see also the draft legislation of Burundi (*ibid.*, § 425).

Rule 152. Commanders and other superiors are criminally responsible for war crimes committed pursuant to their orders.

Practice

Volume II, Chapter 43, Section B.

Summary

State practice establishes this rule as a norm of customary international law applicable in both international and non-international armed conflicts.

International and non-international armed conflicts

The rule that persons are responsible for war crimes committed pursuant to their orders is contained in the Geneva Conventions and the Hague Convention for the Protection of Cultural Property and its Second Protocol, which require States to prosecute not only persons who commit grave breaches or breaches respectively but also persons who order their commission.[27] The Statutes of the International Criminal Court, of the International Criminal Tribunals for the Former Yugoslavia and for Rwanda and of the Special Court for Sierra Leone and UNTAET Regulation No. 2000/15 for East Timor, all of which apply in both international and non-international armed conflicts, also contain this rule.[28]

Many military manuals provide that commanders and other superiors are responsible for war crimes committed pursuant to their orders.[29] This rule is also set forth in the legislation of many States.[30] There is national case-law dating from the First World War to the present day which confirms the rule

---

[27] First Geneva Convention, Article 49 (*ibid.*, § 457); Second Geneva Convention, Article 50 (*ibid.*, § 457); Third Geneva Convention, Article 129 (*ibid.*, § 457); Fourth Geneva Convention, Article 146 (*ibid.*, § 457); Hague Convention for the Protection of Cultural Property, Article 28 (*ibid.*, § 458); Second Protocol to the Hague Convention for the Protection of Cultural Property, Article 15 (*ibid.*, § 461).

[28] ICC Statute, Article 25(3) (*ibid.*, § 460); ICTY Statute, Article 7(1) (*ibid.*, § 467); ICTR Statute, Article 6(1) (*ibid.*, § 468); Statute of the Special Court for Sierra Leone, Article 6 (*ibid.*, § 463); UNTAET Regulation No. 2000/15, Section 14(3) (*ibid.*, § 472).

[29] See, e.g., the military manuals Argentina (*ibid.*, § 473), Australia (*ibid.*, § 474), Belgium (*ibid.*, § 475), Cameroon (*ibid.*, § 476), Canada (*ibid.*, §§ 477–478), Congo (*ibid.*, § 479), France (*ibid.*, §§ 480–481), Germany (*ibid.*, § 482), Italy (*ibid.*, § 483), New Zealand (*ibid.*, § 4843), Nigeria (*ibid.*, § 485), South Africa (*ibid.*, § 486), Spain (*ibid.*, § 487), Switzerland (*ibid.*, § 488), United Kingdom (*ibid.*, §§ 489–490), United States (*ibid.*, §§ 491–492) and Yugoslavia (*ibid.*, § 493).

[30] See, e.g., the legislation of Argentina (*ibid.*, § 494), Armenia (*ibid.*, § 496), Azerbaijan (*ibid.*, § 497), Bangladesh (*ibid.*, § 498), Belarus (*ibid.*, § 499), Belgium (*ibid.*, §§ 500–501), Cambodia (*ibid.*, § 503), Costa Rica (*ibid.*, § 504), Ethiopia (*ibid.*, § 505), Germany (*ibid.*, §§ 506–507), Iraq (*ibid.*, § 508), Luxembourg (*ibid.*, § 511), Mexico (*ibid.*, § 512), Netherlands (*ibid.*, §§ 513–514), Russia (*ibid.*, § 516), Switzerland (*ibid.*, § 517) and Yugoslavia (*ibid.*, § 518); see also the draft legislation of Argentina (*ibid.*, § 495), Burundi (*ibid.*, § 502), Jordan (*ibid.*, § 509), Lebanon (*ibid.*, § 510) and Nicaragua (*ibid.*, § 515).

that commanders are responsible for the war crimes committed pursuant to their orders.[31] Further practice is contained in official statements.[32]

The UN Security Council, UN General Assembly, UN Secretary-General and UN Commissions of Experts Established pursuant to Security Council Resolutions 780 (1992) and 935 (1994) have recalled this rule.[33]

This rule has been reaffirmed in various cases before the International Criminal Tribunals for the Former Yugoslavia and for Rwanda.[34]

While some practice refers specifically to orders issued by commanders,[35] or superiors,[36] other practice refers more generally to orders issued by any person.[37] International case-law has held, however, that while no formal

---

[31] See, e.g., Argentina, National Court of Appeals, *Military Junta case* (*ibid.*, § 519); Canada, Military Court at Aurich, *Abbaye Ardenne case*, Statement by the Judge Advocate (*ibid.*, § 520); Canada, Court Martial Appeal Court, *Seward case* (*ibid.*, § 521); Croatia, District Court of Zadar, *Perišić and Others case* (*ibid.*, § 522); Germany, Reichsgericht, *Dover Castle case* (*ibid.*, § 523); United States, Military Commission at Rome, *Dostler case* (*ibid.*, § 524); United States, Federal Court of Florida, *Ford v. García case* (*ibid.*, § 526).

[32] See, e.g., the practice of Slovenia (*ibid.*, § 531), United Kingdom (*ibid.*, §§ 532–533) and United States (*ibid.*, §§ 534–535).

[33] See, e.g., UN Security Council, Res. 670 (*ibid.*, § 536), Res. 771 (*ibid.*, § 537), Res. 780 (*ibid.*, § 538), Res. 794 (*ibid.*, § 539), Res. 808 (*ibid.*, § 540), Res. 820 (*ibid.*, § 541) and Res. 1193 (*ibid.*, § 542); UN Security Council, Statements by the President (*ibid.*, §§ 543–546); UN General Assembly Res. 50/193 (*ibid.*, § 547); UN Secretary-General, Report pursuant to Paragraph 2 of Security Council Resolution 808 (1993) (*ibid.*, § 548); UN Commission of Experts Established pursuant to Security Council Resolution 780 (1992), Final report (*ibid.*, § 549); UN Commission of Experts Established pursuant to Security Council Resolution 935 (1994), Final report (*ibid.*, § 550).

[34] See, e.g., ICTR, *Akayesu case*, Judgement (*ibid.*, § 553) and *Kayishema and Ruzindana case*, Judgement (*ibid.*, § 554); ICTY, *Martić case*, Review of the Indictment (*ibid.*, § 556), *Karadžić and Mladić case*, Review of the Indictments (*ibid.*, § 557), *Rajić case*, Review of the Indictment (*ibid.*, § 558), *Delalić case*, Judgement (*ibid.*, § 559), *Blaškić case*, Judgement (*ibid.*, § 560), *Kordić and Čerkez case*, Judgement (*ibid.*, § 561) and *Krstić case*, Judgement (*ibid.*, § 562).

[35] See, e.g., the military manuals of Australia (*ibid.*, § 474), Cameroon (*ibid.*, § 476), Congo (*ibid.*, § 479), France (*ibid.*, §§ 480–481), New Zealand (*ibid.*, § 484), Nigeria (*ibid.*, § 485), Switzerland (*ibid.*, § 488), United Kingdom (*ibid.*, § 489) and United States (*ibid.*, § 491); Argentina, *Military Junta case* (*ibid.*, § 519); United States, Military Commission at Rome, *Dostler case* (*ibid.*, § 524); United States, Federal Court of Florida, *Ford v. García case* (*ibid.*, § 526); the practice of the United States (*ibid.*, §§ 534–535); the reported practice of Pakistan (*ibid.*, § 530); ICTY, *Delalić case*, Judgement (*ibid.*, § 559)

[36] See, e.g., the military manual of Belgium (*ibid.*, § 475), Germany (*ibid.*, § 482) and Switzerland (*ibid.*, § 488); Germany, Reichsgericht, *Dover Castle case* (*ibid.*, § 523); ICTY, *Delalić case*, Judgement (*ibid.*, § 559).

[37] See, e.g., First Geneva Convention, Article 49, second paragraph (*ibid.*, § 457); Second Geneva Convention, Article 50, second paragraph (*ibid.*, § 457); Third Geneva Convention, Article 129, second paragraph (*ibid.*, § 457); Fourth Geneva Convention, Article 146, second paragraph (*ibid.*, § 457); Hague Convention for the Protection of Cultural Property, Article 28 (*ibid.*, § 458); ICC Statute, Article 25(3) (*ibid.*, § 460); Statute of the Special Court for Sierra Leone, Article 6(1) (*ibid.*, § 463); ICTY Statute, Article 7(1) (*ibid.*, § 467); ICTR Statute, Article 6(1) (*ibid.*, 468); UNTAET Regulation No. 2000/15, Section 14(3) (*ibid.*, § 472); the military manuals of Argentina (*ibid.*, § 473), Canada (*ibid.*, § 477), Italy (*ibid.*, § 483), South Africa (*ibid.*, § 486), Spain (*ibid.*, § 487), United Kingdom (*ibid.*, § 490) and Yugoslavia (*ibid.*, § 493); the statement of Slovenia (*ibid.*, § 531); UN Security Council, Res. 670 (*ibid.*, § 536), Res. 771 (*ibid.*, § 537), Res. 780 (*ibid.*, § 538), Res. 794 (*ibid.*, § 539), Res. 808 (*ibid.*, § 540), Res. 820 (*ibid.*, § 541) and Res. 1193 (*ibid.*, § 542).

superior-subordinate relationship is required, "ordering" implies at least that a superior-subordinate relationship exists *de facto*.[38]

Interpretation

With respect to the actions undertaken by subordinates in accordance with an order to commit war crimes, three situations must be distinguished. First, in case the war crimes are actually *committed*, State practice is clear that there is command responsibility, as stated in this rule. Secondly, when the war crimes are not actually committed but only *attempted*, State practice tends to indicate that there is also command responsibility. The Statute of the International Criminal Court and UNTAET Regulation No. 2000/15 for East Timor specify that there is command responsibility for ordering the commission of a war crime when the crime in fact occurs or is attempted.[39] Some national legislation specifies that a commander who gives an order to commit a crime is guilty, even if the subordinate only attempts to carry out the crime.[40] Thirdly, in case the war crimes are neither carried out nor attempted, a few States do attribute criminal responsibility to a commander merely ordering the commission of a war crime.[41] But most practice indicates no command responsibility in such cases. It is clear, however, that if a rule consists of a prohibition on giving an order, for example, the prohibition on ordering that there be no survivors (see Rule 46), then the commander who gives the order is guilty, even if the order is not carried out.

Rule 153. Commanders and other superiors are criminally responsible for war crimes committed by their subordinates if they knew, or had reason to know, that the subordinates were about to commit or were committing such crimes and did not take all necessary and reasonable measures in their power to prevent their commission, or if such crimes had been committed, to punish the persons responsible.

Practice

Volume II, Chapter 43, Section C.

[38] See, e.g., ICTR, *Akayesu case*, Judgement (*ibid.*, § 553) and *Kayishema and Ruzindana case*, Judgement (*ibid.*, § 554); ICTY, *Kordić and Čerkez case*, Judgement (*ibid.*, § 561); see also Croatia, District Court of Zadar, *Perišić and Others case* ("persons who were in a position to issue orders for combat") (*ibid.*, § 522); ICTY, *Martić case*, Review of the Indictment ("persons who, through their position of political or military authority, are able to order the commission of crimes") (*ibid.*, § 556).

[39] ICC Statute, Article 25(3)(b) (*ibid.*, § 460); UNTAET Regulation No. 2000/15, Section 14(3) (*ibid.*, § 472).

[40] See, e.g., the legislation of Belgium (*ibid.*, § 501), Germany (*ibid.*, § 507), Luxembourg (*ibid.*, § 511) and Netherlands (*ibid.*, § 513).

[41] See, e.g., the legislation of Belgium (*ibid.*, § 501), Luxembourg (*ibid.*, § 511) and Netherlands (*ibid.*, § 513).

Summary

State practice establishes this rule as a norm of customary international law applicable in both international and non-international armed conflicts.

International armed conflicts

The criminal responsibility of commanders for war crimes committed by their subordinates, based on the commanders' failure to take measures to prevent or punish the commission of such crimes is a long-standing rule of customary international law. It is on this basis that a number of commanders were found guilty of war crimes committed by their subordinates in several trials following the Second World War.[42]

This rule is to be found in Additional Protocol I, as well as in the Statutes of the International Criminal Court and of the International Criminal Tribunal for the Former Yugoslavia.[43] It has also been confirmed in several cases before the International Criminal Tribunal for the Former Yugoslavia.[44]

Military manuals, military instructions and the legislation of a number of States specify the responsibility of commanders for the crimes of their subordinates, including States not, or not at the time, party to Additional Protocol I.[45]

This rule was recalled in resolutions on the conflict in the former Yugoslavia adopted by the UN General Assembly and UN Commission on Human Rights.[46]

Non-international armed conflicts

Practice with respect to non-international armed conflicts is less extensive and more recent. However, the practice that does exist indicates that it is

---

[42] See, e.g., United Kingdom, Military Court at Wuppertal, *Rauer case* (*ibid.*, § 656); United States, Military Tribunal at Nuremberg, *Von Leeb (The High Command Trial) case* (*ibid.*, § 657) and *List (Hostages Trial) case* (*ibid.*, § 658); United States, Supreme Court, *Yamashita case* (*ibid.*, § 659); IMT (Tokyo), *Case of the Major War Criminals* (*ibid.*, §§ 693–700) and *Toyoda case* (*ibid.*, § 701).

[43] Additional Protocol I, Article 86(2) (adopted by consensus) (*ibid.*, § 569); ICC Statute, Article 28 (*ibid.*, § 574); ICTY Statute, Article 7(3) (*ibid.*, § 581).

[44] See, e.g., ICTY, *Martić case*, Review of the Indictment (*ibid.*, § 705), *Karadžić and Mladić case*, Review of the Indictments (*ibid.*, § 706), *Delalić case*, Judgement (*ibid.*, § 707), *Aleksovski case*, Judgement (*ibid.*, § 708), *Blaškić case*, Judgement (*ibid.*, § 709), *Kunarac case*, Judgement (*ibid.*, § 711), *Kordić and Čerkez case*, Judgement (*ibid.*, § 712), *Krstić case*, Judgement (*ibid.*, § 713) and *Kvočka case*, Judgement (*ibid.*, § 714).

[45] See, e.g., the military manuals of the United Kingdom (*ibid.*, § 613) and United States (*ibid.*, §§ 614–618); see also the practice of Italy (*ibid.*, § 669) and the legislation of Azerbaijan (*ibid.*, § 623), Bangladesh (*ibid.*, § 625), France (*ibid.*, § 633), Italy (*ibid.*, § 635), Luxembourg (*ibid.*, § 638), Netherlands (*ibid.*, § 640), Spain (*ibid.*, § 643), Sweden (*ibid.*, § 645), Philippines (*ibid.*, §§ 604–606).

[46] See, e.g., UN General Assembly, Res. 48/143, 50/192 and 51/115 (*ibid.*, § 680) and Res. 49/205 (*ibid.*, § 681); UN Commission on Human Rights, Res. 1994/77 (*ibid.*, § 683).

uncontroversial that this rule also applies to war crimes committed in non-international armed conflicts. In particular, the Statutes of the International Criminal Court, of the International Criminal Tribunals for the Former Yugoslavia and for Rwanda and of the Special Court for Sierra Leone and UNTAET Regulation No. 2000/15 for East Timor explicitly provide for this rule in the context of non-international armed conflicts.[47] The fact that this rule would also apply to crimes committed in non-international armed conflicts did not occasion any controversy during the negotiation of the Statute of the International Criminal Court.

In the *Hadžihasanović and Others case*, the International Criminal Tribunal for the Former Yugoslavia held that the doctrine of command responsibility, as a principle of customary international law, also applies with regard to non-international armed conflicts.[48] This rule has also been confirmed in several cases brought before the International Criminal Tribunal for Rwanda.[49]

There is national case-law applying this rule to situations outside international armed conflicts. A US Federal Court in Florida applied it in the *Ford v. García case* in 2000, which concerned a civil lawsuit dealing with acts of extra-judicial killing and torture committed in El Salvador.[50] The Ad Hoc Tribunal on Human Rights for East Timor applied it in the *Abilio Soares case* in 2002 in which the Tribunal considered that the conflict in East Timor was an internal one within the meaning of common Article 3 of the Geneva Conventions.[51] In the *Boland case* in 1995, Canada's Court Martial Appeal Court found a superior guilty of having neglected to prevent the death of a prisoner even though he had grounds to fear that his subordinate would endanger the prisoner's life.[52] In the *Military Junta case*, Argentina's Court of Appeal based its judgement on the failure of commanders to punish perpetrators of torture and extra-judicial killings.[53]

Other practice to this effect includes the report of the UN Commission on the Truth for El Salvador in 1993, which pointed out that the judicial instances failed to take steps to determine the criminal responsibility of the superiors of persons guilty of arbitrary killings.[54]

---

[47] ICC Statute, Article 28 (*ibid.*, § 574); ICTY Statute, Article 7(3) (*ibid.*, § 581); ICTR Statute, Article 6(3) (*ibid.*, § 582); Statute of the Special Court for Sierra Leone, Article 6(3) (*ibid.*, § 577); UNTAET Regulation No. 2000/15, Section 16 (*ibid.*, § 585).

[48] ICTY, *Hadžihasanović and Others case*, Decision on Joint Challenge to Jurisdiction (*ibid.*, § 716). In this respect, the interlocutory appeal filed by the accused was unanimously dismissed by the Appeals Chamber, see ICTY, *Hadžihasanović and Others case*, Decision on Interlocutory Appeal Challenging Jurisdiction in Relation to Command Responsibility, 16 July 2003, Case No. IT-01-47-AR72, § 57 (Disposition on the first ground of appeal).

[49] See ICTR, *Akayesu case*, Judgement (cited in Vol. II, Ch. 43, § 702) and *Kayishema and Ruzindana case*, Judgement (*ibid.*, § 703).

[50] United States, Federal Court of Florida, *Ford v. García case* (*ibid.*, § 661).

[51] Indonesia, Ad Hoc Tribunal on Human Rights for East Timor, *Abilio Soares case* (*ibid.*, § 654).

[52] Canada, Court Martial Appeal Court, *Boland case* (*ibid.*, § 650).

[53] Argentina, Court of Appeal, *Military Junta case* (*ibid.*, § 649).

[54] UN Commission on the Truth for El Salvador, Report (*ibid.*, § 690).

Interpretation

This rule has been interpreted in case-law following the Second World War and also in the case-law of the International Criminal Tribunals for the Former Yugoslavia and for Rwanda. This includes, but is not limited to, the following points:

    (i) Civilian command authority. Not only military personnel but also civilians can be liable for war crimes on the basis of command responsibility. The International Criminal Tribunal for Rwanda, in the *Akayesu case* in 1998 and in the *Kayishema and Ruzindana case* in 1999, and the International Criminal Tribunal for the Former Yugoslavia, in the *Delalić case* in 1998, have adopted this interpretation.[55] It is also contained in the Statute of the International Criminal Court.[56] The Statutes of the International Criminal Tribunals for the Former Yugoslavia and for Rwanda and of the Special Court for Sierra Leone refer in general terms to a "superior,[57] as do many military manuals and national legislation.[58]

    (ii) Commander/subordinate relationship. The relationship between the commander and the subordinate does not necessarily need to be a direct *de jure* one. *De facto* command responsibility is sufficient to occasion liability of the commander. This principle is recognised in various judgements of the International Criminal Tribunals for the Former Yugoslavia and for Rwanda.[59] The Tribunals identified the actual possession of control over the actions of subordinates, in the sense of material ability to prevent and punish the commission of crimes, as the crucial criterion.[60] The same idea is reflected in Article 25 of the Statute of the International Criminal Court.[61]

    (iii) The commander/superior knew, or had reason to know. Practice confirms that command responsibility is not limited to situations where the commander/superior has actual knowledge of the crimes committed or about to be committed by his or her subordinates, but that constructive knowledge is sufficient. The latter idea is expressed in various sources with slightly different formulations: "had reason to know",[62] "had information which should have

---

[55] ICTR Rwanda, *Akayesu case*, Judgement (*ibid.*, § 702) and *Kayishema and Ruzindana case*, Judgement (*ibid.*, § 703); ICTY, *Delalić case*, Judgement (*ibid.*, § 707).

[56] ICC Statute, Article 28 (*ibid.*, § 574).

[57] ICTY Statute, Article 7(3) (*ibid.*, § 581); ICTR Statute, Article 6(3) (*ibid.*, § 582); Statute of the Special Court for Sierra Leone, Article 6(3) (*ibid.*, § 577).

[58] See, e.g., the military manuals of Belgium (*ibid.*, § 588), Netherlands (*ibid.*, § 599), Sweden (*ibid.*, § 610), Uruguay (*ibid.*, § 619) and Yugoslavia (*ibid.*, § 620) and the legislation of Belarus (*ibid.*, § 626), Cambodia (*ibid.*, § 628), Canada (*ibid.*, § 629), Estonia (*ibid.*, § 622), France (*ibid.*, § 633), Germany (*ibid.*, § 634), Netherlands (*ibid.*, § 641), Rwanda (*ibid.*, § 642) and United States (*ibid.*, § 647); see also the draft legislation of Argentina (*ibid.*, § 621), El Salvador (*ibid.*, § 631) and Lebanon (*ibid.*, § 637).

[59] See, e.g., ICTR, *Kayishema and Ruzindana case*, Judgement (*ibid.*, § 703); ICTY, *Delalić case*, Judgement (*ibid.*, § 707), *Aleksovski case*, Judgement (*ibid.*, § 708), *Blaškić case*, Judgement (*ibid.*, § 709), *Kunarac case*, Judgement (*ibid.*, § 711) and *Kvočka case*, Judgement (*ibid.*, § 714).

[60] See, e.g., ICTY, *Delalić case*, Judgement (*ibid.*, § 707), *Aleksovski case*, Judgement (*ibid.*, § 708) and *Kvočka case*, Judgement (*ibid.*, § 714).

[61] ICC Statute, Article 28 (*ibid.*, § 574).

[62] See, e.g., ICTY Statute, Article 7(3) (*ibid.*, § 581); ICTR Statute, Article 6(3) (*ibid.*, § 582) and related case-law (*ibid.*, §§ 702–716); Statute of the Special Court for Sierra Leone, Article 6(3) (*ibid.*, § 577); UNTAET Regulation No. 2000/15, Section 16 (*ibid.*, § 585); Canada, *LOAC Manual*

enabled [the commander/superior] to conclude in the circumstances at the time",[63] the commander/superior "(owing to the circumstances at the time,) should have known",[64] the commander/superior was "at fault in having failed to acquire such knowledge",[65] and the commander/superior was "criminally negligent in failing to know".[66] These formulations essentially cover the concept of constructive knowledge.

For superiors other than military commanders, the Statute of the International Criminal Court uses the language: "consciously disregarded information which clearly indicated".[67] This standard was used by the International Criminal Tribunal for Rwanda in the *Kayishema and Ruzindana case* in 1999 to delineate the meaning of "had reason to know" for non-military commanders.[68]

(iv) Investigation and reporting. Failure to punish subordinates who commit war crimes can result from a failure to *investigate* possible crimes and/or failure to *report* allegations of war crimes to higher authorities. This is set forth in Additional Protocol I and in the Statute of the International Criminal Court.[69] It is also the standard in many military manuals, national legislation, national case-law and other practice.[70] In its final report on grave breaches of the Geneva Conventions and other violations of international humanitarian law committed in the former Yugoslavia, the UN Commission of Experts Established pursuant to Security Council Resolution 780 (1992) recalled this basis of command responsibility.[71]

In its judgement in the *Blaškić case* in 2000, the International Criminal Tribunal for the Former Yugoslavia specified, however, that a commander must give priority, where he or she knows or has reason to know that his or her subordinates are about to commit crimes, to prevent these crimes from being

---

(*ibid.*, § 591); Cambodia, *Law on the Khmer Rouge Trial* (*ibid.*, § 628); UN Secretary-General, Report on the draft ICTY Statute (*ibid.*, § 685).

[63] See, e.g., Additional Protocol I, Article 86(2) (adopted by consensus) (*ibid.*, § 569); the military manuals of Canada (*ibid.*, § 591), Netherlands (*ibid.*, § 599), New Zealand (*ibid.*, § 601), Sweden (*ibid.*, § 610), United Kingdom (*ibid.*, § 613) and United States (*ibid.*, §§ 614–615 and 617–618); Indonesia, Ad Hoc Tribunal on Human Rights for East Timor, *Abilio Soares case*, Indictment and Judgement (*ibid.*, § 654).

[64] See, e.g., ICC Statute, Article 28 (*ibid.*, § 574); the military manuals of Australia (*ibid.*, § 587), Belgium (*ibid.*, § 588), Canada (*ibid.*, § 591) and New Zealand (*ibid.*, § 601); United States, Federal Court of Florida, *Ford v. García case*, Judgement (*ibid.*, § 661); the practice of the United States (*ibid.*, §§ 676–677).

[65] See, e.g., IMT (Tokyo), *Case of the Major War Criminals* (*ibid.*, § 693).

[66] See, e.g., Canada, *Crimes against Humanity and War Crimes Act* (*ibid.*, § 629).

[67] ICC Statute, Article 28(2) (*ibid.*, § 574).

[68] ICTR, *Kayishema and Ruzindana case*, Judgement (*ibid.*, § 703).

[69] Additional Protocol I, Article 87(1) (*ibid.*, § 570); ICC Statute, Article 28(a)(ii) and (b)(iii) (*ibid.*, § 574).

[70] See, e.g., the military manuals of Argentina (*ibid.*, § 724), Australia (*ibid.*, §§ 725–726), Benin (*ibid.*, § 727), Canada (*ibid.*, §§ 728–729), Colombia (*ibid.*, § 730), Dominican Republic (*ibid.*, § 731), El Salvador (*ibid.*, § 732), Germany (*ibid.*, § 733), Netherlands (*ibid.*, §§ 734–735), Nigeria (*ibid.*, § 736), Peru (*ibid.*, § 737), Philippines (*ibid.*, § 738), South Africa (*ibid.*, §§ 739–740), Sweden (*ibid.*, §§ 610 and 741), Togo (*ibid.*, § 742) and United States (*ibid.*, §§ 743–744), the legislation of Argentina (*ibid.*, § 621), Canada (*ibid.*, § 729), Egypt (*ibid.*, § 630), Germany (*ibid.*, § 745), India (*ibid.*, § 746), Ukraine (*ibid.*, § 646), United States (*ibid.*, § 647) and the practice of the United States (*ibid.*, §§ 750–752) and Yugoslavia (*ibid.*, § 753).

[71] UN Commission of Experts Established pursuant to Security Council Resolution 780 (1992), Final report (*ibid.*, §§ 689 and 754).

committed and that "he cannot make up for the failure to act by punishing the subordinates afterwards".[72]

(v) *Necessary and reasonable measures.* In the *Delalić case* in 1998, the International Criminal Tribunal for the Former Yugoslavia interpreted the term "necessary and reasonable measures" to be limited to such measures as are within someone's power, as no one can be obliged to perform the impossible.[73] With respect to necessary and reasonable measures to ensure the punishment of suspected war criminals, the Tribunal held in the *Kvočka case* in 2001 that the superior does not necessarily have to dispense the punishment but "must take an important step in the disciplinary process".[74] In its judgement in the *Blaškić case* in 2000, the Tribunal held that "under some circumstances, a commander may discharge his obligation to prevent or punish an offence by reporting the matter to the competent authorities".[75]

Rule 154. Every combatant has a duty to disobey a manifestly unlawful order.

Practice

Volume II, Chapter 43, Section D.

Summary

State practice establishes this rule as a norm of customary international law applicable to orders given in both international and non-international armed conflicts.

Manifestly unlawful orders

This rule flows from the duty to respect international humanitarian law (see Rule 139) and is also a corollary of the rule that obeying a superior order is not a defence of a war crime, if the subordinate should have known that the act ordered was unlawful because of its manifestly unlawful nature (see Rule 155). In finding that superior orders, if manifestly unlawful, cannot be a defence, several courts based their judgements on the fact that such orders must be disobeyed.[76]

Besides the practice related to the defence of superior orders, practice specifying that there is a duty to disobey an order that is manifestly unlawful or that would entail the commission of a war crime is contained in the military

---

[72] ICTY, *Blaškić case*, Judgement (*ibid.*, § 709).
[73] ICTY, *Delalić case*, Judgement (*ibid.*, § 707).
[74] ICTY, *Kvočka case*, Judgement (*ibid.*, § 714).
[75] ICTY, *Blaškić case*, Judgement (*ibid.*, §§ 709 and 757).
[76] See, e.g., Belgium, Court-Martial of Brussels, *Sergeant W. case* (*ibid.*, § 820); Israel, District Military Court for the Central Judicial District and Military Court of Appeal, *Ofer, Malinki and Others case* (*ibid.*, § 825); Netherlands, Special Court in Amsterdam, *Zühlke case* (*ibid.*, § 827); United States, Army Court of Military Appeals, *Calley case* (*ibid.*, § 829).

manuals, legislation and official statements of numerous States.[77] This rule is confirmed in national case-law.[78]

This practice, together with the fact that a subordinate who commits a war crime pursuant to an order which is manifestly unlawful cannot invoke that order as a defence and remains guilty of that crime (see Rule 155), means that there is a duty to disobey such an order.

Unlawful orders

With respect to the position of a combatant who disobeys an order that is unlawful, but not manifestly so, practice is unclear. Many countries specify in their military law that it is the duty of all subordinates to obey "lawful" or "legitimate" orders and that not to do so is a punishable offence.[79] Although this could be interpreted as implying that subordinates must not obey unlawful orders, no practice was found stating such an obligation. Some practice was found providing for a right to disobey an unlawful order.[80] Disobedience of an unlawful order should not entail criminal responsibility, under domestic law, as subordinates only have a duty to obey lawful orders.[81]

Armed opposition groups

As mentioned above, this rule flows from the duty to respect international humanitarian law (see Rule 139) and is also a corollary to the rule that obeying

---

[77] See, e.g., the military manuals of Australia (ibid., § 765), Belgium (ibid., § 766), Cameroon (ibid., §§ 768–769), Canada (ibid., § 770), Congo (ibid., § 771), Dominican Republic (ibid., § 772), El Salvador (ibid., § 773), France (ibid., § 774), Germany (ibid., §§ 775 and 915), Italy (ibid., § 776), Netherlands (ibid., § 777), New Zealand (ibid., § 778), Rwanda (ibid., § 781), South Africa (ibid., §§ 782–783 and 885), United Kingdom (ibid., § 784) and United States (ibid., § 787), the legislation of Belgium (ibid., § 795), Germany (ibid., § 802), South Africa (ibid., § 813), Spain (ibid., §§ 815 and 931), the reported practice of India (ibid., § 980), Philippines (ibid., § 842), Spain (ibid., § 844), the statements of Israel (ibid., § 984), Italy (ibid., § 837) and Jordan (ibid., § 838) and the practice of Kuwait (ibid., §§ 830 and 986).

[78] See, e.g., Belgium, Court-Martial of Brussels, Sergeant W. case (ibid., § 819); Chile, Santiago Council of War, Guzmán and Others case (ibid., § 821); Colombia, Constitutional Court, Constitutional Case No. T-409 and Constitutional Case No. C-578 (ibid., § 822); Israel, District Military Court for the Central Judicial District and Military Court of Appeal, Ofer, Malinki and Others case (ibid., § 824); Italy, Military Tribunal of Rome, Military Appeals Court and Supreme Court of Cassation, Hass and Priebke case (ibid., § 825); Netherlands, Special Court in Amsterdam, Zühlke case (ibid., § 826); United States, Army Court of Military Appeals, Calley case (ibid., § 828).

[79] See, e.g., the legislation of Armenia (ibid., § 791), Australia (ibid., § 792), Brazil (ibid., § 796), Chile (ibid., § 797), Croatia (ibid., § 798), Egypt (ibid., § 800), India (ibid., § 803), Jordan (ibid., § 804), Kenya (ibid., § 805), Malaysia (ibid., § 806), Nigeria (ibid., § 807), Pakistan (ibid., § 808), Peru (ibid., § 810) and Philippines (ibid., § 780) and the reported practice of Egypt (ibid., § 833), India (ibid., § 843) and Pakistan (ibid., § 841).

[80] See the practice of Argentina (ibid., § 820), Cuba (ibid., § 823) and Egypt (ibid., § 824).

[81] See, e.g., the legislation of Armenia (ibid., § 791), Austria (ibid., § 793), Poland (ibid., § 811), Spain (ibid., § 815) and Tajikistan (ibid., § 817). The practice which makes it a punishable offence not to execute an order, without distinguishing between a lawful and an unlawful order, is unclear. See, e.g., the legislation of Belarus (ibid., § 794, but see § 903), Cuba (ibid., § 799, but see § 832) and Russia (ibid., § 812, but see § 843).

a superior order is not a defence of a war crime, if the subordinate should have known that the act ordered was unlawful because of its manifestly unlawful nature (see Rule 155), both of which apply equally to State armed forces and to armed opposition groups. However, no specific practice was found to confirm this conclusion, as the military manuals, national legislation and case-law referring to this rule relate essentially to members of State armed forces.

Rule 155. Obeying a superior order does not relieve a subordinate of criminal responsibility if the subordinate knew that the act ordered was unlawful or should have known because of the manifestly unlawful nature of the act ordered.

Practice

Volume II, Chapter 43, Section E.

Summary

State practice establishes this rule as a norm of customary international law with respect to war crimes committed in both international and non-international armed conflicts. This rule is without prejudice to the existence of other defences, such as duress, which are not addressed in this study.

International and non-international armed conflicts

The rule that a superior order is not a defence was set forth in the Charters of the International Military Tribunals at Nuremberg and at Tokyo.[82]

During the negotiation of Additional Protocol I, the ICRC submitted a draft article which prohibited the defence of superior orders if the person "should have reasonably known that he was committing a grave breach of the Conventions or of the present Protocol". This proposal was not accepted, although the principle enunciated in the Charters of the International Military Tribunals was not contested.[83] Reasons for not adopting this draft varied, but States mentioned problems with the limitation of the draft rule to grave breaches, which was too narrow, and the fact that subordinates had a duty of obedience, whereas the draft did not limit liability to acts which were manifestly illegal.[84] Practice since the Diplomatic Conference leading to the adoption of the Additional

---

[82] IMT Charter (Nuremberg), Article 8 (*ibid.*, § 854); IMT Charter (Tokyo), Article 6 (*ibid.*, § 862).
[83] See the practice of the CDDH (*ibid.*, § 855).
[84] See, e.g., the statements of Argentina (*ibid.*, § 973), Canada (*ibid.*, § 976), Israel (*ibid.*, § 983), Mexico (*ibid.*, § 987), Norway (*ibid.*, § 990), Poland (*ibid.*, § 991), Spain (*ibid.*, § 994), Syria (*ibid.*, § 996), United Kingdom (*ibid.*, § 998), United States (*ibid.*, § 1001), Uruguay (*ibid.*, § 1003) and Yemen (*ibid.*, § 1005).

Protocols, outlined below, has confirmed the customary nature of the rule that superior orders are not a defence.

The rule that superior orders are not a defence is restated in the Statutes of the International Criminal Court, of the International Criminal Tribunals for the Former Yugoslavia and for Rwanda and of the Special Court for Sierra Leone and in UNTAET Regulation No. 2000/15 for East Timor.[85] Conditions are spelled out in some detail in the Statute of the International Criminal Court: obedience to an order is not a defence when the person knew the order was unlawful or when the order was manifestly unlawful.[86] The Convention against Torture and the Inter-American Convention on the Forced Disappearance of Persons also state that superior orders cannot be a defence.[87]

Several military manuals and the legislation of many States provide that a superior order is not a defence if the perpetrator knew or should have known that the act ordered was unlawful.[88] Other military manuals and national legislation exclude this defence in situations where the act was manifestly unlawful without mentioning a particular mental element.[89] However, it is safe to conclude that if an act is manifestly unlawful the subordinate should at least have known, if he or she did not actually know, that the act ordered was unlawful. Several judgements in recent cases, some of which concerned non-international armed conflicts, reached essentially the same conclusions.[90] There is no

---

[85] ICC Statute, Article 33 (ibid., § 859); ICTY Statute, Article 7(4) (ibid., § 868); ICTR Statute, Article 6(4) (ibid., § 869); Statute of the Special Court for Sierra Leone, Article 6(4) (ibid., 860); UNTAET Regulation No. 2000/15, Section 21 (ibid., 872).

[86] ICC Statute, Article 33 (ibid., § 859).

[87] Convention against Torture, Article 2 (ibid., § 856); Inter-American Convention on the Forced Disappearance of Persons, Article VIII (ibid., § 857).

[88] See, e.g., the military manuals of Germany (ibid., § 880), South Africa (ibid., § 885), Switzerland (ibid., § 888), United States (ibid., §§ 891–892 and 894) and Yugoslavia (ibid., § 896) and the legislation of Belarus (ibid., § 903), Egypt (ibid., § 909), Ethiopia (ibid., § 912), Germany (ibid., §§ 915–917), Iraq (ibid., § 918), Luxembourg (ibid., § 922), Netherlands (ibid., § 923), Poland (ibid., § 928), Slovenia (ibid., § 930), Switzerland (ibid., § 935), Yemen (ibid., § 939) and Yugoslavia (ibid., § 940).

[89] See, e.g., the military manuals of Cameroon (ibid., § 874), Canada (ibid., §§ 875–876), Dominican Republic (ibid., § 878), Peru (ibid., § 884) and South Africa (ibid., § 886) and the legislation of Albania (ibid., § 897), Brazil (ibid., § 905), France (ibid., § 913), Israel (ibid., § 919), Netherlands (ibid., § 924), Peru (ibid., § 926), Rwanda (ibid., § 929) and Spain (ibid., §§ 931–933).

[90] See, e.g., Argentina, National Court of Appeals, Military Junta case (ibid., § 941); Austria, Supreme Court, Leopold case (ibid., § 943); Belgium, Court-Martial of Brussels, Sergeant W. case (ibid., § 944); Belgium Court of Cassation, V. C. case (ibid., § 945); Belgium, Military Court, Kalid case (ibid., § 946); Bosnia and Herzegovina, Republika Srpska, Modrića Municipal Court, Halilović case (ibid., § 947); Canada, Supreme Court, Finta case (ibid., § 948); Germany, Reichsgericht, Llandovery Castle case (ibid., § 953); Germany, Federal Supreme Court, Subordinate's Responsibility case (ibid., § 954); Israel, District Military Court for the Central Judicial District and Military Court of Appeal, Ofer, Malinki and Others case (ibid., §§ 955–956); Israel, Supreme Court, Eichmann case (ibid., § 957); Italy, Military Tribunal at Verona, Schintlholzer case (ibid., § 958); Italy, Military Tribunal of Rome and Supreme Court of Cassation, Priebke case (ibid., § 959); Netherlands, Special Court in Amsterdam, Zühlke case (ibid., § 960); Nigeria, Supreme Court, Nwaoga case (ibid., § 962); Philippines, Supreme Court, Margen case (ibid., § 963); South Africa, Appeal Division, Werner case (ibid., § 964); United Kingdom, Military Court at Lüneberg, Auschwitz and Belsen case (ibid., § 965); United States, Military Tribunal at Nuremberg, Krupp case (ibid., § 966), Krauch (I.G. Farben Trial) case (ibid., § 967) and Von Leeb case (The High

practice to the contrary in relation to acts that are manifestly unlawful. However, practice that solely refers to the unlawfulness of the act ordered, without the requirement of knowledge of such unlawfulness, is not sufficiently widespread and uniform as to establish a rule of customary international law.

Mitigation of punishment

There is extensive practice to the effect that obeying an order to commit a war crime can be taken into account in mitigation of punishment, if the court determines that justice so requires. This practice includes the Charters of the International Military Tribunals at Nuremberg and at Tokyo, the Statutes of the International Criminal Tribunals for the Former Yugoslavia and for Rwanda and of the Special Court for Sierra Leone and UNTAET Regulation No. 2000/15 for East Timor.[91]

In addition, there is extensive State practice to this effect in military manuals, national legislation and official statements.[92] Some States, however, exclude mitigation of punishment for violations committed pursuant to manifestly unlawful orders.[93]

In his report to the UN Security Council on the draft Statute of the International Criminal Tribunal for the Former Yugoslavia in 1993, the UN Secretary-General referred to the possibility of mitigating punishment in the case of obedience to superior orders.[94] A similar point is contained in the final report of the UN Commission of Experts Established pursuant to Security Council Resolution 935 (1994) to examine violations of international humanitarian law committed in Rwanda.[95]

Command Trial) (*ibid.*, § 968); United States, Military Commission in Wiesbaden, *Hadamar Sanatorium case* (*ibid.*, § 969); United States, Army Board of Review, *Griffen case* (*ibid.*, § 970); United States, Army Court of Military Appeals, *Calley case* (*ibid.*, § 971).

[91] IMT Charter (Nuremberg), Article 8 (*ibid.*, § 854); IMT Charter (Tokyo), Article 6 (*ibid.*, 862); ICTY Statute, Article 7(4) (*ibid.*, § 868); ICTR Statute, Article 6(4) (*ibid.*, § 869); Statute of the Special Court for Sierra Leone, Article 6(4) (*ibid.*, § 860); UNTAET Regulation No. 2000/15, Section 21 (*ibid.*, 872).

[92] See, e.g., the military manuals of Canada (*ibid.*, § 875), New Zealand (*ibid.*, § 882), Nigeria (*ibid.*, § 883), Switzerland (*ibid.*, § 888), United Kingdom (*ibid.*, § 889) and United States (*ibid.*, §§ 891–892 and 894), the legislation of Australia (*ibid.*, § 900), Bangladesh (*ibid.*, § 902), Chile (*ibid.*, § 907), Congo (*ibid.*, § 908), Ethiopia (*ibid.*, § 912), France (*ibid.*, §§ 913–914), Germany (*ibid.*, § 915), Niger (*ibid.*, § 925) and Switzerland (*ibid.*, § 935) and the statements of Canada (*ibid.*, § 976), Israel (*ibid.*, § 982) and Poland (*ibid.*, § 991).

[93] See, e.g., the military manuals of Canada (*ibid.*, § 875) and New Zealand (*ibid.*, § 882) and the legislation of Spain (*ibid.*, § 931).

[94] UN Secretary-General, Report pursuant to Paragraph 2 of Security Council Resolution 808 (1993) (*ibid.*, § 1008).

[95] UN Commission of Experts Established pursuant to Security Council Resolution 935 (1994), Final report (*ibid.*, § 1011).

WAR CRIMES

Rule 156. Serious violations of international humanitarian law constitute war crimes.

Practice

Volume II, Chapter 44, Section A.

Summary

State practice establishes this rule as a norm of customary international law applicable in both international and non-international armed conflicts.

International and non-international armed conflicts

The Statute of the International Criminal Court defines war crimes as, *inter alia*, "serious violations of the laws and customs applicable in international armed conflict" and "serious violations of the laws and customs applicable in an armed conflict not of an international character".[1] The Statutes of the International Criminal Tribunals for the Former Yugoslavia and for Rwanda and of the Special Court for Sierra Leone and UNTAET Regulation No. 2000/15 for East Timor also provide jurisdiction over "serious" violations of international humanitarian law.[2] In the *Delalić case* in 2001, in interpreting Article 3 of the Statute of the International Criminal Tribunal for the Former Yugoslavia listing the violations of the laws or customs of war over which the Tribunal has jurisdiction, the Appeals Chamber stated that the expression "laws and customs of war" included *all* laws and customs of war in addition to those listed in the Article.[3] The adjective "serious" in conjunction with "violations" is to be found in the military manuals and legislation of several States.[4]

---

[1] ICC Statute, Article 8 (cited in Vol. II, Ch. 44, § 3).
[2] ICTY Statute, Article 1 (*ibid.*, § 11); ICTR Statute, Article 1 (*ibid.*, § 14); Statute of the Special Court for Sierra Leone, Article 1(1) (*ibid.*, § 5); UNTAET Regulation No. 2000/15, Section 6(1) (*ibid.*, § 16).
[3] ICTY, *Delalić case*, Judgement, (*ibid.*, § 111).
[4] See, e.g., the military manuals of Colombia (*ibid.*, § 21), Croatia (*ibid.*, § 22), France (*ibid.*, §§ 24–25), Italy (*ibid.*, § 30) and Spain (*ibid.*, § 36) and the legislation of Congo (*ibid.*, § 56), New Zealand

There is also practice which does not contain the adjective "serious" with respect to violations and which defines war crimes as any violation of the laws or customs of war.[5] The military manuals and legislation of a number of States similarly do not require violations of international humanitarian law to be serious in order to amount to war crimes.[6] However, most of this practice illustrates such violations in the form of lists of war crimes, typically referring to acts such as theft, wanton destruction, murder and ill-treatment, which indicates that these States in fact limit war crimes to the more serious violations of international humanitarian law.

Serious nature of the violation

A deductive analysis of the actual list of war crimes found in various treaties and other international instruments, as well as in national legislation and case-law, shows that violations are in practice treated as serious, and therefore as war crimes, if they endanger protected persons or objects or if they breach important values.

(i) The conduct endangers protected persons or objects. The majority of war crimes involve death, injury, destruction or unlawful taking of property. However, not all acts necessarily have to result in actual damage to persons or objects in order to amount to war crimes. This became evident when the Elements of Crimes for the International Criminal Court were being drafted. It was decided, for example, that it was enough to launch an attack on civilians or civilian objects, even if something unexpectedly prevented the attack from causing death or serious injury. This could be the case of an attack launched against the civilian population or individual civilians, even though, owing to the failure of the weapon system, the intended target was not hit. The same is the case for subjecting a protected person to medical experiments – actual injury is not required for the act to amount to a war crime; it is enough to endanger the life or health of the person through such an act.[7]

(ii) The conduct breaches important values. Acts may amount to war crimes because they breach important values, even without physically endangering

---

(*ibid.*, § 70) and Nicaragua (*ibid.*, § 71); see also the reported practice of the Netherlands (*ibid.*, § 93).

[5] Report of the Commission on Responsibility set up after the First World War (*ibid.*, § 6); IMT Charter (Nuremberg), Article 6(b) (*ibid.*, § 1); IMT Charter (Tokyo), Article 5(b) (*ibid.*, § 8); Allied Control Council Law No. 10, Article II (*ibid.*, § 7).

[6] See, e.g., the military manuals of Australia (*ibid.*, § 18), Canada (*ibid.*, § 20), Israel (*ibid.*, § 29), Netherlands (*ibid.*, § 32), New Zealand (*ibid.*, § 33), Nigeria (*ibid.*, § 34), South Africa (*ibid.*, § 35), Switzerland (*ibid.*, § 38), United Kingdom (*ibid.*, § 39) and United States (*ibid.*, §§ 40 and 43) and the legislation of Bangladesh (*ibid.*, § 48), Netherlands (*ibid.*, § 69), Spain (*ibid.*, § 73) and United Kingdom (*ibid.*, § 74); see also the reported practice of Iran (*ibid.*, § 91).

[7] See Knut Dörmann, *Elements of War Crimes under the Rome Statute of the International Criminal Court: Sources and Commentary*, Cambridge University Press, 2003, pp. 130 and 233.

persons or objects directly. These include, for example, abusing dead bodies;[8] subjecting persons to humiliating treatment;[9] making persons undertake work that directly helps the military operations of the enemy;[10] violation of the right to fair trial;[11] and recruiting children under 15 years of age into the armed forces.[12]

The Appeals Chamber of the International Criminal Tribunal for the Former Yugoslavia, in the interlocutory appeal in the *Tadić case* in 1995, stated that, in order for an offence to be subject to prosecution before the Tribunal, the "violation must be serious, that is to say, it must constitute a breach of a rule protecting important values, and the breach must involve grave consequences for the victim". It then went on to illustrate this analysis by indicating that the appropriation of a loaf of bread belonging to a private individual by a combatant in occupied territory would violate Article 46(1) of the Hague Regulations, but would not amount to a "serious" violation of international humanitarian law.[13] As seen from the examples of war crimes referred to above, this does not mean that the breach has to result in death or physical injury, or even the risk thereof, although breaches of rules protecting important values often result in distress and anxiety for the victims.

Violations entailing individual criminal responsibility under international law

In the interlocutory appeal in the *Tadić case* in 1995, the Appeals Chamber of the International Criminal Tribunal for the Former Yugoslavia stated that

[8] See, e.g., United States, General Military Government Court at Dachau, *Schmid case* (cited in Vol. II, Ch. 35, § 111) (the mutilation of the dead body of a prisoner of war and refusal of an honourable burial amounted to a war crime); see also Australia, Military Court at Wewak, *Takehiko case* (*ibid.*, § 106); Australia, Military Court at Rabaul, *Tisato case* (*ibid.*, § 107); United States, Military Commission at Yokohama, *Kikuchi and Mahuchi case* (*ibid.*, § 109); United States, Military Commission at the Mariana Islands, *Yochio and Others case* (*ibid.*, § 110).

[9] See United States, Military Commission in Florence, *Maelzer case* (cited in Vol. II, Ch. 32, § 297) (concerning prisoners of war who were forced to march through the streets of Rome as in an ancient triumphal parade); Australia, Military Court at Rabaul, *Tanaka Chuichi case* (*ibid.*, § 3884) (concerning Sikh prisoners of war who were made to cut their hair and beards and in one instance forced to smoke a cigarette, acts contrary to their religion); see also ICC Statute, Article 8(2)(b)(xxi).

[10] See France, General Tribunal at Rastadt of the Military Government for the French Zone of Occupation in Germany, *Roechling case* (cited in Vol. II, Ch. 32, § 1863); Netherlands, Temporary Court-Martial of Makassar, *Koshiro case* (*ibid.*, § 1865); United States, Military Tribunal at Nuremberg, *Krauch (I. G. Farben Trial) case* (*ibid.*, § 1872); United States, Military Tribunal at Nuremberg, *Von Leeb (The High Command Trial) case* (*ibid.*, § 1874); see also ICC Statute, Article 8(2)(b)(xv).

[11] See Australia, Military Court at Rabaul, *Ohashi case* (cited in Vol. II, Ch. 32, § 2958); United States, Military Commission at Shanghai, *Sawada case* (*ibid.*, § 2962); United States, Military Tribunal at Nuremberg, *Altstötter (The Justice Trial) case* (*ibid.*, § 2965); see also ICC Statute, Article 8(2)(a)(vi) and (c)(iv).

[12] See ICC Statute, Article 8(2)(b)(xxvi) and (e)(vii).

[13] ICTY, *Tadić case*, Interlocutory Appeal (cited in Vol. II, Ch. 44, § 106).

"the violation of the rule [of international humanitarian law] must entail, under customary or conventional law, the individual criminal responsibility of the person breaching the rule".[14] This approach has been consistently taken by the International Criminal Tribunals for the Former Yugoslavia and for Rwanda in their case-law concerning serious violations of international humanitarian law other than grave breaches of the Geneva Conventions.[15] For example, with regard to serious violations of Additional Protocol I other than grave breaches, the International Criminal Tribunal for the Former Yugoslavia had to examine whether such violations entail individual criminal responsibility under customary international law or whether Additional Protocol I provides for individual criminal responsibility notwithstanding the fact that the violation is not listed as a grave breach.[16]

This practice does not exclude the possibility that a State may define under its national law other violations of international humanitarian law as war crimes. The consequences of so doing, however, remain internal and there is no internationalisation of the obligation to repress those crimes and no universal jurisdiction.

Earlier practice seems to indicate that a specific act did not necessarily have to be expressly recognised by the international community as a war crime for a court to find that it amounted to a war crime. This point is illustrated by many judgements by national courts which found the accused guilty of war crimes committed in the Second World War which were not listed in the Charters of the International Military Tribunals at Nuremberg and at Tokyo, such as the lack of fair trial,[17] abuse of dead bodies,[18] offending the religious sensibilities of prisoners of war,[19] and misuse of the red cross emblem.[20]

---

[14] See ICTY, *Tadić case*, Interlocutory Appeal (*ibid.*, § 106).

[15] See ICTY, *Tadić case*, Judgement (*ibid.*, § 107), *Blaškić case*, Judgement (*ibid.*, § 112), *Kordić and Čerkez case*, Judgement (*ibid.*, § 120), *Furundžija case*, Judgement (*ibid.*, § 110), *Delalić case*, Judgement (*ibid.*, § 109), *Kunarac case*, Judgement (*ibid.*, § 113), *Kvočka case*, Judgement (*ibid.*, § 114), *Krnojelac case*, Judgement (*ibid.*, § 115), *Vasiljevic case*, Judgement (*ibid.*, § 116), *Naletilić case*, Judgement (*ibid.*, § 117), *Stakić case*, Judgement (*ibid.*, § 118), *Galić case*, Judgement (*ibid.*, § 119); ICTR, *Akayesu case*, Judgement (*ibid.*, § 103), *Musema case*, Judgement (*ibid.*, § 105) and *Rutaganda case*, Judgement (*ibid.*, § 104).

[16] See, e.g., ICTY, *Galić case*, Case No. IT-98-29-T, Judgement and Opinion, 5 December 2003, §§ 113–129.

[17] See, e.g., Australia, Military Court at Rabaul, *Ohashi case* (cited in Vol. II, Ch. 32, § 2958); United Kingdom, Military Court at Wuppertal, *Rhode case* (*ibid.*, § 2964); United States, Military Commission at Rome, *Dostler case* (*ibid.*, § 2961); United States, Military Commission at Shanghai, *Sawada case* (*ibid.*, § 2962) and *Isayama case* (*ibid.*, § 2963); United States, Military Tribunal at Nuremberg, *Altstötter (The Justice Trial) case* (*ibid.*, § 2965).

[18] See Australia, Military Court at Wewak, *Takehiko case* (cited in Vol. II, Ch. 35, § 106); Australia, Military Court at Rabaul, *Tisato case* (*ibid.*, § 107); United States, Military Commission at Yokohama, *Kikuchi and Mahuchi case* (*ibid.*, § 109); United States, Military Commission at the Mariana Islands, *Yochio and Others case* (*ibid.*, § 110); United States, General Military Court at Dachau, *Schmid case* (*ibid.*, § 111).

[19] See Australia, Military Court at Rabaul, *Tanaka Chuichi case* (cited in Vol. II, Ch. 32, § 3884).

[20] See United States, Intermediate Military Government Court at Dachau, *Hagendorf case* (cited in Vol. II, Ch. 18, § 1313).

National practice after the Second World War showed that, whereas States of a common-law tradition tended to try persons on the basis of international law, many States with a civil law tradition – in the absence of special legislation for war crimes – tried the same crimes on the basis of their ordinary criminal legislation.[21] For the latter, therefore, if the act was criminal during peacetime, it could be treated as a war crime when committed during armed conflict, provided that the act was also prohibited by the laws and customs of war. There is also some recent practice to the same effect.[22]

Violations of customary international law or treaty law

The International Military Tribunal at Nuremberg determined that violations of the Hague Regulations amounted to war crimes because these treaty rules had crystallised into customary law by the time of the Second World War. Similarly, the negotiation of the Statute of the International Criminal Court was based on the premise that, to amount to a war crime to be included in the Statute, the conduct had to amount to a violation of a customary rule of international law. Another example of violations of customary international law being used as a basis for war criminality is the resolution adopted by consensus in the UN Commission on Human Rights declaring that Israel's "continuous grave breaches" of the Fourth Geneva Convention and Additional Protocol I were war crimes.[23] As neither Israel nor many of the Commission's members had ratified Additional Protocol I at the time, this statement must have been based on the understanding that these breaches constituted war crimes under customary international law.

However, the vast majority of practice does not limit the concept of war crimes to violations of customary international law. Almost all military manuals and criminal codes refer to violations of both customary law and applicable treaty law.[24] Additional practice specifying treaty provisions as war crimes includes statements to this effect by France, Germany and the United States.[25] The Appeals Chamber of the International Criminal Tribunal for the Former Yugoslavia, in the interlocutory appeal in the *Tadić case* in 1995,

---

[21] See, e.g., the legislation of France (cited in Vol. II, Ch. 44, § 60), Netherlands (*ibid.*, § 67) and Norway (*ibid.*, § 72) and the reported practice of Belgium (*ibid.*, § 83).

[22] See, e.g., the legislation of the Democratic Republic of the Congo (*ibid.*, § 55) and the practice of Germany (*ibid.*, §§ 521–524).

[23] UN Commission on Human Rights, Res. 1982/1 (*ibid.*, § 98).

[24] See, e.g., the military manuals of Australia (*ibid.*, § 18), Belgium (*ibid.*, § 19), Canada (*ibid.*, § 20), Ecuador (*ibid.*, § 23), France (*ibid.*, § 26), New Zealand (*ibid.*, § 33), Switzerland (*ibid.*, § 38), United Kingdom (*ibid.*, § 39) and United States (*ibid.*, §§ 40 and 43) and the legislation of Bangladesh (*ibid.*, § 48), Canada (*ibid.*, §§ 51–52), Congo (*ibid.*, § 56), Finland (*ibid.*, § 59), New Zealand (*ibid.*, § 70) and United States (*ibid.*, § 75); see also the draft legislation of Burundi (*ibid.*, § 50).

[25] See the statements of France (*ibid.*, § 87), Germany (*ibid.*, § 90) and United States (*ibid.*, § 95).

also stated that war crimes can comprise serious violations of both customary rules and applicable treaty provisions, i.e., those that are "unquestion-
ably binding on the parties [to the armed conflict] at the time of the alleged
offence".[26]

Interpretation

Practice provides further specifications with respect to the nature of the
conduct constituting a war crime, its perpetrators and their mental state.

(i) Acts or omissions. War crimes can consist of acts or omissions. Examples
of the latter include failure to provide a fair trial and failure to provide food
or necessary medical care to persons in the power of the adversary.[27] Unlike
crimes against humanity, which consist of a "widespread or systematic" commission of prohibited acts, any serious violation of international humanitarian
law constitutes a war crime. This is clear from extensive and consistent case-
law from the First World War until the present day.

(ii) Perpetrators. Practice in the form of legislation, military manuals and
case-law shows that war crimes are violations committed either by members of the armed forces or by civilians against members of the armed
forces, civilians or protected objects of the adverse party.[28] National legislation typically does not limit the commission of war crimes to members of the armed forces, but rather indicates the acts that are criminal
when committed by any person.[29] Several military manuals contain the
same approach.[30] A number of military manuals, as well as some legislation,
expressly include the term "civilians" among the persons that can commit war
crimes.[31]

---

[26] ICTY, *Tadić case*, Case No. IT-94-1-AR72, Decision on the Defence Motion for Interlocutory
Appeal on Jurisdiction, Appeals Chamber, 2 October 1995, §§ 94 and 143.

[27] As to the failure to provide a fair trial, see the examples in footnotes 11 and 17. As to the failure to
provide food or necessary medical care to prisoners of war, see, e.g., the legislation of Argentina
(cited in Vol. II, Ch. 37, § 60), Australia (*ibid.*, § 61), Bangladesh (*ibid.*, § 63), Chile (*ibid.*,
§ 64), Dominican Republic (*ibid.*, § 65), Ireland (*ibid.*, § 66), Mexico (*ibid.*, § 67), Nicaragua
(*ibid.*, § 68), Norway (*ibid.*, § 69), Peru (*ibid.*, § 70), Spain (*ibid.*, § 72) and Uruguay (*ibid.*,
§ 73).

[28] See Knut Dörmann, *Elements of War Crimes under the Rome Statute of the International Criminal Court: Sources and Commentary*, Cambridge University Press, 2003, pp. 34–
37 and 391–393; see the Second World War trials (cited in Vol. II, Ch. 44, § 78) and
United States, District Court for the Central District of California, *Leo Handel case* (*ibid.*,
§ 79).

[29] See, e.g., the military manuals of Australia (*ibid.*, § 18), Ecuador (*ibid.*, § 23), New Zealand (*ibid.*,
§ 33), United Kingdom (*ibid.*, § 39) and United States (*ibid.*, §§ 40 and 43) and the legislation of
Moldova (*ibid.*, § 66).

[30] See, e.g., the military manuals of Australia (*ibid.*, § 18), Canada (*ibid.*, § 20) and Switzerland
(*ibid.*, § 38).

[31] See, e.g., the military manuals of Ecuador (*ibid.*, § 23), New Zealand (*ibid.*, § 33), United Kingdom
(*ibid.*, § 39) and United States (*ibid.*, §§ 40 and 43) and the legislation of Moldova (*ibid.*, § 66);
see also Jordan, *Draft Military Criminal Code* (*ibid.*, § 62).

(iii) Mental element. International case-law has indicated that war crimes are violations that are committed wilfully, i.e., either intentionally (*dolus directus*) or recklessly (*dolus eventualis*).[32] The exact mental element varies depending on the crime concerned.[33]

List of war crimes

War crimes include the following serious violations of international humanitarian law:

(i) Grave breaches of the Geneva Conventions:
In the case of an international armed conflict, any of the following acts committed against persons or property protected under the provisions of the relevant Geneva Convention:

- wilful killing;
- torture or inhuman treatment, including biological experiments;
- wilfully causing great suffering or serious injury to body or health;
- extensive destruction or appropriation of property, not justified by military necessity and carried out unlawfully and wantonly;
- compelling a prisoner of war or other protected person to serve in the forces of a hostile Power;
- wilfully depriving a prisoner of war or other protected person of the rights of a fair and regular trial;
- unlawful deportation or transfer;
- unlawful confinement;
- taking of hostages.

Basis for the war crimes listed above

This list of grave breaches was included in the Geneva Conventions largely on the basis of crimes pursued after the Second World War by the International Military Tribunals at Nuremberg and at Tokyo and by national courts. The list is repeated in the Statutes of the International Criminal Tribunal for the Former Yugoslavia and of the International Criminal Court.[34] It is also reflected in the legislation of many States.[35] The understanding that such violations are war crimes is uncontroversial.

---

[32] See, e.g., ICTY, *Delalić case*, Case No. IT-96–21-T, Judgement, Trial Chamber II, 16 November 1998, §§ 437 and 439.

[33] See the paper prepared by the ICRC relating to the mental element in the common law and civil law systems and to the concepts of mistake of fact and mistake of law in national and international law, circulated, at the request of several States, at the Preparatory Commission for the International Criminal Court, Doc. PCNICC/1999/WGEC/INF.2/Add.4, 15 December 1999, Annex; see also the Elements of Crimes for the International Criminal Court.

[34] ICTY Statute, Article 2; ICC Statute, Article 8(2)(a).

[35] With respect to wilful killing, see, e.g., the legislation referred to in the commentary to Rule 89. With respect to torture or inhuman treatment, see, e.g., the legislation referred to in the commentary to Rule 90. With respect to biological experiments, see, e.g., the legislation referred

(ii) Other serious violations of international humanitarian law committed during an international armed conflict:

- committing outrages upon personal dignity, in particular, humiliating or degrading treatment and desecration of the dead;
- enforced sterilisation;
- compelling the nationals of the adverse party to take part in military operations against their own party;
- killing or wounding a combatant who has surrendered or is otherwise *hors de combat*;
- declaring that no quarter will be given;
- making improper use of distinctive emblems indicating protected status, resulting in death or serious personal injury;
- making improper use of the flag, the military insignia or uniform of the enemy resulting in death or serious personal injury;
- killing or wounding an adversary by resort to perfidy;
- making medical or religious personnel, medical units or medical transports the object of attack;
- pillage or other taking of property contrary to international humanitarian law;
- destroying property not required by military necessity.

Basis for the war crimes listed above

These violations were the subject of war crimes trials after the Second World War.[36] They are also included in the Statute of the International Criminal Court or, if not replicated in exactly the same terms, are in effect covered, as evidenced by the Elements of Crimes for the International Criminal Court.[37] The war crime "making medical or religious personnel, medical units or medical transports the object of attack" covers aspects of the war crime contained in Article 8(2)(b)(ix) and (xxiv) of the Statute of the International Criminal Court.[38] The identification of these violations as war crimes in the Statute of the International Criminal Court was not controversial. Attacking persons *hors de combat* and the perfidious use of protective emblems or signs are listed in

to in the commentary to Rule 92. With respect to extensive destruction or appropriation of property, not justified by military necessity and carried out unlawfully and wantonly, see, e.g., the legislation referred to in the commentary to Rule 50. With respect to compelling a prisoner of war or other protected person to serve in the forces of a hostile power, see, e.g., the legislation referred to in the commentary to Rule 95. With respect to wilfully depriving a prisoner of war or other protected person of the rights of a fair and regular trial, see, e.g., the legislation referred to in the commentary to Rule 100. With respect to unlawful confinement, see, e.g., the legislation referred to in the commentary to Rule 99. With respect to the taking of hostages, see, e.g., the legislation referred to in the commentary to Rule 96.

[36] See generally Knut Dörmann, *Elements of War Crimes under the Rome Statute of the International Criminal Court: Sources and Commentary*, Cambridge University Press, 2003.

[37] See, e.g., concerning desecration of the dead, Elements of Crimes for the International Criminal Court, Footnote 49 relating to Article 8(2)(b)(xxi) of the ICC Statute.

[38] ICC Statute, Article 8(2)(b)(ix) and (xxiv).

Additional Protocol I as grave breaches.[39] There is also practice which extends the scope of this war crime to the perfidious use of protective *signals*.[40]

(ii) Other serious violations of international humanitarian law committed during an international armed conflict (continued):

- making the civilian population or individual civilians, not taking a direct part in hostilities, the object of attack;
- launching an attack in the knowledge that such attack will cause incidental loss of civilian life, injury to civilians or damage to civilian objects which would be clearly excessive in relation to the concrete and direct military advantage anticipated;
- making non-defended localities and demilitarised zones the object of attack;
- subjecting persons who are in the power of an adverse party to physical mutilation or to medical or scientific experiments of any kind which are neither justified by the medical, dental or hospital treatment of the person concerned nor carried out in his or her interest, and which cause death to or seriously endanger the health of such person or persons;
- the transfer by the occupying power of parts of its own civilian population into the territory it occupies or the deportation or transfer of all or parts of the population of the occupied territory within or outside this territory;
- making buildings dedicated to religion, education, art, science or charitable purposes or historic monuments the object of attack, provided they are not military objectives.

Basis for the war crimes listed above

These violations of customary international law are listed as grave breaches in Additional Protocol I and as war crimes in the Statute of the International Criminal Court.[41] The wording varies slightly between these two instruments, but in essence they are the same violations as indicated in the Elements of Crimes for the International Criminal Court.

(i) Making the civilian population or individual civilians, not taking a direct part in hostilities, the object of attack. In addition to the practice mentioned above, there are numerous examples of national legislation which make it a criminal offence to direct attacks against civilians, including the legislation of States not, or not at the time, party to Additional Protocol I.[42] References to more practice can be found in the commentary to Rule 1.

(ii) Launching an attack in the knowledge that such attack will cause incidental loss of civilian life, injury to civilians or damage to civilian objects which would be clearly excessive in relation to the concrete and direct military

---

[39] Additional Protocol I, Article 85(3)(e) and (f).

[40] See, e.g., the practice of Colombia (cited in Vol. II, Ch. 18, § 1235), Costa Rica (*ibid.*, § 282), France (*ibid.*, §§ 1065, 1150, 1241, 1339 and 1407), Georgia (*ibid.*, §§ 1105, 1190, 1368 and 1428), Spain (*ibid.*, §§ 381, 608, 1302 and 1436) and Tajikistan (*ibid.*, §§ 387, 1115, 1204, 1382 and 1439); see also United States, *Naval Handbook*, § 6.2.5.

[41] Additional Protocol I, Article 85(3) and (4); ICC Statute, Article 8(2)(b).

[42] See legislation (cited in Vol. II, Ch. 1, §§ 217–269), in particular the legislation of Azerbaijan (*ibid.*, §§ 221–222), Indonesia (*ibid.*, § 243) and Italy (*ibid.*, § 245).

advantage anticipated. In addition to the practice mentioned above, numerous States have adopted legislation making it an offence to carry out an attack which violates the principle of proportionality.[43] References to more practice can be found in the commentary to Rule 14.

The definition of the war crime "launching an attack in the knowledge that such attack will cause incidental loss of civilian life, injury to civilians or damage to civilian objects which would be clearly excessive in relation to the concrete and direct military advantage anticipated" follows more closely the wording found in the Statute of the International Criminal Court.[44] The word "overall" is not contained in Articles 51 and 85 of Additional Protocol I, nor in the substantive rule of customary international law (see Rule 14). The purpose of this addition in the Statute of the International Criminal Court appears to be to indicate that a particular target can have an important military advantage that can be felt over a lengthy period of time and affect military action in areas other than the vicinity of the target itself. As this meaning is included in the existing wording of Additional Protocol I and the substantive rule of customary international law, the inclusion of the word "overall" does not add an extra element.[45]

(iii) Making non-defended localities and demilitarised zones the object of attack. In addition to the practice referred to above, it is an offence to attack non-defended localities under the legislation of numerous States.[46] References to more practice can be found in the commentary to Rule 37.

While "making demilitarised zones the object of attack" is a grave breach of Additional Protocol I, it is not mentioned as such in the Statute of the International Criminal Court. Nevertheless, attacks against demilitarised zones are

---

[43] See, e.g., the legislation of Armenia (cited in Vol. II, Ch. 4, § 50), Australia (*ibid.*, §§ 51–52), Belarus (*ibid.*, § 53), Belgium (*ibid.*, § 54), Canada (*ibid.*, §§ 57–58), Colombia (*ibid.*, § 59), Congo (*ibid.*, § 60), Cook Islands (*ibid.*, § 61), Cyprus (*ibid.*, § 62), Georgia (*ibid.*, § 64), Germany (*ibid.*, § 65), Ireland (*ibid.*, § 66), Mali (*ibid.*, § 68), Netherlands (*ibid.*, § 69), New Zealand (*ibid.*, §§ 70–71), Niger (*ibid.*, § 73), Norway (*ibid.*, § 74), Spain (*ibid.*, § 75), Sweden (*ibid.*, § 76), United Kingdom (*ibid.*, §§ 78–79) and Zimbabwe (*ibid.*, § 80); see also the draft legislation of Argentina (*ibid.*, § 49), Burundi (*ibid.*, § 56), El Salvador (*ibid.*, § 63), Lebanon (*ibid.*, § 67), Nicaragua (*ibid.*, § 72) and Trinidad and Tobago (*ibid.*, § 77).

[44] ICC Statute, Article 8(b)(iv).

[45] See Knut Dörmann, *Elements of War Crimes under the Rome Statute of the International Criminal Court: Sources and Commentary*, Cambridge University Press, 2003, pp. 169–173, in particular pp. 169–170.

[46] See, e.g., the legislation of Armenia (cited in Vol. II, Ch. 11, § 279), Australia (*ibid.*, §§ 280–282), Azerbaijan (*ibid.*, § 283), Belarus (*ibid.*, § 284), Belgium (*ibid.*, § 285), Bosnia and Herzegovina (*ibid.*, § 286), Canada (*ibid.*, §§ 288–289), China (*ibid.*, § 290), Congo (*ibid.*, § 291), Cook Islands (*ibid.*, § 292), Croatia (*ibid.*, § 293), Cyprus (*ibid.*, § 294), Czech Republic (*ibid.*, § 295), Estonia (*ibid.*, § 297), Georgia (*ibid.*, § 298), Germany (*ibid.*, § 299), Hungary (*ibid.*, § 300), Ireland (*ibid.*, § 301), Lithuania (*ibid.*, § 304), Mali (*ibid.*, § 305), Netherlands (*ibid.*, § 306–307), New Zealand (*ibid.*, §§ 308–309), Niger (*ibid.*, § 311), Norway (*ibid.*, § 312), Poland (*ibid.*, § 313), Slovakia (*ibid.*, § 314), Slovenia (*ibid.*, § 315), Spain (*ibid.*, § 316), Tajikistan (*ibid.*, § 317), United Kingdom (*ibid.*, §§ 319–320), United States (*ibid.*, § 321), Venezuela (*ibid.*, § 322), Yugoslavia (*ibid.*, § 323) and Zimbabwe (*ibid.*, § 324); see also the draft legislation of Argentina (*ibid.*, § 278), Burundi (*ibid.*, § 287), El Salvador (*ibid.*, § 296), Jordan (*ibid.*, § 302), Lebanon (*ibid.*, § 303), Nicaragua (*ibid.*, § 310) and Trinidad and Tobago (*ibid.*, § 318).

an offence under the legislation of numerous States.[47] In addition, such attacks would arguably constitute the war crime of "making civilian objects, that is, objects that are not military objectives, the object of attack" or "making the civilian population or individual civilians, not taking a direct part in hostilities, the object of attack" contained in the Statute.[48]

References to more practice can be found in the commentary to Rule 36.

(iv) Subjecting persons who are in the power of an adverse party to physical mutilation or to medical or scientific experiments of any kind which are neither justified by the medical, dental or hospital treatment of the person concerned nor carried out in his or her interest, and which cause death to or seriously endanger the health of such person or persons. In addition to the practice referred to above, numerous military manuals specify the prohibition of physical mutilation, medical or scientific experiments or any other medical procedure not indicated by the state of health of the patient and not consistent with generally accepted medical standards.[49] The prohibition is also found extensively in national legislation.[50] References to more practice can be found in the commentary to Rule 92.

(v) The transfer by the occupying power of parts of its own civilian population into the territory it occupies or the deportation or transfer of all or parts of the population of the occupied territory within or outside this territory. In addition to the practice referred to above, numerous military manuals prohibit the deportation or transfer by a party to the conflict of parts of its civilian population into the territory it occupies.[51] This rule is included in the legislation of numerous States.[52]

---

[47] See, e.g., the legislation of Armenia (cited in Vol. II, Ch. 11, § 133), Australia (*ibid.*, §§ 134–135), Azerbaijan (*ibid.*, § 136), Belarus (*ibid.*, § 137), Belgium (*ibid.*, § 138), Bosnia and Herzegovina (*ibid.*, § 139), Canada (*ibid.*, § 140), Cook Islands (*ibid.*, § 141), Croatia (*ibid.*, § 142), Cyprus (*ibid.*, § 143), Czech Republic (*ibid.*, § 144), Estonia (*ibid.*, § 146), Georgia (*ibid.*, § 147), Germany (*ibid.*, § 148), Hungary (*ibid.*, § 149), Ireland (*ibid.*, § 150), Lithuania (*ibid.*, § 153), Netherlands (*ibid.*, § 154), New Zealand (*ibid.*, § 155), Niger (*ibid.*, § 157), Norway (*ibid.*, § 158), Slovakia (*ibid.*, § 159), Slovenia (*ibid.*, § 160), Spain (*ibid.*, § 161), Tajikistan (*ibid.*, § 162), United Kingdom (*ibid.*, § 163), Yemen (*ibid.*, § 164), Yugoslavia (*ibid.*, § 165) and Zimbabwe (*ibid.*, § 166); see also the draft legislation of Argentina (*ibid.*, § 132), El Salvador (*ibid.*, § 145), Jordan (*ibid.*, § 151), Lebanon (*ibid.*, § 152) and Nicaragua (*ibid.*, § 156).

[48] ICC Statute, Article 8(2)(b)(i) and (ii).

[49] See, e.g., the military manuals of Argentina (cited in Vol. II, Ch. 32, §§ 1434–1435), Australia (*ibid.*, §§ 1436–1437), Belgium (*ibid.*, § 1438), Bosnia and Herzegovina (*ibid.*, § 1439), Burkina Faso (*ibid.*, § 1440), Canada (*ibid.*, § 1441), Ecuador (*ibid.*, § 1442), France (*ibid.*, §§ 1443–1445), Germany (*ibid.*, § 1446), Israel (*ibid.*, § 1447), Italy (*ibid.*, § 1448), Morocco (*ibid.*, § 1449), Netherlands (*ibid.*, § 1450), New Zealand (*ibid.*, § 1451), Nigeria (*ibid.*, §§ 1452–1453), Russia (*ibid.*, § 1454), Senegal (*ibid.*, §§ 1455–1456), South Africa (*ibid.*, § 1457), Spain (*ibid.*, § 1458), Sweden, (*ibid.*, § 1459), Switzerland (*ibid.*, § 1460), United Kingdom (*ibid.*, §§ 1461–1462) and United States (*ibid.*, §§ 1463–1466).

[50] See, e.g., the legislation (cited in Vol. II, Ch. 32, §§ 1467–1535).

[51] See, e.g., the military manuals of Argentina (cited in Vol. II, Ch. 38, §§ 346–347), Australia (*ibid.*, § 348), Canada (*ibid.*, § 349), Croatia (*ibid.*, § 350), Hungary (*ibid.*, § 351), Italy (*ibid.*, § 352), Netherlands (*ibid.*, § 353), New Zealand (*ibid.*, § 354), Spain (*ibid.*, § 355), Sweden (*ibid.*, § 357), Switzerland (*ibid.*, § 357), United Kingdom (*ibid.*, § 358) and United States (*ibid.*, § 359).

[52] See, e.g., the legislation of Armenia (cited in Vol. II, Ch. 38, § 361), Australia (*ibid.*, §§ 362–363), Azerbaijan (*ibid.*, §§ 364–365), Bangladesh (*ibid.*, § 366), Belarus (*ibid.*, § 367), Belgium (*ibid.*, § 368), Bosnia and Herzegovina (*ibid.*, § 369), Canada (*ibid.*, §§ 371–372), Congo (*ibid.*,

In addition, numerous military manuals specify the prohibition of unlawful deportation or transfer of civilians in occupied territory.[53] It is an offence under the legislation of many States to carry out such deportations or transfers.[54] There is case-law relating to the Second World War supporting the prohibition.[55]

References to more practice can be found in the commentaries to Rules 129–130.

(vi) Making buildings dedicated to religion, education, art, science or charitable purposes or historic monuments the object of attack, provided they are not military objectives. In addition to the practice referred to above, it is a punishable offence to attack such objects under the legislation of numerous States.[56]

With respect to attacking religious or cultural objects, the Statute of the International Criminal Court uses as the basis for this war crime the fact that such

§ 373), Cook Islands (*ibid.*, § 374), Croatia (*ibid.*, § 375), Cyprus (*ibid.*, § 376), Czech Republic (*ibid.*, § 377), Germany (*ibid.*, § 379), Georgia (*ibid.*, § 380), Ireland (*ibid.*, § 381), Mali (*ibid.*, § 384), Moldova (*ibid.*, § 385), Netherlands (*ibid.*, § 386), New Zealand (*ibid.*, §§ 387–388), Niger (*ibid.*, § 390), Norway (*ibid.*, § 391), Slovakia (*ibid.*, § 392), Slovenia (*ibid.*, § 393), Spain (*ibid.*, § 394), Tajikistan (*ibid.*, § 395), United Kingdom (*ibid.*, §§ 397–398), Yugoslavia (*ibid.*, § 399) and Zimbabwe (*ibid.*, § 400); see also the draft legislation of Argentina (*ibid.*, § 360), Burundi (*ibid.*, § 370), Jordan (*ibid.*, § 382), Lebanon (*ibid.*, § 383) and Trinidad and Tobago (*ibid.*, § 396).

[53] See, e.g., the military manuals of Argentina (cited in Vol. II, Ch. 38, §§ 39–40), Australia (*ibid.*, §§ 41–42), Canada (*ibid.*, § 43), Colombia (*ibid.*, § 44), Croatia (*ibid.*, § 45), Ecuador (*ibid.*, § 46), France (*ibid.*, §§ 47–49), Germany (*ibid.*, § 50), Hungary (*ibid.*, § 51), Italy (*ibid.*, § 52), Netherlands (*ibid.*, § 53), New Zealand (*ibid.*, § 54), Nigeria (*ibid.*, § 55), Philippines (*ibid.*, § 56), South Africa (*ibid.*, § 57), Spain (*ibid.*, § 58), Sweden (*ibid.*, § 59), Switzerland (*ibid.*, § 60), United Kingdom (*ibid.*, § 61) and United States (*ibid.*, §§ 62–64).

[54] See, e.g., the legislation (cited in Vol. II, Ch. 38, §§ 65–156).

[55] See, e.g., China, War Crimes Military Tribunal of the Ministry of National Defence, *Takashi Sakai case* (cited in Vol. II, Ch. 38, § 159); France, General Tribunal at Rastadt of the Military Government for the French Zone of Occupation in Germany, *Roechling case* (*ibid.*, § 157); Israel, District Court of Jerusalem, *Eichmann case* (*ibid.*, § 161); Netherlands, Special Court of Cassation, *Zimmermann case* (*ibid.*, § 166); Poland, Supreme National Tribunal at Poznan, *Greiser case* (*ibid.*, § 157); United States, Military Tribunal at Nuremberg, *Krauch (I.G. Farben Trial) case* (*ibid.*, § 157); United States, Military Tribunal at Nuremberg, *Krupp case* (*ibid.*, §157); United States, Military Tribunal at Nuremberg, *Milch case* (*ibid.*, § 157); United States, Military Tribunal at Nuremberg, *List (Hostages Trial) case* (*ibid.*, § 157); United States, Military Tribunal at Nuremberg, *Von Leeb (The High Command Trial) case* (*ibid.*, § 157).

[56] See, e.g., the legislation of Argentina (cited in Vol. II, Ch. 12, § 105), Armenia (*ibid.*, § 107), Australia (*ibid.*, §§ 108–109), Azerbaijan (*ibid.*, § 110), Belarus (*ibid.*, § 111), Belgium (*ibid.*, § 112), Bosnia and Herzegovina (*ibid.*, § 113), Bulgaria (*ibid.*, § 114), Canada (*ibid.*, §§ 116–117), Chile (*ibid.*, § 118), China (*ibid.*, § 119), Colombia (*ibid.*, §§ 120–121), Congo (*ibid.*, § 122), Cook Islands (*ibid.*, § 123), Croatia (*ibid.*, § 124), Cuba (*ibid.*, § 125), Cyprus (*ibid.*, § 126), Czech Republic (*ibid.*, § 127), Dominican Republic (*ibid.*, § 128), Estonia (*ibid.*, § 130), Georgia (*ibid.*, § 131), Germany (*ibid.*, § 132), Hungary (*ibid.*, § 133), Ireland (*ibid.*, § 134), Italy (*ibid.*, § 135), Jordan (*ibid.*, § 136), Kyrgyzstan (*ibid.*, § 138), Latvia (*ibid.*, § 139), Lithuania (*ibid.*, § 141), Mali (*ibid.*, § 142), Mexico (*ibid.*, § 143), Netherlands (*ibid.*, §§ 144–145), New Zealand (*ibid.*, §§ 146–147), Nicaragua (*ibid.*, § 148), Niger (*ibid.*, § 150), Norway (*ibid.*, § 151), Paraguay (*ibid.*, § 152), Peru (*ibid.*, § 153), Poland (*ibid.*, § 154), Romania (*ibid.*, § 155), Russia (*ibid.*, § 156), Slovakia (*ibid.*, § 157), Slovenia (*ibid.*, § 158), Spain (*ibid.*, §§ 159–160), Sweden (*ibid.*, § 161), Switzerland (*ibid.*, §§ 162–163), Tajikistan (*ibid.*, § 164), United Kingdom (*ibid.*, §§ 166–167), United States (*ibid.*, § 168), Uruguay (*ibid.*, § 169), Venezuela (*ibid.*, § 170), Yugoslavia (*ibid.*, § 171) and Zimbabwe (*ibid.*, § 172); see also the draft legislation of Argentina (*ibid.*, § 106), Burundi (*ibid.*, § 115), El Salvador (*ibid.*, § 129), Jordan (*ibid.*, § 137), Lebanon (*ibid.*, § 140), Nicaragua (*ibid.*, § 149) and Trinidad and Tobago (*ibid.*, § 165).

an attack is a violation of customary international law, in particular because the objects referred to are civilian and this prohibition is included in the Hague Regulations.[57] Additional Protocol I provides that attacks on religious or cultural objects are grave breaches if such objects have been accorded special protection.[58] In practice this refers to the special protection regime created by the Hague Convention for the Protection of Cultural Property.[59] The Second Protocol to the Hague Convention for the Protection of Cultural Property also subjects such specially protected cultural objects ("placed under enhanced protection") to the grave breaches regime, as it provides that the attack on such objects or the use of such objects for military purposes is subject to the obligation to prosecute or extradite on the basis of universal jurisdiction.[60] Although an attack on religious or cultural property is a war crime under customary international law, the obligation to prosecute or extradite on the basis of universal jurisdiction for grave breaches defined in this respect in Additional Protocol I and in the Second Protocol to the Hague Convention is only binding on the parties to those treaties. This is true for all the war crimes listed here and which constitute grave breaches of Additional Protocol I (see commentary to Rule 157).

References to more practice can be found in the commentary to Rule 38.

(ii) Other serious violations of international humanitarian law committed during an international armed conflict (continued):

- making civilian objects, that is, objects that are not military objectives, the object of attack;
- using starvation of civilians as a method of warfare by depriving them of objects indispensable to their survival, including by impeding relief supplies;
- making persons or objects involved in a humanitarian assistance or peacekeeping mission in accordance with the Charter of the United Nations the object of attack, as long as they are entitled to the protection given to civilians or civilian objects under international humanitarian law;
- launching an attack in the knowledge that such attack will cause widespread, long-term and severe damage to the natural environment which would be clearly excessive in relation to the concrete and direct military advantage anticipated;
- using prohibited weapons;
- declaring abolished, suspended or inadmissible in a court of law the rights and actions of the nationals of the hostile party;
- using human shields;
- conscripting or enlisting children under the age of 15 into armed forces, or using them to participate actively in hostilities;
- committing sexual violence, in particular rape, sexual slavery, enforced prostitution and enforced pregnancy.

---

[57] Hague Regulations, Article 27.   [58] Additional Protocol I, Article 85(4)(d).
[59] Hague Convention for the Protection of Cultural Property, Article 8.
[60] Second Protocol to the Hague Convention for the Protection of Cultural Property, Article 15.

Basis for the war crimes listed above

This group of war crimes is listed in the Statute of the International Criminal Court.[61] With the exception of the war crime of "declaring abolished, suspended or inadmissible in a court of law the rights and actions of the nationals of the hostile party", these crimes reflect the development of customary international law since the adoption of Additional Protocol I in 1977.

(i) Making civilian objects, that is, objects that are not military objectives, the object of attack. The customary nature of the war crime of making civilian objects the object of attack has been recognised in several judgements of the International Criminal Tribunal for the Former Yugoslavia.[62] Many States have adopted legislation making it an offence to attack civilian objects during armed conflict.[63] This war crime is in effect a modern formulation based on the rule in the Hague Regulations which prohibits destruction of enemy property unless imperatively demanded by the necessities of war.[64] This would also cover the deliberate destruction of the natural environment. References to more practice can be found in the commentary to Rules 7 and 50.

(ii) Using starvation of civilians as a method of warfare by depriving them of objects indispensable to their survival, including by impeding relief supplies. The prohibition of using starvation of civilians as a method of warfare was considered a new rule at the time of the adoption of Additional Protocol I. However, practice since then has not only made this a customary rule, but its inclusion in the Statute of the International Criminal Court as a war crime if committed in an international armed conflict was not controversial. Destroying objects indispensable to the survival of the civilian population also reflects a customary prohibition. There had, in fact, been a prosecution relating to a case of destruction of crops in a scorched earth operation during the Second World War, although the basis of the prosecution was the destruction of property not required by military necessity.[65] The prohibition of starvation is set forth in numerous military manuals.[66] Many States have adopted legislation

---

[61] ICC Statute, Article 8(2)(b).

[62] See, e.g., ICTY, *Blaškić case*, Judgement (cited in Vol. II, Ch. 2, § 181) and *Kordić and Čerkez case*, Judgement (*ibid.*, § 182).

[63] See, e.g., the legislation of Australia (cited in Vol. II, Ch. 2, § 119), Azerbaijan (*ibid.*, § 120), Canada (*ibid.*, § 122), Congo (*ibid.*, § 123), Croatia (*ibid.*, § 124), Estonia (*ibid.*, § 126), Georgia (*ibid.*, § 127), Germany (*ibid.*, § 128), Hungary (*ibid.*, § 129), Ireland (*ibid.*, § 130), Italy (*ibid.*, § 131), Mali (*ibid.*, § 132), Netherlands (*ibid.*, § 133), New Zealand (*ibid.*, § 134), Norway (*ibid.*, § 136), Slovakia (*ibid.*, § 137), Spain (*ibid.*, § 138), United Kingdom (*ibid.*, § 140) and Yemen (*ibid.*, § 141); see also the draft legislation of Argentina (*ibid.*, § 118), Burundi (*ibid.*, § 121), El Salvador (*ibid.*, § 125), Nicaragua (*ibid.*, § 135) and Trinidad and Tobago (*ibid.*, § 139).

[64] Hague Regulations, Article 23(g).

[65] See United States, Military Tribunal at Nuremberg, *List (Hostages Trial) case* (cited in Vol. II, Ch. 16, § 225) and *Von Leeb (The High Command Trial) case* (*ibid.*, § 226).

[66] See, e.g., the military manuals of Argentina (cited in Vol. II, Ch. 17, § 9), Australia (*ibid.*, §§ 10–11), Belgium (*ibid.*, § 12), Benin (*ibid.*, § 13), Canada (*ibid.*, § 14), Colombia (*ibid.*, § 15), Croatia (*ibid.*, § 16), France (*ibid.*, §§ 17–18), Germany (*ibid.*, § 19), Hungary (*ibid.*, § 20), Indonesia (*ibid.*, § 21), Israel (*ibid.*, § 22), Kenya (*ibid.*, § 23), South Korea (*ibid.*, § 24), Madagascar (*ibid.*,

making starvation of civilians as a method of warfare an offence.[67] References to more practice can be found in the commentary to Rules 53–55.

(iii) Making persons or objects involved in a humanitarian assistance or peacekeeping mission in accordance with the Charter of the United Nations the object of attack, as long as they are entitled to the protection given to civilians or civilian objects under international humanitarian law. The prohibition of attacking peacekeeping troops has developed with the greater use of such forces over the last few decades. The criminalisation of such behaviour was first introduced in the Convention on the Safety of UN and Associated Personnel.[68] Although this Convention is not yet widely ratified, its characterisation of attacks on such personnel, or objects belonging to them, as war crimes was accepted without difficulty during the negotiation of the Statute of the International Criminal Court. It is an offence under the legislation of many States to attack personnel and objects involved in a peacekeeping mission.[69]

As shown by the formulation "as long as they are entitled to the protection given to civilians or civilian objects under international humanitarian law" in the Statute of the International Criminal Court,[70] this war crime is a special application of the war crimes of making the civilian population or individual civilians the object of attack and making civilian objects the object of attack. In the case of attack on troops, the act would only be criminal if, at the time, the troops had not become involved in hostilities and had not thereby lost the protection afforded to civilians under international humanitarian law (see Rule 6). The reference to humanitarian assistance is intended to refer to such assistance being carried out either in the context of peacekeeping operations by troops or civilians, or in other contexts by civilians. References to more practice can be found in the commentary to Rules 31 and 33.

(iv) Launching an attack in the knowledge that such attack will cause widespread, long-term and severe damage to the natural environment which would be clearly excessive in relation to the concrete and direct military

---

§ 25), Netherlands (*ibid.*, § 26), New Zealand (*ibid.*, § 27), Nigeria (*ibid.*, § 28), Russia (*ibid.*, § 29), Spain (*ibid.*, § 30), Sweden (*ibid.*, § 31), Switzerland (*ibid.*, § 32), Togo (*ibid.*, § 33), United Kingdom (*ibid.*, § 34), United States (*ibid.*, § 35) and Yugoslavia (*ibid.*, § 36).

[67] See, e.g., the legislation of Australia (cited in Vol. II, Ch. 17, §§ 37–38), Azerbaijan (*ibid.*, § 39), Belarus (*ibid.*, § 40), Bosnia and Herzegovina (*ibid.*, § 41), Canada (*ibid.*, § 43), China (*ibid.*, § 44), Congo (*ibid.*, § 45), Côte d'Ivoire (*ibid.*, § 46), Croatia (*ibid.*, § 47), Ethiopia (*ibid.*, § 48), Georgia (*ibid.*, § 49), Germany (*ibid.*, § 50), Ireland (*ibid.*, § 51), Lithuania (*ibid.*, § 52), Mali (*ibid.*, § 53), Netherlands (*ibid.*, §§ 54–55), New Zealand (*ibid.*, § 56), Norway (*ibid.*, § 57), Slovenia (*ibid.*, § 58), United Kingdom (*ibid.*, § 60) and Yugoslavia (*ibid.*, §§ 61–62); see also the draft legislation of Burundi (*ibid.*, § 42) and Trinidad and Tobago (*ibid.*, § 59).

[68] Convention on the Safety of UN and Associated Personnel, Article 9.

[69] See, e.g., the legislation of Australia (cited in Vol. II, Ch. 9, § 15), Azerbaijan (*ibid.*, § 16), Canada (*ibid.*, § 18), Congo (*ibid.*, § 19), Georgia (*ibid.*, § 20), Germany (*ibid.*, § 21), Mali (*ibid.*, § 22), Netherlands (*ibid.*, § 23), New Zealand (*ibid.*, §§ 24–25) and United Kingdom (*ibid.*, §§ 27–28); see also the draft legislation of Burundi (*ibid.*, § 17) and Trinidad and Tobago (*ibid.*, § 26).

[70] ICC Statute, Article 8(2)(b)(iii).

advantage anticipated. The protection of the natural environment is a value that has considerably developed since the adoption of Additional Protocol I. The description of the war crime relating to the environment in the Statute of the International Criminal Court, combining as it does the high threshold of damage and lack of proportionality,[71] is more restrictive than the customary prohibitions relating to the environment (see Rules 43 and 45). The inclusion of this war crime was not controversial during the negotiation of the Statute of the International Criminal Court. In addition, a deliberate attack on the environment, not required by military necessity, would also amount to a war crime because it would in effect be an attack on a civilian object (see Rule 7).

(v) Using prohibited weapons. States negotiating the Statute of the International Criminal Court did so on the basis that the list of war crimes in the Statute reflected customary law rules, including the list of weapons whose use was subject to the Court's jurisdiction. As well as the specific weapons listed in Article 8(2)(b)(xvii)–(xix) of the Statute, weapons that are of a nature to cause superfluous injury or unnecessary suffering or which are inherently indiscriminate are listed in Article 8(2)(b)(xx), which adds that they must also be subject to a "comprehensive prohibition" and listed in an annex to the Statute.[72]

Several military manuals provide that the use of prohibited weapons constitutes a war crime.[73] In addition, the use of weapons that are prohibited under international law is a criminal offence under the legislation of numerous States.[74] This practice is both widespread and representative.

(vi) Declaring abolished, suspended or inadmissible in a court of law the rights and actions of the nationals of the hostile party. This prohibition goes back to the Hague Regulations.[75] It was included without controversy in the Statute of the International Criminal Court, as it was considered part of customary international law.[76]

---

[71] ICC Statute, Article 8(2)(b)(iv).   [72] ICC Statute, Article 8(2)(b)(xx) (*ibid.*, § 405).

[73] See, e.g., the military manuals of Australia (cited in Vol. II, Ch. 20, §§ 408–409), Ecuador (*ibid.*, § 411), Germany (*ibid.*, § 412), South Korea (*ibid.*, § 413), Nigeria (*ibid.*, § 414), South Africa (*ibid.*, § 415), Switzerland (*ibid.*, § 416), United Kingdom (*ibid.*, § 417) and United States (*ibid.*, §§ 418–420).

[74] See, e.g., the legislation of Belarus (cited in Vol. II, Ch. 20, § 422), Bosnia and Herzegovina (*ibid.*, § 423), Bulgaria (*ibid.*, § 424), Colombia (*ibid.*, § 425), Croatia (*ibid.*, § 427), Czech Republic (*ibid.*, § 428), Denmark (*ibid.*, § 429), El Salvador (*ibid.*, § 430), Estonia (*ibid.*, § 431), Ethiopia (*ibid.*, § 432), Finland (*ibid.*, § 433), Hungary (*ibid.*, § 434), Italy (*ibid.*, § 435), Kazakhstan (*ibid.*, § 436), Lithuania (*ibid.*, § 437), Moldova (*ibid.*, § 438), Mozambique (*ibid.*, § 439), New Zealand (*ibid.*, § 440), Nicaragua (*ibid.*, §§ 441–442), Norway (*ibid.*, § 443), Poland (*ibid.*, § 444), Russia (*ibid.*, § 445), Slovakia (*ibid.*, § 446), Slovenia (*ibid.*, § 447), Spain (*ibid.*, §§ 448–449), Sweden (*ibid.*, § 450), Tajikistan (*ibid.*, § 451), Uzbekistan (*ibid.*, § 452), Vietnam (*ibid.*, § 453) and Yugoslavia (*ibid.*, § 454); see also the draft legislation of Argentina (*ibid.*, § 421).

[75] Hague Regulations, Article 23(h).   [76] ICC Statute, Article 8(2)(b)(xiv).

(vii) Using human shields. Using human shields is prohibited under customary international law (see Rule 97) but has also been recognised as a war crime by the International Criminal Tribunal for the Former Yugoslavia, either as inhuman or cruel treatment,[77] or as an outrage upon personal dignity.[78] Its inclusion in the Statute of the International Criminal Court was uncontroversial.[79] Using human shields constitutes a criminal offence under the legislation of many States.[80] References to more practice can be found in the commentary to Rule 97.

(viii) Conscripting or enlisting children under the age of 15 into armed forces, or using them to participate actively in hostilities. The prohibition of enlisting children under 15 years of age into the armed forces, or using them to participate actively in hostilities, was introduced in Additional Protocol I.[81] Although this is a relatively recent prohibition, the inclusion of such acts as war crimes in the Statute of the International Criminal Court was uncontroversial. The recruitment of children is prohibited under the legislation of many States.[82] Using children to participate actively in hostilities is also prohibited under the legislation of many States.[83] References to more practice can be found in the commentary to Rules 136–137.

(ix) Committing sexual violence, in particular rape, sexual slavery, enforced prostitution and enforced pregnancy. The explicit listing in the Statute of the International Criminal Court of various forms of sexual violence as war crimes

---

[77] See, e.g., ICTY, *Blaškić case*, Case No. IT-95-14-T, Judgement, Trial Chamber I, 3 March 2000, § 716; *Kordić and Čerkez case*, Case No. IT-95-14/2-T, Judgement, Trial Chamber III, 26 February 2001, § 256; see also *Karadžić and Mladić case*, Review of the Indictments (cited in Vol. II, Ch. 32, § 2366).

[78] See, e.g., ICTY, *Aleksovski case*, Case No. IT-95-14/1-T, Judgement, Trial Chamber I, 25 June 1999, § 229.

[79] ICC Statute, Article 8(2)(b)(xxiii).

[80] See, e.g., the legislation of Australia (cited in Vol. II, Ch. 32, § 2287), Azerbaijan (*ibid.*, §§ 2288–2289), Bangladesh (*ibid.*, § 2290), Belarus (*ibid.*, § 2291), Canada (*ibid.*, § 2293), Democratic Republic of the Congo (*ibid.*, § 2294), Congo (*ibid.*, § 2295), Germany (*ibid.*, § 2296), Georgia (*ibid.*, § 2297), Ireland (*ibid.*, § 2298), Lithuania (*ibid.*, § 2299), Mali (*ibid.*, § 2300), Netherlands (*ibid.*, § 2301), New Zealand (*ibid.*, § 2302), Norway (*ibid.*, § 2303), Peru (*ibid.*, § 2304), Poland (*ibid.*, § 2305), Tajikistan (*ibid.*, § 2306), United Kingdom (*ibid.*, § 2308) and Yemen (*ibid.*, § 2309); see also the draft legislation of Burundi (*ibid.*, § 2292) and Trinidad and Tobago (*ibid.*, § 2307).

[81] Additional Protocol I, Article 77(2).

[82] See, e.g., the legislation of Australia (cited in Vol. II, Ch. 39, § 407), Azerbaijan (*ibid.*, § 408), Bangladesh (*ibid.*, § 409), Belarus (*ibid.*, §§ 410–411), Canada (*ibid.*, § 413), Colombia (*ibid.*, §§ 414–415), Congo (*ibid.*, § 416), Georgia (*ibid.*, § 418), Germany (*ibid.*, § 419), Ireland (*ibid.*, § 420), Jordan (*ibid.*, § 421), Malawi (*ibid.*, § 422), Malaysia (*ibid.*, § 423), Netherlands (*ibid.*, § 425), New Zealand (*ibid.*, § 426), Norway (*ibid.*, § 427), Philippines (*ibid.*, § 428), Spain (*ibid.*, § 429), Ukraine (*ibid.*, § 431) and United Kingdom (*ibid.*, § 432); see also the draft legislation of Argentina (*ibid.*, § 406), Burundi (*ibid.*, § 412) and Trinidad and Tobago (*ibid.*, § 430).

[83] See, e.g., the legislation of Australia (cited in Vol. II, Ch. 39, § 529), Belarus (*ibid.*, §§ 530–531), Canada (*ibid.*, § 533), Colombia (*ibid.*, §§ 534–535), Congo (*ibid.*, § 536), Germany (*ibid.*, § 537), Georgia (*ibid.*, § 538), Ireland (*ibid.*, § 539), Jordan (*ibid.*, § 540), Malaysia (*ibid.*, § 541), Mali (*ibid.*, § 542), Netherlands (*ibid.*, § 543), New Zealand (*ibid.*, § 544), Norway (*ibid.*, § 545), Philippines (*ibid.*, § 546) and United Kingdom (*ibid.*, § 548); see also the draft legislation of Burundi (*ibid.*, § 532) and Trinidad and Tobago (*ibid.*, § 547).

reflects changes in society in recent decades, in particular the demand for greater respect for and recognition of women. Although rape was prohibited by the Geneva Conventions, it was not explicitly listed as a grave breach either in the Conventions or in Additional Protocol I but would have to be considered a grave breach on the basis that it amounts to inhuman treatment or wilfully causing great suffering or serious injury to body or health. It was not the subject of war crimes trials after the Second World War, even though the practice of sexual violence was widespread. However, since then, not only has there been recognition of the criminal nature of rape or sexual assault in armed conflict in the legislation of many States,[84] but there have also been a number of prosecutions and convictions on this basis by the International Criminal Tribunals for the Former Yugoslavia and for Rwanda.[85]

The inclusion of crimes of sexual violence in the Statute of the International Criminal Court was not of itself controversial. There was, however, some controversy concerning two of the crimes of sexual violence, namely, "forced pregnancy" and "any other form of sexual violence". "Forced pregnancy" was introduced as a crime in the Statute of the International Criminal Court following the suggestion of Bosnia and Herzegovina and others because of the incidence of such acts during its armed conflict.[86] Some delegations, however, feared that this crime might be interpreted as imposing on States a duty to provide forcibly impregnated women access to abortion.[87] Given that the crime involves two other war crimes, namely, rape and unlawful confinement, the customary nature of the criminality of this behaviour is not in doubt. Characterising "any other form of sexual violence" as a war crime caused some difficulty for some delegations as they felt it to be somewhat vague. It was solved by introducing the words "also constituting a grave breach of the Geneva Conventions". Although the intention of some of the groups that pressed for the inclusion of this crime was to stress that any form of sexual violence should be considered to be a grave breach, this phrase has been interpreted by States in the Elements of Crimes for the International Criminal Court as requiring that

---

[84] See, e.g., the legislation of Armenia (cited in Vol. II, Ch. 32, § 1620), Australia (ibid., §§ 1621–1623), Azerbaijan (ibid., §§ 1624–1625), Bangladesh (ibid., § 1626), Belgium (ibid., § 1627), Bosnia and Herzegovina (ibid., § 1628), Canada (ibid., § 1630), China (ibid., § 1631), Colombia (ibid., § 1632), Congo (ibid., § 1633), Croatia (ibid., § 1634), Estonia (ibid., § 1636), Ethiopia (ibid., § 1637), Georgia (ibid., § 1638), Germany (ibid., § 1639), South Korea (ibid., § 1643), Lithuania (ibid., § 1644), Mali (ibid., § 1645), Mozambique (ibid., § 1646), Netherlands (ibid., §§ 1648–1649), New Zealand (ibid., § 1650), Paraguay (ibid., § 1653), Slovenia (ibid., § 1654), Spain (ibid., § 1656), United Kingdom (ibid., § 1658) and Yugoslavia (ibid., §§ 1659–1660); see also the draft legislation of Argentina (ibid., § 1619), Burundi (ibid., § 1629) and Trinidad and Tobago (ibid., § 1657).

[85] See, e.g., ICTY, Nikolić case, Review of the Indictment (cited in Vol. II, Ch. 32, § 1731), Delalić case, Judgement (ibid., § 1733), Furundžija case, Judgement and Judgment on Appeal, (ibid., §§ 1734–1735) and Kunarac case, Judgement (ibid., § 1736).

[86] ICC Statute, Article 8(2)(b)(xxii).

[87] See Knut Dörmann, Elements of War Crimes under the Rome Statute of the International Criminal Court: Sources and Commentary, Cambridge University Press, 2003, pp. 329–330.

"the conduct was of a gravity comparable to that of a grave breach of the Geneva Conventions".[88]

References to more practice can be found in the commentary to Rule 93.

(ii) Other serious violations of international humanitarian law committed during an international armed conflict (continued):

- slavery and deportation to slave labour;
- collective punishments;
- despoliation of the wounded, sick, shipwrecked or dead;
- attacking or ill-treating a *parlementaire* or bearer of a flag of truce;
- unjustifiable delay in the repatriation of prisoners of war or civilians;
- the practice of apartheid or other inhuman or degrading practices involving outrages on personal dignity based on racial discrimination;
- launching an indiscriminate attack resulting in loss of life or injury to civilians or damage to civilian objects;
- launching an attack against works or installations containing dangerous forces in the knowledge that such attack will cause excessive incidental loss of civilian life, injury to civilians or damage to civilian objects.

Basis for the war crimes listed above

These war crimes are not referred to as such in the Statute of the International Criminal Court. However, they are criminal either by virtue of the fact that such acts in practice amount to one or more of the crimes listed in the Statute, or because they are violations of customary international law, the criminal nature of which has been recognised by the international community.

(i) *Slavery and deportation to slave labour.* Slavery and deportation to slave labour are violations of customary international law (see Rules 94–95), and their practice in armed conflict amounts to a war crime. The legislation of many States prohibits slavery and the slave trade, or "enslavement".[89] Deportation of civilians to slave labour is listed as a war crime in the Charter of the International Military Tribunal at Nuremberg.[90] "Enslavement" and deportation to slave labour were the basis for several war crimes trials after the Second World War.[91] References to more practice can be found in the commentary to Rules 94–95.

---

[88] See Knut Dörmann, *Elements of War Crimes under the Rome Statute of the International Criminal Court: Sources and Commentary*, Cambridge University Press, 2003, pp. 331–332.

[89] See, e.g., the legislation of Armenia (cited in Vol. II, Ch. 32, § 1817), Australia (*ibid.*, § 1820), Belgium (*ibid.*, § 1825), Canada (*ibid.*, § 1828), China (*ibid.*, § 1829), Congo (*ibid.*, § 1831), Croatia (*ibid.*, § 1833), France (*ibid.*, § 1835), Ireland (*ibid.*, § 1836), Kenya (*ibid.*, § 1839), Mali (*ibid.*, § 1843), Netherlands (*ibid.*, § 1844), New Zealand (*ibid.*, § 1846), Niger (*ibid.*, § 1848), Norway (*ibid.*, § 1849), Philippines (*ibid.*, § 1851), United Kingdom (*ibid.*, § 1855) and United States (*ibid.*, §§ 1856–1857); see also the draft legislation of Burundi (*ibid.*, § 1827) and Trinidad and Tobago (*ibid.*, § 1853).

[90] IMT Charter (Nuremberg), Article 6 (*ibid.*, § 1761).

[91] See, e.g., Canada, Federal Court of Appeal, *Rudolph and Minister of Employment and Immigration case* (*ibid.*, § 1861); Netherlands, Special Court of Cassation, *Rohrig and Others case* (*ibid.*, § 1866); Poland, Supreme National Tribunal of Poland at Poznan, *Greiser case* (*ibid.*, § 1867);

(ii) Collective punishments. Collective punishments amount to depriving the victims of a fair trial and are listed as a war crime in the legislation of numerous States.[92] Depending on the nature of the punishment, it is likely to amount to one or more other war crimes, as found, for example, in the *Priebke case* in 1997, which concerned reprisal killings in the Second World War.[93] References to more practice can be found in the commentary to Rule 103.

(iii) Despoliation of the wounded, sick, shipwrecked or dead. In the *Pohl case* in 1947, the US Military Tribunal at Nuremberg stated that robbing the dead "is and always has been a crime".[94] Such behaviour generally amounts to either pillage or to the taking of property in violation of international humanitarian law. The behaviour is also specifically characterised as a criminal act in the legislation of numerous States.[95]

The 1906 Geneva Convention for the Amelioration of the Condition of the Wounded and Sick in Armies in the Field requires that "the necessary measures to repress, in time of war, individual acts of robbery and ill treatment of the sick and wounded of the armies" be taken.[96] In particular, many manuals prohibit pillage of the wounded, sick and shipwrecked, sometimes referred to as "marauding", or specify that it constitutes a war crime.[97]

United States, Military Tribunal at Nuremberg, *List (Hostages Trial) case (ibid.,* § 1870), *Milch case (ibid.,* § 1871), *Krauch (I. G. Farben Trial) case (ibid.,* § 1872) and *Krupp case (ibid.,* § 1873).

[92] See, e.g., the legislation of Argentina (cited in Vol. II, Ch. 32, § 3777), Australia (*ibid.,* § 3778), Bangladesh (*ibid.,* § 3779), Bosnia and Herzegovina (*ibid.,* § 3780), China (*ibid.,* § 3781), Democratic Republic of the Congo (*ibid.,* § 3782), Côte d'Ivoire (*ibid.,* § 3783), Croatia (*ibid.,* § 3784), Ethiopia (*ibid.,* § 3785), Ireland (*ibid.,* § 3786), Italy (*ibid.,* § 3787), Kyrgyzstan (*ibid.,* § 3788), Lithuania (*ibid.,* § 3789), Norway (*ibid.,* § 3790), Romania (*ibid.,* § 3791), Slovenia (*ibid.,* § 3792), Spain (*ibid.,* § 3793) and Yugoslavia (*ibid.,* § 3794).

[93] Italy, Military Tribunal of Rome, *Priebke case* (cited in Vol. II, Ch. 32, § 3796).

[94] United States, Military Tribunal at Nuremberg, *Pohl case (ibid.,* § 235).

[95] See, e.g., the legislation of Albania (cited in Vol. II, Ch. 35, § 165), Algeria (*ibid.,* § 166), Argentina (*ibid.,* § 167), Armenia (*ibid.,* § 168), Australia (*ibid.,* § 169), Azerbaijan (*ibid.,* § 170), Bangladesh (*ibid.,* § 171), Bosnia and Herzegovina (*ibid.,* § 172), Botswana (*ibid.,* § 173), Bulgaria (*ibid.,* § 174), Burkina Faso (*ibid.,* § 175), Canada (*ibid.,* § 176), Chad (*ibid.,* § 177), Chile (*ibid.,* § 178), Colombia (*ibid.,* § 179), Côte d'Ivoire (*ibid.,* § 180), Croatia (*ibid.,* § 181), Cuba (*ibid.,* § 182), Czech Republic (*ibid.,* § 183), Denmark (*ibid.,* § 184), Egypt (*ibid.,* §§ 185–186), El Salvador (*ibid.,* § 187), Ethiopia (*ibid.,* § 188), France (*ibid.,* § 189), Gambia (*ibid.,* § 190), Georgia (*ibid.,* § 191), Ghana (*ibid.,* § 192), Guinea (*ibid.,* § 193), Hungary (*ibid.,* § 194), Indonesia (*ibid.,* § 195), Iraq (196), Ireland (*ibid.,* § 197), Italy (*ibid.,* § 198), Kazakhstan (*ibid.,* § 199), Kenya (*ibid.,* § 200), South Korea (*ibid.,* § 201), Latvia (*ibid.,* § 202), Lebanon (*ibid.,* § 203), Lithuania (*ibid.,* § 204), Malaysia (*ibid.,* § 205), Mali (*ibid.,* § 206), Moldova (*ibid.,* § 207), Netherlands (*ibid.,* § 208), New Zealand (*ibid.,* § 209), Nicaragua (*ibid.,* §§ 210–211), Nigeria (*ibid.,* § 212), Norway (*ibid.,* § 213) Romania (*ibid.,* § 214), Singapore (*ibid.,* § 215), Slovakia (*ibid.,* § 216), Slovenia (*ibid.,* § 217), Spain (*ibid.,* §§ 218–219), Switzerland (*ibid.,* § 220), Tajikistan (*ibid.,* § 221), Togo (*ibid.,* § 222), Trinidad and Tobago (*ibid.,* § 223), Uganda (*ibid.,* § 224), Ukraine (*ibid.,* § 225), United Kingdom (*ibid.,* §§ 226–227), Uruguay (*ibid.,* § 228), Venezuela (*ibid.,* § 229), Vietnam (*ibid.,* § 230), Yemen (*ibid.,* § 231), Yugoslavia (*ibid.,* § 232), Zambia (*ibid.,* § 233) and Zimbabwe (*ibid.,* § 234).

[96] 1906 Geneva Convention for the Amelioration of the Condition of the Wounded and Sick in Armies in the Field, Article 28.

[97] See, e.g., the military manuals of Burkina Faso (cited in Vol. II, Ch. 34, § 417), Cameroon (*ibid.,* § 418), Canada (*ibid.,* § 420), Congo (*ibid.,* § 422), France (*ibid.,* § 423), Israel (*ibid.,* § 425), Italy (*ibid.,* § 426), Lebanon (*ibid.,* § 428), Mali (*ibid.,* § 429), Morocco (*ibid.,* § 430), Philippines

References to more practice can be found in the commentary to Rules 111 and 113.

(iv) Attacking or ill-treating a parlementaire *or bearer of the flag of truce.* This is a violation of the Hague Regulations and of customary international law (see Rule 67). It amounts to an attack on either a civilian or a combatant who at that moment is *hors de combat* and therefore constitutes a war crime. Several manuals consider that attacks against a *parlementaire* displaying the white flag of truce constitutes a war crime.[98] Breach of the inviolability of *parlementaires* is an offence under the legislation of many States.[99] References to more practice can be found in the commentary to Rule 67.

(v) Unjustifiable delay in the repatriation of prisoners of war and civilians. This war crime is listed as a grave breach in Additional Protocol I.[100] So far, no prosecutions of this war crime have been noted, nor is this crime specifically listed in the Statute of the International Criminal Court. However, the criminal nature of this violation has been accepted by the 161 States party to Additional Protocol I. The legislation of numerous States specifies that it is a war crime, including Azerbaijan, which is not party to Additional Protocol I.[101] In case a delay in the repatriation of prisoners of war or civilians is unjustifiable, in practice there would no longer exist a legal basis for their deprivation of liberty and it would amount to unlawful confinement (see commentary to Rule 99).

(vi) The practice of apartheid or other inhuman or degrading practices involving outrages on personal dignity based on racial discrimination. This war crime is listed as a grave breach in Additional Protocol I.[102] It does not appear in exactly these terms in the list of war crimes in the Statute of the International

---

(*ibid.*, § 434) ("mistreat"), Romania (*ibid.*, § 435), Senegal (*ibid.*, § 436), Switzerland (*ibid.*, § 437), United Kingdom (*ibid.*, § 438) and United States (*ibid.*, § 442) ("mistreating").

[98] See, e.g., the military manuals of Australia (cited in Vol. II, Ch. 19, §§ 161–162), Canada (*ibid.*, § 167), Ecuador (*ibid.*, § 169), South Korea (*ibid.*, § 175), New Zealand (*ibid.*, § 179), Nigeria (*ibid.*, § 180), South Africa (*ibid.*, § 185), Switzerland (*ibid.*, § 189), United Kingdom (*ibid.*, § 190) and United States (*ibid.*, §§ 192–195).

[99] See, e.g., the legislation of Argentina (cited in Vol. II, Ch. 19, § 197), Bosnia and Herzegovina (*ibid.*, § 199), Chile (*ibid.*, § 200), Croatia (*ibid.*, § 201), Dominican Republic (*ibid.*, § 202), Ecuador (*ibid.*, § 203), El Salvador (*ibid.*, § 204), Estonia (*ibid.*, § 205), Ethiopia (*ibid.*, § 206), Hungary (*ibid.*, § 207), Italy (*ibid.*, § 208), Mexico (*ibid.*, §§ 209–210), Nicaragua (*ibid.*, § 211), Peru (*ibid.*, § 212), Slovenia (*ibid.*, § 213), Spain (*ibid.*, §§ 214–216), Switzerland (*ibid.*, § 217), Venezuela (*ibid.*, §§ 218–219) and Yugoslavia (*ibid.*, § 220); see also the draft legislation of Argentina (*ibid.*, § 198).

[100] Additional Protocol I, Article 85(4)(b).

[101] See, e.g., the legislation of Australia (cited in Vol. II, Ch. 37, §§ 664–665), Azerbaijan (*ibid.*, § 666), Belarus (*ibid.*, § 668), Belgium (*ibid.*, § 669), Canada (*ibid.*, § 671), Cook Islands (*ibid.*, § 672), Croatia (*ibid.*, § 673), Cyprus (*ibid.*, § 674), Czech Republic (*ibid.*, § 675), Estonia (*ibid.*, § 677), Georgia (*ibid.*, § 678), Germany (*ibid.*, § 679), Hungary (*ibid.*, § 680), Ireland (*ibid.*, § 681), Lithuania (*ibid.*, § 684), Moldova (*ibid.*, § 685), New Zealand (*ibid.*, § 687), Niger (*ibid.*, § 689), Norway (*ibid.*, § 690), Slovakia (*ibid.*, § 691), Slovenia (*ibid.*, § 692), Spain (*ibid.*, § 693), Tajikistan (*ibid.*, § 694), United Kingdom (*ibid.*, § 695), Yugoslavia (*ibid.*, § 696) and Zimbabwe (*ibid.*, § 697); see also the draft legislation of Argentina (*ibid.*, § 662), El Salvador (*ibid.*, § 676), Jordan (*ibid.*, § 682), Lebanon (*ibid.*, § 683) and Nicaragua (*ibid.*, § 688).

[102] Additional Protocol I, Article 85(4)(c).

Criminal Court, but such conduct would amount to a war crime as an outrage on personal dignity, as well as humiliating and degrading treatment. Apartheid in the application of international humanitarian law is a crime under the legislation of numerous States.[103] In addition, respect for all persons *hors de combat* without adverse distinction is a fundamental guarantee provided for in customary international law (see Rule 88).

(vii) Launching an indiscriminate attack resulting in loss of life or injury to civilians or damage to civilian objects. The prohibition of indiscriminate attacks is part of customary international law (see Rule 11). Launching an indiscriminate attack constitutes an offence under the legislation of numerous States.[104] Although not listed as such in the Statute of the International Criminal Court, an indiscriminate attack amounts in practice to an attack on civilians, as indicated by the International Court of Justice in the *Nuclear Weapons case* in 1995 and in several judgements of the International Criminal Tribunal for the Former Yugoslavia.[105]

The description of "intention" of the Statute of the International Criminal Court includes the perpetrator being "aware that [the consequence] will occur in the ordinary course of events".[106] It is clear that launching an attack knowing that civilian casualties are likely to occur does not in itself necessarily amount to an indiscriminate attack, because incidental injury or damage is not as such prohibited. However, launching an attack without attempting to aim properly at a military target or in such a manner as to hit civilians without any thought or care as to the likely extent of death or injury amounts to an indiscriminate attack. Launching such an attack knowing that the degree of incidental civilian

---

[103] See, e.g., the legislation of Australia (cited in Vol. II, Ch. 32, §§ 601–602), Azerbaijan (*ibid.*, § 603), Belgium (*ibid.*, § 604), Bulgaria (*ibid.*, § 605), Canada (*ibid.*, § 607), Colombia (*ibid.*, § 609), Cook Islands (*ibid.*, § 611), Cyprus (*ibid.*, § 612), Czech Republic (*ibid.*, § 613), Georgia (*ibid.*, § 615), Hungary (*ibid.*, § 616), Ireland (*ibid.*, § 617), Moldova (*ibid.*, § 621), New Zealand (*ibid.*, § 623), Niger (*ibid.*, § 626), Norway (*ibid.*, § 627), Peru (*ibid.*, § 628), Slovakia (*ibid.*, § 629), Spain (*ibid.*, § 630), Tajikistan (*ibid.*, § 631), United Kingdom (*ibid.*, § 633) and Zimbabwe (*ibid.*, § 635); see also the draft legislation of El Salvador (*ibid.*, § 614), Jordan (*ibid.*, § 618), Lebanon (*ibid.*, § 619) and Nicaragua (*ibid.*, § 625).

[104] See, e.g., the legislation of Armenia (cited in Vol. II, Ch. 3, § 33), Australia (*ibid.*, § 34), Belarus (*ibid.*, § 35), Belgium (*ibid.*, § 36), Bosnia and Herzegovina (*ibid.*, § 37), Canada (*ibid.*, § 38), China (*ibid.*, § 39), Colombia (*ibid.*, § 40), Cook Islands (*ibid.*, § 41), Croatia (*ibid.*, § 42), Cyprus (*ibid.*, § 43), Estonia (*ibid.*, § 45), Georgia (*ibid.*, § 46), Indonesia (*ibid.*, § 47), Ireland (*ibid.*, § 48), Lithuania (*ibid.*, § 51), Netherlands (*ibid.*, § 52), New Zealand (*ibid.*, § 53), Niger (*ibid.*, § 55), Norway (*ibid.*, § 56), Slovenia (*ibid.*, § 57), Spain (*ibid.*, § 58), Sweden (*ibid.*, § 59), Tajikistan (*ibid.*, § 60), United Kingdom (*ibid.*, § 61), Yugoslavia (*ibid.*, § 629) and Zimbabwe (*ibid.*, § 63); see also the draft legislation of Argentina (*ibid.*, § 33), El Salvador (*ibid.*, § 44), Jordan (*ibid.*, § 49), Lebanon (*ibid.*, § 50) and Nicaragua (*ibid.*, § 54).

[105] See ICJ, *Nuclear Weapons case*, Advisory Opinion (cited in Vol. II, Ch. 3, § 243); ICTY, *Galić case*, Case No. IT-98-29-T, Judgement and Opinion, 5 December 2003, § 57 ("indiscriminate attacks, that is to say, attacks which strike civilians or civilian objects and military objectives without distinction, may qualify as direct attacks against civilians"), with further references to the *Blaškić case*, Judgement, and the *Martić case*, Review of the Indictment; see also *Tadić case*, Interlocutory Appeal (cited in Vol. II, Ch. 3, § 134), *Karadžić and Mladić case*, Review of the Indictments (*ibid.*, § 135), *Kordić and Čerkez case*, Decision on the Joint Defence Motion (*ibid.*, § 136) and *Kupreškić case*, Judgement (*ibid.*, § 137).

[106] ICC Statute, Article 30(3).

deaths, injuries or damage will be excessive is categorised as a grave breach in Additional Protocol I.[107] References to more practice can be found in the commentary to Rule 11.

(viii) Launching an attack against works or installations containing dangerous forces in the knowledge that such attack will cause excessive incidental loss of civilian life, injury to civilians or damage to civilian objects. This war crime is listed as a grave breach in Additional Protocol I.[108] It covers attacks against works or installations which are themselves military objectives, or attacks against military objectives located at or in the vicinity of such works, resulting in excessive incidental civilian casualties or damage.[109] Such an attack is a violation of customary international law and is also covered, in practice, by the Statute of the International Criminal Court ("launching an attack in the knowledge that such attack will cause incidental loss of life, injury to civilians or damage to civilian objects which would be clearly excessive in relation to the concrete and direct overall military advantage anticipated").[110] References to more practice can be found in the commentary to Rule 42.

(iii) Serious violations of common Article 3 of the Geneva Conventions:

In the case of an armed conflict not of an international character, any of the following acts committed against persons taking no active part in the hostilities, including members of armed forces who have laid down their arms and those placed *hors de combat* by sickness, wounds, detention or any other cause:

- violence to life and person, in particular murder of all kinds, mutilation, cruel treatment and torture;
- committing outrages upon personal dignity, in particular humiliating and degrading treatment;
- taking of hostages;
- the passing of sentences and the carrying out of executions without previous judgement pronounced by a regularly constituted court, affording all judicial guarantees which are generally recognised as indispensable.

Basis for the war crimes listed above

Common Article 3 of the Geneva Conventions has crystallised into customary international law, and the breach of one or more of its provisions has been recognised as amounting to a war crime in the Statutes of the International Criminal Tribunal for Rwanda, of the Special Court for Sierra Leone and of the International Criminal Court, as well as by the International Criminal Tribunal for the

---

[107] Additional Protocol I, Article 85(3)(b).   [108] Additional Protocol I, Article 85(3)(c).
[109] It should be noted that an attack, intentionally directed against a work or installation which does not constitute a military objective, would constitute the war crime of making civilian objects the object of attack, independent of the civilian casualties or damage caused.
[110] ICC Statute, Article 8(2)(b)(iv).

Former Yugoslavia.[111] Its inclusion in the Statute of the International Criminal Court was largely uncontroversial. It should be pointed out that, although some of the wording is not the same as the equivalent crimes in the grave breaches applicable to international armed conflicts, there is no difference in practice as far as the elements of these crimes is concerned. This is borne out by the Elements of Crimes for the International Criminal Court and by the case-law of the International Criminal Tribunal for the Former Yugoslavia.[112]

(iv) Other serious violations of international humanitarian law committed during a non-international armed conflict:

- making the civilian population or individual civilians, not taking a direct part in hostilities, the object of attack;
- pillage;
- committing sexual violence, in particular, rape, sexual slavery, enforced prostitution, enforced sterilisation and enforced pregnancy.

Basis for the war crimes listed above

These violations of customary international law are included in the list of war crimes in the Statute of the International Criminal Court and, for the most part, in the Statutes of the International Criminal Tribunal for Rwanda and of the Special Court for Sierra Leone (see *infra*).

(i) *Making the civilian population or individual civilians, not taking a direct part in hostilities, the object of attack.* The International Criminal Tribunal for the Former Yugoslavia has referred to this prohibition as a war crime in non-international armed conflicts.[113] The war crime is not listed in the same terms in the Statute of the International Criminal Tribunal for Rwanda, but the Statute refers in general terms to serious violations of Additional Protocol II, Article 13 of which prohibits attacks against civilians.[114] To direct attacks against civilians is an offence under the legislation of numerous States.[115] References to more practice can be found in the commentary to Rule 1.

---

[111] ICTR Statute, Article 4; Statute of the Special Court for Sierra Leone, Article 3; ICC Statute, Article 8(2)(c); see, e.g., ICTY, *Tadić case*, Interlocutory Appeal (cited in Vol. II, Ch. 32, § 928); ICTY, *Jelisić case*, Judgement (*ibid.*, § 934).

[112] Elements of Crimes for the International Criminal Court (relating to Article 8(2)(c) of the ICC Statute); ICTY, *Delalić case*, Case No. IT-96–21-T, Judgement, Trial Chamber II, 16 November 1998, §§ 422–423 (in relation to murder), § 552 (in relation to cruel treatment), § 443 (in relation to torture) and § 187 (in relation to the taking of hostages).

[113] See ICTY, *Tadić case*, Case No. IT-94-1-AR7, Decision on the Defence Motion for Interlocutory Appeal on Jurisdiction, Appeals Chamber, 2 October 1995, §§ 100–118 and *Martić case*, Case No. IT-95–11-R61, Review of the Indictment Pursuant to Rule 61 of the Rules of Procedure and Evidence, Trial Chamber I, 8 March 1996, § 11.

[114] ICTR Statute, Article 4.

[115] See, e.g., the legislation of Armenia (cited in Vol. II, Ch. 1, § 218), Australia (*ibid.*, § 220), Azerbaijan (*ibid.*, §§ 221–222), Belarus (*ibid.*, § 223), Belgium (*ibid.*, § 224), Bosnia and Herzegovina (*ibid.*, § 225), Canada (*ibid.*, § 228), Colombia (*ibid.*, § 230), Democratic Republic of the Congo (*ibid.*, § 231), Congo (*ibid.*, § 232), Croatia (*ibid.*, § 234), Estonia (*ibid.*, § 239), Georgia (*ibid.*, § 240), Germany (*ibid.*, § 241), Ireland (*ibid.*, § 244), Lithuania (*ibid.*, § 248), Netherlands (*ibid.*, § 250), New Zealand (*ibid.*, § 252), Niger (*ibid.*, § 254), Norway (*ibid.*, § 255), Slovenia (*ibid.*,

(ii) Pillage. With respect to the war crime of pillage, the International Criminal Tribunal for the Former Yugoslavia, in the *Jelisić case* in 1999, convicted the accused of "plunder", a term sometimes used instead of "pillage", under Article 3 of its Statute.[116] Pillage is an offence under the legislation of many States.[117] References to more practice can be found in the commentary to Rule 52.

(iii) Committing sexual violence, in particular, rape, sexual slavery, enforced prostitution, enforced sterilisation and enforced pregnancy. With respect to sexual violence, the Statute of the International Criminal Court specifies in particular rape, sexual slavery, enforced prostitution, enforced sterilisation and enforced pregnancy.[118] The Statutes of the International Criminal Tribunal for Rwanda and of the Special Court for Sierra Leone define this war crime as "outrages upon personal dignity, in particular humiliating and degrading treatment, rape, enforced prostitution and any form of indecent assault".[119] In the *Furundžija case* in 1998 and *Kunarac case* in 2001, the International Criminal Tribunal for the Former Yugoslavia convicted the accused of rape in the context of a non-international armed conflict.[120] Sexual violence is an offence under the legislation of numerous States.[121] The comments above in relation to the

---

§ 257), Spain (*ibid.*, § 259), Sweden (*ibid.*, § 260), Tajikistan (*ibid.*, § 261), United Kingdom (*ibid.*, § 265), Vietnam (*ibid.*, § 266), Yemen (*ibid.*, § 267) and Yugoslavia (*ibid.*, § 268); see also the legislation of Czech Republic (*ibid.*, § 237), Hungary (*ibid.*, § 242), Italy (*ibid.*, § 245) and Slovakia (*ibid.*, § 256), the application of which is not excluded in time of non-international armed conflict, and the draft legislation of Argentina (*ibid.*, § 217), Burundi (*ibid.*, § 226), El Salvador (*ibid.*, § 238), Jordan (*ibid.*, § 246), Nicaragua (*ibid.*, § 253) and Trinidad and Tobago (*ibid.*, § 262).

[116] See ICTY, *Jelisić case*, Case No. IT-95-10-T, Judgement, Trial Chamber I, 14 December 1999, § 49.

[117] See, e.g., the legislation of Australia (cited in Vol. II, Ch. 16, § 559), Azerbaijan (*ibid.*, § 561), Bosnia and Herzegovina (*ibid.*, § 563), Canada (*ibid.*, §§ 569–570), Colombia (*ibid.*, § 576), Democratic Republic of the Congo (*ibid.*, § 577), Congo (*ibid.*, § 578), Croatia (*ibid.*, § 580), Ecuador (*ibid.*, § 582) El Salvador (*ibid.*, §§ 584–585), Estonia (*ibid.*, § 586), Ethiopia (*ibid.*, § 587), Gambia (*ibid.*, § 589), Georgia (*ibid.*, § 590), Germany (*ibid.*, § 591), Ghana (*ibid.*, § 592), Guinea (*ibid.*, § 593), Ireland (*ibid.*, § 599), Kazakhstan (*ibid.*, § 605), Kenya (*ibid.*, § 606), Latvia (*ibid.*, § 608), Moldova (*ibid.*, § 614), Netherlands (*ibid.*, § 620), New Zealand (*ibid.*, §§ 621–622), Nicaragua (*ibid.*, § 623), Nigeria (*ibid.*, § 624), Norway (*ibid.*, § 625), Paraguay (*ibid.*, § 627), Russia (*ibid.*, § 631), Singapore (*ibid.*, § 633), Slovenia (*ibid.*, § 635), Spain (*ibid.*, §§ 637–638), Switzerland (*ibid.*, § 642), Tajikistan (*ibid.*, § 643), Trinidad and Tobago (*ibid.*, § 645), Uganda (*ibid.*, § 648), Ukraine (*ibid.*, § 649), United Kingdom (*ibid.*, § 652), Uzbekistan (*ibid.*, § 657), Venezuela (*ibid.*, § 658), Yemen (*ibid.*, § 661), Yugoslavia (*ibid.*, § 663), Zambia (*ibid.*, § 664) and Zimbabwe (*ibid.*, § 665); see also the legislation of Bulgaria (*ibid.*, § 565), Burkina Faso (*ibid.*, § 566), Czech Republic (*ibid.*, § 581), Hungary (*ibid.*, § 594), Italy (*ibid.*, §§ 602–603), South Korea (*ibid.*, § 607), Mozambique (*ibid.*, § 616), Paraguay (*ibid.*, § 626), Peru (*ibid.*, § 628), Slovakia (*ibid.*, § 634) and Togo (*ibid.*, § 644), the application of which is not excluded in time of non-international armed conflict, and the draft legislation of Argentina (*ibid.*, § 556), Burundi (*ibid.*, § 567) and Trinidad and Tobago (*ibid.*, § 646).

[118] ICC Statute, Article 8(2)(e)(vi).

[119] ICTR Statute, Article 4(c) (cited in Vol. II, Ch. 32, § 1579); Statute of the Special Court for Sierra Leone, Article 3(e) (*ibid.*, § 1571).

[120] See ICTY, *Furundžija case*, Judgement (cited in Vol. II, Ch. 32, § 1735) and *Kunarac case*, Judgement (*ibid.*, § 1736).

[121] See, e.g., the legislation of Armenia (cited in Vol. II, Ch. 32, § 1620), Australia (*ibid.*, §§ 1622–1623), Azerbaijan (*ibid.*, §§ 1624–1625), Bangladesh (*ibid.*, § 1626), Belgium (*ibid.*, § 1627), Bosnia and Herzegovina (*ibid.*, § 1628), Canada (*ibid.*, § 1630), Colombia (*ibid.*, § 1632), Congo

crime of sexual violence in international armed conflicts also apply. References to more practice can be found in the commentary to Rule 93.

(iv) Other serious violations of international humanitarian law committed during a non-international armed conflict (continued):

- ordering the displacement of the civilian population for reasons related to the conflict and not required for the security of the civilians involved or imperative military necessity;
- subjecting persons in the power of the adversary to medical or scientific experiments of any kind not necessary for the health of the persons concerned and seriously endangering their health;
- declaring that no quarter will be given;
- making medical or religious personnel or objects the object of attack;
- conscripting or enlisting children under the age of 15 into the armed forces or groups, or using them to participate actively in hostilities;
- making religious or cultural objects the object of attack, provided that they are not military objectives.

Basis for the war crimes listed above

These are violations of Additional Protocol II and of customary international law, and have been listed as war crimes in the Statute of the International Criminal Court.

(i) Ordering the displacement of the civilian population for reasons related to the conflict and not required for the security of the civilians involved or imperative military necessity. This act is a violation of Additional Protocol II,[122] and of customary international law (see Rule 129). Such acts are often, in practice, linked to policies of "ethnic cleansing" or similarly abusive treatment of certain groups. Such displacement is listed as a war crime under the Statute of the International Criminal Court.[123] It is also a criminal offence under the legislation of numerous of States.[124] There have been many condemnations of

(*ibid.*, § 1633), Croatia (*ibid.*, § 1634), Estonia (*ibid.*, § 1636), Ethiopia (*ibid.*, § 1637), Georgia (*ibid.*, § 1638), Germany (*ibid.*, § 1639), Lithuania (*ibid.*, § 1644), Netherlands (*ibid.*, § 1649), New Zealand (*ibid.*, § 1650), Slovenia (*ibid.*, § 1654), Spain (*ibid.*, § 1656), United Kingdom (*ibid.*, § 1658) and Yugoslavia (*ibid.*, § 1660); see also the legislation of South Korea (*ibid.*, 1643), Mozambique (*ibid.*, § 1646) and Paraguay (*ibid.*, § 1653), the application of which is not excluded in time of non-international armed conflict, and the draft legislation of Argentina (*ibid.*, § 1619), Burundi (*ibid.*, § 1629) and Trinidad and Tobago (*ibid.*, § 1657).

[122] Additional Protocol II, Article 17.   [123] ICC Statute, Article 8(2)(e)(viii).

[124] See, e.g., the legislation of Armenia (cited in Vol. II, Ch. 38, § 66), Australia (*ibid.*, § 69), Azerbaijan (*ibid.*, § 70), Belarus (*ibid.*, § 73), Belgium (*ibid.*, § 74), Bosnia and Herzegovina (*ibid.*, § 75), Bulgaria (*ibid.*, § 77), Cambodia (*ibid.*, § 79), Canada (*ibid.*, § 81), China (*ibid.*, § 82), Colombia (*ibid.*, § 84), Democratic Republic of the Congo (*ibid.*, § 85), Congo (*ibid.*, § 86), Côte d'Ivoire (*ibid.*, § 88), Croatia (*ibid.*, § 89), Czech Republic (*ibid.*, § 92), Estonia (*ibid.*, § 95), Ethiopia (*ibid.*, § 96), Georgia (*ibid.*, § 99), Germany (*ibid.*, § 100), India (*ibid.*, § 103), Ireland (*ibid.*, § 104), Kazakhstan (*ibid.*, § 108), Latvia (*ibid.*, § 110), Mali (*ibid.*, § 117), Moldova (*ibid.*, § 120), New Zealand (*ibid.*, § 124), Nicaragua (*ibid.*, § 125), Niger (*ibid.*, § 127), Norway (*ibid.*, § 129), Paraguay (*ibid.*, § 131), Poland (*ibid.*, § 133), Portugal (*ibid.*, § 134), Romania (*ibid.*, § 135), Russia (*ibid.*, § 136), Slovakia (*ibid.*, § 139), Slovenia (*ibid.*, § 140), Spain (*ibid.*, § 141), Tajikistan (*ibid.*, § 143), United Kingdom (*ibid.*, § 148), Uzbekistan (*ibid.*, § 152) and Yugoslavia (*ibid.*, § 154); see also the draft legislation of Argentina (*ibid.*, § 65), Burundi (*ibid.*, § 78), El Salvador (*ibid.*, § 94) and Trinidad and Tobago (*ibid.*, § 144).

such behaviour by the UN Security Council, UN General Assembly and UN Commission on Human Rights in the non-international armed conflicts in Afghanistan, Bosnia and Herzegovina, Burundi, Iraq, Liberia, Rwanda, Sudan and Zaire.[125] References to more practice can be found in the commentary to Rule 129.

(ii) Subjecting persons in the power of the adversary to medical or scientific experiments of any kind not necessary for the health of the persons concerned and seriously endangering their health. This act is a violation of Additional Protocol II,[126] and of customary international law (see Rule 92). It is listed in the Statute of the International Criminal Court as a war crime, if such experimentation results in death or seriously endangers the health of the persons concerned.[127] It is also considered criminal under the legislation of numerous States.[128] Such behaviour is a violation of the respect due to persons in the power of the adversary and is likely also to amount to cruel treatment or an outrage upon personal dignity (see Rule 90). References to more practice can be found in the commentary to Rule 92.

(iii) Declaring that no quarter will be given. This war crime is listed in the Statute of the International Criminal Court.[129] It is not referred to in these terms in Additional Protocol II but is in practice the same as the prohibition of ordering that there be no survivors in Article 4(1) as well as in Article 4(2)(h), which prohibits threats to kill persons *hors de combat*. The actual carrying out of such threats would be a violation of common Article 3 of the Geneva Conventions. It is an offence under the legislation of numerous States to order that no quarter be given.[130]

---

125 See UN Security Council, Res. 752 (cited in Vol. II, Ch. 38, § 193), Res. 822, 874 and 884 (*ibid.*, § 195) and Res. 918 (*ibid.*, § 196); UN Security Council, Statements by the President (*ibid.*, §§ 200–203); UN General Assembly, Res. 46/134 (*ibid.*, § 208) and Res. 50/193 (*ibid.*, § 210); UN Commission on Human Rights, Res. 1994/87 (*ibid.*, § 211), Res. 1995/77 (*ibid.*, § 212) and Res. 1996/73 (*ibid.*, § 213).

126 Additional Protocol II, Article 5(2)(e).   127 ICC Statute, Article 8(2)(e)(xi).

128 See, e.g., the legislation of Australia (cited in Vol. II, Ch. 32, § 1470), Azerbaijan (*ibid.*, §§ 1471–1472), Belarus (*ibid.*, § 1475), Belgium (*ibid.*, § 1476), Bosnia and Herzegovina (*ibid.*, § 1477), Bulgaria (*ibid.*, § 1479), Cambodia (*ibid.*, § 1481), Canada (*ibid.*, § 1482), Colombia (*ibid.*, § 1484), Congo (*ibid.*, § 1485), Côte d'Ivoire (*ibid.*, § 1487), Croatia (*ibid.*, § 1488), Ethiopia (*ibid.*, § 1492), Georgia (*ibid.*, § 1493), Germany (*ibid.*, § 1494), Ireland (*ibid.*, § 1496), Lithuania (*ibid.*, § 1500), Mali (*ibid.*, § 1504), Moldova (*ibid.*, § 1506), New Zealand (*ibid.*, § 1509), Niger (*ibid.*, § 1512), Norway (*ibid.*, § 1514), Paraguay (*ibid.*, § 1516), Poland (*ibid.*, § 1517), Romania (*ibid.*, § 1518), Slovenia (*ibid.*, § 1521), Spain (*ibid.*, §§ 1522–1523), Tajikistan (*ibid.*, § 1525) and Thailand (*ibid.*, § 1526); see also the legislation of the United Kingdom (*ibid.*, § 1530), Yemen (*ibid.*, § 1533) and Yugoslavia (*ibid.*, § 1534), the application of which is not excluded in time of non-international armed conflict, and the draft legislation of Argentina (*ibid.*, § 1466), Burundi (*ibid.*, § 1480), El Salvador (*ibid.*, § 1491), Jordan (*ibid.*, § 1497), Lebanon (*ibid.*, § 1499), Nicaragua (*ibid.*, § 1511) and Trinidad and Tobago (*ibid.*, § 1527).

129 ICC Statute, Article 8(2)(e)(xi).

130 See, e.g., the legislation of Australia (cited in Vol. II, Ch. 15, § 56), Bosnia and Herzegovina (*ibid.*, § 57), Canada (*ibid.*, § 59), Congo (*ibid.*, § 61), Croatia (*ibid.*, § 62), Ethiopia (*ibid.*, § 63), Georgia (*ibid.*, § 64), Germany (*ibid.*, § 65), Ireland (*ibid.*, § 66), Netherlands (*ibid.*, § 71), New Zealand (*ibid.*, § 72), Norway (*ibid.*, § 73), Slovenia (*ibid.*, § 74), United Kingdom (*ibid.*, § 75) and Yugoslavia (*ibid.*, § 79); see also the legislation of Italy (*ibid.*, § 67), the application of which is not excluded in time of non-international armed conflict, and the draft legislation of Burundi (*ibid.*, § 57) and Trinidad and Tobago (*ibid.*, § 76).

The order that no quarter be given is a war crime whether or not the order is carried out. References to more practice can be found in the commentary to Rule 46.

(iv) Making medical or religious personnel or objects the object of attack. Such persons and objects are protected under Additional Protocol II.[131] Attacks on them are listed as a war crime under the Statute of the International Criminal Court in slightly different terms, namely "directing attacks against buildings, material, medical units and transport, and personnel using the distinctive emblems of the Geneva Conventions in conformity with international law".[132] Despite this wording, it should be noted that the distinctive emblem does not of itself confer protected status, and therefore the crime is actually attacking persons or objects knowing that they are medical personnel, units and transports and religious personnel, irrespective of whether or not they are using the emblem.[133]

Religious personnel, whether military or civilian, are entitled to the same respect as military or civilian medical personnel. Attacks on such persons are recognised as criminal in the legislation of many States.[134]

The UN Commissions of Experts Established pursuant to Security Council Resolutions 780 (1992) and 935 (1994) investigated violations of international humanitarian law in the conflicts in the former Yugoslavia and Rwanda respectively, on the understanding that these violations amounted to war crimes.[135] Similarly, attacks on hospitals, medical units and transports are criminalised by the legislation of many States.[136]

Attacks on protected persons or objects in Rwanda, Somalia and the former Yugoslavia have been condemned by the UN Security Council and UN

---

[131] Additional Protocol II, Articles 9 and 11.   [132] ICC Statute, Article 8(2)(e)(ii).

[133] See Knut Dörmann, *Elements of War Crimes under the Rome Statute of the International Criminal Court: Sources and Commentary*, Cambridge University Press, 2003, pp. 447–451.

[134] See, e.g., the legislation of Croatia (cited in Vol. II, Ch. 7, § 340), Estonia (*ibid.*, § 342), Georgia (*ibid.*, § 343), Ireland (*ibid.*, § 344), Nicaragua (*ibid.*, § 346), Norway (*ibid.*, § 438), Poland (*ibid.*, § 349), Slovenia (*ibid.*, § 350), Spain (*ibid.*, §§ 351–352), Tajikistan (*ibid.*, § 353), Yugoslavia (*ibid.*, § 354); see also the legislation of Italy (*ibid.*, § 345), the application of which is not excluded in time of non-international armed conflict, and the draft legislation of Argentina (*ibid.*, § 338), El Salvador (*ibid.*, § 341) and Nicaragua (*ibid.*, § 347).

[135] See the final reports of the UN Commissions of Experts Established pursuant to Security Council Resolution 780 (1992) (cited in Vol. II, Ch. 7, §§ 144 and 546) and to UN Security Council, Res. 935 (1994) (*ibid.*, § 145).

[136] See, e.g., the legislation of Argentina (cited in Vol. II, Ch. 7, § 453), Australia (*ibid.*, §§ 455–456), Azerbaijan (*ibid.*, § 457), Bosnia and Herzegovina (*ibid.*, § 459), Canada (*ibid.*, § 461), Chile (*ibid.*, § 462), Colombia (*ibid.*, § 464), Congo (*ibid.*, § 465), Cuba (*ibid.*, § 467), Dominican Republic (*ibid.*, § 468), Estonia (*ibid.*, §§ 471 and 716), Georgia (*ibid.*, §§ 473 and 717), Germany (*ibid.*, §§ 474 and 718), Guatemala (*ibid.*, § 475), Iraq (*ibid.*, § 476), Ireland (*ibid.*, §§ 477 and 719), Lithuania (*ibid.*, §§ 479 and 721), Mexico (*ibid.*, § 480), Netherlands (*ibid.*, § 482), New Zealand (*ibid.*, § 483), Nicaragua (*ibid.*, §§ 484 and 722), Norway (*ibid.*, §§ 486 and 724), Peru (*ibid.*, § 487), Poland (*ibid.*, § 489), Portugal (*ibid.*, § 490), Romania (*ibid.*, §§ 491 and 725), Slovenia (*ibid.*, § 492), Spain (*ibid.*, §§ 493 and 726), Sweden (*ibid.*, § 494), Tajikistan (*ibid.*, §§ 495 and 728), United Kingdom (*ibid.*, § 498), Venezuela (*ibid.*, §§ 501 and 729) and Yugoslavia (*ibid.*, § 502); see also the draft legislation of Argentina (*ibid.*, §§ 454 and 712), Burundi (*ibid.*, § 460), El Salvador (*ibid.*, §§ 470 and 715), Nicaragua (*ibid.*, §§ 485 and 723) and Trinidad and Tobago (*ibid.*, § 496).

Commission on Human Rights.[137] The protection of medical aircraft is subject to more specific conditions than other objects (see commentary to Rule 29). References to more practice can be found in the commentary to Rules 25–30.

(v) Conscripting or enlisting children under the age of 15 into the armed forces or groups, or using them to participate actively in hostilities. This practice is listed as a war crime in the Statute of the International Criminal Court.[138] The inclusion of this war crime was not controversial during the negotiation of the Statute of the International Criminal Court. The crime has also been included in the Statute of the Special Court for Sierra Leone.[139] Recruiting children under the age of 15 years into the armed forces or groups or using them to participate actively in hostilities was first prohibited by treaty in non-international armed conflicts in Additional Protocol II.[140] Since then, the unlawfulness of this behaviour has gained universal recognition and is re-affirmed in the Convention on the Rights of the Child, to which virtually all States are party.[141] The use of children under 15 in various non-international armed conflicts has been repeatedly and vigorously condemned by the international community.[142] This war crime is also set forth in the legislation of many States.[143]

References to more practice can be found in the commentary to Rules 136–137.

(vi) Making religious or cultural objects the object of attack, provided that they are not military objectives. This practice is prohibited by Additional Protocol II,[144] and by customary international law (see Rule 38). It is listed as a war crime, using wording taken from the Hague Regulations, in the Statute of the International Criminal Court.[145] The attack of such objects in non-international armed conflicts is criminalised in the Hague Convention for the Protection of Cultural Property,[146] to which the Second Protocol adds more detail.[147] The particular importance attributed to this prohibition by the international community is evidenced by the condemnation of such attacks in

---

[137] See, e.g., UN Security Council, Res. 771 (cited in Vol. II, Ch. 7, § 534) and Res. 794 (*ibid.*, § 535); UN General Assembly, Res. 40/139 (*ibid.*, § 538) and Res. 41/157 (*ibid.*, § 538); UN Commission on Human Rights, Res. 1992/S-1/1 (*ibid.*, § 542).

[138] ICC Statute, Article 8(2)(e)(vii).

[139] Statute of the Special Court for Sierra Leone, Article 4(c).

[140] Additional Protocol II, Article 4(3)(c).

[141] Convention on the Rights of the Child, Article 33(3).

[142] See, e.g., the statements of Italy (cited in Vol. II, Ch. 39, § 559) and United States (*ibid.*, § 569); UN Security Council, Res. 1071 and 1083 (*ibid.*, § 572); UN Security Council, Statement by the President (*ibid.*, § 576); UN Commission on Human Rights, Res. 1998/63 (*ibid.*, § 464), Res. 1998/75 (*ibid.*, § 465) and Res. 1998/82 (*ibid.*, § 467).

[143] See *supra* footnotes 82 and 83.   [144] Additional Protocol II, Article 16.

[145] ICC Statute, Article 8(2)(e)(iv).

[146] Hague Convention for the Protection of Cultural Property, Articles 19 and 28.

[147] Second Protocol to the Hague Convention for the Protection of Cultural Property, Articles 15(1) and 22.

Afghanistan and the former Yugoslavia.[148] This practice constitutes an offence under the legislation of numerous States.[149] The crime is also listed in the Statute of the International Criminal Tribunal for the Former Yugoslavia.[150] In the *Tadić case* in 1995, the International Criminal Tribunal for the Former Yugoslavia found that it applied to non-international armed conflicts.[151] References to more practice can be found in the commentary to Rule 38.

(iv) Other serious violations of international humanitarian law committed during a non-international armed conflict (continued):

- making civilian objects the object of attack;
- seizing property of the adverse party not required by military necessity;
- making persons or objects involved in a humanitarian assistance or peacekeeping mission in accordance with the Charter of the United Nations the object of attack, as long as they are entitled to the protection given to civilians or civilian objects under international humanitarian law;
- killing or wounding an adversary by resort to perfidy.

Basis for the war crimes listed above

These are violations of customary international law, listed as war crimes in the Statute of the International Criminal Court.[152]

(i) *Making civilian objects the object of attack.* This is not the expression used by the Statute of the International Criminal Court, but it is essentially the same as the war crime of "destroying the property of an adversary unless such destruction . . . be imperatively demanded by the necessities of the conflict".[153] The prohibition of attacking civilian objects is contained in many military

---

[148] See, e.g., the practice of Cape Verde (cited in Vol. II, Ch. 12, § 181), Croatia (*ibid.*, § 185), Germany (*ibid.*, § 194), Iran (*ibid.*, § 202), Pakistan (*ibid.*, § 215), United Arab Emirates (*ibid.*, § 219) and Yugoslavia (*ibid.*, §§ 237–239); UN General Assembly, Res. 47/147, 49/196 and 50/193 (*ibid.*, § 245); UN Commission on Human Rights, Res. 1994/72 (*ibid.*, § 248) and Res. 1998/70 (*ibid.*, § 249); UNESCO, General Conference, Res. 4.8 (*ibid.*, § 251); OIC, Res. 1/5-EX (*ibid.*, § 261).

[149] See, e.g., the legislation of Argentina (cited in Vol. II, Ch. 12, § 105), Australia (*ibid.*, §§ 108–109), Azerbaijan (*ibid.*, § 110), Belarus (*ibid.*, § 111), Belgium (*ibid.*, § 112), Bosnia and Herzegovina (*ibid.*, § 113), Bulgaria (*ibid.*, § 114), Canada (*ibid.*, §§ 116–117), Chile (*ibid.*, § 118), Colombia §§ 120–121), Congo (*ibid.*, § 122), Croatia (*ibid.*, § 124), Cuba (*ibid.*, § 125), Czech Republic (*ibid.*, § 127), Dominican Republic (*ibid.*, § 128), Estonia (*ibid.*, § 130), Georgia (*ibid.*, § 131), Germany (*ibid.*, § 132), Hungary (*ibid.*, § 133), Ireland (*ibid.*, § 134), Kyrgyzstan (*ibid.*, § 138), Latvia (*ibid.*, § 139), Lithuania (*ibid.*, § 141), Mexico (*ibid.*, § 143), New Zealand (*ibid.*, § 147), Nicaragua (*ibid.*, § 148), Niger (*ibid.*, § 150), Norway (*ibid.*, § 151), Paraguay (*ibid.*, § 152), Peru (*ibid.*, § 153), Poland (*ibid.*, § 154), Romania (*ibid.*, § 155), Russia (*ibid.*, § 156), Slovakia (*ibid.*, § 157), Slovenia (*ibid.*, § 158), Spain (*ibid.*, §§ 159–160), Sweden (*ibid.*, § 161), Switzerland (*ibid.*, §§ 162–163), Tajikistan (*ibid.*, § 164), United Kingdom (*ibid.*, § 167), Uruguay (*ibid.*, § 169), Venezuela (*ibid.*, § 170) and Yugoslavia (*ibid.*, § 171); see also the draft legislation of Argentina (*ibid.*, § 106), Burundi (*ibid.*, § 115), El Salvador (*ibid.*, § 129), Jordan (*ibid.*, § 137), Nicaragua (*ibid.*, § 149) and Trinidad and Tobago (*ibid.*, § 165).

[150] ICTY Statute, Article 3(d).

[151] ICTY, *Tadić case*, Interlocutory Appeal (cited in Vol. II, Ch. 12, § 268).

[152] ICC Statute, Article 8(2)(e).   [153] ICC Statute, Article 8(2)(e)(xii),

manuals applicable in non-international armed conflicts.[154] Numerous States have adopted legislation making it an offence to attack civilian objects during armed conflict.[155]

The criminal nature of the violation, indicated in the Statute of the International Criminal Court and the legislation referred to above, is based on the importance the international community attaches to the need to respect civilian objects. The International Criminal Tribunal for the Former Yugoslavia, in the *Blaškić case* in 2000, found the accused guilty of "unlawful attack[s] on civilian objects" in violation of Article 3 of the Tribunal's Statute.[156]

References to more practice can be found in the commentary to Rule 7.

(ii) Seizing property of the adverse party not required by military necessity. In addition to pillage, seizing property not justified by military necessity is listed as a war crime in the Statute of the International Criminal Court.[157] The Statute of the International Criminal Tribunal for the Former Yugoslavia lists "plunder of public or private property" as a war crime.[158] In the *Jelisić case*, the International Criminal Tribunal for the Former Yugoslavia convicted the accused of plunder under Article 3(e) of its Statute.[159] Seizing property not justified by military necessity is an offence under the legislation of many States.[160] References to more practice can be found in the commentary to Rule 50.

(iii) Making persons or objects involved in a humanitarian assistance or peacekeeping mission in accordance with the Charter of the United Nations the object of attack, as long as they are entitled to the protection given to civilians or civilian objects under international humanitarian law. This war

---

[154] See e.g. the military manuals of Benin, Croatia, Germany, Nigeria, Philippines and Togo (cited in Vol. II, Ch. 2, § 7), Benin, Colombia, Croatia, Ecuador, Germany, Italy, Kenya, Lebanon, Madagascar, South Africa, Togo and Yugoslavia (*ibid.*, § 115).

[155] See, e.g., the legislation of Australia (cited in Vol. II, Ch. 2, § 119), Azerbaijan (*ibid.*, § 120), Canada (*ibid.*, § 122), Congo (*ibid.*, § 123), Croatia (*ibid.*, § 124), Estonia (*ibid.*, § 126), Georgia (*ibid.*, § 127), Germany (*ibid.*, § 128), New Zealand (*ibid.*, § 134), Norway (*ibid.*, § 136), Spain (*ibid.*, § 138) and United Kingdom (*ibid.*, § 140); see also the legislation of Hungary (*ibid.*, § 129), Italy (*ibid.*, § 131) and Slovakia (*ibid.*, § 137), the application of which is not excluded in time of non-international armed conflict, and the draft legislation of Argentina (*ibid.*, § 118), Burundi (*ibid.*, § 121), El Salvador (*ibid.*, § 125), Nicaragua (*ibid.*, § 135) and Trinidad and Tobago (*ibid.*, § 139).

[156] ICTY, *Blaškić case*, Judgement (cited in Vol. II, Ch. 2, § 181).

[157] ICC Statute, Article 8(2)(e)(xii).   [158] ICTY Statute, Article 3(e).

[159] ICTY, *Jelisić case*, Judgement (cited in Vol. II, Ch. 16, § 740).

[160] See, e.g., the legislation of Armenia (cited in Vol. II, Ch. 16, § 122), Australia (*ibid.*, § 125), Azerbaijan (*ibid.*, § 126), Belarus (*ibid.*, § 129), Belgium (*ibid.*, § 130), Bosnia and Herzegovina (*ibid.*, § 131), Cambodia (*ibid.*, § 135), Canada (*ibid.*, § 138), Congo (*ibid.*, § 142), Croatia (*ibid.*, § 144), El Salvador (*ibid.*, §§ 149–150), Estonia (*ibid.*, § 151), Georgia (*ibid.*, § 154), Germany (*ibid.*, § 155), Latvia (*ibid.*, § 166), Lithuania (*ibid.*, § 168), Moldova (*ibid.*, § 177), Netherlands (*ibid.*, § 180), New Zealand (*ibid.*, § 182), Nicaragua (*ibid.*, § 184), Niger (*ibid.*, § 185), Portugal (*ibid.*, § 193), Slovenia (*ibid.*, § 199), Spain (*ibid.*, §§ 200–201), Tajikistan (*ibid.*, § 205), United Kingdom (*ibid.*, § 211), Uzbekistan (*ibid.*, § 215) and Yugoslavia (*ibid.*, § 219); see also the legislation of Bulgaria (*ibid.*, § 133), Czech Republic (*ibid.*, § 147), Italy (*ibid.*, §§ 161–162), Mozambique (*ibid.*, § 178), Nicaragua (*ibid.*, § 183), Paraguay (*ibid.*, § 190), Peru (*ibid.*, § 191), Romania (*ibid.*, § 194) and Slovakia (*ibid.*, § 198), the application of which is not excluded in time of non-international armed conflict, and the draft legislation of Argentina (*ibid.*, § 121), Burundi (*ibid.*, § 134), Jordan (*ibid.*, § 164) and Trinidad and Tobago (*ibid.*, § 206).

crime is contained in Article 4 of the Statutes of the Special Court for Sierra Leone and of the International Criminal Court.[161] It was included on the basis that such acts amount to attacks on civilians or civilian objects. It is an offence under the legislation of many States to attack personnel and objects involved in a peacekeeping mission.[162] It is also significant that such operations take place in all types of conflicts and the nature of the conflict does not change in any way the respect that the international community expects to be accorded to such personnel and their equipment. References to more practice can be found in the commentary to Rules 31 and 33.

(iv) Killing or wounding an adversary by resort to perfidy. This war crime is listed in the Statute of the International Criminal Court.[163] It is an offence under the legislation of many States, especially if it involves the perfidious use of the red cross or red crescent emblem.[164] The criminal nature of this act in non-international armed conflicts was also confirmed by the Appeals Chamber of the International Criminal Tribunal for the Former Yugoslavia in the *Tadić case* in 1995.[165] References to more practice can be found in the commentary to Rule 65.

(iv) Other serious violations of international humanitarian law committed during a non-international armed conflict (continued):

- using prohibited weapons;
- launching an indiscriminate attack resulting in death or injury to civilians, or an attack in the knowledge that it will cause excessive incidental civilian loss, injury or damage;
- making non-defended localities and demilitarised zones the object of attack;
- using human shields;
- slavery;
- collective punishments;
- using starvation of civilians as a method of warfare by depriving them of objects indispensable to their survival, including by impeding relief supplies.

Basis for the war crimes listed above

These violations are not listed in the Statute of the International Criminal Court as war crimes. However, State practice recognises their serious nature

---

[161] Statute of the Special Court for Sierra Leone, Article 4; ICC Statute, Article 8(2)(e)(iii).

[162] See *supra* footnote 69.

[163] ICC Statute, Article 8(2)(e)(ix).

[164] See, e.g., the legislation of Argentina (cited in Vol. II, Ch. 18, § 1267), Azerbaijan (*ibid.*, § 1270), Belgium (*ibid.*, § 1271), Bolivia (*ibid.*, § 1272), Bosnia and Herzegovina (*ibid.*, § 964), Canada (*ibid.*, § 1274), Colombia (*ibid.*, § 1275), Congo (*ibid.*, §§ 968 and 1276), Costa Rica (*ibid.*, § 1278), Croatia (*ibid.*, § 969), Ethiopia (*ibid.*, § 1282), Georgia (*ibid.*, §§ 970 and 1283), Germany (*ibid.*, §§ 971 and 1284), Guatemala (*ibid.*, § 1285), Kyrgyzstan (*ibid.*, § 1289), Liechtenstein (*ibid.*, § 1291), Moldova (*ibid.*, §§ 1293–1294), New Zealand (*ibid.*, § 976), Niger (*ibid.*, § 1300), Norway (*ibid.*, §§ 977 and 1301), Slovenia (*ibid.*, § 978), Spain (*ibid.*, § 1302), Sweden (*ibid.*, §§ 979 and 1303), Switzerland (*ibid.*, § 1304), Tajikistan (*ibid.*, § 1305), Togo (*ibid.*, § 1306), United Kingdom (*ibid.*, § 981), Yemen (*ibid.*, § 1310) and Yugoslavia (*ibid.*, § 983); see also the draft legislation of Burundi (*ibid.*, § 966), El Salvador (*ibid.*, § 1280), Jordan (*ibid.*, § 1282), Lebanon (*ibid.*, § 1290), Nicaragua (*ibid.*, § 1298) and Trinidad and Tobago (*ibid.*, § 980).

[165] ICTY, *Tadić case*, Interlocutory Appeal (cited in Vol. II, Ch. 18, §§ 920 and 1503).

and, as a result, a court would have sufficient basis to conclude that such acts in a non-international armed conflict are war crimes.

(i) Using prohibited weapons. Recent treaties prohibiting the use of certain weapons in any type of conflict require that such use be subject to criminal sanctions. This is the case for the Chemical Weapons Convention, Amended Protocol II to the Convention on Certain Conventional Weapons and the Ottawa Convention banning anti-personnel landmines.[166] The Statute of the International Criminal Court does not include the use of prohibited weapons in the sections dealing with non-international armed conflicts, but this issue was not openly debated during the Rome Diplomatic Conference.

Several military manuals provide that the use of prohibited weapons constitutes a war crime.[167] The national legislation criminalising the use of prohibited weapons does so in general terms. None limits such criminality to international armed conflicts and several explicitly criminalise the use of prohibited weapons in non-international armed conflicts.[168] As most States define a "war crime" as being a "violation" or a "serious violation" of international humanitarian law (see *supra*), it is reasonable to conclude that they would consider the use of prohibited weapons in non-international armed conflicts to fall within this category.

The UN Secretary-General's Bulletin on observance by United Nations forces of international humanitarian law, which is not limited to international armed conflicts, provides that violations of its rules – including those requiring respect for treaties prohibiting the use of certain weapons – be treated as criminal offences.[169]

The use of prohibited weapons may also amount to another war crime, in particular attacking civilians or launching indiscriminate attacks. This would be the case, for example, for the use of biological weapons. References to more practice can be found in the commentaries to Rules 70–79 and Rule 86.

(ii) Launching an indiscriminate attack resulting in death or injury to civilians, or an attack in the knowledge that it will cause excessive incidental

---

[166] Chemical Weapons Convention, Articles I(1)(b) and VII(1)(a); Amended Protocol II to the Convention on Certain Conventional Weapons, Articles 3 and 14; Ottawa Convention, Articles 1 and 9.

[167] See, e.g., the military manuals of Australia (cited in Vol. II, Ch. 20, § 408), Ecuador (*ibid.*, § 411), Germany (*ibid.*, § 412), South Korea (*ibid.*, § 413) and South Africa (*ibid.*, § 415).

[168] See, e.g., the legislation of Belarus (cited in Vol. II, Ch. 20, § 422) (limited to weapons "prohibited by international treaties"), Bosnia and Herzegovina (*ibid.*, § 423), Colombia (*ibid.*, § 425), Croatia (*ibid.*, § 427), Estonia (*ibid.*, § 431), Ethiopia (*ibid.*, § 432) (limited to weapons "forbidden by international conventions"), Finland (*ibid.*, § 433), Kazakhstan (*ibid.*, § 436) (limited to weapons "prohibited by an international treaty"), Lithuania (*ibid.*, § 437), Moldova (*ibid.*, § 438) (limited to weapons "prohibited by international treaties"), Nicaragua (*ibid.*, §§ 441–442), Poland (*ibid.*, § 444), Russia (*ibid.*, § 445) (limited to weapons "prohibited by an international treaty"), Slovenia (*ibid.*, § 447), Spain (*ibid.*, §§ 448–449), Sweden (*ibid.*, § 450), Tajikistan (*ibid.*, § 451), Uzbekistan (*ibid.*, § 452), Vietnam (*ibid.*, § 453) and Yugoslavia (*ibid.*, § 454); see also the legislation of Bulgaria (*ibid.*, § 424), Czech Republic (*ibid.*, § 428), Hungary (*ibid.*, § 434), Italy (*ibid.*, § 435), Mozambique (*ibid.*, § 439) and Slovakia (*ibid.*, § 446), the application of which is not excluded in time of non-international armed conflict, and the draft legislation of Argentina (*ibid.*, § 421).

[169] UN Secretary-General's Bulletin, Section 6(2) (*ibid.*, § 407).

civilian loss, injury or damage. Launching indiscriminate attacks in non-international armed conflicts has been so frequently and vigorously condemned by the international community as to indicate the customary nature of this prohibition, which protects important values and is aimed at preventing unwarranted death and injury. As such, this violation falls into the general definition of war crimes. Launching an indiscriminate attack is an offence under the legislation of numerous States.[170] The International Criminal Tribunal for the Former Yugoslavia referred to this violation in the context of non-international armed conflicts in the *Tadić case* in 1995 and, in general terms, in the *Kupreškić case* in 2000.[171]

The same consideration is true for the launching of attacks in the knowledge that they will cause excessive incidental civilian damage, injury or death. In particular, launching such attacks is an offence under the legislation of many States.[172]

Both indiscriminate and disproportionate attacks can be likened to attacks on civilians if the perpetrator was aware that this would be the effect of the attack in the ordinary course of events. This was in effect confirmed by the UN Commission on Human Rights when it condemned the "disproportionate use of military force" in the conflict in Chechnya based on Additional Protocol II, which prohibits attacks on civilians but does not specifically refer to indiscriminate or disproportionate attacks.[173]

References to more practice can be found in the commentary to Rules 11 and 14.

(iii) Making non-defended localities and demilitarised zones the object of attack. This practice amounts to a war crime because such attacks are either attacks on the civilian population or on civilian objects, namely destruction of an adversary's property not imperatively demanded by the necessities of the conflict (see Rule 50).[174] This crime constitutes an offence under the legislation of numerous States.[175] References to more practice can be found in the commentary to Rules 36–37.

---

[170] See, e.g., the legislation of Belarus (cited in Vol. II, Ch. 3, § 35), Belgium (*ibid.*, § 36), Bosnia and Herzegovina (*ibid.*, § 37), Colombia (*ibid.*, § 40), Croatia (*ibid.*, § 42), Estonia (*ibid.*, § 45), Georgia (*ibid.*, § 46), Indonesia (*ibid.*, § 47), Lithuania (*ibid.*, § 51), Niger (*ibid.*, § 55), Slovenia (*ibid.*, § 57), Spain (*ibid.*, § 58), Sweden (*ibid.*, § 59), Tajikistan (*ibid.*, § 60) and Yugoslavia (*ibid.*, § 62); see also the draft legislation of Argentina (*ibid.*, § 32), El Salvador (*ibid.*, § 44), Jordan (*ibid.*, § 49), Lebanon (*ibid.*, § 50) and Nicaragua (*ibid.*, § 54).

[171] ICTY, *Tadić case*, Interlocutory Appeal (cited in Vol. II, Ch. 3, § 134) and *Kupreškić case*, Judgement (*ibid.*, § 137).

[172] See, e.g., the legislation of Armenia (*ibid.*, § 50), Belarus (*ibid.*, § 53), Belgium (*ibid.*, § 54), Colombia (*ibid.*, § 59), Germany (*ibid.*, § 65), Niger (*ibid.*, § 73), Spain (*ibid.*, § 75) and Sweden (*ibid.*, § 76); see also the draft legislation of Argentina (*ibid.*, § 49), Burundi (*ibid.*, § 56), El Salvador (*ibid.*, § 63) and Nicaragua (*ibid.*, § 72).

[173] See UN Commission on Human Rights, Res. 2000/58 (cited in Vol. II, Ch. 3, § 116).

[174] See ICC Statute, Article 8(2)(e)(xii).

[175] See, e.g., the legislation of Azerbaijan (cited in Vol. II, Ch. 11, §§ 136 and 283), Belarus (*ibid.*, §§ 137 and 284), Belgium (*ibid.*, §§ 138 and 285), Bosnia and Herzegovina (*ibid.*, §§ 139 and 286), Croatia (*ibid.*, §§ 142 and 293), Czech Republic (*ibid.*, §§ 144 and 295), Estonia (*ibid.*, §§ 146 and 297), Georgia (*ibid.*, §§ 147 and 298), Germany (*ibid.*, §§ 148 and 299), Hungary (*ibid.*, §§ 149 and 300), Lithuania (*ibid.*, §§ 153 and 304), Niger (*ibid.*, §§ 157 and 311), Poland

(iv) Using human shields. This practice has been recognised as a war crime by the International Criminal Tribunal for the Former Yugoslavia, either as a form of cruel treatment,[176] or an outrage upon personal dignity.[177] The legislation of several States criminalises the use of human shields in non-international armed conflicts.[178] The use of human shields in non-international armed conflicts has been condemned by States and by the United Nations, for example, with respect to the conflicts in Liberia, Rwanda, Sierra Leone, Somalia, Tajikistan and the former Yugoslavia.[179] References to more practice can be found in the commentary to Rule 97.

(v) Slavery. Slavery is prohibited by Additional Protocol II,[180] and customary international law (see Rule 94). The military manuals and the legislation of many States prohibit slavery and the slave trade, or "enslavement".[181] In addition, this practice constitutes a war crime because it amounts to cruel treatment or an outrage upon personal dignity (see Rule 90). Slavery and slave labour are also prohibited under the legislation of numerous States.[182] References to more practice can be found in the commentary to Rule 94.

(vi) Collective punishments. Collective punishments are prohibited by Additional Protocol II,[183] and customary international law (see Rule 103). This prohibition is also set forth in the legislation of many States.[184] This war crime is listed in the Statutes of the International Criminal Tribunal for Rwanda and of the Special Court for Sierra Leone.[185] In addition, collective punishments

---

(*ibid.*, § 313), Slovakia (*ibid.*, §§ 159 and 314), Slovenia (*ibid.*, §§ 160 and 315), Spain (*ibid.*, §§ 161 and 316), Tajikistan (*ibid.*, §§ 162 and 317), Venezuela (*ibid.*, § 322), Yemen (*ibid.*, § 164) and Yugoslavia (*ibid.*, §§ 165 and 323); see also the draft legislation of Argentina (*ibid.*, §§ 132 and 278), Burundi (*ibid.*, § 287), El Salvador (*ibid.*, §§ 145 and 296), Jordan (*ibid.*, §§ 151 and 302), Lebanon (*ibid.*, §§ 152 and 303) and Nicaragua (*ibid.*, §§ 156 and 310).

[176] See, e.g., ICTY, *Blaškić case*, Case No. IT-95–14-T, Judgement, Trial Chamber I, 3 March 2000, § 716; *Kordić and Čerkez case*, Case No. IT-95–14/2-T, Judgement, Trial Chamber III, 26 February 2001, § 256; see also *Karadžić and Mladić case*, Review of the Indictments (cited in Vol. II, Ch. 32, § 2366).

[177] See, e.g., ICTY, *Aleksovski case*, Case No. IT-95–14/1-T, Judgement, Trial Chamber I, 25 June 1999, § 229.

[178] See, e.g., the legislation of Azerbaijan (cited in Vol. II, Ch. 32, §§ 2288–2289), Belarus (*ibid.*, § 2291), Democratic Republic of the Congo (*ibid.*, § 2294), Germany (*ibid.*, § 2296), Georgia (*ibid.*, § 2297), Lithuania (*ibid.*, § 2299), Poland (*ibid.*, § 2305) and Tajikistan (*ibid.*, § 2306); see also the legislation of Peru (*ibid.*, § 2304) and Yemen (*ibid.*, § 2309), the application of which is not excluded in time of non-international armed conflict, and the draft legislation of Burundi (*ibid.*, § 2292).

[179] See, e.g., the statements of Chile (cited in Vol. II, Ch. 32, § 2312), Tajikistan (*ibid.*, § 2328) and Yugoslavia (*ibid.*, § 2348); the reported practice of Rwanda (*ibid.*, § 2325); UN Commission on Human Rights, Res. 1995/89 (*ibid.*, § 2350); UN Secretary-General, Progress report on UNOMIL (*ibid.*, § 2351), Progress report on UNOMSIL (*ibid.*, § 2352) and Report pursuant to paragraph 5 of Security Council resolution 837 (1993) on the investigation into the 5 June 1993 attack on the UN forces in Somalia conducted on behalf of the UN Security Council (*ibid.*, § 2353).

[180] Additional Protocol II, Article 4.   [181] See *supra* footnote 89.

[182] See, e.g., the legislation of Albania (cited in Vol. II, Ch. 32, § 1816), Australia (*ibid.*, § 1819), Azerbaijan (*ibid.*, § 1821), Belgium (*ibid.*, § 1825), Bosnia and Herzegovina (*ibid.*, § 1826), Democratic Republic of the Congo (*ibid.*, § 1830), Côte d'Ivoire (*ibid.*, § 1832), Croatia (*ibid.*, § 1833), Ireland (*ibid.*, § 1836), Norway (*ibid.*, § 1849), Paraguay (*ibid.*, § 1850), Slovenia (*ibid.*, § 1852), Uzbekistan (*ibid.*, § 1854) and Yugoslavia (*ibid.*, § 1859); see also the draft legislation of Burundi (*ibid.*, § 1827).

[183] Additional Protocol II, Article 4.   [184] See *supra* footnote 92.

[185] ICTR Statute, Article 4(b); Statute of the Special Court for Sierra Leone, Article 3(b).

constitute a war crime because they consist of the deprivation of the right to fair trial (see Rule 100) and may also constitute cruel treatment (see Rule 90). References to more practice can be found in the commentary to Rule 103.

(vii) Using starvation of civilians as a method of warfare by depriving them of objects indispensable to their survival, including by impeding relief supplies. This practice is a violation of Additional Protocol II,[186] and customary international law (see Rule 53). In addition, there is very extensive State practice expressing outrage at acts in non-international armed conflicts, including the impediment of relief supplies which caused the starvation of civilians. This practice proves that such behaviour is not only a violation of customary international law, but also, in the eyes of the international community, a very serious violation.

The UN Commission on Human Rights characterised the deliberate impeding of humanitarian relief supplies to Sudanese civilians as "an offence to human dignity".[187] It is particularly noteworthy that the UN Commission of Experts Established pursuant to Security Council Resolution 935 (1994) included a breach of Article 14 of Additional Protocol II in its interim report on violations of international humanitarian law in Rwanda.[188]

Several States specifically criminalise the use of starvation of civilians as a method of warfare.[189] In addition, these violations in practice amount to killing civilians, in itself a war crime, because each violation consists of deliberate acts that in the normal course of events lead to their death. They may also be considered to be inhuman treatment (see Rule 87).

References to more practice can be found in the commentary to Rules 53–55.

Composite war crimes

It should also be noted that certain conduct, not listed above, is nevertheless criminal because it consists of a combination of a number of war crimes. These so-called composite war crimes are, in particular, enforced disappearances and ethnic cleansing. Enforced disappearance amounts in practice to depriving a person of a fair trial and often also to murder (see commentary to Rule 98). Ethnic cleansing comprises various war crimes, such as murder, rape, unlawful deportation or ordering the displacement of the civilian population for reasons relating to the conflict and not required for the security of the civilians nor for reasons of imperative military necessity, and outrages on personal dignity based on racial discrimination and inhuman or degrading treatment (see commentary to Rule 129).

---

[186] Additional Protocol II, Articles 14 and 18.
[187] UN Commission on Human Rights, Res. 1996/73 (cited in Vol. II, Ch. 17, § 631).
[188] UN Commission of Experts Established pursuant to Security Council Resolution 935 (1994), Interim report (cited in Vol. II, Ch. 17, § 113).
[189] See, e.g., the legislation of Azerbaijan (cited in Vol. II, Ch. 17, § 39), Belarus (*ibid.*, § 40), Bosnia and Herzegovina (*ibid.*, § 41), Croatia (*ibid.*, § 47), Ethiopia (*ibid.*, § 48), Germany (*ibid.*, § 50), Lithuania (*ibid.*, § 52), Slovenia (*ibid.*, § 57) and Yugoslavia (*ibid.*, § 61).

Rule 157. States have the right to vest universal jurisdiction in their national courts over war crimes.

Practice

Volume II, Chapter 44, Section B.

Summary

State practice establishes this rule as a norm of customary international law with respect to war crimes committed in both international and non-international armed conflicts. The universality principle is additional to other bases of criminal jurisdiction: territoriality principle (based on where the crime occurred);[190] active personality principle (based on the nationality of the perpetrator);[191] passive personality principle (based on the nationality of the victim);[192] and protective principle (based on the protection of national interests or security).[193]

International and non-international armed conflicts

The right of States to vest universal jurisdiction in their national courts for war crimes is supported extensively by national legislation.[194] There have also been a number of cases of suspected war criminals being tried by national courts on the basis of universal jurisdiction.[195] Over the last decade, several persons have been tried by national courts for war crimes committed in non-international

---

[190] See, e.g., the military manuals of New Zealand (cited in Vol. II, Ch. 44, § 152), Switzerland (*ibid.*, § 156) and United States (*ibid.*, § 161) and the legislation of Australia (*ibid.*, § 165), Bangladesh (*ibid.*, § 169), Canada (*ibid.*, § 177) and Côte d'Ivoire (*ibid.*, § 183); see also the draft legislation of Nicaragua (*ibid.*, § 218).

[191] See, e.g., the military manuals of New Zealand (*ibid.*, § 152), Switzerland (*ibid.*, § 156), United States (*ibid.*, §§ 159–161) and Yugoslavia (*ibid.*, § 162) and the legislation of Australia (*ibid.*, § 165), Azerbaijan (*ibid.*, § 168), Canada (*ibid.*, §§ 177–178), Germany (*ibid.*, § 196), Kyrgyzstan (*ibid.*, § 205), Mexico (*ibid.*, § 213), Netherlands (*ibid.*, § 214), Russia (*ibid.*, § 224) and United States (*ibid.*, § 243).

[192] See, e.g., the military manuals of New Zealand (*ibid.*, § 152), Switzerland (*ibid.*, § 156) and United States (*ibid.*, §§ 159–161) and the legislation of Canada (*ibid.*, § 178), Chile (*ibid.*, § 179), Côte d'Ivoire (*ibid.*, § 183), France (*ibid.*, § 193), Germany (*ibid.*, § 196), Mexico (*ibid.*, § 213), Netherlands (*ibid.*, § 214), Slovenia (*ibid.*, § 228) and Sweden (*ibid.*, § 231).

[193] See, e.g., United States, *Naval Handbook* (*ibid.*, § 161); the legislation of Azerbaijan (*ibid.*, § 168), Chile (*ibid.*, § 179) and Netherlands (*ibid.*, § 214); Israel, District Court of Jerusalem, *Eichmann case* (*ibid.*, § 258).

[194] See, e.g., the legislation of Australia (*ibid.*, § 165), Azerbaijan (*ibid.*, § 168), Bangladesh (*ibid.*, § 169), Belarus (*ibid.*, § 171), Belgium (*ibid.*, § 172), Canada (*ibid.*, §§ 177–178), Colombia (*ibid.*, § 180), Costa Rica (*ibid.*, § 182), Ecuador (*ibid.*, § 188), El Salvador (*ibid.*, § 189), Ethiopia (*ibid.*, § 190), France (*ibid.*, § 195), Germany (*ibid.*, §§ 196 and 198), Luxembourg (*ibid.*, § 208), New Zealand (*ibid.*, § 217), Niger (*ibid.*, § 219), Slovenia (*ibid.*, § 228), Sweden (*ibid.*, § 231), Switzerland (*ibid.*, § 232), Tajikistan (*ibid.*, § 234), United Kingdom (*ibid.*, §§ 238–240) and United States (torture) (*ibid.*, § 242); see also the draft legislation of Lebanon (*ibid.*, § 206), Sri Lanka (*ibid.*, § 230) and Trinidad and Tobago (*ibid.*, § 235).

[195] In addition to the cases cited in footnote 207, see also Australia, High Court, *Polyukhovich case* (*ibid.*, § 247); Canada, High Court of Justice, *Finta case* (*ibid.*, § 250); Netherlands, Special

armed conflicts on the basis of universal jurisdiction.[196] It is significant that the States of nationality of the accused did not object to the exercise of universal jurisdiction in these cases. Several military manuals further support the rule that war crimes jurisdiction may be established on the basis of the principle of universal jurisdiction.[197]

The right of States to vest universal jurisdiction in their national courts for war crimes is also supported by treaty practice. The Second Protocol to the Hague Convention for the Protection of Cultural Property states that it does not affect "the exercise of jurisdiction under customary international law", which was intended by delegates at the negotiation of the Protocol to refer to the right of States to vest universal jurisdiction in their national courts for war crimes.[198] The Genocide Convention, which refers explicitly to territorial jurisdiction, has been interpreted as not prohibiting the application of the principle of universal jurisdiction to genocide.[199] While the Statute of the International Criminal Court does not oblige States to establish universal jurisdiction over the war crimes it lists, several States have incorporated the list of war crimes contained in the Statute in their national legislation and vested jurisdiction in their courts to prosecute persons suspected of having committed such war crimes on the basis of the principle of universal jurisdiction.[200]

Link to the prosecuting State

Practice is not uniform with respect to whether the principle of universal jurisdiction requires a particular link to the prosecuting State. The requirement that some connection exist between the accused and the prosecuting State, in particular that the accused be present in the territory or has fallen into the hands of the prosecuting State, is reflected in the military manuals, legislation

---

Court of Cassation, *Ahlbrecht case* (*ibid.*, § 262); Netherlands, Special Court of Cassation, *Rohrig and Others case* (*ibid.*, § 263); United Kingdom, Supreme Court of Judicature, Court of Appeal, *Sawoniuk case* (*ibid.*, § 271); United States, Court of Appeals, *Demjanjuk case* (*ibid.*, § 273).

[196] See, e.g., Belgium, Court of Cassation, *The Four from Butare case* (*ibid.*, § 249); France, Court of Appeal, *Munyeshyaka case* (*ibid.*, § 253); Netherlands, Supreme Court, *Knesević case* (*ibid.*, § 264); Switzerland, Military Tribunal at Lausanne, *Grabež case* (*ibid.*, § 267) and *Niyonteze case* (*ibid.*, § 269).

[197] See, e.g., the military manuals of Australia (*ibid.*, § 144), Netherlands (*ibid.*, § 150), United Kingdom (*ibid.*, § 157) and United States (*ibid.*, § 161) ("certain war crimes").

[198] Second Protocol to the Hague Convention for the Protection of Cultural Property, Article 16(2)(a). See also Jean-Marie Henckaerts, "New Rules for the Protection of Cultural Property in Armed Conflict", *International Review of the Red Cross*, No. 835, September 1999, p. 617.

[199] Genocide Convention, Article VI (cited in Vol. II, Ch. 44, § 109); Germany, Higher Regional Court at Düsseldorf, *Jorgić case* (*ibid.*, § 255); Israel, District Court of Jerusalem, *Eichmann case* (*ibid.*, § 258).

[200] See, e.g., the legislation of Belgium (*ibid.*, § 172), Canada (*ibid.*, § 178), Germany (*ibid.*, § 198), New Zealand (*ibid.*, § 217) and United Kingdom (*ibid.*, § 240); see also the draft legislation of Trinidad and Tobago (*ibid.*, § 235).

and case-law of many States.[201] There is also legislation and case-law, however, that does not require such a link.[202] The Geneva Conventions do not require such a link either.

In 2000, the Democratic Republic of the Congo instituted proceedings before the International Court of Justice challenging an international arrest warrant issued by a Belgian judge against the Congolese Minister of Foreign Affairs. In its pleadings before the Court in 2001, the Democratic Republic of the Congo did not object in principle to the existence of States' right to vest universal jurisdiction in their national courts over war crimes, but argued that the indicted person needed to be in the territory of the State exercising such jurisdiction. The judgement of the International Court of Justice turned on the question of immunity of heads of State and foreign ministers and therefore no decision was taken on the extent of universal jurisdiction.[203] In their separate and dissenting opinions, the judges were divided on the issue of whether universal jurisdiction could be exercised when the accused was not present in the territory of the prosecuting State, but the majority did not contest the right to try a suspected war criminal on the basis of universal jurisdiction.[204]

Obligation to establish universal jurisdiction

The right of States to vest universal jurisdiction in their national courts over war crimes in no way diminishes the obligation of States party to the Geneva Conventions and States party to Additional Protocol I to provide for universal jurisdiction in their national legislation over those war crimes known as "grave breaches".[205] Numerous States have given effect to this obligation in their

---

201 See the military manuals of Canada (*ibid.*, § 146), Ecuador (*ibid.*, § 147), Netherlands (*ibid.*, § 151), New Zealand (*ibid.*, § 152) and United States (*ibid.*, § 161); the legislation of Australia (*ibid.*, § 165), Bosnia and Herzegovina (*ibid.*, § 173), Canada (*ibid.*, §§ 177–178), Colombia (*ibid.*, § 180), France (*ibid.*, §§ 194–195), Germany (*ibid.*, § 196), India (*ibid.*, § 201), Switzerland (*ibid.*, §§ 232–233), United Kingdom (*ibid.*, §§ 239–240) and United States (torture) (*ibid.*, § 242); Canada, High Court of Justice, *Finta case* (*ibid.*, § 250); France, Tribunal de Grande Instance de Paris, *Javor case* (torture) (*ibid.*, § 252); Germany, Supreme Court of Bavaria, *Djajić case* (*ibid.*, § 254); Germany, Higher Regional Court at Düsseldorf, *Jorgić case* (*ibid.*, § 255); Germany, Supreme Court of Bavaria, *Kusljić case* (*ibid.*, § 257); Netherlands, Special Court of Cassation, *Rohrig and Others case* (*ibid.*, § 263).

202 For explicit references to the possibility of commencing (extradition) proceedings against a suspected war criminal who is not present in the territory of the prosecuting State, see the legislation of Canada (*ibid.*, § 176), Luxembourg (*ibid.*, §§ 207–209) and New Zealand (*ibid.*, § 217); Germany, Higher Regional Court at Düsseldorf, *Sokolović case* (*ibid.*, § 256); United States, Court of Appeals, *Demjanjuk case* (*ibid.*, § 273).

203 ICJ, *Arrest Warrant case*, Judgement, (*ibid.*, § 305).

204 ICJ, *Arrest Warrant case*, Judgement, (*ibid.*, § 305).

205 First Geneva Convention, Article 49; Second Geneva Convention, Article 50; Third Geneva Convention, Article 129; Fourth Geneva Convention, Article 146; Additional Protocol I, Article 85(1).

legislation.[206] Several suspected war criminals have been prosecuted for grave breaches on the basis of universal jurisdiction.[207]

In addition to the Geneva Conventions and Additional Protocol I, a number of other treaties oblige States party to provide for universal jurisdiction over certain crimes, including when they take place during armed conflict. These are, in particular, the Convention against Torture, the Inter-American Convention on Forced Disappearances, the Convention on the Safety of UN Personnel and the Second Protocol to the Hague Convention for the Protection of Cultural Property.[208]

Rule 158. States must investigate war crimes allegedly committed by their nationals or armed forces, or on their territory, and, if appropriate, prosecute the suspects. They must also investigate other war crimes over which they have jurisdiction and, if appropriate, prosecute the suspects.

Practice

Volume II, Chapter 44, Section C.

Summary

State practice establishes this rule as a norm of customary international law applicable in both international and non-international armed conflicts. This rule, read together with Rule 157, means that States must exercise the criminal jurisdiction which their national legislation confers upon their courts, be it limited to territorial and personal jurisdiction, or include universal jurisdiction, which is obligatory for grave breaches.

---

[206] In addition to the legislation referred to in footnote 194, the legislation of the following countries is based on, or refers to, the grave breaches regime of the Geneva Conventions (and Additional Protocol I where applicable): Australia (cited in Vol. II, Ch. 44, § 166), Austria (*ibid.*, § 167), Azerbaijan (*ibid.*, § 168), Bangladesh (*ibid.*, § 169), Barbados (*ibid.*, § 170), Belarus (*ibid.*, § 171), Belgium (*ibid.*, § 172), Botswana (*ibid.*, § 174), Bulgaria (*ibid.*, § 175), Canada (*ibid.*, § 176), Cook Islands (*ibid.*, § 181), Cuba (*ibid.*, § 184), Cyprus (*ibid.*, §§ 185–186), Denmark (*ibid.*, § 187), Finland (*ibid.*, § 191), France (*ibid.*, § 194), Germany (*ibid.*, § 197), Guatemala (*ibid.*, § 199), Israel (*ibid.*, § 203), Kenya (*ibid.*, § 204), Luxembourg (*ibid.*, § 209), Malawi (*ibid.*, § 210), Malaysia (*ibid.*, § 211), Mauritius (*ibid.*, § 212), New Zealand (*ibid.*, § 216), Nigeria (*ibid.*, § 220), Papua New Guinea (*ibid.*, § 221), Paraguay (*ibid.*, § 222), Poland (*ibid.*, § 223), Russia (*ibid.*, § 224), Seychelles (*ibid.*, § 226), Singapore (*ibid.*, § 227), Spain (*ibid.*, § 229), Switzerland (*ibid.*, § 233), Uganda (*ibid.*, § 236), United Kingdom (*ibid.*, § 237), Vanuatu (*ibid.*, § 244) and Zimbabwe (*ibid.*, § 245); see also the draft legislation of Sri Lanka (*ibid.*, § 230).

[207] See, e.g., Denmark, High Court, *Sarić case* (*ibid.*, § 251); Germany, Supreme Court of Bavaria, *Djajić case* (*ibid.*, § 254); Germany, Higher Regional Court of Düsseldorf, *Jorgić case* (*ibid.*, § 255); Germany, Higher Regional Court of Düsseldorf, *Sokolović case* (*ibid.*, § 256); Germany, Supreme Court of Bavaria, *Kusljić case* (*ibid.*, § 257); Israel, District Court of Jerusalem and Supreme Court, *Eichmann case* (*ibid.*, §§ 243–244); Switzerland, Military Tribunal at Lausanne, *Grabež case* (*ibid.*, § 252).

[208] Convention against Torture, Article 5; Convention on the Safety of UN Personnel, Article 10; Inter-American Convention on Forced Disappearances, Article 4; Second Protocol to the Hague Convention for the Protection of Cultural Property, Article 16(1).

International and non-international armed conflicts

The Geneva Conventions require States to search for persons alleged to have committed, or ordered to have committed, grave breaches and to try or extradite them.[209] The obligation to investigate and prosecute persons alleged to have committed crimes under international law is found in a number of treaties that apply to acts committed in both international and non-international armed conflicts.[210] The preamble to the Statute of the International Criminal Court recalls "the duty of every State to exercise its criminal jurisdiction over those responsible for international crimes".[211]

The rule that States must investigate war crimes and prosecute the suspects is set forth in numerous military manuals, with respect to grave breaches, but also more broadly with respect to war crimes in general.[212] Most States implement the obligation to investigate war crimes and prosecute the suspects by providing jurisdiction for such crimes in their national legislation, and there have been numerous national investigations and prosecutions of suspected war criminals.[213] It is not possible, however, to determine whether this practice was pursuant to an obligation or merely a right. An obligation to investigate and prosecute is, however, stated explicitly in a variety of other State practice, such as agreements and official statements.[214]

In addition, the obligation to investigate war crimes and prosecute the suspects has been reaffirmed on several occasions by the UN Security Council in relation to attacks on peacekeeping personnel and in relation to crimes committed in the non-international armed conflicts in Afghanistan, Burundi,

---

[209] First Geneva Convention, Article 49; Second Geneva Convention, Article 50; Third Geneva Convention, Article 129; Fourth Geneva Convention, Article 146.

[210] Genocide Convention, Article VI; Hague Convention for the Protection of Cultural Property, Article 28; Convention against Torture, Article 7; Chemical Weapons Convention, Article 7(1); Amended Protocol II to the Convention on Certain Conventional Weapons, Article 14 ; Ottawa Convention, Article 9; Second Protocol to the Hague Convention for the Protection of Cultural Property, Articles 15–17.

[211] ICC Statute, preamble (cited in Vol. II, Ch. 44, § 134).

[212] In addition to those which refer to the grave breaches regime, see the military manuals of Australia (*ibid.*, § 356), Cameroon (*ibid.*, § 359), Canada (*ibid.*, § 362), Colombia (*ibid.*, § 363), Ecuador (*ibid.*, § 365), Germany (*ibid.*, § 369), Italy (*ibid.*, § 370), Netherlands (*ibid.*, § 373), Switzerland (*ibid.*, § 381), United Kingdom (*ibid.*, § 382), United States (*ibid.*, §§ 383–384 and 387) and Yugoslavia (*ibid.*, § 388).

[213] See, e.g., the practice of Algeria (*ibid.*, § 533), Germany (*ibid.*, § 540), Italy (*ibid.*, § 541), South Africa (*ibid.*, § 544), United Kingdom (*ibid.*, § 547), United States (*ibid.*, §§ 550–555) and Yugoslavia (*ibid.*, § 556).

[214] See, e.g., Memorandum of Understanding on the Application of International Humanitarian Law between Croatia and the SFRY, Article 11 (*ibid.*, § 343); Agreement on the Application of International Humanitarian Law between the Parties to the Conflict in Bosnia and Herzegovina, Article 5 (*ibid.*, § 345); Comprehensive Agreement on Human Rights in Guatemala, Article III (*ibid.*, § 347); the statements of Australia (*ibid.*, § 534), German Democratic Republic (*ibid.*, § 538), Germany (*ibid.*, §§ 539–540), Italy (*ibid.*, § 541), Slovenia (*ibid.*, § 543), South Africa (*ibid.*, § 544), United Kingdom (*ibid.*, § 547), United States (*ibid.*, §§ 550–554) and Yugoslavia (*ibid.*, § 523); the reported practice of Algeria (*ibid.*, § 533), Bosnia and Herzegovina (*ibid.*, § 536) and United States (*ibid.*, § 555).

Democratic Republic of the Congo, Kosovo and Rwanda.[215] In 1946, in its first session, the UN General Assembly recommended that all States, including those not members of the United Nations, arrest persons who allegedly committed war crimes in the Second World War and send them back for prosecution to the State where the crimes were committed.[216] Since then, the UN General Assembly has, on several occasions, stressed the obligation of States to take measures to ensure the investigation of war crimes and crimes against humanity and the punishment of the perpetrators.[217] With respect to sexual violence in situations of armed conflict, the UN General Assembly has adopted several resolutions without a vote calling upon States to strengthen mechanisms to investigate and punish all those responsible for sexual violence and to bring the perpetrators to justice.[218]

The UN Commission on Human Rights has adopted a number of resolutions, most of them without a vote, requiring the investigation and prosecution of persons suspected of having committed violations of international humanitarian law in the context of the conflicts in Burundi, Chechnya, Rwanda, Sierra Leone, Sudan and the former Yugoslavia.[219] In a resolution on impunity adopted without a vote in 2002, the Commission recognised that persons suspected of war crimes should be prosecuted or extradited.[220]

In relation to crimes committed in non-international armed conflicts, a number of States have issued amnesties for war crimes, but these have often been found to be unlawful by their own courts or by regional courts and were criticised by the international community (see commentary to Rule 159 on the granting of amnesty).[221] There is, however, sufficient practice, as outlined

---

[215] UN Security Council, Res. 978 (*ibid.*, § 558), Res. 1193 (*ibid.*, § 559) and Res. 1199 (*ibid.*, § 560); UN Security Council, Statements by the President (*ibid.*, §§ 561–569).

[216] UN General Assembly, Res. 3 (I) (*ibid.*, § 570).

[217] UN General Assembly, Res. 2583 (XXIV) and 2712 (XXV) (*ibid.*, § 571), Res. 2840 (XXVI) (*ibid.*, § 572) and Res. 3074 (XXVIII) (*ibid.*, § 573). These resolutions attracted substantial abstentions and a few negative votes. This was due, however, to States' concern that there was insufficient clarity regarding the definition of war crimes and crimes against humanity and not, it seems, to any objection to the principle that war crimes be investigated and prosecuted.

[218] UN General Assembly, Res. 50/192 and 51/77 (*ibid.*, § 575) and Res. 52/107 (*ibid.*, § 576).

[219] UN Commission on Human Rights, Res. 1994/77 (*ibid.*, § 578), Res. 1995/77 (*ibid.*, § 583), Res. 1995/91 (*ibid.*, § 584), Res. 1996/71 (*ibid.*, § 580), Res. 1996/76 (*ibid.*, § 584), Res. 1999/1 (*ibid.*, § 585), Res. 1999/10 (*ibid.*, § 586) and Res. 2000/58 (*ibid.*, § 587). All resolutions were adopted without a vote, except Res. 1995/77 and Res. 2000/58, which attracted some negative votes and abstentions. It appears, however, that the reason for this does not lie in the inclusion of the duty to investigate and prosecute war crimes, as the other resolutions, which were adopted without a vote, also contained this duty.

[220] UN Commission on Human Rights, Res. 2002/79 (*ibid.*, § 589).

[221] See, e.g., Argentina, Federal Judge, *Cavallo case* (*ibid.*, § 700); Chile, Supreme Court, *Saavedra case* (*ibid.*, § 701); Chile, Appeal Court of Santiago, *Videla case* (*ibid.*, § 702); Ethiopia, Special Prosecutor's Office, *Mengistu and Others case* (*ibid.*, § 704); Spain, Sala de lo Penal de la Audiencia, *Pinochet case* (*ibid.*, § 706); Inter-American Commission on Human Rights, *Case 10.287 (El Salvador)* (*ibid.*, § 755); Inter-American Commission on Human Rights, *Case 10.480 (El Salvador)* (*ibid.*, § 757); UN Security Council, Res. 1315 (*ibid.*, § 725); UN Commission on Human Rights, Res. 2002/79 (*ibid.*, § 734); UN Secretary-General, Report on the establishment of a Special Court for Sierra Leone (*ibid.*, 738); UN Secretary-General, Report on the protection of civilians in armed conflicts (*ibid.*, § 739).

above, to establish the obligation under customary international law to investigate war crimes allegedly committed in non-international armed conflicts and to prosecute the suspects if appropriate.

Trial by international or mixed tribunals

States may discharge their obligation to investigate war crimes and prosecute the suspects by setting up international or mixed tribunals to that effect, a fact commented upon in military manuals, national case-law and official statements.[222] This is evidenced in particular by the creation of the International Military Tribunals at Nuremberg and at Tokyo after the Second World War and, more recently, by the establishment by the UN Security Council of the International Criminal Tribunals for the Former Yugoslavia and for Rwanda. The Special Court for Sierra Leone and the Extraordinary Chambers in the Courts of Cambodia for the Prosecution of Crimes Committed during the Period of Democratic Kampuchea were established pursuant to an agreement between the United Nations and Sierra Leone and Cambodia respectively. The International Criminal Court is the first international tribunal to be established by an international treaty which bears no relation to war crimes committed in a specific armed conflict. The Statutes of the International Criminal Court, of the International Criminal Tribunal for Rwanda, of the Special Court for Sierra Leone and of the Extraordinary Chambers for Cambodia expressly include within their jurisdiction war crimes committed during non-international armed conflicts.[223]

Refugee status

It is generally accepted that persons suspected of having committed war crimes are not entitled to refugee status. This is provided for, in particular, in the Convention on the Status of Refugees, and there is State practice to this effect.[224]

---

[222] See the military manuals of Argentina (*ibid.*, § 355), Australia (*ibid.*, § 144), France (*ibid.*, § 148) South Korea (*ibid.*, § 149), Switzerland (*ibid.*, §§ 156 and 381), United Kingdom (*ibid.*, § 15744), United States (*ibid.*, §§ 159–160 and 369) and Yugoslavia (*ibid.*, §§ 162 and 388); United Kingdom, House of Lords, *Pinochet Extradition case* (Opinion of Lord Phillips of Worth Matravers) (*ibid.*, § 270); United States, Military Tribunal at Nuremberg, *Altstötter (The Justice Trial) case* (*ibid.*, § 272); statements of Egypt (*ibid.*, § 613), Iran (*ibid.*, § 613), Pakistan (*ibid.*, § 613), Saudi Arabia (*ibid.*, § 613), Senegal (*ibid.*, § 613), Turkey (*ibid.*, § 613) and United Kingdom (*ibid.*, § 287).

[223] ICC Statute, Article 8(2)(c) and (e) (*ibid.*, § 3); ICTR Statute, Article 4 (*ibid.*, § 15); Statute of the Special Court for Sierra Leone, Articles 3 and 4; Law on the Establishment of the Extraordinary Chambers in the Courts of Cambodia for the Prosecution of Crimes Committed during the Period of Democratic Kampuchea, Articles 6–7.

[224] Refugee Convention, Article 1(F)(a). See, e.g., Australia, *Defence Force Manual* (cited in Vol. II, Ch. 44, § 636); Netherlands, Council of State, Administrative Law Division, *Ahmed case* (*ibid.*, § 638); United States, Court of Appeals, *Demjanjuk case* (*ibid.*, § 639); the reported practice of Netherlands (*ibid.*, § 640) and United States (*ibid.*, § 641).

In 1994, with respect to Rwanda, the UN Security Council stressed that "persons involved in [serious breaches of international humanitarian law] cannot achieve immunity from prosecution by fleeing the country" and that "the provisions of the Convention relating to the status of refugees do not apply to such persons".[225] Exclusion from asylum of suspected war criminals has also been supported by the UN General Assembly in the Declaration on Territorial Asylum and in Resolution 3074 (XXVIII) on principles of international cooperation in the detection, arrest, extradition and punishment of war criminals.[226]

Rule 159. At the end of hostilities, the authorities in power must endeavour to grant the broadest possible amnesty to persons who have participated in a non-international armed conflict, or those deprived of their liberty for reasons related to the armed conflict, with the exception of persons suspected of, accused of or sentenced for war crimes.

Practice

Volume II, Chapter 44, Section D.

Summary

State practice establishes this rule as a norm of customary international law applicable in non-international armed conflicts.

Non-international armed conflicts

The obligation of the authorities in power to endeavour to grant the broadest possible amnesty at the end of hostilities is set forth in Additional Protocol II.[227] Since then many States have granted amnesty to persons who have taken part in a non-international armed conflict, either by special agreement,[228] legislation,[229] or other measures.[230]

---

[225] UN Security Council, Statement by the President (*ibid.*, § 642).
[226] UN General Assembly, Res. 2312 (XXII) (*ibid.*, § 643) and Res. 3074 (XXVIII), § 7 (*ibid.*, § 644).
[227] Additional Protocol II, Article 6(5) (adopted by consensus) (*ibid.*, § 651).
[228] See, e.g., the Esquipulas II Accords (*ibid.*, § 652), Quadripartite Agreement on Georgian Refugees and Internally Displaced Persons (*ibid.*, § 653), Agreement on Refugees and Displaced Persons annexed to the Dayton Accords (*ibid.*, § 634), Agreement between the Parties to the Conflict in Bosnia and Herzegovina (*ibid.*, § 656), Cotonou Agreement on Liberia (*ibid.*, § 657), General Amnesty Proclamation Order annexed to the Sudan Peace Agreement (*ibid.*, § 659), Moscow Agreement on Tajikistan (*ibid.*, § 661), Peace Agreement between the Government of Sierra Leone and the RUF (*ibid.*, § 668) and Protocol II to the Arusha Peace and Reconciliation Agreement for Burundi (*ibid.*, § 669).
[229] See, e.g., the legislation of Algeria (*ibid.*, § 673), Bosnia and Herzegovina (*ibid.*, §§ 678–680), Burundi (*ibid.*, § 681), Chile (*ibid.*, § 682), Colombia (*ibid.*, § 683), Croatia (*ibid.*, § 684), El Salvador (*ibid.*, § 685), Guatemala (*ibid.*, § 688), Peru (*ibid.*, § 690), Russia (*ibid.*, § 691), South Africa (*ibid.*, § 693), Tajikistan (*ibid.*, §§ 694–696) and Zimbabwe (*ibid.*, § 699).
[230] See, e.g., the statements of the Former Yugoslav Republic of Macedonia (*ibid.*, § 709), Rwanda (*ibid.*, § 711) and Philippines (*ibid.*, §§ 713–715) and the reported practice of Malaysia (*ibid.*, § 710) and Rwanda (*ibid.*, § 712).

The UN Security Council has encouraged the granting of such amnesties, for example, in relation to the struggle against apartheid in South Africa and the conflicts in Angola and Croatia.[231] Similarly, the UN General Assembly adopted resolutions encouraging the granting of such amnesties in relation to the conflicts in Afghanistan and Kosovo.[232] Furthermore, the UN Commission on Human Rights adopted resolutions to this effect in relation to Bosnia and Herzegovina and Sudan.[233] Some regional bodies have welcomed such amnesties, for example, the European Union and NATO in relation to the Former Yugoslav Republic of Macedonia and the OSCE in relation to Tajikistan.[234] It is noteworthy that the resolutions adopted by the United Nations were in relation to States not party to Additional Protocol II (South Africa, which did not ratify the Protocol until 1995, Angola, Afghanistan and Sudan), and that not all of the States voting in favour of these resolutions were themselves party to Additional Protocol II.

With the exception of the UN Security Council resolutions, which called on the South African government to grant amnesties for opponents of apartheid, the other resolutions adopted by the United Nations and statements by regional bodies take the form of encouragement to grant amnesty or approval of amnesties adopted. This shows that authorities are not absolutely obliged to grant an amnesty at the end of hostilities but are required to give this careful consideration and to endeavour to adopt such an amnesty.

Exception

When Article 6(5) of Additional Protocol II was adopted, the USSR stated, in its explanation of vote, that the provision could not be construed to enable war criminals, or those guilty of crimes against humanity, to evade punishment.[235] The ICRC shares this interpretation.[236] Such amnesties would also be incompatible with the rule obliging States to investigate and prosecute persons suspected of having committed war crimes in non-international armed conflicts (see Rule 158).

Most amnesties specifically exclude from their scope persons who are suspected of having committed war crimes or other specifically listed crimes

---

[231] UN Security Council, Res. 190 and 191 (*ibid.*, § 719), Res. 473 (*ibid.*, § 720), Res. 581 (*ibid.*, § 721), Res. 1055 (*ibid.*, § 722), Res. 1064 (*ibid.*, § 723) and Res. 1120 (*ibid.*, § 724); UN Security Council, Statements by the President (*ibid.*, §§ 726–727).

[232] UN General Assembly, Res. 47/141 (adopted without a vote), Res. 48/152 (adopted without a vote) and Res. 49/207 (adopted without a vote) (*ibid.*, § 729) and Res. 53/164 (adopted by 122 votes in favour, 3 against and 34 abstentions) (*ibid.*, § 730).

[233] UN Commission on Human Rights, Res. 1996/71 (adopted without a vote) (*ibid.*, § 732) and Res. 1996/73 (adopted without a vote) (*ibid.*, § 733).

[234] EU, Secretary General/High Representative CFSP, Communiqué No. 0039/02 (*ibid.*, § 747); NATO, Statement (*ibid.*, § 748); OSCE, Press Release (*ibid.*, § 749).

[235] USSR, Statement at the Diplomatic Conference leading to the adoption of the Additional Protocols (*ibid.*, § 716).

[236] See the practice of the ICRC (*ibid.*, §§ 759–760).

under international law.[237] In the *Videla case* in 1994, Chile's Appeal Court of Santiago held that offences which it considered to constitute grave breaches were unamenable to amnesty.[238] In the *Mengistu and Others case* in 1995, the Special Prosecutor of Ethiopia stated that it was "a well established custom and belief that war crimes and crimes against humanity are not subject to amnesty".[239] This was confirmed in the *Cavallo case* in 2001 by Argentina's Federal Judge with respect to crimes against humanity.[240] In the *Azapo case* in 1996, however, concerning the legality of establishment of the Truth and Reconciliation Commission, South Africa's Constitutional Court interpreted Article 6(5) of Additional Protocol II as containing an exception to the peremptory rule prohibiting an amnesty in relation to crimes against humanity.[241] It should be noted, however, that the work of the Truth and Reconciliation Commission in South Africa did not involve the granting of blanket amnesties as it required full disclosure of all the relevant facts.[242]

In resolutions on Croatia and Sierra Leone, the UN Security Council confirmed that amnesties may not apply to war crimes.[243] In a resolution on impunity adopted without a vote in 2002, the UN Commission on Human Rights made the same point,[244] as did the UN Secretary-General in several reports.[245] Some regional bodies have also stated that amnesties may not cover war crimes, in particular the European Parliament in relation to the former Yugoslavia.[246]

There is international case-law to support the proposition that war crimes may not be the object of an amnesty, in particular the judgement of the

---

[237] See, e.g., the Quadripartite Agreement on Georgian Refugees and Internally Displaced Persons (*ibid.*, § 653), the Agreement on Refugees and Displaced Persons annexed to the Dayton Accords (*ibid.*, § 654), Statute of the Special Court for Sierra Leone (*ibid.*, § 655) and Agreement between Parties to the conflict in Bosnia and Herzegovina on the Release and Transfer of Prisoners (*ibid.*, § 656); see also the legislation of Algeria (*ibid.*, § 673) (exempting terrorist or subversive acts), Argentina (*ibid.*, § 676) (exempting crimes against humanity), Bosnia and Herzegovina (Federation) (*ibid.*, § 679), Colombia (*ibid.*, § 683), Croatia (*ibid.*, § 684), El Salvador (*ibid.*, § 685) (exempting assassinations of Mgr Romero and Herbert Anaya, kidnapping for personal gain or drug trafficking), Ethiopia (*ibid.*, § 687) (exempting crimes against humanity), Guatemala (*ibid.*, § 688), Russia (*ibid.*, § 691), Tajikistan (*ibid.*, § 695) and Uruguay (*ibid.*, § 697) and the draft legislation of Argentina (*ibid.*, § 677) and Burundi (*ibid.*, § 646); see also the practice of Bosnia and Herzegovina (*ibid.*, § 707), Former Yugoslav Republic of Macedonia (*ibid.*, § 709) and Philippines (*ibid.*, § 715).
[238] Chile, Appeal Court of Santiago, *Videla case* (*ibid.*, § 702).
[239] Ethiopia, Special Prosecutor's Office, *Mengistu and Others case* (*ibid.*, § 704).
[240] Argentina, Federal Judge, *Cavallo case* (*ibid.*, § 700).
[241] South Africa, Cape Provincial Division, *Azapo case* (*ibid.*, § 705).
[242] See South Africa, *The Promotion of National Unity and Reconciliation Act*, 26 July 1995, Chapter 2, Article 3(1) ("The objectives of the Commission shall be to promote national unity and reconciliation in a spirit of understanding which transcends the conflicts and divisions of the past by . . . (b) facilitating the granting of amnesty to persons who make full disclosure of all the relevant facts relating to acts associated with a political objective and comply with the requirements of this Act."), see also Articles 4(c) and 20(1)(c).
[243] UN Security Council, Res. 1120 (cited in Vol. II, Ch. 44, § 724) and Res. 1315 (*ibid.*, 725).
[244] UN Commission on Human Rights, Res. 2002/79 (*ibid.*, § 734).
[245] See, e.g., UN Secretary-General, Report on the establishment of a Special Court for Sierra Leone (*ibid.*, § 738) and Report on the protection of civilians in armed conflict (*ibid.*, § 739).
[246] European Parliament, Resolution on human rights in the world and Community human rights policy for the years 1991/1992 (*ibid.*, § 746).

International Criminal Tribunal for the Former Yugoslavia in the *Furundžija case* in 1998 with respect to torture.[247]

Human rights bodies have stated that amnesties are incompatible with the duty of States to investigate crimes under international law and violations of non-derogable human rights law, for example, the UN Human Rights Committee in its General Comment on Article 7 of the International Covenant on Civil and Political Rights (prohibition of torture).[248] In a case concerning El Salvador's 1993 General Amnesty Law for Consolidation of Peace, the Inter-American Commission on Human Rights found that law to be in violation of the American Convention on Human Rights, as well as of common Article 3 of the Geneva Conventions and Additional Protocol II.[249] In its judgement in the *Barrios Altos case* in 2001 concerning the legality of Peruvian amnesty laws, the Inter-American Court of Human Rights held that amnesty measures for serious human rights violations such as torture, extrajudicial, summary or arbitrary executions and enforced disappearances were inadmissible because they violated non-derogable rights.[250]

Rule 160. Statutes of limitation may not apply to war crimes.

Practice

Volume II, Chapter 43, Section E.

Summary

State practice establishes this rule as a norm of customary international law applicable in relation to war crimes committed in both international and non-international armed conflicts.

International and non-international armed conflicts

The non-applicability of statutory limitations to war crimes and crimes against humanity is provided for by the 1968 UN Convention on the Non-Applicability of Statutory Limitations to War Crimes and Crimes against Humanity and by the 1974 European Convention on the Non-Applicability of Statutory Limitations to Crimes against Humanity and War Crimes.[251] In the discussions

---

[247] ICTY, *Furundžija case*, Judgement (*ibid.*, § 751).
[248] UN Human Rights Committee, General Comment No. 20 (Article 7 of the International Covenant on Civil and Political Rights) (*ibid.*, § 752).
[249] Inter-American Commission on Human Rights, *Case 10.480* (*ibid.*, § 757).
[250] Inter-American Court of Human Rights, *Barrios Altos case* (*ibid.*, § 758).
[251] UN Convention on the Non-Applicability of Statutory Limitations to War Crimes and Crimes against Humanity, preamble (*ibid.*, § 763) and Article 1 (*ibid.*, § 764) (the UN Convention has been ratified by 48 States); European Convention on the Non-Applicability of Statutory Limitations to Crimes against Humanity and War Crimes, Article 1 (*ibid.*, § 765) and Article 2 (*ibid.*, § 766) (the European Convention has been ratified by 3 States).

leading to the adoption of the UN Convention, some States considered the prohibition of statutes of limitation for war crimes to be a new rule,[252] while other
States considered that it was already established.[253] The main objection of the
States which considered it a new rule was that the Convention would apply
retroactively and thus violate the principle of non-retroactivity of criminal law
and that statutory limitation was a general principle of their domestic criminal
law at that time.[254] But many States argued that war crimes were of an exceptional character and should not, therefore, be subject to the ordinary regime of
criminal law and to the operation of statutes of limitation and/or that they had
already implemented the principle of non-applicability of statutory limitations
to war crimes.[255]

Between 1969 and 1973, the UN General Assembly adopted several resolutions calling on States to ratify the UN Convention on the Non-Applicability
of Statutory Limitations to War Crimes and Crimes against Humanity and, in
1970, welcoming its entry into force.[256] These resolutions attracted substantial
abstentions and a few negative votes. During the debates on these resolutions,
States' main concern was the lack of clarity regarding the definitions of war
crimes and crimes against humanity as used in the Convention.[257]

The recent trend to pursue war crimes more vigorously in national and international criminal courts and tribunals, as well as the growing body of legislation giving jurisdiction over war crimes without time-limits, has hardened the
existing treaty rules prohibiting statutes of limitation for war crimes into customary law. In addition, the operation of statutory limitations could prevent
the investigation of war crimes and the prosecution of the suspects and would
constitute a violation of the obligation to do so (see Rule 158).

---

[252] See, e.g., the statements of Brazil (*ibid.*, § 836) and Greece (*ibid.*, § 845); see also the statements
of Belgium (*ibid.*, § 834), Cyprus (*ibid.*, § 841), Honduras (*ibid.*, § 846), India (*ibid.*, § 848),
Norway (*ibid.*, § 851) and Sweden (*ibid.*, § 855).
[253] See, e.g., the statements of Bulgaria (*ibid.*, § 837) and Czechoslovakia (*ibid.*, § 842).
[254] See the statements of Brazil (*ibid.*, § 836), Cyprus (*ibid.*, § 841), Greece (*ibid.*, § 845), Honduras
(*ibid.*, § 846) and Sweden (*ibid.*, § 855).
[255] See the statements of Bulgaria (*ibid.*, § 837), Czechoslovakia (*ibid.*, § 842), France (*ibid.*, § 843),
Hungary (*ibid.*, § 847), India (*ibid.*, § 848), Israel (*ibid.*, § 849), Poland (*ibid.*, § 853), Romania
(*ibid.*, § 854), Ukraine (*ibid.*, § 856), USSR (*ibid.*, § 857), United Kingdom (*ibid.*, § 858), United
States (*ibid.*, § 860), Uruguay (*ibid.*, § 862) and Yugoslavia (*ibid.*, § 864).
[256] UN General Assembly, Res. 2583 (XXIV) (*ibid.*, § 868), Res. 2712 (XXV) (*ibid.*, § 869) and
Res. 2840 (XXVI) (*ibid.*, § 870).
[257] Only a few objections were raised with regard to the principle of the non-applicability of statutory limitations, which are similar to those expressed in the discussions leading to the adoption of the Convention (see footnotes 252–255 and accompanying text). Norway and Colombia
announced that they would abstain in the vote on Res. 2583 because they objected to the
principle as such owing to their domestic legislation (UN Doc. A/C.3/SR.1723, 3 December
1969, UN Doc. A/C.3/SR.1724, 3 December 1969 and UN Doc. A/C.3/SR.1725, 4 December 1969). France and Turkey also explained that they had to abstain for reasons related to
their domestic legislation (UN Doc. A/C.3/SR.1724, 3 December 1969, §§ 36 and 60). Bolivia
stated that it would abstain because "the non-applicability of statutory limitations was clearly
abhorrent" and was "at variance with...the principles of non-retroactivity of penal law"
(UN Doc. A/C.3/SR.1725, 4 December 1969, § 19).

The Statute of the International Criminal Court provides that the crimes within the jurisdiction of the Court are not subject to any statute of limitation, and this provision was not a matter of controversy, in part because the International Criminal Court only has jurisdiction in relation to acts committed after the Statute enters into force for the State concerned.[258] UNTAET Regulation No. 2000/15 for East Timor also states that war crimes may not be subject to any statute of limitation.[259]

The principle that statutes of limitation do not apply to war crimes is set forth in many military manuals and in the legislation of many States, including those of States not party to the UN or European Conventions on the Non-Applicability of Statutory Limitations to War Crimes or Crimes against Humanity.[260] There are also official statements to this effect. For example, in 1986, the United States wrote a note to Iraq (also not party to the UN Convention) to the effect that individuals guilty of war crimes could be subject to prosecution at any time, without regard to any statute of limitations.[261] In a letter to the UN Secretary-General in 1993, Yugoslavia stated that war crimes were not subject to statutes of limitation.[262] In 2000, upon signature of the Statute of the International Criminal Court, Egypt stated that it was a "well established principle that no war crime shall be barred from prosecution due to the statute of limitations".[263] There is also case-law of States not party to the UN or European Conventions in which the courts concerned ruled that statutes of limitation do not apply to war crimes.[264] It is significant that several States that objected earlier to a prohibition of statutory limitations, or whose legislation was not clear on this point, have now ratified the Statute of the International Criminal Court or the UN Convention on Non-Applicability of Statutory Limitations thus recognising the principle that statutes of limitation do not apply to war crimes.[265]

---

[258] ICC Statute, Article 29 (cited in Vol. II, Ch. 44, § 767).
[259] UNTAET Regulation No. 2000/15, Section 17(1) (ibid., § 772).
[260] See, e.g., the military manuals of Australia (ibid., § 773), Italy (ibid., § 775) and United States (ibid., §§ 777–778); the legislation of Argentina (ibid., § 780), Belgium (ibid., § 786), Congo (ibid., § 789), Germany (ibid., § 797), Luxembourg (ibid., § 805), Mali (ibid., § 807), Niger (ibid., § 810), Switzerland (ibid., § 819), Tajikistan (ibid., § 820) and Uzbekistan (ibid., § 821); see also the draft legislation of Burundi (ibid., § 787), Jordan (ibid., § 802) and Lebanon (ibid., § 803).
[261] United States, Department of State, Diplomatic Note to Iraq (ibid., § 861).
[262] Yugoslavia, Deputy Prime Minister and Minister of Foreign Affairs, Letter to the UN Secretary-General (ibid., § 865).
[263] Egypt, Declarations made upon signature of the ICC Statute (ibid., § 768).
[264] See Chile, Appeals Court of Santiago, Videla case (ibid., § 827); Ethiopia, Special Prosecutor's Office, Mengistu and Others case (ibid., § 828); Italy, Military Tribunal of Rome, Hass and Priebke case (ibid., § 832); Italy, Military Appeals Court, Hass and Priebke case (ibid., § 832); Italy, Supreme Court of Cassation, Hass and Priebke case (ibid., § 832).
[265] See the legislation of Austria (ibid., § 783), Colombia (ibid., § 788), Greece (ibid., § 878), Malaysia (ibid., § 806), Malta (ibid., § 878), Norway (ibid., § 878), Portugal (ibid., § 878), Spain (ibid., §§ 817–818), Sweden (ibid., § 878), Turkey (ibid., § 878) and Uruguay (ibid., § 862) and the statements of Brazil (ibid., § 836), Cyprus (ibid., § 841), Greece (ibid., § 845), Honduras (ibid., § 846) and Sweden (ibid., § 855). However, Austria, Brazil, Colombia, Cyprus, Greece,

Ethiopia's Constitution provides that statutes of limitation do not apply to crimes against humanity, without mentioning war crimes.[266] However, in the *Mengistu and Others case* in 1995, the Special Prosecutor of Ethiopia stated that "it is...a well established custom and belief that war crimes and crimes against humanity are not...barred by limitation".[267] France's Penal Code provides for the non-applicability of statutes of limitation for genocide and "other crimes against humanity".[268] In the *Barbie case* in 1985, France's Court of Cassation held that in contrast to crimes against humanity, war crimes committed during the Second World War were subject "to the time-limits imposed by statute".[269] However, France was also a member of ECOSOC when Resolution 1158 (XLI) was adopted in 1966, which considered it desirable to affirm, in international law, "the principle that there is no period of limitation for war crimes and crimes against humanity" and which urged all States "to take any measures necessary to prevent the application of statutory limitations to war crimes and crimes against humanity".[270] France subsequently supported the non-applicability of statutes of limitation to war crimes in a debate in the United Nations in 1967 leading to the adoption of the UN Convention on Non-Applicability of Statutory Limitations to War Crimes and Crimes against Humanity, and it signed the European Convention on the Non-Applicability of Statutory Limitations to Crimes against Humanity and War Crimes.[271] In addition, France has ratified the Statute of the International Criminal Court.

Israel's Nazis and Nazi Collaborators (Punishment) Law provides that there shall be no period of limitation for prosecution of war crimes, but this law only covers war crimes committed by Nazis in the Second World War.[272] However, Israel subsequently supported the general principle that statutes of limitation do not apply to any war crimes.[273] Some other States have similarly vested jurisdiction in their courts over war crimes committed during the Second World War,[274] but these States also support the general principle that statutes of limitation may not apply to any war crimes.[275] There have also been some recent

---

Honduras, Malta, Norway, Portugal, Spain, Sweden and Uruguay have in the meantime ratified the ICC Statute. Spain, in addition, amended its Penal Code to provide explicitly that statutory limitations do not apply to war crimes. Uruguay, in addition, ratified the UN Convention on the Non-Applicability of Statutory Limitations to War Crimes and Crimes against Humanity.

[266] Ethiopia, *Constitution* (ibid., § 794).
[267] Ethiopia, Special Prosecutor's Office, *Mengistu and Others case* (ibid., § 828).
[268] France, *Penal Code* (ibid., § 795).
[269] France, Court of Cassation, *Barbie case* (ibid., § 829).
[270] ECOSOC, Res. 1158 (XLI) (adopted by 22 votes in favour, none against and 2 abstentions) (ibid., § 872).
[271] See the practice of France (ibid., §§ 765 and 843).
[272] Israel, *Nazis and Nazi Collaborators (Punishment) Law* (ibid., § 800).
[273] See the statement by Israel (ibid., § 849).
[274] See the legislation of Australia (ibid., § 392), China (ibid., § 409), Luxembourg (ibid., § 449), Russia (ibid., §§ 812 and 479), United Kingdom (ibid., § 498) and United States (ibid., §§ 501–503).
[275] See the practice in support of this rule of Australia (ibid., § 773), Luxembourg (ibid., § 805), Russia (ibid., §§ 813 and 857) and United States (ibid., §§ 777–778). No contrary practice was

convictions for war crimes committed during the Second World War.[276] Insufficient evidence may often amount to an obstacle to successful prosecution of war crimes that took place several decades before proceedings were instituted. Such practical considerations do not undermine the principle that statutes of limitation are not applicable to war crimes.

Rule 161. States must make every effort to cooperate, to the extent possible, with each other in order to facilitate the investigation of war crimes and the prosecution of the suspects.

Practice

Volume II, Chapter 44, Section F.

Summary

State practice establishes this rule as a norm of customary international law applicable in relation to war crimes committed in both international and non-international armed conflicts.

International and non-international armed conflicts

Additional Protocol I and the Second Protocol to the Hague Convention for the Protection of Cultural Property provide that parties to a conflict shall afford to one another the greatest measure of assistance in connection with investigations and criminal proceedings, including extradition, brought in respect of the war crimes listed in those treaties.[277] Similar provisions are to be found in the European Convention on Mutual Assistance in Criminal Matters, the OAU Convention against Mercenarism, the UN Mercenary Convention and the United States–Soviet Memorandum of Understanding on the Pursuit of Nazi War Criminals.[278]

---

found with respect to China. The statement in the UK Military Manual that it is "open to two or more belligerents to agree in a peace treaty, or even in a general armistice, that no further war crimes trials will be instituted by them after a certain agreed date or as from the date of the treaty of the armistice" (*ibid.*, § 776) can be interpreted as contrary practice but it dates from 1958, i.e., before the adoption of the UN and European Conventions on the Non-Applicability of Statutory Limitations to War Crimes and Crimes against Humanity, and the United Kingdom has now ratified the ICC Statute and thus recognises that statutes of limitation do not apply to war crimes, at least not to those war crimes codified in the Statute.

[276] See, e.g., Australia, High Court, *Polyukhovich case* (*ibid.*, § 515); Canada, High Court of Justice, *Finta case* (*ibid.*, § 250); Canada, Supreme Court, *Finta case* (*ibid.*, § 250); United States, Court of Appeals, *Demjanjuk case* (*ibid.*, § 273).

[277] Additional Protocol I, Article 88 (adopted by consensus) (*ibid.*, § 886); Second Protocol to the Hague Convention on the Protection of Cultural Property, Article 19 (*ibid.*, § 890).

[278] European Convention on Mutual Assistance in Criminal Matters, Article 1(1) (*ibid.*, § 885); OAU Convention against Mercenarism, Article 10 (*ibid.*, § 887); UN Mercenary Convention, Article 13 (*ibid.*, § 888); United States–Soviet Memorandum of Understanding on the Pursuit of Nazi War Criminals, Article 1 (*ibid.*, § 889).

In 1989, the UN Security Council urged States to cooperate with each other in the context of the prohibition of hostage-taking,[279] and in 1998 it urged States to cooperate with the governments of the Democratic Republic of the Congo and Rwanda in the investigation and prosecution of those guilty of violations of international humanitarian law.[280] The UN General Assembly adopted several resolutions between 1970 and 1973 calling on States to cooperate in the investigation and prosecution of suspected war criminals.[281] It should be noted that these UN General Assembly resolutions attracted substantial numbers of abstentions, mainly, however, because the crimes covered by those resolutions were not clearly defined.[282] In two resolutions adopted unanimously and without a vote respectively, the UN Commission on Human Rights also urged States to take necessary measures to cooperate in order to ensure the prosecution of persons guilty of war crimes and crimes against humanity.[283] The voting record of the General Assembly resolutions, together with the fact that the UN Security Council and UN Commission on Human Rights *urged* States to cooperate rather than calling on them to do so, indicates that there does not seem to be, in customary international law, an absolute obligation to cooperate, but rather an expectation that States should make efforts in good faith to do so, to the extent possible. It is significant that the United States, which is not party to Additional Protocol I, stated in 1987 that it supported the principle that appropriate authorities "make good faith efforts to cooperate with one another".[284]

There appears to be, therefore, general acceptance of the principle that States must make every effort to cooperate with each other, to the extent possible, in order to facilitate the investigation and trial of suspected war criminals and, in this regard, no distinction has been made by States between war crimes committed in international armed conflicts and war crimes committed in non-international armed conflicts. The forms of cooperation mentioned in the various resolutions include investigations, exchange of documents, arrest, prosecution and extradition.

Extradition

There is uniformity of practice, both in treaty law and national law, to the effect that war crimes are subject to extradition under extradition treaties. However, there does not appear to be an *obligation* to extradite persons suspected of war crimes. Additional Protocol I states that "when circumstances permit, [States]

---

[279] UN Security Council, Res. 683 (*ibid.*, § 913).
[280] UN Security Council, Statement by the President (*ibid.*, § 914).
[281] UN General Assembly, Res. 2712 (XXV) (*ibid.*, § 915), Res. 2840 (XXVI) (*ibid.*, § 916), Res. 3020 (XXVII) (*ibid.*, § 917) and Res. 3074 (XXVIII) (*ibid.*, § 918).
[282] See footnotes 217 and 257 and accompanying text.
[283] UN Commission on Human Rights, Res. 3 (XXI) (*ibid.*, § 919) and Res. 1988/47 (*ibid.*, § 920).
[284] United States, Remarks of the Deputy Legal Adviser of the Department of State (*ibid.*, § 909).

shall co-operate in the matter of extradition". It adds that they "shall give due consideration to the request of the State in whose territory the alleged offence has occurred".[285] All extradition agreements include conditions required for extradition (typically, the offence has to be a crime in both States with a minimum punishment provided for) and it should also be noted that it would be a violation of international law to extradite a suspect to a country where the person risks being subjected to torture or cruel or inhuman treatment or punishment. While there are examples of extraditions, such as in the *Priebke case* in 1995 and the *Cavallo case* in 2001, there have also been instances of refusal to extradite, *inter alia*, because of the absence of an extradition treaty with the requesting State, such as the *Barbie extradition case* in 1974.[286] A number of States specifically provide that they will not extradite their own nationals.[287]

Many bilateral and regional extradition treaties, as well as national legislation, specify that there cannot be extradition for "political offences" but that this exception cannot apply to crimes under international law.[288] This principle is also set forth in other treaties.[289] It has been applied in national case-law.[290]

This practice appears to show that cooperation in prosecuting suspected war criminals should include extradition when requested, but potentially subject to conditions. There is no indication that this rule is considered any differently for crimes committed in the context of international or non-international armed conflicts. If extradition is refused, then, in the case of grave breaches or other crimes where multilateral treaties provide for an obligation to try or extradite on the basis of universal jurisdiction, the requested State is required to

---

[285] Additional Protocol I, Article 88(2) (*ibid.*, § 936).

[286] Argentina, Supreme Court of Justice, *Priebke case* (*ibid.*, § 971); Mexico, Federal Court of the First Circuit, *Cavallo case* (*ibid.*, § 974); Bolivia, Supreme Court, *Barbie extradition case* (*ibid.*, § 972). It should be noted, however, that Klaus Barbie was subsequently expelled from Bolivia to France.

[287] See, e.g., the practice of Belgium (*ibid.*, § 1024), Croatia (*ibid.*, § 1010), Lithuania (*ibid.*, § 1015), Mongolia (*ibid.*, § 1003), Russia (*ibid.*, § 1017), Rwanda (*ibid.*, § 1018), Spain (*ibid.*, § 1019), Yemen (*ibid.*, § 1020) and Yugoslavia (*ibid.*, § 1021); see also the bilateral extradition treaties that make a specific exception for a State's own nationals (*ibid.*, § 994), although there are others that exclude this exception (*ibid.*, §§ 995, 996, 999, 1001 and 1004).

[288] See, e.g., Extradition Treaty between Brazil and Peru, Article IV (*ibid.*, § 1030); European Convention on Extradition, Article 3(1) (*ibid.*, § 1032), Extradition Treaty between Venezuela and Chile, Article 4(5) (*ibid.*, § 1034); Additional Protocol to the European Convention on Extradition, Article 1 (*ibid.*, § 1036); Extradition Treaty between Spain and Argentina, Article 5(1) (*ibid.*, § 1037); Extradition Treaty between Peru and Spain, Article 5 (*ibid.*, § 1038); Extradition Treaty between Chile and Spain, Article 5(1) (*ibid.*, § 1039); Extradition Treaty between Australia and Chile, Article IV(1) (*ibid.*, § 1040); Extradition Treaty between Argentina and the United States, Article 4 (*ibid.*, § 1042); the legislation of Argentina (*ibid.*, § 1047), Luxembourg (*ibid.*, § 1052), Netherlands (*ibid.*, § 1053), Peru (*ibid.*, § 1054), Portugal (*ibid.*, § 1055) and Spain (*ibid.*, § 1057).

[289] See, e.g., Genocide Convention, Article 7 (*ibid.*, § 1031); International Convention on the Suppression and Punishment of the Crime of Apartheid, Article 11 (*ibid.*, § 1035); Inter-American Convention on the Forced Disappearance of Persons, Article V (*ibid.*, § 1041); Second Protocol to the Hague Convention for the Protection of Cultural Property, Article 20 (*ibid.*, § 1043).

[290] See, e.g., New Zealand, *Military Manual* (*ibid.*, § 1045) (referring to Ghana, Court of Appeal, *Schumann Extradition case* (1949)); Argentina, Supreme Court of Justice, *Bohne case* (*ibid.*, § 1059).

try the alleged criminal itself. In case of other war crimes, the State is required to proceed with investigation and prosecution in accordance with Rule 158.

Cooperation with international tribunals

There are specific provisions for cooperation in the context of the statutes of international tribunals. Such cooperation must be undertaken either by virtue of the treaty, as in the case of the Statute of the International Criminal Court, or in order to implement binding UN Security Council resolutions, as in the case of the tribunals set up under Chapter VII of the Charter of the United Nations.[291]

---

[291] ICC Statute, Articles 86–101, in particular Article 86 (*ibid.*, § 1070) and Article 93 (*ibid.*, § 1071); UN Security Council, Res. 827 (*ibid.*, § 1125) (concerning cooperation with the ICTY) and Res. 955 (*ibid.*, § 1127) (concerning cooperation with the ICTR).